A CONSTITUTIONAL HISTORY
OF THE
UNITED STATES

A—
CONSTITUTIONAL HISTORY OF THE UNITED STATES

BY ANDREW C. McLAUGHLIN
PROFESSOR EMERITUS OF HISTORY
UNIVERSITY OF CHICAGO

STUDENT'S EDITION

APPLETON-CENTURY-CROFTS

EDUCATIONAL DIVISION

MEREDITH CORPORATION   NEW YORK

JH
31
M3

108C7

"For who are a free people? Not those, over whom government is reasonably and equitably exercised, but those, who live under a government so constitutionally checked and controuled, that proper provision is made against its being otherwise exercised."—John Dickinson, *Letters From a Farmer in Pennsylvania* (1768).

PREFACE

The purpose of this volume is to present briefly and clearly the constitutional history of the United States during nearly two centuries. I have no special ambition to write a long and learned work—so long as to deter a prospective reader from the task of scanning its pages, and so technical that only the learned expert, to whom I can give no valuable information, will occasionally turn its pages. I have attempted, therefore, to include essentials and those alone, to discuss those matters which in my own judgment the American citizen, not highly trained in the law, should know familiarly.

But the writing of a short history of a long and complex period furnishes its special difficulties. The author is under continuous obligation to practice self-restraint. He must exercise unremitting care in selecting the materials that he wishes to include in his story. This process of choice makes unrelenting demand and requires the use of discriminating judgment; the results may not satisfy the wisely critical reader. Conclusions, though they may be based on extensive exploration, must often be summed up in a sentence or two, without cautious modification or elaborate exposition. But one can only do his best, and choose the things he believes to be the most significant and useful.

This volume does not pretend to be in the main a history of constitutional law as announced by the courts. I have sought above all to make it concrete and not abstract, to associate constitutional principles with actual political and social conditions and with actual controversies reaching far beyond the court-room. But in many cases this association had to be presented briefly or to be plainly indicated only by inference. The great controversies, however, needed to be treated with sufficient detail. After all, the most important question, during the first three-fourths of a century under the Constitution, was the question whether the nation would survive, continue to live as an undivided whole. The most significant and conclusive constitutional decision was not rendered by a court of law but delivered at the famous meeting of General Grant and General Lee at Appomattox. This is only an illustration of the fact that, not judicial pronouncements, but great controversies, discussed and rediscussed by statesmen and the common people, are, or may be, the crucial matters.

It may seem that I have given disproportionally brief attention to the first third of the present century. If that be a just criticism, it may, nevertheless, be pointed out that, when we view the occurrences within our own memories, we are in danger of forcing unduly our own prejudices upon the reader. Only the greatest historians have ever succeeded in writing objectively of their own times. Furthermore, in discussing recent events it is difficult or impossible to get perspective; and perspective is for the historian his one necessity. And yet the apparent brevity of treatment of the later years is partly not real. Constitutional decisions, rendered in the early decades of this century, are often cited or briefly discussed in connection with problems arising in the more distant past. Frequently—and I hope with due caution—problems of early years are appraised by the principles laid down at a later time. Among the 342 cases referred to in the course of the book, 112 were decided in the twentieth century. Perhaps I ought to add that I have not attempted to trace constitutional developments after 1932.

I wish to acknowledge the suggestions furnished by some of my colleagues and others: Professor Arthur H. Kent; Professor Edward W. Hinton; Professor Avery O. Craven; Professor Quincy Wright; Professor Rodney L. Mott; Professor Edward S. Corwin; Professor James G. Randall; Dr. Howard K. Beale. I wish also to give full recognition to the patient and intelligent labors of my assistant, Miss Marjorie L. Daniel.

The reprinting of this volume has given me the opportunity to make a few changes, chiefly because of the appearance of new data. It may be well also to add here a few words to the preface of the earlier edition, especially to expose more clearly the method of treatment that I followed in the composition of this volume. My intention, when I planned the book, was not to continue the narrative beyond 1900. But I found it undesirable to stop abruptly; the interpretation of the fourteenth amendment necessitated continuation into the early decades of the present century; and the reader will find, I think, the main principles of interpretation and application of the amendment as far as they were announced before about 1925. It seemed desirable also to present at least briefly in a final chapter some of the more conspicuous problems of the early twentieth century. Of the 112 cases that were

decided in the present century and referred to in this volume, seventy-
five are mentioned and in some instances briefly discussed in chapters
before the last. For example, it did not seem necessary, when the
draft act of the Civil War was under discussion, to omit reference
to the Selective Service Act and the Court's decision in 1918. It seemed
proper in a discussion of the Jacksonian period to call attention to
the development of the presidential office and to differences of opinion
in the early twentieth century. There appeared to be no violent dis-
tortion of historical method, if, when discussing a case decided in 1793,
attention be given to decisions bearing on the subject though they
were rendered in 1904 and 1907. In the debates on the Missouri Compromise of 1820, the equality of the states in the Union was one of the
main subjects of dispute; and it seemed unwise to omit in that connection the judicial pronouncement of 1911. When the Alien and Sedition Acts were considered in the text, it seemed wise to mention decisions rendered over a century afterward.

Throughout the book I have not refrained, when discussing controversies of an early date, to notice, in text or footnote, principles that
were announced in later years; important decisions of the later nineteenth century are mentioned in connection with judicial determinations
or events of earlier decades. For example, when dealing with Marshall's
decisions, the text calls attention to principles announced in 1878; to
leave the Dartmouth College Case without a brief presentation of later
interpretations or modifications, appears to me undesirable.

In other words, the method is in some measure topical; at least,
there is no attempt to be bound by strict adherence to chronology. Such
adherence is likely to leave the reader in some confusion or possibly
with misconception of actual constitutional order. I hope that the reader
will gather not only a proper knowledge of the constitutional movement of the more distant past but also some appreciation of the constitutional system as it was at the end of the first quarter of the present
century. The method of treatment seems to me to be helpful in bringing
out the continuity of constitutional development and the vital connection between the earlier and the later years.

Andrew C. McLaughlin

CONTENTS

CONTENTS   xiii

A CONSTITUTIONAL HISTORY
OF THE
UNITED STATES

CHAPTER I

INTRODUCTION

To find a beginning of American constitutional history is a difficult or impossible task. Certain important principles of constitutional government were in existence long before the United States was founded; some of these principles are commonly, though rather loosely, said to have had their origin in Magna Charta. This means only that, to know fully the forces and ideas which are embodied in our constitutional system, it is necessary to know the main course of English constitutional history. There are—to choose a simple example—in the Constitution of the United States terms and provisions which disclose their full meaning only when studied as a part of English constitutional history—habeas corpus, bill of attainder, common law, trial by jury, and other phrases. Moreover, the institutions and the elementary, though all-important, constitutional principles were not suddenly begotten in the America of the eighteenth century. Even in recent years the courts of this country have found it necessary to examine the laws and constitutional principles of England which were very old when the Federal Convention met in Philadelphia in 1787.

Furthermore, institutional forms as distinguished from principles were the product of long growth; to some extent their developments can be traced in English history. They are, however, more distinctly seen in the American colonies. When these colonies became states, their institutions were patterned in very large measure on the actual institutions of the colonies as they had developed in preceding decades. The framers of the federal Constitution were in their turn guided by the state constitutions; they did not enter upon their great task by ignoring the past; they did not seek in any large degree to invent what was new and untried. A complete constitutional history of the United States would include, therefore, at least a full outline of colonial development. Indeed, the states as they stand to-day are a part of our system of government, and an exhaustive treatment of our history would necessarily deal with the origin and development of state insti-

3

tutional forms; it would, for instance, deal with the bicameral system and the position and authority of the governor. But if one is to compress his work within manageable and readable limits, he must begin somewhere and curb his anxiety to seek origins and to portray the forces which worked through the earlier centuries. The purpose of this work is to trace the main lines of constitutional development for more than a hundred and fifty years, beginning with the middle of the eighteenth century. State history must be largely neglected, but not totally lost to view.

Constitutional history, moreover, when viewed in its entirety, is of almost limitless extent, because to comprehend it fully one must have in mind social and industrial change and movement. Institutions and principles do not develop or move in a vacuum; they bear the impress of actual social need and of imperative adjustment, even though the waves of time often seem to dash in vain against the walls of habit and of established practice. But here again, there is so much to be taken into account that one must exercise continuous restraint. He must be satisfied by only occasional references to the pulsations of the social and economic life which cause constitutional controversies and account for important determinations by voters, legislatures, and courts.

In discussing the earlier period covered by this work, the purpose of the writer is to dwell upon the emergence of the constitutional system as embodied in the Constitution of the United States. Some attention must be paid to the transformation of colonies into self-governing commonwealths, and to the principles on which state constitutions were founded, for that was the heart of the Revolution. But I do not expect to enter upon more than incidental study of the growing irritation between the colonies and the home country. There is no need of prolonged examination of the dispute as a mere prelude to war. The causes of the conflict by arms which broke the empire in twain have been often told by competent scholars. Our main purpose must be to look for ideas, the announcements of doctrines, the unfolding of principles, which are of significance because they entered into the American constitutional system, when that system came into tangible existence.

There are two main thoroughfares which may be traced in traversing the three decades before 1788: (1) one of these marks the course of developing principles of limited government which was supposed to guard individual liberty. Legally limited governments were the impressive products of the generation which formed state constitutions and brought the United States as a body politic into being. (2) The other main thoroughfare is that which led on to the particular form which the United States assumed; with the adoption of the federal Constitution, a federal state was founded. This was a state almost, if not quite, new to the world, though to-day states of similar structure dot the earth. As a system of political order, federalism is characterized by a distribution of essential powers of sovereign authority among governments; each government has its distinct share of powers; and as long as the system remains unchanged by some constitutional process, each has its inviolable hold upon its field of activity. To put the case concretely—the United States is a federal state, because it is a composite or complex system of political organization; it has the quality of diversification, not of concentration or complete consolidation.[1] The central government on the one hand and each state on the other have their respective spheres of legal authority. The United States differs from a mere league of totally sovereign states and from a totally unitary state.

If we look upon the Revolutionary period as a period in which constitutional principles developed and found expression, and in which institutions were produced, if we are not content with the war and the cleavage of the old empire, if we examine the years to discover their creative character, we find the two main achievements which have already been mentioned—the establishment of limited government and the founding of the federal state. These were the products of discussion and aspiration. Every period in history must be evaluated by its results; only thus can its actual life be comprehended. The Revolutionary period, which lasted for a generation and ended with the adoption of the federal Constitution, was peculiarly prolific in ideas, principles, and political philosophy of a practical character; it ended in the successful building of a political structure which has survived.

Much of what is important to us as evidence of the creative forces of the Revolutionary period comes to light in an examination of the arguments used in the years before the war. Probably we can see better

---

[1] It would be easier to describe the United States as a body in which sovereignty is divided between state and nation. And that would probably be the definition of the men of the late eighteenth century. But that brings up the question whether sovereignty can be divided; and the vaguer definition given above seems therefore preferable here. If sovereignty is complete political authority, then there seems to be only one possessor of sovereignty in our system, viz., the power that can amend the Constitution of the United States.

than did the statesmen of the time the full significance of the contest, because we know the results; we realize the implications of what was said and done as history brings them into the light. Our interest in those discussions is not due to any desire to discover whether, on the basis of the constitutional system of the old empire, the position taken by the colonists was legally sound or not. We must bear in mind the historical processes of preceding decades and also the immediate character of the controversy; but we must select those things which we find leading up to the end—the establishment of institutions and the crystallization of principles in the American constitutional system.

As one examines the speeches and pamphlets and resolutions which were put forth to support the colonial position, he discovers, quite naturally, that the lines which led on the one hand to limited government and were designed to protect individual liberty, and the lines which, on the other hand, led to the final foundation of the federal state—that is to say, the two lines of progress selected for special attention in this work—were interlaced; the arguments and pronouncements were mutually supporting. The declarations against parliamentary taxation included a demand for protection of the individual from arbitrary taxation and also the right of the colonies as constituent parts of the empire to tax themselves; they included, therefore, the striving for personal rights and for the recognition of colonial competence. The rights of the individual and the rights of each colony appeared, though logically distinguishable, to rest in some respects on a common foundation.

If chronological order is to be followed, rather than purely logical order, we may expect to find this interweaving; and in general it may be necessary to leave to the reader the comparatively easy task of determining whether the facts and arguments as presented point to the coming of limited governments guarded by written constitutions or give evidence of the principle of diversification which is embodied in the federal state. In the minds of the men of the time, the inevitable and fully-developed results of their own words were not of course perfectly plain. They were participants in a great movement, the full products of which could not be entirely appreciated.

CHAPTER II

THE OLD EMPIRE

In the middle of the eighteenth century Britain had a wide-reaching empire. It was beset with difficulties, for there were enemies of long standing who were not content. The empire was powerful and prosperous. Studious efforts had been made on the basis of mercantilism to build up a self-sustaining empire. Rigorous enactments were passed to ward off invasion by commercial rivals and to hold the profits of the empire within its own hands. There had been some attempts to simplify the colonial system, which was, however, still very complex; for things had moved along under no well-defined and consistent plan. There were two types of colonies: corporate colonies and the provinces. The corporate colonies chose their own officials and had charge, without substantial interference from Westminster, of their own internal affairs. There were two kinds of provinces: proprietary, with a charter granting to the proprietor considerable authority, which, however, in the course of time proved to be not easily or independently exercised; and royal provinces (only one, Massachusetts, having a charter), in which the royal governor as the Crown's agent was supposed to carry out the royal behests. It is quite apparent that the royal colonies were most directly, effectively, and immediately controlled from Westminster.

Each colony had an assembly, in which at least one chamber was elective. And these assemblies were not lacking in self-respect or in activity. Royal governors complained of headstrong legislatures desirous of having their own way and ready to ignore the orders sent from across the ocean. In large degree, the colonies managed their own internal affairs, occasionally hampered by royal instructions and disallowance of colonial acts. Their external affairs were in the hands of the Crown. Acts of Parliament, especially sundry measures directing the course of external commerce, had been passed and were more or less obeyed. Nothing like complete analysis of the situation can be presented here and none is here attempted. The salient fact is the reality of diversity, complexity, and the existence of an imperial system in which there was a large measure of colonial self-government. The colonies were daily growing in self-assurance, in economic well-being, and in political competence; and the time was near when they were prepared to announce their rights or to demand assurance as to what their rights were.

Not that there was a spirit of disloyalty or intentional independence; but the colonies had been living their own lives, not without restraint, but with considerable freedom. Virginia, for instance, had managed her internal affairs for over a century; her political capacity was high; any attempt to change the political system by encroaching upon the colonial field, especially in matters of taxation, was sure to awaken opposition. Connecticut, a corporate colony, complacent in her possession of self-government, serves as another example. Resentment was certain to be aroused by the intrusion of the hand of the British government, if it should roughly disturb the habits and the rights of the colony. The essential matter is this colonial competence which had been strengthened by decades of experience. The right or the propriety of interference with an established régime was not decided and cannot be decided on the basis of mere logic or abstract governmental theory.

In a general view of imperial administration and control, certain elements stand forth with some distinctness. Great officers of state were the agencies through which royal management was actually exercised. Among these ministers the Secretary of State for the Southern Department had chief charge of American affairs. The Privy Council had wide and in some respects effective authority. The Board of Trade was a body engaged in gathering information, in consultation, advice, and recommendation rather than in issuing direct and authoritative orders; but its influence was of importance and its views upon questions of colonial policy and management were often determinative. The royal authority was chiefly and most conspicuously exercised by (1) appointment and commissioning of the royal governor; (2) instructions which the governor was directed to carry out, and which were likely to include orders for the use of the gubernatorial veto or directions to see that certain policies were followed in the colony; (3) disallowance by the king in council of colonial statutes, probably the most effective and far-reaching method of control;[1] (4) review of

---

[1] Some evidence of the extent of the use of disallowance can be seen from the following statement: "Of 8,563 acts submitted by the continental colonies, 469 or

the decisions of colonial courts by the Privy Council acting in its judicial capacity.

As a general rule, the royal control was not exercised heedlessly. The investigations of the Board of Trade were commonly painstaking and were conducted fairly and intelligently. There was little ill-considered and hasty interference with colonial affairs; and this appears to be especially true of the exercise of disallowance and judicial review. Power was used, on the whole, not for the purpose of rude intrusion, but for essentially non-local purposes, or for ends which appeared to be of imperial scope and interest.[2] But disallowance, though the most effective means of retaining imperial authority and building up a homogeneous empire, was often a source of annoyance to the colonies, more, it seems, because of delay and uncertainty before actual use of the power than because of its objects or effects. While the colonies legislated and colonial courts sat and issued decisions, the Board of Trade and the Privy Council strove, not altogether without result, to maintain and build up a common system of law—or at least a colonial recognition of certain principles. The colonies did not absorb in all respects the forms and procedure of the common law; but especially in those matters which dealt with civil rights and liberties, the history of English constitutionalism was by no means ignored. It is not easy to distinguish those elements in the common law which can safely be placed within the realm of constitutional prin-

5.5 per cent. were disallowed by orders in council." E. B. Russell, *The Review of American Colonial Legislation by the King in Council* (Columbia University *Studies in History*, etc., LXIV, no. 2), p. 221. "The royal disallowance was an executive rather than a legislative act, performed not by the king but by the Council as his executive agent. It was an exercise of the royal prerogative, an expression of the king's supreme authority in the enacting of laws by inferior law-making bodies, whose right to make laws at all rested on the king's will. . . . The royal disallowance was, therefore, not a veto but an act of regulation and control, in the same sense that a royal letter and instruction was an act of regulation. In fact, disallowance and instruction were synonymous, for both expressed in different forms the royal will." C. M. Andrews, "The Royal Disallowance," Am. Antiq. Society *Proceedings*, new series, XXIV, p. 343.

[2] Professor Andrews classifies the actual purposes of disallowance as follows: "The policy which governed the board and its advisers had four leading aspects. First, to defend the law and custom of the British constitution; secondly, to guard the interest and welfare of British subjects; thirdly, to protect the colonies or any of their inhabitants from ill-advised legislation; and lastly, to prevent the passing of laws that were extraordinary, oppressive, improper, or technically defective." The first group, Andrews says, was the largest, but "Probably the most important of all the reasons for disallowance was that an act affected the trade and shipping of the kingdom or the privileges and prerogatives of British subjects." *Ibid.*, pp. 349, 354. See also, O. M. Dickerson, *American Colonial Government 1696-1765*, ch. V.

ciples and those elements which have to do only with relationships and responsibilities of individuals. But it is plain that those elements of constitutional right, not commonly catalogued as belonging within the field of common law, were common, in large measure, to the empire, if we use the term to include England and the continental colonies.

During the century ending in 1780, 265 cases were carried from colonial courts to the Privy Council.[3] It is, of course, difficult to say how much emphasis should be laid on the exercise of judicial control and how much it affected later events and the establishment of American institutions. There is no very tangible evidence indicating that the American system of appeals from state to federal courts was a direct inheritance from the old imperial system; but one would not dare to deny its influence; institutional principles and practices do not spring out of nothingness; they are not self-creative. Though there appears to have been only a few cases in which the scope of the legislative authority of a colony was passed upon by the Privy Council in a manner to suggest plainly a complete parallel between the power of the Privy Council and the power of our courts in declaring an act void, the practice of judicial review, we are justified in assuming, was not without its influence upon later times.

The decisions of the Council in exercising the power of disallowance often involved constitutional principles in a very broad sense; there was an attempt to maintain the general principles of the common law and of the law of Britain, which thus became, if we use general terms, in a sort of way the law of the empire. Disallowance of colonial acts, though technically to be distinguished from judicial decisions, often in reality was exercised in such a manner as to keep the colonies within their own sphere and to preserve parliamentary acts, notably the navigation acts, from violation or impairment.[4] In other words,

[3] A. M. Schlesinger, "Colonial Appeals to the Privy Council," *Pol. Sci. Quart.,* XXVIII, p. 446. "The king in council reversed the colonial courts 76 times and affirmed their decisions 57 times. . . . In 77 cases no decision is recorded; 45 cases were discharged for non-prosecution. Only eleven appeals are noted in the records as having been heard *ex parte." Ibid.,* p. 448.

[4] The discussion in the Constitutional Convention of 1787 concerning the proposal to give Congress the authority to negative state acts will be spoken of in a later chapter. The proposal bore a distinct resemblance to the old disallowance. Madison mentioned the resemblance. It is interesting to see the men founding the American system considering, some of them advocating, the institutional practice which had been used by Britain for the maintenance of an empire. But it is even more interesting to see that the framers of the Constitution finally recognized the distinction between disallowance because of the undesirability of an act, on the one hand, and on the other, *judicial determination* of the illegality of an act.

if a colonial law were disallowed because it exceeded the power of the legislature under a charter, or because it disregarded the principle that the colony should not pass an act contrary to the law of Britain, the disallowance really involved the question of the extent of legislative authority. There is therefore a certain resemblance between such disallowance and a decision, which, under our constitutional system, may be rendered by an American court passing upon the validity of state legislation which is asserted to be in violation of laws, treaties, or the Constitution of the United States.

The rôle of Parliament, beyond the passage of navigation acts and acts of trade, had not been conspicuous. If a thoughtful colonist had been asked concerning the extent of parliamentary power, his answer presumably would have been that Parliament was the supreme legislative authority in the empire; but the admission would have been qualified, as Jeremiah Dummer had at one time qualified it, by saying, "And shall not the supreme Judicature of all the Nation do right?" [5] Here again it is impossible to speak with complete accuracy in a few words, or to show with absolute certainty the extent to which parliamentary statutes had invaded or affected internal colonial concerns. But the main fact is the absence rather than the plenitude of parliamentary legislation. The colonists had lived for years in most respects unaffected by such legislation, and must have thought of the legislature at Westminster as far away from their own immediate interests.

There were a few enactments which more or less directly affected the internal legislation and freedom of action of the colonies. The conspicuous ones are the following: the Piracy Act (1700) may perhaps be thus classified though in general it appears plainly an imperial matter; but more important are the acts fixing the rates at which foreign coins should circulate (1708), establishing the post office (1710), making colonial real estate and slaves chargeable with debts (1732), providing for naturalization (1740), extending the Bubble Act to the colonies (1741), and forbidding the issue of paper money in New England (1751). But these acts were not of a purely local character;

---

[5] "It's true, the legislative Power is absolute and unaccountable, and King, Lords and Commons may do what they please; but the Question is not about Power, but Right: And shall not the supreme Judicature of all the Nation do right? One may say, that what the Parliament can't do justly, they can't do at all. *In Maximis minima est licentia.* The higher the Power is, the greater Caution is to be us'd in the Execution of it, because the Sufferer is helpless and without Resort." Italics of the original omitted. Jeremiah Dummer, *Defence of the New-England Charters* (Boston, 1745), pp. 40-41.

considerations of the general welfare entered into them; and at all events the very fact that such acts were passed and thus brought within the purview of actual imperial control is a matter of some consequence. This field of parliamentary legislation was occupied because of the teachings of experience or because of apparent need. And it is from the real, rather than the formal or theoretical scope of imperial power, that the empire was taking shape—a matter of importance to anyone seeking the historical foundations of the American constitutional system.

It ought to be said that, in addition to the acts referred to above which appear to have the essential quality of acts passed for general imperial interests—at all events, not to be intrusions on colonial management of internal affairs—there were certain other acts which were passed to check American manufacturing and thus to protect British interests. These measures, such as those restricting the making of woolens and, at a later time, hats and iron, rested on the assumption that the insular interests of Britain should receive particular support. But, we should notice, there were other acts or provisions of acts which were not peculiarly for British advantage.[6] Most of these matters which Parliament had actually dealt with do not appear, in the light of our own system, to be suitable subjects for local legislatures alone in a well-articulated system in which powers are distributed between the central government and the states.[7]

For a hundred years, parliamentary acts had with greater or less earnestness and success regulated the external commerce of the empire. Against the barriers set up, the colonists had at times complained. The extent to which the acts were broken is not for us a subject of extreme importance. The fact is that such acts were passed, the colonists were accustomed to the regulations. One act, the West India Act or Molasses Act of 1733, was systematically avoided; it was designed by high duties to force the colonies to purchase the products of the British insular possessions and not those of the foreign West Indian colonies, especially the commodity which was one of the main articles of colonial

---

[6] "Some of the interests sacrificed for the good of the Empire were British, some colonial." G. L. Beer, *British Colonial Policy 1754-1765*, p. 196.

[7] Notice the provisions in our own Constitution concerning piracy, the post office, paper money, naturalization, bankruptcy, and rates of foreign coins. The act making real estate chargeable with debts was intended to prevent a colony from releasing persons who came to settle in the colony from their obligations to the creditors to whom they owed money before their migration; it may be looked upon as an enforcement of the principles of reasonable comity.

commerce; in the mid-eighteenth century and before that date, the rum made from West Indian molasses formed the basis of many profitable New England voyages. The policy of mercantilism pointed unerringly to the regulation of trade as a main function of an imperial government, a function second only to providing for defense. The activity of Parliament in this particular was very real; every colonist, though only slightly interested in traffic on the high seas, must have been conscious of this fact.

Once again, for purposes of emphasis, it is desirable to remind the reader that the colonial assemblies managed their own "internal police." They levied taxes for local purposes; they had in reality defended themselves as parts of the empire—more or less inadequately and without concert, it is true, but fairly successfully; their local trade was in their own hands; and they in short did the many things—sometimes under pressure from the representatives of the royal authority—that concerned the daily life of the colonies. Even in the royal colonies, the legislative assemblies had little by little worn away the actual authority of the Crown. The old method of opposition, by which the royal power in England had been gradually diminished, was often used successfully by colonial assemblies, for possession of the purse strings enabled the assemblies to reach their goal.[8]

But in certain aspects the scope of the imperial power stood forth conspicuously. Parliament regulated trade beyond the confines of any single colony. The Crown had charge of the post office, foreign affairs, war and peace, the army and navy, leaving the subordinate military forces, the militia, to the individual colony; it was in the mid-century beginning to take active general charge of Indian affairs and trade with the Indians; it had ownership of the Crown lands within the royal colonies and was soon to become busily interested in the whole western question; it had taken some part in the establishment of the colonies, though they had been begun by private enterprise; it was prepared soon after the mid-century to enter upon plans of founding and organizing new settlements. Now, every colonist must have been

---

[8] "Despite the refusal of the home government to accept the inevitable, the fact remains that before 1760 the royal control of the colonies was largely destroyed. . . . Thus colonial government was no longer in the hands of the royal officials; the authority of the royal and proprietary governors relaxed; they lost their patronage, their control over the military, their ability to employ secret funds, to check riots and revolts, to manage a police or to take any adequate measures to ensure security at home, or to protect the frontiers against the French and Indians." C. M. Andrews, *The Colonial Period*, pp. 174-175.

familiar with the main features of the picture of the empire. Some conspicuous and important powers of imperial scope must have been taken for granted; to their existence and the need of their existence the colonists were accustomed.

In the whole picture of the imperial system we see plainly the fact that each colonist was living under two governments; the colonial government which was peculiarly his own was not in possession of complete authority. The colonists at no time were wonted to the sight of a single government exercising more than limited power. If one insists that in theory the government at Westminster had complete and unalloyed power, the fact, nevertheless, if practice and habits are properly taken into account, is that the government allowed colonial governments to function. Should we admit that in theory Parliament was supreme, we must nevertheless say also that this supreme power encroached but little upon internal colonial affairs; and if we recognize the continuing power of the Crown, we must see in addition the unremitting activity of colonial assemblies. The Crown, through disallowance and judicial review, brought into light the fact of colonial subordination and the existence of a central government controlling certain matters of general importance.

This rough sketch of the empire, the reader must be warned, presents only a general picture, subject to modification or enlargement in details. But anyone even slightly familiar with the American constitutional system will see at once the similarity between the general scheme of the old empire and the American political system of federalism. Plainly enough in essentials, if we look at the actual *practice,* the empire of the mid-eighteenth century was a diversified empire; powers were actually distributed and exercised by various governments. And if we consider the conspicuous powers exercised by the central government, we find the list strikingly like the list confided by the Constitution of the United States to the national government. If we add to the powers exercised by imperial authority the single power to obtain money by taxation, the similarity is even more evident. It is quite impossible to estimate with detailed accuracy the measure of influence of this system in the days when the Americans were called upon to organize their own empire, but that the Americans were not influenced by their own experiences and by well-known relationships appears to be an impossible supposition; such a supposition would compel us to think that the American system of federalism was a sudden creation, unbegotten by historical forces and unguided by teachings and habits of the past.

Britain had, therefore, in the mid-eighteenth century an empire characterized in actual practice by the principle of distribution and not by concentration of authority. If Great Britain in 1760 had reached out her hand and said, "This is the law of the empire; thus the system is formed," she would have recognized herself as the most considerable member of an empire with the pivotal characteristic of federalism —many governments, each possessing its legal sphere of authority. If the empire could have been hardened or petrified into the form then existing, it would have been in essential and important particulars a federal empire.[9] This system, we must notice, was the product of growth largely unintended and unplanned. Its value came from that very fact, from opportunistic effort, from allowing, often heedlessly, spontaneous growth. Developments had been the product of natural forces and conditions.

A narrative account of colonial history would relate a series of controversies, not violent but argumentative in character, between the representative assemblies and the royal or proprietary governors. If these are made to stand forth, the impression is left of a steady movement forward to independence; but there was no real purpose of breaking the ties of allegiance. Disputes do disclose, however, a fairly continuous development of the sense of self-dependence and the desire of the colonists, especially the politicians, to have their own way; political controversy was laying the foundations for future action because of the steady growth of competence and the influence of practical experience. We are dealing in these pages, however, not with the causes of disruption but with a general scheme of empire, as it actually took shape and persisted; we are dealing with actual distribution of powers in a

[9] In an earlier paper ("The Background of American Federalism," *Am. Pol. Sci. Rev.*, XII, pp. 215-240), I said that Great Britain by the middle of the eighteenth century had a working federal empire. To this statement Professor G. B. Adams, though not criticizing the main contents of the paper, objected on the ground that an empire with a central government free from control by the empire as a whole was not a federal empire. The criticism may be sound. The important idea is, however, that the chief quality of federalism—distribution of powers—appeared in the working practices of the old empire, and that distribution, as a practical fact, does more than merely *suggest* the scheme of distribution in the American constitutional system of a later day. The similarity between actual distribution in the old empire and the distribution provided for by the Constitution of the United States is apparent and discloses the evident fact of a family relationship; in essentials American federalism was the child of the old empire.

complex imperial system. The colonists might occasionally object to the power of a royal or proprietary governor, and they occasionally fretted under the prohibitions of the navigation acts and acts of trade; but the general system continued. Any attempt to overthrow the system, or to alter its essentials, any attempt, above all, to encroach upon that sphere of authority which had developed under the play of natural forces, was sure to awaken resentment and alarm.

We shall see, as we go on, various evidences of the effect produced by the dualistic structure of the old empire. The practice of that empire, as the colonists knew it and felt it, must be appreciated for an understanding of the rise and establishment of American federalism. In the succeeding chapters, covering the years before the federal Constitution was framed and adopted, this work has in mind two things: the emergence of federalism as a legal system and the protection of individual right and freedom under limited government.[10]

[10] In addition to the references cited in this chapter, see E. B. Greene, *Provincial America 1690-1740* (*Am. Nation Series,* VI) ; E. B. Greene, *The Provincial Governor in the English Colonies of North America* (*Harvard Historical Studies,* VII) ; M. W. Jernegan, *The American Colonies 1492-1750;* H. L. Osgood, *The American Colonies in the Seventeenth Century,* III; H. L. Osgood, *The American Colonies in the Eighteenth Century,* I-II.

CHAPTER III

THE PROBLEM OF IMPERIAL ORGANIZATION.
THE ALBANY PLAN

By the middle of the eighteenth century Britain was faced with the problem of imperial organization. We cannot say that her leaders were fully conscious of the fact; but looking back upon those years it is plain to us that, if her empire was to survive undamaged, a problem of great difficulty presented itself. And this problem, as we now view the facts, was central and insistent in its demands. Even if the blind could not see it, the question was there. Could the empire be so organized and arranged that it could find adequate means of preserving and using its strength? Could actual conditions be so envisaged that colonial valor and colonial enterprise would, without diminution of colonial self-government, contribute their vigor to the essential unity and development of the empire? The pressing and immediate question appeared to be means of securing men and money for imperial defense; but the necessity of the case demanded the establishment of a system which would not only recognize imperial unity but conserve local rights and local self-respect. Principles of self-government, consonant with the actual competence and experience of the colonies, must find their place in the system; principles of individual liberty, the outgrowth of English constitutionalism—and deeply cherished by the colonists— must be watchfully guarded; and all arrangements and plans must be adjusted to the needs of a powerful and developing general system of empire.

That Britain failed to find a solution of the problem the reader need not be told. The story of conflict and failure is of immense consequence in the history of British imperial growth; but we are entering upon the study of events which produced the United States; and our attention is called to the fact that essentially the problem was passed on to the American states when they became free to organize their own empire. To solve the problem of imperial organization, therefore, grounded as it was in the history of the old empire, was the central, dominating, irrepressible task of a generation (1750-1788).

If there had been no danger to Britain because of the menace of France and her Indian allies, events might have moved on quietly for a time; the old easy-going system of imperial management might have continued undisturbed, save by the recurring evidence of unrest characteristic of a people on this side of the water who were not easily content. And if in any crisis the colonists had freely, generously, and thoughtlessly turned over their funds to be spent in defense, the problem of imperial order, we may well imagine, would not have been pressing. But this is only saying that if responsibility, expense, and coöperation had been assumed voluntarily, there would have been no need of law or compulsion. The cold fact was, however, that the colonies would not work together, and if there was one thing they disliked more than granting money—a dislike common to humanity in general—it was the pain of being deprived of the right to argue about the matter and of spending the money themselves, if spend they must.[1] Hesitation, debate, and delay are among the pains and penalties of popular government.

So varied were the colonies, so different in their social and industrial life, so far-removed one from the other, that any scheme of voluntary coöperation or systematic union presented enormous difficulty. Each colony had a fixed sense of its own importance and not much interest in its neighbors or sympathy with its neighbors' needs. In one view of the case, this readiness of each colony to look out for itself, this sentiment of local allegiance, this sense of self stands forth as the salient feature in the picture of the mid-century. So evident were the conditions that it appears to-day as a remarkable fact that the colonies were later, under pressure of common danger, brought to coöperation and union. And still, underlying all this reality of variation and of local loyalty, political institutions were strikingly similar;

---

[1] Franklin writing in 1754 portrayed the situation: ". . . some Assemblies being before at variance with their governors or councils, and the several branches of the government not on terms of doing business with each other; others taking the opportunity, when their concurrence is wanted, to push for favourite laws, powers, or points, that they think could not at other times be obtained, and so creating disputes and quarrels; one Assembly waiting to see what another will do, being afraid of doing more than its share, or desirous of doing less, or refusing to do any thing because its country is not at present so much exposed as others, or because another will reap more immediate advantage; from one or other of which causes, the Assemblies of six out of seven colonies applied to, had granted no assistance to Virginia, when lately invaded by the French, though purposely convened, and the importance of the occasion earnestly urged upon them. . . ." Franklin, *Writings* (A. H. Smyth, ed.), III, p. 203.

grumble as the colonists might over navigation acts or disallowance, they had worked out their system of self-government on the basis of a common tendency and desire; they all cherished the principles of English liberty, as they conceived it. From one end of the land to the other they spoke the same political language, cherished the same ideas, believed in the same fundamental doctrines; in these respects—omitting differences in religion and in habits of life and industry which militated against a feeling of common interest—there existed a real unity, a unity which was based on possession of certain principles and aspirations. Contradictions often appear to be the core of life; and so we find the principles of self-government and of self-control making for segregation, and yet the very desire for political self-determination constituted a common quality and made for coöperation when political interests and economic needs were at stake. In the long run, coöperation and ultimate union were found to be necessary for the preservation of the separate colonies and states.

Long before the mid-eighteenth century, various suggestions or plans of union had been put forth as well as attempts on the part of the royal authority to simplify the colonial system. But it is difficult to trace with assurance the influence of these proposals upon later movements. The New England Confederation which was established in 1643 and lasted for forty years, most of the time in a state of desuetude, had some effect in suggesting a general scheme of union when that problem in the eighteenth century demanded an answer.

After the peace of Aix-la-Chapelle, which was in reality only a truce, it was apparent that a new struggle with France was likely to come, a contest for dominion in the great valley beyond the mountains and also, it might well be, for the very existence of the coast colonies. What part were the colonies prepared to play in this encounter? Would they freely enlist their men and open wide their purses, or would they hesitate and talk and insist upon their privileges when danger was at their very doors? Their general attitude furnished little hope or consolation. It was especially necessary to hold the Iroquois Indians and in general to handle the Indian question with discretion. Recognizing the need of effective coöperation, the Board of Trade planned a conference of colonial governors, and in 1753 instructions were sent to the governors of royal and proprietary colonies [2] north of the Caro-

---

[2] Virginia and New Jersey did not send representatives. The Lieutenant-Governor of New York seems to have represented Virginia. Representatives from Rhode Island and Connecticut attended.

linas directing them to see that commissioners were sent to treat with
the Six Nations and to renew the "Covenant Chain" with them. The
formation of some kind of union appears to have had the sanction of
the British authorities.

The outcome was the Albany Congress of 1754. After the Indian
matters were disposed of, the commissioners entered upon consideration of the need for union and coöperation. They unanimously decided
that a union was absolutely necessary for security and defense, and
they drew up a plan of union which appears to have been based on
"Hints" furnished by Franklin and, though seemingly the product of
considerable discussion, was probably largely his own handiwork. The
plan deserves careful examination for various reasons, but especially
because it points unerringly to certain distinct elements in the general
problem of union; and those matters came to the fore and pressed for
consideration not only then but in later years; it plainly discloses the
nature of the task of imperial organization and it points to certain
definite powers which were of common interest and needed to be confided to some central authority. It marks the beginning of an effort
to single out the things that should be turned over to a central government or an agency of central administration. Any effort to formulate
a basis of classification and distribution of powers is of commanding
interest to the student of the American political system as it came to be.

By the terms of the plan, a Grand Council was provided for, the
members to be chosen by the representative assemblies in the colonies.[3]
The general executive authority was given to a President General who
was to be appointed and supported by the Crown, and who had the
right to negative all acts of the Council; with the advice of the Council, he was to make all Indian treaties which concerned the colonies
generally, and he was to make peace or declare war with the Indians.
The President and the Council were authorized to regulate Indian
trade, and to "make all purchases from Indians for the Crown, of
lands [now] not within the bounds of particular Colonies, or that
shall not be within their bounds when some of them are reduced to
more convenient dimensions." They were to have charge of founding
new settlements on such purchases and of providing laws for them,
until the Crown should "think fit to form them into particular
Govern^{ts}." To this central authority also was confided the right to

---

[3] No representation from Georgia was provided for. There were to be not less
than two nor more than seven representatives from any one colony. *Documents
Relative to the Colonial History of the State of New-York*, VI, p. 889.

raise armies and pay them, to equip vessels of war, and "for these purposes" to levy "duties, imposts or taxes. . . ." A General Treasurer was to be appointed and also a particular treasurer in each colony when necessary; and the President General and the Council were to have the extraordinary power of ordering the sums in the treasuries of each government into the General Treasury, or of drawing on them "for special payments. . . ." All laws were to be, as near as might be, agreeable to the laws of England and should be transmitted to the king for approbation. The President General could nominate for the approval of the Council all military officers, while all civil officers could be nominated by the Council for approval by the executive.

The plan, therefore, granted to the proposed central government a method and the power of raising money; it marked out a fairly definite sphere of action; and it bestowed ample authority over four subjects of supreme importance—Indian affairs, war, purchase of wild lands, and control, for a time at least, of western settlement. The commissioners even ventured to provide for proportional rather than equal representation of the several colonies in the Grand Council and to suggest quite plainly the desirability of limiting the extent of the larger colonies, some of which had claims to a vast territory beyond the mountains. Both of these latter proposals were sure to arouse opposition and in later years proved to be especially perplexing obstacles in the way of forming a federal union.

The document, as we read it to-day, appears remarkably precocious. It foreshadowed the anxieties, aspirations, disputes, and achievements of the years ahead. We need not be astonished that thirty-five years later, after the debates, trials, and tribulations of a generation, Franklin declared that in his judgment, if this plan or something like it had been adopted and carried out, "Separation of the Colonies from the Mother Country might not so soon have happened, nor the Mischiefs suffered on both sides have occurred perhaps during another Century." [4] But the significance of these proposals lies not so much in their suggestions for a method of saving the old empire as in their indication of the route that was to be followed in later years.

There was small ground for hope that the plan would be favorably received on either side of the ocean. It received short shrift in England. The Board of Trade had its own ideas and drafted a plan, but it need not detain us; it is significant, however, as proof of the fact

[4] Franklin, *Writings* (A. H. Smyth, ed.), III, p. 226, note 1.

that the home authorities were seriously considering the problem of empire and chiefly the need of acquiring and controlling means of defense. No colony accepted the Albany proposals.[5] Franklin said the plan was not favored in the colonies because it allowed too much to prerogative and the Crown disapproved it because it "placed too much Weight in the Democratic Part of the Constitution. . . ." [6]

The plan indeed was ahead of the time; though measures for defense were imperative, any general plan of union, in which the colonies would have a large share, and which would be political in character and not calculated for defense alone, was objectionable to Britain, and on the other hand, colonial self-esteem and caution looked askance at intrusion upon hard-won preserves. How disconcerting to the average colonist was the proposal to establish a central government—even a central government in which the colonies would be represented—which could put its hand into the colonial treasury and draw forth funds even for war against a common enemy! "Every Body," said Franklin, "cries, a Union is absolutely necessary; but when they come to the Manner and Form of the Union, their weak Noddles are perfectly distracted." [7] The task was to distract weak and strong noddles alike for several decades to come. This was no job for puny minds. Something, the shrewdest heads on both sides of the water believed, had to be done. The Board of Trade declared that if the colonies would not acquiesce in some such arrangement as the one proposed by the Board, there was no alternative but an act of Parliament.

Eager and anxious for imperial stability and for success in the war with France, Franklin wrote the next year (1755) that a plan of union ought to "take Place" and be established by king and Parlia-

[5] Nothing could more amply bring before us the watchful regard for colonial pence than the instructions of Connecticut to her commissioners at the Albany Congress. She desired the commissioners to join with others in representing to the king the defenseless state of his governments in America, to make evident the great expense Connecticut had assumed in comparison with southern colonies in former wars, and to be sure that the obligation on Connecticut was "no greater than of necessity." The commissioners were to "agree to no proportion of expence save for the present occasion," to make no presents to the Indians unless necessary, and to oppose as far as possible everything of that nature. They were to see to it that Connecticut troops served with eastern and not western troops, if there were any such distinction, and they must be careful not to bind the colony in any way before ratification by "this Hon. Assembly." *Public Records of the Colony of Connecticut,* X, p. 268 note.

[6] Franklin, *Writings* (A. H. Smyth, ed.), III, p. 227 note.

[7] *Ibid.,* III, p. 242.

ment. "'Till it is done never expect to see an American War carried on as it ought to be, nor Indian Affairs properly managed." [8] Colonial governors were beginning to think that the only way to get money for defense was parliamentary taxation and some of them advised it. Governor Shirley of Massachusetts declared the behavior of the colonies showed the necessity not only of "a Parliamentary Union, but taxation. . . ." [9] The ministry during these years must have received ample assurance [10] that the colonies would not act of themselves and that some sort of compulsion was necessary.[11] The course of the war probably hardened this belief, and yet some of the colonies participated with a good deal of vigor, especially under the inspiring leadership of Pitt. And it is an interesting example of the apparent perversity of human nature that the freer colonies, those most fully in command of themselves, were the readiest to do their part. In the royal colonies, where affairs were most directly under royal control, bickerings and disputes with the governor were prominent and almost continuous. The proprietary colonies indulged in enjoyable disputes with the representative of the proprietary authority and yielded with ill grace to any demands for effective coöperation. The spirit of indi-

[8] *Ibid.*, III, p. 267.

[9] *Documents Relative to the Colonial History of the State of New-York*, VI, p. 940.

[10] See the "Sharpe Correspondence," I, *Archives of Maryland*, VI, pp. 96, 99, 203. "This perverseness of the Virginia Assembly has induced the Gover[r] to apply home as I am told some other Governors have also done for an Act of the British Legislature to be obligatory upon all the Govern[ts] equally, & compel them to contribute their Quotas for the Defence & Protection of their Properties & His Majesty's American Dominions. . . ." Sharpe to Calvert, September 15, 1754, in *Ibid.*, p. 99. Sharpe made his own proposals—a poll tax, or a duty on wines and liquors, or a stamp duty. ". . . or can I now think we can have any Dependence on the Assemblies of the different Colonies with't a B. Act of Parliam't to raise a gen'l Tax on all his M'y's Subjects on this Cont't. . . . I much want to know if any Thing is done in regard to the Union of the Colonies. The Scheme from Albany on y't head is by no means agreeable to our people, and I dare not give my Opinion thereon, as I hear it lies with his M'y in Council; but it will be very agreeable if any Thing can be done to bring the wrong-headed People in this Part of the World to a proper Understand'g of their pres't Danger, and to rouse an Emulat'n among them for their Safety in rais'g proper Supplies for defeat'g the Designs of the Com'n Enemy." Governor Dinwiddie to the Earl of Halifax, February 12, 1755, in "Dinwiddie Papers," I, Va. Hist. Soc. *Collections*, new series, III, pp. 496-497. See also Governor Dinwiddie to the Lords of Trade, February 23, 1756, in "Dinwiddie Papers," II, Va. Hist. Soc. *Collections*, new series, IV, p. 340.

[11] For references, see G. L. Beer, *British Colonial Policy 1754-1765*, pp. 44-46 note. For an account of conditions, see E. I. McCormac, "Colonial Opposition to Imperial Authority During the French and Indian War," University of California *Publications in History*, I, no. 1, pp. 1-98.

vidual right and an insistence on colonial privileges were marked features of the situation. Despite all of the difficulties, Britain triumphed in the war, but the embarrassment resulting from incoherence and from the absence of a thoroughly articulated empire was apparent.

In some respects the war probably brought forth a certain sense of imperial unity, and it may have developed a recognition of identity of interests between one colony and another. But we must not speak with too much assurance. Each colony was quite conscious of itself and of its own right to guard what it deemed to be its privileges. The war gave special opportunity for the exercise of political craftsmanship. At the end, if the need of coöperation was more evident than it had been at an earlier time, and if there was glorification of British prowess and exultation over the victory, nevertheless imperial unity, organization on any viable basis suitable to the conditions, and the establishment of any effective system were even more remote, to all appearances, than before hostilities began.[12] If one is inclined to blame the British statesmen for not working out a scheme of imperial order then or at a later time, he must surely also perceive the herculean nature of the task; and, moreover, the background of colonial incoherence and of colonial self-sufficiency must be taken into account in any attempt to appreciate the job which the Americans faced, not only in 1754 but in later years, when, for their own well-being, there was imperative need of coöperation and continental organization. The casual reader is probably inclined to overemphasize the single feature of the individual's belief in his personal liberties and his readiness to defend them, and is likely to underestimate the sense of self which was cherished by each colony as a constituent part of an empire. And we must remember that the empire had grown up without any consistent and adequate political system, the eyes of the British administration being fixed largely on trade, while Britain watched her enemies and her commercial rivals in Europe. A commercial rather than a well-articulated political empire had received the weight of attention.

---

[12] "Despite the coöperation of many colonies in a common military undertaking, which, it may be, smoothed the way to an eventual understanding, the dislike and even the enmity of colony for colony were as great in 1763 as in 1750, while the absorption of each in its own affairs was as profound as at any time in its history." C. M. Andrews, *The Colonial Period*, pp. 232-233.

CHAPTER IV

THE WRITS OF ASSISTANCE AND THE REVENUE ACT

Let us now take up the course of events in the years beginning about the end of the French war. In giving this chronological narrative, we shall be concerned chiefly with detecting the statement of principles of government. We shall find some confusion and some inconsistency; we shall find a shifting from one position to another, and we should err if we assumed that the Americans had at the beginning a perfectly clear line of thought which was finally triumphant. But we shall see from the experiences of the fifteen years before independence was declared some fairly definite ideas emerging; and we shall have in mind, amid the confusion, those principles that finally became domesticated and firmly seated in our institutional system; especially we shall look for two essentials of American constitutionalism: (1) that governments have only limited power; (2) that governmental power may be distributed among governments; in other words, we shall find the two most salient ideas of the American system: the written Constitution, binding on governments, and the American federal system.

In 1761 an event took place that John Adams declared marked the birth of the American Revolution—"Then and there", he said, of the famous speech of James Otis against writs of assistance, "the child Independence was born." The circumstances were these. Massachusetts merchants had been in the habit of treating with a lofty disdain the navigation act burdening their trade with the foreign colonies in the West Indies. Just how common and grave was this habit of disobedience (vulgarly known as smuggling) is of no considerable importance. Soon after the death of George II (1760), an application was made to the superior court of Massachusetts for the issuance of writs of assistance; for it appears that old writs ceased to be good six months after the death of a monarch. The writ in question gave to the persons to whom it was issued general authority to search for smuggled goods, and its terms were very comprehensive and sweeping. In opposition to the granting of such authority by the issuing of the writ, James Otis appeared before the court. He and his associates were faced by able lawyers on the other side. The subject of dispute was significant. The brilliant oratory of Otis was called into being to denounce a process which, he contended, threatened the sanctity of one's dwelling and the security of property.

We do not know very much of what Otis said. John Adams, then a young lawyer, present at the argument, wrote in later years an extended account; but that account was written nearly sixty years after the speech; and, quite plainly, Adams included in his statement a sort of summary of the Revolutionary argument; it probably differs in many ways from the line Otis followed. However that may be, Adams did put down at the very moment, certainly practically contemporaneously, a brief outline of what Otis did say; and that brief outline is full of significance. Otis denounced the dangerous character of the writ as an infringement of an Englishman's right of "House"; he dwelt upon the extensive authority given by the writ and declared it to be "against the fundamental Principles of Law." ". . . all Precedents," he declared, were "under the Control of the Principles of Law." He had in mind, presumably, the fundamental principles of British freedom, and he probably used the word "Constitution" as that word was and is used in Britain; but he went further, declaring that Parliament was incapable of enacting legislation providing for such a writ. As the question before the court was the lawfulness of the writ, he would not stop by endeavoring to discover whether parliamentary authority sanctioned it; for not even Parliament could lawfully go beyond the constitution. Furthermore, the court must uphold the constitution even against Parliament itself; the court must "pass such acts into disuse." [1]

We find here, therefore, more than fervid eloquence appealing to the sacred rights of Englishmen; we find American doctrines, startling probably to the solemn judges who heard them. Even an act of Parliament might be no law, and if so, it was the duty of the court so to declare. It seems almost incredible that Otis comprehended the full import of his own words; for in after years such an elementary principle in American law was not clearly seen by even keen-minded men.

---

[1] "As to Acts of Parliament. An act against the Constitution is void; an act against natural equity is void; and if an act of Parliament should be made, in the very words of this petition, it would be void. The executive Courts must pass such acts into disuse. 8 Rep. 118 from Viner. Reason of the common law to control an act of Parliament." The words "executive Courts" distinguish the judicial tribunals from the General Court, which was the legislature of the province.

But there stands his assertion. So, to Otis at least, the British constitution must have been something real and tangible, fairly direct and conclusive in its limitations. The logical conclusion from his statement is that an unconstitutional law is not necessarily a bad law, or an inappropriate law, or even a law running counter to endeared traditions; an unconstitutional law is not a law at all; it is void; and a court must so declare. One inevitable result of this reasoning he did not state and, as far as we know, perhaps he did not see; if the act in question was no law, no one was under obligation to obey it. He did, however, say that the court must not treat the act as law and thus aid in enforcing obedience.[2]

Otis's argument is so impressive and so prophetic of the constitutional system which was to come that we are in danger of overestimating its actual effect or of thinking of him as the creator of a fundamental American doctrine. We can well believe, however, that the doctrine was as precocious as it was prophetic, though it was by no means altogether without historical background. It was for the moment ahead of its time, but the days were soon to come when the refuge of Americans was to be found in the declaration that some things were beyond the power of Parliament, and if Parliament exceeded its power, it acted illegally. We should not overstress the appeal to judicial authority as a relief from unconstitutional enactment, but notice the thought on which that appeal rested: there are limits, constitutional limits, to power. That was the staff on which developing revolution was to rest, and that was the foundation on which American constitutionalism was to be reared. In light of what went on and of what men said in succeeding years, it is not so much judicial duty as this fundamental idea of limited as over against unlimited power that is of chiefest significance. Judicial authority must wait upon the developing principle that limited government is possible and that unlimited government is tyranny.

[2] Logically of course, if an act is not a law, *no one* is legally bound by it; he can simply refuse to obey the lawbreaker. Perhaps Otis saw it all, though later words from him make doubtful his full grasp of it. But it is to be noticed that he did summon judicial support to the constitution, and did announce a judicial power; and thus he helped to bring in the American conception of the Constitution as a law to be recognized by courts. And still, the fact is not so much the extent of Otis's influence as the inference we are entitled to make concerning a condition of affairs or an attitude of mind which would account for the doctrine. Possibly we should also take into account the fact that in this case Otis was a lawyer arguing for his client. It is by no means impossible for a lawyer to announce as undoubted law principles which he scarcely hopes the court will accept, and to which under less demanding conditions he would scarcely adhere himself.

This belief that there were legal limits, beyond which Parliament must not go, was associated with the belief in natural law and the unchanging principles of reason and justice; "natural equity" were Otis's words. And of similar import were "Reason of the common law"—those fundamental principles were supposed to be established in English constitutionalism. In this connection he referred to Coke,[3] having in mind Coke's dictum in the famous Doctor Bonham case.[4] It thus appears that Otis, and others that thought like him, believed their position was founded on revered legal authority; for had not Lord Coke himself plainly spoken? ". . . it appears in our books, that in many cases, the common law will control Acts of Parliament, and sometimes adjudge them to be utterly void: for when an Act of Parliament is against common right and reason, or repugnant, or impossible to be performed, the common law will control it, and adjudge such Act to be void." Had not other British judges announced the same doctrines? But withal—and this is important—Otis was asserting that *Britain had a fixed constitution* and its limits were applicable, indeed must be observed, in the empire. Thus he was announcing that there already existed what in reality the Americans were to create as a tangible fact. This tendency to assert the undeniable existence of principles, which were to find institutional expression, is a significant quality of the American Revolutionary process, of which we shall find other proof.

We do not and cannot know just how much effect these declarations of Otis had on the popular mind, though we do know that the mind of the average New Englander was prepared for them. The writs were issued after some delay, and we need not follow their history. Other events were in progress which brought in new objections and similar doctrines concerning the exercise of British authority. These events now claim attention.

In 1764 Parliament passed, at the suggestion of George Grenville, First Lord of the Treasury and Chancellor of the Exchequer, the Sugar Act, part of a general plan for enforcing the acts of trade and navigation and for obtaining some revenue from the colonies.[5] It is

[3] That is the significance of his reference to "8 Rep. 118 from Viner."
[4] All this is elaborately treated by Horace Gray, afterwards Justice Gray of the federal Supreme Court, in an appendix to Quincy (Mass.) *Reports* (1761-1772).
[5] "It was the first statute distinctly taxing the colonies, and marked a radically new departure in colonial policy." G. L. Beer, *British Colonial Policy 1754-1765*, p. 277.

not our business to look into Grenville's purposes minutely. However great the temptation to obtain relief for the financial burdens of Britain by getting money from America, whatever justification there might appear to be in compelling America to pay at least a portion of the expense incurred for her defense, the means and method proposed by Grenville proved to be obnoxious. They were, furthermore, innovations upon long-established practices. That the sums received from certain duties in the colonies had fallen far short of meeting the cost of collection, producing, it was said, about one-fourth of the cost,[6] was not necessarily a reason for attempting to make the customs remunerative. The acts of navigation were not for revenue, but for regulation, restriction, or prevention of trade.

The purposes for which such acts were passed might have been obtained, even if no revenue at all reached the public coffers. It is not our affair to scrutinize the violation of law or to examine the ineptitude or corruption of certain officials, though the story is an interesting, if rather sordid, tale. The facts are that the plan of enforcing the acts of navigation and at the same time using them or parts of them for revenue was a most serious innovation; and it was an innovation likely, not only to affect seriously the commercial practices of the colonies, but also to arouse colonial opposition because it involved new principles. At a later date Burke put the thing in a nutshell: "Whether you were right or wrong in establishing the colonies on the principles of commercial monopoly, rather than on that of revenue, is at this day a problem of mere speculation. You cannot have both by the same authority. To join together the restraints of an universal internal and external monopoly with an universal internal and external taxation is an unnatural union,—perfect, uncompensated slavery."[7] Men had borne the burdens of trade regulations, "Because men do bear the inevitable constitution of their original nature with all its infirmities. The Act of Navigation attended the colonies from their infancy, grew with their growth, and strengthened with their strength. They were confirmed in obedience to it even more by usage than by law."[8] Burke thus saw not only what he called "uncompensated slavery" in the joining of taxation and burdensome restriction, but that the colonies were used to the regulations of trade but not used to the imposi-

---

[6] George Grenville, *The Regulations Lately Made concerning the Colonies* (London, 1765), p. 57.

[7] Edmund Burke, *Works* (revised ed.), II, p. 35.

[8] *Ibid.*, II. p. 33.

tion for revenue.[9] An examination of the West India Act—the Molasses Act of 1733—shows that its purpose was to compel the colonies to forego trade in certain commodities with the French and Spanish colonies in the Caribbean. The Sugar Act lowered the duties, plainly to get revenue.

This act of 1764, adding in some respects rather grievous restrictions on colonial trade and onerous red tape for their enforcement, provided that trials might be instituted in any colonial court, or in any vice-admiralty court which might be appointed over all America, as the informer or prosecutor might elect. This provision was naturally unwelcome to the colonial mind, for it might involve a trial in a distant court with all the accompanying burdens and inconveniences. But objectionable as such new regulations were, they were not more ominous than the announcement in the act that the purpose was to improve the revenue, that "the commons of Great Britain, . . . being desirous to make some provision . . . towards raising the said revenue in America, have resolved to give and grant unto your Majesty the several rates and duties herein after-mentioned. . . ." [10]

We can pass over the outcries against the burdensome character of the act as a restriction on trade, and against the unwisdom of interfering with a commerce beneficial to the colonies and to Britain herself, significant though those outcries were as indications of colonial feeling or provocative as they might be of later rebellion. There appeared little or no opposition, as far as I am aware, to the general right of Parliament to regulate the trade of the empire. There was opposition to the revenue plan as well as combative argument breaking out into open violence when the proposals for raising revenue were further carried out in the Stamp Act the next year (1765). The opposition to the revenue-raising feature of the Sugar Bill was especially presented by Otis in his *Rights of the British Colonies Asserted and Proved,*[11] a pamphlet of such popularity that it deserves special examination.

The author begins in the orthodox fashion of those questioning

---

[9] It is no answer to say that the colonists would have objected to furnishing revenue, even if the whole navigation system had been abolished. Nor is it an answer to say that some acts, the West India or Molasses Act chiefly, had been in reality sedulously disobeyed. The principles of the act were essentially new.

[10] Italics and capitalization of the original omitted. For the details of this act, see *The Statutes at Large,* 4 Geo. III, c. 15.

[11] This pamphlet was mentioned in Parliament in the debates on the repeal of the Stamp Act.

the authority of government; he considers the origin of government, and finds its "everlasting foundation in the unchangeable will of God, the author of nature, whose laws never vary." [12] There must be in every society a sovereign, absolute, and uncontrollable power, "from whose final decisions there can be no appeal but directly to Heaven." [13] This power was originally and ultimately in the people, who did not make nor can they rightfully make an absolute unlimited renunciation of their essential right. As people are the origin of power, and as government obtains such authority as it has from the people, "There is no one act which a government can have a *right* to make, that does not tend to the advancement of the security, tranquility and prosperity of the people." There remains still in the people a supreme power to remove, or alter the legislative, when they find the legislative act contrary to the trust reposed in them.[14] But though the reasoning will support revolution and though it contains the essence of democratic thinking as far as the ultimate authority in the state is concerned, this pamphlet was not intended to preach revolution. Otis probably believed that Britain would accept its fundamentals without alarm. He pointed out that the colonists, having endured the hardships of settling a new country, did not renounce their natural liberty, for the gift of God cannot be annihilated.

The powers of Parliament, the supreme legislature of the kingdom and its dominions, Otis expressly acknowledges. Parliament has the right to make acts for the general good and by naming the colonies to bind them as well as the subjects within the realm.[15] No authority,

---

[12] "It is by no means an arbitrary thing, depending merely on compact or human will for its existence." But he resorts to compact as the formal method of setting up human authority. ". . . the form and mode of government is to be settled by compact, as it was rightfully done by the convention after the abdication of James II. . . ." Italics of the original omitted.

[13] The distinction here between Locke and Otis is noteworthy. Otis emphasizes the power of a people before government is set up; he seems to see a people as a real preëxisting authority.

[14] Cf. John Locke, *Two Treatises on Civil Government* (Henry Morley, ed.). bk. II, sec. 149.

[15] He asserted that to his personal knowledge this principle had been held to for twenty years in Massachusetts. "The act of navigation is a good act, so are all that exclude foreign manufactures from the plantations, and every honest man will readily subscribe to them." In the years after the war a number of changes and additions were made to the system for the regulation of trade; these were in part aimed to encourage certain branches of colonial industry. There was some indication of an appreciation of the fact of the unity of imperial interests. See G. L. Beer, *The Commercial Policy of England Toward the American Colonies* (Columbia University *Studies in History*, etc., III, no. 2), p. 145.

however, has a right to make itself arbitrary nor can any supreme power "take from any man any part of his property, without his consent in person, or by representation." [16] In other words, the principles of representation must apply in the empire.

To solve this problem, or as a partial solution, he commits himself to the idea of representation in Parliament, a proposal never taken very seriously by any number of persons on either side of the ocean; the proposal, nevertheless, is in itself proof beyond cavil that Otis was not then merely a revolutionary firebrand, and in succeeding portions of his paper he gives us visions of a really free and glorious empire. [17] We mistake the whole character of the work if we see in it only a pamphlet making for rebellion. Doubtless he is at times vague; he was as a matter of fact troubled by the same perplexing problem that vexed Locke and others presenting the idea of natural law as a restraint upon governmental authority. Could order be based on the right to disobey? So Otis acknowledges openly the authority of Parliament, for "There would be an end of all government, if one or a number of subjects or subordinate provinces should take upon them so far to judge of the justice of an act of parliament, as to refuse obedience to it." What then is to be done, if on the one hand government has no right to exceed certain limits and, on the other, people have no right to disobey? [18] This is his answer; this is the peaceful solution: "If the reasons that can be given against an act, are such as plainly demonstrate that it is against natural equity, the executive courts will adjudge such acts void." [19] Thus, for unauthorized acts of government, Otis finds a remedy in the organs of government itself.

The appendix to this *Rights of the British Colonies Asserted and Proved* [20] contains the substance of a memorial presented to the Massachusetts house in pursuance of the instructions of the town of

[16] Italics of the original omitted.

[17] The whole argument through this portion of the pamphlet is enough to show that Otis in those days was not a mere declamatory malcontent or mischief-maker. His main idea after all was the liberty of Englishmen and the building up of a free empire based on the lasting foundations of unchanging law.

[18] I am not at all sure I should say that people, according to Otis, have no right to disobey. But he was here, after flatly announcing popular right, showing that there was a remedy short of revolution and disorder, short of an "appeal . . . to Heaven." He was putting forth a constructive argument.

[19] Italics of the original omitted.

[20] I cannot be absolutely sure that this appendix appeared in the original edition. There were several editions or reprints. The one I have had access to is the Boston edition, 1764.

Boston to its representatives, and by the house ordered to be sent to the colony's agent in London. " 'Tis hoped," said these men of Boston, "it will not be considered as a new doctrine, that even the authority of the parliament of Great-Britain is circumscribed by certain bounds, which if exceeded their acts become those of meer power without right, and consequently void. The judges of England have declared in favour of these sentiments, when they expresly declare; that acts of parliament against natural equity are void. That acts against the fundamental principles of the British constitution are void." [21] In a footnote to this memorial, quotations are made from English judicial decisions to the effect that acts against natural equity are void.

Concerning natural rights Otis of course refers to Locke and makes incidental reference to certain writers of continental Europe. Connected with the memorial there appears a striking passage from Vattel, the influence of which is easily discerned in the later developments of American law: "It is here demanded whether, if their power [legislative power] extends so far as to the fundamental laws, they may change the constitution of the state? The principles we have laid down lead us to decide this point with certainty, that the authority of these legislators does not extend so far, and that they ought to consider the fundamental laws as sacred, if the nation has not in very express terms given them the power to change them. For the constitution of the state ought to be fixed. . . ." [22] In the same passage from which these words are taken, Vattel says that the legislators cannot change the constitution without thereby destroying their own foundation.

In this pamphlet Otis does not let loose his thunderbolts against the acts of trade, as Adams many years later asserted that Otis did in the writs of assistance case. On the contrary, he accepts the navigation act as "a good act. . . ." He admits that Parliament has the right as well as the power to bind both Ireland and America, but "whether this can be extended to an indefinite taxation of both, is the greater question." He asserts that Parliament has on the whole not taxed; for the Molasses Act was intended as a prohibition, "and 'tis pity it had not beem [sic] so expressed, as there is not the least doubt of the just and equitable right of the parliament to lay prohibitions

[21] Italics of the original omitted.
[22] Emeric de Vattel, born in Neuchâtel, 1714. His *Droit des gens* was published in 1758, and published in English in 1760. The edition to which I have had access is dated 1811, where the reading is the constitution of the state "ought to possess stability. . . ." *The Law of Nations,* bk. I, p. 11.

thro' the dominions, when they think the good of the whole requires it. But as has been said, there is an infinite difference between that and the exercise of unlimited power of 'taxation [*sic*], over the dominions, without allowing them a representation. . . ." [23]

[23] Otis here distinguished between taxation and regulation, but the idea was not as yet brought out distinctly.

CHAPTER V

THE STAMP ACT

Grenville's general scheme for obtaining revenue from the colonies culminated in the Stamp Act (1765)—of unhappy memory.[1] It provided for a burdensome tax upon the colonies and was of course immediately resented, and that too with an approach to unanimity. How could the colonies declaim against the tax? What routes could they follow? (1) They might object in general to the grievous financial burden, and this they did. (2) They denied not only the justice but the legality of the legislation—or at least they denounced it as violation of elementary principles of English liberty; they asserted that as British subjects they were immune from taxation because they were not represented; they set forth their rights as Englishmen. (3) They declared that the colonies, as corporate parts of the empire, had their own governments possessed of the power to tax and to regulate internal concerns. The resolutions of public assemblies and the arguments in pamphlets did not of course clearly distinguish between the various modes of opposition. The contentions, though mutually supporting, were different; we find them on the one hand asserting the rights of individuals under government; and on the other announcing, even when men did not see the full nature and could not see the product of their argument, that the British empire was in reality not a simple empire but a composite empire in which each commonwealth had its share of duty and authority.

This fact is well illustrated by the resolutions offered by Patrick Henry to the Virginia House of Burgesses. They appear to have been scattered broadcast through the colonies, as broadcasting was done in

[1] Not merely a provision for an occasional halfpenny stamp. Newspapers or pamphlets contained in half a sheet carried "a stamp duty of one halfpenny, for every printed copy thereof." Every advertisement carried a tax of two shillings; admission to the bar, ten pounds, though a license to retail spirituous liquors, only twenty shillings; a diploma or certificate of any degree taken in a college, university, academy, or seminary, two pounds. These are but indications of the character and the weight of the tax. The act provided for stamps on legal documents, playing cards, etc.

those simple days. They declare that the Stamp Act encroached on the fundamental rights of Englishmen and that Virginia had its own assembly which from time immemorial had possessed the right to tax Virginians. In other words, the people had a twofold protection—the fundamental constitutional immunity belonging to Britons and also the constitution or structure of the empire.[2]

To protest against the Stamp Act, a Congress assembled in New York in October, 1765. The resolutions of the Congress are possibly not quite so plainly and forcibly constructed as those of Henry, but they follow the same general lines: His Majesty's liege subjects in the colonies are entitled to the inherent rights of natural-born subjects within the kingdom; it is essential to the freedom of a people, and is the undoubted right of Englishmen, that no taxes be imposed on them without their consent, given personally, or by their representatives; the colonists cannot be represented in Parliament; the only representatives of the people are those chosen by the people of the colonies, and no taxes ever have been or can be imposed on them but by their legislatures.[3] They acknowledge not only the same allegiance to the Crown that is owing from His Majesty's subjects within the realm but "all due subordination to that august body the parliament of Great-Britain."

The debates in the House of Commons on the repeal of the Stamp Act are illuminating because they disclose the nature of the controversy, and it seems well to discuss them before passing on to a fuller

[2] Some of the resolutions were not passed by the assembly; but all except one appear to have been in the set that was widely spread abroad. See the resolutions and notice the critical discussion by M. C. Tyler in his *Patrick Henry* (revised ed.), pp. 69-76 and especially p. 75, note 1. The resolutions assert first, that the colonists are entitled to all the privileges ever held by the people of Great Britain; second, that the royal charters declare that they are entitled to all immunities of natural-born subjects of England; third, that taxation by the people or persons chosen by themselves to represent them is the distinguishing characteristic of British freedom; fourth, that the Virginians have "uninterruptedly enjoyed the right of being thus governed by their own Assembly in the article of their taxes and internal police"; fifth, that the general assembly have the only and sole exclusive right and power to lay taxes and impositions; sixth, that the people of Virginia are not bound to yield obedience to any law imposing taxes on them except the laws of the general assembly of their province; seventh, that any person maintaining that any other person or persons have the right to tax the people of that colony shall be deemed an enemy of the colony.

[3] The above condensation does not give the full content of the resolutions, but it is sufficient to show their character. For the Congress and its resolutions, see H. Niles, *Principles and Acts of the Revolution in America*, p. 451 ff.; *Select Charters* (William MacDonald, ed.), pp. 313-315.

consideration of the American arguments. We find the parliamentarians, then as later, taking refuge in an absolute announcement of complete control over the colonies. The mere statement of this authority, these men seem to have thought, scarcely allowed room for protest or needed the support of elaborate argument, though ere long detailed defense of Britain's power was presented by countless pamphleteers and eager penmen. Parliamentarians scorned distinctions and refinements; Parliament, sovereign in the empire, necessarily had the right to tax. And it is desirable, in passing, to note the last resort of noble minds—an insistence upon naked legal rights; to surrender under compulsion would lower the dignity and honor of the kingdom. The duty to maintain parliamentary dignity, to wrest from the colonists an acknowledgment of parliamentary power, even though no one might intend to use it or at least to use it harshly, was first and last of supreme consequence.[4]

William Pitt, who was then the idol of America and for years to come was hailed as the founder of the empire and the friend of freedom, vigorously attacked the Stamp Act and denied that Parliament possessed the power to tax the colonies. Asserting the authority of the "kingdom over the colonies, to be sovereign and supreme, in every circumstance of government and legislation whatsoever", he denied that taxation is a part of the governing or legislating power. "The distinction between legislation and taxation is essentially necessary to liberty."[5] Grenville scouted any difference between internal and external taxation, declaring that "this kingdom has the sovereign, the supreme legislative power over America," that taxation is "one branch of the legislation", and it is, and has been, exercised over those who are not and never were represented.[6] In reply to Grenville, Pitt

[4] The position of Mr. Nugent, afterwards Lord Clare, is characteristic of a "diehard"—a man willing to let all else go, if he can secure the acknowledgment of what he calls a principle. ". . . a pepper-corn," declared this gentleman, "in acknowledgment of the right, was of more value, than millions without." *Parliamentary History*, XVI, col. 97.

[5] *Ibid.*, XVI, cols. 99-100. This may appear to the reader an impossible distinction, and I have no wish to defend it. One might see, however, the mere fact that the Commons had taxation fully or nearly in their control in the kingdom; and as a practical fact, taxation *was* singled out as a particular power *in the constitution of the kingdom*. Might not such a distinction be applied to the empire? Any such argument as this of Pitt is of interest in this study because it illustrates the nature of the problem. Were there limits on the power of Parliament? Could you make distinctions between powers, or must you rest content with asserting that all powers and authorities are necessarily an undivided whole?

[6] *Ibid.*, XVI, col. 101.

struck another key: "If the gentleman does not understand the difference between internal and external taxes, I cannot help it; but there is a plain distinction between taxes levied for the purposes of raising a revenue, and duties imposed for the regulation of trade, for the accommodation of the subject; although, in the consequences, some revenue might incidentally arise from the latter." [7]

The examination of Benjamin Franklin at the bar of the House was dramatic, one might also say humorous, for the Yankee from Philadelphia was even then a man of mark, and if his customary humor was not in evidence at the time, it appears to us now as we read the pages of the proceedings. But the examination was, after all, confusing in some respects, if one aim of the witness was to bring out clear distinctions between what Parliament could and what it could not do. He seems at one time to distinguish between external and internal taxation, at another to distinguish between taxation and duties or impositions laid for the regulation of commerce; the net result was probably to instill in the minds of his hearers the opposition in America to internal taxes.[8] Although he fumbled his argument a bit, he must have impressed upon the Commons the seriousness of the occasion, and he made one especially wise and humorous statement; it contained the elements of prophecy: "Does the distinction between internal and external taxes exist in the words of the charter?" he was asked. "No, I believe not." "Then may they not, by the same interpretation, object to the parliament's right of external taxation?" "They never have hitherto. Many arguments have been lately used here to shew them that there is no difference, and that if you have no right to tax them internally, you have none to tax them externally, or make any other law to bind them. At present they do not reason so, but in time they may possibly be convinced by these arguments." [9] If parliamentarians would not recognize distinctions, but insisted on absolute and complete power, then the colonists would be driven to deny that Parliament possessed any power whatsoever.

[7] *Ibid.,* XVI, col. 105. Pitt may have got this distinction from Otis, though Otis did not make the distinction so clear as it was to be made later. It more likely came from Dulany's *Considerations,* etc., a pamphlet discussed later.

[8] The reasons for the confusion in the minds of a good many persons doubtless were, first, the difficulty which human beings find in being logical, especially in practical politics; second, almost invariably those endeavoring to maintain that the colonists really did help to support the empire were led off into statements of the burdens of regulations which in their effect put money into the hands of British merchants and finally into the coffers of Britain.

[9] *Parliamentary History,* XVI, cols. 158-159.

The speech of Lord Lyttelton in the House of Lords [10] admirably illustrates how cleverly men may reason to reach foolish conclusions; and the results showed how unwise it is for statesmen to bandy raw logic. The noble lord accepted as fundamental "The last great maxim of this and every other free government . . . that 'No subject is bound by any law to which he is not actually or virtually consenting' ", and he then proceeded to announce that "If the colonies are subjects of Great Britain, they are represented and consent to all statutes"— equivalent to saying that, inasmuch as you admit that the foundation of British government is consent, as long as you remain subject you do consent to have money taken from your pockets whether you like the operation or not. There is no difference between internal and external taxes, he further declared; the Americans make no such distinction and Mr. Otis himself, "their champion, scouts such a distinction. . . ." By declaring the colonists exempt from one statute, he solemnly warned the assembled Lords, "you declare them no longer subjects of Great Britain. . . ." All of this is a pretty piece of legalism, but a very poor basis for practical statesmanship. Lord Mansfield [11] spoke much to the same effect as Lyttelton. No wonder that Pitt in the Commons exclaimed that he did not come into the House with law books doubled down in dog's-ears to defend the cause of liberty, and that Burke at a later time, scorning finespun theories, said, "The question with me is, not whether you have a right to render

[10] February 24, 1766, *Ibid.*, XVI, cols. 166-168.

[11] *Ibid.*, XVI, col. 172 ff. As illustration of the fact that in some considerable degree the British argument, at least in the ensuing years, was made not so much for money as for authority—for the recognition in theory of imperial might—see Chatham's statement in 1775: ". . . and when men are driven for want of argument, they fly to this as their last resource . . . 'acts of parliament (say their advocates) are sacred, and should be implicitly submitted to . . . for if the supreme power does not lodge somewhere operatively, and effectually, there must be an end of all legislation.'" *Lord Chatham's Speech on the 20th of January 1775. Taken by a Member* (London, 1775), p. 9.
The attitude of the more conservative Britons appeared in the protest or dissenting opinion of a number of the Lords (March 11, 1766), with respect to the repeal of the Stamp Act. These Lords contended that repeal in the face of tumults would make the Parliament ridiculous; that it was not only right, but expedient, for Parliament to exert its authority to lay a general tax on the colonies; that the American reasons for disobeying the Stamp Act extended to other laws, and, if admitted, would set the colonies absolutely free from any obedience to the power of the British legislature; and that concessions would lessen the respect of all His Majesty's subjects and throw the whole empire into confusion. In addition to the debates on the Declaratory Act and the repeal of the Stamp Act found in the *Parliamentary History*, XVI, important reports on these debates may be found in the *Am. Hist. Rev.*, XVII, pp. 563-586.

your people miserable; but whether it is not your interest to make them happy? It is not what a Lawyer tells me I may do, but what humanity, reason, and justice, tell me I ought to do." [12]

Nevertheless, we must take facts as they were. The British lawyers laid down absolute doctrines, unbending principles. And it is also a fact that there was serious difficulty in seeing the possibility of reconciling the power of Parliament with a reasonable or moderate freedom and self-dependence of the colonies. Instead of ridiculing British statesmen because they could not see the possibility of modified or incomplete authority, we may notice a similar blindness among many Americans. The truth is, the problem was in many aspects a perplexing one; and its final solution grew out of the nature of things and out of the necessities of the case rather than out of early and continuously clear perception of principles. But this is equally true: the defenders of American liberties in Parliament announced that there were limits to parliamentary authority; at least some of them saw that the colonies could have the right of self-taxation without dismemberment of the empire. The debates of 1766 showed fairly clearly that the gist of dispute was whether Parliament had in theory limited or unlimited authority; and that continued to be the source and center of disagreement.

Parliament repealed the Stamp Act, coupling it, however, with a fatuous Declaratory Act, the announcement of a principle, a warning that the government would not by one jot or one tittle abate its supreme authority.[13] The colonists accepted the olive branch and ignored the threatening rod; more accurately, they rejoiced in the repeal of the Stamp Act and paid little apparent heed to the announcement of power; but they never forgot Parliament's assertion of unlimited power to bind them "in all cases whatsoever." It is unnecessary to repeat that the validity of that assertion was the center of the Revolutionary controversy.

Let us leave the colonists rejoicing over their victory (a victory doubtless achieved more because of the fear or distress of British merchants than because of the weight of American resolutions and

---

[12] "Mr. Burke's Resolutions for Conciliation With America," *American Archives* (Peter Force, ed.), fourth series, I, col. 1760.

[13] The act, after stating that the colonies were "subordinate" and "dependent", went on to say "that the King's majesty, by and with the advice and consent of the lords spiritual and temporal, and commons of Great Britain, in parliament assembled, had, hath, and of right ought to have, full power and authority to make laws and statutes of sufficient force and validity to bind the colonies and people of America ... in all cases whatsoever." Italics of the original omitted.

arguments), and return to view more fully than we have yet done the nature of American opposition while the Stamp Act was still in force. Let us look first at certain pamphlets, selected not altogether at random, but chosen as indicative of able, fairly conservative, and influential expositions of America's case. In *The Grievances of the American Colonies Candidly Examined*,[14] Stephen Hopkins, Governor of Rhode Island, protested against the wisdom of the Sugar Act as an unwholesome interference with colonial trade, a trade beneficial to both Britain and the colonies.[15] He was far from a rebellious state of mind, though he pointed out that to tax the colonies as the Stamp Act did was to deprive them of long-established rights, and that "one who is bound to obey the will of another, is as really a slave, though he may have a good master, as if he had a bad one. . . ." Of greater interest was his acknowledgment of the power of Parliament to regulate trade and, furthermore, although each colony had a legislature, "there are many things of a more general nature, quite out of the reach of these particular legislatures, which it is necessary should be regulated, ordered and governed. . . . Indeed, every thing", he said, "that concerns the proper interest and fit government of the whole commonwealth, of keeping the peace, and subordination of all the parts towards the whole, and one among another, must be considered in this light. . . ." There must be this general power, superintending and ordering the whole, and that power "every man of the least knowledge of the British constitution, will be naturally led to look for, and find it in the parliament of Great Britain. . . ." Here, then, we find a conservative and calm presentation of an idea, so conservative and calm that it fails, perchance, in driving power: there is a whole, but there are also parts, and these parts have their own particular interests. To guard and upbuild those interests is the duty of Parliament; but that duty does not involve the right to disregard the legitimate rights of the colonies and their respective legislatures. What Hopkins sees or comprehends is an empire, within its limits are colonies possessed of their share of authority, and over all is one general superintending body whose business it is to care for the interests of the whole.

The next pamphlet to be examined came from the pen of Daniel

[14] London, 1766. The first edition had the title, *The Rights of Colonies Examined*.

[15] Hopkins's attack on the breaking up of the trade with the West Indies is not oratorical but damaging, a severe attack, in reality, on the unwisdom of the restrictive system. The attack came naturally from a Rhode Islander, for the rum, molasses, and slave trade of the Rhode Island merchants was large and lucrative, and to break it down spelled something like disaster.

Dulany of Maryland.[16] Here again we find the distinctions already mentioned. The colonies are dependent upon Great Britain; and the authority of Parliament may be justly exercised to preserve their dependence; but from that fact does not come the right to seize the property of the colonists. "In what the Superior may *rightfully* controul, or compel, and in what the Inferior ought to be at Liberty to act without Controul or Compulsion, depends upon the Nature of the Dependance, and the Degree of the Subordination. . . . May not then the Line be distinctly and justly drawn between such Acts as are necessary, or proper, for preserving or securing the Dependance of the Colonies, and such as are not necessary or proper for that very important Purpose?" [17] He speaks of the fact that the colonies are "impowered to impose internal Taxes", but he does not in reality make the distinction between internal taxes and external, or grant Parliament the right to levy the external. On the contrary, conceding to Parliament the right "to *regulate the Trade of the Colonies*," for "a Denial of it would contradict the Admission of the Subordination, and of the Authority to preserve it," [18] he declares that "there is a clear and necessary Distinction between an Act imposing a Tax for *the single Purpose of Revenue,*[19] and those Acts which have been made for the *Regulation of Trade,* and have produced some Revenue *in Consequence of their Effect and Operation as Regulations of Trade.*" [20]

[16] *Considerations on the Propriety of Imposing Taxes in the British Colonies, for the Purpose of Raising a Revenue, by Act of Parliament.* This pamphlet, like that of Hopkins, did not bear the author's name. I have used the second edition (London, 1766). Tyler says the first edition issued from the press in October, 1765. M. C. Tyler, *The Literary History of the American Revolution* (one volume ed.), p. 101.

[17] *Ibid.*, pp. 16-17.

[18] *Ibid.*, p. 47. Italics mine.

[19] *Ibid.*, p. 46. See also p. 48. Italics in the original.

[20] *Ibid.*, p. 46. Part of the italics mine. I do not mean to assert that in this respect Dulany's argument is all the way through so perfectly clear as to be plain even to the stupid or perverse. He admits, for example, that the imposition of a duty may in some instances be the "proper Regulation." But on the whole, he plainly distinguishes between the right to regulate and the right to tax. To the unwary reader he is also confusing because he argues that the colonies have paid taxes in Great Britain; but as a matter of fact he is dealing with the incidence of taxation—on whom does the burden of a tax ultimately fall? As well might we argue that if the United States to-day levies a duty on British steel rails, the people of Great Britain are taxed to the amount of the duty.

It is rather sad to recall that the writer of this able pamphlet, unable to follow the colonists into rebellion, was later vehemently denounced as a Tory and his property confiscated. This is one of many examples of the loss to America of men of active minds and distinguished ability whose services were much needed in later years.

This pamphlet is of undoubted significance. Dulany was a lawyer, educated in England, with a reputation on both sides of the Atlantic, a man of very remarkable mental gifts and learning. His insistence that the British Commons had no right to *"Give and Grant* the Property of the Commons of *America"* may have suggested to William Pitt the center of his argument in the House of Commons a few months after Dulany's pamphlet was published. ". . . what Right", asks the writer of the *Considerations,* "had the Commons of *Great Britain* to be thus munificent at the Expence of the Commons of *America?"* His argument against "virtual representation" is overwhelming and convincing.

In the pamphlets which have been mentioned as especially significant, we find objections to parliamentary authority and also evidence of a desire to single out certain measures as beyond parliamentary control. The distinction between taxation and regulation of trade is made or implied, and even if the distinction between internal and external taxes appears not very sound, it indicates a problem, an attempt to separate and distinguish one power from another; internal government and taxation belonged to the colonies.

In October, 1765, the house of representatives of Massachusetts, in answer to the Governor's speech, made a significant announcement of principles in a document attributed to the flowing pen of Sam Adams.[21] We are forced to present only a portion of the document, though the whole deserves careful reading. It was at once courteous, dignified, and cutting. "You are pleased to say, that the stamp act is an act of Parliament, and as such ought to be observed. This House, sir, has too great a reverence for the supreme legislature of the nation, to question its just authority: It by no means appertains to us to presume to adjust the boundaries of the power of Parliament; but boundaries there undoubtedly are. . . . Furthermore, your Excellency tells us that the right of the Parliament to make laws for the American colonies remains indisputable in Westminster. Without contending this point, we beg leave just to observe that the charter of the province invests the General Assembly with the power of making laws for its

---

[21] Samuel Adams, *Writings* (H. A. Cushing, ed.), I, p. 13 ff. *Massachusetts State Papers,* p. 43 ff. How much, especially in the earlier days, Sam Adams owed to Otis, is an interesting though for us not a very important question. Otis at one time said to John Adams, "I have drawn them all up, and given them to Sam to *quieu whew* them", at least so John declared. There is little doubt in my own mind that, whoever wrote the first draft of some important papers, the hand or the ideas of Otis are to be found in some of the papers commonly and perhaps rightly attributed to Sam Adams.

internal government and taxation; and that this charter has never yet been forfeited. The Parliament has a right to make all laws within the limits of their own constitution; they claim no more. Your Excellency will acknowledge that there are certain original inherent rights belonging to the people, which the Parliament itself cannot divest them of, consistent with their own constitution: among these is the right of representation in the same body which exercises the power of taxation." The most significant words are "boundaries there undoubtedly are", but we should notice the claim, based on the charter, of the right of the colony to make laws for internal government as well as taxation, and we should notice, too, the use of the word "constitution" and the apparent influence of Vattel.

A few days after this answer, the house drew up a series of resolutions declaring "That there are certain essential rights of the British Constitution of government, which are founded in the law of God and nature, and are the common rights of mankind. . . ." Then followed a number of declarations of their rights as Britons, the announcement that such a representation as the subjects in Great Britain enjoyed was "impracticable for the subjects in America", that the "several subordinate powers of legislation in America were constituted upon the apprehensions of this impracticability", and that "the only method whereby the constitutional rights of the subjects of this Province can be secure, consistent with a subordination to the supreme power of Great Britain, is by the continued exercise of such powers of government as are granted in the royal charter, and a firm adherence to the privileges of the same." [22]

To accuse one's opponents of harboring the most extreme views, and especially to charge them with advocating the conclusions which relentless logic may extort from their actual words, is a common practice of politicians and of all persons who indulge in heated controversy. We must therefore not take too seriously the assertions of royal officials or other informers who found the colonists even in 1765 or 1766 determined upon independence; nor need we give full credit to the announcements that the colonists were even then declaring their

---

[22] Samuel Adams, *Writings* (H. A. Cushing, ed.), I, pp. 23-25. Italics of the original omitted. In this connection it is well to quote a passage from a letter of Sam Adams, written November 13, 1765: ". . . the only way to preserve to the Colonists their rights as British Subjects, consistent with their acknowledgd Subordination to the supreme Legislature of Great Britain, . . . is to continue to them the same powers of Governmt, which they have hitherto been used to, with the same Checks & no other: This is all they desire:" *Ibid.*, I, p. 39.

complete freedom from parliamentary control. Perhaps some extremists went this far; for the people were indignant, and it is easy for indignant people to utter threats or indulge in extravagant expressions. "All of a sudden," wrote Thomas Hutchinson of Massachusetts in February, 1766, ". . . we have it advanced that acts of parliament of England or Great Britain have no more relation to us than acts of parliament of Scotland had before the Union." [23]

No one can know just how widely such opinions were held. Some persons, it appears, besides the ready-tongued, did have some such theory in mind as early as 1766. Richard Bland of Virginia toyed with the idea; but his pamphlet is confusing.[24] He seems not only to make an able defense of colonial right to self-taxation, but also to lay a fairly good basis for looking upon the colonies as dominions of the king free from parliamentary supervision. His main reliance, however, appears to be upon the principle of natural rights, but he does not proclaim sharply that natural rights are a legal limitation upon authority. On the whole, we are justified in concluding that the Americans in no formal way, and probably few in their own minds, were asserting their complete freedom from parliamentary authority. The day for such pronouncement lay some distance ahead. The fact is, the empire was in existence and Parliament had a share in its management; and that share had actually consisted largely in passing acts for the maintenance of the trade of the empire and for matters of general rather than local concern. Though thoughtful men believed portions of the navigation acts to be a hardship, and there were manifestations of a lawless and even turbulent spirit among the restless traders and watermen of the New England seaports, there is little evidence that there was objection to the form or workings of the imperial system as it had been in the past.

Probably many Americans, though I speak only of those capable of thinking connectedly on a principle of government, were troubled by

---

[23] Quoted in Quincy (Mass.) *Reports* (1761-1772), p. 443. "The King of Great Britain indeed is our Sovereign, but we have no representation in parliament, & strictly speaking, not meerly those acts which lay taxes upon us, but no other acts any further than we adopt them, are binding upon us." Thus Hutchinson presented the opinions of 1766.

[24] Richard Bland, *An Inquiry Into the Rights of the British Colonies* (Williamsburg, Virginia, 1766; reprinted in Richmond, 1922). See also Tyler, *The Literary History of the American Revolution* (one volume ed.), pp. 230-231. A reader of Bland's pamphlet is inclined to agree with Jefferson that it is "a singular one", not leading by a direct and simple route to a definite goal.

the difficulty of reconciling the freedom of the colonies, or their possession of certain powers of government, with the fact of parliamentary control in certain rather imposing aspects. It was an easy mental exercise to accept the complete and unalloyed authority of Parliament, and it was easy to deny the existence of such authority in toto; but to envisage the composite or multiple empire was not so easy. The significant fact, therefore, is not the readiness of the colonists to announce the total incapacity of Parliament, but the tardiness of such an announcement. And it should be noticed that the great powers of empire in the hands of the Crown—foreign affairs, war, peace, and the like—were not challenged.

For our constitutional history the important fact is this: however many persons were ready to proclaim the total absence of parliamentary power over the colonies, writers and debaters were struggling for years more or less successfully with the conception of restricted governmental power and the organization of a politically-diversified empire. Such success as they had in reaching the conception of distributed authority was due to their own experiences with an actual, not a theoretical, British empire, an empire of which each colony was an integral part, an integral part of an actual whole. It may not be necessary to remind the reader that the question is not whether any one principle involving the legal structure of the empire was sound in logic or law; the important thing is the situation and the argument, be it good or bad. It is not even necessary to be confident concerning just how many persons held a single doctrine. Knowing as we do the products of the time, recognizing theories foreshadowing the coming of a diversified American "empire", we must take special interest in the emergence of the idea and the nature of the problem.

In Massachusetts, at all events, thanks to the preaching of the ministers, thanks to the doctrines which the ministers had long been heralding, and thanks also to the teachings of James Otis, it is plain enough that at the Stamp Act crisis men did not devote their nimble wits to working out an idea of an empire based wholly on the Crown and the power of the Crown. They surely began by admitting the authority of Parliament and denying its omnipotence—"boundaries there undoubtedly are". Those "boundaries" were the fundamentals of the British constitution. No matter how many other arguments they might have, or how many theories as to the structure of the empire they might put forth, the colonists never lost sight of what they claimed to be the elementary rights of Englishmen. Hutchinson himself said in 1765, "The prevailing reason at this time is, that the Act of Parliament is against Magna Charta, and the natural Rights of Englishmen, and therefore, according to Lord Coke, null and void." [25] When the town of Boston presented to the Governor in council a memorial asking for the opening of the courts, stamps or no stamps, James Otis, John Adams, and Jeremy Gridley appeared in support of the memorial. Otis opened an eloquent harangue with tears; he quoted Molloy: [26] "When there are no Courts of Law to appeal to, it is then we must have Recourse to the Law of Nature. . . ." Adams, not so tearful apparently, declared the Stamp Act "utterly void, and of no binding Force"—not, it seems, because Parliament had no authority over the colonies, but because the act was contrary to "certain Principles fixed unalterably in Nature." [27]

A Virginia court, doubtless under the influence of the same kind of reasoning as that used by Otis and Adams, did not hesitate to take a decided stand. The court "unanimously declared it to be their opinion that the said act did not bind, affect, or concern the inhabitants of this colony, in as much as they conceive the same to be unconstitutional,

[25] Quoted in an appendix to Quincy (Mass.) *Reports* (1761-1772), p. 527. Italics of the original omitted. The whole note on pp. 527-528 is worth studying carefully. Even Justice Cushing, in a letter to Chief Justice Hutchinson, dated "In a hurry Feby. 7, 1766," said, "Its true It is said an Act of Parliament against natural Equity is void. It will be disputed whether this is such an Act. It seems to me the main Question here is whether an Act which cannot be carried into execution should stop the Course of Justice, and that the Judges are more confined than with respect to an obsolete Act." *Ibid.,* p. 528 (quoted from 25 *Mass. Archives,* 55).

[26] *De Jure Maritimo et Navali.*

[27] Quincy (Mass.) *Reports* (1761-1772), p. 198 ff. Otis also referred to Grotius, *De Jure Belli et Pacis.* Again, the whole discussion is illuminating. It is true that Adams said, "A Parliament of Great Britain can have no more Right to tax the Colonies than a Parliament of Paris." And this sort of thing Adams in later years based on a view of the empire in which the Parliament had no authority whatever over the colonies; but his argument in 1765 was the invalidity of the act because the colonies were not represented, and was based on "our Rights as Men, and our Priviledges as Englishmen." *Ibid.,* pp. 201, 200.

It is a noteworthy fact that the Governor, Francis Bernard, in replying to Otis and Adams, and possibly simply to escape discussion, shrewdly asserted that their arguments indicated that it was not the business of the Governor in council but of the court to determine the very question at issue: "The Arguments made Use of, both by Mr. Adams and you, would be very pertinent to induce the Judges of the Superiour Court to think the Act of no Validity, and that therefore they should pay no Regard to it; but the Question with me is, whether that very Thing don't argue the Impropriety of our Intermeddling in a Matter which solely belongs to them to judge of in their Judicial Department." *Ibid.,* p. 206.

and that the said several officers may proceed to the execution of their respective offices without incurring any penalties by means thereof. . . ." [28]

We have thus far seen several distinct but not contradictory ideas, all of them important to one wishing to see the emergence of American constitutionalism. Some of these ideas were as yet rather vague; some of them appeared more sharply outlined in later discussions. (1) There were certain fundamental rights which government could not take away from its subjects. (2) Those rights were embedded in the British constitution. (3) Men were not called upon to obey an act depriving them of their rights. An unconstitutional act was not binding. This doctrine was perhaps implicit rather than explicit. (4) There was a British constitution limiting governmental authority, a constitution, in the American way of viewing it, more definite, not to say rigid, than any conception of it held by Britons. (5) Furthermore, the colonies, as parts of the empire, had functions and powers. (6) There could be and there was a clear distinction between one "power" and another; the "power" to tax was distinguishable from other powers. Parliament might have one power and not another. (7) The charters and immemorial custom gave sanction to the right, the legal right, of the colonies to manage their taxation and internal government. (8) Reason and a just regard for the interests of the whole sanctioned the authority of Parliament to legislate for the maintenance of the empire and for the coöperation of its parts. I am not intent upon forcing the conclusion that every man speaking this language beheld clearly all its logical consequences; I am intent only upon showing that these theories, if not so plain that the thoughtless man could think them, were actually part of the practical politics of the early Revolutionary period. And we should notice also that the discussion at that time as well as later was within the field of law.[29] If one is desirous of tracing the

---

[28] *Virginia Gazette*, March 21, 1766. This decision, the first probably of any court in America and probably in the world to declare an act void because of unconstitutionality, was given by a court held for Northampton County, February 11, 1766. We need not comment here at length on the significance of all this. The thing to be stressed in this connection is not the action of the court as a court—we shall have more to say of that hereafter—but the use of the word "unconstitutional" and the principles on which it was undoubtedly based: there were certain fundamentals of the constitution, there *was* a constitution, and the legislature of Great Britain could not violate its principles. The thought of a constitution not to be tampered with in its fundamental principles must come before any court could act.

[29] This matter will be discussed somewhat more fully in the next chapter. As indicated at the beginning of this chapter, the Americans had more than one way

development of the American argument, he is compelled to see that, in 1765 and for a year or two thereafter, the emphasis was laid on the principles of individual liberty under the British constitution rather than on the freedom of the colonies as constituent parts of the empire; but there was reliance, not only on the rights of colonists as Englishmen, but also on the right to colonial self-government in the empire.

The colonists, someone may say, had no right to set up the principles of the English system as their defense, when they were claiming more than the English system actually contained; they could not properly declare that men's property could not be taken from them without their own consent given in a representative assembly of their own choosing. But the fact of their making the claim, not its theoretical justification, was the important thing. The British system of representation as it existed, and as it continued to exist until 1832, was far from recognizing the populace or the body of voters as the source of authority. No taxation could be levied save by the consent of Parliament; thus far had English constitutionalism progressed. Representation, especially borough representation, was, however, nearly farcical. Old Sarum, almost utterly without human habitation, had the privilege of sending two members to Parliament, while large and populous cities sent no member at all. And this was but one example of prevailing conditions.[30] Elections were rather a method of filling the benches of the House of Commons than a mode of ascertaining the wishes of voters or a mode of exercising their will. But again we must remind ourselves that Englishmen, though some of them were soon to fret under the system, did have something called representation which distinguished their government from the big and little autocracies of Europe. The Parliament had many able members, some of whom were the beneficiaries of the owners of pocket boroughs. The worth of English representation is not to be entirely ignored.[31]

of attacking the Stamp Act. Their objections were not entirely confined to the hardship entailed. Furthermore, they might have said, "This is the law; Parliament has the legal power, but we will not obey." It is of primary importance to notice that they did not say this, but denied the legal validity of this act as they came to deny the legal validity of other acts. That fact is what gave distinction to the Revolution.

[30] Samuel Curwen, an American who was in England from 1775 to 1783, wrote that the spot which formerly was the site of Old Sarum contained about sixty acres without one house on it. But on the lower plain stood one house where a family dwelt. See Edward and A. G. Porritt, *The Unreformed House of Commons*, I, p. 36.

[31] George Grenville, in his *Regulations*, gives an able argument in behalf of British representation: "All British Subjects," he says, ". . . are virtually represented

The Americans, on the other hand, thanks to the colonial conditions, and thanks to the acquiescence, and, in part, to the magnanimity of the home authorities, had developed a system of representation fairly worthy of the name. It was not theoretically perfect, if judged by the doctrines of modern democracy; but it did in considerable degree recognize the right of popular voice in government, and it included the thought that the representative carried with him the desires and behests of his constituents. Suffrage was limited, and moreover there was no proper and proportional adjustment of representation to the numbers of the respective communities; the back-country suffered from discrimination. But withal, the fact is that the colonies had a system so far in advance of British practices that it is almost amusing to see Patrick Henry insisting upon the undoubted right of Englishmen not to be taxed without their own consent given personally or by their representatives. When, therefore, Britain and America entered upon any discussion of representation, they were separated farther than mere ocean space could divide them. Rightly or wrongly, the Americans were announcing principles which they had partly and effectively put into operation, principles to which in later years they gave fuller institutional expression and which are the basis of modern popular government.

Why did the Americans not continually cry out against the rotten and pocket boroughs, and why did they not vociferously denounce the bribery and the spoils practices so evident in the home country? Some of them did this occasionally. Otis, for example, at one time spoke impatiently of the everlasting changes rung upon the fact that large cities sent no members to Parliament; if they are not represented, he said, "they ought to be." [32] Bland spoke of the "Work worthy of the best patriotick Spirits in the Nation to effectuate an Alteration in this putrid

in Parliament; for every Member of Parliament sits in the House, not as a Representative of his own Constituents, but as one of that august Assembly by which all the Commons of Great Britain are represented." ". . . they [Birmingham and Manchester] and the Colonies and all British Subjects whatever, have an equal Share in the general Representation of the Commons of Great Britain, and are bound by the Consent of the Majority of that House, whether their own particular Representatives consented to or opposed the Measures there taken, or whether they had or had not particular Representatives there." p. 109. Italics of the original omitted. So the men of Boston were "represented" by the ploughed fields of Old Sarum and by the pigsties and the pigeon-lofts of Richmond!

[32] *Considerations on Behalf of the Colonists. in a Letter to a Noble Lord* (2nd ed.; London, 1765), p. 6

Part of the Constitution. . . ."[33] But the Americans as a rule were not casting aside as unworthy the whole British system; they made no pretense of having pushed onward to higher ground. They based their arguments on what they thought to be old and well-established principles; they saw in British constitutionalism the basis for their claim.

Thus, the very method of approach is significant; it was legalistic rather than revolutionary; and it is difficult to overestimate the importance of this fact. The Americans setting forth the constitutional rights of Englishmen on both sides of the water, as they claimed those rights to be, did not appear to be engaged in destruction, but in conservation. The character of the formal documents which issued from America during the whole contest is a matter of consequence; they do not seem to breathe forth the air of revolution; they help us to understand how and why it was that even war did not beget thorough social disintegration, and how and why it was that the men of that generation did more than any other single generation to institutionalize principles of government and to perform the difficult task of constructive statesmanship; for in the end the movement was constructive; the institutions and principles, the establishment of which is the theme of these pages, rested not on imaginings—though men cannot move on without imagination—but on history.[34] It is easy, however, to see why the Britons did not feel comfortable, though abundant references were made to Britain's own past by the argumentative colonists. If a member of the House had acknowledged the ethics of the American position, and had not clouded the issue by what he called "virtual representation", he would have denied his right to his own seat; and a general acceptance of American principles would have shaken the British constitution to its foundations.

[33] *Inquiry*, p. 12. ". . . I cannot", Bland also said, "comprehend how Men who are excluded from voting at the Election of Members of Parliament can be represented in that Assembly, or how those who are elected do not sit in the House as Representatives of their Constituents." *Ibid.,* p. 6.

[34] By this statement I do not mean that the Americans were right in their claims, nor do I mean that their arguments and their institutions were entirely the product of historical forces. It is the method of approach that is significant. Though actually creating what was in some respects new, and developing the old, American thinking was strikingly conservative. I refer, of course, not to the crowds that burned effigies and coerced stamp men, but to studied pronouncements of leaders.

CHAPTER VI

AFTER THE STAMP ACT

American satisfaction, induced by the repeal of the Stamp Act, did not long endure, for new troubles were in store. The politicians and placemen at Westminster had no proper appreciation of American sentiment; they had no sense of the enormous difficulty of managing an empire, especially an empire containing some two million colonists who were shrewd, determined, and peculiarly restless under restraint. The Rockingham ministry, in whose administration the stamp tax had been withdrawn, was succeeded in the summer of 1766 by a ministry a number of the members of which were followers of Pitt, who at the same time accepted a peerage and entered the Lords as Earl of Chatham; "the Great Commoner" was to be heard no more in the House where he had electrified his hearers and led the nation. Illness, moreover, soon came upon him, and such influence as he otherwise might have exerted was thus denied him; he could have done little to shape events. Britain was in no mood to listen to the sort of doctrine he was prepared to advocate; above all, the men who had their hands on the offices and on the treasury coffers, the men who were the leaders in politics and those who were the bright stars in the social firmament, were not inclined to emphasize the principle of freedom in the empire.

The new cabinet was a strange compound, the "mosaic" ministry Burke called it, "a very curious show, but utterly unsafe to touch and unsure to stand on." Charles Townshend, the Chancellor of the Exchequer, a nimble-witted and eminently clever man, who had a strange capacity for amusing the Commons by his audacity and trivial sallies, took matters in hand and proposed to collect a revenue in America. He could do it, he seems to have thought, without ruffling the easily-ruffled tempers of those strange people who made a nonsensical distinction between internal and external taxation; if they loved the distinction, he would make the most of it. The scheme which he carried through provided for the appointment of commissioners to superintend the collection of duties in the colonies; there were to be no more shuffling and unmannerly avoidance. Taxes were laid on glass, tea, painters' colors, and paper; the old navigation acts were to be enforced and duties were to find their way into the treasury. Furthermore, writs of assistance were elaborately provided for; and, as if intent on making the medicine as unpalatable as possible, the preamble of the Revenue Act (1767) announced the expediency of raising revenue to make a more certain "provision for defraying the charge of the administration of justice, and the support of civil government, in such provinces where it shall be found necessary; and towards further defraying the expences of defending, protecting, and securing the said dominions. . . ."[1]

Though it is not our job to discern the cumulative irritations that finally provoked rebellion, or to discuss at length the expediency of ministerial conduct, it is scarcely possible to pass over these acts or their enforcement without comment. Here was an expensive and troublesome method of enforcing the acts of trade and navigation, a method proving to be exceedingly trying, though on the whole effective. The colonists did not like to pay taxes; they especially disliked the show of power, the ceaseless surveillance. They did not like writs of assistance, those general warrants which in the hands of unmannerly or corrupt officials appeared to menace the very sanctity of their households. They were accustomed to a wide freedom of legislation in their own assemblies; what was to become of self-government, if Parliament with a word could let loose upon them a whole flock of revenue-collecting locusts? But more distasteful than all else, more distasteful at least to the colonial politicians, was the intent or the threat of placing the courts of justice under the control of the Crown. Officers of civil government were to be paid or might be paid from the revenue thus collected. Were the royal governors to be relieved from their old fear, the fear that they might not receive their salaries, if they did not behave themselves?

Whatever argument may be made in behalf of the naked legal right of Parliament to extort money, it is plain that the cunning Charles Townshend and the clamoring official claquers at Westminster were running counter to the practices of a century and were disregardful of what Americans deemed their privileges. If the colonists had an unusual dislike of taxes, they were also proud and sensitive; and there were among them not only merchants and men of com-

[1] Italics of the original omitted.

merce, but astute players in the game of politics. If money could be raised only by such means as the agile-witted Townshend adopted, then revenue might be no blessing to anybody. The net results appear to have been, on the fiscal side, the collection of no inconsiderable revenue and the expenditure of the funds to enforce the acts; [2] on the purely human side, the exasperation of the British subjects in America; in other words, the whole thing was somewhere below the lowest limit of statesmanship. Finally, the revenue was to be used for *"protecting, and securing the said dominions. . . ."* It was to be used or might be used to pay the soldiery; and though the colonists were still unwavering in their loyalty, there was no love lost between them and the British men-at-arms. True, the Britons had sent troops to fight the French and Indians; Canada had been conquered; but there must have been something humorous in the anxiety to defend colonists who for a hundred and fifty years had been gradually though surely pushing their way westward and had, almost entirely by their own exertions and brave persistence, built up an empire, the advantages of which were now supposed to accrue to the Parliament and merchants of the mother country. [3]

That the colonists were vexed is not a matter for wonder; the wonder is that they did not immediately take arms, at all events the arms of counter argument, against the whole system of trade restrictions; for the acts of navigation, though modified in some particulars for revenue purposes, were now enforced as never before, and one would be inclined to think that the system of regulating colonists "on the maxims of the counter" would have called forth maledictions on its head. But the colonists were used to the navigation acts, though in part the restrictions were honored more in the breach than the observance. And again we recall Burke's later words that "men do bear the inevitable constitution of their original nature with all its infirm-

---

[2] In about seven years the commissioners collected over £200,000 sterling; a large portion was paid out in salaries. See Edward Channing, *A History of the United States,* III, p. 91. "Actually there was no return whatever because the cost of the soldiers and sailors and vessels required to enforce these revenue acts far exceeded the gross returns." *Ibid.,* p. 91, note 1.

[3] I have not taken up in these pages the justice or injustice of taxing the colonies; but it may be said, as the colonists distinctly said, that they did pay taxes, though not directly into the British treasury; they supported their own governments; the colonists paid the governors' salaries, though only in two colonies did they choose them. They had taken part in the wars of the empire and some of the colonies were then burdened with heavy taxes. Their trade was in some respects made secondary to the interests of West Indian planters and to the pockets of British merchants.

ities." Colonies were "confirmed in obedience . . . even more by usage than by law." [4]

We must now turn to what is for us the important matter. How did the colonists take up opposition to the Townshend Acts? What principles of government did they announce? Their most important spokesman was John Dickinson of Pennsylvania. He had taken an important share in the Stamp Act Congress of 1765 and earned in the course of the coming years the title of the "Penman of the American Revolution." Like other colonial leaders, he was a lawyer by training, for lawyers were now coming into their own; he had studied law at the Middle Temple in London; like some leaders, and more than most, he could write with clearness and he knew what he was talking about —a happy, if unusual, combination of abilities. In 1767 and 1768, his "Farmer's Letters" were printed in a Philadelphia newspaper.[5] The attention they received was remarkable; they were reproduced in the American press and were soon published in pamphlet form, not only in America but abroad.[6] None but the illiterate or the remote frontiersman could have been ignorant of the case presented by the "Farmer", and the wide acclaim justifies us in believing that he stated the American cause as the people wished it to be stated.[7]

[4] Edmund Burke, "Speech on American Taxation" (1774), *Works* (revised ed.), II, p. 33.

[5] The full title was "Letters From a Farmer in Pennsylvania, to the Inhabitants of the British Colonies."

[6] Tyler, *The Literary History of the American Revolution* (one volume ed.), pp. 236-237, says the "Letters" were reproduced in all but four of the twenty-five newspapers then published in America. Editions appeared in England and Ireland, and there was also a French edition. Dickinson was applauded by Voltaire, and on the continent of Europe his essays "became . . . the fashion." See also, John Dickinson, *Writings* (P. L. Ford, ed.; *Memoirs of the Hist. Society of Pa.*, XIV), I, p. 279 ff.

[7] For a statement of the popularity of Dickinson's "Letters", see C. J. Stillé, *The Life and Times of John Dickinson* (*Memoirs of the Hist. Society of Pa.*, XIII), pp. 90-92. Thomas Hutchinson stated the position the colonies had come to occupy (1767): "The authority of Parliament to pass any acts whatever affecting the interior polity of the Colonies is, he says, challenged, as destroying the effect of the charters, to which great sacredness is attached. People have been induced to settle in the plantations on the strength of the charters, relying on the continuance of the privileges. King, Lords, and Commons form the legislature of Great Britain: the Governor, who is the King's representative, the Council, and the Assembly form the legislature of the Colony. But as Colonies cannot make laws to extend further than their respective limits, Parliament must step in in all cases to which the legislative power of the Colonies does not extend. Parliament ought to go no farther than this: all beyond is infringing upon the domain of the colonial legislatures. From Virginia to Massachusetts this has now come to be the accepted doctrine." J. K. Hosmer, *The Life of Thomas Hutchinson*, p. 122. This statement Hosmer bases upon Hutchinson's own words in his *History of Massachusetts Bay*, III, p. 172.

Of first importance is the fact that Dickinson, while writing with real eloquence and with literary power, did not indulge in declamation or wild denunciation. There was no intent of arousing the passions of the multitude. He was himself, as Tyler has said, "a man of powerful and cultivated intellect, with all his interests and all his tastes on the side of order, conservatism, and peace, if only with these could be had political safety and honor." [8] While he defended the principles of English liberty, he spoke for an empire of justice.

Dickinson had a difficult task, for he had really to present in broad outline a scheme of empire. He spoke as an Englishman claiming the birthright of an Englishman, as the possessor of privileges won for him and for others by Englishmen who had dared to struggle for their rights; but he spoke also as a citizen of a wide empire in which the rights of Englishmen must be maintained. His argument was not wholly new, but it presented with elaboration and with clarity important views of the constitutional structure of the empire.[9] He envisaged a composite or decentralized system regardful of individual liberty and colonial privilege. He seemed at times to be more insistent upon the unity of the empire than upon the rights of the colonies; or, if that be an over-statement, this is beyond cavil—he spoke not as a disgruntled colonist, cherishing rebellion, but as a citizen of the British empire who gloried in its symmetry and strength. The general applause which his words received is striking proof that people did not wish independence but freedom; and those capable of following his argument must have seen that his picture of the empire embraced both freedom and authority.[10]

The most signal contribution made by Dickinson, if we except his strong portrayal of imperial unity consonant with local rights, was his sharp definition of taxation and the distinction between taxation and the regulation of commerce. As we have already seen, others had made

[8] Tyler, *The Literary History of the American Revolution* (one volume ed.), p. 235.
[9] As we have seen, Hopkins and Dulany had a view of empire, and the view is not to be denied to others.
[10] "The parliament unquestionably possesses a legal authority to regulate the trade of Great-Britain, and all her colonies. Such an authority is essential to the relation between a mother country and her colonies; and necessary for the common good of all. He, who considers these provinces as states distinct from the British Empire, has very slender notions of justice, or of their interests. We are but parts of a whole; and therefore there must exist a power somewhere to preside, and preserve the connection in due order. This power is lodged in the parliament; and we are as much dependent on Great-Britain, as a perfectly free people can be on another." John Dickinson, *Writings* (P. L. Ford, ed.; *Memoirs of the Hist. Society of Pa.,* XIV), I, p. 312. Italics of the original omitted.

the distinction; but even Dulany had not left a clear-cut impression. Dickinson defined taxation as an imposition for raising revenue. The difference between internal and external taxation, he scorned and rejected. He quite properly denied that the Americans had ever committed themselves to such a classification; "all taxes are founded on the same principles; and have the same tendency." [11]

Why is Dickinson's position important? It is important because he believed that in the British empire powers had been distributed; because he made a sharp distinction between one "power" and another; and because our system of government rests on the distribution of "powers" among governments. Every schoolboy knows that we now, in the United States, distinguish the "power" to tax from the "power" to regulate commerce. Anyone knowing the simplest rudiments of American constitutional law as America produced it knows that "powers" are singled out and deposited in one government or another. Everybody knows that this essential characteristic of our system has caused legal discussion in Congress and courts of law and that perplexing problems have arisen in actual practice. Without distribution of powers, American federalism would be non-existent. The important thing now is to see Dickinson portraying an empire in which the central government could exercise wide authority for the whole, while the colonies maintained their freedom; for the Parliament could not tax.

The English pamphleteers could have a merry time with the "Farmer", but their merriment and their serious attempts at refutation were a tribute to the strength of his appeal. If forsooth, said the pamphleteers, you can lay impositions for trade regulations and not for taxation, then, to be sure, a light tax would be unconstitutional while an imposition, so heavy as to be prohibitory and intended to prohibit, would be constitutional; could anyone in his senses defend such a legal system? As a matter of cold fact, such refinements are now simple and crude in comparison with those constantly made by our own courts in laying down constitutional principles. Any person, even the brilliant scoffers at the "Farmer's" scheme of empire, insisting that Parliament must have all power or none,[12] ought to have

---

[11] *Ibid.*, I, p. 332. Italics of the original omitted.

[12] "There is no alternative: either the Colonies are a part of the community of Great Britain, or they are in a state of nature with respect to her, and in no case can be subject to the jurisdiction of that legislative power which represents her community, which is the British parliament." See William Knox, *The Controversy Between Great Britain and Her Colonies Reviewed* (London, 1769), pp. 50-51. We find

known that even in the application of private law, distinctions are often to be drawn which are so tenuous as to be almost undiscernible to the untrained mind. So if you are to have a legal structure of empire, you may expect to find finely-drawn distinctions.

The whole controversy, we may remind ourselves, was over the problem of whether Parliament was absolute or not. Was it absolute in its authority over every British subject? Was it possessed of full and unqualified competence in the empire—in other words, was the empire a centralized empire or was it on the contrary a legally diversified empire? Dickinson proved, or thought he did, that Parliament had regulated trade and had not taxed. There can be no question of the fact that in a very large degree the empire had been a commercial empire, not a lawmaking empire for all its subjects. And if we did not know the perversity of human nature and the ease with which men believe what they want to believe, we should be puzzled by the men who so emphatically denied the possibility of there being legal recognition of what had in reality been a working practice for a hundred years. If Parliament had in the past regulated trade and had not taxed, why was it impossible to conceive the make-up of an empire in which Parliament could legally regulate trade and could not legally tax?[13] However once again, too, the theories of centralization and the absolute authority of Parliament. Nothing could more fully discredit legalism, so shortsighted that it could not see any possibility of change. Knox was denying that Parliament or common reason could recognize the illegality of doing what it had not done and what the passing years showed it could not do.

[13] To-day those persons finding Dickinson's argument full of inconsistencies and sweeping it aside as one of those heated blunderings dear to the colonial heart seem to forget the rudiments of the American constitutional system. Dickinson was speaking in the terms of American constitutionalism as it came to be. His argument, while distinguishing between taxation and regulation of commerce, rested partly on the purpose of the legislation. He saw the difficulty of making the purpose absolutely effective. He relied on the good sense of the British people, if once the distinction was recognized. He might, theoretically, have gone further, and as James Otis had called upon the court to check legislation in violation of natural equity, so Dickinson might have declared that courts would recognize the fact of the purpose or effect and would declare void an act, which, though on its face a regulation, was intended to collect revenue.

For an attempt of Congress, under cover of a granted power, to accomplish ends not within the scope of its authority, see Hammer v. Dagenhart, 247 U. S. 251 (1918). In this case the Court declared an act which purported to regulate interstate commerce was an encroachment upon the powers of the states: "The purposes intended must be attained consistently with constitutional limitations. . . ." 276. The necessary effect of the act, the Court declared, was "by means of a prohibition against the movement in interstate commerce of ordinary commercial commodities, to regulate the hours of labor of children in factories and mines within the States. . . ." Ibid. See also Bailey v. Drexel Furniture Company, 259 U. S. 20 (1922), for a somewhat

this may be, the American colonists of 1768, eagerly devouring the "Farmer's Letters" and toasting the author in public houses up and down the land,[14] were, in appearance at least, accepting the theory of an empire guided by a Parliament with authority to guard the whole and to regulate intercolonial and foreign trade, and with the obligation not to tax the colonies or reduce their legislatures to impotence.

What was Massachusetts to say to the Townshend Acts and the new customs commissioners? Where Sam Adams lived, there something would be said. In the early days of 1768 the Massachusetts representatives were busily at work. Various letters were drawn up and sent to England, all of them announcing the same principles, all of them couched in polite, but unmistakable language.[15] The appeal was chiefly to the British constitution in which were placed and guarded the fundamental rights of men. Over and over again appeared in one form or another the declarations that "The supreme legislative, in every free state, derives its power from the constitution; by the fundamental rules of which, it is bounded and circumscribed." [16] "It is an essential, natural right, that a man shall quietly enjoy, and have the sole disposal of his own property. This right is adopted into the constitution." "Property is admitted to have an existence, even in the savage state of nature." "In all free states, the constitution is fixed; it is from thence, that the legislative derives its authority; therefore it cannot change the constitution without destroying its own foundation." "The security of right and property, is the great end of government." Such sentiments were often repeated, but there was no denial of parliamentary control; even in the petition to the king there was an acknowledgment of "the supreme Legislative power of the whole Empire" and its "superintending authority . . . in all Cases,

similar decision. In McCulloch v. Maryland, 4 Wheaton 316, 423 (1819), Chief Justice Marshall said: "Should Congress, in the execution of its powers, adopt measures which are prohibited by the constitution; or should Congress, *under the pretext* of executing its powers, pass laws for *the accomplishment of objects not entrusted to the government*, it would become the painful duty of this tribunal, should a case requiring such a decision come before it, to say that such an act was not the law of the land." Italics mine.

14 A town-meeting in Boston in March, 1768 passed a vote of thanks to "the ingenious author. . . ." See Stillé, *op. cit.*, p. 91.

15 Most of them were written to the friends of America in Britain, and are attributed to the pen of Sam Adams. See Samuel Adams, *Writings* (H. A. Cushing, ed.), I, pp. 134-199. Concerning authorship, see p. 152, note 2. One letter was a petition to the King; one letter was addressed to the Lords Commissioners of the Treasury.

16 *Ibid.*, I, p. 134. See also, *Ibid.*, I, p. 135 ff.

that can consist with the fundamental Rights of Nature & the Constitution. . . ."

Among these documents the most important was a circular letter sent by the Massachusetts house to the speakers of other houses of representatives. It gave utterance to the principles just quoted, declaring that the constitution is fixed, that the legislative power cannot overleap the bounds of it, and that it "ascertains & limits both Sovereignty & allegiance. . . ." This letter was of course the common property of the colonists. It was made especially conspicuous by the action of Hillsborough, the Colonial Secretary, who ordered the house to rescind; this the house promptly refused to do.

We have, then, in the "Farmer's Letters" and in these documents from the Massachusetts house definite evidence of American opinion in 1768. No doubt there were other opinions even more advanced, for some men were more rebellious in spirit; and doubtless, too, some persons were ready to assert their total freedom from parliamentary control; but almost to the days of the outbreak of war, these more radical positions cannot be considered the opinions of America. How did the principles of the "Farmer" differ from those of Sam Adams and his followers, and what did the two writers have in common? Neither one denied the authority of Parliament as the superintending power of the empire; neither denied the authority of Parliament to regulate trade. Dickinson, however, spoke more plainly than Adams of the empire; that empire was built on the foundations of English liberty; in this empire there was a distinction between powers. Adams, in denying the right to tax, relied upon the argument of natural rights, insisted that the constitution was fixed, and emphasized the right to property as fundamental. The British statesmen might announce the supreme and unlimited authority of Parliament; Adams was prepared to deny the existence of absolute authority in any free state, above all in the constitution of Britain. Briefly, one brought out clearly the possibility of distinguishing "powers" of government and presented to view a diversified empire; the other emphasized the limits on all free governments and stressed the fundamental, unchangeable bounds of the constitution; and this is only to say that the two, mutually supporting, brought forward the two chief foundations of the American constitutional system—a diversified state or empire and a fixed constitution superior to legislative authority. The constitution, as Adams and others viewed it, was fixed and, at least in certain respects, was beyond the touch of legislative authority because within it were embodied fundamental natural rights which were eternal and unalterable. The principles of Adams and of Dickinson coincided in this: both believed in the right and the necessity of living under governments constitutionally limited.

Though Dickinson dwelt chiefly on the difference between taxation and other powers, plainly the superintending power of the Parliament included more than the regulation of commerce. A full examination of the discussion would reveal the colonial acceptance, in theory at least, of the distribution of powers in the empire as the empire had been. I say "in theory at least", for lasting satisfaction with acts of trade, or humble acquiescence in the activities of customs commissioners and of a swarm of spoilsmen let loose from the hives of Westminster, would have been impossible. The Revolution might have come before many years because of diverging interests, ineptitude of British administration, and the willfulness of the colonists; in fact, however, the Americans set forth the old empire as the one with which they were content, and that empire was in practice an empire in which the colonial governments had their share of authority.

So much has been said of the justice or injustice of taxation that we do not always see that the very existence of the colonial governments was at stake. True, the eager legalists in Britain had no intention of banishing the colonial assemblies altogether; but the colonists were afraid, and justly so, for the empire in the British view was a unitary empire and a centralized empire; all power was gathered at the center and the subordinate governments existed only by sufferance. While the colonials resisted the injustice and illegality of taxation, they must have been stupid indeed not to see that the choice lay between a diversified or decentralized empire on the one hand and a unitary, centralized empire on the other.

The discussion was legal discussion; it concerned the structure of the empire and the authority of government. It will not do to dwell upon the number of shillings collected as revenue, or even upon the vexing intrusions of the royal officials, and lose sight of the peril to the assemblies and to the whole political structure of the colonies. If the colonists are not to be charged with political incapacity and a remarkable obtuseness, it is folly to declare that the Revolution was only an economic movement in its causes, operations, and results. No people, possessed of self-respect and a glimmering of political sagacity, could listen unmoved while pamphleteers proclaimed a doctrine, which, if carried out in detail and wrought out to its theoretical end, would deprive them of their own institutions of government. Without the citation of countless references, we can be confident that the American colonists, more strongly than any other people on earth, were imbued with an instinct for practical politics; they, too, were legal-minded, and they, too, even more than the obedient servants of King George, were sensitive and proud, even when not rebellious.[17]

Almost, if not quite, from the beginning of the dispute—in the Stamp Act dispute as well as later—discussion was within the realm of law. Certainly not entirely for any immediate, practical, financial gain, but from a desire to establish a system and a settled legal authority, royal officers in the colonies had spoken of remodeling colonial governments. Francis Bernard, writing in the summer of 1764, said, "It seems to me that the affairs of America are becoming very critical; that common expedients would soon begin to fail; and that a general reformation of the American Governments would become not only a desirable but a necessary measure." [18] Bernard was against mere opportunism. "The patchwork government of America will last no longer: the necessity of a parliamentary establishment of the governments of America upon fixed constitutional principles, is brought on with a precipitation which could not have been foreseen but a year ago. . . ." This he wrote in 1765.[19] Soon after this, Hutchinson wished "to see known established principles, one general rule of subjection. . . ." [20] ". . . while the rules of law are vague and uncertain, especially in such fundamental points, our condition is deplorable. . . ." [21]

The brusque British pamphleteers laid down their final conclusion as the starting-point for their argument, and what they desired was an acknowledgment by America of parliamentary power; they desired the acceptance of a constitutional theory. We need not deny the British landowner's anxiety for a reduced tax upon his acres; but he also desired to see an acknowledgment of the authority of the Parliament

---

[17] Some of the words in the sentences above sound like mere patriotic exclamations of an older day than this. There is no reason for denying the influence of economic causes in the Revolution; but men have and had their pride as well as thrift, and it is folly not to see the immense significance of a struggle for constitutional liberty.

[18] Francis Bernard, *Select Letters on the Trade and Government of America; and the Principles of Law and Polity, Applied to the American Colonies* (London, 1774), p. 24. Capitalization and italics of the original omitted.

[19] Letter of November 23, 1765, in *Ibid.,* pp. 33-34. Italics of the original omitted.
[20] Letter of April 21, 1766, quoted in Quincy (Mass.) *Reports* (1761-1772), pp. 443-444.
[21] Letter of December 31, 1766, quoted in Hosmer. *Hutchinson.* p. 121.

in which he or men like him sat and legislated. The Americans in their turn, though many would be content with negligence, were now insisting on the necessity of maintaining their privileges and the legal basis on which they rested. They were not quite satisfied, now that the issue was raised, to accept the principles of absolute power with the assurance that a kindly king and a well-intentioned Parliament would not abuse the power: "In all free states, the constitution is fixed. . . ." Dickinson eloquently phrased the central idea: "For who are a free people? Not those, over whom government is reasonably and equitably exercised, but those, who live under a government so constitutionally checked and controuled, that proper provision is made against its being otherwise exercised." [22] Freedom, then, there was none, if there was no constitutional restraint upon authority. This, again, is American doctrine.

Both sides were technical and legalistic. The parliamentarians were the victims of certain dogmas curiously similar to the doctrine of indivisible sovereignty, and they cherished the august power of Parliament. The Americans were legal-minded and argumentative; if Parliament asserted its supremacy, announcing that it was, so to speak, *above* the law, the colonists were eager to assert the supremacy of the constitution, their indefeasible, legal rights in their own institutions. They asserted that the law was above Parliament.

Soon after 1768, in light of the objection raised in America, there appears to have been no real hope in Britain of raising revenue in America. It is true that the acts regulating trade were more vigorously enforced and that more revenue was collected than in earlier days. To some considerable extent from 1766, but especially after 1768, the question was not so much whether the colonists would pay taxes as whether they would acknowledge their legal obligation to pay. To avoid misunderstanding, this should be said: the measures taken to enforce the laws of Parliament were annoying and irksome, provocative of rebellion; the colonists of Massachusetts resented troops sent to overawe them, and disliked ships of war, informers, and all the panoply of power. They resented the show of British authority and they, or many of them, had no taste for taxes or for the strict enforcement of navigation laws. That they would have flown to arms against a naked declaration of British supremacy, unaccompanied by actual acts and threats against their government, we have no reason to suppose.

[22] John Dickinson, *Writings* (P. L. Ford, ed.; *Memoirs of the Hist. Society of Pa.* XIV), I, p. 356. Capitalization and italics of the original omitted.

CHAPTER VII

AN OBDURATE PARLIAMENT AND OBSTINATE COLONIES, 1769-1773. THE GREAT CONTROVERSY BETWEEN GOVERNOR AND LEGISLATURE IN MASSACHUSETTS

We cannot watch the gathering clouds of trouble in the empire without seeing the essence of the difficulty. The problem of managing an empire in which were colonists possessed of political skill and the spirit of freedom was too big for the brain and temper of British politicians. It is easy enough to heap blame on wrong-headed ministers and an obstinate king, but the reality to be grasped is that the social and political order of Britain still tolerated a government of that particular mental density, unsuited to the job which an empire of freedom presented. "Magnanimity in politics," said Burke, "is not seldom the truest wisdom; and a great empire and little minds go ill together." The classes ruling in society and the state had a firm grasp on the government, and to those classes the essential principles of America were obnoxious. But withal, two things need to be remembered: as we have already pointed out, the problem was inherently difficult; and Britain, if she had nothing else to be proud of, could well indulge in self-glorification, had she so minded, at the sight of colonists, the fruit of her own loins, who were so capable in politics and in reality so free—and that freedom was the product of her own liberality. Decades had to pass before Britain was in condition to yield in her own insular structure to the ever-growing forces of popular government. The tone of public life, the very principles and practices of the kingdom, though even then there were symptoms of disquietude, lay beneath parliamentary and ministerial arrogance. We must be content here with a few facts, briefly related, which will help in bringing to light the nature of the American position.

One source of trouble was the British army. Justify as you may the need or the advisability of its presence in America, the fact remains that a regiment or two of soldiers in an American town were not considered agreeable companions. The Quartering Act, which was passed about the time of the Stamp Act, aroused special opposition in New York where the legislature was calmly ordered to provide housing and to make provision for the support of the troops. The situation, when General Gage settled down in the province with his soldiery, was next to intolerable. The legislature refused to comply fully with the demands made upon it (1766), and saw fit to debate the question; but that would never do, and the next year, along with Townshend's revenue acts, came an act of Parliament suspending the functions of the legislature until it carried out the terms of the Quartering Act. Even before the news of the measure reached the colony, the legislature yielded, "saving its face by not itemizing the 'salt, vinegar, beer or cyder' which were in dispute." [1] But cider and beer were not the whole of the matter; the measure of repression had done incalculable harm. It was the natural result of an attitude toward a social problem; the way to secure obedience is not by conciliation, not by consideration and affection, but by punishment and above all by steady adherence to a policy, lest yielding diminish dignity. And this fear and belief that America was taking advantage of indulgence took possession of many Britons who were not natively imbued with the qualities of recalcitrant Toryism. But the Americans, in their turn, were led to inquire whether their legislatures were, within their customary fields, independent bodies or only agencies of a government across the sea which could order them to make appropriations as it saw fit.

Then Hillsborough, indignant at the Massachusetts Circular Letter, sent out to the other twelve colonies a letter of his own.[2] He would have none of these efforts to create "unwarrantable combinations" and "unjustifiable opposition to the constitutional authority of Parliament"; and the Massachusetts legislature was ordered to rescind its "rash and hasty proceeding." [3] When the House of Representatives, by a vote of 92 to 17, refused to rescind, the legislature was dissolved; and the next General Court when chosen contained not 17 but 10 supporters of the prerogative.[4] Other legislatures hastened in loyal addresses to announce their adherence to the principles of Massachusetts. Hillsborough's conduct only strengthened American opposi-

[1] C. H. Van Tyne, *The Causes of the War of Independence*, p. 278.

[2] George Bancroft, *History of the United States* (last revision), III, p. 284. For Hillsborough's letter as addressed to Rhode Island, see John Almon, *Prior Documents*, p. 220.

[3] Hillsborough to Governor Bernard, April 22, 1768, in *Ibid.*, pp. 203-204.

[4] Edward Channing, *A History of the United States*, III, p. 99.

tion, brought the doctrines of the Circular Letter into clearer light, and helped to unify opinion. Thus, thanks to these unseemly quarrels with the colonial legislatures, the detached question of the right of Parliament to levy taxes had risen, or degenerated, into the question whether legislatures could even pass resolutions expressing in calm and uninflammatory fashion their opinion of the constitution of the empire.[5] "If the votes of the House", said the Massachusetts assembly, "are to be controlled by the direction of a minister, we have left us but a vain semblance of liberty." [6]

Still, despite all this unnecessary and dangerous disputation, it is conceivable that Britain might have succeeded; for the revenue acts were being enforced, though not without difficulty and occasional lawlessness. But Parliament was impatient; it is the nature of fatuous high-handedness to be impatient. In an address to the throne in 1768 appeared an ominous proposal. Passed by the Lords, the address went to the Commons (1769) where there was a debate which was declared to be "very fine indeed", and the address was finally passed. It suggested the advisability of procuring full information "touching all treasons, or misprision of treason," and the appointment of a special commission for "enquiring of, hearing, and determining, the said offences within this realm, pursuant to . . . the statute of the 35th year of the reign of king Henry the eighth. . . ." A most astounding proposal—to try the "traitors" of Massachusetts in Britain! The threat aroused opposition in America. In a series of resolutions, the House of Burgesses in Virginia asserted once again that the sole right to impose taxes on Virginians was vested in that house, and that trials for treason ought to be held within the colony; sending suspected persons across the sea for trial would rob them of the "inestimable privilege of being tried by a jury from the vicinage. . . ." [7]

The next step taken by Parliament was the repeal of duties levied by the Townshend Acts, except a duty on tea (1770). Lord North, who had just come to the head of the ministry, where he remained for years the obedient servant of the king, advocated repeal. The acts were "preposterous"; [8] he would gladly take steps to soothe the angry Americans, but lenience did not seem to encourage a spirit of obedience; it

---

[5] Consider, for example, the sentiments of South Carolina. Was an assembly a mere gathering of schoolboys, if such sentiments were to be held as impertinent or unlawful? See D. D. Wallace, *The Life of Henry Laurens*, p. 155.

[6] *Massachusetts State Papers*, p. 150.

[7] See the Constitution of the United States, amendment VI.

[8] "Preposterous". it seems, chiefly because they were injurious to British commerce.

led to further insult of "our authority". The tax on tea must be retained. "The properest time to exert our right of taxation, is, when the right is refused." But there were British soldiers in America. Boston did not like them; their presence awakened unpleasant reflections. On the very day that North advocated the repeal of the Townshend duties, occurred the Boston "massacre"; and the next day came the stern demand of the citizens that the soldiers be removed to the castle in the harbor. The spirit of rebellion was waxing strong in the Puritan town.

In 1769, as the legislature refused to carry on business at Boston in the presence of troops, it was adjourned to meet at Cambridge. Governor Bernard soon departed for England, and Lieutenant-Governor Hutchinson, who shortly thereafter was given the full title, was left to meet the waves of discontent. When he summoned the legislature to Cambridge, the storm broke—not the storm of riot, but the more trying deluge of argument.[9] Samuel Adams was on hand to inquire by what authority the Governor acted. Both the council and the house objected, though on somewhat differing grounds, and contested at length the Governor's position; for he simply declared that as an officer of the Crown he could do no other; he must obey instructions. Did instructions, then, coming from a ministry three thousand miles away give full justification for the Governor's doing everything that a minister might desire? If so, what was the value of a charter and wherein lay the authority of the legislature?

The discussion [10] lasted for months and the months lengthened

[9] The methods and the words of the Massachusetts leaders may appear to the reader, as he reads over the documents, exceedingly trying, and he certainly cannot wonder at the irritation or dismay of the Crown's representatives. But irritation and dismay on the one side and continuing, skillful, persistent opposition to authority on the other are for us as students of constitutional history not the center of the matter. Take as just one example the answer of the house to a statement by Bernard when removing the General Court to Cambridge. He lamented the "waste of time and treasure to no purpose." The house replied, "No time can better be employed, than in the preservation of the rights derived from the British constitution, and insisting upon points, which, though your Excellency may consider them as non essential, we esteem its best bulwarks. No treasure can be better expended, than in securing that true old English liberty, which gives a relish to every other enjoyment." We should notice they were defending *English* liberty, defending the principles of the *English* constitution. *Massachusetts State Papers*, pp. 172-173.

[10] The same kind of discussion had arisen in 1728 when Governor Burnet called the legislature to meet at Salem. He gave as one reason the fact that the inhabitants of Boston had in town-meeting declared against "Setling a Salary". Such "forwardness" set an example to the towns in the country and was "better adapted to the Republick of Holland than to a British Constitution." The house contested the right

into years, ending only in 1772, when the legislature was allowed to meet again at Boston. And so, because of a needless order from an incompetent ministry, Massachusetts was taught to consider over and over again the nature of her institutions and her property in her principles of self-government. Hutchinson declared that the people who had previously disowned the power of Parliament now allowed little or no share of government to the king. But this indictment appears to have been false or at least extravagant in both counts; certainly, whatever may have been openly said by the irresponsible or covertly by the more radical leaders, it can hardly be declared that the colonists had come to these ultimate positions. They had not definitely reached the point of announcing in any formal and tangible way that Parliament had no power. Hutchinson himself was to bring them nearly, if not quite, to that declaration. And the time had not yet come when they were prepared to say that the king had degenerated into a tyrant. They were, however, easily to be persuaded; but, while it may to us appear in theory to be a short step from denying the binding effect of instructions to the denial of royal power, the distance in reality was considerable. If the colonists were not prepared to renounce allegiance, petty interference and nagging were likely to arouse the spirit of real rebellion almost as quickly as would acts of cruelty and tyranny.[11]

The year 1772 is for some reasons deserving of special notice; it cannot be passed over without comment. This is true especially because of the activity of Sam Adams, who, whether he was purposely working for complete independence or not, was certainly intent upon keeping alive the spirit of resistance to measures endangering his conception

of the Governor to remove the legislature, but, though protesting, did its work. *Journals of the House of Representatives of Massachusetts 1727-1729*, p. 362 ff. Italics of the original omitted. The discussions furnish an interesting illustration of the irritation caused by the superior tone of the Governor, and an illustration also of the determination of the colonists to maintain their rights and to guard their purses. The principles of the Revolution did not suddenly flock upon the scene in bright and unknown colors in 1765.

[11] Evidence of the fact that the colonial leaders were not at this time (1770-1771) bent upon total disruption of the empire is seen in the fact that in 1773 even the Massachusetts house hurled its arguments not against the king but against the Parliament, and the papers that came from the pens of leaders in 1774 were intended to establish the legal position of the colonies as dominions of the king. Jefferson, it is true, in his "Summary View" (1774), spoke to King George in no humble tones and found fault with His Majesty's conduct, but the time had not yet come to declare that the monarch had at no time legal authority over the colonies. Indeed, the time did not come at all, for the final charge (1776) was to the effect that the king had abused his authority and acted illegally by giving his consent to acts of "pretended legislation", and he had thus degenerated into a tyrant.

of American liberty.[12] Many times he used the arguments of which he was fond; he referred to Montesquieu, and Vattel, and Locke. Of chief interest was his work for the establishment of committees of correspondence in the towns of Massachusetts, a means of arousing a common action and sentiment and a common fear of peril. The document adopted by the town of Boston (November 20, 1772), seemingly the work of Adams, giving "the Rights of the Colonists and of this Province in particular, as Men, as Christians and as Subjects", is an able one, sprinkled with plentiful quotations from the philosophers and asserting the right to freedom to be inalienable. All this is of consequence to us because it brings out so clearly, once more, those fundamental notions which were widely held as the basis of free government —individual right to freedom and property and the necessity of limited rather than unlimited government.

In 1773, thanks to threats that persons accused of offenses committed in America should be sent beyond the sea for trial, another important step was taken, this time by Virginia. That colony recommended the formation of intercolonial committees of correspondence, and thus on a continental scale prepared the system which made opposition effective. The union of the colonies which later became a union of states rested thus at first on community of ideas fostered, though not begotten, by committees—extra-legal, if not illegal, bodies—which could present forcibly the spirit of discontent. Important in our history as opposition is, of importance also is the development of the mechanism and the practices which secured a degree of political unity or coöperation.[13]

In this same year (1773) Governor Hutchinson entered upon a perilous undertaking. Clothed with wisdom of the law and of history, he dared to argue with the Massachusetts legislature, to measure

---

[12] It is often stated that Adams was set upon independence much earlier than 1772, but his own published writings do not give proof of that assertion. Perhaps he was so determined, but if so, he kept it well out of sight, if we can properly judge from the written word. If he was so determined, his apparent reticence is evidence of the essential loyalty of those to whom he appealed. To show that his reasoning led or would lead to independence, because there was no halting place, is not enough. To reason so would be to attribute to him the very line of reasoning he emphatically denounced. "This is Chronus's 'method of reasoning', to prove that because it is necessary that the parliament should enact laws for the regulation of trade, about which there has as yet been no dispute that I know of, . . . Therefore, the parliament hath a right to make laws imposing duties or taxes. . . ." Samuel Adams, *Writings* (H. A. Cushing, ed.), II, p. 314. Italics of the original omitted.

[13] See Van Tyne, *op. cit.*, p. 427 ff.; J. M. Leake, *The Virginia Committee System and the American Revolution.*

swords in reality with Sam Adams, who in some measure was coached by John Adams, an able and learned lawyer. The Governor dared to bring forcibly to the attention of an eager populace the essential nature of the controversy between Great Britain and the colonies. He was vigorous, talented, and determined, but we still wonder at his folly. A number of impressive state papers [14] lie before us to-day, the weapons and the products of the dispute. The Governor's speeches are perhaps the best single presentation of Britain's case, the ablest arguments for parliamentary authority. Hutchinson believed he could conquer by argument. He believed he could convince by reasoning; but where did his reasoning lead? To the conclusion that the colonists had no rights, no institutions, no security, if Parliament wished to take them away; all were held by the insecure tenure of parliamentary grace. Once more the theory of parliamentary omnipotence must be acknowledged. No self-respecting people, accustomed to manage their own affairs, could accept such conclusions.

The council's second answer to the Governor is a memorable document; it is cogent and compelling. What possibilities had Hutchinson's cleverness conjured up! The councilors insisted on freedom from parliamentary taxation, but they were not to be drawn by the Governor's forensics to a denial of all authority. "What is usually denominated the supreme authority of a nation, must nevertheless be limited in its acts to the objects that are properly or constitutionally cognizable by it." Thus, they seem to say, in any constitutionally-organized nation there are legal duties and legal limitations. There is, in the nature and practices of government, no impossibility of recognizing those duties and those obligations. This is not quite the old argument from natural rights and the existence of a constitution that must be fixed; the council saw the possibility of distributed authority in an organized empire. The council plainly grasped the principle which in its reasonings had so far been only reached after, not seized. It referred to Hutchinson's statement that, "although . . . there must be one supreme authority . . . , this constitution will admit of subordinate powers, with legislative and executive authority, greater or less, according to local and other circumstances." "This is very true," the council replied, "and implies that the legislative and executive authority granted to the subordinate powers, should extend and operate, as far as the grant allows; and that, if it does not exceed the limits prescribed

---

[14] They are to be found in J. K. Hosmer, *The Life of Thomas Hutchinson,* p. 249 ff. and in *Massachusetts State Papers,* p. 336 ff.

to it, and no forfeiture be incurred, the supreme power has no rightful authority to take away or diminish it, or to substitute its own acts, in cases wherein the acts of the subordinate power can, according to its constitution, operate. To suppose the contrary, is to suppose, that it has no property in the privileges granted to it; for, if it holds them at the will of the supreme power, . . . it can have no property in them. . . . But, as in fact, the two powers are not incompatible, and do subsist together, each restraining its acts to their constitutional objects, can we not from hence, see how the supreme power may supervise, regulate, and make general laws for the kingdom, without interfering with the privileges of the subordinate powers within it? And also, see how it may extend its care and protection to its colonies, without injuring their constitutional rights? What has been here said, concerning supreme authority, has no reference to the manner in which it has been, in fact, exercised; but is wholly confined to its general nature."

Here we see a fairly firm grasp of the essentials of federalism. Plainly the central principle—the distribution of powers among governments—was taking definite shape in some colonial minds. Though the Parliament was spoken of as "supreme", we are not justified in supposing that the council meant by that word complete and all-embracing authority. Such authority was the very object attacked. The demand was for the recognition of "property" possessed by the colony —legal security within its legal sphere of government. And if to the reader this argument seems neither conclusive nor altogether clear, the fact remains that distribution of authority in the empire and the recognition of the rights of the colonies as constituent portions of the empire were asserted. If Hutchinson's reasoning and his conclusions were legally sound, he nevertheless thrust them unwisely into the faces of a politically-minded people who had practiced freedom; to dare such a thrust was a negation of cautious statesmanship. If the colonists, convinced by his reasonings, were forced to choose between unlimited submission to Parliament and complete freedom from control, which horn of the dilemma would they choose?

In the course of his argument, Hutchinson laid down a principle which he thought was beyond the reach of all denial: "I know of no line that can be drawn between the supreme authority of Parliament and the total independence of the colonies: it is impossible there should be two independent Legislatures in one and the same state; for, although there may be but one head, the King, yet the two Legislative bodies will make two governments as distinct as the kingdoms of England and Scotland before the union." Thus he handed out a principle of political science or philosophy; but men are not always willing to be governed by the principles of philosophy. Hutchinson, be it noticed, could not conceive of a government that possessed only limited authority; he could not conceive of two independent legislatures, not to say two independent governments, in one and the same state; one must be so distinctly subordinate to the other as to have no legally indefeasible property in its own authority.

When Hutchinson boldly threw down the gauntlet, the house eagerly took it up and, after discussing the general question of the powers of Parliament over the province, reached the critical point to which the Governor's speech had forced it. "Your Excellency tells us, 'you know of no line that can be drawn between the supreme authority of Parliament and the total independence of the colonies.' If there be no such line, the consequence is, either that the colonies are the vassals of the Parliament, or that they are totally independent. As it cannot be supposed to have been the intention of the parties in the compact, that we should be reduced to a state of vassalage, the conclusion is, that it was their sense, that we were thus independent. 'It is impossible,' your Excellency says, 'that there should be two independent Legislatures in one and the same state.' May we not then further conclude, that it was their sense, that the colonies were, by their charters, made distinct states from the mother country? . . . there is more reason to dread the consequences of absolute uncontroled power, whether of a nation or a monarch, than those of a total independence. . . . If your Excellency expects to have the line of distinction between the supreme authority of Parliament, and the total independence of the colonies drawn by us, we would say it would be an arduous undertaking, and of very great importance to all the other colonies; and therefore, could we conceive of such a line, we should be unwilling to propose it, without their consent in Congress."

The house appears to admit the possibility of a line of distinction between complete parliamentary power and the total absence of it, but the net result was a denial of any authority at all. Cleverly also the hint was given that the colonies acting together might be able to work out a scheme which would distinguish between powers and save some remnant of parliamentary jurisdiction; and what could be more ominous in the eyes of Westminster than a continental congress? The assertions made by the men of England in their discussions over the Stamp Act repeal, the declarations continually made that the denial of one power necessarily involved the denial of all, had now brought their legitimate and inevitable fruit. The direct and inescapable crisis was induced under provocation from a cocksure Governor who believed that he could do more than English pamphleteers, parliamentary orators, and loyalist newspaper writers had been able to accomplish; he thought that by sheer weight of metal he could sink the tiny shallop of provincial assumption and could overwhelm the great incendiary, its commander. Logic may have been on his side and references to precedent may not have been unavailing; but more than logic and theory were needed. And on their side, the cohorts of Sam Adams had the historical fact, even though here and there it was weakened by precedent, that the Massachusetts legislature did exist, had existed, had legislated, and had acted as a competent legislative body.

One or two other facts require brief statement. Hutchinson endeavored with some success to show that the Massachusetts legislature, in times gone by, had acquiesced in parliamentary legislation. But this, if it be in all respects true, could not, the house replied, destroy colonial rights, for the "fundamentals of the constitution" were stipulated in the charter, and they could not be altered by the legislature. Reference was made to the old favorite doctrine and to the favorite sentiment which was gathered from Vattel: for the authority of the legislature— the house maintained—" 'does not extend so far as the fundamentals of the constitution. They ought to consider the fundamental laws as sacred, if the nation has not in very express terms, given them the power to change them. For the constitution of the state ought to be fixed; and since that was first established by the nation, which afterwards trusted certain persons with the Legislative power, the fundamental laws are excepted from their commission.' " Thus once again appeared the doctrine of fundamental law and an unchanging constitution.[15]

[15] The reader will remember that in the memorial appended to Otis's *Rights of the British Colonies Asserted and Proved*, this passage from Vattel was referred to, and that the house, in the Circular Letter and in other letters of 1768, had made repeated use of this sentiment. My reason for calling attention to it here is that I am desirous of making very plain that this doctrine of fundamental law superior to all governmental authority had taken hold of the Revolutionary mind. It was, however, by no means a new or unfamiliar belief.

In the preceding pages attention has been given to the developing conception of federalism; but the treatment is incomplete. The author presented the subject and considerable evidence in a paper already referred to—"The Background of American Federalism", *Am. Pol. Sci. Rev.*, XII, pp. 215-240. The evidence there given (though again there was no attempt to present everything) appears to be enough to bring out the fact that the principle of federalism was at stake, at least so far as it embodied the idea of the distribution of authority; and it appears plain (1) that the forms and practices of the old empire were a distinct foreshadowing of the American constitutional system of federalism; (2) that the colonists almost to the last were content with what they had been accustomed to under the old imperial system which had never been formulated or diagrammed. "Every advantage that could arise from commerce they have offered us without reserve; and their language to us has been —'Restrict us, as much as you please, in *acquiring* property by regulating our trade for your advantage; but claim not the disposal of that property after it has been acquired.—Be satisfied with the authority you exercised over us before the present reign.'" Richard Price, *Additional Observations on the Nature and Value of Civil Liberty, and the War With America* (London, 1777), p. 76. Notice also the position of the Pennsylvania convention of 1774. See *American Archives* (Peter Force, ed), fourth series, I, cols. 561-562. These are illustrations of what I believe to be the main fact.

CHAPTER VIII

THE INTOLERABLE ACTS. THE ARGUMENTS IN DENIAL OF PARLIAMENTARY AUTHORITY

At the end of the great controversy between Hutchinson and the political leaders to whom he had sought to read a lesson in constitutional law, certain colonial positions were fairly plain. The colonial argument rested on two main pillars: the first was the doctrine of natural rights; the English constitution was supposed to embody natural rights and to make them secure; and closely associated with these principles was the belief that the only free government is restricted government—one that is constitutionally and legally limited. The second was the assertion that the colonies were possessed of an indefeasible portion of governmental power, that the empire was not a centralized or unitary empire, but was decentralized and diversified. Probably the Revolution had already advanced too far not to have very positive results, but on the face of the formal arguments the colonists were content with what had been their privileges and their rights ten years before, in other words, content with the old empire; [1] for it will be noticed, though the Massachusetts house was driven nearly, perhaps we should say fully, to the point of announcing total freedom from parliamentary control, it referred at length to the history of the colony and sought to prove from history its right to freedom from parliamentary interference; it did not assert its independence of the king, but complained of innovations made by Parliament and its agents in America. The council insisted on the reality of the system of distributed powers, the system which had grown up in the empire.

Here, therefore, we can see foundation for the statements made on

[1] When I say "content", I do not mean to say that there were not a good many men ready or, it may be, anxious to go beyond the old régime. I mean that in open public argument, in what we may call the formal presentment of their case, they relied ostensibly and probably honestly on the practices and what they believed to be the real structure of the empire and the real liberties of Englishmen. Whether they were legally right in their claims or not, this historical and legal or semilegal state of mind is important, as we have already said, despite no small amount of lawlessness and turbulence.

an earlier page of this volume. The reasoning of the colonists was wanting in some of the essentials of revolutionary thinking—that is to say, wanting in an attitude of rebellion toward established institutions, lacking an attitude of mind which would welcome an overturning and would sweep away the past and build new structures on its ruins. Colonial reasoning was both abstract and concrete. It was concrete and historical because it referred definitely to actual working institutions; it was in a measure abstract because it laid stress upon natural rights that were postulates of argument. But, it must always be remembered, those rights, as the colonists viewed them, were embodied in British citizenship; they had been given a degree of actuality in British constitutional doctrine; they had been announced time and again by revered British thinkers and political leaders, and, in part at least, were woven into the history of the "glorious revolution" of 1688, which was as near to the colonists as the days of Lincoln are to the men and women of the fourth decade of the twentieth century. It would be folly, of course, to deny that there was nothing in the spirit and history of English constitutionalism on which the colonists could base their demands.

One other thing we can see clearly: the Americans were arguing that they already possessed what in reality they were about to create—of course, only partly create, if create at all, because men, however wise, cannot make something from nothing. It is more nearly accurate to say that from the depths of history, from their own practical experiences, from the lessons of a practical exigency, they were being led forward to the time when they would establish their own institutions, and these institutions were to embody, more tangibly than ever before, adequate representation, limited government, and a diversified "imperial" or widely-extended political system. They were also to find an approach to democracy—some expression for the belief that government exists for man and is legitimately authorized to govern for his good.

The trouble was a fundamental one. The Revolution, even if we are thinking only within the rather narrow limits of constitutional history, gets its chiefest significance as a successful protest against superimposed government, a protest founded on ideas and principles which, active among the American colonists, were to find a wider expression in institutions and to shock and disturb the placid rule of the chosen few, until, in the course of time, the whole foundation on which authority rested was replaced and democracies took upon themselves the burden, the trials, and the anxieties of popular government in a troubled world. Even America, advanced as her principles were, had still to embody fully, in her thinking and her acts, the essentials of popular control—a consummation, if devoutly to be wished, not even yet actually and completely realized.

The action of Parliament (1773) in giving the British East India Company what amounted to a monopoly of the tea trade in America aroused opposition. Resistance was widespread. The most dramatic expression of resentment was the Boston Tea Party. That particular drama brought down upon the heads of the inhabitants of that uneasy town the vengeance of Parliament.[2] The destroyers of valuable property were to be adequately punished for their lawlessness until they paid for the fragrant weed they had cast upon the waters of the harbor. Indignant orators at Westminster then shouted *"delenda est Carthago."* Burke and a few others kept their heads, and that great statesman declared, "This dignity of yours is a terrible incumbrance to you." But the defenders of parliamentary authority were in no mood to listen to his chiding; for underneath all their exclamations was, as ever, the feeling of dignity; Parliament must be obeyed. So Parliament passed the Boston Port Bill shutting up Boston harbor, removing the customhouse to Salem, and leaving the townsmen to ponder on their poverty and their sins until the East India Company was repaid. The outraged parliamentarians might have known, had they stopped to think (an unusual exercise for some of them), that there might be serious trouble; for in other colonies the people had shown equal determination not to pay the duty, admit the principle of taxation, and drink the East India Company's tea. Not that all the colonists were determined and rebellious, far from it; but the disaffection was not confined to the uneasy and truculent Bostonians, who, if they had "to take their medicine", were not willing to take it in taxed tea. Harsh measures for the punishment of Boston were sure to awaken the resentment of the extremists from one end of the continent to the other.

Then came the Massachusetts Government Act. No more should

---

[2] The destruction of the tea aroused much opposition. The friends of America in Britain were taken aback. Chatham could not defend the unwarrantable conduct, and even Franklin hoped for a voluntary reparation and that soon. It is not the purpose of the text to glorify the Tea Party or to depreciate the difficulty of Britain's task. A man like Franklin still hoped to make American freedom secure by reason and diplomatic methods. And it is always a question whether riotous conduct furthers a cause.

the province be in the hands of common folks who knew nothing about politics. There is something really humorous in the statements of these men, who were about to lose an empire partly as the result of their ineptitude, denouncing the incapacity of the Boston men for politics.[3] But they had their way. The Governor of the province was by the bill given more authority; the king was to appoint the councilors of Massachusetts; and the noisy town-meetings—save for the election of town officers and representatives—were not to be held without permission of the Governor. The practical politicians of Westminster supposed they could prevent men from coming together and talking— call their meetings what you will—and supposed that these institutions, which were the very heart and center of New England life and thought, would be snuffed out at the word of a body of wisemen three thousand miles away.

To make matters worse, if it were possible, other bills were passed; one, euphoniously called a bill for the "impartial administration of justice", provided that under certain circumstances, at the word of the royal Governor, with the advice and consent of the council, the trial of an officer or soldier might be transferred to another colony or to England. Lord North might have stopped to remember, if he knew the fact, that the British soldiers charged with the crime of firing on innocent citizens at the Boston "massacre" had been defended by two able colonial lawyers,[4] and that only two were punished, and then not severely. But it was no time for thought or memory. Another act, the Quartering Act, directed the Governor, when the need arose, to provide suitable accommodations for the royal troops. The army, whose presence had done so much to keep the Bostonians irritated, was thus not to be housed and confined in the castle, but placed, if thought best, where its constant presence would curb the people, and, it might be said, provoke them to new outbreaks. These acts were so extreme, so far beyond the ordinary processes of government, that they were nearly in the field of martial law; they looked like war, a war by an army and a Governor responsible only to kingly authority, and directed against a town and a province.

These were four of the five "intolerable acts" of 1774. They were directed against Massachusetts and against disobedient and naughty

---

[3] "I would not have men of a mercantile cast, every day collecting themselves together and debating about political matters. . . ." Lord George Germain, as quoted by Van Tyne, *op. cit.*, pp. 396-397.

[4] No less persons than John Adams and Josiah Quincy.

Boston. The fifth, the Quebec Act, though in the American mind classed with the others, was really an act apart; it provided for greater fairness and justice in the administration of Canada, especially by the recognition of French law and by assuring a degree of liberty for Roman Catholics. In New England, religious animosity was pushed to the fore, and hatred of Catholicism gained new heights. More than once in these pages attention has been called to the incapacity of British statesmen in the task of solving the problems of empire; the irony of the situation is apparent, for, when Parliament did pass an act which breathed the spirit of liberality, the air of the colonies was filled with cries of denunciation.

There was also a provision for extending the boundaries of the Canadian province to the Ohio in the region beyond the mountains; and thus the colonies, some of them claiming under their charters the right to control large areas in the west, were deprived of any right or authority in the vast region toward which certain seaboard easterners were beginning to look with more than languid interest. The measure, heartily disapproved of by many colonials, was denounced as one more measure of tyranny. It should, however, be associated with the king's Proclamation of 1763, with various other plans, with the proposals of the Albany Congress, and with British interest in the Indian trade. The time was coming when the Americans must themselves tackle the western problem; the time was not far distant when they must face the task of working out the principles upon which their own empire should be extended and their own colonies established.

Boston was locked up; but her spirit was indomitable. The colonists were now not prepared to submit to measures which even to-day a person knowing the difficulties of imperial control and administration must consider harsh and intemperate. There was from colony to colony a flash of resentment and a wave of indignation. Not all of the colonists were aroused; there were still many who were acquiescent, believing that liberty could best be secured under Britain, and fearing, too, the radicals, dreading the rise of unpropertied classes—"the mob". The story of the struggle between conservatives and radicals is important, for in America there were differing views, many shades of opinion; but of greater moment in this connection was the awakened public sentiment, the realization, along the line of the colonies from north to south, of a common danger. The issue had passed beyond the mere disputed right of parliamentary taxation; for if Britain, in any emergency, could pass such acts as those which were directed against

Massachusetts, the whole fabric of colonial self-government was in peril. So while many still held back, and while there was unity in no single colony, the "intolerable acts" created sympathy, fellow feeling, the sense of a common interest among the colonies as a whole; and thus, as never before, there was the basis of a national feeling, or, if nationalism is too strong a word, the basis of colonial union.

Advanced thinkers in the colonies were by 1774 ready to move on to a new position. That was natural and inevitable. Events, humorously and ironically announced by Franklin to the Commons eight years before, had run their course. That Parliament was totally without authority over them, the colonists had not at first asserted;[5] but the lofty tone of Britain and the dignified assurance of men like Hutchinson had done their work. Not merely thoughtless and irresponsible, but sober-minded men, who were far from being temperamental rebels, were now at the point of denying that they owed obedience to Parliament in any respect. In preparing the second answer to Hutchinson, the men of the Massachusetts house had been coached on some technical legal points by John Adams, and when that controversy ceased for want of words, Adams, in a pamphlet war, announced definitely and at length his theory of the empire: the union with Britain was only a personal union; the British and the Americans owed allegiance to the same king; there were many kingdoms under the headship of George III; as one of these kingdoms, Massachusetts possessed her own Parliament.[6]

The "Summary View",[7] written by Thomas Jefferson in 1774, also contains the same theory of colonial right; it contains a spirited attack on Parliament and its acts, "acts of power, assumed by a body of men, foreign to our constitutions, and unacknowledged by our laws. . . ." America would no longer listen to meddlesome interference. But significant as is this denunciation of Parliament, of even greater significance are the admonition to King George himself and the declaration

[5] Again it may be wise to say there is some evidence of opinion at a much earlier date to the effect that the colonies were not subject to Parliament. The statement of the text refers to what on the whole appears to have been formal colonial opinion.

[6] In a series of papers signed "Novanglus", published in *The Boston Gazette,* 1774. See John Adams, *Works* (C. F. Adams, ed.), IV, pp. 11-177. These papers were answers to Daniel Leonard ("Massachusettensis").

[7] "A Summary View of the Rights of British America. Set Forth in Some Resolutions Intended for the Inspection of the Present Delegates of the People of Virginia. Now in Convention." Printed at Williamsburg, reprinted in Philadelphia and in London. See Thomas Jefferson, *Works* (federal ed.), II, pp. 47-89.

of certain formal principles of democratic or popular government Revolutionary thinking was moving fast toward a goal, natural to a free people who had in large degree looked after themselves and handled their own affairs. Jefferson was familiar with the arguments so often used : the origin of government in consent, the right of revolution when tyranny becomes intolerable, and all the rest of it; he well knew the great writers on law and politics; but his first notable utterance in the cause of America was more than a repetition of seventeenth-century law and philosophy, dear as they were to him.

His voice was the voice of the more radical Virginia.[8] And it is a signal fact that this young man, gifted with rare literary skill, a man of cultivation and learning, though as yet without much experience save that furnished by rural Virginia, was reading a lecture to His Majesty King George on elementary ideas of government and the duties of rulers to their superiors, the people. The big planters of the tidewater region of the Old Dominion, tenacious as they were of American rights when threatened by Britain, must have read Jefferson's words with misgivings, almost with dread, for in fact they foretold trouble for themselves and their privileges. Though they may not then have been fully aware of it, the spirit of a coming democracy was calling to them. His Majesty was warned "that he is no more than the chief officer of the people, appointed by the laws, and circumscribed with definite powers, to assist in working the great machine of government, erected for their use, and consequently subject to their superintendance. . . . kings are the servants, not the proprietors of the people. Open your breast, sire, to liberal and expanded thought. Let not the name of George the third be a blot in the page of history. . . . The whole art of government consists in the art of being honest." [9]

Jefferson's arraignment of parliamentary power went far—farther than had the ordinary complaints—in criticizing the actual acts familiar to the colonists. He attacked the acts of trade and disallowance of colonial laws as actually practiced; even the post office, he declared, seemed "to have had little connection with British convenience, except that of accommodating his majesty's ministers and favourites with the

---

[8] Of special interest is H. J. Eckenrode, *The Revolution in Virginia*. This study brings out the social and political differences in that important colony.

[9] How pleasing this would have been to George, if he had read it, as he probably did not. Had he accepted such admonitions, he would have been tempted to abandon his practice of buying seats for his supporters in the Commons. In truth, the idea that kings were servants, not masters, was startling enough. To be shocked by such sentiments one did not need to wear a crown.

sale of a lucrative and easy office." "A Summary View" was therefore a harbinger of the Declaration of Independence; and in it we can see some of those principles of Jeffersonism which in still later years were to be influential in American politics.

I have no intention of entering upon the question of the validity of the arguments which were put forth with elaborate legalism by John Adams and more briefly and passionately by Jefferson. They are important as indicative of a growing opposition; they are important as items in the position taken by the colonial Congress in 1774 and in the Declaration of Independence which arraigned George III for giving his consent to acts of "pretended legislation"; they are of interest to the students of the history of the British empire; but they are of strangely little significance to anyone studying, not the causes of war, but the emergence of American constitutionalism. Even under the system advocated by John Adams and others, the Crown of course retained its functions, and those, as we have already indicated, need not be neglected by anyone seeking to find precedents for the grant of certain powers to the central government under the American Constitution when that was formed. But the creative or constructive effect of the arguments as a whole does not appear, save as Jefferson's statements may have been productive of American democracy. By dwelling on the separate independence of each colony, attention was in reality called away from interdependence, the actual need of coherence, and the need of a central administration in certain particulars. Scholars of unquestioned skill and learning are to-day at variance on the question of the legality of parliamentary control, in this respect reproducing the attitudes of Thomas Hutchinson on the one hand and of John Adams on the other; and this very difference of opinion is of more significance than any definite assurance concerning the indubitable legal correctness of either position.[10] Any discussion of this problem in these pages, sufficient to be of any use, would lead us away from the developments we are attempting to trace, and any dictum as to the correctness of one side or the other would be only another assertion. As in a good many other cases, the important fact is that men at a given time did differ.[11]

[10] See C. H. McIlwain, *The American Revolution: a Constitutional Interpretation;* R. L. Schuyler, *Parliament and the British Empire; Some Constitutional Controversies Concerning Imperial Legislative Jurisdiction.*

[11] To put the matter flatly, the present writer simply cannot be enticed by his own curiosity to pass upon a controversial question when the answer does not lead him to a more distinct view of the emergence of institutional forms and the principles underlying them in the American constitutional system. If that be treason, one must make the best of it.

CHAPTER IX

THE CONGRESSES OF 1774-1775

The treatment of Boston aroused the colonists to a new pitch of resentment and to new unity of action. The first step for a continental congress seems to have been taken by Virginia, but the idea was variously proposed. The call or suggestion of Virginia was acted upon in the summer of 1774.[1] Delegates were chosen by different methods, but largely through the agency of the committees of correspondence, those irregular but effective bodies fitted for the task of maintaining popular rights and, if need be, for bringing on revolution.[2] Formal procedure by the colonial legislature was, in nearly every case, not taken and would have been difficult, for there was not only official opposition in most of the colonies, but among the timid or conservative much objection to radical measures. The Congress was therefore decidedly and obviously an extra-legal body; save that it was not chosen to foster revolution, it might well be considered a revolutionary body—composed as it was of representatives who in most instances were not even chosen by the popular branch of the colonial legislatures.[3] In no formal sense, therefore, was the gathering representa-

---

[1] See C. R. Lingley, *The Transition in Virginia From Colony to Commonwealth,* pp. 81-82; A. M. Schlesinger, *The Colonial Merchants and the American Revolution, 1763-1776* (Columbia University *Studies in History,* etc., LXXVIII), p. 363.

[2] "When the Continental Congress met, there is good reason to believe that it was looked upon as a meeting of the committees of correspondence of the several colonies. . . ." Van Tyne, *op. cit.,* pp. 427-428.

[3] In New Hampshire, delegates were chosen by "a meeting of the deputies appointed by the several towns" assembled for the purpose; in Massachusetts, by the house, after locking the door to prevent notice of dissolution by the Governor; in Rhode Island, where there were no royal officers in political control, by the general assembly; in Connecticut (likewise a free corporate colony), by the house which authorized the committee of correspondence to appoint delegates; in New York, "By duly certified polls, taken by proper persons, in seven wards of New York City and County," and by sundry other committees of outlying districts; in New Jersey, by a convention; in Pennsylvania, by the house; in Delaware, by a convention of the "Representatives of the freemen"; in Maryland, by a convention or a "Meeting of the Committees" from the counties; in Virginia, by a provincial convention; in North Carolina, by "a general meeting of deputies of the Inhabitants"; in South

tive of existing colonial governments; it represented the people, the dissatisfied elements of the people, such persons as were sufficiently interested to act, despite the strenuous opposition of the conservatives and, in general, the obstruction or disfavor of the governors.

When the Congress met in Carpenters' Hall, Philadelphia, in early September,[4] what were its tasks? The country was by no means united. The conservatives were growing fearful; many of those who strongly objected to Britain's measures were anxious to reach some means of reasonable adjustment of difficulties; the radicals were active and skillful. But the instructions or declarations of opinions which were drafted by the gatherings that sent the delegates were by no means inducements to precipitate rebellion. One question had to be solved: what principles were to be proposed that would, to use the words of Rhode Island, "establish the rights and liberties of the Colonies, upon a just and solid foundation"?

Even those delegates who were intent upon opposition to parliamentary taxation and were indignant at the treatment of Boston were not in accord concerning methods of procedure or concerning any theory of the constitution of the empire, if the empire was to exist at all. But the time had come when there must be more than complaint; there was need of a fairly decisive statement of constitutional order. The more advanced were ready and anxious to go the whole road, short of casting off the power of the king; but others held back.

John Adams tells us more clearly than the *Journals,* and probably

Carolina, by "a general meeting of the inhabitants" whose action was ratified by the house.

It is interesting to note that the basis of representation in the Congress came up for consideration as soon as the members began the task of organization. Should each colony have one vote or should the principles of proportional representation be adopted? A proposal "to establish an equitable representation according to the respective importance of each Colony", was not carried, and in its place it was decided that "each Colony or Province shall have one Vote.—The Congress not being possess'd of, or at present able to procure proper materials for ascertaining the importance of each Colony." September 6, 1774. *Journals of the Continental Congress* (W. C. Ford, ed.), I, p. 25. Hereafter referred to as *Journals.* Each colony should have "one voice; but as this was objected to as unequal, an entry was made on the journals to prevent its being drawn into a precedent." Connecticut Delegates to Governor Trumbull, October 10, 1774. Quoted in *Ibid.,* I, p. 25, note 1.

[4] September 5, 1774; 44 delegates were present the first day; 45 the second. Representatives from North Carolina appeared later, as did a few additional delegates from colonies represented at the beginning. The first volume of the *Journals* gives the proceedings with copious and learned notes by the editor. The "Autobiography" and "Diary" of John Adams published in the second volume of his *Works* are interesting and valuable for side lights on the meeting.

quite as accurately, what the difficulties were. In the committee of which Adams was a member there was much discussion concerning the basis of American rights. Should it "recur to the law of nature, as well as to the British constitution, and our American charters and grants"?[5] This problem did not, however, prove supremely difficult; it was easy enough to lay claim to all these foundations of freedom; but that did not end the matter; for, as Adams says, "The other great question was, what authority we should concede to Parliament; whether we should deny the authority of Parliament in all cases; whether we should allow any authority to it in our internal affairs; or whether we should allow it to regulate the trade of the empire with or without any restrictions." A subcommittee of which Adams was a member met and debated the pivotal questions. Seemingly without great difficulty all the articles of its report were agreed upon "excepting one, and that was the authority of Parliament, which was indeed the essence of the whole controversy. . . ." [6] Finally, the agreement appearing in the fourth resolution of the "Declaration and Resolves" was reached. It declared that the colonies were "entitled to a free and exclusive power of legislation in their several provincial legislatures . . . in all cases of taxation and internal polity, subject only to the negative of their sovereign, in such manner as has been heretofore used and accustomed. But, from the necessity of the case, and a regard to the mutual interest of both countries, we cheerfully consent to the operation of such acts of the British parliament, as are bona fide, restrained to the regulation of our external commerce, for the purpose of securing the commercial advantages of the whole empire to the mother country, and the commercial benefits to its respective members; excluding every idea of taxation, internal or external, for raising a revenue on the subjects in America, without their consent." [7]

This resolution appears to be essentially a compromise; [8] it did not

[5] The resolutions as finally adopted declared that the colonists "by the immutable laws of nature, the principles of the English constitution, and the several charters or compacts, have the following Rights".

[6] John Adams, *Works* (C. F. Adams, ed.), II, p. 374.

[7] *Journals*, I, pp. 68-69.

[8] Of course, whether or not they denied in toto the authority of Parliament depends on the scope the reader may give to the words "internal polity". If those words are interpreted as excluding entirely from parliamentary control such subjects as naturalization, coinage, the post office, etc.—in other words, those pieces of legislation which we now in our own system recognize as powers within the natural field of general government—then perhaps the conclusion must be reached that the colonies asserted their position as dominions of the king, utterly free, legally, from

acknowledge the legal power of Parliament even to regulate trade, but it consented to the operation of acts for that purpose. Furthermore, it did not repudiate control by the royal prerogative, which was indeed explicitly acknowledged in the address to the king a few days later.[9] There was a distinct acknowledgment of the "negative of their sovereign," which presumably meant disallowance by the king in council. In the "address to the people of Great-Britain", the Congress said, "Place us in the same situation that we were at the close of the last war, and our former harmony will be restored."[10] Thus, as far as constitutional theory was concerned, a continental Congress could not go much further than had the Congress of nine years before. There were, it is true, many who were willing to go further; but the Congress was not prepared to pass on to a total and explicit denial of parliamentary authority; and, be it noticed, the old fact and the old practices were still on the whole dominating.

That the colonists, so far as Congress represented their true feelings, were in a temper easily to be changed into actual rebellion is apparent from the proceedings at Philadelphia. But it was still a rebellion against abuses of parliamentary authority, a rebellion to retain, in the empire and under the king, the constitutional rights which were claimed on the basis of the colonial charters and the English constitution. If, however, the British government should persist, the colonists

other control. But, it will be noticed, there was no *definite* declaration to the effect that Parliament at no time had any authority over them; and the absence of any such statement is to me indicative of hesitation to lay down absolutely plain legal theory. Cf. McIlwain, *op. cit.*, pp. 116-117. Some writers and students may be misled by the wording of the first resolution as given in *Select Charters* (William MacDonald, ed.), pp. 358-359, the resolution there reading "they have never ceded to any foreign power whatever, a right to dispose of either [life, liberty, and property] without their consent." The word "foreign" should be "sovereign". *Journals*, I, p. 67; *Journals of Congress* (1823 ed.), I, p. 20. To object to "sovereign", in any complete sense, was characteristic of the colonial position. MacDonald's work is in general painstaking and accurate.

[9] "We wish not a diminution of the prerogative, nor do we solicit the grant of any new right in our favour." *Journals*, I, p. 119.

[10] *Ibid.*, I, p. 89. The matter presented above is important for our purpose of following the main line of constitutional argument; but it should be noticed that certain essential rights of Englishmen were also asserted by the Congress: rights to the common law and trial by jury, the right peaceably to assemble and petition, and the right to be freed from the presence of a standing army in time of peace, except by consent of the legislature of the colony. It also asserted that it is necessary to good government that the constituent branches of the legislature be independent of each other and that the exercise of legislative power in the colonies by a council appointed, during pleasure, by the Crown, was unconstitutional and dangerous.

must soon deny the authority of Parliament altogether and soon move on to rebellion against the king himself.

The Congress did not present any theory of empire or set forth any scheme of empire, though Joseph Galloway of Pennsylvania presented one.[11] But the resolutions did assert the legal title of the colonies to certain powers and privileges. Probably at that time, when men's minds were inflamed, it would have been impossible to do any piece of constructive work; for the organization of the empire required long and candid consideration and calm discussion. What the Congress did was to assert rights; it provided no real answer to the critical problem of the whole dispute—what plan could be arranged whereby there would be legal obligation, in freedom, upon the outlying parts of the empire to contribute to the defense and support of the empire? While it is not at all strange that such constructive work was not undertaken, we can reasonably assume that some men were considering it. The hope of having a legal system in which the colonies would have a legal share of power and a legal title to their rights was still in men's minds.

Of great consequence was the "Association", "a non-importation, non-consumption, and non-exportation agreement," [12] solemnly entered into by the colonial delegates before the Congress adjourned. If this could be loyally taken up and rigidly enforced, Britain, it was thought, would feel fully the force of American anger. Some portions of the undertaking were not to be put into effect at once. Throughout the colonies, from one end to the other, efforts to carry out the agreement were made, and contests of strength as well as of opinion were frequent. So nearly thorough were the provisions for the execution of the agreement that we may justly consider that the system of committees and the whole machinery constituted in a very marked degree the unification of the radical or the determined forces of the continent.

---

[11] *Journals,* I, p. 43 ff. Galloway especially pointed out the need of having some general authority in the empire with power to regulate commerce. See John Adams, *Works,* II, pp. 390-391.

[12] Adopted October 20, 1774. It was a most imposing and thoroughgoing document. Far more than a mere agreement, it provided for execution by calling for committees in every county, city, and town, for inspection by committees of correspondence, and for enforcement by the boycotting of profiteering merchants. It proposed to encourage frugality and to promote agriculture, to discountenance extravagance and dissipation, "especially all horse-racing, and all kinds of gaming, cock-fighting . . . and other expensive diversions and entertainments. . . ." Restraint even on the wearing of "mourning-dress" was called for.

Here was union reaching out more widely and further down than previous schemes; and here was a method of securing results through the operation of committees.[13]

The winter of 1774 and 1775 was filled with distraction and with some uncertainty. We have been discussing the conflict of opinion between Britain and America; but that conflict was not all. Every colony, as we have seen, had its differences of opinion;[14] each had its own problems and its own experiences, and it is difficult therefore to use any terms of description quite applicable to all alike; and indeed the Revolutionary movement, the social and economic disturbances, the emergence of new leaders, the gleam of new aspirations among classes of men hitherto inactive or negligible in politics—all these are in some ways the most interesting and significant facts in the whole struggle.

Much more than separation from Britain or resistance to "intolerable acts" of a government across the sea was contained in the Revolution. Much social and political history is to be found in those disputes and controversies among the colonists during the years between the adoption of the "Association" and the outbreak of war and the final acceptance of independence.[15] It is not well to tell here the story of American resistance as if the colonies, each working smoothly within its own limits and in accord with the other colonies, presented a united

[13] Had the Congress without interruption continued to sit and direct the activity of the various colonies, the method of organization and of action would have been strikingly like the present organization of a national political party—that organization which brings into harmonious coöperation on a national scale the interests and the activities of the remotest hamlet and the wards and precincts of the large metropolis; that impressive manifestation of political union of continent-wide dimensions, a manifestation of machinery and of articulated organs more indicative of vital nationalism than the mechanism and operation of what we call the government.

[14] In 1774, the "Association" met determined opposition from the mercantile and moderate classes who disliked the violence and the democratic arguments of the radicals. See Schlesinger, op. cit., p. 432 ff.

"It should never be forgotten that in the eyes of the older men the Revolution was a conservative movement, an effort to uphold their liberties against the encroachments of imperialism. Eighteenth-century liberalism had little touched this older generation. . . . They wanted the gods to nod on Parnassus—or even to snore—but they wanted the gods. They thought English thoughts and upheld English institutions and condescendingly looked down on dissenters and democrats as not of themselves." Eckenrode, op. cit., pp. 158-159. See also, p. 160. The author is speaking chiefly of Virginia, but his words may be given a somewhat wider application.

[15] Attention is called to Eckenrode, op. cit.; C. H. Lincoln, The Revolutionary Movement in Pennsylvania 1760-1776; C. L. Becker, The History of Political Parties in the Province of New York, 1760-1776; J. F. Jameson, The American Revolution Considered as a Social Movement.

front to Britain. Each one was internally undergoing very vital and on the whole life-giving though distracting experiences. Save in the self-governing colonies of Connecticut and Rhode Island, the actual management of the Revolutionary movements was passing into the hands of conventions or committees or provincial gatherings—governments outside of the legal government of each colony.[16] During two years or so before independence, therefore, essentially revolutionary governments had partially displaced the purely legal authorities; not that these governments, these extra-legal bodies, necessarily thought of themselves as revolutionary in character; for until toward the end they were not necessarily committed to the task of breaking the empire. They were determined to use popular power to maintain their rights against parliamentary exactions and misgovernment. The thought of complete independence was still almost frightful to many a man earnest in his advocacy of boycott and of hostility to the obnoxious laws of Britain.

Such a condition of affairs could not long continue. Peculiarly hard was the situation in Boston where British forces maintained their hold. There was much that was disorderly about the Revolutionary movement everywhere, but on the whole the calmness and the regularity with which the people of that stern old commonwealth persisted in rebellion without suddenly breaking into tempestuous and profitless rioting is impressive and very conclusive proof of their capacity for self-government. More acts came from Parliament to be heaped on their sullen heads [17] without drawing them into thoughtless outbreaks which might have ruined their cause. The crisis came on the nineteenth of April, 1775; Lexington and Concord, and the hurried retreat of the British troops—such of them as were not killed on the way—back to the protection of their comrades at Boston signaled the beginning of war. At last, to use the pleasing phrase of Locke, there was an "appeal to Heaven".

When the Continental Congress gathered at Philadelphia on the tenth of May, 1775, war had already begun. The Massachusetts men

[16] Georgia was still largely outside of the general movement. It was represented by a delegate from one parish in the Congress of 1775, and later (September) by others chosen by a provincial congress.

[17] An act restraining the trade of New England was passed March 30, 1775, and later extended to the other colonies. In December, a bill cutting off all trade with America was enacted. As the Americans wanted to indulge in non-importation Lord North thought they should have their desire to the utmost. ". . . as the Americans," he is reported to have said, "had refused to trade with Great Britain, it was but just that they be not suffered to trade with any other nation."

had gathered about Boston and the British forces. What was Congress to do? It prepared for war and prayed for peace; it organized an army, appointed Washington commander-in-chief, and sent off to George III a new address asking for justice. The hope of obtaining a redress of grievances without disruption of the empire was daily dwindling; there was a steady though varying forward movement toward independence. Lord North's "Conciliatory Resolution", passed by the Commons (February 27, 1775), was presented to the Congress in May; but it came too late; probably it would have been at no time satisfactory, because there was no abandonment of parliamentary power to "bind the colonies and people of *America* . . . in all cases whatsoever." The proposals were rejected in July, and in August the king issued a "Proclamation of Rebellion".

The autumn and winter passed. In the spring (April 6, 1776) the Continental Congress passed resolutions which substantially established freedom of trade with all the world save Great Britain. The old navigation acts and with them the whole system of parliamentary control and regulation of trade were cast into the discard. With the passing of such resolutions, independence could not be far away.

CHAPTER X

THE PHILOSOPHY OF THE REVOLUTION AND THE DECLARATION OF INDEPENDENCE

America was the child, the developed child, of seventeenth-century England. She had grown strong and self-reliant. She had breathed the air of a new world; she had been shaped in part by her experiences on a virgin continent; but to understand her character, we need to understand her inheritance almost as much as the environment in which she matured. There is truth in the exaggerated assertion that in the Revolution (1765-1776) the England of the seventeenth century arose to combat the England of the eighteenth; and there is truth in the declaration that America separated from Britain in the seventeenth century rather than in the second half of the next century. The simpler statement is that America was influenced in the course of her development by the thinking and by the struggles to liberalize government in the days of the Stuarts, days which saw a rebellion based on an announcement of rights beyond the reach of kingly prerogative, days which saw the execution of one king, and saw also the dethronement of another because he had broken the original contract between king and people. We are not likely to overemphasize either the fact of the English rebellion and the later peaceful revolution (1688) or the thinking that underlay revolt.

Though in the later days its most popular utterances came from a son of Virginia, and though much of its philosophy was a possession common to America as a whole, this seventeenth-century thinking was especially cherished by the New England colonists. This was so in part because the early New Englanders were the offspring of the protest against Stuart absolutism; perhaps also because Massachusetts peculiarly thought of herself as self-founded and not a child of the empire; but certainly because the thinking of the seventeenth century was embedded in church polity and in theology.

Fundamental in New England religious thought were the following: (1) there is a divine law superior to all other and binding on every creature, on ruler and ruled; (2) the individual man before entering church relationship is an individual separate and distinct; (3) churches are formed by the consent and agreement of men; the basis of the church is covenant; churches and church government are not superimposed but created by the people composing the churches; (4) the Ruler of the universe, the embodiment and source of unvarying justice and duty, had bound Himself by covenants, by promises. The interlacing of political and religious thinking was very marked; it would be more nearly correct to say that the two modes of thought were in reality only two manifestations of one. Elementary principles of political philosophy were kept alive, not alone by recollection of the seventeenth-century struggles for liberty or by the actual methods of forming churches, but also by the sermons of the preachers, inculcating political and ecclesiastical doctrine.[1]

During the seventeenth century in England there was so much practical as well as purely theoretical presentation of doctrines concerning the origin of state and government, that it is misleading to select any one writer or politician or any one series of events as illustrative.[2] But among all the writers of that century, John Locke stands out above the rest. He did not, however, originate his doctrines, far from it; doctrines of like character had been put forth in previous centuries; for, as a matter of fact, men had often questioned the basis of governmental authority, and they had announced the all-prevailing divine law as superior to human enactment. Especially, in the hundred years before Locke wrote his famous second essay on government, Englishmen had been talking about and for a time fighting about those very problems.[3] Locke's argument in his

---

[1] Very valuable is A. M. Baldwin, *The New England Clergy and the American Revolution*. One must weigh the fact that two treatises, published in the early part of the eighteenth century from the pen of John Wise, which contained distinct and detailed presentation of the theory of compact, were republished in Boston in 1772, "and so eager was the perusal of them, and so extensive the demand for their clear reasoning in favor of democracy as the best government, that another edition, of which more than one thousand copies were bespoken before its issue, was put to press in the same city in the same year." H. M. Dexter, *The Congregationalism of the Last Three Hundred Years, As Seen in Its Literature*, pp. 501-502.

[2] Of special usefulness in this matter is T. C. Pease, *The Leveller Movement*.

[3] The long effort, though at times only an effort of a secluded closet philosopher, to answer the great question—are there limits on human authority?—is especially interesting to American students of constitutional law. The Revolution and the formation of American institutions should be seen as part of the history of political thought. It is not the intention of these pages to declare that the philosophy of the American Revolution was new; it is not the intention to assert that it came wholly from Locke

second essay, written just after the "glorious revolution" of 1688, had continuing effect, partly because of its directness and simplicity, and partly because it came, for England at least, at the end of a controversy and furnished the basis of parliamentary authority as opposed to divine right of kings. His essay deserves our attention because it was used by the men of our Revolution. When men at that crisis thought and spoke in the terms of Locke, they naturally supposed they were relying on an authority, one of the fathers, whose words could not be meaningless to the men of England in the later eighteenth century. In fact, though a parliamentarian, to refute colonial assumptions, could refer to Locke with approval—as the Scripture is said to be cited by the arch-enemy of mankind—he could not have been entirely at ease when the philosophy of the renowned essay was quoted against him.

A reference by a colonist to Locke's writings must not be considered a mere reference to a bookman who had been speculating about government; he was thought of as the expositor of the foundations of English constitutionalism, an authority on constitutional law. When the colonists of the Revolutionary days referred to him, they thought of him as putting forth, not theories of what *ought* to be, but pronouncements of what actually *was;* in his words and in the words of many other liberal thinkers of the seventeenth century they saw pronouncements of the *real* basis on which the rights of Englishmen were founded. And all this is important because it is a matter of great consequence that the American Revolution had, despite much social turmoil, the quality of conserving the old and not merely blasting it; it is important above all because the Revolutionists did more than announce doctrines and quote authorities; they took the theories of the philosophers and the declarations of men like Locke and wove them into an actual constitutional structure. Locke and others like him were to the Americans more than visionaries.[4]

or from the polity and theology of Puritanism. There was little that was new in the American doctrines, perhaps nothing. But we do find that Americans were ready to institutionalize their principles and not merely to fight for them. For a discussion of the antiquity of the doctrines, see James Sullivan, "The Antecedents of the Declaration of Independence," Am. Hist. Asso. *Report* for 1902, I, pp. 65-81. Sullivan finds all of the doctrines of the Declaration, though many parts were much older, in the philosophy of Nicolas of Cusa, of the early fifteenth century.

[4] Even after, long after, our Constitution was founded, American lawyers not only spoke in the philosophy of Locke, but quoted him or referred to him. See, as an example, T. M. Cooley, *The General Principles of Constitutional Law* (4th ed.), p. 138 and note 1, referring to Locke to show the unconstitutionality of delegation of power by a legislative body.

Seeking the source of government, as a method of ascertaining the extent of its authority, Locke started, as did many others before and after him, by declaring that there was a time when men lived in a state of nature in which there was no government. All men were in "a state of perfect freedom to order their actions, and dispose of their possessions and persons" as they saw fit. Men were also in a state of equality; there was no precedence. And yet it was not a state of license, though it was a state of liberty; for there was a law of nature which taught that no man should harm another "in his life, health, liberty or possessions. . . ." But each man was judge in his own case; and so men turned to the establishment of government to avoid the inconveniences by which they were beset. They did not, however, set up government to be absolute over them; "he who attempts to get another man into his absolute power does thereby put himself into a state of war with him. . . ." Man had liberty in nature, and had only the law of nature for his rule; the "liberty of man in society is to be under no other legislative power but that established by consent in the commonwealth. . . ." As liberty existed before government, and as the right of man to his life existed before government, so also property antedated government. Property, therefore, had natural or divine sanction.

But when man leaves his natural state, "he authorizes the society, or which is all one, the legislative thereof, to make laws for him as the public good of the society shall require," and this "puts men out of a state of Nature into that of a commonwealth. . . ." Though Locke was intent upon upholding the legislative power, his main theme was established security for fundamental natural rights under government. "If man in the state of Nature be so free as has been said, if he be absolute lord of his own person and possessions, equal to the greatest and subject to nobody, why will he part with his freedom, this empire, and subject himself to the dominion and control of any other power? To which it is obvious to answer, that though in the state of Nature he hath such a right, yet the enjoyment of it is very uncertain and . . . the enjoyment of the property he has in this state is very unsafe, very insecure. This makes him willing to quit this condition . . . and it is not without reason that he seeks out and is willing to join in society with others who are already united, or have a mind to unite for the mutual preservation of their lives, liberties and estates, which I call by the general name—property. The great and chief end, therefore, of men uniting into commonwealths, and putting themselves under government, is the preservation of their property. . . ." [5]

Power, Locke declares, "in the utmost bounds of it is limited to the public good of the society. . . . Thus the law of Nature stands as an eternal rule to all men, legislators as well as others." [6] Having in mind the security of person and possessions, he also declares that not even the legislature can assume the power to rule by "extemporary arbitrary decrees, but is bound to dispense justice and decide the rights of the subject by promulgated standing laws, and known authorized judges." [7] "Absolute arbitrary power, or governing without settled standing laws, can neither of them consist with the ends of society and government. . . ." [8] He was thinking of the eternal and unvarying law of nature and of nature's God, and, in addition, the need of established and open principles as a means of giving security. [9]

How far Locke goes in indicating the principles of legally limited government can especially be seen in his reference to a well-recognized principle of the common law—an administrative officer, acting beyond his warrant, may be resisted—and he inquires why this principle is not applicable to the highest magistrate in the land. We find in this the kernel of the doctrine later firmly embedded in American constitutionalism: no one has a right to enforce an unconstitutional law. There are legal bounds to governmental authority. Though we should err in attributing to Locke alone the origin of this idea, we do not err in finding in his philosophy—closely associated as it was with practical politics and with certain established principles of English

[5] Locke, op. cit., bk. II, secs. 123-124.
[6] Ibid., bk. II, sec. 135.
[7] Ibid., bk. II, sec. 136.
[8] Ibid., bk. II, sec. 137; see also secs. 22, 124.
[9] Locke's summary of his chapter, "Of the Extent of the Legislative Power", presents some of the ideas just discussed: "These are the bounds which the trust that is put in them by the society and the law of God and Nature have set to the legislative power of every commonwealth, in all forms of government. First: They are to govern by promulgated established laws, not to be varied in particular cases, but to have one rule for rich and poor, for the favourite at Court, and the countryman at plough. Secondly: These laws also ought to be designed for no other end ultimately but the good of the people. Thirdly: They must not raise taxes on the property of the people without the consent of the people given by themselves or their deputies. And this properly concerns only such governments where the legislative is always in being, or at least where the people have not reserved any part of the legislative to deputies, to be from time to time chosen by themselves. Fourthly: Legislative neither must nor can transfer the power of making laws to anybody else, or place it anywhere but where the people have." Ibid., bk. II, sec. 142.

liberty—a popularization of certain essential principles which were prominent at the time of the American Revolution and of great subsequent importance. That a law contrary to natural right and justice is no law at all was no new doctrine.[10]

It may be at times necessary to transcend the law. The power to act "according to discretion for the public good . . , is called prerogative. . . ."[11] But "Wherever law ends, tyranny begins, if the law be transgressed to another's harm. . . ."[12] To go beyond the law for the good of the people, is, then, prerogative; to do so for the injury of the people is tyranny. Who is to judge what is good and what is harmful? That is the pivotal question. To determine this, there must under some circumstances be an "appeal to Heaven", and the people have the right to determine whether this appeal to the final arbitrament of force is justified or not. This right of determination they cannot surrender, "God and Nature never allowing a man so to abandon himself as to neglect his own preservation."[13]

Locke's argument leads him to the right of revolution, but it must not be conceded that the end is turmoil. May then the prince be opposed, may he be resisted as often as anyone shall find himself aggrieved? This would leave "nothing but anarchy and confusion."[14] But no such consequence is admissible because man has the right to oppose only "unjust and unlawful force." This right of revolution, this final resort to force, this right to rise not against law but against lawlessness, to rise not against legitimate but illegitimate authority, naturally was and remained a cardinal doctrine.[15]

And still, someone may declare that, as the people may dissolve a government, as this is their final right, the very hypothesis lays a

[10] See, for example, Thomas Aquinas, *Summa Theologica*, part 2, no. 3, q. 95, art. 2, p. 57 (1915 ed.) : "Every human law has just so much of the nature of law, as it is derived from the law of nature. But if in any point it deflects from the law of nature it is no longer a law; it is but a perversion of law."

[11] Locke, *op. cit.*, bk. II, sec. 160.

[12] *Ibid.*, bk. II, sec. 202.

[13] *Ibid.*, bk. II, sec. 168. The reader thinking in the terms of modern politics would now answer the question by saying, "The people must judge." But it is to be noticed that Locke means their right to fight, their right to "appeal to Heaven." To constitutionalize and institutionalize this right to judge was to be part of the work of the American Revolution.

[14] *Ibid.*, bk. II, sec. 203.

[15] Rebels in behalf of the great ends of society were not rebels; the tyrant was the lawbreaker, a rebel against law superior to himself. "In whatsoever he has no authority, there he is no king, and may be resisted: for wheresoever the authority ceases, the king ceases too. . . ." *Ibid.*, bk. II, sec. 239.

foundation for frequent rebellion. The answer to this assertion is: "cry up" your governors as much as you will "for sons of Jupiter" —adopt, that is to say, your theory of divine right—and you shall still have rebellion, because people will not endure the extreme of misery; furthermore, revolutions do not occur on account of mere "slips of human frailty"; but "a long train of abuses, prevarications, and artifices, all tending the same way," may arouse the people to put the rule into hands that will secure to them the ends "for which government was at first erected. . . ." [16] Thus we see, when once it be admitted that there are limits on government, a critical question remains: who is to judge whether the limits have been exceeded or not? That proved to be in reality a perplexing question, not to be forgotten in the history of American constitutional doctrine. Locke did not foresee the development of popular government and its mechanism; nor did he see the full implication of his assertions; but implications there were; and in the later developments of American institutions we discover a partial solution of this pressing and imperative question in the full recognition of judicial authority as well as in the right by institutional processes to reorganize government.

The idea that an act contrary to the fundamentals of the constitution (natural justice, natural equity, the law of God, and the law of nature) was no law played its part in the American Revolution. It was notably influential in New England where the ministers had frequently preached the doctrine of covenant and the limits of governmental power. A cardinal illustration is the sermon of Jonathan Mayhew which he preached in 1749-1750, the anniversary of the death of Charles I; [17] the bold young minister ridiculed the attribution of sainthood to the executed monarch, and denied the propriety of calling the great rebellion of the seventeenth century by the name of rebellion, for it surely was not unlawful to oppose acts of tyranny or to refuse to obey a monarch who had *"unkinged"* himself by his own acts.

In looking over this revolutionary thinking of Locke and his disciples, we discover some things especially notable in addition to those already selected for comment: (1) though his whole line of argument grew out of historical necessities and though it was applied to a practical problem, it was at the same time in its nature very artificial, making no great effort to find out whether government really did

16 *Ibid.,* bk. II, sec. 225. Cf. the Declaration of Independence.
17 *A Discourse Concerning Unlimited Submission* (Boston, 1750), p. 38 ff.

originate in compact. The artificial as opposed to the realistic method is evident at every turn. (2) The basic assumption is that men did make the state, that man existed as an individual and that, by the conscious purpose of unrelated beings, a new comprehensive being, a new entity, can come into existence. (3) As man existed in a state of nature under natural law, as he was an abstracted being, it is possible to build upon certain principles which are abstractly true, forever unchangeable; those principles are not the product of experience; they are not of relative validity but of absolute validity. We need not descant upon the value, in any argument, of having absolutes to deal with—unchanging and unchangeable principles. (4) There is in Locke's reasoning no conception of a body politic—that is to say, a conception agreeable to modern metaphysical political philosophy—a single coherent though not fully-organized body laying down its will authoritatively concerning its own structure and the limits of government.

Now, central in all this thinking is the foundation or source of authority by consent of the governed. By inevitable logic, as well as by pious thinking, governments were bound by the purposes of the compact. The whole idea of limited government, bound by law, is implicit, if not absolutely obvious, in the whole theory. We have already noticed the announcement of natural rights in sundry American arguments of the Revolutionary period. Natural and fundamental rights are conspicuous in the declarations of the Massachusetts representatives (1768). The extent to which they were to be taken seriously, when the people came to found their new institutions, will be spoken of later. At the present, the purpose is to point out briefly the nature and the logical effect of the assumption that men existed before government and had rights which were not granted by government (one of the conspicuous principles of American constitutionalism).[18] These doctrines were used as the basis of resistance to Britain, but they are to be taken into account not simply because they partly explain the American Revolution. It is, in fact, rather difficult —though perhaps the learned may succeed—to interpret the course of American constitutional history or American constitutional law without an understanding of the compact philosophy. One illustration must suffice: in a decision rendered by the Supreme Court of the United

[18] This subject of covenant, compact, and binding law is briefly treated in the author's *The Foundations of American Constitutionalism,* a series of lectures delivered in New York University. The purpose of those lectures was to show the origins of American constitutional doctrines, especially as indicated by New England history.

States in 1875 we find these words : "The theory of our governments, State and National, is opposed to the deposit of unlimited power anywhere. . . . There are limitations on such power which grow out of the essential nature of all free governments. Implied reservations of individual rights, without which the social compact could not exist, and which are respected by all governments entitled to the name."[19]

By the spring of 1776, the pretense or the appearance of waging war as subjects of the king was scarcely tenable; many there were who still shrank from formal announcement of independence; but when the Continental Congress adopted resolutions recommending the establishment of governments in the various colonies, it was apparent that they were to be considered as no longer colonies but states. The transmutation of colonies into totally self-governing commonwealths was the heart of the Revolution as a practical fact.

In May a convention in Virginia—an extra-legal body—instructed the colony's delegates in Congress to propose the declaration that the colonies were free and independent and to give the assent of the colony to such a declaration. They were also directed to give assent to any measures which might be thought proper for forming foreign alliances and a "Confederation of the Colonies," with the distinct proviso, however, that "the power of forming Government for, and the regulations of the internal concerns of each Colony, be left to the respective Colonial Legislatures." [20]

Richard Henry Lee of Virginia, offered in Congress, June 7, 1776, the following resolutions : "*Resolved,* That these United Colonies are, and of right ought to be, free and independent States, that they are absolved from all allegiance to the British Crown, and that all political

---

[19] Loan Association *v.* Topeka, 20 Wallace 655, 663. The word "reservations" deserves special attention. It unquestionably implies the existence of rights before governments were established, and it is similar to, if not identical with, the theory of a body of natural rights under natural law anterior to the constitution of social order. We may well notice also the principles often announced in federal court decisions two hundred years and more after Locke, which declared acts void because they violated principles of right and justice; the supposition is that there is a *standard* of justice beyond which legislation must not go and which is protected by the due process clause of the fourteenth amendment.

[20] Journal of the convention in *American Archives* (Peter Force, ed.), fourth series, VI, col. 1524. See also, H. B. Grigsby, *The Virginia Convention of 1776,* pp. 8, 17-18. It is interesting to notice that the Pennsylvania assembly, when consenting to the compacts between the colonies in 1776, spoke of "reserving to the people of this Colony the sole and exclusive right of regulating the internal government and police of the same." *American Archives,* fourth series, VI, col. 755

connection between them and the State of Great Britain is, and ought to be, totally dissolved.

"That it is expedient forthwith to take the most effectual measures for forming foreign Alliances.

"That a plan of confederation be prepared and transmitted to the respective Colonies for their consideration and approbation."

Not all the delegates were as yet convinced that the time had come to take this final and irrevocable step. If New England was restless and its leaders out of patience with discussion and delay, and if Virginia and one or two other colonies were ready and eager to move on, the large and powerful colonies of New York and Pennsylvania were still hesitating. Without unanimity of sentiment and without coöperation among the colonies from one end of the land to the other, the announcement of independence would be peculiarly bold and perhaps foolhardy.

In other colonies there were controversies; there were still differing elements in each; one element was anxious for advanced measures; another was holding back, afraid of independence or dreading the radicals and all their works; a third was lukewarm, undecided, or even uninterested. No complete picture of the situation is possible; any general statement is inexact. On the whole, this is true: the naturally conservative elements of the population, the well-to-do, the people who had most to lose from unsuccessful or perhaps from successful rebellion, many of the merchants fearing "the mob" and the total annihilation of their industry, were inclined to oppose the more eager and radical elements.[21]

On the first day of July the subject of immediate announcement of independence was discussed in the committee of the whole; the debate took up most of the day but it was, John Adams said, "an idle mispence of time," because nothing was said that had not been said a hundred times before. Only nine colonies were then prepared to take the final step. New York refused to vote; South Carolina and Pennsylvania voted in the negative; the vote of Delaware was divided. The Pennsylvania delegates were in a state of uncertainty because their authority came from the legal assembly of the colony, while the resolution favoring independence was passed by another body. In South Carolina the advocates of separation from the mother country were met by strong opposition, and the colony's delegates in Congress could not be sure of their right to vote for separation or of the sup-

---

[21] See Becker, *op. cit.;* Lincoln, *op. cit.;* Schlesinger, *op. cit.,* especially p. 591 ff.

port of the colony should they do so. The next day, however, the situation cleared. Caesar Rodney had hurried from Delaware to Philadelphia in time for the crucial vote. A majority of the Pennsylvania delegates decided to vote for independence, and the South Carolina delegates made up their minds that they could take the same stand. So when on July 2 the final vote was taken, only three delegates [22] are known to have cast their votes in the negative. New York did not vote at all. The formal Declaration was adopted July 4, and at a later time, August 2, it was signed by the members of Congress.[23]

The Declaration was naturally and inevitably directed against George III—inevitably because the time had come to break the bonds of allegiance between king and subjects. Moreover, there was absolutely no reason for getting involved once again in a confusing argument about the old question of parliamentary authority. The supposition underlying the Declaration was that the colonies then were and always had been free from any legal control by Parliament. The king was charged in the Declaration with having given his consent to "acts of pretended legislation". In light of the long preceding contest concerning constitutional authority, there was no other reasonable basis for the announcement of independence;[24] there were certainly men in the Congress—John Adams and Jefferson for example—who would not be ready to confess that it was necessary or proper to declare the overthrow of parliamentary power.

The document is of very great moment in American history because of the philosophy of government set forth in the opening paragraphs. Of that philosophy we have already spoken. It was the philosophy—the political thinking—of compact and natural rights, the

[22] These were Willing and Humphreys of Pennsylvania and Read of Delaware. John Dickinson and Robert Morris of Pennsylvania were absent when the vote was taken. Dickinson appears to have been influenced by the belief that, before actual declaration of independence, state governments should be set up and that there should be agreement on the terms of confederation. It was not unreasonable to contend that substantial governmental union should precede separation or that the two be practically contemporaneous.

[23] "The declaration of independence being engrossed and compared at the table was signed. . . ." *Journals*, V, p. 626. See Herbert Friedenwald, *The Declaration of Independence*, ch. VI. Some of the signers whose names were on the list were not members of Congress on July 4. One member is known to have signed as late as 1781.

[24] Of course, Congress might have discussed at length the problem of just how much power Parliament had had; but there would have been disagreement, and the whole declaration, if one had ever been reached, would have been ineffective. Thus Parliament was ignored as a body "foreign to our constitutions, and unacknowledged by our laws. . . ."

philosophy which justified rebellion or revolution against tyranny, which announced the principle of the popular origin of government and proclaimed the doctrine that governments were possessed of *derived* authority—a doctrine, then and now, of pivotal importance in American constitutionalism. The passages in which these principles were proclaimed were clear and powerful; they expressed the beliefs and the theories held by the American people. Jefferson merely made use of commonly accepted ideas concerning the origin and nature of government.[25] It was not his duty to create a new system of beliefs; and therefore to charge him with having no originality and with indulging in airy phrases is, of course, quite foolish.

George III is stigmatized in the Declaration as a prince "whose character is thus marked by every act which may define a Tyrant. . . ." How, it has been asked, can such a charge be justified? George was an obstinate, perilously active, wrong-headed monarch, but no one can justly call him a "Tyrant". In answer, one may ask a question in return—what, under the circumstances, could Jefferson and his colleagues have said? Certainly not that the king was a kindly father of his people. But in reality the propriety of using the term "Tyrant" depends on the meaning of the word, and its meaning was clearly defined in the very political philosophy which was embodied in the Declaration: a tyrant is a ruler who goes beyond the law to the injury of the people. With that definition in mind, no one desirous of independence would strain and strangle over the word "Tyrant".[26] The Americans then, according to this theory, were not lawbreakers; the king had become a lawbreaker by disregarding the very ends for which government was established—the good of the people.[27]

[25] By this I do not mean that there were no persons who rejected the doctrines of compact and natural rights; but these beliefs were so widely held that they may with some confidence be ascribed even to many who were not ready to act upon them by rebellion.

[26] "As usurpation is the exercise of power which another hath a right to, so tyranny is the exercise of power beyond right, which nobody can have a right to. . . ." Locke, *op. cit.,* bk. II, sec. 199. "Wherever law ends, tyranny begins, if the law be transgressed to another's harm. . . ." *Ibid.,* bk. II, sec. 202. Doubtless the American patriots were willing in their excitement to use terms of denunciation fitting a Borgia or a Caligula. But without reference to that fact, the philosophy of the Declaration is consistent. It is tyranny that justifies revolution, and surely Jefferson piled up a rather large series of specific indictments.

[27] Notice that John Milton (quoted without reference by J. W. Thornton in *The Pulpit of the American Revolution,* pp. 67-68 note) pointed out that to resist authority acting contrary to what St. Paul makes the duty of those in authority is not to "resist the power nor the magistracy" but to "resist a robber, a tyrant, an enemy." Jared Eliot, in his Connecticut election sermon, 1738, said, "Arbitrary

Earlier pages of this chapter contain a brief summary of the political philosophy of Locke and of the Revolution; and that philosophy was presented in condensed form and with astonishing skill in the Declaration. One aspect of the subject merits special attention: "We hold these truths to be self-evident, that all men are created equal, that they are endowed by their Creator with certain unalienable Rights, that among these are Life, Liberty and the pursuit of Happiness." These words would strike few men in those days as novel or absurd. It remained for men of later times to ridicule the assumption of natural equality. But doubtless Jefferson, like Locke, did not intend to assert that each man was as strong, virtuous, and competent as every other; nor was he desirous of announcing social, economic or political equality. There were, however, certain great rights which man had in a state of nature—before there was a government to which he must be obedient; of these rights, certain ones were not surrendered and could not be surrendered. But this is not by any means the whole of the matter; for the main thesis of Jefferson is that governmental power is derived from the consent of the governed; government has not inherent or intrinsic authority, but only granted or delegated authority. The most important word in the Declaration is "deriving".[28]

In a state of nature there was equality; no one had the right to say yea or nay to his neighbor; no one had the right to bid his neighbor do this or not to do that. But government and political order were established by consent, and the system of the original state of nature and of original equality disappeared. Men must continue to be equal in the possession of fundamental natural rights, for they would not have given up equality and freedom to put themselves under absolute, arbitrary, and merciless rule; but, as the result of compact, a *superior* came into existence; there existed one man or body of men with authority to command; and those commands should be obeyed so long

Despotick Government, is, When this Sovereign Power is directed by the Passions, Ignorance & Lust of them that Rule. And a Legal Government is, When this Arbitrary & Sovereign Power puts itself under Restraints, and lays itself under Limitations, in all Instances where they see it Either possible or probable, that the Exercise of this Sovereign Power may prove or have proved Prejudicial or Mischievous to the Subject: Even this is an Act of Sovereign Power. This is what we call a Legal Limited & well Constituted Government. Under such a Government only there is true Liberty." Quoted in Baldwin, *op. cit.*, p. 176.

[28] "The Power of the greatest Potentate on Earth is not Inherent in him, but is a Derivative. . . ." Ebenezer Pemberton, *On the Power and Limitations of Magistrates.* Massachusetts election sermon. 1710. Quoted in *Ibid.*, p. 174.

as government kept itself within the limits which the original compact implied.[29] Jefferson was not bent upon announcing to people who were then engaged, or soon to be engaged, in framing constitutions that they must provide for universal suffrage or must grant equality of either political or economic power. He was primarily intent upon presenting a basis for overthrowing the authority of King George.

The critical question, we may repeat, was how it came about that one man, a monarch, or one set of men had been placed above other men with power to issue orders, laws, and decrees; if governmental power was derived, if men voluntarily and by consent had surrendered their *original* equality, then, unquestionably, government was authoritative only when acting within the limits of the compact and when guarding the natural rights of life, liberty, and property. *Before* government was established, men were in a state of equality; *after* government was established they were not; they gave up their equality and subjected themselves to a superior; but this superior must rule for the common good. This is the sum and substance of the philosophy of Locke and of the Declaration of Independence.

The Declaration is not to be read as if it had no meaning for us save as it permitted an excuse or a reason for separating America from Britain. It contains doctrines which on their peculiarly theoretical side have partly lost their cogency. The notion that the only way in which men can be legitimately bound is by a promise, or something akin to promise and contract, is to-day not quite orthodox political philosophy or quite the thinking of the common man. We do not postulate a pre-social state of existence in which man was an isolated, absolutely

---

[29] In a pamphlet ascribed to Elisha Williams and issued in 1744, we find this: "Reason teaches us that all Men are naturally equal in Respect of Jurisdiction or Dominion one over another. . . . But it [natural freedom] consists in a Freedom from any superior Power on Earth, and not being under the Will or legislative Authority of Man, and having only the law of Nature (or in other Words, of its Maker) for his Rule. . . ." Quoted in *Ibid.,* p. 176. The writer goes on to consider why men gave up the original state of nature and he refers to Locke.

". . . 'Tis not indeed pretended that any one man or number of men have any natural right or superiority, or inherent claim of dominion or governmental authority over any other man or body of men. All men are by nature free and equal and independent in this matter. It is in compact, and in *compact alone*, that all just government is founded." Jonas Clark, Massachusetts election sermon, 1781. Quoted in *Ibid.,* p. 180.

"But though men when they enter into society give up the equality, liberty, and executive power they had in the state of Nature into the hands of the society . . . yet . . . the power of the society . . . can never be supposed to extend farther than the common good. . . ." Locke, *op. cit.,* bk. II, sec. 131. See also secs. 4, 54.

independent, and segregated atom. We think historically; we know how governments did arise; we think of society as a living fact, even if it does in some way establish a government by votes of individuals. But the significance of the Revolution is lost if one does not see the Americans taking this "compact" philosophy seriously, and if he does not see that the elementary principle—the existence of individual rights which governments were established to protect—has not lost its force in American constitutional law.   .

This interpretation of the thinking of the Declaration should not imply the absence of more radical or more advanced doctrines or impulses and desires among the men of the Revolution, especially among those who in some of the colonies had been most active in protesting against the established order of things. Jefferson himself was prepared to attack the intrenchments of privilege secured by law in the Old Dominion. Everywhere men who hitherto had been ignored in colonial politics were forging to the front; they were pushing ahead to new positions, in some cases demanding or assuming further political rights. Some persons were envious of the more fortunate, and probably quite justly so; they envied the possessors of large landed estates and they disliked the economic domination of their owners. The Revolution, in part begotten by social and economic discontent within the individual colonies, was moving on to its inevitable conclusion—not to immediate social equality or to complete economic equality, but to a greater degree of power and confidence in the main body of the people. But that is a long story; its end was not reached in the days of the war or for some decades thereafter. The movements that produced the downfall of British rule, probably also the very philosophy on which the Revolution was based as well as the struggle itself, broke down old traditions and helped in carrying forward the principles of political equality and a fuller realization of the worth and competence of the common man. Revolution was working out its natural consequences; there lay ahead the inevitable diminution of that presumption of superiority which was the dear possession of social and economic leaders.

CHAPTER XI

EARLY STATE CONSTITUTIONS

The Declaration of Independence involved the necessity of estab-lishing state governments. Separation from the mother country meant that the colonies were no longer colonies in the British empire, but independent states. The early stages of the process of transition were distinctly a part of the conflict with Britain. The Revolutionary move-ment, while it was still only a rebellion and before there was any defi-nite intention to break with Britain altogether, necessarily produced some form of extra-legal government; royal and proprietary governors were ignored or steps were taken to overcome or circumvent their power. Provincial congresses or conventions or committees chosen in the various communities contrived, as best they might, to get their way. The growth of the power of these conferences, especially of the com-mittees having in charge the whole management of resistance, was as a rule gradual; but it began before the fourth of July, 1776.

The Continental Congress was naturally interested in the establish-ment of substantial governments in the rebellious colonies. Some of the members were at an early day quite aware of what such an estab-lishment would imply, and if they were eager for independence, they were keenly desirous of seeing the colonies enter upon the job of fashioning governments capable not only of resistance but of doing the work of self-dependent commonwealths.

The first important step was taken by the provincial congress of Massachusetts. That colony sent a formal letter (dated May 16, 1775) to the Continental Congress asking for explicit advice "respecting the taking up and exercising the powers of civil government," and promis-ing to submit to such "a general plan" as Congress might direct for the colonies.[1] Early in June Congress answered the inquiry: inasmuch

[1] The letter, in the form of a resolution, was presented to Congress June 2. An essential paragraph is as follows: "We are happy in having an opportunity of laying our distressed state before the representative body of the continent, and humbly hope you will favour us with your most explicit advice respecting the taking up and exercising the powers of civil government, wᶜʰ we think absolutely necessary for

106

as no obedience was due to the act of Parliament for altering the charter, and no obedience to a governor or lieutenant-governor endeavoring to subvert the charter, those officers should be considered as absent and their offices vacant; it was resolved that "in order to conform, as near as may be, to the spirit and substance of the charter, it be recommended to the provincial Convention, to write letters to the inhabitants of the several places, which are intituled to representation in Assembly, requesting them to chuse such representatives, and that the Assembly, when chosen, do elect counsellors; which assembly and council should exercise the powers of Government, until a Governor, of his Majesty's appointment, will consent to govern the colony according to its charter."

In the latter part of the same year New Hampshire sent a somewhat similar request, which was answered in substantially the same manner.[2] Soon afterwards, like recommendations were made to South Carolina[3] and Virginia.[4] In these three cases, however, the advice of Congress, more clearly than in the reply to Massachusetts, brought out the idea of an independent representative body capable of setting up a government; it more nearly approached the conception of a representative constitutional convention. Indeed, that idea in its fundamentals is plain.[5]

The next spring (May, 1776) a resolution with a very expressive and conclusive preamble was passed in Congress. It declared it necessary that the exercise of every kind of authority under the Crown should be totally suppressed, that all of the powers of government should be exerted under the authority of the people, and that it be

the Salvation of our country and we shall readily submit to such a general plan as you may direct for the colonies, or make it our great study to establish such a form of government here, as shall not only most promote our advantage but the union and interest of all America." *Journals,* II, p. 77. This was a very wise and shrewd approach. It took for granted that the matter was of continental concern; it was becomingly submissive to the opinion of Congress, and it indicated the desirability of a general plan for "America". But the general plan had to wait, for not all the colonies were so far along the road to independence as was Massachusetts.

[2] Laid before Congress October 18, 1775. Answered November 3, 1775.

[3] November 4, 1775.

[4] December 4, 1775.

[5] *"Resolved,* That it be recommended to the provincial Convention of New Hampshire, to call a full and free representation of the people, and that the representatives, if they think it necessary, establish such a form of government, as, in their judgment, will best produce the happiness of the people, and most effectually secure peace and good order in the province, during the continuance of the present dispute between G[reat] Britain and the colonies."

recommended to the assemblies and conventions of the united colonies, where no government sufficient to the exigencies of their affairs had been established, to adopt such government as should, in the opinion of the representatives of the people, best conduce to the happiness and safety of their constituents and of America in general.[6] Thus nearly a year had passed between the advice to Massachusetts and the general recommendation to the colonies. The hesitant might still persuade themselves that the governments established were to be but temporary, lasting only until the unfortunate dispute with the mother country should be settled, but this general advice meant that the colonies were henceforth to be free and independent states.

In the transmutation of colonies into commonwealths the principles on which these new states were to be founded were a matter of transcendent importance. And, as principles have reality and stability only when made actual, the method and the machinery whereby the states were established and organized are of signal significance. Many times in the past, writers on government had asserted that the people were the original possessors of power and the source of governmental authority. Such declarations had been announced as the corner stone of the American argument against Britain. Now that the Americans had the opportunity to set up governments, how nearly would their conduct accord with this doctrine? An intelligent people, a reading people, a people well-schooled by orators, pamphleteers, lawyers, and preachers, and instructed by the political discussions of a decade, had the chance to rear governments and to fix the limits of their power by legal and authoritative commandments. Adams tells us that he declared that the people "must be all consulted, and we must realize the theories of the wisest writers, and invite the people to erect the whole building with their own hands, upon the broadest foundation." [7] The principles of political philosophy were to be put to the test.

What then was necessary if the theories of "the wisest writers" were to be actualized with an exactness they themselves could not have conceived? It was necessary (1) to bring into political action the main body of the people; (2) to produce an organ representing the people,

---

[6] In the above sentences the resolution of May 10 and the preamble adopted on May 15 to accompany the resolution are abbreviated and woven together. We can see in these resolutions the basis of the conversation reported by John Adams: "Mr. Duane called it to me, a machine for the fabrication of independence. I said, smiling, I thought it was independence itself, but we must have it with more formality yet." John Adams, *Works* (C. F. Adams, ed.), III, p. 46.

[7] *Ibid.*, III, p. 16.

the duty of which would be to describe the government and to define, if need be, the limits of its power; (3) to give the people, the original of power, the opportunity of passing definitely upon the proposed constitution and of bestowing upon the government the legal right to govern; (4) so to proceed that the body drawing up the constitution should be sharply distinguished from the legislature—the legislature acting as a temporary revolutionary government and the legislature to be reëstablished under the new system; this was necessary because there must be no obscuring the derivative power of government as distinguished from the inherent power of the people. The body that drafted the constitution must not, therefore, legislate in the ordinary sense of the word. If the convention should not only draft a constitution but also act as a legislative body, then legislation and the constitution might appear to be on the same plane; the convention must not act as if it were a government; it must in all respects consider itself as a body representing the people for the specific purpose of preparing a government. If the constitution emanated from the convention and was not formally ratified by the people, the derivative character of the government might not stand forth so adequately and conclusively that even the blind could see. Only by the most careful observance of process in accord with elementary principles could it be made perfectly evident that to secure life, liberty, and the pursuit of happiness governments are instituted among men and derive their just powers from the consent of the governed.[8]

[8] These ideas and the elements of the process flowed naturally and inevitably from the whole theory of the compact-origin of government as set forth by "the wisest writers" and announced over and over again during the preceding century by the New England preachers. How well Adams and others knew written pronouncements concerning a constitutional convention which were put forth in England in the middle of the seventeenth century, we do not know. They knew the theory, and some of them probably knew Sir Henry Vane's *Healing Question.* They may not have known an interesting document of that earlier century which very distinctly presented the fundamental character of a constitutional convention. I refer to a plan drawn up in 1648: "That some persons be chosen by the Army to represent the whole Body; and that the well-affected in every County (if it may be) chuse some persons to represent them: And those to meet at the Head-Quarters.

"That those persons ought not to exercise any Legislative power, but onely to draw up the foundations of a just Government, and to propound them to the well-affected people in every County to be agreed to: Which Agreement ought to be above Law; and therefore the bounds, limits, and extent of the peoples Legislative Deputies in Parliament, contained in the Agreement to be drawn up into a formall contract, to be mutually signed by the well-affected people and their said Deputies upon the dayes of their Election respectively. . . ." *Legal Fundamentall Liberties,* p. 34. Quoted in Pease, *op. cit.,* p. 261. Notice the character of the body to meet at headquarters and the popular ratification by signing. It appears that deputies elected

The constitutional convention is a familiar American institution, so familiar, in fact, that we find difficulty in realizing its fundamental character. Use of the process of representation for gathering a body of people with authority to draft a constitution appears so simple that we naturally think of the representative convention, the primary body subject only to the people themselves, as if the men of the Revolution created it without engaging in serious perplexity. But of course such was not the case; there was perplexity as well as failure in some cases to adopt methods plainly demonstrating the theory of popular government. But the statesmen of the day had the advantages of experience with representation as a working system and did not need to rely on theory alone. Even the provincial congresses and gatherings which had assumed control in the various colonies, though generally very irregularly constituted and irregularly chosen, were at the worst ostensibly representative; and thus the idea of a body based on systematic representation rather naturally adapted itself, under the wise guidance of Congress, to the existing practices.

In Massachusetts, after much discussion, the method which was followed showed so perfectly the theory of popular power and the nature of a constitution, that the work of that state merits our special attention although the constitution was the last of the strictly Revolutionary constitutions.[9] In May, 1777, the body which, formed on the analogy of the old charter, was the revolutionary but also the actual government of the state, recommended that the towns at the coming election empower their representatives to take part as members of a constituent convention for making a constitution which should be submitted to the towns for adoption and be instituted by the General Court, if approved by two-thirds of the freemen of the state over twenty-one years of age.[10] Upon the authorization of the towns thus secured, the assembly resolved itself into a convention, drew up a con-

to Parliament under this fundamental instrument were, *when elected,* to sign, a provision similar to our provision requiring officers elected as well as others to take oath to abide by the Constitution.

[9] In New Hampshire, where the general methods of operation were likely to resemble those of Massachusetts, a constitution was adopted in 1776 by a body not chosen for that special task and that alone. In 1778 a convention properly constituted drafted a constitution which was defeated by popular vote. Other conventions met and framed constitutions which met with a like fate. One was finally approved in 1783.

[10] H. A. Cushing, *History of the Transition From Provincial to Commonwealth Government in Massachusetts* (Columbia University *Studies in History,* etc., VII, no. 1), p. 207.

stitution and submitted it to the people (March 4, 1778). It was not accepted. There were several objections to it; especially noteworthy was the objection based on the absence of a bill of rights.[11]

If one wishes to see the literalness with which the men of those days took the theories of the origin of government in compact and the original possession of power by the people, he should read the *Essex Result,* the product of a convention of Essex County but largely the work of Theophilus Parsons.[12] "Over the class of unalienable rights", the *Result* declared, "the supreme power hath no controul, and they ought to be clearly defined and ascertained in a BILL OF RIGHTS, previous to the ratification of any constitution. The bill of rights should also contain the equivalent every man receives, as a consideration for the rights he has surrendered." [13]

After the defeat of the constitution in 1778, steps were taken to prepare another and to follow methods in all respects theoretically correct. The temporary government asked the voters to vote on two questions: did they desire a new constitution, and if so, would they empower their representatives to summon a convention for the sole purpose of framing one? As two-thirds of the towns were favorable, the towns were then called upon to select delegates who should form a constitution to be established by the vote of two-thirds of the free male inhabitants twenty-one years old, acting in town-meetings called

[11] There is probably no need of attempting to decide exactly when and where the idea of the character of the full-fledged constitutional convention came to light. We have already noticed the appearance of the idea in England over a hundred years before the American states acted. The origin of the institution, perfectly envisaged, has been attributed to Concord, Massachusetts, by R. S. Hoar ("When Concord Invented the Constitutional Convention," *Boston Transcript,* July 3, 1917). The resolutions of the town-meeting (October 21, 1776) are full of interest: they declare the legislative is no body proper to form a constitution—"first Because we conceive that Constitution in its proper Idea intends a system of principals established to secure the subject in the Possession of, and enjoyment of their Rights & Privileges against any encrouchment [*sic*] of the Governing Part. Secondly Because the same Body that forms a Constitution have of Consequence a power to alter it—thirdly Because a Constitution alterable by the Supreme Legislative is no security at all to the subject against the encrouchment [*sic*] of the Governing part on any or on all their Rights and Privileges." It is quite plain that such principles underlie the great body of American constitutionalism. Edward Rutledge suggested a special congress of new members to draw up articles of confederation (August 19 ?, 1776). *Letters of Members of the Continental Congress* (E. C. Burnett, ed.), II, p. 56. It would seem, however, that the reason was chiefly grounded on the fact that Congress was busy.

[12] Cushing, *op. cit.,* pp. 221-226. Concord cast 111 votes against the constitution and none in its favor. Hoar, *op. cit.*

[13] *Result of the Convention of Delegates Holden at Ipswich in the County of Essex,* p. 15.

for that purpose.[14] The convention thus provided for met (September, 1779), framed a bill of rights and a constitution, submitted its handiwork to the people, then adjourned and awaited the popular verdict. In due time the convention once again assembled, canvassed the votes, decided that the constitution was adopted, and arranged for the inauguration of the new government.[15] The process was perfect; no one could doubt that the people were the source of governmental authority, that their will was superior to the government which was their creature, or that the government and the state were not the same.

This constitution of 1780 was carefully worked out with patient thought and under able, scholarly guidance. It conclusively ended the struggle, centuries old, of enmity between government and the people; the old enemy, government, was made the servant of the politically-organized people.[16] The question for the future was whether the people possessing power would wisely use it and develop laws and political processes suitable to new needs.

The methods of Massachusetts have been here presented in some detail because of the precision with which the work was done. We must content ourselves with a summary of the action of other states. The Virginia constitution, which was drawn up before the adoption of the Declaration of Independence, was framed by a convention acting as the temporary revolutionary government but not expressly authorized to undertake the task of constitution-making. This was true also of South Carolina (1776) and New Jersey. The congresses or conventions of all the other states were expressly authorized to act,

[14] Cushing, op. cit., pp. 227-229. It cannot be said that there is anything sacred in the proportion of two-thirds.

[15] As to the difficulty in determining the full meaning and effect of the returns from the towns, see S. E. Morison, "The Struggle Over the Adoption of the Constitution of Massachusetts, 1780", Mass. Hist. Society Proceedings, L, p. 396 ff. (October, 1916-June, 1917). He says, " '. . . the plain people of the state, in town meeting assembled, were able to point out the principal flaws that time and experience would find in the constitution drafted by John Adams, and adopted by a Convention that included among its members Samuel Adams, James Bowdoin, Theophilus Parsons, John Lowell, George Cabot, and Robert Treat Paine.' "

[16] This statement may appear an exaggeration in light of the fact that there were qualifications for voting, qualifications for holding office, religious provisions, and other matters in the constitution that needed to be altered in later years; the constitution of 1780 was not altogether in accord with twentieth-century democracy. But nevertheless, one does not mistake in seeing in this constitution and the method of its adoption the logical end of a long epoch; men had found a manner of creating a government and making it subject to their will; they had found a method not only of granting power but of preserving liberty. As far as political liberty was concerned, the government was in the people's hands.

but these bodies were not chosen for the *single* purpose of framing constitutions. When constitutions were put into operation without being submitted to the people, there was a good deal of objection in a number of the states to the establishment of a constitution without direct popular sanction.[17]

A word on the subject of submission of the constitution to the people is appropriate here, though we must look into the decades after the Revolution for the development of the practice. Only gradually was the principle of submission taken up by the various states; the first state outside of New England to take this step was New York, in 1821. By the time of the Civil War, the practice seemed to be fairly well established. In a later period, however, various constitutions were drawn up and established without popular ratification. For example, the Mississippi constitution of 1890, the first of a series of constitutions drawn up by southern conventions, the purpose of which was to get rid of certain inconveniences of the constitutions forced upon the states during Reconstruction,[18] was not submitted.

The Revolutionary constitutions were framed in time of war, and the strange fact is, not that they failed in some particulars to carry out the perfect theoretical procedure, but that they so nearly approached it. Although in a number of the states there was a confusion of legis-

---

[17] "Jefferson always denied the power of the convention to adopt a permanent frame and intended that his draft, if adopted, should be referred to the people." Lingley, *op. cit.*, p. 174. "Resolutions in New York and North Carolina expressed strongly the demand for a popular voice in the approval of constitutions, but here too it is probably the case that the popular participation was less than might have been desired because of the critical condition of affairs and of the necessity for prompt action. Even under these conditions action was taken in a number of states which amounted to an informal submission of constitutions to the people (Maryland, Pennsylvania, North Carolina, South Carolina, 1778), but the proposed Massachusetts constitution of 1778 is the first instrument of government which was formally submitted to a vote of the people." W. F. Dodd, "Constitutional Convention," *Cyclopedia of American Government*, I, p. 425.

[18] South Carolina, 1895; Louisiana, 1898; Virginia, 1902. The Delaware constitution of 1897 was not submitted, and the Kentucky constitution of 1891 was altered by the convention after it had been ratified. See W. F. Dodd, *The Revision and Amendment of State Constitutions*, pp. 67-68. The author, after a careful examination of precedents, points out that the "more usual procedure" (not universal practice) includes three popular votes: (1) the vote of the people authorizing a convention; (2) the election by the people of delegates; (3) the submission of the constitution for adoption or rejection. *Ibid.*, p. 71. It should be noticed, however, that he brings out the fact that constitutions are "elaborated by constitutional conventions chosen for this express purpose, and distinct both in organization and election from the ordinary legislative bodies." *Ibid.*, pp. 70-71. Amendments not formulated by conventions are frequently made by popular vote.

lation and constitution-making, a confusion that necessarily obscured in some degree the fundamental distinction between ordinary legislation and the constitution as the supreme will of the state, the necessity of popular authorization seems to have been pretty fully recognized and the nature of a constitution, if not the full qualities of a convention, was in a general way clearly presented.

Although in the whole process of constitution-making there was a fairly complete recognition of the principles of popular government and of Revolutionary doctrines—more plainly so in some states than in others—there was not much in the way of sentimental theorizing unaffected by experience; and the institutions which were actually established were in large measure essentially those to which the people were accustomed. The constitutions provided for a governor and generally for a bicameral legislature. Pennsylvania and Georgia established unicameral legislatures, but soon fell into line with the practice of the other states.[19] The old colonial council was reëstablished in some cases; in some of the states a board of censors was provided for. Suffrage was limited in various ways, so variously in fact that no generalization is possible; and there were also sundry qualifications for holding important offices—not only property qualifications but religious and theological as well.[20]

These early constitutions show a general distrust of the executive and, relatively, a confidence in the legislative—another direct product of colonial experiences. Some decades had to pass before executive authority was widened. Compared with modern constitutions, the early documents were brief. Their brevity can be easily accounted for: the people trusted in the ordinary rectitude and good sense of the legislature; they had not as yet learned the need of embodying in the constitution detailed directions and explicit restrictions; they had not gained that confidence in themselves which at a later day led them to place in their constitutions various provisions not of a fundamental character, but rather in the nature of statutory enactments. Life was comparatively simple and comparatively free from social and economic problems; the later development of constitutions mirrors the increasing complexity of the social and economic order.

Some of the early constitutions did not contain provisions for amendment, and the omission is not easily explained; certainly, if the right of revolution were to be legalized, there should be legal means

---

[19] Pennsylvania in 1790. Georgia in 1789.
[20] Something is said about this in a later chapter of this work.

for altering the form and the foundation of government. The failure to make such provision is probably attributable to haste and partly to the attention given by the framers to the fundamental character of their work; they did not realize how quickly and how often the need of change would arise.[21]

Including Vermont, which began to assume and assert statehood in the period under review, eight states adopted bills of rights (New Hampshire, Vermont, Massachusetts, Pennsylvania, Delaware, Maryland, Virginia, and North Carolina).[22] They accept the theory that government rests on consent and exists for the protection of rights. The Virginia bill of rights, largely the work of George Mason, contains the same philosophy as the Declaration of Independence and it was passed in the state before the Declaration was passed. It announces the doctrine of "inherent" rights of the people and the doctrine that all power is derived power. It then outlines in a masterly way the principles upon which free government rests. Associated with the announcement of the fundamental principle that power springs from the people and that the people have the right to alter and abolish government are certain other declarations of secondary rather than primary importance; they are of service in maintaining the more elementary and fundamental rights. The announcement of religious liberty in the Virginia bill is especially significant as an indication of the liberalizing effect of the Revolutionary movement. The first and most elementary principle of bills of rights is that men possessed rights before government was formed. Though it is now an elementary principle of constitutional law that the legislature of a state in the union has all power not forbidden either expressly or by implication, no man in appearing before a court of justice needs to set forth the essentials of individual liberty as a grant made to him by government; human rights are supposed to have existed before the establishment of government or state.

One well-known principle of the American constitutions is the separation of the powers of government. The legislative, executive,

---

[21] "The absence of provision for alteration in the constitutions of 1776-77, should not be taken as an indication that their framers thought the regular legislatures competent to alter or establish constitutions, but rather that they did not consider the matter at all." Dodd, *The Revision and Amendment of State Constitutions*, p. 27.

[22] For the Delaware bill of rights, see *Am. Hist. Rev.*, III, p. 641 ff. For illustrations of the prevalence of compact thinking, see the preamble of the Massachusetts constitution, 1780, the preamble of the New Jersey constitution, 1776, and the Maryland declaration of rights, 1776.

and judicial branches of government are distinct, and each branch is possessed of its peculiar and particular authority. We have carried that principle to an extent not known to the modern states of Europe; it is applicable to both our state and national governments; countless questions involving the interpretation and the application of the principle have come before the courts for decision. When the federal Constitution was framed, it seems to have been taken for granted as an elementary doctrine that separation of powers was one of the main safeguards of liberty. The idea was associated with the need of checks and balances which would keep each department within its proper sphere. Not all of the early state constitutions [23] plainly provided for separation, nor did the federal Constitution explicitly do so, but only by fairly conclusive implication.

The origin of this principle is not easily determined. Like many others, it is in some respects of hoary antiquity. The influence of Locke is probable.[24] In this matter, as in others, the Americans carried doctrine to the logical ultimate. The most influential writer was Montesquieu, whose *Esprit des Lois* was known in Revolutionary days. John Adams, a lover of checks and balances, seems to have been affected by James Harrington.[25] But American experience strengthened, if it did not create, the principle. Men do not commonly —if they are wise, and the early American statesmen cannot be denied the attribute of wisdom—enthusiastically adopt a disembodied idea from beyond the field of practical acquaintanceship. The colonists had not lived under a system in which separation of the powers was fully recognized; but they had been engaged in a series of debates and disputes concerning the extent of the authority of different branches of government. It is true that in some instances, perhaps commonly, they were really desirous of asserting the supremacy of the legislative branch, but the idea of separation and distinction was in some instances brought fairly clearly to light.[26]

23 "Of the twelve commonwealths which, prior to 1787, had adopted constitutions, six had inserted . . . a general distributing clause. . . ." William Bondy, *The Separation of Governmental Powers* (Columbia University *Studies in History,* etc., V, no. 2), p. 19. Most states now have distributing clauses, and in all the general principle is recognized.

24 Locke spoke of three powers—legislative, executive, and federative—but did not emphasize the necessity of separation on the lines known to our constitutions.

25 See H. F. Russell Smith, *Harrington and His Oceana a Study of a 17th Century Utopia and Its Influence in America,* especially pp. 63-66, 192-194.

26 "Indeed, the doctrine of the separation and balance of powers was proclaimed in Massachusetts before the *Esprit des Lois* saw the light. In 1742 the house of

Associated with the doctrine of separation of powers is the principle that granted power cannot be delegated. And this principle brought up in the course of time a good many constitutional problems. Important as the principle of separation is, constitutions do not provide for complete isolation of the departments of government. For example, the fact that a bill requires the signature of the executive, unless it is passed over his veto, gives him a participation in legislation; and executive influence over legislation has greatly increased in the passing decades.

If it be asked why people were so unwise—and the question is often asked—as to hamper government by division of authority and by checks and balances, the answer is simple: such was the kind of government the leaders and probably men in general wanted. Who are a free people? Those who live under a government so constitutionally checked as to make life, liberty, and property secure. That would have been the explicit answer of the Revolutionary days. In some ways the most marked development of the idea of popular government from that time to this has been the development of the belief that governments, strongly directed by popular opinion, should be competent and active—a change from the belief that governments should not do things to the belief that they should do things.

representatives in Massachusetts rejected the demands of Governor Shirley for a permanent salary on the ground that it 'would greatly tend to lessen the just weight of the other two branches of the government, which ought ever to be maintained and preserved; especially since the governor has so great authority and check upon them.' " W. S. Carpenter, "The Separation of Powers in the Eighteenth Century," *Am. Pol. Sci. Rev.*, XXII, p. 37.

CHAPTER XII

THE ARTICLES OF CONFEDERATION

When Lee introduced into Congress the resolution for independence (June 7, 1776), it was accompanied by a resolution that steps be taken for the formation of a confederation of the states. The need of organization had long been in the minds of certain leaders, and Franklin the year before had brought in a plan based in some degree on the Albany Plan of 1754.[1] With his plan nothing of importance was done, though it evidently had influence on later proceedings; but after independence was declared, Congress began debating at length articles brought in by a committee[2] and commonly called the Dickinson draft. Pressure upon Congress, as well as some inherent difficulties in the problem, delayed the completion of the task, and consequently not until November, 1777, were the Articles finally adopted by Congress and submitted to the states.

With the announcement of independence, the problem of imperial organization crossed the ocean; it was no longer the problem of organizing the British empire or of ascertaining its constitutional structure, but of organizing America. Nevertheless, in many respects the problem was the old one; reduced to the lowest terms, it was at least the problem of arranging some practicable scheme in which the states would work together for common ends. For there was need of coherence in the war; and as time was soon to show, coherence in peace was quite as necessary and possibly more difficult to maintain. What were the elements in the task, if we take for granted that complete unification, complete absorption of the states into a unitary system, was impossible? The most troublesome problems were again the

[1] Presented to Congress July 21, 1775. For Franklin's use of the New England Confederation and the Albany Plan of Union, see L. K. Mathews, "Benjamin Franklin's Plans for a Colonial Union, 1750-1775," *Am. Pol. Sci. Rev.*, VIII, pp. 393-412.

[2] The committee was appointed June 12, 1776. It reported July 12, and the reported articles were discussed for some time thereafter. The committee of the whole, after discussing the report, submitted the amended scheme to Congress on August 20

118

familiar ones; and central among them was the pivotal question of supply, of finding means of assurance that the states would furnish properly the men and the money for the general needs of the union. If they were to retain a large share of self-government, and of course that was inevitable, what authority should be allowed to the body representing them all? Everybody cried, as he had done twenty years before, that union was absolutely necessary; but when it came to plans of union, there was still distraction.[3]

It is possible that, if a system of union could have been decided upon immediately after independence was announced, the Articles of union would have contained no announcement of state sovereignty. In neither the Dickinson draft (July 12, 1776) nor the draft presented to Congress by the committee of the whole (August 20) was the sovereignty of the states specified; the articles submitted on the latter day declared: "Each State reserves to itself the sole and exclusive regulation and government of its internal police, in all matters that shall not interfere with the articles of this Confederation." [4] The opening paragraphs, it is true, might be construed to signify that nothing was contemplated but a working union of sovereign states. Such glimpses as we can get of the work of construction in the succeeding months, especially in 1777, appear to indicate that, when the Articles were made distinctly to conform to the idea of a coöperative system of sovereignties, the change was the product of a developing

[3] Edward Rutledge wrote to John Jay as early as June 29, 1776: "I have been much engaged lately upon a plan of a Confederation which Dickenson has drawn; it has the Vice of all his Productions to a considerable Degree; I mean the Vice of Refining too much. Unless it's greatly curtailed it never can pass, as it is to be submitted to Men in the respective Provinces who will not be led or rather driven into Measures which may lay the Foundation of their Ruin. . . . The Idea of destroying all Provincial Distinctions and making every thing of the most minute kind bend to what they call the good of the whole, is in other Terms to say that these Colonies must be subject to the Government of the Eastern Provinces. . . . I am resolved to vest the Congress with no more Power than that is absolutely necessary. . . ." Letters of Members of the Continental Congress (E. C. Burnett, ed.), I, pp. 517-518 (hereafter referred to as Burnett, Letters).

August 19 (?), 1776, Rutledge wrote to Robert Livingston: "We have done nothing with the Confederation for some Days, and it is of little Consequence if we never see it again; for we have made such a Devil of it already that the Colonies can never agree to it. If my opinion was likely to be taken I would propose that the States should appoint a special Congress to be composed of new Members for this purpose—and that no Person should disclose any part of the present plan. If that was done we might then stand some Chance of a Confederation, at present we stand none at all." Ibid., II, p. 56. This latter statement is interesting in light of what came eleven years later.

[4] The article in the Dickinson draft was slightly longer, but to the same effect.

sense of separate independence or of growing suspicion. The finished Articles, as submitted to the state legislatures for adoption, announced in plain language the retention of sovereignty by the states.[5]

There were three points on which differences of opinion especially centered: (1) whether the states should have equal voting power in the Congress of the Confederation or should vote in proportion to their population or wealth or some such indication of importance and strength; (2) what should be the basis for determining how much each state should pay into the common coffers; (3) whether the states claiming vast stretches of western lands should continue to hold them in their possession; and this included the subordinate question— whether or not Congress should be given authority to limit the dimensions of the states.[6]

The debates on the first two questions are of interest to us because they brought out a number of the crucial problems that vexed

[5] "Each State retains its sovereignty, freedom and independence, and every power, jurisdiction, and right, which is not by this confederation expressly delegated to the United States, in Congress assembled."

Of the article regarding sovereignty of the states, Thomas Burke of North Carolina wrote, "It stood originally the third article; and expressed only a reservation of the power of regulating the internal police, and consequently resigned every other power. It appeared to me that this was not what the States expected, and, I thought, it left it in the power of the future Congress or General Council to explain away every right belonging to the States and to make their own power as unlimited as they please. I proposed, therefore, an amendment, which held up the principle, that all sovereign power was in the States separately, and that particular acts of it, which should be expressly enumerated, would be exercised in conjunction, and not otherwise; but that in all things else each State would exercise all the rights and power of sovereignty, uncontrolled. This was at first so little understood that it was some time before it was seconded, and South Carolina first took it up. The opposition was made by Mr. Wilson of Pennsylvania, and Mr. R. H. Lee of Virginia; in the end however the question was carried for my proposition, eleven ayes, one no, and one divided. The no was Virginia; the divided New Hampshire. . . . In a word, Sir, I am of opinion, the Congress should have power enough to call out and apply the common strength for the common defence: but not for the partial purposes of ambition. . . . The inequality of the States, and yet the necessity of maintaining their separate independence, will occasion dilemmas almost inextricable." Thomas Burke to the Governor of North Carolina, April 29, 1777, in Burnett, Letters, II, pp. 345-346. Thus Burke clearly stated the gist of the problem of imperial organization.

"Since my last we have made no progress in the business of Confederation. A difficulty occurs, which, I fear, will be insuperable: that is how to secure to each State its separate independence, and give each its proper weight in the public Councils. So unequaled as the States are, it will be nearly impossible to effect this; and after all it is far from improbable that the only Confederation will be a defensive Alliance." Thomas Burke to the Governor of North Carolina, May 23, 1777. in Ibid., II, pp. 370-371.

[6] Burnett, Letters, II, p. xvi.

the men who labored to form a union a decade later; [7] the larger states wished proportional representation; the smaller states wished equal representation. Were the states to be unequally taxed but to have equal voting power in Congress? The debate appears to have been earnest and searching. The outcome of the discussion was the provision that each state should have one vote in Congress, thus securing the complete equality of the states in voting power; but charges of war and all other expenses were to be supplied by the states in proportion to the value of land within each state granted to or surveyed for any person, and the improvements on such land. In other words, equality of the states was accepted as the basis of voting power in Congress, inequality was accepted as the basis for contributions to the treasury. This arrangement was sure to be distasteful to many, and in the long run it proved unsatisfactory. Franklin said in the course of the debates, as John Adams noted them: "Let the smaller Colonies give equal money and men, and then have an equal vote. But if they have an equal vote without bearing equal burthens, a confederation upon such iniquitous principles will never last long." [8]

The western land question presented special difficulty. A suitable solution of the problem was of immense importance. The Congress was engaged in a peculiarly difficult task; under any circumstances, the establishment of a union of states, each cherishing its own interests,

[7] As showing the interstate and intersectional jealousies, a letter of Richard Henry Lee (May 26, 1777) is especially illustrative: "Our enemies, and our friends too, know that America can only be conquered by disunion. The former, by unremitting art had endeavored to create jealousy and discord between the Southern and Eastern Colonies, and in truth Sir, they had so far prevailed, that it required constant attention, and a firmness not to be shaken, to prevent the malicious act [art?] of our enemies from succeeding." Richard Henry Lee to the Governor of Virginia, in *Ibid.*, II, p. 374. See also Burke's letter of February 10 (or 16), 1777, to the Governor of North Carolina, in *Ibid.*, II, p. 257; Benjamin Harrison to Robert Morris, January 8, 1777, in *Ibid.*, II, p. 208; Carter Braxton to Landon Carter, April 14, 1776, in *Ibid.*, I, p. 421, a letter of an earlier date but not without significance for later times. From the notes of discussion in Congress taken by Jefferson, and from reports of certain speeches, we find Samuel Chase of Maryland distinctly asserting the cleavage between the larger and the smaller states on the subject of representation. See especially, *Journals*, VI, p. 1102. John Witherspoon of New Jersey said, "if an equal vote be refused, the smaller states will become vassals to the larger. . . ." *Ibid.*, VI, p. 1103. The problem of taxation and representation was rendered more difficult by the fact that the southern states had large numbers of slaves. One article in the earlier drafts of the Articles (July 12, 1776 and August 20, 1776) provided that all charges of war and other expenses should be defrayed out of a common treasury supplied by the several colonies in proportion to the number of inhabitants, except Indians not paying taxes.

[8] July 30, 1776. *Journals*, VI, p. 1079.

must present serious obstacles. And if a union could be formed, what were the prospects that it would endure? In the days when the Confederation was under debate, the critical question was whether a union could be formed at all; and the difficulty of finding an affirmative answer seemed to turn in considerable measure on the dread of the landless states that the landed states would become wealthy and powerful and would overawe and mayhap impoverish their lesser neighbors. But if land were surrendered, it must be governed by somebody; so here again the states, seeking to form a union, were confronted by an essential part of the problem of imperial organization—the problem of imperial expansion. Some of the states claimed that their sea-to-sea charters gave them territory in the west; and New York made assertions of ownership of a considerable region. Other states were within definite limits; Rhode Island, New Jersey, Delaware, and Maryland were comparatively small in area. It is not strange that they should look with jealousy upon their neighbors claiming vast territory, the source of both wealth and power.

It seems remarkable now that the ownership of the transmontane region should have been so hotly contested during those perilous days when the real question was whether the British army would not beat down resistance and the rebellion against the mother country totally fail. But discussed it was; for this western question was a perplexing one, involving much more than merely fixing the western limits of the states. With the question of boundaries went the control of land purchases and the fixing of a land policy as well as direction and control of settlements that might be made beyond the mountains. From the beginning of colonial history, the frontier policy had been for each colony a matter of difficulty, and it was not so easy as it might now seem to cast aside traditions and at once transfer the whole—policy, hopes, plans, government, and lands—into the hands of a central authority as yet untried and indeed unformed. It was characteristic of American optimism, probably, to begin the counting of chickens before they had emerged from the shells.

The problem of the west was an old one, and, like so many others, was associated with the experiences of the old empire. The Albany Plan of Union had proposed a solution. The plan which Franklin presented to Congress in 1775 declared that purchases from the Indians should be made for the general advantage and benefit of the united colonies. The Dickinson draft of a confederation, presented in July, 1776, included even more definite proposals, but they were not included in the draft of the Articles submitted by the committee of the whole the next month. Among the states without large landed possessions, Maryland was the most critical of a system of union which would leave some of the states in possession of western territory. When the Congress was discussing the Articles in the autumn of 1777 —for little had been done during many months preceding—a proposal was offered for which Maryland alone voted (New Jersey's vote was divided): "That the United States, in Congress assembled, shall have the sole and exclusive right and power to ascertain and fix the western boundary of such states as claim to the Mississippi or South Sea, and lay out the land beyond the boundary, so ascertained, into separate and independent states, from time to time, as the numbers and circumstances of the people thereof may require".

The principle of the resolution is significant: the western settlements were not to be held in permanent subordination, but were to become in the course of time independent states, presumably members of the union with equal rights. The proposal, however, was unacceptable, at least as far as it contemplated giving at once to Congress the power to fix boundaries for the large landholding states. Instead of adopting the resolution, Congress added to that paragraph of the Articles which provided for the adjudication of controversies between states the following brief but peremptory statement: "provided, also, that no State shall be deprived of territory for the benefit of the United States." [9]

The Articles were adopted by the Congress, November 15, 1777, and two days later they went forth to the states. Some of the states accepted them fairly promptly, and their delegates signed the Articles under authorization of their respective states. Various amendments were proposed, but the most important dealt with the necessity of settling the western question and especially securing for the use of the United States the crown lands from which revenue could be obtained for paying the debts incurred for the common cause.[10] Maryland

[9] For Maryland's position, see H. B. Adams, *Maryland's Influence Upon Land Cessions to the United States* (Johns Hopkins University *Studies in Hist. and Pol. Science*, third series, III, no. 1). The whole western question and the land cessions are ably discussed by B. A. Hinsdale, *The Old Northwest*. Burnett, *Letters*, II, contains valuable material.

[10] Rhode Island asked that all lands which before the war were the property of the Crown should be considered as the property of the United States, reserving to the states, however, within whose limits such crown lands might be, the jurisdiction thereof. New Jersey's wish was similar to that of Rhode Island. *Journals*, XI, pp. 639, 650.

renewed her request for power in Congress to ascertain and restrict the boundaries of the large landholding states, and this was supported by Rhode Island, New Jersey, Pennsylvania, and Delaware—none of them having claims to territory in the west. By midsummer of 1778 most of the states had given their assent to the Articles. New Jersey took the step later in the year and was followed by Delaware in May, 1779. Maryland was still obdurate.

The months went by. A union of all the states was highly desirable, not to say imperative; delay was dangerous. Some concession or compromise was necessary. New York, whose claims seemed rather more nebulous than those of the states which asserted rights under sea-to-sea charters, passed a legislative act (February 19, 1780) empowering her delegates "to limit and restrict" her western boundaries. Congress now (September 6, 1780) declared this act was calculated to "accelerate the federal alliance"; the states with western land claims were asked to remove the only obstacle to a final ratification of the Articles. October 10, 1780, Congress passed a momentous resolution: all unappropriated lands ceded to the United States should be disposed of for the common benefit of the United States, "and be settled and formed into distinct republican states, which shall become members of the federal union, and have the same rights of sovereignty, freedom and independence, as the other states". Early in the following year Virginia consented to cede her territory northwest of the Ohio River. She laid down certain conditions and these raised some difficulties which do not need consideration here. Maryland could now feel fairly certain that her chief purpose was attained, and her delegates were authorized to sign the Articles. When this was done (March 1, 1781), the Confederation was complete.

Of great consequence was the final organization of the union, defective though it proved to be; and important also was the spirit of conciliation and national sentiment on which the union rested. Of some consequence, too, was the fact that the thirteen commonwealths, bound in "perpetual" union, jointly possessed a large, unsettled region; such possession probably helped in the development of a sense of common interest and common responsibilities. But of supreme importance was the discovery of the principle of expansion, of nation-building. The principle announced by Congress in 1780 was carried into effect by the famous Ordinance of 1787. Passed in the last months of the dying Confederation, the Ordinance is to-day a lasting memorial, a proof that the Americans had learned a great lesson from their own history. In the building of an empire—though for the time the empire was a confederation of sovereignties—the new settlements should not be permanently treated as dependents unfit to associate on terms of equality with the older members of the union.

It is unnecessary to recount the steps by which the various cessions of western lands were made by the states. In the course of time, those steps were taken. It is significant, however, that the Articles did not contain a provision authorizing the Congress of the Confederation to hold and manage the common territory thus granted or to lay down laws and ordinances for the government of the western settlements. Such powers may, perhaps, be inferred from the general acquiescence in the fact of possession and the circumstances under which the Articles were adopted.

A further view of the Articles is necessary. In Congress and in the states, there appears to have been less discussion concerning the powers delegated to Congress than one might have supposed. Taught by experience in the old empire, by the necessity of carrying on the war, and by earlier plans or discussions of union, the delegates in Congress were enabled to work out the distribution of powers between the central authority and the states with some approach to precision. The powers granted to Congress bear a general resemblance to those exercised by the Crown and Parliament in the old colonial system in which the colonies had grown to maturity; and if one compares the Articles with the Constitution adopted at Philadelphia in 1787, he will find a considerable similarity in the scheme of distribution.[11] Time was to show the defects of the system; but the actual merits of the system agreed upon are noteworthy. No power to lay taxes was bestowed on Congress, and no power to regulate commerce, the two things about which there had been so much dispute in the preceding decade. These omissions were largely instrumental in bringing into existence the Constitutional Convention of 1787.

Without the consent of Congress, the states were expressly forbidden to send an embassy to a foreign state, receive an embassy, enter into any agreement with a foreign power, form any treaty of combination among themselves, maintain ships of war or troops in time of peace—though a militia must be provided and sufficiently armed—, or engage in war unless actually invaded or in immediate danger of

11 Reference has already been made to the Albany Plan of 1754, to Franklin's evident study of the New England Confederation of 1643, which did not expire until 1684, as well as to the actual practice of the old empire.

Indian attack. All charges of war and other expenses incurred for the common defense and general welfare were to be defrayed out of a common treasury supplied by the several states. To Congress was given, among other powers, the general powers of determining on war and peace, carrying on foreign affairs, though with some restrictions, regulating the alloy and value of coin, fixing the standard of weights and measures, regulating the trade and managing all the affairs with the Indians "not members of any of the States", establishing and regulating post offices from one state to another, appointing important army officers and all naval officers, borrowing money, building and equipping a navy, and making requisitions upon the states for troops. For doing the most important things, the vote of nine states in Congress was required, practically a three-fourths vote of the thirteen, a restriction certain to make effective action difficult. No alteration of the Articles could be made unless it be agreed to in Congress and confirmed by the legislatures of all the states. A "committee of the states" could, in the recess of Congress, exercise powers intrusted to it by Congress with the consent of nine states, provided that no power for which the voice of nine states was necessary should be delegated to the committee. One of the delegates could be appointed "to preside"— the predecessor, in fact, of the president of the United States, who does not preside at all.

While the Articles granted to Congress considerable authority, its powers were qualified, in some respects carefully, for the protection of the states' rights. Although Congress was given power to enter into treaties, the states were not totally forbidden to lay imposts, but they were forbidden to levy such duties as might interfere with "stipulations in treaties entered into by the United States . . . in pursuance of any treaties already proposed by Congress to the courts of France and Spain." Congress could make no treaty of commerce whereby the states should be restrained from imposing such imposts on foreigners as their own people were subjected to; and apparently the states could freely prohibit the exportation or importation of any kind of goods. The failure to grant Congress complete power to regulate commerce rendered it difficult or impossible to make a commercial treaty with a foreign nation and to have assurance that the states would comply with its provisions. The years that followed disclosed the fact that the want of authority to make treaties which would bind the states was one of the cardinal defects of the system.

This "firm league of friendship", which was declared to be "perpetual", contained significant provisions for mutual friendship and coöperation among the states. While, it appears, the states were separate sovereignties, or possibly it is more correct to say, *because* they were separate sovereignties, the Articles contained explicit provisions concerning the rights of the "free inhabitants" of one state within the limits of another state. Such persons were declared to be "entitled to all privileges and immunities of free citizens in the several states", to have free ingress and egress to and from the respective states, and to enjoy privileges of trade and commerce. Extradition was provided for, and full faith and credit were to be given in each state to the records, acts, and judicial proceedings of every other.

The importance of these provisions for interstate relationships is this: (1) they proposed a substantial basis for a league of friendship that might in reality be perpetual; without such conditions of reciprocal consideration and recognition of common rights and interests, no league could endure. (2) They appear in similar though not identical words in the Constitution of the United States. This latter fact makes it especially important to notice that the provisions in the Articles, later transferred to the Constitution and made law, are based on the supposition that the states stand in relation of one to the other as distinct sovereignties. Extradition, for example, is in general an international matter and based on treaty provisions; no nation is bound, by any principle of "good neighborhood", to turn over to another nation, on demand or request, a fugitive from justice. The Articles embrace this international provision; it is included in the Constitution as a legal obligation.[12] The quasi-international relationship of the states of the union is most plainly illustrated by the fact that the writs issued in one state do not run in another.

More important than all else is the provision, already referred to (which became constitutional law with the adoption of the Constitution), concerning the rights and privileges of the free citizens of each state in the several states. This provision rests on the supposition of state sovereignty—in the Constitution on partial or quasi-sovereignty. The rights of the "nationals" of one state when sojourning in another state are similar to those generally recognized by the principles of international comity. Thus, again, because the states of the American union passed through a period in which they were, or thought

---

[12] The courts have not held that the federal authorities are under obligation to compel or to seek to compel rendition of a fugitive by one state to another at the latter's request.

they were, separate sovereignties, interstate relations, as far as rights of individuals are concerned, are, under the Constitution as it stands to-day, in some important respects not unlike the relations between separate national states of the world. Certain fundamental civil rights and privileges which are commonly recognized by the civilized nations of the world at large and are accorded to their own citizens are also accorded to foreigners sojourning within their limits. A citizen of America going to Britain or France expects to find, and he does find, the same degree of protection to his person and property as that enjoyed by citizens of those nations; he may, for example, make use of the courts of a foreign nation for the assertion and maintenance of his rights. And in these respects the Constitution of the United States makes such protection and such privileges legally obligatory upon the states of the union in their treatment of citizens of the several states.

No nation, no national state, enforces the penal laws of another. The same principle is true of the members of the American union. In civil matters, however, every civilized nation does recognize in its courts the rights of an individual which are based upon the law or spring from the law of a foreign state. The same general principles obtain in interstate law of the American union. Some of these principles of international comity are made legally obligatory by our constitutional system. Full faith and credit are by constitutional provision accorded in each state to the public acts, records, and proceedings of every other state.[13] But in the world at large the same recognition is commonly given (and given on the same principles) by one nation to the acts and judicial proceedings of another nation. Furthermore, the general principles of jurisprudence—within the field of what is called private international law or the "conflict of laws"—are recognized and applied when questions arise concerning the rights of a citizen of one state suing or sued in the courts of another, or concerning the rights which are based on the law of a state not the state of the forum. A right established under the law of Ohio, for example, will be recognized as a right when a suit is instituted for its protection in Great Britain.[14] The principles applied in a foreign state are similar to those which will be applied in a court of an American state in passing upon the rights of litigants, when the rights so claimed spring from the law of a member of the American union. "The judiciary

13 See Constitution, Art. IV, sec. 1.
14 A somewhat unique relationship in such matters exists between France and America, but it serves as an exception to prove the rule.

power of every government", said Hamilton, "looks beyond its own local or municipal laws, and in civil cases, lays hold of all subjects of litigation between parties within its jurisdiction, though the causes of dispute are relative to the laws of the most distant part of the globe." [15] In making this statement, Hamilton was explaining the relationship between the federal and state courts, but he was also stating a general principle of jurisprudence. The thing to be emphasized here is the application of these principles to the interstate law of the American union in which the members stand in a quasi-international relationship.[16]

Among the duties assigned to Congress by the Articles of Confederation was that of acting as the last resort on appeal in disputes between two or more states. Under any conditions such disputes might arise, and in fact they did arise. If, as the Articles stated, the states were sovereign, and if there were no method for peaceful settlement, disputes might have to be settled by war, the time-worn method of trial by battle. The supervising authority of the Privy Council of the old empire, familiar to the men of America, may have had direct influence on the framers of the Articles; if so, it is one more evidence of the effects of the old colonial system. For carrying out this duty, Congress was authorized to act when any state should apply for a hearing. The states in disagreement might under the supervision of Congress appoint, by joint consent, commissioners or judges for hearing and deciding the controversy; but if such a method failed, because

[15] *The Federalist* (1818 ed.), no. LXXXII, p. 446. See also John Marshall's speech in the Virginia convention, June 20, 1788. *The Debates in the Several State Conventions, on the Adoption of the Federal Constitution* (Jonathan Elliot, ed.), 1866 ed., III, p. 556. Hereafter referred to as Elliot, *Debates*.

[16] An illustration of the quasi-international relationship follows. In 1829, Justice Washington, giving the opinion and decision of the federal Supreme Court, said: "For all national purposes embraced by the Federal Constitution, the States and the citizens thereof are one, united under the same sovereign authority, and governed by the same laws. In all other respects the States are necessarily foreign to and independent of each other. Their constitutions and forms of government being, although republican, altogether different, as are their laws and institutions. This sentiment was expressed with great force by the President of the Court of Appeals of Virginia, in the case of *Warder* v. *Arrell* (2 Wash., 298); where he states that in cases of contracts, the laws of a foreign country where the contract was made must govern; and then adds as follows: 'The same principle applies, though with no greater force, to the different States of America; for though they form a confederated government, yet the several States retain their individual sovereignties, and, with respect to their municipal regulations, are to each other foreign.' " Buckner *v.* Finley, 2 Peters 586, 590-591. In this case the question was whether a bill of exchange drawn in Maryland upon a drawee in Louisiana was a "foreign bill". The Supreme Court decided that it was.

the states could not agree upon the tribunal, Congress was authorized to appoint, by a formal and cumbersome method, commissioners or judges with power to reach a "final and conclusive" decision. This provision for peaceful settlement of controversies between sovereign states was one of the most important provisions in the Articles; it at least proposed some method other than war. It foreshadowed one of the signally significant provisions of the third article of the Constitution of the United States.[17]

This fortunate and wise provision in the Articles was not allowed to lie idle. Pennsylvania and Connecticut had long indulged in acrimonious controversy over Connecticut's claim to territory in what is now northern Pennsylvania. On the petition of Pennsylvania, a court was set up at Trenton which in 1782 unanimously decided that the state of Connecticut had no right to the lands in controversy.

During the larger portion of the war and before the Articles went into effect, appeals of prize cases were passed upon by committees of Congress. The Articles gave Congress express authority to appoint courts for the trial of piracies and felonies committed on the high seas and to establish courts for determining appeals in all cases of captures. The states were making admiralty decisions in their own courts; and

[17] For an interesting discussion of this subject, see R. G. Caldwell, "The Settlement of Inter-state Disputes," *Am. Jour. of Int. Law,* XIV, p. 38 ff.; A. H. Snow, *The Development of the American Doctrine of Jurisdiction of Courts Over States, Publications* of the American Society for Judicial Settlement of International Disputes no. 4 (May, 1911); also other pamphlets issued by the same society. Concerning the authority of the Privy Council, Caldwell has this to say: "It is safe to say that from the authority of this administrative body is derived the quasi-international authority of every federal court in the world, except the German Bundesrath whose power to settle the disputes of the members of the German Empire has a wholly distinct origin in the Diets of the Confederation and of the Holy Roman Empire." *Op. cit.,* p. 39. He also mentions nine chief cases coming somewhat formally before the Privy Council in colonial days. *Ibid.* Only one of these, Penn *v.* Lord Baltimore, "came before an ordinary court in a fashion at all comparable to a modern case between two States in the Supreme Court of the United States." *Ibid.,* p. 41. "These early settlements were evidently not in any sense international arbitrations, but had all the paternal character of administrative determinations both in their nature and results." But this "habit of looking to this common administrative court . . . became a real though reluctant habit until almost the moment of war." *Ibid.,* p. 41. Six disputes came before Congress before the Constitution was adopted. See *Ibid.,* pp. 53-54 and J. C. B. Davis, "Federal Courts Prior to the Adoption of the Constitution," in an appendix to 131 U. S. Supreme Court *Reports.* In two of these controversies a court was agreed upon but it did not sit and render a decision in either case. But in the Pennsylvania-Connecticut case the court did sit and it rendered a decision. Since the adoption of the Constitution forty-five interstate controversies have come before the federal Supreme Court (to 1932). This statement is based upon data afforded by Professor Caldwell, in a personal letter, March 18, 1932.

an appellate tribunal, if established under the authority granted by the Articles, was to have jurisdiction of cases appealed from the states. In 1780 Congress resolved to establish a court "for the trial of all appeals from the Courts of Admiralty in these United States". Judges were appointed. This Court in its day was the highest Court in the country, and the only appellate tribunal with jurisdiction over the whole United States.[18] Between the middle of September, 1776, and May, 1787, there were, it would appear, 109 cases which were referred to the Congress committee or brought directly to the Court of Appeals. Of this number fifty-six were lodged with the Court.[19] As a basis or a precedent for the Supreme Court of the United States and for the admiralty jurisdiction of the federal judiciary, the old Court of Appeals was doubtless of influence.

"Each State", said the Articles of Confederation, "retains its sovereignty, freedom and independence. . . ." Were, then, the states sovereign? Did they have any sovereignty to be retained? Few questions in the world's history have been so thoroughly debated; debated chiefly by public men in practical political discussion, but discussed also by historians. The reason for the emphasis upon this question is not attributable to historical curiosity, but rather to the fact that it appeared to be of supreme consequence in any endeavor to decide whether the states, after the Constitution was established, were or were not sovereign. If the states were not sovereign in the years *before* the adoption of the federal Constitution, no one could reasonably assert their possession of sovereignty *after* adoption; but if they were sovereign before such adoption, then one may find the starting-point for an argument in behalf of state sovereignty afterwards.

A treatise on constitutional history may be expected to examine this problem and reach conclusions, but in any presentation of the subject there are difficulties to be met. Even if we should decide upon a definition of "sovereignty", we might be still faced with the difficulty of deciding where sovereignty actually resides at a given time; and this difficulty is especially evident in the period of the Confederation. In the course of American history men have differed, and still differ, in their opinions concerning the nature of sovereignty; they have not

---

[18] Davis, *op. cit.*, pp. XXV-XXVI. The difficulty arising from the fact that the duty or the power to carry out the Court's decisions rested with state authorities is commented on by Davis. *Ibid.*, p. XXIX. Cf. also, J. F. Jameson, "The Predecessor of the Supreme Court," *Essays in the Constitutional History of the United States* (J. F. Jameson, ed.), p. 1 ff.

[19] Davis, *op. cit.*, p. XXXIV.

always known wherein their differences lay. They have often engaged in disputes concerning the question whether at a given time the states were or were not sovereign; this fact is for the historian of more real significance than is any rigid verdict which he may reach for his own edification or for the doubtful gratification of his readers.

In any attempt to decide where at a given moment sovereignty resides in any nation, the investigator is engaged in an historical task; he is using historical data; but his conclusion is within the field of law. Though he be a mere historian, he is under no obligation to withhold from his readers his own conclusion which is a necessary product of his historical study. To give a very simple, concrete example, he may assert or assume the obvious, viz.: that the United States has been a sovereign state since 1865, one of the sovereign national states of the world; the fundamental principle of its legal structure is that it is a single, legally-competent and self-contained body politic; as an historian, he is profoundly interested in discovering how this legal structure came to be and in showing the difficulties encountered in creating or maintaining it. In studying the course of American history, the historian will find his chief task not to establish a conclusion concerning which theory of the nature of the United States was right (legally speaking) and which was wrong, but to present actual differences of opinion as they arose and to mark out the presence of conflicting forces and tendencies.

The word "sovereignty" is still often used with little respect for any rigid definition. If we should, in obedience to the definition now commonly found in books on political theory, declare sovereignty to be the supreme and absolute power by which a state is governed or to be the authority to do anything and everything of a political nature, we should still be constrained to inquire whether the men of the Revolution thus used the term and accepted all its implications. And, indeed, as we shall see more fully later on, the historian will find that very many, if not all of the men of those days, did not have this conception of sovereignty. Thus, the history of the very idea of sovereignty enters into any proper discussion. If sovereignty implies the possibility of limited authority, if sovereignty, in other words, can be divided and still remain sovereignty, then a definition connoting completeness is inappropriate and inapplicable, if applied to the words of men of a century and a half ago.

Sovereignty, whatever it may be, is often, if not always, in conflict with actual conditions in the world. The word, certainly when used in the domain of international relations, implies that each member of the family of nations has complete freedom in determining its course of action; and yet, of course, no nation is in reality completely free, but only theoretically free or free legally speaking. One sovereign nation is supposed to be the equal of every other; but again this is a convenient (or inconvenient) supposition or an accepted fiction; one state can be equal with another only in legal competence, and often the facts go far toward invalidating even this presumption of equality. But, whether the above assertions concerning the difference between realities and legal suppositions be accepted or not, sovereignty can most properly be looked upon as *authority,* the possession of legal right, and not as actual *power;* one cannot say that a sovereign acts illegally or beyond its legal capacity, if sovereignty connotes unrestrained authority. This is true not only of a sovereign nation but also of the possessor of sovereignty within a given nation. In other words, actual *power* to do all political acts may be beyond the capacity of the sovereign, though he has the *authority.*

Though sovereignty is authority and the legal right to act, it is, nevertheless, sometimes necessary to consider actual capacity. It is sometimes necessary to find out from events, from real conditions, where sovereignty rests; in the course of a revolt within a nation, for example, one may wish to discover whether a revolution has taken place and sovereignty has changed its dwelling; or, if a separation of a people into two states is attempted by rebels, it is necessary to discover whether in the course of time they have ceased to be rebels and must be held to have established a new national state. Thus the legal theory as to where sovereignty resides may be damaged or overthrown by consideration of what really is.

Adhering to our belief that sovereignty belongs within the field of law, we may study the years between 1776 and 1788 with the intent to discover where, as America was then organized, sovereignty resided. Accepting for the moment the definition of sovereignty as complete authority, full legal right, can we decide where it rested? The evidence is confusing; at least able and honest men have differed in their conclusions. Even in the Constitutional Convention of 1787, there was a difference of opinion, some men holding that the states did not become sovereign when independence was declared, others seemingly (and one member plainly) asserting that the states did become separate sovereigns.[20]

Now the truth appears to the writer to be just this: it was a time of revolution and of reconstruction; and in consequence there was and is some uncertainty about the nature of the governmental system. The states frequently acted as if they had real authority and not merely nominal sovereignty. In the Articles of Confederation they announced their separate sovereignty, but their actual incapacity to act as independent sovereignties was often at variance with their presumption. The necessities of the situation indicated plainly that safety was in union, in coöperation; and so one may believe, if one chooses to do so, that the reality of interdependence was sufficient to overthrow any legal fiction of independence and separate existence.[21] There were, furthermore, strong ties that bound the states together, forces working through the social and economic order, forces that were powerful and likely to become dominant; certain realities were ignored by declarations concerning separate sovereign existence; and the real problem of the time, a compelling problem, was to bring political forms into accommodation with actual needs and with the dominating fact of interdependence and identity of interests. Again, whatever may be said

[20] See the statements of Luther Martin, James Wilson, Alexander Hamilton, and Rufus King, June 19; of Martin, June 20. Charles C. Pinckney, who had been a member of the Federal Convention, speaking to the South Carolina legislature, January 18, 1788, declared that the "separate independence and individual sovereignty of the several states were never thought of by the enlightened band of patriots who framed this Declaration [of Independence]. . . . Let us, then, consider all attempts to weaken this Union, by maintaining that each state is separately and individually independent, as a species of political heresy. . . ." Elliot, *Debates* (1863 ed.), IV, p. 301.

Among the many discussions of this subject the following may be especially useful: A. W. Small, *The Beginnings of American Nationality* (Johns Hopkins University *Studies in Hist. and Pol. Science*, eighth series, VIII, nos. 1-2); C. H. Van Tyne, "Sovereignty in the American Revolution," *Am. Hist. Rev.*, XII, p. 529 ff.; A. H. Stephens, *A Constitutional View of the Late War Between the States*, I (the classic argument for continued state sovereignty, written by the Vice-President of the southern Confederacy); J. C. Calhoun, *Works* (R. K. Crallé, ed.), I; J. I. C. Hare, *American Constitutional Law*, I (opening discussion); Alexander Johnston, "Declaration of Independence," *Cyclopaedia of Political Science* (J. J. Lalor, ed.), I, p. 743 ff.; Alexander Johnston, "State Sovereignty," in *Ibid.*, III, p. 788 ff.; and E. S. Corwin, *National Supremacy*.

[21] This is what Alexander Johnston means when he says, ". . . calling themselves sovereign did not make them so." "State Sovereignty," *loc. cit.*, p. 791. If this sentence is at all reconcilable with the idea that sovereignty is legal authority, not full power to exercise it, we shall have to construe it as meaning that the states were so far incapable of acting as separate full-governing bodies that the assumption that they possessed sovereignty was invalidated.

on this harrowing question, another unavoidable fact is this: there had been union, a greater or less degree of coöperation, even though all the communities had, in contemplation of law, not been absorbed into one body politic. If anyone wishes to assert that the years between 1775 and 1789 were a period of transition, and that the difficulty of deciding upon the residence of sovereignty in the period in question is insurmountable—if anyone wishes to make such an assertion, the writer lays no indictment against him.

But someone may say that all this is avoidance or an apology for not answering the question whether the states were separately sovereign. To this it may be answered, the historian is under no obligation to answer the question. Could he fully present his evidence, his facts, he would be entitled, should it so please him, to leave the verdict to his readers. If, however, one *must* state an opinion, the writer of these lines is compelled to say that, if one adheres strictly to the conception of sovereignty as implying legal authority, then the only bodies whose doings must be held to be law, because those bodies did them, were the states; they possessed the technical legal authority. If such a conclusion is of value to anyone, he is welcome to it.[22] One cannot very well ignore the word "sovereignty" in the Articles; but one cannot be absolutely sure of the meaning of the word in the minds of men that used it; and one cannot, on the other hand, blind one's eyes to the fact that the states announcing their sovereignty were incompetent to act individually as completely self-reliant members of the family of nations.

In the days of the Revolution and the Confederation, the reigning philosophy was in conflict with the idea that complete unlimited authority could exist anywhere or be possessed by anybody. The conception of the organic or vital character of a body politic was not in accord with "social compact" thinking. Only when in later years men began to think of the state—meaning by the word "state" a body politic, or as we often now say, a nation—as a being possessed of life and will, only when they began to think of the vital source of au-

---

[22] What will one do with a statement like this, which plainly declares that by the Confederation the people became one people? "AGAIN, the formation and completion of that social compact among these States, which is usually stiled *the Confederation,* is another instance of the great things our God has done for us. This is that which gives us a *national existance and character.* . . . By this event, the Thirteen United States . . . became ONE PEOPLE." More than once the states together are spoken of by this author as constituting a "nation". John Rodgers, *The Divine Goodness displayed, in the American Revolution* (New York, 1784), p. 28 ff.

thority behind all mandates, all agreements, all governments, did they begin to conceive with any clarity and definiteness of a complete and indivisible power. Some things were said in the Constitutional Convention of 1787 which appear consistent with the idea of indivisible sover-eignty; but on the whole, it appears just to say, the idea in the minds of the men of that body was that compelling legal authority was to be exercised within given fields; one field was to belong to the national government, one to the states.

CHAPTER XIII

THE TRIBULATIONS OF THE CONFEDERATE PERIOD. THE CHIEF PROBLEM OF THE TIME

The vicissitudes of the years from the adoption of the Articles to the formation of the federal Constitution deserve more attention than can be given in these pages. Almost everything points in only one direction—toward the need of a competent central government and the necessity of finding a system of union which could maintain itself. Elaborate presentation of details is therefore for our purposes not required. The whole story is one of gradually increasing ineptitude; of a central government which could less and less function as it was supposed to function; of a general system which was creaking in every joint and beginning to hobble at every step. The men who came to Philadelphia in the spring of 1787 had learned the lessons taught by the failings of the Confederation.

One source of the difficulty was the Revolution itself. For the Revolution involved war; it started as a revolt against authority. It had deeply affected the old social order, and although, as we have pointed out, the philosophy on which the movement was founded had within it elements of stability and sobriety, the war left, as war always does, the combatants in a state of mental disquietude; social and economic foundations had been shaken; the full hopes of the conflict could not in the twinkling of an eye be gathered into reality. If a war is fought for liberty, why is it necessary to forge chains of perpetual union and obedience to government? Tom Paine's philosophy, which was permeated by the real spirit of real revolution, had gone beyond the limits of the older doctrines on which the social and political order was supposed to rest; for that ardent propagandist was not fond of picturing the state of nature as a place from which men had emerged for their own greater comfort and security; if his most widely-trumpeted sayings are to be taken at their face value, all things which had grown up since the age of primeval bliss and serenity could have no real sanction for their existence, not even the sanction and support of time—"Government like dress, is the badge of lost innocence; the palaces of kings are built on the ruins of the bowers of paradise." Just how far this new state of nature and all the emanations of this tragic philosophy influenced the average man of those days, no one can say; but their presence is plain enough.

Furthermore, there was the age-old feeling that government is inevitably the enemy of man and not his servant. We cannot neglect the effect of the long struggle in history to curb government lest it act the tyrant. Government in America was not as yet securely in the hands of the people-at-large (if there be any such security anywhere at any time), but a long step forward had been taken. "It takes time", however, as John Jay remarked, "to make sovereigns of subjects"—a wise saying. It took time for the people to realize that the government was their own.

Interstate jealousy did not fail to add to the complexities of the situation.[1] The contest for local rights under the old imperial system had strengthened the sense of state reality; men were conscious of their states; the states were in a sense their own creation. It was difficult, after the strain of war had gone, to feel acutely the reality of America and the dependence of its members one upon another; and as the days went by disorganization rather than integration seemed to be gathering headway, until the more serious patriots and watchers of the night feared for the safety of their country. States with commodious harbors had an advantage over their neighbors, and they did not shrink from using it. Madison, speaking of this condition, declared that at one time "New Jersey, placed between Phil^a. & N. York, was likened to a Cask tapped at both ends: and N. Carolina between Virg^a. & S. Carolina to a patient bleeding at both Arms." [2] The experience of those years brought clearly home to thinking men the need of some general regulation of commerce.

The industrial and commercial conditions after the war were in considerable confusion. Readjustments were necessary, especially for

---

[1] "Il règne dans la formation de ces Etats un vice radical qui s'opposera toujours à une union parfaite, c'est que les Etats n'ont ré-ellement aucun intérêt pressant d'être sous un seul chef." Otto, French chargé d'affaires, to comte de Montmorin, April 10, 1787. See *The Records of the Federal Convention of 1787* (Max Farrand, ed.), III, p. 16.

[2] See Madison's preface to the debates in the Federal Convention, *Documentary History of the Constitution,* III, p. 7. The preface was written at a later time but Madison's general description of conditions is valuable. See also a letter from Madison to Jefferson, March 18, 1786, in Charles Warren, *The Making of the Constitution,* p. 16.

the resuscitation of the New England shipping industry. Some improvement came fairly quickly, and there is evidence that by 1786 the clouds of depression were beginning to lift. But it was hard to make much headway, especially as Britain was not ready to treat her former colonies as if they deserved particular favors or consideration; they had made their own beds, now let them lie there—a condition of retirement not suited to the restless spirit of the New England skippers whose ships were soon plowing the seas, even on to the Orient as well as to the ports of continental Europe. Commercial treaties were desirable, and some steps were taken in that direction; but it was hard to do anything effectively as long as the individual states could not be relied on to fulfill their obligations. Foreign nations naturally queried whether America was one or many, or, perhaps, one to-day and thirteen to-morrow.

The treaty of peace was not carried out. Britain still held the western posts from Lake Champlain to Mackinaw and thus retained control of the northern fur trade and influence over the Indians. Spain holding the mouth of the Mississippi was unwilling to allow free navigation through her territory. Trouble was brewing because of American treatment of the loyalists and because the stipulation in the treaty, that there should be no lawful impediment to the collection of debts due British creditors, received no particular attention. John Jay declared in 1786 that the treaty had been constantly violated by one state or another from the time of its signing and ratification. The Barbary powers, eager to take advantage of a helpless country, to seize American seamen, and to hold them for ransom, entered upon the game with lusty vigor. A nation which was not yet a nation in terms of law and political authority could do nothing to resist scorn and humiliation.

The pivotal problem, the immediate and unrelenting problem, was how to get revenue for the pressing needs of the Confederation. Financial affairs were in a pitiful shape and conditions daily grew worse. At the end of active hostilities the situation was bad enough. "Imagine", wrote Robert Morris who had charge of the newly-created office of superintendent of finance, "the situation of a man who is to direct the finances of a country almost without revenue (for such you will perceive this to be) surrounded by creditors whose distresses, while they increase their clamors, render it more difficult to appease them; an army ready to disband or mutiny; a government whose sole authority

consists in the power of framing recommendations." [3] Conditions did
not improve; gloom deepened into darkness. The continental paper
money ere long became a joke; and the returns from requisitions upon
the states soon were lamentably inadequate. A committee of Congress
reported in 1786 that the amount received in fourteen months was not
sufficient for the "bare maintenance of the federal government on the
most economical establishment, and in time of profound peace." [4] The
sums due for interest on the domestic and foreign debts were piling
up to staggering heights and even the principal of the debts—for,
strange as it may seem, Congress had succeeded in borrowing—was
increasing ominously. Morris had by this time resigned; he did not
wish to be a "minister of injustice." Congress was at its wit's end.
". . . the crisis has arrived," a committee announced, "when the
people of these United States, by whose will, and for whose benefit the
federal government was instituted, must decide whether they will support their rank as a nation, by maintaining the public faith at home
and abroad; or whether, for want of a timely exertion in establishing
a general revenue, and thereby giving strength to the confederacy,
they will hazard not only the existence of the union, but of those great
and invaluable privileges for which they have so arduously and so
honourably contended." [5]

At the very beginning, indeed before the Articles had been signed
by the delegates from Maryland, Congress submitted to the states an
amendment (February 3, 1781) vesting in Congress a power to levy
a duty of five per cent. on imported goods, with a few exceptions, and
a like duty on "prizes and prize goods". The monies arising from the
duties were to be used for discharging the principal and interest of the
public debts. The amendment was not adopted, one state, Rhode Island,
failing to ratify. Two years later a similar attempt to obtain revenue
was made. In an amendment proposed at this time, certain commodities
were designated with various rates of duties; on all other goods a five
per cent. duty was provided for; the proceeds were to be applied to
the discharge of the debts, but the duties were not to be continued for
more than twenty-five years. The states were also recommended to
take steps for appropriating annually for a like term of years the sum
of $1,500,000, the amount to be apportioned among the states. This
amendment met the same fate as its predecessor.

[3] Letter from Morris to Franklin, January 11, 1783, in *The Revolutionary Diplomatic Correspondence of the United States* (Francis Wharton, ed.), VI, p. 203.
[4] February 15, 1786. *Journals of Congress* (1823 ed.), IV, pp. 619-620.
[5] February 15, 1786. *Ibid.*, IV, p. 620.

In 1784, an amendment was submitted to the states which, if it had been ratified, would have given Congress certain powers over the regulation or restraint of foreign commerce. "Unless the United States in Congress assembled", it was declared, "shall be vested with powers competent to the protection of commerce, they can never command reciprocal advantages in trade; and without these our foreign commerce must decline & eventually be annihilated. . . ." The amendment was ratified by only two states.

Within the individual states, paper money added to the confusion and made recovery of economic stability difficult. Some of the states refused to be drawn down into the whirlpool; but seven of the thirteen had entered upon the scheme. The wise and proper way to get out of debt was to resort to the printing-press; for what forsooth did free government exist? "Choose such men", said one voice crying from the wilderness of poverty and debt, "as will make a bank of paper money, big enough to pay all our debts, which will sink itself (that will be so much clear gain to the state)".[6] Without question, the debtor was in a bad way; but associated with this sort of appeal for relief were all the uneasy spirits whose attitudes of mind, when minds they used, were inimical to steady economic well-being and to stable and competent government. Whether one approves or disapproves the content and the agitation of the whole controversy, the fact remains that conditions were fraught with peril, a peril enhanced by the poverty of debtors and by the mental and spiritual disquietude which, as we all know, are the fruits of war and the companions of the ensuing peace.

Social unrest passed beyond the grumbling stage in Massachusetts where Shays's rebellion broke out and aroused the anxieties of the conservatives from one end of the continent to the other. Its chiefest interest to us lies in the fact that it unquestionably had the effect of prompting men of mind as well as men of property to strengthen the union and to create self-respecting government. "There are combustibles in every State," Washington wrote in 1786, "which a spark might set fire to." "Good God!" he exclaimed, lamenting the disorder, "Who, besides a Tory, could have foreseen, or a Briton predicted them?" John Marshall, writing to James Wilkinson early in 1787, said, "I fear, and there is no opinion more degrading to the dignity of man,

---

6 *New Haven Gazette,* March 22, 1787. Quoted in O. G. Libby, *Geographical Distribution of the Vote of the Thirteen States on the Federal Constitution, 1787-8* (*Bulletin* of the University of Wisconsin, Economics, Political Science, and History Series, I, no. 1), p. 58.

that these have truth on their side who say that man is incapable of governing himself. I fear we may live to see another revolution." [7]

After this hurried view of the conditions during the so-called "critical period", we may now turn to a consideration of the political system to discover what the leaders of the time believed to be the trouble and especially to see what remedies they proposed. We have already seen that Congress had proposed amendments to the Articles authorizing the collection of customs duties to be used by Congress for defraying the debts of the union, and we have seen that in each case the amendment failed of ratification. These proposals showed the necessity of congressional income, not dependent on state caprice; a conspicuous defect in the Articles was the absence of congressional authority to obtain necessary funds; the old trouble of the taxing power in an imperial system remained. At sundry times the rights and authority of Congress and the character of the Confederation were discussed in Congress and beyond its doors. The proposals and announcements disclose the compelling nature of a serious problem and they bring before us the question of national existence as that question appeared to leading statesmen of the time. [8]

Almost immediately after Maryland's delegates had signed the Articles, a committee of Congress reported that by article thirteen a general and implied power was vested in Congress to carry all the Articles into effect against any state refusing or neglecting to abide by them; that no particular provision had been made for that purpose, and that therefore an amendment should be added fully authorizing Congress to use "the force of the United States" to compel a "State or States to fulfil their federal engagements. . . ." At that early date the need of compulsion was seen by a congressional committee including James Madison who presented the report. This report, sent to a grand committee, resulted in a full presentation (August 22, 1781) of what were believed to be requisites for "execution" of the Confederation; it was also recommended that certain additional powers should be given to Congress, notably the authority "To distrain the property of a state delinquent in its assigned proportion of men and money." Thus again,

[7] Letter from Marshall to Wilkinson, January 5, 1787, in *Am. Hist. Rev.,* XII, p. 348. This coincidence of Washington's and Marshall's sentiments is instructive, if one would understand the later career of each. Marshall seems never to have forgotten the privations of Valley Forge or the menace of Shays's rebellion.

[8] A very useful collection of proposals of this kind is *Proposals to Amend the Articles of Confederation, 1781-1789* (*American History Leaflets,* A. B. Hart and Edward Channing, eds., no. 28).

the central problem of imperial organization—how to secure supplies for the maintenance of the system—came up for solution, and the proposed solution was the use of force, or at least the seizure of property. These proposed amendments were not presented to the states for ratification.

Men interested in public affairs were actively discussing the nature and the defects of the union. Pelatiah Webster, an able publicist, issued *A Dissertation on the Political Union and Constitution of the Thirteen United States* in which he pointed out the necessity of vesting the power of taxation in what he called "The supreme authority"; this authority should have sufficient power to enforce obedience to treaties and alliances. "No laws of any State whatever," he declared, "which do not carry in them a force which extends to their effectual and final execution, can afford a certain or sufficient security to the subject". With this in mind, he proposed naïvely that every person, "whether in public or private character, who shall, by public vote or other overt act, disobey the supreme authority, shall be amendable [*sic*] to Congress," and shall be haled before that body to be fined or imprisoned, "on due conviction".[9] Hamilton in 1783 drafted resolutions "Intended to be submitted to Congress, but abandoned for want of support." He enumerated at length the defects of the Confederation, and made a severe arraignment of the system. The first defect consisted in "confining the power of the Federal Government within too narrow limits". The whole discussion or criticism is extremely interesting to anyone wishing to study the nature of Hamilton's political thinking as well as the critical problem of the time. He plainly objected not only to the inconsistencies of the Articles, but to the impracticability of their effective operation. In 1785, Noah Webster, in his *Sketches of American Policy,* announced a doctrine which by that time must have been fairly familiar, at least to those willing to think: ". . . in all the affairs that

9 This plan of Webster contained much more than is indicated in the text above; but the declaration concerning the necessity of force is the thing I wish to stand out clearly. Some other statements, however, are interesting as indications of his idea of sovereignty: "A number of sovereign States uniting into one Commonwealth, and appointing a supreme power to manage the affairs of the union, do necessarily and unavoidably part with and transfer over to such supreme power, so much of their own sovereignty [*sic*], as is necessary to render the ends of the union effectual. . . . In like manner, every member of civil society parts with many of his natural rights, that he may enjoy the rest in greater security under the protection of society." Italics of the original omitted. Thus Webster thinks a commonwealth can be made by the uniting of sovereign states; but these sovereign states may give up only a portion of their sovereignty (in other words, sovereignty is divisible); and the "supreme power" is evidently only supreme in the powers thus granted.

respect the whole, Congress must have the same power to enact laws and compel obedience throughout the continent, as the legislatures of the several states have in their respective jurisdictions." [10]

Of most significance, however, is the report (August, 1786) of a grand committee of Congress of which Charles Pinckney of South Carolina was chairman.[11] It is important because Pinckney was an influential member of the Convention which met a few months later and drew up the Constitution of the United States. Early in 1786 Congress, in the manifesto mentioned on a previous page, had in a most solemn manner exposed the deplorable and perilous condition of the union. "Oh! my country!" said Jeremy Belknap, "To what an alarming situation are we reduced, that Congress must say to us, as Joshua did to Israel, 'Behold, I set before you life and death.' " [12]

The report of the committee is a sad commentary on the moribund Confederation, for if the proposed remedies had been administered, the result might well have been sudden demise in the place of lingering death. Congress was to be given the power to regulate interstate and foreign trade, with the consent of nine states, and the power of levying additional requisitions in the way of punishment upon any state not promptly complying with requisitions for men or money. If the delinquent and disobedient state should persist in its conduct, while the majority had lived up to their obligations, then Congress should have power to levy and collect taxes and in the last extremity compel the local officers in the delinquent state to do their duty; should such a step prove ineffective, then Congress might itself appoint assessors and collectors. If there were further opposition to congressional authority, the conduct on the part of the state should be considered "an open violation of the federal compact." All this is an exposition of a desperate condition, for the ultimate remedy must be no remedy at all,

[10] A sentiment of almost exactly the same character came from Washington—one of those indications of the clearness with which he could sum up a situation without mincing phrases: "I do not conceive we can exist long as a nation without having lodged some where a power, which will pervade the whole Union in as energetic a manner as the authority of the State governments extends over the several States." George Washington, *Writings* (W. C. Ford, ed.), XI, pp. 53-54. The emphasis of Webster's document was on the need of effective power. To each state, in his opinion, might be left its "sovereign right of directing its own internal affairs; but give to Congress the sole right of conducting the general affairs of the continent." He thus advocated by the division of sovereignty an organization with effective force at the center.

[11] George Bancroft, *History of the Formation of the Constitution,* II, pp. 373-377.

[12] Letter of March 9, 1786, in Mass. Hist. Society *Collections,* fifth series, II, part I, p. 431.

but only a solemn declaration that a disobedient state had broken its promises; and yet the amendments contained provisions for compulsion upon the states by using every conceivable means of coercion short of sending troops into the state—if perchance the troops could be found ready to seize the property of citizens. The committee also proposed as amendments to the Articles that Congress be granted the power to institute a federal judiciary and to provide for securing the attendance of delegates in Congress; if such delegates did not attend, or if they withdrew, they should under certain circumstances be "proceeded against", provided punishment should extend no further than disqualifications to be delegates or to hold any office under the United States or any state.

Nothing could more amply demonstrate the feebleness and distraction of Congress and the necessity for energetic reform, if the union was to last many days. The cumbersome methods proposed for getting money, the practical admission of a continuing and probably inescapable refusal of the states to comply with reasonable requests to defray the absolutely necessary common expenses, and above all, the more pitiful suggestion of measures which might induce members from the states to come to Congress and attend to business, were a confession of masterly incapacity.

Another source of anxiety was the light-hearted way in which treaties were regarded by the states. John Jay, the Secretary for Foreign Affairs, on whose shoulders rested much of the wearying responsibility of the time, persuaded himself, or tried to, that treaties, when once made, were binding on the states and were part of the "laws of the land"—a significant expression. "Your secretary considers the thirteen independent sovereign states as having, by express delegation of power, formed and vested in Congress a perfect though limited sovereignty for the general and national purposes specified in the confederation. In this sovereignty they cannot severally participate (except by their delegates) or have concurrent jurisdiction. . . . When therefore a treaty is constitutionally made, ratified and published by Congress, it immediately becomes binding on the whole nation, and superadded to the laws of the land, without the intervention, consent or fiat of state legislatures." [13] In March, 1787, resolutions

[13] *Secret Journals of the Acts and Proceedings of Congress*, IV, pp. 203-204. Cf. Constitution, Art. VI, para. 2. A committee report to the Congress of the Confederation, discussed March 26, 1784, contained the following provision: " 'That these United States be considered in all such treaties, and in every case arising under them, as one nation, upon the principles of the federal constitution' ". A motion

were passed by Congress declaring treaties "constitutionally made" were "part of the law of the land"; the states were called upon to repeal acts violating the treaty with Britain and to direct the state courts to adjudge cases in accord with the treaty, "any thing in the . . . acts to the contrary . . . notwithstanding." [14]

But what was the very center of the difficulty? What was the chief problem of the time? The trouble and confusion were manifestly caused by the failure of the states to abide by their obligations. The problem was to find a method, if union was to subsist at all, for overcoming the difficulty, to find therefore some arrangement, some scheme or plan of organization wherein there would be reasonable assurance that the states would fulfill their obligations and play their part under established articles of union and not make mockery of union by willful disregard or negligent delay. That was the *chief problem* of the day. The need of granting certain powers to Congress was plain; in other words, the distribution of powers between the center and the parts was imperfectly provided for in the Confederation. The distribution of powers, however, did not constitute the radical difficulty. If additional "powers" were granted Congress, could there be any assurance that the old trouble would not immediately arise? To the men of 1786—such men as were anxious for national stability—the real remedy appeared to be some application of force, the coercion of recalcitrant states, something more than the grant of naked authority to the central organ of union. The problem of imperial order had been reduced in some respects to fairly simple terms; if the task of distinguishing between powers was no longer especially troublesome, the question remaining was perplexing: could the states be held together in a firm and effective union and what arrangement could be made for securing or assuring obedience to their obligations as members of the union? Plainly enough the men of the time—the men of course who really thought—were troubled and perplexed; but few of them could even then see much further than the need of compulsion—the use of force against disobedient states.[15]

was made to strike out this instruction. On the question, shall it stand, the vote stood: New Hampshire, Massachusetts, New York, New Jersey, Pennsylvania, Maryland, Virginia, North Carolina, South Carolina, aye; Rhode Island, Connecticut, no. *Secret Journals of the Acts and Proceedings of Congress,* III, pp. 452-454.

[14] *Journals of Congress* (1823 ed.), IV, pp. 730, 737.

[15] Perhaps some of them did. Washington's statement quoted in note 10 (*ante*) may possibly be so interpreted. Noah Webster appears to me to have been nearest a grasp of a solution of the problem. But the way in which that solution was finally found is a most interesting study; and the study awaits us on the succeeding pages

But the year of gloom was not allowed to pass utterly without hope or light. Virginia and Maryland had been discussing troublesome questions concerning the navigation of the Potomac. But if two states could consult upon matters of mutual interest, why not more than two? Out of these conferences, therefore, came the Annapolis convention in the autumn of 1786. Five states were represented, and a report was drawn up proposing a convention "to meet at Philadelphia on the second Monday in May next, to take into consideration the situation of the United States, to devise such further provisions as shall appear to them necessary to render the constitution of the federal government adequate to the exigencies of the Union. . . ." The proposal, submitted to the states, was sent to Congress which (February 21, 1787) passed a resolution in substantial accord with the recommendation from the Annapolis gathering. A method was thus found for stabilizing the union and for saving it from complete disintegration, saving the new-born United States from becoming "one of the most contemptible nations on the face of the earth." [16] Eager nationalists were anxiously at work during the months that followed; and when May came, the prospect of effective results appeared bright; at least there was ground for hope.

of this work. If the rule of apportioning requisitions were made "plain and easy," and if "refusal were then to follow demand," Richard Henry Lee declared, "I see clearly, that no form of government whatever, short of force, will answer. . . ." "Do you not think, sir, that it ought to be declared, by the new system, that any State act of legislation that shall contravene, or oppose, the authorized acts of Congress, or interfere with the expressed rights of that body, shall be *ipso facto* void, and of no force whatsoever?" Letter from Lee to George Mason, May 15, 1787, in K. M. Rowland, *The Life of George Mason,* II, pp. 105, 107. Jefferson wrote to Madison from Paris, June 20, 1787, suggesting appeals from state courts to a federal court. Jefferson, *Works* (federal ed.), V, p. 285. See also a letter from Richard Henry Lee to Madison, November 26, 1784, in *The Letters of Richard Henry Lee* (J. C. Ballagh, ed.), II, p. 307.

[16] Letter from William Grayson to Madison, March 22, 1786. Quoted in George Bancroft, *History of the Formation of the Constitution,* I, p. 258.

CHAPTER XIV

THE FEDERAL CONVENTION

I: Determination to Found a National Government

Seventy-four delegates were appointed to the Convention;[1] nineteen for one reason or another did not attend; thirty-nine signed the document which resulted from nearly four months of discussion. Rhode Island did not deign to participate, and the delegates from New Hampshire did not come until July 23, after the Convention had decided some of its most difficult problems. The early and, indeed, the conspicuously troublesome questions were therefore passed upon by delegations from eleven states. Many of the members had had political experience. Even at that time, when men were not affected as we are likely to be by tradition, there was a general acknowledgment of the ability and rectitude of the delegates. America, in a crisis, had chosen her best.

One fact is very evident in the Convention's work—results were reached by debate, by interchange of opinion, by deliberate but earnest consideration of problems. There was little or no declamation for its own sake. Conclusions were the product of discussion; and the reader of the debates can to-day see the gradual unfolding of principles and institutional forms as the weeks went by. This means, of course, that no faction worked its will and no leader dominated the rest. Not one delegate envisaged in advance the whole system and all the fundamental principles on which it rested. For once at least in the course of history, opinions were formed and changed as the result of argument. The most conspicuous, and perhaps the most influential, member

---

[1] This number includes those who declined to serve and the substitutes who in some cases took their places. *Records of the Federal Convention* (Max Farrand, ed.; hereafter referred to as Farrand, *Records*), III, p. 557 ff. See also J. F. Jameson, "Studies in the History of the Federal Convention of 1787," Am. Hist. Asso. *Report* for 1902, I, p. 157 and note a. Charles Warren, *The Making of the Constitution*, p. 55, gives the following details: thirty-nine of the delegates had served in Congress; eight had signed the Declaration of Independence; eight had helped to form state constitutions; five had been members of the Annapolis convention; seven had been chief executives of their states; twenty-one had fought in the Revolution.

of the Convention was Washington. He had hesitated to accept the appointment, but had finally done so; his presence gave prestige to the Convention and calmed apprehensions of people who feared a plot or some ruthless attack upon their liberties. He was no great student of political theory or of history, but he had grasped the essentials of the problem of national organization as few others had done. ". . . my wish is," he wrote Madison, before the Convention met, "that the convention may adopt no temporizing expedients, but probe the defects of the constitution to the bottom, and provide a radical cure, whether they are agreed to or not." America, then in the process of construction, was his country. Though he spoke but once on the floor, of his position on certain essential and critical questions there is no doubt. He allied himself with the national party and appears to have supported Madison's views in particular.[2]

The leader on the floor and in some ways the most effective man in the Convention was Madison. For a considerable time his mind had been absorbed with the problem of national reorganization; he came prepared for his work. Without eloquence, as the word is commonly used, he could speak with cogency and skill. No one saw more clearly into the complexities of the problem or the general nature of the solutions that must be reached. He had examined the ancient leagues and pondered the lessons of their history. He had analyzed the defects of the Confederation and found no sanction, no compelling power. "A sanction", he said, "is essential to the idea of law, as coercion is to that of Government." He believed in the need of framing a new constitution, not merely amending the Articles, and in a letter to Washington, written a month before the Convention met, he used these especially significant words: "Conceiving that an individual independence of the States is utterly irreconcileable with their aggregate sovereignty, and that a consolidation of the whole into one simple republic would be as inexpedient as it is unattainable, I have sought for middle ground, which may at once support a due supremacy of the national authority, and not exclude the local authorities wherever they can be subordinately useful." In a letter to Jefferson, then in Europe, he spoke of the expediency of laying "the foundation of the new system in such a ratification by the people themselves of the several States as will render it clearly paramount to their Legislative authorities." [3] In

---

[2] Of special value on this subject is Max Farrand, "George Washington in the Federal Convention," *Yale Review*, XVI, p. 280 ff.

[3] March 19 (18 ?), 1787. Madison, *Writings* (Gaillard Hunt, ed.), II, p. 326.

letters to others [4] he outlined with a remarkable approach to accuracy the main features of the Constitution as it finally came from the hands of the framers.

In the Pennsylvania delegation were two men who labored ably for union and competent government. James Wilson, a Scotchman by birth who had studied in the universities of his native country, had a remarkably clear, critical mind; he was strongly national in his sympathies and stands beside Madison as one of the two strongest thinkers in the Convention. On more than one occasion he marked out with special clarity the nature of the Convention's task and the general principles on which the new system should rest. Gouverneur Morris, eloquent, active-minded, at times caustic and aggressive, played a prominent rôle. He, too, toiled valiantly for an effective national government. Madison in later years spoke of the "brilliancy of his genius" and of his readiness to surrender hastily-formed opinions. To him Madison also ascribed the *"finish* given to the style and arrangement of the Constitution" in its final form; but there is evidence of Wilson's participation in this task of final revision, and perhaps his share was even greater than that of Morris.[5]

The New York delegation was composed of three men; two of them, Yates and Lansing, were anxious to guard the states against encroachment. They were associated in their beliefs and fears with Governor Clinton of New York and the group who were charged, not unjustly, with setting up an "idol of State Sovereignty".[6] A third member was Alexander Hamilton, an able advocate of efficient government and a coherent union. Seven years before the Convention met he had spoken of the necessity of "a solid coercive union",[7] and somewhat later he said, "there is something . . . diminutive and contemptible in the prospect of a number of petty States, with the appearance only of union, jarring, jealous, and perverse, without any determined direction, fluctuating and unhappy at home, weak and insignificant by their dissensions in the eyes of other nations." [8] His views in certain respects were so extreme—some of them perhaps put forth in the Convention

---

[4] See letter to Edmund Randolph, April 8, 1787, in *Ibid.*, II, p. 336 ff.; letter to Washington, April 16, 1787, in *Ibid.*, II, p. 344 ff.

[5] See Warren, *op. cit.*, pp. 687-688; Max Farrand, *The Framing of the Constitution*, p. 181.

[6] Warren, *op. cit.*, p. 339.

[7] Letter to James Duane, September 3, 1780, in Alexander Hamilton, *Works* (J. C. Hamilton, ed.), I, p. 157.

[8] July 4, 1782. See *Ibid.*, II, p. 201.

chiefly to arouse discussion—that they had little if any effect. A proof of his amazing genius is seen in his defense of the Constitution when it was finished and presented to the states for ratification, and especially in the articles of supreme power and intelligence which he contributed to *The Federalist;* but his work in the Convention itself was not significant.[9] His colleagues in the New York delegation disagreed with him; with the apparent exception of one day he was absent for six weeks (June 29 to August 13); when he returned, his colleagues had left the Convention (July 10), and the vote of the state was not cast.

Connecticut sent three able men, Roger Sherman, Oliver Ellsworth, and William S. Johnson. In the earlier days they took a stand against the radical or advanced plans and purposes of the nationalist leaders, but they were not narrow-minded men hemmed in by local patriotism or petty state jealousy. William Paterson was the most important delegate from New Jersey. When the great principle of nationalism was under discussion and the leaders of the Convention seemed to be on the verge of carrying out their will without effective opposition, he became the prominent protagonist for the cause of the smaller states and the advocate of the principles of the Confederation. The Maryland delegation was so made up that on certain critical questions the votes of its members were equally divided; Luther Martin, a lawyer of marked ability, an active defender of the states, labored valiantly against what proved to be the Convention's will. From Delaware came John Dickinson, the "Penman of the American Revolution". Of the South Carolina delegates John Rutledge and Charles Pinckney were the more effective men. The latter, then only twenty-nine years of age, had had valuable experience in Congress and had taken particular interest in the establishment of a competent government.[10]

The Convention was summoned to meet on the second Monday of

[9] Warren says, "Ten men stand out as chiefly responsible for the form which the Constitution finally took—Madison, Randolph, Franklin, Wilson, Gouverneur Morris, King, Rutledge, Charles Pinckney, Ellsworth, and Sherman." Warren, *op. cit.*, p. 57. Probably this is as good a selection as anyone can make, though it necessarily ignores valuable work by others. Franklin's work was rather that of peacemaker than of contributor to the actual structure of the Constitution. Randolph did some effective speaking, at first appeared as a leader, but finally refused to sign. Furthermore, the list leaves out Washington. Farrand, *The Framing of the Constitution,* gives a brief sketch of the members. p. 14 ff.

[10] Gouverneur Morris made 173 speeches; Wilson, 168; Madison, 161; Sherman, 138; Mason, 136; Gerry, 119. See Warren, *op. cit.,* p. 125. On a good many occasions the votes of one or more states were divided. "There were twenty-three occasions when, had there been no divided vote, the result of the vote might have been altered." Maryland's vote was evenly divided twenty-seven times.

May, which fell on the fourteenth. Only a few of the delegates arrived promptly. While waiting for the arrival of other delegates and the organization of the Convention, the members from Virginia set to work on a plan for new articles of union. Virginia felt especially responsible for the meeting and her representatives thought it best to have definite proposals for presentation.[11] Whatever others might think, they were not content with mere amendments for patching up the Confederation. To James Madison, it is fair to assume, we owe a good part of the first plan that was drawn up for the Convention's deliberations.

Eleven days after the time appointed for meeting, seven states were represented and the Convention was organized (May 25), electing George Washington as the presiding officer. Soon after formal organization, rules of procedure were adopted providing, among other things, that nothing spoken in the house should be printed or otherwise published or communicated without leave, and that no copy be taken of any entry on the journal during the sitting of the house without its leave. This injunction of secrecy was obeyed with a remarkable fidelity. Rumors concerning the Convention's labors circulated occasionally beyond the statehouse walls, but the actual work of the assembly went forward undisturbed by popular clamor and apparently uninfluenced by the curiosity of the public. The reason for this secrecy is obvious; it enabled the members to speak plainly, if they would; it prevented tentative or vaguely-formed proposals from going forth to the press; it precluded the likelihood of prejudice or opposition based on incomplete evidence, and it allowed the Convention to present its conclusions. Though leaders proposed at the beginning to correct and enlarge the Articles of Confederation, the plan they entered upon was so different from that of the Articles that they might well have feared an outcry of protest from the public had their purpose been fully exposed to view.

The journal of the Convention, kept by the Secretary, William Jackson, was meager; in some respects he was an untidy workman. If

---

[11] "On the arrival of the Virginia Deputies at Philadelphia it occurred to them that from the early and prominent part taken by that State in bringing about the Convention some initiative step might be expected from them. The Resolutions introduced by Governor Randolph were the result of a Consolidation on the subject. . . ." "James Madison: Preface to Debates in the Convention of 1787," in Farrand, *Records*, III, p. 549. See also Randolph's remarks, May 29. To facilitate reading, the writer has taken the liberty to spell out abbreviations, to modernize certain eighteenth-century spellings, and to omit certain parentheses which appear in the Farrand edition of the *Records*.

we had nothing else but this official journal on which to rely, we should to-day be almost as uncertain as were the people of that earlier day concerning the nature of the discussions, and we should have only a dim idea of what went on behind the closed doors and under the seal of secrecy. Fortunately the indefatigable Madison was at hand. Day by day with great patience and with consummate skill he wrote down not only motions and votes, but also the arguments of the various speakers. All of it was done with clarity and precision and—what is more remarkable—with candor and freedom from petty jealousy.

In addition to Madison's *Notes* we have other sources of information, but they are relatively unimportant. Yates of New York made fairly full notes, but he was not present after July 10. His minutes were published in 1821. Luther Martin, reporting to the Maryland legislature, gave in his *Genuine Information* an account of what took place and presented his interpretation of the proceedings of the Convention and the purposes of its leaders; this statement was printed soon afterwards. In later years Madison criticized the statements of both Yates and Martin. Yates, he said, was inaccurate and in some cases did injustice to the arguments and opinions of particular members; and still, when later revising his own manuscripts, he added a few of Yates's statements. Martin's report betrayed "feelings which had a discolouring effect on his statements." The criticisms seem to be essentially just; there is value in the work of both of these men, but no one probably would suspect Martin, an able, determined, and rather truculent advocate, of possessing a high degree of objectivity, the quality which gives Madison's *Notes* peculiar worth. Within recent years, a few notes and other papers, some of them apparently rather hastily written or prepared as memoranda for debate, have been made available—notes by King of Massachusetts, McHenry of Maryland, Pierce of Georgia, Paterson of New Jersey, Hamilton of New York, and Mason of Virginia—; not one of them adequately covers any considerable portion of the Convention's proceedings; they do, however, throw light on episodes in the Convention's work. To this list should be added certain papers showing the work of the important committee of detail. There are a few other stray papers of no great significance.

Thirty years after the Convention met, John Quincy Adams, then Secretary of State, was assigned the task of preparing for publication the formal official journal—and a task it proved to be. The volume was printed in 1819. Though inaccurate in some respects (most of the inaccuracies being of slight importance), and though extremely brief, it remained for years the only continuous and authoritative statement of the Convention's proceedings. After Madison's death, which occurred in 1836, his papers were purchased by the government and the *Notes* were printed four years later. We find, therefore, this very important fact: during fifty years of our history, politicians, statesmen, and judges relied (if they relied on any source at all) on entirely insufficient, partial, and in some respects prejudiced accounts of the proceedings and debates. The great decisions of John Marshall, the speeches of Hayne and Webster, the theories and pronouncements of Calhoun, were all made with nothing like the information that might have been gained had Madison's *Notes* been published. Story's *Commentaries* appeared in their first edition three years before Madison's death. Important as these facts are, it may be even more interesting to notice how little intelligent use was made of the invaluable information furnished by the *Notes* after they had appeared in print.[12]

If the Convention's job had been confined to the formation of a thoroughly competent government, theoretically sound and capable; had its problem been only that of establishing a completely centralized system, the difficulties would have been sufficient to tax the intelligence of statesmen. But in this instance the problem to be solved was more subtle and more complex. The members found themselves engaged in the task of constructing a new kind of body politic, neither a centralized system on the one hand nor a league or confederation on the other. Certain minor problems, as we shall see, were perplexing and to them was given much discussion—for example, the method of choosing the executive—, but the really difficult job was to form a strong and infrangible union without destroying the states as integral, and, in many respects, autonomous parts of an integral system. The solution of this problem was the signal contribution of the Convention to the political life of the modern world. To aid them, the members

---

[12] *The Records of the Federal Convention,* in three volumes, edited by Max Farrand, contain practically all available sources for the study of the Convention's proceedings. The volumes contain not only Madison's *Notes* and the others mentioned above, but also statements made in later years by men who had been members of the Convention. Some day, possibly, further notes may come to light, but this collection is practically definitive and is rendered more valuable by the critical scholarship of the editor. There are various other editions of Madison's *Notes,* sometimes improperly called Madison's *Journal.* (The word *Notes* is put in italics for convenience, not as a book title.) References to the notes will be cited: Madison's *Notes* (with the date and without specific page references).

had the practices of the old empire, as we have already seen; they had in addition their own experiences in the Revolution and under the Articles of Confederation; their most immediate source of knowledge was the failure of the Confederation to function; to this failure the delegates in the Convention frequently referred; it furnished the most convincing lesson.

In one matter—the distribution of powers between the states on the one side and the central government on the other—the old empire and the Articles furnished them with lessons of organization. But the principle of union and the method of its maintenance had to be worked out, hammered out, in the processes of debate. Our first and most important work, therefore, is to point out in the course of the succeeding pages how that particular task was done. The great achievement was to solve the problem of imperial order, the problem which Parliament had found itself incapable of solving and which now remained for the Americans themselves, a problem calling for supremely intelligent statesmanship and no longer to be avoided.

The "main business" of the Convention was opened by Randolph, who made an effective speech and presented a plan of union which had been sketched by the Virginia delegates.[13] He pictured the existing situation and especially showed the defects of the Confederation and the necessity of change in certain essential respects. The fourth and fifth defects, as Madison noted them, are peculiarly important—"the foederal government could not defend itself against the incroachments from the states", and "it [presumably the Articles] was not even paramount to the state constitutions, ratified as it was in may [sic] of the states." It is difficult to find any interpretation of this brief statement except one signifying the belief of the Virginia delegation that the new scheme of union was to be based on a constitution, which, as far as it went, was to be superior to the state constitutions.

Though skillfully prepared, the Randolph or Virginia plan, which was soon taken as the basis of the Convention's work, was in some respects only a fairly elaborate outline. It declared the need of correcting and enlarging the Articles of Confederation, and then at once announced "that the rights of suffrage in the National Legislature ought to be proportioned to the Quotas of contribution, or to the number of free inhabitants. . . ." It provided for a bicameral legislature, the members of the first branch to be elected by the people, the members

[13] See letter from Madison to Noah Webster, October 12, 1804, in Farrand, *Records*, III, p. 409.

of the second to be chosen by those of the first, out of a number of persons "nominated by the individual Legislatures. . . ." The assignment of powers to the national legislature was stated in general but fairly comprehensive, though indefinite, terms. Its general principle was clear: "the National Legislature ought to be impowered to enjoy the Legislative Rights vested in Congress by the Confederation and moreover to legislate in all cases to which the separate States are incompetent, or in which the harmony of the United States may be interrupted by the exercise of individual Legislation. . . ." The plan provided for a national executive and a national judiciary; the executive and a convenient number of the judiciary were to form a "council of revision", empowered to examine every act of the national legislature before it should "operate, and every act of a particular Legislature before a Negative thereon shall be final;" the dissent of this council was to "amount to a rejection," unless the legislature passed the act a second time or the act of a state legislature was "again negatived by [   ] of the members of each branch."

Other portions of the plan need not be recited; but it is important to notice that the "amendments" made to the Confederation by the Convention were, after approbation of the Congress of the Confederation, to be passed upon by an assembly or assemblies of representatives, "recommended by the several Legislatures to be expressly chosen by the people. . . ." In other words, the work of the Convention was to be presented as offering amendments to the existing system; but it was to stand on the will of the people and not on the authority of the state governments. This plan evidently proposed the establishment of something more than a union of sovereign states acting through a body of delegates to an international conference. The provision for proportional representation from the states was of signal importance. The idea was not new; it was to be found in the Albany Plan; it had been discussed in the Continental Congress; and now because of the fears and forebodings of the small states, it was certain to become a center of controversy. Viewed as a whole, the Randolph plan makes plain the intention of the Virginia delegates not to be content with mere "temporizing expedients".

The proposal to establish a national government with power to do all things which the states were incompetent to do may be considered in itself an answer to what I have called the "chief problem", as conditions appeared to the thoughtful men of the day anxious for union and peace. If such a government could be founded on the popular will, the customary readiness of the states to disregard their obligations might be obviated. But in addition to the distinct establishment of a national system, the *Virginia plan contained three explicit answers to the problem:* (1) the national legislature was empowered "to negative all laws passed by the several States, contravening", in its opinion, "the articles of Union. . . ." (2) It was empowered "to call forth the force of the Union against any member of the Union failing to fulfill its duty under the articles thereof." (3) The "Legislative Executive and Judiciary powers within the several States ought to be bound by oath to support the articles of Union".

Of these three explicit proposals for means of assuring the obedience of the states to their obligations, only one, the third, found its way into the finished Constitution; there it stands to-day, as it has for a century and more, as a sign of moral and legal obligation to maintain the federal system. The fate of the other two provisions will be presented in subsequent pages. The three together furnish conclusive evidence of the fear of dissolution of the union, and fear that the union would be but a shadow as the old one had proved to be, because the states had refused or neglected to perform their duties.

When Randolph had finished, with an exhortation not to suffer the opportunity of establishing peace and harmony to go by unimproved, his plan was referred to a committee of the whole. A "draught of a federal Government", prepared by Charles Pinckney, was also presented and was likewise referred. Just what this latter plan contained we do not know. What has been frequently printed as the Pinckney plan is certainly not what the ardent young statesman of South Carolina actually laid before the Convention.[14] When John Quincy Adams was editing the Secretary's notes thirty years after the Convention adjourned, he wrote to Pinckney and received from him a document which Adams placed in the edited journal as the Pinckney plan. It is quite inconceivable that Pinckney, or anyone else, could have presented to the Convention at the beginning a series of proposals so closely

[14] J. F. Jameson, in his "Studies in the History of the Federal Convention of 1787," *loc. cit.,* not only demolishes the pseudo-Pinckney plan, but by very clever and scholarly work brings out from the study of the debates in the Convention fairly clear indication of what the real plan was. A paper which he found among the Wilson papers proved to be a portion of the real plan and seems to demonstrate that it was elaborate. The author of this volume, relying on the substantial character of Jameson's work, found what is evidently an outline of the original plan. This outline is printed in *Am. Hist. Rev.,* IX, pp. 735-747, with notes and comments. A "reconstructed" plan, based on the outline and on other sources, is to be found in Farrand, *Records,* III, p. 604 ff.

resembling the finished Constitution as does the pseudo-plan which Adams inserted in the journal. The paper on which the "plan", as Adams received it, was written, bore the watermark of the year 1797, and therefore no great amount of historical criticism is needed to decide the document to be not the original but at the best a copy. Pinckney himself, a year after the adjournment of the Convention, wrote to a correspondent that he had no copy of his plan in his possession. From available authentic materials we can reach reasonably certain conclusions concerning the character of the original plan; it proposed not mere amendments to the Confederation, but the establishment of a real government and one, at least in some particulars, endowed with powers and authority.

The committee of the whole went in session the next day (May 30) and immediately took up the Virginia plan as the basis of deliberation. At the beginning of those deliberations a significant step was taken. There were some members who thought it wise to commit the Convention at the outset to fundamental principles.[15] The first resolution of the Virginia plan, indicating the purpose of the Convention, declared the need of correcting and enlarging the Articles of Confederation. Randolph, on the suggestion of Gouverneur Morris, moved the postponement of this resolution in order that three new resolutions might be considered which would announce in general but explicit terms the intention of the Convention. Postponement was agreed to. The first two of these resolutions were strangely similar; each in substance repeated the other: no union of states "merely federal", no treaty or treaties among the states as individual sovereignties would be sufficient to accomplish the objects "proposed by the articles of Condeferation [sic], namely common defence, security of liberty, and general welfare." These two resolutions were passed over without much discussion; but the third, which indeed stated affirmatively the

---

[15] According to McHenry, Hamilton had said, before the close of the previous session (May 29), that it struck him as a necessary and proper preliminary to inquire whether the United States "were susceptible of one government, or required a separate existence connected only by leagues offensive and defensive and treaties of commerce." See Farrand, *Records*, I, p. 27. There is no reference in the journal or in Madison's *Notes* that Hamilton made any such statement in the open Convention, and it seems likely that it was not made during formal proceedings. The incisive young statesman from New York evidently wished to cut the main problem to the heart and to perform the operation at once. So now it was determined to test the sense of the whole body as to whether or not a mere league of sovereignties was sufficient.

principle of the earlier two, was taken up for more careful consideration. Though possibly its full import can be seen only when examined
by the side of the other two, the meaning of the third resolution is
perfectly plain: "that a *national* Government ought to be established
consisting of a *supreme* Legislative, Executive and Judiciary." [16]

Discussion of the third resolution followed, less however, Madison
tells us, "on its general merits than on the force and extent of the
particular terms *national* and *supreme.*" Charles Pinckney asked Randolph whether he meant to abolish the state governments. Randolph
replied "that he meant by these general propositions merely to introduce the particular ones which explained the outlines of the system he
had in view." The question and answer are significant: just what did
the establishment of a supreme national government imply? Did it
involve the disappearance or the total absorption of the states? In the
weeks following that problem proved to be, as we have already indicated, difficult and perplexing.[17]

"Mr. Gouverneur Morris explained the distinction between a
federal and *national, supreme,* Government; the former being a mere
compact resting on the good faith of the parties; the latter having a
compleat and *compulsive* operation." The word "federal", which we
now use as synonymous with "national", was then used in its original
sense (Latin, *foedus*, treaty). Mason at once struck at an essential
fact; admitting the deficiency of the Confederation in not providing
for coercion and punishment of delinquent states, he "argued very
cogently that punishment could not in the nature of things be executed
on the States collectively, and therefore that such a Government was
necessary as could directly operate on individuals, and would punish
those only whose guilt required it." By "States collectively" he evidently meant states in their corporate characters as distinguished from
the individuals composing them. Sherman was hesitant; acknowledging that the Confederation was defective and that additional powers
were necessary, he stated—and the statement is important—that in no
case ought the general and particular jurisdictions to be concurrent; he

[16] For some indication of the reason for not taking action on the first two resolutions, see *Ibid.,* I, p. 39.

[17] At a much later time Gouverneur Morris stated the problem thus: "there was
a serious discussion on the importance of arranging a national system of sufficient
strength to operate, in despite of State opposition, and yet not strong enough to
break down State authority." Morris to W. H. Wells, February 24, 1815, in *Ibid.,*
III, p. 421.

was indisposed to make too great inroads on the existing system, "intimating as one reason, that it would be wrong to lose every amendment, by inserting such as would not be agreed to by the States".

The third resolution, as given above, was adopted; six states voted in the affirmative; one, Connecticut, in the negative; New York was divided. So at the very beginning, the Rubicon was passed. The Convention decided not merely to add powers to the Congress of the Confederation but to frame a government national in scope and character. Long days of discussion followed; but there is not a scintilla of evidence that the Convention turned its back upon the purpose distinctly laid down on the thirtieth of May. State jealousies and anxieties, local pride, and fear of an overawing national authority were still to be dealt with; but the majority adhered to its purpose of establishing a system which would not be a mere league of sovereigns.

Difficulty, however, lay immediately ahead; to vote for an efficient government and even for one founded on national principles was one thing; but if nationalism meant unequal representation of the states in the national legislature, any plan of proportional representation was certain to arouse the *amour propre* of the small states; the old fears and jealousies would be awakened. There arose therefore not only the question of the independence and sovereignty of the states, but also the natural unwillingness of some of the delegates to favor a plan which would diminish the consequence and prestige of their respective states. A small and weak state wished to hold up its head as the equal of a richer and more powerful neighbor.[18] This dread lest the stronger states oppress the weaker was of long standing; it had shown itself especially in the formation of the Confederation, when states, notably Maryland, had hesitated to sign the Articles because of the power and influence of their larger landholding neighbors; it proved to be of consequence in the Convention's labors. The grouping of the states

[18] The significance of the opposition of the small states, which is to be considered more fully in later pages, is thus stated in the text above because it seems possible to overemphasize the idea that the small states were influenced only by their desire to conserve their complete sovereignty. The subject of sovereignty was discussed and the discussion was connected with the question of representation—for if sovereignty necessarily included equality, the states could not surrender equality of representation without diminishing their sovereignty. But there were differences among the delegates from the small states. Some of them were insistent upon the retention of the complete sovereignty of the states. Others appear to have objected to the abandonment of complete equality of representation in Congress, not so much because inequality indicated the surrender of sovereignty as because inequality lowered the prestige of the states. Of course, as we have indicated, the old jealousies were still active; the small states feared the strength of their powerful neighbors.

was not quite the same as it had been ten years before; but in general the same feeling of state pride and the same feeling of foreboding on the part of the less populous or less powerful states rendered the task of forming an effective union a difficult one.

The full meaning and implication of proportional representation were however clearly brought forth in this early discussion, for "Mr. Madison observed that whatever reason might have existed for the equality of suffrage when the Union was a federal one among sovereign States, it must cease when a national Government should be put into the place." But the Delaware delegates were restrained by their commission "from assenting to any change of the rule of suffrage. . . . " And so the matter was postponed for later consideration.

During the next few days the discussion—still in the committee of the whole—was devoted to various points of interest. The Virginia resolutions were taken up one by one and conclusions were reached which, however, had to be debated again and in some respects modified in later days. The subjects debated in these early days we may pass over with only a few words of comment, though some of them were of crucial importance. Wilson made a number of especially able speeches from which we can cull a few significant sentences: "If we are to establish a national Government, that Government ought to flow from the people at large." "Federal liberty is to States, what civil liberty, is to private individuals. And States are not more unwilling to purchase it, by the necessary concession of their political sovereignty, that [sic] the savage is to purchase Civil liberty by the surrender of the personal sovereignty, which he enjoys in a State of nature." Pointing to a principle which proved to be fundamental in the scheme of imperial order ultimately agreed upon in the Convention, he said, "All interference between the general and local Governments should be obviated as much as possible."

The resolution providing for the adoption of the new Constitution by conventions of the people was not debated at length, but in the course of the discussion Madison presented the necessity for this method of ratification, if the new government was to have substantial authority: "he thought it indispensable that the new Constitution should be ratified in the most unexceptionable form, and by the supreme authority of the people themselves." [19] The resolution for popular

---

[19] At a later day (July 23) Madison pointed out "the difference between a system founded on the Legislatures only, and one founded on the people, to be the true difference between a *league* or *treaty*, and a *Constitution*."

ratification was passed (June 12), six states voting in the affirmative; Connecticut, New York, and New Jersey in the negative. Delaware and Maryland were divided.[20] That ratification by the people would place the Constitution above state laws was clearly presented, and, it would seem, thoroughly understood. Thus by the very force called into operation for establishing the Constitution, the chief problem of the period found a partial answer: the new union arising immediately from the people was no longer to be a submissive and humble suitor dependent on the whims, negligence, and changeful humors of state governments.

But the basis of representation in the national legislature could not be indefinitely postponed; that particularly difficult bridge had to be crossed. Despite opposition which had not, however, reached its most formidable stage, a decision was reached not to follow the old rule of equal votes in the legislature; proportional representation in both branches of the legislature was decided upon. Franklin's assertion, at an earlier time, that a system founded on injustice could not last, was in process of fulfillment. The alignment of the states on this question is significant: on the question of proportional representation "in the first branch", seven states voted in the affirmative—Massachusetts, Connecticut, Pennsylvania, Virginia, North Carolina, South Carolina, Georgia. New York, New Jersey, and Delaware voted in the negative. Maryland was divided. The vote of Connecticut is specially significant because it is plain that as early as this her delegation was ready to accept proportional representation in one house, if equal representation in the other should be granted. Dickinson had expressed belief in the advisability of a similar adjustment.[21] When the question of representation in the second branch came to be voted on, the states were grouped much as before; but Connecticut voted for equal representation, as did Maryland, no longer divided.

Quite plainly, at the end of two weeks of debate the Convention contained two groups differing in opinion on certain pivotal if not absolutely essential matters. On the one side were Massachusetts and Pennsylvania and the four states south of the Potomac. They favored a system involving the principle of nationalism and they defended a method of representation and a mode of ratifying the Constitution which were consistent with the existence of a national government.

[20] The journal omits Pennsylvania, but see Madison's *Notes*, June 12.
[21] Madison's *Notes*, June 2, 6, 7. For Sherman's opinion, see his speech at the opening of the session of June 11. Farrand, *Records*, I, p. 196.

Made up of states large in population or area, this group had shown a certain degree of solidarity and unity of purpose. They objected to a system of equality in representation which would allow the inhabitants of a state like Delaware as much power in the government as that of its more powerful neighbors. If all were to be citizens of the United States under a common government, then the number of citizens within a given area should naturally indicate the proportional number of representatives in the national legislature.

The small-state group—Connecticut, New Jersey, Maryland, Delaware, New York—gradually hardening into a fairly efficient opposition was less coherent and less clear in its views than was the other. The vote of Maryland had so far proved to be uncertain. As Hamilton could make no headway against the two other delegates from New York, the vote of that state was frankly against the purpose and designs of the nationalists. Connecticut was open to reason, but its members were determined not to accept a plan of organization which would belittle the states or leave them helpless.[22] New Jersey stood for the principles of the Articles of Confederation.

In the course of the first fortnight many fundamental questions were touched upon—in fact nearly all of the most essential principles and differences of opinion were brought into view, though not fully discussed. On the whole, the nationalists had had their own way. Much remained to be done; but the leaders had some ground for expecting a speedy and successful conclusion of their labors. Unanimity, however, could scarcely have been hoped for. There were differences of opinion which must be reconciled and harmonized to save the Convention from shipwreck.

II: Controversy and Compromise; the Essentials of Federalism; Coercion of Law and Not of Arms

The committee of the whole presented to the Convention (June 13) nineteen resolutions, the product of its consideration of the Virginia plan. These resolutions provided for a national government, a bicameral

[22] Madison in a footnote, added probably at a much later time to his notes taken in the Convention, says, "Connecticut and New York were against a departure from the principle of the Confederation. wishing rather to add a few new powers to Congress than to substitute, a National Government." This does not appear to be a proper statement of the Connecticut position, unless in the earlier days, and especially May 30 when, as we have seen, on the resolution to establish a national government, Connecticut voted in the negative and New York was divided, the six other states voting in the affirmative.

legislature based on proportional representation in both branches, a national executive, a national judiciary to consist of one supreme tribunal, power being given to the national legislature to appoint inferior tribunals, and submission of the Convention's work to assemblies chosen by the people. There were other not unimportant provisions. The whole, though still general in its terms, constituted a substantial scheme for a lasting and workable union. The resolutions included the proposal to grant to the legislature the power to negative state laws "contravening in the opinion of the National Legislature the articles of Union, or any treaties subsisting under the authority of the Union." The proposal of the Virginia plan to bestow upon the national legislature the authority to coerce the delinquent states was not included in the committee's resolutions.

At this juncture, the report of the committee of the whole having been presented, Paterson told the Convention that it was the wish of "several deputations, particularly that of New Jersey," to have further time to consider the committee's report, and "to digest one purely federal, and contradistinguished from the reported plan." The request having been granted, he laid before the Convention (June 15) a set of resolutions which he wished to be substituted for the plan "proposed by Mr. Randolph." The delegates from Connecticut, New York, New Jersey, Delaware, and "perhaps", says Madison, "Mr Martin from Maryland",[23] appear to have participated in the preparation of these resolutions. The defenders of this "federal" scheme of organization—the word "federal" being used to signify a plan of confederate organization—differed, as we have already said, in their main purposes. Dickinson said to Madison: "you see the consequence of pushing things too far. Some of the members from the small States wish for two branches in the General Legislature, and are friends to a good National Government; but we would sooner submit to a foreign power, than submit to be deprived of an equality of suffrage, in both branches of the legislature, and thereby be thrown under the domination of the larger States."[24] He had at an earlier time opposed "consolidation of the States into one great Republic", and had advocated equal representation in one branch of the legislature.[25] Plainly there was no unity

[23] That Martin participated appears to be highly probable; first, because of the significance of the sixth resolution, which contained a principle he later proposed to the Convention in almost the same identical words; second, because he was a truculent, or at least an aggressive and unrelenting, advocate of state sovereignty.
[24] A footnote by Madison, placed under the date of June 15.
[25] In committee of the whole. June 1.

or agreement in the small-state group in behalf of the whole scheme of maintaining the essential principle of the Confederation, the political equality and unimpaired sovereignty of its members. Some of the small-state men were ready for *national* government, provided the states were not destroyed. Could the problem be solved?

The small-state plan proposed to amend the Articles of Confederation by giving additional powers to Congress. It bestowed upon that body authority to regulate foreign and interstate commerce, to levy import and stamp duties, and to make rules and regulations for their collection. In this way it proposed adding to the existing government—if Congress can be called a government—the two essential powers without which any system of union would be weak and probably helpless. Congress, by this plan, was also authorized to resort to the old method of making requisitions upon the states and "to direct the collection thereof" in any state not complying within a specified time; the requisitions were to be in proportion to the whole number of white and other free inhabitants and three-fifths of all other persons except Indians not paying taxes. There was a provision for a federal executive and a judiciary. But even this scheme of bolstering up the old federal union had to face the vexing possibility of a state's disregard of obligations—"the chief problem" once more. What answer did the New Jersey plan contain? It contained a declaration, which will be discussed later, that the acts of Congress and treaties should be "the supreme law of the respective States so far forth as those Acts or Treaties shall relate to the said States or their Citizens, and that the Judiciary of the several States shall be bound thereby in their decisions, any thing in the respective laws of the Individual States to the contrary notwithstanding. . . ." But the plan included another answer—the use of force; *coercion,* appearing at first in the Virginia plan, but abandoned after brief discussion in the committee of the whole, was embodied in the New Jersey plan: "if any State, or any body of men in any State shall oppose or prevent the carrying into execution such acts or treaties, the federal Executive shall be authorized to call forth the power of the Confederated States, or so much thereof as may be necessary to enforce and compel an obedience to such Acts, or an Observance of such Treaties." Even the small-state party saw that the union could not survive, if reliance were based entirely on the whims or the temperamental inclinations of the several states. Both the national plan, when first presented, and the state sovereignty plan contemplated the use of force to maintain the union

One may inquire whether even the plan of the small states, purporting only to amend the Articles, really conserved the principle of the Articles and left the Confederation a union of sovereignties. But the mere grant of powers to Congress and even the authority to collect requisitions would not necessarily imply the transformation of the Confederation into something more, something in essence quite different. Furthermore, though the proposal of the particularists authorizing coercion of states is important, it does not imply legal nationalism; the use of armed force against a state as a corporate body was *thoroughly consistent with the principle of state sovereignty.*

The debates of the next three days (June 16, 18, 19) were crucial and critical. Would the committee of the whole adhere to nationalism or be content with modification of the Confederation? The issue was by no means entirely new. At an earlier session, Paterson had declared the Convention's powers were limited to amendment of the Articles. Referring to the wishes of the people, the commissions under which the delegates acted, and the sentiments of the states, he said: "The idea of a national Government as contradistinguished from a federal one, never entered into the mind of any of them. . . . We have no power to go beyond the federal scheme, and if we had the people are not ripe for any other. . . . A confederacy supposes sovereignty in the members composing it and sovereignty supposes equality." To this Wilson had replied, "If New Jersey will not part with her Sovereignty it is in vain to talk of Government." [26] That was the issue in these three eventful days of debate.

The advocates of state sovereignty made an able defense. The Paterson plan, said Lansing, "sustains the sovereignty of the respective States, that of Mr. Randolph distroys it. . . ." And Paterson declared, "If the sovereignty of the States is to be maintained, the Representatives must be drawn immediately from the States, not from the people : and we have no power to vary the idea of equal sovereignty. The only expedient that will cure the difficulty, is that of throwing the States into Hotchpot"—equalizing the states or making one geographic and political whole as the basis of political nationalism. Meeting the assertions of the small-state group, Randolph declared in a powerful and appealing speech, "The true question is whether we shall adhere to the federal plan, or introduce the national plan. . . . We must resort therefore to a national *Legislation over individuals,* for which Congress are unfit. . . . A National Government alone, properly con-

[26] Madison's *Notes,* June 9.

stituted, will answer the purpose; and he begged it to be considered that the present is the last moment for establishing one. After this select experiment, the people will yield to despair." Madison and Wilson subjected the Paterson proposals to searching analysis and criticism, pointing to their radical defects.

The issue was clearly stated. On the question whether the Randolph plan "should be adhered to as preferable" to that of Paterson, seven states voted in the affirmative—Massachusetts, Connecticut, Pennsylvania, Virginia, North Carolina, South Carolina, Georgia. New York, New Jersey, and Delaware voted in the negative; Maryland was again divided. So by a conclusive majority, but in the face of strong opposition, once again the committee of the whole decided in favor of a national system. The vote of the Connecticut delegates shows once more the readiness to favor an effective government, and more than that, a system avowedly national. If they had participated in drafting the state sovereignty plan, they cast aside their own handiwork; as we shall see, however, they were still determined not to allow the states to be overwhelmed. The report of the committee of the whole was now before the Convention, and in the following sessions all its parts and all its principles were vigorously debated.

The day after the critical vote was taken and the nationalists had won a victory, which, as far as principle was concerned, appeared decisive, Ellsworth (June 20), seconded by Gorham of Massachusetts, moved that the first resolution of the plan, which was then before the Convention, be changed so as to read: " 'the Government of the United States ought to consist of a supreme legislative, Executive and Judiciary'." This change, he explained, "would drop the word *national*, and retain the proper title 'the United States.' . . . He wished also the plan of the Convention to go forth as an amendment to the articles of Confederation, since under this idea the authority of the Legislatures could ratify it. If they are unwilling, the people will be so too. . . . He did not like these [state] conventions. . . . They were better fitted to pull down than to build up Constitutions." To this proposal Randolph replied that he "did not object to the change of expression, but apprised the gentleman who wished for it that he did not admit it for the reasons assigned; particularly that of getting rid of a reference to the people for ratification." The Ellsworth resolution was thereupon unanimously adopted.[27]

[27] "One reason why the Connecticut delegates disliked ratification by Conventions was that, in that State, a Convention had assembled at Middletown in December,

This dropping of the word *"national"* was in after years cited as positive proof of the Convention's change of heart—proof that the members had decided to abandon the aim of the nationalists and to form a constitution on the basis of state sovereignty. Such an assertion could not, with any show of reason, have been made except on the basis of the published journal (1819) and Yates's minutes, which gave only in the meagerest possible terms the fact of the formal omission of the word so objectionable later to the ardent apostles of state sovereignty. But even these sources of information, when the time and the circumstances are considered, should have led one to doubt the sudden alteration of the Convention's purpose. The national plan had just been accepted by seven states of the eleven present, the vote of one state being divided. To suppose immediate retraction and sudden yielding to the particularistic group is to suppose the impossible; and Madison's *Notes,* already quoted, prove that there was no such retraction or surrender. Furthermore, the plan of ratification by the people was later adopted, and as a matter of fact, though this is not important, the word "national" was used in debate, but not of course in formal resolutions.

The rejection of the Paterson plan did not entirely discourage the small-state party. At intervals during the next fortnight the vexed subject of proportional representation arose, a subject, it will be remembered, which involved theoretically the surrender, or the diminution, of state sovereignty, but also touched the *amour propre* of the smaller states. Some members, who were not localists by prejudice and principle, feared lest the states be totally submerged.

The question of representation became connected with the resolution, already passed by the committee of the whole and in accordance with the Virginia plan, to establish a legislature of two branches. Declaring that "the true question here was, whether the Convention would adhere to or depart from the foundation of the present Confederacy", Lansing proposed (June 20) that the powers of legislation be vested in the United States in Congress—that is to say, in a single body similar to the Congress of the Confederation. To this Mason

---

1783, which had violently opposed the votes of Congress as to commutation of pay for officers of the Continental army—and other subjects, and the action of this Convention had caused considerable disturbance in other States." Warren, *op. cit.,* p. 348, note 1. Of course, the impressive fact is not the hesitation among some members to refer their work to the people, but the readiness to rely upon popular decision, and the necessity, for legal and constitutional reasons, to obtain basic authority for the Constitution.

objected, saying that the mind of the people was well-settled in an attachment to republican government and to more than one branch in the legislature. Sherman, however, though supporting Lansing, expressed a willingness to compromise: "If the difficulty on the subject of representation can not be otherwise got over, he would agree to have two branches, and a proportional representation in one of them, provided each State had an equal voice in the other." This proposal was not, as we have seen, original with Sherman, nor was it confined to the Connecticut delegation, though that delegation seems to have been specially interested in it.

Obviously, some of the men fearing the larger states and quite unwilling to see the smaller states totally robbed of equal power in the national councils might be content with something less than complete victory. Lansing's proposal as given above—that legislative power be vested in the United States in Congress—was defeated by the customary majority—the six large states voting against it. Connecticut, New York, New Jersey, and Delaware voted in its favor; Maryland was divided. This vote registered the decision of at least six states not to be content with a unicameral legislature; and on the true question underlying it all—whether the Convention would or would not depart from the fundamental principle of the Confederation—the particularists had once more suffered defeat. But the question still remained whether the Convention, by direct affirmative vote, would decide upon two legislative branches in the proposed national system. The very next day (June 21) the affirmative resolution to establish a legislature of two branches was passed by a vote of seven to three (Maryland again divided). This time Connecticut voted with the large states.

Though much remained to be done and anxious days were ahead, the Convention had now reached a position—as yet perhaps not fully seen by its members—which deserves careful examination. The problem of representation was not fully disposed of. The large-state or national party had been moving victoriously forward. Were its plans to be carried through to the end? And, if carried through, just what did that success imply? The Convention was now approaching the center of the complicated problem of imperial organization. As we have already pointed out several times, the task of forming a national government and of bestowing upon it powers sufficient to guarantee effective life to the system was naturally troublesome and perplexing;

but the critical matter was to provide not only for an effective government but also for the preservation of the states as political bodies which would be more than administrative districts.

The problem of establishing a federal republic, as distinguished from one purely national, could not be solved by destroying the states. So thoroughly had the Convention determined upon a national system that before the end of June the question was not whether the states should be united in an integral union but whether they should be placed at the mercy of a central government. At least one member of the Convention saw the real nature of the problem and was able to state it clearly. Probably others were equally aware of the difficulty and recognized its critical character, but Johnson of Connecticut stated it exactly: "On a comparison of the two plans which had been proposed from Virginia and New Jersey, it appeared that the peculiarity which characterized the latter was its being calculated to preserve the individuality of the States. The plan from Virginia did not profess to destroy this individuality altogether, but was charged with such a tendency. One Gentleman alone (Colonel Hamilton) in his animadversions on the plan of New Jersey, boldly and decisively contended for an abolition of the State Governments. Mr. Wilson and the gentleman from Virginia who also were adversaries of the plan of New Jersey held a different language. They wished to leave the States in possession of a considerable, though a subordinate jurisdiction. They had not yet however shewn how this could consist with, or be secured against the general sovereignty and jurisdiction, which they proposed to give to the national Government. If this could be shewn in such a manner as to satisfy the patrons of the New Jersey propositions, that the individuality of the States would not be endangered, many of their objections would no doubt be removed. If this could not be shewn their objections would have their full force. He wished it therefore to be well considered whether in case the States, as was proposed, should retain some portion of sovereignty at least, this portion could be preserved, without allowing them to participate effectually in the General Government, without giving them each a distinct and equal vote for the purpose of defending themselves in the general Councils." [28]

[28] Madison's *Notes,* June 21. See in addition Johnson's brief statement, June 25, and especially his words on June 29, when, with other pronouncements of a similar character, he said: "Does it not seem to follow, that if the States as such are to exist they must be armed with some power of self-defence. . . . On the whole he thought that as in some respects the States are to be considered in their political capacity, and in others as districts of individual citizens, the two ideas embraced on

Whatever we may think of Johnson's suggestion of state participation in the general government, he comprehended clearly the problem of preserving the states as political entities.

Wilson and Madison tried to answer Johnson's question. Neither believed the states were in danger. "The General Government", said Wilson, "will be as ready to preserve the rights of the States as the latter are to preserve the rights of individuals. . . ." Madison concluded that "Guards were more necessary against encroachments of the State Governments—on the General Government than of the latter on the former. . . . Were it practicable for the General Government to extend its care to every requisite object without the cooperation of the State Governments the people would not be less free as members of one great Republic than as members of thirteen small ones." Evidently Madison was still impressed with the danger of dissolution, the product of state heedlessness and willful pride.

The Convention had been in session for a month and the crucial question of representation was not yet disposed of. It was brought up for settlement June 27, on a resolution for proportional representation in the first branch of the national legislature. In opposition, we need to remember, were the proponents of state sovereignty, those not especially addicted to a principle but because of state pride unwilling to surrender equality, and others like Johnson fearing lest the states be totally submerged. So critical did the situation seem to be that after the debate had continued some time, Franklin, asserting his belief *"that God governs in the affairs of men"*, proposed that the Convention henceforth open its sessions with prayers "imploring the assistance of Heaven. . . ." But the members feared "disagreeable animadversions"; the public might believe the calling in of divine guidance due to embarrassments and dissensions. Within the Convention Williamson remarked, however, that "the true cause of the omission could not be mistaken. The Convention had no funds." Could no minister be unearthed in Philadelphia who would pray for his country without price?

Opening the discussion on this salient matter of representation in Congress, Martin, in a speech which lasted three hours on one day and was continued on the day following (June 27, 28), presented "at great length and with great eagerness" the cause of state sovereignty. ". . . an equal vote in each State was", he said, "essential to the fed-

different sides, instead of being opposed to each other, ought to be combined; that in *one* branch the *people*, ought to be represented; in the *other*, the *States*."

eral idea, and was founded in justice and freedom, not merely in policy . . . that the States being equal cannot treat or confederate so as to give up an equality of votes without giving up their liberty. . . ." Hamilton, who was about to leave the Convention (June 29) and not participate in its debates for a considerable time,[29] pleaded for effective union, and pointed out the distinction between the "carrying and non-carrying States", which would hold the largest states apart one from the other rather than give harmony and group activity.[30] Madison made two exceptionally able speeches; and he spoke, as did Hamilton, of the improbability of combination between such states as Virginia, Massachusetts, and Pennsylvania, which, different in manners and religion and in point of the staple productions, "were as dissimilar as any three other States in the Union." These two men were thus presenting the true situation; there was and could be no real antithesis between the small states and their powerful neighbors; the real danger, if danger should ever come, would be caused by differences of economic interests or diversities of manners and attitudes of mind, and not by the wealth or power of the respective states.

On the third day of debate (June 29) it was voted that in the first branch of the legislature the rule of suffrage should not be according to that of the Articles of Confederation. The six large states of course voted in the affirmative; the others—Connecticut, New York, New Jersey, Delaware—in the negative; Maryland was again divided. At the opening of that day's session, Johnson had strongly expressed again the opinion to which we have already given special attention; something must be done to save the states from annihilation. And now that proportional representation in the lower house had been decided upon, his colleague, Ellsworth, rose to advocate equal representation in the second chamber. He was not sorry on the whole, he said, that the vote just passed had registered the Convention's decision against that rule of suffrage in the first branch. He hoped it would become the basis of a compromise: "We were partly national; partly federal. The proportional representation in the first branch was conformable to

---

[29] "Attended on May 18; left Convention June 29; was in New York after July 2; appears to have been in Philadelphia on July 13; attended Convention August 13; was in New York August 20–September 2." Farrand, *Records,* III, p. 588.

[30] It is very interesting to notice that Read of Delaware, who had pointed out that the instructions of the Delaware delegates precluded their accepting anything but equal representation, advocated nationalism and even expressed approval of Hamilton's plan of centralization. See Madison's *Notes,* June 6, June 11, June 29. He "wished it to be considered by the small States that it was their interest that we should become one people as much as possible. . . ." *Ibid.,* June 26.

the national principle and would secure the large States against the small. An equality of voices was conformable to the federal principle and was necessary to secure the Small States against the large."

In the Convention we must notice—if repetition may be pardoned —that Johnson was, to all appearances, not greatly interested in the controversy between large states and small, but in the danger that nationalism would entirely submerge the states. Ellsworth, it is true, if we can judge from his argument at this juncture, feared large-state domination; and still, how, in the absence of modern terms of description, could the men then forming a new kind of body politic, which we now call a "federal state" and which the men of the day soon came to call a "confederated republic", have better expressed the nature of that political system than in Ellsworth's words—a system "partly national; partly federal"? [31] Toward the end of a long day (June 30), filled with acute argument and with a fervor verging upon acrimony, Ellsworth declared: "Under a National Government he should participate in the National Security, as remarked by Mr. King but that was all. What he wanted was domestic happiness. The National Government could not descend to the local objects on which this depended. It could only embrace objects of a general nature. He turned his eyes therefore for the preservation of his rights to the State Governments." King's answer to Ellsworth is noteworthy: "In the establishment of Societies the Constitution was to the Legislature what the laws were to individuals. As the fundamental rights of individuals are secured by express provisions in the State Constitutions; why may not a like security be provided for the Rights of States in the National Constitution."

These quotations are given here to demonstrate, as far as a few words can, that in the minds of some of the men—how many we do not know—the aim was *not* to prevent nationalism, but to assure the existence of the states; in other words, to solve the problem of imperial federalism and not allow nationalism to become consolidation. It is interesting to see Ellsworth, who some ten days previously had

[31] Compare Madison in *The Federalist,* no. XXXIX. Bancroft speaks of this arrangement—proportional representation in one branch, equal representation in the other—as the "Connecticut compromise". The propriety of the appellation has been questioned, but much is to be said for it. It is true the idea was not confined in its inception or in the course of discussion to the Connecticut men. But that they saw the situation, were not afraid of effective government provided it did not crush the states, and were largely influential in bringing about the conclusion they desired, seems unquestionable.

moved to change the opening resolution of the committee of the whole's report, so as to omit the word *"national"*, now speaking of a "National Government" and assuming the establishment of such a government. But the idea, possibly the hope, of maintaining state sovereignty, as such, was not entirely dead; Martin, of course, was adamant. Bedford of Delaware "contended that there was no middle way between a perfect consolidation and a mere confederacy of the States." The large states, he declared, dared not dissolve the confederacy, and if they should, the small states would find some foreign ally to take them by the hand.

In the debate on Ellsworth's motion for equal representation in the second branch, Wilson and Madison gave elaborate expositions of their doctrine of nationalism and defended the organization of a government which they believed to be consonant with nationalism. Though not advocating destruction of the states, they were determined to prevent equality of representation in the second legislative chamber as well as in the first; they believed the danger to the small states to be imaginary only; and they thought an equality, which disregarded facts, was unwise. "If the minority of the people of America", said Wilson, "refuse to coalesce with the majority on just and proper principles, if a separation must take place, it could never happen on better grounds. . . . We talk of States, till we forget what they are composed of." Madison now declared the division of interests did not in fact lie between the large and the small states but between northern and southern. King, ably and eloquently speaking in behalf of the cause of nationalism, declared he was filled with astonishment at the sight of men, who, if they were convinced that every individual was secured in his rights, "should be ready to sacrifice this substantial good to the phantom of *State* sovereignty".

The vote on the resolution for equality of suffrage in the second branch came at the opening of the session on July second. The result was a tie—five votes to five.[32] Georgia, which had steadily voted with the large-state party, was now divided—Baldwin voting for equal representation, and Houstoun against it. Baldwin was a Connecticut man who had not long before removed to Georgia, and we may well suppose he was influenced by the old, seasoned politicians of the northern

[32] Massachusetts, Pennsylvania, Virginia, North Carolina, and South Carolina voted against equal representation. Connecticut, New York, New Jersey, Delaware, and Maryland voted for equal representation.

state to support their cause and perhaps save the Convention from dissolution and failure. The vote of Maryland, which had been so often tied, was cast by Martin alone because of the tardiness of his colleague Jenifer in coming to the meeting. If Baldwin had continued to vote as he had previously voted, and if Jenifer had been prompt in attendance on that eventful morning, the large-state party would have been successful once more. On this narrow margin did the fateful decision—or evidence of inability to reach decision—depend.[33]

The Convention was now, as Sherman said, "at a full stop. . . ." Evidently the small-state men were beyond persuasion; and if they were defeated, the Convention would be a failure. Concession was inevitable. General Pinckney proposed the appointment of a committee to report a compromise. Madison and Wilson were opposed to the commitment. But Martin warned the Convention that no modifications whatever could "reconcile the Smaller States to the least diminution of their equal Sovereignty." A committee of one from each state was agreed upon. That the result would be a report recommending compromise was foreseen; and the committee was so constituted as to make at least partial victory for the small-state men a foregone conclusion; not one of the steadiest objectors to equality in the Senate was named a member. The Convention adjourned to allow time for the committee's work.

Those were anxious days, though in fact the crisis was actually passed; no committee report could shatter the fundamentals of the national system already agreed upon. The committee's report—constituting the great compromise on the subject which had vexed the Convention for weeks—provided that in the first branch of the legislature each state should be allowed one member for every 40,000 inhabitants; in the second branch, each state should have an equal vote; all bills for raising or appropriating money and for fixing salaries must originate in the first branch and not be altered or amended by the second.

The more strenuous members of the large-state party protested;

[33] Martin, reporting to the Maryland legislature, said, "Immediately after the question had been taken, and the President had declared the votes, Mr. Jenifer came into the convention, when Mr. King, from Massachusetts, valuing himself on Mr. Jenifer to divide the State of Maryland on this question, as he had on the former, requested of the President that the question might be put again; however, the motion was too extraordinary in its nature to meet with success." See Farrand, *Records,* III, p. 188 note.

they were not content. Madison did not regard the power of the lower house to originate money bills as any concession, and he "was not apprehensive that the people of the small States would obstinately refuse to accede to a Government founded on just principles. . . ." Morris made a peculiarly vigorous appeal to the sense of the assembly. He came there, he said, as a representative of America, "in some degree as a Representative of the whole human race; for the whole human race will be affected by the proceedings of this Convention." If the small states should refuse to consent to a system essentially sound, they might, he declared, make "a noise for a time," but eventually they would find ties of interest, kindred, and common habits too strong to be broken. "This Country", he exclaimed, "must be united. If persuasion does not unite it, the sword will." He appears to have had clearly in mind a thought which we have seen Madison expressing before, that groups of like economic and social interests would come to the fore, and that the antithesis between the large and small states was unreal; at all events, the future proved (and is proving to-day) the essential truth of that position.

For more than a week the debate went on; the report of the committee was taken up piecemeal; it was discussed and rediscussed; changes and additions were made, but the essentials of the committee's recommendations, including the crucial clause which gave equal representation in the Senate, stood unaltered. The question of agreeing to the whole report as amended was carried by a vote of five to four (July 16). Pennsylvania, Virginia, South Carolina, and Georgia voted in the negative; Massachusetts was divided. Once again by the narrowest of margins a momentous decision was reached; but the importance of the decision consists not so much in the content of the resolution as in the fact that a decision was reached at all and that the break-up of the Convention was avoided.

The truth is, the nationalists had lost little or nothing, though some of them were for the moment discouraged. Equal representation of the States in the Senate neither injured the large states as such nor destroyed the principle of nationalism; in the long run it probably had no appreciable effect in preserving the states from being compounded into a consolidated republic; it did not protect the smaller states against their larger neighbors. The Senate has at no time stood as a guardian of the weaker members of the union. Nationalism, though endangered by sectionalism, brought into play the loyalties and the coöperation of groups irrespective of the size or material wealth of the particular states. Such nationalism as we now know—a nationalism of patriotism and loyalty—had to grow by degrees; and the development of the central government, produced by the industrial and social changes of the passing decades, was not hindered by the Senate of the United States.

Only one week after the settlement of the great dispute by the acceptance of compromise, a motion was made that the members of the second branch, the Senate, should vote per capita (July 23). Ellsworth said he always had been in favor of such a provision. But it was a momentous change. Martin pointed out that it meant a departure from "the idea of the *States* being represented. . . ." Possibly the small-state men—such of them as remained—supposed the senators from any one state would act together on any matter directly affecting the interests of their state; but the resolution was at variance with the idea that the senators came as ambassadors to express the will of their master; and in fact, Gerry, a few days earlier, had suggested per capita voting because it would prevent delays and inconveniences which had been experienced in the old Congress, "and would give a national aspect and Spirit to the management of business."

By the adoption of the great compromise neither party in the Convention was entirely satisfied. Lansing and Yates had left before the crucial vote was taken, reporting to Governor Clinton that the Convention was proceeding along lines beyond the powers of the delegates and that it was impracticable to establish a general government pervading every part of the United States, certain in a short time to "be productive of the destruction of the civil liberty of such citizens who could be effectually coerced by it".[34] Luther Martin remained, though he left before the end to make an attack upon the Convention's work. But others went on with the job. "From the day when every doubt of the right of the smaller states to an equal vote in the senate was quieted, they—so I received it from the lips of Madison, and so

[34] Farrand, *Records*, III, pp. 244-247. Warren justly calls our attention to various contents of the Constitution as it was at the time of the compromise, and says: ". . . the small States were entirely right in believing that no such form of Government as the Nationalists, at that stage in the Convention, were supporting would ever be accepted by the people of the States. . . ." Warren, *op. cit.*, p. 310. But we should notice that he is speaking of the fact that, as it then stood, the Constitution gave large and undefined power to the national legislature, including the right to veto state laws. He does not declare that the principle of nationalism, under properly-guarded assignment of governmental authority, would have defeated the Constitution.

it appears from the records—exceeded all others in zeal for granting powers to the general government. Ellsworth became one of its strongest pillars." [35]

It is expedient to mention here a discussion concerning treason which arose a month after the great compromise. There was no doubt about the possibility of treason against the United States, but could there be treason against a state? A clause of the resolution of the committee of detail declared treason to consist "only in levying war against the United States, or any of them; and in adhering to the enemies of the United States, or any of them." Differences of opinion developed, and the nature of the discussion cannot be ascertained with assurance from Madison's treatment. Johnson, who two months before had stated so clearly the necessity of preserving the states, now declared there could be no treason against a particular state. Mason said the United States would have a qualified sovereignty only; the individual states would retain a part. "An Act may be treason against a particular State which is not so against the United States." But Johnson answered, "That case would amount to Treason against the Sovereign, the supreme Sovereign, the United States". The trouble plainly arose in part from the difficulty of determining the nature and extent of the sovereignty which the states retained, if they retained any at all. Ellsworth maintained the existence of divided sovereignty, the United States being sovereign on one side of the line dividing the jurisdictions, the states on the other: "each", he said, "ought to have power to defend their respective Sovereignties." But in the end the decision was to leave out reference to the states and define treason against the United States. Whether or not this conclusion implies and was meant to imply that there can be treason against a state is uncertain; beyond all doubt, however, it recognizes the sovereign character of the union, perhaps on the theory of a sovereignty divided between states and nation. [36]

---

[35] George Bancroft, *History of the Formation of the Constitution of the United States*, II, p. 88.

[36] It is interesting and important to notice, in light of the supremely important controversy concerning the nature of the union in the decades ahead and the ending in civil war, that Luther Martin advocated a clause declaring that no act done by one or more states against the United States or by any citizen of any one of the United States under the authority of any one or more states should be deemed treason or punished as such; " 'but, in case of war being levied by one or more of the States against the United States, the conduct of each party towards the other, and their adherents respectively, shall be regulated by the *laws of war* and of *nations.*' " Martin reported to his legislature that this proposal was "opposed to the great

Thus far we have followed the main line of the Convention's work and have attempted to make clear the struggle over the nature of the union. The contest had centered on the question of representation, because, if the union was to be a national union, people, citizens, should be the basis of representation, not states as corporate bodies. The advocates of state equality and equal representation of the states had met with successive defeats; but those who were anxious to pre- serve the states, though not averse to a national system, attained their goal, as they believed, by providing equal representation in the Senate.

It had been at least partly taken for granted that the establishment of a national government logically and properly implied the operation of that government directly on individuals. King and Madison had announced (July 14) the principle with especial plainness. There never will be a case, said King, in which the general and national govern- ment "will act as a federal Government on the States and not on the individual Citizens." Madison "called for a single instance in which the General Government was not to operate on the people individ-- ually." [37] Wilson, moreover, had brought forth with great clearness that there should be little or no contact between the central government and the states: "The same train of ideas which belonged to the rela- tion of the Citizens to their State Governments were applicable to their relations to the General Government and in forming the latter, we ought to proceed, by abstracting as much as possible from the idea of State Governments. With respect to the province and objects of the General Government they should be considered as having no exist- ence." [38]

Quite obviously, if there were to be spheres of authority, there was need of marking out the political domain of each with considerable distinctness. And here, let us notice, is not only *a central principle of the American federal state, but the real answer to the anxieties which had burdened the hearts of the small-state men who feared de- struction of the states;* the answer to their anxieties did not in reality rest on equal representation in the Senate, but on granting to the na--

object of many of the leading members of the convention, which was, by all means to *leave the States* at the *mercy* of the *general government*, since they could not succeed in their *immediate* and *entire* abolition." See Farrand, *Records*, III, p. 223.

[37] See also Madison's statement (June 19) where he pointed out that "in a *federal* Government [as distinguished from a national government], the power was exercised not on the people individually; but on the people *collectively*, on the *States.*"

[38] June 25. Farrand, *Records*, I, p. 406. Very early in the debates (May 30) Sherman had "admitted also that the General and particular jurisdictions ought in no case to be concurrent." See *Ibid.*, I, pp. 34-35.

tional government clearly-stated and clearly-recognizable powers. Only on such a principle, could freedom from friction between governments be avoided; and only in this way could the states have reasonable assurance of their continuance as efficient and effective members of an integral union.

Now, it is an interesting fact that this question of exact distribution of powers between the states on the one hand and the central government on the other did not receive much consideration during the first two months. When the Convention turned over to the committee of detail a series of resolutions to be fashioned into a constitution, the statement of distribution was still general and indefinite.[39] Why this delay in making explicit assignment of powers? The delegates were particularly interested in the establishment of a permanent union, and not until that troublesome question was answered were they ready for details. But most important of all was the fact that the assignment of powers did not present an intricate and novel difficulty; the men of those days, though engaged in a task requiring great wisdom and discretion, were not dependent on mere theory concerning this essential matter. Behind them lay the practices of the old empire, the experiences of the Revolution, and the provisions of the Articles of Confederation. Historical facts pointed the way.[40]

The assignment of explicitly enumerated powers was first worked out not in open Convention but by the committee of detail.[41] In its report the powers of Congress were named in eighteen brief paragraphs. The new government was to have prescribed powers. Such was the inevitable presumption, but it was made clear beyond all presuming when, after the ratification of the Constitution, the tenth amend-

[39] "Resolved That the Legislature of the United States ought to possess the legislative Rights vested in Congress by the Confederation; and moreover to legislate in all Cases for the general Interests of the Union, and also in those Cases to which the States are separately incompetent, or in which the Harmony of the United States may be interrupted by the Exercise of individual Legislation." *Ibid.*, II, pp. 131-132.

[40] Reference has been made in an earlier chapter to the structure of the old empire which in its actual practices foreshadowed the structure of the federal organization of the American union.

[41] This committee was composed of Rutledge of South Carolina, Randolph of Virginia, Gorham of Massachusetts, Ellsworth of Connecticut, and Wilson of Pennsylvania. Working on the task of framing the submitted resolutions into a constitution, they arranged the materials into articles and sections, and presented the results of careful organization. To the committee had been referred not only the resolutions adopted by the Convention but the Pinckney and Paterson plans. At the end of ten days they made their report, and this—which was in the form of a constitution—was then discussed item by item for about six weeks by the Convention.

ment was adopted. The powers thus granted were stated in broad and rather generous terms, without niggardly precision. The vitality of a federal republic—its continuance as a working system—depends on the accuracy with which powers are distributed; those that can be most effectively administered by the central government, without undue encroachment on local affairs, should be deposited with that government; those powers adapted to local needs and properly subject to local authority should be left to the individual commonwealth. Changes in the social and industrial order, such changes as came in the last half of the nineteenth century and after, may make advisable a reassortment of powers; but the principle of distribution based on the capacity for serving the needs of society must remain, if the federal state is to continue, preserve its essential character, and not be lost in centralized nationalism.

We have seen how, despite fears and jealousies, a national government with extensive powers was decided upon. This was an essential part of the solution of the problem of which the reader has often been reminded—the problem of establishing a system in which the states would abide by their obligations and not destroy the union. But, so far, we have not seen what became of two provisions which were put forth at an early stage as solutions of this problem—the proposals to give the national legislature authority to coerce a recalcitrant state and the authority to negative state laws. Coercion fell by the wayside in the early days of the Convention as the plan of forming a national government operating directly on individuals took shape; as the implications of the plan became apparent, coercion was abandoned.[42] Not only did war upon a state, because of the misdeeds of its government, inflict suffering on individual citizens, but it was really a method —a method inherited from barbarism—of settling disputes between nations in the absence of enforceable law.[43] The Constitution in its

[42] In comment on the Paterson plan, Mason said (June 20): "The most jarring elements of nature; fire and water themselves are not more incompatible that [sic] such a mixture of civil liberty and military execution. Will the militia march from one State to another, in order to collect the arrears of taxes from the delinquent members of the Republic? . . . Rebellion is the only case in which the military force of the State can be properly exerted against its Citizens." Farrand, *Records,* I, pp. 339-340.

[43] Soon after the Convention adjourned Madison wrote to Jefferson: "It was generally agreed that the objects of the Union could not be secured by any system founded on the principle of a confederation of Sovereign States. A *voluntary* observance of the federal law by all the members could never be hoped for. A *compulsive* one could evidently never be reduced to practice, and if it could, involved equal calamities to the innocent & the guilty, the necessity of a military force both obnoxious

final form gave Congress the power to call forth the militia to execute the laws of the union, suppress insurrections, and repel invasions, but coercion of delinquent states in their corporate capacity was abandoned because coercion of individual citizens, disobedient to the law, was consistent with real nationalism and consistent too with the prospect of a permanent, smoothly-working union.

The proposal to give the national legislature authority to veto state laws, which, like coercion, was thought to be a proper method for preserving the union and solving "the chief problem", was for a considerable time ably defended by some of the eager nationalists. It was accepted without dissent or debate (May 31).[44] But objections arose, and six weeks later (July 17) the matter came up for final decision. Madison still believed the negative as essential "to the efficacy and security of the General Government"; the necessity of such a government proceeded, he said, from the propensity of the states to pursue their particular interests. Gouverneur Morris, on the other hand, said such a power would be "terrible to the States, and not necessary, if sufficient Legislative authority should be given to the General Government." Then Sherman made a most significant statement: the negative, in his opinion, was unnecessary, "as the Courts of the States would not consider as valid any law contravening the Authority of the Union, and which the [national] legislature would wish to be negatived." A law that ought to be negatived, Morris now declared, would be set aside by the judiciary department, and if that security should fail, the law might be repealed by a national law. The

& dangerous, and in general a scene resembling much more a civil war than the administration of a regular Government. Hence was embraced the alternative of a Government which instead of operating, on the States, should operate without their intervention on the individuals composing them; and hence the change in the principle and proportion of representation." October 24, 1787. Madison, *Writings* (Gaillard Hunt, ed.), V, p. 19. Ellsworth, addressing the Connecticut convention, said: "Hence we see how necessary for the Union is a coercive principle. No man pretends the contrary: we all see and feel this necessity. The only question is, Shall it be a coercion of law, or a coercion of arms? [Hamilton had used the same expression in the Convention at Philadelphia, June 18] . . . I am for coercion by law—that coercion which acts only upon delinquent individuals." Elliot, *Debates*, II, p. 197.

[44] "The other clauses giving powers necessary to preserve harmony among the States to negative all State laws contravening in the opinion of the National Legislature the articles of Union down to the last clause, the words 'or any treaties subsisting under the authority of the Union', being added after the words 'contravening &c. the articles of the Union'; on motion of Doctor Franklin, were agreed to without debate or dissent." Farrand, *Records*, I, p. 54. The wording of this leaves it uncertain whether the provision concerning treaties was in the original Randolph plan or not. Probably it was not.

principle was, however, firmly grasped and most clearly stated by Sherman, who asserted that the power proposed to be given to Congress involved "a wrong principle, to wit, that a law of a State contrary to the articles of the Union, would if not negatived, be valid and operative." In other words, a state act contrary to the Constitution could not be law; it had no validity.

Immediately after the vote on the power of negativing was taken, Martin rose and presented a resolution which had first appeared in the small-state party plan and was probably his own handiwork.[45] Reference to it has already been made. It deserves repetition here: "that the Legislative acts of the United States made by virtue and in pursuance of the articles of Union, and all treaties made and ratified under the authority of the United States shall be the supreme law of the respective States, as far as those acts or treaties shall relate to the said States, or their Citizens and inhabitants—and that the Judiciaries of the several States shall be bound thereby in their decisions, any thing in the respective laws of the individual States to the contrary notwithstanding". The resolution was adopted without dissent (July 17).

A month and more after the adoption of this resolution, it was amended (August 23), and the amendment is of signal interest; it added at the beginning the words "This Constitution". Thus, not only laws and treaties of the United States, but the Constitution itself was declared to be the supreme law of the respective states and of their citizens and inhabitants. The wording of this provision, as it appeared in the final draft of the Constitution, differs slightly from that just given: "This Constitution, and the laws of the United States which shall be made in pursuance thereof, and all treaties made, or which shall be made, under the authority of the United States, shall be the

---

[45] Of course such a resolution was quite out of place in the Paterson plan with its principle of maintaining the Confederation. Its presence there is an evidence of the hurried preparation of the plan, and impressive evidence also of how fully it was recognized that the states must be held to their obligations. But how could the idea of state sovereignty be reconciled with an arrangement which authorized the central government to make "supreme law of the respective States"? Possibly the super-astute mind can conceive such a reconciliation. But the resolution, at all events, would make of the Confederation, if it remained a Confederation, a strange and rather anomalous one. Calhoun, in his most competent days, could, probably, show the consistency between state sovereignty and law binding on state judges; the even stronger provisions of the Constitution did not prove insuperable for him. Why Martin should have favored the resolution as a special child of his own, we do not know. He was a very able lawyer. Looking about for a principle which would counteract the weakness of a union of sovereignties, perhaps he instinctively turned to courts.

supreme law of the land; and the judges in every State shall be bound thereby, anything in the Constitution or laws of any State to the contrary notwithstanding." The people of a state, acting even in their primary capacity when forming their own constitution, cannot legally violate the Constitution, laws, or treaties of the United States. This declaration, therefore, taken on its face, does not leave a shred of state sovereignty as a legal theory of the union—if, of course, we mean by state sovereignty the undiminished authority of a fully-competent body politic.

It is difficult to overemphasize the importance of this declaration in the Constitution. The significant word is not "supreme", but "law". If the Constitution is law, nothing contrary to it can also be law. There can be no such thing as illegal law. Furthermore, to make the declaration explicit beyond all chance of misunderstanding, the judges in their court-rooms are bound to recognize and apply the Constitution. Courts—acting as all courts are expected to act in distributing justice to litigants—must treat the Constitution as law. The very structure of the union, the very essentials of the federal system were thus intrusted to courts. No special tribunal was set up, no body of censors, no board of review; judges in the quiet of their own court-rooms must maintain the authority of government and the binding effect of the Constitution on which the federal system rests.

The resolution, when it was first presented, imposed responsibility upon the state courts, and the article as finally adopted especially mentions state judges. But we can hardly suppose the framers' intention not to include the federal courts. Logically at least, they also must treat the Constitution as law, and this logic is supplemented by the words of the third article giving to the federal courts jurisdiction of cases arising under the Constitution, laws of the United States, and treaties. This brings up the question whether or not the courts of the United States and the courts of the state were assumed to have the right to declare an act of Congress void. That the courts must interpret the Constitution and determine its particular applications before they can decide certain kinds of controversies, seems an inevitable conclusion; and in doing so they may be called upon to uphold the Constitution and ignore an act. This subject will be considered somewhat more fully in later pages of this work; it is sufficient to point here to the cardinal fact that the Constitution is *plainly declared to be law, enforceable in courts,* to be handled as other law is handled, to be treated with the respect with which other laws are treated, to be enforced as other laws are enforced; for the duty of any court is to announce and apply law. That the Constitution was to be binding and legally infrangible is a matter of immense importance; but here we are considering the right to judge whether an act violates it; and in this connection the significant fact is that courts and judges are mentioned at all and that the courts are called upon to treat the Constitution as *law*.

We must add that the principle of judicial authority to declare a legislative act void was mentioned in the Convention at various times. Martin, for example,—perhaps the ablest technical lawyer of them all —objecting to the association of the judges with the executive as a council of revision, declared, "And as to the Constitutionality of laws, that point will come before the Judges in their proper official character. In this character they have a negative on the laws." Some of the delegates were, it is true, not prepared to accept this principle; and in fact, though the duty of state judges to treat the Constitution as law was made perfectly plain, there was no complete and definite announcement by the Convention of a court's duty to pronounce congressional acts void. And still, it may be fair to say, the existence of this judicial power was by most of the delegates taken for granted.[46] The delegates knew the principle well enough; they did not need to create an idea entirely new. They were, moreover, not likely to be especially affrighted by the spectacle of a court's ignoring a congressional act. Though anxious to establish an effective government and an indestructible union, they were not desirous of so arranging the system that an unfettered democracy might have its way or that a government might move on without check or hindrance—quite the contrary.[47]

III: Sectional Diversity; Slavery; the Presidency; the Philosophy of the Fathers

During the first two months, while the Convention was engaged in discussing the nature of the new union and in seeking to adjust the differences between the large and the small-state factions, various

[46] An extended examination of this question is ably made by C. A. Beard, *The Supreme Court and the Constitution*.

[47] It is impossible here to discuss in detail the origin of this idea, so critically significant; all great ideas have a long history in their growth to maturity. We should, however, be at a loss in any endeavor to discover the origin of the idea that courts might declare an act void unless we appreciate the philosophy of the Revolution and, indeed, of history preceding. Central in that philosophy and in the practical politics of the Revolution was the principle that a government transcending its assigned powers acts illegally.

other subjects were debated and at times the serious fact of sectional diversity came into view. The differences between east and west and between north and south were real. Should new states when admitted to the union be allowed representation on the same terms as those provided for the other states? In other words, in a developing empire, was the union to be one of equal states or not? And if the principle of proportional representation were adopted, should slaves be counted in the enumeration of inhabitants?

Proposals to limit the power of the west were advocated especially by Gouverneur Morris, who believed "The Busy haunts of men not the remote wilderness, was the proper School of political Talents." [48] For once, the mild-mannered Madison forgot to be gentle. Morris, he said, on the one hand recommended to the southern states implicit confidence in the northern majority, and at the same time "was still more zealous in exhorting all to a jealousy of a Western majority. To reconcile the gentleman with himself it must be imagined that he determined the human character by the points of the compass." [49]

Before Morris had announced his fears, Mason proclaimed his antagonism to discrimination against the frontier: "Strong objections", he said, "had been drawn from the danger to the Atlantic interests from new Western States. Ought we to sacrifice what we know to be right in itself, lest it should prove favorable to States which are not yet in existence." So here was a strange antithesis: Morris, representing the freemen of a state which had been a wilderness only a hundred years or so before, speaking words of disparagement concerning the frontiersmen; Mason, a master of many slaves, the ruler of a large plantation, the owner of a magnificent estate where his daily wants were ministered to by a retinue of black servitors, insisting upon the principle of democratic equality. The counsels of liberality prevailed. The Convention refused to provide for limited and inferior representation of the west.[50]

[48] See Madison's *Notes*, July 11. See also July 5.

[49] It is interesting to notice that while the subject was under discussion, the old decrepit Congress at New York was engaged in enacting the Ordinance of 1787 (July 13), which provided for equality of the new states of the old northwest when they should be admitted into the union. Randolph remarked in the Convention (July 11): "Congress have pledged the public faith to New States, that they shall be admitted on equal terms." This reference was, of course, to the resolution of Congress passed seven years before.

[50] In this connection it should be noted that the western question was involved in the whole difficult problem of determining the basis of representation. "The majority

But when provision for the admission of new states was under consideration, Morris returned to the idea of protecting the east. He did not succeed in securing definite decision in favor of inequality, but he was successful in obtaining the abandonment of an explicit provision for the admission of new states "on the same terms with the original States". The decision of the Convention, as it appears in the finished Constitution, simply reads, "New States may be admitted by the Congress into this Union. . . ."[51] It is difficult to escape the conclusion that this was a vague and inexplicit compromise which left to Congress the right at its discretion to prescribe such terms of admission as would make the new states inferior to the old.[52] Certainly the principle of equality was not plainly and definitely announced.

Connected with the question of the west and its proportionate participation in the new government was the question whether slaves should be counted in fixing the basis of representation. In the earlier days the proposal to enumerate three-fifths of the slaves appeared to be acceptable, but at a later time objections arose. Certain men from the far south declared in favor of enumerating all the slaves. Some of the northern members, on the other hand, could see no propriety in counting any of them. "Are they admitted as Citizens?" asked Wilson. "Then why are they not admitted on an equality with White Citizens? Are they admitted as property? then why is not other property ad- mitted into the computation?" Morris declared "he verily belived [sic] the people of Pennsylvania will never agree to a representation of Negroes." The problem was complicated by the belief that prop- erty should be taken into consideration as a basis of representation, of people", said Wilson, "wherever found ought in all questions to govern the minority. If the interior Country should acquire this majority they will not only have the right, but will avail themselves of it whether we will or no. This jealousy misled the policy of Great Britain with regard to America. . . . Again he could not agree that property was the sole or the primary object of Government and Society. The cultivation and improvement of the human mind was the most noble object." A vote passed at one time to take as a basis both wealth and population was finally changed by striking out "*wealth*". The question to strike out "*wealth*" was adopted with practical unanimity—nine states voted in the affirmative, Delaware divided (July 13).

51 The whole subject of the expansion of the union was complex and perplexing. Vermont was likely to be admitted ere long. Furthermore, the problem of admitting as new states certain portions of the old states made a statement of general principles difficult. For the conclusion see Constitution, Art. IV, sec. 3, para. 1.

52 The chapter in this work on the Missouri Compromise discusses this subject. See Max Farrand, "Compromises of the Constitution," *Am. Hist. Rev.*, IX, p. 479 ff.; Warren, *op. cit.*, p. 595 ff.

and negro labor was apparently supposed to be less productive of wealth than free labor.[53]

Davie of North Carolina insisted upon counting at least three-fifths of the blacks. Without such recognition of slave property and numbers, North Carolina would never "confederate". Morris proposed that the basis of taxation and representation be the same, and this proved to be the way out of the maze; the proposal was adopted. Direct taxation and representation stood together; in assigning representation and direct taxation, three-fifths of the slaves were to be counted. If a slaveholding state had more wealth, as judged by its population, let it pay more taxes. We should notice that the resolution as finally phrased refers to direct taxes, by which, it is probable, the Convention meant something in the nature of a requisition, something at least different from an excise or a tax on imports; but in the course of the following years indirect taxation was the mode commonly used for revenue.

Toward the end of August, after three months of labor, new diffi-

[53] "Mr. Mason could not agree to the motion [to strike out the words "three fifths" and therefore count *all* the slaves], notwithstanding it was favorable to Virginia because he thought it unjust. It was certain that the slaves were valuable, as they raised the value of land, increased the exports and imports, and of course the revenue, would supply the means of feeding and supporting an army, and might in cases of emergency become themselves soldiers. . . . He could not however regard them as equal to freemen and could not vote for them as such." "Dr. Johnson, thought that wealth and population were the true, equitable rule of representation; but he conceived that these two principles resolved themselves into one; population being the best measure of wealth. He concluded therefore that the number of people ought to be established as the rule, and that all descriptions including blacks *equally* with the whites, ought to fall within the computation." Farrand, *Records,* I, pp. 581, 593. Professor Farrand is quite right in pointing out that the whole subject of slavery did not occupy as much attention in the Convention as was later ascribed to it. He objects to calling the adoption of the three-fifths rule a compromise at all. See Farrand, *The Framing of the Constitution,* pp. 107-108; Farrand, "Compromises of the Constitution," *Am. Hist. Rev.,* IX, pp. 479-481. This contention is based partly on the fact that the proportion had been proposed before that time and even before the Convention met. Moreover, the discussion arose in connection with the great compromise, the report of the committee of July 5; the counting of slaves as the basis of representation did not form the most critical problem under discussion. Though of considerable importance in later days, in the course of the Convention it was one of the minor adjustments. There seems no doubt, however, that Morris's proposal smoothed the troubled waters. "The purpose of this provision [connecting direct taxation with representation] was to lessen the inducement to the Southern States to seek to increase their representation; since, by so doing, they would proportionally increase their share of the tax burdens. It is important to note, however, that Morris and some other delegates from the North were actuated quite as much by their fears of conditions which might arise in the West, as by their anxiety over the South." Warren, *op. cit.,* p. 290.

culties arose and brought the existing sectional diversities sharply to the light. Serious though not prolonged debate arose over the proposal to deny to Congress the power to levy duties on exports. "To deny this power", Wilson declared, "is to take from the Common Government half the regulation of trade". The discussion brought differing economic interests to the light, but sectional lines were not sharply drawn and concession was reached without great difficulty. The proposal to deny the power was adopted.[54]

The greater trouble, however, was presented by the slave-trade. Here there was not only diversity of sectional interests—for the far south demanded the right to import slaves—but also a moral problem. Georgia and South Carolina wanted more slaves to till their fields; the men of the middle region protested against the trade. Some of the New England men thought it better to allow the importation of slaves than to abandon the hope of a constitution; they believed slavery was disappearing and could not endure. Morris had at an earlier day bitterly attacked slavery, and now Mason, a slave-owner, with great feeling and intense earnestness, passed judgment upon its iniquities: "Every master of slaves is born a petty tyrant. They bring the judgment of heaven on a Country. As nations can not be rewarded or punished in the next world they must be in this. By an inevitable chain of causes and effects providence punishes national sins, by national calamities." [55]

As some of the delegates from the south declared that, if the right to import slaves were denied, their states would not accept the Constitution, the Convention had to do something to settle the difficulty. The draft of the Constitution reported by the committee of detail (August 6) denied to Congress the authority to levy a tax on the migration or importation of such persons as the several states should think proper to admit, and denied the authority to prohibit such migration or importation; the committee had also reported a provision

---

[54] For obvious reasons the states were later also forbidden to levy duties on exports without the consent of Congress. For a full statement see Constitution, Art. I, sec. 10, para. 2.

[55] Mason "lamented that some of our Eastern brethren had from a lust of gain embarked in this nefarious traffic." It may be that such New Englanders as were willing to allow the slave-trade to continue, because of the demand of the far south were influenced by the interest of their section in the trade. Their very distance from the plantation region probably influenced them. Ellsworth said, "As population increases; poor laborers will be so plenty as to render slaves useless. Slavery in time will not be a speck in our Country." August 22. See also Sherman's remarks, August 22.

requiring a two-thirds vote for the passage of a navigation act. Thus an opportunity for compromise was offered; and so the final agreement was reached: the slave-trade was not to be prohibited before the first of January, 1808, but in the meantime a tax not exceeding ten dollars per person might be imposed; the proposal requiring a two-thirds vote for the passage of a navigation act was abandoned. In the course of the discussion Madison complained that twenty years would produce all the mischief that could be apprehended from the liberty to import slaves. New Jersey, Pennsylvania, Delaware, and Virginia, voted against allowing importation for twenty years.[56]

In later years the Constitution was spoken of as if it were a compact or agreement between the slave states and the free. Nothing can be more false to the fact. The opposition to slavery was by no means confined to the northern states. The right to continue the slave-trade was extorted from the Convention by the delegates of two or three states,[57] and by reluctance of others to see the hope of union shattered. Slavery was openly condemned, and no one but Charles Pinckney ventured upon an elaborate defense of it; he presented briefly an argument with an aroma similar to the philosophy of Calhoun fifty years later.[58] Though the New Englanders later voted in favor of allowing importation for a time, they appear to have been influenced, as has been suggested, by the belief that slavery would not last. Alas! Before a decade had passed, Eli Whitney had invented the cotton gin.

No single problem was more perplexing than that presented by the presidency. The chief magistrate, with extensive executive powers, must be effective but not clothed with the majesty of monarchical authority; he must not appear to the people, when the veil should be lifted from the Convention's handiwork, as only another king and perhaps an incipient despot. He must be dependent and not autocratic, but he must also have sufficient though not dangerous independence.

[56] The position of Maryland is uncertain though the vote was cast for allowing the importation during the period. Martin had earlier opposed importation as "dishonorable to the American character. . . ."

[57] Probably North Carolina should be added to South Carolina and Georgia. The opposition of the North Carolina delegates appears, however, to have been directed against complete restriction. North Carolina's position can be seen, though only indistinctly, from remarks by Williamson, August 22 and 25. See also remarks by Morris and Mason, August 25, and by Rutledge, August 22.

[58] And still, he thought the southern states, if left to themselves, would probably stop the importation of slaves. He, as a citizen of South Carolina, would vote for it. Madison's *Notes*, August 22.

The principle of the separation of powers must be made secure; the executive must not be the mere creature of the legislature.

But if the Convention was to succeed in establishing an executive clothed with authority and still so held in leash that he could do no serious harm, some suitable method of election must be discovered. Wilson said, as the Convention neared the end, "This subject has greatly divided the House, and will also divide people out of doors. It is in truth the most difficult of all on which we have had to decide." [59] If there had been complete confidence in the intelligent will of the people-at-large, possibly popular election might have solved the problem; but this is merely a vague hypothesis, and we need not look askance at the Convention's attitude of mind when we think of the America of those days, without good roads, with no telegraph, no railroads, no newspapers of general circulation, no adequate means of knowing who were the suitable men to be intrusted with the leadership of the nation; there were no national parties and no national party machines; in short, men were living in the eighteenth century. There appears in general to have been some confidence in the process of successive filtrations : a chosen few selected for the ultimate task would have the requisite wisdom to elect to high office men of superior ability and virtue.

The decision was at length in favor of choice by electors. This arrangement, however, brought up new objections, for, by the plan proposed, if the electors should fail to give any one person a majority, the duty of choice would fall to the Senate. Mason declared that "nineteen times in twenty the President would be chosen by the Senate, an improper body for the purpose." To allow the Senate this power of choice appeared unendurable because the president had already been made subservient to the Senate in certain vital particulars. ". . . the President", Wilson said, "will not be the man of the people as he ought to be, but the Minion of the Senate. He cannot even appoint a tide-waiter without the Senate". But other difficulties were to be met : by the proposed method of election each state was to appoint as many electors as it had representatives and senators; this was an advantage

---

[59] "On twenty-one different days this subject was brought up in the Convention. Over thirty distinct votes were taken upon different phases of the method of election. Five times they voted in favor of appointment by the national legislature, and once against it. Once they voted for a system of electors chosen by the state legislatures, and twice they voted against such a system. Three times they voted to reconsider the whole question." Farrand, "Compromises of the Constitution," *loc. cit.*, pp. 486-487

to the large states. But if the Senate would frequently have the duty of electing when no one person had received the majority of votes for the presidency, then the small states would profit. Once again, the delegates must take into consideration the old differences, imaginary rather than real, between the large states and the small. Finally, the right of choice, in case the electoral vote was not conclusive, was transferred to the House, where, however, the votes must be taken by states, the representatives from each state having one vote. Thus the undue influence of the Senate was avoided and the small states retained their share of power.

When the engrossed copy of the Constitution had been read, Franklin, the weather-beaten statesman who had been interested for thirty years and more in an effective union, offered a speech which was read by Wilson. Confessing his disapproval of several parts of the Constitution, he was not sure he never should approve them. ". . . the older I grow," he said, "the more apt I am to doubt my own judgment, and to pay more respect to the judgment of others." And he told of "a certain french lady, who in a dispute with her sister, said 'I don't know how it happens, Sister but I meet with no body but myself, that's always in the right'—*Il n'y a que moi qui a toujours raison.*" Evidently the Convention had some prospects of ending its days in an atmosphere of humor. Franklin then moved that the Constitution be signed by the members, and offered as a convenient form of statement: " 'Done in Convention, by the unanimous consent of *the States* present. . . .' " "This ambiguous form had been drawn up by Mr. Gouverneur Morris in order to gain the dissenting members, and put into the hands of Doctor Franklin that it might have the better chance of success." [60]

Probably no one found every portion of the Constitution to his liking; but the work was finished, the result of patient toil and amicable accommodation. Refusal to accept the document with hopes for the future could mean nothing but folly; the choice lay between the hopeful chance of a national system and reversion to a confusion which might be little less than disaster. [61] Of the fifty-five delegates

[60] At least one member, Blount, was willing to sign under the terms proposed; he would attest the fact that the Constitution was "the unanimous act of the States", but he would not pledge his own support.

[61] Hamilton asked: "is it possible to deliberate between anarchy and Convulsion on one side, and the chance of good to be expected from the plan on the other." Gouverneur Morris said, "The moment this plan goes forth all other considerations

who had taken part in the Convention, thirty-nine signed the finished instrument; three, Mason, Gerry, and Randolph refused to sign. Martin left a few days before the end of the Convention and did not sign. Of the remaining twelve regular members who were not in attendance at the end and did not sign, seven are known to have approved and three are known to have disapproved of the Constitution.[62]

The Constitution was turned over to Washington to be sent to the Congress, with recommendations that it be submitted to the states. A letter to Congress was prepared by the Convention: "the consolidation of our Union," the letter declared, "the greatest interest of every true American," had been kept steadily in view and the Constitution was "the result of a spirit of amity. . . ." There is in the letter one especially significant statement: "It is obviously impracticable in the foederal government of these States, to secure all rights of independent sovereignty to each, and yet provide for the interest and safety of all —Individuals entering into society, must give up a share of liberty to preserve the rest." In other words, the old philosophy of natural rights and of contract was here made to apply to the organization of the new system; the sovereignty of the states was to be diminished; a portion was to be surrendered.[63]

The federal state which these men succeeded in formulating had the following salient features: (1) sovereign powers were distributed between the states and the national government; (2) the national government had only the powers granted it explicitly or by implication; the states individually retained the residue; (3) each government

will be laid aside—and the great question will be, shall there be a national Government or not?"

[62] Jameson, "Studies in the History of the Federal Convention of 1787," *loc. cit.*, p. 157. Dickinson was absent, but at his request his name was put down by his colleague, Read. Farrand, *Records,* III, p. 81.

[63] The toil and trouble were passed. Washington's own words from his diary are of interest:

"Monday — 17th.

Met in Convention when the Constitution received the unanimous assent of 11 States and Colonel Hamilton's from New York (the only delegate from thence in Convention) and was subscribed to by every Member present except Governor Randolph and Colonel Mason from Virginia—and Mr. Gerry from Massachusetts. The business being thus closed, the Members adjourned to the City Tavern, dined together and took a cordial leave of each other.—after which I returned to my lodgings—did some business with, and received the papers from the secretary of the Convention, and retired to meditate on the momentous work which had been executed, after not less than five, for a large part of the time six, and sometimes 7 hours sitting every day, sundays and the ten days adjournment to give a Committee opportunity and time to arrange the business for more than four months." Farrand, *Records,* III, p. 81.

within its sphere of authority operated immediately over the individual citizen; (4) neither government was to be inferior to the other or in ordinary operation to come into contact with the other; (5) the constitutional system was established as law enforceable in courts and was superior to the authority of every state acting either through its government or by convention of its citizens; (6) the national government recognized and made applicable the principle of the separation of powers with certain modifications.

When we remember that the Convention met before the shadow of the Shays rebellion had been lifted, and that conservatives had been distressed by the tribulations of the Confederate period, the liberality of the Constitution and the broad-mindedness of the delegates are particularly impressive. There was no decision to limit the suffrage or to prescribe property or religious qualifications for office. In these respects the delegates were more liberal than the makers of the state constitutions ten years before. Many of the members appear to have been holders of public securities; [64] but had they been penniless, they could scarcely have shown less interest in the obligation of the new government to pay the debts of the old—unless they had been quite without respect for public faith. An amendment declaring that the legislature " 'shall fulfil the engagements and discharge the debts of the United States,' " was objected to by Butler, "lest it should compel payment as well to the Blood-suckers who had speculated on the distresses of others, as to those who had fought and bled for their country." Mason objected to the term " 'shall' " as too strong, declaring "There was a great distinction between original creditors and those who purchased fraudulently of the ignorant and distressed." Randolph moved that " 'All debts contracted and engagements entered into, by or under the authority of Congress shall be as valid against the United States under this constitution as under the Confedera-

---

[64] I say "appear", because, though Professor C. A. Beard in his *An Economic Interpretation of the Constitution,* a product of toilsome research, has shown that a large number of the delegates presented bonds in 1791, in accordance with Hamilton's funding plan, we cannot be entirely certain that these men owned the certificates in 1787. Furthermore, it is more than likely that in some cases the former members of the Convention acted, when they presented their certificates, as agents of other persons. An incomplete examination of the data, carried on at my suggestion by the Department of Historical Research of the Carnegie Institution at Washington, appears to justify this statement. A number of the more influential delegates presented no certificates in 1791. The fact remains that many of the delegates in all probability were creditors of the states and of the Congress.

tion' ". The motion was adopted by a vote of ten to one, Pennsylvania alone voting in the negative.[65]

Two provisions in the Constitution were, in a way, directed toward the protection of property: no state shall emit bills of credit, and no state shall pass a law impairing the obligation of contracts. Both of these prohibitions resulted from the experiences of the Confederate period. Forty years later, John Marshall, who had lived through the critical years and had taken great interest in the adoption of the Constitution, said of the impairment of contracts: "The mischief had become so great, so alarming, as not only to impair commercial intercourse, and threaten the existence of credit, but to sap the morals of the people, and destroy the sanctity of private faith." [66]

Some of the delegates feared the rise of classes or, indeed, believed the stratification of society to be inevitable. Gouverneur Morris was ready on all occasions to inculcate the political depravity of men, and he pointed to the necessity of checking one vice or interest by an opposing vice or interest.[67] Madison, himself, though impatient with the cynicism of Morris, feared lest in the long run, as the numbers of the unpropertied classes increased, they might combine to endanger property and public liberty, or would become the tools of opulence and ambition. But, though the members of the Convention were rich men according to the standards of the time, there was practically no inclination to give special protection to wealth. There was not then, it is true, confidence in the wisdom of the common people (the confidence characteristic of the professed democracy of the next century) ; but on the other hand, the grievous influences of the rich and the rise of a plutocratic aristocracy were especially feared.[68] The men of those

[65] The Constitution says "All debts contracted and engagements entered into before the adoption of this Constitution shall be as valid against the United States under this Constitution as under the Confederation." Art. VI, para. 1. This statement leaves out the words " 'under the authority of Congress' " of the Randolph resolution, and may indicate a purpose to allow the assumption of state debts.

[66] Dissenting opinion in Ogden *v.* Saunders, 12 Wheaton 213, 355 (1827).

[67] Morris's philosophy is illustrated by his speech on July 2; see also, his remarks on August 7. He said on July 6: "As to the alarm sounded, of an aristocracy, his creed was that there never was, nor ever will be a civilized Society without an Aristocracy. His endeavor was to keep it as much as possible from doing mischief." Note Madison's comments, August 7 and 10. Madison in general desired proper protection for minorities. Mason's position is stated August 8 and 14 and September 15; Gerry's, August 14; Williamson's, September 5; Randolph's, September 5; Wilson's, September 6.

[68] Various announcements indicate this. Dickinson "doubted the policy of interweaving into a Republican constitution a veneration for wealth. He had always

days believed in liberty; liberty and property were not considered mutually opposed. We may have forgotten for how many decades the word "liberty" was the chosen symbol of American life. A government with powers of ruthless interference with property would not have been considered a government to be endured by a free people.

Liberty was to be assured by a government so checked and balanced as to curb the sway of malign influences and to prevent the exercise of tyrannical authority. Just how much the delegates were affected by writings of John Adams, the supreme advocate of checks and balances, we do not know. But the desire of men, realizing as these men did the need of an effective national government, was to have a government so organized as to make liberty secure and to make difficult or impossible the despotism of faction or of passion.[69]

But on the whole the Convention was not ruled by abstract theories —doctrines quite abstracted from the teachings of history and from the facts well-known to the Convention's members. References to the ancient world were occasionally indulged in; lessons from the failures of other nations were mentioned; the fundamental principles of constitutional rights and the elements of English liberty were in the minds of the men who made the Constitution. That generation, of which these men were the flower, had been steeped in the discussion of political principles and had been engaged in the actual construction of governments and constitutions. The greatest single teacher was experience, and the state constitutions were the chief source of governmental forms. The framers were now giving institutional reality to the ideas which the course of colonial history, the practices of the old empire, their own struggle for independence, and their earlier attempts to establish union had inculcated. All through the Revolutionary struggle, until the Revolution was made complete by the adoption of the Constitution, the men of that generation—though some engaged in the vaporings of self-created philosophy—did not bring many absolutely new ideas to birth. They were in fact tremendous realists. Had they set forth to create a new system free from the shackles of history, they must have failed. To call into being a constitutional system

understood that a veneration for poverty and virtue, were the objects of republican encouragement." Franklin declared, "Some of the greatest rogues he was ever acquainted with, were the richest rogues."

[69] For Adams's philosophy, see his *Defence of the Constitutions of Government of the United States;* "Three Letters to Roger Sherman, on the Constitution of the United States," *Works* (C. F. Adams, ed.), VI, p. 427 ff. See especially C. M. Walsh, *The Political Science of John Adams.*

which has lasted for over a century, a system which has withstood perplexing diversities and conflicting sectional interests, the development of democracy, the increase of population from four million to thirty times that number, is a notable achievement.

CHAPTER XV

THE ADOPTION OF THE CONSTITUTION

Congress received the Constitution with no unseemly expression of pleasure; indeed, as Bancroft says, it had been in reality invited "to light its own funeral pyre." No body can be expected to decree gladly its own demise; but there seems to have been no special desire on the part of the moribund Congress to prolong its own futile life. On the twenty-eighth of September, 1787, a resolution without words of commendation was unanimously adopted [1] transmitting the Constitution to the several legislatures to be submitted by them to the state conventions.

The reception of the Constitution by the people at first appeared favorable. Gouverneur Morris wrote a characteristic letter to Washington: "The states eastward of New York appear to be almost unanimous in favor of the new Constitution, (for I make no account of the dissension in Rhode Island). . . . Jersey is so near unanimity in her favorable opinion, that we may count with certainty on something more than votes, should the state of affairs hereafter require the application of pointed arguments." He thought parties in New York were nearly balanced, but as the state was "hemmed in between the warm friends of the Constitution" there was ground for hoping that the "federal party" would prove successful. Of Pennsylvania he had fuller knowledge and entertained doubts. "True it is, that the city and its neighborhood are enthusiastic in the cause; but I dread the cold and sour temper of the back counties, and still more the wicked industry of those who have long habituated themselves to live on the public, and cannot bear the idea of being removed from the power and profit of state government. . . ." [2]

Randolph reported favorable reception of the Constitution in Baltimore and Virginia, while Madison gathered a like impression

[1] Members from eleven states were present, "and from Maryland Mr Ross". Rhode Island was not represented. *Documentary History of the Constitution*, II, p. 22.

[2] October 30, 1787. See Elliot, *Debates* (1866 ed.), I, pp. 505-506.

concerning New York City and most of the eastern states. But the ratification had dangerous foes to meet, and as the days went by the contest became more serious. It will be remembered that Yates and Lansing, of New York, had left the Convention at an early day; and in a letter to Governor Clinton they forcibly expressed their objections to the proposed system of government, for they believed any general government, however guarded by declarations of rights, would be "productive of the destruction of . . . civil liberty. . . ." Clinton and his immediate retinue were particularly hostile and sought by correspondence with leaders of the opposition in some of the other states to create a coöperative resistance. Luther Martin of Maryland, who had declaimed vehemently against the new system, went home to attack it. Gerry played a similar rôle in Massachusetts; he declared in a letter to the legislature that the "liberties of America were not secured by the system. . . ." He believed that in many respects the Constitution had merits and by proper amendments might be "adapted to the 'exigencies of government, and preservation of liberty' "; the document as proposed had "few, if any, federal features," but was "rather a system of national government." [3] George Mason proved a valiant opponent of the new system to which he had himself contributed.[4] Randolph, who had labored earnestly in the Convention itself but had refused to sign, wrote the speaker of the Virginia house, not condemning the Constitution but suggesting its failings, the need of amendments, and the propriety of making changes "while we have the Constitution in our power. . . ." [5] Fortunately, however, perhaps under the persuasion of Washington, he decided to favor adoption and worked to that end in the Virginia convention. It was soon evident that there would be strong opposition in three very important states, Massachusetts, New York, and Virginia, and without them a union would be useless and impracticable. A letter of Richard Henry Lee, written as early as October 16, expressed the opinion of one who was prepared to battle with unstinted persistence against ratification; a new convention ought to be summoned: "It cannot be denied, with truth, that this new Constitution is, in its first principles, highly and dangerously oligarchic. . . ."

[3] See Elliot, *Debates*, I, p. 493.
[4] The letters of Yates and Lansing, of Gerry, Mason, and Randolph are in Elliot, *Debates*, I. They give exceedingly good indication of the nature and extent of objections to the Constitution. This volume also contains Martin's "Genuine Information". See also Farrand, *Records*, III, especially p. 151 ff; p. 172 ff.
[5] See Elliot, *Debates*, I, p. 490.

In the course of the public discussion few portions of the Constitution escaped scathing criticism. Dangers were found lurking in one clause after another and they were gleefully brought to light to confound the friends of the new order. To meet such opposition naturally proved a difficult matter; for it appeared not infrequently that every power granted was certain to be abused and to involve the destruction of American liberties. The dread of granting power filled many minds with foreboding; this dread was the most formidable obstacle to be overcome. The new government seemed something extraneous and distinct, as if it were not to be in the hands of the same people as those choosing the state governments and not to be subject to popular control. The patience, wisdom, and skill with which objections were met call forth deep admiration as one reads to-day the pamphlets and debates of those trying years. Hamilton and Madison deserve the greatest credit, probably, for masterly management and skillful argument. But it is safe to say that the character of George Washington secured the adoption of the Constitution; there was one man known to be strongly in favor of the new system in whom the masses of men had faith. Some persons feared the presidential authority under the new government; as Patrick Henry said, "Your President may easily become King." [6] Many foolish and extravagant attacks appeared in the newspapers. The delegates in the conventions appreciated the magnitude and solemnity of their task; and if the criticisms of the Constitution appear now to be the offspring of unnecessary fear of tyranny, the earnestness and the general intelligence of the discussion furnish marked evidence of political capacity. No mere analysis of the arguments can present the impression gathered by any thoughtful reader from the discussion, an impression of shrewdness and sagacity and common sense.[7]

[6] Richard Henry Lee's powerful opposition to the Constitution, expressed in his *Observation . . . of the system of government, proposed by the late Convention. . . . In . . . Letters from the Federal Farmer to the Republican,* which was one of the most popular and widely-distributed pamphlets of the day, called forth the following stinging rebuke from Oliver Ellsworth in his "Letters of a Landholder": "The factious spirit of R. H. L., his implacable hatred to General Washington, his well-known intrigues against him in the late war . . . is so recent in your minds it is not necessary to repeat them. He is supposed to be the author of most of the scurrility poured out in the New-York papers against the constitution." See *Essays on the Constitution* (P. L. Ford, ed.), p. 161. Ellsworth hit hard and did not belabor his opponents—Martin, for example—with gloves.

[7] The remarks of a Mr. Smith in the Massachusetts convention are worth quoting at length, as showing how one plain man could look at the problem. We must be content with only a few of his sentences: "Mr. President, I am a plain man, and get

In some of the central states, conventions soon gathered and acted promptly. Before the first of the year, the Constitution was ratified by Delaware, New Jersey, and Pennsylvania, the two former unanimously giving a favorable vote. In Pennsylvania, though the final vote was two to one for acceptance, the debates lasted three weeks and were marked by the persistence of a determined opposition sufficient to call for the full strength of Wilson and McKean in advocacy of the new government.

Wilson's defense of the Constitution was very able. He had to meet two main objections—the absence of a bill of rights and the charge that the Constitution established a consolidated government. In answer to the former objection he declared a bill of rights would be "highly imprudent". "In all societies, there are many powers and rights which cannot be particularly enumerated. A bill of rights annexed to a constitution is an enumeration of the powers reserved. If we attempt an enumeration, every thing that is not enumerated is presumed to be given." [8] He considered at length the assertion "that the boasted state sovereignties will, under this system, be disrobed of part of their power"; [9] he spoke of the new system as a "confederated republic". "I consider the people of the United States as forming one great community; and I consider the people of the different states as forming communities, again, on a lesser scale." [10] Denying that the states would be obliterated, he asserted there would be consolidation so far as the

my living by the plough. I am not used to speak in public, but I beg your leave to say a few words to my brother ploughjoggers in this house. . . . I had been a member of the Convention to form our own state constitution, and had learnt something of the checks and balances of power, and I found them all here. I did not go to any lawyer, to ask his opinion; we have no lawyer in our town, and we do well enough without. I formed my own opinion, and was pleased with this Constitution. . . . But I don't think the worse of the Constitution because lawyers, and men of learning, and moneyed men, are fond of it. I don't suspect that they want to get into Congress and abuse their power. . . . I don't know why our constituents have not a good right to be as jealous of us as we seem to be of the Congress; and I think those gentlemen, who are so very suspicious that as soon as a man gets into power he turns rogue, had better look at home." Elliot, *Debates* (1863 ed.), II, pp. 102-103. One may make a shrewd guess to the effect that this plowman's direct appeal won as many votes as did many more labored addresses; men such as Mr. Smith were able to found and perpetuate free government.

[8] *Ibid.*, II, p. 436. Italics of the original omitted.

[9] *Ibid.*, II, p. 443. Italics of the original omitted.

[10] *Ibid.*, II, p. 456. "The United Netherlands are, indeed, an assemblage of societies; but this assemblage constitutes no new one, and therefore it does not correspond with the full definition of a confederate republic." *Ibid.*, II, p. 422. Italics of the original omitted.

general objects of the union were concerned: "so far it was intended to be a consolidation, and on such a consolidation, perhaps, our very existence, as a nation, depends." [11] Though Wilson's statement concerning the essential nature of a bill of rights is not without theoretical foundation, practically there could be no sound objection to the announcement of certain principles in the amendments to the Constitution, provided it was made perfectly clear that the denial of certain powers did not imply that powers not denied to Congress were granted. The opponents of the Constitution were working for delay, and they wanted amendments to be offered to Congress and "taken into consideration by the United States" before the Constitution should be finally ratified.[12] To this there was of course objection; the convention decided against the proposal by a vote of forty-six to twenty-three, and the Constitution was ratified by the same vote.[13] After adoption public agitation and discussion ensued. Nearly nine months after the ratifying convention had adjourned, a gathering at Harrisburg proposed amendments to the Constitution and advocated a revision by a general convention from the several states of the union.[14] But the discontented elements, here as elsewhere, were not intransigent; they advised the people of the state to acquiesce in the organization of the government.

January saw the adoption of the Constitution by Georgia and Connecticut; the next month it was adopted by Massachusetts after a prolonged and serious discussion. Maryland and South Carolina soon fell into line. Before the first of June, therefore, eight states had ratified. The New Hampshire convention, meeting in February, was adjourned to a later time, but finally adopted the Constitution, June 21, 1788. But the all-important states of New York and Virginia were still in doubt.

[11] *Ibid.*, II, p. 461.

[12] J. B. McMaster and F. D. Stone, *Pennsylvania and the Federal Constitution,* p. 424.

[13] Philadelphia broke forth into rejoicing. At a dinner celebrating ratification thirteen toasts were proposed and drunk. Among them were the following: "The *People* of the United States." "May order and justice be the pillars of the American Temple of Liberty." "The virtuous minority of Rhode Island." Noteworthy, too, as indicative of a belief in the mission of America to enlighten the world and to bring freedom to Europe were the toasts: "May the flame, kindled on the Altar of Liberty in America, lead the nations of the world to a knowledge of their rights and to the means of recovering them." "May America diffuse over Europe a greater portion of political light than she has borrowed from her." "Peace and free governments to all the nations in the world." *Ibid.*, pp. 428-429.

[14] *Ibid.*, p. 558 ff.

Massachusetts, as we have seen, voted for ratification early in the winter, but a brief presentation of the convention's debates may now be given, as well as some account of the controversies in Virginia and New York. In the first of these states there was opposition from the interior region,[15] where Daniel Shays had found his support, where people were still smarting under a sense of unjust treatment, and still disliking the social and economic power of Boston and the eastern section in general. Added to this smoldering discontent was the fear, common to the opponents of the Constitution everywhere, of a new government on which was bestowed vast authority endangering the well-being of the states and the liberty of the individual man. Hancock and Samuel Adams, both of them possessors of considerable influence among the plain people, were reticent at first, seemingly the prey of misgiving and uncertainty. Adams indeed wrote Richard Henry Lee in December: ". . . I stumble at the Threshold. I meet with a National Government, instead of a Federal Union of Sovereign States." Hancock was chosen chairman of the convention but for a time did not attend the sessions because of an illness which some persons thought would be cured when he discovered which way the winds of popular favor were blowing. But ere long his uncertainty vanished. Ratification was secured in Massachusetts, and it seems the anxiety of Hancock and Adams was banished by a letter from Washington, which had been printed in Virginia and Pennsylvania and was published in a Boston paper while the convention was in session:[16] ". . . and clear I am if another Federal Convention is attempted, the sentiment of the members will be more discordant. . . . I am fully persuaded . . . that it [the Constitution] or disunion, is before us. If the first is our choice, when the defects of it are experienced, a constitutional door is open for amendments and may be adopted in a peaceable manner without

---

[15] See O. G. Libby, *The Geographical Distribution of the Vote of the Thirteen States on the Federal Constitution, 1787-8* (*Bulletin* of the University of Wisconsin, Economics, Political Science, and History Series, I, no. 1), p. 12. Libby says the eastern section was 73 per cent. for ratification and 27 per cent. against; the middle section was 14 per cent. for and 86 per cent. against; the western section was 42 per cent. for and 58 per cent. against.

[16] See letter from Washington to Charles Carter, December 14, 1787, in Washington, *Writings* (W. C. Ford, ed.), XI, pp. 210-211 note. See also, George Bancroft, *History of the United States* (last revision), VI, pp. 401, 380. Earlier than the date of the letter to Carter, Washington's private letters show he had advocated ratification, and, if it seemed necessary, the submission of amendments after ratification. See especially, *Writings*, XI, p. 185. For the Massachusetts convention, see S. B. Harding, *The Contest Over the Ratification of the Federal Constitution in the State of Massachusetts* (*Harvard Historical Studies*, II).

tumult or disorder." This was a plain solution of the perplexities of the anxious and earnest men who, like Adams, were stumbling at the threshold and saw their dearly-won liberties surrendered to a new and dreadful government.

The plan of ratifying the Constitution and recommending amendments was followed. Nine amendments were proposed, and the representatives of the state in Congress were enjoined to exert their influence to obtain adoption of the amendments in the manner prescribed by the Constitution. But the victory was a narrow one. Of the 355 delegates, 168 refused to yield even to the lure of subsequent amendments. By a change of ten votes from the affirmative to the negative, the Constitution would have been defeated in Massachusetts. What the consequence would have been we can only imagine; but our imagination calls forth a picture of confusion and, mayhap, strife. Union might have resulted from arms, not from peaceful agreement.

And still, there was a readiness to acquiesce in a decision reached after long and fair discussion.[17] Delegates who had objected earnestly to the Constitution went back to their constituents to say that the new system, ratified after free debate, would receive their support. To anyone knowing anything of the career of "irreconcilables" in modern European history, the most conspicuous thing in the struggle over the adoption of the American Constitution is found in this readiness to accept defeat and not to cherish undying animosities. The readiness of a minority to accept a fair defeat is necessary for successful democracy and popular government; the right of the majority to govern, subject to the necessity of a consideration for minority rights, is no more a part of democracy than is the duty of the minority to coöperate in the acknowledgment of majority power.

In the Virginia convention there was fervid and declamatory attack upon the proposed Constitution. Patrick Henry led the attack ably and eloquently. Richard Henry Lee was not in the convention, but the depth of his opposition to the new system was known and his influence in the state and in the land at large was not slight. George Mason was chosen to the convention and ably supported Henry's oratorical attacks, while James Monroe gave such assistance as he could. But Madison was also there, and without Madison the federal Constitution would have stood no chance of surviving. He was aided by John Marshall, then a young man of thirty-two, by George Nicholas, and by Randolph, who, as we have seen, had finally decided to advocate

[17] See, for example, Elliot, *Debates*, II, pp. 182-183.

adoption. Madison bore the brunt of the fight. Quietly, almost placidly, meeting the assaults of Henry's waves of oratory with arguments, facts, and logic—in short, in his own gentle way—he performed feats of forensic skill in one of the great debates of history.[18]

One subject of dispute—the extent of the treaty-making power—was particularly important in Virginia and added to the difficulty of securing ratification; the western part of the state feared that free navigation of the Mississippi would be surrendered or that some humiliating agreement with Spain would be entered into.[19] But there were many other objections to the Constitution. Henry left no stone unturned in his effort to defeat ratification; his ingenuity was as clever as his oratory was bold and defiant. The men at Philadelphia, he declared, had no authority to do more than amend the Confederation, and yet they had proceeded to draw up plans for a consolidated government: ". . . What right had they to say, *We, the people?* . . . Who authorized them to speak the language of, *We, the people,* instead of, *We, the states?* States are the characteristics and the soul of a confederation. If the states be not the agents of this compact, it must be one great, consolidated, national government, of the people of all the states. . . . Even from that illustrious man who saved us by his valor, I would have a reason for his conduct. . . ." [20] As the days went by, ably supported by Mason and a few others, he assaulted—there is no better word—provision after provision of the new Constitution.

[18] As E. P. Smith properly says, "Now it is not easy for us to make the comparison fairly." "The Movement Towards a Second Constitutional Convention in 1788," *Essays in the Constitutional History of the United States* (J. F. Jameson, ed.), p. 83. We irresistibly side with Madison and see the telling quality of his arguments. Even acknowledging the disadvantage arising from the passing of a century and more, we need not deny ourselves the pleasure of admiring the quality of Madison's skill. Henry was doubtless a very great orator, one of the most commanding in a century of great orators among the English-speaking peoples; his prestige was large, his manner often, as is the wont with orators of the Chatham type, intimidating; but Madison won the victory.

[19] George Nicholas referred to the tendency of the opposition to harp upon this matter: "Gentlemen recurred to their favorite business again—their scuffle for Kentucky votes." Elliot, *Debates* (1863 ed.), III, p. 502. For some time past Jay had been engaged on behalf of the Confederation in negotiations with the Spanish minister.

[20] *Ibid.,* III, pp. 22-23; see also, pp. 156, 171, 395. George Mason declared: ". . . it is a national government, and no longer a Confederation. . . . The assumption of this power of laying direct taxes does, of itself, entirely change the confederation of the states into one consolidated government." *Ibid.,* III, p. 29. In the Philadelphia convention he had not taken a stand, especially in the earlier days, in opposition to the establishment of a national system. See especially his remarks on May 30, June 7, June 20, July 23.

In the course of the debates Madison found it necessary to describe the nature of the new union. Here, it will be noticed, he had to meet the assertion that the Constitution provided for a "consolidated government", one of the main charges of his opponents: "In some respects it is a government of a federal nature; in others, it is of a consolidated nature. . . . Thus it is of a complicated nature; and this complication, I trust, will be found to exclude the evils of absolute consolidation, as well as of a mere confederacy. If Virginia was separated from all the states, her power and authority would extend to all cases: in like manner, were all powers vested in the general government, it would be a consolidated government; but the powers of the federal government are enumerated; it can only operate in certain cases; it has legislative powers on defined and limited objects, beyond which it cannot extend its jurisdiction." [21] This did not satisfy Henry: "This government is so new, it wants a name. I wish its other novelties were as harmless as this." [22] But the sneer was unjustified; even to-day one might find it difficult to give an untechnical description more satisfactory than Madison's.[23]

Henry's dislike of the whole document was so intense, if one may justly gather his opinion from the debates, that one has difficulty in seeing how he could give his adherence to ratification under any condition; but toward the end his chief demand was for the adoption of amendments before the acceptance of the Constitution. Here, however, as in Massachusetts, the convention decided to ratify the Constitution and to associate with ratification a series of amendments for adoption after the establishment of the new system. So after these weeks of strenuous and orderly, but heated, controversy, the Federalists won by the narrow margin of eleven votes.[24]

[21] Elliot, *Debates,* III, pp. 94-95. The whole of Madison's defense against the charge of consolidation is important. Cf. Wilson's statement referred to on a previous page.

[22] *Ibid.,* III, p. 160.

[23] He discussed the same subject in *The Federalist,* no. XXXIX.

[24] June 25, 1788. The vote is given in the *Debates* as eighty-nine to seventy-nine, but the count of ayes and noes is eighty-nine to seventy-eight. See Elliot, *Debates,* III, pp. 654-655. Henry at one time treated with eloquent contempt the proposals for subsequent amendments. Such proposals, he declared, were made "only to lull our apprehensions. . . . Will gentlemen tell me that they are in earnest about these amendments? I am convinced they mean nothing serious." *Ibid.,* III, pp. 649-650. Libby points out that the eastern section of Virginia was 80 per cent. favorable to adoption. The middle region, the region of small farmers, was 74 per cent. against adoption. The third district, including the Shenandoah valley, chiefly Scotch-Irish and German in population, was 97 per cent. for adoption. The Kentucky district was 90

In New York, as in Virginia, the advocates of the Constitution met vigorous opposition—so vigorous and so ably led that for a long time ratification seemed to be quite impossible. The Clinton faction, led by a leader who had the confidence of large numbers of the people, were determined to prevent ratification of the Constitution as it was presented, and they prosecuted their attack unrelentingly. Taking the name of the Federal Republicans, they brought to bear all possible forces of persuasion and influence. In other states men appeared to be chiefly concerned with the danger to individual liberty; in New York this fear was not absent; appeals could be made to sentiment as well as to economic interest. But the localists were playing a dangerous game; New York, as yet not one of the most populous states, could not safely play a lone hand. There was a considerable sense of self-sufficiency, a reliance on the state's own strength, but its frontiers were open to attack; it was not safe, either as a member of a distracted and incompetent Confederation or standing quite alone, to face with its own feeble strength a world hungry for power. The Clinton men wanted a union not sufficiently strong to prevent the state from having its own way in certain essential particulars. And Clinton himself of course declared, as did men in other states, that the Constitution in the end would establish a consolidated government. We find therefore an atmosphere of personal ill feeling, based in part on animosities, or less vehement feeling, which had been developing for some time, and based also on a desire for a large degree of economic or commercial freedom. New York City possessed a magnificent harbor which gave to the state commercial advantages over its neighbors, and the leaders of the Clinton group, seeing in prospect a development which the coming decades turned into achievement, looked with misgivings upon any scheme of government likely to rob the state of its peculiar strength. ". . . the constitution called forth in New York the fiercest resistance that selfish interests could organize." [25]

John Jay, a mild-tempered man, capable of taking a strong position but not given to the use of bitter words, writing before the state convention met, thus placed the facts before the people: "We have unhappily become divided into parties; and this important subject has been handled with such indiscreet and offensive acrimony, and with

per cent. against adoption. This was the region fearing the closure of the Mississippi, and it was also the region of the "Spanish conspiracy". Libby, *op. cit.,* pp. 34-35.

[25] George Bancroft, *History of the United States* (last revision), VI, p. 454. We may question, however, whether one side was more influenced by its interests than the other

so many little, unhandsome artifices and misrepresentations, that pernicious heats and animosities have been kindled, and spread their
flames far and wide among us." [26] He did not charge the Clintonians
alone with being the victims of party zeal and acrimony; he was pleading for sane and reasonable consideration of the Constitution and for
freedom from vindictive strife. New York City and the more immediate neighborhood favored ratification. The small farmers in general,
it appears, were arrayed against the large landowners.[27] So there was
not only a clash of pecuniary interests but something like class antagonism. The geographical differences were plain and the feeling was
acute—so plain in fact that it was even rumored that the region in and
about New York City might venture to separate from the rest of the
state.[28]

The *Letters from the Federal Farmer,* written by Richard Henry
Lee, the implacable foe of the Constitution, were circulated freely in
New York. But able defenders of the Constitution were at hand.
Robert R. Livingston and Jay, men of character and influence,
strongly advocated ratification. And one continentalist, peculiarly
fitted by temperament and intelligence for forensic conflict, entered
the lists with enthusiasm; Hamilton, now reaching the height of his
intellectual power and filled with zeal for a cause he had long cherished,
saved the union and the Constitution in New York.

In explaining and defending the Constitution, Madison, Hamilton,
and Jay published essays in the New York press. They were signed
by the pen-name of "Publius" and later published under the title of
The Federalist. These essays were probably of service in winning
support of the Constitution; but the extent of that service we naturally cannot measure. For much immediate practical effect they were
perhaps too learned, too free from passion. Not often are many people
converted by plain logic and unadorned presentation of facts and principles; and doubtless those vehemently detesting the new system were
not convinced. We do know, however, that the essays then published
are among the few great treatises on government ever published by

[26] Elliot, *Debates,* I, p. 500.

[27] "We must conclude, then, that although the better part of Antifederal New York
was indeed infested with great estates which monopolized the best lands as late as
1788, the opposition to the Constitution came from the small farmer, generally *t*
tenant on a large manor or patent, not from the manor lord or proprietor." E. W.
Spaulding, *New York in the Critical Period 1783-1789,* p. 83. Cf. Libby, *op. cit*
p. 26.

[28] *Ibid.,* p. 19; Bancroft, *History of the United States* (last revision), VI, p. 455.

political philosophers or statesmen. The traditional treatise had been more or less vague, distant, theoretical, and written not infrequently in a style quite beyond the grasp of any but the learned, and the specially learned at that. But *The Federalist* was not clouded by the mists of needless abstractions or darkened by a heavy and opaque style. The articles were directed toward one great question—the worth of the proposed Constitution—and this fact gave them a certain coherence; but, withal, they were filled with wise discussions of the principles of government. No one can read them to-day without admiration for the learning and skill of these young men engaged in one of the most momentous political struggles in all history. One additional fact is to be noted: *The Federalist* probably had more effect after the new government went into operation than in the days of uncertainty when the fate of the union seemed to hang in the balance; its learned and logical and yet concrete interpretation of the Constitution long continued to be influential in solving the practical problems of law and government.

When the New York convention met, the advocates of ratification faced an opposition so strongly intrenched, so ably generaled, and so capable of offensive attack, that the task of the constitutionalists must have seemed well-nigh hopeless. Hamilton himself is authority for the statement that two-thirds of the elected delegates were hostile. Could the known opposition, supported by combined interests astutely managed, be overcome by the weapons of argument and persuasion? Governor Clinton, chosen as the president of the convention, had not much to say in the discussion upon the floor. The Anti-Federalists were led by Lansing and Melancthon Smith; the Federalists by Hamilton, Jay, and Robert R. Livingston. We do not find in the debates announcement that union was unnecessary or even that the Confederation was sufficient without modification; but as in other states the Constitution was subjected to criticism in many details and was held forth as destructive of the states [29] and the liberties of the people. The opponents of the proposed system, though continuous in their attacks, came ere long to the point where they were willing to accept some sort of conditional ratification.

At one stage in the anxious days of debate Hamilton seems almost

---

[29] Melancthon Smith said: "He was pleased that, thus early in debate, the honorable gentleman [Livingston?] had himself shown that the intent of the Constitution was not a confederacy, but a reduction of all the states into a consolidated government." Elliot, *Debates*, II, p. 224.

to have yielded to despair. Complete and unqualified ratification appeared unlikely, if not quite impossible. He wrote Madison asking his opinion of a conditional ratification with "the *reservation* of a right to recede" in case amendments were not obtained. "My opinion is," Madison wrote in reply, "that a reservation of a right to withdraw, if amendments be not decided on under the form of the Constitution within a certain time, is a *conditional* ratification; that it does not make New-York a member of the new Union, and consequently that she could not be received on that plan." [30] It was no time to abandon the contest.

Toward the end of the convention, Smith moved that the Constitution ought to be ratified *"upon condition, nevertheless, That until a convention shall be called and convened for proposing amendments"* certain powers granted to Congress should not be exercised. Lansing moved to postpone the various propositions before the house in order to take into consideration a draft of a conditional ratification, with a bill of rights prefixed and with amendments. Mr. Jones, to whom honor is due, moved that the words *"on condition"* in Smith's motion be obliterated, and that the words *"in full confidence"* be substituted. This motion was carried. The crisis was passed; Melancthon Smith himself voted for unconditional ratification, as did Gilbert Livingston, who had complained bitterly against the menacing specter of the new government.[31] But the margin of victory was narrow; thirty-one voted for unconditional ratification, twenty-nine against it. The next day (July 24) Lansing, not to be overcome, moved to adopt a resolution announcing the reservation of the right of the state to withdraw within a certain number of years, unless proposed amendments should previously be submitted to a general convention. "The motion was negatived" is the brief but sufficient statement in the records of debate. The final ratification was agreed upon July 26 by a vote of thirty to twenty-seven. Two votes, changed from affirmative to negative, would have changed the result, and New York would have refused to accept the Constitution, except under embarrassing conditions and qualifica-

---

[30] Hamilton, *Works* (J. C. Hamilton, ed.), I. pp. 464-465; see also, A. C. McLaughlin, *The Confederation and the Constitution*, pp. 310-311.

[31] "What will be their [the Senate's] situation in a federal town? Hallowed ground! Nothing so unclean as state laws to enter there, surrounded, as they will be, by an impenetrable wall of adamant and gold, the wealth of the whole country flowing into it." At this someone asked what wall was meant and Livingston answered, "A wall of gold—of adamant, which will flow in from all parts of the continent"— a reply which caused "a great laugh in the house." Elliot, *Debates*, II, p. 287.

tions. Nine states had ratified the Constitution before Virginia and New York acted.

It appears to have been the hope of Clinton and his cohorts from the beginning rather to insist on a new convention and amendments than to advocate outright the rejection of the Constitution, and, after the vote was taken, the convention unanimously adopted a circular letter addressed to the governors of the several states requesting them to secure action by the legislatures in order that Congress might speedily summon a convention.[32] Madison declared this letter to be of "a most pestilent tendency"; but it was the only way to secure New York's acceptance, and it was a cheap price to pay. The prospect of another convention gave some encouragement to North Carolina and Rhode Island, both of which still held back.[33] The Virginia legislature, dominated by Henry, hastened to make application to Congress and to issue a circular letter to the other states. But the movement for the new convention failed; the people were doubtless weary of prolonged discussion. In Connecticut it received no support; Massachusetts thought a second convention might endanger the union; and the Pennsylvania house announced that it could not consistently with its duty to the good people of the state, or with its affection to the citizens of the United States, concur with Virginia in asking for a convention.[34]

As we have seen, the objections to the Constitution by its opponents were plentiful. Possibly the most frequent charge was the absence of a bill of rights. The Federalists endeavored to defend the failure to lay down the fundamental principles and reservations because the Constitution was a grant of power, and, in consequence, the new government would have no authority except what was actually bestowed. This argument, while technically correct, did not assuage the fears of the opponents; they desired to have some limitations expressly laid down. The history of the Constitution after adoption is evidence of the wisdom of these demands.[35]

[32] Elliot, *Debates*, II, pp. 413-414.
[33] Space does not allow extended discussion of the debates in North Carolina or Rhode Island. Both states did not ratify until after the Constitution had gone into operation. See L. I. Trenholme, *The Ratification of the Federal Constitution in North Carolina*, and F. G. Bates, *Rhode Island and the Formation of the Union*, chs. V-VI.
[34] Smith, "The Movement Towards a Second Constitutional Convention in 1788," *loc. cit.*, pp. 101-103, 109-110.
[35] *The Federalist*, no. LXXXIV, argues there are in the Constitution certain definite restrictions, e.g., provision for habeas corpus, provision against bills of attainder, etc. But such an assertion militates against the succeeding theoretical

The single most serious objection, with the possible exception of the one just mentioned, was the overthrow of the Confederation and the alleged complete "consolidation" of the union.[36] But there were many others : the reëligibility of the president and the danger of monarchy; the vast power of the president, who was neither checked nor assisted by a council; the treaty-making power of the president and Senate, especially dwelt upon in Virginia and North Carolina; the power of the Senate and length of the senatorial term; the authority of Congress over the seat of government; the power of Congress to regulate the time, place, and manner of electing representatives, a power which would be used to vex and enslave the people; the two-year term for representatives; the small number of representatives; the regulation of commerce; and the absence of provision for jury trial in civil cases. Even the vice-presidency—though not receiving much attention—was spoken of as a useless office. Patrick Henry, proclaiming the common detestation of slavery, but asserting the ruinous consequences of manumission, held up to view the awful thought that Congress, legislating for the common defense and general welfare, might call for the emancipation of slaves.[37]

In the system established by the Constitution, the courts were

argument. If there were need of some restrictions to protect liberty, why not of others? "Here," says the writer, "in strictness, the people surrender nothing; and as they retain every thing, they have no need of particular reservations. . . . I go further, and affirm, that bills of rights, in the sense and to the extent they are contended for, are not only unnecessary, in the proposed constitution, but would even be dangerous.—They would contain various exceptions to powers not granted; and on this very account, would afford a colourable pretext to claim more than were granted." Wilson's argument already referred to is of like character.

[36] In speaking of this objection, Rufus King in the Massachusetts convention said: "The introduction to this Constitution is in these words: 'We, the people,' &c. The language of the Confederation is, 'We, the states,' &c. The latter is a mere federal government of states." Elliot, *Debates*, II, p. 55. Nason said: "Let us, sir, begin with this Constitution, and see what it is. And first, 'We, the people of the United States, do,' &c. If this, sir, does not go to an annihilation of the state governments, and to a perfect consolidation of the whole Union, I do not know what does. . . . How, then, can we vote for this Constitution, that destroys that sovereignty?" *Ibid.*, II, p. 134.

[37] Warren quite properly points out that a "fair survey of the situation will satisfy one that the Antifederalist party had its share of 'men distinguished alike for their integrity and ability'." He quotes a letter written by Madison from New York, October 30, 1787: " 'I am truly sorry to find so many respectable names on your list of adversaries to the Federal Constitution. The diversity of opinion on so interesting a subject among men of equal integrity and discernment is at once a melancholy proof of the fallibility of the human judgment and of the imperfect progress yet made in the science of government.' " Warren, *The Making of the Constitution*, pp. 751-752.

called upon to exercise wide authority. Probably few fully appreciated how important a part they were destined to play; for, as we have seen, on the courts—state and national—rests much of the obligation of maintaining the constitutional system. The fear of judicial methods and processes dangerous to individual liberty was often manifest in the debates; and the provisions of the sixth, seventh, and eighth amendments, which were adopted after the ratification of the Constitution, give evidence of this fear and of the need of restrictions for the protection of individual rights. But of special significance was the opposition to the broad jurisdiction of the federal courts, for they, it was alleged, would absorb all judicial authority and would leave none for the state tribunals, or, at the best, leave them but the puny rôle of passing upon trivial local disputes.

There was not much debate on the power of the federal Court to declare a law of Congress void;[38] the right of the courts to do this could scarcely alarm those who were filled with fear of congressional tyranny. There was some objection to the clause making the Constitution, laws, and treaties the supreme law of the land; but it is probably right to say the objection bore rather upon the fact or the principle of federal supremacy than upon its maintenance by courts. The more serious objection, as said above, was directed to inclusive and widely-extended federal jurisdiction.

On this subject Hamilton's discussion in *The Federalist* is especially interesting and impressive. The doctrines which he laid down may have helped the men, who, after the new government went into effect, marked out the judicial system. Of chief consequence is his use of fundamental principles of jurisprudence, particularly those within what the lawyers call the "conflict of laws". He applied those principles to the new federal system.[39] Here, he seems to say, is no strange and fantastic novelty, nothing revolutionary; these fundamental doctrines are well-seasoned and need create no great perplexity. There are few things more important than the acceptance and the continuation of the principles of the common law and the principles of general jurisprudence in our constitutional system.

Quieting the fears of those who saw the state courts relegated

<hr/>

[38] Hamilton ably discussed this in no. LXXVIII of *The Federalist*. James Iredell discussed the general principles of judicial review most illuminatingly in 1787. See G. J. McRee, *Life and Correspondence of James Iredell*, II, p. 172 ff.

[39] Marshall made a similar statement in the Virginia convention. See Elliot, *Debates*, III, p. 556. Notice Mason's attack upon article III of the Constitution. *Ibid.*, p. 551. Note Wilson's description of the judiciary. *Ibid.*, II, p. 486 ff.

to a condition of insignificance, Hamilton appears to intimate that they might have more duties rather than less: ". . . I hold that the state courts will be divested of no part of their primitive jurisdiction, further than may relate to an appeal; and I am even of opinion, that in every case in which they were not expressly excluded by the future acts of the national legislature, they will of course take cognizance of the causes to which those acts may give birth. This I infer from the nature of judiciary power, and from the general genius of the system." [40] This means that the setting up of a system of courts with their special and limited jurisdiction will not in itself lessen the previous jurisdiction and authority of other courts; furthermore, as there is a new lawmaking power, there will be additional laws to be recognized and applied by the courts already in existence. In Hamilton's statement there is only one word to which one might take exception; that is "expressly".

The exposition in *The Federalist* discloses to clear view the nature of our federal judicial system. State laws are (in accord with principles of general jurisprudence) recognized and applied in federal courts; federal laws are recognized and applied in state courts, and the Constitution, of course, is law in both.[41]

It is of course an interesting and critical question whether the men of 1787-1788 intended to establish a government and a new

[40] In no. XXXII of *The Federalist* Hamilton lays down general principles which he believes applicable to the legislative authority of the new government. Especial attention is paid to the question whether Congress will necessarily have *exclusive* authority over fields of legislation granted to it by the Constitution. The line of thought he proposes in this number is followed as a basis of the learned discussion of the judicial power, which he treats in no. LXXXII.

[41] It is unnecessary to point out here the instances in which the federal courts have exclusive jurisdiction. The *general* principle is as stated in the text. "The laws of the United States are laws in the several States, and just as much binding on the citizens and courts thereof as the State laws are. The United States is not a foreign sovereignty as regards the several States, but is a concurrent, and, within its jurisdiction, paramount sovereignty. Every citizen of a State is a subject of two distinct sovereignties, having concurrent jurisdiction in the State,—concurrent as to place and persons, though distinct as to subject-matter. Legal or equitable rights, acquired under either system of laws, may be enforced in any court of either sovereignty competent to hear and determine such kind of rights and not restrained by its constitution in the exercise of such jurisdiction. Thus, a legal or equitable right acquired under State laws, may be prosecuted in the State courts, and also, if the parties reside in different States, in the Federal courts." Claflin *v.* Houseman, 93 U. S. 130, 136 (1876). For a plain announcement that rights arising under congressional acts may be enforced in state courts, see Second Employers' Liability Cases, 223 U. S. 1, 55-59 (1912).

political system totally different in essential character from that provided by the Articles of Confederation. Did they purpose to abandon a union of sovereign states? That they had no such purpose is often asserted to-day; but the reader of the contemporary literature will find insurmountable difficulty in reaching this conclusion. He will find abundant assertion by friends, and even more by enemies of the new order, that a *national* system was being founded; the advocates of ratification felt called upon to stress the fact that the states were not being *entirely* robbed of powers and utterly doomed to destruction. It is sometimes said, and has been said by historians, that the people would have firmly refused to adopt the Constitution had they not supposed that a state could at any time withdraw. Such an assertion needs evidence to support it. Of the intention of the framers to establish a national government and to abandon a Confederation of sovereign states there is no possibility of doubt. Madison's statement to Jefferson (October 24, 1787) is fully supported by all the evidence: "It appeared to be the sincere and unanimous wish of the Convention to cherish and preserve the Union of the States. . . . It was generally agreed that the objects of the Union could not be secured by any system founded on the principle of a confederation of Sovereign States." The people of that generation had been making constitutions; they knew what the very word involved. The prolonged discussion in the conventions and in the controversial literature of 1787-1788 appears all to have been based on the belief that the people were engaged in a most solemn undertaking, and that its consequences could affect their happiness and welfare for generations. They were certainly well warned: "It is to be observed", said Richard Henry Lee in the *Letters from the Federal Farmer,* "that when the people shall adopt the proposed constitution it will be their last and supreme act; it will be adopted not by the people of New Hampshire, Massachusetts, &c., but by the people of the United States. . . ."[42]

[42] See *Pamphlets on the Constitution* (P. L. Ford, ed.), p. 311. "The 'Letters of the Federal Farmer' was one of the most popular of arguments against the new government, 'four editions (and several thousands) of the pamphlet . . . being in a few months printed and sold in the several states' ". Note in *Ibid.,* p. 277. There were so many declarations that the new system did not maintain the principle of the Confederation that references are hardly necessary, but see Gerry's statement as another example. Farrand, *Records,* III, pp. 128-129. A letter of "Cato" (George Clinton), printed in *The New York Journal,* represented the strong opposition to the Constitution in New York: "what have they done? . . . This Convention have exceeded the authority given to them, and have transmitted to Congress a new political fabric, essentially and fundamentally distinct and different from it, in which

The argument for state sovereignty will be discussed on later pages, but it may be said here that the argument rests upon a notion of sovereignty different from that commonly if not universally held by the men of 1788. The position so elaborately portrayed and defended by Calhoun and his disciples was not based essentially on concrete *evidence of the purposes of the people,* certainly not on direct testimony. The state sovereignty argument in general does not rest on direct testimony expressed contemporaneously with the adoption of the Constitution to the effect that the people believed they were establishing a system and intended to establish a system from which any state, when it so desired, might withdraw.[43]

The demand for a second convention before the adoption of the Constitution is in itself an evidence (perhaps not conclusive, but evidence nevertheless) of a belief by the opponents of the proposed system that the states were irretrievably bound and could not withdraw at any time when they found the new yoke oppressive. It is significant, too, that there was no successful effort, like that made when the Articles of Confederation were under discussion, to announce in the Constitution the retention of sovereignty by the states. If anyone knew the character of the new document, it was Oliver Ellsworth; he had struggled valiantly in the Convention to save the identity of the states and to keep them from being submerged in the national system; he was an able lawyer and later a chief justice of the United States. Advocating the adoption of the Constitution, he pointed to the authority of the judiciary to declare void any law unauthorized by the Constitution, whether passed by the national legislature or by the states. "Still, however, if the United States and the individual states will quarrel, if they want to fight, they may do it, and no frame of government can possibly prevent it. It is sufficient for this Constitution, that, so far from laying them under a necessity of contending, it pro-

the different states do not retain separately their sovereignty and independency, united by a confederate league—but one entire sovereignty, a consolidation of them into one government. . . ." See *Essays on the Constitution* (P. L. Ford, ed.), p. 253. Cf. a letter of Roger Sherman, printed in *The New Haven Gazette,* in which he pointed out that each state retains "its sovereignty in what concerns its own internal government. . . ." *Essays on the Constitution,* p. 238.

[43] The ablest and most elaborate exposition of historical evidence in favor of state sovereignty is in A. H. Stephens, *A Constitutional View of the Late War Between the States,* I. There is no space here to examine his treatment, but it is fair to say that he conspicuously stresses certain phrases or words from which the *inferences* may be drawn that the states retained complete sovereignty and the right to secede.

vides every reasonable check against it. But perhaps, at some time or other, there will be a contest; the states may rise against the general government. If this do take place, if all the states combine, if all oppose, the whole will not eat up the members, but the measure which is opposed to the sense of the people will prove abortive. In republics, it is a fundamental principle that the majority govern, and that the minority comply with the general voice. How contrary, then, to republican principles, how humiliating, is our present situation! A single state can rise up, and put a *veto* upon the most important public measures. . . . Hence we see how necessary for the Union is a coercive principle. No man pretends the contrary: we all see and feel this necessity. The only question is, Shall it be a coercion of law, or a coercion of arms? There is no other possible alternative. Where will those who oppose a coercion of law come out? Where will they end? A necessary consequence of their principles is a war of the states one against the other. I am for a coercion by law—that coercion which acts only upon delinquent individuals. This Constitution does not attempt to coerce sovereign bodies, states, in their political capacity. No coercion is applicable to such bodies, but that of an armed force. . . . But this legal coercion singles out the guilty individual, and punishes him for breaking the laws of the Union." [44] No one searching for belief among the fathers that any state might legally withdraw from the union and that its citizens might legally refuse to obey the laws of the union can obtain from these words much satisfaction.

At a later day, fifty years or so after the adoption of the Constitution, the advocates of the right of the states to secede from the union cited certain resolutions and declarations made by the state ratifying conventions. But these assertions, depended on to indicate the right of a state at any time to withdraw, were in reality the commonplaces of the compact philosophy, entirely out of harmony with the idea that a state of the union, as if it were an international body, acting upon its sovereign authority, could withdraw from a treaty relationship. They announce the fundamental principles of free government. Resolutions of Virginia, New York, and Rhode Island are those commonly cited.

In ratifying the Constitution the Virginia convention used the following words: "We the Delegates of the People of Virginia . . .

---

[44] Elliot, *Debates*, II, pp. 196-197. This statement of Ellsworth should be studied in connection with the question in 1860-1861 whether the states could be coerced. He here states clearly that individuals in states can be forced to obey national law.

Do in the name and in behalf of the People of Virginia declare and make known that the powers granted under the Constitution being derived from the People of the United States may be resumed by them whensoever the same shall be perverted to their injury or oppression and that every power not granted thereby remains with them and at their will: that therefore no right of any denomination can be cancelled abridged restrained or modified by the Congress by the Senate or House of Representatives acting in any Capacity by the President or any Department or Officer of the United States except in those instances in which power is given by the Constitution for those purposes: & that among other essential rights the liberty of Conscience and of the Press cannot be cancelled abridged restrained or modified by any authority of the United States." [45]

New York and Rhode Island adopted resolutions which were substantially alike. The first New York declaration is: "That all Power is originally vested in and consequently derived from the People, and that Government is instituted by them for their common Interest Protection and Security." The third declaration reads: "That the Powers of Government may be reassumed by the People, whensoever it shall become necessary to their Happiness; that every Power, Jurisdiction and right, which is not by the said Constitution clearly delegated to the Congress of the United States, or the departments of the Government thereof, remains to the People of the several States, or to their respective State Governments to whom they may have granted the same. . . ." [46] After these expressions appear statements concerning freedom of religion, the right to keep and bear arms, and similar pronouncements. In this respect the Rhode Island resolutions were of a similar character.

The Rhode Island convention, adopting the Constitution in 1790, declared "That all power is naturally vested in, and consequently derived from the People. . . . That the powers of government may be reassumed by the people, whensoever it shall become necessary to their

---

[45] *Documentary History of the Constitution*, II, p. 145.

[46] *Ibid.*, II, pp. 190-191. It is specially singular that New York should be mentioned as a state reserving the power to withdraw from the union, for in the ratifying convention, as we have seen, a proposal to retain that power was voted down. Is it possible to believe that, when the great question had been thus settled, the defenders of the Constitution in New York would have quietly accepted a resolution declaring the right to secede? For Rhode Island, see *Ibid.*, p. 310 ff. The resolutions are more like bills of rights than anything else. The Rhode Island resolutions, for example, begin with the declaration "That there are certain natural rights, of which men when they form a social compact, cannot deprive or divest their posterity. . . ."

happiness. . . ." [47] All this is orthodox enough in the philosophy of social compact. But perhaps of more interest is the fact that, after making sundry statements concerning the guaranties and principles of safe government, the convention enjoined the senators and representatives who were to be elected to Congress to prepare certain amendments. The first of these is as follows: "The United States shall guarantee to each State its sovereignty, freedom and independence, and every power, jurisdiction and right, which is not by this constitution expressly delegated to the United States." [48] These words are almost an exact copy of the second article of the Articles of Confederation. Did Rhode Island suppose she was entering into a new confederation of sovereignties? Washington had at an earlier day expressed the hope that the scales were "ready to drop from the eyes, and the infatuation to be removed from the heart" of the people of that state.[49] Evidently some of the scales were still in place. But the nearest approach—and it was rather a rejection than an approach—to the resolution recommended by Rhode Island guaranteeing sovereignty, was the important principle announced in what became the tenth amendment: "The powers not granted to the United States by the Constitution, nor prohibited by it to the States, are reserved to the States respectively or to the people." This statement was intended to safeguard the rights of the component parts of an integral union.

It is sometimes said that, if the people of the whole country in primary meetings or by individual votes had had the opportunity of passing upon the Constitution, it would have been rejected.[50] But of course no one can positively know whether such assertions are true or not.

[47] Only such portions of the resolutions of Virginia, New York, and Rhode Island as might be conceived to be assertions of the right to secede are given here. They in reality contain the principles of the compact philosophy—government has derived and not indigenous authority. Some of these doctrines are discussed in A. C. McLaughlin, *The Foundations of American Constitutionalism* and *The Courts, the Constitution and Parties.*

[48] *Documentary History of the Constitution,* II, p. 316.

[49] Washington, *Writings* (W. C. Ford, ed.), XI, p. 287. Italics of original omitted.

[50] Libby says, ". . . there is sufficient proof of a general correspondence between the sentiment of the constituency and the vote of the delegate at the state convention to warrant the conclusion, that the votes of these representatives registered the public sentiment in each state on the question of ratifying the Federal Constitution." Libby, *op. cit.,* p. 70. Hildreth questions whether "upon a fair canvass," a majority of the people, even in the ratifying states, were in favor of the Constitution. He appears to rely chiefly on the dissent by the minority of the Pennsylvania convention. *The History of the United States* (revised ed.), second series, IV, pp. 28-29. See also, Smith, "The Movement Towards a Second Constitutional Convention in 1788," *loc. cit.,* p. 111.

There was strong opposition. It was most intense in the back-country, in those sections where people felt less keenly than in the seashore towns the need of national organization and government; opposition was not unnatural among persons living the free life of the frontier. One cannot, however, go studiously through the debates without seeing the impracticability, or at least the difficulty, of properly discussing such matters as were involved by any other method than that actually followed. The proposed system was attacked and defended, caricatured and lauded in the newspapers; pamphlets were issued and were widely distributed; learned treatises were written and read; hand-to-hand debates tested the strength of argument. Had Henry's passionate oratory been addressed to crowds of listeners at the county courthouses, his eloquence might have won a sweeping victory; but in the quiet of the assembly hall it proved no match for Madison's relentless and unemotional logic. If the New York voters had been subjected only to the cleverness of Clinton and the skillful arguments of Melancthon Smith, they would perhaps have failed to read *The Federalist;* but the arguments of Hamilton were too strong for the opponents of ratification under conditions in which arguments counted.

The debates in Massachusetts, a critical state, were, as already suggested, impressive; fears and forebodings and prejudices were met frankly; over 350 delegates from a population of about half a million discussed and debated for a month the alleged dangers and the probable value of the proposed system. And this sort of thing, we are sometimes told, was a conspiracy to rob the people of their rights![51] The action of New Hampshire is especially interesting. When the convention assembled, a majority, including many members from the remote parts of the state, opposed the Constitution. Some of the delegates were instructed by their towns to vote against ratification. But, as has already been noticed, the convention adjourned; there was further discussion and time for consideration, and when it met again the Constitution was adopted by a vote of fifty-seven to forty-seven.[52]

Just how many people voted for the delegates to the state conventions of ratification cannot be told. It seems all but certain that only

---

[51] In Pennsylvania the opponents of adoption continued in an ill humor for some time. The region in which the "whisky rebellion" afterwards occurred (1794) was especially hostile to the new system. In Pennsylvania the suffrage was widely distributed and, though the adoption of the Constitution was accomplished quickly, perhaps hurriedly, the people had every chance that a public press afforded.

[52] See especially, Libby, *op. cit.,* pp. 70-75, with quotations from newspapers; J. B. Walker, *A History of the New Hampshire Convention.*

a small portion voted and only a fraction of those qualified to vote. The residents of the more thickly-populated regions could and probably did vote in greater proportions than those in the sparsely-settled regions. This may have given the towns or the commercial areas an advantage. The unavoidable fact is that the men of those days did not eagerly participate in elections when they had the right and the opportunity. In Philadelphia only about five per cent. of the population voted for delegates,[53] though one would gather from the papers and pamphlets that there was much excitement. In Boston where 2700 were entitled to vote, only 760 electors participated in the election of delegates to the ratifying convention, about one-half as many as voted in the next gubernatorial election.[54]

Several conclusions seem reasonably well-founded : the majority of the people, even when the issue was important and had been much discussed, were apathetic; the "better classes", the "well-born", had had influence and they long continued to exercise it. The new government was set up by men who were sufficiently interested to take the trouble to vote. The democracy of the nineteenth century had not yet arrived.

It is quite impossible to classify accurately the opponents or the advocates of the Constitution. Economic influences of course played their part. If generalizations must be indulged in, it is probably correct to say that on the whole the well-to-do—especially the commercial elements of the population—favored ratification; the sections remote from the centers of trade were inclined to be opposed to it. But even this classification needs modification. Not all of the back-country —the region naturally less affected by government and in some instances bearing a traditional grudge against domination by the eastern section—was opposed to ratification; and by no means were all of the prosperous planters or men of property advocates of the new system. No attempt to draw lines sharply dividing the people into classes can be successful. Geographical and sectional conditions were of considerable influence in determining the attitudes of men; some differences of opinion were apparently due to special economic interests. If one thinks of the struggle in Virginia, where Washington and Mason repre-

[53] C. A. Beard, *An Economic Interpretation of the Constitution*, pp. 246-247. For New York, see Spaulding, *op. cit.*, p. 230.
[54] Beard, *op. cit.*, p. 244. Voting in the early days has been painstakingly presented by J. F. Jameson, "Did the Fathers Vote?" *New England Magazine*, new series, I, p. 484 ff. See also C. O. Paullin, "The First Elections Under the Constitution." *The Iowa Journal of History and Politics*, II, p. 3.

sented opposite sides, the difficulty of classification is plain. Richard Henry Lee, after referring to debtors and also to aristocrats desirous of power, said: "these two parties are really insignificant compared with the solid, free, and independent part of the community." [55] Though the areas favorable to ratification, in a number of instances, lay along routes of trade, it is quite possible, of course, that this attitude toward the Constitution was due, at least in a measure, to the fact that the people of those areas could be reached by information emanating from the east, and were not solely guided by economic influences or geographical environment.[56]

Certain it is that the fear lest the states be submerged, lest personal liberty be endangered, lest one section or group of states should tyrannize over another (in other words, sectional jealousy that was only partly due to any particular sectional economic interests) embodied the great list of objections to the Constitution. The first amendment to the Constitution provided for religious liberty; not one amendment proposed to the Constitution struck at the prohibition of paper money [57] or at the provision against the impairment of the obligation of contracts.

The adoption of the Constitution was a great event in history; the representatives of a numerous people living in various communities, along a coast a thousand miles and more in length, met in their respective gatherings and there, generally without bitter partisan strife and totally without uproar, debated the nature of the government which they proposed to establish over half a continent.[58]

---

[55] Quoted in Warren, *The Making of the Constitution*, p. 747.

[56] Warren, after speaking of the natural hesitation of men of the back-country to grant to a new government extensive powers, and of the fact that they were necessarily ignorant of the legislation of other states which had produced political evils, says, "And in addition to all these considerations, a division between the Western and Eastern portions of the States, in 1787, represented, to some extent, a division between the less well-informed and the better informed, rather than a division between the poor and the well-to-do." *Ibid.*, pp. 749-750.

[57] There must have been a good deal of opposition on this ground, though it did not come prominently to the fore. Madison, writing to Jefferson, October 17, 1788, declared that the articles relating to treaties, to paper money, and to contracts created more enemies than all the errors in the system positive and negative together. Henry announced in the Virginia convention his detestation of paper money. Elliot, *Debates*, III, p. 156. He protested, however, against undue infringement upon state competence: "If we cannot be trusted with the private contracts of the citizens, we must be depraved indeed." *Ibid.*

[58] To lament, as some appear to do, that the Constitution was not adopted by a method which might perhaps be suitable at the present day, is to lose sight of the momentous character of the undertaking which must be viewed with an apprecia-

The Constitution was ratified by the states in the following order:

Delaware, December 7, 1787. Unanimous.
Pennsylvania, December 12, 1787. 46-23.
New Jersey, December 18, 1787. Unanimous.
Georgia, January 2, 1788. Unanimous.
Connecticut, January 9, 1788. 128-40.
Massachusetts, February 6, 1788. 187-168.
Maryland, April 26, 1788. 63-11.
South Carolina, May 23, 1788. 149-73.
New Hampshire, June 21, 1788. 57-47.
Virginia, June 25, 1788. 89-79 (89-78).
New York, July 26, 1788. 30-27.
North Carolina, November 21, 1789. August 2, 1788, refused by a vote of 184-83 to ratify until a bill of rights and other amendments were put forth. Ratified November 21, 1789, by a vote of 195-77.
Rhode Island, May 29, 1790. 34-32.
Vermont, whose entry into the union was contemplated by the Federal Convention, adopted the Constitution January 10, 1791, and was admitted March 4.

---

tion of the background of preceding centuries. Jefferson wrote, March 18, 1789, "The example of changing a constitution by assembling the wise men of the State, instead of assembling armies, will be worth as much to the world as the former examples we had given them." Jefferson, *Works* (federal ed.), V, pp. 469-470.

CHAPTER XVI

ORGANIZATION OF THE GOVERNMENT. HAMILTON'S FINANCIAL POLICY. IMPLIED POWERS. THE JUDICIAL SYSTEM

To put the Constitution into effect and the government into operation, the old Congress named the first Wednesday in January for the appointment of presidential electors, the first Wednesday in February for the election of the president, and the first Wednesday in March, which was the fourth day of the month, for the establishment of the new government at New York, then the meeting-place of Congress. The new legislature met with the deliberation characteristic of those days. A quorum of the House was not in attendance until the first of April and of the Senate not until some days later. Washington was declared elected President and Adams Vice-President; the President took the oath of office April 30, 1789. Even before the inauguration of the President the House had gone to work upon a revenue bill, which was passed after some weeks of discussion, and after modification by the Senate the act became a law; the new government had means of getting revenue. At an early date provision was made for the organization of executive departments. Washington named to the important offices provided for by the congressional act, Thomas Jefferson, Secretary of State; Alexander Hamilton, Secretary of the Treasury; and Henry Knox, Secretary of War. The office of Attorney-General, not strictly an executive office, was given to Edmund Randolph.[1] Some months passed, however, before these offices were filled and the executive branch of the government was in working order.

The new government went into operation quietly. Those who had opposed the adoption of the Constitution were prepared to accept the results of the long discussion and not to prevent the peaceful inauguration of the system. There were, it is true, many who still retained certain fears and forebodings—fears lest under cover of the Consti-

---

[1] The office of attorney-general was provided for by the Judiciary Act of 1789. Among other duties the attorney-general was to be legal adviser to the president and the heads of departments. See H. B. Learned, *The President's Cabinet*, p. 105.

tution personal rights would be ignored or even a counter-revolution be brought to pass. Such opposition, if opposition it may be called, was, as we shall see, confined practically to a determination not to allow the Constitution to be maltreated by the men charged with the duty of making it operative. The Constitution marked the limits of governmental power; those limits must not be crossed. We need to bear in mind that the Constitution was actualized as a living fact by translation into tangible institutions. To comprehend now the importance of this early transmutation is not easy; but the fact is plain; every step taken, every principle announced or acted upon, was important in giving life to words; conduct was creative; practice and procedure soon became constitutional reality.

As we have seen, some of the states when ratifying the Constitution had advocated and proposed amendments. At the first session of the first Congress twelve amendments were proposed, ten of which were in the course of time ratified by the requisite number of states. These amendments are restrictions on the powers of the national government, not on the powers of the states.[2]

Finance was the crucial problem of the time. How were the debts of the country to be provided for? Any attempt to establish a thorough financial system, indeed anything likely to give effectiveness to the new government, was sure to meet with objection. In the autumn of 1789 Congress directed the Secretary of the Treasury to prepare a plan for the support of the public credit. Hamilton entered joyously upon the task and in January presented his report. The whole paper richly rewards reading, if anyone desires to know the principles for which Hamilton stood and the basis on which the financial system of the new government was made to rest. By what means, he asked, is the maintenance of public credit to be effected? "The ready answer to which question is, by good faith; by a punctual performance of contracts." The answer appears simple enough now, but its importance thus announced at the beginning, in days of poverty when at least partial repudiation was thinkable, was of great moment. It involved the establishment of the national character. The proper and honest handling of the debts meant more than financial stability or economic well-being in any narrow sense; there was a moral obligation. There

---

[2] See Barron v. Baltimore, 7 Peters 243 (1833). This is perfectly in accord with the general principles of constitutional construction and with the history of the proposal and adoption of the amendments.

was, the Secretary declared, a general belief that the credit of the United States would be established on "the firm foundation of an effectual provision for the existing debt." ". . . among ourselves," he said, "the most enlightened friends of good government are those whose expectations are the highest. To justify and preserve their confidence; to promote the increasing respectability of the American name; to answer the calls of justice; to restore landed property to its due value; to furnish new resources, both to agriculture and commerce; to cement more closely the union of the States; to add to their security against foreign attack; to establish public order on the basis of an upright and liberal policy;—these are the great and invaluable ends to be secured by a proper and adequate provision, at the present period, for the support of public credit."

He deprecated making any discrimination between the "original holders of the public securities, and present possessors, by purchase".[3] Against such a proposal he presented vigorous objections. In this connection he referred to the constitutional provision concerning the validity of the debt. The state debts, too, he believed should be assumed: "Indeed, a great part of the particular debts of the States has arisen from assumptions by them on account of the Union. And it is most equitable that there should be the same measure of retribution for all." The total foreign and domestic national debt, including arrears of interest, he placed at $54,124,464.56; the state debts he estimated to be about $25,000,000, making in the aggregate nearly $80,000,000.

The discussion in the House disclosed distrust and divergence of opinion. Concerning the debt owed to foreign governments, there was not much to be said; but the domestic debt was another matter. Why pay the present holders the face value of the certificates, when, as everyone knew, many of these certificates had been secured for a small fraction of their face value? Why put money in the pockets of the speculators and the money-changers? Some members probably wished a definite depreciation of the debt. Madison, not edified by the eagerness of the bondholders to reap their unexpected reward, proposed in the House to pay to the holders of the certificates the highest price which the certificates had up to that time reached in the market, and to pay the remainder to the original holders. Such a plan was of

---

[3] "Those who advocate a discrimination are for making a full provision for the securities of the former at their nominal value, but contend that the latter ought to receive no more than the cost to them, and the interest." Hamilton, "First Report on the Public Credit," *Works* (H. C. Lodge, ed.), II, pp. 236-237.

course impracticable, and is here mentioned only because it gives evidence of Madison's separation from Hamilton and his failure to identify himself with the elements that were gathering about the Secretary of the Treasury and applauding his plans. And all this is important for constitutional history because opposition based upon constitutional argument arose and conflicting theories of constitutional construction concerning the powers of the national government were put forth. The debates in the House were sufficiently earnest and excited to give warning of the struggle to come. Madison's proposal received only thirteen out of forty-nine votes.

The assumption of the state debts had a particularly hard road to travel. Over that matter the debate was heated, vehement. The root of the difficulty was that some of the states, and notably Virginia, had considerably reduced their debts, while others had not. The debt of Massachusetts was burdensome, as was that of South Carolina. The members from the states with large debts and all holders of state securities were naturally impressed with the wisdom of Hamilton's proposal for assumption; but it was at first not acceptable to Congress. Hamilton did not despair. Jefferson had recently appeared in New York to take up the duties of office, and partly through his assistance a bargain was struck whereby enough votes were obtained to secure assumption, and it was arranged that the seat of government should be for ten years at Philadelphia and thereafter on the Potomac. The bill for the funding of the debt, including the debts of the states at specified amounts, was passed in August, 1790. Jefferson later lamented that for "This game", as he called it, ". . . I was most ignorantly & innocently made to hold the candle." ". . . the more debt Hamilton could rake up, the more plunder for his mercenaries."

Hamilton's reasons for desiring assumption were fairly plain. By this as by other plans he doubtless desired to attract the interest of those "enlightened friends of good government" of whom he had spoken. Assumption would be of value to security-holders and would be approved by all or many who desired stability and good order in financial affairs. If such persons were drawn to support the new government, it would have real and substantial strength. Probably of great moment in his mind was the effect of having creditors look to the national government rather than to the states for payment of their claims.[4]

---

[4] It should be noticed that in his report he mentions that in countries in which the public debt is properly funded it answers most of the purposes of money:

The question of assumption had arisen in the Constitutional Convention,[5] and Hamilton's plan therefore could have been no new and startling proposal to a good many members of Congress. Disintegration of the union was a real danger, to men like Hamilton, the greatest danger. If there should be but one debtor—the nation—the creditors would be deeply interested in the national stability. A creditor is always interested in the well-being of his debtor. Why the seat of government should be considered such a weighty matter is less easy to understand. Whatever the reason, it appeared to be a thing of vital importance. The site of the national government had been discussed before there was any government worthy of the name, and at a time when men might properly doubt whether there would be a nation; of course state pride and jealousy played their parts, and that very jealousy was fraught with peril. Though of trivial importance in comparison with Hamilton's wide and deeply-laid plans, it was one of those tangible questions which are wont to arouse men's combative local patriotism.[6]

Did Hamilton's assumption measure really help to strengthen the union? One cannot be sure. Doubtless anything making for financial and commercial stability and for strengthening the public credit helped to create national vitality and to develop national sentiment. But enmities were aroused, sectional differences appeared, and the agrarian opposition to the certificate-holders and speculators quickened suspicions and alarms. Hamilton's plans for developing political unity and strengthening the new government were not altogether promoted by assumption. Ere long Jefferson was bitterly hostile to all the devices which seemed calculated to enrich the speculators. The agrarian elements were not ready to balance financial stability and commercial prosperity over against the ready-made fortunes of the few; the whole funding process appeared to be begotten of evil.

Hamilton's plans included the levying of an excise tax on distilled liquors as well as an increase in customs duties. In the spring of 1791,

". . . stock, in the principal transactions of business, passes current as specie." When one considers the monetary conditions of that day the advantage of stock that might thus pass current is obvious. He also points out that under the new government a principal branch of revenue "is exclusively vested in the Union;" and the states, for various reasons, would always be checked in the levying of taxes on articles of consumption.

[5] See Farrand, *Records*, II, p. 327; III, p. 361.

[6] The Pennsylvania convention at the time of adopting the Constitution, though eleven states had still to act, appointed a committee which actually reported on the proposal to cede to Congress a seat of government. See McMaster and Stone. *op. cit.*, p. 430.

the Excise Act was passed. There could be no reasonable objection to it on constitutional grounds, for the right to levy excises is explicitly mentioned in the Constitution, but it provoked indignant opposition. The objectors in the back-country, who had been accustomed to use this liquid currency for more than their own delectation, carried their opposition so far that it was necessary at a later time (1794) to call forth troops to suppress the "whisky rebellion" in western Pennsylvania. Men claimed the natural right to drink freely without having their simple joys disturbed, and they doubtless failed to see the humor in the suggestion that they might be drinking down the national debt.

Of most importance from the viewpoint of the constitutional historian was Hamilton's plan for a national bank. On that subject he made a separate report in December, 1790. To justify the measure the Secretary had to show the advantages of a bank and its service to the government. The principal advantages he declared were the augmentation of active or productive capital, the greater facility of the government in obtaining pecuniary aids, especially in emergencies, and lastly, the increased facility in the payment of taxes. A capital of ten million dollars was proposed, one-fourth payable in specie and the remainder in certificates of the public debt; one-fifth of the capital stock was to be subscribed for by the government, that sum to be borrowed of the bank.

The proposal was of course sharply attacked. A large portion of the American people have never felt affection for banks; in those days the mysteries of the banking business were to many persons as hateful as they were obscure. In Congress Madison furnished the arguments against the constitutionality of the measure, and as usual he spoke with ability and precision.[7] Doubtless he found himself in an awkward position. He had ardently desired the organization of a real

---

[7] He called attention to the rejection in the Convention of granting Congress the power of incorporation, declaring in addition: "It appeared on the whole that the power exercised by the bill was condemned by the silence of the Constitution; was condemned by the rule of interpretation arising out of the Constitution; was condemned by its tendency to destroy the main characteristics of the Constitution; was condemned by the expositions of the friends of the Constitution whilst depending before the people; was condemned by the apparent intentions of the parties which ratified the Constitution; was condemned by the explanatory amendments proposed by Congress themselves to the Constitution." Quoted in D. R. Dewey, *Financial History of the United States,* pp. 99-100. See also Gaillard Hunt, *The Life of James Madison,* p. 202. It may be noticed that a quarter of a century later Madison signed the bill creating the Second Bank of the United States.

union; more than any other man he could be credited with the honor of forming the system which was now going into effect. But was the document which he had so ably defended in Virginia against the blasts of Henry's eloquence to be distorted by clever interpretation? We may assume his dislike of seeing nationalism and governmental authority attained by indirection; and if we think he was over-precise, we need to remember also that in Hamilton's deft, but not too delicate hands, the Constitution might be transmuted into a document quite unlike that intended by its makers.[8] Madison's opposition to Hamilton's ideas and proposals, an opposition which soon grew in intensity, has often been commented upon. He was now plainly drawing away from his companion in the recent titanic struggle for the establishment of a national government and an efficient union. In him those elements of the people who dreaded the extension of the governmental power and saw no need for banks or bonds, and who looked with foreboding upon a huge national debt, found an able and conscientious leader.

In full sympathy with Madison was the Secretary of State, a man with a strange and exceptional capacity for popular leadership, and with a decided objection to overhead government. It used to be not uncommon to attribute Madison's retirement from active coöperation with Hamilton to the machinations or the uncanny influence of Jefferson. How much we can fairly ascribe to such influence, no one can say. But it is not quite fair to assume that, because Madison favored a strong government during days of disorder when the union seemed to be in process of disintegration, he could not, unless he were converted by secret and selfish counsels, have taken a stand against what appeared to be an extravagant and unexpected interpretation of governmental authority. The government was established; that was the salient fact; it had gone into operation; and no one can now find cause for wonder in discovering differences of opinion concerning constitutional construction. Some men, anxious to keep faith, or fearing, as many did, the rise of a dominating and dictatorial government, were

---

[8] In this connection the ruminations of a contemporary are illustrative. William Maclay, a Senator from Pennsylvania, filled with the suspicions and forebodings which were by no means peculiar to himself, wrote in his *Journal*, April 4, 1790: "Hence appears plainly how much the assumption of the State debts was made a point of by the court party. In fact, the reduction of the State governments was the object in theory in framing both the Constitution and the Judiciary and in as many laws of the United States as were capable of taking a tincture of that kind. But it won't do." *Journal of William Maclay*, p. 232. ". . . I clearly see," he wrote in 1791, "that the poor goddess of liberty is likely to be hunted out of this quarter as well as the other quarters of the globe." *Ibid.*, p. 402.

not ready at once to acquiesce silently in the exercise of every power which the acute Secretary of the Treasury thought advisable. Madison's opposition was not an entirely new attitude or based on unreasoning jealousy or foolish foreboding. The Constitutional Convention had refused to grant even a restricted and limited power to create a corporation.[9] It would have been strange indeed, had Madison openly advocated under the Constitution a power which he knew the Convention had refused to consign to the new government.

The bank bill passed both houses in the early days of 1791, and was approved by the President (February 25). But before signing, Washington asked for the opinion of others, and this request brought forth two able state papers which presented two conflicting principles of constitutional construction. Jefferson, finding the bill unconstitutional, laid down the doctrine of strict construction; Hamilton advocated broad or liberal construction. Each paper may properly be considered the classical exposition of the respective theories set forth. All the ingenuity of later days fell short of discovering more cogent or adroit argument.

Jefferson quoted the tenth amendment and declared that the incorporation of a bank was not one of the delegated powers; it was not one of those specially enumerated powers; nor was it within the "general phrases" of the Constitution wherein authority is granted to impose taxes to provide for the general welfare and to make all laws necessary and proper for carrying the enumerated powers into execution. He pointed out that the general welfare clause bestowed on Congress power, not to do anything it might please to provide for the general welfare, but only to lay taxes for that purpose.[10] The necessary and proper clause he interpreted by an emphasis on "necessary"; all the enumerated powers could be carried into execution without a bank, and it was therefore not necessary and consequently not authorized. Bank bills might be a more convenient vehicle for payment

[9] Madison, in the Convention, moved that Congress be given power " 'to grant charters of incorporation where the interest of the U. S. might require & the legislative provisions of individual States may be incompetent'." Farrand, *Records*, II, p. 615.

[10] "To lay and collect taxes, duties, imposts, and excises, to pay the debts and provide for the common defense and general welfare of the United States. . . ." Art. I, sec. 8, para. 1.
"To make all laws which shall be necessary and proper for carrying into execution the foregoing powers. . . ." Art. I, sec. 8, para. 18.
This must be held to-day a position theoretically sound, though it sometimes seems as if the theory were lost in the mists of practical politics.

of taxes than treasury orders; but a little difference in the degree of convenience could not constitute the necessity which the Constitution mentioned. In this last statement we find the dangerously weak link in his whole argument; if a government cannot use means which it considers suitable for exercising its powers, and if it cannot be guided by considerations of convenience and of ease in the management of its undoubted authority, then it is almost hopelessly restricted. For the captious critic might without difficulty find that any or every proposed measure is unnecessary and hence unconstitutional because some other measure or proceeding might be used. No government strictly confined by such a doctrine could function.

Hamilton's argument was a masterly exposition of the theories of a broad and liberal interpretation of the Constitution. His general conclusions were those on which the government has acted from its foundation and which are still supposed to be effective. He did not dare to announce what appears in these latter days to be the opinion of no inconsiderable number of people: that the federal government can legally do anything and everything thought to be for the general welfare. He did not deny, of course, that the government is one of enumerated powers. At the outset, the astute young Secretary laid down the principle, which he declared to be inherent in the very definition of government, "That every power vested in a government is in its nature *sovereign,* and includes, by *force* of the *term,* a right to employ all the *means* requisite and fairly applicable to the attainment of the *ends* of such power, and which are not precluded by restrictions and exceptions specified in the Constitution, or not immoral, or not contrary to the *essential ends* of political society."

The critical question concerned the right to erect a corporation; Hamilton contended, as it is "unquestionably incident to *sovereign power* to erect corporations," it is consequently incident "to *that* of the United States, in *relation* to the *objects* intrusted to the management of the government." In this portion of the argument he was approaching dangerously near to the idea that, if other governments had the power to establish corporations, the United States government must be supposed to have it. But he did not pass over into that forbidden territory. He found in the Constitution implied as well as express powers, and for the sake of accuracy he declared there were also *"resulting powers",* which he defined as those resulting from the whole mass of the powers of government and from the nature of political society.[11] ". . . *necessary*", he maintained, "often means no more than *needful, requisite, incidental, useful,* or *conducive to.* . . . The *degree* in which a measure is necessary, can never be a *test* of the legal right to adopt it; that must be a matter of opinion, and can only be a *test* of expediency." He then propounded his doctrine of implied powers in words that needed no addition in the future, when men defended liberal construction. Speaking of the test of the constitutionality of an act, he said, "This criterion is the *end,* to which the measure relates as a *mean.* If the *end* be clearly comprehended within any of the specified powers, and if the measure have an obvious relation to that *end,* and is not forbidden by any particular provision of the Constitution, it may safely be deemed to come within the compass of the national authority." [12]

These two doctrines or principles of constitutional interpretation underlay many of the debates and controversies in the decades that followed their first pronouncement. It is sometimes said that they constituted the continuing foundations and principles of parties; that the line of cleavage between contesting parties was the line marking off the advocates of broad construction from the defenders of the outer ramparts of narrow construction. But obviously such a generalization is not tenable. Devotion to either one of these doctrines, even if it seems to occupy a particular shrine and be worshiped by the faithful of a party, must at best be of secondary, not primary, importance; for men do not swear fealty to a mode of constitutional interpretation for its own sake; they do not bow down to an abstraction of constitutional law. Jefferson, for example, was a strict constructionist (at least

[11] Hamilton mentioned as an example of resulting powers the right of the United States to possess sovereign jurisdiction over conquered territory. Compare Marshall's opinion in The American Insurance Co. *v.* Canter, 1 Peters 511 (1828).

[12] Note the following from the opinion of the Court in Kansas *v.* Colorado, 206 U. S. 46 (1907): "The last paragraph of the section which authorizes Congress to make all laws which shall be necessary and proper for carrying into execution the foregoing powers, and all other powers vested by this Constitution in the Government of the United States, or in any department or office thereof, is not the delegation of a new and independent power, but simply provision for making effective the powers theretofore mentioned." *Ibid.,* 88. "But, as our national territory has been enlarged, we have within our borders extensive tracts of arid lands which ought to be reclaimed, and it may well be that no power is adequate for their reclamation other than that of the National Government. But if no such power has been granted, none can be exercised." *Ibid.,* 91-92. This case appears to repudiate the doctrine, which had certain advocates in the early twentieth century, to the effect that an object not within the competence of any one state is, in consequence, within the scope of federal authority.

part of the time), not because he was a narrow-minded technician, but because he had definite ideas of social needs and because he had a social philosophy. Hamilton wanted to do things; he was not primarily burning candles before the altar of a disembodied principle of constitutional interpretation. Parties, furthermore, have the qualities of a chameleon; they easily change color; and when a party is in power, things which shocked its constitutional conscience when it was in opposition appear harmless and beneficial. It is so easy to transfer the lares and penates of daily worship from one niche to another.

Almost from the very beginning of the government the Constitution was vigorously defended both by those who believed that granted power should be used freely and by those who feared lest constitutional limits be exceeded; no one seriously criticized it. Both groups, differing in their opinion as to the limits of constitutional authority, buckled on the armor of orthodox righteousness in defense of the Constitution itself. All this, of course, was of tremendous influence in conserving, and, on the whole, in stabilizing constitutional government. This "worship of the Constitution", this apotheosis of a sheet of parchment, has often aroused the curiosity and the wonder of the outside world; but man must, it seems, worship something, and the American man soon paid reverence to the document which symbolized to him union, the product of stress and storm, a noble achievement of which he was fully prepared to boast. Debates and quarrels about construction of the Constitution made for permanency by lifting the document itself beyond the reach of ordinary party evaluation and beyond the assaults of malignant malcontents.

At the very beginning of the government Congress took up the task of establishing the judicial system. The framers of the Constitution had left to Congress a large measure of discretion. The general principles are laid down in the Constitution but the details are not given. The extent of the judicial power is stated in broad and comprehensive terms; the power is "vested in one Supreme Court, and in such inferior courts as Congress may from time to time ordain and establish";[13] but the Constitution does not state the number of judges and does not make it obligatory on Congress to establish inferior

[13] The absence of explicit provision for inferior courts is doubtless due to the uncertainty of the framers about the advisability of explicitness. Then there was a difference of opinion in regard to the need for any inferior courts. See the discussion in the Convention, June 5, 1787.

courts. The task lay with Congress to work out a system of courts and to establish the system by law. The duty was one of great importance, and especially important was the task of designating the relationship between the state courts and the federal courts, a subject on which there had been considerable discussion in the past. The Judiciary Act, which is attributed chiefly to the skill of Oliver Ellsworth, was passed in September, 1789. It remained for over a century without vital alteration, and the more general and critical principles are still in force.

The Supreme Court, as established by the act, consisted of one chief justice and five associate justices. Thirteen districts were established, in each of which there was to be a district court.[14] Three circuits were provided for; in each was to be held a court consisting of any two justices of the Supreme Court and the district judge. To the district courts was assigned cognizance of crimes of an inferior order and they were given exclusive original cognizance of all civil causes of admiralty and maritime jurisdiction.[15] The circuit courts were to have original jurisdiction, concurrent with the courts of the states, of all suits of a civil nature at common law or in equity, where the sum involved was more than five hundred dollars, and the suit was between a citizen of a state in which the suit was brought and a citizen of another state. To the circuit courts was assigned exclusive cognizance of crimes and offenses cognizable under the authority of the United States, except where the act otherwise provided, and also concurrent jurisdiction with the district courts of criminal cases which might be there instituted. Provision was made for removal of causes from a state court to a circuit court under certain conditions.[16] Appeals might be made, by writ of error, from a district to a circuit court, and by like process from a circuit court to the Supreme Court.[17]

Of paramount significance are the provisions of the act concerning review by the federal Supreme Court of judgments and decrees of state tribunals. This subject, which is covered by section twenty-five of the act, was in later years the center of acute and bitter controversy. The Constitution does not *explicitly* grant to the federal judiciary any

---

[14] There were then eleven states in the union. Each was made a district. Maine, then a part of Massachusetts, was also made a district, as was the Kentucky region, then a part of Virginia.

[15] *Statutes at Large,* I, ch. 20, sec. 9.

[16] The reader should notice that this does not refer to an *appeal* from a state court, but for removal of a cause at an early stage in the proceedings. *Ibid.,* sec. 12.

[17] *Ibid.,* sec. 22. The text above does not attempt to give in detail the extent and character of the jurisdiction prescribed by the statute; such portions of the act as appear especially important are selected.

such right to examine, review, or affirm the decisions of state courts. The Judiciary Act established this authority in the following manner: a case could be carried to the Supreme Court for review (1) when a decision of the highest state court "in which a decision in the suit could be had" was against the validity of a treaty or statute of the United States, or an authority exercised under the United States; (2) when the validity of a statute of a state or an authority exercised by a state had been drawn into question on the ground of its being repugnant to the Constitution, laws, or treaties of the United States, and the decision of the state court be in favor of the validity; (3) when there was drawn into question the construction of any clause of the Constitution or of a treaty or statute of the United States, and the decision was against the title, right, privilege, or exemption claimed by either party.

An examination of this statement, which at first sight appears perplexing, shows that the purpose was to provide that a state decision could be carried to the Supreme Court for review only if the state court was charged with failing to give full effect to the Constitution, laws, or treaties of the United States. And this fact carries us back again to what I have called the chief problem of the critical period, the problem of finding a method by which there would be assurance that the states would fulfill their obligations. The obligation to uphold the Constitution and the structure of the union was specifically thrown upon state judges. But how could there be any certainty that the judges would not uphold a state law, even though it be contrary to the "law of the land", or would not deny to a litigant at the bar a privilege claimed to belong to him under the federal Constitution, law, or treaty? To establish such certainty, or at least to provide for such assurance as federal judicial oversight would furnish, the Judiciary Act included the system of review of state decisions.

The Judiciary Act does not indicate any objection to a decision by a state court refusing to recognize the validity of a federal statute; but it does provide for a review to test the legality of the decision; it seems, indeed, to take for granted that such a decision might properly be rendered, and from this we are led to conclude that the federal Supreme Court could agree with the state tribunal as well as disagree; therefore the Judiciary Act, even though it makes no specific declaration of the power, assumes the right of a court, either state or national, to declare congressional acts void. As this fundamental statute was enacted by men, some of whom had been active in the

Federal Convention, we are entitled to gather from it evidence of the intention of the framers to recognize this important judicial power. That fact should be taken into consideration by those who even to-day question the constitutional right of any court to declare an act void, or, to use the words of James Otis of an earlier day, pass it "into disuse".[18]

[18] See C. A. Beard, *The Supreme Court and the Constitution,* where this subject is treated at length.

CHAPTER XVII

THE ESTABLISHMENT OF THE EXECUTIVE DEPART-MENTS AND THE DEVELOPMENT OF THE CABINET

We must now briefly present the main facts and influences which produced the president's cabinet. This body, though it is not provided for by the Constitution, is now and has been almost from the beginning of the government a conspicuous portion of the actual political system. For an understanding of its rise, it is necessary to go back to the time of the Revolution and the old Congress and also to see the experiences of the Confederate period, which gave their lessons to the men of that generation. Even a brief examination of the rise of the cabinet as an advisory council brings into view the very character of the presidency, as the office and its duties emerged and as it took fairly definite form and being in the early years.

During nearly the whole course of the Revolution, the general business of the government had been carried on by committees and boards, or possibly one might better say, not carried on. The clumsy and inefficient methods taught their lesson, however; by 1781 Congress from its own ineptitude had learned enough to provide for departments, each in charge of a single officer.[1] The titles of these officials were Secretary for Foreign Affairs,[2] Superintendent of Finance, Secretary at War, and Secretary of Marine. The system suffered various lapses and

---

[1] Secretary for Foreign Affairs, January 10, 1781; Superintendent of Finance, Secretary at War, and Secretary of Marine, February 7, 1781. *Journals of Congress* (1823 ed.), III, pp. 564, 575. The marine department did not last long, its duties being turned over to the Superintendent of Finance. *Ibid.,* III, p. 665. "It is positively pathetic to follow Congress through its aimless wanderings in search of a system for the satisfactory management of its executive departments. At no period between 1774 and 1781 can we find it pursuing any consistent line of action with reference to them. A humble committee served as the common origin of all. With the exception of the Committee of Foreign Affairs, they developed independently into ,boards, and afterwards each was tossed about and tinkered at different times and under different circumstances." J. C. Guggenheimer, "The Development of the Executive Departments, 1775-1789," *Essays in the Constitutional History of the United States* (J. F. Jameson, ed.), p. 148.

[2] Changed in 1782 to Secretary to the United States of America for the Department of Foreign Affairs. H. B. Learned, *The President's Cabinet,* pp. 53-54.

238

modifications, partly caused by the difficulty in getting suitable persons to accept or carry on the offices. But, in an uncertain way, experience had proved the desirability of individual responsibility in administrative work.

Robert Morris held the office of Superintendent of Finance from May, 1781 until November, 1784. About the time of Morris's retirement, John Jay became Foreign Secretary and held the position until after the establishment of the new government. Henry Knox, becoming Secretary at War in 1785, was also in office when the Confederation expired. The services of Morris and especially of Jay must have made fairly clear the idea of executive officers, with administrative assistants, and with considerable independence in the ordinary conduct of their duties.[3] When Washington assumed office there were only two department heads holding positions inherited from the old régime —Jay and Knox.

The Constitution contains no more than incidental references to executive departments. The president is authorized to "require the opinion in writing of the principal officer in each of the executive departments upon any subject relating to the duties of their respective offices. . . ." The other reference is found in the clause granting Congress the power to vest the appointment of inferior officers "in the President alone, in the courts of law, or in the heads of departments." [4] It follows by necessary implication that departments with a principal officer in each are contemplated by the Constitution; but the number and duties of such departments are left to the determination of Congress at its discretion.

The words of the Constitution and the experiences of the Confederation were a sufficient guide to Congress. By acts passed in 1789, state, war, and treasury departments, and the office of attorney-general [5] were established. At the head of each department was a secretary. The departments of state and war were called executive departments, and the secretaries were directed to perform such duties as should be intrusted to them by the president. The treasury was not

<hr>

[3] See *Ibid.*, p. 59.

[4] Reference may also be made to the Constitution, Art. I, sec. 8, para. 18.

[5] The attorney-general was considered a member of the cabinet when it got well under way; but not before 1870 did he become the head of the department of justice. The post office went on at first on about the same basis as under the Confederation. Samuel Osgood was appointed Postmaster-General in 1789 and the office was more fully provided for in 1794. The postmaster-general was not at first admitted as a regular member of the cabinet; the department was not explicitly called an executive department until 1874.

called an executive department; the secretary, it seems, was thought of as standing in a peculiar relationship to Congress; he was to perform all such services relative to the finances as he should be directed to perform, and he was to "make report and give information to either branch of the Legislature, in person or in writing, (as he may be required,) respecting all matters referred to him by the Senate or House of Representatives, or which shall appertain to his office. . . ." If it were intended to place the treasury under the special guardianship of Congress, such intention was doubtless due to the experience of colonial days. In the royal and proprietary colonies, the executive and the legislative branches of the legislature were not unlikely to be in opposition, or at least to have different points of view, especially on fiscal matters; and little by little the assemblies had gained a large degree of control over the colonial treasuries.

The wording of the act establishing the treasury department indicates, therefore, the possibility of the development of a system in which the secretary would be very directly responsible to Congress or subject to some sort of very immediate control. On the other hand—though this seems rather fanciful—he might have become a minister directing or attempting to direct the course of financial legislation. Had the early Congress summoned the secretary or allowed him to appear in person, the intimacy between his office and the legislature would, presumably, have been greater than any association based on written reports. The first Secretary was eager enough to lead; but he was not given the opportunity of advocating his measures on the floor. He appears at times to have looked upon his office as that of minister extraordinary, and he had great influence on the development of the executive power; in the early years he shaped in considerable measure the financial policy of Congress. We are not dealing with mere shadows when we contemplate the possibility of the establishment of practices, growing out of the intimacy between Congress and the treasury, which would have affected the strength and character of the presidency; a divided or far from unified executive might have been the result.[6]

---

[6] Learned points out that there are three underlying principles of the American presidency: (1) unity in the executive power; (2) responsibility to the people for the execution of the law; (3) discretionary power in the president to direct and remove his assistants. Learned, *op. cit.*, p. 379. Each one of these is in some measure the result of developing practices. The second obtained its special significance forty years and more after the Constitution was adopted. The third, now generally accepted, was not established without some verbal turmoil. The three are mutually or reciprocally supporting.

Hamilton and Jefferson, the two leading men among Washington's advisers, deserve special attention. Around them and their opinions gathers in considerable measure the constitutional and political history of the last decade of the century. They also represent with very peculiar distinctness certain differences of mind and underlying principles of action—such attitudes and tendencies, be they of one kind or the other, as commonly affect men and women in their political and social relations. Of Hamilton something has already been said in these pages. At the time of life when most boys are engaged in the aimless frivolities of adolescence, Hamilton was deeply interested in the cause of the Revolution. He was a man of very marked mental gifts, an able lawyer, with a decided capacity for financial affairs. He was indefatigable and earnest, striking direct and unerring blows, leading his followers with no apparent misgivings and with no doubt of the validity of his considered opinions. For years he had been deeply concerned by the distress and the inefficiency of the Confederation; his anxiety was caused by a native dislike for confusion and a native talent for system, and withal he belonged to that small body of wide-visioned men whose country was America and who did not enshroud themselves in the clouds of petty local politics. He was a continentalist, a nationalist, by temperament and by training. In some ways he was a natural leader, but, though not without a degree of personal charm, there was within him a certain headstrong determination, a product, it may be, of his own logical talent. His assurance and the very qualities of his genius appear to have made him incapable of wide and appealing popular leadership. As so often happens in human life, his strength was his weakness.

Of Jefferson, too, only a word can be said, though many words would be insufficient because his character was so complex and his interests so varied. Primarily he was not of the administrative temper; a learned lawyer and a practical politician, he was fundamentally a philosopher. He, too, was profoundly interested in the success of America, but he did not see success in a smoothly-working governmental system or in administrative devices; he had come to distrust governmental machinery and to place his confidence in the primary impulses of his fellow men. This confidence, it may be the part of caution to say, was a part, the creative part, of his philosophy; but in practice he was at times not confiding, but suspicious; his philosophy taught him confidence in man; his experience or, it may be, a sensitive temperament, sometimes made him suspicious of men, the actual men of affairs with whom he had to deal. Though reared in the solitudes of Virginia, he was, after some years of residence at Paris, a man of the world. He had given his mind to the study of human affairs, not so much to the science of orderly and stable government, as to the science or philosophy of human well-being. Conditions in Europe shocked and antagonized him. In the early days of the Revolution he had arrayed himself with a radical anti-British element, and in the years before he went to France he had been engaged in the task of freeing Virginia from the hold of the big plantation owners. To class him with Clinton or any of the other localists, whose minds were glued to immediate interests and who were incapable of seeing beyond state limits, is a radical blunder; what he feared was the establishment in America of a burdensome, expensive, overhead government, aping, in its manners and in its attitude toward the common man, the governments of Europe, against whose impositions his whole nature and its accordant philosophy were arrayed. His thinking was national—or international —rather than provincial; but because he had no liking for elaborate legalism, he failed at times to see with proper clarity that the very success of popular government depended upon the stability of the American union.

Comparisons are odious; and they may be especially so when great men are compared. Hamilton and Jefferson were, by any standards, great men. The country needed both of them. It needed Hamilton's talent for organization, his conception of national authority and of efficiency. It needed Jefferson and his sympathy for the genius of the young, fresh country just breaking away from the bonds of colonialism and entering upon the perils and trials of democratic government. It needed Hamilton's administrative skill and his fervid nationalism; it also needed Jefferson's vision, his comprehension of the needs and the aspirations of the common folks, the farmers, the plain people, who never to the end lost confidence in him because he continued confident of them. We cannot see how America could have become the America we know without both of them. One can scarcely over-emphasize the influence of Hamilton in the establishment of the governmental system. Jefferson—or Jeffersonism—embodied the hopeful and adventurous America which was coming into existence and gaining a consciousness of itself.

So far we have been concerned with the organization of executive departments distinctly provided for by the Constitution. A consideration of the origin and development of the cabinet as we know it to-day must now command our attention. In the Constitutional Convention there had been considerable discussion about the desirability of a council of revision, a privy council, a council of state—some advisory body to act with the president.[7] Such plans were natural accompaniments of an unwillingness to establish an executive free from oversight and dangerously competent. The institutions of the colonies, the provisions of some of the state constitutions, and perhaps also the royal council of Britain, probably influenced those members of the Convention who desired a check upon presidential power. The Senate, because of its share in appointments and in the making of treaties, constituted to some extent a check on the executive and was, probably, especially in treaty-making, supposed to furnish advice and consent. But nothing that we may term a cabinet council was provided for in the Constitution. From actual conditions, therefore, and from the practical necessities of the case as problems of government presented themselves, the cabinet came into existence.

The cabinet is a well-known political institution in America; or, to speak more correctly, the term is one in common use. If we mean by the word "cabinet" a council or advisory body—and that is the ordinary connotation—the institution is entirely unknown to formal law, either to constitutional or statute law; it is a product of history, a part of our unwritten constitutional system. The term "cabinet" in a congressional enactment first appeared in 1907;[8] but the word was then used almost incidentally and cannot be considered as indicating the intention to establish the cabinet as a body—in any technical sense a legal institution.[9] Concerning some of its customary characteristics, one has to speak with caution. It is to-day made up of the heads of the various executive departments; it meets frequently and discusses matters of general interest and policy. Its conclusions, if it reaches any, are not binding upon the president; he is not under any legal necessity of calling the members together or of asking their opinions; but the habit of group consultation is an established habit, and a president neglecting consultation and acting quite without advice would be considered as violating tradition, possibly one should say good manners. No one would venture to say that there must be unanimity of opinion; but

[7] See especially the discussion on September 7, 1787, and the approval of the provision to give the president authority to call for the opinions of the heads of departments.

[8] Learned, *op. cit.*, p. 157.

[9] It may be questioned whether Congress could establish a cabinet by law.

there is a certain or uncertain degree of general loyalty to the purposes of the president; there is a distinct or nebulous administrative policy or tendency which no member is expected openly to flout. The members are the president's appointees and are naturally expected to work harmoniously with him. A cabinet officer can, of course, in the seclusion of the cabinet meetings, express his opposition to a proposed line of conduct; but public opposition, even if it should have no serious consequences, is looked upon with disfavor. If he finds himself in substantial disagreement with the president and has conscientious objections to the presidential policy, he is expected to retire from office. The essential unity of the executive forces must be maintained. Congress cannot by legislation place any official in the cabinet, though when a department is created the secretary is by tradition and custom a member of the body; [10] the president can do without cabinet meetings, refuse to summon some secretaries, invite the vice-president to participate, in short, legally speaking, do as he thinks best.

The fact of meeting, the giving of advice and the interchange of opinions, though these things are important, are not the matters of most consequence. The most significant thing is the most intangible— the expression of the vague and indefinable need of administrative or executive coherence. This need, as we shall see in a moment, came clearly, though gradually, to view in the course of the first twelve years; when we enter upon Jefferson's administration we find ourselves in the presence of a body of men with similar views and enthusiasms, not merely a number of executive officers, but a body of councilors with a common loyalty. This, of course, could not have come to very full realization until there were policies calling for executive judgment and discretion, marking off one set of men from another, until, in other words, there were parties, even if the parties were not fully equipped with all the paraphernalia and common loyalties of the modern party system.

Washington, it is sometimes said, strangely appointed to his cabinet two men, Jefferson and Hamilton, representing different parties—an unfortunate statement, for at the beginning there was no cabinet and there were no parties, at least no parties fully-organized and recognized. The President could have had no idea that he was to have a cabinet. In his administrations both of these institutions began to take form, both of them the product of the new tasks and the new opportunities of popular government. Theoretically, the heads of the

[10] The postmaster-general was first made a cabinet member by Jackson (1829).

various departments, though subject to the President's orders, could have gone along independently and separately; theoretically, too, the new government could have operated without parties; as a matter of fact, the men making the Constitution were apparently ignorant of the party as we now use the term. But as issues arose, as violent differences of opinion developed, as the possibilities of popular contention—the garrulous companion of democratic government—came upon the scene, the need of something like unity in the executive came to light. On the surface, heads of the departments were executive officers, and only executive officers, with the duty of giving separate advice or information when it was called for; but the President needed counsel and he needed support; he needed it more than he did the haggling and disputatious argument of men whom he called together for advice.

We must not suppose that at the beginning Washington thought of the chief executive officers as his sole advisers; much less did he consider them as a council with fairly consistent or tangible policies. In the very early years of his presidency he consulted various people, some of them not in executive office. In 1790, he asked for written opinions not only from the three secretaries but also from John Adams and John Jay—the Vice-President and the Chief Justice. Thereafter he occasionally asked Adams for written advice.[11] He even asked Madison to prepare for him a veto of the bank bill (1791), which he might use if he decided against the measure. The President naturally needed expert assistance in solving difficult questions of constitutional construction. Concerning problems of foreign affairs, over which the Constitution gave him great authority, there was abundant opportunity for differences of opinion, and there was need of deciding upon a policy, even the need of deciding upon the extent and character of the President's power. It was necessary to take affirmative action and not merely to carry out legislative orders. Amid the perplexities arising from the French treaties in 1793, Washington requested the federal judges to give their opinions on the legal problems involved. The judges, however, declined to answer the questions propounded.

During the absence of the President from the seat of government

[11] Learned, *op. cit.*, pp. 120-121. Learned's accumulation of evidence on the early growth of the cabinet is particularly helpful. See ch. V. See also M. L. Hinsdale, *A History of the President's Cabinet.* It is noteworthy that when Jefferson became Vice-President he declared privately that he considered his office "as constitutionally confined to legislative functions" and that he could not take part "in executive consultations, even were it proposed. . . ." Letter from Jefferson to Elbridge Gerry, May 13, 1797. See Jefferson, *Works* (federal ed.), VIII, p. 284.

there was special need of interchange of opinions among members of what we now call the "administration". Accordingly we find Washington writing (April 4, 1791) to the secretaries—the Attorney-General not being mentioned—asking them to consult together upon any serious and important cases that might arise, and to determine whether his own presence was necessary. He suggested the advisability of calling upon Adams to participate in the consultation, if Adams had not left the seat of government. The three secretaries and the Vice-President met and discussed various matters. Jefferson sent a report to Washington.[12] This was the beginning, as far as we know, and the first of what before long were called cabinet meetings.

In the next year (1792) there were other meetings. Of one, Jefferson says: "Mar. 31. A meeting at the P's, present Th: J., A.H., H.K. & E.R. The subject was the resoln of the H. of Repr. of Mar. 27. to appt a commee to inquire into the causes of the failure of the late expdn under Maj. Genl. St. Clair. . . ." In 1793, consultations were sufficiently frequent to justify us in saying that the habit had been established. For another year or two the opinion of the Vice-President was occasionally asked, but the cabinet normally consisted of the secretaries and the Attorney-General. In 1793 the word "cabinet" began to be used with more or less frequency.

Harmony and a common understanding among the members of the cabinet did not prevail. The differences between Hamilton and Jefferson developed into animosities. The latter surrendered his office at the end of 1793. Hamilton and Knox remained about a year longer. Thereafter there appears to have been comparative peace, though Randolph, who had become Secretary of State, made his contributions to the President's vexations and anxieties. After his disappearance from the scene (1795), there was no occasion for much unbecoming quarreling or clandestine intrigue. Washington wrote (September 27, 1795): "I shall not, whilst I have the honor to administer the government, bring a man into any office of consequence knowingly, whose political tenets are adverse to the measures, which the general government are pursuing; for this, in my opinion, would be a sort of political suicide."

This pronouncement is often taken as a declaration of Washington's recognition of parties and even of his conscious affiliation with the Federalists. That may be so; but the conclusion must be reached only with suspicion of its correctness. Certainly, however, he had come

[12] See Jefferson, *Works* (federal ed.), VI, p. 243 ff.

to see that a reasonable degree of harmony and common purpose among his chief advisers was a necessity. After his experiences with Randolph, the need of having men in the principal offices who would support and not mangle his policies is to us so plain that there is no necessity of accounting for his sentiment by attributing it to party devotion or to a newly-awakened belief in the party system. The time had come when the presidential office must be considered to have a policy which it must attempt to follow consistently as issues arose. In carrying out that policy, the president must be able to rely on the loyalty and the intelligent coöperation of those with whom he consulted and who had the duty of carrying out the policies determined upon. Washington's tolerance of varying opinion and his desire to call into requisition the intelligence of others were characteristic of him. And probably tolerance was safer in those early days than any set determination to have no one about him but those in all respects determined to see only one side of every question; but the executive, a unified executive, was at all events taking shape, created by the compelling necessities of the case. The disturbances in Adams's cabinet and the need, once more displayed, of coherence and essential harmony, it is not necessary to dwell upon here. Those conditions brought forth again the fact that the president must have about him men in personal sympathy with him and his policies and ready to carry his program faithfully into operation.

CHAPTER XVIII

THE ESTABLISHMENT OF THE AUTHORITY OF THE EXECUTIVE IN FOREIGN AFFAIRS

The provision in the Constitution concerning the power to make treaties was the product of considerable discussion in the Federal Convention. The problem of determining where this important power should rest presented serious difficulty. At that time the fisheries and our relations with Spain were matters of immediate interest; there was anxiety, especially in some portions of the south, lest the navigation of the Mississippi be surrendered and lest the government be too complaisant in dealing with Spanish claims and ambitions.[1] One cannot say just how much the anxieties or misgivings of the moment influenced the delegates; but they probably did influence them to some extent. However that may be, checks upon the free exercise of the treaty-making power were inevitable.[2] The committee of detail, reporting August 6, bestowed the power upon the Senate alone; but this provision was at length changed, and the power was granted to the president by and with the concurrence of two-thirds of the Senate. This provision was placed in the second article of the Constitution, the article dealing with the executive authority. That the Senate should serve as a guard or check upon the president, lest he act ignorantly or

[1] See, for example, the speeches of Gouverneur Morris and Hugh Williamson on September 8, 1787. See also, Charles Warren, *The Making of the Constitution*, p. 656 ff.

[2] A grant of this exceedingly important power to the president alone was, for that time, quite impossible. There was too much fear of one-man power. In the Convention James Wilson even proposed joining the House with the Senate. He also declared that the requirement of a two-thirds vote in the Senate would put it into the power of a minority to control the will of a majority, and that the same provision would allow a minority to perpetuate war (September 7, 8). In the state conventions there was considerable contention over the treaty-making provision. "In view of the sentiment which has developed in recent years against requiring more than a majority of the Senate to ratify a treaty, it is interesting to notice that, in 1788, much of the opposition to the treaty clause was based on the feeling that the two thirds requirement was too small." Warren, *op. cit.*, p. 658. Virginia proposed an amendment requiring for certain kinds of treaties "the concurrence of three fourths of the whole number of the members of both Houses respectively."

corruptly, is plain; to what extent he was expected to treat the Senate as an advisory council, which he should continually consult and which he should at all times keep informed of the progress of negotiations, is not so evident.

It is common now to think of the Senate's right to concur or to refuse when a treaty is laid before it. The extent to which the president may take the Senate, or more usually the committee on foreign relations, into his confidence, formally or informally, during the processes of negotiations, depends upon circumstances and, indeed, upon the president's inclination. The president carries on diplomatic correspondence; and this duty necessarily involves the power of communicating with foreign governments during all the proceedings preliminary to the formal concurrence of the Senate. He discusses with the foreign government, a party to the proposed treaty, any modifications which the Senate may have insisted upon, in case he consents to renew negotiations after such modifications are proposed. Ratification, when the terms of the treaty are agreed upon, is also a presidential prerogative. It is hardly necessary to add that the negotiations with foreign governments are, in practice, carried on by the secretary of state, or by a minister or a commission, all of whom are the president's servants. These practices and principles, which we now accept as part of the constitutional system, are the products of interpretation as the necessity for interpretation and action arose. The main principles came out fairly clearly during Washington's presidency.

At the beginning Washington believed oral communications with the Senate indispensable; but his first attempt brought forth difficulties. In the summer of 1789 he appeared before the Senate, accompanied by the Secretary of War. He wished to advise with them on the terms of the treaty to be negotiated with the southern Indians, which the Secretary was prepared to explain. William Maclay, a Senator from Pennsylvania, on whose *Journal* we are largely dependent for our knowledge of the activities of the Senate in the early days, says that Washington "told us bluntly that he had called on us for our advice and consent. . . ." Just what the bluntness consisted in we do not know, but probably it was a product of Maclay's own suspicions. He and presumably some others who were not so critical and so absurdly sensitive were fearful lest they be trodden upon. Some portions of the treaty were postponed for later consideration. Robert Morris, at the suggestion of Maclay, moved reference of the matter to a committee, and that method of procedure the Senate decided upon. Washington, so Maclay records, "started up in a violent fret" and said, "This defeats every purpose of my coming here"—which was indeed the fact. He therefore soon withdrew "with a discontented air. Had it been any other man than the man whom I wish to regard as the first character in the world, I would have said, with sullen dignity." [3] Two days later the discussion was continued and the business was concluded. But thereafter neither Washington nor any of his successors undertook to obtain advice and consent by personal consultation.

If the senators wished to follow legislative methods, to appoint a committee, and in fact refuse to consult with the President for fear lest their own dignity be infringed upon, there was nothing to be done about it; and if they must make speeches, nothing could prevent them. But as a result, presidents have been left free to carry forward the whole process of negotiations and of treaty-making until the finished document is laid before the Senate for its concurrence. Maclay, cherishing a super-heated fear of executive power, would have been surprised probably, had he been told that the Senate was in fact surrendering in considerable measure its right to be consulted at various stages, and that the president was to be left a large amount of unhampered freedom. After this encounter with the Senate, Washington endeavored, by sending communications, though not appearing in person, to treat the Senate as an advisory body in the ordinary sense of the word. But conditions were making against the establishment of the practice as a formal necessity. The most critical treaty of his administration, the Jay treaty of 1794, seems to have been submitted without previous consultation or communication. [4] The conditions of that eventful year were fraught with peril; and the danger of war and internal commotion was too imminent to admit of long delay, interminable harangues, and ill-natured strife.

When war between France and Britain broke out in 1793, grave problems arose. The treaties with France, which had been made during the Revolution, contained embarrassing commitments. If they should be carried out with scrupulous regard for all their obligations, the

[3] *Journal of William Maclay*, pp. 128-131. Italics of the original omitted.

[4] A brief treatment of the treaty-making power may be found in J. M. Mathews, *The Conduct of American Foreign Relations*. See especially pp. 140-148. In later years, the president in a few instances communicated with the Senate before negotiations were completed, and even consulted the Senate, though not personally present. President Wilson went before the Senate to give a formal address July 10, 1919. *Congressional Record*, 66 Cong., 1 sess., p. 2336 ff. See, for examples of consultation, S. B. Crandall, *Treaties, Their Making and Enforcement* (Columbia University Studies in History, etc., XXI, no. 1), p. 59 ff.

country would find itself at war with Britain, the main result of which, we may justly assume, would be ruin. We do not need to consider at any length the ethical propriety of disregarding a treaty; it is not a question for constitutional history; but anyone knowing the plans brought by Genêt, the French minister, will realize that conditions prevailed which appeared, and appear even more strongly now, to relieve the administration from any reasonable accusation of bad faith and stubborn ingratitude.

In reaching a decision concerning the stand to be taken by the administration, differences arose in the cabinet. Sympathies with one combatant or the other were too intense to allow complete objective and unimpassioned consideration of the problem. But as a matter of fact, despite differences, there was substantial agreement on certain essentials. The cabinet unanimously agreed that a minister from the French Republic should be received and that a proclamation, now commonly called a proclamation of neutrality, should be issued; that was the heart of the matter. Jefferson put forward an able statement of the inviolability of treaties; he cited plentiful authorities; but even he confessed that "if performance becomes *self-destructive* to the party, the law of self-preservation overrules the laws of obligation to others." [5] He believed renunciation or open disregard of the French treaties should be postponed at least until actual peril was manifest. Hamilton believed the United States would be justified in ignoring the treaties on sundry grounds, especially because the government of France was quite different from the one with which the treaties had been made, and because the French were quite plainly the aggressive combatants. At first he did not advocate the complete and open renunciation of the treaties, but desired that before the French minister should be received, he should be apprised of the intention to reserve for future consideration the question whether the operation of the treaties should be suspended. [6] The Constitution expressly gives the

---

[5] *Works* (federal ed.), VII, p. 286. "The danger which absolves us must be great, inevitable & imminent." *Ibid.,* p. 287.

[6] "Jefferson . . . disapproved of connecting the reception of the minister with any reservation on the treaties, even if it should be decided to make such a reservation. In the latter case he thought the suspension should be a separate act. He denied that the reception of the minister had anything to do with the applicability of the treaties, and that such a qualified reception was necessary to protect the interest of the United States." C. M. Thomas, *American Neutrality in 1793,* pp. 72-73. It is worthy of note that Washington decided to receive the French minister without any qualifications. "We are not permitted to know the relative influence which the various arguments had in determining this decision; whether it was due entirely to a con-

president authority to receive ambassadors, and though this might not necessarily be construed to include the authority to receive, when reception in fact constitutes the recognition of a new government, such has been the established interpretation, and it probably depends in part on Washington's reception of the French minister. Genêt was received and immediately proceeded to make himself disagreeable—not to the more excited populace, but to those anxious lest the country be thrown into war as a companion in arms of the French Republic;[7] such a possibility had already affrighted the souls of the conservatives. But the conduct of the French minister eased the situation by the middle of the summer, and the cabinet decided to request his recall.

Regarding the actual position to be taken when the question first arose concerning the treaties, there was, as we have said, no really critical diversity between the two secretaries, though they do not appear to have been quite calm and merely placidly argumentative. The truth is, a decision to remain neutral and announce the fact settled the matter, if all the inevitable consequences of neutrality were to be adhered to. But Jefferson seems to have objected to the word "neutrality"[8] as indicating a decision of the executive concerning the future, and because the authority of Congress to declare war should not be encroached upon by a declaration that there was to be no war. And the proclamation when issued did not contain the word "neutral" or "neutrality".

Washington's proclamation is considered to-day an important docu-

viction that a suspension of the treaties was unwise, or whether it was due partly to a persuasion that there was no reason for joining such an announcement to the reception of a minister, and this being the case, that the announcement could well await the development of events. Whatever reasons may have appealed to the President, it is clear that he accepted the position of the Secretary of State and rejected the advice of the Secretary of the Treasury." *Ibid.*, p. 76. The treaties were formally declared no longer legally obligatory in 1798. This was done by act of Congress. The constitutional authority of the president to interpret a treaty and to determine its application in a given instance is passed over intentionally in the text above without comment. For the termination of treaties, denunciation and abrogation by Congress, and denunciation by the president, etc., see Quincy Wright, *The Control of American Foreign Relations*, pp. 256-262.

[7] Jefferson wrote to Monroe (July 14, 1793) declaring Genêt's "conduct is indefensible by the most furious Jacobin." Jefferson, *Works* (federal ed.), VII, p. 449.

[8] "The proclamn as first proposed was to have been a declaration of neutrality. It was opposed on these grounds. 1. That a declaration of neutrality was a declaration there should be no war, to which the Executive was not competent. 2. That it would be better to hold back the declaration of neutrality, as a thing worth something to the powers at war, that they would bid for it, & we might reasonably ask a price. . . ." Letter from Jefferson to Madison, June 23, 1793, in *Ibid.*, VII, pp. 407-408.

ment in the history of international law. The discussions that arose concerning the President's authority are important in constitutional history. Despite what seems to have been a degree of superficial harmony in the cabinet, there was bitterness underneath, and the public was more than uneasy.[9] Still the constitutional controversy might, we may suppose, have been kept to some extent under cover, had not Hamilton, always combative, decided to show his whole hand. He published articles in the press under the pen name of "Pacificus", and spread out his doctrines for popular consumption. With customary ability and incisiveness, he defended the President's right to issue the proclamation. But why he should have thought it necessary to add to the public indignation by outlining at length his full theory of the executive power, is not plain. He was no friend of halfway measures and he probably believed it was time that the people should know the scope of the president's power; if they were shocked by the picture, they would recover.

One statement in defense of the proclamation was of crushing force, and had it stood alone, it might be held conclusive; possibly it might have silenced opposition, or, if that were quite impossible, it might have had a quieting effect: "If, on the one hand, the Legislature have a right to declare war, it is on the other, the duty of the executive to preserve peace till the declaration is made". But Hamilton did not content himself with this assertion. The executive was, he declared, the department to which the Constitution intrusted intercourse with foreign nations; the legislature was "charged neither with *making* nor *interpreting* treaties." The authority to issue a proclamation of neutrality belonged to the executive: "As the *organ* of intercourse between the nation and foreign nations; as the *interpreter* of the national treaties, in those cases in which the judiciary is not competent—that is, between government and government; as the *power* which is charged

---

[9] "Every Gazette I see (except that of the U. S.) exhibits a spirit of criticism on the anglified complexion charged on the Executive politics. . . . The proclamation was in truth a most unfortunate error. . . . It wounds the popular feelings by a seeming indifference to the cause of liberty. And it seems to violate the forms & spirit of the Constitution, by making the executive Magistrate the organ of the disposition the duty & the interest of the Nation in relation to War & peace, subjects appropriated to other departments of the Government." Letter from Madison to Jefferson, June 10, 1793. See Madison, *Writings* (Gaillard Hunt, ed.), VI, p. 127 note. Madison thought it "mortifying" to the real friends of the President to see his fame and influence unnecessarily made to depend on "political events in a foreign quarter of the Globe. . . ." We can scarcely refrain from the conclusion that the usually cautious Madison was not thinking very soberly in some particulars.

with the execution of the laws, of which treaties form a part; as that which is charged with the command and disposition of the public force."

Such assertions as these, while they seem to us quite ordinary and orthodox, were not likely to be received joyfully by the Jeffersonians and the crowds then shouting for France and liberty; but Hamilton did not stop there; he proceeded to lay down statements concerning the scope and character of the executive powers which were certain to awaken resentment and dismay. He quoted from the Constitution: "the EXECUTIVE POWER shall be vested in a President of the United States"; and he referred to certain presidential powers which the Constitution specially mentioned. This enumeration of specified powers was, however, "merely to specify the principal articles implied in the definition of executive power; leaving the rest to flow from the general grant of that power, interpreted in conformity with other parts of the Constitution, and with the principles of free government. The general doctrine of our Constitution, then, is, that the *executive power* of the nation is vested in the President; subject only to the *exceptions* and *qualifications* which are expressed in the instrument." These exceptions he mentioned: the participation of the Senate in the appointment of officers and in the making of treaties, and the right of Congress to declare war and grant letters of marque and reprisal. "With these exceptions, the *executive power* of the United States is completely lodged in the President." He took occasion also to dwell on the president's power to receive ambassadors and other public ministers: "This right includes that of judging, in the case of a revolution of government in a foreign country, whether the new rulers are competent organs of the national will, and ought to be recognized or not".

Here was the picture of no supine official, humbly awaiting the public behests or meekly carrying legislative orders into execution. One cannot wonder at the consternation produced by these pronouncements, as men, fearful of executive power and dreading the group whom Jefferson called the "monocrats", looked upon the large outlines of the sturdy figure of the presidency, even though at that moment Washington himself held the office.[10] Hamilton's words are of interest because it would be nearly impossible even now to draw the outlines of the executive in more sweeping and comprehensive terms than those he

---

[10] "How far *the President* considers himself as committed with respect to some doctrines. He is certainly uneasy at those grasped at by *Pacificus.* . . ." Letter from Jefferson to Madison, August 3, 1793, in Jefferson, *Works* (federal ed.), VII, p. 464.

laid down. Especially in very recent decades, the leadership of the president in legislative matters has greatly grown; but it is difficult to say just how much of Hamilton's view of the scope of the executive office has been substantiated by the passing years.

As in many cases, the propriety of a statement depends on the interpretation of a word or two; if "executive" meant what Hamilton declared it meant, then for his argument that was enough.[11] He had in his mind, whether quite conscious of the fact or not, many of the lineaments of the executive as that figure appeared in the British system; consequently, under our constitutional system, whatever might be justly, perhaps traditionally, considered executive power belonged, with few explicit exceptions, to the president, who was a constitutional reproduction of a monarchical prototype. The executive had all "executive" power not by the Constitution denied him! We may still find it difficult to acquiesce in all these broad and unrestrained assertions of executive authority, and we may perchance especially question Hamilton's assumption that full power is granted subject only to a few express limitations; but whether we acquiesce or not, Hamilton drew the outlines of a vigorous and competent official, and the influence of this opinion and of Washington's general attitude were doubtless of effect.

But the men who feared the development of autocratic authority in America were not content. "For God's sake, my dear Sir, take up your pen," Jefferson wrote to Madison, "select the most striking heresies and cut him to pieces in the face of the public." Madison, writing under the pseudonym "Helvidius", entered upon a long (and one might justly say tiresome) attack, and his criticism of the pronouncements of "Pacificus" frustrates any attempt at successful condensation. He naturally objected to Hamilton's method of argument; and we must acknowledge that in one respect his animadversions were pertinent: whence, he asks, can the propounder of the theories of executive power under the Constitution have borrowed his ideas? "There is but one answer to this question. The power of making treaties and the power of declaring war, are *royal prerogatives* in the *British government,*

---

[11] Hamilton may have had in mind the statements of Montesquieu and Locke. Montesquieu spoke of three sorts of power: "the legislative; the executive, in respect to things dependent on the law of nations; and the executive in regard to things that depend on the civil law." Locke distinguished executive, legislative, and federative powers. He said that though the executive and federative powers are distinct, they are hardly to be placed in the hands of distinct persons. See Wright, *op. cit.*, pp. 141-142.

and are accordingly treated as *executive prerogatives* by *British commentators.*" [12] This statement cannot be fairly considered as a purely partisan attack intended to quicken the animosity of the multitude. Once admit, Madison said, the theories of the executive put forth by "Pacificus", and you admit inferences and consequences against which no constitutional ramparts could defend the public liberty; "no citizen could any longer guess at the character of the government under which he lives".

What would have happened if Congress had been in session during that anxious spring and summer when mobs were grumbling in the streets,[13] we cannot know and fortunately do not need to imagine. In August, the President wrote asking the opinion of his advisers as to whether Congress should be summoned. Differences of opinion appeared. "Knox s[ai]d we sh[oul]d have had fine work if Congress had been sitting these two last months. The fool thus let out the secret. Hamilton endeavored to patch up the indiscretion of this blabber, by saying 'he did not know; he rather thought they would have strengthened the Executive arm.' " This is Jefferson's story. But if Knox, like an *enfant terrible,* had let the cat out of the bag, how fortunate for Hamilton that he had been able to get his ideas of the executive authority put into public expression without congressional uproar.

The year 1793, as we have seen, was replete with perplexities that sorely distressed Washington and his advisers; but the following year was more difficult still. Had there been a united nation, or had the politicians been fairly reasonable, the situation would still have been perilous. But the country was sharply divided in its sympathies for the warring nations of Europe; politicians were loquacious and contentious; and under such conditions Washington had to meet difficulties that would have tested the wisdom and the courage of any government. The country, just accustoming itself to its new institutions, was in no condition for a conflict, which almost surely would have included civil tumult. In addition to the discord among the people and the inflamma-

---

[12] Madison, *Writings* (Gaillard Hunt, ed.), VI, p. 150.

[13] "You certainly never felt the terrorism excited by Genet in 1793 when ten thousand people in the streets of Philadelphia day after day threatened to drag Washington out of his house and effect a revolution in the government to compel it to declare war in favor of the French Revolution and against England." Letter from John Adams to Jefferson, many years afterwards, quoted in C. D. Hazen, *Contemporary American Opinion of the French Revolution* (John Hopkins Univ. *Studies in Hist. and Pol. Science,* extra volume XVI), p. 186. Italics of the original omitted. We may credit the figures, "ten thousand", probably to Adams's flowing pen. But the situation was serious.

tory declarations of the "democratic societies", there were four serious problems needing solution, to be solved peaceably if possible; for, however much some bold people might speak of American prowess, Washington must have seen that a foreign war would be disastrous. (1) Spain had not acquiesced in the treaty of 1783, but insisted on claiming territory north of the thirty-first parallel; a claim coupled with control of the southern Mississippi was especially obnoxious to the men in the new settlements beyond the mountains, and there were a few miscreants in that region who were not above plotting with Spaniards and receiving bribes from the Spanish treasury. (2) The Excise Act was openly flouted in western Pennsylvania where men bitterly resented a tax upon their customary beverage. (3) Great Britain, retaining the frontier posts within the American border and retaining also the fur trade with the northern Indians, was believed to be encouraging the red men in their warfare against the western settlers.[14] (4) The war upon the sea had opened to Britain opportunities for harassing American commerce, which were peculiarly irritating.

The settlement of these problems—the weathering of the storms of that perilous year, probably the most menacing time between the treaty of peace and the war of 1861—we must pass over hastily; but they belong in constitutional history because upon their wise solution depended the character, perhaps the very existence, of the new government. A treaty was made with Spain, fixing the southern boundary (1795). A force much larger than Washington had had at his command many times during the Revolution was sent against the insurgents in western Pennsylvania, and the insurrection ceased. Washington appears to have believed that the lawlessness was a natural result of the activities of "self-created societies", those imitation Jacobin clubs which had been making so much vocal disturbance for some little time.[15] He doubtless welcomed the opportunity of testing the strength

[14] In this year Lord Dorchester made a speech to the Indians which our government naturally and properly resented. This subject of the frontier posts is a large one. See S. F. Bemis, *Jay's Treaty;* A. C. McLaughlin, "The Western Posts and the British Debts", Am. Hist. Asso. *Report* for 1894, pp. 413-444; Theodore Roosevelt, *The Winning of the West,* especially IV.

[15] In his address to Congress, November 19, 1794, he spoke of "certain self-created societies". The Senate's address of November 21, is unmistakable. "Our anxiety arising from the licentious and open resistance to the laws in the Western counties of Pennsylvania, has been increased by the proceedings of certain self-created societies, relative to the laws and administration of the Government; proceedings, in our apprehension, founded in political error, calculated, if not intended, to disorganize

of the new government and finding whether it could enforce its laws; if he were successful, he would demonstrate to the public that they had a government whose behests must be obeyed. Fortunately, the fervor of the "democratic societies" was nearly burning out; though perils were not yet passed, the emotional tumults were beginning to subside; common sense was reasserting itself. The end of that eventful year marked the decline of the kind of declamation and parade which in its essence endangered the stability or even the existence of the government—at all events the existence of the kind of government Washington was seeking to strengthen.[16]

In 1794, the Indians of the northwestern region were for the time thoroughly beaten, and the next year a treaty with them settled the major difficulties. But the relations with Britain were serious in the extreme; in the spring of 1794 war appeared to be imminent; Congress provided for an embargo and other measures of defense were taken. Washington decided to send Jay to Britain to make a treaty that would preserve the peace. The result was the famous treaty of 1794, which, whatever its defects and however heated the demonstration by the ardent friends of France, at least saved America from war. But the fury of the malcontents, when the treaty was known, was unbounded; no other government than one under the direction of George Washington could have stood the strain.

The President called a special session of the Senate (June, 1795)[17] and submitted the treaty for acceptance; there was no previous con-

our Government, and which, by inspiring delusive hopes of support, have been influential in misleading our fellow citizens in the scene of insurrection." The address of the House on the President's speech, adopted after long discussion, is significant. The House felt, with the President, "the deepest regret at so painful an occurrence in the annals of our country"; it had learned with the greatest concern of misrepresentations of the government and its proceedings; but the crisis had demonstrated to a candid world that the great body of the American people were "attached to the luminous and vital principle of our Constitution, which enjoins that the will of the majority shall prevail". *Annals of Congress,* 3 Cong., 2 sess., cols, 788, 794, 947-948.

[16] The prominent fact is that the American people did keep their heads. As one reads of the silly extravagances of the populace he may forget that the world was on fire, and that the American people, though they had just passed through a Revolution and a succeeding period of uncertainty and disorder, went forward without devastating insurrection, and, under the guidance of wise architects, built up a substantial government. Those days in America can be understood only by remembering conditions in England and in Europe generally. One may well recall how deeply the intellectuals of Britain—many of them—were stirred as nothing before or perhaps since has stirred that class of the people; those were the days when, as Wordsworth tells us, it was bliss to be alive, but to be young were very heaven.

[17] Called March 3, 1795 to convene June 8.

ference or discussion between the Senate and the President; advice and counsel were limited in practice to assent or dissent. The Senate decided for acceptance on condition that there be added to the treaty an article suspending the operation of a clause concerning the trade with the British West Indies. But the trouble was not yet over; the House had something to say when a bill was introduced for carrying the treaty into effect. The debate was long and earnest. Inasmuch as the treaty, when once made, was "the supreme law of the land", was the House under legal obligation to take the necessary step to make it in all respects operative? Could the House inquire into the merits of the treaty and, for that purpose, must it be furnished with information from the Executive? A resolution passed the House asking for Jay's instructions and for the correspondence and other papers relative to the treaty, "excepting such of said papers as any existing negotiation may render improper to be disclosed." The President refused the request, denying the right of the House "to demand, and to have, as a matter of course, all the papers respecting a negotiation with a foreign Power". The power of making treaties, he asserted, is exclusively vested in the president by and with the advice and consent of the Senate, provided two-thirds of the senators present concur; every treaty so made and promulgated is the law of the land. It naturally follows from Washington's assertion that the House is under constitutional obligation to pass the necessary measures for making a treaty effective. Hamilton, in a communication to Washington, had declared "the House of Representatives have no moral power to refuse the execution of a treaty, which is not contrary to the Constitution, because it pledges the public faith; and have no legal power to refuse its execution because it is a law, until at least it ceases to be a law by a regular act of revocation of the competent authority."

Though disavowing any claim to a share in the making of treaties, the House, by a very decided majority, asserted, after Washington's refusal, its full right and duty to deliberate on the expediency of carrying a treaty into effect, when it "stipulates regulations on any of the subjects submitted by the Constitution to the power of Congress" and its execution depends on the passage of a law or laws. The bill carrying the appropriation for the execution of the treaty was finally passed by the House. It thus appears that Washington carefully guarded the executive power, and the House recognized the validity of his position in certain respects. But it did not admit that its sole duty was to stand blindfolded and pass any or every act necessary for the execution of a treaty. The theory of the matter, if treated abstractly, may give some room for dispute, and has indeed been subjected to minute consideration at various times in the past.

One or two things are now fairly well established: a treaty may be self-executing, that is to say, it may need no congressional act to bring it to full execution; but if it does require such an act, the House cannot be coerced; and to declare as a general principle that the House is legally bound to pass necessary legislation is a principle which the House has many times rejected. Probably no one would assert that, if a treaty be manifestly unconstitutional, the House must nevertheless pass legislation to make it operative; and furthermore, if it be founded on bribery or some other form of rascality, the House cannot be expected to ignore the fact. In other words, there are *some* limits on the obligation of the House. There may seem to be a certain degree of folly in asserting, when a political body is independent, that it cannot use discretion in the exercise of its power. But there are doubtless both moral and legal obligations upon Congress which it cannot properly ignore. Naturally, as a matter of practical fact, there must be reasonable accommodation; for when all is said, it takes common sense, quite as much as acute logic and forensic argument, to make a constitutional system actually work. In the course of years, there have appeared certain practices indicative of an appreciation of the sensitiveness of the House and a readiness to recognize the rights and duties of the House, especially in fiscal matters.[18]

During the debates on the Jay treaty, Albert Gallatin, defending the rights of the House, as he conceived them, made an exceedingly able speech,[19] in the course of which he referred to some especially

[18] Cf. Mathews, *op. cit.*, pp. 201-212, and references there cited. "Resolved, That it is the sense of this House that the negotiation by the Executive Department of the Government of a commercial treaty whereby the rates of duty to be imposed on foreign commodities entering the United States for consumption should be fixed would, in view of the provision of section 7 of article I of the Constitution of the U. S. be an infraction of the Constitution and an invasion of one of the highest prerogatives of the House of Representatives." Hinds, *Precedents,* II, 989, quoted in *Ibid.*, p. 204, note 2. "It thus appears that in the case of treaties relating to certain matters which, under the Constitution, are delegated to the legislative control of Congress, the treaty-making power has conceded that a treaty should not be put into effect until it has been approved by Congress. This has been agreed to particularly in relation to the regulation of customs revenue. . . ." Mathews, *op. cit.*, p. 211. See also, as an indication of the position of the House, *Statutes at Large*, XXXIII, ch. I, sec. 1. The act in question declared that nothing herein contained "shall be held or construed as an admission on the part of the House of Representatives that customs duties can be changed otherwise than by an Act of Congress, originating in said House."

[19] *Annals of Congress*, 4 Cong., 1 sess., col. 464 ff.

interesting and perplexing questions. He discussed the constitutional extent of the treaty-making power: "A Treaty is unconstitutional if it provides for doing such things, the doing of which is forbidden by the Constitution; but if a treaty embraces objects within the sphere of the general powers delegated to the Federal Government, but which have been exclusively and specially granted to a particular branch of Government, say to the legislative department, such a Treaty, though not unconstitutional, does not become the law of the land until it has obtained the sanction of that branch." He declared that a law could not repeal a treaty or a treaty repeal a law; but this is a statement which we must now say is not sound; the exact reverse is the accepted constitutional principle.[20] In some respects his most interesting remarks bore upon the question as to whether or not there were any limits upon the authority of the treaty-making power. His chief purpose was to defend the legislative branch of the House in particular, but if he had mentioned the possibility of the treaty-making power's so acting as to rob the states of their reserved constitutional rights, he would have touched upon a subject more disturbing and more perplexing than encroachment on the particular functions of either house or both houses of Congress.

On this general subject a few words may be appropriate here, though the principles involved were by no means made clear in 1796. The right to make a treaty which will affect the field of state legislative authority, and even take from the state a right and freedom which it might otherwise freely exercise, was early upheld by the Supreme Court.[21] Only a moment's attention is needed to convince anyone that, if every power in the hands of the states were to be immune from the slightest encroachment by the treaty-making power, the scope of that power would be slender indeed. If a state, which normally has control of internal police in a very full sense of the word, could continue to enforce its regulations without reference to any treaty stipulations, some of the most important matters commonly dealt with in international agreements could not be handled at all.

[20] ". . . it is well settled that in case of a conflict between an act of Congress and a treaty—each being equally the supreme law of the land—the one last in date must prevail in the courts." Justice Harlan in Hijo v. United States, 194 U. S. 315, 324 (1904).

[21] "We do not have to invoke the later developments of constitutional law for this proposition. . . ." Justice Holmes giving the opinion of the Court in Missouri v. Holland, 252 U. S. 416, 434 (1920). He cites among other cases, Hopkirk v. Bell, 3 Cranch 454; Ware v. Hylton, 3 Dallas 199; Chirac v. Chirac, 2 Wheaton 259—all fairly early cases.

Unquestionably, therefore, the domain of states' rights cannot be considered as bounded by an impassable wall; but the question remains to what extent or under what circumstances can the barrier be passed. It may now be accepted as established, that if a treaty requires legislation for its execution, Congress has constitutional authority to pass such legislation, even if without the treaty there should be no such authority. The fact that such a treaty interferes with the powers commonly exercised by the states, and considered to be within their sphere of reserved power, does not make the treaty or the law for its execution unconstitutional. In a recent case (1920)[22] these principles are clearly laid down. "We do not mean to imply", said Justice Holmes, giving the opinion of the Court, "that there are no qualifications to the treaty-making power;" but the opinion does not, naturally, tell us what the qualifications or limits are.[23] "No doubt the great body of private relations usually fall within the control of the State, but a treaty may override its power." The opinion contains one statement which is very illustrative of the broad interpretation of the Constitution with which we are now familiar, and though it is specially inapplicable to the days of 1796, when the Jay treaty was discussed, it may well be given here: ". . . when we are dealing with words that also are a constituent act, like the Constitution of the United States, we must realize that they have called into life a being the development of which could not have been foreseen completely by the most gifted of its begetters. It was enough for them to realize or to hope that they had created an organism; it has taken a century and has cost their successors much sweat and blood to prove that they created a nation. The case before us must be considered in the light of our whole experience

---

[22] Missouri v. Holland, 252 U. S. 416. This is the "migratory bird case" involving the constitutionality of an act of Congress carrying into effect a treaty for the protection of migratory birds. The fact that game laws and similar legislation have been considered within the police power of the state, and would be within such power in the absence of treaty regulations, did not make the treaty or the act for its execution unconstitutional. So the principle holds that the treaty-making power justifies Congress in passing legislation which without a treaty would be unconstitutional.

[23] The Court in some instances has said that there are limits. "The treaty power . . . is in terms unlimited except by those restraints which are found in that instrument [the Constitution] against the action of the government or of its departments, and those arising from the nature of the government itself and of that of the States." Geofroy v. Riggs, 133 U. S. 258, 267 (1890). See, for a discussion of this principle, W. W. Willoughby, *Principles of the Constitutional Law of the United States* (2nd ed.), p. 241. This author believes that *dicta* of the Supreme Court which would appear to restrict the treaty-making power from infringing upon the reserved rights of the states will sooner or later be finally repudiated by the Court.

and not merely in that of what was said a hundred years ago. The treaty in question does not contravene any prohibitory words to be found in the Constitution. The only question is whether it is forbidden by some invisible radiation from the general terms of the Tenth Amendment. We must consider what this country has become in deciding what that Amendment has reserved." [24]

[24] For a discussion of the extent of the treaty-making power, see E. S. Corwin, *National Supremacy,* especially ch. VI, "Treaty-Power Versus Police Power".

CHAPTER XIX

THE ALIEN AND SEDITION ACTS

The House passed the bill for carrying the Jay treaty into effect in the spring of 1796, and in the summer of that year Britain gave up the western posts. Washington must have breathed more easily and with deep satisfaction. The most trying and perilous crisis was passed. For two years he had been without the aid of first-rate advisers; Jefferson had retired from office at the end of 1793, Hamilton a year later.[1] While these two men were his official advisers he could feel confident that, however much they might differ, or even because of their differences, he was getting material on which to base his own judgment. Factious disputes were peculiarly annoying to him, but he seems to have had natural aptitude for choosing his course when alternatives were clearly and ably presented. After Hamilton's withdrawal, Washington occasionally appealed to him for assistance, which was given with usual precision and positiveness.[2] But on the whole, the President had to get on as he best could with advisers of mediocre quality.

When Washington retired to Mount Vernon, hoping to enjoy the labor and the ease of plantation life, Adams came to the presidency, with Jefferson as Vice-President—a combination indicative of the imperfect organization of parties. Adams was a lonely figure; he did not stand with the Hamilton group, whose leaders did not like him; nor was he more of a favorite with the Jefferson group or with that great body of voters and politicians who were beginning to form a real party with an organization capable of waging successful partisan warfare. He retained for a time in the executive offices the men who had been serving under Washington, but they looked to Hamilton as their leader. Not without executive ability, though with marked in-

[1] Jefferson, December 31, 1793. Hamilton, January 31, 1795.
[2] The above remark is especially applicable to the argument concerning the propriety or obligation to send information on the Jay treaty to the House. On two or three other occasions, including the preparation of the famous farewell address, Hamilton served the President.

capacity for holding men to himself by bonds of personal attachment and confidence, Adams finally took the reins into his own hands, accepted the resignation of McHenry, his Secretary of War, and dismissed Pickering, the Secretary of State. This was in 1800; for the previous three years, however, the President had struggled along with advisers on whose general loyalty and sympathy he could not thoroughly rely. Washington, as we have said, had a signal facility in reaching conclusions when conflicting opinions were proposed; and so in theory might a president pursue his way. But Adams was in no such position and had no such aptitude.

Washington might well feel not only relieved but gratified at the end of his term; he had performed services of inestimable value to his country, though doubtless he was the last man to appraise at their true worth his own influence and his own wisdom. Anxious though he was, unduly anxious, about factious party strife, he had good reason to believe that the government would live. But there were dangerous breakers ahead. If the Jay treaty had solved for the time the perilous disputes with Britain, it irritated France; and that country was making things unpleasant for America and was playing the bully. There resulted the well-known X.Y.Z. controversy; commissioners (Charles C. Pinckney, John Marshall, and Elbridge Gerry) sent by Adams to Paris to settle the dispute were treated with disrespect, confronted with humiliating terms at the very beginning, and, to crowd insult upon injury, were informed by insolent emissaries that if they desired attention, the members of the Directory must be properly bribed.

The publication of the X.Y.Z. correspondence (sent to Congress by Adams April 3, 1798) had very immediate effect. Old party antagonisms were for the moment forgotten or nearly forgotten. Preparations were made for war, and Washington was summoned from retirement to take charge of the army. Adams, often charged with being hot-headed and impetuous, in the emergency was wise and cautious. Receiving a hint that new negotiations could be conducted with decency, he named a commission (1799) which succeeded in making a treaty and quieting the disturbance. Adams's decision was sensible and prudent; indeed, he acted throughout the period with good judgment, but his decision to approach France and reach a peaceful solution of the difficulties made the Federalist leaders almost frantic.

The political events of the decade under discussion—the decade during which the government was established, parties were formed, and practices of enduring effect were begun—have been passed over rapidly in the preceding pages; but we have now come to a crisis and a controversy demanding careful examination. The French trouble in 1798 and 1799 produced legislation of a radical nature and, on the other hand, led the Republican leaders to the announcement of principles which were very far-reaching, much farther reaching than the politicians expected or probably intended, for political leaders are likely to have a very immediate goal in view; and even Madison and Jefferson could not, of course, see the far distant future.

The Federalists, irritated by the scandalous assaults of journalists and pamphleteers, fearing the effects of abuse and misrepresentation when war with France appeared inevitable, having no patience at the best with the clamor of the common folks, angered by the mouthings of the aliens who took advantage of a free country to heap abuse upon its rulers, the kind of abuse that would not have been tolerated in their native land—the Federalists were now beside themselves. Congress, despite serious and able opposition, passed important and eventful acts. (1) The Naturalization Act (June 18, 1798) provided for fourteen years' residence before the granting of full citizenship and required registration of resident aliens as well as new arrivals. (2) The Alien Enemies Act (July 6, 1798) provided that whenever a proclamation by the president announcing war or predatory invasion was issued, alien enemies should be liable to apprehension and removal; the president was authorized "to direct the conduct to be observed, on the part of the United States, towards the aliens who shall become liable. . . ." (3) The Alien Act (June 25, 1798) authorized the president to order such aliens as he might deem dangerous or to be engaged in "treasonable or secret machinations" against the government to depart from the country; if anyone so ordered should be "found at large" and without a license to remain, he should "on conviction thereof" be imprisoned for not more than three years and become ineligible to citizenship. The president might in his discretion grant a license to remain in the country, but he was on the other hand given full authority to send forth any alien already in prison under the provisions of the act; and if any alien so dismissed should return without permission, he should "on conviction thereof" be imprisoned so long as in the opinion of the president the public safety might require. Both this act and the Alien Enemies Act allowed an alien to remove his property, and there were other provisions which respected his property rights. (4) The Sedition Act (July 14, 1798) was directed against unlawful combination or conspiracy purposing to oppose governmental measures or impede their operation. In sweeping and comprehensive language, it further provided for punishing anyone publishing or causing to be published scandalous and malicious writings against the government, or either house of the Congress, or the president, with intent to defame them or to bring them "into contempt or disrepute", or to stir up sedition, or excite unlawful combinations for resisting any law of the United States or any act of the president done in pursuance of such laws. A person accused under the act might be brought before "any court of the United States having jurisdiction thereof," and punished by a fine not exceeding two thousand dollars, and by imprisonment not exceeding two years.[3]

The question of the constitutionality of these acts which were soon vehemently attacked must now be examined. But the reader should be warned that it is in some measure improper, in an historical investigation, to present as criteria judicial decisions and pronouncements of a later time.

Little need be said of the Naturalization Act. The portion dealing with the term of residence before admission to citizenship is of course unquestionably constitutional; and, though the provision for registration of aliens and, under some circumstances, for their giving surety for good behavior might even now raise questions of propriety, the constitutionality of the act can be passed by without serious comment. The act was, however, reactionary in character, certain to awaken hostility toward the party responsible for it.

The Alien Enemies Act likewise does not demand much attention There can be no doubt of the right of Congress to authorize the president to take such steps as seem necessary to protect the country against the machinations of enemies; indeed one might say that in all probability the president, as commander-in-chief, might go far in this direction without formal statutory authorization. It is true, he might act tyrannically and might abuse his power. Possibly we might criticize the act because no provision was made for the proper protection of those persons who were alleged to be enemy aliens but asserted they were citizens; but on the face of the act itself one cannot find the assignment of unconstitutional authority.[4]

[3] The Naturalization Act was repealed in 1802 and five years were established as the term of residence. The Alien Enemies Act was not repealed. The Alien Act was limited by its terms to two years and was not renewed. The Sedition Act expired in 1801 and was not renewed.

[4] Referring to the deportation of aliens under the General Immigration Act of 1917, the Supreme Court said, "Jurisdiction in the executive to order deportation

The Alien Act and the Sedition Act were drastic and extravagant pieces of legislation. "Let us not", wrote Hamilton at the time, "establish a tyranny. Energy is a very different thing from violence." [5] The former act authorized the president without the shadow of a trial to order out of the country any alien judged dangerous, no matter how long he had been a resident; it thus offered plentiful opportunity for injustice and harsh treatment. The assignment of such power was certain to arouse intense opposition and awaken public alarm. Assertion of the Jeffersonians that alien friends were within the care of the states and the states alone can now be dismissed as untenable. The act, as we have seen, provided that any alien who was ordered to depart and "found at large" without a license should "on conviction thereof" be punished. The offense appears to be failure to obey the command of the executive. Was personal liberty properly safeguarded? We can leave that question unanswered, only referring once more to the possibility of tyrannical administration. But the courts in comparatively recent days have gone so far in upholding the right to deport aliens that one must hesitate to condemn the Alien Act as a positive infringment of constitutional liberty because of its provisions granting wide executive power in this respect. The critical question is whether judicial trial is imperative, a trial, that is to say, with the usual formalities of a court of justice. Because of traditional habits of thought, we naturally at first sight react against the theory that personal rights, even though the person may be alleged to be a foreigner, should be passed upon outside of a court of law; but necessity has given rise to more expeditious, and perhaps we should say, more summary methods; executive tribunals and officials have been allowed great authority, and their decisions considered final. The courts have reserved the right to determine whether or not a fair hearing has been allowed by the administrative officials; but they have not denied, that, as a principle, the officials have the power to act, if reasonable and suitable methods of conduct have been followed.[6]

exists only if the person arrested is an alien. The claim of citizenship is thus a denial of an essential jurisdictional fact." The Court referred to a similar situation when proceedings are taken against a person under the military service and he denies that he is in the military service. "It is well settled that in such a case a writ of habeas corpus will issue to determine the status." Ng Fung Ho v. White, 259 U. S. 276, 284 (1922).

[5] Letter from Hamilton to Oliver Wolcott, June 29, 1798, in Hamilton, *Works* (H. C. Lodge, ed.), X, p. 295.

[6] "That Congress may exclude aliens of a particular race from the United States", said the Supreme Court in a comparatively recent case, "prescribe the terms and

The Sedition Act presents more serious difficulties. Suppression of freedom of speech and the press must under all circumstances be looked upon with misgivings. And this is so not so much because any specific words in the Constitution may perhaps be violated or given improper construction, as because the very vitals of free government are endangered or maltreated when freedom of thought and discussion are crudely interfered with. One of the chief attacks upon the Sedition Act immediately after its passage was founded on the assertion that it took for granted that the federal courts had jurisdiction of common law crimes. It is perfectly true, as the Supreme Court later declared,[7] that there is no such jurisdiction; but as a matter of fact, the Sedition Act established a statutory crime; and the question is whether Congress had the authority to announce the crime and provide for its punishment. In general, of course, libel and slander are matters within the province of the states. If statements, which would be commonly regarded as criminally libelous, were di-

conditions upon which certain classes of aliens may come to this country; establish regulations for sending out of the country such aliens as come here in violation of law; and commit the enforcement of such provisions, conditions, and regulations exclusively to executive officers, without judicial intervention,—are principles firmly established by the decisions of this court." Yamataya v. Fisher, 189 U. S. 86, 97 (1903). See also United States v. Ju Toy, 198 U. S. 253 (1905) and cases there quoted and referred to. In Fong Yue Ting v. United States, 149 U. S. 698 (1893), the right to expel or deport foreigners who have not been naturalized or taken any steps toward becoming citizens is specifically upheld. Concerning right to a hearing, consult Chin Yow v. United States, 208 U. S. 8 (1908). Concerning punishment without judicial trial see Wong Wing v. United States, 163 U. S. 228 (1896).

[7] See United States v. Hall, 8 Otto 343 (1879) and cases cited, particularly United States v. Hudson and Goodwin, 7 Cranch 32 (1812). In the former case Justice Clifford said, "Such courts possess no jurisdiction over crimes and offences committed against the authority of the United States, except what is given to them by the power that created them; nor can they be invested with any such jurisdiction beyond what the power ceded to the United States by the Constitution authorizes Congress to confer,—from which it follows that before an offence can become cognizable in the Circuit Court the Congress must first define or recognize it as such, and affix a punishment to it, and confer jurisdiction upon some court to try the offender." 345. In United States v. Hudson and Goodwin, the Court held that the circuit courts could not exercise common law jurisdiction of criminal cases. There may be implied powers in the government to preserve its own existence and promote its ends; but if such powers do exist, "The legislative authority of the Union must first make an act a crime, affix a punishment to it, and declare the court that shall have jurisdiction of the offence." 33-34. The constitutionality of these acts has been attacked on the ground that there was no proper designation of the court or assignment of jurisdiction; but such criticism appears to be without thorough basis because of the general provision of the Judiciary Act of 1789 assigning criminal jurisdiction to the circuit courts. As to there being a common law of the United States, see Western Union Tel. Co. v. Call Pub. Co., 181 U. S. 92 (1901) and references.

rected against John Adams or any member of Congress as a private individual, and if such an attack could have no reasonably assignable or conceivable connection with the safety of the government and its operation, then the United States could not punish the culprit in its courts. We cannot now doubt that the government—quite plainly, in times of peril—can protect itself against verbal attack, either upon its officials or its policies, if the attack is of such a character as to endanger its safety or reasonable security in the conduct of its affairs; an act providing for the trial of an alleged culprit cannot be considered under such circumstances an assumption of authority totally belonging to the states.

The question remains how far Congress may go without violating the first amendment, which guarantees freedom of speech and the press. Once more we are aided by judicial decisions of much later date. This subject in some of its aspects was passed upon by the courts in considering the constitutionality of certain parts of the Espionage Act of 1917. It appears to be a safe conclusion to say that whether an act is a violation of the amendment depends upon the scope of the act, perhaps more evidently upon its application, and also, as is so often the case, upon actual circumstances and conditions. Freedom of speech does not mean unlimited liberty to say anything and everything, under any and all conditions; there are limits: "The most stringent protection of free speech would not protect a man in falsely shouting fire in a theatre and causing a panic. . . . The question in every case is whether the words used are used in such circumstances and are of such a nature as to create a clear and present danger that they will bring about the substantive evils that Congress has a right to prevent. It is a question of proximity and degree. When a nation is at war many things that might be said in times of peace are such a hindrance to its effort that their utterance will not be endured so long as men fight and that no Court could regard them as protected by any constitutional right." [8] It is difficult, therefore, to pass any

[8] Justice Holmes giving the opinion of the court in Schenck v. United States, 249 U. S. 47, 52 (1919). In another case, Justice Holmes, dissenting, said: "I had conceived that the United States through many years had shown its repentance for the Sedition Act of 1798, by repaying fines that it imposed. Only the emergency that makes it immediately dangerous to leave the correction of evil counsels to time warrants making any exception to the sweeping command, 'Congress shall make no law . . . abridging the freedom of speech.'" Abrams v. United States, 250 U. S. 616, 630-631 (1919). Professor Corwin has summed up a discussion of freedom of speech by saying, ". . . Congress is not limited to forbidding words which are of a nature 'to create a clear and present danger' to national interests, but it may forbid words

sweeping judgment on the constitutional validity of the Sedition Act; so much must depend upon the interpretation of its more extreme provisions and upon the question of the application of its provisions by the courts in concrete cases. But we must remember that any act which gives opportunity to officials for punishing the innocent must be considered as approaching the verge of unconstitutionality; for, when all is said, the protection of an innocent and peaceful citizen is quite as important as the rapid and condign punishment of the guilty; and reasonable assurance of such protection and safety should appear on the surface of the act.

The more important question remains whether, technicalities being cast aside, the acts of 1798 were contrary to the spirit of the Constitution and appear in essence to be at variance with the elementary principles of free and liberal government. Without a great degree of actual liberty to express opinion and to criticize authority, democratic government cannot exist; it is in danger of being hidden in the mists and miasmic vapors which obscure normal vision in time of war; and this fact of course points to the antagonism between war, which rests on force, and popular government, which demands argument. That the acts which we are considering breathe on the whole a spirit of arrogance and intolerance, and that such a spirit was noxious and menacing, appears to be beyond doubt.[9]

which are intended to endanger those interests if in the exercise of a fair legislative discretion it finds it 'necessary and proper' to do so. . . . In short, the cause of freedom of speech and press is largely in the custody of legislative majorities and of juries, which, so far as there is evidence to show, is just where the framers of the Constitution intended it to be." E. S. Corwin, "Freedom of Speech and Press Under the First Amendment," *Yale Law Journal,* XXX, p. 55.

[9] In the earlier years of the twentieth century and especially after the world war there was much discussion concerning this subject. An illustration of the position of the more "liberal" opinion on the bench is the dissenting opinion of Justice Holmes in Gitlow *v.* New York, 268 U. S. 652, 673 (1925): "It is said that this manifesto was more than a theory, that it was an incitement. Every idea is an incitement. . . . If in the long run the beliefs expressed in proletarian dictatorship are destined to be accepted by the dominant forces of the community, the only meaning of free speech is that they should be given their chance and have their way." See also the concurring opinion of Justice Brandeis (in which Justice Holmes concurred) in Whitney *v.* California, 274 U. S. 357, 376-377 (1927): "Fear of serious injury cannot alone justify suppression of free speech and assembly. Men feared witches and burnt women. It is the function of speech to free men from the bondage of irrational fears. . . . Only an emergency can justify repression. Such must be the rule if authority is to be reconciled with freedom. Such, in my opinion, is the command of the Constitution. It is therefore always open to Americans to challenge a law abridging free speech and assembly by showing that there was no emergency justifying it."

CHAPTER XX

THE VIRGINIA AND KENTUCKY RESOLUTIONS

Jefferson and Madison thought it high time that there be some public protest against the Alien and Sedition Acts, and against the whole doctrine of constitutional interpretation wantonly made use of by the Federalists to justify their ends. The government, still young, still without established principles, might be so carried on as to become in reality a government of unlimited authority, doing as it listed without respect for constitutional restraint. In any attempt to evaluate or understand the protests that came from these two men, we must bear in mind not only their desire to defend individual liberty, but (perhaps chiefly) their antagonism to a Federalist system of constitutional interpretation which they feared would make of the Constitution nothing but a scrap of paper. They determined to call the attention of the country to the fact that, on proper constitutional principles, the government was a limited government, not to be magnified into omnipotence by processes of cunning construction. That was the central assertion.

Jefferson drew up resolutions which were passed in somewhat softened form, but without very material alteration, by the Kentucky legislature, November 16, 1798. Their authorship was not known until long afterwards. Madison prepared resolutions which were adopted by a majority of the Virginia legislature after earnest debate, December 24, 1798. Appeal was made for the coöperation of the other members of the union. The Kentucky resolutions expressed the belief that the "co-States, recurring to their natural right in cases not made Federal, will concur in declaring these acts void and of no force, and will each unite with this Commonwealth in requesting their repeal at the next session of Congress." The Virginia resolutions expressed confidence that the other states would concur in declaring the obnoxious acts unconstitutional, and that each would take necessary and proper measures for coöperating with Virginia in maintaining "the authorities, rights, and liberties reserved to the States respectively, or to the people." After hearing from various states, Kentucky passed a second set of resolutions (November 22, 1799) which indicated no repentance, but contained the word "Nullification" which in the course of time came to have dramatic if not tragic connotations in American history: "That a Nullification by those sovereignties, of all unauthorized acts done under color of that instrument is the rightful remedy".[1] The words "nullification" and "the rightful remedy" appeared in Jefferson's draft of the previous year.[2] The Virginia legislature (1800) considered an elaborate and very able report prepared by Madison, presenting what in his opinion were the fundamentals of the constitutional system and forcefully declaring that in the last resort the states must judge of the extent of the government's powers. After this consideration, the legislature reaffirmed its adherence to the principles previously announced.

The resolutions of 1798—the first sets which were sent forth by the two protesting states—are the most important. The Kentucky resolutions at considerable length skillfully arraigned the constitutionality of the Alien and Sedition Acts; they declared that the Congress of the United States, having been granted power to punish certain crimes, such as treason and piracy, had no power to punish other crimes; that this power belonged to the respective states; that alien friends were under the jurisdiction of the state wherein they reside; that no power over freedom of speech and of the press was delegated to Congress; that authorizing the president to remove an alien without a shadow of a judicial trial was a palpable violation of the Constitution. The Virginia resolutions were briefer and less specific but of the same general tenor.

In each of the first series of resolutions, we find one paragraph laying down certain general principles concerning the nature of the union; and those general principles were in later years often quoted and rehearsed; their sentiments were loudly proclaimed and applauded by tens of thousands who doubtless had never seen or read the documents for which they expressed so much reverent affection. The resolutions of 1798 were held to contain the creed of the Democratic-Republican party, and they were, in fact, the classic expression of the states' rights doctrine. Furthermore, at a later time, especially when

---

[1] Italics of the original omitted.
[2] Jefferson had said, ". . . in cases of an abuse of the delegated powers, the members of the general government, being chosen by the people, a change by the people would be the constitutional remedy; but, where powers are assumed which have not been delegated, a nullification of the act is the rightful remedy." *Works* (federal ed.), VIII, p. 471.

Calhoun took up the task of defending South Carolina against the tariff (1828-1833), they were used to support the doctrine of state sovereignty, a doctrine far in advance of mere states' rights.[3] These particular paragraphs—the third in the Virginia set, the first in the Kentucky—require our special attention, for it will be noticed that the main contention of the resolutions, viz., the unconstitutional character of the Alien and Sedition Acts as encroachments on individual liberty, was in the course of time lost from sight and attention was paid to the general principles which were laid down as introductory to the argument.

The third paragraph of the Virginia resolutions is as follows: "That this Assembly doth explicitly and peremptorily declare that it views the powers of the Federal Government as resulting from the compact to which the States are parties, as limited by the plain sense and intention of the instrument constituting that compact; as no further valid than they are authorized by the grants enumerated in that compact; and that, in case of a deliberate, palpable, and dangerous exercise of other powers not granted by the said compact, the States, who are parties thereto, have the right and are in duty bound to interpose for arresting the progress of the evil, and for maintaining within their respective limits the authorities, rights, and liberties appertaining to them."

The first paragraph of the Kentucky resolutions reads: "*Resolved, that the several States composing the United States of America, are not united on the principle of unlimited submission to their general government; but that by compact under the style and title of a Constitution for the United States and of amendments thereto, they constituted a general government for special purposes, delegated to that government certain definite powers, reserving each State to itself, the residuary mass of right to their own self-government; and that whensoever the general government assumes undelegated powers, its acts are unauthoritative, void, and of no force: That to this compact each State acceded as a State, and is an integral party, its co-States forming, as to itself, the other party: That the government created by this compact was not made the exclusive or final judge of the extent of*

---

[3] "States' rights" and "state sovereignty" are often used as synonymous expressions; but a distinction should be made. One may well hold, and indeed must hold, that under our constitutional system the states have rights of government beyond the reach of the central government; but he need not hold that the states are sovereign, certainly he need not believe them possessed of the unalloyed and undiminished sovereignty which Calhoun asserted belonged to them.

the powers delegated to itself; since that would have made its discretion, and not the Constitution, the measure of its powers; but that as in all other cases of compact among parties having no common Judge, each party has an equal right to judge for itself, as well of infractions as of the mode and measure of redress."

What was the constitutional theory of these documents? As far as the remedy for unconstitutional exercise of authority is concerned, it may perhaps be that they were intended to mean and did mean only that the states in coöperation could lay down authoritative interpretation of the Constitution, either by amendment or by some such process. It may be that the purpose of the resolutions was only to call upon the states to recognize and announce a principle; possibly the chief immediate purpose was to persuade the people to choose congressmen who would register dissent from Federalist doctrine. That these various methods were in Madison's mind seems the inevitable conclusion from his words in the report of 1800.[4] But there are a few words, especially those of Jefferson, which militate against this gentle and favorable construction.[5]

"Nullification" as used by Jefferson presents more difficulty then does "bound to interpose." Jefferson's pen ran swiftly and with perilous ease. But we need not ignore the latter portion of his resolutions —the set adopted with modifications by Kentucky in 1798—which con-

[4] Elliot, *Debates*, IV, p. 546, and especially pp. 578-579. Twenty-five years later (1823), Jefferson wrote: "The ultimate arbiter is the people of the Union, assembled by their deputies in convention, at the call of Congress, or of two-thirds of the States." *Works* (H. A. Washington, ed.), VII, p. 298.

[5] Alexander Johnston made an excellent study of the constitutional phases of the resolutions, especially in regard to "nullification". See Alexander Johnston, "Kentucky and Virginia Resolutions," *Cyclopaedia of Political Science* (J. J. Lalor, ed.), II, pp. 672-677. By way of summary, Johnston says that ". . . the resolutions of both series are a protest against a supposed intention of the federalists to place some restrictions upon any attempt of state legislatures to demand a national convention to sit in judgment upon the acts of the federal government; that the belief in such an intention was fostered by the federalists' use of the then novel word 'sovereign,' as applied to the federal government, and by their constant assertions that the federal government was the 'final' judge of the extent of its own powers, thus seeming to exclude any such power in a new national convention; that both Jefferson and Madison intended, 1, to appeal to public opinion, and 2, to rouse the states for a prompt call for a national convention upon the first appearance of an attempt by congress and the president to make such legislative action penal under a new sedition law. . . ." p. 676. Johnston states that the word "compact" in the resolutions is unessential; that Madison clearly did not use the word "in its full sense", and that the case is much more doubtful in regard to Jefferson. By "compact" "in its full sense" Johnston evidently means what Calhoun at a later date meant by it, i.e., an agreement or contract which did not establish a new and authoritative body politic.

tained an eloquent denunciation of tyranny. His main assumption in this connection appears to be sufficiently orthodox, at least for his day. Just as individuals when they enter society and set up government may surrender certain rights which were theirs in a state of nature and reserve the rest, so states entering the union could grant away a portion of their sovereign rights. What was to be done in case the reserved rights were encroached upon? Possibly he meant that each state could separately resist and, if necessary, retire. Neither he nor Madison would be willing to acknowledge that men could not in times of supreme danger resist government.[6] This so-called right of revolution was, however, quite different from the right of a sovereign body politic to act upon its absolute, legal, sovereign authority under any and all circumstances and refuse to be bound by an international engagement. We must remember also that we are almost certain to be misled, if we insist upon interpreting the words "nullification" or "bound to interpose" as meaning exactly what they did after Calhoun and South Carolina had given visible and objective lessons in the subject. This fact must give us pause. We must stop to realize the likelihood, if not the certainty, of our erring, if at the outset we apply to words of 1798 the connotations with which words were clothed thirty years later, after John Taylor and John C. Calhoun had let the light of their intellects play upon the subject of sovereignty, and after Calhoun had elaborated a metaphysical philosophy.

It is well to recall the object of the resolutions. The framers and advocates of these resolutions had no intention of breaking up the union, though they may have feared the dissolution of the union as the result of Federalist aggression. Nor did they wish to announce that the central government had no power; they wished to assert that it did not have *all* power; that its authority was limited by the plain sense and intention of the Constitution;[7] that there were limits on

---

[6] In 1832 Madison, writing to C. E. Haynes, said: "It is true that in extreme cases of oppression justifying a resort to original rights, and in which passive obedience & non-resistance cease to be obligatory under any Government, a single State *or any part of a State* might rightfully cast off the yoke." Italics mine. *Writings* (Gaillard Hunt, ed.), IX, p. 483. This, it will be noticed, is the right of self-preservation and the right to *resist* government which any individual or group is supposed to have, and not the right of a sovereign body to retire from a league.

[7] If the reader will refer to the Virginia resolution quoted above, and will substitute the word "Constitution" for "compact", he will probably not find much contrary to orthodox constitutional interpretation; he will probably find nothing to affront him, however nationalistic his opinions, until he reaches in his reading that

congressional power; and that, if Congress overstepped those limits, its acts were void. Now there is no more elementary principle of American government than this; it is the very first foundation-stone of our whole system; government has only delegated authority. But if it has only delegated authority, what is to be done in case it oversteps the prescribed bounds? Who is to judge whether the bounds have been passed or not? Jefferson declared the states—perhaps an individual state—were to judge of the infraction of the Constitution; Madison believed they had the right to "interpose"; Jefferson emphatically announced that the national government was not the exclusive and final judge of the powers delegated to itself. There, in other words, stood the old question: granted that government, founded on consent, has only delegated authority, who is to judge whether further authority has been seized? It is the old question which Locke and the advocates of derived government had to meet; they justified opposition only when "a long train of abuses" (to quote both Locke and the Declaration of Independence) dangerously infringed upon natural rights. The critical problem of constitutional history, therefore, was not whether the states were possessed of unqualified sovereignty, but whether it was theirs to pass judgment concerning an alleged deliberate, palpable, and dangerous encroachment upon their reserved rights. In the course of time, but only in the course of time, the right of the national government to judge of its own powers, subject to revision by amendment to the Constitution, became, from the practical necessity of the situation, the accepted constitutional principle. But for the first forty years of the Constitution's life the problem most frequently appearing and giving the most anxious attention was this very question—the right to judge.

The more important question remains: what theories of the nature of the union were held by the framers of these documents and by those giving the resolutions their support? A common, almost universal, method of interpretation begins by ignoring the argument for individual liberty and the very able presentation of constitutional limitation; the main content of the resolutions is held to be a declaration that the union is a system of sovereign states, a confederation from which each state can retire at any moment at its discretion; nullification—refusal to be bound by any objectionable act—is within the

portion of the resolution referring to the right of the states to "interpose". And what does "interpose" mean?

rights of any state; and if an attempt is made to enforce the act, secession is the natural remedy.[8] Jefferson and Madison, then,—the one "the founder of the Democratic party", the other "the father of the Constitution"—were also the founders and fathers of state sovereignty, forcible nullification, and secession. This method of interpretation, which finds in the resolutions the full-blown doctrine of state sovereignty and secession, depends upon the significance attributed to certain words, the most important being "compact", "parties", and "sovereign". If the Constitution is a compact, and if parties by entering into a compact cannot thereby form a new body politic and establish a legal authority, then of course it follows, as night the day, that the states are not legally bound by the Constitution, that they are not members of *a body,* and that they can withdraw from the system in which they have temporarily aligned themselves. If the states are "sovereign", as the second Kentucky resolutions declare, and if sovereignty means complete political authority, then, naturally, the union is not sovereign or partly sovereign; the individual states are totally self-determining; they cannot do anything illegal because any step they may take is legal. But on the other hand, if a compact *is* binding, if by a compact a body politic can be formed, then to call the Constitution a compact does *not* mean that a body politic was not formed; it does not mean that the Constitution is not binding. If sovereignty is divisible, then to call the states sovereign does not necessarily mean that they have undiminished sovereignty. In other words, if you insist on making certain words mean what you want them to mean, you can reach the conclusion you wish to reach.

The discussion just given brings to our attention the nature of the thinking of the men of 1798. The pivotal doctrines announced in the resolutions were those written by Jefferson in the Declaration of Independence; the philosophy was the philosophy of the American Revolution. Is it necessary to repeat the substance of that philosophy? All free and rightful government rests on consent, on agreement; all rightful governmental authority is delegated authority; if government exceeds the bounds of delegated authority, its acts are unauthoritative and of no force. The latter portion of the ninth resolution of Kentucky

[8] The best example of this kind of interpretation is H. von Holst, *The Constitutional and Political History of the United States,* I, ch. IV. According to this writer, Madison and Jefferson meant the same thing; Madison was a bit more wily or circumspect; but "bound to interpose" and "nullification" meant exactly the same thing; the resolutions meant everything that came out in the South Carolina troubles of 1832, and meant the constitutional doctrine that underlay secession.

brings out the idea succinctly: ". . . the co-States, recurring to their natural right in cases not made Federal, will concur in declaring these acts void and of no force. . . ." The Virginia and Kentucky resolutions rest on a political philosophy which at a later day Calhoun and the advocates of state sovereignty positively rejected. No long disquisition should be necessary for the student of eighteenth-century politics. There was no more solemn word in the political vocabulary of the eighteenth century than the word "compact"; all decent government rested on compact; every free state rested on compact; social relations rested on compact; kingship and the once-revered English constitution rested on compact; governments derived their just power from the consent of the governed. Furthermore, the men of the eighteenth century believed sovereignty could be divided.[9]

Madison's letters of a later day, when Calhoun and South Carolina issued their pronouncements, were complete answers to the declaration, or rather the assumption, that his theories of 1798 were identical with those of the great Carolinian: "Were this a mere league, each of the parties would have an equal right to expound it; and of course, there would be as much right in one to insist on the bargain, as in another to renounce it. But the Union of the States is, according to the Virg^a. doctrine in 98-99, a *Constitutional Union;* and the right to judge *in the last resort,* concerning usurpations of power, affecting the validity of the Union, referred by that doctrine to the parties to the compact.

[9] "It has hitherto been understood, that the supreme power, that is, the sovereignty of the people of the States, was in its nature divisible, and was in fact divided, . . . that as the States, in their highest sov. char., were competent to surrender the whole sovereignty and form themselves into a consolidated State, so they might surrender a part & retain, as they have done, the other part. . . . Of late, another doctrine has occurred, which supposes that sovereignty is in its nature indivisible; that the societies denominated States, in forming the constitutional compact of the U. States, acted as indivisible sovereignties, and consequently, that the sovereignty of each remains as absolute and entire as it was then. . . . In settling the question between these rival claims of power, it is important to keep in mind that all power in just & free Gov^ts. is derived from compact. . . ." Madison, *Writings* (Gaillard Hunt, ed.), IX, pp. 568-569. See *Letters and Other Writings of James Madison* (1865 ed.), IV, pp. 61, 75, 293-294, 393, 419. See also, Kohl *v.* United States, 91 U. S. 367, 372 (1876).

In Gaillard Hunt, *The Life of James Madison,* there is an interesting and valuable chapter on "The Madison Doctrine and Nullification". "When the nullification doctrine [of 1828 and after] appeared the Virginia Legislature resolved by a vote almost unanimous that the Virginia resolutions of 1798 did not support it, and Madison wrote to Edward Livingston: 'The doctrine of nullification [is] as new to me as it was to you.' The conclusion is inevitable that these public men who were personally concerned in the movement of 1798 and who saw the South Carolina doctrine appear in 1828 did not believe that the former furnished a fair foundation upon which to build the latter." p. 263.

On recurring to original principles, and to extreme cases, a single State might indeed be so oppressed as to be justified in shaking off the yoke; so might a single county of a State be, under an extremity of oppression. But until such justifications can be pleaded, the compact is obligatory in both cases." [10] There is nothing more interesting, and, in the history of constitutional construction, more important, than the controversies that arose when men had forgotten the meaning of words. Madison had not forgotten.

Someone may say that the theory that the states could judge of encroachments on their reserved rights menaced in plain everyday reality the stability of the union quite as much as did the doctrine of complete sovereignty. But there is an obvious distinction (and for everyday practical purposes a useful distinction) between the assertion that the states are wholly sovereign—no more bound than England or France or Spain would be if they entered into a treaty—and the assertion that they have the duty of protecting their reserved rights. If we are interested in the history of constitutional interpretation, such a distinction is vital.

The resolutions brought forth answers from the legislatures of sister states.[11] The question could not be divorced from the violence and prejudice of party politics. The chief topic under consideration was the constitutionality of the Alien and Sedition Acts. Some of the answers deserve attention because they explicitly declare that it is not the duty of state legislatures to decide on the constitutionality of federal laws, for such power has been bestowed upon the judiciary. Furthermore, the failure of the states to deny that the Constitution was a compact is illuminating.[12] This failure may be considered as

---

[10] Letter from Madison to J. C. Cabell, September 7, 1829, in *Writings* (Gaillard Hunt, ed.), IX, pp. 347-348.

[11] Elliot, *Debates,* IV, p. 532 ff. Certain additional materials, contributed by F. M. Anderson, are in *Am. Hist. Rev.,* V, pp. 45-63; 225-252.

[12] "This fundamental doctrine received no attention in any of the replies or the discussions over them, so far as the latter have been preserved, except in the reply of Vermont to Kentucky." F. M. Anderson, "Contemporary Opinion of the Virginia and Kentucky Resolutions, II," *Am. Hist. Rev.,* V, p. 237. Professor Anderson also says, "Thus, according to Madison's further reasoning, the people of each state instead of the people of the United States *en masse,* were the parties to the Constitution. In the counter-resolutions offered by the Federalists this interpretation of the parties to the Constitution is accepted entirely. The conclusion which the Federalists drew from this premise, as applied to the particular question at hand was quite different from that drawn by Madison, but the agreement between them is significant, for it shows that many of the Federalists as well as the Republicans accepted the fundamental doctrine of state sovereignty." *Ibid.,* p. 242. Probably the vast majority

indicating that they accepted the idea that each state was absolutely sovereign and bound only by treaty, that no state was legally bound. But the very absence of this failure indicates just the contrary. No one was likely to be shocked by a reference to the Constitution as a "compact"; to the men of that day the word did not have the connotations which the men in later years put upon it. Massachusetts, who in adopting her own state constitution called it a "compact", declared through her senate in 1799: ". . . that . . . they cannot admit the right of the state legislatures to denounce the administration of that government to which the people themselves, by a solemn compact, have exclusively committed their national concerns. . . . That the people, in that solemn compact which is declared to be the supreme law of the land, have not constituted the state legislatures the judges of the acts . . . of the federal government. . . ."

Virginia, it is often said, prepared for forcible resistance in 1798.[13] The charge, resting on almost no evidence which can be considered as real evidence, has been pretty thoroughly demolished. It should no longer be cited as proof that the resolutions of 1798 were intended to be a declaration of a single state's right to resist in arms or of an intention, if need be, to resort to war and a dissolution of the union.[14]

of people in 1798-1799, if they thought at all, believed that the Constitution was a compact and was adopted by the states; but did they place upon the word the meaning with which Calhoun invested it thirty years later? In one respect I cannot agree with Professor Anderson: the fundamental doctrine of state sovereignty, I should say, is not that the Constitution is a compact, but that, because it is a compact it is not binding law, and that if it was adopted by the states, then it was only an agreement. John Marshall also believed that the people of the states adopted the Constitution.

[13] See the evidence cited in A. J. Beveridge, *The Life of John Marshall*, II, pp. 399-400; see von Holst, *op. cit.*, I, pp. 156-158.

[14] See P. G. Davidson, "Virginia and the Alien and Sedition Laws," *Am. Hist. Rev.*, XXXVI, pp. 336-342. In fact, anyone reading carefully through the debates in the Virginia legislature will find it difficult or impossible to believe that armed conflict was preparing. That a state by legislative act could prepare for war, build an arsenal and the like, and do all this in almost complete and profound secrecy at the time, is too great a strain upon one's power of credence.

CHAPTER XXI

THE ELECTION OF 1800.
THE REPEAL OF THE JUDICIARY ACT OF 1801

The trouble with France, which had gone so far that battles had actually been fought on the sea, was in process of settlement by the capable diplomacy and common sense of the President. But as the excitement cooled, the Federalists appeared not to have won laurels. The war, it is true, had for a time given Adams popularity and appeared to revivify the Federalist party. Reaction was however inevitable, a reaction made more intense by the acts that sought to suppress discussion, by the taxation which was of course unpopular, and by the arrogance of the Federalist leaders. The party was ill-managed; its leaders found difficulty in working together in harmony; there were in fact too many leaders and too few privates in the array. Hamilton did not like or trust Adams and sought to prevent his reëlection to the presidency. The popular tide had turned against the party whose leading members had done much to give the new government strength and stability. In the election of 1800 Adams was defeated; but to the consternation of many and to Jefferson's discomfort he and Aaron Burr received the same number of electoral votes.

As the Constitution then stood, each elector voted for two persons; the person having the highest number of votes, if such number was a majority of the whole, was to be president. If there should be more than one person with such a majority, and with an equal number of votes, then the House of Representatives, after the counting of the votes in the presence of both houses, should immediately choose one of them for president, but in such choice the votes should be taken by states, each state having one vote. The framers of the Constitution had supposed that the electors, appointed by the states, would act as free agents, each giving by his ballot his personal opinion as to the man best fitted for the presidency. The fathers foresaw neither parties, as we know parties, nor the formal processes of nomination and of intricate and effective party machinery. It was understood among the Republicans of 1800 that Jefferson was the candidate for the presidency, Burr the candidate for the vice-presidency. But the natural working of the party system resulted in every Republican elector's voting for both candidates; and the simplest mathematical product was the embarrassing tie.

When the result was seen, rumors began to fly. The House was made up of men elected during the excitement of the trouble with France. Would the Federalist members acting as automatons, without prejudice, quietly register what might be considered the desire of their opponents, choose Jefferson and leave the vice-presidency to Burr? To many Federalists, Jefferson was anathema; party spirit was acute, flaming, intolerant. The situation was disclosed by the first ballot taken in the House (February 11, 1801). There was no choice. The Federalists had on the whole decided to support Burr, the man whose elevation Hamilton said could "only promote the purposes of the desperate and profligate." From New England he received four votes; from the south he received the support of South Carolina and Delaware. Eight states voted for Jefferson, one less than a majority; one member from New Jersey who Jefferson at an earlier date had thought would "come over",[1] and the only member from Georgia (the other member having died) had made it possible to cast the vote of those two states for the man whom the Republicans considered their candidate. Vermont and Maryland were divided.

If this situation should continue, the election might be delayed indefinitely and the end of Adams's term would see the land without a chief magistrate. Various proposals were discussed; danger of an interregnum or conflict and chaos appeared imminent.[2] If there were no choice, could some officer, perhaps John Marshall, then Secretary of State, or some other person selected by the Federalist Congress, be authorized to assume the presidential office? The Republicans, to put the case mildly, were wroth; to any such measure they were not prepared to accede. Conditions are best presented in Jefferson's own words: "If they [the Federalists] could have been permitted", he wrote Monroe (February 15, 1801), "to pass a law for putting the government into the hands of an officer, they would certainly have

---

[1] Letter from Jefferson to Madison, December 19, 1800, in Jefferson, *Works* (federal ed.), IX, p. 158.

[2] That the crisis was trying is indicated by the following item from *The National Intelligencer* (February 16, 1801), as the situation disclosed itself: "All the accounts received from individuals at a distance, as well as the feelings of citizens on the spot, concur in establishing the conviction that the present is among the most solemn eras which have existed in the annals of our country."

prevented an election. But we thought it best to declare openly and firmly, one & all, that the day such an act passed, the middle States would arm, & that no such usurpation, even for a single day, should be submitted to. This first shook them; and they were completely alarmed at the resource for which we declared, to wit, a convention to re-organize the government, & to amend it. The very word convention gives them the horrors, as in the present democratical spirit of America, they fear they should lose some of the favorite morsels of the constitution." [3]

Conditions were, however, not hopeless or so fraught with danger of civil tumult as the Jeffersonians feared. Hamilton was known to be unfavorable to Burr, and his influence still had some weight. Common sense, and probably a fear of serious consequences, began to take the place of besotted partisanship. So, after a week of anxiety, an end was reached (February 17, 1801). The Maryland Federalists put in blanks and the rest of the delegation voted for Jefferson. The same result was brought about in the Vermont delegation by the withdrawal of one of the members. Bayard, the only representative from Delaware, cast a blank ballot, and the South Carolina delegation did the same. Jefferson was thus chosen by a vote of ten states to four, the minority votes coming from the four old New England states.

Unquestionably the Federalists were justified constitutionally in voting for Burr. Technically their conduct was irreproachable. No one, however, can defend them, if they seriously thought of preventing an election by delay; and it is quite possible to impugn their judgment in preferring Burr to Jefferson. The significance of the situation lies in the fact that the Federalists acted as they did for party ends; that party candidates, distinctly so considered, had been presented; and that a question could actually arise whether or not individual members of the House could use their own judgment or must consider themselves bound in some vague way to recognize the intention of the electors, the intention also of those who had chosen the electors, and of those who had selected the candidates. Obviously the party system had wrought a change. If electors chosen to support candidates would vote for the party nominees, a tie was not only possible but inevitable; at every election, unless party machinery were so developed that word would go out from some central party organ to the electors, directing one of them not to cast his vote for the vice-presidential candidate, a

---

[3] Jefferson, *Works* (federal ed.), IX, p. 179. See also, James Monroe, *Writings* (S. M. Hamilton, ed.), III, pp. 256-257.

tie would occur. Even then complications might arise. The one most obvious fact is that there were candidates; and each elector of a party would vote for both.

The method of choosing the president, which had been the subject of so much discussion in the Constitutional Convention, had broken down in one particular. Some modification which would adjust the Constitution to facts was necessary. The subject had been brought to attention four years before this, when Adams and Jefferson were chosen, though they were of differing political faiths. Proposals for amendment had been made in Congress at various times, but nothing had been done. Even after the election of 1800-1801 there was delay, caused in part by party dispute; but in December, 1803, the twelfth amendment providing for separate electoral ballots for president and vice-president was adopted by Congress and sent to the states for ratification. It was proclaimed in force September 25, 1804. Three states rejected it: Massachusetts, Connecticut, and Delaware. The New Hampshire legislature ratified it but the Governor vetoed the ratification.[4] The veto, however, probably did not invalidate the ratification, for the Constitution plainly gives the authority to the legislatures of the states.[5] The opposition of the Federalists to the amendment is an interesting example of sectional suspicion and petty partisanship.[6]

[4] H. V. Ames, *The Proposed Amendments to the Constitution of the United States During the First Century of Its History* (Am. Hist. Asso. *Report* for 1896, II), p. 79, note 7.

[5] On this matter there is no authoritative decision; but probably, on the whole, both reason and practice indicate that the governor's consent is not necessary. "It is believed that the framers of the Constitution did not anticipate that the chief executives of the States would participate with the legislative bodies in the approval or disapproval of amendments submitted, for at the time the Constitution was framed but one of the States conferred upon the governor the veto power." *Ibid.*, p. 297. The reason above given is only one of the reasons for thinking the governor does not participate. The same principle appears to obtain with reference to the president, whose signature to a proposed amendment is unnecessary. *Ibid.*, pp. 295-296. See Hollingsworth *v.* Virginia, 3 Dallas 378, 381, note 1 (1798). In that case Justice Chase appears to have said, "The negative of the President applies only to the ordinary cases of legislation. He has nothing to do with the proposition, or adoption, of amendments to the Constitution." In this connection it is interesting to notice that the opponents of the twelfth amendment in the federal House declared the resolution not constitutionally passed in the Senate because not two-thirds of the senators but only two-thirds of those present voted for it. Ames, *The Proposed Amendments, loc. cit.*, p. 79. In the National Prohibition Cases, 253 U. S. 350 (1920), the Court held that the required two-thirds vote is two-thirds of the members present. For an excellent survey of the amending process, see H. V. Ames, "The Amending Provision of the Federal Constitution in Practice," Am. Philosophical Society *Proceedings*, LXIII, pp. 62-75.

[6] After the twelfth amendment to the federal Constitution no other was passed

The defeat of the Federalists may be attributed to quite obvious causes; in part at least, it may be accounted for by impulsive reaction, one of those changes in public sentiment, sometimes quite unexpected, which have often come in our political history. But there were doubtless more serious and more meaningful reasons. The Federalist party had been a great party; its leaders were able men; under them the Constitution had been translated into an actual working system; but the party had its weakness in a country where the common voter had power. This power he was beginning to appreciate. The Federalist leaders were deficient because of a native inability to appeal, by and large, to the masses of the people. If they were wise statesmen, they were not very competent politicians. Their fundamental philosophy was benevolent leadership, accompanied by a distrust of those whom they would command. The capacity of their opponents, the Jeffersonians, to reach out to the people and, in the next few years after 1800, to form a party organization of a comprehensive character, was one which the Federalists did not possess, partly no doubt because of the very nature of their party and its social philosophy. Something new was coming into being, a well-articulated institution, the national party with its tentacles reaching out to the remotest hamlet, nationalistic in its character and influence. There was a new and growing loyalty, a sense of devotion to the party. The developing power of the Republicans came partly from the fact that their principles were in accord with the sentiments of the people, and partly from skill in the establishment and the management of party machinery.[7] There is something amusing, no doubt, in the sight of this party advocating local self-government and the right of the individual to fight his own way to comfort and happiness, and, nevertheless, creating an elaborate and powerful national organization; for nationalism and local rights are by nature hardly companionable bedfellows; and organization is hourly in opposition to actual individualism. But such are the processes of history; human affairs do not go forward in obedience to logic.

and accepted by the states until the thirteenth, the immediate product of the Civil War. Two amendments proposed by Congress were not accepted—one proposed in 1810 and one in 1861, the latter being intended to protect slavery in the states.

[7] The skill with which the Republicans so organized their forces as to give the appearance of carrying out popular behests, and at least to gather popular backing, is to be distinguished from the Federalist system, which appeared to consist in talking down to the plain people and pointing the way they should go. The more elaborate organizing was done early in the nineteenth century. Of great interest in this connection is G. D. Luetscher, *Early Political Machinery in the United States.*

Jefferson in later years spoke of the election as the "revolution of 1800". But to what extent and in what respects there was a revolution is not evident on the surface. Events soon showed that when necessity arose the government was not conducted with loving adherence to the doctrine of strict construction, nor did it always show anxiety lest the rights of the states be encroached upon. It is difficult to find any material change in the character or activities of the government. But if we consider imponderable elements, the passing of the Federalist régime is of decided significance. Jefferson's idealistic political philosophy, his belief in the essentials of individualistic democracy, his confidence in the power and character of the common man, were, in essence, diametrically opposed to the political thinking and social attitude of the Federalists. Democracy was to make tremendous strides forward in the early decades of the new century; Jeffersonism was in many respects in keeping with the developing social forces of the time.

If the history of America is the history of a people entering upon the great adventure of popular government and marching forward with a considerable degree of achievement, nothing can be much more important than the accession to the presidency of a man who had faith and foresight. Jefferson's inaugural address was a great state paper, and can be read to-day as an incomparable presentation of the spirit and the essential meaning of democracy, especially democracy resting upon confidence in man's individual right to seek his own salvation. We must remember that America had to do more, or was to do more, than found a government, provide laws, establish order, and maintain national dignity. The land was to be the home of a confident, buoyant, and powerful people whose destiny was in their own hands. We cannot lose sight of the fact that for many decades, perhaps even to the present time, America meant to Europe a land in which people were seeking to build up a new political and social system, free from the stratifications of the old world; it was in the eyes of the European man, be he of high or low degree, a land whose success in democracy, if success be won, threatened and more than threatened the stability of privilege, superimposed authority, and all those suppositions concerning the superiority of upper class domination which the old world had inherited from a feudal past. In the opening months of the nineteenth century there came to the presidential chair a man who was permeated with confidence in the brightness of an alluring future.

In December, 1800, nearly three months before the end of Adams's administration, a bill was introduced in Congress, still in the hands of the Federalists, proposing extensive changes in the Judiciary Act of 1789. There were some good reasons for these changes; in fact, the year before, President Adams had recommended revision and amendment of the act, and a committee of the House had reported a bill. Under the existing system, the justices of the Supreme Court were obliged to hold circuit courts; and in those days traveling was neither comfortable nor expeditious; the duty involved actual hardship. ". . . the First Magistrate," said Gouverneur Morris, "in selecting a character for the bench, must seek less the learning of a judge than the agility of a post-boy." Under the prevailing system, too, a justice sitting in the Supreme Court might be called upon, unless he voluntarily refrained, to take part in the decision of a controversy on which he had already delivered an opinion when holding circuit court. Something also may be said for the need of increasing the number of districts and thereby making the federal courts more easily accessible— a consideration, however, which did not pleasantly affect the average Republican congressman.

The bill, which was enacted less than three weeks before Adams's retirement and the end of the Federalist régime, provided that from and after the next vacancy, the number of justices of the Supreme Court should be five, instead of six, and it relieved the justices of their duties as postboys. It increased the number of district courts and provided for circuit judges, sixteen in number, with corresponding marshals and attorneys. Here was a golden opportunity for the office-seeker and for the extension of party influence. The indignation of the Republicans might have been tempered, had they been given the chance of filling the new offices with their own party adherents. But no such opportunity was granted them. With an eye for detail, Adams patiently proceeded to appoint to the new positions none but members of his own party before he hurried away in his carriage, not lingering until the new President had taken the oath and delivered his inaugural address.[8] John Marshall, who had been appointed Chief Justice some

---

[8] Channing says that Adams's yielding to the pressure for office in the last two months of his administration was "most unfortunate, but it should be attributed to the goodness of his heart rather than to any selfish desire to defraud Jefferson of any of his rights." See Edward Channing, *A History of the United States*, IV, p. 241. If Adams's heart was on the right side, it was the Federalist side! Channing also says that the recent death of his son was the reason for Adams's "seemingly discourteous departure" before Jefferson's inauguration. *Ibid.*, IV, p. 243, note 2.

time before, was left to bear the brunt of Republican suspicion and opprobrium.

The new Judiciary Act, however admirable it may appear, was passed at a most inopportune time. The Republicans were nursing their dislike of the judiciary, a dislike begotten by the harshness and arrogance of certain judges, notably Chase, in the sedition trials, and by the tendency to recognize the common law as a part of the national body of law. They could not quietly accept the new act; they were irritated at the sight of a party, beaten in the election and deprived of control in the political branches of the government, now taking refuge in the judiciary where they would be free from popular pressure and might be able to perpetuate their obnoxious and unpopular doctrines. So bitter was the feeling, so extreme the partisanship, that the freedom and the independence of the judiciary were endangered. "We have been asked," said Senator Jackson of Georgia, in a debate on the repeal of the act establishing the new courts, "if we are afraid of having an army of judges? For myself, I am more afraid of an army of judges, under the patronage of the President, than of an army of soldiers. . . . Have we not seen sedition laws? Have we not heard judges crying out through the land, sedition!" [9]

Jefferson was not willing to acquiesce in this extension of the judicial system. He had by no means recovered from his hostility to the Alien and Sedition Acts. He distrusted the judiciary in the hands of the Federalists. His message to Congress (December, 1801) contained this passage: "The judiciary system of the United States, and especially that portion of it recently erected, will of course present itself to the contemplation of Congress, and, that they may be able to judge of the proportion which the institution bears to the business it has to perform, I have caused to be procured from the several States and now lay before Congress an exact statement of all the causes decided since the first establishment of the courts, and of those which were depending when additional courts and judges were brought in to their aid." This was plainly a gentle hint of the needlessness of more courts and more judges. Senator Breckenridge [10] of Kentucky offered a motion to repeal the new Judiciary Act. For two months the subject was before Congress. The debate is of importance, not as a mere exhibition of party strife, though that was conspicuous, but because

[9] *Annals of Congress*, 7 Cong., 1 sess., col. 47.
[10] There is some variation in the spelling of this name. The form used here is that which appears in the *Annals of Congress*.

certain fundamental constitutional problems were discussed with earnestness and ability.

The arguments of those who advocated repeal and defended the right of Congress to take such action amounted to this : legislation for the removal of a judge from office would be illegal, but there was a plain distinction between a removal from office and the abolition of the office itself; there were in the Constitution certain limitations of congressional competence in dealing with the judiciary, but there were only three : there must be one and only one Supreme Court, the judges should not be removed from office during good behavior, and their compensation while in office should not be diminished. The advocates of repeal, when they discussed constitutional authority at all, also laid special emphasis upon the right of Congress to establish inferior courts; such courts, they claimed, being created by Congress could be abolished at the discretion of the body which created them. This argument can scarcely be considered totally unreasonable and only the offspring of party passion and prejudice. Concerning the general validity of this reasoning, no dogmatic assertion is desirable. The opponents of repeal stoutly maintained the constitutional impropriety of destroying the office, and thus by indirection removing the newly-appointed judges. But the Federalists may be charged with their full share of partisanship and with the sin of disregarding the spirit of the Constitution; for to use judicial positions for purely partisan purposes or for some ulterior reason is an offense against the spirit. The Constitution plainly does not contemplate making the judiciary the plaything of party politics.[11]

In the course of the debate, the right of a court to declare a congressional act void was discussed. This matter was brought into the

---

[11] One has to confess that there *may* be at times sound reason for filling judicial positions with men who have certain theories of the Constitution. Like so many other questions, this is not purely an abstract constitutional matter. In recent days we have seen senators opposing the appointment to judicial positions of men who have particular attitudes toward matters of pressing interest; we have seen men, like Lincoln in 1858, declaring that a certain tendency in the Supreme Court must be checked or counteracted. In all such matters, the degree of impropriety needs to be taken into consideration. If we say that all such plans and purposes are unconstitutional, if we contend that only a man's personal honor and legal learning need be considered, we are demanding as constitutional standards what conditions of practical statesmanship will probably make untenable. At all events, we are faced with a problem of ethics rather than one of constitutional power. And as long as men continue to be political beings and as long as judges are thought of as human, presidents and senators will be likely to consider more than mere intellectual acumen in appointees for the bench.

debate chiefly, not from the expressed announcement by the Federalists that the Supreme Court would declare the repeal of the Judiciary Act void, but as evidence of the independence of the judiciary, an independence which would be destroyed if the inferior judges should be considered as only the creatures of Congress, and if, to promote the will of a majority of Congress, judicial positions could be abolished. "On examination," said Senator Mason of Massachusetts, "it will be found that the people, in forming their Constitution, meant to make the judges as independent of the Legislature as of the Executive. Because the duties which they have to perform, call upon them to expound not only the laws, but the Constitution also; in which is involved the power of checking the Legislature in case it should pass any laws in violation of the Constitution." [12]

In the Senate, Breckenridge clearly and cogently gave the basis for repudiating this doctrine: "My idea of the subject . . . is, that the Constitution intended a separation of the powers vested in the three great departments, giving to each exclusive authority on the subjects committed to it. . . . That those who made the laws are presumed to have an equal attachment to, and interest in the Constitution; are equally bound by oath to support it, and have an equal right to give a construction to it. That the construction of one department of the powers vested in it, is of higher authority than the construction of any other department; and that, in fact, it is competent to that department to which powers are confided exclusively to decide upon the proper exercise of those powers: that therefore the Legislature have the exclusive right to interpret the Constitution, in what regards the law-making power, and the judges are bound to execute the laws they make." [13]

When Breckenridge closed, Gouverneur Morris rose and congratulated the Senate and America "that we have at length got our adversaries upon the ground where we can fairly meet [them]. . . ."

---

[12] *Annals of Congress*, 7 Cong., 1 sess., col. 32. "To my mind, these considerations are satisfactory, that, from the very constitution of our courts, from the practice and admission of our State courts and State Legislatures, and Federal courts, and Federal Legislature, that the judges of the United States, sitting in court, have the power, and by oath are bound to pronounce, that an act contrary to the Constitution, is void. . . . The concentrating the branches of power either Executive and Legislative, or Legislative and Judiciary, in the same hands, is the very essence of tyranny. . . ." John Stanley in the House. *Ibid.*, col. 576.

[13] *Ibid.*, col. 179. How this principle could be accepted, if the question was whether or not a president was to be the sole judge of his own authority and quite free from judicial restraint, it is not easy to see.

". . . the honorable member last up has told us in so many words, that the Legislature may decide exclusively on the Constitution, and that the judges are bound to execute the laws which the Legislature enact. . . . If this doctrine be sustained . . . what possible mode is there to avoid the conclusion that the moment the Legislature of the Union declare themselves supreme, they become so? . . . The sovereignty of America will no longer reside in the people, but in the Congress, and the Constitution is whatever they choose to make it." [14] In the House, John Randolph, with characteristic vehemence, announced principles similar to those of Breckenridge: "Here", he exclaimed, "is a new power. . . . But, sir, are we not as deeply interested in the true exposition of the Constitution as the judges can be? With all the deference to their talents, is not Congress as capable of forming a correct opinion as they are?" [15]

In these discussions, it should be noticed, those denying the power of a court to pronounce an act void did not suggest that the Constitution was not binding on both Congress and the courts. Their strongest pronouncement was in defense of the right of the legislators, in wielding powers confided to them by the Constitution, to judge, without judicial interference or check, of the extent of those powers. The winter passed before the final vote was taken; the debating was earnest and intelligent. In early March (1802) the act of repeal was passed and signed by the President. It provided that acts in force before the enactment of the Judiciary Act of 1801 were revived and in full operation.

Near the end of April an amendatory act was passed which made sundry alterations in the existing system; it provided that there should be but one term of the Supreme Court each year, which should begin on the first Monday in February. No session of the Court could be held, therefore, until some nine months had passed. If John Marshall and his colleagues should contemplate finding the repeal of the Judiciary Act of 1801 void, they would have to wait for a time, and meanwhile the public excitement would be abated. That this was the purpose of the Republicans in passing the act is by no means certain, though it is often asserted; but the act contained many other provisions, and there was comparatively little attention paid in the debates to the postponement of the Court's session. At all events, delay made a declaration of the unconstitutionality of the repeal difficult, perhaps

14 *Ibid.*, cols. 180-181.
15 *Ibid.*, col. 661.

impossible; [16] it also postponed the decision of a case to be discussed on later pages—the famous case of Marbury *v.* Madison.

[16] "The chief alterations made from the old system consist in the holding the Supreme Court only once a year by four justices, and the establishment of six circuits, within each district of which circuit courts are to be holden twice a year, composed of one justice of the Supreme Court and the judge of the district, in which said court is held." *Annals of Congress,* 7 Cong., 1 sess., col. 1160. It is often said that the act in question postponed a session for fourteen months: ". . . the Supreme Court . . . was practically abolished for fourteen months." A. J. Beveridge, *The Life of John Marshall,* III, p. 97. As a matter of fact, *after* the passage of the act of April, 1802, about nine months passed without a session of the Court. It is true that about fourteen months passed between the meeting of the Court, which had been held in December, 1801, and the meeting in February provided for by the act of April, 1802. That the act was passed by the Republicans with the intention of preventing a decision by the Court on the validity of the repeal of the Judiciary Act of 1801, may be true, as has been suggested; that motive was touched on in the debates in the House by Bayard and was denied by Nicholson. The chief attack of the Federalists was against the impropriety of providing only one session per year.

CHAPTER XXII

THE ANNEXATION OF LOUISIANA

In the early nineteenth century the most important event in American history, an event important too in the world's history, was the annexation of Louisiana—a vast territory which Napoleon with a magnificent gesture threw into the laps of the American envoys at Paris, receiving in return fifteen million dollars that his coffers might be filled for fighting the obstinancy of Britain. However much Napoleon might still cherish a grandiose scheme for a colonial empire in the Americas, he had surrendered a region which added to the United States an area larger than the land bounded by the treaty of 1783. For a time the accession gave excuse for further bitterness in the hearts of New England malcontents; but its great and lasting effect was to build up and strengthen the young republic. The central valley of the continent, with all its potential riches, a great geographical unit, destined to be the heart of a powerful nation, was brought under the American flag.[1] The old Mississippi question which had vexed the country from the earliest days of the Revolution was to vex it no more; almost unlimited space for expansion under national protection was furnished; and the spirit of nationalism, the feeling and sentiment of strength, vitality, and destiny, were given new and dominant energy.

This extension of the American domain was brought about by the Republican party under the leadership of Thomas Jefferson. If Jefferson was a localist, intent upon saving the states from the power of an overtowering national government, his purpose was badly dam-

[1] The Mississippi River, the central line of a magnificent valley, flowed henceforth through American territory. If we look for the bonds that held the American states and American sections together, we may find the strongest bond, not to have been laws and courts, but water, the river system of the Mississippi valley. When Mr. Russell, the correspondent of the *London Times*, was introduced to Lincoln, the President put out his hand and said, "Mr. Russell, I am very glad to make your acquaintance, and to see you in this country. The *London Times* is one of the greatest powers in the world,—in fact, I don't know anything which has much more power,— unless perhaps it's the Mississippi." Quoted in Abraham Lincoln Association *Papers* (1931), p. 21.

aged when he reached out his hand for the treaty which Livingston and Monroe had signed at Paris. Of course states' rights were not affected as a mere theory; but the extension of the national domain tended to develop national interests and to add to national responsibilities. Jefferson was not, it is true, at any time anything less than an American; his advocacy of states' rights was primarily in defense of individual liberty; his affections and hopes extended far beyond the confines of his native state.

Jefferson had been vigorously opposed to a free and easy interpretation of the Constitution. When faced by imperative necessity, he put his constitutional scruples aside. The matter of Jefferson's inconsistency, because of his willingness to annex territory when no such power appeared to be given by the Constitution, does not need many words of sardonic comment. He was not alone in his inconsistency; in fact, the leaders of neither party appeared to honor consistency as a factor of statesmanship. The Federalist leaders showed no marked inconsistency with the inner spirit of their party—instinctively it was a party believing in the right of superiors to rule; it did not shrink from imperialism—, but they of course objected to the treaty, partly no doubt because they were faithfully carrying out the doctrine that the duty of a party of opposition is to oppose.

The constitutional difficulties gave Jefferson anxiety and he thought it advisable to amend the Constitution, though that might have granted authority after the deed was done. "I had rather", he wrote, "ask an enlargement of power from the nation, where it is found necessary, than to assume it by a construction which would make our powers boundless. Our peculiar security is in possession of a written Constitution. Let us not make it a blank paper by construction." [2] His proposals, however, met with cold reception even from those who had been the warmest exponents of strict construction and states' rights. He drafted constitutional amendments and submitted them to members of his cabinet. [3] Gallatin, to whom one copy was sent, and who had already expressed his opinion that "the United States as a nation have an inherent right to acquire territory", [4] barely acknowledged its receipt and appears to have made no comments. From other quarters the worried President received slight help or consola-

[2] Jefferson to Wilson Cary Nicholas, September 7, 1803, in Jefferson, *Works* (federal ed.), X, p. 10 note.
[3] One was drawn in July and the other in August.
[4] Gallatin to Jefferson, January 13, 1803, in Albert Gallatin, *Writings* (Henry Adams, ed.), I, p. 113.

tion. No way out of the trouble was open to him but to acquiesce, "confiding, that the good sense of our country will correct the evil of construction when it shall produce ill effects." [5] He alone and unaided could not amend the Constitution, nor, in light of the emergency—for Napoleon might not forever await ratification of the treaty and payment of the price—was it wise to linger and delay. His party was against him, and a handful of Federalists were eager for the fray. But with the annexation of Louisiana, strict, narrow, construction was badly damaged; it might be again dragged to the light for party or sectional service; but for the time being it was useless in the hands of those who had begotten it.

The debate over measures for carrying the treaty into effect brought forth Federalist opposition and Republican support in both houses of Congress. The Federalist party did not haggle over the fact of annexation but dwelt chiefly upon certain provisions of the treaty and their implications. The framers of the Constitution, declared Gaylord Griswold of New York, "carried their ideas to the time when there might be an extended population; but they did not carry them forward to the time when an addition might be made to the Union of a territory equal to the whole United States, which additional territory might overbalance the existing territory, and thereby the rights of the present citizens of the United States be swallowed up and lost." [6] Here was the old fear lest the east be shorn of its powers; and yet the consequences of this extensive scope of the treaty-making power might have caused anyone, if he looked into the future, to hesitate and indulge in misgivings. The Federalist position, however, was most clearly presented by Roger Griswold of Connecticut: "A new territory and new subjects may undoubtedly be obtained by conquest and by purchase; but neither the conquest nor the purchase can incorporate them into the Union. They must remain in the condition of colonies, and be governed accordingly." [7]

[5] Jefferson to Wilson Cary Nicholas, September 7, 1803, in Jefferson, *Works* (federal ed.), X, p. 11 note.

[6] *Annals of Congress,* 8 Cong., 1 sess., col. 433. The third article of the treaty read: "The inhabitants of the ceded territory shall be incorporated in the Union of the United States, and admitted as soon as possible, according to the principles of the Federal constitution, to the enjoyment of all the rights, advantages, and immunities of citizens of the United States; and in the mean time they shall be maintained and protected in the free enjoyment of their liberty, property, and the religion which they profess."

[7] *Ibid.,* col. 463. Griswold also objected to great powers in the hands of the President and the Senate. "It is, in my opinion, scarcely possible for any gentleman

The opposition made no serious impression on the House; the resolutions for establishing a provisional government and paying France were referred to committees. On the critical resolution, that provision ought to be made for carrying the treaty into effect, the vote was ninety to twenty-five,[8] two-thirds of the minority being from New England.

In the Senate a few members did not hesitate to attack the constitutionality of the treaty; it was not however the validity of annexation which they denied, but the right to incorporate people, and to absorb them into the United States. No such act could be effected, declared Pickering of Massachusetts, without an amendment of the Constitution which should be made not by the concurrence of two-thirds of both houses and ratification by three-fourths of the states, but by all the members of the union, "in like manner as in a commercial house, the consent of each member would be necessary to admit a new partner into the company. . . ." [9] He did not doubt the right to acquire territory, either by purchase or by conquest, and to govern the territory so acquired as a dependent province.[10] With these doctrines, Tracy of Connecticut substantially agreed.[11] Extreme Federalism, then, had reduced the Constitution to a partnership in which the original influence and authority of each member could not be diminished without its express consent.

And what a change had swept over the advocates of states' rights! The two senators from Virginia, John Taylor [12] and Wilson Cary Nicholas, as well as Senator Breckenridge of Kentucky, all of whom had been prominent advocates of the resolutions of 1798, now looked with sorrow upon the Federalist doctrines of national incompetency. They appeared to have no misgivings; they were not inclined to indulge, as did their leader in the White House, in lamentation over the necessity of assuming powers.

on this floor to advance an opinion that the President and Senate may add to the members of the Union by treaty whenever they please, or, in the words of this treaty, may 'incorporate in the union of the United States' a foreign nation who, from interest or ambition, may wish to become a member of our Government. Such a power would be directly repugnant to the original compact between the States, and a violation of the principles on which that compact was formed." *Ibid.,* col. 461. Concerning the significance of incorporation, see Downes *v.* Bidwell, 182 U. S. 244 (1901).

   [8] *Annals of Congress,* 8 Cong., 1 sess., cols. 488-489.
   [9] *Ibid.,* col. 45.
   [10] *Ibid.*
   [11] *Ibid.,* cols. 55-58.
   [12] See especially, *Ibid.,* col. 50. Taylor's position is significant because of the nature of his writings and theories at a later date.

Both parties agreed on one point: foreign territory could be annexed. But the Federalist spokesmen looked with favor upon a union which would narrowly guard the balanced powers of the states— parties to the constitutional compact—, while the Republicans scorned meagerly technical views of the constitutional system and of national authority. The Federalists granted the possibility of an empire over a vast area and over a dependent people; the Republicans wanted Louisiana and gave their sanction not only to the annexation but to the ultimate absorption of people into the United States, a step which made certain the creation of a new union and was sure to cast reproach upon any doctrine of state sovereignty, as far as that doctrine rested for support upon the sovereignty of the original thirteen states when they ratified the federal compact.[13]

While the New England opposition was fostered by provincialism and by partisanship, we cannot look upon the Federalist argument itself as only a piece of intellectual perversity. Certainly men might well stop at least to question the advisability of incorporation of an extensive area and its people into the United States. The extent of the treaty-making power as exemplified by the treaty raised a question of much perplexity; the interpretation of the clause concerning incorporation presented difficulties. The impressive fact is that (whether the impulse sprang merely from national land-hunger or not) nationalism had so far developed by 1803 that a treaty doubling the area of the United States met with little opposition—a treaty promising the people of the annexed region admission as soon as possible into the advantages and immunities of citizens of the United States. Impressive too is the Federalist doctrine of empire. Neither party could look upon the United States as a mere collection of impotent sovereignties.[14]

---

[13] I do not understand that the Republican leaders plainly committed themselves to an interpretation of the treaty which would involve the right of the treaty-making power to provide for admission of annexed territory into the union as a state without congressional action.

[14] Jefferson doubted at this time whether new states could be formed out of annexed territory. "But when I consider that the limits of the U S are precisely fixed by the treaty of 1783, that the Constitution expressly declares itself to be made for the U S, I cannot help believing the intention was to permit Congress to admit into the Union new States, which should be formed out of the territory for which, & under whose authority alone, they were then acting." Jefferson to Wilson Cary Nicholas, September 7, 1803, in Jefferson, *Works* (federal ed.), X, p. 10 note.

CHAPTER XXIII

JOHN MARSHALL, CHIEF JUSTICE. THE EARLY HISTORY OF THE SUPREME COURT. MARBURY v. MADISON

Before Adams left office he appointed John Marshall Chief Justice of the United States. This office Marshall held for more than three decades (1801-1835), and his influence in shaping the foundations of American constitutional law can hardly be overestimated. Presidents were elected and retired from office; parties were broken up and reconstituted; changes in social and economic conditions were wrought by time; the population of the land greatly increased in numbers; the boundaries of the republic were extended; new states were formed; old ideas and mental attitudes of the eighteenth century passed away; but Marshall in the quiet of the court-room continued to give forth decisions from the bench and to win for himself fame as one of the great judges of all time. He had a unique opportunity. He was called upon to construe the fundamental law of a nation, to lay down principles which were to be of supreme consequence in securing national stability and national development. No other justice in the course of the past ages had such an opportunity and such responsibilities. The Constitution which he was called upon to interpret and apply was the Constitution, moreover, of a federal, not of a unitary or centralized state; in consequence, judicial problems were novel, and little help could be gained from precedent, especially in deciding those controversies which were most vital and significant. If not always free from emotional strain, he was peculiarly judicial in his outward attitude; he was decisive without being overbearing. His literary style, especially in his more important opinions in the years when he had reached the summit of his intellectual power, was clear, simple, and eloquent, if the occasion made eloquence appropriate. The layman as well as the learned practitioner can read his words and grasp their meaning.[1]

[1] "To the accomplishment of that task [of laying down the legal principles of nationalism] Marshall brought the master-mind of American constitutional govern-

His early training and preparation for his task were not very thorough; he had had none of the prolonged drill to which the modern student is subjected; but his experiences in the army and in political life had given him an insight into practical problems and had furnished him with stern convictions. The years spent in the Revolutionary army, where he had suffered the slings and arrows of out rageous fortune, had left their deep impressions; and if we seek the basic depths of his devoted nationalism, we can doubtless find them in the privations of Valley Forge; these privations, he well knew, were the product of incompetent government, an imperfect union of the states, and the absence of national patriotism. In his greatest and most powerful opinions, as we read them to-day, he appears to us to be speaking not in the terms of technical law but as one of Washington's soldiers who had suffered that the nation might live. Had he been more of a technical lawyer, thoroughly steeped in the history and entangled in the intricacies of the law, he might not have been so great a jurist; for his duties called for the talent and the insight of a statesman capable of looking beyond the confines of legal learning and outward onto the life of a vigorous people entering upon the task of occupying a continent and soon to be confronted with new and imperious problems.[2]

There appears to be a tendency among modern writers to attribute to Marshall the creation of the elementary principles of constitutional construction. This is true of both those who extol and those who criticize or lament his work, especially his great decisions which expounded the principles of nationalism. But as a matter of plain fact, his predecessors in the Court, when passing on questions which involved the general nature of the Constitution and the structure of the union, viewed the Constitution in much the same way as Marshall did. From the very beginning to the present there has been no variation from the main line of construction which Marshall in successive cases drew with a firm and strong hand; the decisions made by the

ment, hardly the perfection of legal reasoning and learning, but so sound a common-sense for the practical working of legal theory, so just an instinct for the national welfare, and so austere and unswerving a judicial fairness and openness of mind that no judge since may be compared with him." Introduction to *The Constitutional Decisions of John Marshall* (J. P. Cotton, Jr., ed.), I, p. xxxvi.

[2] It is doubtless this quality of Marshall's work which has occasionally induced some writers (in the present writer's judgment) to overstress his political purposes as distinguished from the compulsion of purely legal or, we might say, abstract principles of disembodied law—if there be such a thing.

Court in the first decade of the Constitution's life furnished solid foundation for later constructions embodying legal nationalism.

The most important of the early decisions, that were rendered before Marshall came to the bench, was Chisholm v. Georgia.[3] The question at issue was whether one of the states of the union was suable by a citizen of another state. As the Constitution then stood, the judicial power of the United States extended to controveries "between a State and citizens of another State", and therefore at first sight the question appeared easily answerable in the affirmative. And still, if the states were supposed to retain even partial sovereignty, their suability presented difficulties.[4] Moreover, the prospect of a state's being brought before the Court and ordered to pay its debts was not alluring. The dignity of the state would be affronted; and its treasure, if it had any, diminished. The Court discussed the question at great length and decided that a state could be sued.

In giving their opinions the justices considered not only the clause directly involved but also the nature of the union. Justice Iredell dissented, holding that in the absence of explicit legislation by Congress a state could not be sued, and said that his "present opinion" was against any construction of the Constitution which would "admit, under any circumstances, a compulsive suit against a State for the recovery of money." [5] He declared that every state "in every instance where its sovereignty has not been delegated to the *United States,* I consider to be as completely sovereign, as the *United States* are in respect to the powers surrendered." [6] This was the doctrine of divided sovereignty which appeared in other opinions as the doctrine of the Court. Justice Wilson construed the Constitution in terms of decided nationalism: "As a Judge of this Court, I know, and can decide upon the knowledge, that the citizens of *Georgia,* when they acted upon the large scale of the *Union,* as a part of the 'People of the *United States,'* did *not* surrender the Supreme or sovereign Power to that State; but, *as to the purposes of the Union,* retained it to themselves.

[3] 2 Dallas 419 (1793).
[4] Marshall in the Virginia convention of 1788 said, "I hope that no gentleman will think that a state will be called at the bar of the federal court. . . . It is not rational to suppose that the sovereign power should be dragged before a court." Elliot, *Debates,* III, p. 555. Madison said, "It is not in the power of individuals to call any state into court." *Ibid.,* p. 533. See also Hamilton, in *The Federalist,* no. LXXXI.
[5] 2 Dallas 419, 449.
[6] "The *United States* are sovereign as to all the powers of Government actually surrendered". 2 Dallas 419, 435.

As to the purposes of the Union, therefore, *Georgia is* NOT *a sovereign State."* Chief Justice Jay said, "Every State Constitution is a compact made by and between the citizens of a State to govern themselves in a certain manner; and the Constitution of the *United States* is likewise a compact made by the people of the *United States* to govern themselves as to general objects, in a certain manner." His general position was that "the sovereignty of the nation is the people of the nation, and the residuary sovereignty of each State, in the people of each State. . . ." The people of the United States, he declared, "acting as sovereigns of the whole country", established "a Constitution by which it was their will, that the State Governments should be bound, and to which the State Constitutions should be made to conform."

Georgia indulged in loud lamentation; its house of representatives passed a bill "declaratory of certain parts of the retained sovereignty of the state" and subjecting to death "without benefit of clergy" any officer or other person levying on the property of the state by virtue of the authority of any court. It is impressive, this tender sense of sovereign self-sufficiency,[7] in a state of about 80,000 inhabitants including slaves. But Georgia was not alone. Suits had been begun against Maryland, New York, and Massachusetts;[8] and those states, as well as others, were eager to banish the danger of being compelled to pay their debts. An amendment was drawn up by Congress and proposed to the states for their acceptance in 1794, but not until January 8, 1798, was announcement made of complete ratification:[9] "The judicial power of the United States shall not be construed to extend to any suit in law or equity, commenced or prosecuted against one of the United States by citizens of another State, or by citizens or subjects of any foreign State."

The amendment did not by these words explicitly exclude a suit brought against a state by one of its own citizens. The question arose nearly a century after the decision in the Chisholm case. In the later case,[10] the Supreme Court solemnly declared Iredell's position to be

---

[7] But it is not plain that the act meant that Georgia retained *full* sovereignty.

[8] Ames, *The Proposed Amendments, loc. cit.,* p. 156.

[9] *Messages and Papers of the Presidents* (J. D. Richardson, compiler; hereafter referred to as Richardson, *Messages and Papers*), I, p. 260.

[10] Hans *v.* Louisiana, 134 U. S. 1, 16 (1890). An important early case in interpreting the amendment is Osborn *v.* Bank of the United States, 9 Wheaton 738 (1824). See also, Cohens *v.* Virginia, 6 Wheaton 264, 412 (1821).

right, and that of the other judges wrong: "The suability of a State without its consent was a thing unknown to the law. This has been so often laid down and acknowledged by courts and jurists that it is hardly necessary to be formally asserted. It was fully shown by an exhaustive examination of the old law by Mr. Justice Iredell in his opinion in *Chisholm* v. *Georgia;* and it has been conceded in every case since, where the question has, in any way, been presented. . . ." [11]

In the case of Calder *v.* Bull [12] the term *"ex post facto"* was interpreted as applying only to criminal laws. The Court also indicated what provisions in an act would be considered *ex post facto* in character. In addition, the announcement was clearly made that the state legislatures retain all powers delegated to them by the state constitutions which are not taken away by the federal Constitution, and that the federal Court had no jurisdiction to determine that any law of a state contrary to the constitution of such state is void. Of special interest is one statement of Justice Chase: "An act of the Legislature (for I cannot call it a law) contrary to the great first principles of the social compact, cannot be considered a rightful exercise of legislative authority." [13] Justice Iredell, on the other hand, declared that, while an act violating constitutional provisions is void, the Court cannot pronounce it void merely because in the opinion of the judiciary it is

[11] Naturally one may inquire (1) whether the states in adopting the Constitution including the third article did not thereby *consent* to suits; (2) whether the states retained their fundamental character or quality of sovereignty, for the jurists of 1793 and 1890 really agreed that the states retained only modified sovereignty. In the Hans *v.* Louisiana case Justice Harlan dissented as to the disapproval of Chisholm *v.* Georgia. He said that comments made upon the decision in Chisholm *v.* Georgia were not necessary to the determination of the present case and besides, "the decision in that case was based upon a sound interpretation of the Constitution as that instrument then was." In 1907 (Kawananakoa *v.* Polyblank, 205 U. S. 349, 353), we find this: "A sovereign is exempt from suit, not because of any formal conception of obsolete theory, but on the logical and practical ground that there can be no legal right as against the authority that makes the law. . . ." In 1883 the Court declared that a state, by assuming the prosecution of debts owing to its citizens by another state, cannot create a controversy with another state within the meaning of the term as used in the Constitution. New Hampshire *v.* Louisiana, and New York *v.* Louisiana, 108 U. S. 76. In 1904, the question arose as to whether one state can sue another and be entitled to recover, when claims of individuals have passed absolutely into the hands of the state. The Court decided that the suit can be instituted: "Obviously that jurisdiction is not affected by the fact that the donor of these bonds could not invoke it." Four justices dissented. South Dakota *v.* North Carolina. 192 U. S. 286, 312.

[12] 3 Dallas 386 (1798).

[13] *Ibid.,* 388. Capitalization and italics of the original omitted.

contrary to the principles of natural justice.[14] In this matter Iredell's opinion coincides with principles later followed by the courts;[15] but the due process of law clause in the fifth and fourteenth amendments of the federal Constitution, and like provisions in state constitutions, as judicially construed in later years, make the distinction not very important, if there be any distinction at all.

An important decision was rendered concerning the binding effect of the treaty of peace and especially of the provision which declared that "creditors on either side shall meet with no lawful impediment to the recovery . . . of all bona fide debts heretofore contracted." The Court held that the treaty nullified the sequestering act of Virginia which was passed during the Revolution, and that, as the Constitution declared that all treaties "made, or which shall be made, under the authority of the United States, shall be the supreme law of the land", the treaty was binding upon the states and must be recognized and applied by the judiciary. "A treaty", said Justice Chase, "cannot be the supreme law of the land, that is of all the United States, if any act of a State Legislature can stand in its way."[16] The nationalistic interpretation of the Constitution stands forth conspicuously in this opinion.

In this same year (1796) the Court, passing upon the question whether a tax on carriages was or was not a direct tax as the term appears in the Constitution,[17] declared such a tax could be levied without apportionment among the states. Members of the Court expressed the opinion that only two taxes could be classified as direct—a capitation tax and a tax on land. But this opinion, though at times referred to in later cases, did not finally settle the question concerning the actual limits of direct taxation. A century afterwards the Court declared unconstitutional an act levying taxes on incomes.[18] The nature of that decision will be discussed in later pages of this work.

[14] *Ibid.*, 399.
[15] But see Loan Association *v.* Topeka, 20 Wallace 655, 663 (1875), in which the Court speaks of "Implied reservations of individual rights, without which the social compact could not exist, and which are respected by all governments entitled to the name."
[16] Ware *v.* Hylton, 3 Dallas 199, 236 (1796). Italics of the original omitted.
[17] Hylton *v.* the United States, 3 Dallas 171 (1796). The Constitution says "Representatives and direct taxes shall be apportioned among the several States . . . according to their respective numbers. . . ." Art. I, sec. 2, para. 3. "No capitation or other direct tax shall be laid, unless in proportion to the census or enumeration herein before directed to be taken." Art. I, sec. 9, para. 4.
[18] Pollock *v.* Farmers' Loan and Trust Co., 157 U. S. 429; 158 U. S. 601 (1895).

Even while the discussions which ended in the repeal of the Judiciary Act of 1801 were going on, a very important case came before the Supreme Court. William Marbury, who had been appointed by Adams to be a justice of the peace in the District of Columbia, had not received his commission. Marshall, who had acted as Secretary of State until the end of Adams's term, had neglected, because of the hurry of the later days, to attend to the transmission of the commission, and Marbury sought the aid of the Court. Motion was made in the December term of 1801 for a rule requiring the Secretary of State, Madison, to show cause why a mandamus should not issue directing him to deliver the commission. The rule was issued, but Madison ignored it. On motion for a mandamus, Marshall gave an opinion and the Court made a decision in which for the first time a congressional enactment was declared by the Supreme Court to be unconstitutional and of no effect (1803).[19]

The Chief Justice first passed upon the question of Marbury's right to receive the commission, and then, having decided in favor of that right, proceeded to declare invalid a portion of the Judiciary Act of 1789 which granted to the Court the power to issue a mandamus; he thereupon dismissed the application for the mandamus because the Court had no constitutional authority to issue it, and had, indeed, no jurisdiction of a case of this kind. It thus appears that the Court announced the duty of the administration and the rights of Marbury in a case which constitutionally it had no authority to entertain. This method of procedure appears to-day most extraordinary.

Can it be reasonably said that a court can lay down an authoritative decision concerning the merits of a controversy over which it has no jurisdiction? And if the Court in this instance had no jurisdiction, why was it not proper to make that declaration at once and without further ado, and without announcing Marbury's right to his commission? Certainly there is no obligation upon a court to decide whether

19 Marbury v. Madison, 1 Cranch 137 (1803). In the case of Cooper v. Telfair, 4 Dallas 14, 19 (1800), Justice Chase said that "although it is alleged that all acts of the legislature, in direct opposition to the prohibitions of the constitution, would be void; yet, it still remains a question, where the power resides to declare it void? It is, indeed, a general opinion, it is expressly admitted by all this bar, and some of the Judges have, individually, in the circuits decided, that the supreme court can declare an act of congress to be unconstitutional, and, therefore, invalid; but there is no adjudication of the supreme court itself upon the point. I concur, however, in the general sentiment. . . ." In this case the question was whether an act of Georgia was constitutional, and therefore the power to declare an act of Congress void was not really the question before the Court.

rights have been violated before it considers its own capacity. In this case, according to Marshall's own theories, the want of jurisdiction was plain on the very face of the pleadings.[20]

The ire of the Republicans had already been aroused by what they considered the gross impropriety of ordering the Secretary of State to show cause; they resented the assumption of power in a court to call a high executive officer before it; they were not in a mood to view temperately the sight of a court, not only declaring an act void, but, before doing so, casting opprobrium upon high executive officers—members and leaders of their own party. Had Marshall had the temerity—perhaps it is fortunate that the opportunity did not arise—to declare the repeal of the Judiciary Act of 1801 unconstitutional, the result might have been disastrous to judicial independence.

What Marshall succeeded in doing was (1) to condemn his political opponents, (2) to exhibit the power of the Court to declare legislative acts void, and (3) to refuse to issue the mandamus; he thus avoided a contest with the President in which he would have been inevitably worsted, because Jefferson would have paid no attention either to him or to his writ. Steps were soon to be taken for testing by impeachment the sanctity of judicial tenure and the immunity of partisan justices; the impeachments which will be considered on later pages must be borne in mind, if we wish to appreciate how critical were the problems and how sensitive the temper of the time. There is no evidence that the Marbury case was trumped up for the purpose of giving Marshall the opportunity to declare an act void, but we can well assume his pleasure in discovering that he had the chance to do so and could exercise the power without bringing on a perilous dispute.

We must now turn to the more important part of Marshall's opinion, a declaration that a certain portion of the thirteenth section of the Judiciary Act of 1789 was void. That section assigned to the Supreme Court the power to issue "writs of mandamus . . . in cases warranted by the principles and usages of law, to any courts appointed,

[20] Chief Justice Taft in Myers *v.* United States, 272 U. S. 52 (1926), said the opinion of Marshall in the Marbury case, as far as it bore on the right of a president to dismiss an officer, was *obiter dictum.* Justice McReynolds upheld the procedure of Marshall in every particular. Why he should do so, the lay mind fails to understand. If the Court in this instance had declared Marbury not entitled to his commission, would the decision have been conclusive of his rights? Can a conclusive decision concerning personal rights be laid down by a court in a case over which it has no jurisdiction? And if the Court had no authority to pass upon the rights involved, why could not Marshall say so and go on to another job?

or persons holding office, under the authority of the United States." [21] The Constitution says that the Supreme Court shall have original jurisdiction in two classes of cases: those affecting ambassadors, other public ministers, and consuls, and those in which a state shall be a party. In all the other cases to which the federal judicial power extends, the Supreme Court is given appellate jurisdiction. The Marbury case, instituted as an original proceeding in the Supreme Court, was plainly not within the original jurisdiction of the Court.

But there was, nevertheless, no need of declaring the provision of the Judiciary Act void. If we read the whole section of the act, a few words of which are quoted in the preceding paragraph, we find no *distinct* and obvious intention to grant to the Supreme Court the right to issue writs of mandamus, except where it had jurisdiction of the case—that is to say, when the Court was exercising its appellate jurisdiction or its original jurisdiction under the terms and restrictions of the Constitution. The Chief Justice could have properly said that, though the words of the act might be construed as an attempt to grant unconstitutional authority to the Court, they were quite capable of another construction; and this construction should be placed upon them —that is to say, such a construction as would signify the right to issue a writ of mandamus "in cases warranted by the principles and usages of law," and in connection with controversies over which the Court, by the Constitution, had jurisdiction.[22]

[21] *Statutes at Large,* I, ch. 20, sec. 13. Italics of the original omitted.

[22] See A. C. McLaughlin, "Marbury vs. Madison Again," *American Bar Association Journal,* XIV, pp. 155-159. It has long been an established principle—not always conscientiously adhered to—that a court will adopt a construction of a statute, which, without doing violence to its fair meaning, will bring it into harmony with the Constitution. This principle offers opportunity for escaping the necessity of declaring an act void. See United States *v.* D. and H. Co., 213 U. S. 366 (1909), and Knights Templars' Indemnity Co. *v.* Jarman, 187 U. S. 197, 205 (1902), and cases there cited. A court often will so interpret a statute that it will not conflict with a fundamental or important principle of the common law. This statement may appear to the reader to have no bearing on the problem we are considering. But as a matter of fact, at least historically speaking, there is a close association between the attitude of courts toward the common law and their attitude in America toward the Constitution. The famous Doctor Bonham case, to which James Otis paid attention in his speech on the writs of assistance, was just this kind of a case; Coke was upholding the principles of the common law and he insisted on so construing a parliamentary act as not to violate the common law and fundamental principles of justice. In any attempt to understand the development of judicial power, we should not lose sight of the fact that there were supposed to be fundamental rights which government should not encroach upon; and if an act could bear a construction

Before further discussion of the principle involved in this famous decision, and before looking for its historical basis, it is well to disabuse our minds of the notion, if the notion be there, that it is the peculiar function of the Supreme Court to pronounce legislative acts void; that Court stands in no peculiar relationship to Congress and is not charged with the special and exclusive duty of upholding the Constitution which is law. It is the duty of any and every court to announce the law and to apply the law in distributing justice to litigants. No matter how lowly a court may be, such is its duty; that is its ordinary and daily job; and in strict theory it proceeds no differently, when deciding whether a legislative act is law or not law, from the way it proceeds when it passes on any other legal problem. Naturally and inevitably an inferior court will hesitate to pronounce a legislative act void; but in theory it has the right and the duty, for the Constitution is the law. We have recently seen a judge of an inferior federal court practically declare an amendment to the Constitution void; and though the Supreme Court, passing upon the question when the case was carried up on appeal, overruled the decision of the lower court, it did not even remotely suggest that the judge was guilty of presumption.[23] Furthermore, we must remember, this judicial power has been used for a hundred and fifty years by state courts; it has been used hundreds of times when those courts have been called upon to consider the constitutionality of state statutes and to decide whether they were or were not contrary to the state constitution or to the Constitution of the United States.[24] The Judiciary Act of 1789, as we have seen, plainly took for granted the right and the possibility of a state court's declaring an act of Congress void; and provision was therefore made for a review in the Supreme Court of the United States to determine whether the decision of the state court should stand.

In giving the famous opinion, Marshall, referring to the distinc-

which would make it consistent with common law and with the essential justice supposed to be embodied in the common law, then that construction would be adopted by the court. The same principle obtains to-day in an American court; a statute will not receive a construction violating fundamental common law and old, established principle, if another construction can be reasonably made use of. See Marshall's statement declaring that an act of Congress ought not to be construed to violate the law of nations, "if any other possible construction remains. . . ." Murray v. Schooner Charming Betsy, 2 Cranch 64, 118 (1804).

[23] United States v. Sprague et al., 282 U. S. 716 (1931).

[24] W. F. Dodd says that in Illinois alone the state supreme court "during the period from 1870 to 1913 passed upon 789 cases involving the constitutionality of statutes, and in more than a fourth of these cases statutes were declared invalid." W. F. Dodd, *State Government* (1922 ed.), p. 147.

tion between governments which are limited and those which are unlimited, said the distinction was abolished if the limits did not confine the persons on whom they were imposed, and if acts prohibited and acts allowed were of equal obligation. "The constitution is either a superior paramount law, unchangeable by ordinary means, or it is on a level with ordinary legislative acts, and, like other acts, is alterable when the legislature shall please to alter it. . . . Certainly all those who have framed written constitutions contemplate them as forming the fundamental and paramount law of the nation, and, consequently, the theory of every such government must be, that an act of the legislature, repugnant to the constitution, is void." He declared this theory to be essentially attached to a written constitution. He also declared, "It is emphatically the province and duty of the judicial department to say what the law is. . . . If two laws conflict with each other, the courts must decide on the operation of each." This argument was buttressed by the statement that, inasmuch as the judicial power of the United States extends to all cases arising under the Constitution, the courts must examine the Constitution : "In some cases, then, the constitution must be looked into by the judges. And if they can open it at all, what part of it are they forbidden to read or to obey?"

Now, the critical question was not whether the Constitution was or was not binding. The question was whether Congress, though acknowledging the obligation to observe constitutional limitations of its power, had the right to decide what the limits were.[25] As a basis for the power of a court to disagree with the legislature and declare an act void, it is not enough to point to a written Constitution. We now know that a country may have a written constitution and the courts may nevertheless have no such power. A court, however, is not without justification in giving weight to historical forces, principles which may have been begotten, and fundamental theories upon which constitutions and laws must be supposed to rest. In fact, this

---

[25] The classical presentation of the right of the legislature to decide on the extent of its own authority was given by Justice Gibson in Eakin v. Raub, 12 Sergeant and Rawle (Pennsylvania) 330, 350 (1825) : "But, in theory, all the organs of the government are of equal capacity; or, if not equal, each must be supposed to have superior capacity only for those things which peculiarly belong to it; and as legislation peculiarly involves the consideration of those limitations which are put on the law-making power, and the interpretation of the laws when made, involves only the construction of the laws themselves, it follows, that the construction of the constitution, in this particular, belongs to the legislature, which ought, therefore, to be taken to have superior capacity to judge of the constitutionality of its own acts." Justice Gibson was speaking of the right of a state court to declare a state act void.

particular judicial power rests so *plainly on purely historical forces,* rather than on any piece of formal logical argument from a document, that anything less than a discussion of historical influences leaves one in doubt concerning the Court's authority. We can recognize the basic principle of the decision only if we know the developments of American thought and of American constitutional principles during forty years and more before Marbury asked for the mandamus. Even should we find in state and federal constitutions the *explicit* announcement of such extraordinary judicial power (and there is no such announcement), we would be led to inquire into the origin of the principle and to examine the nature of the forces that brought such power into existence.

Although the Marbury case was the first in which the Supreme Court declared a congressional act void, there had been various expressions of opinion and dicta by federal justices and some important decisions which need to be taken into consideration as a preparation for Marshall's decision. This examination will lead us over ground already traversed and give us opportunity to review facts and theories already presented. If we begin with the date of Marshall's opinion and work our way backward, seeking to find the origin of the principle on which he acted, we shall find ourselves, even in a hasty and cursory search, studying not only the immediate antecedents of the Marbury case but reaching farther back and looking once more at the doctrines and philosophy of the American Revolution. The doctrine of what is now called "judicial review" is the last word, logically and historically speaking, in the attempt of a free people to establish and maintain a non-autocratic government. It is the culmination of the essentials of Revolutionary thinking and, indeed, of the thinking of those who a hundred years and more before the Revolution called for a government of laws and not of men.

In Calder *v.* Bull, the statements of Justice Chase and Justice Iredell concerning the power of the Court are noteworthy.[26] Two years earlier, in the case of Hylton *v.* the United States,[27] a federal act was attacked as unconstitutional, and, though the Court did not so decide, the suit was brought on the supposition that the Court had the power to declare the act invalid. In Van Horne's Lessee *v.* Dorrance, Justice Paterson said: ". . . if a legislative act oppugns a constitutional principle, the former must give way, and be rejected on the score of

[26] 3 Dallas 386 (1798).
[27] 3 Dallas 171 (1796).

repugnance. . . . It is an important principle, which, in the discussion of questions of the present kind, ought never to be lost sight of, that the Judiciary in this country is not a subordinate, but co-ordinate, branch of the government." [28] This latter statement is especially to be noticed, because, if we should examine carefully all of the early decisions, both state and national, we would find frequent emphasis on the coördinate authority of departments and the independence of the judiciary; a court had power to review and reject an act, not because it was superior to the legislature, not because the court was set up as a body of censors, but because it was entitled to its own independent judgment concerning the meaning of the Constitution and the extent of legislative competence. In the so-called "First Hayburn Case", it appears that certain federal justices in a circuit court declared void a portion of an act requiring judges to sit as pension commissioners.[29]

If we look beyond judicial dicta and decisions, we find similar announcements of the principle. It was by no means novel in 1803. In replies to the Virginia and Kentucky resolutions, several states spoke of the national judiciary as the final interpreter of the Constitution. In 1791 and 1792, James Wilson delivered a series of lectures to the students of the University of Pennsylvania in which he fully developed the doctrine of the Court's independent right to construe the Constitution, and, if necessary, to reject a legislative act. Time and again this subject was touched on in Congress in the first decade after the establishment of the government, and with one exception the speaker took for granted the authority of the Court to ignore unconstitutional legislation.[30] Hamilton's discussion of judicial authority in *The Federalist* is extensive and explicit; he took issue with those who

[28] 2 Dallas 304, 309 (1795).

[29] Max Farrand, "The First Hayburn Case, 1792," *Am. Hist. Rev.*, XIII, pp. 281-285. Professor Farrand seems to demonstrate that Wilson, Blair, and Peters actually met the issue and declared the law unconstitutional. Notice also United States *v.* Yale Todd, referred to in a note appended to United States *v.* Ferreira, 13 Howard 40, 52-53 (1851). For further announcement of the doctrine, see Ogden *v.* Witherspoon, 3 North Carolina 227 (1802), and *Federal Cases*, no. 10, 461, where Marshall declared a state act void because it violated the principle of the separation of powers; see Chase's words in United States *v.* Callender, *Federal Cases*, no. 14,709 (1800), and Iredell's opinion in Minge *v.* Gilmour, *Federal Cases*, no. 9,631 (1798).

[30] A careful examination of the records so far as printed discloses the fact that, "in every Congress from 1789 to 1802, the power of the Court to hold Acts of Congress invalid was not only recognized but endorsed by members of both political parties . . . and that there is but one specific recorded objection . . . namely by Charles Pinckney . . . in 1799. . . ." Charles Warren, *Congress, the Constitution, and the Supreme Court.* p. 97.

had fallen into "perplexity respecting the right of the courts to pronounce legislative acts void, because contrary to the constitution . . . from an imagination that the doctrine would imply a superiority of the judiciary to the legislative power." [31] He referred with approval to the integrity of the state judiciary—evidently having in mind instances in which state judges had declared acts void—and said, "they must have commanded the esteem and applause of all the virtuous and disinterested." In the state conventions which ratified the Constitution this power of the courts was referred to on several occasions; their right to declare acts void was held forth as a safeguard against improper extension of the legislative power.[32]

If we examine the decisions of state courts, passing upon the construction or the validity of state acts, we find a number of instances in which the principle we are here considering was applied or announced. Again we must remind ourselves that the right of the judiciary to independent judgment concerning legislative competence is not confined to federal courts or to judges of any particular description when the question of the constitutionality of legislation arises. The early exercise of this power by state courts to declare such state acts void as they believed to be in conflict with the principles of the state constitutions is especially impressive because no constitution contained the specific statement that it was law.[33] Pronouncements of the principle which we are considering were made both before and after the federal Constitution was adopted.[34]

[31] *The Federalist* (1818 ed.), no. LXXVIII, p. 421. The importance of this idea of equality and independence, rather than superiority, I have already referred to, but I again call attention to it because that was one of the chief foundations for the doctrine we are considering.

[32] Note Oliver Ellsworth in the Connecticut convention. Elliot, *Debates,* II, p. 196. Wilson, in the Pennsylvania convention, announced that the courts would have this power "as a consequence of their independence, and the particular powers of government being defined. . . ." McMaster and Stone, *op. cit.,* p. 354. Note also Marshall in the Virginia convention. Elliot, *Debates,* III, p. 553. See Luther Martin, "Genuine Information," in *Ibid., I,* p. 380. It will be recalled that Hamilton, Ellsworth, Wilson, and Martin had been members of the Federal Convention.

[33] On this phase of the subject, as indeed of the whole, a scholarly and able treatment will be found in C. G. Haines, *The American Doctrine of Judicial Supremacy,* second ed. A briefer statement is in A. C. McLaughlin, *The Courts, the Constitution and Parties.*

[34] The following are examples of state cases in which state legislative acts were declared unconstitutional by state courts or in which the principle of judicial review was announced: Whittington v. Polk, 1 Harris and Johnson (Maryland) 236, 241 (1802); Lindsay and others v. the Commissioners, 2 Bay (South Carolina) 38, 61-62 (1796); State v. ———, 1 Haywood (North Carolina) 28, 29, 40 (1794); Bowman and others v. Middleton, 1 Bay (South Carolina) 252, 254 (1792), a conspicuous

As already said, the Constitution contains no explicit grant of power to declare acts void, and the debates in the Convention do not banish all doubt—if anyone wishes or is anxious to doubt—concerning the intention of the framers or their assumption that this power, not explicitly granted, would nevertheless be exercised. A careful examination of the debates will, however, probably convince the skeptic that men of the Convention made that assumption. Some delegates, at one stage of the Convention's work, disapproved of the exercise of such power; but the general trend of the discussion appears to indicate the general assumption that the power would be exercised in cases over which the courts had jurisdiction.[35]

case, the court declaring an act void because it was against "common right" and "*magna charta*"; Kamper *v.* Hawkins, 1 *Virginia Cases* 20 (1793); Stidger *v.* Rogers, 2 Kentucky 52 (1801); State *v.* Parkhurst, 4 Halsted (New Jersey) 427 (1802); Austin *v.* University of Pennsylvania, 1 Yeates (Pennsylvania) 260, 261 (1793); Respublica *v.* Duquet, 2 Yeates (Pennsylvania) 493 (1799); Turner *v.* Turner's Executrix, 4 Call (Virginia) 234 (1792); Cases of the Judges, 4 Call (Virginia) 135 (1788). See also, Austin Scott, "Holmes vs. Walton: the New Jersey Precedent," *Am. Hist. Rev.*, IV, pp. 456-469. The case was decided in 1780. Commonwealth *v.* Caton et al., 4 Call (Virginia) 5 (1782) contains an announcement of the theory. Rutgers *v.* Waddington (1784), often referred to, is important but is not a clear precedent. See J. B. Thayer, *Cases on Constitutional Law*, part 1, pp. 63-72. The two most conspicuous and influential cases are Trevett *v.* Weeden (Rhode Island, 1786) and Bayard and Wife *v.* Singleton (North Carolina, 1787). For the former case, see the argument of J. M. Varnum, in P. W. Chandler, *American Criminal Trials*, II, p. 281 ff., and in Brinton Coxe, *Judicial Power and Unconstitutional Legislation*, p. 236 ff. Reference should also be made to W. P. Trent, "The Case of Josiah Philips" (1778), *Am. Hist. Rev.*, I, pp. 444-454, which is not a substantial precedent in all respects. The newspapers in July, 1787, when the Federal Convention was in session, contained a notice that the General Court of New Hampshire had repealed a certain act "and thereby justified the conduct of the Justices of the Inferior Court who have uniformly opposed it as unconstitutional and unjust." Quoted in Warren, *The Making of the Constitution*, p. 337 and note 1.

[35] Farrand, *Records*, II, pp. 73-80. See also *Ibid.*, II, pp. 27-28. At a later date, Mercer of Maryland, who was present in the Convention for only a few days altogether, disapproved of the doctrine; and Dickinson said he was impressed by Mercer's statement and thought no such power ought to exist, but he was "at a loss what expedient to substitute." *Ibid.*, II, pp. 298-299. See also debates of June 4 in Madison's *Notes* in *Ibid.*, I, p. 97; and Pierce's notes in *Ibid.*, I, p. 109. This subject is briefly discussed in Charles Warren, *The Making of the Constitution*, p. 331 ff., and also in his *Congress, the Constitution, and the Supreme Court*, ch. IV. See also, F. E. Melvin, "The Judicial Bulwark of the Constitution," *Am. Pol. Sci. Rev.*, VIII, pp. 167-203. A longer discussion is in Charles Beard, *The Supreme Court and the Constitution*, where the author, in an attempt to answer the question whether the Court usurped power to declare laws void, presents not only the words used in the Convention but also other evidence. Among other things he cites the Judiciary Act of 1789, and points to the number of men in the Congress passing that act who had been members of the Convention. Reference is also made to the fact that certain

Special attention should be paid to the words of the Constitution which declare that the Constitution is law. The fact that a constitution, like any other law, is to be interpreted and applied in courts is the salient and cardinal idea. If anyone argues that the quality of the Constitution as law does not necessarily imply the right to judge of the constitutionality of a congressional act, when Congress has exercised its own power to judge, he must nevertheless see that, if the Constitution were not law, the courts could not exercise the power we are discussing;[36] upon the state courts was placed the explicit obligation to handle the federal Constitution as *law,* to pronounce, if need be, portions of their own state constitutions void. Courts—that is the central fact—were to be used to preserve the constitutional system. Again—the repetition needs no apology—the principle and the practice of enforcing either a state or a national constitution as *law* is the pivotal matter which needs explanation and understanding.

We have already called attention to the principle of the separation of the powers of government, a principle widely held and in some state constitutions given explicit expression. With this was included, of course, the independence of the judiciary, which was supposed to make for the preservation of liberty. If this spirit or fact of independence were carried far enough, the courts would (and they did) announce their independent right to declare what the law is and to disregard the judgment of the legislature concerning the extent of its own authority. This independence, like so many other things, takes its roots in English history; no judges of England, had, it is true, gone further than to declare that "the common law will control Acts of Parliament and adjudge them to be utterly void. . . ." But English courts had a considerable degree of independence in fact and, on the whole, much independence in spirit in endeavoring to maintain what they might possibly have called the *law* of the constitution,[37] certainly the essential rights of civil liberty.

delegates in the Convention had direct knowledge of the exercise of this power by the state judges.

[36] The courts carried the principle and the philosophy on which it was based to its logical conclusion.

[37] Certainly worthy of special attention is the fact that the ordinary judiciary in Britain entertains cases involving the rights of a litigant who claims that his rights have been violated by an official; there is and was no special court having jurisdiction of cases involving the authority of officials; questions are passed upon by the ordinary courts of law in distributing justice to individuals. In other words, the courts did recognize as law the principles of the constitution protecting civil liberty, though they did not go so far as to pronounce parliamentary acts void.

The old Congress of the Confederation was especially tried by the readiness of the states to disregard the treaty of peace. The result of such conduct was confusion; in the conduct of foreign affairs it caused ineptitude, demoralizing incompetence. We have noticed in a preceding chapter that even in the time of the Confederation the Congress saw the desirability of courts' upholding treaties; when treaties are "constitutionally made" they become "part of the law of the land. . . ." Resolutions of Congress called upon the state legislatures to repeal their objectionable acts and to authorize the courts to decide cases in accordance with the treaty and to disregard a state law in conflict with the treaty. The declaration, it is true, was not made that a court should disregard a distinct legislative enactment; but the statement nevertheless cannot be considered of no value in any attempt to discover the rise of judicial power.[38] This fact is significant chiefly as indicative of a tendency or a state of mind in the days immediately before the Federal Convention met.

In connection with the cases decided before the adoption of the federal Constitution, we find references to the reasoning of Vattel, to whose influence on the men of the Revolution attention was called on preceding pages of this volume. These pronouncements, restating the principles of the Revolution, were the product of a period of stress and storm in which elementary or fundamental doctrines—more important than institutional forms—were the common possession of the people; the courts were prepared to make those doctrines real in the law; they institutionalized a theory by acting on it. James Iredell, of North Carolina, who later became a member of the federal Supreme Court, said (1786, 1787), "We were not ignorant of the theory *of the necessity of the legislature being absolute in all cases,* because it was the great ground of the British pretensions." "Without an express Constitution the powers of the Legislature would undoubtedly have been absolute (as the Parliament in Great Britain is held to be), and any act passed, *not inconsistent with natural justice* (for that curb is avowed by the judges even in England), would have been binding on the people. The experience of the evils which the American war fully disclosed, attending an absolute power in a legislative body, suggested the propriety of a real, original contract between the people and their future Government, such, perhaps, as there has been no instance of in the world but in America." [39] This transmutation of Revolutionary

[38] See *Journals of Congress* (1823 ed.), IV, pp. 730, 737.
[39] G. J. McRee, *Life and Correspondence of James Iredell,* II, pp. 146, 172-173.

doctrine into judicial decisions, in which the state courts took their stand against the authority of the legislature and maintained the state constitution, as the judges conceived the constitution to be, was not in all instances hailed with approval.[40] But the courts, as we have seen, gradually developed and asserted their power.

In some of the early state constitutions provisions were made for checks upon legislative powers. Had the duty of the courts been fully understood, those provisions, it may be, would not have been made. But on the whole, they bring out in strong light the fundamental thought of the time: there is danger in unchecked legislative power; absolute government is not free government; legislators must obey the law. And thus, if we are looking for a state of mind, for a philosophy of government, for basic principles on which courts act in refusing to recognize unconstitutional legislation, these attempts of the early constitution-makers to find methods of limiting legislative discretion rather strengthen than weaken the position and the theory of the courts, when they definitely carried into operation (without clearly assigned instruction from the people) this belief that only constitutionally-restrained government is free and safe.

To the reader who has been patient enough to follow the writer in discussing the principles of the Revolution as given on earlier pages, further discussion may seem unnecessary. But a word or two may not be amiss. The colonists flatly opposed parliamentary acts on the ground that such acts were unconstitutional and hence not binding. And after all, the essential principle is this: *no one* is bound to obey an act which is not law. In our anxiety to discover why a court can declare an act void, we may lose sight of this primary principle; the courts only recognize the supremacy of that principle and make it operative; the individual litigant declares an act void and asks the court to agree with him. We need to remember also the formal announcement of the Revolutionary days, "In all free states, the constitution is fixed", the constant use of Locke's second essay, and the repetition of Vattel's assertion that legislators cannot change the constitution without destroying the foundation of their own authority. Locke points out that according to the elementary principles of the common law, an officer

---

[40] Madison said in the Federal Convention: "In R. Island the Judges who refused to execute an unconstitutional law were displaced, and others substituted, by the Legislature who would be willing instruments of the wicked & arbitrary plans of their masters." Farrand. *Records,* II, p. 28. This case must have been well known.

acting without authority may be resisted.[41] Over and over again in the Revolutionary argument we find assertion that Parliament was bound and limited by the constitution; the colonists attributed to Britain a principle which they were to make actual in their own constitutions; and the courts, when opportunity arose, assumed the right, in their independence, to act upon that principle and make the Revolutionary doctrine as real as their own position permitted. If we look back through the ages, we see constantly arising the question: are there no limits on governmental power? The framers of our written constitutions sought to answer that question; they established bills of rights referring to rights which government did not create and which no government could violate. Once again, "who are a free people?" The courts carried the principle of inviolable law into practical effect in their administering of justice.[42]

The right of a court to declare an act of Congress void was acted upon only twice before the Civil War. Fifty-four years after Marbury v. Madison, the Supreme Court declared the Missouri Compromise beyond congressional competence and hence invalid. In these two cases, the Supreme Court might have avoided the issue of constitutionality altogether: in the Marbury case, Marshall could have properly construed the act of 1789 in such a way as to deny the jurisdiction of the Court without declaring a portion of the act void; Taney

[41] It may seem strange to the reader that one should call attention to the common law of a country in which the theory holds that Parliament possesses sovereign authority and that what it does must be law. It is unnecessary to cite again the dicta of English judges. The essential fact is this: common law judges were and are engaged in announcing principles not laid down in formal legislative enactments. They may refer to precedents, but they make no pretense, in enforcing the common law, of carrying out the mandates of a government, mandates laid down in legislation. The principles they announce are supposed to have existed before governments, to be founded in custom and in substantial justice; such was the source of the belief that the English constitution embodied certain fundamental principles of common right— the colonists said natural right and justice. Had courts been accustomed only to interpret and apply legislative acts, they would have found it more difficult, more at variance with their habits of thought and their method of approach, to declare a legislative act void and of no effect. Furthermore, even the elementary common law principles, announced by Locke as justifying opposition to officials, were made the basis, by his own reasoning, of a *constitutional* right for opposition to unwarranted governmental action.

[42] The foundation for this power as *an historical fact* rested on the general assumptions that underlie compact and natural rights thinking: government is founded on compact; rights existed before government; governments are established to protect rights. See E. S. Corwin, "The 'Higher Law' Background of American Constitutional Law," *Harvard Law Review*, XLII, pp. 149-185, 365-409; A. C. McLaughlin, *The Foundations of American Constitutionalism*, especially ch. V.

could have avoided any declaration concerning the constitutionality of the Missouri Compromise, and it seems fairly if not conclusively certain that his decision was unwarranted. The salient facts are, therefore, (1) the principle took its rise in the state courts; (2) the state courts have used the power freely in a multitude of cases; (3) especially for the first seventy years the most important power of the federal Supreme Court, in viewing the constitutionality of legislation, was the power to declare state acts invalid, if they violated the federal Constitution, laws, or treaties; this power preserved the federal system from disintegration.[43]

The judicial authority we are here considering may have gained strength from colonial conditions and the institutional practices of the old empire; for we cannot explain the rise and establishment of the principle in American constitutional structure without recognizing it, as we have said, as the product of history, the result of a developing attitude of mind toward government and authority. It may be well, therefore, to notice that there never had existed in America a legislature free from external restraint; in some colonies there had been charters granting and limiting colonial power. The early settlements had been made in some instances by corporations, and beyond the powers assigned to the corporation it of course could not go. The influence of the corporation has probably not received sufficient attention in our studies of the growth of American constitutionalism. Furthermore, the king in council exercised the right to disallow colonial acts, and the same body entertained appeals from colonial courts. Probably these experiences and these institutional practices had their effect in making clear to the American mind that a legislature need not necessarily have complete authority or be the ultimate and conclusive judge of its own power. But when all is said, the main line of argument and the main ideas announced by the courts arose during the course of the Revolutionary discussion. Those ideas took their beginning chiefly in the history of seventeenth-century England—the century in which America took her birth. The *conscious* line of approach to the principle of judicial independent right to protect civil

---

[43] "The United States would not come to an end if we lost our power to declare an Act of Congress void." Speech of Holmes, February 15, 1913, *Speeches of Oliver Wendell Holmes,* quoted in Charles Warren, *The Supreme Court in United States History,* I, p. 17 and note 2. The power certainly appears of no supreme significance before the Civil Rights Cases, 1883, though the important principle of that case had been announced in earlier cases. There has been a marked increase in the number of cases since 1865.

liberty, the line followed in the early state decisions, rested on the basis of fundamental law (a principle distinctly stated and an ideal striven for during the Cromwellian period, especially 1647-1653) [44] and on doctrines of natural justice and natural right which were thought to be inviolable.

Before leaving this subject and passing on to consider the historical events of the early nineteenth century, attention may be called again to the relation of the courts to executive authority. The connection between the power to ignore unconstitutional legislation and to treat executive acts as valid, only if they be legal and constitutional, is evident; it is evident at least, if we are looking for fundamental principles. This power is of tremendous significance, one of the most important in our whole constitutional system. The right of a court in its ordinary distribution of justice to punish the agents of the highest executive power, if they act beyond the law, took its rise in English law; it is a primary principle of the British-American system of law and of British-American constitutionalism. Is it more than a narrow step from this right and this principle, which keeps the executive within constitutional limits, to the right and the principle which restrain the legislature by refusing to treat unconstitutional enactments as law? Even if the two principles or rights be kept distinct and be without necessary logical connection, nevertheless the authority of a court—and of course this is true within the state constitutional system as well as within the federal—to restrain or hold in check executive power cannot be considered less important than the right to ignore unconstitutional legislation.

[44] "The idea of limiting government by law was in the air. A reëstablishment of the constitution in such form that it could not again be set aside by the rivalry of king and Parliament was probably the one thing that men of all parties desired." T. C. Pease, *The Leveller Movement*, p. 194. The author is speaking here of 1647, but in a measure the idea continued beyond that year.

CHAPTER XXIV

THE IMPEACHMENT OF PICKERING AND CHASE.
THE BURR CONSPIRACY

Even before the decision in Marbury v. Madison, Jefferson sent
to the House (February 3, 1803) documents and a message calling
attention to the conduct of John Pickering, a federal district judge in
New Hampshire, and saying that "proceedings of redress" were within
the powers of the House, "if they shall be of opinion that the case
calls for them." The House speedily took action for impeaching Pickering before the Senate, but the trial was not begun until the next
winter (January, 1804). He was charged with malfeasance and unlawful conduct in the handling of one particular case, and of being a
man of loose morals and intemperate habits who had appeared upon
the bench "in a state of total intoxication", and had "frequently, in
a most profane and indecent manner, invoke[d] the name of the Supreme Being".

Difficult questions of constitutional interpretation arose. The Constitution provides for the removal of civil officers from office "on impeachment for and conviction of treason, bribery, or other high crimes
and misdemeanors." Could an officer be convicted only for an indictable offense, or could he be convicted and removed from office because
of gross misconduct? Judge Pickering, it appeared from a petition
from his son, had for some time been insane; and Robert G. Harper,
representing the petitioner, asked for an opportunity to show this fact.
Evidence was admitted and it established the Judge's insanity and
habitual drunkenness—the latter, we may charitably suppose (it was
indeed so asserted in one deposition), the result of the former condition. Harper declared "that to constitute any crime a vicious will is
necessary, and that a man insane cannot be put upon his trial. . . ."
The Senate, thus faced by an awkward problem, finally voted, not
without protest from some of its members, that Pickering was "guilty,
as charged". By using this form of verdict the Senate took refuge in a
subterfuge, avoiding an explicit announcement of its right to remove

an officer for acts not technically criminal. The final vote did not establish a precedent of much value.[1]

But a more worthy and valiant foeman to meet the steel of the excited Republicans was Justice Samuel Chase of the Supreme Court, a man of imperious and domineering temper whose zeal was not always moderated by discretion. His shameful conduct in the Fries, Callender, and Cooper cases, the latter two under the Sedition Act, had aroused justifiable resentment.[2] But those matters were of the past and might possibly have been ignored, had he not in 1803, in charging a grand jury at Baltimore, taken occasion to make a political harangue of an objectionable character. For political discourses from the bench there were some notable precedents, but in this instance Chase exceeded moderation. In a non-technical sense his misbehavior seems unquestionable.[3] Was his misconduct such as to justify removal from office? Did it constitute a misdemeanor, in the constitutional sense of the word?

In a series of eight articles Chase was charged with various offenses, among them conducting himself in the Fries trial "in a manner highly arbitrary, oppressive, and unjust"; unbecoming conduct and disregard of law in the Callender case; stooping "to the level of

[1] The senators, said Senator Dayton, "were simply to be allowed to vote, whether Judge Pickering was guilty as charged—that is, guilty of the facts charged in each article—aye or no. . . . There were members who were disposed to give sentence of removal . . . who could not, however, conscientiously vote that they [the facts alleged and proved] amounted to high crimes and misdemeanors, especially when committed by a man proved at the very time to be insane, and to have been so ever since. . . ." Annals of Congress, 8 Cong., 1 sess., col. 365. Senator White declared that such procedure would give warrant for removing anyone from office; every officer of government would be "at the mercy of a majority of Congress. . . ." Ibid. The vote of "guilty, as charged" stood nineteen yeas, seven nays. Ibid., col. 367. Proceedings are found in Ibid., cols. 315-367. The Pickering impeachment was the second to come before the Senate. William Blount of Tennessee, a Senator, was not convicted, his defense being that a senator was not a civil officer of the United States; furthermore, he had already been expelled from the Senate.

[2] "In short, the assaults upon the National Judiciary were made possible chiefly by the conduct of the National judges themselves." A. J. Beveridge, The Life of John Marshall, III, p. 30.

[3] To the grand jury Chase commented upon the repeal of the Judiciary Act: "The independence of the national Judiciary is already shaken to its foundation, and the virtue of the people alone can restore it." Universal suffrage, he said, will "rapidly destroy all protection to property, and all security to personal liberty; and our republican constitution will sink into a mobocracy, the worst of all possible governments." ". . . the modern doctrines by our late reformers, that all men in a state of society are entitled to enjoy equal liberty and equal rights, have brought this mighty mischief upon us. . . ." The address is given in full in Annals of Congress, 8 Cong., 2 sess., cols. 673-676.

an informer" by refusing to discharge a grand jury at Newcastle, and indulging in other objectionable procedure, thereby "degrading his high judicial functions"; and addressing the grand jury at Baltimore in a "highly indecent" manner, "tending to prostitute the high judicial character with which he was invested. . . ."[4] The trial opened January 2, 1805; various delays ensued, time being given for the preparation of Chase's answer; and so not until February 4, 1805, did the Senate proceed to the actual trial on the charges submitted.

The proceedings were solemn and dignified; the crisis was real. Perhaps in imitation of the famous trial of Warren Hastings, when, as Macaulay tells us, "The gray old walls were hung with scarlet", the Senate chamber was "fitted up in a style of appropriate elegance. Benches, covered with crimson, . . . were assigned to the members of the Senate."[5] The managers appointed by the House were led by John Randolph, who not long before had begun his meteoric career in Congress. The accused was defended by an array of able lawyers— Robert G. Harper, Joseph Hopkinson, and Luther Martin, the "Federalist bulldog", for Martin was now an implacable Federalist. He was not only a brilliant speaker, quite capable if need be of vehement attack, but also learned and skillful in the presentation of his argument. His speech toward the end of the trial occupied the greater part of two days and was a powerful defense of his client's rights.

The critical question was what constituted an impeachable offense. The counsel for Chase insisted that the offense must be an indictable one, not merely reprehensible conduct of which the senators might disapprove. The controversy on this particular question may be summed up in the words of Martin: ". . . no judge or other officer can . . . be removed from office but by impeachment, and for the violation of *some law*, which violation must be, not simply a crime or misdemeanor, but a *high* crime or misdemeanor." He called attention to the statement of Rodney, one of the House managers, that a judge holds his office during good behavior and that misbehavior and misdemeanor are synonymous. Martin shrewdly admitted the identity of meaning, declaring that only such misbehavior as constituted a misdemeanor, "a violation of some law punishable", could be considered

---

[4] *Ibid.*, cols. 85-88.
[5] *Ibid.*, col. 100. ". . . a new gallery was raised, and fitted up with peculiar elegance, intended primarily for the exclusive accommodation of ladies. But this feature of the arrangement, made by the Vice President, was at an early period of the trial abandoned, it having been found impracticable to separate the sexes!"

misbehavior in the constitutional sense.[6] Had the House managers been as adroit, as well-prepared, and as consistent as their adversaries, the result might have been the same; but the reader of the arguments has an unwonted feeling of compassion for Randolph, whose copious vocabulary was an insufficient defense against the assaults of his opponents. The verdict for acquittal was pronounced March 1. Thirty-four members were in attendance; twenty-three votes were necessary for conviction. The highest number voting "guilty" on any one article —the eighth, which referred to the Baltimore harangue—was nineteen.

What might have ensued had Chase been convicted, no one can say. It is difficult to believe that Marshall would have been the next victim; he had not indulged in unbecoming behavior or treated attorneys in a manner which they at least thought contemptuous; he had not declared the repeal of the Judiciary Act of 1801 void; his greatest error or ground for partisan attack was his method of handling the Marbury case, not his exercising the right of the Court to declare an act unconstitutional.[7] Such right had been so often acknowledged that impeachment on that ground could have been maintained only by the most extreme and violent partisanship. In the high excitement of the time, however, a general assault upon the judiciary might have followed. John Quincy Adams wrote to his father: "The attack by impeachment upon the Judicial Department of our National Government began two years ago, and has been conducted with great address as well as with persevering violence. . . . The assault upon Judge Chase . . . was unquestionably intended to pave the way for another prosecution, which would have swept the Supreme Judicial Bench clean at a stroke. . . ."[8] Certainly the most important matter was not the legal basis for impeachment but the attack upon the judiciary, which, if successful, might have made the courts political footballs; the attack upon the judiciary must have made it plain that justices were engaged in a dangerous practice when they displayed violent partisan temper on

[6] *Ibid.,* col. 436. A detailed and valuable account of the impeachments is given in Henry Adams, *History of the United States,* II, chs. VII, X.
[7] See Charles Warren, *The Supreme Court in United States History,* I, pp. 243-244. Beveridge says, ". . . Marshall had actually proposed to his associates upon the Supreme Bench that they refuse to sit as circuit judges, and 'risk the consequences.'" Beveridge, *op. cit.,* III, p. 122.
[8] March 8, 1805. Quoted in Charles Warren, *The Supreme Court in United States History,* I, pp. 294-295.

the bench. As a result of this trial the basis of impeachment still remained indefinite. Neither the Senate nor the House committed itself to the doctrine laid down by Martin. There is, however, much space open to occupancy between the right to convict an officer for purely partisan purposes or for immediate particular interests, on the one hand, and the right to do so for only a penal offense, on the other. We have no reason to suppose that a Senate, thoroughly convinced of the serious misconduct of a judge on the bench or of any other official, will be deterred by technical interpretation of "high crimes and misdemeanors" from pronouncing sentence against him.[9]

Hardly was the Chase trial out of the way when a new excitement took its place. Newspapers and partisan orators were given another opportunity to display their talents. Few events in our history have been so theatrical, so well-supplied with all the features of melodrama, as the conspiracy of Aaron Burr and his trial for treason. It is a long, intricate, and perplexing story; and before it ends we find the names of many men, playing one rôle or another, who are famous in American history: Aaron Burr, the central figure, a debonair, conscienceless adventurer; James Wilkinson, who had for years been in the pay of Spain, ready for any safe intrigue with money in it; poor Blennerhasset, who fell a prey to Burr's gracious cajoleries only to lose his fortune and find his romantic hero "a vulgar swindler"; Samuel Swartwout, afterwards appointed by President Jackson to be collector at the port of New York where he stole more than a million dollars; John Randolph of Roanoke, acting as the foreman of the grand jury; Andrew Jackson, who, incapable of treason, had been approached by Burr for his own purposes; Jonathan Dayton, a framer of the federal Constitution and one of Burr's active confederates; William Wirt, representing the government at the trial, an orator of the first rank; Luther Martin, one of Burr's able attorneys through many days of strenuous and violent debate; Thomas Jefferson, who had at first taken lightly the story of intrigue and treason but finally used the authority of his office for conviction with an amazing intensity of purpose, as if the credit of his administration and his party were hanging in the balance; John Marshall, imperturbable, realizing that

[9] "By the liberal interpretation of the term 'high misdemeanor,' which the Senate has given it, there is now no difficulty in securing the removal of a judge for any reason that shows him unfit. . . ." Ex-President Taft, speaking to the American Bar Association in 1913. American Bar Association *Report* for 1913, XXXVIII, p. 432.

more was at stake than the conviction of a worthless prisoner, prepared laboriously to expound the law and defend the Constitution. And so, as the facts developed, as the trial came on and wound its way along, the court and the Chief Justice were once more in the limelight, once more the objects of denunciation.

What Burr was trying to do, or thought he was trying to do, is still a matter of conjecture. Recent investigators have come to the conclusion that he was not intent upon separating the west from the union, but was planning to make use of strained relations between Spain and the United States to win glory and wealth for himself, basing his hopes on the traditional dislike for the Spaniards especially among the southwesterners. But to reach this conclusion Burr's own words must be cast aside as a mere attempt to obtain money from foreign governments by false pretenses; in fact, there was so much secrecy and so much lying that to reach a positive opinion is difficult. [10]

Just what Burr had in mind we do not need to determine. Whatever it was, the conspiracy added fuel to sectional and party controversies already sufficiently aglow. The government was in the midst of severest perplexities in its relations with foreign nations, for Great Britain was impressing our seamen, and at the beginning of this exciting summer news came that a British man-of-war had poured a broadside into an American frigate. Our claim to West Florida raised delicate questions of our relations with Spain. The New England leaders were seriously discontented and openly grumbling. Burr's plans, even if they were intended to be but a joyful attack upon the despised Spaniard, imposed a new and maddening burden upon a sorely-perplexed administration. But it was not the administration alone that was in danger; the stability and safety of the nation were imperiled by foreign aggression and domestic discontent.

In the course of the multiple hearings, disputes, arguments, and opinions arising from Burr's escapade, a series of significant constitutional questions arose and important decisions were rendered. Two young men, Bollman and Swartwout,[11] who had been brought under

---

[10] Henry Adams, *History of the United States,* II, ch. VIII; III, chs. X-XIV, XIX, gives a full narrative. W. F. McCaleb, *The Aaron Burr Conspiracy,* attempts, perhaps successfully, to establish the fact that Burr did not plan to dismember the union. Beveridge, *op. cit.,* III, chs. VI-IX, agrees with McCaleb and develops his thesis. Adams, writing before McCaleb's studies, relies in part for his condemnation of Burr on statements made by Burr which were not improbably pure fiction.

[11] Ex parte Bollman and ex parte Swartwout, 4 Cranch 75 (1807).

the spell of Burr and used for his own ends, having been committed by a circuit court and charged with treason, applied to the Supreme Court for a writ of habeas corpus. The Constitution defines treason as levying war against the United States or adhering to their enemies and giving them aid and comfort. The Chief Justice, delivering the opinion of the Court, found no evidence sufficient to justify the commitment of the prisoners on the charge of treason. In reaching this conclusion he said, "To conspire to levy war, and actually to levy war, are distinct offenses. The first must be brought into open action by the assemblage of men for a purpose treasonable in itself, or the fact of levying war cannot have been committed. . . . It is not the intention of the court to say that no individual can be guilty of this crime who has not appeared in arms against his country. On the contrary, if war be actually levied, that is, if a body of men be actually assembled for the purpose of effecting by force a treasonable purpose, all those who perform any part, however minute, or however remote from the scene of action, and who are actually leagued in the general conspiracy, are to be considered as traitors."

This statement appeared to give considerable basis for finding Burr guilty, when his turn came, though of course the question remained whether or not the famous assemblage at Blennerhassett's Island was an assemblage for a treasonable purpose. On the other hand, a letter from Burr to Wilkinson, which was presented in the Bollman case to show that a treasonable enterprise was on foot, was declared by Marshall to contain not one syllable having "a natural reference to an enterprise against any territory of the United States." [12] This belief of course cast doubt upon the treasonable character of the whole undertaking.

The next step was taken against Burr himself. When the question of his indictment was under consideration by the grand jury at Richmond, Marshall took the extraordinary step of issuing a writ of *subpoena duces tecum* to Jefferson. It was of course disregarded and only added to the fury of Jefferson's dislike of the Chief Justice and to his own wrathful determination to bring Burr to the gallows. The struggle appeared in reality not so much a contest over the question of Burr's guilt as a passage-at-arms between the President and the man holding the highest judicial office. As to whether Marshall was technically justified in issuing the writ, there still appears to be a difference

---

[12] 4 Cranch 75, 132-133. Documents bearing on the question can be found in 4 Cranch, appendixes A and B.

of opinion.[13] But it certainly added fuel to the flame of partisan controversy; and the heat engendered remained long after Burr himself had dwindled into appropriate obscurity, leaving behind him his grandiose conspiracy for the tender ministrations of the historian.

In the summer of 1807, Burr was finally indicted for treason and, in a separate indictment, for misdemeanor. The list of attorneys for the government and for the defense included men of ability and distinction. William Wirt fought valiantly for conviction. Luther Martin, defending Burr, had the time of his life, for nothing was dearer to his heart than a controversy with Jefferson; "as great a scoundrel as Tom Jefferson" is said to have been his customary method of denouncing a particularly obnoxious person.

The Constitution provides that no person shall be convicted of treason "unless on the testimony of two witnesses to the same overt act, or on confession in open court." The crisis of the trial arose in connection with the question of the admissibility of certain evidence offered by the prosecution. The attorneys for the defense objected on the ground that Burr was not present with the forces at Blennerhassett's Island, that he was at a great distance and in a different state, and that the testimony offered to connect him with those who committed the overt act was totally irrelevant. Marshall's ruling against the admission of the kind of evidence which proposed to show Burr's connection with the assemblage was decisive. The verdict of the jury was that Burr was "not proved to be guilty under this indictment by any evidence submitted to us"—a form of verdict which perhaps tells its own story. The court decided that the verdict should remain as found by the jury; and that an entry should be made on the record of "not guilty".[14]

Marshall's opinion was long and elaborate; the questions involved were difficult and intricate. However learned and acute his argument may be, it appears to be wanting in the clarity, simplicity, and convincing force so apparent in his later decisions. If this be so, the want may be chargeable to the intricacy of the problem, or, perhaps, to the

[13] "The course of recent criticism has usually been to support Marshall in this matter of the subpoena. It is confessed that the court had no authority to enforce this command against the President, and it must be admitted that the issuing of futile orders is not conducive to the dignity of the court. And again, it seems a curious conception of the judicial function to call the head of the nation from his official duties to give testimony. The incident seems best explained as an honest mistake of judgment. . . ." *The Constitutional Decisions of John Marshall* (J. P. Cotton, Jr., ed.), I, p. 99.

[14] David Robertson, *Reports of the Trials of Colonel Aaron Burr*, II, pp. 446-447.

fact that the Chief Justice had not as yet reached the pinnacle of his powers; but his position was a delicate one; political and personal passions were involved; any precise and sweeping opinion not laboriously exposing his position, any opinion appearing to be dogmatic and peremptory, would have been fraught with danger to his authority and the dignity of the court.

He referred to the opinion in the Bollman and Swartwout case and to the words already quoted: "if war be actually levied, . . . all those who perform any part however minute or however remote from the scene of action and who are actually leagued in the general conspiracy are to be considered as traitors." But he declared: "This opinion does not touch the case of a person who advises or procures an assemblage and does nothing further. The advising certainly, and perhaps the procuring is more in the nature of a conspiracy to levey [sic] war than of the actual levying of war." This was a crucial position because it made a distinction between actual presence with an armed force, or actual participation in the levying of war, on the one hand, and advice and like services, on the other.

The pivotal statements in the opinion cannot easily be selected, but the following pronouncement is especially important: "If in one case the *presence* of the individual make the guilt of the assemblage his guilt, and in the other case the *procurement* by the individual make the guilt of the assemblage his guilt, then presence and procurement are equally component parts of the overt act, and equally require two witnesses. . . . The presence of the party, where presence is necessary, being a part of the overt act must be *positively* proved by two witnesses. No presumptive evidence, no facts from which presence may be conjectured or inferred will satisfy the constitution and the law. If *procurement* take the place of *presence* and become part of the overt act, then no presumptive evidence, no facts from which the procurement may be conjectured or inferred, can satisfy the constitution and the law." ". . . the fact itself [the procurement] must be proved by two witnesses, and must have been committed within the district." [15] This means, in simple phraseology, that the fact of Burr's

[15] *Ibid.*, II, pp. 436-437. Italics mine. "The present indictment charges the prisoner with levying war against the United States, and alleges an overt act of levying war. That overt act must be proved, according to the mandates of the constitution and of the act of congress, by two witnesses. It is not proved by a single witness. The presence of the accused has been stated to be an essential component part of the overt act in this indictment, unless the common law principle respecting accessories should render it unnecessary; and there is not only no witness who has proved his

responsibility for the assembling of the armed forces had to be established by two witnesses who could testify to the same overt act. The prosecution despaired of securing the necessary testimony.

This mode of reasoning has been strongly attacked,[16] and our own judgment is uncalled for. Though the Chief Justice made abundant references to English authorities, the opinion leaves the impression of a determination not to allow English history or law to dull his belief in the liberal provisions of a free Constitution. Certainly he gave the fullest effect to the words which were intended to guard against the establishment or punishment of constructive treason. Actual participation in a treasonable enterprise had to be established by competent testimony of the nature provided by the Constitution. Doubtless the decision makes it difficult to establish the guilt of one who may be the real leader in a treasonable movement; for, while an actual assembling in arms and the presence of a single person with the armed forces may be easily susceptible of proof, it is difficult to establish the guilt of one who carries on his machinations in secret, where secrecy is the *sine qua non* of success. To such objections Marshall made answer: "If it be said that the advising or procurement of treason is a secret transaction, which can scarcely ever be proved in the manner required by this opinion, the answer which will readily suggest itself is, that the difficulty of proving a fact will not justify conviction without proof. Certainly it will not justify conviction without a direct and positive witness in a case where the constitution requires two. The more correct inference from this circumstance would seem to be, that the advising of the fact is not within the constitutional definition of the crime. To advise or procure a treason is in the nature of conspiring or plotting treason, which is not treason in itself." [17]

Withal we cannot lament the determination of the Chief Justice so to construe the Constitution that treason is not to be inferred from any amount of conjecture or surmise. Furthermore, Burr's intentions were too uncertain to furnish any assurance that a verdict of guilty would have been just, had all the facts been exposed. Marshall's reflec-

---

actual or legal presence, but the fact of his absence is not controverted. The counsel for the prosecution offer to give in evidence subsequent transactions at a different place and in a different state, in order to prove—what? the overt act laid in the indictment? that the prisoner was one of those who assembled at Blannerhassett's [*sic*] island? No: that is not alleged. It is well known that such testimony is not competent to establish such a fact." *Ibid.,* II, p. 443.

[16] See E. S. Corwin, *John Marshall and the Constitution,* ch. IV.

[17] Robertson, *op. cit.,* II, p. 437.

tion on Wilkinson's letter, when he was passing on the matter of Boll-man and Swartwout, leads us to think he had grave doubts about the actual treasonable nature of the whole enterprise. And we may well imagine that he was glad, when interpreting the Constitution as a new and positive safeguard of freedom, to find a method whereby the critical question of Burr's essential intent and purpose was avoided and was not passed on by the jury with insufficient if not misleading evidence at its command.

Further proceedings against the alleged culprit broke down and came to naught. When Burr was released, the air reeked with maledictions. Jefferson was piqued; he was indignant. His message to Congress, though certain especially truculent sentences were stricken out of the first draft, displayed his discontent. Why should he, the popular leader, the head of a victorious party, be once again balked by the Chief Justice, a crafty manipulator of the law? Once more the strange and fascinating contradiction: Jefferson, the foe of tyranny, the apostle of freedom and individual rights, was angry because the Chief Justice, an advocate of strong and effective government, had so interpreted the Constitution as to protect a prisoner alleged to be guilty of treason against the nation. Marshall's decision partook of the character of Jeffersonian liberalism and modernism; and Jefferson lamented.

CHAPTER XXV

FEDERAL AND STATE DIFFERENCES.

FEDERALIST OPPOSITION. THE EMBARGO.
THE OLMSTEAD CASE

Why did the Federalist leaders object to the terms of the Louisiana treaty? Partly because they would have objected to the annexation of paradise, if the arrangements had been made by Thomas Jefferson; partly because they were growing bitter at the sight of Virginia's domination; partly because they were afraid of the south and were perhaps more afraid of the west where new states were growing up and would ere long rob New England of her powers and influence. To some of the New Englanders, and doubtless to others as well, the specter of democracy appeared menacing and frightful. Government was intended for the wise, the good, and the rich, and the future held nothing but desolation for a country ruled by Jacobins and an ignorant populace.[1]

Then began deliberate but secret whisperings of secession.[2] We shall probably never know just how definite the conspiracy was and just who were implicated. The irascible Pickering, "honest Tim", was foremost and the most confident. "I do not know *one reflecting* Nov-Anglian", he wrote to Rufus King in 1804, "who is not anxious for the GREAT EVENT at which I have glanced." [3] The difficulty in

---

[1] "Like death it [a democracy] is only the dismal passport to a more dismal hereafter", wrote Fisher Ames, who was probably the most doleful of all the malcontents. Letter from Ames to Christopher Gore, October 3, 1803, in Fisher Ames, *Works* (Seth Ames, ed.), I, p. 324. "Our country is too big for union, too sordid for patriotism, too democratic for liberty. . . . Its vice will govern it, by practising upon its folly." Letter from Ames to Thomas Dwight, October 26, 1803, in *Ibid.*, I, p. 328. "The federalists must entrench themselves in the State governments, and endeavor to make State justice and State power a shelter of the wise, and good, and rich, from the wild destroying rage of the southern Jacobins." Letter from Ames to Christopher Gore, December 13, 1802, in *Ibid.*, I, p. 310.

[2] The chief sources are Henry Adams, *Documents Relating to New-England Federalism. 1800-1815;* H. C. Lodge, *Life and Letters of George Cabot; Works of Fisher Ames* (Seth Ames, ed.), I; J. C. Hamilton, *History of the Republic of the United States*, VII; W. P. and J. P. Cutler, *Life, Journals and Correspondence of Rev. Manasseh Cutler*, especially II, pp. 86-87, 140.

[3] Adams, *New-England Federalism*, p. 352.

331

appraising this declaration as evidence arises from a suspicion of Pickering's judgment, about which no words of praise would be justified. Furthermore, no one would be capable of reflection except a person viewing the world in general and the vices of democracy as Pickering did. George Cabot kept his head, though he was also depressed by the awful spectacle of democracy: *"We are democratic altogether"*, he told Pickering, "and I hold democracy, in its natural operation, to be *the government of the worst*." [4] But nothing, he believed, could be done until the people felt something real and serious, such as a war with Great Britain, "manifestly provoked by our rulers." [5] The people were not in a state of distress; they were not greatly disturbed or anxious; and yet some of these wise, good, and rich leaders actually seemed to think New England could be led by her fears and forebodings to dissolve the union, although the strongest ground for taking the step must be the democratic theories of the Virginians. It was much like saying to the people, "The Virginians, under the tutelage of Jefferson, trust the people; we do not; therefore all of you should coöperate with us in destroying the union." The truth appears to be that the conspiracy, despite Pickering's words, was confined to a few; but outside of this rather narrow circle a considerable number were restless and grumbling. When serious hardship arose, many were ready to join in denunciation of the government (1808-1814); then the wise and the good had more material to work with.

In 1804, the plan of the conspiracy leaders included the enticing of New York into the camp of the malcontents; they hoped to do this by bringing Aaron Burr into the fold. In its most positive form this scheme appears to have consisted of making Burr the leader in a secession movement; New York and the New England states were to form a new confederacy. There is really not much evidence of the sober intent to carry this plan to its final consummation. Perhaps the purpose—at all events as a beginning—was to consolidate the northern interests for effective resistance to the Jeffersonian party. The plan, whatever it was, failed. Burr was defeated in the campaign for the governorship of New York, though supported by no small number of Federalists; and when he shot Alexander Hamilton his career and even his capacity for mischief were badly shattered. That the conspirators would have been willing to separate the northern states is fairly certain; but it appears likely that success in building up a northern party

---

[4] *Ibid.*, p. 346.
[5] *Ibid.*, p. 347.

by the capture of New York and perhaps other middle states would have satisfied or dulled their ambition for secession until an extreme emergency arose.[6]

There is something peculiarly unattractive in the conduct of these conspiring New Englanders; they were victims of bigoted partisanship. Some of them were attached to the cause of England without sufficient respect for America's own dignity and rights. They were planting their feet to resist movements that were to sweep all obstacles aside from the pathway of democracy, expansion, union, and nationalism. It is not our business, as mere historians, to pronounce democracy, expansion, and nationalism essentially wise and noble; but those opposing these movements were placing themselves outside the currents of the nineteenth century. We must remind ourselves, however, that patriotism was necessarily of slow growth; democratic ideals and the early and emphatic rejection of the doctrines of the wise, the good, and the rich are altogether too much to expect from any set or group who were themselves comfortably established in social position.

At a later day (1828-1829) the career of the Federalist party in the early years of the century was strongly, perhaps one should say stridently, described by John Quincy Adams. The description was the result of a dispute with certain gentlemen of New England who resented his charging Federalist leaders with entertaining plans for dissolving the union:

"This coalition of Hamiltonian Federalism with the Yankee spirit had produced as incongruous and absurd a system of politics as ever was exhibited in the vagaries of the human mind. It was compounded of the following prejudices:

"1. An utter detestation of the French Revolution and of France, and a corresponding excess of attachment to Great Britain, as the only barrier against the universal, dreaded empire of France.

[6] For a succinct statement, see S. E. Morison, *The Life and Letters of Harrison Gray Otis*, I, pp. 264-267. Hamilton's opinion was as follows: the election of Burr would reunite the scattered fragments of the Democratic party and reënforce it by a detachment of Federalists under his leadership; in New England the ill opinion of Jefferson and jealousy of the ambition of Virginia were leading men to think of dismembering the union. "It would probably suit Mr. Burr's views to promote this result, to be the chief of the Northern portion. . . ." Hamilton, *Works* (H. C. Lodge, ed.), VIII, pp. 374-375. Cabot believed in 1804 that a war with Britain might be a signal for the break-up of the union. See *ante*, note 5. ". . . but, if they had involved us by their folly and baseness in a war with Great Britain, I believe New England might be roused to do *any thing* which her leading men should recommend." Letter from Cabot to King, March 17, 1804, in Adams, *New-England Federalism*, p. 363. But see a letter from Cabot to Pickering, October 5, 1808, in *Ibid.*, p. 373.

"2. A strong aversion to republics and republican government, with a profound impression that our experiment of a confederated republic had failed for want of virtue in the people.

"3. A deep jealousy of the Southern and Western States, and a strong disgust at the effect of the slave representation in the Constitution of the United States.

"4. A belief that Mr. Jefferson and Mr. Madison were servilely devoted to France, and under French influence." [7]

The relations of America with the warring powers of Europe, especially after 1805, were replete with difficulty. There is no need of our trying to estimate the comparative weight of insults and injuries which the United States suffered on the one side from Britain's ruthless disregard of neutral rights and, on the other, from the sly and insidious attacks of Napoleon. But after the Chesapeake affair (1807) conditions were almost intolerable, though Jefferson continued to bear them—not with light heart and a sunny smile, but to bear them none the less. It is easy enough for us to criticize and to lament the weakness of the administration and the frailty of a divided country; but it is not so easy to say what ought to have been done to preserve the semblance of national self-respect and to preserve it in the presence of virulent partisanship and sectional bitterness. Of course, the elementary difficulty was the absence of thoroughgoing national consciousness, the impelling sense of common interest. Before the trouble was over, the continuity of the union was seriously threatened. And still, as we shall see, when after years of tribulation war actually came, the union did hold together; there was still enough nationalism and patriotism to assure its survival.

In the latter part of 1807 Jefferson saw that something must be done. He decided upon an embargo. When, as a result of French de-

[7] Adams, *New-England Federalism*, p. 284. Pickering, who was ready to believe anything sufficiently damaging to his opponents, said in 1812 that he had no doubt that French money had been distributed to bring on the war against Britain. Letter from Pickering to Edward Pennington, July 12, 1812, in *Ibid.*, p. 388. On the secession movements, 1804-1814, Morison makes the following comments: "The secession movement of 1804 was a select conspiracy, confined to a handful of extremist leaders; the movements of 1808 and 1814 were entered into by the entire Federal party in New England, and their object was not disunion, but, in the one case, relief from the embargo, and in the other, peace and protection to New England interests. Pickering, indeed, attempted to steer the Hartford Convention into a disunion course, but failed. The conspiracy of 1804 was an isolated affair, the real significance of which is personal—the example it offers of the manner in which political jesuits throw aside every scruple to attain their ends." Morison, *op. cit.*, I, pp. 269-270.

crees and Britain's orders in council, American ships were in danger of either being quietly confiscated or blown out of the water, was it not wise to hold them safe in their own harbors and allow the shipmasters to fret their souls away in idleness and discontent? [8] He therefore entered upon a terrapin policy; America should withdraw within her shell and look forth from this calm security upon the tribulations of the world.[9] The rapidity with which Congress responded illustrates the authority which Jefferson still wielded, an authority to be rather severely crippled after the embargo had been tried and found wanting. The Senate agreed to the proposal after a few hours of debate. John Quincy Adams exclaimed, "The President has recommended the measure on his high responsibility. I would not consider, I would not deliberate; I would act!" [10] The House took time for consideration but acted promptly. The final vote in the Senate was twenty-two to six; in the House, eighty-two to forty-four.

The act was passed and was signed by the President on December 22, 1807. Early in the next year two supplementary acts were passed to make the measure more sweeping and effective. In the succeeding months preparations were made for armed defense of the country. Money was appropriated for Jefferson's toy gunboats and for fortifications, and provisions were made for building up a small army and for equipping the militia. But it can hardly be said that the days of the embargo were energetically used to prepare for inevitable war. The President hoped that under the peaceful policy of restriction the warring nations of Europe would be brought to their senses, learn to leave American commerce alone, permit the merchantmen to traverse the ocean with their cargoes unmolested, and allow them to reap the fruits which the old world's war provided for an energetic neutral.

[8] Jefferson's special message (December 18, 1807) indicates at least this main purpose. Jefferson, *Works* (federal ed.), X, pp. 530-531.

[9] "When the great American tortoise", declared John Randolph, with characteristic venom in a speech, at a later date, "draws in his head, as this nation laying an embargo has been compared to this animal, you do not see him trotting along; he lies motionless on the ground; it is when the fire is put on his back, that he makes the best of his way, and not till then." April 5, 1808. *Annals of Congress,* 10 Cong., 1 sess., col. 1963.

[10] So Timothy Pickering reported, at a somewhat later time. "The words were spoken in secret session, but Senator Pickering noted them for future use. Among the antipathies and humors of New-England politics none was more characteristic than this personal antagonism, beginning a new conspiracy which was to shake the Union to its foundations." Henry Adams, *History of the United States,* IV, p. 173. Adams's treatment of the mission of George Rose is especially entertaining, and the presentation of Pickering's subterraneous operations is illuminating. *Ibid.,* IV, p. 178 ff.

All through the weary months of 1808 opposition to the embargo increased; there was occasional violence; the heart of New England gradually hardened. The shipmasters and traders were not prepared placidly to endure the sight of their vessels tied up at the wharves or anchored in the harbors; and the wrath of the men of the northern region, when the embargo interfered with trade across the Canadian border, was not less ominous. The opposition became each day more serious. Jefferson's efforts at enforcement led him on to a position which in some respects resembled that of a dictator in war rather than that of a peaceful leader whose main desire was to allow and secure the placid development of his country. The following is an illustration: "Yours of July 27th", Jefferson wrote to General Dearborn, "is received. It confirms the accounts we received from others that the infractions of the embargo in Maine & Massachusetts are open. . . . The tories of Boston openly threaten insurrection if their importation of flour is stopped. The next post will stop it. I fear your Governor [Sullivan, himself a Jeffersonian Republican!] is not up to the tone of these parricides, and I hope, on the first symptom of an open opposition to the laws by force, you will fly to the scene and aid in suppressing any commotion." [11]

But perhaps the most significant indication of how nearly the embargo resembled war itself, with many of war's privations and dislocations, or how its enforcement necessitated such orders as might have been endured with courage had a foreign enemy blockaded the coast, is shown by a statement of the harried President when it must have seemed to him that peaceful coercion of the foreigner was proving a failure and was repelling even his own former followers in New England. Writing of conditions at Buckstown, he said to Gallatin: "This is the first time the character of the place had been brought under consideration as an objection. Yet a general disobedience to the laws in any place must have weight towards refusing to give them any facilities to evade. In such a case we may fairly require positive proof that the individual of a town tainted with a general spirit of disobedience, has never said or done anything himself to countenance that spirit." [12]

Gallatin had already written to the President his opinion that if the embargo was to be persisted in, two determinations must be

[11] August 9, 1808. Jefferson, *Works* (federal ed.), XI, pp. 40-41.
[12] November 13, 1808. Jefferson, *Writings* (H. A. Washington, ed.), V, pp. 386-387.

adopted: one, no vessel should be allowed to move without the special permission of the Executive; and, two, the collectors should be given "the general power of seizing property anywhere, and taking the rudders or otherwise effectually preventing the departure of any vessel in harbor, though ostensibly intended to remain there; and that without being liable to personal suits." In other words, customary and essential safeguards for personal property and liberty and the right of individual redress in courts of law must be abandoned.

Such conditions could not continue. The presidential election resulted in the choice of Madison as Jefferson's successor. Jefferson's last annual message (November, 1808) indicates how great a change had, in at least one respect, come over his dream. He actually pointed with a measure of pride and gratification to the fact that the situation "into which we have thus been forced has impelled us to apply a portion of our industry and capital to internal manufactures and improvements." The embargo, as if it were a prohibitory tariff, had in fact driven the Americans, and especially the New Englanders, to enter upon manufacturing; and Jefferson, whose ideal had been a country flourishing in simple productive labor of the farm and plantation, free from the debasing influence of the factory and the scarcely less degrading effect of the countingroom, now looked with satisfaction upon the consoling prospect of an industrial and self-sustaining nation. But once more, flinging stones at Jefferson's inconsistencies serves no purpose. His readiness, however, to see the possibility of a self-sufficient country, with "home manufactures" and internal improvements, is noteworthy because it foreshadowed the efforts and the controversies which arose after the war of 1812 and became the center of heated controversy and constitutional dispute.

Jefferson knew the embargo to be a failure, thanks to the implacable hostility of New England—a hostility which appears not to have been modified by the fact that restriction was laying foundations for new industries. The winter months (1808-1809) were filled with debate and with attack and counterattack; but after more than a year of anxiety and hatred the embargo policy was doomed. In the last trying months Jefferson made little effort to exercise leadership; Madison had been elected to take office in March and Gallatin's skillful hand was still at the helm of the treasury. Josiah Quincy, as if to exemplify the sweetness of Federalist temper, spoke of the retiring President still in office as "a dish of skim-milk curdling at the head of our nation". Some portions of the embargo were temporarily retained, but it was in effect succeeded by nonintercourse with Britain and France. More trouble lay ahead of a country distracted by sectional and factious opposition. War appeared scarcely less perilous than peace.

The constitutional questions which arose during the embargo days now demand brief attention. One objection to the measure was the absence of a time limit. Could prohibition of commercial intercourse be enacted without any provision for termination? The dispute does not merit any agonizing examination. Congress which passed the measure could repeal it. The failure to fix the life of an act does not make it unconstitutional. Of more significance was the denial of congressional power to prohibit commerce under pretense of regulating it. The conclusion laid down by Judge John Davis of the federal district court of Massachusetts appears irrefutable: "Power to 'regulate,' it is said, cannot be understood to give a power to annihilate. . . . It will be admitted that partial prohibitions are authorized by the expression; and how shall the degree or extent of the prohibition be adjusted but by the discretion of the national government, to whom the subject appears to be committed. . . . Further, the power to regulate commerce is not to be confined to the adoption of measures exclusively beneficial to commerce itself, or tending to its advancement; but in our national system, as in all modern sovereignties, it is also to be considered as an instrument for other purposes of general policy and interest." [13] Nothing can better illustrate the contradictions of politics than the contention of Federalists that a court should take a stand contrary to their own traditions.

The opposition to the embargo, wherever and however that opposition displayed itself, is important in constitutional history because it brings to our attention the frailty of the union and the danger lest the constitutional system be overthrown. But we are now called upon to consider the nature of the arguments and the declarations put forth in Congress and by state officials; we must endeavor to discover what theory of the union and of the constitutional order was commonly presented by those who attacked the constitutionality of the measure.

Before entering upon a brief presentation of a few important documents in this embargo controversy, it may be well to put forth this general thesis: during the years from the adoption of the Constitution, and notably from the Virginia and Kentucky resolutions, until the close of the war of 1812, and indeed for some time later, the

[13] See Adams, *History of the United States,* IV, pp. 268-269.

central constitutional controversy was not concerning state sovereignty but states' rights; and it was particularly concerned with the question whether the states as individual bodies had the right to judge of their own authority and its extent, or, on the other hand, whether the central government was the judge of its own powers and the states must quietly accept the conclusions of that government. We can, in the writer's opinion, scarcely overemphasize the weight of the fact that the dissatisfied legislatures, under Federalist control, insisted upon the right of the states to judge; their position is associated closely with the philosophy of the Revolution, with the idea of divided sovereignty, and with the principle of legally limited government. The statement of Jefferson in the Kentucky resolutions was bearing fruit—now, in practice, not quite to his own taste—that the parties to the compact were the ultimate judges of the extent of delegated authority. The Constitution did not in so many words declare where the right to judge rested; controversy and dispute were inevitable; because of the self-consciousness of the individual states, the adherents of the old compact philosophy, as well as the more thoughtless and acrimonious partisans, were intent upon the right of the parties to the compact to decide.

It appears a wrong interpretation, though it is the common one, to find in these protests and denunciations the full embodiment of the doctrine of state sovereignty. Only a careful examination of the doctrines, elaborately outlined by John Taylor and Calhoun at a later day, can bring to light the difference between them and the prevailing political thinking of the earlier decades under the Constitution. Certainly such an examination will disclose how far were the men of the first four decades from *fully* envisaging the doctrines of state sovereignty as later exposed to view. If there is this essential difference, then we are led astray or are wandering from the path, if we find in every announcement of opposition to national authority a threat of secession as the natural consequence of sovereignty, which remained without modification in the separate states. Any resolution by a state legislature impugning national authority is now looked upon as a piece of presumption; and if we so look upon it, we lose sight of the signal importance of the discussions in our history bearing on the question of the right to judge.[14]

If, when a legislative resolution calls a state a "sovereign" state, we must conclude that it means to assert the state's full and unqualified

[14] See the chapter on the Virginia and Kentucky resolutions, *ante.*

authority in every particular, then we must believe that in some instances the states did look upon the union as a league and not as a
body politic. Much depends upon what was meant by "sovereignty";
and anyone who is to-day at all conversant with the word and its history will not be dogmatic and impose a definition upon the consciousness of state legislators of a century and more ago. We must bear in
mind the easy fluency with which at the present time a state is spoken
of as "sovereign"; and we must also remember that the doctrine of
divided sovereignty was, and probably is, orthodox in the legal creed
of constitutionalists.[15] One of the results of loose speech, the prerogative of practical politics, is a confusion of the terms state sovereignty and states' rights.

There can be no question that there were threats of rebellion as
well as whisperings about the desirability of breaking away from the
contaminating influence of Virginia and Jeffersonism. But the main
thought seems to have been that if rebellion should come, it would be
a rebellion justified by the national government's violation of legal
authority; it would be based in part on the right of individuals to life,
liberty, and the pursuit of happiness, and in part on the right of the
states to protect their liberty which in certain essentials had not been
surrendered by the establishment of a national government with
limited powers. We must recognize a clear distinction between opposition to illegal acts and secession from the union on the ground that
secession is based upon unalloyed sovereignty. The impressive fact is
the absence of a distinct and frank assertion of the legal right to
break the union at any time and without demonstration of illegality
by the central government. Still it may be that at this time there was
coming into the mind of the discontented New Englanders the conception of the Constitution as a treaty, rather than as a compact

[15] "To deny, therefore, a limited sovereignty to a State of the Union, under the
Constitution, is, forensically and historically, as incorrect and mischievous as to
assert more than a limited sovereignty for the United States under the Constitution.
Each is sovereign; but each is sovereign only within the limits traced by the Constitution." D. H. Chamberlain, "The State Judiciary," *Constitutional History of the
United States as Seen in . . . American Law,* p. 247. This book is a series of addresses
by T. M. Cooley and other eminent jurists. Just how this able lawyer would define
"sovereignty" may awaken our curiosity; but he could not—if he thought a moment—
define it as *complete* political authority. Cooley, referring with approval to Jay's
opinion in Chisholm *v.* Georgia, says, "And the deduction was irresistible: the sovereignty of the nation was in the people of the nation, and the residuary sovereignty of
each State in the people of each State." *Ibid.,* p. 48.

analogous to the social compact. But during the embargo period the writer has found only slight evidence of that fact.

It is impossible to present here in any detail illustrations of the sort of assertions which were made by the querulous New Englanders during the months that sorely tried their patience. Demonstration by ample quotation, if demonstration be possible, would require not only plenteous quotations, but studious examination of words and phrases within their context. We must be content with only a few brief examples. In Congress, Josiah Quincy, who cannot be looked upon as a timid soul shrinking from announcement of convictions, admitted that the embargo laws were the laws of the land, but he asked, ". . . who shall deny to a representative of the people the right, in their own favorite tribunal, of bringing your laws to the test of the principles of the Constitution?" Asking what should be the remedy for unconstitutional legislation, "so oppressive upon the mass of the people that it is impossible to wait upon the slow processes of the Judiciary", he answered by saying that the people and the state legislatures were in duty bound not to rebel or to break the union, "but to take the Constitution, that great charter of their liberties, into their consideration, and to strengthen and support its principles by vindicating them from violation."

In January, 1809, in reference to a speech from the Governor of Massachusetts in which he condemned lawless disregard of the embargo, the state senate declared the union "is a confederation of equal and independent states with limited powers. . . ." "We beg leave to observe," the response also said, "that those rights, which the people have not chosen to part with, should be exercised by them with delicacy —only in times of great danger—not with 'distraction and confusion' —not to oppose the laws, but to prevent acts being respected as laws, which are unwarranted by the commission given to their rulers." [16] The house gave similar opinions: "We are unwilling to believe that any division of sentiment can exist among the New England States or their inhabitants as to the obvious infringement of rights secured to them by the Constitution of the United States; and still more so that any man can be weak or wicked enough to construe a disposition to support that Constitution and preserve the union by a temperate and firm opposition to acts which are repugnant to the first principles

[16] *State Documents on Federal Relations* (H. V. Ames, ed.; hereafter referred to as Ames, *State Documents*), no. 1, p. 28.

and purposes of both, into a wish to recede from the other states. . . . If ever such suspicions existed they can have arisen only in the minds of those who must be sensible that they had adopted and were persisting in, measures which had driven the people to desperation, by infringing rights which the citizens of Massachusetts conceive to be unalienable, and which they fondly hoped had been inviolably secured to them by the federal compact. . . . Nothing but madness or imbecility could put at hazard the existence of a 'balanced government, capable of operating and providing for the public good,' unless the administration of that Government, by its arbitrary impositions had endangered or destroyed the very objects for the protection of whch [*sic*] it had been instituted." [17]

A report and resolutions drawn up by the Massachusetts legislature the next month are somewhat more extreme. The most advanced and threatening assertions are as follows—though only a reading of the whole document can bring out its full meaning: "While the laws continue to have their free course, the judicial courts are competent to decide this question, and to them every citizen, when aggrieved, ought to apply for redress. It would be derogatory to the honour of the commonwealth to presume that it is unable to protect its subjects against all violations of their rights, by peaceable and legal remedies. While this state maintains its sovereignty and independence, all the citizens can find protection against outrage and injustice in the strong arm of the state government." The resolutions declare the embargo and supplementary acts unjust and unconstitutional and not legally binding on the citizens of the state, and announce the willingness of the legislature to coöperate with any of the other states "in all legal and constitutional measures" for procuring such amendments to the Constitution as would protect commerce and afford permanent security.[18] The resolutions conclude with a reference to the necessity of rescuing "our common country" from impending ruin and of preserving inviolate the union of the states.[19]

No attempt has been made in this chapter to do more than sketch

[17] *Ibid.*, no. 1, pp. 29-31. Notice also an additional statement to the effect that when a man's liberty is infringed, "if not absolved from his allegiance, he may demand redress, and take all lawful measures to obtain it." p. 32.

[18] February 15, 1809. *Ibid.*, no. 1, pp. 34-35.

[19] The report and resolutions were to be transmitted "to the legislatures of such of our sister states, as manifest a disposition to concur with us in measures to rescue our common country from impending ruin, and to preserve inviolate the union of the states." *Ibid.*, no. 1, p. 36.

the outlines of a dangerous situation—dangerous to the continuity of the union and to the effective authority of the government. So much depends on the connotation of words that opportunities are offered for differences of opinion concerning the extent to which the theory of unalloyed state sovereignty was held or proclaimed. But one thing is probably evident: the center of the controversy was the question of the state's right to preserve its reserved authority and to resist intrusions upon its field of sovereign power.[20] In the writer's opinion, the fully-equipped doctrine of state sovereignty or the belief in it was, to say the least, not prominent; and we in some respects lose sight of the nature of the controversies during the first forty years of our history under the Constitution unless we appreciate, as already said, the continuity and the persistence of this question as to who had the right to pass final judgment on the extent of a governmental power.

During the years in which there was much dangerous discontent among the New England Federalists, an old controversy broke out anew in Pennsylvania. The dispute began during the Revolution when the committee of appeals of the old Congress, reviewing the decision of a Pennsylvania court, decided that prize money arising from the sale of the sloop *Active* and her cargo belonged to Gideon Olmstead and other claimants. Pennsylvania refused to abide by the decision. A portion of the proceeds of the sale, in the form of loan-office certificates, subsequently passed into the hands of David Rittenhouse,[21] the state Treasurer, who, however, did not formally commit them to the

[20] Notice even Timothy Pickering writing, "Pray look into the Constitution, and particularly to the 10th article of the amendments. How are the powers reserved to the States respectively, or to the people, to be maintained, but by the respective States judging for themselves and putting their negative on the usurpations of the general government?" Letter from Pickering to Christopher Gore, January 8, 1809, in Adams, *New-England Federalism*, p. 378. Italics of the original omitted. When the Constitution was before the people for adoption, Pickering (December 24, 1787) made assertions concerning the nature of the Constitution which were orthodox at that time, i.e., that there was "partial consolidation": "The 'Federal Farmer' admits the necessity of the 'partial consolidation,' as the only plan of government which can secure the freedom and happiness of this people; and yet, when the Convention have proposed a *partial* consolidation, he says they evidently designed thereby to effect ultimately an *entire* consolidation!" Quoted in C. W. Upham, *The Life of Timothy Pickering*, II, p. 355.

[21] The certificates were afterwards "funded by him, in his own name, under the act of Congress making provision for the debt of the United States. . . . These certificates remained in the private possession of David Rittenhouse . . . and after his death they remained in possession of his representatives. . . ." United States *v.* Judge Peters, 5 Cranch 115, 138 (1809).

treasury, and they later passed into the possession of the executrixes of the Rittenhouse estate. In 1803, the federal district court gave personal judgment against the executrixes; but the state was still obdurate; the legislature ordered the Governor to protect the "rights of the state" and the "persons and properties" of the executrixes. The executrixes finally turned the disputed sum into the state, which promised them protection from liability by giving "a sufficient instrument of indemnification. . . ." Olmstead was as persistent as a Connecticut Yankee is entitled to be, and he and his fellows secured in 1809 a mandamus from the federal Supreme Court directing Judge Peters to issue process for carrying out the judgment previously awarded.

In giving the opinion [22] Chief Justice Marshall used the following forceful and characteristic words: "If the legislatures of the several states may, at will, annul the judgments of the courts of the United States, and destroy the rights acquired under those judgments, the constitution itself becomes a solemn mockery, and the nation is deprived of the means of enforcing its laws by the instrumentality of its own tribunals." The state was not compliant; the militia was called out to prevent service and execution. Armed conflict between federal officers and state troops appeared inevitable; but the federal marshal by a clever ruse succeeded in serving his writ. By this time the state was ready to retreat. The federal authority was amply sustained, for General Bright, who had commanded the militia, and others with him were haled before the federal court, convicted, and sentenced to pay fines and suffer imprisonment for obstructing the court. Madison, who had upheld the national authority, pardoned the condemned men, probably wisely, because they had acted under a mistaken sense of duty.[23]

Resolutions which were passed by the Pennsylvania legislature (April 3, 1809) are especially illuminating.[24] They express a desire that the other states, "who are equally interested in the preservation of

[22] *Ibid.*, 136.
[23] The historical incidents are discussed by J. F. Jameson, "The Predecessor of the Supreme Court," *Essays in the Constitutional History of the United States* (J. F. Jameson, ed.), p. 17 ff.; by J. C. B. Davis, in an appendix to 131 U. S., p. XXIX ff.; Richard Hildreth, *The History of the United States of America* (revised ed.), VI, pp. 155-164. Of interest in this connection is a similar incident, which called forth protest from New Hampshire against the findings of the federal judiciary. Penhallow et al. *v.* Doane's Administrators, 3 Dallas 54 (1795). New Hampshire's protests are in Ames, *State Documents,* no. 1, pp. 11-15. The contention plainly was that by the adoption of the Constitution the state did not then intend to admit that the "confederation was in force prior to March, 1781, or that the federal constitution existed with respect to New Hampshire before June, 1788."
[24] Ames, *State Documents,* no. 2, pp. 2-4.

the state rights", should understand the position taken by Pennsylvania, and also that the government of the United States should see "that the Legislature, in resisting encroachments on their rights, are not acting in a spirit of hostility to the legitimate powers of the United States' courts; but are actuated by a disposition to compromise, and to guard against future collisions of power, by an amendment to the constitution. . . ." They declare "That, as a member of the Federal Union, the Legislature of Pennsylvania acknowledges the supremacy, and will cheerfully submit to the authority of the general government, as far as that authority is delegated by the constitution of the United States." The senate and house trust "they will not be considered as acting hostile to the General Government, when, as *guardians of the State rights,* they can not permit an infringement of those rights, by an unconstitutional exercise of power in the United States' courts." Powers are granted to the general government and rights are reserved to the states, but "it is impossible, from the imperfections of language, so to define the limits of each, that difficulties should not some times arise from a collision of powers. . . ." What is needed, therefore, is an amendment to the Constitution establishing a tribunal for the purpose of settling disputed jurisdiction of state and national governments: "To suffer the United States' courts to decide on STATE RIGHTS will, from a bias *in favor of power,* necessarily destroy the FEDERAL PART of our Government: And whenever the government of the United States becomes consolidated, we may learn from the history of nations what will be the event."

How was this proposal received by the other states? There were then seventeen states in the union, and at least eleven of them disapproved.[25] Virginia's answer is worth noting: a tribunal was already provided for—"the Supreme Court, more eminently qualified . . . to decide the disputes aforesaid in an enlightened and impartial manner, than any other tribunal which could be erected." This reply was drawn up twelve years after the famous resolutions of 1798; but Virginians were now in the saddle; a Virginian was President, a Virginian was

---

[25] New Hampshire, Massachusetts, Vermont, New Jersey, Maryland, Virginia, North Carolina, Georgia, Ohio, Kentucky, Tennessee. *Ibid.,* no. 2, p. 5. See Pennsylvania's further declaration in behalf of an impartial tribunal, 1810. *Ibid.,* no. 2, pp. 7-8. Various resolutions are in the journals of the Pennsylvania senate and house, 1809-1810. Of special interest are the resolutions in the *Journal of the Senate,* XX, p. 376 ff., and in the *Journal of the House,* XX, pp. 250-254, 403-424. We should notice, however, that a minority of the legislature strongly attacked the doctrine of the right to resist the federal courts. But the minority likewise accepted the principle of divided authority.

the Chief Justice, and though Jefferson and other sturdy citizens of the Old Dominion fretted under Marshall's hand, and, before another decade passed, were pouring out vials of their wrath upon him, still it must have been some consolation to Virginians to think that, when all was said, he was one of their own blood. So much depended on local pride, on partisan prejudice, on personal passion, that varieties of constitutional interpretation, instead of a single simple one, came continually to the fore. But the contest in this particular was obviously over the power to judge.

The following year, the Pennsylvania legislature, adopting resolutions in opposition to the renewal of the United States Bank charter, made certain pronouncements more nearly in accord with the idea of complete state sovereignty than did any other state during this period: "The act of union thus entered into being to all intents and purposes a treaty between sovereign states, the general government by this treaty was not constituted the exclusive or final judge of the powers it was to exercise; for if it were so to judge then its judgment and not the constitution would be the measure of its authority." These phrases, though more extreme in their connotations than those of the Kentucky resolutions of an earlier day, are plainly sippings from that perennial fountain. Here, the reader may say, we find the complete and authoritative doctrine of state sovereignty in native nudity. But a careful examination of even this document awakens doubt of that interpretation, if it does not actually strengthen the belief that the critical matter was the right to judge. The resolutions speak of the federal Constitution's adoption by the "people of the United States", [26] of the establishment of a general government for special purposes, of the reservation of rights not delegated, and of the anxiety "to secure an administration of the federal and state governments, conformably to the true spirit of their respective constitutions. . . ." [27] One is left, therefore, with at least a vague impression that these legislators looked upon the Constitution of the United States as a constitution.

The admission of Louisiana into the union (1812) called forth bitter opposition from the New Englanders who feared the growing

[26] The one expression which Calhoun abhorred was this. The acknowledgment that there was a people of the United States violated his principles.

[27] Ames, *State Documents*, no. 2, pp. 8-10; *American State Papers, Finance*, II, p. 467. Virginia was opposed to the Bank. The stand taken by W. B. Giles in Congress deserves attention. His natural inclination was not toward nationalism. His stand was distinctly upon the idea of divided sovereignty. See *Annals of Congress*, 11 Cong., 3 sess., col. 181 ff.

ascendancy of the south and the increase of western power. The easterners saw their own section submerged by the rising tide of other sections; they saw their influence and authority flouted and their interests subjected to slave-owners and intellectual incompetents. The speech of Josiah Quincy, delivered while admission was under discussion, is well-known: ". . . if this bill passes," he exclaimed, "the bonds of this Union are virtually dissolved; that the States which compose it are free from their moral obligations, and that, as it will be the right of all, so it will be the duty of some, to prepare definitely for a separation—amicably if they can, violently if they must." [28] He spoke of the analogy between a political partnership and an ordinary business partnership; he did not desire to see a new partner admitted; he did not believe the people adopting the Constitution intended to grant political power to the people of Louisiana. It appears rather unwise to take too seriously the exclamations of excited forensic oratory, though on this occasion the arguments against the right of Congress to admit states from territory, which was not held by the union when the Constitution was adopted, are not totally absurd and unreasonable. At a later date (June 16, 1813), a committee of the Massachusetts senate drew up a report [29] which strongly set forth objections to the admission of states "created in territories, beyond the limits of the old United States. . . . It is, in truth, nothing less than the power to create in foreign countries, new political sovereignties, and to divest the old United States of a proportion of their political sovereignty, in favor of such foreigner." [30]

[28] January 14, 1811. *Annals of Congress*, 11 Cong., 3 sess., col. 525. Edmund Quincy, writing his father's biography in 1867, says of this speech "that the secessionism it contains is a very different doctrine from that preached in later times." This may appear a pious example of wishful thinking; but an examination of the whole speech will lead the reader to think that there was some ground for the statements of the biographer. See *Life of Josiah Quincy*, p. 213.

[29] Ames, *State Documents*, no. 2, pp. 21-24.

[30] Though the writer has been over the main documents time and time again and examined them critically, he should acknowledge the aid of a thesis by M. C. Kennedy, *States Rights, 1807-1815* (*MS.* in the library of the University of Chicago), an able and careful examination of the available material.

CHAPTER XXVI

THE WAR OF 1812

After long years of vexation and dispute, after attempts at peaceful coercion of the warring nations of Europe, after diplomatic controversy and failure of formal protest, war finally came. It was brought on partly by the "war hawks" of the south and west under the leadership of Henry Clay. It found its main support in the western regions from New Hampshire to Georgia; it was supported by an enthusiastic group in the farther south;[1] and it made its special appeal to the younger men of a new generation who were less timid than their elders, more appreciative of national dignity, and less influenced by a pet prejudice against one or the other of the European belligerents. The congressional vote disclosed a dangerous absence of unanimity. In the House, seventy-nine voted for war; forty-nine for peace. In the Senate, nineteen voted for war, thirteen for peace. Furthermore, the voting disclosed sectional diversity; representatives of the states north and east of New Jersey opposed the war; the far south and the west were solidly for war.[2] In other words, the sections suffering the least from the British navy and having little commerce to be protected were ready for a conflict to avenge attacks upon American rights on the seas. Some of the more sanguine spirits were out for conquest and expansion.

In a war thus begun there was bound to be trouble. Sectionalism and partisan suspicion were prevalent and were soon made perilously evident.[3] New England provincialism was prepared to display itself;

[1] J. W. Pratt, *Expansionists of 1812*, pp. 10-11, 48-49.

[2] In the House, Massachusetts voted six for and eight against; Connecticut and Rhode Island voted unanimously against, and New York voted three for and eleven against.

[3] Attention is called to "An Address . . . to their Constituents, on the subject of the war with Great Britain", which was drawn up by thirty-four members of Congress after the declaration of war. Niles, *Weekly Register*, July 11, 1812. It appears to have been written by Josiah Quincy. See Edmund Quincy, *Life of Josiah Quincy*, p. 260. Of interest also are addresses to the people by the houses of the Massachusetts legislature, which, taken on the whole, may perhaps be considered indicative of a fairly conservative temper. The senate said the union was threatened,

the privations of the struggle added to the discontent which soon became clamorous and denunciatory. Complaints were directed against a war which the New Englanders believed was actuated by an unreasonable hatred of Britain and a detestable devotion to France. In the minds of the angry malcontents there lurked the suspicions and forebodings which have already been mentioned: dislike of Jeffersonian democracy and all its progeny; distrust of the south and the west; objection to restrictions which appeared to be totally devastating to commerce; and in addition, the rank injustice of enumerating three-fifths of the slaves as the basis of representation, for that gave the southerners power in the government to be used in combating the interests of the free states.

We shall have to confine ourselves to a study of the few leading protests of the New England states during the war with the purpose of considering their constitutional theory. A critical question arose almost as soon as war was declared. Did the President of the United States, or anyone by his order, have the legal authority to summon the state militia and place it under national military officers? Who was to judge when the emergency had arisen justifying the summons? In Massachusetts the problem was turned over to the supreme judicial court for an opinion (August 5, 1812).[4] The judges, in reply, referred to the constitutional right of the federal government to use the state militia for three specific purposes—executing the laws of the union, suppressing insurrections, and repelling invasions; "but no power is given," they said, "either to the President or to Congress, to determine that either of the said exigencies do in fact exist." As this power was not delegated to the federal government and not prohibited to the states, it was reserved to the states. The President, the justices concluded, may exercise the command of the militia, when

and asked each person to fulfill his duty as a member of the social compact by "support of the government of his choice." Niles, *Weekly Register,* July 11, 1812. The house declared the people of Massachusetts were citizens of one common country and were bound to support all constitutional laws until the obnoxious ones were repealed by a change of men. *Ibid.,* August 29, 1812.

4 " '1st. Whether the commanders in chief of the militia of the several states have a right to determine, whether any of the exigencies contemplated by the constitution of the United States exist; so as to require them to place the militia, or any part of it, in the service of the United States, at the request of the President, to be commanded by him pursuant to acts of Congress?'

" '2nd. Whether, when either of the exigencies exist, authorizing the employing the militia in the service of the United States, the militia thus employed, can be lawfully commanded by any officer, but of the militia, except by the President of the United States?' " Ames, *State Documents,* no. 2, p. 13.

properly and lawfully acting in the service of the United States, but they knew "of no constitutional provision authorizing any officer of the army of the United States to command the militia, or authorizing any officer of the militia to command the army of the United States." [5]

A similar position was taken by other New England states. Connecticut [6] declared that that state was a free, sovereign, and independent state, that the United States were a confederacy of states, and that "we are a confederated and not a consolidated republic. The governor of this state is under a high and solemn obligation, 'to maintain the lawful rights and privileges thereof, as a sovereign, free and independent state,' as he is 'to support the constitution of the United States'. . . . The same constitution, which delegates powers to the general government, inhibits the exercise of powers, not delegated, and reserves those powers to the states respectively." The reader may know exactly what all this implies; the writer cannot be sure. What is meant, for example, by "a confederated . . . republic"? He can but suggest that possibly the free, sovereign state had surrendered a portion, but only a portion, of her sovereignty. Rhode Island followed; the Governor, having summoned a council of war—at least he so named it— asked who was to be the judge, and the council, without a dissenting voice, decided that the power belonged to the Executive of the state.[7]

The Governor of Vermont, the next year (1813), emphatically denied that the "whole body of the militia" could "by any kind of magic" at once be transformed "into a regular army for the purpose of foreign conquest. . . ." But there were some persons who disapproved of these doctrines, peculiarly dangerous in the winter of 1813-1814; the Governor's position was supported by only a narrow majority in the Vermont assembly (96 to 89), and when he attempted to recall the militia which had been ordered from "our frontiers", the troops refused to obey his orders and sent back a defiant reply: "We will not obey, but will continue in the service of our country till discharged." [8] Commenting upon this state of affairs, the legislature of New Jersey viewed with contempt and abhorrence the "ravings of an infuriated faction," whether they came from a "maniac governor" or from "discontented or ambitious demagogues. . . ." [9]

---

[5] *Ibid.*, no. 2, pp. 13-15.
[6] August 25, 1812. *Ibid.*, no. 2, pp. 15-18. Italics of the original omitted.
[7] *Ibid.*, no. 2, pp. 18-19.
[8] *Ibid.*, no. 2, pp. 19-21; see J. B. McMaster, *A History of the People of the United States,* IV, p. 226.
[9] February 12, 1814. Ames, *State Documents,* no. 2, p. 20.

In opposition to the new embargo (1813) the Massachusetts General Court adopted a report of a committee, known as "Lloyd's Report", and a series of resolutions.[10] Here we find assertions similar to those already quoted. The whole document deserves more careful study than can be presented here. "The sovereignty reserved to the States," the report declares, "was reserved to protect the Citizens from acts of violence by the United States, as well as for purposes of domestic regulation. We spurn the idea that the free, sovereign and independent State of Massachusetts is reduced to a mere municipal corporation, without power to protect its people, and to defend them from oppression, from whatever quarter it comes." Reference is made to the remedy proposed by Madison, when he led the "Legislature of Virginia into an opposition, without any justifiable cause;" he was supposed to "understand the principles of our concurrent Sovereignty. . . ." What was meant by "sovereignty reserved to the States"? What was meant by "concurrent Sovereignty"? Did it mean sovereignty held concurrently by state and national governments, or held concurrently by the several states?

The proposed conscription bill brought forth denunciation from Connecticut; the measure was attacked as "subversive of the rights and liberties of the people of this state, and the freedom, sovereignty, and independence of the same, and inconsistent with the principles of the constitution of the United States." [11] An act was passed by the state (January, 1815) authorizing and directing judges to discharge on habeas corpus all minors enlisted without the consent of their parents or guardians under the terms of the Enlistment of Minors Act.[12] We may notice here that at a much later date (1827) the question of the right to call forth the militia was passed on by the Supreme Court of the United States, and, as far as judicial decision can give sanction, established the president's right to judge. The constitutionality of conscription was formally announced in 1918.[13]

Conditions were distressing in the year 1814; so incapable was the government to wage war effectively when it had to meet distrust and state jealousy at every turn, that some of the states took measures for building up state armies for their own defense against British

10 February 22, 1814. *Ibid.*, no. 2, pp. 25-31.
11 October, 1814. *Ibid.*, no. 2, p. 32.
12 *Ibid.*, no. 2, p. 32. The Enlistment of Minors Act was passed December 10, 1814. *Ibid.*
13 Martin *v.* Mott, 12 Wheaton 19 (1827) ; Selective Draft Law Cases, 245 U. S. 366 (1918).

forces.[14] The end of the incoherence and vociferous complaint came only with the end of the war; but before it closed, discontent had reached such a state in New England that Massachusetts asked for a convention of the New England states at Hartford to consider methods of defense and to discuss the advisability of proposing amendments to the Constitution. "This Legislature", said the Massachusetts legislature's circular letter of October 17, 1814, "is content, for its justification to repose upon the purity of its own motives, and upon the known attachment of its constituents to the national union, and to the rights and independence of their country." [15] When the convention met (December 15, 1814), twenty-five delegates were in attendance. Massachusetts, Connecticut, and Rhode Island were officially represented, and two counties in New Hampshire sent delegates. One delegate from a Vermont county was later admitted.

The result of the convention was a series of resolutions. They began by recommending to the legislatures of the states represented in the convention to pass measures to protect their citizens from the operation of unconstitutional acts subjecting the militia or other citizens to forcible drafts or impressments. They recommended that the legislatures request the government of the United States to consent to some arrangement whereby the said states could separately or in concert be empowered to defend themselves against the enemy, and a reasonable portion of the taxes collected within the states be paid into their treasuries. The states represented in the convention were advised to prepare their militia for effective service and to employ them, upon the request of the governor "of either of the other States", in assisting "the State . . . making such request to repel any invasion thereof which shall be made or attempted by the publick enemy."

Seven amendments to the federal Constitution were proposed. All of these proposals were mild and gentle rather than imperious demands from self-sufficient, totally sovereign states. Some of them were the expression of New England's distrust of Virginia and the west; but there was no flat assertion of the right to break up the union, no

[14] McMaster, *op. cit.,* IV, pp. 243-245, refers to steps taken by New York, Connecticut, Massachusetts, Maryland, Virginia, South Carolina, Kentucky, and Pennsylvania.

[15] Ames, *State Documents,* no. 2, pp. 35-36. John Lowell wrote Timothy Pickering, December 3, 1814: "I would have it a *treaty,* not a *constitution.* The latter is mere paper, violated at pleasure by interested or ambitious men. But, when a treaty is broken, you know your remedy." Adams, *New-England Federalism,* p. 414. This is only an interesting piece of evidence that Lowell considered the Constitution to be a constitution and not a treaty.

threat of such intention, no direct declaration of a state's right to judge
of constitutional power, no announcement of sovereignty or even qualified sovereignty, but rather an appeal for modification of those constitutional provisions which, just then, seemed to bear with peculiar
severity upon the New England states.[16] When the messengers bearing
these plaintive resolutions reached Washington, the crisis had passed;
peace was at hand; amid the general hysterical rejoicing the proposals
of the Hartford envoys appeared already antiquated; no one was in a
mood for lamentation or desired to be reminded of the part played
by the discontented and the mutinous. The very name of Hartford
convention came ere long to be a term of reproach.

The resolutions of the convention, because of what they did not
say, are a strong argument for the assertion that the states did not
consider themselves sovereign, legally free from all restraint. It is
quite impossible to conceive of sovereign members of the family of
nations presenting their complaints and proposals in any such manner
and in any such terms. But be this as it may, the whole course of New
England opposition during the war and the ten years preceding disclosed how feeble were the sentimental bonds holding the sections
together. Patriotism is a sentiment, not a legal contrivance; and the
simple fact is that America had not as yet developed a degree or quantity of sentimental devotion fitting it to meet great crises with calm
assurance and bravery. The days of deeper and more resolute patriotism were ahead; but, strangely—though no more strangely than
other paradoxes in history—, the war had the effect of nationalizing
the people. The anxieties and the bickerings of the war were soon forgotten; at least they were not remembered as reflections on the loyalty
of the people-at-large and the effectiveness of the nation; the reproach

[16] 1. Representatives and direct taxes to be apportioned according to free population.

2. A two-thirds vote of Congress to be required for the admission of new states.

3. Embargoes to be limited to sixty days.

4. A two-thirds vote of Congress to be required to interdict the commercial intercourse between the United States and any foreign nation.

5. A two-thirds vote of Congress to be required to declare war or authorize
hostilities, except in case of invasion.

6. The exclusion of persons "hereafter" naturalized from Congress and any civil
office of the United States.

7. Provision against the election of the same person a second time to the
presidency and against electing the president from the same state for two successive
terms.

Nine states passed resolutions of nonconcurrence. Ames, *State Documents*, no. 2,
pp. 40-42.

and the stigma attaching to opposition indicated a newly-awakened zeal and a new appreciation of obligation to country.

The position taken by the New England states during the war appears to be more advanced than the stand taken against the embargo. Suffering and irritation brought forth stronger assertions concerning the rights of the states and the restrictions upon the federal government. It may be that various pronouncements were meant literally to assert complete and unmodified sovereignty. Perhaps the excerpts appearing in the preceding pages may convince the reader of such intention. Though only a few excerpts from resolutions have been given, they probably present the most extreme and downright statements concerning the character of the union and the limits of federal authority. No attempt is here made to enter into the question of how far the more radical malcontents, whispering their grievances one to another, were actually wishing or plotting for secession. It has seemed wise to take formal resolutions and public pronouncements as indicative of a more or less common opinion. But would the men of New England, even during the war, have asserted that they were not bound by acts of Congress which were plainly within its constitutional authority? Did they mean by their strident phrases more than the right to judge of the extent of federal authority and the duty to protect that portion of sovereignty which had not been surrendered? Is there much evidence of a theory essentially different from the old Revolutionary doctrine— the right to refuse obedience to illegal acts? [17]

[17] For interesting excerpts from newspapers during the war, see F. M. Anderson, "A Forgotten Phase of the New England Opposition to the War of 1812," Mississippi Valley Historical Association *Proceedings,* VI, pp. 176-188. In some of these excerpts we find declarations concerning state sovereignty which are unusually explicit. A notable statement is an article entitled "A State cannot Rebel," which was presented in the *Connecticut Spectator,* August 3, 1814. It goes to the limit in proclaiming state sovereignty: ". . . the state is sovereign, and any attempt to control that sovereignty, is a usurpation." "State sovereignty excludes the possibility of State rebellion: a sovereign state may infract its treaties, but can never rebel. . . ." *Ibid.,* pp. 180-181. Such words are practically in accord with the definition and the conception of sovereignty as later expounded. It may be that even when a writer speaks of the division of sovereignty he believes that the portion surrendered may be recalled. See for example articles in the *Columbian Centinel* (Boston), November 21, 24, 28, 1814. *Ibid.,* pp. 186-187. Asserting that the states are "'free, sovereign and independent' nations", the writer declares "each State has entered into a solemn compact with all the other States, by which, *to a certain extent, and for certain purposes,* a portion of State sovereignty is ceded to a general government formed by this union. To that *extent,* and for those *purposes,* we owe obedience to the general government; to them our allegiance is *secondary, qualified* and *conditional;* to our State sovereignties it is *primary, universal* and *absolute.*" It is difficult to agree with Professor Anderson in all respects. If, as it appears, he believes the doctrines of

The technical constitutional questions discussed in this chapter may well be considered as of slight importance in comparison with the actual danger of a destruction of the union. That danger is of course a salient constitutional fact; but of even more consequence is the actual continuity of the union; there was enough strength in the structure, shaken though it was to its foundation, to enable it to endure the blasts.

Calhoun and Jefferson Davis are to be found in the articles of 1814, he can hardly consistently say (*Ibid.*, p. 188) that the writers of the radical articles "applied without qualification and in a very rigid way the doctrines and conceptions of the social compact political philosophy." The social compact philosophy conceives of divided sovereignty, of the binding effect of compact, and of the founding of *a* body politic by compact and consent. One of the highly significant facts of Calhoun's philosophy was his total abandonment of the social compact doctrines.

CHAPTER XXVII

CONDITIONS AFTER 1815. THE RISE OF THE NEW WEST. INTERNAL IMPROVEMENTS

After the war, the most noteworthy features of American life were the spirit of nationalism, the rapid building up of the new west, the extension and the expression of a buoyant and confident democracy. These three conditions or developments were interrelated and interdependent. In both Europe and America, the nineteenth century was marked by the growth of the spirit of nationalism, the integration of peoples, expansion, and the increase of popular power. Our story has to do with America, but it is well to notice, before entering upon the story with more detail, that American history follows, or leads, along the lines familiar to students of European affairs.

The sources of the sentiment of nationalism cannot, of course, be fully discovered. Before the war began, in spite of a good deal of petty sectional and state jealousy, men were not devoid of patriotism; the war itself was brought on largely by the younger men who were tired of bickering when national honor was at stake; and when the struggle was over there was a wider outlook. Even the New Englanders, sullen as many of them had been, took pride in the victories at sea, for there had been victories as well as disasters; and the smoke of the battle of New Orleans cast a mellow glow upon a war not otherwise the subject of much exultation.

The men of the generation after the war were devoted to the union; and to gather the significance of that one word—union—as it appealed to them, we need to bear in mind the distractions preceding the war and the humiliating and perilous distractions in the midst of the war itself. The former partisan bitterness, based on hatred for one or the other of the warring nations of Europe, had now ceased to be a matter of great consequence. Peace in Europe helped to still the old-fashioned partisan strife in America. Men were looking westward to the Pacific, not with foreboding across the Atlantic.

Sectionalism did not disappear entirely; a country of an extensive area embracing differing interests and differing modes of life was certain to be troubled by sectionalism; and indeed the wonder is, not that there were conflicting interests, but that the union was held together at all, to be tested at length by one supreme effort at secession nearly three-quarters of a century after the Constitution was framed. But for a time after the second war with Britain this sectionalism was not obtrusive; and, though a state occasionally broke out in resolutions and indulged in lamentation over banks or internal improvements or tariff, the lamentation was not inconsistent with a feeling of pride in the nation. Though a nationalistic interpretation of the Constitution is a natural consequence of national sentiment, we do not need to conclude that every defense of states' rights is an evidence of absence of affection for the nation. Those years then—the fifteen years or so after the war—were very significant as they expressed and built up this affection which in later decades was to withstand the disintegrating effects of slavery and the conflicting interests of free and slave labor.

When the Revolution ended, only a few hardy woodsmen had pushed beyond the mountains into the great valley. But the migration went steadily on. Kentucky entered the union in 1792, Tennessee in 1796, Ohio in 1803. In the face of protests from the northeastern Federalists, who saw the union shattered by the admission of a new partner, Louisiana entered in 1812. Immediately after the war, people began to pour over the mountains; regions that had been nothing but untracked wilderness, or wilderness tracked only by river-highways, were turned, in a lustrum or less, into farms and villages; the people were lustily engaged in the task which chiefly absorbed their energies, the task of occupying the continent. The union stretched away to the Mississippi and beyond; and in that region men were born and reared: new leaders of men, Lincoln and Jefferson Davis, and scores of others only less important were children of the west. The nation was no longer a string of republics along the Atlantic coast.

Of the effect of this new west much can be said. The spirit and character of the frontiersman—the spirit and character created by the job of peopling the wilderness—made themselves felt even within the field of constitutional history. The west was naturally nationalistic. Expansion and nationalism are boon companions. The men who crossed the mountains, devoted as they may have been to the state from which they came, no longer had an undivided affection for the place of their birth; they were making new states and developing a new affection; the older provincialism was lost. In some regions, as in the old northwest, they settled on national land; they were protected at times by national troops; their officials in early days were national officials; and as wards of the nation their settlements grew into territories and finally into states. Provincialism requires time and quiet for development; the west had no time and did not know repose. Men who are engaged in the extension of empire are not naturally puny-minded. The river system and the essential unity of the great valley made interdependence of sections an obvious and dominating fact; geography itself taught the evident lesson of union. In the hastily-made states of the west, state sovereignty, as a doctrine, based on a sense of the individual character of the state, had infertile soil for growth. This is not saying there was no sectionalism, born of particular interests and prejudices. The westerner has never been modest about laying down his demands and setting up his economic needs. But his demands and his laments have as a rule not dimmed the luster of his affection for his country.

The rise of the west brings before us with renewed force the fact that our constitutional system had to adapt itself to a developing, not to a stagnant, country, or to one growing within a narrowly-limited area. Formed for thirteen seaboard states, the Constitution had to be fitted to the needs of a continent. There were within the same nation not only the free-labor states and slave-labor states, but also regions old and new, sections well along in commercial and industrial life and sections undeveloped, still living in a primitive though rapidly-changing industrial condition. The contrast between north and south, between two industrial systems, was perilous, and the contrast ended in conflict and war; but quite as important, perhaps, were the continuous adjustments necessitated by national expansion and by the varying views of east and west. In any broad view of constitutional history, such fundamental and elementary facts must always be kept in mind.

But what of the southern section of the Mississippi basin? Into some portions of that region masters went with their slaves; big, flourishing plantations were scattered along the rich bottom-lands and reproduced the social and industrial life of the old south. There too, in the earlier days, the people were influenced by western conditions, and some portions of the far southern states long remained western in their sympathies and habits. A flourishing region, raising before long great quantities of cotton, did not for many years feel any strong temptation to acquire sectional forebodings. And yet, in the Mississippi valley, as along the coast, there were two differing systems of industry, slave labor and free labor; the slave-owning region gave new life to slavery. In the west itself there was the basis for serious divergence that might ripen into hostility.

As the Europeans in crossing the Atlantic to America dropped from their shoulders some of the habits of mind and the social customs of the old world, so the eager immigrants into the Mississippi basin cast aside, as they passed the mountains, something of the thinking and most of the social barriers and burdens which they had known in the east. They did not start all over again entirely free from traditions, but, unhampered by social cleavage and marked differences of economic conditions, they could rear their political communities without fear of molesting any vested prestige of social and political superiors.

The old scruples about constitutional authority were, in the years after the war, partly discarded by the men who had especially nourished them. The old fear of monarchy was of course forgotten. The Republicans, it was said, had "out-federalized" the Federalists. Madison and Monroe, though occasionally struggling with old misgivings, were generous in their interpretation of national power—as generosity went a hundred years and more ago. Madison recommended protection for manufactures, the building of roads and canals, the establishment of a national university, an army, and a well-provided navy. He vetoed a bank bill (1815), but signed the bill creating a new Bank in 1816. Monroe, in his turn, was not beset with fears and forebodings, though he was less venturesome than John Quincy Adams, who, when he took the presidency, had no hesitation in presenting large schemes of national activity. Some men, it is true, still wrestled anxiously with constitutional scruples; when their economic interests were unfavorably affected, they did not fail to criticize and complain; but all this was not destructive or fatal. The main fact is clear beyond all cavil: if the nation was to move on and prosper as a vital whole, it must be held together, not by laws and congresses and courts alone, nor by principles of constitutional interpretation, but by the *spirit* of union, by sentiment.

With this temporary disappearance or subsidence of strict construction, a tendency which indeed began its course soon after Jefferson took the presidential chair, it might seem that Jeffersonism was wholly discredited. But Jefferson himself never gave up in theory his belief in the value of local self-government. Believing that the nation was safe if the people in the states were possessed of power to manage unmolested the great body of their own affairs, he clung to states' rights, dreaded consolidation, and disapproved of the tendency of the judiciary to establish national authority by constitutional construction. But fate and the way of the world were against localism. The heart of Jeffersonian principles, however, was not dying, but triumphant; the essentials of democratic government were daily more actively alive. Telling a buoyant westerner that the government must be in the hands of the wise, the good, and the rich would have been an extravagant indulgence in humor. As Taine has said of the men who made France a thousand years ago, these sturdy westerners had no need of ancestors, for they were ancestors themselves.

Even within the limited field of constitutional history the development of the new democracy, sure of itself, confident of its power, has its conspicuous place. America, someone has said, was bred in a cabin —a suitable place for the birth and upbringing of a democratic people. In those years after the war, clearly appeared the America we know, the America of the nineteenth century, in some respects bearing peculiarly the stamp of frontier self-reliance and frontier individualism. If that America could not make a democracy and carry it on, the failure would not be due to want of confidence in her own prowess.[1]

In the period under consideration (1815-1830) opposition to the acts of the federal government was chiefly directed against the national Bank, internal improvements, and the tariff. Opposition to the Bank can best be studied in connection with certain decisions rendered by the Supreme Court, and we shall omit that topic until we discuss those decisions. The tariff question, which by 1830 had become the center of serious and alarming dispute, will be taken up in connection with the pronouncements of South Carolina and the theories of Calhoun concerning state sovereignty (1828-1833). The earliest controversies arose in connection with proposals for expenditures for internal improvements.

The development of transportation, of means of communication, has been effective in building up nationalism and beating down localism. The nation was to attain and in the course of time did attain industrial integrity; without it, mere legal integrity would have been a shadow, should it survive at all. In the early west the steamboats—

[1] Reference should of course be made to F. J. Turner, *The Frontier in American History*, and *Rise of the New West*.

the old, but then brilliantly new, flat-bottomed steamboats—puffing their way up and down the countless rivers of the Mississippi basin made it possible to people the land quickly and to carry on with comparative comfort the task of winning the wilderness; they helped to bring the western communities together. But adequate ties with the east were lacking.

The waterways of the west were not enough. The westerners wanted roads. Late in Jefferson's administration, Gallatin, the Secretary of the Treasury, had mapped out a comprehensive plan for roads and canals, and a few years later a beginning was made on the Cumberland Road, which was intended to be a great highway connecting the east with the transmontane region. After the war the need of proper overland connection was stronger; if the western farmers were to market their own products with profit or were to obtain with any ease the products of eastern factories, there was need of more than the river systems. The easterners, too, might have felt more strongly than many appeared to do the advantage to be gained from cheaper food from the west.[2]

A number of the states entered separately upon plans for developing routes of communication within their own borders; but the problem of interstate communication and especially of highways across the mountains was replete with difficulties. The individual states were incompetent—at least they were incompetent unless they banished all thoughts of economic rivalry, and that was of course impossible. This whole matter was of importance, not so much because it involved technical interpretation of the Constitution as because constitutional or institutional unity naturally rested on actual economic interdependence. The west was beginning to demand expenditures from the national government for western roads, and the demand continued.

But plans for road-building encountered sectional opposition as well as constitutional scruples. The seaboard states found as a rule no legal obligation preventing the government from attending to the seacoast harbors; but to build roads within the states was another matter. The westerners were aroused by the readiness with which money was granted for the coast and by the reluctance or refusal to make appropriations for the west. Clay in a forceful speech (1824), lauding the patriotism and devotion of the west to the union, presented an able

---

2 "When wheat brought twenty-five cents a bushel in Illinois in 1825, it sold at over eighty cents in Petersburg, Virginia, and flour was six dollars a barrel at Charleston, South Carolina." Turner, *Rise of the New West*, p. 106.

argument for liberal interpretation of the Constitution and for a policy which did not confine its tender attention to the states bordering on the ocean. "Yes," he exclaimed, "any thing, every thing, may be done for foreign commerce; any thing, every thing, on the margin of the ocean. But nothing for domestic trade; nothing for the great interior of the country!" ". . . not one stone has yet been broken, not one spade of earth has been yet removed in any Western State." [3]

In his annual message of 1816, Madison called the attention of Congress "to the expediency of exercising their existing powers, and, where necessary, of resorting to the prescribed mode of enlarging them, in order to effectuate a comprehensive system of roads and canals. . . ." As he had already signed a bill for the establishment of the national Bank, he might well have been expected to sign the "bonus bill", which provided for using the Bank bonus and the dividends for internal improvements; but his older scruples prevailed, and on the last day of his public life (March 3, 1817) he vetoed the bill. He declared his belief in the great importance of roads and canals and the improvement of watercourses, "and that a power in the National Legislature to provide for them might be exercised with signal advantage to the general prosperity"; but such power was not given by the Constitution and could not be deduced from it. ". . . the permanent success of the Constitution," he said, "depends on a definite partition of powers between the General and the State Governments"; and he objected to any "constructive extension" of the powers of Congress.[4] In 1822, Monroe took much the same position as his predecessor. In an elaborate paper accompanying his veto of an internal improvements bill, he descanted at length upon the nature of the union.

[3] *Annals of Congress*, 18 Cong., 1 sess., cols. 1035, 1040.

[4] Perhaps no better evidence of the perplexities and the difficulties of interpreting the written Constitution of a federal state and of maintaining federalism, and at the same time responding to actual insistent need for national activity and legislation, can be found than in Madison's own career and the apparent agitations of his own mind. A sincere nationalist, in the sense that he was not possessed by a loyalty to his own province but thought in national terms with real patriotism, he nevertheless believed in a large degree of states' rights as conducive to the public welfare and the maintenance of the union as he conceived that union to be. On the one hand, the states existed; the union existed under a national government with limited authority; the principle of local self-government was inherent in the nature and scheme of the union. On the other hand, the needs of the nation as a whole were real, active, persistent, increasing. To Madison, of utmost concern was the sanctity of the written word, even when the limitations it imposed were inconvenient. And if he was inconsistent, his course must be accounted for by the intrinsic difficulty of maintaining states' rights, strict construction, a regard for the limits of constitutional authority, and also the realities of national life.

Concerning the particular problem then under discussion he declared an amendment necessary before Congress could enter upon any control of internal improvements.

Both Madison and Monroe touched upon the meaning of the so-called "welfare clause" of the Constitution.[5] Madison's position must be considered sound theoretically; Congress is granted the authority to tax; but the words to "provide for the common defense and general welfare" do not constitute a separate and substantive grant of authority.[6] Congress has authority to raise money that it may exercise the powers authorized specifically, and these are conveniently summarized as providing for the common defense and general welfare. Monroe asserted the right of Congress to appropriate freely for any purpose of a general character, even when it cannot control the object for which the money is spent;[7] what he feared was the hand of the national government thrust within the borders of the state. This was not an unimportant announcement; it furnished a way whereby the federal government could spend money without anyone's questioning whether the object for which the money was provided was constitutionally subject to congressional control and management. It helped, in the course of the ensuing decades, to create a vast bureaucratic system at Washington which is to-day a subject of wonder if not always of admiration.

Money was appropriated for repairs of the Cumberland Road.[8] But the opposition in the south was beginning to stiffen, and New England was not willing to see money spent for the west. The subject of internal improvements was logically or practically associated with the tariff, a part of Clay's "American System"; and new sectional forces made themselves felt. The general attitude toward the constitutional power to provide for internal improvements in 1818 is illustrated by votes in the House; the opinion was then expressed that Congress could appropriate money for various improvements, but it

[5] The Congress shall have power "To lay and collect taxes, duties, imposts, and excises, to pay the debts and provide for the common defense and general welfare of the United States. . . ." Art. I, sec. 8, para. 1.

[6] See Jefferson's argument on the bank act discussed *ante*. In a vague paragraph of his veto message, Madison seems to imply that the power to appropriate money for general purposes may perhaps be constitutional.

[7] Richardson, *Messages and Papers*, II, p. 173.

[8] In his annual message of December 3, 1822, Monroe said: "Should Congress, however, deem it improper to recommend such an amendment, they have, according to my judgment, the right to keep the road in repair by providing for the superintendence of it and appropriating the money necessary for repairs."

did not have the authority to construct post-roads and military roads or canals for interstate commercial communication or even canals for military purposes. The sectional alignment in 1824 is shown by the vote on the proposal for a general survey bill, which was carried. It showed New England representatives casting twelve votes for and twenty-six against; the middle states thirty-seven for and twenty-six against; the south twenty-three for and thirty-four against; the west including the southwest forty-three for and none against.[9]

The intricacies of minute constitutional construction, which have been presented altogether too briefly in these last pages, may seem almost trivial to the eyes of the modern student of public affairs. The common man has forgotten, or almost forgotten, that Congress has only limited powers. He has seen the government engaged in legislation of such sweeping general character that he is almost unaware of the technical necessity for discovering authority to act. No one would now question the right to improve and maintain harbors, to have oversight of the improvement of roads for which federal money is expended, to build roads, to retain and maintain forest reserves within a state, or even to grant money freely for agriculture. But to look upon the scruples of the early days as evidence of stupid statesmanship is quite unnecessary. The desire to hold the central authority strictly within the assigned bounds does not imply either feeble-mindedness or criminal perversity.

The contrast between misgivings of these early years of the last century and the actual extent of national authority in recent times may be illustrated by the statement of the Supreme Court in California v. Central Pacific Railroad Company (1888).[10] It was there held that Congress has authority to authorize corporations to construct railroads and other highways across the states: "Without authority in Congress to establish and maintain such highways and bridges, it would be

[9] See Turner, *Rise of the New West,* pp. 229, 235. Professor Ames thus sums up the important position of the states toward constitutional principles in the period under consideration: "Opposition to the doctrine of broad construction led those who objected to a protective tariff on constitutional grounds to oppose also the other important feature of the so-called 'American System,' namely, national aid to internal improvement. This was necessary on ground of consistency, if for no other. It is not surprising therefore to find generally in the series of resolutions passed by the Southern States, during the period 1825-1832, condemnation of both the protective tariff and internal improvement acts. This was especially true to 1827. In fact, contemporary evidence indicates that more emphasis was placed upon the opposition to federal internal improvement measures than to the protective tariff bills prior to that date." Ames, *State Documents,* no. 4, p. 1.

[10] 127 U. S. 1 (1888). See also In re Debs, 158 U. S. 564 (1895).

without authority to regulate one of the most important adjuncts of commerce." It would appear as a natural consequence from this right to build and maintain that Congress would have authority for exercising such control as to make the roads serviceable and to preserve them from injury—in other words, to exercise, if need be, general public protection of such property within state limits. When this decision was rendered, the old-time tender solicitude for the states and narrow interpretation of the Constitution had faded into the mists of antiquity.[11]

[11] The general welfare clause of the Constitution was interpreted and applied by the Supreme Court for the first time in 1936: United States *v.* Butler, 297 U. S. 1. The Court rejected Madison's interpretation (see p. 363 of this volume). Its interpretation does not vary materially from Monroe's. "The power to tax and spend is a separate and distinct power; its exercise is not confined to the fields committed to Congress by the other enumerated grants of power; but it is limited by the requirement that it shall be exercised to provide for the general welfare of the United States." (Syllabus of the case p. 2.) The Court, holding the Agricultural Adjustment Act unconstitutional, declared that the act encroached upon the reserved rights of the states. "Congress has no power to enforce its commands on the farmer. . . . It must follow that it may not indirectly accomplish those ends by taxing and spending to purchase compliance." (*Ibid.,* p. 74.) Three justices dissented. Justice Stone, speaking for the dissenters, said: "If the expenditure is for a national public purpose, that purpose will not be thwarted because payment is on condition which will advance that purpose. . . . If appropriation in aid of a program of curtailment of agricultural production is constitutional, and it is not denied that it is, payment to farmers on condition that they reduce their crop acreage is constitutional." (*Ibid.,* p. 86.)

The Court distinguished the case from Massachusetts *v.* Mellon (p. 789 of this book) : "It was there held that a taxpayer of the United States may not question expenditures from its treasury on the ground that the alleged unlawful diversion will deplete the public funds and thus increase the burden of future taxation" (p. 58). As the opinion points out, such expenditures had not been challenged because no remedy was open for testing their constitutionality in the Courts (p. 73).

In light of this decision and the fact that various learned commentators have rejected Madison's interpretation of the general welfare clause, the author of this volume should retract the statement on page 363 that Madison's position was sound theoretically. His own opinion should not be considered as of importance. The reprinting of this volume (1939) furnishes opportunity to make this modification of the text.

CHAPTER XXVIII

THE DEVELOPMENT OF STATE CONSTITUTIONS

If we should confine ourselves to a consideration of the events and constitutional controversies in the national field, we would not get a very satisfactory or correct appreciation of the developments of popular government in the first half century after independence. Such a story would omit the evidences of the most essential thing in the life of a state moving continually forward toward popular control. More important than legal institutions are the capacity of the people and their readiness to assume the responsibilities of self-government. The development of this readiness, the growth of essential democracy, is not easily traced; but its results are obvious: the common man became more self-reliant. In the first fifty years, the social leaders of the older type lost their position of leadership. A study of the history of those years will free the mind of the reader from the idea that the American man started in 1776 wholly free and has gradually been wound about by chains of privilege.

All through our history the state constitutions furnish an excellent index of the prevailing political thinking. Alterations in the constitutions mark developments or tendencies in political life. More clearly, on the whole, than any other class of documents, they show results of economic and social movement. From even a cursory examination, we find plain proof that great and essential changes took place in the first half century. The changes in the constitutions were not merely technical or formal; in many cases they marked a decided movement in the direction of a wider and stronger democracy. Most significant of all was the widening of the suffrage, and, it must be remembered, the national Constitution left the right to determine the qualifications for suffrage to the states; if the number of those qualified to vote for members of the "most numerous branch" of the state legislature was increased, the number allowed to vote for congressmen was likewise increased; and if presidential electors were chosen by popular vote, any enlargement of the popular electorate added to the number qualified to vote for presidential electors.

It is difficult to outline in general terms, and still with accuracy, the limits placed on the suffrage by the early constitutions, for the qualifications varied from state to state. Only one state, Vermont (1777), permitted manhood suffrage; every other state laid down restrictions. In South Carolina (1778) a voter must acknowledge the "being of a God," believe in a future state of rewards and punishments, and, equipped with these beliefs, must have a freehold estate of fifty acres or pay a tax equal to the tax on fifty acres of land. In New Jersey (1776) a voter must be worth fifty pounds of proclamation money, while in Virginia (1776), as in some of the other states, at least a small freehold was necessary. In Massachusetts (1780) a voter must have a freehold estate "of the annual income of three pounds" or other property of sixty pounds value. To vote for representatives in New York (1777) one must have a twenty-pound freehold or a small leasehold estate; but to vote for governor or senators one must have a freehold of one hundred pounds value. Pennsylvania (1776) and New Hampshire (1784) were less exacting, the former giving the suffrage to taxpayers and to sons of freeholders, the latter to taxpayers.

The tendency to lighten or remove suffrage restrictions appeared even before the new century began. South Carolina (1790) retained a property qualification, but gave up the religious requirements; twenty years later the property test was abandoned.[1] New Hampshire (1792) took steps in the same direction. In the same year Delaware substituted the payment of a tax for the property test appearing in her earlier constitution, and allowed sons of taxpayers to vote. In the next century Maryland (1810) adopted manhood suffrage. As might be expected, the western states entered the union with liberal provisions, manhood suffrage being provided for by Kentucky (1792), Indiana (1816), Illinois (1818), Alabama (1819), and Missouri (1820). Maine, separating from Massachusetts, adopted manhood suffrage in 1819; Mississippi (1817) and Louisiana (1812) were almost as liberal.[2]

Massachusetts and New York held constitutional conventions, the former in 1820, and the latter in 1821, in which property qualifica-

---

[1] The amendment (1810) is a bit confusing, but the above seems to be a reasonable interpretation.

[2] In speaking of manhood suffrage, I have not attempted to point out how far the states admitted negroes to the suffrage, on the whole not an extremely important question until later years. The tendency appears to have been in the direction of the exclusion of colored men, if any modification was made in suffrage requirements. In some cases, soldiers and sailors were disqualified.

tions for suffrage were ably debated. The conservatives there took their stand, almost the last stand at the north, against the tide of democracy which was sweeping the country. The New York debates deserve more than passing notice because they illustrate so well the fear of popular suffrage, the belief in the sobering influence of property, and also something of the old belief that property itself should claim representation. A proposal earnestly debated was one restricting the right to vote for state senators to those who, in their own or their wives' rights, had a freehold estate of a certain value. "Life and liberty", said one speaker, "are common to all, but the possession of property is not. Hence the owners of property have rights which, in relation to those who are destitute, are separate and exclusive." ". . . a fair representation of every class of citizens in the administration of government, requires that the right of suffrage should be so arranged, as to give due weight to property, as well as to personal rights." [3] Such arguments were by that time rather old-fashioned. Their disappearance is significant; they had little breathing-space after 1825.

James Kent, the learned Chancellor, depicted with great earnestness the dangers of universal suffrage. Those pursuing that *"ignis fatuus"*, he declared, ought to be awakened and startled by the growth of New York City. He pictured the condition of France and England with millions of unpropertied people. "The radicals in England," he said, "with the force of that mighty engine, would at once sweep away the property, the laws, and the liberties of that island like a deluge." Martin Van Buren was more hopeful; he asked the convention to move on in accord with other states and to forget the forebodings which the framers of the Constitution had entertained nearly forty years before. "Experience," he asserted, "the only unerring touchstone, had proved the fallacy of all those speculations. . . ." [4] But even Van Buren halted when it came to the question of granting complete and universal suffrage; he, too, had his fear of the rabble; free voting in New York City, he asserted, would drive from the polls all sober-minded people. Finally the convention granted the suffrage to taxpayers, though even from this requirement certain persons were exempted, and gave to men of color the privilege of voting if they possessed a two hundred and fifty-dollar freehold and paid a tax on it. Five years later the state, by an amendment, swept all restrictions away from the path of the white voter.

[3] *Reports of the Proceedings and Debates of the Convention of 1821*, p. 226.
[4] *Ibid.*, p. 261.

In Massachusetts there was a similar discussion; the defenders of property succeeded in limiting the suffrage to taxpayers,[5] but the qualifications of the first constitution were abandoned. The action of two populous and influential states like New York and Massachusetts was of course significant of what had been going on in the land, and no less significant was the act of Connecticut summoning a convention and supplanting her old charter with a modern constitution (1818).

The early constitutions commonly laid down qualifications for office-holding which were thought to insure the hold of the prosperous and the virtuous upon the powers of office. By the constitution of Massachusetts (1780) no one could be a senator unless he possessed a freehold of three hundred pounds value or a personal estate of six hundred pounds, or both to the amount of the latter sum; no one could be a representative unless he had a freehold of one hundred pounds or a ratable estate of twice that amount; and a governor must be blessed with a thousand-pound freehold. Such officers must take an oath that they believed in the Christian religion. It followed, therefore, that any voter properly qualified might vote for a Christian sufficiently rich to be a safe guardian of the state. In Delaware (1776) the office-holders must be trinitarians and believe in the divine inspiration of the Scriptures; members of the legislature must be not only orthodox but freeholders. In Pennsylvania (1776) a representative must declare his belief in one God, the creator and governor of the universe, the rewarder of the good and the punisher of the wicked, and must acknowledge the divine inspiration of the Scriptures. In South Carolina (1778) only Protestants, possessed of considerable property, could be members of the legislature; the governor and certain other officials must each have in his own right a settled plantation or a freehold worth at least ten thousand pounds currency. New York (1777) and Virginia (1776) managed to get on without religious tests for office-holding and provided only a freehold qualification for holding some positions; but some kind of religious and property qualifications was common to most of the other states.

That such requirements for office-holding should be laid down in the constitutions of Revolutionary days need not surprise us, though the constitutions, on the whole, mark a very decided step forward in popular government. The movement toward liberalism began before

---

[5] Reference was made in the third article of the adopted amendments to certain citizens "who shall be by law exempted from taxation. . . ." *Journal of Debates and Proceedings*, p. 618.

the end of the century and thereafter went slowly forward. Massachusetts abandoned the religious restriction in the early nineteenth century; the Connecticut constitution of 1818 made a declaration of complete religious equality. In the west, there was from the beginning freedom from religious tests except in three states where atheists were excluded from certain offices.[6] Property qualifications for office-holding also gradually gave way, but only slowly. Even the new states in some cases laid down such requirements.[7] But gradual though the movement was, it was continuous, and marked (as did the abandonment of the suffrage restrictions) growing liberality, less faith in orthodox religious belief and in the sacred superiority of property, and more faith of men in themselves and in their fellows. There was also some advance in the direction of popular apportionment of representation, and this was of great significance, for it marked, as did other changes, growing recognition of the fact that people were the basis of government and that privileged areas must give way.

In the south, where the western non-slaveholding regions of a state were likely to be underrepresented, this movement for reapportionment was of extreme importance. In the Virginia convention of 1829-1830, which contained a number of conspicuous and able men— John Marshall, James Madison, and William B. Giles among them—, a great debate was staged.[8] The outcome, something of a compromise, was unsatisfactory to the free farmers of the western region, and left a sense of injustice in their minds; but disruption of the Old Dominion was not consummated until over thirty years later, when the nation was shaken by civil war.

In the early days, it was common to trust the legislature; except as its powers were limited or checked by a few direct commands and by the general principles of the constitution, it possessed full legislative

[6] In Arkansas (1836) no person who denied the being of a God, in Tennessee (1796) and in Mississippi (1817) no person who denied the being of a God or a future state of punishments and rewards could hold any office in the civil department of the state, though the Arkansas and Tennessee bills of rights declared against religious tests.

[7] Ohio (1802), Indiana (1816), and Illinois (1818) required legislators to be taxpayers, not a burdensome requirement, on the whole.

[8] Something of the attitude of the conservatives may be gathered from the remarks of one delegate: ". . . if any plague originate in the North, it is sure to spread to the South and to invade us sooner or later: the influenza—the small-pox—the varioloid—the Hessian fly—the Circuit Court system—Universal Suffrage—all come from the North—and they always cross above the falls of the great rivers". Only, it appears, the old tidewater region was in itself immune from infection. *Proceedings and Debates of the Virginia State Convention, of 1829-30*, p. 407.

authority. The governor, on the other hand, was not trusted; and this distrust was probably due to the fact that the name and the office recalled to the popular mind the colonial official with whom there had been controversy and dispute. In the Revolutionary constitutions, except in four states,[9] he was chosen by the legislature. This method of choice is an evidence of lack of faith in the capacity of the people to choose men qualified for high office, and a belief in the greater wisdom of the legislature. In some states he was guided or advised by a council, another relic of the past; he had as a rule no veto and little or no power of appointment.[10] But in these respects, as in others, changes came: the council began to disappear; the veto was granted; popular election was substituted for election by the legislature. The development of the governor's independence and his immediate dependence upon the people show that the people were no longer in fear of the executive; they were confident of their own authority and their own strength; timidity was not becoming in a people who had now come to the stage of growth when they looked upon an officer not as a superior but as a servant. This changed attitude of mind, so clearly exposed by the development of state constitutions, underlies and explains the qualities of the Jacksonian era and can be seen in the field of national as well as state politics. In fact, without appreciation of it, Jackson and Jacksonism are incomprehensible.

Beyond the governor and the executive council, little was said in the early constitutions about executive officers. When they were provided for at all, they were commonly chosen in some manner by the state government, not by the people. The drift away from appointment toward popular election was slow; not until the nineteenth century was well advanced was there a marked demand, in accord with the spirit of Jacksonian democracy, for the possession of full elective power by the people. That change, when it was finally adopted, was of immense significance and influence on the character of state governments. But the lengthening of the ballot and the consequent burdens which were thus placed on the uncomplaining shoulders of the average voter probably did not make government really more democratic, more just, or more efficient.

[9] New Hampshire, Vermont, Massachusetts, and New York.
[10] In Massachusetts he had a veto that might be overcome by a two-thirds vote of the legislature. There too, he had considerable powers of appointment. The South Carolina constitution of 1776 provided that the governor could assent to or reject bills. In New York a council of revision, of which the governor was a member, had a qualified veto.

CHAPTER XXIX

THE MISSOURI COMPROMISE

The peopling of the Mississippi valley proceeded so rapidly that in 1818 the territory of Missouri, beyond the river, was asking admission to the union. And now it was apparent that expansion of the republic was inextricably entangled with the slavery problem. Was slavery to be carried into the public domain and were new states to be formed in which slaveholding was to be perpetuated? Thus, even slavery as a moral and industrial question was complicated because of the opportunities of a new continent; the slavery problem was part of the western problem; slavery could not be dealt with as an institution fixed within narrow boundaries and not subject to a rapidly-developing civilization.

The wiser statesmen of earlier days appreciated to some extent the dangers resulting from the differences between the north and the south. It is true that when the Constitution was adopted there were slaves in most of the northern states;[1] but to no great extent was northern industry founded on slave labor; and steps had already been taken for gradual emancipation in nearly all of those states where the institution still existed.[2] Furthermore, in the early years there was, both north and south, a feeling of opposition or disapproval of slavery, a disapproval plainly exhibited by leaders of Virginia, though that state contained a quarter of a million of bondsmen on her semi-baronial estates. As the earlier years of the new century went by, the slavery problem did not play a large rôle in men's minds, nor were the early constitutional problems associated with the rights or wrongs of the matter. Opposition to slavery did not disappear; indeed it is evident that by 1820 it had grown rather than decreased at the north; and at the south opposition was neither quite dead nor silent.[3] It was

[1] A trifle over 40,000 north of Delaware, the largest number in New York (21,193). Virginia contained 292,627 out of a total of 697,624 in the whole union.

[2] No slavery in Vermont, New Hampshire, and Massachusetts. Gradual emancipation was provided for in Pennsylvania, Connecticut, and Rhode Island.

[3] In the congressional debates on the admission of Missouri, we find Reid of

not uncommon for southerners to deplore the institution as a burden under which they labored. And so, though the clash of interests and the bitterness of dispute are now seen to have been quite inevitable, the struggle arising over the admission of Missouri brought dismay; thirty years of national existence had not prepared men for the intensity and bitterness of sectional strife.

The intensity of feeling and the vehemence of discussion would have been less marked, no doubt, if there had not been certain sectional jealousies—though that may be too strong a word—which were not directly connected with the slavery question. When the federal Constitution was framed, the population of the states north of Mason and Dixon's line (the northern line of Delaware and Maryland) was nearly the same as that of the southern states. But the northern population had increased more rapidly than the southern; and, furthermore, as only three-fifths of the slaves were counted for determining representation in the House, that chamber was soon securely in the hands of the free states. After the admission of Alabama in 1819 the Senate was evenly divided between the sections, eleven free and eleven slave states.[4] If the balance were to be disturbed, one section would of course have the advantage in the Senate, and should the disturbance be caused by the admission of a free state, the north, as far as sectional interests went, would have a majority in both houses.

It is quite impossible to know just how much the south—or the north for that matter—was influenced in 1820 by a conscious desire to protect sectional interests by the preservation of an equal voice in the Senate. The south was not as yet a self-conscious section; that con-

Georgia declaring, "For my own part, surrounded by slavery from my cradle to the present moment, I yet
    'Hate the touch of servile hands;
    'I loathe the slaves who cringe around:'
and I would hail that day as the most glorious in its dawning, which should behold, with safety to themselves and our citizens, the black population of the United States placed upon the high eminence of equal rights, and clothed in the privileges and immunities of American citizens!" But he denied the right of Congress to place a condition on the admission of Missouri assuring the disappearance of slavery in that state. *Annals of Congress,* 16 Cong., 1 sess., col. 1025 ff.

    [4] The slave states were: Delaware, Maryland, Virginia, North Carolina, South Carolina, Georgia, Kentucky, Tennessee, Louisiana, Mississippi, Alabama. The free states were: New Hampshire, Vermont, Massachusetts, Connecticut, Rhode Island, New York, Pennsylvania, New Jersey, Ohio, Indiana, Illinois. The balance remained substantially equal until the admission of California in 1850, though there were short intervals of inequality: Arkansas was admitted in 1836 and Michigan in 1837; Florida in 1845 and Iowa in 1846; Texas in 1845 and Wisconsin in 1848.

dition came later. The debates of 1819 strengthened the sense of soli-darity of southern interests, but to what extent this feeling directed and governed the purposes of southern political leaders at that time, one cannot be sure. It seems probable that resistance to the admission of Missouri as a free state was due to a natural dislike of a restric-tion which would hem slavery within existing limits, and due also to an instinctive reaction against any step which would appear to deprive the southern slave-owner of what he deemed his rights; it appears improbable that, when the Missouri question arose, the south-ern politicians were already determined to maintain for all future time a protective balance in the Senate.[5]

A very brief story of the main facts is a sufficient background for understanding the constitutional problems. After the admission of Louisiana as a state in 1812, the territory of Missouri covered the remainder of the territory acquired from France in 1803. The people of the southern part of the territory asked for the division of the territory, and in 1819 that region was organized as the territory of Arkansas, but only after there had been a decided effort on the part of many members in the House to provide for the exclusion of slaves or the gradual disappearance of slavery. Meanwhile, steps were taken to admit another portion of the territory—Missouri—as a state in the union. When the bill came up in the House, Tallmadge of New York offered to the enabling act an amendment providing that there should be no further introduction of slavery, and that all children born within the state should be free at the age of twenty-five years. This amendment was agreed to by the House, February 16, 1819, with a small majority in its favor, and the next day the bill was passed. The Senate, however, dropped the amendment and passed the bill; the House refused to concur in the Senate's action. The end of the session was at hand, and when Congress assembled in December (1819) a new factor was added to the problem; Maine, hitherto a part of Massachusetts, had, with the consent of the parent state,

---

[5] The distinctions, perhaps not made with sufficient sharpness in the text, are laid down for this reason: it must not be taken for granted that the south in 1820—the south which contained Kentucky, Tennessee, and the newer states of the southern Mississippi valley—was consciously a section with sectional interests clearly envisaged. In one way it was a section; there was slavery in every state, and when slavery was touched there were likely to be similar reactions throughout the whole south; there was the basis, in other words, for the development of a large degree of sectional consciousness; on this basis of a common institution sectional self-consciousness grew, especially after 1835. New England also felt and had felt her particular interests and doubtless cherished them.

formed a constitution and asked admission into the union—another free state. An act for admission was passed by the House; but the Senate joined the admission of Missouri to the act for admitting Maine and made no provision for the exclusion or emancipation of slaves. It did, however, add what is known as the Thomas amendment, which finally proved the basis of compromise: "in all that territory ceded by France to the United States, under the name of Louisiana, which lies north of thirty-six degrees and thirty minutes north latitude, excepting only such part thereof as is included within the limits of the State contemplated by this act, slavery and involuntary servitude, otherwise than in the punishment of crimes whereof the party shall have been duly convicted, shall be and is hereby forever prohibited".

The House, discussing the whole subject at length, finally passed a bill for admitting Missouri, but prohibiting slavery there (March 1, 1820). The Senate, considering the House bill, struck out the anti-slavery clause but attached the Thomas amendment. The Senate, in short, stood for the admission of Missouri without slavery restriction within the state. The House insisted on the exclusion of slavery. The outcome was the admission of Maine [6] and the passage by both houses of an enabling act for Missouri, not excluding slavery from the state when admitted, but dedicating to free labor the remainder of the Louisiana territory north of thirty-six thirty—the Thomas amendment, the famous Missouri Compromise. We should notice that it referred only to the Louisiana territory and that it did not constitute a condition or a limitation upon Missouri. By the bargain thus struck, while Missouri came in as a slave state, slavery was "forever prohibited" in the larger portion of the territory remaining.[7]

During the months of the debate the whole slavery question received an airing, both within and without the halls of Congress. The southerners did not on the whole defend the institution in the abstract, but they emphatically insisted that they should not be deprived of the right to move with their slaves into the west. Some of them, though deploring slavery, maintained the value of dispersion, of mitigating

[6] Maine was admitted March 3, and an act authorizing Missouri to form a constitution was passed March 6, 1820.

[7] By treaty with Great Britain in 1818 the northern line of the territory westward to the mountains was fixed at 49°. The treaty with Spain (1819-1821) fixed the southern and western limits as far as 42°. The Louisiana region not included within the states of Louisiana, Arkansas, and Missouri may be roughly described as a large triangle with its apex at the south.

the evil by spreading it over a wider area. On the other hand, the opponents of slavery-extension insisted on preserving the western regions from the blight of slavery. Among the public-at-large there was deep interest, active debate, and intense feeling. An occasional southerner spoke of breaking up the union; at the north voices were heard denouncing the whole institution of slavery.

There was much able debating in Congress; men were sufficiently in earnest to give up mere wordy harangues; they were not content with tickling the ears of the groundlings and arousing partisan rancor. The main constitutional arguments were many times repeated. For directness, vigor of expression, and clarity of reasoning, the speeches of Rufus King of New York and William Pinkney of Maryland in the Senate are conspicuous. King, thirty-three years before, had been a delegate from Massachusetts at the Philadelphia convention, and was noted then as a speaker of grace and ability. He had long been opposed to slavery and he brought to the Missouri debate experience as a public man, knowledge of his subject, maturity of judgment, and profound convictions. Perhaps too, he represented in some measure the old-time Federalist and New-England jealousy of southern and western power. Pinkney was one of the leading lawyers in America— perhaps standing actually at the head of the bar—, a finished and effective speaker, a master of the old-fashioned oratory; probably even Webster was not quite his peer.

It was contended by opponents of restriction that the Louisiana treaty imposed the obligation to admit the inhabitants into the union as a state. The treaty provided that "The inhabitants of the ceded territory shall be incorporated in the Union of the United States, and admitted as soon as possible, according to the principles of the Federal constitution, to the enjoyment of all the rights, advantages, and immunities of citizens of the United States. . . . " This clause did not necessarily establish the right of the inhabitants at that time or later to be admitted into the union as a state.[8] If the treaty did so stipulate, it would be a far cry from such stipulation to the position

[8] Taylor of New York, in an able speech in the House, declared that without such a provision the inhabitants of the ceded territory would have stood as aliens in relation to the United States; and, if that assertion is too extreme, the following words are probably not: "The object of the article doubtless was to provide for their admission to the rights of citizens, and their incorporation into the American family. The treaty made no provision for the erection of new States in the ceded territory." *Annals of Congress*, 15 Cong., 2 sess., col. 1172. King, in the Senate, said there was want of precision in the treaty. But he held that the claim in question did constitute a stipulation for admission. This did not imply admission without condition.

that Congress was precluded from placing a condition on the admission of Missouri, provided that Congress had such constitutional authority. Furthermore, a treaty can be overridden by a law.[9] Taylor of New York not only pointed out that Congress had in the past made conditions for the admission of the state of Louisiana into the union, but exclaimed: "The unconstitutional doctrine had not then been broached, that the President and Senate could not only purchase a West Indian island or an African principality, but also impose upon Congress an obligation to make it an independent State, and admit it into the Union. . . . The treaty, therefore, has no operation on the question in debate." [10]

The main discussion and the most important argument arose concerning the right to place conditions upon the admission of a state. The discussion, it must be remembered, came up with reference to the prohibition of slavery in the state, not with reference to its exclusion from portions of the territory beyond the limits of the state. That the problem may be brought forward distinctly, let us first consider the argument of Rufus King. This we have in a condensed form in "The Substance of Two Speeches" [11] which he delivered in the Senate. He showed at length that Congress had exercised the power of placing conditions on admission, and had even made the exclusion of slavery a condition. The power to admit new states was conferred, he maintained, without limitation; the discretion of Congress was complete. After the state came into the union, it could not annul the article by which slavery was excluded; the judiciary of the United States would on proper application deliver from bondage any person held as a slave in the state.

William Pinkney's oration, as we read it to-day, appears as an impressive exhibition of dialectic cleverness. Flowing grace and ease of style are almost too evident, seeming to overshadow the argument; [12] but the argument is very able. Denying the power to place

The whole subject of the status of annexed territories, the significance of incorporation, etc., is treated in Downes *v.* Bidwell, 182 U. S. 244 (1901). An analysis of the Louisiana treaty "fails to disclose any reference to a promise of statehood. . . ." *Ibid.,* 325. See also the chapter on the annexation of Louisiana in this volume.

[9] Chae Chan Ping *v.* United States, 130 U. S. 581 (1889) ; Head Money Cases, 112 U. S. 580 (1884).

[10] *Annals of Congress,* 15 Cong., 2 sess., cols. 1172-1173.

[11] *The Life and Correspondence of Rufus King* (C. R. King, ed.), VI, p. 690 ff.

[12] His speech is in *Annals of Congress,* 16 Cong., 1 sess., cols. 389-417. It is worth noticing that he adhered to the orthodox theory concerning sovereignty, i.e., orthodox for the early decades of the century. "The parties [the states] gave up a portion of that sovereignty to insure the remainder." col. 397.

the proposed condition on admission, he exclaimed, "No man can contradict me when I say that, if you have this power, you may squeeze down a new-born sovereign State to the size of a pigmy, and then taking it between finger and thumb, stick it into some nitch of the Union, and still continue, by way of mockery, to call it a State in the sense of the Constitution." Congress, he said, was given power to admit new states into the union. "What is that Union? A confederation of States equal in sovereignty, capable of every thing which the Constitution does not forbid, or authorize Congress to forbid." Even if Congress has the power to admit and the power to refuse, such discretion does not necessarily involve a power to exact terms. "You must look to the *result*, which is the declared object of the power"; that result must be the preservation of the union of equal states and the establishment of new states in the constitutional sense of the word. He did not explicitly deny the right to impose restrictions or conditions, but he did declare, "You can prescribe no conditions which, if carried into effect, would make the new State less a sovereign State than, under the Union as it stands, it would be." [13]

By the aid of judicial decisions of later years,[14] we can now pass upon the validity of these arguments. Congress can prescribe condi-

[13] We can easily see how much the hearts of the antislavery men were moved by the assertion that the power of the free states in Congress could not be exercised by placing limitations on new states and thus prevent the union from becoming a union of slaveholding states. "The territory of Missouri is beyond our ancient limits, and the inquiry whether slavery shall exist there, is open to many of the arguments that might be employed, had slavery never existed within the United States. It is a question of no ordinary importance. Freedom and slavery are the parties which stand this day before the Senate: and upon its decision the empire of the one or the other will be established in the new state which we are about to admit into the Union." *The Life and Correspondence of Rufus King* (C. R. King, ed.), VI. p. 702.

[14] Coyle *v.* Smith, 221 U. S. 559 (1911). The act (1906) admitting Oklahoma provided that the state capital should be at Guthrie until 1913, and that meanwhile no public money, except so far as necessary, should be voted for erection of buildings for capitol purposes. The Oklahoma convention adopted an ordinance to that effect, but in 1910 the state passed an act removing the capital and appropriating money for buildings. The Supreme Court emphatically denied the continuous binding effect of such a condition after admission. See also references to other opinions in the opinion cited above. In Hogg *v.* Zanesville Canal and Manufacturing Co., 5 Ohio 410 (1832), a certain provision in the Ordinance of 1787 was held binding as an article of compact. A later decision of the federal Supreme Court said, referring to Illinois, "Whatever the limitation upon her powers as a government whilst in a territorial condition, whether from the ordinance of 1787 or the legislation of Congress, it ceased to have any operative force, except as voluntarily adopted by her, after she became a State of the Union." "She was admitted, and could be admitted, only on the same footing" with the original states. Escanaba Co. *v.* Chicago, 107 U. S. 678, 688, 689 (1883).

tions precedent—conditions that can be fulfilled before admission. But a congressional act purporting to impose a political obligation or restriction on the state after admission, to which other states are not subject, is in fact not a condition at all; it is an attempt to make a law which is beyond congressional competence.[15] The states of the union are equal in their possession of political authority.

That the framers intended to provide for the admission of new states on terms of equality with the old is open to doubt. In light of the discussions in the Convention, it is quite possible to look upon the words "New States may be admitted by the Congress into this Union" as a compromise between those delegates wishing to place limits on new states and those favoring complete equality; the resolution adopted by the Convention did not make equality mandatory.[16]

The compromise providing for Missouri's entrance into the union, with no restriction on her power over slavery but with a declaration against slavery in the remainder of the Louisiana purchase north of thirty-six thirty, probably appealed to the masses of people as settling the question of slavery-extension. After controversy and excitement, there is always a readiness to react and to accept a settlement as a release from emotional strain, even if the settlement be not entirely satisfactory. But probably some of the more ardent antislavery advocates felt as King did, that the banishing of slavery north of the prescribed line did not amount to anything, because the act in that particular could be revoked at pleasure and because the "Spanish Province of Texas" would be brought into the union as a slave state— two lugubrious prophecies which later years fulfilled.[17] The end was not yet.[18] The first crisis was passed, but the danger had been im-

---

[15] "As to requirements in such enabling acts as relate only to the contents of the constitution for the proposed new State, little need to be said. The constitutional provision concerning the admission of new States is not a mandate, but a power to be exercised with discretion. From this alone it would follow that Congress may require, under penalty of denying admission, that the organic laws of a new State at the time of admission shall be such as to meet its approval." Coyle v. Smith, 221 U. S. 559, 568.

[16] See Max Farrand, "Compromises of the Constitution," *Am. Hist. Rev.*, IX, pp. 483-484. See also, Farrand, *Records,* II, pp. 454-455. King was a member of the Convention. If he had had Madison's *Notes,* he could have strengthened his position.

[17] I have given above but a word or two from King's letter to Oliver Wolcott, March 3, 1820. The whole is interesting. See *The Life and Correspondence of Rufus King* (C. R. King, ed.), VI, pp. 287-288.

[18] ". . . the struggle indicated," says Professor J. A. Woodburn, "a notable change in the southern mind on the slavery question, and that a slave power was forming which would attempt to control all legislation of the federal Union affecting slavery."

minent; thinking men could see the difficulty of maintaining a union of sections differing in their conceptions of political and economic interests. The controversy sounded, said Jefferson, "like an alarm bell rung at midnight."

The exclusion of slavery from territories north and west of Missouri was not put forward by the determined advocates of the proposal to exclude slavery from Missouri; it was presented and used to obtain the support of the less aggressive opponents of slavery-extension. It was the price offered for the admission of the state with slavery and for the settlement of a wearying controversy.[19] Though the provision for exclusion found its place in the Missouri bill, it was not in any sense a condition on the state. It was a declaration of a policy, in the form of enactment, and was an exercise of the authority of Congress over the territories. Concerning that authority there was little real question.[20] When the bill came up for consideration in Monroe's cabinet, the members were asked their individual opinions concerning the constitutional right to prohibit slavery in a territory. No one of them denied the right. Three southerners in the cabinet, W. H. Crawford of Georgia, John C. Calhoun of South Carolina, and William Wirt of Virginia, signed statements declaring Congress possessed that power.[21]

The Missouri trouble was not altogether disposed of by the passage of the famous compromise; another struggle and another compromise lay immediately ahead. Authorized to form a constitution, the Missouri convention proceeded to do so, and incorporated in it a declaration that it should be the duty of the legislature to pass laws to prevent free negroes and mulattoes from coming to and settling in the state. If Missouri was intent on stirring up strife, she had her way. Were free negroes citizens in the state of their domicile? If they were, to prevent their entrance into Missouri would be a violation of the federal

"The Historical Significance of the Missouri Compromise," Am. Hist. Asso. *Report* for 1893, p. 292.

[19] Woodburn, who has made a thorough study of the whole debate, agrees with Greeley: "It was, in effect, an offer from the milder opponents of slavery restriction to the more moderate and flexible advocates of that restriction." Woodburn, *op. cit.*, p. 264, quoting Greeley, *Political Text Book, 1860*, p. 63.

[20] ". . . no considerable body of opinion appeared to combat, with any approach to success, the sovereign power of the nation to control the Territories." Woodburn, *op. cit.*, p. 291. It was asserted by extreme advocates of slavery that that kind of property must be protected like other kinds in the territories; but the precedents of previous years, the course of the debate, and finally the act itself were overwhelmingly against them.

[21] John Quincy Adams, *Writings* (W. C. Ford, ed.), VII, pp. 1-2.

Constitution, which declares that the citizens of each state shall be entitled to all the privileges and immunities of citizens in the several states. The Constitution means that a citizen of one state is entitled to go into any other, and there, retaining his original citizenship, to enjoy the privileges and immunities of the citizens of the state into which he goes. But there is no need of our examining the question, for the status of free negroes was a matter discussed at length in later years.[22]

It is plainly the duty of Congress to refuse the admission of a state if its constitution is in conflict with the Constitution of the United States. Even William Pinkney would be logically bound to accept that verdict. But the outcome was another compromise; its passage was brought about by the persuasive management of Henry Clay. It provided for the admission of Missouri on an equal footing with the original states upon the fundamental condition that the objectionable clause should not be construed to authorize the passage of any law, and that no law ever should be passed, by which any citizen of a state in the union would be excluded from the enjoyment of any privileges or immunities to which he is entitled under the Constitution, and that the legislature should solemnly declare its assent to this fundamental condition (March 2, 1821). The legislature made the prescribed pledge, preceding it with an announcement that Congress could not legally place a condition on the admission of the state and that the Constitution of the United States and of the state would re-

---

[22] As a matter of fact, other states had on their statute books acts excluding free negroes, and still other states later made similar enactments. Free negroes were considered undesirable neighbors. For example, Delaware had such a law (1811), South Carolina (1820), North Carolina (1826), and Illinois (1853). Missouri in 1847 passed a statute to carry into effect the provision in her constitution against admission of free negroes, despite the condition prescribed twenty-seven years before.

The State v. Claiborne, 19 Tennessee 331 (1838) is an exceedingly interesting case. The Attorney-General in his argument states with accuracy the nature of the union as "a State", and proceeds to lay down the principle of the first clause of the first section of the fourteenth amendment adopted thirty years later. But having done this, he excludes negroes from citizenship and thus anticipates Taney's opinion in the Dred Scott case (1857). The court in its decision likewise excludes the negro from citizenship: "But in reference to the condition of the white citizen, his condition is still that of a degraded man. . . ." He is not entitled to the protection of the "privileges and immunities" clause.

We ought also to note that at a later time there was the problem whether a state had the right in the exercise of its police powers to exclude all persons who were deemed likely to be injurious to the well-being of the state. See the Passenger Cases, 7 Howard 283 (1849), and the discussion in a later chapter of this work, especially the treatment post, pp. 469-471.

main "as if the said resolution had never passed, and the desired declaration was never made. . . ." [23]

While Congress was still debating the admission of Missouri in the winter of 1820-1821, a question arose concerning the counting of the electoral vote for president. Should Missouri's vote be counted? [24] If Missouri was a state, her vote must be counted. The result was a third compromise. The vote was counted in the alternative: the President of the Senate, pursuant to a resolution adopted by the two Houses, announced that, if the vote of Missouri was counted, Monroe had 231 votes; if not counted, he had 228; but in either event he was elected. The strife in the winter of 1821, involving the right of Missouri to exclude free negroes and the right of having her vote counted in the election, was more intense than the previous controversy.

Though some years passed before further angry controversy arose on slavery, the results of the dispute and the conclusions finally agreed upon were of much consequence. Slavery, it was apparent, was not gradually disappearing, and though as yet there was little open defense of the system, the basis for serious controversy endangering the union was evident to the anxious onlooker. Two labor systems faced each other across a definite line. "North" meant in common parlance, or soon came to mean, free labor; "south" meant slave labor. "The old schism of federal and republican threatened nothing," wrote Jefferson, "because it existed in every State, and united them together by the fraternism of party. But the coincidence of a marked principle, moral and political, with a geographical line, once conceived, I feared would never more be obliterated from the mind; that it would be recurring on every occasion and renewing irritations, until it would kindle such mutual and mortal hatred, as to render separation preferable to eternal discord." [25]

<hr/>

[23] June 26, 1821.

[24] There were some declamatory assertions to the effect that Missouri was already a state, waiting plaintively outside the pale. As to the question when a territory becomes a state, there is some information, though not elaborate or conclusive. See Scott v. Jones, 5 Howard 343 (1847). The proper principle would seem to be that the state does not exist as a member of the union until its admission is formally declared by Congress.

[25] Letter to William Short, April 13, 1820, in Jefferson, *Writings* (H. A. Washington, ed.), VII, p. 158. That Jefferson even in 1820 did not mean that the "old schism" amounted to nothing is plain from his letter to Charles Pinckney, September 30. In *Ibid.*, VII, p. 180. He saw the old views of the Federalists in a new attack. His recognition of the unifying effect of national parties is interesting. Actually, the parties soon to be reconstituted were national parties; they crossed the geographic line; they helped to maintain nationalism and the union.

CHAPTER XXX

CONSTITUTIONAL LAW

UNDER CHIEF JUSTICE MARSHALL

In the period we are discussing, characterized on the whole by a sentiment of nationalism and of expansion, a number of disputes concerning national power came before the federal Court and gave to John Marshall and his colleagues the opportunity for laying down principles of immense importance. The opinions in these cases were based on reasoned and emphatic announcements of national authority or they marked with distinctness certain limits on the authority of the states. That these discussions and these opinions should have come in those formative days, before sectionalism and state sovereignty grew really menacing, is of much consequence; nationalism, appearing in various other ways, was thus buttressed by judicial decision; in the settlement of concrete controversies the very foundations of the constitutional system were exposed, as only Marshall could expose them.

If America was to live and grow as a nation, if conflicting sectional interests were to be reconciled, if natural forces, both geographic and economic, which were making for nationalism, were to prevail, then no trivial and constricted construction of the Constitution should stand in the way. One can easily see how a narrow-minded literalist with no comprehension of the magnitude of America might have fastened upon the basic law of the land a construction in harmony with localism and provincialism; how easy it would have been to place such legal obstacles in the way that the developing sense of national unity and of sectional interdependence would have been hampered. Any puny and pedantic construction would have held the young giant in legalistic swaddling-clothes. Natural facts would have been in conflict with the frame and form of the law. Neither Marshall nor anyone else created nationalism by means of constitutional construction; but by taking a broad, forward-looking view of realities, he and others maintained and built up a Constitution suitable for a nation, and a developing nation at that.[1] ". . . a constitution", the Chief Justice said in one of his greatest decisions, "is framed for ages to come, and is designed to approach immortality as nearly as human institutions can approach it."

In 1810, Marshall delivered a significant opinion in the case of Fletcher v. Peck.[2] The controversy arose out of the Yazoo land scandal of an earlier day (1795) which continued to thrust itself into the light. Some 35,000,000 acres of land claimed by Georgia were sold by the legislature of that state for $500,000. Every member of the legislature, save one, voting for the measure got a share of the plunder. The state was aroused, and the next legislature declared the act of cession to be unconstitutional and void.[3] But could a legislature of a state, when once a grant was made, rescind it? Marshall said no, in the case under consideration. The Constitution of the United States declares that no state shall pass a "law impairing the obligation of contracts"; Marshall declared that contracts were of two kinds, executory and executed. "A contract executed is one in which the object of contract is performed; and this, says Blackstone, differs in nothing from a grant." This grant of land, then, was a contract, and the provision of the Constitution against invalidation of contracts

---

[1] It is difficult to measure exactly the influence of able lawyers like Webster and Pinkney on constitutional development, but it must have been very great. If we wish a written rule of law binding on government, that end is attained by the presentation to courts of actual and concrete controversies; and in reaching decisions, the courts are aided by the arguments of lawyers who have laboriously examined the law and legal precedent. Marshall did not need to traverse unknown territory with no direction from guides who knew the terrain at least as thoroughly as he did. "The arguments in M'Culloch vs. Maryland occupied nine days." A. J. Beveridge, The Life of John Marshall, IV, p. 288. Marshall is said to have declared Pinkney to be the greatest man he had ever seen in a court of justice. Pinkney was connected with the Dartmouth College case and for a time with Gibbons v. Ogden; he made great and impressive arguments in McCulloch v. Maryland and in Cohens v. Virginia. His arguments in the Maryland case and in Cohens v. Virginia were masterly expositions of the authority of Congress and the Court. In the latter case he pointed out the permanent importance of the right of the courts of the union to entertain appeals from state tribunals on questions involving constitutional construction. If this appellate power were taken away, he declared, ". . . every other branch of federal authority might as well be surrendered. To part with this, leaves the Union a mere league or confederacy." Webster was counsel in the Dartmouth College case, McCulloch v. Maryland, Cohens v. Virginia, Osborn v. the Bank, and Gibbons v. Ogden. Arguments for the rights of the states were made by attorneys of brilliance and ability. Ibid., passim.

[2] 6 Cranch 87.

[3] U. B. Phillips, Georgia and State Rights, Am. Hist. Asso. Report for 1901, II, pp. 31-32.

applied not only to contracts made by individuals but to those made by the state itself.

Two years after the Fletcher case, the Supreme Court in New Jersey *v.* Wilson decided that a contract made by the state with an Indian tribe, in which it was provided that certain lands purchased for the Indians should not be taxed, was binding on the state; the state could not therefore repeal the original act exempting the lands from taxation [4] even when they had passed with the consent of the state into the hands of purchasers.

A controversy involving a question of somewhat similar nature was presented in the famous Dartmouth College case (1819).[5] By a charter received from the Crown during colonial days, the trustees of Dartmouth College were created a body corporate. The state legislature in 1816 passed acts to amend the charter and to enlarge and improve the corporation; the number of trustees was increased, the governor of the state was empowered to appoint the additional members, and provision was made for a board of overseers to inspect and control the trustees in certain particulars. These legislative enactments were but one incident, though an important one, in a controversy which had long been waging, had awakened personal animosities, and had become entangled in state politics and stained with religious rancor. As might perhaps have been expected from Marshall's earlier decisions, the charter of incorporation was declared by Marshall to be a contract, and its obligations were in consequence protected by the contract clause of the Constitution. There were serious objections to be overcome before such a decision could be reached. Was not the college a public corporation, and should not such an institution be subject to legislative control in the public interest? "A corporation," the Chief Justice of the New Hampshire court had said, "all of whose franchises are exercised for public purposes, is a public corporation." [6] But Marshall declared that Dartmouth College was "an eleemosynary institution, incorporated for the purpose of perpetuating the application of the bounty of the donors, to the specified objects of that bounty"; that the trustees or governors were "not public officers,"

---

[4] 7 Cranch 164 (1812). See also Terrett *v.* Taylor, 9 Cranch 43 (1815). Notice the remark of the Court in Stone *v.* Mississippi, 101 U. S. 814, 820 (1880) : "While taxation is in general necessary for the support of government, it is not part of the government itself. . . . No government dependent on taxation for support can bargain away its whole power of taxation. . . ."

[5] Trustees of Dartmouth College *v.* Woodward, 4 Wheaton 518 (1819).

[6] 1 New Hampshire Reports 111, 117 (1817).

nor was the college "a civil institution, participating in the administration of government. . . ."

This is the most famous of Marshall's decisions [7] though not the most far-reaching in its constitutional effects. It has not escaped criticism, but it has stood from that day to this. It is an accepted principle, therefore, that a charter of a private corporation is a contract as that word is used in the Constitution. The decision, announcing limitation on a state's authority, was of importance in industrial history; for it gave assurance of the inviolability of corporation charters and gave stability to those great industrial agencies.

Had Marshall's decision stood unmodified, or, let us say, had it stood in all its apparent strength, the corporation, with its untouchable charter, might have been beyond the reach of legislative regulation or control. The principle, as we have said, still stands; but it has not prevented the state from exercising reasonable control over corporations. This result is due (1) to the recognition of the right of a state in granting charters to reserve, by constitutional provision or in some other legal manner, the right to amend or recall; [8] (2) to a principle later announced by the Court, that charters are not to be construed as giving by implication more than the plain terms indicate; [9] (3) to a principle laid down, fifty years and more after the Dartmouth College case, that a business "affected with a public interest", whether it be carried on by a corporation or by an individual, is subject to legislative control in certain particulars; [10] (4) to the principle that a state cannot by charter, or otherwise, devest itself of the power and the duty to preserve the public health and safety; in other words, it cannot surrender the exercise of the police power.[11] Of all this we

[7] "This is one of Marshall's most celebrated decisions. It is often cited as the one which established the inviolability of contracts under the Constitution. But the actual controversy, as the Chief-Justice remarked, turned, not so much upon the true construction of the Constitution, in the abstract, as upon its application to the case, and upon the true construction of the charter of Dartmouth College; whether that was a grant of political power which the State could resume or modify at pleasure, or a contract for the security and disposition of property bestowed in trust. . . ." Henry Hitchcock, "Constitutional Development in the United States as Influenced by Chief-Justice Marshall," *Constitutional History of the United States as Seen in the Development of American Law*, p. 104.

[8] The amendment or revocation, however, is not held to be totally without limitation.

[9] Charles River Bridge *v.* Warren Bridge, 11 Peters 420 (1837).

[10] Munn *v.* Illinois, 94 U. S. 113 (1877).

[11] In Boston Beer Co. *v.* Massachusetts, 97 U. S. 25, 32 (1878) the Court held that, though a corporation was chartered for the manufacture of malt liquors and "although this right or capacity was thus granted in the most unqualified form, it

shall have something to say hereafter; but it is well to point out here that with the increase of corporations in number and in scope of activity, and with the development of complex social and industrial order, the need of controlling corporations and subjecting them in very large degree to the authority of the state in the course of time was fully recognized.

The currency and banking conditions of the country were responsible for two important decisions of the Supreme Court: McCulloch v. Maryland (1819) [12] and Osborn v. Bank of United States (1824).[13] It is impossible to give briefly anything like an effective picture of the financial and commercial confusion in which the people were laboring, particularly after the disappearance of the old Bank which had been established in 1791 and the charter of which had not been renewed in 1811. So many kinds of notes were in circulation, so many banks were issuing notes without specie to support them, that one wonders how business could be conducted at all. In 1816 the second Bank of the United States was founded with a federal charter; but for a time it did not appear to furnish an adequate remedy for the prevailing trouble. Especially in the newer regions of the country, the rage against the national Bank and its branches was almost boundless; to weary and discontented folk it appeared to be only an instrument for carrying out the schemes of money sharks, for collecting debts from the helpless, and for drying up the sources of money. Several states proceeded to overcome the evil by levying taxes upon the branch banks —Maryland, North Carolina, Ohio, Tennessee, and Kentucky.

The Maryland tax law was tested in the federal Supreme Court. The opinion of Marshall in the case has been called his greatest opinion, partly because it laid down and supported by elaborate argument the broad powers of the national government. This appraisal may be questioned, for the principle as well as the practice of broad

cannot be construed as conferring any greater or more sacred right than any citizen had to manufacture malt liquor; nor as exempting the corporation from any control therein to which a citizen would be subject, if the interests of the community should require it. . . . All rights are held subject to the police power of the State." "No Legislature can bargain away the public health or the public morals." Stone v. Mississippi, 101 U. S. 814, 819 (1880). "The rule of construction in this class of cases is that it shall be most strongly against the corporation." Northwestern Fertilizing Co. v. Hyde Park, 97 U. S. 659, 666 (1878). It should be noticed that Marshall in the Dartmouth College case said that "the framers of the constitution did not intend to restrain the states in the regulation of their civil institutions, adopted for internal government. . . ." 4 Wheaton 518, 629.

[12] 4 Wheaton 316.
[13] 9 Wheaton 738.

construction had been fully presented before; and at least one other case (Cohens *v.* Virginia), bearing on the nature of the union and the authority of the government, was of equal importance and the opinion of the Chief Justice in that case was at least equally able. But the Maryland opinion came at a peculiarly critical time; it ran counter to widely-extended, though by no means universal, public opinion; and its importance cannot well be overestimated.

The facts in the case are simple: Maryland had passed a law providing that if a branch bank should be established without authority from the state, its notes must be printed on stamped paper unless the bank relieved itself of the obligation by paying a specified tax. The branch bank in Baltimore refused to comply; McCulloch, the cashier, was sued for debt. The question was at length brought before the Supreme Court. In giving the decision Marshall thought it necessary to consider the Constitution "in its most interesting and vital parts. . . ." He began with a discussion of the union and the origin of the Constitution. "The powers of the general government, it has been said, are delegated by the states, who alone are truly sovereign; and must be exercised in subordination to the states, who alone possess supreme dominion." In response to this assertion he referred to the method by which the Constitution was adopted, viz., by the people in conventions chosen for the purpose. "It is true, they assembled in their several states—and where else should they have assembled? No political dreamer was ever wild enough to think of breaking down the lines which separate the states, and of compounding the American people into one common mass. Of consequence, when they act, they act in their states. But the measures they adopt do not, on that account, cease to be the measures of the people themselves, or become the measures of the state governments." [14] "The government of the Union,

[14] Such a statement as this could not satisfy the proponents of state sovereignty when that doctrine found full expression. John Taylor was beginning to make clear that the state government was not the state, and that the conventions in adopting the Constitution were decidedly the agents of the states acting in their sovereign capacity; if the people, though meeting within the geographical limits of their respective states, were not acting as part of the people of the United States as a whole—as a single political entity—, then the Constitution emanated from thirteen separate sovereignties. Elsewhere in the opinion Marshall says: "Much more might the legitimacy of the general government be doubted, had it been created by the states." 4 Wheaton 316, 404. His opponents would naturally retort, "But that is just the way it was established—by the states in their highest sovereign capacity." The Chief Justice announced the orthodox doctrine of divided sovereignty: "The creation of a corporation, it is said, appertains to sovereignty. . . . But to what portion of sovereignty does it appertain? . . . In America, the powers of sovereignty are divided between

then", he declared, ". . . is, emphatically, and truly, a government of the people. In form and in substance it emanates from them. Its powers are granted by them, and are to be exercised directly on them, and for their benefit."

Asserting that the government of the union, though limited in its powers, is supreme within its sphere of action, he proceeded to develop at length the doctrine of implied powers. A government must have the authority to use the means for effectively exercising the powers bestowed upon it: "Let the end be legitimate, let it be within the scope of the constitution, and all means which are appropriate, which are plainly adapted to that end, which are not prohibited, but consist with the letter and spirit of the constitution, are constitutional." This is the classical definition of "implied powers", and is the doctrine of broad construction essentially like that pronounced by Hamilton nearly thirty years before. If a corporation, therefore, is a suitable means of carrying out delegated authority, Congress can establish a corporation; and it may establish a bank as a suitable means for performing the fiscal operations of the government.

But the more immediate question remained. Could Maryland tax the branch bank? The Court decided that the state had not the right: "The sovereignty of a state extends to everything which exists by its own authority, or is introduced by its permission; but does it extend to those means which are employed by Congress to carry into execution—powers conferred on that body by the people of the United States? We think it demonstrable that it does not." The basis of this assertion was, in part, that "the power to tax involves the power to destroy; that the power to destroy may defeat and render useless the power to create. . . ." The act of Maryland was therefore unconstitutional.[15]

The decision in the Maryland case announced the law; but amid the excitement and discontent of those days it was not looked upon as the final and authoritative word. The nature of the union, the position of the states, and the authority of the Supreme Court were the government of the Union, and those of the States. They are each sovereign, with respect to the objects committed to it. . . ." *Ibid.*, 410.

[15] *Ibid.*, 429, 437. See also Dobbins v. Commissioners, 16 Peters 435 (1842), holding that the salaries of federal office-holders could not be taxed by a state. It was later held that a like constitutional principle prevented the federal government from taxing agencies of state governments. Collector *v.* Day, 11 Wallace 113 (1871). Thus salaries of state officers are not taxable by the United States. The dissenting opinion of Justice Bradley is of interest: "I cannot", he said, "but regard it as founded on a fallacy, and that it will lead to mischievous consequences." *Ibid.*, 129.

still matters of dispute. The enemies of the Bank raged and imagined many vain things. That is what makes the decision and Marshall's opinion so important in constitutional history in the broadest sense. It came at a time when the tide of feeling ran high and when theories of national rights and character, very different from the theories of Marshall, were current among the disaffected. On March 29, 1819, the Pennsylvania legislature asked for an amendment to the Constitution prohibiting Congress from establishing any bank except within the District of Columbia. This resolution was disapproved by at least nine states, but was approved by the legislatures of Tennessee, Ohio, Indiana, and Illinois.[16] South Carolina apprehended "no danger from the exercise of the powers which the people of the United States have confided to Congress," while New York declared that "the dignity, the welfare, the prosperity and the permanency of that government (which is our pride and our admiration) forbid the adoption of the proposed amendment. . . ."

Kentucky was much excited over a decision by the Supreme Court in the case of Green v. Biddle,[17] a decision which held inviolable a contract entered into between Kentucky and Virginia when the former state was organized. The Court declared a Kentucky statute void on the ground that it impaired the obligations of that contract. The legislature of the state was filled with wrath. "Any judicial act," said Governor Adair in a message to the legislature, "that tends to alienate the minds, and consequently the affections, of large portions of the citizens . . . must in the same degree weaken the power and render less secure the stability of the government. I need not be told that the general government is authorized to use physical force to put down insurrection and enforce the execution of its laws. I know it; but I know, too, with equal certainty that the day when the government shall be compelled to resort to the bayonet, to compel a State to submit to its law, will not long precede an event of all others most to be deprecated." [18]

[16] Ames, *State Documents*, no. 3, pp. 1-3.

[17] 8 Wheaton 1 (1823). Justices Story and Washington delivered the opinion of the Court.

[18] Ames, *State Documents*, no. 3, p. 18. The Kentucky legislature passed resolutions (December 29, 1823) against the "erroneous, injurious and degrading doctrines of the opinion of the Supreme Court of the United States" and resolved that it ought to request Congress so to organize the Court that no constitutional question involving the validity of a state law should be decided unless two-thirds of the members of the Court should concur in the decision. *Ibid.*, pp. 19-20. Notice the refusal of the Kentucky court to be bound by an opinion of the Supreme Court of

Ohio, not overawed by the decision in the Maryland case, went on her way. A few weeks before that decision was rendered, the legislature had passed an act (February 8, 1819) to levy a tax of $50,000 on any bank doing business within the state without being allowed to do so by law. When the agents of the state proceeded to seize the money in the vault of the branch bank at Chillicothe, the bank sought the protection of the federal court in Ohio. The court at length ordered the return of the money and the order was ignored. Resolutions, preceded by a committee report breathing defiance, were adopted by the legislature and forwarded to the President and both houses of Congress (1821).[19] They were able if not convincing. They approved the doctrines of the Virginia and Kentucky resolutions; they asserted the right of the state to tax the property of any private corporation created by Congress and doing business within the state; and they protested vigorously against the doctrine that the "political rights" of the separate states that compose the American union and their powers as sovereign states could be finally settled and determined by the Supreme Court[20] in cases contrived between individuals. Shortly after this an act was passed "to withdraw from the Bank of the United States the protection of the laws of this State in Certain Cases." The bank was to be practically an outlaw in Ohio.

the United States when the opinion was not concurred in by a majority of the Court. Bodley v. Gaither, 3 T. B. Monroe's Reports 57, 58-59 (1825). See also the discussion in Hawkins v. Barney's Lessee, 5 Peters 457 (1831), and the request of the Kentucky house for advice in resistance to "the decisions and mandates" of the United States Supreme Court (1825). Ames, *State Documents*, no. 3, p. 23. Before this date, Senator Johnson of Kentucky, later Vice-President of the United States, had proposed (1821) in the Senate an amendment to the Constitution which would make the Senate the final court of appeal in all cases to which a state was a party or should desire to be a party in consequence of having its constitution or law questioned. He declared that the federal Constitution did not give the federal judiciary authority to declare a state act void. H. V. Ames, *The Proposed Amendments to the Constitution of the United States*, Am. Hist. Asso. *Report* for 1896, II, pp. 161-163. Ames also calls our attention to a proposal by Senator Davis of Kentucky, in 1867, which would provide for a tribunal composed of one member from each state to decide all questions of constitutional power that should arise in the government of the United States and all conflicts of jurisdiction between the federal government and the states. He made a similar proposal in 1871. *Ibid.*, p. 163.

[19] Ames, *State Documents*, no. 3, p. 5 ff. The reader should notice especially the resentment during these years against the Supreme Court. The feeling was strong, vehement. What right had the Court to thrust in its hand and decide upon state competence?

[20] Massachusetts, in resolutions, emphatically combated Ohio's position. *Ibid.*, no. 3, pp. 13-15. Virginia was at the same time much wrought up over the power of the Court. See *Ibid.*, no. 3, pp. 15-16.

The validity of the decree of the lower court directed to Osborn, the auditor of Ohio, and others, was not brought up and decided in the Supreme Court until 1824.[21] The case gave Marshall one more chance to lay down the principles of the Constitution and to defend the federal judiciary. This he did with his usual consummate skill. The most difficult question to be decided, technically speaking, and one of vast importance, was whether the suit was an action against the state and therefore not within the jurisdiction of the federal judiciary because of the eleventh amendment, or, on the contrary, whether the agents employed by the state were personally responsible. In discussing this problem, Marshall characteristically began by disclosing the inevitable results of adopting the theories of those against whom he was prepared to rule: the denial of jurisdiction of the Court is, in effect, to maintain "that the agents of a state, alleging the authority of a law void in itself, because repugnant to the constitution, may arrest the execution of any law in the United States. . . . The carrier of the mail, the collector of the revenue, the marshal of a district, the recruiting officer, may all be inhibited, under ruinous penalties, from the performance of their respective duties. . . . Each member of the Union is capable, at its will, of attacking the nation, of arresting its progress at every step, of acting vigorously and effectually in the execution of its designs, while the nation stands naked, stripped of its defensive armor, and incapable of shielding its agent or executing its laws, otherwise than by proceedings which are to take place after the mischief is perpetrated, and which must often be ineffectual, from the inability of the agents to make compensation." ". . . if the courts of the United States cannot rightfully protect the agents who execute every law authorized by the constitution, from the direct action of state agents in the collection of penalties, they cannot rightfully protect those who execute any law." [22] The suit, the Court declared, was not a suit against a state, because the state was not the actual party on the record; [23] that is to say, though the state might have an interest in the matter, actually on the face of the proceeding, the suit was against Osborn and not against the state. The Court therefore held that the money seized by Osborn should be returned

[21] Osborn v. Bank of United States, 9 Wheaton 738.
[22] Ibid., 847-849.
[23] "Consequently, the 11th amendment, which restrains the jurisdiction granted by the constitution over suits against states, is, of necessity, limited to those suits in which a state is a party on the record." Ibid., 857.

to the bank. The remainder of the decision was chiefly a reannouncement of the principles of McCulloch v. Maryland.

The significance of this case is apparent. It announced with clearness and definiteness the authority of the United States at a time when doctrines were abroad which menaced the efficiency of the union or threatened to undermine it altogether. It upheld a principle of supreme importance, a principle which may be said to underlie and support all constitutional law in a free state, viz., that an agent cannot take refuge behind the directions of a superior, if that superior is acting without legal right. If a state government is acting unconstitutionally in passing an act and in directing its execution, the officials engaged in the attempt to carry the law into effect are personally responsible for the injury inflicted. That is the way in which constitutional order and personal liberty are protected; governments or legislatures cannot be sued for torts; but their agents can be. An administrative officer cannot be entitled to do an unconstitutional act because some higher governmental authority directs him to do so. The principle is at the very basis of English and American free government. In private law, as distinguished from constitutional law, the principle holds that every man is responsible for the wrongs he inflicts; he cannot set up immunity by asserting that he acted only as an agent of some other person; this superior person may be himself liable for damages; but the agent who actually inflicts the wrong cannot shift the responsibility. In fact, once adopt the principle that an unconstitutional law is no law, it follows that the agent attempting to carry out a law of that kind is without any authority; he is therefore individually liable, and by the ordinary principles of the common law he is responsible for wrongs inflicted.[24] Without this principle it is difficult to see how our constitutional system could be worked at all. At a later time the Supreme Court modified that portion of Marshall's decision which declared the question whether a suit came within the purview of the eleventh amendment and was therefore not within the jurisdiction

---

[24] "If, therefore, an individual, acting under the assumed authority of a State, as one of its officers, and under color of its laws, comes into conflict with the superior authority of a valid law of the United States, he is stripped of his representative character, and subjected in his person to the consequences of his individual conduct." In re Ayers, 123 U. S. 443, 507 (1887). See also United States v. Lee, 106 U. S. 196 (1882); Poindexter v. Greenhow, 114 U. S. 270, 290-291 (1885). I have omitted from the text above any consideration of the extent to which an officer executing a writ of a court may be exempt from personal liability.

of the federal Court depended only on whether or not the state was on the record a party.[25]

In discussing the Bank cases we have passed over other matters of great interest and importance. In 1816 Justice Story gave the opinion of the Supreme Court on a question involving the right of that Court to review the decisions of state courts.[26] The Virginia court of appeals had refused to be bound by an earlier federal decision, and had declared the twenty-fifth section of the federal Judiciary Act of 1789 to be unconstitutional. When the Virginia court made this announcement, the controversy was again brought before the Supreme Court and Justice Story, in an elaborate and powerful opinion, maintained the Court's appellate jurisdiction.

The politicians and the pamphleteers of Virginia broke forth in argument; the discussion lasted for years. The chief defenders of a state's right, not only primarily, but finally and conclusively, to pass upon the validity of its own legislation, were Justice Spencer Roane and John Taylor of Caroline. Taylor's position was rather more advanced or extreme in its doctrine of states' rights than was that of Roane. Roane asserted, not so much absolute and undiminished sovereignty of the state, as the right of the state to guard the *portion* of sovereignty which it possessed; nothing in the Constitution, he declared, justified Congress in bestowing upon the federal judiciary the right of final judgment concerning the extent of a state's powers. If the federal Court could pass authoritatively upon the validity of federal acts, so a state court could pass conclusively upon the validity of state acts, in cases properly coming before it. If, on the other hand, the decision of the validity of both federal and state acts rested with the federal Supreme Court, then in effect the states were at the mercy of the national government, were shorn of their power and were devoid of dignity.

The importance of this contention can scarcely be overestimated;[27]

---

[25] "It is, therefore, not conclusive of the principal question in this case, that the State of Virginia is not named as a party defendant. Whether it is the actual party . . . must be determined by a consideration of the nature of the case as presented on the whole record." In re Ayers, 123 U. S. 443 (1887). See also Cunningham *v.* Macon and Brunswick R.R. Co., 109 U. S. 446 (1883) ; Hagood *v.* Southern, 117 U. S. 52 (1886) ; State of North Carolina *v.* Temple, 134 U. S. 22 (1890).

[26] Martin *v.* Hunter's Lessee, 1 Wheaton 304.

[27] Justice Johnson pointed to the "momentous importance" of the problem. The states must be preserved; but "the general government must cease to exist whenever it loses the power of protecting itself in the exercise of its constitutional powers." *Ibid.,* 304, 363.

it came at a time when other states, or large numbers of people within them, were clamoring against the Court and its nationalizing tendencies; some of the arguments of states' rights were exceedingly able; party politics, state pride, personal animosities, and real or assumed economic interests aggravated the quarrel and added to the discontent. The theory which was set up and strongly defended by the Virginians denied to the federal Court the authority to maintain the federal Constitution and laws and to protect them from state aggression. Was the union under such conditions more than a shadow, a thing of shreds and patches?

The difficulty was that Roane had an arguable case. This does not mean that he was right, but that his position could be defended by far more than declamation and ill humor, which were the weapons frequently used by the opponents of the Court. Roane went to the heart of the matter. The Constitution did not contemplate a centralized and consolidated union, but a system in which authority was divided; there was nothing to be found in the Constitution expressly authorizing the central government to be the judge of the extent of its own power, nor did the Constitution expressly deny the power of the state courts to pass finally upon the validity of state legislation. At this very time, it will be remembered, Ohio was putting forth its own powerful and highly-elaborated doctrine against judicial encroachment upon the states' preserves.

If we attempt to pass upon this matter, we are led back to a consideration of the discussions in the Federal Convention. When the Constitution was being worked out by its framers, they turned to courts as the instrument for preserving the federal system. The critical problem arose from the willfulness of the states, from their readiness to disregard federal obligations. The Convention placed in the Constitution a declaration that the Constitution, laws, and treaties of the United States were the supreme law of the land, and the judges in *every state* were to be bound thereby. The primary obligation, in a case brought before a state court, was to recognize the binding effect of the supreme law. There the framers left the matter, as far as explicit statement was concerned. The Judiciary Act of 1789 provided for appeal to the federal Supreme Court, when a litigant put forth a claim to protection or privilege under the "supreme law" and such alleged protection or privilege were denied him; that section of the act was now declared by the Virginians to be unconstitutional; Congress, they said, had no legal right to provide for such appeal; the

Supreme Court in exercising such jurisdiction was usurping authority.[28]

The Judiciary Act was almost contemporaneous with the organization of the government and was passed by a Congress containing men who were in the Convention;[29] and that fact certainly adds weight to any argument in favor of the constitutionality of the act. There is one thing further which may seem technical and of slight moment, but it is actually neither: the Constitution gives authority to Congress but does not *require* Congress to establish inferior courts. The constitutional provision was a compromise between those delegates of the Convention who thought that the Constitution should explicitly provide for inferior federal courts and those delegates who feared lest such courts, if established, would exercise extensive jurisdiction and rob the state courts of their jurisdiction.[30] If therefore there could be no appeal from state courts, and if no inferior federal courts were established by Congress, the Supreme Court would have no appellate jurisdiction of any kind, although the Constitution plainly contemplates that it should be chiefly an appellate tribunal. It seems therefore an unavoidable conclusion that the framers of the Constitution took for granted that there could and should be an appeal from a state court to the federal Court on constitutional questions.

Not until five years after Martin *v.* Hunter's Lessee did Marshall have his opportunity to reply from the bench to the Virginia pamphleteers.[31] This he did in the case of Cohens *v.* Virginia.[32] The

---

[28] It is impossible to emphasize too strongly the importance of this question. The reader will remember that in the Federal Convention of 1787 the proposal to use force against a delinquent state was abandoned and the maintenance of the union was intrusted in large measure to courts.

[29] Marshall referred to this in his opinion in Cohens *v.* Virginia, 6 Wheaton 264, 420 (1821).

[30] See Farrand, *Records,* I, pp. 124-125. Luther Martin, "Genuine Information," *Ibid.,* III, pp. 206-207. Rutledge declared in the Convention "that the State Tribunals might and ought to be left in all cases to decide in the first instance the right of appeal to the supreme national tribunal being sufficient to secure the national rights and uniformity of Judgments". Wilson and Madison argued that the national legislature should be empowered to institute federal tribunals, and observed that "there was a distinction between establishing such tribunals absolutely, and giving a discretion to the Legislature to establish or not establish them." *Ibid.,* I, pp. 124-125.

[31] For an account of the relations of Marshall to the Virginia group, see W. E. Dodd, "Chief Justice Marshall and Virginia, 1813-1821," *Am. Hist. Rev.,* XII, pp. 776-787.

[32] 6 Wheaton 264 (1821). Marshall did not sit in the case of Martin *v.* Hunter's Lessee because at an earlier day he had been involved in the general subject under dispute, the ownership of certain confiscated lands in Virginia.

facts of the case are simple. Cohens was fined by a Virginia court for selling lottery tickets in Virginia. He maintained that he was deprived of his legal and constitutional rights inasmuch as the lottery was authorized by Congress; he carried his case on appeal to the Supreme Court. The center of the dispute was the nature of the union and the authority of the federal judiciary to determine whether a state court had rendered a decision contrary to the "supreme law of the land". The lawyers for Virginia denied the constitutional authority of the Court to review the finding of the state court. Marshall defended the jurisdiction of the Court. His opinion was able, searching, and eloquent. The situation was critical; the great Chief Justice, who was also a great Virginian, appreciated the gravity of the issue. The counsel for his native state were attempting to carry by assault the central fortress of nationalism.

He elaborately and eloquently discussed the nature of the union. "That the United States form," he said in a forceful passage, "for many, and for most important purposes, a single nation, has not yet been denied. In war, we are one people. In making peace, we are one people. . . . In many other respects, the American people are one; and the government which is alone capable of controlling and managing their interests in all these respects, is the government of the Union. . . . The constitution and laws of a state, so far as they are repugnant to the constitution and laws of the United States, are absolutely void. These states are constituent parts of the United States. They are members of one great empire—for some purposes sovereign, for some purposes subordinate." [33]

It was necessary in the course of the discussion to pass upon the eleventh amendment which declares that "The judicial power of the United States shall not be construed to extend to any suit in law or equity, commenced or prosecuted against one of the United States by citizens of another State, or by citizens or subjects of any foreign State." Marshall asserted that this suit was not commenced or prosecuted against a state: "It is clearly in its commencement the suit of a state against an individual, which suit is transferred to this court, not for the purpose of asserting any claim against the state, but for the purpose of asserting a constitutional defense against a claim made by a state." [34]

The opinion we have been discussing was given when the Virginia

[33] 6 Wheaton 264, 413-414.
[34] 6 Wheaton 264, 409.

counsel moved to dismiss the writ of error bringing the suit before the federal Court on the ground that the federal Court was without jurisdiction. That motion, as we have seen, was overruled; but when the case came up for decision on the merits, the Court decided that the law of Congress should not be so construed as to give the right to sell lottery tickets outside of the corporate limits of Washington. So Cohens had to pay his fine after all. But his effort to maintain what he believed to be his constitutional rights had brought forth a momentous and learned disquisition on the government of the union and the nature of the judicial system.[35]

Two other cases deserve more than passing mention. The first leading decision on the subject of interstate commerce—Gibbons v. Ogden—disclosed Marshall's wisdom in his determination not to fasten limitations on national authority by the application of minute definitions. In 1824 there came before the Court the question of the validity of a New York act granting to certain persons the exclusive right to navigate New York waters in steamboats.[36] The immediate issue of concern was whether or not a state had in its power the right to lay down exclusive regulations concerning instruments of transportation; but the main issue was in fact greater. Could a single state, asserting its complete authority over transportation on waters within its limits, obstruct the natural routes of communication between that state and every other and even shut its harbors to foreign vessels? If so, the United States might theoretically continue to exist as a political whole; but the development of industrial integrity would be almost impossible.

State sovereignty or any extreme doctrine of states' rights, carried to the point of preserving economic isolation for each and every state, could have but one result—the disintegration of the union.[37] Almost at the beginning of his opinion in the case Marshall swept aside all narrow definitions of commerce: "Commerce, undoubtedly, is traffic, but it is something more; it is intercourse." [38] While the completely inter-

---

[35] This is an excellent illustration of the way in which the constitutional system itself is preserved by the insistence of the individual citizen upon his own personal rights.

[36] Gibbons v. Ogden, 9 Wheaton 1.

[37] "The power over commerce, including navigation, was one of the primary objects for which the people of America adopted their government. . . ." Ibid., 190. See the Constitution, Art. 1, sec. 8, par. 3; sec. 9, par. 6; sec. 10, par. 2.

[38] The powers involved in the right to regulate commerce, said the Supreme Court at a later day, "keep pace with the progress of the country, and adapt them-

nal commerce of a state is subject to state regulation, interstate and foreign commerce is within the control of Congress. The power to regulate it does not stop with the boundaries of states. This power "is vested in Congress as absolutely as it would be in a single government, having in its constitution the same restrictions on the exercise of the power as are found in the constitution of the United States."

No subject in constitutional law has presented more difficulties than the regulation of interstate commerce; and a difficult problem has been that of determining how far a state can go in commercial regulation in the absence of congressional enactment. Many decisions have been rendered since Marshall's time, and it would be too much to say that Gibbons *v.* Ogden in 1824 by any means fully announced the law as it was to be. What it did do was to give the commerce clause a broad construction, which assured general and national control when later conditions made such control and regulation desirable.

Three years after the decision in the steamboat case, Marshall delivered another important decision on the law of foreign commerce, again marking out a restriction on state authority.[39] He denied the right of a state to require importers of foreign goods to pay a license fee. This is the "original package" case, and its interpretation and application in later years raised perplexing questions. The critical question was at what time do the articles imported become subject to the taxing power of the state? "It is sufficient", said the Court, "for the present to say, generally, that when the importer has so acted upon the thing imported that it has become incorporated and mixed up with the mass of property in the country, it has, perhaps, lost its distinctive character as an import, and has become subject to the taxing power of the state; but while remaining the property of the importer, in his warehouse, in the original form or package . . . , a tax upon it is too plainly a duty on imports to escape the prohibition in the con-selves to the new developments of time and circumstances. They extend from the horse with its rider to the stage-coach, from the sailing-vessel to the steamboat, from the coach and the steamboat to the railroad, and from the railroad to the telegraph, as these new agencies are successively brought into use to meet the demands of increasing population and wealth." Pensacola *v.* Western Union Telegraph Co., 96 U. S. 1, 9 (1878). In this case the Court declared that Congress could regulate the telegraph as a means of interstate communication. In a comparatively recent case it was decided that correspondence schools were engaged in interstate commerce. International Textbook Co. *v.* Pigg, 217 U. S. 91 (1910). A similar decision was made concerning electric current. See Public Utilities Commission *v.* Attleboro Steam and Electric Co., 273 U. S. 83 (1927).

[39] Brown *v.* Maryland, 12 Wheaton 419 (1827).

stitution." [40] This principle was at a much later time declared to be applicable to interstate commerce as well as foreign.[41]

The general nature and effect of Marshall's constitutional decisions are apparent. They asserted and defended, by broad principles of construction, the competence of the national government within the field of sovereignty assigned to it. They laid down decisively the fact of limitations on the states. They conclusively upheld the power of the Supreme Court to review state decisions, and in this way protected the Constitution from infringement. That Marshall was intent upon defending the interests of property from rude interference by state legislatures is less easily demonstrated, but that he was determined to support what he deemed to be constitutional restrictions is plain. His main doctrines were doubtless those of the Federalists, which had been so eloquently presented by Hamilton, but that his chief decisions ran counter to the hopes and purposes of the framers of the Constitution, who sought to build a lasting and effective national government, cannot be successfully maintained.

[40] *Ibid.*, 441-442.
[41] Leisy *v.* Hardin, 135 U. S. 100 (1890).

CHAPTER XXXI

THE PARTY SYSTEM AND PARTY MACHINERY. THE DEATH OF KING CAUCUS

At the end of the first quarter of the nineteenth century the American people were in certain respects a very different people from what they were forty years before. They had become democratic; the nation was a democratic nation. The word "democracy" has too many connotations to be used lightly; but plainly, as shown by the changes in the state constitutions, the people-at-large were entitled to take a much larger share than were the men of the earlier generation in the management of their own political affairs. Self-confidence in the wisdom and capacity of the common run of men was manifest—especially of course in the west—, and we may remind ourselves again that a democracy distrusting itself is not a democracy justifying the trust of others, if indeed it be a democracy at all. If the individualism of Jeffersonian democracy was not plainly manifest in all respects, the average person had nevertheless no difficulty in assuming his own worth and preparing to act upon it. To maintain and manage democratic institutional forms, a nation must be democratic-minded; forms are not of so very much consequence in and of themselves; the development, therefore, of this spirit and sense of popular power and of popular competence is of more real significance even for the constitutional historian than are the formalities of the law—of more real significance because the most important constitutional question in the history of a free, self-governing nation is whether it can be really free, actually self-governing, capable of living.

This spirit of self-confidence was sufficiently present by 1824 to resent the prevailing system of nominating candidates for public office. In a number of the states, the method of the earlier days had already been abandoned; the representative convention—or a convention ostensibly representative—had taken the place of the legislative caucus for the selection of leading state officials. This change means simply that the people were not content with voting for candidates selected by an

401

inner circle of politicians and chiefly office-holders. In 1824, the dis-satisfaction was extended to national politics. This leads us to an examination of the party system as it had developed up to that time. And we are also called upon to examine for a moment the character of the party as an instrument of government. This cannot be done without a general description of the party system as it has developed during the last century and more; and we may, therefore, well begin with commenting briefly on the nature and effect of this institution which has played such an important rôle in American political life.

The political party is essentially an instrument of government. It is one of the methods whereby men in the popular state manage their political affairs; it is an institution through which they seek to con-trol the formal, legal government and to direct the workings of the constitutional system. We might even call it a constitutional institu-tion, if we look at the Constitution not as a formal document but as the combination of institutional forms, practices, and principles which constitute the structure and the actual political activities of the state. The very fact that the people are divided into two great armies, each with its officers, history, traditions, *esprit de corps,* character, treasure, and power, is in itself of significance. In any study of the party, we should see that the important thing is not its principles, but the fact that it exists at all and that it is used as a means of conducting public affairs, of doing—or failing to do—the tremendously difficult job of carrying on popular government. The political party, as we now see it, is an essentially modern thing; and in some ways we obscure its char-acter if we use the word "party" indiscriminately to describe old-time factions, hostile groups, or social cliques which had their many exits and entrances in the long drama of history before the rise of the mod-ern popular state. Certainly what we now call a "party" was begotten by the duties and the opportunities of democracy; it came into being as the result of an attempt to actualize popular government.

In America, the party has for the historian particular interest be-cause the constitutional system, at the beginning at least, appeared peculiarly ill-adapted to the party system. The clashing factions of the Revolutionary period and of the years immediately following bore some resemblance, it is true, to the modern party; but when the Con-stitutional Convention met, the fathers had no knowledge of parties as we now know them; a party appeared to be a quarreling faction, en-dangering the stability of the government. They had little or no con-ception of a party as a means whereby issues could be discussed, the people could decide on questions of policy, men could be chosen for office according to popular desire, and unity in governmental plans and procedure could in a measure be secured. And thus, when the Constitution was signed and adopted and the document was safely locked away, there remained still unprovided for the two supreme jobs of democracy—the placing in office of the men whom the people wish to have in office and the transferring of the people's desires into legislation and administration. Representation and elections were, it is true, recognized and provided for in general terms; but, as we now know, these are not enough if the people are to have institutional forms and practices for actually carrying on popular government.

And so, after the new government was established, parties arose and assumed the new duties and responsibilities of making democracy real. This does not mean that men were quite conscious of the significance of what they were doing; but it can hardly be denied that the party as an institution took upon itself the two duties already referred to; the extent to which it performed those duties and the extent to which it proved unfaithful are a long and wearying story, an important, indeed the central, theme in the confusing and distracting history of a nation which has prided itself on being democratic but has often questioned whether its democracy was real or pretended. Certain it is, when once parties and the government of parties were established and operative, the job of the people, desiring to be their own governors, was to control this new institution which, like all living institutions, sought to develop and strengthen its own life; the job within each party, if men could only see it, was the job of making the government of the party—the machine—subject to the will of the party as a whole. Thus in the course of the passing decades emerged the new task—to control the government that would control the government, actually to use the party and the government of the party as means of putting into office men whom the people wish to put into office and as means of insuring reality to the popular state.

It is often difficult to distinguish cause from effect. One may hesitate to say whether essential national unity, that is to say, a degree of harmony on fundamental matters and a nation-wide readiness to coöperate, made the party or the party made the nation. Certainly the party organization gave expression to common interests and created ties holding together men of various sections; it held them by a loyalty to a national, not to a sectional interest; it made for coöperation; it tended to subject local interests to a wider and more comprehensive system. In the course of time, party loyalty appeared to be stronger than any other influence in the actual maintenance of the union; the time came when the dissolution of the Democratic party implied the dissolution of the union itself. Even on the slavery question, for more than a decade before the Civil War, opinions and irritations were held in check by the unceasing pressure of party. Thus as a general rule— for we can and must admit exceptions—, the party has reacted against sectionalism and has aided the process of adjustment or compromise which must always be conspicuous in the tasks of a people occupying half a continent.

Did democracy make the party or did the party make democracy? Democracy, unless we insist on mere individualism, connotes solidarity; a people divided into cliques and factions, separated into groups, each sharking for its own booty, each unconscious of community of interest, each unwilling to yield its own pet opinions, cannot function as a democracy. Willingness to work and act together for a common end is the heart and center of the democratic spirit, and without the spirit the body has no life. If you answer to this that there were two parties and they were often at daggers drawn, nevertheless it must be admitted that each held its own adherents; and moreover, whenever a party seeks popular support and wishes to place its own men in office, it reaches out after the "vote"; it must accommodate its action and propensities to a fairly general desire or inclination. Seldom, if ever, has a party openly and in its own consciousness, sought to banish public good and attain only selfish ends; such a tendency is characteristic of a faction rather than of a party. Furthermore, the eagerness to win and the struggle for votes make ostensible class-selfishness a practical menace to party success and reasonable longevity.

If these reflections appear to be fanciful, the reader will surely confess that party machinery has furnished means for popular action. If we have outgrown all this, if the whole system of committees and leaders and managers and all the intricate mechanism appear now antiquated and more than humanly vulgar, the historian nevertheless finds in the earlier days the development of a system which helped to make the people articulate. If in reality the directive force was at the top, if it did not spring from the people-at-large, if orders, though carefully concealed, went out from a centralized bureau of astute politicians, yet on the whole, without mechanism, nothing would have been left but confusion or at least nothing but incoherence. And if this statement meets with objection because it has lost its force in these days of the radio, and the telegraph, and a public press hungry for readers, it stands true of the earlier days when the party mechanism linked the people together and gave them a method of expressing an opinion which they thought was their own.

No one can discuss the party without falling into contradictions or paradoxes; no one can doubt, for instance, that the mechanism of the party and the passions of party loyalty have often distorted public purposes or at least inhibited popular desires; and furthermore, great changes in legislation and even in the written Constitution itself have come about, not through the agitation of parties or the use of party machinery, but by the development of popular sentiment created and expressed in the countless ways familiar to us whereby sentiment and purpose are impressed on the public mind.[1]

The party has made inroads upon the very structure of federalism. In principle, a federal state is characterized by the distribution of powers among governments. But the unremitting influence of national parties has tended to obscure the states and to rob them of their significance. State issues have been subordinated to the needs of national parties. Governors and legislators and road commissioners have been chosen, not because of their attitude toward state problems, but because of their affiliation with the national party. Nationalism in the very real sense has been created by the development of communication, by the actual interdependence of states and sections. But we cannot disregard the integrating effect of the party system which has been national, not federal; the incongruity of *national* organizations' managing or trying to manage a *federal* state is evident. Moreover, all the elaborate system of checks and balances so dear to the heart of John Adams has been affected though not destroyed by the party system; for the party is not troubled by self-imposed inhibitions set up for the express purpose of preventing effective action.

The choosing of men for office is the most important activity of the popular state. If the people, through majority decision, can place in office the men they want in office, they have in one main respect succeeded in the task of democracy. If they cannot, "popular government" is a misnomer. All the methods, therefore, used for the selection of candidates and for choosing between them are of prime

---

[1] I have in mind all the amendments to the Constitution that have been added since 1870. I mean also the mass of national and state legislation, some of which is of immense consequence, such as workingmen's compensation acts and a vast amount of welfare legislation.

significance in the history of a people who would be, and thought they were, self-governing. And this leads us to see the importance in the would-be popular state of the methods and the mechanism of election. But the most difficult and perplexing problem has been that of finding methods of nominating rather than of electing. In the very early days, state officers of higher rank were nominated by caucuses of the party men in the state legislatures. For the presidential election there was no formal method of nomination, but by 1800 processes were beginning to appear. In that year the Republicans held two caucuses made up of party adherents in Congress; one selected Jefferson as candidate for the presidency and the other added the name of Burr.[2] In the same year, the Federalists followed the caucus method of nomination for the first and last time. For the next twenty-four years the party caucus at Washington exercised the privilege and the responsibility of naming the Republican candidates.[3] The system, as we have already said, had been disappearing in the states; a representative convention took its place and before 1824 it was a fairly well-recognized method of nominating state officers. The change was due in part doubtless to the improvement of roads, which made it easier for delegates to come together; it was due also to the development of the party and to the growing sense of power in the common people. The time was passing when the voter, if interested in politics at all, was willing to acquiesce in the decisions of a group of legislators at the state capital.[4] By 1824 men were prepared to ask, why should congressmen in solemn conclave choose the person to be voted for by the people? Were not the people capable of nominating the candidate for the presidency as well

---

[2] Whether Burr was proposed distinctly as candidate for the vice-presidency is not entirely plain. It is said that Burr insisted on receiving equal support with Jefferson. But the fact, if it be a fact, is not of supreme importance in this connection.

[3] It appears that in 1820 the caucus was called but found it unnecessary to make a choice. See J. B. McMaster, *A History of the People of the United States,* IV, pp. 515-516.

[4] One writer has wisely said: "The nominating convention is an incident in the effort of the masses to pull down authority from the top and place it on the ground—an instrument by which they try to get vital control of the business of governing." Carl Becker, "Nominations in Colonial New York," *Am. Hist. Rev.,* VI, pp. 270-271. This article deals with revolutionary activities and methods and treats of tendencies which I have had to ignore in the condensed treatment of the text. But it is well to notice Professor Becker's clear statement of the connection between the rise of democracy and "the transition from absolutist or autocratic methods of nomination to democratic methods."

as casting their final ballots? Did they need somebody to guide their faltering steps?

Had there been two or more competing parties in 1824, the old practice might have continued untouched for a time. In that year, however, there were many favorites, all Republicans; if the nominee of the congressional caucus were to be accepted, and if he were to be considered the regular candidate for the presidency, nomination was equivalent to election. William H. Crawford was named by the congressional caucus, and the friends of Andrew Jackson, Henry Clay, and John Quincy Adams, were not inclined mildly to acquiesce. The battle was on; "king caucus" no longer held the scepter. Tennessee had already through her legislature named Jackson, and in due course the other aspirants for the presidency were formally or informally listed and their claims defended.

No one of these men received the majority of electoral votes. Jackson received ninety-nine votes, Adams, eighty-four, Crawford, forty-one, and Clay, thirty-seven. The election devolved upon the House, the choice to be made "from the persons having the highest numbers, not exceeding three, on the list of those voted for as President. . . ."[5] The House voting by states elected Adams. At that time, in six of the states the legislature appointed the electors, and therefore it is practically impossible to get anything like a definite idea of the desires of the people-at-large. No one can say, or could have said, with certainty what the result would have been, had Adams and Jackson been the only candidates. Of course the action of the House was entirely constitutional. The Constitution-makers of 1787 had no intention of giving the main body of voters the right of choice; and if the electors did not give a majority of their votes to any one man, the right to choose was left to the untrammeled decision of the House.

The heavens rang with declamation against this desecration of what Benton called the *"Demos Krateo"* spirit; the will of the people had been violated; the fundamentals of popular rule had been profaned. The old activities of "king caucus" had been attacked and scorned, but here, forsooth, the House had elected the President and acted with unbecoming independence! Adams's presidency was sure to be strewn with difficulties. There was a widespread determination to give the voice of the "people" its full effect. Here, then, is a fact of profound importance: the "people" have appeared upon the scene;

[5] Constitution, amendment XII.

they are (or think they are) the real rulers. It is impossible to put down in words the exact significance of the word "people" as it came to be used and as we still use it. Certainly we should err, if we intimated that before the second quarter of the century the wishes of the people-at-large had not been considered; but certainly also there had been a rise of self-consciousness in the masses of men, a growing belief in their own capacity; there was a very real though intangible power, the will of the people—not the will to be expressed by ballots alone, but nevertheless real and always to be obeyed. And this marks, not so much in technical law as in deeper reality, the fuller emergence of the popular state. Democracy, though still subject to the freaks and follies of adolescence, was coming of age.

In 1828, the names of Jackson and Adams were put forward in various ways, but for the next presidential election the representative convention was used for nominations.[6] This gathering, taken in connection with the disappearance of "king caucus", must be looked upon as an effort in the main body of the voters to select their own candidates, an effort to reach out and to control the mechanism of selection. The presidential convention has lasted until the present day, modified in some degree by the use of the presidential preference primary which was established in some of the states early in the twentieth century. It still stands, though the states have commonly established, for the nomination of candidates for state and local office, the direct primary, the product of a popular revolt against the corruption or the inadequacy of the convention system.

But it is needless to tell the reader that the dethronement of "king caucus" did not mean that the people had actually succeeded in wresting the power from the party operatives; they had not succeeded in reaching the throne themselves. Popular government is not so easily obtained, or, if obtained in a momentary fit of enthusiasm, it is not easily made permanent and secure. Under the worst conditions, the convention was held safely within the hands of the machine; it was not infrequently manipulated by political traders and those ready to indulge in corruption; at its best, the whole system was managed by the professional politician, who, however skillful and unvenal, was not the pliant servant of his constituents. And there, as a living thing, stood the party, holding men by ties of tradition and loyalty; it held within its ranks thousands and, in later years, millions of men; it was by its inner instincts prompted to perpetuate and strengthen

[6] The Anti-Mason party held a nominating convention in 1831.

itself. Constitutional problems and even sectional interests must not be allowed to endanger party stability or to sap its vigor. Is it necessary to say again that if the people cannot place in office men of their own choice, they are not living in a democracy?

CHAPTER XXXII

JACKSON AND THE BANK. THE EMERGENCE OF THE MODERN PRESIDENCY

Three years and more of Jackson's first term in office had passed before the problem of the national Bank arose and became a subject of acute and bitter controversy. It remained, in one way or another, a subject of dispute for years, even indeed until after his second administration and his successor in office had come and gone. Representing the western or frontier spirit, Jackson did not come to the presidency with any natural affection for a great moneyed institution controlled in general by eastern capitalists. After his accession his suspicions were augmented by party strife, but they were natural and inevitable. Early in his administration he openly questioned the constitutionality and expediency of the Bank,[1] and he mentioned the subject again in his second annual message; but the friends of the Bank seem not to have measured the strength of his real hostility. When a bill to recharter the Bank passed Congress in the summer of 1832, the President promptly vetoed it. The bill, returned to the Senate with the veto, did not receive the necessary two-thirds vote, and therefore failed.

For various reasons the veto message is an interesting document. The Bank Act of 1816, it will be remembered, had been declared constitutional by the Supreme Court; and that, said the defenders of the Bank, settled the matter; there was no further room for controversy. But this position Jackson stoutly combated: "Mere precedent is a dangerous source of authority, and should not be regarded as deciding questions of constitutional power except where the acquiescence of the people and the States can be considered as well settled. So far from this being the case on this subject, an argument against the bank

---

[1] "Both the constitutionality and the expediency of the law creating this bank are well questioned by a large portion of our fellow-citizens, and it must be admitted by all that it has failed in the great end of establishing a uniform and sound currency." Jackson's first annual message. Richardson, *Messages and Papers,* II, p. 462. T. P. Abernethy has shown that Jackson was in some respects allied with the more well-to-do and conservative elements in Tennessee. See *From Frontier to Plantation in Tennessee.*

might be based on precedent. One Congress, in 1791, decided in favor of a bank; another, in 1811, decided against it. One Congress, in 1815, decided against a bank; another, in 1816, decided in its favor. Prior to the present Congress, therefore, the precedents drawn from that source were equal. If we resort to the States, the expressions of legislative, judicial, and executive opinions against the bank have been probably to those in its favor as 4 to 1. There is nothing in precedent, therefore, which, if its authority were admitted, ought to weigh in favor of the act before me.

"If the opinion of the Supreme Court covered the whole ground of this act, it ought not to control the coördinate authorities of this Government. The Congress, the Executive, and the Court must each for itself be guided by its own opinion of the Constitution. Each public officer who takes an oath to support the Constitution swears that he will support it as he understands it, and not as it is understood by others. It is as much the duty of the House of Representatives, of the Senate, and of the President to decide upon the constitutionality of any bill or resolution which may be presented to them for passage or approval as it is of the supreme judges when it may be brought before them for judicial decision. The opinion of the judges has no more authority over Congress than the opinion of Congress has over the judges, and on that point the President is independent of both. The authority of the Supreme Court must not, therefore, be permitted to control the Congress or the Executive when acting in their legislative capacities, but to have only such influence as the force of their reasoning may deserve." [2]

The President commented upon the Court's decision: the Court had upheld the Bank Act as constitutional on the ground that a bank was an appropriate method of carrying the enumerated powers of Congress into effect; but, he declared, inasmuch as by the Court's own statement the question of whether Congress should use this method of exercising its power was left to the discretion of Congress, the degree of necessity of a bank was exclusively a matter for legislative consideration.

The outcry of the Bank's defenders was loud and prolonged; the reverberations are distinguishable to this day—or almost to this day. Histories and biographies dealing with the "reign of Andrew Jackson" reproduced in later years the essence of the cartoons of a century ago representing King Andrew as a monarch in ermine waving the

[2] Richardson, *Messages and Papers*, II, pp. 581-582.

veto and trampling on the Constitution. The lampoons of Colonel Jack Downing, the popular satirist and humorist of Jackson's day, appear to have been prolonged in sober discussions many decades after the Bank question had passed out of memory. That Jackson was peremptory and dictatorial, no one needs to announce or deny. He was not by temperament or by training a legalist; he was not zealous in defending a narrow interpretation of constitutional authority, when narrowness would interfere with his desires. But so much of the denunciation as was based on this veto message was in large degree unjustified and unintelligent. The denunciation of Jackson's own time came from the partisans who were beaten and exasperated; it was partly due to suspicion of a frontiersman and Indian-fighter, not one of the socially elect, who dared to interpret the Constitution and oppose the opinions of mighty statesmen like Webster and Clay.[3]

A good deal of the opposition was due to the bold announcement of presidential authority; for in this as in other respects Jackson was exhibiting the scope of the presidential office; he was doing much to make the presidency what we know it to be to-day; or, if this statement be too strong, he brought to light the scope of the office, because, relying on popular support, he was prepared to exercise his power; and, by using his veto, he made plain that the president occupied a position of authority as well as influence in the field of legislation. He did not bow humbly before Congress or listen obediently to the orators of the Senate. That he acted impetuously or even unwisely, that he too readily entered into controversy, that he had only slight appreciation of the delicate and intricate character of financial affairs, are probably justifiable assertions. But these facts have little to do with the question of the legal validity or invalidity of his conduct or with his success in maintaining the authority and strengthening the influence of his office.

The President's veto was attacked as being unconstitutional. But his opponents could do nothing but declaim, unless they resorted to impeachment. The bill was vetoed, and the veto prevented the passage of the law. How then could the veto be declared unconstitutional? It was unconstitutional, said his opponents, because such an exercise of the veto power was not contemplated by the framers of the Constitu-

[3] "I look upon Jackson as a detestable, ignorant, reckless, vain & malignant tyrant. . . . This American elective monarchy frightens me. The experiment, with its foundations laid on universal suffrage & an unfettered & licentious press, is of too violent a nature for our excitable people." James Kent to Joseph Story, April 11, 1834, Mass. Hist. Society *Proceedings,* second series, XIV, p. 418.

tion. It was to be used only on extraordinary occasions.[4] Clay complained that members frequently heard during the progress of measures through Congress the statement that the President would veto them, and the prospective veto was spoken of as an objection to their passage. Jackson had no fear of his own authority and no hesitation about using it; but the notion that he used the veto power like a swashbuckler is rather absurd. Before the Bank bill he had vetoed only four bills; all of them involved the old troublesome question of internal improvements; in two of these cases the veto was a pocket veto. Twelve times in the course of eight years his signature was withheld; of these twelve cases seven were pocket vetoes.[5] Fifty years later Cleveland vetoed over a hundred bills in a single year. And still, Jackson made it plain that the president held legislative authority and was ready to use it.

The President's right to question the constitutionality of the Bank bill, despite the Supreme Court's decision upholding the constitutional authority of Congress to establish a bank, scarcely deserves serious discussion in these days. On the whole, the important fact is not so much the position he assumed as that he found it necessary to take the position at all. The controversy at least indicates the position and the authority to which the Supreme Court had attained under the leadership of Marshall. If we consider the slow growth of judicial authority, it is significant that in 1832 men should put forward a judicial decision as conclusive, not only in determining the validity of a measure already passed, but as finally and peremptorily binding on the legislative when a new measure is presented for passage.

---

[4] "The veto is an extraordinary power, which, though tolerated by the constitution, was not expected, by the convention, to be used in ordinary cases. It was designed for instances of precipitate legislation, in unguarded moments. . . . The veto is hardly reconcileable with the genius of representative government. It is totally irreconcileable with it, if it is to be frequently employed in respect to the expediency of measures, as well as their constitutionality. It is a feature of our government borrowed from a prerogative of the British king." Henry Clay, in the Senate, July 12, 1832. *The Life and Speeches of Henry Clay* (1843 ed.), II, pp. 89-90. Complaints of this kind bring before us clearly the difference between the time of Jackson and the last few decades. No one would now think of denouncing the idea that the president's wishes should be considered. He is now a powerful influence in directing the course of legislation. The desires of the president and the possibility of a veto are always taken more or less fully into consideration. Indeed, his plans and even the measures for which he distinctly stands are influential, and may be compelling. This note was written, it is well to say, before the fourth of March, 1933.

[5] E. C. Mason, *The Veto Power*, pp. 143-145.

Bills must receive the president's signature; and in signing or refusing to sign he is free to follow his own judgment, as members of Congress are free when the measure is before them. A question, possibly answered with difficulty, would, or might be, whether the president or a congressman can constitutionally and properly vote for a measure when a substantially identical bill has been judicially proclaimed unconstitutional. But there would seem in principle to be no doubt of such a right in the legislative body, which includes the president. The propriety and wisdom of such action is a different matter and must be decided by circumstances. Obviously, a studied determination by the legislators to pass measures which the courts will not recognize as law may be nothing more than a proof of obstinate stupidity; and on the whole, the important fact is that decisions by the Supreme Court have come to be considered, as a practical fact, determinative of what the Constitution is.

In considerable degree, the courts in their earlier opinions, when announcing their authority to pronounce acts void, rested that authority on their *independence*. In the course of time there has come, as already said, the tendency and the common, if not quite universal, practice of considering the principles laid down by the Supreme Court as final. Thus if we can, because of the principle of the separation of powers, defend judicial authority to declare acts void, we must also see that in matters of constitutional interpretation this principle has largely broken down; or, we may more properly say, in this case as in others, it has been modified by practical considerations and thus made workable.[6]

A more difficult question, however, still confronts us. Did Jackson really believe, as some of his words may imply, that a decision of the Court is not binding on the president acting in his executive capacity? Granted that he accepts a decision, as far as he may be called on to do so, as deciding the particular controversy passed upon by the judicial department, is he under obligation to consider the whole question of constitutionality settled? An attempt to answer that inquiry would lead us into a discussion of a problem theoretically interesting but

[6] Ex-President Taft, questioning Jefferson, Jackson, and Lincoln, in their assertions concerning the limitation of judicial authority, contents himself with saying, "It is sufficient to say that the Court is a permanent body, respecting precedent and seeking consistency in its decisions, and that therefore its view of the Constitution, whether binding on the Executive and the legislature or not, is likely ultimately to prevail as accepted law." *Our Chief Magistrate and His Powers*, p. 138.

practically of no use. The fact is, Jackson did not carry his reasoning so far as to treat the Bank as an outlaw.[7]

But we cannot escape quite so easily. Is there anything to be said for Jackson's announcement of every officer's right to support the Constitution "as he understands it"? That Jackson intended to assert the right of independent and final judgment of every official, one may doubt, if his words are read with their context. And of course, any such position, if commonly acted upon, would spell confusion worse confounded. But withal it must be remembered that no one is bound by an unconstitutional act; such an act is not law; in strictest theory, it binds no official and no person whatever; and if no one objected to a law, it would be difficult or impossible for a court to pass upon its validity; an officer carrying out an unconstitutional act, before as well as after a judicial declaration of unconstitutionality, may be held personally liable for invasion of private liberty or property. Any private person has the right and it may be his duty to refuse to obey an unconstitutional act; but if he is held by the court to be wrong in concluding that an act is unconstitutional and therefore to be disregarded, he has to take the consequences.[8] This same principle may be applicable to the president, but in his case the tribunal qualified to condemn him would probably be the Senate sitting as a court of impeachment.

The portions of Jackson's veto message which are not at all technical are quite as important as the legal argument in defense of his right to veto. He attacked "artificial distinctions" and the granting of "gratuities, and exclusive privileges, to make the rich richer and the potent more powerful. . . ." He stood for the interests of the common man and against the tendency of the rich to use the government for their own advantage; he stood forth as the champion of the rights

[7] President Johnson took steps to test the validity or the proper interpretation of some of the provisions of the Tenure of Office Act.

[8] Webster's argument against the veto was partly taken up with the financial or economic effects of the veto. His constitutional argument was able; it attacked Jackson's arguments which would lead to the conclusion that the existing Bank was established without constitutional authority. He did not deny the President's right to veto a bill on the ground of unconstitutionality, but he assailed Jackson's reasoning. He also said: "The President is as much bound by the law as any private citizen, and can no more contest its validity than any private citizen. He may refuse to obey the law, and so may a private citizen; but both do it at their own peril, and neither of them can settle the question of its validity." That is a clear statement of sound principle. *Works,* III, p. 433. Webster attacked those portions of the message which implied, as Webster believed, the possession of dispensing power.

of the people; they had in him a single national leader. This was his belief, and in any attempt to see the presidential office as it has grown to be, we must grasp the fact, vague as it may appear, that the president's power largely rests on this direct and immediate contact with the main body of the people. Some presidents have known how to use this relationship effectively and thus secure power and influence commensurate with the possibilities of the office; others have not. But nothing would be more distinct from reality than a view of the president as a person obediently fulfilling, as a mere executive and administrative official, the behests of Congress. A policy plainly put forth by the president and apparently supported by popular sympathy has, as we now know well, tremendous influence. Unluckily for Jackson's opponents, they did not appreciate the new presidency which he was establishing or the strength of his appeal; and they appeared to forget that he was not only an executive but also a legislative official with a nation-wide constituency.

But Jackson, after succeeding in the election of 1832, was not content with victory at the polls or with his veto of the Bank bill. The Bank in his mind was a menace; its power for mischief must be curtailed in the interest of popular safety. In the early summer of 1833 he made a tour extending into the northeastern states and received the degree of Doctor of Laws from Harvard—a ceremony which gave the wits of the day a chance to display their cleverness. He was coldly received by the rich and powerful of Boston; but probably he did not grieve overmuch. His work lay before him. He returned to Washington and proceeded to carry out his plans against the Bank; no longer should it profit from the deposits of the public money in its vaults. He was determined to strangle "this hydra of corruption". This was no sudden decision, however; it had been in his mind for months.[9]

The Bank charter (1816) provided that the money of the United States should be deposited in the Bank or its branches unless the secretary of the treasury should at any time otherwise order; if such an order were issued, the secretary should immediately lay before Congress, if in session, and if not, immediately after the commencement of the next session, the reasons for the order. Jackson had already found difficulty in carrying out his designs. Louis McLane, who held

[9] It is not within the scope of this work to discuss the question of the propriety of Jackson's conduct or the truth of his suspicions and beliefs about the Bank. That question belongs in financial and economic history. Furthermore, I make no pretense here of passing upon political and personal controversies.

the office of Secretary of the Treasury, was opposed to the removal of the deposits—i.e., ceasing to deposit the public funds in the Bank. In May, 1833, he was transferred to the state department, and to the vacant secretaryship Jackson appointed William J. Duane. If the President wished to have his policy adopted quietly, he made a serious blunder, for Duane refused to give the desired order. As the members of the cabinet continued to be divided in opinion, Jackson read to them a paper giving reasons for the removal of the deposits (September 18, 1833).

This paper is a noteworthy document. It had been revised by Taney and it revealed the skill and the acumen of an able lawyer.[10] "Upon him", the President said, "has been devolved by the Constitution and the suffrages of the American people the duty of superintending the operation of the Executive Departments of the Government and seeing that the laws are faithfully executed. In the performance of this high trust it is his undoubted right to express to those whom the laws and his own choice have made his associates in the administration of the Government his opinion of their duties under circumstances as they arise." [11] He disclaimed any intention of dictation, hoping that the facts he disclosed would produce uniformity of opinion in the cabinet. But of most consequence was his declaration that the proposed measure was his own. He is said to have declared, "I take the responsibility." Certainly that was his position. Duane refused to follow the President's advice or instructions and would not resign. Jackson dismissed him and turned over the office to Taney, who thereupon ordered the public money to be deposited in selected state banks and sent to Congress, when it assembled, the reasons for his action.

When the Senate asked for a copy of the paper read to the cabinet, already published, Jackson replied courteously but firmly that his own self-respect and his sense of the rights secured to the executive branch of the government constrained him to decline compliance. What he said to the "heads of Departments acting as a Cabinet council" [12] was, he declared, no concern of the Senate.

The heavens rang with oratory and the depths with denunciation. Who was this man, Jackson, who was willing to defy the law and as-

---

[10] Under Taney's hand, "it became a proper state paper and not a 'combative Bulletin,' as Van Buren pronounced the first draft." J. S. Bassett, *The Life of Andrew Jackson*, II, p. 644.

[11] Richardson, *Messages and Papers*, III, pp. 18-19.

[12] *Ibid.*, III, p. 36.

sume responsibility? "We are in the midst of a revolution," declared Clay at the beginning of a powerful speech in the Senate, "hitherto bloodless, but rapidly tending towards a total change of the pure republican character of the government, and to the concentration of all power in the hands of one man. . . . Many of our best citizens entertain serious apprehensions that our Union and our institutions are destined to a speedy overthrow." [13] He denied the power of the President to order removal of the deposits, declared that the secretary of the treasury was, by the act establishing the office, constituted the agent of Congress, and announced that the treasury department was not one of the executive departments of the government; that department stood on a different footing from all others.

After a winter of heated oratory and argument, the Senate adopted (March, 1834) resolutions declaring Taney's reasons unsatisfactory and insufficient, and "That the President, in the late Executive proceedings in relation to the public revenue, has assumed upon himself authority and power not conferred by the constitution and laws, but in derogation of both. . . ." In reply came Jackson's famous "Protest",[14] another state paper of importance in American constitutional history. If the majority in the Senate thought he would be incapable of prompt and effective retort, they were badly mistaken.

The "Protest" is a vigorous announcement of presidential power, and to-day it stands substantially unshaken. There was, however, one peculiarly difficult point involved in the dispute: was the secretary of the treasury an executive officer? Was he responsible to the president and subject to his orders? There is some reason for thinking that Congress, by the act establishing the office (1789), intended to put the office on a different plane from that of the secretaryships of state and

[13] *The Life and Speeches of Henry Clay* (1843 ed.), II, pp. 177, 179. "We behold", said Clay in a fervid peroration, "the usual incidents of approaching tyranny. The land is filled with spies and informers; and detraction and denunciation are the orders of the day. People, especially official incumbents in this place, no longer dare speak in the fearless tones of manly freemen, but in the cautious whispers of trembling slaves. The premonitory symptoms of despotism are upon us; and if Congress do not apply an instantaneous and effective remedy, the fatal collapse will soon come on, and we shall die—ignobly die! base, mean, and abject slaves—the scorn and contempt of mankind—unpitied, unwept, unmourned!" *Ibid.*, p. 230. Webster's speeches, both on the veto message and the removal of the deposits, are able and less melodramatic than Clay's.

[14] Richardson, *Messages and Papers*, III, p. 69 ff. Benjamin F. Butler, appointed Attorney-General in place of Taney, now Secretary of the Treasury, is said to have given chief assistance on the legal side. Bassett, *op. cit.*, II, p. 650.

war.[15] It is also possible that the first Congress in providing for the departments supposed the system of the new government would be a decentralized system; the president would have nothing to do with ordinary administration. In short, the national governmental system was, by this view, if such a view were really held, to be similar in its make-up to the state governments as we know them. In the state system the governor has as a rule no authority to direct the ordinary administrative conduct of the chief state officials; they are not appointed by him; they are as a rule not removable by him.[16] They may go on their own way regardless of his desires.

The federal executive was saved from this decentralized system partly by the fact, doubtless, that it was not possible and apparently not intended by the first Congress to deprive the president of control over the departments of state and war. He has by the Constitution great authority in the conduct of foreign affairs. He is the commander-in-chief of the army and navy, and in his duty to see that the laws are faithfully executed it may be necessary to use the military forces. Centralized executive and administrative authority was also secured by the desirability or necessity of the president's having a policy. Centralized responsibility, however, rested primarily on the authority to

[15] For discussion, see F. J. Goodnow, *Comparative Administrative Law*, I, p. 62 ff. Not until 1873 was the treasury department defined by law as an executive department. H. B. Learned, *The President's Cabinet*, p. 373. See the chapter in this work on the development of the cabinet.

[16] The state system differs so much from state to state that it is difficult to describe it accurately except at great length. The outstanding fact is that the executive is decentralized. "However, although the governor is coming to have a much larger control over that part of the state administration created by statute, his power in most of the states is slight over the officers of the state executive department who are elected by popular vote or by the two houses of the state legislature." W. F. Dodd, *State Government* (1922 ed.), p. 286. "In some cases constitutions expressly vest in the governor supervision over other elective state officers. Legally these officers are in such an independent position that, if they decline to act, the governor's remedy is to apply to the courts to compel action, in the same manner as a private individual may do." *Ibid.*, p. 240. One can hardly imagine the government of the United States with a headless executive and administrative system. The confusion and the absence of centralized responsibility in the state system have been productive of a number of recent attempts at betterment. We may talk in awe-struck tones of the danger to the cause of liberty, if authority is centralized in a single individual, a governor or a president; but no one, probably, is now fearful that popular government will fall because of Caesarism, based on legal authority. Nothing is likely to discredit and endanger democracy more than a system in which there is no sense of personal responsibility, and in which there is such complexity in government that official responsibility cannot be easily determined.

appoint and to remove officials. If all executive and administrative officials may at will be removed from office, the authority to direct their conduct in office flows as a natural consequence; an office-holder must either obey or retire.[17]

In the early discussions in the House (1789) the question of the president's right to remove officers was debated in connection with the provision for the establishment of the state department, first called the department of foreign affairs. The debate is not easily analyzed, but the conclusion appears to be in favor of the right to remove. In the Senate, the vote of the vice-president in favor broke a tied vote.[18] The practice and the assumed authority in the president has on the whole been fairly constant; but not until 1926 was this matter fully and elaborately discussed by the Supreme Court.[19] The decision concerning the right of the president to remove a postmaster, appointed by him with the advice and consent of the Senate, was given by a divided Court, with able dissent. The decision rendered by the majority of the Court upheld the presidential right to remove without consulting the Senate, though the dissenting justices strongly objected to the view that the president can approve a statute and act under it and then disregard the restriction contained in it.[20] The Court reached this de-

---

[17] Ex-President Taft pointed out that "Congress may repose discretion in appointees of the President, which the President may not himself control." *Our Chief Magistrate and His Powers,* p. 125. But if the president can remove an official, this principle is not of tremendous consequence.

[18] This debate and the value of the decision, if such it may be called, is considered at length in the opinion of the Supreme Court rendered by Chief Justice Taft and in the opinions rendered by McReynolds and Brandeis, two of the dissenting justices. Plainly men of wisdom may differ concerning the meaning and value to be attributed to the discussion. Myers v. U. S., 272 U. S. 52 (1926).

[19] *Ibid.*

[20] "With such power over its own creation [the office], I have no more trouble in believing that Congress has power to prescribe a term of life for it free from any interference than I have in accepting the undoubted power of Congress to decree its end." Justice Holmes, dissenting. *Ibid.,* 177. This decision of the Court is noteworthy in that the Chief Justice declared that certain portions of Marshall's decision in Marbury v. Madison were either *obiter,* i.e., not essential parts of the decision, or had been overruled by a later decision. He also declared that the Tenure of Office Act of Johnson's time (to be discussed later in this work) was unconstitutional. See the able criticism by E. S. Corwin of the Chief Justice's opinion in the Myers case. "Tenure of Office and the Removal Power Under the Constitution," *Columbia Law Review,* XXVII, p. 353 ff. For an early case bearing on removal, see ex parte Hennen, 13 Peters 230 (1839). See also, Parsons v. U. S., 167 U. S. 324 (1897). The decision left at least one question not definitely decided; can the president remove officials appointed by heads of department? But see the Hennen case, pp. 259, 260. The comptroller general (according to the Act of 1921) is not removable

cision partly on the ground of early interpretation by Congress (1789), partly on unbroken or practically continuous practice, partly on independent constitutional interpretation; and it based the power, in a measure, on the president's duty to see that the laws are faithfully executed.

In the "Protest" so ably conceived, Jackson reminded the Senate of its constitutional authority to sit as a court of impeachment, but he denied its authority as an independent chamber to declare his acts illegal. That he was entirely justified in this announcement is questionable. No one would dare say unhesitatingly that the Senate has no authority to pass such resolutions of opinion as it chooses. Perhaps the only conclusion is that the senators acted in ill temper. The Senate declared the "Protest" a breach of its privileges and refused to enter the paper on the journals.

There is something almost amusing in the senatorial outburst of impatience. Had the senators forgotten they were only a part of the legislative body? Their chief duty was to pass acts; the President had authority in final determination somewhat less than that of two-thirds of both chambers acting separately. Not even the whole Congress, except by passing a joint resolution over the presidential veto, could order the Secretary to replace the deposits. The Senate was helpless; and considering its helplessness, one must not criticize too harshly its resort to oratory.

Though the purely constitutional questions are now easily disposed of, we should not too readily decide that they were quite so easy a century ago. The right to dismiss an official was not a totally-assured prerogative of the president; neither was it perfectly plain that the president could direct the performance of certain prescribed duties. Jackson's position is of consequence because he might have yielded; a constitutional precedent might have been established, which, if followed, would have made it possible or obligatory for certain departments to carry on their duties without direct responsibility to the president. The immense powers of the presidential office were being disclosed; we need not wonder that men, some of them passionately, others calmly, questioned and feared.

In one further respect, Jackson assumed a position which has often been ridiculed. He claimed to be the possessor of all executive authority not taken from him or limited by specific restriction. But such

by the president. In 1935 the Court upheld an act limiting the power to remove a federal trade commissioner.

a theory appears in some respects not wholly at variance with modern conceptions of the presidential office. Indeed, Hamilton's own doctrines were not substantially different; and if we should pass on to later times, we would find support for this theory. Theodore Roosevelt wrote in his *Autobiography:* "The most important factor in getting the right spirit in my Administration, next to the insistence upon courage, honesty, and a genuine democracy of desire to serve the plain people, was my insistence upon the theory that the executive power was limited only by specific restrictions and prohibitions appearing in the Constitution or imposed by the Congress under its Constitutional powers. My view was that every executive officer, and above all every executive officer in high position, was a steward of the people bound actively and affirmatively to do all he could for the people, and not to content himself with the negative merit of keeping his talents undamaged in a napkin. I declined to adopt the view that what was imperatively necessary for the Nation could not be done by the President unless he could find some specific authorization to do it. . . . In other words, I acted for the public welfare, I acted for the common well-being of all our people, whenever and in whatever measure was necessary, unless prevented by direct constitutional or legislative prohibition." [21]

[21] Theodore Roosevelt, *An Autobiography,* p. 357. Ex-President Taft in this connection said he disagreed with his predecessor in office. He referred to the decision of the Supreme Court in the case of the Floyd Acceptances, 7 Wallace 666 (1869), where Justice Miller said: "The answer which at once suggests itself to one familiar with the structure of our government, in which all power is delegated, and is defined by law, constitutional or statutory, is, that to one or both of these sources we must resort in every instance. We have no officers in this government, from the President down to the most subordinate agent, who does not hold office under the law, with prescribed duties and limited authority." *Our Chief Magistrate and His Powers,* pp. 142-144. Taft quite disagreed with Roosevelt's authority to act as Roosevelt said he proposed to act in the crisis of the anthracite coal strike of 1902. *Ibid.,* pp. 145-147. But though the spirit of Jackson was not dissimilar to that of Roosevelt, the former made no claim of acting as he saw fit for the benefit of the people without constitutional authority or law. He did claim his right to see that the law was enforced and that his constitutional authority to care for the interest of the people should be respected and obeyed. He specifically announced that he was solicitous that he be not supposed to claim for himself or his successors any power or authority not clearly granted by the Constitution and laws to the president. He did not deny that Congress by law (a law that had to be signed by the president or passed over his veto) might state exactly where money or any other property must be placed. Such a law he must obey and see that others obeyed it. He did deny emphatically that he could legally be deprived of his authority over his secretaries or other officers. If the secretary of the treasury could be removed from presidential direction, so might any other officer, and the president would thus be left as "powerless as he would be useless—the shadow of authority after the substance had departed."

Jackson's belief that he stood for the interests of the nation as a whole, his feeling that the people gave him a mandate, and that they were the supreme authority are apparent throughout his "Protest" and in other pronouncements. Thus we find the spirit or fact of nationalism. There was in existence a body of people, an authoritative body (authoritative in fact if not in theory), not simply a coöperative system of sovereign or even partly sovereign states; the President was the direct and immediate representative of the whole people.

As a matter of plain fact, we only exaggerate and overemphasize when we say that Jackson was in stark reality the first President of the American people. How can such a statement be supported? There was a "people" in a fuller sense than ever before; the word "people" had a new significance; it signified the existence of a public consciousness and sense of power. The word itself, as we now use it, is the most meaningful word in the American political vocabulary. Furthermore, when Jackson entered the presidency a larger number of people could actually participate in political affairs, and a larger number did vote than in earlier years. Moreover, a much larger number voted directly for the presidential electors, because the old system of appointment of electors by the state legislature had been abandoned in every state save one by 1828.[22]

There had developed the feeling that a man of the people should guard the interests of the people; the old feeling of fear of government, fear lest government do things, fear lest individual liberty be crushed had in considerable measure disappeared. The new state constitutions, it is true, indicated a certain or uncertain distrust of legislative competence, but they show also a readiness to allow the governor a considerable measure of power; they were not afraid of him. If Jackson commonly assumed that what he wished the people wished also, he was not far wrong. His conception of his office, his assertion of his constitutional power, his recognition of the immediate contact between the chief magistrate and the people, his readiness to assume responsibility and leadership—all these give ground for calling him the maker of the modern presidency.[23]

[22] An examination of the election data in the years following 1824 discloses the rapid development of popular interest and participation in elections, significant of developing democracy. In 1824 the popular vote for the presidency was about five per cent. of the population; 1828, nine and one-half per cent.; in 1832 ten per cent.; in 1844, sixteen and one-half per cent. The data on which these figures are based are probably sufficiently exact to justify these statements.

[23] It is desirable to refer here to the development of the office in Washing-

The removal of the deposits did not end the bank question. The state banks scrambled for their share of the public deposits. Reckless speculation in western lands, greedy and unintelligent banking methods, clouds of paper money, all foretold a disastrous panic, though men, as usual, could not read the signs. The crash came immediately after Jackson's retirement (1837), and Van Buren had to bear the burdens of a desperate situation. The Whigs did not give up the struggle for a national bank, and that matter did not find its end until a Whig President, Tyler, with finely-drawn constitutional scruples, refused to sign a bank bill that did not quite meet his requirements (September 9, 1841).[24]

There is something almost pathetic in the sight of the heated and partisan rancor of parties during the eight years of Jackson's presidency. It is true, the fiscal practices of the states and the nation-at-large needed serious and intelligent attention; but the problem was incrusted with partisan strife. The Whig leaders were wedded to their idol and the people-at-large would have none of it, though they did sweep a Whig President into office in 1840 on a tide of emotional resentment resulting from the hard times of the preceding three years. They thought that in Harrison they had found a new leader of the populace, a man like unto themselves. But Harrison died after a brief month of office and Tyler came into the presidency, a Whig in name, but really a strict constructionist out of sympathy with the passionate purposes of the party.[25] There were enough troublesome problems to

ton's time, and the degree to which the President directed foreign affairs. It is also well to notice Jefferson's activities. He brought to light the fact or the possibility of presidential leadership.

[24] Tyler's objections do not need extended comment. Primarily he appears to doubt the constitutionality of a bank to be engaged in ordinary banking activities outside of the District of Columbia. "It operates *per se* over the Union by virtue of the unaided and, in my view, assumed authority of Congress as a national legislature, as distinguishable from a bank created by Congress for the District of Columbia as the local legislature of the District. . . . If this proposed corporation is to be regarded as a local bank of the District of Columbia, invested by Congress with general powers to operate over the Union, it is obnoxious to still stronger objections. It assumes that Congress may invest a local institution with general or national powers." Richardson, *Messages and Papers,* IV, p. 70.

[25] Jackson's term ended in 1837. Van Buren succeeded him. Harrison was elected in 1840 in the famous log-cabin and hard-cider campaign. In April, 1841, John Tyler of Virginia, upon Harrison's death, succeeded to the presidency and the Whig leaders were soon disappointed and exasperated. One thing deserves special attention, indeed more attention than I can here give to it. Tyler assumed the presidency; he did not and would not go upon the supposition that he was merely acting-President, that indeed he was in any way different from an official originally chosen to the office.

be solved, above all others, the slavery problem with the constitutional and human perplexities involved in it; but as far as party controversies went, men vehemently debated matters which had in reality lost their vitality. Bitter struggles there were in Congress over the slavery question, especially between 1835 to 1840, but there was little partisan strife on that subject—an apt illustration of the way in which parties often, perhaps generally, avoid direct difference and dispute on the greatest social problems and seem frequently to be unaware of their existence.

It is necessary now to turn back and take up the story of the controversy concerning the constitutional structure of the union. That story has already been told as it appeared in the Virginia and Kentucky resolutions of 1798, in the New England resolutions and pronouncements of the early years of the nineteenth century, in the writings of Roane and Taylor, and in the decisions of the Supreme Court under Marshall. We must now discuss the attempt of John C. Calhoun and South Carolina to establish a doctrine of state sovereignty.

This assumption established a constitutional fact. That the vice-president succeeding to the presidency has the title of president and thus is clothed with the full dignity of office as well as the power is in itself a matter of some consequence.

CHAPTER XXXIII

GEORGIA AND STATES' RIGHTS. SOUTH CAROLINA RESORTS TO NULLIFICATION. THE THEORIES OF JOHN C. CALHOUN

During the administration of John Quincy Adams, whose path was not strewn with roses, a serious difficulty arose with the state of Georgia, which claimed, in accord with a treaty entered into in 1825, full jurisdiction and authority over certain Indian lands. Before the time set by the treaty for the surrender of the lands, the state took steps to survey them; and the Indians asserted that the treaty had not received the consent of the tribe. The national government objected to the action of the state, but Georgia wished no interference from the President and did not hesitate to announce her rights in the boldest fashion. It is unnecessary to enter here upon the tangled skein of the controversy. The salient fact is Georgia's insistence upon her rights and the declarations of her intention to defend them. "The Executive of Georgia", said the Governor in a letter to the Secretary of War, "has no authority in the civil war with which the State is menaced to strike the first blow, nor has it the inclination to provoke it; that is left to those who have both the inclination and the authority, and who profess to love the Union best. The Legislature will, on their first meeting, decide what, in this respect, the rights and interests of the State demand. In the meantime, the right to make the survey is asserted, and the reference of the treaty to Congress, for revision, protested against without any qualification." [1]

[1] August 15, 1825. Ames, *State Documents,* no. 3, p. 31. The impressive thing about Troup's letters is the tone of ill temper and arrogance. In one letter to the war department he said, "the President of the United States may rest contented that the Government of Georgia cares for no responsibilities in the exercise of its right and the execution of its trust, but those which belong to conscience and to God, which, thanks to Him, is equally our God as the God of the United States." June 25, 1825. In *Ibid.,* no. 3, p. 30. If Georgia was a sovereign state, connected only with others in an international arrangement (the Constitution of the United States), then her authorities were using language not quite consistent with diplomatic courtesy; and if such methods were to be followed, they were sure to produce war in any kind of

426

The legislature supported the Governor. But President Adams was not content with the treaty to which the Indians strongly objected, and a new treaty was entered into (January, 1826). Georgia insisted upon her rights and the validity of the first treaty. The legislature claimed the soil and jurisdiction of all territory within the "present chartered and conventional limits" of the state, and admitted the right of the general government only to regulate commerce with the Indian tribes. It announced the abrogation of the earlier treaty, in so far as it devested Georgia of any right acquired under it, to be illegal and unconstitutional, and it declared the protest of the President against any measure of the state in the exercise of an "essential part of her sovereignty" to be an instance of dictation and of unwarranted federal supremacy.[2] About the same time the Governor declared that the Supreme Court was not made the arbiter in controversies involving rights of sovereignty between the states and the United States. There was danger of civil war. The President was determined to prevent the survey of the lands and he warned Troup that the government would, if need be, use force; the Governor, not intimidated by such pronouncements, called out the state militia. Congress was not willing to support the President. A few months later (November, 1827) a treaty was entered into for the final surrender of the Creeks' lands to the state.

Even more difficult questions arose in connection with Georgia's demand for the lands of the Cherokees. The tribe was far removed from simple savagery. In 1827 they adopted a constitution asserting that the Cherokees constituted one of the sovereign and independent nations of the earth. To Georgia this was intolerable, and the legislature declared all white persons in the Cherokee territory to be subject to the laws of the state, and after June 1, 1830, all laws of the Chero-

international arrangement. In other words, even if Georgia were a completely sovereign state, a reasonable degree of good manners would be a desirable possession.

[2] The legislature in 1827, objecting to an appropriation by Congress for the aid of the African Colonization Society, declared the "Federal compact" was made between independent sovereignties by which each relinquished "portions and like portions of its sovereign power. . . ." See U. B. Phillips, *Georgia and State Rights*, Am. Hist. Asso. *Report* for 1901, II, p. 115. This is noteworthy as an example of the adherence, even in those times of excitement, to the doctrine of the idea of divided sovereignty. Troup, in a letter to the Georgia congressmen, referring to the Indian dispute, said: "I consider all questions of mere sovereignty as matter for negotiation between the States and the United States, until the proper tribunal shall be assigned by the Constitution itself for the adjustment of them." February 21, 1827. Quoted in *Ibid.*, p. 64.

kee nation were to be void.[3] A Cherokee Indian named Tassel [4] was convicted of murder in a Georgia court. But Georgia defied a writ of error allowed by the Chief Justice of the federal Court—a flagrant insult to the sovereignty of Georgia. The legislature authorized the Governor "with all the force and means, placed at his command, . . . to resist and repel, any and every invasion, from whatever quarter, upon the administration of the criminal laws of this State." It declared that the state of Georgia "will never so far compromise her sovereignty as an independent State, as to become a party to the case sought to be made before the Supreme Court of the United States, by the writ in question." Tassel was promptly and effectively executed.

But other steps were already being taken to have the question of Georgia's jurisdiction determined. On behalf of the Cherokees, an injunction was asked for to restrain the state from executing "certain laws of that State, which, as is alleged, go directly to annihilate the Cherokees as a political society, and to seize, for the use of Georgia, the lands of the nation which have been assured to them by the United States in solemn treaties repeatedly made and still in force." The Supreme Court "after mature deliberation" declared that "an Indian tribe or nation within the United States is not a foreign state in the sense of the Constitution, and cannot maintain an action in the courts of the United States." [5]

Another opportunity arose for the Court to render an opinion, for Marshall to express himself clearly, and for Georgia to defy the judicial authority. Several missionaries, among them one Samuel

[3] *Acts of the General Assembly* (1828), p. 89.
[4] Tassel is the spelling used in Cherokee Nation *v.* Georgia, 5 Peters 1, 12 (1831).
[5] Cherokee Nation *v.* Georgia, 5 Peters 1, 15, 20 (1831). The Constitution gives the federal courts jurisdiction of suits and controversies "between a State, or the citizens thereof, and foreign states, citizens, or subjects." Art. III, sec. 2, para. 1. Cf. United States *v.* Kagama, 118 U. S. 375 (1886), where the Court announced the rather obvious facts that the relation of the Indian tribes to the people of the United States had always been "an anomalous one and of a complex character", and that the tribes had been "regarded as having a semi-independent position" not as states or nations but as a separate people, with the power of regulating their internal concerns and thus far not brought under the laws of the union or of the state within the limits of which they resided. In this case the Court recognized the right of Congress to enact legislation providing for the punishment of crimes committed by Indians on an Indian reservation. It sustained federal authority chiefly by asserting that the Indian tribes were "wards of the nation" and "communities *dependent* on the United States." For discussion of the problem, see J. B. Thayer, "A People Without Law," *Legal Essays*, p. 91 ff. The truth seems to be that the Court has upheld as constitutional what the political branches of the federal government have actually undertaken to do in their handling of this difficult problem.

Worcester, were haled before a state court and charged with violating a law of the state forbidding whites to reside within the Cherokee limits without a license. They were found guilty and sentenced to four years of imprisonment at hard labor. Worcester appealed to the United States Supreme Court; Georgia denied the Court's jurisdiction and relied upon her own sovereign rights. Marshall rendered a forceful opinion, pronouncing the Georgia law void and declaring the judgment of the state court should be reversed and annulled.[6] Georgia smiled in derision and Worcester remained in prison. The next year, having indicated their willingness to acknowledge the power of the state, he and his companion in trouble were pardoned by the Governor.[7]

All this is of interest in constitutional history because it illustrates the difficulty of handling the Indian question and gives an idea of difficulties inevitably confronting the government of a nation rapidly extending its settlements. It is of course chiefly of importance because of Georgia's attitude of defiance and her successful opposition to the government. Only a few of her protests, resolutions, and exclamations have been quoted here, but enough to show the general facts. Of interest also is the calm manner in which the Chief Justice and his colleagues on the federal bench analyzed the problem and announced the law. That Georgia could not be brought to terms by judicial announcement of her iniquities, and that the decision of the Court would never be carried out did not deter the justices; but to think of their position as undignified, fruitless, and vain is a mistake. In fact, there is something impressive and compelling in the quiet dignity with which the Court proclaimed its opinion. Jackson is said to have remarked, "Well, John Marshall has made his decision, now let him enforce it." Possibly Jackson said this, and said it with a sneer; but the Court did not ask the President to enforce its decision or order its own officials to do anything of the kind. The President in a few months was face to face with the nullifiers in South Carolina, and he then did not shrink or falter in the performance of what he believed to be his duty.

[6] Worcester v. Georgia, 6 Peters 515, 561 (1832). "The Cherokee Nation . . . is a distinct community, occupying its own territory, with boundaries accurately described, in which the laws of Georgia can have no force, and which, the citizens of Georgia have no right to enter but with the assent of the Cherokees themselves or in conformity with treaties and with the acts of Congress. . . . The act of the State of Georgia under which the plaintiff in error was prosecuted is consequently void, and the judgment a nullity."

[7] Nine of the prisoners availed themselves of the Governor's pardon before Worcester's case came before the Court. See Phillips, op. cit., pp. 80, 83.

Anyone studying the fact and the influence of sectionalism in American history will hesitate to emphasize the feeling or the peculiar interests of any one section as compared with others; but he cannot forget the southern sense of a common southern cause which came in the course of time to produce secession. This sentiment grew after slavery had furnished plainly a common ground for the south to stand upon, and this growth took place more conspicuously after 1835 than at any earlier day. And still, as we see a degree of uniformity in opposition to the tariff, after about 1824, and see also the pronouncement that southern interests were the victims of northern aggression, we get an impression of a coming trouble based on a feeling of a real, though perhaps still vague, sectional solidarity. The doctrines of states' rights and state sovereignty have already been often mentioned in this work; state sovereignty is to be the special topic of this chapter; but as a matter of fact the doctrine was a weapon of defense, not so much for protecting the peculiar interests of a particular state, as for defending a section and a sectional economic interest. Therein lay the danger to the union—sectional diversity and sectional sentiment, aided, if need be, by constitutional argument which was based upon the individuality of the states.

No one more clearly than Calhoun, who became the high priest of state sovereignty, saw the menace of diversity based upon rivalry of economic interests; and he saw this before he put forth his theory of state sovereignty and before he looked out upon the union as only a combination of states each clothed with the full panoply of power. Writing in 1827 concerning a proposed gathering of manufacturing interests at Harrisburg, he pointed to the disruptive influence of such movements and naturally descried an intention to promote sectional desires and ambitions: "thus the dangerous example is set of seperate [sic] representation, and association of great Geographical interests to promote their prosperity at the expense of other interests, unrepresented, and fixed in another section, which, of all measures that can be conceived, is calculated to give the greatest opportunity to art, and corruption, and to make two of one nation." [8] To Calhoun the thought of Clay, that the tariff was national, helpful to all, planter, farmer, and manufacturer alike, now made no appeal; he saw dangerous sectional ambition thrusting itself forward at the expense of a weaker region.

[8] Letter to J. E. Calhoun, August 26, 1827. *Correspondence of John C. Calhoun,* Am. Hist. Asso. *Report* for 1899, II, p. 250.

The third decade was not far advanced when South Carolina showed signs of uneasiness and, indeed, of restlessness and resentment. To what was this due? It was largely due no doubt to economic causes, but those causes were not simple or easily remedied. There is evidence that the coastal or tidewater region of the old south had long been declining in economic welfare. Loud laments had issued from the eastern plantation region of Virginia. Wasteful methods of agriculture and the washing away of the soil were having their effect. The cotton-raising area now extended into the interior of South Carolina, and soon after the war of 1812 planters had moved to the rich and alluring lands of the lower Mississippi basin. In the first quarter of the nineteenth century cotton had become of immense importance. In 1801 South Carolina had raised twenty million pounds; in 1821 her crop was fifty million pounds. At the beginning of the third decade, the southwest, including Tennessee, had become a serious competitor; and when the fourth decade came, that region was actually producing more cotton than the old south.[9] The price of cotton fell ominously. "In 1816 the average price of middling uplands in New York was nearly thirty cents, and South Carolina's leaders favored the tariff; in 1820 it was seventeen cents, and the south saw in the protective system a grievance; in 1824 it was fourteen and three-quarter cents, and the South-Carolinians denounced the tariff as unconstitutional. When the woollens bill was agitated in 1827, cotton had fallen to but little more than nine cents, and the radicals of the section threatened civil war." [10]

The south was plainly falling behind the north in population. New England's population was not increasing rapidly, but New England was shifting her emphasis from commerce to manufacturing and was no longer in a complaining mood. Between 1820 and 1830 the population of New York was increased by 545,796, while the increase in the whole of the old south was less than 400,000. In that decade ove‫־‬ 1,100,000 persons were added to the population of the northern states, not including the new states west of the mountains, and that was over three times as much as the total growth of all the old states south of the Pennsylvania line. In 1790 South Carolina contained 107,094 slaves; forty years later, 315,401. Between 1820 and 1830 the slave population of the state increased 56,926 and the white popu-

---

[9] F. J. Turner, *Rise of the New West*, p. 47. Turner says these figures are illustrative rather than exact.
[10] *Ibid.*, p. 325.

lation about 22,000. To the population of Pennsylvania in the same decade were added about 300,000 persons—more than three-fourths as many as the total increase of the old south, including both slave and free.[11]

It is difficult to say just how much the south or the whole of the old slaveholding region was suffering from industrial depression. Measurements are, however, not necessary; the general condition is plain enough: while the north was moving ahead and the west was growing with astonishing rapidity, the older south was falling behind. For us, the important fact is that the feeling of irritation and the sense of being treated unjustly resulted in the announcement of constitutional theories and the elaboration of intricate political and philosophic doctrines, which developed and continued to be of immense influence until those supporting them were crushed by civil war.

We cannot, naturally, discover to what extent the decline of the old south's prosperity was due to the protective tariff. The decline had been going on for years and there was more than one influence at work in the older tidewater region. But in the third decade of the century the value of the average annual exports of the three staple products of the south—tobacco, cotton, and rice—largely exceeded in value all other domestic exports.[12] And one cannot wonder at southern antagonism to a protective system under which planters did the exporting, paid the import duty, and bought goods of northern make at a price artificially maintained by the tariff. But the general situation was complex; various influences were at work—slave labor, soil erosion, the competition of the new west, immigration of foreigners into the northern states, the extension of factory production. As we have already seen, strict construction of the Constitution had displayed itself in opposition to internal improvements, an opposition in some instances directed rather against the legal authority than against the desirability of proposed measures; the southerners were now, however, opposed to the expenditure of money for the development of industry in which they had no part; they were opposed to

[11] In these figures, Delaware is included in the middle states, Maryland and the District of Columbia in the old south. I have followed in this respect the tables in *A Century of Population Growth,* published by the Bureau of the Census, 1909. Kentucky and Tennessee I have not included in the old south. Pennsylvania's increase in population was 298,775 and the increase of the population of the old south was 377,218.

[12] Timothy Pitkin, *A Statistical View of the Commerce of the United States* (1835 ed.), p. 518. In 1828 Calhoun estimated the annual exports at $53,000,000, over two-thirds being raised on southern plantations.

both tariff and internal improvements—the twin brothers of Clay's "American System" which would bring the farm to the factory and the factory to the farm.[13]

South Carolina was now entering upon a new experience; for, from the very beginning of the government the state had not wearied in her sympathy for national principles. In all the earlier years most of the other states at one time or another had broken forth in expostulation and in announcements of constitutional principles of states' rights. But South Carolina's page was clean and clear.[14] In 1817 Calhoun defended the "bonus bill", which proposed using the bonus and subsequent dividends received from the Bank for internal improvements: "We are great, and rapidly—I was about to say fearfully—growing. . . . We are under the most imperious obligation to counteract every tendency to disunion. . . . Those who understand the human heart best know how powerfully distance tends to break the sympathies of our nature. . . . Let us, then, bind the republic together with a perfect system of roads and canals. Let us conquer space. . . . I am no advocate for refined arguments on the constitution. The instrument was not intended as a thesis for the logician to exercise his ingenuity on."[15]

In 1820 when certain resolutions were introduced into the house of representatives of South Carolina, a committee, to which the resolutions were referred, announced opposition to the tariff, but objected strongly to the tendency, becoming too common, of arraying the states as distinct sovereignties in opposition to the national authority, and recommended that the house "adhere to those wise, liberal

---

[13] "We must speedily adopt a genuine American policy. Still cherishing a foreign market, let us create also a home market, to give further scope to the consumption of the produce of American industry." "Are we doomed to behold our industry languish and decay yet more and more? But there is a remedy, and that remedy consists in modifying our foreign policy, and in adopting a genuine American system. We must naturalize the arts in our country, and we must naturalize them by the only means which the wisdom of nations has yet discovered to be effectual—by adequate protection against the otherwise overwhelming influence of foreigners." Henry Clay in the debate on the tariff of 1824. *Annals of Congress,* 18 Cong., 1 sess., cols. 1970, 1978. It is impossible here to consider the attitude of the different sections toward the tariff in the decade from 1820 to 1830. For discussion, see F. J. Turner, *Rise of the New West,* pp. 145-147, 236 ff.; F. W. Taussig, *The Tariff History of the United States* (7th ed. revised), p. 68 ff.

[14] See, for example, a speech of Langdon Cheves of South Carolina. *Annals of Congress,* 12 Cong., 1 sess., cols. 734-735.

[15] Calhoun, *Works* (R. K. Crallé, ed.), II, pp. 190, 192. The speech as given in the *Annals of Congress,* 14 Cong., 2 sess., cols. 854-855, differs in some respects from that given in the *Works.*

and magnanimous principles by which this state has been hitherto so proudly distinguished." [16] The next year George McDuffie, who afterwards played a conspicuous rôle as an advocate of state sovereignty, published a pamphlet in which he declared that the "general government is as truly the government of the whole people, as a state government is of part of the people. Its Constitution, in the language of its preamble, was ordained and established by 'the People of the United States.'" [17] James Hamilton, in an introductory statement to the pamphlet, proclaimed the truths unfolded by McDuffie to be in their nature essentially imperishable. A few years later both of these men were defending extreme antinational doctrine.[18]

Discontent with the policies of internal improvements and protection was disturbing South Carolina in 1824 and 1825, but ill feeling had not as yet run to ominous heights. The Governor, in a message to the legislature, lamented the extent to which the federal judiciary and Congress had gone toward the establishment of a great consolidated government; but the house announced that "Every citizen of these United States owes a double allegiance; namely to the government of the United States, and to the government of the individual State to which he may belong." The resolutions of the house declared that "the People have conferred no power upon their State Legislature to impugn the Acts of the Federal Government or the decisions of the Supreme Court of the United States", and that "any exercise of such a power by this state would be an act of usurpation." [19]

In the summer of 1828 the state was seething with discontent. Certain radicals had reached a perilous stage of exclamatory resent-

[16] The report seems to have been adopted by the house. See Ames, *State Documents*, no. 4, pp. 2-3.

[17] *Defence of a Liberal Construction of the Powers of Congress*, pp. 7-8.

[18] Gaillard Hunt, in his *John C. Calhoun*, p. 75, quotes from the *Southern Patriot and Commercial Advertiser* (1822) an interesting statement of the difference between South Carolina and Virginia: "The former believe that when all the departments of the general government have affirmed the constitutionality of an act of Congress, no state has a right to oppose it by penal laws any more than certain other states had a right to oppose, positively or negatively, the late war with Great Britain; whereas, the latter contend that a state, being sovereign, has a right to decide for herself whether the general government has exceeded its power or not, and to refuse to yield obedience to its laws accordingly." This statement must be read in light of South Carolina's remaining antagonism to New England's opposition in the war of 1812, and it is also a bit severe on Virginia, but it does not on the whole misrepresent South Carolina's history.

[19] This, it may be said, was not necessarily and *entirely* inconsistent with the doctrine of state sovereignty as Calhoun later exposed it. Under that doctrine, the state, not the legislature, is the final judge.

ment against the tariff. But then, as at a later time, not all were ready to move forward and resort to force or to secession. There was then, and there long continued to be, a strong and able union party, though comparatively few of the conservatives failed to condemn the tariff. The debates, the public speeches, the articles in the press, went merrily onward; and presumably the agitator, sure of himself and zealous in his cause, had at that time, as probably he must always have, a decided advantage over the advocate of calmness, delay, and careful weighing of consequences. An appeal to calm reason is not well-fitted to fire the heart. These differences of opinion in the state, the fierce disputes between the radical elements and the union party, are an interesting story but must be passed over here with but a single word: when we speak of South Carolina's opinions and announcements, we need to remember that a substantial minority was not willing to proclaim thoroughgoing state sovereignty and to accept its inevitable results.

In the midsummer of 1828, Calhoun, though strongly feeling the injustice of the tariff, was not quite ready to give utterance to extreme doctrines.[20] He was then Vice-President, was a candidate in the election of that year, and still entertained the ambition of becoming president. It is unnecessary to ascribe to him selfish anxiety about his own future, but he was for the moment holding back. Sometime during that summer or autumn he determined to take a hand, draw up a strong attack upon the injustice of the tariff, and indicate briefly the state's right to protect her interests. His uncertainty had disappeared. As Jefferson, when Vice-President, had drafted the Kentucky resolutions and kept his authorship a secret, so Calhoun's authorship of the South Carolina "Exposition" of 1828 was not then divulged.

We need not examine this paper in detail; it foreshadowed the fuller constitutional doctrines that were later to come from his pen; it announced the right of the state to "interpose" (nullification), and it sketched the theoretical basis on which interposition could rest.

[20] Calhoun, in a letter to Monroe, July 10, 1828, after lamenting the undue burden carried by the south, said: "It seems to me that we have no other check against abuses, but such as grow out of responsibility, or elections, and while this is an effectual check, where the law acts equally on all, it is none in the case of the unequal action to which I refer." *Correspondence of John C. Calhoun*, Am. Hist. Asso. *Report* for 1899, II, pp. 266-267. Too much emphasis may be laid on this letter, but it is difficult to refrain from assuming from it that Calhoun had not then carefully studied the terrain of state sovereignty, or had not made up his mind to enter boldly into its defense.

The important fact is that Calhoun had entered the lists; he had thrown in his lot with his state; the doctrine of state sovereignty had found the ablest and shrewdest of advocates. The "Exposition" was not adopted by the legislature, but copies were printed. For the time being the legislature contented itself with a formal protest against the constitutionality of the protective system.

The right to "interpose"—a word borrowed from the Virginia resolutions of 1798—rested of course on the doctrine of state sovereignty;[21] but the principle of complete and unmodified sovereignty, except as to the right to judge, was not here, at the beginning, brought out so clearly as at a later time.[22] Nor did Calhoun at this juncture speak plainly about secession; he is, in fact, anxious to show the middle way between secession on the one hand and humble acquiescence on the other. It was not necessary to break up the union with a single blow. But the states were competent and in duty bound to preserve their rights and save the Constitution and the union. Interposition should naturally be carried out by the state itself, not by the legislature. In the course of the next four years Calhoun's theories were reiterated and developed.

South Carolina was not alone in her opposition to the tariff and internal improvements, or indeed alone in the announcement of constitutional principles. Georgia, in "her sovereign character", issued a protest against the tariff (December 20, 1828). Virginia proclaimed the Constitution a federal compact between sovereign states, and declared that each state had the right to construe the compact for itself. There were other manifestoes of like character. But some states of course supported the tariff and some repudiated the constitutional theory of interposition. Kentucky's statement of principles is especially

[21] The essential novelty of Calhoun's position consisted in his assumption of the indivisibility of sovereignty; sovereignty was a whole; to mar it or to diminish it was to destroy it. John Taylor had already presented the essential character of sovereignty as Calhoun exposed it. "In the early years of the Republic it had been generally believed that in the United States there existed a divided sovereignty." C. E. Merriam, *A History of American Political Theories*, pp. 278-279. "Up to the time when the theory of Calhoun became influential, the characteristic American doctrine was that in the United States, whatever might elsewhere obtain, the sovereignty had been divided into several portions without the destruction of its life principle." *Ibid.*, p. 260. See also, for discussion and evidence, A. C. McLaughlin *The Courts, the Constitution and Parties*, pp. 189-242.

[22] After saying that "sovereign powers delegated are divided", he declares that "The right of judging . . . is an essential attribute of sovereignty,—of which the States cannot be divested without losing their sovereignty itself,—and being reduced to a subordinate corporate condition." *Works*, VI, p. 41. See also p. 56.

noteworthy: South Carolina, said the state which a generation before had passed the famous resolutions of 1798, cannot derive any aid from the manner in which the Constitution was formed; "whether it was the work of the people of the United States collectively, or is to be considered as a compact between sovereign States, or between the people of the several States with each other, there is, there can be, there ought to be, but one rule, which is, that the majority must govern." [23]

In 1830 the great debate took place in the Senate between Robert Y. Hayne of South Carolina and Daniel Webster of Massachusetts. It began with a resolution introduced by Senator Foot of Connecticut respecting the sale of western lands, a subject which stirred the feelings of men and induced them to charge one section or another with entertaining selfish and narrow-minded opinions concerning the general interests and the growth [24] of the nation. In reply to charges made by Hayne, Webster seized upon the opportunity to justify New England; and then the debate turned into an oratorical controversy concerning the nature of the union and the validity of South Carolina's theories which had already been put forth in the "Exposition" of 1828. The debate is important, not because of the clarity and cogency of argument, but because it aroused popular interest.

Hayne's theories were in the main those of Calhoun; and of state sovereignty he spoke with a certain degree of clarity: "The whole form and structure cf the Federal Government, the opinions of the framers of the constitution, and the organization of the State Governments, demonstrate that, though the States have surrendered certain specific powers, they have not surrendered their sovereignty." He repudiated the old theory of divided sovereignty. Madison, it will be remembered,

---

[23] See Ames, *State Documents,* no. 4, p. 23 ff. This volume contains the most essential documents for the period.

[24] The situation as it was in 1828 is thus presented by Professor Wellington: "The interest of the different sections in these issues, in the order of their importance, was as follows: The Northwest—low-priced public lands, internal improvements, a high tariff; the Southwest—low-priced public lands, a low tariff, internal improvements; the seaboard South—a low tariff, no internal improvements at federal expense, high-priced public lands; the North Atlantic States—a high tariff, high-priced public lands, internal improvements." R. G. Wellington, *The Political and Sectional Influence of the Public Lands 1828-1842,* p. 9. Each section, however, needed the assistance of another or others to get what it specially desired; hence combinations and log-rolling. The whole subject is of great importance, especially in political history rather than in constitutional. Louisiana's interest in sugar helped that state to look with favor on the tariff. See her resolutions of March 15, 1830. Kentucky had hemp for which protection was sought, and Ohio had wool.

about this time announced—and he continued to announce—that the original and commonly-held belief was that the states had given up a *portion* of their sovereignty.[25]

Webster's theories concerning the nature of the union were essentially those of Marshall. In his second reply to Hayne, he briefly discussed the origin of the government: "I hold it to be a popular Government, erected by the people . . . and itself capable of being amended and modified, just as the people may choose it should be. It is as popular, just as truly emanating from the people, as the State Governments. . . . It is not the creature of the State Governments." Such a statement, however, could make no impression on the advocates of state sovereignty, for the people of the state were the state, and consequently an adoption of the Constitution by the people constituted an adoption by the state—that was the main pillar of the vast metaphysical structure of state sovereignty. In the final "Remarks" (January 27, 1830) Webster took a definite step forward, declaring the Constitution to have been ordained and established by the people of the United States in the aggregate. Thus, it appears, Calhoun's theories could be met either by declaring the result of compact between sovereignties to be the establishment of a legal and vital union, or by declaring that the Constitution emanated from a single will, the people as a whole.[26]

It is unnecessary for us to go over the ground already traversed in the preceding pages of this work. The reader is aware of the author's position, namely, that the Federal Convention intended to

[25] "It has hitherto been understood that the supreme power, that is, the sovereignty of the people of the States, was in its nature divisible, and was, in fact, divided . . . ; that as the States, in their highest sovereign character, were competent to surrender the whole sovereignty and form themselves into a consolidated State, so they might surrender a part and retain, as they have done, the other part. . . . Of late, another doctrine has occurred, which supposes that sovereignty is in its nature indivisible. . . ." Madison, *Letters and Other Writings* (1865 ed.), IV, pp. 390-391. See also pp. 61, 63, 75, 294, 395, 419. See the chapter in the present volume on the Virginia and Kentucky resolutions.

[26] It is interesting to notice that Webster, when replying to Calhoun at a later time, February 16, 1833, quoted the words of New Hampshire and Massachusetts in ratifying the Constitution: "They recognize the Divine goodness 'in affording the people of the United States an opportunity of entering into an explicit and solemn compact with each other, by assenting to and ratifying a new Constitution.' You will observe, Sir, that it is the people, and not the States, who have entered into this compact; and it is the people of all the United States." Capitalization and italics of the original omitted. Webster, *Works*, III, p. 476. This speech of Webster, although perhaps not so lofty in diction as the second reply to Hayne, appears on the whole to meet the state sovereignty theory more satisfactorily.

establish a national government in the full sense of the word; that the men ratifying the Constitution took the same view of the document; and that the very fact of silence, the absence of any declaration of a state's right to withdraw, is strong, if not absolutely conclusive, evidence that the people believed they were entering upon a new system different in essentials from the old Confederation of sovereignties. Again it is well to bear in mind that Madison's *Notes* had not been published; and without those notes no one could speak as confidently as we can about the purpose of the Constitution-makers.[27]

There was no action in South Carolina until after the passing of the tariff of 1832; then the leaders prepared to prevent the execution of the tariff act and to preserve the Constitution—as the South Carolina radicals viewed the Constitution.[28] Calhoun, now earnestly consecrated to his doctrines, exposed them clearly. He with his converts believed, or tried to believe, in the efficacy of passive resistance, if it were necessary to resist at all after the state announced her will; the national government could not legally use force against the state, and if attempt at coercion were made, there would still be no way of compelling obedience.[29]

The convention summoned by the legislature met late in November

[27] After the Civil War, Alexander Stephens wrote and published his *Constitutional View of the Late War Between the States*. The argument in favor of state sovereignty is largely taken up with the assertion that the states were sovereign before the ratification of the Constitution. He quotes documents in which the word "confederacy" was used when the union or the Constitution was spoken of in the early days. That fact seems to him to be conclusive. Well, Lincoln in February, 1861, spoke of the union as a confederacy. Did he mean that the states could rightly secede?

[28] The members of the South Carolina delegation in Congress, with three exceptions, before leaving Washington after the passage of the act of 1832, drew up an "Address to the people of South Carolina", in which they declared that all hopes had vanished, the protective system was the settled policy of the country. "They left the question of remedy to the sovereign power of the state." See C. S. Boucher, *The Nullification Controversy in South Carolina*, pp. 170-171.

[29] "In considering this aspect of the controversy, I pass over the fact that the General Government has no right to resort to force against a State. . . . Let it, however, be determined to use force, and the difficulty would be insurmountable, unless, indeed, it be also determined to set aside the Constitution, and to subvert the system to its foundations. Against whom would it be applied? Congress has, it is true, the right to call forth the militia 'to execute the laws and suppress insurrection;' but there would be no law resisted, unless, indeed, it be called resistance for the juries to refuse to find, and the courts to render judgment, in conformity with the wishes of the General Government; no insurrection to suppress; no armed force to reduce; not a sword unsheathed; not a bayonet raised; none, absolutely none, on whom force could be used, except it be on the unarmed citizens engaged peaceably and quietly in their daily occupations." Calhoun to General Hamilton, August 28, 1832. Calhoun, *Works*, VI, pp. 163-164.

and drew up an ordinance of nullification which declared the tariff acts void; it declared that it should not be lawful for any state or federal authority to enforce payment of the duties; that it should be the duty of the legislature to pass laws to carry the ordinance into effect and prevent the enforcement of the tariff acts after the first of February, 1833. It provided that no case involving the authority of the ordinance or the validity of legislative acts in conformity with it should be appealed to the federal Supreme Court. All officers, excepting members of the legislature, and all jurors impaneled in any cause involving the ordinance or any act passed for its execution must take oath to obey the ordinance. Efforts of the federal government to execute the nullified acts by military or naval force, or by shutting the ports of the state, or by harassing her commerce, would be "inconsistent with the longer continuance of South Carolina in the Union. . . ." Addresses were issued by the convention to the people of South Carolina and to the people of the United States. The last of these documents, in which the people of the several states were particularly named, announced the right of South Carolina to judge in the last resort of the extent of her reserved powers; it asserted that the state, any state, in resisting an unconstitutional act, was in reality supporting the Constitution; and it suggested a general convention of the states.[30]

The legislature met November 27 and proceeded to carry out the mandates of the convention. It passed an act authorizing any consignee of goods to replevy them from a federal collector; other methods were provided for protecting the interests of the state and preventing the execution of the tariff acts within the limits of the state; and, on December 18, definite proposals were made to the other states for the summoning of a national convention.

But Jackson, the headstrong and unreasonable Jackson, for whom the state had cast its vote four years before, and in whom the nullifiers themselves had for a time cherished a pleasant confidence, might so far forget himself as actually to resort to arms; in fact, he had already let the nullifiers know his stern opposition to theories and practices meaning disorganization and disunion. The western Indian-fighter, Bank-smasher, and man of the people loved the union and was incapable of discovering in Calhoun's subtle arguments the method

[30] See *State Papers on Nullification*, p. 59 ff. Cf. Calhoun, *Works*, VI, p. 193 ff., especially p. 207.

of reconciling and identifying disobedience and order. Evidently nullification was not likely to be a peaceable procedure. So the nullifiers
provided for an army. Not all of the people of South Carolina, however, were following in Calhoun's footsteps. The union men denounced the ordinance of nullification as the "mad edict of a despotic
majority".[31] They too made preparations for resistance, and "some
cried out 'enough !' 'what have we to fear; we are right and God and
Old Hickory are with us.' "[32]

The most difficult portion of the task awaits us—a critical exposition of Calhoun's theories. It is impossible in these pages to trace
the steps in their development during the twenty years after South
Carolina had given an object lesson in nullification; but fortunately,
though there was development, there was no particular inconsistency,
and we can therefore discuss his principles as a whole. At the outset
this must be said: he sought by all means to find legal basis for his
position. This is significant. He was not content with any "right of
revolution", if we mean by that phrase the right of any man or set
of men to rise against the government and throw it aside because it is
intolerable. The state had the right and the duty to uphold the Constitution and protect it from illegal assault by the general government.
No more characteristic attitude, nothing more consistent with what
was or appeared to be American temperament, could be imagined;
unless people could be convinced that law was on their side, there
was little hope of arousing the spirit of opposition to what was or
seemed to be unfair and hurtful.

He must also make out—and in this, as always, he was doubtless sincere—that state sovereignty and nullification would not involve disorder and war; they were consonant not only with the written Constitution but also with elementary and essential principles
of the American system. He must close his eyes and the eyes of
others to the disorganizing effect of state opposition to a national
act. He must present the whole matter as conservative and preservative; nullification would be carried through calmly, and without tumult.
He was prepared to defend a complicated but, as he would maintain,
thoroughly logical and sound system of preserving the union and the

[31] Boucher, op. cit., p. 244.
[32] Ibid., p. 247, quoting a letter from James O. Hanlon to Jackson, December 20
1832, which tells of a convention of union men.

Constitution; nullification would preserve the union by preventing the perversion of the Constitution at the instance of particular economic or sectional interests.

He did not shrink from upholding the cause of the minority against the majority. As the years went by, this aspect became more pronounced. It was a natural and inevitable position for any region in which the social and industrial system was based on slavery, on the right of one man to own and control fifty. Slavery, it is true, was not uppermost in the minds of men during the nullification controversy of 1832-1833; a few years later the fateful banns of wedlock between slavery and state sovereignty were proclaimed. But, as we have seen, even in 1830 the disadvantage of the south was apparent; the north was outstripping the south in population; and Calhoun had no sympathy for a mere numerical majority. On the contrary, the whole genius of the American system and the very existence of liberty were dependent, he believed, on the right of a minority to be protected or to protect itself against the tyranny of numbers. The cleverness with which he developed this doctrine, especially in later writings, is impressive. It is perfectly true that our institutions are not based on the principle that the majority can and must in all respects have its way; the fathers, fearing the tyranny of an uncontrolled majority, relied in part upon the efficiency of checks and balances as a means of protecting liberty. In this matter, as in others, Calhoun so shrewdly and ably used fundamentally sound notions to build up his extensive and complex theories in defense of local and sectional rights, that one is astonished if not convinced by his skill. How shrewd was his declaration that a negative on governmental action is the heart and center of constitutionalism!

Furthermore, his own state furnished in her own history and her own political institutions an example of recognizing interests and protecting sections. South Carolina herself had contained—and less markedly as the years went by, continued to contain—sectional and diverse interests within her own borders. The politicians of South Carolina were experienced in the art of solving a sectional problem by balancing section against section within the state, or, more properly, of protecting slaveholding interests against the back-country farmers.[33] And thus Calhoun found support for the idea that interests must concur—the doctrine of the "concurrent majority". Of course he did not see,

[33] See W. A. Schaper, "Sectionalism and Representation in South Carolina," Am. Hist. Asso. *Report* for 1900. I, p. 237 ff.

nor did he wish to see, that it really meant the concurrence of a minority, and hence, in all matters affecting the interests of a minority, the determination by a minority.[34]

A letter from Calhoun to Hamilton,[35] written in the summer of 1832, contains within its fifty printed pages the sum and substance of state sovereignty and its corollary, the right to nullify and secede. There was not—that was the core of his position—at that time, nor had there ever been, any such political body as the American people: in that character the people never performed a single political act. Such is his opening declaration; and for his theories it is absolutely fundamental. The union is a union of states as communities, and there is no direct and immediate connection between the individual citizens of a state and the general government. By this he must mean that the right to pass laws directed and applied to individuals resulted from the antecedent consent of the state as a body politic; for the contact between the general government and the individual citizen is too plain for denial, and Calhoun did not as a rule fly in the face of the obvious. It belongs to the state as a member of the union to determine in convention the extent of the obligations into which it has entered and to declare an act void and unconstitutional. The

[34] The doctrine of the "concurrent majority" appears inconsistent with or certainly not in natural harmony with the doctrine of state sovereignty. We should notice that, if it is applicable at all, anywhere or at any time, it is only applicable where there are distinct interests; for the basic theory is that each interest must concur with the other; in other words, each interest must have a veto on the other. It is thus a device not logically associated with the doctrine of the absolute will of the individual sovereign state over its own affairs. "The necessary consequence of taking the sense of the community by the concurrent majority is, as has been explained, to give to each interest or portion of the community a negative on the others." "It is this negative power,—the power of preventing or arresting the action of the government,—be it called by what term it may,—veto, interposition, nullification, check, or balance of power,—which, in fact, forms the constitution. They are all but different names for the negative power. In all its forms, and under all its names, it results from the concurrent majority. Without this there can be no negative; and, without a negative, no constitution." In other words, there must be for constitutional action, in any really constitutional government, the coöperation and consent of distinct interests, not merely a numerical majority, and this right of each to dissent and thus prevent action he quaintly transfuses into "concurrent majority". These excerpts are from "A Disquisition on Government," *Works*, I, p. 35, which was written near the end of his life, but the doctrine was briefly set forth in 1832. See *Works*, VI, p. 181 ff. "Such is the solidity and beauty of our admirable system—but which, it is perfectly obvious, can only be preserved by maintaining the ascendency of the constitution-making authority over the law-making— the concurring over the absolute majority." *Ibid.*, VI, p. 186. Capitalization of the original omitted.

[35] *Works*, VI, p. 144 ff.

general government is the "joint agent" of the states. To support some of his positions Calhoun referred to the journal of the Federal Convention—a weak reed to lean upon. The government has no right to exercise any control over a state, by force, veto, judicial process or in any other way. The government of the United States is unlike the old government of the Articles of Confederation, but the Constitution "is as strictly and as purely a confederation, as the one which it superseded." [36]

A state has a right to nullify a law, but nullification is not secession; nullification is essential for preserving the Constitution; without it, the only remedy for unconstitutional exercise of power by the central government would be the dissolution of the union. The object of nullification by a single state is to compel the agent—the central government—to fulfill the object of its creation.[37] Secession may follow upon nullification, but that step would be taken only in case the other states should undertake to grant or acknowledge the power objected to and uphold the nullified act; then, and only then, if in the judgment of the nullifying state the nature of the granted power defeats the object of the association or union, the dissatisfied state can withdraw. In other words, a state should not withdraw because of the misdeeds of the *agent,* but only because of the misdeeds of the principals. Hence, whether the act in question is unconstitutional, whether the nullifying state is right in its position, is a question for the states, the principals, the contracting parties. The states, if the matter is of great consequence, should meet in a general convention, for in that body rests the power to correct error and repair injury. But even there, in that gathering of sovereign states, a simple majority cannot decide in favor of the act nullified; amendments to the Constitution may be made by three-fourths of the states; that number must then be necessary for decision *adverse* to the *nullifying* state; less than that number cannot declare the nullifying state to be wrong and the act of the national government to be constitutional. In other words, one more than one-fourth of the states can proclaim the invalidity of

[36] *Works,* VI, p. 158. Italics of the original omitted.

[37] "On the contrary, the object of nullification is to confine the agent within the limits of his powers, by arresting his acts transcending them, not with the view of destroying the delegated or trust power, but to preserve it, by compelling the agent to fulfil the object for which the agency or trust was created; and is applicable only to cases where the trust or delegated powers are transcended on the part of the agent." *Works,* VI, pp. 168-169. Italics of the original omitted.

any congressional act.[38] This appears at first sight to be a startling conclusion; but it was entirely in accord with the fundamentals of Calhoun's philosophy; the one intolerable thing would be government by a numerical majority.

We need not upbraid Calhoun for not bringing too clearly into the light the fact that not even three-fourths of the states could finally uphold the law and hold the union together; even after such a vote, it would still be within the right of a state to secede, because the state is sovereign. This right to withdraw is acknowledged briefly by his admitting that secession may follow nullification, but of course the right is not stressed, for he is under the necessity of presenting his system as preservative and not dangerous to the existence of the union.[39] Though he acknowledges constitutional obligations, his whole theory of state sovereignty must be made to include the right of the state to decide, for nothing can legally bind sovereignty. The very essence of sovereignty, as he himself defined and defended sovereignty, is the *complete* right of self-determination. It is almost pitiful, this effort to find order in confusion, this desire to find a way of binding a state that cannot be bound. And yet the elements of the process were on the whole consistent: the states were sovereign, but there was no reason why one state should not discover the opinion of the others before breaking up the union; to give the other states an opportunity to pass upon the question of the constitutionality of an act would be a courteous procedure; and at all events, it looked well; it helped to give the whole theory and process an aspect of legal solemnity.

Nullification, as Calhoun exposed it to view, has often been attacked. I think I am right in saying that it never became a thoroughly acceptable doctrine to the southern people. But it is hard to discover good grounds for the objection, if state sovereignty be the premise.[40]

[38] "The amending power, *in effect*, prevents this danger. In virtue of the provisions which it contains, the resistance of a State to a power cannot finally prevail, unless she be sustained by one fourth of the co-States. . . ." *Works*, VI, p. 175. See also pp. 176-178, and I, p. 290 ff.

[39] In later years he still acknowledged that "by the solemn obligation which it contracted, in ratifying the constitution", the state is bound to acquiesce unless the decision of the amending authorities is inconsistent with the ends for which the Constitution was established. Of this inconsistency the particular state must in the end be the judge. *Works*, I, pp. 300-301.

[40] In the letter to Hamilton, referred to above, Calhoun said: "There are many who acknowledge the right of a State to secede, but deny its right to nullify; and yet, it seems impossible to admit the one without admitting the other." *Works*, VI p. 170.

True, this method of preserving the union and maintaining states' rights was complex, baffling; to the earnest defenders of the union and of the general government it was essentially odious. As the Civil War approached, southern leaders were inclined simply to threaten secession without resort to nullification. As they became more and more irritated they were prepared to say: "Accept our ideas or we leave you; we have the moral right and the constitutional right to abandon you to your sins; we shall look after ourselves." And yet, if the union was in reality a solemn system of actual sovereignties—sovereignties in essence like Holland and France and Spain and other nations of the world—then the principle of nullification was not illogical. Why should not an aggrieved state declare an act void and ask for the judgment of the rest?

Critics and advocates of Calhoun's theories have been wont to speak of them as if they represented the Constitution as only a treaty between sovereignties. It requires no intellectual effort to comprehend the nature of a league of sovereignties or the nature of a treaty, and consequently such words have been used to describe the union and the Constitution. But while Calhoun held the whole structure to be the product of consent and agreement of sovereign bodies, the difference between it and the structure of any common league or any treaty arrangement was obvious. The facts needed to be faced; and he faced them. He pointed to the undeniable fact: the Constitution was ratified and the government was set up by the *same general processes* as those followed in setting up the state constitutions and state governments. People bestowed authority on governments. *The general government rested on the same basis as the state governments.* How could the great logician be also a magician and transmute a Constitution into a contract of alliance? He could, or thought he could, bring the rabbit out of the hat because the states, that is to say, the people acting in separate states, as separate corporate entities, adopted the Constitution. The product of *separate* action could be nothing more than an *agreement;* when the states (the people in conventions) set up a central or a general government they did not by that act destroy their existence as separate sovereignties.[41]

[41] "Thus viewed, the Constitution of the United States, with the government it created, is truly and strictly the Constitution of each State,—as much so as its own particular Constitution and Government, ratified by the same authority,—in the same mode, and having, as far as its citizens are concerned, its powers and obligations from the same source,—differing only in the aspect under which I am considering the subject,—in the *plighted faith* of the State to its co-States, and of which, as far

This of course is thin ice to stand upon; but on such frail support must the highly-elaborated doctrine of state sovereignty stand, if it can stand at all. We have reached here the very heart of the state sovereignty argument: *separate adoption* of the Constitution *does not, cannot, transform the people of the various states into one political body.*[42]

What can be said of such an assertion? It does not belong in the field of history or of law; if it have any truth in it, the dogma must belong in the field of metaphysics. Why cannot thirteen separate peoples, acting separately, fuse themselves by their own determination into a single new state? What prevents them? If the people of Brazil, Argentina, Chile, and Uruguay should, each acting in geographic separation one from the other, decide upon entering into a new whole with its own government, would anyone say that they could not do so? What is there in the nature of terrestrial or celestial verities to prevent their doing that very thing? And if they succeed in doing it, must we still hold it impossible?

The principles of Calhoun almost defy abbreviation, if they be treated justly; and still the basic doctrines, of which perhaps he was not altogether conscious, can be extracted from the many thousands of words he devoted to their defense:

I. Separate action of individual communities cannot create a new being.

    A. The states separately adopted the Constitution.

    B. Therefore the Constitution did not establish a new entity.

II. The result of a *compact* or contract among *equals* is not a law; for law is the mandate of a *superior*.

    A. The states were equal when they ratified the Constitution, therefore the Constitution is not law.

III. Sovereignty is indivisible; and as no one would contend that the states surrendered all of their sovereignty, they must have retained all of it.

In its elements, state sovereignty, begotten by practical economic need and used with astonishing skill in practical politics, was a phi-

as its citizens are considered, the State, in the last resort, is the exclusive judge." *Works,* VI, p. 152. To the same effect is his statement in his "Discourse on the Constitution and Government of the United States." Notice there he also distinguishes between a federal government and a confederacy. *Works,* I, pp. 167-168.

[42] John Taylor had plentifully labored the same idea. Calhoun insisted on it: there was not a single creative whole—an American people in 1788; therefore the Constitution was not the expression of a *common* will.

losophy. How could the assertions of such a philosophy be met? The fact is that the very statement of the doctrine of state sovereignty, if coldly analyzed, manifests its inherent weakness. It is too metaphysical, too detached from the realities of politics, to be convincing. If people, north or south, did actually read the documents, could the readers understand them? We are entitled to doubt it. And still, this theory, with all its subtlety and elaborateness, gave strength to those wishing to believe.

Need we point out again that the theory of state sovereignty does not rest on statements made when the Constitution was framed and adopted (1787-1788)?—that is to say, it does not rest on contemporary *testimony* to the effect that a state could withdraw from the union. No such testimony has been found.[43] The omission of the word "national" by the Philadelphia Convention and the failure to provide in the Constitution for the use of force against a state are spoken of by Calhoun,[44] but in his early papers he had to rely on the published journal and from that he could get no clear idea why the Convention did not decide for the coercion of states as corporate entities and why the word "national" was omitted.

The state sovereignty argument could be met and was met by two different lines of assertion. (1) If the Constitution was a compact, it nevertheless was binding and was law. This was in accord with earlier political philosophy, the philosophy of the eighteenth century, the philosophy of the men who made the Constitution: all free governments rest on compact; all authority springs from consent. (2) The Constitution was ratified by the people of the United States in their aggregate capacity, though they met in geographically-separated areas. Both of these lines of attack were used; in the earlier days the first was chiefly relied upon. We have already seen Webster beginning to use the latter theory. Doubtless, however, the declaration most satisfying to the average person was to the effect that the Constitution meant exactly what it said—that it was "law", because it said so, and no state or person could deny its binding effect.[45]

[43] See the chapter in this work on the Federal Convention. Reference has been made in a preceding chapter to resolutions passed by certain states when they ratified the Constitution; they do not uphold Calhoun's theories. If Calhoun had studied, really studied, Madison's *Papers,* when they were published in 1840, and had he known the elements of the compact philosophy, he would have had a more difficult task to maintain his theories.

[44] *Works,* I, pp. 113-114, VI, p. 154 ff.

[45] For fuller discussion, see A. C. McLaughlin, *The Courts, the Constitution and Parties,* pp. 189-242, or "Social Compact and Constitutional Construction," *Am.*

Jackson replied to the ordinance of South Carolina with his famous proclamation. It was ably written. There has been some discussion over its authorship, but it is saturated with Jackson's spirit, with his own indomitable and imperative nature. It was dignified and stern, but not wanting in a certain kindly, or to use his own word, "paternal" quality. No one can overestimate the importance and continuing effect of Jackson's influence; that he of all men, the embodiment of frontier nationalism, the man of the plain people, the leader of the new democracy and the new party, took a decisive stand against disorganization was of the utmost consequence for the future. He not only used words, he was ready to fight.[46] He spoke of his belief in the Constitution; he deplored "the threat of unhallowed disunion"; he appealed to love of country; he begged the men of South Carolina to retrace their steps; and he announced his duty to enforce the law: "The laws of the United States must be executed. I have no discretionary power on the subject; my duty is emphatically pronounced in the Constitution. Those who told you that you might peaceably prevent their execution

Hist. Rev., V, pp. 467-490; *The Foundations of American Constitutionalism.* The truth is there was at that time a shifting away from the compact philosophy and the coming in of a new organic or vital or social philosophy, and men of course did not see it. Calhoun himself was speaking in terms of the new; he applied it to the state; the state was a living being with a will, built up by historical and social forces. But he would not see that perhaps the same could be said of the United States. What was to hinder one from seeing the Constitution as the product of social forces, seeing it as the will of a people really existing, though they met in sections and used existing political machinery to record their will? If one rejects as metaphysically impossible the notion that *separate* action can beget unity and create a new whole out of diversity, why not recognize at least the possibility of there being a single vital force in 1788 beneath the phenomenon of separate action? Had Calhoun done so, his own political philosophy would have been consistent and in line with the developing fact and theory of society as a living, forceful thing. For the new philosophy looks always below phenomena, below and beyond mere surface acts, to the deeper reality; and it can find unity in apparent diversity. The historian, for example, and the plain citizen of the present day, though unlearned in history, is not content with phenomena, but seeks the eternal and underlying truth, the vital force, of which men themselves are not quite aware.

[46] See Boucher, *op. cit.,* ch. VII, for Jackson's determination. Van Buren, in his *Autobiography,* Am. Hist. Asso. *Report* for 1918, II, p. 544, says of Jackson, "He had at this time, it must be admitted, one feeling which approached to a passion and that was an inclination to go himself with a sufficient force, which he felt assured he could raise in Virginia and Tennessee, as '*a posse comitatus*' of the Marshal and arrest Messrs. Calhoun, Hayne, Hamilton and McDuffie in the midst of the force of 12,000 men which the Legislature of South Carolina had authorized to be raised and deliver them to the Judicial power of the United States to be dealt with according to law. The reader will find this project more than once stated in his letters to me written *currente calamo.*"

deceived you; they could not have been deceived themselves. . . . Their object is disunion. But be not deceived by names. Disunion by armed force is *treason.*" Those were fateful words.

Jackson had no misgivings about the Constitution and the nature of the union. His peculiarly straightforward statement must have satisfied many persons bewildered by Calhoun's words and the announcements of the nullifiers. He was not to be led away and deluded by metaphysics.[47] "The Constitution of the United States, then, forms a *government*, not a league; and whether it be formed by compact between the States or in any other manner, its character is the same. . . . Because the Union was formed by a compact, it is said the parties to that compact may, when they feel themselves aggrieved, depart from it; but it is precisely because it is a compact that they can not. A compact is an agreement or binding obligation." And thus we see the conflict of ideas: on one side the assertion that, as the Constitution was a compact, it was not binding; on the other, the announcement that because it was a compact it was binding.

The various states of the union answered South Carolina. Those answers are interesting documents and they disclose an interesting situation, for not one state supported South Carolina's contention— strange fact, if Calhoun's and Hayne's theories were the old and hence technically sound, and Webster's, Jackson's, and Marshall's the new. It is not quite clear whether every state would have denounced secession as distinguished from nullification; but none of them upheld nullification. Georgia proclaimed her abhorrence of nullification as neither a peaceful nor a constitutional remedy; Alabama resolved that nullification was "unsound in theory and dangerous in practice", and that it was "unconstitutional and essentially revolutionary. . . ." North Carolina declared the doctrine was "revolutionary in its character" and "subversive of the Constitution"; Mississippi acknowledged herself in hearty accord with the political sentiments of the President

---

[47] "Now, is it possible that even if there were no express provision giving supremacy to the Constitution and laws of the United States over those of the States, can it be conceived that an instrument made for the purpose of '*forming a more perfect union*' than that of the Confederation could be so constructed by the assembled wisdom of our country as to substitute for that Confederation a form of government dependent for its existence on the local interest, the party spirit, of a State, or of a prevailing portion in a State? Every man of plain, unsophisticated understanding who hears the question will give such an answer as will preserve the Union. Metaphysical subtlety, in pursuit of an impracticable theory, could alone have devised one that is calculated to destroy it." Richardson, *Messages and Papers*, II, p. 643.

and deplored nullification as contrary to the letter and spirit of the Constitution. Virginia adhered to the resolutions of 1798 as the true interpretation of the Constitution, but denied that the resolutions upheld either South Carolina on the one hand or the President on the other—a statement leaving us in doubt, but certainly not advocating the theories of South Carolina. Of the northern and western states it is unnecessary to speak; they condemned the revolutionary doctrines. Maine approved the spirit and tone of the President's address but upheld states' rights without giving any distinct evidence of supporting state sovereignty.[48]

The report of the Massachusetts joint select committee is especially illuminating as an example of the application of the old "compact" thinking. The committee saw that nullification rested on this assumption: the states were independent of each other when they formed the Constitution; therefore they were independent afterwards. ". . . there can be no doubt," the committee said, "that independent States are morally as capable of forming themselves into a body politic, as independent individuals." Thus the answer to the assertion that the Constitution is a compact and therefore not a binding law, is to assert that, if the Constitution is a compact, it *is* a binding law.

In his annual message of December, 1832, Jackson had recommended a reconsideration of the tariff, saying that "the policy of protection must be ultimately limited to those articles of domestic manufacture which are indispensable to our safety in time of war." In a special message to Congress (January 16, 1833) he proposed the passage of such federal legislation as would insure the protection of persons and property by the federal courts, and, in case there should be forcible resistance, would fully authorize the use of land and naval forces of the United States.[49] This latter proposal was embodied in

[48] For the situation in Georgia, see Phillips, *op. cit.*, ch. V. Phillips says that the editor of *Niles's Register*, in noting political events in Georgia from 1819 to 1833, declared many times that it was impossible to understand Georgia politics. We may take refuge in the same ignorance. In truth, conditions were confusing. There were personal factions and geographical sections and other perplexing differences. But both houses of the state legislature by a decided majority repudiated nullification as being neither a peaceful nor a constitutional remedy (November 20, 1832). *Ibid.*, pp. 127, 130-131.

[49] January 24, 1833, Jackson wrote Poinsett, union leader in South Carolina, that if Congress failed to act, and he was informed of "illegal assemblage" to oppose the revenue acts, he would issue a warning to disperse, and if the assemblage did not comply he would call into the field a force sufficient to "overawe resistance, put treason and rebellion down without blood, and arrest and hand over to the judiciary for trial and punishment, the leaders, exciters and promoters of this rebellion and

a measure mildly called *"An Act further to provide for the collection of duties on imports"*, but commonly called the "force bill" or the "bloody bill". While a new tariff act and the "force bill" were under consideration in Congress, South Carolina postponed the application of the measures for enforcing the nullification ordinance.

The "force bill" and the measure for reducing the tariff proceeded together. The Senate passed the "force bill" on February 20 and the tariff bill on March 1. The House passed the tariff bill on February 26 and the "force bill" on March 1. The so-called "compromise tariff" provided for gradual reduction of duties, during the succeeding years, until by the middle of 1842 a general level of twenty per cent was reached.

South Carolina had succeeded; so the enthusiastic nullifiers believed.[50] The state repealed the ordinance of nullification and passed a new ordinance nullifying the "force bill". Accepting the olive branch of the tariff, the convention rejected with scorn the rod of national authority. And yet, on the surface at least, Calhoun's theories had failed. They had received no substantial support from any one of the legislatures of the other states—even from those hostile to the tariff. The votes in Congress are significant. There were forty-eight senators; their vote on the "force bill" stood thirty-two in favor and one opposed; fifteen members did not vote. The one Senator voting in the negative was John Tyler of Virginia. Among those voting in the affirmative were one Senator from Virginia, one from Georgia, two from Louisiana. In the House 149 members voted in favor of the "force bill", forty-seven against.[51] It is possible that some of these

---

treason." Poinsett MSS., quoted by J. B. McMaster, *A History of the People of the United States,* VI, p. 163 note.

[50] McMaster says that the *Columbia Telescope* (March 12, 1833) declared: "This little State has defied the swaggering giant of the Union. Thirteen thousand Carolinians have not only awed the wild West into respect, compelled Pennsylvania stolidity into something like sense, New York corruption into something like decency, Yankee rapacity into a sort of image of honesty, but they have done all this loftily and steadily and in the face of seventeen thousand betrayers of the liberty of their own State." McMaster, *op. cit.,* VI, p. 169. This was the spirit that finally brought devastation upon the state and decades of attempted recuperation.

[51] *Journal of the Senate,* 22 Cong., 2 sess., pp. 198-199; *Journal of the House,* 22 Cong., 2 sess., pp. 453-454. See also, *Congressional Debates,* 22 Cong., 2 sess., appendix, p. 1. Eight of the states then in the union seceded in 1861; but in 1833 twenty-seven of their sixty-three representatives voted for the "force bill". All this furnishes a pretty strong support of the prevalent belief that the government was a real government and could enforce its laws even though a state *in convention* attempted to nullify them.

men voting to uphold the authority of the government by force and arms would have declared that a state could secede but could not nullify; until it was out of the union its citizens must obey the law. But such a position appears quite unlikely.

CHAPTER XXXIV

CHIEF JUSTICE TANEY AND THE SUPREME COURT

Chief Justice Marshall died in 1835, leaving to his country the example of a distinguished service. His task had not been easy or his life free from anxiety. The greatest task of all had been the establishment of the Court as the recognized final authority in determining the extent of state powers; he had not failed; but almost to the very end of his life he found one state or another denying the Court's authority or even, as in the case of Georgia, flouting it. South Carolina had put forth a doctrine contrary to all his philosophy and all his pronouncements. He had reason for fearing that the union might not survive.

The appointment of a successor was a matter of moment. Jackson named for the position Roger Brooke Taney. He had been Attorney-General in Jackson's cabinet and later Secretary of the Treasury; the latter position he had to surrender because the Senate refused to confirm the appointment. He had remained in office long enough, however, to carry out Jackson's scheme for the removal of the deposits and had effectively aroused the enmity of the Whigs. The conservatives looked upon him as a dangerous character, unfit to wear the robe of justice which had been so ably and gallantly borne by his great predecessor. The Whig newspapers burst forth in lamentation. Clay's mighty wrath was not held in perfect control. Webster of course was dissatisfied. Justice Story, who had served with Marshall for more than twenty years and ardently admired his chief, agreed with Webster that the Supreme Court was *"gone"*.[1] The Senate hesitated to confirm the appointment, but finally consented after the passing of a winter which must have been filled with gloom for all those who believed the

[1] See *The Letters of Daniel Webster* (C. H. Van Tyne, ed.), p. 198. Webster's letter was written January 10, 1836, and Story's belief that the Court was *"gone"* may have been due to Marshall's death and to other changes and not alone to Taney's being named. In the winter of 1837 Story wrote favorably of the new Chief Justice. In the spring of that year he wrote: "I am the last of the old race of judges. I stand their solitary representative with a pained heart and subdued confidence." See B. C. Steiner, *Life of Roger Brooke Taney*, p. 189.

land unable to bear the burden of incompetent democracy. To carry the load of a Democratic President was bad enough, but a Democratic Chief Justice, who might well undo all the achievements of the past, was a tribulation hard to be endured. And yet the judgment to-day is that the new Chief Justice proved capable; the high office did not lose its distinction. In the later years, it is true, his name was darkened by the decision in the Dred Scott case and by his disapproval of Lincoln's suspension of habeas corpus; but during his term of service, at least up to the time of the Dred Scott decision, the influence of the Court probably increased rather than diminished. In a series of very important cases Taney displayed unquestionable ability and learning.

The Court had already undergone significant changes in membership, but some of the old members continued to serve. Of these Joseph Story was the most conspicuous, and no history of American law would touch upon the vitals of the subject without mention of his name. His *Commentaries on the Constitution of the United States* appeared in 1833, to be labored over by law students during half a century and more. It is difficult to measure the influence of works of that kind and especially of this one, but it was unquestionably very great. It naturally presented with definite emphasis the fundamental precepts which Marshall's career had exemplified. In many respects, the second quarter of the century was of marked importance in the development of American law, and Story of course did not toil alone. Kent's *Commentaries on American Law* was published only a few years before Story published his *Commentaries.* Somewhat later Theophilus Parsons published his *Treatise on the Law of Contracts* (1853), and on the bench of the Massachusetts court Lemuel Shaw expounded the law in a series of influential decisions. There were able jurists at the bar, and we need to ask ourselves again whether the courts or, on the other hand, the lawyers at the bar create the law and direct its course. A competent authority, speaking of the sixty years before the Civil War, asserts that the achievements during that period compare favorably with any other period of growth and adjustment in legal history; in its many characteristics it was analogous to "the classical period in England—the age of Coke." [2] We need not suppose, therefore, that the years which we are entering upon with the accession of Taney were uneventful or unproductive; America was still in the making; able and learned publicists were clarifying and

---

[2] Roscoe Pound, "The Place of Judge Story in the Making of American Law," Cambridge Hist. Society *Publications,* VII, p. 39.

enlarging the law; and in the field of constitutional law questions of vital importance had to be met and solved.

The Court was now safely in the hands of the Democrats.[3] And that fact implies much. Though the justices were not limited and constrained by the bonds of a narrow partisanship, their outlook upon the problems and the movements of the day was not quite the same as under the previous order of things. It is sufficient to say that the justices breathed the air of their time. Taney, especially, had sympathy for the aspirations of the common people and for their zeal to manage their own affairs. If in the past there had been, as is frequently said, anxiety lest the rights of property and vested interests be trampled under the feet of an eager populace, that anxiety disappeared or was now not regnant. Despite the extravagant doctrines of Calhoun and his ardent followers, the Court was not agitated by dread lest the union crumble. From the very beginning of the government state sovereignty had found no shadow of recognition in the judicial councils of the nation; [4] nor did it find any support after the accession of Taney. The Chief Justice was not willing, however, that the Constitution should be so interpreted by implication and assumption as unduly to hamper the states in the performance of their duties; the right and the opportunity of the states to act within their sphere and to function within the union seemed to him quite as important as anything else.

The country was entering upon a new era; in fact it had already

[3] Jackson appointed McLean of Ohio, 1829, Wayne of Georgia, 1835, Barbour of Virginia, 1836, and Taney of Maryland, 1836. Van Buren appointed Catron of Tennessee, 1837, and McKinley of Virginia, 1837. Daniel of Virginia succeeded Barbour in 1841. Story died in 1845.

[4] It is a strange fact, on the whole, that the advocates of the doctrine of state sovereignty and secession never seem to take much notice of the continuity of judicial opinion from the beginning. It is possible that Justice Campbell, because of his opinion in the Dred Scott case (1857), deserves to be called an exception to the rule. But it is not absolutely plain that his opinion necessarily bears this interpretation. He resigned and joined the Confederacy in 1861. Justice McLean said, in Wheaton and Donaldson v. Peters and Grigg, 8 Peters 591, 658 (1834): "The federal government is composed of twenty-four sovereign and independent States, each of which may have its local usages, customs and common law." Did he mean to use the word "sovereign" as Calhoun used it? That appears to be impossible. Marshall was still on the bench, though I do not know that he sat in the case. Story was on the bench, and had just published his *Commentaries*. The statement by McLean is a pure *obiter dictum*. The question was not whether the states were sovereign, in the full sense, but whether they had their own system of law, and whether there was a common law of the United States. The former question can be answered in the affirmative to-day and the latter in the negative; but no one supposes the states have more than limited sovereignty.

entered. The period of Jacksonian democracy was not characterized solely by declamation and noisy announcements of popular power. There was enthusiasm for social betterment. Reform was in the air. Governments were no longer considered merely necessary burdens to be endured; they were expected to obey the popular will. Commerce was expanding, railroads were coming on the scene, new industrial activities were productive of political and legal problems. Corporations were forming for new enterprises. Not many of the judicial questions resulting from all these changes and all this vitality came before the highest Court; but a number of cases did arise where the decisions were of epochal importance.[5] In later years, beginning about the end of Reconstruction, like problems flocked to the Court in plentiful numbers; for that period also, the permanence of the union being assured, was a time of expansion, of new corporations, of new social needs and demands, of industrial development. But in this later period the Court had the fourteenth amendment to deal with; that amendment placed restrictions upon the states, and the duty of enforcing those restrictions fell to the courts. In Taney's time the Constitution contained a few explicit prohibitions upon the states—notably not to impair the obligation of contracts, not to pass *ex post facto* laws, and not to emit bills of credit; and there were non-explicit but real prohibitions resulting from the grant of powers to the national government. The effect and extent of those grants inevitably depended upon the interpretation given to the words.

There was no attempt in the new Court to overthrow the great decisions of Marshall's day and to begin anew. That is not the way of courts. They move on from precedent to precedent, but as the times change, as new needs arise, as the social outlook is enlarged or modified, the courts are affected. The justices have the skill to adapt, construe, and apply the older formulas, and to defy the layman to discover how the course has altered or the current of the stream has shifted. Indeed, in that way the common law itself has been developed

[5] "It was this change of emphasis from vested, individual property rights to the personal rights and welfare of the general community which characterized Chief Justice Taney's Court. And this change was but a recognition of the general change in the social and economic conditions and in the political atmosphere of that period, brought about by the adoption of universal manhood suffrage, by the revolution in methods of business and industry and in means of transportation, and by the expansion of the Nation and its activities." Charles Warren, *The Supreme Court in United States History*, II, p. 309. Especially valuable is E. S. Corwin's able article: "The Doctrine of Due Process of Law Before the Civil War," *Harvard Law Review*, XXIV, pp. 366-385, 460-479.

and adapted to an advancing and ever more intricate civilization in spite of the fact (or because of the fact) that the law is supposed to rest on unchanging foundations of everlasting justice. The Constitution, too, has been fitted to a new world under the gentle ministrations of bench as well as bar. If occasionally or frequently judges appear adamant, or if the courts seem to lag hopelessly behind social needs, the onlooker, glancing back through decades, will probably be convinced that they only delay the modification of the old.

The main problems of the time, as far as they concerned constitutional history, involved the task of adjustment and accommodation, the task of giving such recognition to the powers of the states and such acknowledgment of the authority of the national system that the whole intricate structure of federalism would work and not break down. The states, Taney believed with all his heart, had not only rights but duties. It was the business of the states and their governments—and not merely their technical right under the Constitution— to care for the safety and to promote the happiness of their people; for such purposes they existed. In carrying out these duties, they should not be hindered by vague implications and presumptions gathered from the Constitution by clever interpretation. Though the national government should be protected in secure possession of undoubted authority and not be obstructed by petty scruples, the courts were under no obligation to view the national power as an object of special solicitude. After all, the union was a union of states. That the tendency arose from an attitude of mind which was not the possession of a particular judge or a particular court is evidenced by the fact that the state courts were moving in the same direction. In those tribunals we find a readiness to accept enactments of legislatures and an unwillingness to throw obstacles in their path.[6]

If we look forward from the second quarter of the century to the fourth quarter and to the interpretation of the fourteenth amendment, the tendencies in the courts during the quarter of a century before the

---

[6] "The right of courts to invalidate legislative enactments, after the first wave of enthusiasm which brought its adoption, was indeed scarcely used before the Civil War in any but a few states as an effective check upon legislative power. The practice of judicial review was confined during this period mainly to four states, North Carolina, Massachusetts, New York, and New Hampshire." C. G. Haines, *The American Doctrine of Judicial Supremacy* (2nd ed.), p. 340. "But what was happening on the Supreme Bench was the index of what was happening also in the state judiciaries, where popular sovereignty and states' rights united to force a recognition of the plenitude of legislative power." Corwin, "The Doctrine of Due Process of Law Before the Civil War," *loc. cit.*, p. 462.

Civil War have peculiar significance. For in some respects the cases coming before the state courts in the earlier period presented the problems which were so conspicuous in the last years of the nineteenth century and in the early years of the twentieth. This statement is not meant to imply that the tendency of the judicial decisions after 1875 was similar to the tendency of the earlier period, but that the problems were similar; we see in the later period as well as in the earlier the influence of social need, and, on the other hand, the pressure of propertied interests appealing to the conservative instincts of the courts. In both periods the question arose as to whether wide opportunity should be allowed for social experiment or whether, on the other hand, legislatures should be bound by what the courts thought ought to be done. What principle or philosophy should be accepted in determining the scope and character of state legislative powers?

Before 1868, when the fourteenth amendment was adopted, the state courts, passing upon the validity of state legislation, were in the main free to interpret their constitutions as they chose. The legislatures, feeling the impact of popular demand, passed acts of social legislation which brought to the fore fundamental questions concerning personal rights to property, and, less conspicuously, to liberty. What should be the basis of decisions? If it were definitely and consistently held that the people, when drafting a constitution and setting up a government, bestowed upon that government all powers not denied to the government, or, in other words, if the legislature had all powers not specifically or by *obvious* implication denied it, would the courts enforce only the plainly-stated prohibitions and limitations? Or were there principles, not patent on the face of the document, which constituted restrictions on legislative competence? Could the legislature be restrained by the spirit of free institutions, by the doctrine of natural rights, by the implications of the social compact, or by any other similar method of approach?[7]

On the whole, the tendency of the state courts was to look upon the state legislation as the expression of popular will; they were not ready to determine the constitutionality of legislation by deciding whether or not there were extraneous principles binding on the legis-

---

[7] The best-known opinion largely based on this philosophy was given by Justice Miller in Loan Asso. *v.* Topeka, 20 Wallace 655 (1875). The case, be it remembered, came after the Civil War; it was a federal and not a state case. It was decided after the fourteenth amendment was adopted, but before the federal Court had developed the theories of the due process clause of the amendment. It illustrates admirably the kind of philosophic approach of which the text speaks.

lature, though they lay beyond the region of the plain words and prohibitions of the constitution itself. The philosophy of the Revolution, a popular philosophy which was used to resist tyrannical government, was not to be freely utilized to prevent the people from achieving their purposes. Who could better determine what was best for the people than the people themselves? This conclusion was not reached, however, without argument and litigation.[8]

It is apparent, too, that, despite the general tendency to recognize legislative enactments as law and not to throw up obstacles in addition to those erected by the people themselves in their own constitutions, the courts were subjected to constant pressure; litigants and lawyers hoped for the judicial pronouncement of a principle or a method of construction whereby the legislatures could be checked and property could be protected from intrusion.

If certain words in a constitution could be so construed as to embody the principle of natural justice, then the doctrine that ex-

[8] The issue is admirably presented in a decision of the Michigan court in 1856. Speaking of the arguments which were presented against the validity of a statute, and indicating the court's unwillingness to accept them, the court said: "It is not denied but that the legislative department possesses this discretionary power, to a very great extent; but it is insisted that, when this power shall be improvidently exercised, it becomes the duty of the court to declare the act void. That is to say, that all the acts of the legislature while representing the sovereignty of the people as a law-making power, which, from the nature of things, must involve the power of a choice, founded upon the wants and necessities of the public, are to be reviewed and passed upon by the judiciary before they can be considered as of binding force." Asking by what authority the courts could exercise this supervisory power, the court replied: "Certainly not by anything contained in the constitution, nor by anything that is capable of definition, except, perhaps, in the language of one of the eminent judges above cited, that it is derived from a fundamental principle of right and justice inherent in the nature and spirit of the social compact, and the character and genius of our government. . . ." The court refused to be governed by that sort of thing. The opinion of the dissenting judge in the case is an especially clear statement of this doctrine that the legislature was bound by the principles of free government and of the social compact. The People v. Gallagher, 4 Michigan 244, 255-256 (1856). Another example is the following: "The legislature having full power to pass such laws as is [sic] deemed necessary for the public good, their acts cannot be impeached on the ground, that they are unwise, or not in accordance with just and enlightened views of political economy, as understood at the present day." ". . . arguments against their policy must be addressed to the legislative department of the government." Mobile v. Yuille, 3 Alabama 137, 143 (1841). A very interesting case, because of the liberality of its outlook, is Goddard v. Jacksonville, 15 Illinois 588, 590 (1854) : "The framers of Magna Charta, and of the constitutions of the United States and of the state, never intended to modify, abridge or destroy the police powers of government." The court upheld an ordinance of the town declaring the sale of liquor a nuisance, and refused to be bound by reference to natural rights.

traneous principles constituted limitations on legislative power need not be openly applied. The principle or something analogous, though not so named, would then appear in the constitution as an *express* limitation on governmental power. A conservative political philosophy, fearing the incursion of legislative enactments into the field of personal rights, late in the period under consideration, sought to find refuge in the constitutional provision against depriving a person of life, liberty, or property without due process of law. Could those words be so interpreted as to constitute an express prohibition of legislation which would encroach upon what the courts would deem substantial rights of the individual to hold and enjoy property?

In the earlier years that clause, appearing in state and federal constitutions, was interpreted, if interpreted at all, as applying to the preservation or the recognition of *procedure,* i.e., to the actual *process,* and not to the substance of the right alleged to be involved. It had been held, however, that the mere establishment of procedure by legislative enactment did not necessarily make the procedure due and legal. Toward the end of the period preceding the Civil War, there was at least one conspicuous case in which the very substance of an act was examined and the act declared void because it violated rights guaranteed and secured by the due process clause. In other words, no matter what the *procedure,* no matter how formal the legislative enactment, property had rights beyond the reach of the legislature and was distinctly protected by the due process clause of the constitution itself. That fact marks a decided development in American constitutional law. Henceforward, if this interpretation of the due process clause were commonly accepted, not the will of the legislature, but the sense of right and justice residing in the bosom of the courts would be decisive of the constitutionality of social and economic legislation.[9]

The salient case, mentioned in the preceding paragraph, was decided in New York in 1856 where the court held an act void as a

---

[9] It is interesting and important to notice that the doctrine of natural right continued to have vitality. It was the child of centuries, lauded and sanctified by time. Before the mid-nineteenth century it had begun to lose its place of privilege in political philosophy and the words themselves were used less and less; but the age-old belief that there were permanent principles of right embodied in the nature of things— a belief on which even the philosophy of the common law reposed—continued to have its effect. Especially after the Civil War it was found by the courts, though they did not thus declare, to be covered and protected by the due process clause of the constitutions. Of this we shall see more in later pages of this work.

violation of the due process clause and a deprivation of property.[10] The case deserves special attention because the decision was rendered only a few months before Taney gave his opinion in the Dred Scott case where he used—though rather incidentally—the due process clause of the federal Constitution as a basis for the protection of slavery. Strangest of all strange contradictions and developments from the Revolution to the Civil War! Strange that Taney of all men should have reached out his hand for the new doctrine based on implication and assumption, and strange that doctrines of liberty, beloved by the fathers and the fathers of the fathers, should be used to protect property in slaves. It is a matter of acute interest that amid the agitation for social reform which swept over large portions of the land in the thirties—the humanitarian movement—two purposes stand forth with some distinctness: zeal for the abolition of slavery and determination to control or even extirpate the liquor traffic. Both had to meet the objection that property and vested rights would be encroached upon. In the New York case, referred to above, property in liquor was protected by construction of the due process clause; in the Dred Scott case, slavery in the territories was given judicial protection. Opposition to slavery soon overshadowed all other social objectives and finally brought on civil war; other ambitions for social betterment were thus crowded from the field, to be taken up again in later years.

We must now turn to a brief consideration of some of the leading cases decided in the first twenty years after the accession of Taney. In his very first term, three decisions were rendered which exemplify the difference between the older point of view and the new. In 1830 the Supreme Court had passed upon an act of Missouri providing for the issue of certificates in various denominations which would be receivable in payment of taxes and could be loaned to citizens of the state. The law was held invalid on the ground that it contravened the explicit prohibition in the Constitution against a state's emitting bills of credit. Marshall in giving the opinion said: "To 'emit bills of credit,' conveys to the mind the idea of issuing paper intended to

---

[10] Wynehamer v. New York, 13 New York 378 (1856). "That the prohibitory act, in its operation upon property in intoxicating liquors existing in the hands of any person within this state when the act took effect, is a violation of the provision in the constitution of this state which declares that no person shall be 'deprived of life, liberty or property, without due process of law.'" This statement is taken from the reporter's summary. *Ibid.*, 486. See also R. L. Mott, *Due Process of Law*, pp. 317-318. "This decision was recognized as epoch-making almost as soon as it was rendered." *Ibid.*, p. 318.

circulate through the community for its ordinary purposes, as money, which paper is redeemable at a future day." [11]

Shortly before Marshall's death another case of somewhat similar character arose.[12] Arguments were presented but no decision was rendered, and after the accession of Taney it was reargued. Kentucky had established a bank declared to be the exclusive property of the commonwealth, which was in fact the sole stockholder; it was authorized to issue notes. The Court sustained the act, the opinion being given by Justice McLean. Justice Story vigorously dissented, asserting that, when the cause had been formerly argued, a majority of the justices were decidedly of the opinion that the act was unconstitutional and amounted to an authority to issue bills of credit. "Among that majority", he said, "was the late Mr. Chief Justice Marshall—a name never to be pronounced without reverence." [13] It was not a trifling matter in those days to interfere with a community anxious for paper money. McLean declared: "There is no principle on which the sensibilities of communities are so easily excited, as that which acts upon the currency; none of which States are so jealous as that which is restrictive of the exercise of sovereign powers." [14] It is not our business to criticize the Court, but the layman to-day cannot help thinking that the tender regard for the rights of the states and for the feelings of the western people had some influence; and at all events he is entitled to believe that the Kentucky bank gave ample opportunity for the spread of the evils—the natural progeny of paper money— which the framers of the Constitution had hoped to prevent.[15] But

[11] Craig v. Missouri, 4 Peters 410, 432.

[12] Briscoe v. the Bank of Kentucky, 11 Peters 257 (1837).

[13] Ibid., 328. See, however, Justice Baldwin's statement, where he points out that there were differences in the two cases, and that if the issue of the Briscoe case had been involved in the Craig case, Chief Justice Marshall's opinion would not have carried his Court. Ibid., appendix, p. 113.

[14] Ibid., 312. Reference should be made to Darrington v. the Bank of Alabama, 13 Howard 12 (1851), where the Court held definitely to the doctrine of the Briscoe case, declaring bills issued by a bank were not bills of credit although the state was the sole stockholder and pledged its faith for the ultimate redemption of the bills. When one remembers the importance of the paper money issue in the days when the Constitution was formed and adopted, he is tempted to inquire whether the fathers could have imagined that their purpose could be so easily avoided.

[15] The distinction between the Craig case and the Briscoe case is that in the latter the notes were held not to circulate on the faith of the state: "To constitute a bill of credit within the Constitution, it must be issued by a State, on the faith of the State, and be designed to circulate as money. It must be a paper which circulates on the credit of the State, and is so received and used in the ordinary business of life." Briscoe v. the Bank of Kentucky, 11 Peters 257, 318.

the Court thought otherwise. The decision is a clear indication of the reaction against the extreme nationalistic interpretation which had won its victories under the earlier régime.

Of even greater importance is the Charles River Bridge case.[16] It is of significance not only because it is an indication of the new attitude toward the rights and prerogatives of the states, but also because it announced a doctrine of fundamental importance in connection with the development of social and economic conditions of the time—and indeed of future time. The question brought up for decision was the validity of a Massachusetts act which chartered a corporation, the Warren Bridge Company, and gave it the power to build a bridge across the Charles River, from Charlestown to Boston. The bridge competed for traffic with another bridge, owned and managed by the Charles River Bridge Company, a corporation created by the state about fifty years before. Did the later act of incorporation impair the obligation of the contract embodied in this earlier charter? That charter contained no explicit grant of exclusive rights to the company. Should it nevertheless be so interpreted? The Chief Justice, supported by his colleagues, with the exceptions of Story and Thompson, answered in the negative and upheld the act establishing the Warren Bridge Company.

The Chief Justice first made clear that the Charles River Bridge Company could not support its case upon the principle that the act in question devested vested rights: "It is well settled by the decisions of this court that a State law may be retrospective in its character, and may devest vested rights, and yet not violate the Constitution of the United States. . . ." ". . . it is apparent that the plaintiffs in error cannot sustain themselves here . . . upon the ground that vested rights of property have been devested by the Legislature." [17] This was a momentous announcement, for it held, what was in theory plain enough, viz., that the states were at liberty to manage their own internal affairs; but in addition it swept aside any and all suppositions that the federal courts were to interpret the Constitution and especially the contract clause (unless that clause had been plainly violated) so as to protect property from assaults by state legislation—place property, indeed, under judicial guardianship.

But the main assertion of the Chief Justice was to the effect that

---

[16] Charles River Bridge v. Warren Bridge, 11 Peters 420 (1837).

[17] Ibid., 539-540. The Court cited two decisions: Satterlee v. Matthewson, 2 Peters 380 (1829) ; Watson et al. v. Mercer, 8 Peters 88 (1834).

public grants should be construed strictly and in favor of the state: ". . . in grants by the public nothing passes by implication."[18] The opinion was not simply a guarding of the state from intrusion upon its reserved rights. The principle was one of general application; the state had not only rights but duties; no vague or presumed restriction should be allowed to hamper or retard the performance of those duties. Implicit in the decision—if not plainly and emphatically announced— was the right of a people through their government to meet by legislation the necessities of a developing social structure: ". . . the object and end of all government is to promote the happiness and prosperity of the community by which it is established, and it can never be assumed that the government intended to diminish its power of accomplishing the end for which it was created. And in a country like ours, free, active and enterprising, continually advancing in numbers and wealth; new channels of communication are daily found necessary, both for travel and trade, and are essential to the comfort, convenience, and prosperity of the people. A State ought never to be presumed to surrender this power, because, like the taxing power, the whole community have an interest in preserving it undiminished. . . . The continued existence of a government would be of no great value, if by implications and presumptions, it was disarmed of the powers necessary to accomplish the ends of its creation, and the functions it was designed to perform, transferred to the hands of privileged corporations."[19] A quarter of a century before this, Marshall had announced that a state could impose upon itself the obligation not to tax certain property.[20] Taney was decidedly averse to the extension of a principle which might by implication be used to restrict a state's power to manage its own affairs.

We have already referred to the fact that the Dartmouth College case might have been so applied and so rigorously enforced that the states would have been bereft of powers essential for the management and control of corporations;[21] and we have noticed the way in

[18] Charles River Bridge v. Warren Bridge, 11 Peters 420, 546, referring to United States v. Arredondo, 6 Peters 691, 738, and the cases there cited.
[19] Charles River Bridge v. Warren Bridge, 11 Peters 420, 547-548. It must not be supposed that the Court manufactured the principle that public grants should be construed strictly. The cases cited and the references made to both English and American law forbid such a conclusion. See *Ibid.*, 544-547.
[20] New Jersey v. Wilson, 7 Cranch 164 (1812).
[21] "In truth the principle of the Dartmouth College case, perhaps correct enough when limited as it was applied to a private grant, had been pushed by its advocates to an extreme that would have left our State governments in possession of little

which the states succeeded in maintaining their right of control. In later decades, and especially in the last quarter of the century, when the problem of corporation control was of major importance, the principle laid down by Taney did not need alteration. The courts went much further, asserting the powers of the states and denying that a legislature can "bargain away the public health or the public morals." [22] The states *must* preserve their essential powers.

It is hard to conceive of anything, except the preservation of the union itself, more important than the preservation of the states' right to control corporations and to manage their own affairs unless the control and management be in plain violation of the Constitution; and yet able lawyers a century ago were in a state of consternation. Story declared that he believed a great majority of the ablest lawyers were against the decision. "There will not," he wrote, "I fear, ever in our day, be any case in which a law of a State or of Congress will be declared unconstitutional; for the old constitutional doctrines are fast fading away, and a change has come over the public mind from which I augur little good."

Before the decisions in the Kentucky bank case and the bridge case were rendered, the Court had passed upon another critical question. In the mind of the conservative, clinging stoutly to the doctrines and tendencies of the old régime, it was classed with the others as an example of dangerous doctrines, likely to undermine the foundations of the supreme judicial authority. This case [23] involved the validity of a New York act requiring the master of every vessel arriving in New York from any other state or foreign country to report the name, age, and last legal settlement of every person who had been with him during the voyage. The effect or at least the purpose of the decision was to preserve the police power of the states in order that they might, with a certain degree of freedom, perform the duty of caring for the well-being and happiness of the people. The Court planted itself on what it called "impregnable positions" : "that a State has the same undeniable and unlimited jurisdiction over all persons and things within its territorial limits, as any foreign nation, where that jurisdiction is not surrendered or restrained by the Constitution of the

more than the shell of legislative power." G. W. Biddle, "Constitutional Development in the United States as Influenced by Chief Justice Taney," *Constitutional History of the United States as Seen in the Development of American Law*, p. 132.

[22] Stone *v.* Mississippi, 101 U. S. 814, 819 (1880).

[23] New York *v.* Miln, 11 Peters 102 (1837). The opinion of the Court was delivered by Justice Barbour. Story naturally dissented.

United States. That, by virtue of this, it is not only the right, but the bounden and solemn duty of a State, to advance the safety, happiness and prosperity of its people, and to provide for its general welfare, by any and every act of legislation which it may deem to be conducive to these ends; where the power over the particular subject, or the manner of its exercise is not surrendered or restrained, in the manner just stated. That all those powers which relate to merely municipal legislation, or what may, perhaps, more properly be called internal police, are not thus surrendered or restrained; and that, consequently, in relation to these, the authority of a State is complete, unqualified and exclusive." [24]

That the states possess the police power and have the right to exercise it is an elementary principle of constitutional law; but it is equally true that in the exercise of the power, as the Court declared, a state has no right to encroach upon the field of congressional authority. It was not enough simply to proclaim in any given instance that the act in question was within the police power of the state and therefore valid. The nature and effect of the act had to be examined to ascertain whether in the exercise of the power the state had intruded upon congressional authority. Some general formula, more adequate and applicable than the pronouncements in the Miln case, had ere long to be found.

Ten years after the Miln case, the question we have just been considering arose and presented its difficulties plainly. But before considering the case then arising it is well to recall the fact that in 1827, the Supreme Court, Chief Justice Marshall giving the opinion in the "original package" case,[25] had laid down an important principle and announced the unconstitutionality of a state act requiring importers to pay a license fee. In 1847 the Supreme Court was called upon to consider the validity of acts of three New England states placing certain impositions and restrictions upon the sale of spirituous liquors. The acts were upheld.[26] Various opinions were presented by the justices. The Chief Justice stated the grounds upon which the decision rested. Two of the three cases (the Massachusetts and the Rhode Island cases) did not present serious difficulties; they did not in reality run counter to the "original package" decision. But the New

---

[24] *Ibid.*, 139. Though Justice Barbour gave the opinion, the above may be considered the main plank in Taney's platform.
[25] Brown *v.* Maryland, 12 Wheaton 419.
[26] License Cases, 5 Howard 504.

Hampshire case was different; in that case a barrel of gin which had been purchased in Boston was brought to Dover and there sold in the cask in which it had been transported; and for this sale the sellers were indicted and convicted. Taney contended that there was no congressional legislation on the subject and therefore the state legislation was valid.[27] Admitting the supreme power of Congress over interstate and foreign commerce, he declared that the state, nevertheless, acting for the safety or convenience of trade or for the protection of its citizens, could make regulations for its own ports and for its own territory, and that state regulations of that character were valid unless they came in conflict with a law of Congress. He distinguished this case from the "original package" case by pointing out that the former arose out of commerce with foreign nations which Congress had regulated by law.[28] Forty years after this decision the Court said that the principle laid down in the New Hampshire case—that the law of the state was valid because Congress had made no regulation on the subject—must be regarded as having been distinctly overthrown by numerous cases.[29]

In the License Cases, which we have just considered, Taney indicated that there was a field within which the states could act in the absence of congressional legislation. But in reality no general formula or general principle was clearly announced. If it were admitted that the power of Congress over interstate commerce was not in all cases necessarily exclusive, there still remained a question of how far a state could go. Could a principle or formula be laid down indicating the scope and character of local legislation which might be held valid in the absence of congressional enactment? The answer was given in a decision in 1851, four years after the License Cases, and that decision, though very general in its terms, is so simple that one wonders why it had not been announced before. The Court upheld a pilotage act of Pennsylvania.[30] The opinion was given by Justice Curtis. He referred to existing differences of opinion and then said: "Now, the

[27] The question in Taney's opinion was "whether the grant of power to Congress is of itself a prohibition to the States, and renders all State laws upon the subject null and void." *Ibid.*, 578.

[28] *Ibid.* Taney did not give weight to what was perhaps a dictum in the Brown case: "It may be proper to add, that we suppose the principles laid down in this case, to apply equally to importations from a sister state." Brown *v.* Maryland, 12 Wheaton 419, 449. See, however, Woodruff *v.* Parham, 8 Wallace 123 (1869), where the Court placed a significant limitation on the "original package" doctrine.

[29] Leisy *v.* Hardin, 135 U. S. 100, 118 (1890).

[30] Cooley *v.* Port Wardens, 12 Howard 299, 319.

power to regulate commerce, embraces a vast field, containing not only many, but exceedingly various subjects, quite unlike in their nature; some imperatively demanding a single uniform rule, operating equally on the commerce of the United States in every port; and some, like the subject now in question, as imperatively demanding that diversity, which alone can meet the local necessities of navigation. . . . Whatever subjects of this power are in their nature national, or admit only of one uniform system, or plan of regulation, may justly be said to be of such a nature as to require exclusive legislation by Congress." This was a step forward in the clarification of the subject, and it formed the basis for further exposition at a later time: ". . . where the subject upon which Congress can act under its commercial power is local in its nature or sphere of operation, . . . the State can act until Congress interferes and supersedes its authority; but where the subject is national in its character, . . . and requires uniformity of regulation, . . . Congress can alone act upon it. . . . The absence of any law of Congress on the subject is equivalent to its declaration that commerce in that matter shall be free." [31] The principle was clear; its application often presented difficulty.[32]

To the student of constitutional history the Passenger Cases are of peculiar interest.[33] They came up for decision in 1849, only two years after the License Cases, and involved a similar problem—once again the national control over commerce and on the other hand the power and the duty of the state to protect its citizens. But in this instance the controversy was even more intense than before. Statutes of New York and Massachusetts imposed taxes upon alien passengers

[31] Concurring opinion of Justice Field in Bowman v. Chicago etc. Railway Co., 125 U. S. 465, 507-508 (1888). See also Leisy v. Hardin, 135 U. S. 100 (1890).

[32] "The power to authorize the building of bridges is not to be found in the Federal Constitution; it has not been taken from the States. The States may exercise concurrent or independent power in all cases but three: 1. Where the power is lodged exclusively in the Federal Constitution. 2. Where it is given to the United States and prohibited to the States. 3. Where, from the nature and subjects of the power, it must necessarily be exercised by the National Government exclusively. The power to build bridges over navigable rivers does not fall within either of these exceptions. Until the dormant power of the Constitution is awakened and made effective by appropriate legislation, the reserved power of the States is plenary; and its exercise, in good faith, cannot be made the subject of review by this court." From the syllabus of Gilman v. Philadelphia, 3 Wallace 713 (1866). This general statement of the principles of construction is essentially that of Hamilton in The Federalist, no. XXXII. See Houston v. Moore, 5 Wheaton 1, 49 (1820), where Justice Story, dissenting, laid down a principle similar to this.

[33] 7 Howard 283 (1849). The statutes of the two states were not in all respects the same, but the statement as given in the text sets forth the essential fact.

arriving in the ports of those states. The Court declared them unconstitutional as illegal interference with foreign commerce, but on what reasoning it is difficult to say. The arguments of counsel and the opinions of various justices occupy nearly three hundred pages, and, as the reporter said in his introductory note, there was no opinion of the Court as a body. Four justices dissented from the decision. The Chief Justice in dissent said it must "rest with the State to determine whether any particular class or description of persons are likely to produce discontents or insurrection in its territory, or to taint the morals of its citizens, or to bring among them contagious diseases, or the evils and burdens of a numerous pauper population." [34] The significance of the case is in part indicated by the variety of the opinions rendered and by the intensity of their tone.

The elementary issues in the controversy were in fact entangled with the slavery question. How much the justices were consciously influenced by that fact it is impossible to say. But that slavery was casting its shadow over the Court seems undeniable. Were the members already aware of the likelihood of their being called upon to settle the problems arising from the proposed expansion of slavery into the new west? It is not unlikely, though no expression of opinion from the justices themselves is known to the present writer. Only the year before, the Senate had passed a bill providing that all cases involving property in slaves within the new western territories, which the bill proposed to establish, could be appealed to the Supreme Court. This provision does not, it is true, have any positive and logical connection with the issue before the Court in the Passenger Cases. Plainly present, however, was the question whether each state could exclude free negroes, and—only less plainly—whether the state and the state alone could pass upon the admission of slaves within its borders; furthermore, the right of Congress to regulate and even prohibit interstate traffic in slaves was a matter not without poignant interest.[35]

[34] *Ibid.*, 467. Interesting in this connection is Hannibal and St. Joseph Railway Co. *v.* Husen, 95 U. S. 465 (1878), where the Court held that a state law forbidding the entrance of Texan, Mexican, or Indian cattle during a certain period of the year was unconstitutional. But the Court admitted the right of the state to prevent the entrance of persons and animals suffering from contagious diseases, and to establish quarantine laws; but "it may not interfere with transportation into or through the State, beyond what is absolutely necessary for its self-protection." *Ibid.*, 472.

[35] In his dissenting opinion, Justice Daniel—coming from a state which had a vital interest in the interstate slave traffic—spoke of "the extraordinary doctrine that the States of this Union can have no power to prohibit the introduction of slaves

There had recently been a heated discussion in Congress over the propriety of admitting Florida into the union with a constitution forbidding the entrance of free negroes. Various other states had passed legislation to that effect.[36] An acrimonious dispute had arisen between Massachusetts and South Carolina because of the enforcement of the "negro seamen act" of the latter state, which provided in effect that any negroes employed aboard a vessel entering the state should be confined while the ship was in harbor. Samuel Hoar, a distinguished citizen of Massachusetts, had been expelled from South Carolina when he went thither to institute legal proceedings to test the constitutionality of this act. The legislature announced the right to exclude seditious persons whose presence might be dangerous to the peace of the state, and objected to the presence of an "emissary sent by the State of Massachusetts" with the purpose of interfering with the institutions of South Carolina.

In the case of the Propeller Genesee Chief (1851) the Chief Justice, delivering the opinion of the Court, upheld an act of Congress extending the jurisdiction of the federal district courts to certain cases upon the lakes and navigable waters connecting them. He declared that the act did not intend to regulate commerce; the jurisdiction of the courts could not be made to depend on regulations of commerce. But to justify the authority of Congress in this instance it was necessary for the Court to modify the old law as to the extent of admiralty and maritime jurisdiction. According to English law, admiralty jurisdiction was confined to the ebb and flow of the tide.[37] Taney cited decisions rendered by the Court which appeared to rest on the English definition; but he declared that rule inapplicable to America—as indeed in common sense it was. And still, here was a case which the Chief Justice decided on the basis of a broad and liberal interpretation, on the basis of implied congressional power.[38] It was not quite in accord

within their territory when carried thither for sale or traffic, because the power to regulate commerce is there asserted to reside in Congress alone." *Ibid.*, 498.

[36] Van Buren in argument referred to the laws of fifteen states forbidding or regulating the admission of free people of color. Justice Woodbury referred to the same subject. *Ibid.*, 374, 526. See the chapter on the Missouri Compromise in this work.

[37] 12 Howard 443. "And this definition in England was a sound and reasonable one, because there was no navigable stream in the country beyond the ebb and flow of the tide. . . ." *Ibid.*, 454. The Chief Justice even said that when the Constitution was adopted the English definition was equally proper here.

[38] Justice Daniel naturally dissented: ". . . now, without there having been engrafted any new provision on the Constitution, without the alteration of one letter

with his doctrine that congressional power should not be allowed to rest upon mere implication, a doctrine which he had in sundry other instances forcibly upheld.[39] In this instance geographic facts were too strong for academic theory, and the police power of the state was not endangered.

Two more cases of importance must be given passing notice. In Luther v. Borden (1849), a case arising from the so-called Dorr Rebellion in Rhode Island, the Court refused to pass upon some of the critical issues, declaring that it was not its function to settle political questions—a distinctly significant conclusion.[40] The Wheeling Bridge case (1851)[41] illustrates once more the difficulty of finding the limits of state authority and the bearing of the commerce clause of the Constitution. The question at issue was the right of the state of Virginia to authorize the bridging of a navigable stream wholly within her limits. The Court decided against the right. Taney and Daniel dissented. The former said: "The Ohio being a public navigable stream, Congress have undoubtedly the power to regulate commerce upon it. . . . But this power has not been exercised. . . . The bridge in question is entirely within the Territory of Virginia. Prior to the adoption of the Constitution of the United States, she had an unquestionable right to authorize its erection. She still possesses the same control over the river, subject to the power of Congress, so far as concerns the regulation of commerce."[42] The principle laid down by the Chief Justice was in later years practically upheld by the Court.[43]

of that instrument . . . the jurisdiction of the admiralty is to be measured by miles, and by the extent of territory which may have been subsequently acquired. . . ." *Ibid.*, 465.

[39] The decision was foreshadowed in Waring v. Clarke, 5 Howard 441 (1847). In that case, as in so many others, there was dissent. Woodbury, Grier, and Daniel dissented. The first two came from the north, Daniel from Virginia. Wayne of Georgia rendered the decision.

[40] 7 Howard 1.   [41] Pennsylvania v. the Wheeling Bridge Co., 13 Howard 518.
[42] *Ibid.*, 579-580, 583.

[43] Willamette Iron Bridge Co. v. Hatch, 125 U. S. 1 (1888). In 1829 the Court, Chief Justice Marshall giving the opinion, had held that a dam stopping a navigable creek "must be supposed to abridge the rights of those who have been accustomed to use it. But this abridgment, unless it comes in conflict with the constitution or a law of the United States, is an affair between the government of Delaware and its citizens. . . ." Willson v. Black-bird Creek Marsh Co., 2 Peters 245, 251. See also Gilman v. Philadelphia, 3 Wallace 713 (1866). It seems as if a distinction might properly be made between the Wheeling Bridge case, on the one hand, and the Gilman and Willamette Bridge cases, on the other, because in the first of these cases the river was not in its whole course confined to a single state, and an obstruction would interfere with free use of the river by other riparian states.

CHAPTER XXXV

EARLY CONTROVERSIES OVER THE SLAVERY PROBLEM (1833-1842)

Nullification had been called into action and state sovereignty with all its mysteries had been exhibited in opposition to the tariff. There was at the beginning no open connection between state sovereignty and slavery. But the wedlock was soon to be consummated.[1] As slavery reached out westward, taking up new areas in the old states and extending into the Mississippi basin, an economic basis was laid for sectional sentiment. State sovereignty and local pride could then rely on a developing sense of sectional interest. The doctrine, inaugurated against the tariff, was soon used to deny the right to interfere with the slaveholder; but the real danger to the union was not so much the "interposition" of a single state, as the development of a sectional consciousness, a consciousness based on the possession of a "peculiar" institution which was daily becoming more peculiar.

The rise of the abolitionists is of importance;[2] but the abolition movement cannot properly be isolated and treated as altogether separate from certain main movements and qualities of the day. In reality,

[1] Benton, speaking of earlier conditions in the south and comparing them with the situation in the thirties, wrote: "A real change had come, and this change, the effect of many causes, was wholly attributed to one—the unequal working of the Federal Government—which gave all the benefits of the Union to the North, and all its burdens to the South. And that was the point on which Southern discontent broke out—on which it openly rested until 1835; when it was shifted to the danger of slave property." T. H. Benton, *Thirty Years' View*, II, p. 133.

[2] For the early history of the antislavery movement in America, see Hart, *Slavery and Abolition*, ch. XI. For a fuller study, see A. D. Adams, *The Neglected Period of Anti-Slavery in America (1808-1831)*. "When Jackson became president, in 1829, anti-slavery seemed, after fifty years of effort, to have spent its force. The voice of the churches was no longer heard in protest; the abolitionist societies were dying out; there was hardly an abolitionist militant in the field; the Colonization Society absorbed most of the public interest in the subject, and it was doing nothing to help either the free negro or the slave; in Congress there was only one anti-slavery man, and his efforts were without avail. It was a gloomy time for the little band of people who believed that slavery was poisonous to the south, hurtful to the north, and dangerous to the Union." Hart, *op. cit.*, pp. 165-166.

473

if we study the abolitionists carefully, we find that by the very extravagance or intensity of their zeal they gave conspicuous evidence of the social mind, or of social tendencies, not so readily discovered in more restrained efforts or more placid movements. Great social movements do not thrive in shallow or infertile soil. The decade beginning with 1830, in western Europe as well as in America, was preëminently the era of humanitarianism, of social and political reform, of movement toward a wider and freer democracy.[3] "It was now the day of ideals in every camp," wrote John Morley in his *Life of Richard Cobden*. "The general restlessness was as intense among reflecting Conservatives as among reflecting Liberals. . . . A great wave of humanity, of benevolence, of desire for improvement,—a great wave of social sentiment, in short,—poured itself among all who had the faculty of large and disinterested thinking." Morley was writing of England but this tumult of new—and yet not new—emotions showed itself in America; it appeared conspicuously among the intellectuals of New England. Emerson's essay on "New England Reformers" should be read by anyone desiring to understand the agitation of the reforming mind. "What a fertility of projects for the salvation of the world! One apostle thought all men should go to farming, and another that no man should buy or sell, that the use of money was the cardinal evil; another that the mischief was in our diet, that we eat and drink damnation. These made unleavened bread, and were foes to the death to fermentation. . . . Others devoted themselves to the worrying of churches and meetings for public worship; and the fertile forms of antinomianism among the elder puritans seemed to have their match in the plenty of the new harvest of reform. . . . A restless, prying, conscientious criticism broke out in unexpected quarters. Who gave me the money with which I bought my coat? Why should professional labor and that of the counting-house be paid so disproportionately to the labor of the porter and woodsawyer?"

There were many movements or new social activities in various

---

[3] ". . . the general humanitarian movement was by no means solely an American movement; it showed itself in Europe as well as on this side of the water. Furthermore, it was closely associated with, or it embodied within itself, the fundamental philosophy of developing democracy, even political democracy; it helped toward the enlargement of the suffrage, the growing appreciation of man's right to self-government, and it made for an improvement in the conditions of labor. . . . There was a general trend toward social reform, which in succeeding years swept strongly onward and has by no means spent its force at the present moment." A. C. McLaughlin, *Steps in the Development of American Democracy*, pp. 118-119.

fields: temperance, religion, newspapers, public education, missionary societies, and labor. Even nationalism—involving a sense of unity combined with individual responsibility—was a mark of the developing social sense. In these movements we find in general two tendencies that were, or appear to be, mutually antithetical: revolt against the formalism of the social order or zeal for personal freedom and, on the other hand, the establishment of communities or associations—individual liberty coupled with a sense of responsibility for one's fellows. For the newer humanitarianism was in essence different from the individualistic doctrine of an earlier day. Democracy, indeed, contains within itself these two elementary ideas which superficially appear to be in conflict.

If we accept these statements, we are freed from the notion that the antislavery movement was isolated and essentially peculiar and that even Garrisonian abolitionism was distinct and entirely isolated from the main movements of the time. The real nature of the tragic controversy which began in the fourth decade of the century to menace the union is seen only when we recognize the developing forces of occidental civilization—or what we still call civilization. It is necessary to see the south seeking to maintain a worn-out system of economic order and battling against a resistless tide of social progress, or, if progress be denied, of social change. The struggle to maintain the old was long, brave, able, hopeless, foredoomed to failure.

Garrisonian abolitionism was permeated with religious zeal. To the followers of this intrepid leader, slavery was not a misfortune or a wrong, but a sin, a corroding sin. Like all other sins, it should be cast forth; to delay was to indulge in willful wickedness. No excuse for moral iniquity could be based on historical forces or on the danger and the difficulty of immediate emancipation. Sympathy with the slaveholders, caught in a net which they had not themselves cast, played small part in the drama of the abolitionist's denunciation of wrongdoing. Once again appear the diversity and the contradictions of this amazing life of ours: here was Garrison filled with zeal for the welfare of the blacks, but filled with everything but pity for the whites who held the blacks in bondage. Ere long, while he and his fellows were proclaiming no union with slaveholders, they announced their devotion to a greater union: "Our country is the world—our countrymen are all mankind." Though the maintenance of the Constitution and the union was necessary for the success of democracy and its mission, the Garrisonian abolitionist scorned the Constitution as a covenant with death and an agreement with hell.[4]

The abolitionists of the Garrison type were at no time a very large number; nor were they a very large portion of the earnest opponents of slavery. Among the antislavery forces there were, naturally, all degrees of activity and interest; some were opposed to slavery on principle, but were content with their mental disapproval; others were outspoken and vigorous; comparatively few were committed to the doctrine of sin and instant repentance or to other ideals cherished by the Garrisonian cult. The advanced abolitionists had no patience with mere remedial measures; ere long they refused to vote under a government which recognized slavery. Equally earnest but more worldly-minded and practical souls were desirous of doing what could be done, and after a time many of them joined actively in political and party movements. Acrid attack upon the slave-owner and demands for his immediate repentance could not bring about emancipation, and it did not.

It is often said that the violence of the abolitionists—their scathing and maddening attack alone—aroused the southerners to bitterness and made certain the direful antagonism which ended in war and forcible manumission. This may be true. Undoubtedly Garrison's words did not turn away wrath. A slaveholder did not relish being held up as a sinner and the embodiment of evil. But no one of us can know that if Garrison had used gentler manners, slavery would have peaceably disappeared. We know that certain southerners had before 1830 worked out a philosophy of slavery [5] which was doubtless strengthened in its appeal by vehement attack and also by less vociferous but irritating disapproval. The slaveholding system was so strongly intrenched, so influential, so dominant, that strenuous defense, even reaching into philosophy and religion, was inevitable. At all events, the south, especially the older lower south, quickly reacted against criticism.[6]

---

[4] "And your covenant with death shall be disannulled, and your agreement with hell shall not stand. . . ." Isaiah, XXVIII, 18. Garrisonian abolitionism outran itself; so anxious was Garrison for freedom for everyone that he despised the nation and nevertheless reached out for a world of brotherhood.

[5] See A. O. Craven, *Edmund Ruffin Southerner*, pp. 124-125; W. E. Dodd, *The Cotton Kingdom*, pp. 48-70.

[6] There had been a good deal of opposition to slavery in the southern states. Still we find the Governor of South Carolina recommending a "firm determination to resist, at the threshold, every invasion of our domestic tranquillity, and to preserve our sovereignty and independence as a state, . . . and, if an appeal to the first principles of the right of self-government be disregarded, and reason be successfully

The north was not at ease. Despite a widespread disapproval of slavery in the abstract, the northern people in the thirties disapproved of agitation. Antislavery sentiment grew, partly by the very effort to suppress discussion; and after a time the chief crusader was allowed to talk and write in peace—such peace as his own tumultuous spirit allowed him. Every passing year made more difficult the solution of the great problem by some process of gradual improvement, a process by which the two sections could work harmoniously.

The preceding paragraphs, brief and inadequate though they are, may explain in some degree why and how it was that America was slow and backward in the task of casting off slavery. Other nations moved on, but America had to crush slavery by force, to pay the enormous price of civil war. In explaining or extenuating our tardiness and our final resort to bloodshed, it is necessary to remember the tremendous importance of cotton, the fact that slavery was not, as in the case of the British empire, in colonies, but in the very midst of the nation, that the industrial and social fabric of a large section and of millions of people was built upon it, that the slaves were members of a backward race, and that our union was not a centralized unitary state, but a confederated republic. It is not, however, the task of this work to depict the play of the conflicting forces of freedom and slavery except as the contest involved constitutional discussion. This must now be briefly traced.

The new activity of the antislavery forces and the rise of new sentiment brought before Congress a number of questions involving constitutional power. Should the slaves be emancipated in the District of Columbia, or, at least, should the slave trade be there forbidden? What should be done with the antislavery petitions submitted to Congress? Could and should antislavery propaganda, the so-called incendiary publications, be excluded from the mails? Before 1835 there was not much discussion of either the right of petition or of slavery in the District. In the latter part of that year, the debate began. Peti-

combatted by sophistry and error, there would be more glory in forming a rampart with our bodies on the confines of our territory, than to be the victims of a successful rebellion, or the slaves of a great consolidated government." The South Carolina senate and the house passed resolutions. Governor Troup of Georgia in 1825 said, "Temporize no longer—make known your resolution that this subject shall not be touched by them, but at their peril. . . ." Words of this kind were brought forth not by abolitionism, but by opposition to the Negro Seamen Act, by resolutions of the Ohio legislature advocating gradual emancipation and favoring colonization of free negroes, and by a bill introduced by Senator King for using funds from land sales to aid in emancipation and removal of slaves. Ames, *State Documents*, no. 5, p. 11 ff.

tions praying for the abolition of slavery and the slave trade in the District were presented in the House by Fairfield of Maine, and one of them was summarily laid on the table. Discussion arose because of the motion of Slade of Vermont that Fairfield's second petition be printed. He defended briefly the desirability of printing. The Speaker interposed with the ruling that, on the motion to print, it was not in order to go into the merits of the petition. The motion to print, as well as the petition, was laid on the table by large majorities.

Two days later (December 18, 1835) another petition was presented, and Hammond of South Carolina moved that it be not received. "He could not sit there and see the rights of the southern people assaulted day after day, by the ignorant fanatics from whom these memorials proceed." [7] Discussion followed concerning procedure under the rules of the House. Thomas of Maryland, who had previously voted to lay petitions on the table, now declared petitions should be received and the announcement distinctly made that they were unreasonable and ought not to be granted. And yet he saw what was coming: "Without our agency, indeed in defiance of all precautions on the part of Congress, the power and purpose of the General Government to interfere with the question of slavery has been, and will be, discussed in every newspaper, in every periodical publication, from Maine to Missouri. It is a gross error to suppose that this House can, by a mere *sic volo,* give law to the people of the United States." The petition, on the second day of debate, was laid on the table by a vote of 140 to 76. On the negative side were arrayed such strange companions as John Quincy Adams of Massachusetts and Hammond and Pickens of South Carolina.

But the matter was not so easily decided. Immediately another question arose and gave further opportunity for debate. Adams, who had been chosen to Congress soon after his retirement from the presidency, now entered the lists and began the long contest for freedom of petition. The right could have found no abler or more earnest advocate. And still, at the beginning at least, he hoped discussion would be avoided; he believed that orderly and respectful treatment of memorials on the dread subject would not foment debate, but an attempt at suppression would inevitably have that result. This old, experienced statesman, speaking freely, irrepressible, saw one thing most clearly: the way to arouse the people was to attempt a policy of enforced silence. At first, therefore, he advocated submission of memorials to

[7] *Congressional Debates (Register of Debates).* 24 Cong., 1 sess., col. 1967.

a committee and the unanimous acceptance of its report: [8] "And what will the discussion amount to? A discussion upon the merits of slavery. . . . Well, sir, what becomes of these incendiary pamphlets, the speeches in this House, if they go to the public? . . . The newspapers report these speeches; every speech is circulated through your whole country; and how can you arrest it? Will you introduce a resolution that members of this House shall not speak a word in derogation of the sublime merits of slavery? . . . Well, sir, you begin with suppressing the right of petition; you must next suppress the right of speech in this House; for you must offer a resolution that every member who dares to express a sentiment of this kind shall be expelled, or that the speeches shall not go forth to the public—shall not be circulated." [9]

During the winter the vexed subject would not down. January 4, Adams presented a petition from certain citizens of Massachusetts praying for the abolition of slavery and the slave trade in the District. He appeared willing to accept the course recently followed and to move that it be laid on the table. A Virginia member asked if the petition had been received and the Speaker said it had not; whereupon a Georgia member moved that it be not received. Evidently the proslavery leaders had decided upon final and conclusive measures; for the Speaker, James K. Polk of Tennessee, now said that, upon looking up authorities, he had formed the opinion that the first question to be decided upon the motion of a member was whether the petition should be received.[10] This was a magnificent blunder; discussion followed discussion, not only on the rules but also on slavery. Adams appealed from the decision of the chair.[11] Not until three weeks later was the decision rendered, the House supporting the Speaker's ruling. "Mr. Adams said he was glad the question had been at last decided. By the decision, every member of the House, having a petition to present, is authorized to debate, as long as he shall think proper, the question of reception, whether on slavery or any other subject." [12]

8 *Ibid.*, col. 2001.
9 *Ibid.*, col. 2002.
10 *Ibid.*, col. 2129.
11 "Mr. Hardin rose to a question of order. It was not in order, in his estimation, to discuss the motion of the gentleman at this time. The order of business now seemed to be, first, prayers, then the journal was read, and afterwards, on almost every morning, the gentleman from Massachusetts [Mr. Adams] made a speech." *Ibid.*, col. 2315.
12 *Ibid.*, col. 2316. It is to be noticed that a Maine member, Leonard Jarvis, in January, 1836, offered a resolution declaring that the subject of the abolition of

In May, the fatal step was taken, fatal because the effort to prevent discussion and to quiet the rising fever increased agitation beyond the walls of Congress. A committee made a report and introduced resolutions announcing that Congress had no authority to interfere with slavery in the states and ought not to interfere with slavery in the District of Columbia; that it was extremely important that the agitation of the subject should be finally arrested to restore tranquillity to the public mind; and that "all petitions, memorials, resolutions, propositions, or papers, relating in any way, or to any extent whatsoever, to the subject of slavery, or the abolition of slavery, shall, without being either printed or referred, be laid upon the table, and that no further action whatever shall be had thereon." These resolutions were passed, May 25-26, 1836. Adams, when called upon to vote on the final resolution, said, "I hold the resolution to be a direct violation of the constitution of the United States, the rules of this House, and the rights of my constituents."

Of course this did not restore tranquillity to the public mind; the "gag resolutions" awakened popular opposition and they did not altogether prevent discussion in Congress. The earnest advocates of the full right of petition, like Adams, as well as stern and more radical opponents of slavery, such as Slade, could find a loophole somewhere by which to intrude the hated subject. On February 6, 1837, Adams rose, said he had a petition from twenty-two slaves, and asked if it came under the rule. Vociferous confusion followed. There were demands for censure of the presumptuous member. But nothing like that could be done without debate; and Adams had his day. The scene reminds the reader of the famous lines of Macaulay about the boys ranging the woods to start a hare.[13] He reminded his excited accusers that he had only asked the Speaker for his opinion; he had presented no petition; and, to throw oil on the fire, he remarked that in reality the petition asked not for the emancipation of the slaves but for their continuance in bondage.[14] The ironic humor of the whole affair would have stirred any normal-minded body to laughter; but on this subject

slavery in the District ought not to be entertained, and petitions ought to be laid on the table and not referred or printed. *Ibid.*, col. 2241.

[13] "All shrank, like boys who, unaware,
Ranging the woods to start a hare,
Come to the mouth of the dark lair
Where, growling low, a fierce old bear
Lies amidst bones and blood."

[14] *Congressional Debates (Register of Debates)*, 24 Cong., 2 sess., col. 1611.

the House was no longer normal; it was more nearly so after Adams had finished his scathing counter-attack and his defense of free speech. We may pass over the debates and the developing irritation during the next two or three years to notice that on January 28, 1840, the House adopted as a standing rule "That no petition, memorial, resolution, or other paper praying the abolition of slavery in the District of Columbia, or any State or Territory, or the slave trade between the States or Territories of the United States in which it now exists, shall be received by this House, or entertained in any way whatever." Nearly five years later this rule was repealed (December, 1844). It had worked immeasurable harm to the proslavery cause, had aroused intense opposition at the north, had linked in men's minds the repression of free speech and petition with the slavery cause, had widened and deepened the chasm between north and south; it had helped to place the whole dreadfully perplexing problem beyond the point where peaceful and considered plans of restriction or gradual emancipation could be carefully and calmly examined.[15]

The purely technical question of the right to refuse all attention to a petition, as well as the authority to deal with emancipation or the slave trade in the District, sinks into comparative insignificance when compared with the consequences of suppression and the worse than futile attempts to preserve silence. But a word is needed. Any legislative body is justified in refusing to consider petitions concerning a topic over which it has no authority. Arguments were put forth to the effect that Congress had no constitutional power to deal with slavery in the District, but such arguments will scarcely bear inspection. Congress had as much authority as had any state to deal with emancipation within its own limits.[16] Again, no legislative body can justly allow

---

[15] For discussions of those fateful five years, see H. von Holst, *The Constitutional and Political History of the United States*, II, especially pp. 475-478 on "Adams's 'Trial.'"

[16] Arguments on constitutional power to emancipate can be found in *Congressional Debates (Register of Debates)*, 24 Cong., 1 sess., cols. 2020-2021. Of special interest is the speech of Wise of Virginia. *Ibid.*, col. 2024 ff. He reached the conclusion that Congress was without technical authority; by this reasoning slavery, it would appear, was riveted forever on the District and hence on the nation. For Slade's speech and reply to Wise, see *Ibid.*, col. 2042 ff. Slade effectively showed that but recently the subject of slavery and emancipation had been openly discussed in Virginia and Kentucky. *Ibid.*, cols. 2058-2060. Much has been made of the extreme position of the abolitionists; and one should read Wise's speech, which, aside from the constitutional argument, illustrates the sort of declamatory denunciation which was bound to awaken resentment at the north. It was not enough to complain of Garrisonian taunts and vituperation; anyone proposing emancipation in the District, however

itself to be smothered by countless petitions and ensuing discussion on a subject with which it does not care to deal. Justification for refusal to discuss is thus dependent on the extent of the troublesome intrusion. But such consideration at once leads us into a broader view of constitutional right. To refuse to receive, to reject utterly without notice, a petition dealing with matters vitally interesting to many people is in practical effect to nullify in that particular the whole sacred right of petition. Free popular government does not consist only of periodical elections or of setting up for two or more years a hermetically-sealed legislature without avenues of contact with the people during the term for which officials are chosen.

Thus far we have omitted the discussion in the Senate. But the speeches there are of great interest and deserve attention. That body at no time went quite so far as the House. No general rule was adopted against reception, but petitions were summarily laid on the table and the effect on the public mind was much the same as that produced by the more extreme procedure of the other chamber. Debates in the winter of 1836 are of special interest. There was keen argument, but very little defense of the purpose of the petitions, yet much serious declamation about the danger of discussion, as the discussion went on from week to week.

One, and only one, quotation can be given, and that from Calhoun, disclosing as it does his fervent anxiety to bring the south to a common position on this one subject of slavery. He seemed in his fervor actually to have thought the outright refusal to accept petitions would have the effect or some effect in silencing northern opposition. "The Senators from the slaveholding States, who most unfortunately have committed themselves to vote for receiving these incendiary petitions, tell us that whenever the attempt shall be made to abolish slavery, they will join with us to repel it. . . . I announce to them that they are now called on to redeem their pledge. The attempt is now making. The work is going on daily and hourly. The war is waged, not only in the most dangerous manner, but in the only manner it can be waged. Do they expect that the abolitionists will resort to arms, and commence a crusade to liberate our slaves by force? Is this what they mean when they speak of the attempt to abolish slavery? If so, let me tell our friends of the South who differ from us, that the war which the

courteously, was in southern eyes heaping insult on the south and endangering the very foundations of society. Further constitutional arguments may be found in *Ibid.*, 2070 ff.

abolitionists wage against us is of a very different character, and far more effective. It is a war of religious and political fanaticism, mingled, on the part of the leaders, with ambition and the love of notoriety, and waged, not against our lives, but our character. . . . How can it be successfully met? . . . There is but one way: we must meet the enemy on the frontier, on the question of receiving; we must secure that important pass—it is our Thermopylae." [17] Never did he speak more wisely; and never more inadequately; slavery could not be saved by enforced silence; and yet only by silence—as he clearly saw— could it be saved. If that appear to be an insoluble paradox, it must stand at that.

Calhoun's words are significant because there was already at the south, as has been pointed out, a fairly well developed philosophy of slavery, though of recent origin, and there was growing up, not only a social philosophy but a religious, as well as a Biblical, defense of the system. Religious agitation against slavery had to be met by religious pronouncements and by the awakening of religious fervor.[18] You cannot, by passing resolutions and rules in Congress, stem the tide of social movement, supported by religious enthusiasm. After all, the great conflicts are conflicts of opinion and often of opinion inflamed by religious devotion—"religious" in a very general sense, meaning enthusiastic and emotional response to a cause believed to be right and just, a cause, in this case, based on conscientious beliefs and scruples.

While the petition debates went on, another problem thrust itself upon Congress and the country: the right to exclude "incendiary"

[17] March 9, 1836. *Ibid.*, cols. 774-775. Clay objected to receiving and immediately rejecting a petition. "He thought that the right of petition required of the servants of the people to examine, deliberate, and decide, either to grant or refuse the prayer of a petition, giving the reasons for such decision." *Ibid.*, cols. 778-779. For a later presentation of Clay's position (1839) on the right to provide for emancipation, see *The Life and Speeches of Henry Clay* (1843 ed.), II, p. 395 ff. Lest one get the opinion that the objection to the abolition petitions came solely from the south, it is well to notice resolutions passed by the Maine legislature and presented to the federal Senate (April 8, 1836). They were passed unanimously by the Maine senate and almost unanimously by the house. They asserted that the government of the United States is one of enumerated, limited, and defined powers, that the power of regulating slavery within the states does not belong to Congress, that the states, "with certain defined exceptions," are, with respect to each other, distinct and sovereign states; any interference by a state, or by the citizens of a state, with the domestic concerns of another state, "tends to break up the compromises of, and to disturb, the Union." *Congressional Debates (Register of Debates)*, 24 Cong., 1 sess., col. 1109.

[18] I am not implying by these sentences that the southerners were insincere or hypocritical. I am speaking of a natural tendency to develop a philosophy and, if need be, a religious enthusiasm to support a cause.

publications from the mail. Under fear awakened by the Turner insurrection in Virginia (1831) the south was greatly excited by the prospect of similar disorders. In the summer of 1835 there was much excitement in South Carolina over the discovery of a considerable quantity of inflammatory matter.[19] The Charleston post office was broken into and the obnoxious material carried off and burned on the Parade Ground. The postmaster brought the subject of the use of the mails to the attention of Postmaster-General Kendall, who replied that he had no authority to exclude matter from the mails; he said, however, to the New York postmaster: ". . . you and the other postmasters who have assumed the responsibility of stopping these inflammatory papers, will, I have no doubt, stand justified in that step before your country and all mankind."

In his annual message of December, 1835, Jackson referred to incendiary material and expressed the belief that doubtless no respectable portion of the people could feel anything but "indignant regret at conduct so destructive of the harmony and peace of the country, and so repugnant to the principles of our national compact and to the dictates of humanity and religion." He suggested the passing of a law to prohibit, "under severe penalties, the circulation in the Southern States, through the mail, of incendiary publications intended to instigate the slaves to insurrection." In the Senate, the subject, on the motion of Calhoun, was referred to a committee of five; its members consisted of four from the slaveholding states and one from the north. But the committee could not reach agreement. It finally introduced a report and proposed a bill, all the terms of which satisfied only a minority of the committee.[20] The constitutional questions raised in the discussion are still of unusual interest.

The bill, it should be noted, did not carry out the President's suggestion, for the bill provided for the punishment of any deputy

---

[19] In 1835, a circular from the American Anti-Slavery Society was sent to the auxiliary societies asking for money for agents, periodicals, and distribution of tracts. Many tracts and papers were printed and sent into the south. None, it was said, were sent to negroes; but of course the south took alarm not to be wondered at. Alarm was followed by violence. For some details, see J. B. McMaster, *A History of the People of the United States*, VI. p. 272 ff. The Anti-Slavery Society of Massachusetts indignantly denied that it had been "guilty of circulating incendiary publications among the southern slaves." Nor, it believed, was any antislavery society guilty. "We have never advocated the right of physical resistance, on the part of the oppressed." Reference should be made to "Walker's Appeal" which pictured "wretchedness in consequence of slavery" and found its way to the south (1829).

[20] *Congressional Debates (Register of Debates)*, 24 Cong., 1 sess., col. 385.

postmaster who knowingly received or put into the mail "any pamphlet, newspaper, handbill, or other paper . . . touching the subject of slavery, addressed to any person or post office in any State, . . . where, by the laws of the said State, . . . their circulation is prohibited." [21] The President's plan implied the right of the government to decide what was objectionable and what not; it might indeed have tacitly admitted that the government was not under obligation to act at all; but the bill placed the duty on the government to recognize and give effect to the laws of the states. Calhoun was now prepared to use his sovereignty doctrine as a shield for slavery. The course of the debate, we unfortunately cannot follow in detail; the yellow pages of *The Globe* or the *Register of Debates* furnish interesting reading to-day.[22]

Of particular consequence was Calhoun's position.[23] The federal government was under obligation to protect the states, and "Though the power of the general Government over the mail is delegated, it is not more clear and unquestionable than the rights of the States over the subject of slavery—a right which neither has been nor can be denied. In fact, I might take higher grounds, if higher grounds were possible, by showing that the rights of the States are as expressly reserved as those of the general Government are delegated. . . . Will any rational being say that the laws of the States of this Union, which are necessary to their peace, security, and very existence, ought to yield to the laws of the general Government regulating the Post Office,

[21] *Ibid.,* col. 383.

[22] "Who is to determine, and in what manner, whether the constitution of Massachusetts, which declares that all men are born free and equal, or the declaration of independence . . . touch the subject of slavery, or are incendiary? . . . if I wish to send a letter, a paper; yes, sir, the declaration of independence itself, through the Post Office, it must first be scrutinized by a clerk, to ascertain whether it violates the laws of Alabama, Carolina, or some other State; and if, in his opinion, the subject of slavery is touched, so as to offend one of these sweeping laws, I am denied the privilege of the mail." Davis of Massachusetts, *Ibid.,* col. 1106.

[23] "But the principle of the message goes still farther," Calhoun pointed out. "It assumes for Congress jurisdiction over the liberty of the press. The framers of the constitution (or rather those jealous patriots who refused to consent to its adoption without amendments to guard against the abuse of power) have, by the first amended article, provided that Congress shall pass no law abridging the liberty of the press, with the view of placing the press beyond the control of congressional legislation. But this cautious foresight would prove in vain, if we should concede to Congress the power which the President assumes of discriminating in reference to character what publications shall or shall not be transmitted by the mail. It would place in the hands of the general Government an instrument more potent to control the freedom of the press than the sedition law itself, as is fully established in the report." *Ibid.,* col. 1138.

which at best is a mere accommodation and convenience, and this when this Government was formed *by the States* mainly with a view to secure more perfectly their peace and safety? But one answer can be given. All must feel that it would be improper for the laws of eleven States in such case to yield to those of the general Government, and, of course, that the latter ought to yield to the former. When I say *ought,* I do not mean on the principle of concession. I take higher grounds. I mean under the obligation of the constitution itself." [24]

But, in the opinion of the great Carolinian, the slaveholding states had a constitutional remedy. In closing his great speech of April 12, 1836, Calhoun turned conclusively to "interposition", that is to say, to nullification. "If you refuse co-operation with our laws, and conflict should ensue between your and our law, the southern States will never yield to the superiority of yours. We have a remedy in our hands, which, in such event, we shall not fail to apply. We have high authority for asserting that, in such cases, 'State interposition is the rightful remedy'—a doctrine first announced by Jefferson—adopted by the patriotic and republican State of Kentucky by a solemn resolution, in 1798, and finally carried out into successful practice on a recent occasion, ever to be remembered, by the gallant State which I, in part, have the honor to represent." [25] In other words, what was best for the states in the protection of their reserved rights, and especially in the protection of slavery, was a question for the states to answer; in such a decision the general government must acquiesce. If the general government refused to acquiesce, then nullification and presumably, if need be, secession must follow. But the result was not what Calhoun hoped. The bill introduced in February was defeated in June by a vote of twenty-five to nineteen. A bill was finally passed making it a penal offense for a postmaster unlawfully to detain and not deliver mail-matter to the person addressed.

Naturally there was comment on the freedom of the press and denial of the right of Congress to exclude material from the mail. In light of later construction of the Constitution, we can speedily dispose of some of these problems. Congress can certainly determine that certain matter must not be carried in the mail; in managing the post office it can exercise what is sometimes called (probably improperly) the federal police power—the right, in exercising its granted authority,

[24] *Ibid.,* cols. 1144-1145.
[25] *Ibid.,* col. 1148.

to take into consideration the peace and well-being of society.[26] What limits there may be upon this power of exclusion has not been authoritatively decided, but it has been declared that in the enforcement of an act the protection furnished by constitutional provisions, notably the fourth amendment, is not to be infringed. The Court has also declared that if printed matter be excluded from the mail, its transportation in other ways cannot be forbidden, and that no regulations can be enforced against the transportation of printed matter in the mail so as to interfere in any manner with the freedom of the press.[27] Whether Congress can enforce the right of carrying into the state and delivering mail-matter held by the state to be seditious or dangerous has not been passed upon by the Supreme Court. The question would seem properly to turn upon the moment when the material becomes subject to the state law.[28]

Was Calhoun totally wrong or can Congress recognize in any way the laws of the states and, by acting or refusing to act, support or give effectiveness to those laws? In light of decisions of a later day, there appears now to be no difficulty in answering that question. The problem arose in connection with state prohibition laws; an act of Congress

[26] "The circulation of newspapers is not prohibited, but the government declines itself to become an agent in the circulation of printed matter which it regards as injurious to the people." Ex parte Rapier, 143 U. S. 110, 133 (1892).

[27] The Supreme Court has upheld the right of Congress to exclude lottery circulars and newspapers containing lottery advertisements from the mail. Ex parte Rapier, 143 U. S. 110 (1892). In an earlier case, the Court, upholding a federal statute making it a penal offense to send lottery circulars through the mail, called attention to the obligation to recognize the fourth amendment and said also, "Nor can any regulations be enforced against the transportation of printed matter in the mail, which is open to examination, so as to interfere in any manner with the freedom of the press. Liberty of circulating is as essential to that freedom as liberty of publishing; indeed, without the circulation, the publishing would be of little use. If, therefore, printed matter be excluded from the mails, its transportation in any other way cannot be forbidden by Congress." Ex parte Jackson, 96 U. S. 727, 733 (1878). Under the commerce power the carrying of lottery tickets by an express company from one state to another can be prohibited. See Champion v. Ames, 188 U. S. 321 (1903). For further discussion, see Lewis Publishing Co. v. Morgan, 229 U. S. 288 (1913); Milwaukee Publishing Co. v. Burleson, 255 U. S. 407 (1921).

[28] In 1857 Attorney-General Cushing gave his opinion concerning this matter. The crucial portion of the opinion is as follows: "On the whole, then, it seems clear to me that a deputy postmaster, or other officer of the United States, is not required by law to become, knowingly, the enforced agent or instrument of enemies of the public peace, to disseminate, in their behalf, within the limits of any one of the States of the Union, printed matter, the design and tendency of which are to promote insurrections in such State." He was discussing the act of 1836. *Official Opinions of the Attorneys General*, VIII, p. 501. We are, however, entitled to question this opinion as of present validity.

provided that liquors transported into a state should upon arrival be subject to the police power of the state and should not be exempted therefrom by reason of their being introduced in original packages. If Congress in its discretion can determine what is or is not a suitable regulation of commerce, and can adopt, if it sees fit, regulations intended to give effect to the laws of the state,[29] it can presumably take the same position under the post office power.

But when all is said, the important fact is not the power of Congress, technically considered, but application of the principle of state sovereignty to the slavery question. The union was formed for the sake of the states and their interests; in performing its duties, those interests should be paramount and conclusive; what the states, even in their ordinary legislation, desired, that must be done by Congress in exercise of its delegated powers. Such in essence was the argument; and more: whatever any one state asserted to be its particular interest must be a check on congressional action, and if Congress neglects the interest of a state, nullification is the rightful remedy. Under this interpretation of national authority, what was "the supreme law of the land"?

Here, then, the banns of wedlock between slavery and state sovereignty were formally proclaimed. The announcement was a momentous fact and of great consequence. The master of ceremonies was in deadly earnest; but after all, it was a marriage of convenience, indeed in some ways an unnatural union; for loudly as it might be asserted that slavery was a matter for the south alone, slavery was in danger as long as it attempted to be purely local. As the days went on, the thought that slavery might be confined to the states where it existed, to live actually a local life, cut off from territorial expansion, became a sort of nightmare to the southern leaders. Agriculture, where work was done by slaves, could not thrive except as an extensive industry, and—as the past had shown exhaustion of soil and wasteful methods—new lands, and fresh soils, and virgin opportunities beckoned slavery on to expansion, we might even say conquest.

And still, as we have already seen, there was some bond of natural affection between slavery and state sovereignty. The menace to state autonomy was the increasing population of the free states, and that increase must be met. As already indicated, Calhoun at a later day elaborately developed the whole philosophy of inhibitions on govern-

---

[29] See In re Rahrer, 140 U. S. 545 (1891) ; Clark Distilling Co. *v.* Western Maryland Railway Co., 242 U. S. 311 (1917).

mental action; and he found no sanction for the authority of mere numbers. Slavery and state sovereignty were in some respects bound in a companionate marriage, a marriage of inner sentiment and of mutually supporting emotional responses.

As one watches Calhoun, struggling like a valiant knight in defense of honor and for the colors of his fair lady, slavery, the picture elicits at once admiration and compassion. With superb ability he encountered invincible hosts; he was confronted by the growing spirit of humanitarianism, not confined to America, though strikingly illustrated by waxing antislavery sentiment and extravagantly exhibited by the Garrisonian abolitionists; he was faced by growing nationalism, and by the disconcerting temper of modern life which in some ways was to grow in intensity—a temper which battered at the walls of local privacy and broke down the walls of seclusion of nations.

No one could put the case for slavery more cogently than Calhoun. He chiefly defended *negro* slavery, the fact and the form of slavery as it existed in America. But his arguments must stand as a defense of the few and of the right of the strong and those possessed of assumed superiority to be served by the many, whether the many be black or white. He defended negro slavery because it solved the race problem and the labor problem. It hardly seems possible that in 1836 and 1837 Calhoun saw all this so clearly as it is here presented; but there his words stand to be read by anyone curious enough to take the trouble. Slavery to Calhoun in 1837 was no longer a thing to be regretted or even remotely apologized for, but a thing for which the south would sacrifice its life.

Calhoun's most powerful defense of slavery is in his speech on the reception of abolition petitions, February 6, 1837. "They who imagine that the spirit now abroad in the North, will die away of itself without a shock or convulsion, have formed a very inadequate conception of its real character; it will continue to rise and spread, unless prompt and efficient measures to stay its progress be adopted. . . . By the necessary course of events, if left to themselves, we must become, finally, two people. . . . The conflicting elements would burst the Union asunder, powerful as are the links which hold it together. Abolition and the Union cannot co-exist." Thus did Calhoun anticipate by some twenty years the statement of Lincoln that the nation could not long exist half slave and half free; a house divided against itself cannot stand. "I hold that in the present state of civilization, where two races of different origin, and distinguished by color, and other physical differences, as well as intellectual, are brought together, the relation now existing in the slaveholding States between the two, is, instead of an evil, a good—a positive good." He compared the conditions of the laboring classes of Europe with those of the American slaves and found the verdict in favor of American slavery. With this, however, he was not content: "But I will not dwell on this aspect of the question; I turn to the political; and here I fearlessly assert that the existing relation between the two races in the South, against which these blind fanatics are waging war, forms the most solid and durable foundation on which to rear free and stable political institutions. It is useless to disguise the fact. There is and always has been in an advanced stage of wealth and civilization, a conflict between labor and capital. The condition of society in the South exempts us from the disorders and dangers resulting from this conflict; and which explains why it is that the political condition of the slaveholding States has been so much more stable and quiet than that of the North." Slavery was not only the solution of the labor problem but the surest basis for a developing civilization; the way to promote civilization and, presumably, culture was to rear them upon the backs of labor owned by capital.[30]

Determined to have a duel à outrance with abolitionism and also desiring to force the Senate to accept some of his basic theories, Calhoun introduced into the Senate a series of resolutions, December 27, 1837.[31] They are of consequence because, though Calhoun was then in advance of his time, they show his power as a prophet, his appreciation of the issues which time would make plain. Their substance is as follows:

(1) The Constitution was adopted by independent, sovereign states acting severally, and each state entered the union with a view to its increased security against all dangers, domestic as well as foreign.

(2) The states retained, severally, the sole power over their own domestic institutions and police, and "any intermeddling of any one or more States, or a combination of their citizens, with the domestic

---

[30] Further defense of slavery is in the report of the committee on incendiary publications, February 4, 1836. Calhoun, *Works*, V, p. 190 ff. Here one passage is specially significant. To what extent was it true prophecy? "Social and political equality between them [the two races] is impossible. . . . But, without such equality, to change the present condition of the African race, were it possible, would be but to change the form of slavery. It would make them the slaves of the community instead of the slaves of individuals. . . ." *Ibid.*, p. 205.

[31] *Cong. Globe*, 25 Cong., 2 sess., p. 55.

institutions and police of the others, on any ground, or under any pretext whatever, political, moral, or religious, with the view to their alteration, or subversion, is an assumption of superiority not warranted by the Constitution . . . subversive of the objects for which the Constitution was formed. . . ."

(3) The government was instituted by the several states as a common agent, and it is bound so to exercise its powers as to give increased stability to the domestic institutions of the states.

(4) Slavery is an important part of the domestic institutions of the slaveholding states, inherited from their ancestors and recognized by the Constitution as forming an essential element in the distribution of powers among the states; no change of opinion in other states can justify attacks upon it; such attacks are a violation "of the mutual and solemn pledge to protect and defend each other," are a breach of faith, and a violation of the "most solemn obligations, moral and religious."

(5) The intermeddling of any person, with the intent to abolish slavery in the District or in any of the territories on the ground that it is sinful or immoral, or the passing of any act of Congress with that in view, would be a dangerous attack on the institutions of the slaveholding states.

(6) The union rests on equality. ". . . to refuse to extend to the Southern and Western States any advantage which would tend to strengthen, or render them more secure, or increase their limits or population by the annexation of new territory or States, on the assumption or under the pretext that . . . slavery . . . is immoral . . . would be contrary to that equality of rights and advantages which the Constitution was intended to secure alike to all the members of the Union, and would, in effect, disfranchise the slaveholding States, withholding from them the advantages, while it subjected them to the burthens, of the Government."

The first and second resolutions were passed without modification. It seems scarcely possible that the learned senators comprehended fully the implications of the first, concerning which Calhoun said, "The idea that this Republic was made up of one great aggregate of individuals, tended to increase the zeal of these fanatics, and a more rapid spread of their doctrines. The remedy must be found in the promulgation of opposite doctrines"—the true doctrines of the Constitution. The third and fourth resolutions were passed after slight alteration; the fifth was altered; the sixth was not adopted but there was added to the fifth a statement against abolishing slavery in the territories where it already existed. That anyone, not an earnest and sincere advocate of slavery, should have been willing to vote for the declaration which was embodied in the fifth resolution, as it was finally passed, seems strange; for the declaration was there made that any attempt to abolish slavery in the District would be a violation of the faith implied in the cessions by Virginia and Maryland. Nothing could be more in conflict with historical fact.[32]

So it seemed that, as long as any state maintained slavery, nothing must be done by Congress to detract in any manner from its security; the citizens in every other state must preserve inviolable quietness; the United States must stand alone chained to a system of labor and social order from which the rest of the civilized world was moving rapidly away. Did Calhoun really mean that no man or woman in a remote valley of the White Mountains or a far-off corner of the western prairies should denounce slavery or lament its existence or declare its immorality, because to do so was to break the holy spirit of the compact? Democracy and popular government are founded on the right and the duty of free speech, free discussion, and interchange of opinion; but slavery would have none of it; and so its very presence, with all the much-heralded alarm and apprehension, was contradicting the very essence of free government.

But the slavery problem would not down, despite resolutions. It came up in one place if not in another. In the discussions concerning petitions and the circulation of incendiary materials, there was the assumption or the expressed declaration that meddling of northerners with the subject of slavery was a violation of constitutional obligation. Slavery belonged to the south, and the south must be left alone; slavery was a local matter, so local that to discuss it a thousand miles away endangered its existence; so local that it must be national—at least there was national obligation binding on Massachusetts and Vermont not to discuss the denial of human rights by South Carolina. The time was not far distant when slavery must be considered so local, so distinctly a "peculiar institution", that it must in some degree have recognition even in international affairs.[33]

A series of questions and controversies arose from the domestic slave trade whereby slaves were carried by sea from one American port

[32] Webster answered the faith argument. See *Works*, IV, pp. 374-375.
[33] See Calhoun's position in connection with the annexation of Texas which will be referred to in a later chapter.

to another. Of these, the most important was the case of the brig *Creole*. The slaves on board that ship going from Hampton Roads, Virginia, to New Orleans rose in revolt (November, 1841), took charge of the ship, and brought her into the port of Nassau, in the Bahamas, where slavery had been abolished. Did they become free men when by revolt they obtained their physical freedom? Were they free when they reached free soil and found refuge in a land which did not recognize slavery?

Webster, then Secretary of State, demanded of the British government the return of the negroes as criminals guilty of mutiny and murder. Britain refused. Joshua Giddings, a Representative from the Western Reserve District of Ohio, offered in the House a series of resolutions deserving particular attention: (1) before the adoption of the Constitution, each state had full and exclusive jurisdiction over slavery within its own territory. (2) By adopting the Constitution, no part of this power was delegated to the federal government. (3) All authority over commerce on the high seas was surrendered to the federal government. (4) Slavery, being an abridgment of the natural rights of man, can exist only by force of positive municipal law and is confined to the territorial jurisdiction of the power creating it. (5) When a ship leaves the waters of a state and enters upon the high seas, the persons on board cease to be subject to the slave laws of the state. (6) When the *Creole* left the territorial jurisdiction of Virginia, the persons on board became amenable only to the laws of the United States. (7) In resuming their natural rights of personal liberty, these persons violated no law of the United States and were not justly liable to punishment. (8) All attempts to regain possession of them and re-enslave them are unauthorized by the Constitution and incompatible with national honor. (9) Efforts to exert national influence in favor of the coastwise slave trade, "or to place this nation in the attitude of maintaining a 'commerce in human beings,' are subversive of the rights and injurious to the feelings of the free States, are unauthorized by the Constitution, and prejudicial to our national character."

Thus, at last, the gauntlet was frankly thrown down. It is as if Giddings had said: you claim that slavery is your peculiar institution, that it is nobody's business but your own, that it is purely local; we accept your assertion; we proclaim it a local institution and insist that it be kept at home. You have complained of alarm and of harassed feelings; we also complain, for our pride and our love of national honor are sorely assaulted by your endeavor to make slavery a national institution, subject to national protection, and to be defended by the nation in international disputes.

But passing over the cleverness of Giddings's *tu quoque* argument, the issue was fairly presented—was slavery really a local institution? Did Congress have any authority over the subject at all? Must slavery be protected beyond the limits of the slaveholding state? Could a slave-owner under national protection take his slaves onto the high seas or into the national domain of the west?

In his argument with the British authorities concerning the status of the fugitive blacks, Webster claimed that slavery was recognized by the Constitution and that the slaves on the brig *Creole* continued to be property on the high seas. Not until twelve years later was the dispute decided, when Joshua Bates, an American-born English banker,[34] to whom as arbitrator the subject was submitted, decided in favor of the land of his birth; and the British government paid one hundred and ten thousand dollars because British officials had refused to return the refugees to slavery.

Giddings was censured by a vote of the House of nearly two to one; a two-thirds vote was needed for expulsion. Enough members voted in his favor to indicate a developing sense of self-respect among the northern members.[35] He immediately resigned but he was promptly reëlected by his constituents; henceforth members of Congress were allowed to speak and offer resolutions on the subject of slavery without being harried and browbeaten by an intolerant majority.

Webster, as we have seen, defended property in slaves on the high seas on the ground that the Constitution recognized property in slaves. The pivotal question of the next two decades was this: what was the nature of slavery, constitutionally speaking? To what extent, if at all, did the Constitution recognize slaves as property? The Constitution did not use the words "slaves" or "slavery"; the words were carefully avoided. It provided for the counting of three-fifths of "other persons" in determining the number of representatives assigned to a state. It forbade Congress to prohibit, before the year 1808, the introduction of "such persons" as any of the existing states should think proper to admit before the year 1808. It declared that no person held to service or labor in one state should obtain freedom by flight into a free state,

[34] Hart, *Slavery and Abolition*, pp. 294-295.

[35] The vote indicates clearly that the odium of intolerance is not to be placed upon the south alone. Northern members, with no such provocation as the southerners felt, voted in the affirmative. The excuse for the vote was that the matter was at the time a subject of diplomatic discussion. But that is no excuse at all.

EARLY CONTROVERSIES OVER SLAVERY   495

but should be delivered up on demand to his master. The first of these constitutional provisions recognizes in reality the existence of slavery within some of the states; the second, in placing the limitation on the power of Congress, evidently recognizes prevalent objections to the slave trade and the probability of congressional action; the third—the fugitive slave clause—plainly indicates that slavery is in its nature a local institution; it was not considered necessary to place in the Constitution an announcement that, if horses should escape from Maryland into Pennsylvania, they would remain the property of the person from whom they fled. As a matter of plain, unadorned fact, the Constitution and the debates in the Convention suggest strongly, if they do not actually demonstrate, that slavery was on the whole looked upon with disapproval. To meet the immediate demands of the far southern states, where there was or seemed to be a need of labor, a temporary concession was made; importation of slaves was allowed for twenty years (1788-1808). This and the other provisions of the Constitution already referred to furnish slender basis on which to set up a constitutional and national recognition of property in slaves and the duty of Congress to protect it on the high seas and to defend it in international controversies.

Of course, someone may assert that Congress is under obligation to recognize as property whatever any state by its laws holds to be property. That Calhoun or other zealous advocates of property in men would have been content with such a principle is exceedingly doubtful. Would the government of the United States have been under obligation to protect property in white men and women, if Massachusetts had established white slavery? If the answer is in the negative, then the particular right to have slave property protected by national power had to rest, not upon the mere fact of slave property in one or more states, but either upon express constitutional recognition of property in *black* slaves or upon the presumption that the natural and inevitable condition of *blackness* was a condition of bondage.

CHAPTER XXXVI

THE ANNEXATION OF TEXAS

By 1840, there was a strong antislavery sentiment at the north. The abolitionists were no longer in danger of bodily assault; and the milder advocates of emancipation were at least accorded toleration. A political party opposed to slavery, the Liberty party, cast 7,069 votes in 1840, in the campaign of log-cabins, coons, and hard cider. Trivial as this number was in a total vote of over 2,400,000, it was significant. Thenceforward, the slavery question had to be considered in party politics; it was no longer a matter of merely social and religious agitation.

The Texas question began to loom on the horizon as early as 1836, when Texas announced her independence from Mexico; but for various reasons, partly, probably, because the commercial panic and depression were enough to keep men's thoughts occupied with their own troubles, annexation did not become a matter of serious concern until Tyler's term was fairly well advanced. Until very recent years, northern historians have not uncommonly detected in the movement for annexation little save the slaveholders' longing for more territory to be tilled by slaves, a longing which degenerated into a dark-lantern conspiracy to absorb the great southwest and to be carried forward despite the Constitution itself. This interpretation will, however, not stand examination. By no means all the slave-owners were advocates of western expansion. Furthermore, the spirit of imperialism was coming into vogue. Annexation awakened the enthusiasm of a people not devoid of self-glorification;[1] it appealed to the imagination and the spirit of the American people and especially to the buoyant confidence of the men of the Mississippi valley who had been the vanguard of expansion.

[1] See, for example, the speech of W. J. Brown of Indiana in the House (January 14, 1845). Let the Mexicans discharge one gun, "and Mexico would soon be stricken from the roll of nntions [*sic*], and over her capitol would float the banner of freedom. At the banks of the Del Norte . . . our empire would not cease; but fifty years would not pass before it carried all of Mexico; and a century would not pass before it might be found . . . on the coast of Patagonia." *Congressional Globe,* 28 Cong., 2 sess., p. 137.

But opposition to expansion grew when the form and result of the proposal came into view. The antislavery forces saw nothing to please them in the annexation of more slave territory. The movement for the absorption of Texas was forwarded by the political incompetence of Mexico, by her facility in revolutions, and by her cavalier manner of resisting pressure for the payment of claims against her government. At first Texas desired annexation to the United States, but later she began to face about and appeared to have lost her enthusiasm. In the latter part of Tyler's term (1843), the American administration was stirred by the fear lest Texas succumb to the blandishments of Britain. That, of course, would never do. Rumors spread to the effect that a plan was on foot for bringing about the abolition of slavery with British encouragement or assistance. So the subject of annexation was broached by Upshur, the American Secretary of State. But Texas was coy, and when the Texas President, Houston, hesitated and expressed doubt about the treaty's being agreed to by the Senate, he was assured that there need be no fear on that score. Houston demanded a pledge that American troops would be sent to repel Mexico—for Mexico obstinately refused to recognize the fact of Texan independence —if that country attacked Texas while negotiations were in progress. Such assurance [2] was given. It already looked as if we were annexing a war.

In February, 1844, Upshur was killed by an explosion of a big gun on the *Princeton,* and after a brief interval Calhoun came in as Secretary of State. The stage was now set for annexation. Calhoun told the Texas representatives in Washington that the President had ordered a strong naval force to concentrate in the Gulf, "to meet any emergency", and that similar orders had been issued to move "the disposable military forces on our Southwestern frontier for the same purpose." He further said that "during the pendency of the treaty of annexation," the President would "use all the means placed within his power by the Constitution to protect Texas from all foreign invasion." [3] A treaty of annexation was concluded April 12, 1844. It provided for

---

[2] The American chargé in Texas was charged with suffering his zeal to go too far. But the statement said to be sent on the President's authority was not essentially different: that the President "was not indisposed, as a measure of prudent precaution, and as preliminary to the proposed negotiation, to concentrate in the Gulf of Mexico, and on the Southern borders of the United States, a naval and military force to be directed to the defence of the inhabitants and territory of Texas at a proper time. . . ." *Senate Documents,* 28 Cong., 1 sess., V, no. 349, p. 10. See also *Ibid.,* p. 5.

[3] *Ibid.,* p. 11.

the cession of all the territories of Texas "to be annexed to the said United States as one of their territories, subject to the same constitutional provisions with their other territories." [4]

But to this consummation so devoutly wished by Calhoun and President Tyler disappointing objections arose. The antislavery forces at the north were hostile. There was objection even at the south,[5] and a presidential election was at hand. The question of annexation had received little public attention for a considerable time and it now flashed upon the scene. The senators were not content; the Whig leader, Clay, was not a natural ally of Calhoun and he detested Tyler. Nothing could more fret and irk the proud Kentuckian than a successful coup and a diplomatic victory for the President. So the treaty was rejected (June 8, 1844). Calhoun's pretty house of cards crumbled. Instead of the necessary two-thirds vote in its favor, over two-thirds voted against it.

Beyond peradventure, the impulse of the administration—the zeal of Upshur, Calhoun, and Tyler—was stirred by the menacing prospect of a free Texas.[6] The annexation was not a proslavery conspiracy, in the sense that the slaveholders in general plotted for more slave territory; nor, as we have said, was land-hunger confined to the south; but Calhoun believed the safety of the southern institution was endangered and he resented the assumption of Britain that her duty called upon her to bring freedom to the world. The correspondence which he carried on implied an obligation to defend slavery as a subject of national concern. What had then become of the local character of slavery, an institution for the south alone? [7] As he had shown in earlier years that slavery was endangered and the union imperiled by northern abolitionists, so now he saw the same menace in the establishment of a free state on the borders of the union.

[4] The treaty is in Calhoun, *Works,* V, p. 322 ff., and in *Senate Documents,* 28 Cong., 1 sess., V, no. 341, p. 10 ff.

[5] But not by any means in the whole south. "Even before the treaty was rejected mass-meetings at Ashley and Beaufort [South Carolina] declared in favor of giving up the Union rather than Texas, and called for a convention of the slave states to consider the question of annexing Texas to the Union, or, if the United States would not accept it, to the southern states." G. P. Garrison, *Westward Extension,* pp. 141-142.

[6] *Ibid.,* p. 27 ff.; letter from Calhoun to B. E. Green, April 19, 1844, *Works,* V, pp. 347-348; letter from the same to Edward Everett, April 27, 1844, *Correspondence of John C. Calhoun,* Am. Hist. Asso. *Report* for 1899, II, p. 579; see also, Richardson, *Messages and Papers,* IV, pp. 311-312.

[7] That question was directly asked by *The Democratic Review* in January. 1845. See XVI, p. 8.

By the time the vote on the treaty was taken in the Senate, annexation was involved in partisan politics. Tyler was without a party. The
Whigs, who could not abide him because he had opposed their fiscal
measures and had not been guided by their peerless leader, Clay, were
not willing to give the President the satisfaction of success in his
Texas plans. Before the treaty was rejected by the Senate, the Democrats had nominated James K. Polk for president and demanded the
re-annexation of Texas "at the earliest practicable period. . . ." The
Whigs had nominated Clay on a platform saying nothing about Texas.
Van Buren and Clay had announced their opposition to immediate
annexation. And when Van Buren was not nominated by his party,
some of his partisans were naturally in ill humor. A decision by the
Senate on the merits of annexation was therefore quite impossible;
when the vote was taken, all the affirmative votes but one came from
the Democratic senators.[8]

President Tyler was not to be balked by the rejection of the treaty;
in the early summer, he sent documents to the House and also a message, which suggested the advisability of finding a way to reach the
coveted goal: ". . . while I have regarded the annexation to be accomplished by treaty as the most suitable form in which it could be
effected, should Congress deem it proper to resort to any other expedient compatible with the Constitution and likely to accomplish the
object I stand prepared to yield my most prompt and active cooperation. The great question is not as to the manner in which it shall be
done, but whether it shall be accomplished or not."[9] He thus threw
upon the House the responsibility of deciding the question. There
spoke the arch constitutionalist! A man who had been at various times
extravagantly solicitous about constitutional restraints, and so anxious
and wary that he had broken with his party because of some highly

[8] See Garrison, *op. cit.*, pp. 120-121. Tyler had announced (May 15, 1844) as his
opinion that the United States having by treaty acquired a title to Texas which required only the action of the Senate to perfect it (!), no other power could be permitted to acquire any portion of the territory, pending the Senate's deliberations,
without placing itself in a hostile attitude toward the United States and justifying the use of force to repel the invasion. Thus we find that a situation may be
entirely created by the president and bring on a war; and in such a war the United
States is to be considered the aggrieved and offended party, its territory wantonly and
offensively invaded. These questionings appear rather trivial in comparison with the
main fact of actual annexation; and now that we can see beyond the vapors of sectional and partisan animosities, it seems probable that no nation then—and no nation
now—would tolerate the intrusion of a rival during the process of courtship.

[9] Richardson, *Messages and Papers*, IV, pp. 323-327.

technical objections to a bank measure, now declared the method of annexing an area larger than France was of no consequence provided the act be done.

The election of 1844, with Clay the Whig candidate and Polk the Democratic, resulted in a Democratic victory. Though there was much shouting for the re-annexation of Texas and the re-occupation of Oregon, it is not perfectly evident that the country, by electing Polk, voted for Texas. There were other issues. But the movement for annexation was taken up by the administration with new confidence and assurance. In his final annual message (December, 1844), Tyler recurred to the subject so near to his heart. He declared that Mexico was threatening Texas, though her inability to reconquer the region "had been exhibited . . . by eight (now nine) years of fruitless and ruinous contest", and that it was the will of both the people and the states that Texas be annexed "promptly and immediately." He recommended that the terms of annexation already agreed upon by the two governments be adopted by Congress "in the form of a joint resolution or act to be perfected and made binding on the two countries when adopted in like manner by the Government of Texas." [10]

Before the end of January, after much talk and considerable excitement, the House passed a joint resolution for the admission of Texas as a state, the final vote being 120 to 98.[11] In the course of the debate the idea had grown clearer that Congress was entitled to act under the clause of the Constitution providing that "New States may be admitted by the Congress into this Union. . . ." The resolution announced that Congress consented that the territory properly included within and rightfully belonging to the Republic of Texas might be erected into a state, with the consent of the existing government, in order that it might be admitted into the union. The consent of Congress was based on certain conditions: (1) that such state was to be formed subject to the adjustment by the United States government of all questions of boundary which might arise with other governments; (2) that certain public property was to be ceded to the United States; (3) that additional states, not exceeding four in number, might, with the consent of Texas, be formed out of her territory, and such new states as might be formed south of the parallel thirty-six thirty should be admitted into the union with or without slavery, as the people of

[10] *Ibid.,* IV, p. 341 ff.
[11] January 25, 1845. *Congressional Globe,* 28 Cong., 2 sess., p. 194. Twenty-two northern Democrats voted against it; six southern Whigs voted for it.

each state asking admission should desire, but that in any state formed out of territory north of that line slavery should be prohibited.[12]

The slavery question of course had come into the debate. The most zealous of the antislavery men denounced the whole scheme and plan of annexation as one intended to protect and foster the peculiar institution of the south. "They had been told," said C. B. Smith of Indiana, "by gentlemen themselves who advocated this measure, that it was a southern question—that Texas was to be annexed for the purpose of strengthening and fortifying the institution of slavery—that they demanded that this territory should be annexed as a guaranty for the preservation of their rights. Let him ask, had they any right to make such a demand?" [13] There was also a desire among some of the northern men to gain for the north a share of the new region, not so much, it appeared at times, to save that share from slavery because slavery was evil as to secure a portion of the booty, an area into which free settlers might move.[14]

Soon after the Senate had received the House's joint resolution, the chairman of the committee on foreign relations presented a report and offered resolutions for the rejection of the House's measure. Some of the senators were naturally desirous of safeguarding the special authority of the Senate as part of the treaty-making power. But a treaty needed a two-thirds vote, so something must be done. R. J. Walker of Mississippi now made a clever proposal; it gave the senators still anxious to preserve the senatorial prerogative an opportunity of escape—to appear to hold their position and still in reality to yield. The Walker amendment proposed that, if the President deemed it more advisable to negotiate instead of submitting the resolution of annexation to Texas as an "overture", he might negotiate; and perhaps some of the defenders of senatorial authority may have actually believed that Tyler would adopt that method. The subterfuge was eagerly grasped; the House resolution as amended was passed a few hours

---

[12] This last clause providing for free states north of thirty-six thirty was an amendment presented by Stephen A. Douglas, on the last day. *Ibid.*, p. 193. It is noteworthy because it came from Douglas, and because it did not provide against slavery in a *territory* but laid down a restriction on the admission of a state. That such a provision should have been thus acquiesced in is significant of the anxiety to get Texas without further discussion and delay.

[13] *Ibid.*, p. 109. See, as another example, the speech of E. S. Hamlin of Ohio. *Ibid.*, p. 118. One florid speech from Yancey of Alabama was a powerful defense of Calhoun and of slavery as a national institution. *Ibid.*, appendix, p. 88. See also the speech of J. R. Giddings. *Ibid.*, appendix, p. 342 ff.

[14] See, for example, the speech of Jacob Brinkerhoff of Ohio. *Ibid.*, p. 132.

after the Walker proposal was offered. But the victory was a narrow one: twenty-seven to twenty-five. When the resolution with the Walker amendment was returned to the House for concurrence, it was accepted by a vote of 132 to 76.

The line of cleavage in the House was drawn along partisan boundaries; two southern Whigs voted in the affirmative; two northern Democrats voted in the negative. Thus there appeared again that highly interesting alignment. For, though the issue was not distinctly between freedom and slavery, and was not distinctly sectional, the fact remains that annexation was opposed by many at the north because of opposition to the extension of slaveholding territory, and the movement for annexation came more and more to be looked upon as a movement for the advancement of slaveholders' interests. Some of the northern Democrats were soon to break away from party shackles, but if one desires to explain the character and make-up of the Democratic party, or—if the reader prefers—if one desires to understand the national as distinguished from the sectional character of the party, he is called upon to go as far back in history as the Texas struggle and to account, if he can, for the votes of that eventful winter.

The defense of the treaty-method of annexation rested on the fact that negotiations with a foreign state must be carried on before admission, and also on the federative nature of the union; the Senate representing the states was the suitable body to determine whether a foreign state should be admitted to the privileges of association with the existing members of the union. Extremists were capable of carrying this doctrine further; Massachusetts adopted resolutions declaring that she had never delegated the power to admit into the union states or territories beyond the original territory of the union; that there was no precedent for the admission of a foreign state, and as the power was beyond the competence of Congress, an act of admission would not be binding on the people of Massachusetts.[15]

The southern advocates of annexation, earnest and determined, might have taken more seriously the warnings of Senator Archer: if Congress had the power by a majority vote to admit states and to place stipulations and conditions, might not mere numbers prevail and the malignant spirit of abolitionism have its way? The power of one more than one-third of the senators to prevent annexation of a foreign state should be defended and protected by persons or sections fearing the development of popular power in the union. This position, we may

[15] *Ibid.*, appendix, p. 237.

notice, ought to have been closely adhered to by all persons especially solicitous for the retention of states' rights; there are at least some grounds for asserting that the framers of the Constitution, recognizing the sweep of the treaty-making power, consigned to the Senate participation in treaty-making, partly because in that body the states, large and small, were equally represented.[16]

Furthermore, as Texas was a foreign sovereign state, arrangements or agreement for annexation could be carried on and conclusions reached only by the governmental authority in the American system charged with the duty of conducting foreign affairs. On this point Archer was emphatic. If the results of such negotiations should be the formal consent of both parties to the annexation of the foreign state, could such an understanding and agreement be considered less than a treaty? Even if final admission into the union must be a matter for congressional discretion, must not the terms of agreement with a foreign state be reached by negotiations and formulated in a treaty?

The arguments in favor of annexation by joint resolution rested, as we have seen, on the power of Congress to admit new states. That Texas was at the time a foreign state, and that the resolution for admission stipulated terms, did not bewilder the advocates of congressional power; the grant of power involved the right to make all adequate and incidental provisions. In more than one respect the joint resolution is a curious product. There appears to have been an idea that the Missouri Compromise line would then or ultimately divide the land annexed in such a way as to exclude slavery from a considerable portion.[17] But as a matter of fact no very large portion of the region, actually annexed, was north of thirty-six thirty. The final paragraphs of the resolution are the strangest. So anxious were the senators, as the

16 "The same causes made it indispensable to give to the senators, as representatives of states, the power of making, or rather ratifying, treaties." ". . . the small states would not consent to confederate without an equal voice in the formation of treaties." Speech of W. R. Davie, a member of the Federal Convention of 1787, in the North Carolina convention, July 28, 1788. Elliot, *Debates* (1866 ed.), IV, p. 120. See also, pp. 123-124. And see *Ibid.*, p. 27, for a speech of Spaight in the North Carolina convention, July 24, 1788, and Washington's message to the House, March 30, 1796, in Richardson, *Messages and Papers*, I, pp. 195-196.

17 T. H. Benton, in his *Thirty Years' View*, II, p. 633, calls attention to the prominence given to the Missouri Compromise line. Notice Buchanan's remarks quoted by Benton, *Ibid.*, in which he glories in the solution of the slavery problem by the reëstablishment of the Compromise line of 1820. The sanctity of the line of demarcation was certainly emphasized by the resolution, but it should be noticed, however, that the resolution did not actually deal with slavery in a territory, but with slavery in the states that might be formed.

fourth of March approached, to get through with the whole annexation business, that they seized upon Walker's amendment with avidity; if the president did not wish to present to Texas the resolution as an "overture", he might negotiate. What was or is an "overture"? On its face, the resolution purported to be an enabling act for the admission of a state. Was an enabling act an "overture"? But if instead of overturing, the President negotiated, then he might either submit the results of his labors to the Senate as a treaty or to Congress in the form of "articles". What precise meaning should be assigned to the term "articles"? Doubtless no one knew and doubtless no one knows. Whether the President overtured or treated, Texas was to be admitted —that was the crux of the matter—; Congress was committed to admission.

Probably never was there a stranger hybrid among resolutions. But Tyler did not procrastinate. He hurried off a messenger to Texas to attain the consummation of his long-cherished hopes. Of course Texas was ready to come in. The terms proposed were accepted, a state constitution was ratified in the early autumn, and in December (1845) the final resolution admitting the state was passed by Congress.

The procedure followed in the annexation of Texas did not constitute a conclusive precedent in favor of annexation of territory by joint resolution. Over fifty years later (1898) the Hawaiian Islands were annexed by a joint resolution;[18] but the method of annexing Texas did not constitute a proper precedent for the annexation of a land and people to be retained as a possession or in a territorial condition. Congressional authority for annexation of Texas rested on the constitutional power to admit new states; Hawaii was not and is not a state.

Upon principle, it appears a reasonable conclusion that Con-

[18] Joint resolution for annexing the Hawaiian Islands, July 7, 1898: "Whereas the Government of the Republic of Hawaii having, in due form, signified its consent, in the manner provided by its constitution, to cede absolutely and without reserve to the United States of America all rights of sovereignty of whatsoever kind in and over the Hawaiian Islands and their dependencies, and also to cede and transfer to the United States the absolute fee and ownership of all public, Government, or Crown lands, public buildings or edifices . . . belonging to the Government of the Hawaiian Islands, together with every right and appurtenance thereunto appertaining: Therefore,

"*Resolved by the Senate and House of Representatives of the United States of America in Congress assembled,* That said cession is accepted, ratified, and confirmed, and that the said Hawaiian Islands and their dependencies be, and they are hereby, annexed as a part of the territory of the United States and are subject to the sovereign dominion thereof, and that all and singular the property and rights hereinbefore mentioned are vested in the United States of America."

gress, and not the treaty-making power, has the final authority to bring foreign territories into full participation in the union.[19] To the present writer two steps would seem to be necessary: (1) a treaty for annexation (which ought, if it promises admission into the union, to say, lest the foreign country misunderstand, that actual admission depends upon Congress) and (2) an act of Congress for admission.

[19] In the case of Downes *v.* Bidwell, 182 U. S. 244, 312 (1901) Justice White, accepting the judgment of the Court, gave an opinion in which Justices Shiras and McKenna concurred, and said, ". . . it seems to me impossible to conceive that the treaty-making power by a mere cession can incorporate an alien people into the United States without the express or implied approval of Congress." This did not refer to the admission of a state into the union, but to the incorporation of a people as the consequence of annexation; but the argument against admission of a state by treaty would naturally be much stronger. The treaty-making power, it would appear, can annex but not fully incorporate without the consent of Congress. The right to admit new states is a congressional power. The statement of Senator Huntington of Connecticut in 1845 is noteworthy: "Now, I take leave to say that the power to annex foreign territory by treaty, and the power to admit New States into the Union by an act of Congress, are not concurrent, but distinct powers. Each is independent of the other, and neither can exercise both, nor can one exercise the authority conferred on the other. The one acquires territory; the other admits States." *Congressional Globe,* 28 Cong., 2 sess., appendix, p. 399.

CHAPTER XXXVII

WAR WITH MEXICO. THE WILMOT PROVISO. SLAVERY IN THE TERRITORIES

The acquisition of Texas brought on war with Mexico; the war resulted in the addition of a large area to American territory, and there ensued disputes concerning the extension of slavery into the newly-acquired region. These disputes and differences, growing into animosities, ended in civil war. We now enter therefore on a period of some fifteen years during which the question of slavery in the western territories was always present and always overshadowed all other political controversies.

Fortunately it is not our affair to examine in detail the processes by which the war was brought on, and fortunately, too, there is no need for our concerning ourselves with passing judgment upon the morality or immorality of Polk's conduct. Even to-day, three-quarters of a century and more after the President announced to Congress that war had been begun by the act of Mexico, there is not unanimity of opinion on this matter among American historians. There is, however, a decided tendency to sustain Polk. Without doubt, he was anxious to make as much as he could out of the situation. He wanted to settle the boundary dispute by getting Mexico to recognize the limits which Texas, not too modestly, had laid down. He wanted to get payment of the claims of American citizens,[1] but he knew that the last thing Mexico could or would do was to pay money. Indeed, Mexico's poverty opened up roseate possibilities; it presented the chance of a bargain; if the United States offered to assume the debts and dangled before the eyes of the dazzled Mexicans a sum of some millions of dollars, why should the two countries not be the best of friends, if Mexico would only cede a large area in the west including California

---

[1] In his instructions to Slidell he indicated that he would waive the payment of claims, if Mexico would accept the boundaries of Texas as Texas had announced them—the Rio Grande from its mouth to its source, thence due north to the forty-second parallel. Polk was willing to pay five million dollars in addition to the assumption of American claims.

and the much-to-be-desired harbor of San Francisco?[2] Polk wanted California, and we can imagine that, had he not wanted that fair land so badly, he might have treated Mexico a bit more gently and not have been so ready for stern measures. And yet, had he dallied and delayed, war might have come nevertheless; for Mexico was distracted and irritable; she was unreasoning if not unreasonable. Furthermore, to single out Polk as the "mendacious", to hold him up as an example of imperial designs and of dishonest diplomacy in a decade when American oratory was blazing with coruscating declarations of the glories of manifest destiny and the beauties of a pious imperialism—to select Polk as an example of impropriety in the decade of the roaring forties is to bestow upon him an unmerited degree of distinction.

The President was under moral and legal obligations to negotiate with Mexico before he proceeded to take her property. He tried to negotiate by sending John Slidell to Mexico; but the attempt was unsuccessful. Before Slidell had given up in despair, but after he had reported the probable refusal to receive him, Polk took an eventful step; he ordered American troops to march into the disputed area south of the Nueces (January 13, 1846). In May, he decided on war; and the fates were with him, for, just at the lucky moment, word came of a fight between Mexican and American troops north of the Rio Grande. Polk could therefore solemnly announce the outbreak of a war of defense: "But now, after reiterated menaces, Mexico has passed the boundary of the United States, has invaded our territory and shed American blood upon the American soil."[3]

The chief charge against the President at the time was based upon the occupation of the disputed area south of the Nueces. The resolution annexing Texas spoke of the "territory properly included within, and rightfully belonging to the Republic of Texas. . . ." The con-

---

[2] An able though brief defense of Polk is given by E. C. Barker, "California as the Cause of the Mexican War," *The Texas Review*, II, no. 3, pp. 213-221. The author attacks the assertion, often made, that Polk brought on the war in order to get California.

[3] Message of May 11, 1846. Richardson, *Messages and Papers*, IV, p. 442. "The fact is," says Professor Burgess, adopting Polk's defense in toto, "it was a defensive war at the outset, and if the Mexicans were excited to their move across the Rio Grande by the appearance of United States troops on the northern bank, they had only to thank themselves for bringing them there by previously massing their own troops on the south bank." J. W. Burgess, *The Middle Period*, p. 331. "In the face of Mexico's solemn threats concerning the annexation of Texas, any prudent executive would have ordered troops to Texas in 1845." Barker, "California as the Cause of the Mexican War," *loc. cit.*, p. 220.

sent of Congress, the resolution stated, was given upon certain conditions, among them the adjustment by the United States "of all questions of boundary that may arise with other governments. . . ." That the resolution would have been passed, unless it was taken for granted that a settlement with Mexico would be reached before actual entry upon the region in question, is at least doubtful.

Against the charge of illegal conduct Polk, defending himself, asserted that Congress had recognized that region as part of our territory by including it within our revenue system and by directing the appointment of a revenue officer to reside within the district. But this sort of thing did not please the Whigs who were naturally ready to attack a Democratic President even if they felt compelled to support the war when once it had begun. Congress, said Alexander Stephens of Georgia, after the outbreak of war, had not made any determination of the boundary of Texas, "and I venture to say that no resolution so fixing the boundary could have passed this or the other House. . . . But some one asks me, what was the President to do? How was he to know where to stop, as there was no fixed line? I answer, his duty was a plain one. It was to keep the army within that portion of the territory which 'rightfully belonged to Texas,' or over which she had established her jurisdiction and supremacy, where her laws extended and were enforced, and where the people acknowledged her Government." [4] He contended that Congress alone could determine the boundary in case Mexico would not treat in a friendly manner.[5]

The antislavery men have been charged with wrong-headedness because they could see nothing in the matter but a wicked scheme for the extension of slavery.[6] But it is well to remember that even southern

[4] Speech in the House, June 16, 1846. *Congressional Globe,* 29 Cong., 1 sess., appendix, p. 949. See also Calhoun, *Works,* IV, pp. 377-378.

[5] The orders to General Taylor (August 30, 1845) contain the following: "In case of war, either declared or made manifest by hostile acts, your main object will be the protection of Texas; but the pursuit of this object will not necessarily confine your action within the territory of Texas. Mexico having thus commenced hostilities, you may . . . cross the Rio Grande, disperse or capture the forces assembling to invade Texas, defeat the junction of troops uniting for that purpose, drive them from their positions on either side of that river, and, if deemed practicable and expedient, take, and hold possession of, Matamoras and other places in the country." *Executive Documents,* 30 Cong., 1 sess., VII, no. 60, pp. 88-89. In light of all the facts, there may have been justification of this procedure; but one is inclined to inquire what becomes of the authority of Congress to declare war?

[6] See, for example, Burgess, *op. cit.,* p. 331. Burgess says the attitude of the abolitionists—meaning by the term probably the men opposed to slavery-expansion—was "too narrow and bigoted to win much attention."

Whigs denounced Polk's audacity, and no one can be surprised at the antislavery indignation when one takes into account that those men knew, even as you and I, the correspondence of Calhoun of two years before and the alleged danger lurking in the existence of a free Texas. The technical right, if such there were, to move troops into a disputed area and then to proclaim the opening of a defensive war, begun because of Mexican aggression, need not lead us to proclaim the blindness and perversity of the antislavery men. The whole movement for expansion which resulted in securely gathering in a vast territory was, beyond question, due in large degree to a passion for enlargement and to patriotic pride, augmented by fears and charges of British imperial plans and of plots for dominion or for controlling influence in the far west. Even Calhoun, commonly considered the particular champion of slavery, objected to the methods by which, without congressional approval, the country had been, as he believed, hurried into war; and though later he advocated a line of demarcation running through to the Pacific, he was opposed to the wild schemes for absorbing Mexican territory which were filling the minds of enthusiastic patriots.[7]

The slavery question arose almost as soon as war was begun.[8] Polk wanted money and he hoped to get more territory than was "rightfully belonging" to the state of Texas or than we had claimed.[9]

[7] Calhoun's speech of February 9, 1847, is impressive, especially where he declares that in selecting a "defensive line" it should be "such as would deprive Mexico in the smallest possible degree of her resources and her strength. . . ." *Works,* IV, pp. 306-307. See also his fear of sectional dispute. *Ibid.,* p. 323.

[8] The persistence of the slavery question and the extent to which the subject frayed the nerves of contestants in debate is humorously presented by Benton's speech in the Senate, May 31, 1848. "This Federal Government was made for something else than to have this pestiferous question constantly thrust upon us to the interruption of the most important business. . . . What I protest against is, to have the real business of the country, the pressing, urgent, crying business of the country stopped, prostrated, defeated, by thrusting this question upon us. We read in Holy Writ, that a certain people were cursed by the plague of frogs, and that the plague was everywhere. You could not look upon the table but there were frogs, you could not sit down at the banquet but there were frogs, you could not go to the bridal couch and lift the sheets but there were frogs! . . . Here it is, this black question, forever on the table, on the nuptial couch, everywhere! . . . I remember the time when no one would have thought of asking a public man what his opinions were on the extension of slavery any more than what was the length of his foot. . . ." *Congressional Globe,* 30 Cong., 1 sess., appendix, p. 686.

[9] Message to Congress, August 8, 1846: "It is probable that the chief obstacle to be surmounted in accomplishing this desirable object [a peace just and honorable to both parties] will be the adjustment of a boundary between the two Republics which shall prove satisfactory and convenient to both, and such as neither will hereafter be

In midsummer (August, 1846), the war being then well under way, he asked Congress to make an appropriation to provide for any expenditure which it might be necessary to make in advance for the purpose of settling all difficulties with Mexico. To an appropriation bill framed to carry out the President's wishes, David Wilmot of Pennsylvania proposed a proviso that neither slavery nor involuntary servitude should ever exist within any of the territory to be acquired.[10] The House passed the bill as thus amended and did so without delay, August 8, 1846. But the bill was talked to death in the Senate by an advocate of the proviso who in his loquacious anxiety forgot that the hour ending the session was at hand—a fateful blunder. Of course, to win the Senate to the principle of the proviso would have been difficult, perhaps impossible, anxious as men were to push the appropriation through; but had Congress at that juncture definitely declared in favor of free soil, would it have been possible for the south after annexation to demand the right of taking their slaves into the new west?

The question arose again the next year (1847) in connection with a bill to appropriate three million dollars for the purpose [11] of enabling the President to conclude a treaty of peace with Mexico. The Wilmot proviso was again introduced. In the course of the debate that followed, Douglas moved to extend the line of thirty-six thirty through any territory acquired under the act; but the House would not consent.[12] The same day the antislavery proviso was passed by a vote of 115 to 106, and the bill was passed by a substantially similar vote. The Senate, however, was not of that mind; an attempt to provide for the exclusion of slavery was defeated; and though Wilmot returned to the attack in the House, his proviso was there defeated also (March 3, 1847), and the bill for the appropriation was passed unadorned by an antislavery attachment.[13] The most noteworthy fact is

inclined to disturb. In the adjustment of this boundary we ought to pay a fair equivalent for any concessions which may be made by Mexico." Richardson, *Messages and Papers,* IV, p. 459.

[10] It is noteworthy that this movement was begun by Free Soil Democrats—a warning that there were dissatisfied elements in the party and foreshadowing later opposition to slavery-extension.

[11] *Congressional Globe,* 29 Cong., 2 sess., p. 303 (February 1, 1847).

[12] February 15, 1847. *Ibid.,* 424. The rejection did not mean the abandonment of the purpose to exclude slavery from the *whole* area.

[13] The Senate rejected an antislavery amendment by a vote of thirty-one to twenty-one, March 1, 1847. *Ibid.,* p. 555. Wilmot's amendment of March 3 was lost in the House by a vote of 97 to 102. The appropriation bill was passed by a vote of 115 to 81. *Ibid.,* p. 573.

the size of the antislavery vote in both houses : opposition to the extension of slavery was not confined to an insignificant number, nor was it
the special possession of a small body, who, like the abolitionists, might
be charged with unreasoning enthusiasm. Reasons for passing the
appropriation measure without the proviso were probably not due to
a complete surrender of the principle. The session was nearly at an
end; something must be done if money was to be granted for making
a peace and acquiring territory; congressmen obstructing the government by insisting on the proviso would meet criticism or opposition;
zeal for territorial expansion was daily waxing stronger and reached
extremes of patriotic fervor in the months that followed.[14]

The historian is subject to professional inhibitions; he must not
indulge in inclinations to favor one side or the other; he must not
believe that even the extermination of slavery was a good thing for
the world; he must stand stolid and unmoved in the presence of a great
controversy which was one of the most momentous in the annals of
America and the world. This is supposed to be his attitude; but no
one, unless ceasing to be human, can fail to be stirred by the events
of those years. After all, the nineteenth century is known and will be
known as the century during which slavery disappeared from the
civilized world; and if the United States in 1848 had so far forgotten
herself as to absorb Mexico, and had she been drawn on to further
conquests, America and the world would be—though *ex post facto*
prophecy is also forbidden the historian—quite different from what
they are to-day.

In February, 1848, the treaty of Guadalupe Hidalgo was signed
and transmitted to Washington. An interesting problem was presented.
The treaty had been negotiated by N. P. Trist, an agent sent long
before by Polk. He had been recalled but continued to act, and the
result of his insolent persistence was now in the President's hands.
With many grumblings and much ill-suppressed irritation Polk accepted the treaty and sent it to the Senate where it was found accept-

[14] See E. G. Bourne, "The United States and Mexico, 1847-1848," *Am. Hist. Rev.*,
V, pp. 491-502. This article of Bourne, especially if one supplement it by reading the
debates in Congress, furnishes an astonishing picture of the manifest-destiny fever of
those hectic days. When Congress met in December, 1847, Calhoun introduced resolutions against the extinction of Mexican nationality and declared (December 20)
one could scarcely read a newspaper without finding it filled with speculation on that
subject. An illustration of the high-flown sentimentality is in the speech of Dickinson
of New York who declared in the Senate (January 12, 1848) that it was America's
destiny to include the whole of North America.

able. It provided for compensation to Mexico for the surrender of a great region extending westward to the Pacific. Mexico was to be paid fifteen million dollars and the United States assumed claims against the Mexican government. The treaty with Great Britain in 1846 established our claim to the Oregon country as far north as the forty-ninth parallel. Thus during Polk's presidency a vast area was added to the United States. Was it to be the home of slavery or of free labor?

By the law of Mexico, slavery did not exist in the territory which she surrendered. There was also no slavery in Oregon; and the people of Oregon, several hundreds in number, left to their own devices, formed a temporary government and excluded slavery. Was there any constitutional obligation to establish slavery in these regions? Orators spoke in fervid periods about the glorious forward march of freedom under the banner of liberty and self-government; and yet there were some who asserted that the banner carried slavery with it. By the summer of 1848 various theories had been presented, and we may well give them briefly at this point, omitting for the moment any full consideration of the constitutional questions involved.

(1) Antislavery men declared that slavery should be forbidden; the western land was free and should not be inundated by slavery. Doubtless most of them, though eager to oppose the extension of slavery, were content with a declaration of the duty of Congress to exercise its power to exclude slavery from the newly-acquired territory. Others, taking a more advanced position, denied the authority of Congress to recognize or establish slavery in the public domain; the Free Soil party, organized in 1848, nominated Van Buren and Adams, and on a ringing platform declared Congress had no more power to make a slave than to make a king.

(2) At the opposite extreme stood Calhoun, ably supported by Jefferson Davis of Mississippi in the Senate and by Barnwell Rhett of South Carolina in the House. Congress, according to these defenders of southern rights, was under constitutional obligation to hold the territories for the common use and benefit of the states, and the southerner had as much right to go west with his slaves as the northerner had to go with horses or sheep.

(3) At the end of the year 1847, Lewis Cass of Michigan issued his Nicholson letter.[15] Cass was a Democratic leader, was considered

---

[15] The letter to A. O. P. Nicholson of Tennessee is given in W. T. Young, *Life of General Lewis Cass*, p. 320 ff. A copy was printed in pamphlet form at Washington

a likely candidate of the party for the presidential office, and was in fact nominated in 1848. Congress, he asserted, should leave slavery alone and allow the people of an organized territory to deal with the troublesome problem as they saw fit. This was not literally the beginning of the doctrine of what came to be known as popular sovereignty or, as less politely termed, "squatter sovereignty"; arguments against the power of Congress to deal with slavery had already been put forth in congressional debates,[16] but the letter brought the matter to public attention. Cass's argument in the letter was not so vigorous in its denial of constitutional authority as were some of his speeches at a later day; but it appeared not only to point to the justice and propriety of placing upon the people of the territories the full right of self-government, but also to indicate the constitutional obligation to allow them full control of domestic affairs.

These were the main and outstanding constitutional doctrines. Before taking up these various theories for detailed examination, we should notice a bill introduced by Senator Clayton of Delaware for the establishment of governments in Oregon, California, and New Mexico (July 18, 1848). The bill was intended to embody a compromise and was commonly so-called. It provided for the temporary recognition of the laws in force in Oregon. The governments of California and New Mexico were to have no power to legislate on the subject of slavery. In this way, the right to introduce or prohibit slavery was made to rest "on the Constitution, as the same should be expounded by the judges, with a right of appeal to the Supreme Court of the United States." It was thought, Clayton explained, that Congress would thus "avoid the decision of this distracting question, leaving it to be settled by the silent operation of the Constitution itself. . . ."[17] The measure passed the Senate, but it received short shrift in the

---

(1847) and was probably widely circulated. For discussion of the doctrine of the letter, see A. C. McLaughlin, *Lewis Cass*, p. 232 ff.

[16] See, for example, the remarks of Leake of Virginia in the House, February 17, 1847. Possibly he leaves one in a little uncertainty, but he said, "We [the south] maintain . . . that is a question to be left to the people of this territory to decide, and with which this Government cannot interfere." *Congressional Globe*, 29 Cong., 2 sess., p. 444. This is to be compared with his speech of a few days earlier. *Ibid.*, appendix, pp. 111-113. See also resolutions introduced into the Senate by Dickinson of New York, December 15, 1847. *Ibid.*, 30 Cong., 1 sess., p. 27. For an argument denying congressional authority, see the speech of John Gayle of Alabama in the House, March 28, 1848. *Ibid.*, p. 542.

[17] *Congressional Globe*, 30 Cong., 1 sess., p. 950. It is interesting to notice that Calhoun voted for the measure. *Ibid.*, p. 1002.

House. The proposal of the bill for leaving the slavery question to the Court is of importance in light of certain portions of the Compromise of 1850, which will be discussed later, the Kansas-Nebraska bill of 1854, and the Supreme Court decision in 1857.

In the course of debate, various opinions were expressed about the advisability of this proposed settlement of the vexing problem. Corwin of Ohio declared the bill to be "a rich and rare legislative curiosity"; it did not enact a law, but only a lawsuit. Hale of New Hampshire said the Constitution was interpreted as variously as the Bible. Badger of North Carolina was unwilling to leave the decision "to a court, so large a portion of which were opposed to slavery." Stephens of Georgia, later Vice-President of the Confederacy, was unwilling to turn the matter over to the Court because he believed the Constitution did not carry slavery into a region where it did not exist, and the Court must so decide. Congress should, he believed, acknowledge the equitable right to carry slavery into the western territory and should legislate accordingly; but inasmuch as the southwest was free by the law of Mexico, it must remain free until positive legislation provided for slavery: "The Constitution no more carries the local law of slavery of any State into a State or Territory where, by law, it is prohibited, than it carries any other local law. . . ." [18] A bill organizing Oregon was passed in the summer of 1848; it extended the principle of the Ordinance of 1787 over the territory and thus indicated plainly the belief of Congress that it had the power to exclude slavery.

One feature of the debates in the Senate deserves a word of comment. Stephen A. Douglas was now pushing toward the front and was soon to be the leader of the northern Democracy. As chairman of the Senate committee on territories he had peculiarly good opportunity to fashion legislation. He advocated the extension of the Missouri Compromise line through to the Pacific. All through these debates, though some southerners found fault with the Compromise, and though arguments were brought forth to deny congressional authority to exclude slavery from the national domain, the permanence, even the sanctity, of the Compromise of 1820 appears on the whole to have been taken for granted.

We may now consider more carefully these opposing theories of constitutional obligation. The advanced proslavery doctrine was nat-

---

[18] *Congressional Globe,* 30 Cong., 1 sess., appendix, p. 1106. See a letter written by Stephens in 1854 explaining his opposition to the Clayton Compromise. *Am. Hist. Rev.,* VIII, pp. 91-97.

urally put forward by Calhoun, now nearing the end of his long and laborious life. For twenty years he had been the champion of southern interests, opposing the tariff, defending slavery as a wise and moral institution, announcing his devotion to the union and the Constitution, but holding forth the need of southern unity and the inevitable dissolution of the union if the Constitution were distorted by northern economic greed or by unfairness to the south. Even attacks on the morality of slavery were in his opinion unjust and dangerous; the union must be preserved by a sacred regard for the peculiar institution of the south. Again one is impressed by the vigor and earnestness of this pathetic figure as he argued with consummate skill in behalf of a cause doomed by fate to destruction.

Fundamental in Calhoun's thinking, even more fundamental than state sovereignty, was hostility to majority rule. Of this something has been said in a previous chapter. For this reason he lamented the growing tendency to speak of the United States as a nation. Declaring the devotion of the south to the union, he exclaimed: "Sir, we are as devoted to this Union as any portion of the American people. I use the phrase as meaning the people of the Union. But we see in nationality evils immeasurable to us. Admit us to be a nation, we see where we stand. We are in a minority. We have peculiar institutions; we have peculiar productions; and we shall have to trust to the mere numerical majority of the whole—the unsafest of all Governments— for protection. I would rather trust to a sovereign. I would rather trust to an aristocracy—any form of government, rather than to that." [19]

Clinging closely to the idea of state sovereignty as the basis of constitutional right, Calhoun was fearful lest by the introduction of new free states the rights of the slaveholding states would be utterly destroyed. He was in fact looking upon the union as in reality a union of sections, though he held it to be constitutionally a union of sovereign states. Indeed, much as the northerners might speak of the nation, and far as the idea of nationalism had sunk into their inmost thoughts, even they could not conceal from themselves the fact of sectional divergence. As shown by his "Discourse on the Constitution and Government of the United States," the great southern leader

---

[19] February 20, 1847. *Congressional Globe*, 29 Cong., 2 sess., p. 467. But if mere numbers could not govern, how could a state within its own limits actually manage its own affairs? Calhoun believed restrictions to be the sum of constitutionalism; and, we must remember, he put forth the theory of concurrent majority which he illustrated by the experiences of South Carolina.

was now interested more keenly, if possible, than ever before in preventing a complete breakdown of the balance or of even the constitutional equilibrium of the sections.[20] The very essence of his theory of concurrent majority included fundamentally the existence of contrary interests, each with its own identity. The equilibrium as a practical fact had already been destroyed; a recognition of state sovereignty and of the equal right of the southern slaveholder in the territories without discrimination was the remedy. But could he actually hope that slavery with these safeguards could hold its own, especially if every territory when coming into the union could decide for itself whether it should be free or slave?

Though Calhoun was interested in sectional equality or such a policy as would prevent the southern states from being reduced to an unhappy minority, the immediate question was slavery in the territories. On that matter, he declared, the Constitution furnished a remedy: the public domain "is the common property of the States of this Union. They are called 'the territories of the United States.' And what are the 'United States' but the States united? Sir, these territories are the property of the States united; held jointly for their common use." [21] He introduced resolutions which asserted that the territories belong to the several states and are held by them as their joint and common property; that Congress, as the joint agent of the states, has no right to make any discrimination between the states by which any of them shall be deprived of its equal right in any territory; that an act depriving citizens of any state from emigrating with their property would be a violation of the Constitution and the rights of the states from which the citizens emigrated, and in derogation of the perfect equality which belongs to the members of the union; that a people, in forming a constitution, have the right to adopt a government which they think best suited to their needs, and no condition for admission into the union can be imposed, save that its constitution shall be republican.

Before this speech, Barnwell Rhett of South Carolina had proclaimed the same doctrine in the House.[22] The Constitution, he said,

---

[20] Notice Calhoun's speech of February 19, 1847. *Ibid.*, p. 453 ff.

[21] *Ibid.*, p. 454.

[22] January 15, 1847. *Congressional Globe*, 29 Cong., 2 sess., appendix, pp. 244-247. I am not seeking to establish any priority for either Rhett or Calhoun, but to present the theory as it came from both. Rhett in this speech saw that the "only effect, and probably the only object of their reserved sovereignty is, that it secures to each State

"declares, that the territories belong to the United States. They are tenants in common, or joint proprietors, and co-sovereigns over them. As co-sovereigns they have agreed, in their common compact, the Constitution, that their agent, the General Government, 'may dispose of, and make all needful rules and regulations,' with respect to them; but, beyond this, they are not limited or limitable in their rights. Their sovereignty, unalienated and unimpaired by this mutual concession to each other, exists in all its plenitude over our territories; as much so, as within the limits of the States themselves."

Here then was state sovereignty in its starkest and crudest form. There was nothing of the refinement of earlier argument. The Constitution was a plain contract between individual entities, and they as such own the territories.

Jefferson Davis of Mississippi, in a very able speech, defended the proslavery cause, but he did not, like Rhett and Calhoun, base the right to carry slaves into the territories on the ownership of the territories by the states;[23] nor indeed did he with any fullness put forward the sovereignty of the states as proof of southern rights, although he used some expressions which may bear such an interpretation. He argued from the Constitution and found there no power to exclude slavery. He discovered, on the other hand, a recognition of slaves as property. ". . . territory of the United States," he said, "is the property of all the people of the United States; . . . sovereignty of the territory remains with them until it is admitted as an independent State into the Union. . . ." Congress could not discriminate against one kind of property. He also made one important admission: "but for the Constitution the right to property in slaves could not have extended beyond the State which possessed them."[24]

In one particular, Calhoun agreed with Cass in denying the right of Congress to govern the territories; but he thus agreed only by denying that the power of Congress came from the clause in the Con-

the right to enter the territories with her citizens, and settle and occupy them with their property—with whatever is recognised as property by each State." p. 246.

[23] In this respect Davis, we may notice now, came more nearly than did Calhoun to the announcement of the principles upon which the Supreme Court ten years later decided the question of slavery in the territories.

[24] July 12, 1848. *Congressional Globe*, 30 Cong., 1 sess., appendix, pp. 907-914. An interesting letter to Calhoun written in March, 1848, by John A. Campbell, later a Justice of the Supreme Court, is in the *Miss. Valley Hist. Rev.*, XIX, pp. 568-570. Campbell then insisted upon the local character of slavery.

stitution granting the authority "to dispose of, and make all needful rules and regulations respecting, the territory or other property belonging to the United States;" he could find no direct and unequivocal grant of power. The word "all" may have given him pause. But he declared the United States could acquire territory; the right came from the war and treaty-making powers. The people of the territories thus annexed are subject to the laws of the United States; they are not free to do as they please; in the latter case "they would cease to be the territories of the United States the moment we acquired them and permitted them to be inhabited. The first half-dozen of squatters would become the sovereigns, with full dominion and sovereignty over them. . . ." [25]

But though Congress has power, Calhoun could not admit that Congress has full power; the general government must act for the benefit of the real owners, the states, and furthermore it is limited by certain "general and absolute prohibitions of the constitution" such as the provisions prohibiting *ex post facto* laws, the establishment of religion, and granting titles of nobility.[26] He swept aside the notion that the laws of Mexico against slavery remain in effect after annexation. The Constitution followed the flag, and the flag bore slavery in its folds. There was no need of affirmative legislation to establish slavery; it already existed as a matter of legal fact in acquired territory; Congress would act both unjustly and illegally in attempting to make the territory free. An argument like that presented to the House by Stephens, declaring the territories were free because the law of the country from which they were acquired continued in force, made no impression on Calhoun,[27] who would recognize as law nothing contrary to the Constitution; the Constitution recognized property in slaves. Neither the Ordinance of 1787 nor the Missouri Compromise, as precedents indicative of congressional power to exclude slavery,

[25] Speech in the Senate, June 27, 1848. *Works,* IV, p. 479 ff.

[26] In this latter assertion, the necessity of respecting individual rights to elementary liberty, Calhoun's argument is in some respects distinctly prophetic of the opinions of the Supreme Court which resulted from the perplexities arising out of the acquisition of territory after the Spanish-American War of 1898. See the opinion given by Justice Brown in Downes *v.* Bidwell, 182 U. S. 244, 277 (1901). See also, *Ibid.,* 294-295; Dorr *v.* United States, 195 U. S. 138 (1904), where Justice Day quotes with approval Hawaii *v.* Mankichi, 190 U. S. 197 (1903). This subject is discussed in later pages of this work.

[27] Stephens's speech, in which there was the most formal and explicit announcement of this doctrine, was given later than the long one by Calhoun delivered June 27, 1848, but of course Calhoun knew the theory well and swept it aside.

abashed the sturdy champion of the peculiar institution. Even if they were to be given all the force which could be claimed for them as precedents, "they would not have the weight of a feather against the strong presumption which I . . . showed to be opposed to the existence of the power." [28] He did not have much, if anything, to say about the practical necessity of positive legislation for the protection of slave property in the territories; possibly he intentionally shunned such dangerous and delicate ground, for he may have seen how instinctively the north, now becoming acutely sensitive, would shrink from the idea of affirmative legislation.

Toward the end of a powerful speech which has already been referred to and which elicits our admiration because of its frankness, vigor, and clarity, Calhoun (with as near an approach to humor as he ever showed) denounced the "proposition . . . repeated daily from tongue to tongue," that men are born free and equal: "Men are not born. Infants are born. They grow to be men." But in some respects his warning to the listening Senate is most impressive: "Now, let me say, Senators, if our Union and system of government are doomed to perish, and we to share the fate of so many great people who have gone before us, the historian, who, in some future day, may record the events ending in so calamitous a result, will devote his first chapter to the ordinance of 1787, lauded as it and its authors have been, as the first of that series which led to it. His next chapter will be devoted to the Missouri compromise, and the next to the present agitation." [29]

State sovereignty, Calhoun's beloved, does not in itself, as a matter of pure theory, contradict or deny the right of Congress to exclude slavery from the public domain; whether or not that power was in the hands of Congress must depend on whether or not it had been expressly or impliedly granted by the "sovereign" states; it must depend on the interpretation of the Constitution, call it a compact, if you will. True, Calhoun's statements concerning the southern devotion to slavery sixty years before, [30] if taken at face value, bore upon the question of constitutional interpretation; and the general supposition, which may be ascribed to him, that the government existed to benefit the states and to guard their interests, has its bearing on interpretation. But even if the states were sovereign and had the right of sovereigns to secede for any reason, the authority of Congress to legislate concerning

[28] *Works,* IV, p. 494.
[29] *Ibid.,* p. 507.
[30] *Ibid.,* p. 482.

slavery must rest on a grant to the "agent", as long as the Constitution (the compact) existed.

The doctrine of Cass, though not fully elaborated until somewhat later, deserves attention here, not because of the intricacy of the constitutional problem, but because of its practical importance. It came in the course of time to have a wide popularity. It offered a comfortable escape from any supposed obligation for congressional decision. How thoroughly the constitutional doctrine, which he put forth, was understood or accepted, it is difficult to say. And yet the theory of "squatter" or popular sovereignty rested, in the minds of its advocates, on correct constitutional principles; and furthermore, those principles were in accord with the elemental and sentimental spirit of American government, with the notion that people, and perhaps frontiersmen most of all, should be left alone and not be hampered by intrusion of the strong hand of government. For various reasons these principles appealed to the public—partly of course because they showed the way to avoid responsibility. This announcement that Congress had no authority to manage the domestic affairs of a territory rested not on state sovereignty but on strict construction of the Constitution. Congress had not been assigned the authority, therefore it did not possess the authority. Whence then came the power of the people themselves in the territories to pass upon the question of slavery? From the same source as that from which you yourselves, O conscript fathers, obtained your right to self-government—from Almighty God, from the great and all-controlling principles of justice. All defenders of this doctrine were naturally troubled by the fact that Congress was engaged in the duty of setting up governments in the territories; whence then came the right to do even that much? Cass would limit the right of Congress to the establishment of a government; over matters of domestic concern the people of a territory, with their own government, had complete control. As matters of domestic concern he classed parent and child, husband and wife, master and servant—the last a euphemism for slavery.[31]

As we have seen, Calhoun met such statements with withering scorn. If Congress had a right to annex, it had a right to govern.

---

[31] Cass's doctrine was presented in full in a speech occupying nearly two days, January 21 and 22, 1850. *Congressional Globe,* 31 Cong., 1 sess., appendix, part 1, p. 58 ff. The argument was able and eloquent, but the later exposition, though much fuller than that of the Nicholson letter of two years before and though enlarging on the constitutional foundations for the position, was essentially the same as the earlier statement. In the statement above I have sought to give the fully-developed doctrine.

Control and acquisition went hand in hand, or were one and the same; and the Constitution *ex proprio vigore* at the moment of acquisition covered the whole region. With the Constitution went slavery. If the Constitution recognized slavery, no territorial government, the mere creature of Congress, could do what Congress itself could not do.

Clear as the various announcements of constitutional principles appear to you and me, when they are presented briefly and succinctly, they were capable of causing considerable confusion or uncertainty in the public mind. How many people are likely to read and inwardly digest a senatorial speech? And how easy it is to forget with intentional or unintentional perversity! The Cass doctrine which afterwards paraded at the head of the Democratic procession when Douglas was the master of ceremonies, the doctrine which was later dubbed popular sovereignty, meant this when first pronounced: the people of a territory during the *territorial* time have the right and the constitutional power to establish or prohibit slavery in the *territory*. But to some people the doctrine may have meant simply a proposal to drop the troublesome slavery question from the shoulders of Congress without any miserable haggling about constitutional obligation. Though one cannot altogether resist the inclination to believe that confusion was due to the skill of professional politicians, there was, perhaps at the beginning and more clearly later, some confusion between, on the one hand, the right of the people of the territories to decide the slavery question during their territorial existence—the real doctrine of popular sovereignty—and, on the other hand, their right to decide, when forming a state constitution, whether slavery should be recognized or not. Moreover, the phrase "non-interference with slavery" was coming into favor. Did "non-interference" mean that Congress should just drop the matter and reach no conclusion, or that the territories had the right to decide for themselves, or that nobody, neither Congress nor a territorial legislature, should interfere with a southerner's right to take his slaves to the public domain and hold them there? Slogans are sometimes useful in political controversies, and especially so if they relieve people from the job of thinking.

Concerning the constitutional right to exclude slavery from the territories, the advocates of exclusion were emphatic. Though there were some persons, as we have seen, who denied the right to recognize slavery, the weight of argument in Congress was upon congressional authority to manage the territories; and over and over again historical facts were referred to, showing the actual exercise of authority and disproving the assumption that in the earlier days slavery was the darling of the south. Senator Davis of Massachusetts pointed to the "preposterous" idea that each emigrant from a state carried with him the law of the state from which he came. "Slavery," he said, "unless it can make a law, and support and maintain itself, exists and has existed, and been sustained in these Territories, by the United States. If, then, they can create or sustain it, they can abolish it, unless prohibited by the Constitution." [32]

No one can know how much of acute legal argument had penetrated the mind of the average voter in the campaign of 1848. The Free Soilers, it is true, on the face of their platform, felt no doubt. The Democratic platform indulged in safe platitudes, and Cass's letter of acceptance of the presidential nomination was couched in guarded terms. But it is to be noted that Yancey of Alabama introduced a resolution in the Democratic convention announcing "the true republican doctrine" to be "non-interference with the rights of property of any portion of the people of this confederacy, be it in the States or Territories thereof, by any other than the parties interested in them. . . ." What did he mean by "non-interference" or by the words "parties interested in them"? The resolution was defeated. What did the defeat imply? Probably Yancey meant Calhoun's doctrine of the sanctity of slave property. But the words might possibly be interpreted to mean the doctrine already set forth by Cass, the nominee of the convention, or to mean just leaving the subject alone.[33]

[32] *Congressional Globe*, 30 Cong., 1 sess., appendix, p. 895.

[33] MacDonald, a careful scholar, says Yancey's statement was the doctrine of squatter sovereignty. *Select Documents* (William MacDonald, ed.), p. 378. And yet, Yancey in the Alabama convention of that year moved to declare that doctrine equally false with the doctrine that Congress could exclude slavery from the territories. See Joseph Hodgson, *The Cradle of the Confederacy*, p. 270. See also H. von Holst, *The Constitutional and Political History of the United States*, III, p. 363; M. M. Quaife, *The Doctrine of Non-Intervention With Slavery in the Territories*, pp. 75-76. Quaife thinks Yancey may have intentionally couched his resolution in ambiguous terms.

CHAPTER XXXVIII

THE COMPROMISE OF 1850

The Whigs elected Taylor in 1848, and the defeat of Cass was chargeable partly to the defection of the Free Soil Democrats in New York.[1] The slavery question remained to be dealt with. Taylor was inexperienced in political affairs, but he was by temperament inclined to be judicious, and, though a slaveholder, he was not likely to take an extreme position on slavery. In his inaugural address (March 5, 1849) he scarcely touched upon the great problem, but he did express an intention not to support "any particular section or merely local interest. . . ."

His annual message (December 4, 1849) called the attention of Congress to California, where the people had formed a state constitution and were about to ask admission into the union. He spoke with a degree of uncertainty because word of the final framing and adoption of the state constitution had not as yet reached Washington; "latest advices" gave him reason to suppose the work was finished and he expected the state would apply for admission. He knew well enough, however, what was going on in the western west; the eager gold-hunters wished to govern themselves and were equal to the task. In fact, he announced to Congress that he had sent agents to California and New Mexico, and he "did not hesitate to express to the people of those Territories" his wish "that each Territory should, if prepared to comply with the requisitions of the Constitution of the United States, form a plan of a State constitution and submit the same to Congress. . . ." Denying any intention of interfering with the domestic institutions of the western people, he nevertheless had advised the formation of a constitution, for he was actuated by a "desire to afford to the wisdom and patriotism of Congress the opportunity of avoiding occasions of bitter and angry dissensions among the people of

[1] New York was a "close" state. In 1844, if the Liberty party men had voted for Clay, he would have carried that state, and if the Free Soilers had voted for Cass, he would have carried the state in 1848; but of course not all the Free Soilers were recreant Democrats.

the United States." He believed both territories, if they should present themselves for admission, should be allowed to enter the union.[2]

The Californians formed a constitution which did not recognize slavery. The rest of the territory acquired from Mexico was without territorial government. Would Congress admit California and thus disturb the existing balance between free and slave states; and would it look with any favor on the exclusion of slavery from the territories not yet organized? Those were the critical questions during the fateful months of 1850. There were certain additional problems. What should be done with the western part of Texas which might properly be considered as lying within the general region of New Mexico, if not legally a part of it? The existence of slavery in the District of Columbia still stirred the antislavery forces. The slaveholders, on the other hand, complained because their slaves were escaping from bondage and finding protection at the north.

As we enter upon a brief study of the debates, the constitutional arguments, and the expansive oratory of the session of 1850, the tragedy of the coming civil war seems to cast its shadow upon us. We realize, too, that in some respects we have passed into a new era; Calhoun, Clay, and Webster, who had begun their active political careers some forty years before, were still living and they participated in the debates; but they were reaching the end. They had entered the field when American nationality was endangered by internal dissension and when national dignity was attacked by contemptuous treatment from foreign nations. Each in his own way, southerner and northerner alike, had striven to maintain the union. Calhoun had always asserted his devotion to the union, the union as he conceived it to be; and now at the end, the hand of death upon him, there still burned within him a spark of affection for the nation which he would refuse to consider a nation at all. Clay, a border statesman, who more than any other statesman during those forty years had appealed to the sympathy and loyal affection of all sections, had done valiant service by his real spirit of generous nationalism. "Compromise" is the word usually used in speaking of Clay's statesmanship, but the word need carry no opprobrious meaning; we need to bear in mind the continuing presence of sectional interests and of rivalries which might have become hostilities. Sectionalism, moreover, had not been confined to the controversies between north and south, and adjustment was a continuing necessity. Webster's oratory had enthralled men, and he, too, had cherished the

2 Richardson, *Messages and Papers*, V, pp. 27-28.

union and aroused in his hearers, if they had ears willing to hear, ardent devotion to their country. Now these men, leaders for a generation, were leaving the field of action. But the old question remained: could the nation survive?

The reader of the debates finds himself in a new, though not utterly strange, atmosphere. The younger men—not mere striplings, but already experienced combatants—were prepared to speak with a certain directness; they spoke bluntly; their thinking appears, in a way, more realistic; but the difference between them and the men of the generation then passing from the field is not easily described. The northerners among them recognized the actuality of sectional variations. William H. Seward, Salmon P. Chase, and Stephen A. Douglas cannot be charged with a want of national spirit; but they had not been brought up in a school in which the one motivating principle was the necessity of maintaining the union. Alexander H. Stephens of Georgia was, or had been, a strong unionist; but he was not willing to sacrifice all for the cause. Jefferson Davis, upon whom the mantle of Calhoun fell when the old warrior was summoned by death, contended vigorously for the peculiar interests of the south, but to us he seems to be lacking in the intensity of moral enthusiasm which characterized the great Carolinian, and to be in some ways more sectional in his sympathy than the exponent of the philosophy of sectionalism himself.

Clay, entering upon the last great effort of his life, introduced in January a series of resolutions [3] which became the subject of prolonged controversy. The first resolution provided for the admission of California without any restriction in regard to slavery. The second declared that as slavery did not exist by law and was not likely to be introduced into any of the territory acquired from Mexico, it was inexpedient for Congress to provide either for or against its inclusion, and that suitable territorial governments ought to be established in the region without any restriction or condition on the subject of slavery. The third laid down boundaries for Texas "excluding any portion of New Mexico. . . ." The fourth proposed that the United States should provide for the payment of that portion of the public debt of Texas contracted prior to her annexation—a payment not above a sum to be specified—on condition that Texas relinquish claim to any part of New Mexico. The fifth announced the inexpediency of the abolition of slavery in the District of Columbia except under certain

[3] January 29, 1850. *Congressional Globe,* 31 Cong., 1 sess., pp. 246-247.

conditions. The sixth declared the expediency of prohibiting the trade in slaves brought into the District either to be sold therein as merchandise or to be transported to other markets. The seventh declared that a more effectual fugitive slave law ought to be enacted. The eighth denied the powers of Congress to prohibit or obstruct the trade in slaves between slaveholding states, and asserted the admission or exclusion of slaves brought from one state into another was wholly a subject for state legislation.[4]

These subjects consumed the attention of Congress for months. Speech followed speech. There was much plain speaking and no little bitterness. Threats of secession were not uncommon,[5] and there were fervid declarations of devotion to the union. Some of the southerners were willing to accept the Missouri Compromise line through to the Pacific: "We maintain", said Jefferson Davis, "that it is the right of the people of the South to carry this species of property to any portion of the Territories of the United States; that it rests under the Constitution, upon the same basis as other property; but, when speaking of a compromise, it was the ultimatum I announced. . . . It is a partial recognition of a right we claim to be co-extensive with the Territories of the United States; but which we are willing, in a spirit of compromise, and in compliance with the past acquiescence of the States, to restrict by the parallel of 36° 30′ north." [6]

As we might expect, able and incisive speeches, direct and forceful, not clouding the issue, came from the men who had not been leaders and orators for a generation. Stephen A. Douglas took active part. Salmon P. Chase of Ohio spoke on one occasion for the greater part

[4] Henry S. Foote of Mississippi, after Clay had finished presenting his resolutions and commenting on them, said if other questions connected with the subject of slavery could be satisfactorily adjusted, he saw no objection to admitting all California above the thirty-six thirty line, provided a new slave state could be formed within the existing state of Texas "so as to keep up the present *equiponderance* between the slave and the free States," and provided all was done by way of compromise. *Ibid.*, p. 247. This is another evidence of the determination of southern leaders to maintain a balance between sections. See also *Ibid.*, pp. 166-168.

[5] Even from certain inhabitants of Pennsylvania and Delaware came a petition praying for the immediate and peaceful dissolution of the union. *Ibid.*, p. 311. See also *Ibid.*, p. 414.

[6] *Ibid.*, p. 250. Reference should be made to the speech of Toombs of Georgia, February 27, 1850, *Congressional Globe*, 31 Cong., 1 sess., appendix, p. 199: "We have the right to call on you to give your blood to maintain these thousands and all the rest of the slaves of the South in bondage. . . . This is a pro-slavery Government. Slavery is stamped upon its heart—the Constitution."

of two days, especially disclosing by copious references to historical documents the opposition to slavery in the days of the Revolution. An effective speech was made by George W. Julian, a Representative from an Indiana district peopled largely by Quakers. Anyone desiring a plain, unvarnished presentation of the attitude of common men of the north toward slavery, anyone desiring to read a straightforward statement in reply to the charge that the northern fanatics had vexed the south by their aggression, may well read this sincere speech of a man who felt deeply but did not indulge in unnecessary and acrimonious assaults upon the south.

Three speeches have become famous in American history—those made by Calhoun, Webster, and Seward. Calhoun emphasized the balance of the sections. To an extent quite unsupported by historical fact, he saw the union in reality as a union of sections; he found the equilibrium existing at the time the Constitution was formed, and conveyed the impression, though perhaps unintentionally, that such balancing was the plain purpose of the framers of the Law of the Land. When the government was established "there was nearly a perfect equilibrium between the two, which afforded ample means to each to protect itself against the aggression of the other; but, as it now stands, one section has the exclusive power of controlling the Government, which leaves the other without any adequate means of protecting itself against its encroachment and oppression." [7] It is unnecessary for us to say again that the framers of the Constitution did not intend to establish a union of sections rather than a union of states; but the fact which in Calhoun's mind was fraught with peril was the preponderance of northern power and northern votes.

Webster's seventh of March speech was the most sharply criti-

[7] *Works*, IV, p. 544. This "balance" interpretation of the Constitution is shown with astonishing clearness in a speech by S. W. Inge of Alabama defending the principle of ownership of the territories by the states as separate sovereignties, and announcing that the Constitution not only guaranteed slavery where it existed but provided for its extension. "Will the representatives of the North attempt," he asked, "by the power of numbers, to outrage the Constitution and degrade the South by the the admission of this Territory as a State, without the offer of some equivalent?" This "outrage" was the admission of California as a free state. *Congressional Globe*, 31 Cong., 1 sess., appendix, pp. 103-105. If one also wishes to see the ideas which hardened the northern heart, he may read in Inge's speech the account of southern prosperity which would result from southern independence—the mouth of the Mississippi would be held, Cuba would be ready to spring into the embrace of the south, a field of indefinite extension would invite "us south and west of the Rio Grande." *Ibid.*, p. 105.

cized and was probably the most important. On the whole, he defended the proposed Compromise. "Now, as to California and New Mexico," he said, "I hold slavery to be excluded from those territories by a law even superior to that which admits and sanctions it in Texas. I mean the law of nature, of physical geography, the law of the formation of the earth." He believed the south had been wronged by the northern people and legislators by their "disinclination to perform fully their constitutional duties" in regard to the return of fugitive slaves. He did not enter upon a consideration of technical problems of constitutional law; he seemed to think the time for that had gone by. The speech was an appeal to the spirit of union and nationalism. It was intended to be soothing, and it was inspiring, but it brought down upon him the maledictions of thousands at the north who had expected, or hoped for, support of the antislavery cause.

He sketched the change in the attitude of the south toward slavery from the days of the Revolution. He spoke of the antislavery forces in terms which were at times contemptuous. He found fault with men who thought clearly of their own duty but in the embracement of one truth were led to a disregard of other truths equally important: "As I heard it stated strongly, not many days ago, these persons are disposed to mount upon some particular duty, as upon a war-horse, and to drive furiously on and upon and over all other duties that may stand in the way. . . . They are apt, too, to think that nothing is good but what is perfect, and that there are no compromises or modifications to be made in consideration of difference of opinion or in deference to other men's judgment. . . . They prefer the chance of running into utter darkness to living in heavenly light, if that heavenly light be not absolutely without any imperfection." This characterization, while harsh and unfeeling, was not altogether false as a portrayal of the extremists; but there was little defense, little at least that served as consoling defense, for the conscientious and soberminded men who thought the time had come to stop the spread of slavery.

How Webster's speech affected many thousands at the north, we know well enough. They resented it. To what extent it caused others to hesitate and finally to adopt an attitude of compromise is not so easily determined. Recent investigators are convinced of its effect on the south, where the break-up of the union was openly discussed and by many openly advocated. Webster had made up his mind to save the union, if he could; and there seems good reason for believing that he succeeded.[8] That his words held the south from the last fatal plunge and delayed the attempt at secession for a decade, is at least a possible judgment. Neither at the north nor at the south was the advance-guard satisfied with his pronouncement; but he probably made an impression on the more easily persuaded in both sections. Anything that helped to retard the unification of the south in defense of slavery, and postponed the trial of physical strength of the respective sections, helped to preserve the union; for the northern states were rapidly developing in industrial strength, and railroads were increasing northern industrial integrity.

And still, Webster's main line of appeal and assertion, judged by the light of history, is wanting in moral fervor. Even if he were wise in his declaration that slavery could never obtain a hold in the desolate regions of the southwest, was there to be from him no statesmanlike declaration against the institution of slavery, no mild objection to its expansion?[9] He paid but slight attention to the grounds of northern complaint against the south, and must have left the impression that the main if not the only source of irritation was the excited imagination and the mad impulse of northern fanatics. Could a New England statesman find no word of sympathy for the cause of free labor?

If Webster's words were calculated to tranquilize the excited south, and if, as seems to be the fact, they encouraged a spirit of compromise and stimulated hope for a peaceful country, we are still forced to see that expectations of a united country were ill-founded. After all is said, one is justified in appraising statesmanship by the events of later years. By such appraisal, the speech of William H. Seward of New York must take high rank. Seward was a Whig, still comparatively young, though experienced in political life. From now on he

---

[8] Cf. H. D. Foster, "Webster's Seventh of March Speech and the Secession Movement, 1850," with a foreword by Nathaniel Stephenson, *Dartmouth College Reprints,* series 1, no. 5, p. 5. The main body of this article is in *Am. Hist. Rev.,* XXVII, pp. 245-270. Stephenson says: "Here is the aspect of Webster's great stroke that was so long ignored. He did not satisfy the whole South. He did not make friends for himself of Southerners generally. What he did was to drive a wedge into the South, to divide it temporarily against itself. He arrayed the Upper South against the Lower and thus because of the ultimate purposes of men like Cheves with their ambition to weld the South into a genuine unit, he forced them to stand still, and thus to give Northern pacifism a chance to ebb, Northern nationalism a chance to develop."

[9] In 1848, he had declared, "I shall oppose all slavery extension and all increase of slave representation, in all places, at all times, under all circumstances, even against all inducements, against all supposed limitation of great interests, against all combinations, against all compromise." See James Schouler, *History of the United States,* V, p. 110.

awakened sympathetic response in the hearts of many young men of the north who were looking forward to a new, united, non-slaveholding country. No one, probably, would ascribe to the speech as a whole any degree of emotional appeal; portions were eloquent, and portions, from our present point of view, were just plain sense. There is difficulty in realizing that his words appeared at the time to be radical or dangerous. The world, he pointed out, was giving up slavery. Why debate for a moment the propriety of admitting California as a free state? Not one of the existing free states would think of adopting slavery; why question the right of California to be free? Furthermore, the extinction of slavery must come: "I feel assured that slavery must give way, and will give way, to the salutary instructions of economy, and to the ripening influences of humanity; that emancipation is inevitable, and is near; that it may be hastened or hindered; and that, whether it be peaceful or violent, depends upon the question, whether it be hastened or hindered—that all measures which fortify slavery, or extend it, tend to the consummation of violence—all that check its extension and abate its strength, tend to its peaceful extirpation. But I will adopt none but lawful, constitutional, and peaceful means, to secure even that end; and none such can I or will I forego." [10]

One portion of Seward's speech attracted particular notice and was given an interpretation unjustified by a fair consideration of the words: "The Constitution regulates our stewardship; the Constitution devotes the domain to union, to justice, to defence, to welfare, and to liberty. But there is a higher law than the Constitution, which regulates our authority over the domain, and devotes it to the same noble purposes." [11] This was his famous pronouncement of a "higher law"; pro-slavery sympathizers held this "higher law" doctrine to be a blasphemous declaration requiring men to abjure the law and the Constitution, to push forward to their chosen end, and to be guided only by their own zealous fanaticism. The phrase remained in the public mind to trouble the less vehement opponents of slavery at the north and to furnish the defenders of slavery with proof of the unconstitutional aspirations of northern fanatics. But this interpretation of his words seems quite unfair. Men were asked to act not only on their legal authority but in accordance with right and justice.[12]

[10] *Congressional Globe*, 31 Cong., 1 sess., appendix, p. 268.

[11] *Ibid.*, p. 265.

[12] Seward's interpretation of "higher law" in a speech delivered July 2, 1850, appears to give a more reasonable ground for asserting that he was advocating the application of abstract theories in disregard of constitutional obligations.

Before the presentation of Clay's resolutions, Cass made a long and able defense [13] of his doctrine: the constitutional right of the people of a territory, while it existed as a territory, to decide for themselves whether or not they would have slavery in the territory. So plain is this statement that one finds difficulty in attempting to discover how it came about that the theory of territorial or popular sovereignty was later interpreted by some persons as merely the right of a people in a territory to decide the question of slavery when forming a state constitution. The subject under discussion then, and the subject which continued to be under discussion, was the question of slavery in the territories, not in the states. Perhaps the confusion of partisan controversy, the passing of time, congenital difficulty in understanding constitutional theory, and, it may be, the purposeful desire of the canny politicians all contributed to the transmutation of the Cass doctrine.

Jefferson Davis, though at times apparently excited, on the whole spoke calmly. Not indulging in irritating attack upon the north, he presented a forceful argument in favor of slavery-extension. He did not thoroughly accept the reasoning of Calhoun, but did, more plainly than formerly, place his argument on the basis of state sovereignty; the exclusion of slavery from the western region could rightfully come only from agreement of the states, and the validity of the Missouri Compromise was derived from the acquiescence of the states.[14]

Early in May, a committee, to which the perplexing questions involved in Clay's proposals were submitted, presented a report recommending (1) the postponement of any decision concerning the admission of new states formed out of Texas; (2) the admission of California; (3) the establishment of territorial governments for Utah and New Mexico without the Wilmot proviso, embracing all the territory acquired from Mexico not contained within California; (4)

[13] January 21-22, 1850. It occupies about fifty columns of the *Congressional Globe,* and if anyone wishes to read it, no one will interfere with him. See *Congressional Globe,* 31 Cong., 1 sess., appendix, p. 58 ff.

[14] "The sovereignty rests in the States, and there is no power, save that of the States, which can exclude any property, or can determine what is property, in the Territories so held by the States in common. . . . It is, therefore, that I have held and hold that the Missouri compromise derived its validity from the acquiescence of the States, and not from the act of Congress." *Ibid.,* p. 150. If the states owned the territory in common, then only a unanimous agreement could exclude slavery. Davis attacked the doctrine of Cass, "This vagrant power to govern the Territories. . . ." He denied the existence of the power of "any number of individuals, however small, however unauthorized." to exercise the sovereignty held by the states. *Ibid.*

the combination of the two last-named measures in the same bill; (5) the establishment of a boundary for Texas, and the exclusion of New Mexico from the jurisdiction of Texas ("with the grant to Texas of a pecuniary equivalent") ; (6) a more effectual fugitive slave law; and (7) the prohibition of the slave trade in the District of Columbia. A bill which included the second, third, and fifth proposals, and dubbed the "omnibus bill", was introduced, and the debate went on. The President believed the combination objectionable; [15] but his days of opposition were drawing to a close; in the evening of July 9, 1850 he died. Millard Fillmore assumed the presidency. Seward, who had been friendly with Taylor, had influence in the White House no longer. Webster became Secretary of State; the stage was set for the acceptance of the Compromise.

The senators, undeterred by the heat of a Washington summer, continued with their work and succeeded in carrying through the various measures of the Compromise. Utah and New Mexico were given territorial governments with no pronouncement concerning their authority to deal with slavery; California was admitted as a free state; Texas was presented with ten million dollars to recompense her for surrender of her claims, and the boundaries of the state were drawn as they appear to-day; after the first of the succeeding January it should be unlawful to bring a slave into the District of Columbia "for the purpose of being sold"; a fugitive slave act, more drastic than its predecessor, was adopted.

The measures went through the House without substantial change, but September was well advanced before the great composite Compromise was completed.[16] The slavery question was "settled"; the crisis

[15] "The avowed object of uniting the three questions in one bill was, that the new state should serve as a tow-boat for the two territories." H. von Holst, *The Constitutional and Political History of the United States*, III, p. 525. "General Taylor told me, in the last conversation I had with him, that he preferred that California should not come in at all, rather than that she should come in bringing the territories on her back." Webster, *Private Correspondence*, II, p. 387. There was trouble brewing in Texas and threats of serious opposition, but Taylor's stand was like that of Jackson two decades before. Southern Whigs interviewed Taylor. "Southern officers," one of them told him, "will refuse to obey your orders if you send troops to coerce Texas." "Then," replied Taylor, "I will command the army in person; and any man who is taken in treason against the Union I will hang as I did the deserters and spies at Monterey." See Schouler, *op. cit.*, V, p. 185, referring to Thurlow Weed, *Memoirs*, II, ch. 13, and a conversation with F. W. Seward.

[16] On the passage of the bill in the Senate admitting California, a protest was handed in by ten southern senators. It spoke of the act as contrary to the spirit and intent of the Constitution, and as in effect a declaration that the purpose of excluding slavery was so important that all principles of sound policy and of the Constitution

was passed. The only remaining necessity was—to use Lincoln's words of a later day—that people should cease talking about the vexing problem and care nothing about the very thing they cared most about.[17]

Let us now consider the constitutional principles involved in the settlement, though settlement it proved not to be. Concerning the right to exclude slavery from the territories, the most difficult question—the pivotal question—*no decision* was reached. On that point the Compromise *did not contain a clear principle;* that was the beauty of it. It neither accepted nor rejected the doctrine of territorial power to deal with slavery; it neither set forth nor denied the theory of the right of Congress to exclude slavery; nor did it embody the constitutional right of the southerner to take his slaves into the national domain and hold them there under the protection of the Constitution. The pretense of later years that it contained a principle of constitutional right or of justice was only "window-dressing."

Perhaps it may be contended that the principle involved in the Compromise was the doctrine of "non-intervention". But this doctrine had not then and has not now any distinct and positive meaning. If someone wearily reading the sources reaches the conclusion that the act must be read one way and not another, his conclusions will not be very valuable, because he must decide in the end that the people of 1850 did not and could not follow the constitutional arguments as a modern investigator in his study may do as he turns the number-

itself were disregarded. "Against this conclusion we must now and for ever protest, and it is destructive of the safety and liberties of those whose rights have been committed to our care, fatal to the peace and *equality* of the States which we represent, and must lead, if persisted in, to the *dissolution* of the confederacy, in which the slaveholding States have never sought more than *equality,* and in which they will not be content to remain with less." See T. H. Benton, *Thirty Years' View,* II, pp. 769-770. Two senators from Virginia, two from South Carolina, one from Tennessee, one from Louisiana, one—Jefferson Davis—from Mississippi, one from Missouri, and two from Florida, signed the protest. Here there was **threat** of disunion based on the ground of unconstitutional action because a free state was admitted into the union without provision for a like addition to the slaveholding members of the union. What had become of the idea that admission should not turn upon the question of slavery or freedom, but on whether the constitution of the state was in accord with the Constitution of the United States? The nation was a combination of distinct sections; disturbance of the balance was unconstitutional. At no time was a more preposterous declaration submitted to a candid world. The Senate refused to receive the protest.

[17] "Is it not a false statesmanship that undertakes to build up a system of policy upon the basis of caring nothing about the very thing that everybody does care the most about?—a thing which all experience has shown we care a very great deal about?" Lincoln's reply to Douglas at Alton, October 15, 1858. *Political Debates Between Abraham Lincoln and Stephen A. Douglas,* p. 350. Italics of the original omitted.

less pages of the *Congressional Globe* or as he fingers the correspondence and biographies of the politicians of the mid-century.[18]

One thing more: did the framers of the Compromise expressly intend to leave the constitutional problem undecided, expecting the matter to be brought to the Supreme Court? And was there any distinct pledge or agreement to abide by a judicial decision? There is some indication of such an intention; there is no plain evidence of such a pledge. The indication of an intention arises chiefly from the provision in the acts for Utah and New Mexico that all cases involving the title to slaves, without regard to the value of the matter in controversy, might be carried to the Supreme Court, and also that a writ of error or appeal should be allowed to this supreme tribunal "upon any writ of habeas corpus involving the question of personal freedom. . . ." That this was a clear and precise intention to turn over the sole and final responsibility to the Court is certainly not evident.[19]

We now come to the most fateful measure of the whole Compromise—the Fugitive Slave Act. The advanced and earnest antislavery men at the north were indignant. In such attention as we may give the act, perplexing constitutional problems appear. The Constitution provides that "No person held to service or labor in one State, under the

[18] Of interest is a letter written by Howell Cobb of Georgia, July 17, 1850, to be found in *The Correspondence of Robert Toombs, Alexander H. Stephens, and Howell Cobb,* Am. Hist. Asso., *Report* for 1911, II, p. 196 ff. But this long letter may leave the reader in doubt of Cobb's own opinion of the technical meaning of the Compromise. He apparently firmly believed that Congress could not exclude slavery (though he would have been willing to acquiesce in the Missouri Compromise line through to the mountains of the west), and apparently to him "non-intervention" meant this: he says the Senate bill "virtually repudiates" the doctrine of the Wilmot proviso, "leaving the decision of the subject where we have always desired that it should be left, where the Constitution has put it, in the hands of the people, to be decided by their free and unrestricted will under the operation of those great natural causes and influences to which I have already referred." p. 203. This might be interpreted as meaning popular sovereignty—the right of the people of the territory to exclude slavery; he perhaps meant their right to decide when coming into the union.

[19] It is difficult to conceive that A. H. Stephens construed the Compromise as leaving the decision to the Court, in light of the fact that in 1854 he was still contending that unless Congress positively acted to establish slavery, the territory remained free as it was when admitted, and that the Court would so decide. See his letter of June 15, 1854 in *Am. Hist. Rev.,* VIII, pp. 91-97. E. E. Sharpe, "Slavery in the Territories under the Compromise of 1850," *The Historical Outlook,* XVIII, p. 108: "Statesmen in Congress did not agree as to the meaning of the Compromise of 1850." Cass referred to the possibility or desirability of a Court decision. *Congressional Globe,* 31 Cong., 1 sess., p. 1121. What the authors said after 1850 is not sufficient to show what they intended in 1850, but their words show that the Compromise might mean many things. In considering this matter some weight should probably be given to the proposal of the Clayton Compromise of 1848.

laws thereof, escaping into another, shall, in consequence of any law or regulation therein, be discharged from such service or labor, but shall be delivered up on claim of the party to whom such service or labor may be due." [20] As early as 1793, Congress passed an act authorizing anyone claiming a fugitive slave to carry him before either a federal or a state magistrate. In practice, the fugitive was usually brought before a state official.[21] Some of the northern states began to pass laws which sought to prevent the kidnapping of free negroes and furnished remedies in state tribunals. An important case arose in Pennsylvania where a statute (1826) provided against the seizure of free negroes and for procedure in the state courts to protect the rights of persons claimed as slaves. The case was carried to the federal Supreme Court, which, in a long and learned opinion from the pen of Justice Story, pronounced the seizure and return of fugitives solely a matter of federal, not state concern, and declared that while state officials might act, the state was not under obligation to participate in the reclamation of fugitives.[22]

To discuss the constitutional questions is probably a fruitless task. Like other problems, they are not wholly abstract, for historical facts and attitudes of mind complicate them. Even in 1793 there was recognition of the right of the owner or the agent of the owner of an alleged fugitive to seize him without any formal process; he was to be brought before a judge or magistrate and upon satisfactory proof

---

[20] Art. IV, sec. 2, para. 3. The first two sections of the article deal with interstate relations and interstate comity, i.e., what we may term the international relations of the states.

[21] A. B. Hart, *Slavery and Abolition*, p. 280. Conditions before 1850 are set forth briefly by Hart. See also, M. G. McDougall, *Fugitive Slaves (1619-1865)*, and W. H. Siebert, *The Underground Railroad*. For the use of state courts and state officials in carrying out federal laws, reference may be made to the use of the state courts in naturalizing foreigners, and in condemnation proceedings under the right of eminent domain. United States v. Jones, 109 U. S. 513 (1883).

[22] Prigg v. Pennsylvania, 16 Peters 539 (1842). "Upon this ground we have not the slightest hesitation in holding that, under and in virtue of the Constitution, the owner of a slave is clothed with entire authority, in every State in the Union, to seize and recapture his slave, whenever he can do it without any breach of the peace or any illegal violence." 613. "The clause is found in the national Constitution and not in that of any State. It does not point out any State functionaries or any State action to carry its provisions into effect. The States cannot, therefore, be compelled to enforce them; and it might well be deemed an unconstitutional exercise of the power of interpretation to insist that the States are bound to provide means to carry into effect the duties of the national government, nowhere delegated or intrusted to them by the Constitution." 615-616. Congressional legislation must supersede all state legislation. ". . . State magistrates may, if they choose, exercise . . . authority, unless prohibited by State legislation." 622.

was to be delivered to the claimant. This procedure was decidedly informal and seems more so when compared with the processes of extradition. But the provisions in the Constitution dealing with fugitive slaves and fugitives from justice (both of them in the fourth article) are not alike. In the case of extradition, the fugitive from justice is to be delivered up on demand of the executive of the state from which he fled. There is no such provision for executive demand in the case of a fugitive from labor. He is to be delivered up on claim of the party to whom the labor is due.

There is at least one astonishing provision in the act of 1850. It declared that in no trial or hearing under the act should the testimony of the alleged fugitive be admitted in evidence. It is true that in the case of extradition the fugitive is not necessarily entitled to a hearing.[23] There is a difference between this principle and the distinct declaration in the act of 1850 that a fugitive should *not* be allowed to speak in his own behalf. Furthermore, in the case of the alleged criminal, the governor acts upon formal papers,[24] as we have already indicated—papers emanating from the governor of the state demanding the return.

What prompted such palpably unfair procedure, certain to arouse the animosity of the antislavery people, whether heretofore lukewarm or excited? Probably it was partly due to the belief that a hearing participated in by the alleged slave would be likely, because of northern prejudice, to result in his being freed. Someone may also answer the question by saying that as the slave was property, there was no reason why he should be heard. But such answer only begs the question or asserts that affidavits in the hand of a claimant should be sufficient to decide the question of status; and this sufficiency appears in fact to be the intention of the act. But another question arises and it carries us far into the body of the constitutional problem of slavery. Suppose the man seized as an alleged fugitive were a white man. Could he not deny his bondage? Under the terms of this act, if Jefferson Davis should go to Massachusetts, put his hand on the shoul-

[23] Munsey *v.* Clough, 196 U. S. 364 (1905) and cases cited. "The person demanded has no constitutional right to be heard before the governor on either question, and the statute provides for none." *Ibid.,* 372. "The contention that the Governor of Missouri could not act at all on the requisition papers in the absence of the accused and without previous notice to him is unsupported by reason or authority. . . ." See Marbles *v.* Creecy, 215 U. S. 63, 68 (1909).

[24] "The charge against the accused must be made in some due form of law, in some species of judicial proceeding instituted in the State from which he is a fugitive." T. M. Cooley, *General Principles of Constitutional Law* (4th ed.), pp. 243-244.

ders of Daniel Webster, hale him before a commissioner and produce affidavits, Webster could not deny his obligation to serve Davis as a slave. Of course the ready answer is that the act did not mean to sanction any such procedure against a white man. What then is the interpretation of the Constitution? Is slavery the natural condition of black men? Does the Constitution presume that every black man is a slave? Is the presumption so conclusive that at least in some circumstances a black man cannot even deny his slavery? Was there a general supposition when the Constitution was formed and for decades thereafter that this was a white man's government, and a white man's country, and that the natural and normal protections of the law were not intended to guard black men? The south, at least in later days, so believed the facts to be. But on the face of the Constitution such does not appear to be the fact.[25]

If one objects to the inadequacy of the summary process of the Fugitive Slave Act, he may be answered by the assertion—again, it would seem, a begging of the question—that the processes were intended, not to injure free men, but to make certain the prompt and speedy return of fugitives. But constitutional provisions and legal practices are in many respects directed to the protection of the innocent; an act making it quite legal and possible to deny a free man (indeed, white or black) ordinary protection, and forbidding him to deny his guilt or his alleged status, cannot be looked upon as wholly free from an unconstitutional stain. If such criticism as this affects no one, and if the reader says that a black man, claimed as property, ceases to be a person for the time being and is not protected by the normal safeguards of law, he is entitled to his opinion; but all can agree on the implication of the act. And all can appreciate the wrath of those men at the north who believed a black man was a person, at least to the extent of retaining his ability to deny he was only property. It may be contended that the procedure provided by the act was not essentially different from extradition, and that a negro taken to the south would have the right—mayhap the opportunity—to have his freedom tested in a court. Such a right did not appeal to the northerners as of great practical value; and their inevitable suspicion

<hr/>

[25] Nowhere is the difficulty of maintaining a union made of states with differing underlying presumptions more clearly illustrated than by the words of the attorney representing Pennsylvania in the Prigg case: "Now, in a slaveholding Stae [sic] color always raises a presumption of slavery which is directly contrary to the presumption in a free or non-slaveholding State; for in the latter, *prima facie*, every man is a free man." Prigg v. Pennsylvania, 16 Peters 539, 576 (1842).

was perhaps unjust, for negroes asserting their freedom in southern states were not without remedy on the face of the southern laws, not totally without redress as a practical matter.[26]

The antislavery men denounced the act because judicial duties were assigned to commissioners whose appointment and term of office were not in accord with the constitutional provision concerning judicial officers. The validity of this objection is at least doubtful, especially in the light of recent developments of administrative law and tribunals.[27] The same conclusion must be reached concerning the charge that the act made no provision for the writ of habeas corpus. Even if the writ had been specially provided for, the judge issuing the writ must have decided that the fugitive was legally in custody, if the law was valid.[28]

Under the terms of the act, the southern slave-owner had a right to his escaped slave. He was justified in complaining because obstacles were thrown in his way. The Personal Liberty Laws of the northern states [29] were not illegal in providing against the participation of state officers in the seizure of the fugitive and against the use of state public property. But they were illegal when they sought to obstruct or to prevent the execution of the act. Possibly even the milder laws were at variance with the spirit of interstate comity, a vague term but not without its legal connotation. The laws differed one from another, and an accurate general description is therefore made with difficulty. It is plain that the more objectionable acts were passed after 1850, and particularly after the repeal of the Missouri Compromise in 1854. The statute of Vermont (1850) declared it the duty of the state's attorneys to protect, defend, and secure the release of every person claimed as a fugitive slave. Michigan passed a similar act in 1855, and provided that any person arrested as a fugitive slave should be entitled to the benefits of the writ of habeas corpus and of trial by jury. Similar laws were passed in other states. But as a

26 See Allen Johnson, "The Constitutionality of the Fugitive Slave Acts," Yale Law Journal, XXXI, pp. 179-181.

27 Ibid., pp. 173, 181.

28 J. J. Crittenden discussed this subject in Opinions of the Attorneys General, V, pp. 257-258 (September 18, 1850).

29 For a brief summary of the Personal Liberty Laws, see McDougall, op. cit., ch. V. The author says: "But the action of the State governments in the personal liberty bills, from the time the Fugitive Slave Act of 1793 began to be executed to the outbreak of the Civil War, showed that the dissatisfaction of the North was fundamental, and was not confined merely to the few in the van of the Antislavery movement." p. 65.

matter of fact, though these measures were provocative, they were ineffectual. I see no reason for denying the truth of the remark made by Charles Francis Adams in January, 1861, referring to "The personal liberty laws, which never freed a slave." [30] They were the light darts of the picador, but they were not fatal.

The salient fact was that the slaves were escaping. The underground railroad was in active operation, helping thousands to find shelter in the north or to make their way to Canada.[31] The south resented both this fact and the spirit which actuated the north; and here the southerners found impregnable ground for complaint. The north more and more detested slave-hunting.

The most conspicuous incident, which involved discussion of the constitutionality of the Fugitive Slave Law and brought to view the essential antagonism between north and south, arose out of the arrest of Sherman M. Booth in Wisconsin on the charge of assisting in the escape of a fugitive. A state justice issued a writ of habeas corpus and released Booth from the custody of a federal marshal. The matter dragged its way through the courts; the supreme court of the state declared the act of 1850 void. The controversy finally reached the Supreme Court of the United States where Chief Justice Taney rendered a decision upholding the federal authority.[32] The state indulged in exclamatory protest. The legislature drew up resolutions attacking the presumption of the federal judiciary which had assumed the power to reverse a judgment of a state tribunal involving the personal liberty of a citizen. Using with emphasis and freedom the Kentucky resolutions of 1798 and 1799, Wisconsin now announced that "a *positive defiance* of those sovereignties, of all unauthorized acts done or attempted to be done under color of that instrument [the Constitution], is the rightful remedy." These declarations were made on the eve of a civil war which brought forth national power and expanded national authority, a war in which Wisconsin lost thousands of her men in defense of the union and national enforcement of national law.

In those trying days, when the slavery discussion was at its height,

---

[30] *Congressional Globe,* 36 Cong., 2 sess., appendix, p. 124.

[31] Siebert gives various estimates of the number. He refers to statements of men living at the time of the Compromise to the effect that there were from twenty to fifty thousand escaped slaves living at the north. Siebert, *op. cit.,* pp. 237-238. For estimates of the number escaping to the north, see p. 340 ff.

[32] Ableman *v.* Booth, 21 Howard 506 (1859). Taney's statement of divided sovereignty—the orthodox doctrine—is especially clear and deserves attention.

there was much talk at the south of secession. There were threats and there were arguments. Just how far the principles of Calhoun had permeated the south it is impossible to say; but those principles were active. Against them was arrayed able and sturdy opposition, especially the opposition of Whig leaders. Of course, to sum up a complicated condition in a few words and to state exact truth is quite impossible, but on the whole the fact appears to be this: men of Whig tradition, although that element included a considerable portion, and probably indeed the greater portion, of the large slaveholders, true to the nationalistic spirit of their party, were inclined to attack the theoretical legal right to secede; they rejected Calhounism, the doctrine of state sovereignty.[33] But they were not, many of them at least, opposed to the idea of disunion to protect their interests, if the northern states refused to recognize substantial justice as the south conceived justice to be—principally the right to an equal share of the public domain, the right to carry slavery into the west. Of course the reader may declare that there is no practical difference between (1) the doctrine

[33] "Even those Democrats who saw no justification for recourse to secession in the existing situation, usually defended the doctrine of secession as a remedy against oppressive conditions. The Whigs throughout the South took issue with the Democrats on this point and were nearly united in their denial of any such right. They held that when conditions became intolerably oppressive and all other remedies had been tried and had failed, there remained recourse, in the last resort, to the inalienable right of revolution. This was the burden of the letters and speeches of their candidates, of the editorials of the Whig press, and of the resolutions of local and state Union conventions, besides those which the Mississippi constituent convention and the Tennessee legislature officially adopted under Whig influence." A. C. Cole, *The Whig Party in the South*, pp. 194-195. A letter of Howell Cobb, August 12, 1851, is an interesting and able refutation of secession as a constitutional right based on the suppositions of Calhoun. But even Cobb placed the right of a state to secede upon "just causes", to be determined by itself. The nature of the argument cannot be here presented in full. See *The Correspondence of Robert Toombs, Alexander H. Stephens, and Howell Cobb*, Am. Hist. Asso. *Report* for 1911, II, p. 249 ff. Stephens wrote to Cobb (then classified as a Union Democrat) June 23, 1851: "In reference to the calling out of the militia, etc., maintain the right of the President and duty of the President to execute the law against all factious opposition whether in Mass. or S. C. Maintain the power to execute the fugitive slave law at the North and the power to execute the Revenue or any other law against any *lawless* opposition in S. C. Turn the whole force of this upon the *revolutionary* movement in S. C., and urge all good citizens who value law and order and the rights of liberty and property to stand by the supremacy of the law. This is the life and soul of a republic. Warn the good people of Georgia to beware of revolution—refer to France—and plant yourself against the factionists of S. C., upon the constitution of the country. The right of secession treat as an abstract question. It is but a right to change the Govt., a right of revolution, and maintain that no just cause for the exercise of such right exists. And keep the main point prominent, that the only question now is whether we should go into revolution or not. S. C. is for it. This is the point to keep prominent." *Ibid.*, p. 238.

of unalloyed full sovereignty of the state with the right of secession, (2) the right to revolt—that is to say, the right to break up the union for "just causes"—the justice to be passed upon by the individual state. In the history of constitutional theory, however, the distinction is not unimportant.

CHAPTER XXXIX

THE ELECTION OF 1852 AND THE REPEAL OF THE MISSOURI COMPROMISE

In the election of 1852 both of the main parties announced their adherence to the Compromise. The Free Soilers, still devoted to the antislavery program, cast a smaller vote than they had cast four years before. Franklin Pierce, the Democratic candidate, received an overwhelming electoral majority, so large indeed that it rang the death-knell of the Whigs. A party cannot thrive without offices; neither can it long survive without principles. The Democrats were now looked upon, in the south at least, as sounder than the Whigs on the slavery question; the Whigs, tainted by antislavery doctrine at the north, no longer had a helpful principle for prolonging their life—only an economic policy and a constitutional theory more or less adequately supporting their economic interests; they had no war cries or slogans to arouse and hold enthusiasm. Their greatest leaders had passed from the scene; Clay and Webster died in the election year. The party had, on the whole, represented the conservative tendencies and interests of the nation, and at the south it had taken, in general, an attitude of opposition to the disintegration of the union. But what was to be done now that slavery, the most important of all economic interests, had found shelter under Democratic banners?

The influence of slavery as a dissolvent had already become obvious; religious denominations had broken asunder, and thus an important national bond had been severed.[1] With the disappearance of the Whig party, which after 1854 had few adherents and little vitality, a great political institution holding men together in a common loyalty was gone. But the Democratic party, largely because the northern wing could and would work with the southern, continued to live.

[1] No one saw this or stated it more clearly than Calhoun. Speaking in 1850 he said, "The cords that bind the States together are not only many, but various in character. Some are spiritual or ecclesiastical; some political; others social. . . . The ties which held each denomination together formed a strong cord to hold the whole Union together; but, powerful as they were, they have not been able to resist the explosive effect of slavery agitation." *Works,* IV, p. 557.

If the time should come when this party should split asunder, the union would be without the support of a national institution for which men felt affection and for which they had been willing to check or restrain local and provincial tendencies. The political parties were the tangible expression of coöperation and common purpose; they had been not only national in scope but also nationalizing in effect. No small number of men in both sections began to flock into the American or Know Nothing party, a secret organization, which gave them a chance to change their colors in the dark.

The most significant fact of all was that the Democratic party stood for the moment in a position of towering supremacy. But what kind of a Democratic party?—a party now considered sound in its readiness to support, indirectly if not directly, a great economic and social interest. What had become of the old party which embraced the common man, the small landowner, the backwoodsman, the man who believed primarily in freedom and opportunity and resented the airs of the superior beings? One of the most impressive facts in American history is this transformation. The reader may well deny that the party after 1852 stood forth as the champion of slavery: but in reality, as far as it had a consistent tendency, its influence was directed to the maintenance of slavery interests, because it discountenanced agitation and was satisfied with compromise on the territorial question. The spell of the old party name, hallowed by the shades of Jefferson and Jackson, helped to hold the party together; but, as events were soon to show, many of the plain people of the north were escaping from the fold. How could the plain workmen at the north look placidly at a system of labor which recognized the right of one man to *own* a hundred laborers? The party still held at the north many thousands who wished to work in harmony with southern members and were willing to rely upon the skillful management of Douglas and others who continued to proclaim the principles of free government for territories and states; they found solace and support in a policy which freed them from affirmative support of slavery and assured their faith, or seemed to assure their faith, in the essentials of popular government.

The Congress which was elected in 1852, amid the earnest clamors for the sanctity of the Compromise, assembled thirteen months after the election. And one of the first specters to appear on the horizon was the slavery question which had just been solemnly interred. It was actually proposed to repeal the Missouri Compromise. And one advocate of repeal was Stephen A. Douglas of Illinois. No one could have expected from his previous career that, of all men, he would take a stand reflecting upon the wisdom or the sanctity of the measure which had stood for more than three decades. We shall present in a moment a brief statement of the legislative history of the Kansas-Nebraska bill and notice the changes made in its provisions as the months went by. But it is sufficient to say here that it was passed in the spring of 1854. It provided for two territories west and northwest of Missouri and Iowa—portions of the Louisiana purchase as yet not admitted as states or given territorial government. It repealed the Missouri Compromise explicitly and announced, or appeared to announce, the doctrine of popular sovereignty.

There has been much discussion [2] in recent years concerning the authorship of this movement, and especially concerning the motives of Douglas in advocating, if not originating, the proposal to discard the old Compromise of 1820. In constitutional history it is not a matter of supreme importance whether or not we find the master mind to have been Senator Atchison, or Senator Douglas, or someone else; nor is it of peculiar importance to us that we discover whether Douglas planned to bestow loving favors on the south, secure southern eulogies and win the presidency, or was chiefly enraptured with the prospect of a railroad connecting his own state with the newer regions and tracing its way over the western prairies—even the Pacific railroad question was now a sectional question. That Douglas was quite as much a railroad man as he was a statesman, we must acknowledge; but if there is a problem of bestowing commendation or abuse, one motive appears no holier than the other. Nor is it quite plain that he could not have had both motives, neither interfering with the other. If Douglas was illustrating the propensity of politicians to fish in troubled waters, he soon found the waters turbid and troubled enough to suit the most ambitious angler. It is probably fair to say that he was seriously guided, as was Cass, by his western or frontier inclination to allow people to manage their own affairs; he would let the people of a territory look after their own interests without molestation by the federal government. Certainly he could speak with passion and fervor on that topic. He must retain the allegiance of the

---

[2] See especially P. O. Ray, *The Repeal of the Missouri Compromise;* F. H. Hodder, "Genesis of the Kansas-Nebraska Act," Wis. Hist. Society *Proceedings* for 1912, pp. 69-86; F. H. Hodder, "The Railroad Background of the Kansas-Nebraska Act," *Miss. Valley Hist. Rev.*, XII, pp. 3-22.

common man whose economic interests would be furthered by the opportunities of an open west; he must hold the westerners of his own region. Farmers of the old northwest, it seems, were restless and uneasy and were beginning to think their salvation would lie in the possession of cheap lands beyond the Missouri. But the south must not be antagonized lest everything be lost. The task of recon-- ciling the conflicting interests and sections was enough to test the skill of the most astute political leader.

A bill for the organization of Nebraska had been passed by the House early in 1853, and its passage was advocated by Douglas in the Senate, where it was not adopted. No one, however, supposed the passage of the bill would affect the Missouri Compromise.[3] In De- cember of that year a bill, identical in all respects with the one just mentioned, was introduced into the Senate and referred to the com-- mittee on territories—and this meant referring it to Douglas. On January 4 Douglas presented a report accompanied by a bill providing for the organization of the territory of Nebraska.

The report is a curious affair. We find in it a fairly clear state- ment of the differences of opinion concerning the constitutional status of slavery in the territories. The controverted questions were said to involve the same grave issues as those producing "the fearful struggle of 1850. As Congress deemed it wise and prudent to refrain from deciding the matters in controversy then, either by affirming or re- pealing the Mexican laws, or by an act declaratory of the true intent of the Constitution and the extent of the protection afforded by it to slave property in the territories, so your committee are not prepared now to recommend a departure from the course pursued on that memorable occasion, either by affirming or repealing the 8th section of the Missouri act, or by any act declaratory of the meaning of the Constitution in respect to the legal points in dispute." Having thus asserted the intention to follow the noncommittal policy of 1850, the report declared the Compromise measures of that year to rest on three propositions. The first and most important declared that all questions relating to slavery in the territories should be left to the

[3] "The only reference in the debate to the slavery question was in a speech made by Atchison of Missouri. . . . Atchison was a zealous pro-slavery man and he had hitherto opposed the organization of Nebraska Territory because of the existence of the compromise restriction upon slavery. He now said he favored the passage of the bill. He had investigated the matter and found 'no prospect, no hope of a repeal' of that restriction." M. M. Quaife, *The Doctrine of Non-Intervention With Slavery in the Territories*, pp. 100-101.

people residing in them; the second, that cases involving the title to slaves and questions of personal freedom should be referred to the adjudication of local tribunals, with right of appeal to the Supreme Court of the United States; the third, that the fugitive slave clause of the Constitution should be carried into execution in all the organized territories.

The bill to organize Nebraska, which accompanied the report, was, when first printed in the Washington *Sentinel,* January 7, practically identical in form and content with the Utah and New Mexico acts of 1850, but three days after publication it was explained that by a "clerical error" a portion had been omitted; and this portion provided for territorial control of slavery in accordance with the terms of the report.[4] This principle, however, was too clearly stated, it would seem, to satisfy the proslavery leaders; it really appeared to be a frank acknowledgment of the right of the people of the territories to decide. The southerners wished to see a recognition of the principle of non-intervention, bearing the meaning of no interference with their constitutional right to carry their slaves into the national domain. There was now a demand for the explicit repeal of the Missouri Compromise.

What was Douglas to do? Whatever may have been the cause of his eagerness for territorial organization, he doubtless wished to maintain unity in his party, or (if "unity" be too strong a word) cooperation between the southern and northern wings. Under pressure from southern proslavery interests, but desirous also of meeting the wishes of his western constituents who were eager to have the Nebraska region organized, would he now turn his back upon the famous Compromise? And what induced the southerners to go so far as to demand the repeal? One reason, of course, was their determination to receive from Congress a recognition of their constitutional right. They valued that abstract right, and no wonder, for in their opinion anything less seemed to brand them and their institution as inferior; they resented discrimination. They were now far enough along toward their ultimate goal, they were sufficiently irritated, to demand a principle, even if it should be useless and even though it should overthrow a Compromise which nearly everyone had sup-

---

[4] "All evidence points to the conclusion that Douglas added this hastily, after the bill had been twice read in the Senate and ordered to be printed; but whether it was carelessly omitted by the copyist or appended by Douglas as an afterthought, it is impossible to say." Allen Johnson, *Stephen A. Douglas,* p. 233.

posed to be final and unchangeable. But their policy was dangerous and aggressive, and as we all know, its end was disaster to the cause they had at heart. Here again, however, the burden cannot be placed upon the south alone. Without northern votes, this attack upon the Compromise would have been hopeless.

Senator Dixon of Kentucky proposed the explicit repeal of the Missouri Compromise (January 16, 1854) and the announcement of the distinct right to take slaves into any of the territories of the United States. A few days later (January 23) a reconstructed measure was presented by Douglas. A form had been hit upon which would allow northern and southern Democrats to defend the act. Jefferson Davis later said that it admitted of an interpretation in agreement with southern views of non-intervention.[5] Two territories were provided for instead of one, as in the original measure—the lower one, south of forty degrees and north of thirty-seven, was to be called Kansas; the upper one, Nebraska, ran to the northern boundary of the United States and west to the mountains. Perhaps the south could get possession of Kansas and people it with slaves and supporters of slavery, though to charge Douglas with planning to bring this about is unwarranted.[6] The Missouri Compromise was now declared "inoperative" on the ground that it had been superseded by the Compromise of 1850. And there was also a declaration of what certainly appeared to be a definite pronouncement of the doctrine of territorial sovereignty, or, as Douglas now called it, the doctrine of popular sovereignty.

That the Compromise of 1850 had superseded the Compromise of thirty years before was a statement too preposterous not to arouse intense and declamatory opposition.[7] There were no frank declarations of definite doctrine in the Compromise of 1850. So to smooth out the discontent—to use a mild word—"superseded" was changed to

---

[5] *The Rise and Fall of the Confederate Government,* I, p. 29.

[6] See Johnson, *Stephen A. Douglas,* p. 238. Johnson points out that the provision for two territories was associated with the project for the Pacific railroad. *Ibid.,* pp. 238-239. There is no doubt also that Iowa leaders believed that the establishment of two territories would be an advantage to that state, ". . . otherwise the seat of government and leading thoroughfares must have all fallen south of Iowa." Ray, *op. cit.,* p. 178, note 251, quoting Senator A. C. Dodge of Iowa.

[7] Seward was doubtless right when he said, "I now throw my gauntlet at the feet of every Senator now here, who was in the Senate in 1850, and challenge him to say that he then knew, or thought, or dreamed, that, by enacting the compromise of 1850, he was directly or indirectly abrogating, or in any degree impairing, the Missouri compromise?" Frederic Bancroft, *Life of Seward,* I, p. 347.

"inconsistent with", but the phrase was almost equally objectionable. The resolution, therefore, as now proposed and adopted declared that the eighth section of the act for the admission of Missouri, "being inconsistent with the principle of non-intervention by Congress with slavery in the States and Territories, as recognized by the legislation of eighteen hundred and fifty, . . . is hereby declared inoperative and void; it being the true intent and meaning of this act not to legislate slavery into any Territory or State, nor to exclude it therefrom, but to leave the people thereof perfectly free to form and regulate their domestic institutions in their own way, subject only to the Constitution of the United States. . . ."

Of course, it may be said that "the principle of non-intervention" should be interpreted as meaning that Congress should do nothing, leave the matter to the people of the territories, and, avoiding all theories of constitutional power, allow the question to be passed upon by the Court; and this interpretation may receive some support from the fact that the act included the provision appearing in the Clayton Compromise and in the Compromise of 1850, allowing cases involving the title to slaves to be carried to the Supreme Court of the United States without regard to the value of the matter in controversy. Possibly even the words "subject only to the Constitution of the United States" implied an intention or an agreement to shun the problem and let the judiciary settle it.[8] That there was this intention

[8] That this interpretation was the one in the minds of the men behind the scenes seems possible. Speaking of the days before the reconstructed bill was drafted, Quaife says: "The Democratic Senators met repeatedly in party caucus in the effort to adjust their differences of opinion and agree upon a common course of action. The former proved impossible of attainment; but the latter was realized through following the precedent set by the Clayton Compromise and by the Adjustment measures of 1850. Just as on those occasions, so now, it was agreed to frame the bill in such shape that both Northern and Southern men could support it. . . . The advocates of the Constitutional extension of slavery over the territories on the one hand, the supporters of the doctrine of Territorial Sovereignty on the other, agreed to pass a bill with the understanding that their differences of opinion as to the effect it would have were to be adjudicated by the Courts; when so settled, all were to abide by the decision." Quaife, *op. cit.*, p. 111. Quaife seems to rely for direct testimony chiefly on the statement made by Senator Judah P. Benjamin of Louisiana, in 1860. But to strengthen such testimony one must add the strong likelihood on general principles that the party leaders would discuss the matters many times, seek to reach a compromise, and prepare a measure which was sufficiently ambiguous to obtain support. Benjamin said, "We could not agree. Morning after morning we met, for the purpose of coming to some understanding upon that very point; and it was finally understood by all, agreed to by all, made the basis of a compromise by all the supporters of that bill, that the Territories should be organized with a delegation by Congress of all the power of Congress in the Territories, and that the extent of the power of Congress

and that there was an understanding between the southern advocates of slavery-extension and others was later positively declared; and it seems more than probable that such was the fact. But the debates show a strange absence of an explicit declaration of any such agreement.

Two years after the passage of the Kansas-Nebraska bill, Douglas said, "My opinion . . . has been well known to the Senate for years. . . . I told them it was a judicial question. . . . My answer then was, and now is, that if the Constitution carries slavery there let it go, and no power on earth can take away; but, if the Constitution does not carry it there, no power but the people can carry it there. Whatever may be the true decision of that constitutional point, would not have affected my vote for or against the Nebraska bill. . . . If my colleague [Senator Trumbull] will examine my speeches, he will find that declaration. He will also find, that I stated I would not discuss this legal question, for by the bill we referred it to the courts." [9] Thus, according to Douglas, he did not believe his much-lauded popular sovereignty contained any constitutional principle. By this interpretation, what became of what Benton called a "stump speech, injected in the belly of the bill," as an announcement of popular sovereignty?

At all events, there stood the declaration which appeared on its face to be an announcement of popular sovereignty: the right of the people to decide—or the apparent right—, and that was an idea certain to win applause. In a speech of wrath, Douglas, heaping abuse upon Charles Sumner and Salmon P. Chase, opponents worthy of his steel, vehemently defended the bill, insisted upon his own consistency and apparently advocated the territorial right of self-determination.[10]

Legislative candor never was more thoroughly obscured; it is practically impossible to-day, with letters and biographies of politicians and with the interminable pages of the *Congressional Globe*

should be determined by the courts." May 8, 1860. *Congressional Globe*, 36 Cong., 1 sess., p. 1966. See in addition, Douglas's statement in 1859. *Ibid.*, 35 Cong., 2 sess., p. 1258. For Jefferson Davis's interpretation of the measure, see *The Rise and Fall of the Confederate Government*, I, p. 29. "What was in the background of Southern consciousness was expressed bluntly by Brown of Mississippi, who refused to admit that the right of the people of a Territory to regulate their domestic institutions, including slavery, was a right to destroy. 'If I thought in voting for the bill as it now stands, I was conceding the right of the people in the territory, during their territorial existence, to exclude slavery, I would withhold my vote. . . . It leaves the question where I am quite willing it should be left—to the ultimate decision of the courts.' " Johnson, *Stephen A. Douglas*, p. 247.

[9] *Congressional Globe*, 34 Cong., 1 sess., appendix, p. 797.

[10] March 3, 1854. *Congressional Globe*, 33 Cong., 1 sess., appendix, p. 325 ff. See Cass's defense of popular sovereignty, *Ibid.*, p. 270 ff.

to be ransacked and studied, to know just what was intended by this child of misfortune born in the "Stygian cave forlorn", the secret gathering of the faithful. Once more, that was the beauty of the whole measure; the most conspicuous feature of the landscape was the haze in which it was shrouded. At the north it was represented to be what, indeed, it appeared to be—an enactment distinctly recognizing the principle of territorial sovereignty. The southerners might well accept the bill as better for them than the Missouri Compromise. If they accepted the "stump speech" at all, it may have meant to the shrewdest among them only the right of the people to exercise their will when forming a constitution for admission into the union. How it could have carried that meaning it is difficult to see, because the measure dealt distinctly with the territories, and the subject in controversy was the extent of congressional authority over slavery in the territories. But the act used the blessed word "non-intervention", and that could mean what it might mean. If anyone can believe that Douglas thought the bill announced a distinct constitutional principle, and if anyone can reconcile his defense of popular sovereignty—i.e. territorial sovereignty—with the intention of allowing the Supreme Court to determine the proper constitutional principle, he is entitled to do so; but his intellectual acumen will be heavily drawn upon.

The bill passed the Senate early in March by a vote of thirty-seven to fourteen. For a time it seemed as if it was to be smothered in the House, where it was referred to the committee of the whole; but, thanks to the cleverness of Douglas and to the pressure of party discipline, the bill was extricated from the mass of other bills and was passed by a vote of 113 to 100. In the Senate, two southerners voted against the bill. It was carried by the southern votes with the aid of fourteen northern votes, all cast by Democrats. In the House, nine southern votes were cast in the negative and sixty-nine in the affirmative, while the northern Democratic vote was divided almost equally. No northern Whig voted for the bill in either house.[11] Amendments of no great consequence necessitated its return to the Senate where the bill as amended was passed. On May 30 it received the President's approval.

The measure, after all, was plainly largely a southern measure. Had Douglas held his party together? The result might well fill him with misgivings. At the south, the party was fairly well united, and

[11] See the classification of votes given by J. F. Rhodes, *History of the United States*, I, pp. 475, 489.

on the one critical question of slavery it was now supplemented by accretions from the Whigs. At the north, its condition was perilous. Stragglers by the thousands were drifting from its ranks. But perhaps even there it might be held in working order, for the old loyalty to the party was still strong and the leadership of Douglas was potent. The Democratic party could still pride itself on being a national party as long as Democrats in sufficient numbers voted with the south to insure southern interests.

The Kansas-Nebraska bill aroused furor at the north. The Compromise of 1820 had been looked upon for a generation as dedicating an extensive region to free institutions; it had been looked upon, as Benton said, not as "a mere statute, to last for a day", but as a measure "intended for perpetuity. . . ." Benton was a Democrat from a slaveholding state; his scorn of the fateful bill was intense and bitter; a bill, he said, which was a "bungling attempt to smuggle slavery into the Territory, and all the country out to the Canada line and up the Rocky Mountains."

In the winter, while the Kansas-Nebraska measures were under discussion, a movement was inaugurated to cast aside old party affiliations and to reorganize a new party definitely and unequivocally opposed to the extension of slavery. The first steps were taken at Ripon, Wisconsin. In July, a convention at Jackson, Michigan, made up of former Whigs and Free Soilers, or Free Democrats, adopted the name "Republican"; a state ticket was nominated and a general convention was proposed for the adoption of "measures in resistance to the encroachments of slavery." The movement spread. The old Whig party was practically gone; its members were in great numbers attracted into the new order. The nature of the Republican party of early days can be seen in the fact of the accession of Free Soil Democrats, of men especially in the old northwest believing profoundly in the old watchwords of freedom and the rights of the common man, and of many Whigs with their economic and constitutional inclinations

CHAPTER XL

THE DRED SCOTT CASE

James Buchanan took the oath of office March 4, 1857. His inaugural address deserves brief attention. In studying those times one gets used to indirection or evasion—most of it, perhaps, not intentional. Possibly in Buchanan's case there was no conscious purpose to cover his remarks with a cloak of mist or to mislead his hearers; perhaps his mind worked more easily in a haze; but there is required more than ordinary attention, aided by good will, to find logic and consistency in his discussion of the territorial problem. But the nature of his wanderings need not now trouble us, though the address makes plain the prevailing confusion and the opportunity for ceaseless misunderstanding of vital issues. Just when the people of a territory should decide the slavery question was, Buchanan declared, "a matter of but little practical importance." And yet the question of territorial condition was the actual issue. "Besides," he went on to say, "it is a judicial question, which legitimately belongs to the Supreme Court of the United States, before whom it is now pending, and will, it is understood, be speedily and finally settled. . . . The whole Territorial question being thus settled upon the principle of popular sovereignty—a principle as ancient as free government itself—everything of a practical nature has been decided."

The case which Buchanan had in mind was Dred Scott v. Sandford,[1] the details of which we shall consider in a moment. The decision was given two days after the inauguration. How did the President know the judges would pass upon the question of slavery in the territories? The case had been long before the Court, for it had first been argued in February, 1856, and again in December; but these hearings and arguments gave no conclusive evidence of the Court's intention to take up the fateful question of congressional authority. Buchanan's foreknowledge appeared to indicate some kind of underground in-

---

[1] 19 Howard 393 (1857). Important recent discussions of the case are: E. S. Corwin, "The Dred Scott Decision," *Am. Hist. Rev.*, XVII, p. 52 ff.; F. H. Hodder, "Some Phases of the Dred Scott Case," *Miss. Valley Hist. Rev.*, XVI, p. 3 ff.

trigue and collusion.[2] Before the decision was rendered, however, other persons also were confident that the case would settle the slavery problem.[3] Furthermore, as we now know, there had been communications between two of the justices and the President-elect. Justice Catron (February 19, 1857) actually wrote Buchanan a suggestion of what he might say in his inaugural address; and he asked Buchanan to write to Justice Grier and tell him "how necessary it is—& how good the opportunity is, to settle the agitation by an affirmative decision of the Supreme Court, the one way or the other." [4] Justice Grier (February 23, 1857), acknowledging a letter from Buchanan, wrote a reply giving much information and said: "There will therefore be six if not *seven* (perhaps Nelson will remain neutral) who will decide the compromise law of 1820 to be of *non-effect*." [5] This correspondence, at least by present standards, appears highly improper; but it tends, when fully examined and studied in connection with other facts, to disprove the charge that the Dred Scott case was the final step in a conspiracy beginning with the repeal of the Compromise three years before.

Dred Scott, a negro slave, had been taken by his master, a Dr. Emerson, in 1834, from Missouri into the state of Illinois. Two years later, Emerson, taking Dred with him, removed to Fort Snelling, which was within the region from which slavery was excluded by the terms of the Missouri Compromise. In 1838 Emerson returned to Missouri, carrying with him Dred, a woman Dred had married at Fort Snelling, and a child born of this marriage. Some years later Emerson sold his slave to John F. A. Sandford of New York, who did not, however, remove Dred from Missouri.[6]

[2] See Lincoln's speech of June 16, 1858: "Why", he asked, "was the court decision held up? . . . Why the delay of a reargument? Why the incoming President's advance exhortation in favor of the decision? These things look like the cautious patting and petting of a spirited horse preparatory to mounting him, when it is dreaded that he may give the rider a fall." He spoke of the framed timbers prepared by Stephen, Franklin, Roger, and James.

[3] Alexander H. Stephens wrote in January, 1857: "The decision will be a marked epoch in our history. I feel a deep solicitude as to how it will be. . . . The restriction of 1820 will be held to be unconstitutional." Quoted in R. M. Johnston and W. H. Browne, *Life of Alexander H. Stephens,* p. 318. See also, B. C. Steiner, *Life of Roger Brooke Taney,* pp. 335-336.

[4] James Buchanan, *Works* (J. B. Moore, ed.), X, p. 106, note 1.

[5] *Ibid.,* X, pp. 106-108 note.

[6] The facts above given are those agreed upon by the attorneys in the case, and they form the basis of the Court's decision. J. W. Burgess in his *Middle Period* (p. 449 ff.) has an account differing in some particulars. He relies on statements made to him by A. C. Crane, a clerk in the law office of the attorney who espoused Dred's

A suit for Dred's freedom, resulting in his favor, was started in a lower Missouri court, but when carried for review to the state supreme court the judgment was reversed, the court holding that when the negro was brought back to Missouri he was a slave, no matter what might have been the effect of his sojourn in a free state and a free territory. The case was remanded to the lower court, where it was still pending when an action for assault and battery—trespass *vi et armis*—was begun against Sandford in the federal circuit court for the district of Missouri. If Dred was a citizen of Missouri, the federal court would have jurisdiction, because Sandford was a citizen of New York.

The defendant, Sandford, pleaded that Dred was not a citizen of Missouri because he was a negro of African descent. This was a plea to the jurisdiction of the court, called a plea in abatement. To this plea the plaintiff demurred; in other words, granting the fact alleged, namely, that Dred was a negro, it did not follow that he was not a citizen. The court sustained the demurrer and then, upon the facts of the case, instructed the jury that the law was with the defendant. Judgment was rendered in Sandford's favor. The case was thereupon carried by Dred's attorney to the Supreme Court of the United States.

As we have seen, the case was twice argued and had been before the Court several months before the final decision. The members of the Court differed among themselves on the question of the course to be followed; in their earlier discussions the point chiefly at issue was whether the plea in abatement which had been passed upon by the circuit court should be reëxamined; and there was no unanimity in the end.[7] Even as late as the middle of February, however, the

case. The differences in detail are not important, but it is important to get through this channel evidence to show that the suit was not fictitious, but a genuine effort on the part of antislavery men to obtain freedom for a negro unlawfully, as they believed, held in bondage.

[7] The grounds of disagreement on this matter are seen in the opinions finally rendered. For example, the Chief Justice said, "The plea in abatement and the judgment of the court upon it, are a part of the judicial proceedings in the Circuit Court, and are there recorded as such; and a writ of error always brings up to the superior court the whole record of the proceedings in the court below." Justice Catron said, "The judgment of the Circuit Court upon the plea in abatement is not open, in my opinion, to examination in this court upon the plaintiff's writ. The judgment was given for him conformably to the prayer of his demurrer. He cannot assign an error in such a judgment." Justice Curtis was not willing to accept the principle "that the defendant, by pleading over, after the plea to the jurisdiction was adjudged insufficient, finally waived all benefit of that plea."

justices in conference reached the determination not to raise or decide the question of jurisdiction. The majority were seemingly willing to decide the case simply on the ground that the status of Dred in Missouri had been determined by the Missouri court. If this course were followed, the Court would not discuss at all the problem of slavery in the territories and the competence of Congress. Two of the justices, McLean and Curtis, were prepared, however, to enter upon the whole question of Dred's freedom, and to examine, therefore, the validity and effect of the famous Compromise. This intention may have furnished [8] the other justices with reason and excuse for taking the same course and presenting at length opinions concerning the authority of Congress to exclude slavery from the territories.

So the stage was finally set for a long and inharmonious discussion of the Missouri Compromise. Justice Nelson alone believed the Court should confine its attention to the effect of the Missouri court's decision, which in his judgment fixed Dred's status in Missouri. There were nine justices. The Chief Justice read what may be called the opinion of the Court and rendered the decision. Dred was a slave. With that decision six of the other justices agreed, but each of the nine gave a separate opinion and as a rule followed his own line of reasoning. Grier's opinion was short and did not disclose his reasons. Nelson, as we have seen, confined his attention to a single point. On

[8] Instead of asserting that the dissentients caused the others to enter upon the merits of the controversy, I say "may have furnished", because there seems no doubt that the justices desiring to settle the question were under pressure. Justice Wayne in particular was anxious to have a decision. Hodder ("Some Phases of the Dred Scott Case," *loc. cit.,* p. 11) says, "The opinion of Nelson, which but for the dissent of McLean and Curtis would have been the opinion of the Court, held that when a slave returns to a slave state his status is determinable by the courts of that state." In so saying he may be right, but I cannot help believing, in light of all the evidence, that this statement underestimates the influence brought to bear upon the justices to announce a decision on the whole matter. Attention is called to the correspondence of Catron, Grier and Buchanan referred to on a previous page. See also Steiner, *op. cit.,* pp. 336-337. Justice Catron said that the Court had been forced to pass upon the constitutionality of the Missouri Compromise by the determination of the two dissentients. See Hodder, "Some Phases of the Dred Scott Case," *loc. cit.,* p. 10 and p. 11, note 20, referring to P. G. Auchampaugh, "James Buchanan, the Court and the Dred Scott Case," *Tennessee Historical Magazine,* X, pp. 234-238, giving a letter written on February 19, 1857. To this it may be said, first, that if the justices believed that the question of the Compromise was not before them or properly to be considered, their determination ought not to have been influenced by what the dissentients did, and, we may surmise, they would not have been so influenced in any case not appealing to their emotions or their desire to place a quietus on the slavery controversy; second, that the two dissentients, as they viewed the case, were logically carried on to a consideration of the Compromise and its validity. The others were not.

the vital question McLean and Curtis totally disagreed with the reasoning of the others and with the decision of the Court.

We shall have to content ourselves with a consideration of only two of the opinions, those of Chief Justice Taney and Justice Curtis, as they best disclose the situation. The Chief Justice was a citizen of Maryland, a slave state. No one now would question his learning, ability, and substantial character. Curtis was a citizen of Massachusetts, a state filled with strong antislavery sentiment. The number of opinions and the variety of arguments, as well as the whole history of the case, were bewildering to the average citizen, and this diversity helped to cast disrepute upon the decision and upon the Court.[9] The lowering of the Court's prestige was one of the most lamentable results of the whole affair.

The Chief Justice, after discussing the propriety of taking up the plea in abatement, declared Dred Scott was not a citizen of Missouri within the meaning of the Constitution, and was, therefore, not entitled to sue in the federal courts; the judgment of the circuit court on the plea in abatement was erroneous. The reasoning leading him to these conclusions is simple enough in some respects: the Constitution was made by and for white men; when it was adopted, negroes had for more than a century "been regarded as beings of an inferior order, and altogether unfit to associate with the white race, either in social or political relations; and so far inferior, that they had no rights which the white man was bound to respect. . . ." This opinion was regarded "as an axiom in morals as well as in politics. . . ." [10] It was inconceivable, therefore, that the framers of the Constitution should have intended to include black men as citizens. He elaborately denied that a state could make a citizen. The fact that Dred was a negro was sufficient to dispose of his right to bring suit.

But the Chief Justice was not content to rest there. He asserted the duty of the Court to correct every error made by the lower court. His argument was this: the lower court had given judgment in favor of the defendant, although the question of the jurisdiction of the court had been plainly presented, as shown by the plaintiff's own bill

---

[9] "When, as in this case, the student finds six judges arriving at precisely the same result by three distinct processes of reasoning, he is naturally disposed to surmise that the result may possibly have induced the processes rather than that the processes compelled the result, though of course such surmise is not necessarily sound. . . ." But on an examination of the opinions, Corwin says that one's "suspicion becomes conviction." Corwin, "The Dred Scott Decision," *loc. cit.*, p. 68.

[10] 19 Howard 393, 407.

of exception; Dred had admitted that he and his wife were born slaves, and he had endeavored to show that he became free by being taken to certain places where slavery did not exist; if his sojourn in those regions did not make him free, then he continued to be a slave and, hence, not a citizen; the case ought to have been dismissed (irrespective of the plea in abatement) for want of jurisdiction, and no judgment ought to have been rendered.[11] The Court, therefore, was called upon to consider whether Dred did become free by his stay in the Missouri Compromise territory north of thirty-six thirty.

When the Chief Justice proceeded to inquire whether Dred was a slave or not, and, therefore, whether or not the circuit court acted without jurisdiction, the first thing to be determined, one would naturally suppose, was whether Dred was a slave by the law of Missouri upon his return to that state. If he was a slave, that disposed of the case. But the Chief Justice postponed discussion of that point; he took it up only at the end of his opinion when he briefly decided that the circuit court had no jurisdiction because by the law of Missouri the plaintiff was a slave and not a citizen.[12] The Chief Justice was not quite fair-minded in treating that topic last and after he had treated the constitutionality of the Compromise. Plainly, if he had treated it earlier, he would have found it difficult to enter upon a consideration of congressional authority over the territories. It is a

[11] Note the following statements from the opinion: ". . . but if that plea [the plea in abatement] is regarded as waived, or out of the case upon any other ground, yet the question as to the jurisdiction of the Circuit Court is presented on the face of the bill of exception itself, taken by the plaintiff at the trial. . . . Now, if the removal of which he [Dred] speaks did not give them their freedom, then by his own admission he is still a slave; and whatever opinions may be entertained in favor of the citizenship of a free person of the African race, no one supposes that a slave is a citizen of the State or of the United States." *Ibid.*, 427. ". . . and if, upon the showing of Scott himself, it appeared that he was still a slave, the case ought to have been dismissed, and the judgment against him and in favor of the defendant for costs, is, like that on the plea in abatement, erroneous, and the suit ought to have been dismissed by the Circuit Court for want of jurisdiction. . . ." *Ibid.* "The correction of one error in the court below does not deprive the appellate court of the power of examining further into the record, and correcting any other material errors which may have been committed by the inferior court. *Ibid.*, 428. "We are at a loss to understand . . . by what process of reasoning it can be made out, that the error of an inferior court in actually pronouncing judgment for one of the parties, in a case in which it had no jurisdiction, cannot be looked into or corrected by this court, because we have decided a similar question presented in the pleadings." *Ibid.*, 429.

[12] The Chief Justice and others made reference to Strader et al. *v.* Graham, 10 Howard 82 (1850). In that case the Court had held that the status of negroes, held as slaves, when returning from Ohio to Kentucky depended upon the laws of the latter state.

principle of judicial action now, and was presumably effective then, that a court will not declare a statute void unless it is necessary to the determination of the cause before it. And that Taney, with his history on the bench and his general attitude toward the duties of the courts, should have gone out of his way to declare an act void, is an especially noticeable fact.

The constitutionality of the Compromise was raised in an attempt to determine whether Dred had become free by his sojourn at Fort Snelling. Obviously, if one doubted congressional authority to exclude slavery from the territories, one was confronted by some fairly difficult obstacles, among them the Ordinance of 1787. The Chief Justice disposed of that obstacle by declaring that the Ordinance was a compact entered into by sovereign states, but it was of no binding effect after the states had surrendered "a portion of their independent sovereignty to a new Government. . . ." [13] The constitutional provision giving Congress the power to make all needful rules and regulations respecting the territory or other public property, he said, "applied only to the property which the States held in common at that time [1787], and has no reference whatever to any territory or other property which the new sovereignty might afterwards itself acquire." [14] Did Congress, then, have no authority over the territories? Such authority Taney admitted; but, he contended, it did not flow from the clause just mentioned, but from the right to acquire territory.

All territory so acquired must be held for the benefit of the people of the several states who created the government; [15] this is a crucial point in the opinion because it leads to the basis of the final fatal decision concerning the power to exclude slavery from the territories. The power of Congress over the territories, Taney declared, is plainly

[13] That Taney's views were not those of the state sovereignty protagonists is shown by various statements and positions, and notably when he said, "They [the states in 1787] were about to dissolve this federative Union, and to surrender a portion of their independent sovereignty to a new Government, which, for certain purposes, would make the people of the several States one people, and which was to be supreme and controlling within its sphere of action throughout the United States. . . ." 19 Howard 393, 435. ". . . when the present United States came into existence under the new Government, it was a new political body, a new nation. . . ." *Ibid.*, 441. See also *Ibid.*, 447-448.

[14] Taney's argument through here is unusually obscure, but he holds that as the Ordinance of 1787 was within the competence of sovereign states, the Congress under the Constitution, after the states ceased to be entirely sovereign, regarded the form of government and the principles of jurisprudence which were to be applicable to the region as already determined by the sovereign states. *Ibid.*, 438-439.

[15] *Ibid.*, 448.

limited by the Constitution; it cannot be a mere discretionary power; the amendments of the Constitution distinctly restrict such authority, and one of them expressly protects property; furthermore, property in slaves is "distinctly" affirmed by the Constitution,[16] and slave property, like other property, is protected by the due process of law announced in the fifth amendment—an interpretation of due process at that time almost unknown. It is therefore "the opinion of the court", he said, "that the act of Congress which prohibited a citizen from holding and owning property of this kind in the territory of the United States north of the line therein mentioned, is not warranted by the Constitution, and is therefore void. . . ." Thus the Missouri Compromise, in effect for a generation—accepted and on the whole believed in by men who had no doubt of its validity—, was declared to be a mere usurpation of authority.

Taney's contention that the Constitution was made for white men and that blacks could not be citizens was ably controverted by Curtis, who asserted, first, that all persons who were citizens when the Constitution was adopted must reasonably be considered citizens in purview of that document; second, that at the time of adoption in some of the states negroes were citizens, even having the right to vote. Consequently, mere declaration that a person was a negro was not sufficient to establish want of citizenship;[17] the Court therefore had

[16] "But the power of Congress over the person or property of a citizen can never be a mere discretionary power under our Constitution and form of Government. The powers of the Government and the rights and privileges of the citizen are regulated and plainly defined by the Constitution itself." *Ibid.*, 449. "The powers over person and property of which we speak are not only not granted to Congress, but are in express terms denied, and they are forbidden to exercise them." *Ibid.*, 450. "Now, as we have already said in an earlier part of this opinion, upon a different point, the right of property in a slave is distinctly and expressly affirmed in the Constitution." *Ibid.*, 451. Taney's argument on this point is especially labored; and the word "distinctly" is plainly inappropriate, because it is untrue to fact. Regarding this use of due process, see the chapter on Chief Justice Taney and the Supreme Court and the chapter on the fourteenth amendment in this work.

[17] Taney and Curtis differed radically concerning the source of citizenship. The assertion of the Chief Justice that the framers intended to exclude all negroes from citizenship, Curtis rejected, and his reasons seem conclusive, even when we admit that the right to vote does not necessarily establish citizenship of the possessor of the right. But in Taney's view, citizenship sprang from the nation and from national authority. Concerning the power granted to Congress to establish a rule of naturalization, Taney said it was "by the well-understood meaning of the word, confined to persons born in a foreign country, under a foreign Government. It is not a power to raise to the rank of a citizen any one born in the United States, who, from birth or parentage, by the laws of the country, belongs to an inferior and subordinate class." 19 Howard 393, 417. In Curtis's view, citizenship was, or might be, the gift of the

no right to reverse the decision of the lower court on that ground, and it had no right to deny, on that ground, the possession of jurisdiction by the lower court or its own jurisdiction.

Curtis devoted some attention to the question whether the decision of the state court was conclusive and binding, and whether, therefore, Dred, on returning to Missouri, was by the law of that state a slave. He declared, "The rules of international law respecting the emancipation of slaves, by the rightful operation ot the laws of another State or country upon the *status* of the slave, while resident in such foreign State or country, are part of the common law of Missouri, and have not been abrogated by any statute law of that State." He quoted with approval the dissenting opinion of Chief Justice Gamble of Missouri, delivered in the case already referred to (Scott *v.* Emerson, 15 Missouri Reports 576), in which the Chief Justice said: "In this State, it has been recognised from the beginning of the Government as a correct position in law, that the master who takes his slave to reside in a State or Territory where slavery is prohibited,

state. We are inclined to say that probably both were in some respects wrong. Every person born in the United States and subject to its jurisdiction is a citizen of the United States and of the state in which he resides. This was announced by the fourteenth amendment eleven years after the Dred Scott case. But the amendment in that particular added nothing new. In the case of United States *v.* Wong Kim Ark, 169 U. S. 649, 658 (1898), the Court said: "It thus clearly appears that by the law of England for the last three centuries, beginning before the settlement of this country, and continuing to the present day, aliens, while residing in the dominions possessed by the Crown of England, were within the allegiance, the obedience, the faith or loyalty, the protection, the power, the jurisdiction, of the English Sovereign; and therefore every child born in England of alien parents was a natural-born subject, unless the child of an ambassador . . . or of an alien enemy in hostile occupation of the place where the child was born. . . . The same rule was in force in all the English Colonies upon this continent down to the time of the Declaration of Independence, and in the United States afterwards, and continued to prevail under the Constitution as originally established." If this position is correct, Taney's position was in some respects wrong, unless we assume with him that such principles do not apply under a white man's Constitution. If the statement of the Court in this later case was always the law, then it would appear that, if a free negro should come to America, his child born here would be a citizen of the United States. The mere fact that the child was black would not prevent his being a citizen. Curtis's position was wrong in declaring that anyone recognized by a state as a citizen was a citizen—in other words, that citizenship sprang from the state, though the United States could make aliens citizens by naturalization: "The Constitution has left to the States the determination what persons, born within their respective limits, shall acquire by birth citizenship of the United States; it has not left to them [the states] any power to prescribe any rule for the removal of the disabilities of alienage. This power is exclusively in Congress." Dred Scott *v.* Sandford, 19 Howard, 393, 582.

thereby emancipates his slave."[18] Curtis admitted that a state could "refuse to recognise a change, wrought by the law of a foreign State, on the *status* of a person, while within such foreign State," but he declared that the judiciary had no authority or power to alter the established law of the state.[19]

Having thus disposed of the decision of the Missouri court, and having decided that it was not conclusive, Curtis proceeded to consider the merits of the controversy and the critical and all-important issue: did Dred become free by being taken into territory covered by the Missouri Compromise? Had Congress constitutional authority to exclude slavery from the public domain?

He took up the constitutional clause so much discussed. When Congress is given authority to make *"all* needful rules and regulations", it means *all*. Nothing in the language restricts the operation of these words to territory held by the United States in 1787. Why, he asked, should the Court ignore this express grant of power and found the right to govern on the right to acquire, which was only an implied or inferred power? The purpose of this clause—and here we find his most cogent assertion and argument—being to grant Congress the power to provide for a body of municipal law for the government of settlers, the allowance or prohibition of slavery must be within the scope of the granted power, because, when the Constitution was adopted, such allowance or prohibition was a *recognized subject of municipal legislation.* On this phase of the matter Curtis had history to fortify his argument; he was able to show that Congress almost from the beginning had exercised the power in question; it had recog-

---

[18] Cf. G. W. Biddle, "Constitutional Development in the United States as Influenced by Chief-Justice Taney," *Constitutional History of the United States as Seen in the Development of American Law*: ". . . the courts of Missouri had no right to disregard the law, and to reverse their original decisions, nor was the Federal Supreme Court bound to follow the last decision of the highest court of this State under the circumstances presented." p. 180. Less than one year before the Dred Scott case was decided, Justice Grier had delivered an opinion of the Court in the course of which he said, "When the decisions of the state court are not consistent, we do not feel bound to follow the last, if it is contrary to our own convictions,—and much more is this the case, where, after a long course of consistent decisions, some new light suddenly springs up, or an excited public opinion has elicited new doctrines, subversive of former safe precedent." Pease *v.* Peck, 18 Howard 595, 599 (1856).

[19] The opinion of Chief Justice Gamble, if read in connection with the opinion of the other two justices, seems to demonstrate that under the stress of resentment against antislavery agitation the other two justices were changing the law of the state. Scott *v.* Emerson, 15 Missouri Reports 576, 590 (1852).

nized slavery and it had excluded slavery.[20] He denied that the prohibition to carry slaves into a territory deprived anyone of his property without due process of law. His denial was strongly buttressed by references to historical evidences. We have already noticed, in a previous chapter discussing the development of law during Taney's time, the fact of his use of the due process clause of the fifth amendment. In his opinion in the case he paid attention to that clause. "And an act of Congress", he said, "which deprives a citizen of the United States of his liberty or property, merely because he came himself or brought his property into a particular Territory of the United States, and who had committed no offence against the laws, could hardly be dignified with the name of due process of law."

Curtis's discussion of the essentially local character of slavery was naturally incontrovertible; it could be denied only by finding in the Constitution some positive provision to the contrary. Both McLean and Curtis pointed to the Court's decision in Prigg *v.* Pennsylvania where it was said: "The state of slavery is deemed to be a mere municipal regulation, founded upon and limited to the range of the territorial laws." [21] Possibly the weakest point in the whole opinion of the Chief Justice was his declaration that to prevent a man from taking a slave into a territory and holding him there as a slave was to deprive the owner of his property, when the owner must be supposed to know that the moment the slave passed from the limits of a slaveholding state the law of that state ceased to have effect.[22]

[20] Besides the act of Congress of 1789, giving effect to the Ordinance of 1787 under the new government, Curtis gave a series of instances in which Congress recognized and others in which it excluded slavery. Under the latter head were laws for the government of the territories—Indiana, Michigan, Illinois, Wisconsin, Iowa, Oregon, and of course the Missouri Compromise of 1820.

Seemingly few persons, if any, seriously doubted, twenty years before the Dred Scott case, the power to exclude slavery. "It will not be questioned", said Curtis, "that, when the Constitution of the United States was framed and adopted, the allowance and the prohibition of negro slavery were recognised subjects of municipal legislation; every State had in some measure acted thereon; and the only legislative act concerning the territory—the ordinance of 1787, which had then so recently been passed—contained a prohibition of slavery. The purpose and object of the clause being to enable Congress to provide a body of municipal law for the government of the settlers, the allowance or the prohibition of slavery comes within the known and recognised scope of that purpose and object." Dred Scott *v.* Sandford, 19 Howard 393, 616.

[21] 16 Peters 539, 611 (1842).

[22] Taney, as we have seen, held that the Constitution explicitly recognized "property" in slaves. But, as we have also seen, the fugitive slave clause itself speaks of persons held to service in one state "under the laws thereof. . . ." If property in slaves was like other property—sheep, horses, or oxen—, there would have been no

The Court's decision and the varying opinions made a tremendous impression on the people-at-large. Men could find able argument for the beliefs they already held. But one thing was plain: the highest judicial authority had declared slavery to be a national institution. Slavery followed the flag—not because the public domain belonged to thirteen sovereign states, as Calhoun had contended, but because this was a white man's country and the Constitution specifically recognized property in slaves.

We can dismiss with a word the charge that the Court was "packed", and that to get a proslavery decision a conspiracy to "pack" it had been silently carried on for years. Historians are now not ready to accept this indictment as true. Of the nine justices, five were from slaveholding states. The southern states were overrepresented in the Court, if one takes into consideration the population of the respective sections and the amount of litigation brought to the attention of the circuit courts.[23] This disproportion may not have been caused by the anxiety of the southerners to have a Court friendly to slaveholding interests; presumably it was not so caused; but such a condition aroused suspicion and gave ground for attack upon the Court's decision. The justices were obviously affected by their sympathies; they were influenced by the sentiments and emotions to which human beings are normally subject; they were not demigods, but men with like passions as ourselves. By being lifted to the Supreme Court, they were not translated into a region where only abstract and dehumanized reasonings appealed to them. The majority were sincerely anxious to solve the slavery question and were led into a discussion and a decision by a false hope that they could accomplish the impossible. The case augmented rather than decreased agitation and unrest.

The decision was most vehemently denounced by orators and

need of this special provision in the Constitution. The contention that the Constitution not only protected property but clearly protected slave property as such has been considered on earlier pages. This doctrine had been plainly announced by Jefferson Davis some years before. The only thing to say is that the Constitution recognized slavery as far as it did recognize slavery. Constitution, Art. I, sec. 2, para. 3; Art. I, sec. 9, para. 1 and para. 4; Art. IV, sec. 2, para. 3.

[23] See the speech of J. M. Ashley in the House (1860), *Congressional Globe*, 36 Cong., 1 sess., appendix, p. 365 ff., where it is asserted that the court of one northern circuit—Ohio, Indiana, Illinois, and Michigan—had in 1856 more cases on the docket than the aggregate on the dockets of the five southern circuit courts. Note also the speech of Benjamin Stanton of Ohio in the House (1857), *Congressional Globe*, 34 Cong., 3 sess., p. 300. See in addition Charles Warren, *The Supreme Court in United States History*, III, p. 11, and H. von Holst. *The Constitutional . . . History of the United States*, VI, p. 20 and note 2.

newspaper-writers disagreeing with the reasoning and the conclusion of the Court. The declaration that the Missouri Compromise was unconstitutional was denounced as a mere presumptuous *dictum,* for, after deciding that Scott could not be considered a citizen and had therefore no standing in the Court, why should the Court proceed to pass upon the merits of the controversy? Even the wisest critics appear not to have taken seriously Taney's method of treatment. To many thousands of northern people one fact appeared plain: the Court after denying its own jurisdiction had proceeded to exercise it. For the niceties of constitutional law the ordinary man has no great patience and no great training. And in this particular instance the turning-point in the case was likely to appeal only to the practiced technician—if to anyone.[24]

[24] Among the most vehement denunciations of the decision of the Chief Justice was Seward's speech in the Senate, March 3, 1858. He charged Taney and the President with entering into a dishonorable intrigue. The Court, he said, after deciding it had no jurisdiction, "proceeded with amusing solemnity to pronounce the opinion that, if they had had such jurisdiction, still the unfortunate negro would have had to remain in bondage, unrelieved, because the Missouri prohibition violates rights of general property involved in slavery, paramount to the authority of Congress." "The Supreme Court," he further said, "also, can reverse its spurious judgment. . . . Let the Court recede. Whether it recede or not, we shall reorganize the Court, and thus reform its political sentiments and practices, and bring them into harmony with the Constitution and with the laws of nature." Frederic Bancroft, *The Life of William H. Seward,* I, p. 446 ff.

CHAPTER XLI

THE STRUGGLE FOR KANSAS

Before the Dred Scott case came to the Court for discussion, the struggle for Kansas had begun. Hardly was the ink dry on the Kansas-Nebraska bill when movements were on foot by slavery and antislavery men alike to get possession of the territory. Popular sovereignty, reduced to its lowest and least edifying terms, was a contest of strength; and in such a contest slavery was doomed to failure. If popular sovereignty meant—despite all attempts to rob it of clear meaning—the right of the people to decide, then slavery had no real chance. The north, moving at first more slowly than the border forces, had every advantage—more men, more economic strength, and equal determination. A slave-owner would well hesitate to carry his animate property into a region where it might soon be taken from him; under any circumstances, such a removal was a serious undertaking. And for the job of settling, for the frontiersman's job of enduring privation and of ceaseless attack upon the stubborn glebe of the western prairies, the free individual settlers were immensely superior to a band of slaves. In the long run, the antislavery men must win. It was "a contest in which the Southern oligarchy, much-cumbered and heavily shod, could not cope with freedom in its nimbler movements." [1]

Even before the passing of the Kansas-Nebraska bill, steps were taken at the north to promote migration to the west. The Massachusetts Emigrant Aid Company was formed, receiving a second charter under the title of the New England Emigrant Aid Company in February, 1855. This movement was hailed at the south as a dastardly attempt to seize the new land by force. In the months that followed it was common among the sympathizers with slavery to denounce the "Hessian mercenaries" and "hirelings" who had been hurried to the territory to work the infamous will of northern abolitionists and mischief-makers. [2]

[1] L. W. Spring, *Kansas,* p. 29.
[2] "They are 'a band of Hessian mercenaries,' said a committee of Missourians, in an address to the people of the United States. 'To call these people emigrants is a

The southern cause had to depend at first on restless adventurers from western Missouri who held no slaves, but who hated all abolitionists and loved the rough-and-tumble of conflict. They were the advance-guard, the janizaries of a militant cause. They were at first successful. A governor and other officers selected at Washington appeared in Kansas; a proslavery delegate to Congress was chosen by several hundred invaders from Missouri. The election of the legislature disclosed what might be accomplished by enterprise; in February, 1855 there appeared to be 2,905 voters; in March, 6,307 votes were cast [3]—quite properly called an "astonishing exhibition of popular sovereignty. . . ." When the news reached New England, the people were stirred to deep resentment; that, then, was popular sovereignty! ". . . it has lately been maintained," exclaimed Edward Everett, "by the sharp logic of the revolver and the bowie-knife, that the people of Missouri are the people of Kansas!" [4] The legislature passed a code of slave laws; among them was one making it a crime to deny in speech or writing the right to hold slaves.[5] The territory was ere long the scene of violence, murder, and ruffianism; the story is unappetizing and, fortunately for our purposes, need not be related. It is needless, also, to attempt any nice discrimination between the factions, when once passions of the baser sort were let loose. The free-state men were, however, on the whole wisely led, not in their career of violence, but in political strategy, by Dr. Charles Robinson, who had come to the territory as an agent of the Emigrant Aid Company.[6]

sheer perversion of language. They were not sent to cultivate the soil. . . . They have none of the marks of the old pioneers. If not clothed and fed by the same power which has effected their transportation they would starve. They are hirelings—an army of hirelings. . . . They are military colonies of reckless and desperate fanatics.' " T. C. Smith, *Parties and Slavery*, p. 124, quoting the *Richmond Enquirer*, October 5, 1855.

[3] "We had at least 7,000 men in the territory on the day of the election and one third of them will remain there. We are playing for a mightly stake, if we win we carry slavery to the Pacific Ocean if we fail we lose Missouri Arkansas and Texas and all the territories, the game must be played boldly." D. R. Atchison to R. M. T. Hunter, March 4, 1855, *Correspondence of Robert M. T. Hunter 1826-1876*, A. H. A. *Report* for 1916, II, p. 161.

[4] Edward Everett, *Orations and Speeches on Various Occasions* (1892 ed.), III, p. 347.

[5] Smith, *op. cit.*, p. 129.

[6] "The struggle for the possession of Kansas, the loss of which to the South made secession a certainty, was essentially political and constitutional—not military. . . . In the field of diplomacy and finesse the pro-slavery leaders were outgeneraled. . . . The career of the free-state men under the lead of Governor Robinson, who pro-

The anti-Missouri forces began to organize in the summer of 1855. They were utterly unwilling to recognize the spurious legislature. In October a convention assembled at Topeka. A majority of the members were Democrats; few were radical antislavery men. They prepared to assume statehood and ask for admission to the union. A constitution, prohibiting slavery after July 4, 1857, was drafted and submitted to the people for adoption, and with it was a separate declaration against the admission of free negroes into the state. The constitution was adopted by an overwhelming majority, the proslavery men of course not voting, but looking askance at the presumption of their opponents. It is interesting to notice that the pronouncement against the admission of negroes was likewise adopted, evidence of no sentimental fervor for the black man's companionship. Ridiculous as it may now seem for a few thousand people to prepare for immediate admission to the union—and to do so when the territory was in turmoil and in high dispute—the movement was not totally without precedent. There was in fact no fully substantiated legal procedure in this all-important matter of establishing a state. Steps were taken to put the constitution into operation. Robinson, known to be an earnest opponent of slavery, was chosen to be Governor (January, 1856). Under his guidance there was sure to be patient but unrelenting work for the cause.

The situation was now serious. There were two governments (the territorial government and the state government), one of them legal, recognized at Washington, though resting on violence and fraud, the other a shadow, without validity, and yet bafflingly real and effective. The free-state party had a fair share of reckless and unmanageable characters, but the "state government" could accomplish its ends only by biding its time and contenting itself with being a visible and continuous protest against the fraudulent territorial system; that much it did succeed in doing effectively. It held the antislavery men together and gave them a method of expression, but it made no desperate attempt to make and enforce law; it only masqueraded as a government. It was, after all, as Jefferson Davis said, "a mere town meeting"—but no one will underestimate town-meetings, if he can recognize enemies when he sees them.

When Congress met in December, 1855,—the Congress elected amid the excitement and upheaval that ensued upon the repeal of the

jected and inspired the whole tactical plan of its operations, has no parallel in American history." Spring, *op. cit.*, pp. 266-267.

Compromise—there was confusion for several weeks because there was no party majority and a speaker could not be chosen or the House organized for business. President Pierce's annual message, not delivered until the end of the month, dealt only briefly with Kansas and her troubles; but it did contain a dissertation on the nature of the union and the wrongs suffered by the unoffending south. Even if the charges against the north were justifiable, even if Pierce were justified in deploring sectional agitation, and even if he were totally right in his views of the Constitution and the aggression of northern sectionalism, it remains still a matter of interest that a man from the mountain state of New Hampshire should put forth exactly and at length the views and the arguments that emanated from the plantations of Mississippi: the south was totally right; the northern antislavery forces were sinfully wrong. "The Congress of the United States", Pierce announced, "is in effect that congress of sovereignties which good men in the Old World have sought for, but could never attain. . . . Our cooperative action rests in the conditions of permanent confederation prescribed by the Constitution."

In January, Pierce sent to Congress a special message—another interesting and amazing document. It laid down the principle of territorial control of domestic institutions; and this is noteworthy. How did it escape the careful eyes of his proslavery mentors in the cabinet? [7] For "propagandist colonization", which was designed to prevent "free and natural action" of the inhabitants of the territory, he had words of reproof: such designs, proclaimed through the press "in language extremely irritating and offensive", naturally aroused intense indignation in neighboring states and especially in Missouri. An act of Congress authorizing the people of a territory to form a constitution was not in the President's opinion indispensable, but in every case it must be the people of a territory, not a party among them, who have the power to form a constitution and ask admission to the union. "Inter-

[7] The act to organize the territories of Kansas and Nebraska, he said, "was a manifestation of the legislative opinion of Congress . . . that the inhabitants of any such Territory, considered as an inchoate State, are entitled, in the exercise of self-government, to determine for themselves what shall be their own domestic institutions, subject only to the Constitution and the laws duly enacted by Congress under it and to the power of the existing States [!] to decide, according to the provisions and principles of the Constitution, at what time the Territory shall be received as a State into the Union." Richardson, *Messages and Papers*, V, p. 352. See also, p. 359. To any unguarded reader this must have meant *territorial* control of slavery. What Pierce objected to was any artificial or external interference, any attempt by the people outside to affect by colonization a decision of the people in the territory.

ference on the one hand to procure the abolition or prohibition of slave labor in the Territory has produced mischievous interference on the other for its maintenance or introduction." As a remedy for disorders in Kansas, which were likely to occur with increasing violence, provision should be made for a convention and preparation for admission to the union when the people should so desire and should be of sufficient number. We are forced to inquire why this readiness to admit Kansas. Is it unfair to assume either that the President saw the contest lost or that he hoped to win the land for slavery before it was inundated by antislavery voters? Or was the President's statement only due to a desire to save the face of popular sovereignty, already badly disfigured?

Before leaving Pierce and his opinions, it is well to call attention to his annual message of the following December (1856). This again is an interesting evidence of the assurance with which a northern politician could defend the southern cause and heap the blame upon a fanatical and meddlesome north: "Extremes beget extremes. Violent attack from the North finds its inevitable consequence in the growth of a spirit of angry defiance at the South." The President's attack upon the antislavery forces, possibly intended to be a reproof only for the most extreme abolitionists, appears to be a vitriolic arraignment of the Republicans; and if it is to be thus interpreted, it was a strange and ultrapartisan announcement, especially as it came from the leader of a party which at the last election had cast less than one-half of the popular vote.[8]

This brief presentation of Pierce and his messages, unimportant as both may seem to be, is necessary for an understanding of those hectic years. It discloses the fact that the southern cause was not southern alone; it reveals the readiness of a northern President, presumably speaking for his party, to stand by that cause in every particular; it enables one to understand the intensity of feeling among northern opponents of slavery-extension, for they knew perfectly well that, if the whole country, north and south, was not to be committed to the slavery cause, they must overcome, not alone their opponents at the south, but their political adversaries at the north, and those who, like Douglas, did not care whether slavery was voted up or voted down.

[8] Buchanan had received 1,838,169 votes; Frémont, 1,341,264; Fillmore, 874,534. Edward Stanwood, *A History of the Presidency* (new ed. revised), I, p. 276. Fillmore was nominated by the American or Know Nothing party and was endorsed by the remnants of the Whigs.

And yet the sayings and doings of the President were not a matter of supreme importance. What was Stephen A. Douglas doing and saying? He was the pivot and the center. He was an able and adroit parliamentarian and the most able and ruthless debater of his day. Virile, active, persistent, tireless, he was capable of winning applause from the multitude, not by virtue of a graceful presence or by dint of the old-fashioned, high-flown rhetoric, but by hard blows and stern argument, or by what passed for argument. He was the most conspicuous figure in the Democratic party; for effective party service no other northern Democrat was quite in the same class. If the union was to be saved, the Democrats must hold the north, and no one could do it but Douglas. The time had come when the unity of that party overshadowed every other consideration.[9] Perhaps the leaders saw that fact clearly, as clearly as we do now. If the Democracy was broken, if the south could no longer rely on unflinching support north of Mason and Dixon's line, nothing remained but southern submission or withdrawal from a contaminated union. Douglas's own section and his own state were permeated with antislavery sentiment; in the election of 1856, three of the free states of the old northwest chose Republican electors, while in Illinois the Democratic victory was ominously slender. In New York the opposing candidates received over twice as many popular votes as were cast for Buchanan. If the "Little Giant" could work his will, vigorous opponents of the man and his policy had to be met and overcome—such men as Lyman Trumbull of Illinois, Zachariah Chandler of Michigan, and Benjamin Wade of Ohio. The first two were new combatants in the arena. Trumbull was a statesman not to be browbeaten by Douglas's favorite methods or misled by adroitness into the discussion of unimportant issues. The other two could be as vehement as Douglas himself, and quite as unyielding.

The Kansas question was hotly debated in Congress in the spring and early summer of 1856. The Senate committee on territories, to which the President's special message was referred, made its report in March. Douglas, the chairman, it is fair to assume, was mainly re-

[9] Alexander H. Stephens, addressing the voters of the Eighth Congressional District of Georgia, August 14, 1857, said that but for the course Walker was pursuing, Kansas would certainly have come in as a slave state. "But to whom", he asked, "are we indebted for that policy which was leading so certainly to that result?" His answer was, "to those true and gallant constitution-abiding men at the north. . . ." *The Correspondence of Robert Toombs, Alexander H. Stephens, and Howell Cobb,* A. H. A. *Report* for 1911, II, pp. 418-419.

sponsible for the argument and the language. A minority report, differing in every respect from that of the majority, was offered by Collamer of Vermont. The majority report studiously and cleverly laid the blame upon the shoulders of the New England Emigrant Company—"a vast moneyed corporation . . . a powerful corporation, with a capital of five millions of dollars invested in houses and lands, in merchandise and mills, in cannon and rifles, in powder and lead. . . ." [10] Possibly Douglas may have really supposed, when repealing the Missouri Compromise, the result would be a quiet, decorous movement into the territory and a polite adjustment of the slavery question.[11] But he was now wroth at this attempt to "abolitionize Kansas." [12] His anger at "Black Republicanism" was bitter. The committee presented a bill authorizing the summoning of a convention for the formation of a constitution; such a step was to be taken when the population was equal in number to that required by the then existing ratio of representation for a member of Congress. One real or ostensible objection to a serious consideration of the free-state constitution already adopted was the fact of its being set up by a gathering which did not recognize the territorial government.[13]

[10] ". . . those who were opposed to allowing the people of the Territory, preparatory to their admission into the Union as a State, to decide the slavery question for themselves, failing to accomplish their purpose in the halls of Congress, and under the authority of the constitution, immediately resorted in their respective States to unusual and extraordinary means to control the political destinies and shape the domestic institutions of Kansas. . . ." *Senate Reports,* 34 Cong., 1 sess., no. 34, p. 39. Such conduct was in direct defiance of the rights of the people, and in direct opposition to the principle of allowing them to be *"perfectly free"* to regulate their domestic institutions.

[11] Lincoln, in his speech of October 16, 1854, at Peoria, soon after the repeal of the Compromise, used words that might well have rung long in the ears of Douglas: "In this state of affairs the Genius of Discord himself could scarcely have invented a way of again setting us by the ears but by turning back and destroying the peace measures of the past. The counsels of that Genius seem to have prevailed." *Works* (J. G. Nicolay and John Hay, editors), I, p. 199.

[12] "When the emigrants sent out by the Massachusetts Emigrant Aid Company, and their affiliated societies, passed through the State of Missouri in large numbers on their way to Kansas, the violence of their language, and the unmistakable indications of their determined hostility to the domestic institutions of that State, created apprehensions that the object of the company was to abolitionize Kansas as a means of prosecuting a relentless warfare upon the institutions of slavery within the limits of Missouri." *Senate Reports,* 34 Cong., 1 sess., no. 34, p. 9.

[13] Collamer's minority report deserves a word; indeed, only want of space excuses failure to give here a summary of both reports. "Treating this grievance in Kanzas [sic] with ingenious excuses, with neglect or contempt, or riding over the oppressed with an army, and dragooning them into submission, will make no satisfactory termination. Party success may at times be temporarily secured by adroit

In March, Douglas and Trumbull had a vigorous duel of words and wits in the Senate chamber; and in that meeting we see the real situation and the real issue, for Senator Trumbull, though elected by a combination of anti-Nebraska, anti-Douglas, and Whig legislators in Illinois, had been a life-long Democrat. The vehemence of Douglas, who resisted what he called a personal attack upon himself, was doubtless caused by the maddening spectacle of a colleague, a renegade from the ranks of the true Democracy, daring to engage in hostile criticism and withal to indulge in damaging logic. Was this Senator from a state which was Douglas's own bailiwick to be allowed to question the leader's authority and the sanctity of party creed? We need not wonder at the earnestness—to use a gentle word—of Douglas; for what became of party solidarity, in behalf of which he toiled and planned, and what became of his own leadership, if "Black Republicanism" was to issue in the Senate chamber from the lips of one who declared he advocated no "other doctrines than those which have been handed down to us by the Democratic fathers of the Republic"? [14]

The House appointed a committee to go to Kansas and investigate conditions. They examined over three hundred witnesses and early in July presented "a report, in which a great mass of facts is accumulated wholly creditable to neither side." [15] In the place of the original bill presented by the committee above-mentioned, another, commonly called the Toombs bill, was offered and adopted by the Senate. It provided for a convention and for the admission of Kansas to the union with a constitution thus formed. It was fair on its face, and was probably meant to be fair, but the Republicans could now see lurking dangers in every corner and wayside bush. They distrusted the gift-bearing Greeks when they found the bill providing for a commission to take charge of the preliminaries—a commission to be appointed by Pierce. The House would have none of it, but sent to the Senate a measure of its own for the admission of Kansas under the constitution already framed by the free-state settlers. To this, of course, the Senate refused to give its consent. In the Senate, and in the House too, the determined opponents of slavery were doubtless

devices, plausible pretences, and partisan address; but the permanent preservation of this Union can be maintained only by frankness and integrity." *Senate Reports,* 34 Cong., 1 sess., no. 34, p. 61.
    [14] For Trumbull's speech (March 14, 1856), see *Congressional Globe,* 34 Cong., 1 sess., appendix, p. 200 ff. Trumbull's caustic treatment of popular sovereignty must have made Douglas writhe. See Trumbull's speech of July 2, 1856, *Ibid.,* p. 778 ff.
    [15] Spring, *op. cit.,* p. 108.

moved by such sentiments as those expressed by Seward (July 2, 1856) : "So far as the subject of slavery is concerned, the most which can be claimed for this bill is, that it gives an equal chance to the people of Kansas to choose between freedom and slavery. . . . I recognize no equality, in moral right or political expediency, between slavery and freedom. I hold the one to be decidedly good, and the other to be positively bad." [16] To the southerners this was intolerable, even to the least bitter of them, and, as we shall see more clearly later, it presented the irreconcilable difficulty : slavery was wrong and, because it was wrong, no more slave states should be admitted; slavery should be confined within its ancient limits.

Through the summer of 1856 the disorders in Kansas suffered no abatement. The presidential election, resulting in a Democratic victory, could not settle the problem, much as Pierce might talk about the decision of the people. The Know Nothing or American party, with its passwords and grips and secrets and all the histrionic performances which frequently attract such people as do not like the labor of connected thought, was by this time increasing in numbers; it served to divert attention from the slavery issue and for a brief period gave evidence of vitality, but, as Horace Greeley said, in good racy English, "It would seem as devoid of the elements of persistence as an anticholera or an anti-potato-rot party would be." In 1854, it succeeded in electing forty-three members to the House; and two years later, having nominated Fillmore for the presidency—a nomination concurred in by the remnant of Whigs reluctant to abandon their old name—it cast over 800,000 votes, about one-fifth of the total number of popular votes of that year. Only one state, however,—Maryland—was carried for the party candidate.

The new Republican party showed astonishing strength. The Congress elected in the autumn after the repeal of the Missouri Compromise (1854) contained over a hundred Republicans and anti-Nebraska men. In the presidential election (1856) over 1,300,000 votes were cast for Frémont, the Republican candidate; but of the states which afterwards joined the Confederacy not a single vote was given for the Republican electors, except in Virginia, where an insignificant number supported the Republican ticket. Plainly, the charge that the new party was sectional had ample foundation, and that fact menaced the union.

When Buchanan had taken office, he appointed to the governorship

[16] *Congressional Globe,* 34 Cong., 1 sess., appendix, p. 790.

of Kansas Robert J. Walker of Mississippi, a shrewd and capable man, who could have had no passionate hatred of slavery. But Walker, like his predecessors, found difficulties awaiting him. The territorial legislature, proslavery, had already taken steps for the gathering of a convention and the framing of a constitution. Walker had been told officially, that any constitution, so adopted, must be submitted to the people, and Walker was determined to carry out his instructions. Because the election of delegates to the convention was based on an absurdly insufficient census and registration, the free-state men refused to participate in the choice of delegates, and the result was the selection of proslavery advocates. The convention met at Lecompton in September, but after a brief session adjourned to meet in October. In the meantime, an election of members of the legislature took place, October 5, 1857. The free-state men, influenced by Robinson and by Henry Wilson, the Massachusetts Senator, now decided to vote, believing that Walker's assurance of a fair and free election gave them a chance to show their undoubted majority. They were successful in gaining control of the legislature,[17] and as a consequence the whole face of affairs was changed.

But the convention which met at Lecompton, proslavery to the core, had not finished its work. If a constitution recognizing slavery should be submitted to the people, and if the Free Soil men should vote, it would probably or certainly be scorned; the battle for slavery would be lost. "The convention, after an angry and excited debate, finally determined, by a majority of only two, to submit the question of slavery to the people, though at the last forty-three of the fifty delegates present affixed their signatures to the constitution."[18] The Lecompton constitution was submitted to the people, but in a strange fashion. The people were not allowed to vote for ratification or for rejection, but only for the constitution with slavery or for the constitution with no slavery; if the latter vote prevailed, the slaves then held in the territory were to remain in bondage. Governor Walker was indignant and went to Washington, where he found the President firm in support of the kind of submission which the Lecompton convention had decided upon. Walker resigned and wrote Cass, then the Secretary

[17] The result of the election turned on the vote of two counties. In one, there were 1,266 proslavery votes cast though scarcely anyone lived there. In the other, which had six houses, including stores, there were 1,628 proslavery votes cast. Walker threw out the returns from these two counties. Spring, *op. cit.*, p. 218.

[18] Buchanan's message of December 8, 1857. Richardson, *Messages and Papers*, V, p. 452.

of State, that ". . . any attempt by Congress to force this constitution upon the people of Kansas will be an effort to substitute the will of a small minority for that of an overwhelming majority of the people of Kansas. . . ." [19] The plan was, however, carried through; the constitution with slavery received 6,226 votes, of which, it is asserted, over 2,700 were fraudulent; the votes in opposition were 569, most of the free-state men refusing to vote. The legislature, now in the hands of the antislavery men, took the extraordinary step of submitting the whole constitution, and the result showed 10,226 against ratification and less than 200 in favor.

The Kansas affairs, which have been briefly presented in the preceding pages, are of importance in constitutional history because they disclose the absurdity of popular sovereignty. But there was another and more important result: a rift appeared in the Democratic ranks. Douglas was in vehement opposition to the Lecompton procedure. He had a stormy interview with the President who warned him against defying the administration, but to this Douglas replied, "Mr. President, I wish you to remember that General Jackson is dead." If the President and his southern supporters were on one side, and Douglas and his warm northern admirers were on the other, the long-cherished unity and harmony of the party were gone.

Buchanan favored admission under the Lecompton constitution. In his message of February 2, 1858, he declared that the free-state men had had a fair opportunity "to decide this exciting question" of slavery. Prompt admission to the union he thought highly desirable; if the people, after admission, desired to change their constitution, this they could freely do: "If a majority of them desire to abolish domestic slavery within the State, there is no other possible mode by which this can be effected so speedily as by prompt admission." [20] This plea was not without its appeal to those willing to forgive and forget, and to those anxious above all to smother the slavery question.

The breach between Douglas and the forces of the administration was a serious matter; in reality, and in the long run, it spelled the

[19] *Senate Reports,* 35 Cong., 1 sess., I, no. 8, p. 131.

[20] Buchanan said, among other things, one surprisingly foolish thing: "It has been solemnly adjudged by the highest judicial tribunal known to our laws that slavery exists in Kansas by virtue of the Constitution of the United States. Kansas is therefore at this moment as much a slave State as Georgia or South Carolina." Richardson, *Messages and Papers,* V, p. 479. The foolishness is not diminished by the fact that one could not be certain of the meaning; but the context appears to show that he believed there was a constitutional obligation to admit Kansas with the proslavery constitution.

dethronement of Douglas. His opposition to the methods, by which the constitution had been adopted, preserved the allegiance, we may assume, of many northern Democrats who were indignant at the Lecompton travesty; but that was not enough; he must hold also the southern members of his party; the task proved in the end too hard for even his indomitable spirit. How much he was guided by the natural ambitions of leadership, no one can say. He was not filled with antislavery zeal, but once aroused (and he was aroused a good part of the time) he could be obstinate and unrelenting. Certainly he proved to be so when he was denouncing "a system of trickery and jugglery to defeat the fair expression of the will of the people." We are forced to feel compassion and even admiration for him in those trying years, abandoned by a portion of his followers, upbraided at the south, beset by men like Lincoln and Trumbull in his own state, and still boldly fighting on, trying to protect himself by the garments of popular sovereignty which had proved to assure everything except peace.

As the result of a noisy controversy in Congress, where truculence was more in evidence than placid statesmanship, a bill was passed (April 30, 1858) for resubmitting the Lecompton constitution. It gave the people of Kansas opportunity to accept a proposition granting to the state a considerable area of government land; if the proposition were accepted, the state was to come into the union under the Lecompton constitution; if rejected, no further convention was to be held until the population of the territory equaled or exceeded the number required for a single representative in Congress. The offer to Kansas, termed a mere sordid bribe by its opponents, was spurned by the Kansas voters. The territory remained outside the union until after the election of Lincoln.

What moved the introduction and passage of such a strange measure as the English bill? Probably a desperate hope that peace might thus be obtained; to this must be added the pressure of the administration and the lavish use of patronage,[21] and possibly the still lingering hope that Kansas might come in as a Democratic state. But it is an illuminating disclosure of a frantic and unhappy condition of mind, when lawmakers could actually suppose that the offer of a few thousand acres to a people, who looked out upon almost limitless, unpeopled prairies stretching away to the remote mountains, would induce them eagerly to accept a constitution which they despised. If members of Congress engaged in angry words and resorted to blows, would the

[21] See Rhodes, *History of the United States,* II, p. 300.

people at the center of conflict be quiet and compliant? If men fought in Kansas, would they be unwilling to fight elsewhere? And if the cause of slavery were lost to more powerful forces on the western plains, did that fact simply foreshadow the final outcome in a greater and more terrible conflict?

CHAPTER XLII

THE LINCOLN-DOUGLAS DEBATES

The outstanding event of 1858 was the series of debates between Lincoln and Douglas, in a contest to secure the senatorship in Illinois. After his nomination at Springfield by the Republicans, Lincoln made a famous and oft-quoted speech; its most startling announcement—startling to those opponents of slavery who wished to put on the soft pedal and not shout aloud any principle that might work mischief to party policy or politics—was contained in the opening paragraph: " 'A house divided against itself cannot stand.' I believe this government cannot endure permanently half slave and half free. I do not expect the Union to be dissolved—I do not expect the house to fall—but I do expect it will cease to be divided. It will become all one thing, or all the other. Either the opponents of slavery will arrest the further spread of it, and place it where the public mind shall rest in the belief that it is in the course of ultimate extinction; or its advocates will push it forward till it shall become alike lawful in all the States, old as well as new, North as well as South." This speech contains within itself the kernel of Lincoln's undeviating belief and the center of his unswerving purpose: slavery must not be allowed to expand. It must be placed, as he more elaborately declared at a later time, where the fathers left it, in the belief and the hope that it would in time disappear.[1]

But as far as the "house divided" principle or prophecy is concerned, there was not really much, if anything, new in it—little except its clarity and its peculiar applicability to the existing situation—, for what had Calhoun talked about for years save the irreconcilable enmity between slavery and the fell spirit of abolitionism, the danger to the

---

[1] In his reply to Douglas at Quincy, October 13, 1858. See Abraham Lincoln, *Complete Works* (J. G. Nicolay and John Hay, editors), I, p. 480. This contention is especially elaborated in the Cooper Institute speech of February 27, 1860—a very astute, adroit, and sound use of historical evidence, directed in part to establish that the fathers believed the national government could exclude slavery from national territory. *Ibid.*, I, p. 599 ff.

union if slavery were condemned?[2] Lincoln's use of the Biblical quotation and his clear pronouncement of the essential hostility between slavery and freedom were impressive because of their solemn simplicity. They must have left on the minds of hearers and readers the assurance that mere palliatives or subterfuges could not unite a nation thus divided.[3] He believed that a movement was on foot for unifying the nation by making slavery national. His recognition of the essential strength of conflicting principles is proof of his statesmanship.

The Lincoln-Douglas debates had all the qualities of a stirring drama. Douglas was the leader of his party, still its most conspicuous man despite his quarrel with the administration. He was looked upon with favor by no small number of Republican politicians who were appreciative of his courage and tried to believe that he was their ally.[4] He was impressive by the very force of a strangely dominating personality, and was—to use Harriet Beecher Stowe's words—"the very ideal of vitality." Though prominent in state politics, Lincoln was comparatively unimpressive. But, as Douglas well knew, he could strike hard blows and had unusual skill in insisting upon critical and crucial points, and he could not easily be confounded and lost in the mists with which Douglas loved to enshroud an antagonist. But it is impossible for us to cover those debates or even briefly to outline them. We must content ourselves with one or two main matters of constitutional interest.

In doing this, we may first call attention to Lincoln's announcement of an essential difference between the Democrats and the Republicans: the Democrats did not say slavery was wrong. This may seem a matter quite without the field of constitutional history, but it was, of course, the center and the kernel of the great controversy that ended in the attempted disruption of the union. It would be folly to consider legislative disputes and not to recognize at all the warfare between

---

[2] Calhoun wrote in 1850: "Nothing short of the terms I propose, can settle it [the great question of the day] finally and permanently. Indeed, it is difficult to see how two peoples so different and hostile can exist together in one common Union." Letter to T. G. Clemson, March 10, 1850. *Correspondence of John C. Calhoun,* Am. Hist. Asso. *Report* for 1899, II, p. 784.

[3] Lincoln's speech was made June 16, 1858. Seward's "irrepressible conflict" speech (October 25, 1858) contained the same sentiment and attracted much attention: "It is an irrepressible conflict between opposing and enduring forces, and it means that the United States must and will, sooner or later, become either entirely a slaveholding nation or entirely a free-labor nation."

[4] A brief, clear statement is given in Allen Johnson, *Stephen A. Douglas,* pp. 348-349.

moral principles and social beliefs. The heart of southern hostility to "Black Republicanism" was the Republican belief in the wrongfulness of slavery. "If there be a man in the Democratic party", said Lincoln, "who thinks it is wrong, and yet clings to that party, I suggest to him in the first place that his leader don't [sic] talk as he does, for he never says that it is wrong. In the second place, I suggest to him that if he will examine the policy proposed to be carried forward, he will find that he carefully excludes the idea that there is anything wrong in it. . . . When Judge Douglas says that whoever or whatever community wants slaves, they have a right to have them, he is perfectly logical if there is nothing wrong in the institution; but if you admit that it is wrong, he cannot logically say that anybody has a right to do wrong." [5]

Doubtless among the Democrats there were many who believed slavery a misfortune, if not morally wrong, but who preferred to let matters drift, dreaded sectional agitation, were influenced by the charges of "abolitionism" constantly heaped upon the Republicans, and were persuaded that at the bottom of Republican doctrine was the belief in the social equality of the black and white races. In appraising Lincoln's statement, we must remember he was debating against a party leader who did not announce his opposition to slavery; if there were Democrats who disagreed with Douglas, they were in the wrong party.

No words of mine can so clearly set forth Lincoln's party principles as does his own declaration: "Because we think it [slavery] wrong, we propose a course of policy that shall deal with it as a wrong. We deal with it as with any other wrong, in so far as we can prevent its growing any larger, and so deal with it that in the run of time there may be some promise of an end to it. We have a due regard to the actual presence of it amongst us, and the difficulties of getting rid of it in any satisfactory way, and all the constitutional obligations thrown about it. I suppose that in reference both to its actual existence in the nation, and to our constitutional obligations, we have no right at all to disturb it in the States where it exists, and we profess that we have no more inclination to disturb it than we have the right to do it. We go further than that: we don't propose to disturb it where, in one instance, we think the Constitution would permit us. We think the Constitution would permit us to disturb it in the District of Columbia.

[5] Speech at Quincy, October 13, 1858. Abraham Lincoln, *Complete Works* (J. G. Nicolay and John Hay, editors), I, p. 464.

Still we do not propose to do that, unless it should be in terms which I don't suppose the nation is very likely soon to agree to—the terms of making the emancipation gradual and compensating the unwilling owners. Where we suppose we have the constitutional right, we restrain ourselves in reference to the actual existence of the institution and the difficulties thrown about it. We also oppose it as an evil so far as it seeks to spread itself. We insist on the policy that shall restrict it to its present limits. We don't suppose that in doing this we violate anything due to the actual presence of the institution, or anything due to the constitutional guaranties thrown around it." [6]

To charge a man presenting such principles with being an abolitionist and advocating social equality between blacks and whites might be good tactics for winning votes, especially in southern Illinois, which had been peopled largely from the south; but such charges or insinuations were appeals to prejudices and passions. The people of the southern states saw in Republicanism all that was obnoxious to them in antislavery doctrine; the purpose of the "Black Republicans" was to stop at nothing in their zeal for social upheaval and the equalizing of the races. Was Douglas in any measure responsible for strengthening this conception of Republican doctrine? With this belief which the southerners held—doubtless because by 1858 their passions were so aroused that the time for calm questioning of purpose was passed—, they might well think their only salvation was in breaking the union and building bulwarks against the tide of fanaticism.

The Dred Scott decision naturally entered into the debates. To both combatants it presented difficulties. Lincoln had to find ground for refusing to be bound by the principle of a decision which he held false, for, if the Republicans accepted the decision as a legitimate statement of constitutional right, their calling was gone; their main purpose was no longer a legal purpose, if they advocated opposition to law and authority. On that matter Lincoln's position was as follows: "We do not propose that when Dred Scott has been decided to be a slave by the court, we, as a mob, will decide him to be free. We do not propose that, when any other one, or one thousand, shall be decided by that court to be slaves, we will in any violent way disturb the rights of property thus settled; but we nevertheless do oppose that decision as a political rule, which shall be binding on the voter to vote for nobody who thinks it wrong, which shall be binding on the members of Congress or the President to favor no measure that does not

[6] *Ibid.*, I, pp. 462-463.

actually concur with the principles of that decision. We do not propose to be bound by it as a political rule in that way, because we think it lays the foundation not merely of enlarging and spreading out what we consider an evil, but it lays the foundation for spreading that evil into the States themselves. We propose so resisting it as to have it reversed if we can, and a new judicial rule established upon this subject." [7]

Is it necessary to discuss the legitimacy of this doctrine as a constitutional principle? From the acknowledgment of the Court's right and duty to interpret and apply the Constitution, as the Court views the Constitution, to the declaration that the Court by its decision fixes upon the Constitution an interpretation that must last forever and beyond, is a far cry. As a matter of practical and righteous politics, to "pack" a court in order to obtain a particular decision is, or may be, constitutionally immoral; to make the Court the plaything of party politics would be to vitiate much of what is sound and wholesome in our constitutional system. But can we deny also the right of the people —if necessary, by party agitation—to bring about an amendment to the Constitution? Some aspects of this subject we considered when speaking of Jackson's veto of the Bank bill. The Supreme Court has changed its mind—rarely, it is true, openly reversing a decision, but not so rarely by gradual and almost imperceptible modifications. Is it a constitutional necessity that such change should always be made without any manifest pressure from popular opinion? The result of popular sovereignty in Kansas appeared to demonstrate that the people there would practically outlaw slavery; if the principle of the Dred Scott decision were accepted, Congress would be under obligation to protect slavery in Kansas. Could no congressman, believing the Dred Scott principle false, refuse to vote for legislation affirmatively protecting slavery in Kansas? The question answers itself; and the answer justifies the assertion of a party's right to support congressmen opposing the spread of slavery. Whether the reader accepts this reasoning or not, it was asking a good deal of Lincoln, as matters then stood, to accept the decision, given in the manner we have described, as an unchanging and unchangeable constitutional principle.

Lincoln's position, then, was difficult: he must allay the anxiety of those who respected the Court and were naturally, above all, law-abiding; and he must at the same time announce the right of himself and his party to refuse recognition of a principle which they believed

[7] *Ibid.*, I, p. 463.

constitutionally unsound and politically unwholesome and perilous. It is unnecessary to take up his attack on the fateful decision as part of a conspiracy,[8] a conspiracy which might be aimed even at the authority of free states to maintain freedom. Portions of this attack now seem groundless or unimportant. But despite all Douglas's denials of intrigue, perhaps he was thinking, as he listened to Lincoln's telling indictment, of the fact (or probable fact) that the leaders of the Democratic party in 1854 had agreed on one thing—that the question of slavery in the territories should be relegated to the Court. If this meant that these leaders north and south would abide by a Court decision and accept the principle, the doctrine of popular sovereignty, as announced in the Nebraska bill and vehemently proclaimed by Douglas, was not a party declaration of fixed constitutional principle.[9] Perhaps Douglas had in mind—he might well have had—that the southern leaders would have an excuse for their bitterness, if they found him opposing the Dred Scott decision or so interpreting it as to deprive them of its effect.

If Lincoln and the Republicans were confronted with trouble because of the Dred Scott case, Douglas and the Democrats were in even greater difficulty. To make that difficulty plain to the voters was Lincoln's task. The Court's decision was in direct conflict with the doctrine of territorial sovereignty: the existence of slavery in the territories was legal; no territorial government, the creature of Congress, could do more than Congress itself, and Congress could not invalidate slavery. There followed as a logical consequence the duty of the territorial legislature to protect slavery by positive legislation as it would other property, and the duty of Congress to act similarly, if need be.

The year before the debates began, Douglas had taken a position on this matter: the right to hold slaves in any territory could not be taken away by act of Congress, but it remained "a barren and worthless right, unless sustained, protected, and enforced by appropriate police regulations and local legislation, prescribing adequate remedies

---

[8] Referred to in his speech at Springfield, June 16, 1858, and later.
[9] Notice Douglas's speech (July 2, 1856), *Congressional Globe*, 34 Cong., 1 sess., appendix, p. 797, which has been already referred to in the chapter on the repeal of the Missouri Compromise. Speaking of the Nebraska bill, he said: "I should have supported it just as readily if I thought the decision would be one way as the other." ". . . I stated I would not discuss this legal question, for *by the bill we referred it to the courts.*" Italics mine. If the reader can discover what this statement makes out of popular sovereignty as a principle of constitutional authority, he will do well. See also the speech of J. P. Benjamin in the Senate (May 2, 1856), *Ibid.*, 34 Cong., 1 sess., p. 1093.

for its violation. These regulations and remedies must necessarily depend entirely upon the will and wishes of the people of the Territory, as they can only be prescribed by the local legislatures." [10] Lincoln succeeded in getting Douglas to make this statement again, and the statement is commonly called the Freeport, or "unfriendly legislation", doctrine. Lincoln asked: "Can the people of a Territory in any lawful way, against the wishes of any citizen of the United States, exclude slavery from their limits prior to the formation of a State constitution?" The reply was almost indignant: "I answer emphatically, as Mr. Lincoln has heard me answer a hundred times from every stump in Illinois, that in my opinion the people of a Territory can, by lawful means, exclude slavery from their limits prior to the formation of a State constitution. . . . It matters not what way the Supreme Court may hereafter [!] decide as to the abstract question whether slavery may or may not go into a Territory under the Constitution, the people have the lawful means to introduce it or exclude it as they please, for the reason that slavery cannot exist a day or an hour anywhere unless it is supported by local police regulations." [11] If the people, he said, are opposed to slavery, they will elect representatives to the local legislature who will by "unfriendly legislation" prevent its introduction. An interesting example this, of a method of debate; for why did Douglas say "hereafter"? And how clever the choice of the word "unfriendly"! [12]

This doctrine of "unfriendly legislation" Lincoln attacked in his speech at Jonesboro, but his most telling assault was made later, at Columbus, Ohio (September 16, 1859), when he exposed it free from "the trash, the words, the collateral matter" as "a bare absurdity:—no less than that a thing may be lawfully driven away from where it has

[10] Quoted in Johnson, *op. cit.*, p. 322.
[11] Abraham Lincoln, *Complete Works* (J. G. Nicolay and John Hay, editors), I, p. 315. Trumbull had in 1856 tried to get Douglas to say positively whether in his opinion a territorial legislature had a right to establish or exclude slavery. Douglas replied that it was a "judicial question, left by the bill to the courts for decision." *Congressional Globe,* 34 Cong., 1 sess., pp. 1371, 1374.
[12] This "hereafter" arose to make trouble in the Democratic convention of 1860. See also the platform of the Douglas Democrats in that year. It is interesting to note that a few days later (at Jonesboro, September 15) Douglas said: "I wish to say to you, fellow-citizens, that I have no war to make on that decision, or any other ever rendered by the Supreme Court. I am content to take that decision as it stands delivered by the highest judicial tribunal on earth, a tribunal established by the Constitution of the United States for that purpose, and hence that decision becomes the law of the land, binding on you, on me, and on every other good citizen, whether we like it or not." Abraham Lincoln, *Complete Works* (J. G. Nicolay and John Hay, editors), I, p. 343.

a lawful right to be." [13] Douglas's doctrine of "unfriendly legislation" is commonly considered the death-knell of his prospects for southern support, and that may be true, but his reply to Lincoln's question at Quincy, October 13, was in fact equally damaging, if he hoped to maintain party agreement on slavery. He had been asked, if "a slave-holding citizen of one of the Territories should need and demand a slave code to protect his slaves", he would vote for such a measure. His reply was: "I answered him that a fundamental article in the Democratic creed, as put forth in the Nebraska bill and the Cincinnati platform, was non-intervention by Congress with slavery in the States and Territories, and hence that I would not vote in Congress for any code of laws either for or against slavery in any Territory. I will leave the people perfectly free to decide that question for themselves." [14]

As we have already seen, the vital question for six years after the repeal of the Compromise was the question whether or not the Democratic party could be maintained as an effective body. Douglas had defied the administration on the Lecompton issue; now Lincoln was successful in bringing home to the people the impossibility of reconciling the Dred Scott decision and popular sovereignty; not even the agile Douglas could ride two horses, going in different directions. The southerners were wroth with him. Lincoln stood forth as a national character, associated at the south with the menace of "Black Republicanism", abolition, and racial equality. He was recognized at the north as one able to meet the redoubtable Douglas in debate and as a clear exponent of the resolve not to allow the further spread of slavery. He had perhaps overemphasized the danger of slavery's inundating the free states or bringing them under the domination of slaveholding purposes and ideals; but he accepted the constitutional duty of uphold-

---

[13] *Ibid.*, I, pp. 551-552. It is worthy of note that Douglas, in a speech at Alton, October 15, 1858, quoted the "able and eloquent statesman", Jefferson Davis, as upholding the Freeport doctrine. Davis, it should be pointed out, said that if the inhabitants of a territory should refuse to pass laws and police regulations for securing their property, "it would be rendered more or less valueless in proportion to the difficulties of holding it without such protection." If the property were slave property, "the insecurity would be so great that the owner could not ordinarily retain it. Therefore, though the right would remain, the remedy being withheld, it would follow that the owner would be practically debarred, by the circumstances of the case, from taking slave property into a Territory where the sense of the inhabitants was opposed to its introduction." See *Ibid.*, I, p. 494. We have no right to suppose the south would calmly accept the nullification of a legal right. And we should notice that Douglas's Freeport doctrine was in answer to Lincoln's question whether the exclusion of slavery could be secured in any *lawful* way.

[14] *Ibid.*, I, p. 475.

ing the fugitive slave law, and disclaimed all aim of interfering with slavery where it already existed. He made no announcement of social equality of white and black, quite the contrary; but he asserted that no man could rightly be made a chattel because of his color. He summoned to his aid such Democrats as believed slavery wrong, and he made an appeal to the old-time Whigs by proclaiming Henry Clay his "beau ideal of a statesman".[15] He thus gained adherents for his party and helped also to place it, in a certain degree at least, on a conservative basis. It was a liberal party because it was arrayed against the extension and towering influence of a great economic interest, because it appealed to the primary sources of liberal sentiment and asked for a recognition of fundamental human rights, and because it tended also to frighten the conservative business interests of the north which dreaded disturbing contests. But it was conservative because it made little or no appeal to the extreme antislavery men, and because it placed emphasis on one practical idea—opposition to the spread of slavery, but obedience to law. It was conservative because it summoned to its standard the great body, probably, of northern Whigs, and the Whigs had been socially and temperamentally conservative in their attitude toward authority, finance, and business stability.

Douglas won the election in Illinois. The legislature chose him as his own successor in the senatorship. But in electing the lower house of the legislature, some sixteen thousand more votes were cast by the supporters of Lincoln than were cast by the Douglas supporters. The vote for the state senate disclosed a similar condition, and the Republican candidates for the state offices were elected. Douglas might well have exclaimed with Pyrrhus, "Another such victory and we are lost!"

In the autumn after the election, Douglas, traveling in the south, gave even there his doctrine of "unfriendly legislation" or the practical equivalent. He adhered to the decision of the Supreme Court, he said, and that decision allowed the southerner to take his slave property into a territory, but once there, his property was dependent on local law; if the legislature failed to protect the property, the ownership was of little or no value—"Non-action is exclusion." [16] His apparently

---

[15] For example: "Henry Clay . . . once said of a class of men who would repress all tendencies to liberty and ultimate emancipation, that they must, if they would do this, go back to the era of our independence, and muzzle the cannon which thunders its annual joyous return . . . !" Again, he quoted Clay as lamenting slavery and as saying, "If a state of nature existed, and we were about to lay the foundations of society, no man would be more strongly opposed than I should be, to incorporating the institution of slavery among its elements." *Ibid.*, I, pp. 299, 502.

[16] Johnson, *op. cit.*, pp. 393-394.

frank statements were nothing less than pathetic; and in the following months his failure to reconcile incompatibles became daily more apparent. Brown of Mississippi in the Senate declared the legislature of Kansas must protect slavery, and if it did not do so, Congress must act. Jefferson Davis, now the leader of the southern Democracy, the heir of Calhoun but with a larger and more united constituency, and like the great master a man of intellectual vigor, pointed out plainly the duty of Congress: a territorial legislature, the creature of Congress and its agent, could not exclude slavery, and if slavery was in jeopardy, Congress must see that such property was protected by affirmative legislation.

But there was much more than this mere conflict between theories; Douglas and Davis, one the northern leader, the other the southern Democratic leader, now declared the impossibility of further coöperation. "I tell you, gentlemen of the South," said Douglas, "in all candor, I do not believe a Democratic candidate can ever carry any one Democratic State of the North on the platform that it is the duty of the Federal Government to force the people of a Territory to have slavery when they do not want it." [17] "I should have been glad," Davis declared, "if the Senator, when he appeared in the Senate, had answered the expectation of many of his friends, and by a speech here have removed the doubt which his reported speeches in the last canvass of Illinois created. . . . He has confirmed me, however, in the belief that he is now as full of heresy as he once was of adherence to the doctrine of popular sovereignty, correctly construed. . . ." [18] Driven along by the persistent questioning of Davis, Douglas answered in much the same way as he had previously answered Lincoln.[19] ". . . I will vote against any law by Congress attempting to interfere with a regulation made by the Territories, with respect to any kind of property whatever, whether horses, mules, negroes, or anything else." [20] The "Little Giant", though clad in heavy armor, was in no enviable position when attacked by Lincoln on one side and Davis on the other.

[17] *Congressional Globe*, 35 Cong., 2 sess., p. 1247.
[18] *Ibid.*, p. 1257.
[19] Abraham Lincoln, *Complete Works* (J. G. Nicolay and John Hay, editors), I, p. 367.
[20] *Congressional Globe*, 35 Cong., 2 sess., p. 1259. Davis said in reply, "Then, as I understand the Senator, . . . it is that he offers to us the proposition that the constitutional rights shall be submitted to the Supreme Court, and now announces that, whatever may be the decision of the Supreme Court, he will not legislate for the protection of the rights thus guarantied." *Ibid.* Further light (or darkness) is thrown on Douglas's position by his statement in *Ibid.*, p. 1244.

Lincoln's campaign, as well as the attitude of Douglas on the Lecompton question, was producing results. Douglas was deposed from his position as chairman of the committee on territories. The south saw in him a traitor to the cause. He still could count upon the support of northern admirers, but as a national leader of a united party his reign was over. He continued to write and speak with an impressive cleverness that need not be termed sagacity. The constitutional fact is just this: however Douglas might reason, if the Dred Scott decision were good law, then southerners had the right to carry their slave property into the territories; Congress had full authority over the territories—organized or not—subject to the limitations set down in the Constitution; one of these limitations—the fifth amendment—provided protection for property.

He continued to defend his interpretation of the Kansas-Nebraska Act: "It was agreed [1854] that while we might differ as to the extent of the power of the Territorial Legislature on these questions, we would make a full grant of legislative authority to the Legislature of the Territory, with the right to pass such laws as they chose, and the right of anybody to appeal to the court to decide upon the validity and constitutionality of such laws, but not to come to Congress for their annulment." [21] Douglas (February 23, 1859) quoted at length a speech of Senator Benjamin of Louisiana, made in 1856, in which that Senator pointed to the disagreements between the northern and southern Democrats concerning the Kansas-Nebraska bill, and declared that they had " 'agreed that every question touching human slavery or human freedom should be appealable to the Supreme Court of the United States for its decision.' " [22]

There is no use in wearying the reader with an account of how persistently the "Little Giant" struggled. One or two things are plain: congressmen are not under legal obligation to provide legislation for carrying out a principle of a judicial decision of which they disapprove. But if the Kansas-Nebraska bill really referred the question of territorial slavery to the Supreme Court, it is reasonable to infer that the men who concocted the bill hoped in that way to settle the controversy which threatened the party, and expected that, if judicial determination upheld the legality of slavery in the territories, the makers of the bill would act accordingly. Any assertion of Douglas to the contrary leaves one cold, the prey of consuming skepticism.

21 February 23. 1859. *Ibid.*. p. 1245.
22 *Ibid.*, p. 1258.

CHAPTER XLIII

THE EVE OF THE CIVIL WAR

The Democratic party met in convention at Charleston, April 23, 1860. It was a momentous and dramatic meeting. Was it still possible to hold the party together and present a united front to the enemy at the north? Could some kind of a makeshift arrangement be devised capable of carrying the party through another election? Both portions, north and south alike, must have seen that the break-up of the party might or would mean the dissolution of the union or a serious attempt at dissolution. The southerners, many of them, were not without patriotism, and their devotion to the party had aided in the maintenance of the union; in fact, there were two patriotisms—a lingering affection for the old union and a devotion to the old party—and of the two, party patriotism was by this time probably the stronger.

The northerners believed that no southerner could carry the north and be elected, for the southern defense of slaveholding interests was too extreme and the Republicans were strong and determined. The average southerner had lost patience with Douglas, and indeed the center of the strife was the hard-fighting leader who could count upon northern adherents still faithful and still clamorous. The Anti-Douglas delegates desired a positive statement in the platform to the effect that neither Congress nor a territorial legislature could destroy or impair the rights of persons or property in the territories. And another critical question, as it appeared in the convention's debates, was whether the party platform should explicitly declare it to be the duty of the federal government in all its departments to protect, when necessary, the rights of persons and property in the territories; and that meant the duty to protect slavery by affirmative legislation. The Douglas Democrats desired a more equivocal statement; they did not wish to go to the northern voters with a positive platform in defense of slavery-expansion. A gentle declaration to abide by the decisions of the Supreme

589

Court appeared to the Douglas men quite enough. Just what the abiding would consist of could be left to the imagination of the voters.[1]

In the midst of the dispute, Yancey of Alabama, a silver-tongued orator, made a speech which warmed the hearts of the southern auditors; he spoke of the decision of the venerable justice "clothed in the supreme ermine" who "had made an exposition of constitutional law, which had rolled in silvery cadence from the dark forests of the North to the glittering waters of the Gulf." [2] "He charged that the defeats of the Democracy in the North were to be traced to the pandering by the party in the free States to anti-slavery sentiments; they had not come up to the high ground which must be taken on the subject, in order to defend the South—namely, that slavery was right." [3] The speech of the fire-consuming orator was scarcely finished when Senator Pugh of Ohio, a stalwart supporter of Douglas, "in a condition of considerable warmth" thanked God "that a bold and honest man from the South had at last spoken, and told the whole truth of the demands of the South." "He then traced the downfall of the Northern Democracy, and the causes of that fall, charging the South with it. And now the Northern Democracy were taunted by the South with weakness. And here, it seemed, the Northern Democracy, because they were in the minority, were thrust back and told in effect they must put their hands on their mouths, and their mouths in the dust. 'Gentlemen of the South,' " he exclaimed, " 'you mistake us—you mistake us—we will not do it.' " [4] Whatever the ambiguity of cleverly-woven platforms, here was an issue, the real issue, clearly presented. Irritated by threats and denunciations of the southern delegates, those Douglas

---

[1] The first resolution favored by the Douglas delegates declared that questions of the rights of property in states or territories "are judicial in their character" and that the party "is pledged to abide by and faithfully carry out such determination of these questions as has been or may be made by the Supreme Court of the United States." The "may be" might well indicate an obligation to abide by a decision of later years reversing the Dred Scott decision. The later Douglas resolutions simply declared that the party would abide by the decisions of the Court on questions of constitutional law. The opposition resolutions proclaimed distinctly that neither Congress nor a territorial legislature had power to abolish slavery in the territories; that the territorial legislature had no power to prohibit introduction of slaves, to exclude slavery, or to "impair the right of property in slaves by any legislation whatever", and that it was the duty of the federal government to protect, when necessary, property on the high seas and in the territories.

[2] Murat Halstead, *A History of the National Political Conventions of the Current Presidential Campaign* (1860), p. 49. Halstead was present and wrote highly entertaining accounts of the proceedings.

[3] *Ibid.*, p. 48.

[4] *Ibid.*, pp. 49-50.

men, who had for years been called "doughfaces" at the north and charged with meek subservience to the slavocracy, were now prepared to speak boldly; they would go no further.[5] Yancey was right; the only road to harmony was in the acknowledgment of the morality of slavery.

Amidst the excitement and brilliance of blazing oratory, when there appeared no chance for an acceptance of a platform announcing the duty of protecting slavery in the territories, delegates from the southern south began to withdraw, Alabama leading the secession. The step was taken with full realization that the next move would probably be a dissolution of the union.[6] But after the withdrawal, it was still impossible to nominate Douglas, because under the rules a two-thirds vote of the full convention was required. After vain trials to select a nominee, the convention adjourned to meet in Baltimore in June. Ten days had been passed in the proceedings of the most momentous and fateful party gathering in American history. Meanwhile, the seceding delegates, meeting during the first days of May at Charleston, adopted resolutions, one of them of course declaring it to be the duty of the government in all its departments to protect slavery in the territories. They issued a call for a convention to meet in Richmond the following month. The meeting was held, but, pending the meeting at Baltimore, the convention did nothing of importance.

The Baltimore convention—the adjourned meeting of the regular convention at Charleston—was not a scene of tranquillity, though a decided majority were in favor of Douglas. In the course of the dis-

---

[5] Halstead, writing of what he heard after the split in the party at Baltimore in June, says, "The North-western delegates, on their return home, congratulated themselves upon the presumption, that if they had ripped up the Democratic party, they had shown the Republicans that they, as Democrats, were not doughfaces. The reflection that they were no more to be reproached as serfs of the South seemed sweet and ample consolation for all the struggles and perils through which they had passed, and the pangs they had suffered in the dissolution of the party. . . . The fact is the South was never before quite so well matched in her own game of brag and intolerable arrogance." *Ibid.*, p. 230.

[6] See speeches of the seceding delegates and other quoted remarks in *Ibid.* "Yancey said that, perhaps even now, the pen of the historian was nibbed to write the story of a new Revolution. At this, some one of the crowd cried 'three cheers for the Independent Southern Republic.' They were given with a will." *Ibid.*, p. 75, giving an account of a public gathering on the evening of April 30. On the other side, the rancor against the seceders was bitter. "I never heard", said Halstead, "Abolitionists talk more uncharitably and rancorously of the people of the South, than the Douglas men here. Our North-western friends use language about the South, her institutions, and particularly her politicians, that is not fit for publication, and my scruples in that respect are not remarkably tender. A good many of them will eventually become the most intolerant Republican partisans." *Ibid.*, p. 87.

cussion Douglas dispatched a message beseeching his friends to save "the party and the country" without regard to his individual interests; but the dispatch was not made public.[7] When harmony proved unattainable, another secession of certain southern delegates took place. Douglas and Benjamin Fitzpatrick of Alabama were nominated by the regular convention; the latter withdrew his name, and in his place Herschel V. Johnson of Georgia was nominated by the national committee. The seceders nominated John C. Breckinridge of Kentucky and Joseph Lane of Oregon.[8] To the convention at Richmond the platform and the candidate were acceptable.

The platform adopted by the Douglas Democrats at Baltimore contained the statement already referred to: inasmuch as there were differences of opinion in the party concerning the powers of a territorial legislature and the powers and duties of Congress, the party would abide by the decision of the Supreme Court "upon the questions of Constitutional law." Just before adjourning, a supplementary resolution was adopted to the effect that the measure of restriction on a territorial legislature, "as the same has been or shall hereafter be finally determined by the Supreme Court . . . , should be respected by all good citizens and enforced with promptness and fidelity by every branch of the General Government." Here was apparently a recognition of the duty of Congress to protect slavery in the territories as long as the Dred Scott case should stand unaltered; and it is difficult to find in the words a basis for the legality of "unfriendly legislation". The Breckinridge platform in plain terms announced that neither Congress nor a territorial legislature could destroy or impair the rights of persons or property in the territory, and that it was the duty of the federal government in all its departments to protect these rights when necessary. How do the two statements of the two platforms differ?

---

[7] *Ibid.*, pp. 194-195.

[8] It is worth noticing that the seceding convention at Charleston, in May, was made up almost entirely of delegates from the farther south; the seceding convention at Baltimore contained delegates from the border states. An indication of the difficulties which Douglas was to meet in the coming months was the presence at the Baltimore seceding convention of representatives from New York, California, Pennsylvania, Oregon, Minnesota, Massachusetts, and Vermont. See *Ibid.*, pp. 218, 221-222. Douglas's strength as a candidate in the older west may be seen from the fact that in the election he received about forty-four per cent. of the popular vote from the five states of the old northwest, Lincoln about fifty-two per cent. In New England Douglas received twenty-seven per cent., Lincoln sixty-two per cent. The figures are necessarily only approximate; but they show the hold of Douglas upon his section. In Illinois, Lincoln received only 12,000 more votes than Douglas and only 2,300 more than a moiety of all the votes cast.

The Breckinridge platform was more plain and emphatic in its declaration in favor of territorial slavery; the Douglas platform offered more room for dodging the supreme issue. And still, only an astute practitioner in the art of politics could without considerable difficulty find any difference between them.

If the real issue did not appear quite plainly in the Democratic platforms, the issue was made plain by the discussions at Charleston: the northern Democrats could no longer play the rôle of Sancho Panza to the south's Don Quixote. But above all, there stood Douglas. In southern eyes he had proved himself unworthy of the support of honest men. Certainly he had shown that he could not be relied upon to foster slaveholding interests. The fact of the matter is that the Douglas Democrats, paying lip service to the principle of the Dred Scott decision, had no intention of making it effective; the southerners demanded a recognition of congressional obligation to carry out the principle, but many of them must have known they could not get it, and some of them admitted that there was no pressing need of affirmative legislation for the protection of territorial slavery.[9] No student of history, however, is likely to go so far as to expect men to be consistent after they have reached a state of emotional fervor.

But perhaps platforms are taken too seriously. "I have a declining respect for platforms," said Davis in the Senate, May 17, 1860. "I would sooner have an honest man on any sort of a rickety platform you could construct, than to have a man I did not trust on the best platform which could be made." To this Douglas replied with one of his skillful thrusts, characteristic of the born debater: "If the platform is not a matter of much consequence, why press that question to the disruption of the party? Why did you not tell us in the beginning of this debate that the whole fight was against the man, and not upon the platform?"[10] Douglas pointed out to Davis that the platform, not the candidate, was the bone of dispute at Charleston; but that was in truth only the superficial fact.

[9] Speaking, apparently, of Kansas, Jefferson Davis said, "He [Douglas] can have no apprehension that in that country to which they never would be carried except from necessity, and for domestic purposes, they could ever so accumulate as to constitute a great political element." *Congressional Globe*, 36 Cong., 1 sess., p. 2150. This is an illustration, not a demonstration, of the assertion made in the text. There is other evidence that would seem to make it plain that he was after the acknowledgment of a naked right. See also, A. H. Stephens to J. H. Smith, September 16, 1860, *The Correspondence of Robert Toombs, Alexander H. Stephens, and Howell Cobb*, Am. Hist. Asso. *Report* for 1911, II, p. 498.

[10] *Congressional Globe*, 36 Cong., 1 sess., pp. 2155-2156.

At that moment when the two Senators were glowering at each other in the Senate chamber, certain essentials of the dominating controversy of sections and social systems seemed to be shown by the personalities, and even by the outward appearance, of the two men. The contrast was almost grotesque: Douglas, short, rotund, confident in manner and carriage, his hair long and thrown back in waves from a broad and powerful forehead, his whole being radiating animal and intellectual vigor which was increased rather than diminished in its effect by his air of rough abandon verging at times on uncouthness, appeared to disclose the possibilities, to incarnate the strength and possibly the vulgarity of a vital self-confident democracy. Davis in his look and manner embodied what, one might think, a slave-master should be and was: tall, slender, erect, sinewy, with a certain look of breeding, of refinement, and almost of frailty, with something of arrogance or superciliousness in manner and bearing, possessed of forensic ability of a high order, but not satisfying the appetites of those southerners who liked an interminable flux of words and flowery periods—his very presence filled the common men of the north with dislike of what they deemed the assumed superiority of a man who thought he was better than other folks because he owned black men.

The Republican convention at Chicago was no less exciting and no less noisy than the Charleston meeting of the Democrats; but its troubles were soon over. There was no serious conflict over the platform, for on the main principle all were in substantial agreement. The contest centered upon the choice of candidates. Seward, the natural leader of the party, as far as there was any leadership, led on the first two ballots. But it is often more difficult to nominate a person who has long been prominent than to name one less well-known; for though the experienced leader may have gained adherents, he has likewise created opposition. Lincoln had the advantage of local support and was believed by many able to carry certain doubtful states. So on the third ballot he was chosen as the "available" candidate. The result is profoundly interesting, the product of political forces which were intangible and now not easily appreciated; and yet upon the vote turned the history of the next few years; it gave a statesman to the world; it lifted a man whose powers were not fully known, and indeed not as yet fully developed, into a position from which he emerged the most conspicuous, powerful, and influential statesman of the nineteenth century.

The platform was explicit on the subject of slavery in the territories: "That the new dogma that the Constitution, of its own force, carries slavery into any or all of the Territories of the United States, is a dangerous political heresy. . . . That the normal condition of all the territory of the United States is that of freedom . . . and we deny the authority of Congress, of a territorial legislature, or of any individual, to give legal existence to slavery in any Territory of the United States." This was the old Free Soil doctrine of 1848: Congress had no more power to make a slave than to make a king. It was not in harmony with Curtis's opinion in the Dred Scott case, declaring Congress possessed of full power over slavery in the territories.[11]

Candidates—John Bell of Tennessee and Edward Everett of Massachusetts—were also put in the field by a Constitutional Union convention. Its platform was of no great consequence since it simply discussed sectional and geographical parties, and proclaimed it the part of patriotism to recognize no political principle other than the Constitution, the union, and the enforcement of the laws—all well enough, if there had been no dispute concerning what the Constitution was and what was law, or if the people had been in a mood to sweep aside all question of right and wrong, all question of constitutional principle and morality. The supporters of these mild gentlemen who were content with covering a controversy with sonorous phrases cast less than 600,000 votes in the election—about one-eighth of the total.

The result of the campaign was fairly well assured from the beginning. Douglas fought valiantly, but he knew full well that every vote he received made more probable the election of Lincoln; and yet he seemed to hope that the party might still be saved; he battled the disunionist faction; his words were of great consequence in the darker days that were just ahead. Asked at Norfolk, Virginia, if he would advise or vindicate resistance to a decision of the south to secede in the event of Lincoln's election, he replied, "I answer emphatically, that it is the duty of the President of the United States and of all others in authority under him, to enforce the laws of the United States, passed by Congress and as the Courts expound them; and I, as in duty bound

---

[11] Quoting the clause of the Constitution giving Congress power to make "all needful rules and regulations", Curtis said, "The purpose and object of the clause being to enable Congress to provide a body of municipal law for the government of the settlers, the allowance or the prohibition of slavery comes within the known and recognised scope of that purpose and object." 19 Howard 393, 615-616.

by my oath of fidelity to the Constitution, *would do all in my power to aid the government of the United States in maintaining the supremacy of the laws against all resistance to them, come from whatever quarter it might. . . ."* [12] The influence of Douglas, still the skillful and admired party leader, was of immense influence; he had battled long for party success; he did not care whether slavery was voted up or down; but one sentiment he cherished: he was devoted to the union and to his country. Without the tradition which he left behind him (he died in June, 1861)—a tradition, permeating if not saturating the northern Democracy, of devotion to an integral union—, Lincoln, we may well surmise, could not have saved the nation from dismemberment.

On the main constitutional obligation, the attitudes were as follows: Lincoln denied the principle laid down in the Supreme Court's decision, if it were a decision and not a mere *obiter dictum*; he considered it the duty of everyone to accept the decision as determining the status of Dred Scott; he believed Congress and the people should not be bound by the principle announced by the Court. Davis upheld the principle; it announced the rights of southerners and slave owners in the territories; he asserted the duty of Congress to act accordingly, if such action were needed. Just what the main body of Douglas Democrats believed is not quite entirely plain, but it appears that they believed they could, like their leader, accept the principle but refuse to acknowledge that the principle placed obligation on Congress to act for the maintenance of the principle. Obviously either Lincoln or Davis was right; Douglas's position was untenable in frank party strife.

No congressman is under constitutional obligation to carry out in legislation the principle of a judicial decision; but no politician, however clever he may be, is justified in going before the country and announcing his adherence to the principle of a judicial decision, and at the same time declaring his opposition to the passage of an act for carrying the principle into operation. There were only two alternatives open to a frank party warrior: one was to denounce the Dred Scott case and refuse to participate in carrying out its principle; the other was to accept the principle and to insist upon the duty of Congress to make the principle effective. And still, we must not be intent upon a ruthless condemnation of Douglas or charge him with conscious deceit. The ways of politicians are their own. Douglas, moreover, was fighting for a let-alone policy, a plan of shutting one's eyes to the obvious, that the union might still be saved.

[12] Quoted in Allen Johnson, *Stephen A. Douglas,* p. 433.

Lincoln was elected, receiving 180 electoral votes out of a total of 303. From a total of somewhat more than 4,600,000 popular votes, he received about 1,866,000. In other words, he received nearly 500,000 less than one-half of the total. With an electoral majority, he was a minority president; his total popular vote was over 900,000 less than that received by his opponents—and this does not include, of course, the vote of South Carolina where the electors were chosen by the legislature. The condition is, however, further illuminated by the fact that the southern states—not including South Carolina—, which were soon to enter upon the task of dissolving the union, cast about 850,000 votes and chose eighty electors, while the five states of the old northwest cast half a million more votes than the whole secession south and chose only fifty-eight electors; Ohio, with half as many votes as were cast in the south, chose twenty-three electors. The three-fifths compromise of the Constitution allowing the enumeration of three-fifths of the slaves, who were the personal property of the white owners, helped to provide this marked deviation from the principles of popular government.

When Congress met in December, 1860, it faced the danger of immediate secession. In neither house did the Republicans have a majority.[13] Buchanan's message is a famous document. In the President's opinion the northern states, by their ill-timed and illegal acts, especially by passage of acts to defeat the execution of the Fugitive Slave Law, had done great wrong. Furthermore, those who had appealed from the decision "of our highest constitutional tribunal to popular assemblies would, if they could, invest a Territorial legislature with power to annul the sacred rights of property. This power", the President declared, "Congress is expressly forbidden by the Federal Constitution to exercise." (To this position had the doctrine of popular sovereignty declined!) The election of any one of our fellow citizens to the presidency was not a just cause for the dissolution of the union, especially when he had been chosen by a minority of the people. He expressed the hope that the northern states would repeal their "obnoxious enactments. . . ." "The Southern States, standing on the basis of the Constitution, have a right to demand this act of justice

13 In the Senate there were thirty-six Democrats, two Anti-Lecompton Democrats, two Americans, and twenty-six Republicans. In the House there were ninety-two Democrats, seven Anti-Lecompton Democrats, twenty-four Americans, and one hundred and fourteen Republicans. See T. C. Smith, "Political Parties in Congress of the United States," *Cyclopedia of American Government*, I, p. 391.

from the States of the North. Should it be refused, then the Constitution, to which all the States are parties, will have been willfully violated by one portion of them in a provision essential to the domestic security and happiness of the remainder. In that event the injured States, after having first used all peaceful and constitutional means to obtain redress, would be justified in revolutionary resistance to the Government of the Union." [14]

The President, it will be noticed, spoke of "revolutionary resistance", for he repudiated the right of legal secession. "The right of resistance on the part of the governed against the oppression of their government can not be denied. . . . But the distinction must ever be observed that this is revolution against an established government, and not a voluntary secession from it by virtue of an inherent constitutional right. In short, let us look the danger fairly in the face. Secession is neither more nor less than revolution. It may or it may not be a justifiable revolution, but still it is revolution."

He was greatly troubled. "Has the Constitution delegated to Congress the power to coerce a State into submission which is attempting to withdraw or has actually withdrawn from the Confederacy?" He denied the possession of such power. The upshot of his rumination, therefore, was that a state could engage in revolution; a revolution in this instance was or might be justified; a state could not legally secede, and the government could not coerce it into submission. He quoted Madison's words in the Convention opposing the idea of using force against a state. If the President had looked into the debates of 1787 more closely, he would have found that coercion of a state as a body politic was abandoned, not in order that a state could do as it wished, but because the very principle of a confederation of sovereignties was to be abandoned.[15] If, as has been asserted, President Buchanan

[14] Buchanan said that it was a well-known historical fact that the Constitution could never have been adopted by the Convention without the fugitive slave provision. This is possible, but the real controversy in the Convention arose over the proposed prohibition of the slave trade. A full knowledge of constitutional history would have been beneficial to Buchanan. The statement had however been made before and he is entitled to that excuse.

[15] Buchanan might well have quoted Randolph who opposed the small-state party plan. That plan provided for the continuance of the principle of a confederation of sovereign states and relied on using force against a delinquent state. "The true question is whether we shall adhere to the federal plan, or introduce the national plan. . . . There are but two modes, by which the end of a Gen! Gov't can be attained: the 1st is by coercion as proposed by Mr. P.s plan [the small-state party or confederation plan] 2. by real legislation as prop'd by the other plan. Coercion he pronounced to be *impracticable, expensive, cruel to individuals*. . . . We must resort

made a distinction between coercing states and enforcing the execution of the laws on persons, he succeeded in clothing his utterances with obscurity.[16]

A further question began to trouble Buchanan—could he call forth the militia or summon the army to protect property and overcome resistance to authority? Jeremiah S. Black, the Attorney-General, had given Buchanan an opinion on the subject. A complete analysis of this opinion cannot be given here; the argument is full of difficult problems; we must content ourselves with a few words. "There was," he declared, "undoubtedly a strong and universal conviction among the men who framed and ratified the Constitution, that military force would not only be useless, but pernicious, as a means of holding the States together." [17] He announced the "right of the General Government to preserve itself in its whole constitutional vigor, by repelling a direct and positive aggression upon its property or its officers. . . ." The government has the right to protect its property; but in general it must act on the defensive. It has the right to collect the revenue as provided by law. "You can use force only to repel an assault on the public property, and aid the courts in the performance of their duty." The statutes of 1795 and 1807 he considered briefly; these acts, he maintained, gave the President authority to use the troops when the courts and federal marshals were defied; in case there were no officers, because all had resigned, troops would be "out of place, and their use wholly illegal. If they are sent to aid the courts and marshals, there must be courts and marshals to be aided." This opinion is echoed by Buchanan in his message. All this seems to mean that a little insur-

therefore to a National *Legislation over individuals,* for which Cong^s. are unfit." *The Debates in the Federal Convention of 1787 . . . Reported by James Madison,* June 16. By "Cong^s." he probably meant the Congress of the Confederation or any similar body. The *confederation* or small-state party plan proposed coercion; the *national* plan and the national leaders opposed the coercion of states. See the chapter on the Federal Convention.

[16] Notice G. T. Curtis's defense of the message. *Life of James Buchanan,* II, pp. 327-328. Buchanan quoted Madison as saying in the Convention, "Any government for the United States formed on the supposed practicability of using force against the unconstitutional proceedings of the States would prove as visionary and fallacious as the government of Congress." It is interesting to notice that Farrand (*Records,* I, p. 165) tells us that "unconstitutional proceedings" appeared in the original notes as "misdeeds". This discloses the real situation, because the question in 1787 was whether in every case of delinquency the state should be proceeded against with arms.

[17] *Official Opinions of the Attorneys General,* IX, p. 525. "If it be true that war cannot be declared, nor a system of general hostilities carried on by the Central Government against a State, then it seems to follow that an attempt to do so would be *ipso facto* an expulsion of such State from the Union." *Ibid.*

rection may be put down, and a big one must not be.[18] And yet the statutes themselves, if reasonably construed, appear to declare that, when an insurrection has arisen so great that the ordinary federal civil officers cannot overcome it, the president may take steps to suppress it; and surely an insurrection so extended that there are no officers would justify the use of the president's authority.

That Buchanan declared openly against the legality of secession perhaps had some effect in winning his party to the forcible support of the union when the die was cast. But the more eager defenders of the union and the more ardent opponents of the southern cause found in the message little to encourage them or to fire their hearts. In one respect, it may be noticed, Buchanan cogently and correctly put forth an argument against the constitutional right of secession: "In that mighty struggle between the first intellects of this or any other country it never occurred to any individual, either among its opponents or advocates, to assert or even to intimate that their efforts were all vain labor, because the moment that any state felt herself aggrieved she might secede from the Union. What a crushing argument would this have proved against those who dreaded that the rights of the States would be endangered by the Constitution!" We do not, it is true, know what might have occurred to any individual; but we do know the absence of any such pronouncement.

[18] Black, it will be noticed, took for granted that the President had no independent power, either as executive or as commander-in-chief of the army, to use the army to protect the property and execute the laws. Such power must be bestowed by Congress. His interpretation of the acts of 1795 and 1807 was, to say the least, narrow in the extreme. The act of 1795 provided "That whenever the laws of the United States shall be opposed, or the execution thereof obstructed, in any state, by combinations too powerful to be suppressed by the ordinary course of judicial proceedings, or by the powers vested in the marshals by this act, it shall be lawful for the President of the United States, to call forth the militia of such state, or of any other state or states, as may be necessary to suppress such combinations, and to cause the laws to be duly executed; and the use of militia so to be called forth may be continued, if necessary, until the expiration of thirty days after the commencement of the then next session of Congress." The act of 1807 provided for the use of the army, as well as the militia, under like conditions. I am utterly unable to understand the statement of Curtis to the effect that there was no law under which the President could call out the militia to suppress insurrections against the United States. See James Buchanan, *Works* (J. B. Moore, ed.), XI, p. 48.

Speaking of the power given to Congress by the Constitution, Black mentioned a portion of Article 1, section 8, of the Constitution; but he strangely interpreted it. The power to "provide for calling forth the militia to execute the laws of the Union, suppress insurrections, and repel invasions" he declared, with other provisions, was made "to protect the States, not to authorize an attack by one part of the country upon another. . . ." He does not admit that there may be an insurrection against the United States!

The illegality of coercing states troubled the dreams of unionists and brightened the visions of secessionists. The most essential feature of our constitutional system—the existence of two governments over every individual, each government having compulsive authority in its own sphere—was not plain even to those who ought to have known. Men occupying the positions of statesmen were free from the encumbrance of information concerning elementary principles of law and history. But the Republicans, as the days wore by, came to see and grasp the essentially sound principle and did not surrender it during the war that followed. Everything done in violation of legal national authority was illegal; the war was an insurrection; the government had no intention of coercing a state, but it did propose to enforce its laws against its own citizens and to break up any combinations engaged in essentially illegal and disloyal acts.

In the Senate, Lyman Trumbull, December 20, 1860, made the situation plain: "One of the Senators speaks of declaring war against a State. If there is anybody in this Senate, or in this country, who ever talked of the United States declaring war against one of its States, or of coercing one of its States, or ever entertained such a notion, I know not who it is. I have never seen him. This phrase, 'coerce a State,' is a phrase calculated to mislead the public mind. . . . Nobody proposes to declare war against a State. *That would admit at once that the State was out of the Union—a foreign Government.* Of course, we cannot declare war against a State. Nobody proposes to coerce a State, or to convict a State of treason. You cannot arraign a State for trial; you cannot convict it or punish it; but you can punish individuals. . . . The Government has power to coerce and to punish individuals who violate its laws." [19] "Do you mean by that you are going to march an army to coerce a State?" Trumbull at a later time (March 2, 1861) asked this question only to answer it. "No, sir; and I do not mean the people of this country to be misled by this confusion of terms about coercing a State. The Constitution of the United States operates upon individuals; the laws operate upon individuals; and wherever individuals make themselves amenable to the laws, I would punish them according to the laws. . . . So far as it can be done, I am for executing the laws; and I am for coercion." [20] This was, of course, absolutely sound legal doctrine. [21]

[19] *Congressional Globe*, 36 Cong., 2 sess., p. 156. Italics mine.
[20] *Ibid.*, p. 1382.
[21] Notice the passages on coercion in the chapter on the Constitutional Convention, *ante.*

Andrew Johnson, later elected to the vice-presidency of the United States, said in the Senate in December, 1860: "As a State, the Federal Government has no power to coerce it; but it is a member of the compact to which it agreed in common with the other States, and this Government has the right to pass laws, and to enforce those laws upon individuals within the limits of each State. While the one proposition is clear, the other is equally so. This Government can, by the Constitution of the country and by the laws enacted in conformity with the Constitution, operate upon individuals, and has the right and the power, not to coerce a State, but to enforce and execute the law upon individuals within the limits of a State."

To many persons one thing seems to have been unnecessarily obscure. They did not see that state officers, pseudo state governments, and state armies, opposing the Constitution and laws of the United States, were in consequence acting illegally; they were not, technically and in the eyes of the law, legal authorities, the coercion of which could properly be called coercion of the state. This may appear to be a fine-drawn distinction; but we are here discussing fine-drawn distinctions. If the Constitution and the laws made in pursuance thereof are supreme law, then no person or set of persons, even though pretending to act in virtue of state authority, can rely on the sanctity of their offices, if they act in contravention of the law. Even if all the people of a single state should assume the authority to do illegal things and attempt to support a state government doing unconstitutional and hence illegal acts, such conduct would, technically speaking, not be the action of a state, for a state in the union is a state when performing its functions as a state in the union and acting within its legal field.

In South Carolina, there had been for twenty years and more an active sentiment for disunion; for ten years that sentiment had been strong and aggressive. A fascinating story is unfolded, as we see that little state cherishing the principles of Calhoun and gradually extending her theories of independence, her political and social philosophy, and her devotion to slavery as a sacred institution, until the south had in large measure accepted them and was prepared to act. As soon as the news of Lincoln's election reached the legislature, a state convention was summoned, to meet on December 17. On the twentieth of that month the convention issued "AN ORDINANCE to dissolve the union between the State of South Carolina and the other States united with her under the compact entitled 'The Constitution of the United States

of America' ". The Mississippi legislature, November 30, denounced
the people of the northern states who had "assumed a revolutionary
position towards the Southern States", and declared "The secession of
each aggrieved State is the proper remedy. . . ." A convention adopted
an ordinance of secession on January 9; and thus, as might have been
expected, Mississippi was the first to follow South Carolina in the
effort to dissolve the union.[22]

Delegates from six states of the farther south—South Carolina,
Georgia, Florida, Alabama, Mississippi, and Louisiana—met at Montgomery, Alabama, February 4. They adopted a provisional constitution to continue for one year from the inauguration of the president
or until a permanent constitution was formed and put into operation.
The Constitution of the United States was followed in most particulars, but only one legislative house was provided for, inasmuch as all
legislative power was to remain in "this Congress now assembled until
otherwise ordained." The government of the Confederacy continued
under this provisional system for about a year. The new Congress met
February 18, and Jefferson Davis was inaugurated under the new
constitution February 22, 1862. Before this Congress adjourned, it
drew up a constitution intended to be permanent and submitted it to
the seceding states for adoption. It was speedily accepted by the six
states mentioned above and by Texas. The provisional constitution
provided for the election of the president and vice-president by the
Congress, each state having one vote. In the exercise of legislative
power every state was entitled to one vote and was "represented by
any one or more of its deputies who may be present."

Four other states soon joined the Confederacy. Virginia—the Old
Dominion and the Mother of Presidents—passed an ordinance of
secession April 17 which was submitted to popular vote and accepted
by the people late in May. The roll of the discontented and unfortunate
was thus complete. Western Virginians were not satisfied, however,
and a movement was soon on foot to separate from the eastern portion
—to secede from Virginia—and to set up a new state in the region beyond the Shenandoah.

Jefferson Davis and Alexander H. Stephens were chosen by the

[22] The following dates for the ordinances of secession of the other states may be
useful for reference: Florida, January 10; Alabama, January 11; Georgia, January
19; Louisiana, January 24; Texas, February 1, ratified by the people, February 23;
Virginia, April 17, ratified May 23; Arkansas, May 6; North Carolina, May 20;
Tennessee, May 7, by the legislature, ratified June 8. See Ames, *State Documents*,
no. VI, p. 77.

Congress at Montgomery to be the President and Vice-President of the new system. Stephens was a conservative, believing until almost the last minute that secession was unwise and might, if wisdom prevailed, be avoided.[23] Davis himself, though ready for the great adventure, was considered comparatively conservative and less tempestuous than some of the radical secessionists. In midsummer the Confederate Congress met at Richmond, which had been chosen as the capital of the Confederacy.

The permanent constitution which went into effect the following year (1862) was in most respects a copy of the Constitution of the United States.[24] The preamble, *"invoking the favor and guidance of Almighty God"*, indicated that the constitution was established by the "People of the *Confederate* States, *each State acting in its sovereign and independent character. . . ."* In nearly the same terms as those given in the provisional constitution, the permanent constitution forbade the importation of slaves from any foreign country, except from slaveholding states or territories of the United States, and Congress was given power to prohibit the introduction of slaves from any state or territory not a member of the Confederacy. The citizens of each state were to have the right of transit and sojourn in any state of the Confederacy, with slaves and other property, and the right of property in such slaves was not to be impaired thereby. Congress was forbidden to pass any law denying or impairing the right of property in negro slaves. Provision was explicitly made for the acquiring of new territory, and in all such territory the institution of slavery, as it existed in the south, was to be recognized and protected by Congress and by the territorial government; the inhabitants of the Confederate States and territories were assured of the right to take to the territory any slaves lawfully held by them. The constitution did not, though it would have been logical, perhaps, to do so, provide for voting by states in both branches of the legislature. Congress was empowered to grant a seat upon the floor of either house to heads of executive departments, with the privilege of discussing any measures appertaining to their departments.

[23] J. F. Rhodes says, "As early as 1834 Stephens had arrived at the conviction of the sovereignty of the States and the right of secession." *History of the United States*, III, p. 209. It is hard to reconcile that belief with Stephens's letter to Cobb, June 23, 1851, already quoted. *The Correspondence of Robert Toombs, Alexander H. Stephens, and Howell Cobb*, Am. Hist. Asso. *Report* for 1911, II, p. 238.

[24] Jefferson Davis, *The Rise and Fall of the Confederate Government*, I, p. 648 ff., gives the constitution and the Constitution of the United States in parallel columns.

In December, Buchanan's cabinet began to dissolve. Cass, the Secretary of State, resigned because he believed immediate steps should be taken to defend the forts in Charleston harbor and to provide for the collection of the revenue. He was succeeded by Jeremiah S. Black, who had held the office of Attorney-General. Black was succeeded in the latter office by Edwin M. Stanton, who seems to have supplied Buchanan with some degree of much-needed decisiveness.[25] Cobb of Georgia, the Secretary of the Treasury, resigned a few days before Cass did. He was followed soon by Floyd of Virginia and Thompson of Mississippi.

It is wise to refrain from criticism of Buchanan's failure to threaten the south and his refusal to do anything that would precipitate war. To take the responsibility of initiating open warfare is much to expect of any man. The President's most emphatic action was to send a ship to Charleston harbor with provisions for Major Anderson in command of Fort Sumter; the ship was driven back by the South Carolina batteries. That the President had legal authority to defend the fort and to provision its garrison is beyond question, but that he should have done more than he did may well be doubted. For some weeks after the November election, there were various evidences that the north had suffered a temporary reaction, and there were doubtless many persons who were inclined to agree with Horace Greeley that you could not pin the sections together by bayonets. This reaction, it is true, gradually evaporated after the first of the new year; men were beginning to realize what secession meant; it meant dismemberment of the union and a mutilated country. But the firing on the *Star of the West,* though an act of war, was received at the north almost with indifference. When the issue became clear, however, the possession of the lower regions of the Mississippi River by a foreign and presumably unfriendly nation did not appeal to the thoughtful men of the old northwest. It would have been folly to take positive action and call out the troops while plans for conciliation were being debated in Congress. Only the firing on Sumter, after Buchanan had gone, convinced the north that war was not a matter of debate but a fact.

[25] "Old Buck, at heart, is right and with us, but after Stanton came in, I have seen him gradually giving way. . . ." Jacob Thompson, Secretary of Interior in Buchanan's cabinet, to Howell Cobb, January 16, 1861. *The Correspondence of Robert Toombs, Alexander H. Stephens, and Howell Cobb,* Am. Hist. Asso *Report* for 1911, I, p. 532.

Soon after the opening of Congress in December, proposals for compromise and conciliation were taken up. Discussion went on during the whole of that tragic winter. One by one, senators and representatives from the south bade their colleagues adieu and hurried away to join their fellow citizens in the coming conflict; but the debates went on and hopes for settlement were not entirely abandoned.

John J. Crittenden of Kentucky offered a joint resolution in the Senate (December 18, 1860) for amendments to the Constitution, and, in addition, for declarations to be made by Congress. The amendments declared that there should be no slavery in the territory north of the Missouri Compromise line, and that south of that line slavery should be protected; any territory, either north or south, should be admitted into the union with or without slavery as its constitution should provide. Congress should have no power (1) to abolish slavery in places subject to its jurisdiction within slaveholding states, (2) or in the District of Columbia as long as either Maryland or Virginia retained slavery, or in the District without the consent of the inhabitants and compensation to the owners objecting to emancipation, (3) or to abolish the interstate slave trade. Congress should be under obligation to provide for compensation to the owners of fugitive slaves, if the capture and removal of the slaves were prevented by force, and the government should have the right to sue the county where such violence occurred. Finally, the articles of amendment, thus proposed, provided that other portions of the Constitution (the section providing for counting three-fifths of the slaves and the fugitive slave section) should not be affected by any subsequent amendment and no amendment should be made giving any power to interfere with slavery in any state by whose laws it was permitted. The resolutions which were to be passed by Congress as declaratory of its opinion were chiefly directed against the Personal Liberty Laws. One thing is plain in these Crittenden proposals: slavery was to be protected as securely as laws and the Constitution could protect it, and no future developments could by constitutional means alter that protection; and furthermore, all additions, if any were made, to the national territory south of the boundary should, apparently, be dedicated to slavery.[26] A committee of

---

[26] In the committee appointed to consider the subject, Davis and Toombs and five Republicans voted against the article drawing the Missouri Compromise line. It is not entirely plain that the Republicans realized at this juncture, quite so clearly as they did later, that the game was lost if they allowed extension of slavery into regions that might be later acquired.

thirteen appointed in the Senate (December 20) was hopelessly divided and reached no affirmative results.[27]

The House proceeded in somewhat similar fashion. A committee of thirty-three reached certain recommendations; but recommendations were in vain. After the report had been under consideration for weeks, an amendment to the Constitution was adopted by the House (February 28, 1861) by the narrow margin of 133 votes to 65: "No amendment shall be made to the Constitution which will authorize or give to Congress the power to abolish or interfere, within any State, with the domestic institutions thereof, including that of persons held to labor or service by the laws of said State." [28] The amendment was passed by the Senate without delay and was submitted to the states. It appears to have been ratified legally by two states, Ohio and Maryland.[29] This was the proposed thirteenth amendment—quite different from the one which five years later was added to the Constitution (December, 1865).

A peace conference, called at the suggestion of Virginia, met in Washington on February 4, and continued in session for over three weeks. It proved to be utterly futile and is chiefly noteworthy as representing the interest of the border states in compromise and conciliation. Delegations from twenty-one states were in attendance; [30] some of the delegates were appointed by state legislatures, others by governors; Maine and Iowa were represented by their congressional delegations. The convention succeeded in drawing up a constitutional amendment containing seven sections, which Congress was asked to submit to state conventions. The proposals were similar in various ways to those which had already been debated. There was, however, one especially significant provision: no territory should be acquired, except by discovery and for naval and commercial stations and transit routes, without the consent of a majority of all the senators from the slave states

[27] The committee reported its inability to agree upon any general plan of adjustment, December 31, 1860.

[28] See *Congressional Globe,* 36 Cong., 2 sess., pp. 1284-1285.

[29] A constitutional convention of Illinois ratified it, but this ratification was probably illegal, because Congress had specified ratification by legislatures. See H. V. Ames, *The Proposed Amendments to the Constitution,* Am. Hist. Asso. *Report* for 1896, II, p. 196, note 8; pp. 286, 363. See also Hawke *v.* Smith, 253 U. S. 221 (1920).

[30] For some reason the report of the convention to Congress gives the name of Wisconsin as one of the states represented. But see L. E. Chittenden, *A Report of the . . . Conference Convention,* pp. 465-466, and Doolittle's statement, *Congressional Globe,* 36 Cong., 2 sess., p. 1270.

and a majority of all the senators from the free.[31] But the convention's work went for naught.

Hopes of conciliation were dying. Congress could do nothing and was daily losing patience with vain efforts at compromise and concession while the Confederate Government at Montgomery was entering upon its task, and when the dissolution of the union was declared by secessionists and their sympathizers in Congress to be a fact and not a debatable theory. There were northerners in Congress who believed the time had come for decision, a decision, if need be, reached by war. Senator Zachariah Chandler, one of those men of iron—stern and vehement—whom the crisis had brought into the foreground, a fit match for the Toombses and the Rhetts of the south, had telegraphed the Governor of Michigan "at the request of Massachusetts and New York" to send delegates to the peace conference. "Ohio, Indiana, and Rhode Island", he said, "are caving in, and there is danger of Illinois. . . . I hope you will send *stiff-backed* men, or none. . . . Without a little blood-letting this Union will not, in my estimation, be worth a rush." [32]

To state definitely and accurately the central points of difficulty and disagreement during those trying months is a task beyond the author's power. But this seems fairly clear: the northerners were willing to provide absolutely against the interference with slavery within the states where it then existed; they were willing, if not desirous, to have the Liberty Laws repealed so far as they placed illegal barriers against the reclamation of fugitives; they were even willing, at least the leaders were, to allow the continuance of slavery in New Mexico; they appeared to be ready to acquiesce in the continuance of the interstate slave trade and not to insist upon the abolition of slavery in the District. But the nub of the difficulty was this: they could not rest if slavery was to be protected in regions subsequently annexed, and if it was to be thus extended and fortified. That the fears of antislavery men were not baseless is to-day perfectly obvious.[33] How far some of the abler men were willing to go, and how much

[31] The report was offered February 27. *Congressional Globe,* 36 Cong., 2 sess., pp. 1254-1255.

[32] Chittenden, *op. cit.,* pp. 468-469.

[33] Notice, for example, the Democratic platforms of 1860 favoring the acquisition of Cuba, Buchanan's advocacy of its annexation, and his proposal for moving troops into Mexico. See Richardson, *Messages,* V, pp. 510-511, 561, 642; H. L. Wilson, "President Buchanan's Proposed Intervention in Mexico," *Am. Hist. Rev.,* V, p. 687 ff. Buchanan believed or said he believed that the acquisition of Cuba would kill the foreign slave traffic. Sometimes he was too naïve to be funny.

farther they refused to go, can be seen from the letters of Lincoln and from the speeches of Thomas Corwin and Charles Francis Adams in Congress. While it may be folly to engage in an analysis of a confused situation where passion and suspicion were masterful, we can be fairly certain that if the danger of slavery-extension into regions *to be acquired later* could have been disposed of, every other demand of the south might have been agreed to as a temporary compromise —but, of course, congressional pronouncements, laws, and constitutional amendments could not permanently unite the divided house.

On one point—and that point was the heart of the Republican position, the one thing for which Lincoln had positively and openly stood—Lincoln was unchanging: "I say now, however," he wrote to Seward, February 1, 1861, "as I have all the while said, that on the territorial question—that is, the question of extending slavery under the national auspices—I am inflexible. I am for no compromise which assists or permits the extension of the institution on soil owned by the nation. And any trick by which the nation is to acquire territory, and then allow some local authority to spread slavery over it, is as obnoxious as any other. I take it that to effect some such result as this, and to put us again on the highroad to a slave empire, is the object of all these proposed compromises. I am against it. As to fugitive slaves, District of Columbia, slave-trade among the slave States, and whatever springs of necessity from the fact that the institution is amongst us, I care but little, so that what is done is comely and not altogether outrageous. Nor do I care much about New Mexico, if further extension were hedged against." [34]

[34] Abraham Lincoln, *Complete Works* (J. G. Nicolay and John Hay, editors), I, pp. 668-669. Charles Francis Adams said in the House, January 31, 1861, "I have now considered all the alleged grievances which have thus far been brought to our attention. 1. The personal liberty laws, which never freed a slave. 2. Exclusion from a Territory which slaveholders will never desire to occupy. 3. Apprehension of an event which will never take place. For the sake of these three causes of complaint, all of them utterly without practical result, the slaveholding States, unquestionably the weakest section of this great Confederacy, are voluntarily and precipitately surrendering the realities of solid power woven into the very texture of a Government that now keeps nineteen million freemen, willing to tolerate, and, in one sense, to shelter, institutions which, but for that, would meet with no more sympathy among them than they now do in the remainder of the civilized world."
He pointed out that New Mexico then had twenty-two slaves. "I say, then, in answer to the demand of a constitutional guarantee of protection to slavery in New Mexico, that you are asking for what in substance you enjoy already, and what is good for nothing to you if you get it." "We are called not only to guaranty slavery within our own Territories, but we must provide for it in those of our neighbors, before we get them." Corwin spoke of the region which, southerners claimed, "it would

A brief discussion of the causes and motives which prompted the southern people to break up the union is certain to be unsatisfactory to the reader—and a long discussion is not likely to be more acceptable. The reader has already been warned that dispute had reached a stage where calm reasoning had been displaced by enthusiasm and passion. In the writer's judgment, the slave-owners were especially galled by the assumption of the northern enthusiasts that they represented a superior morality and were on the crest of civilization. The southerners were shocked by the conditions of northern factory workers; the northerners looked upon the slave-owners as aristocrats flaunting their pride in the face of hardy artisans and plain men. The differences between the sections were real and not imaginary; and probably little variations were quite as significant in awakening resentment as were large ones. The south, we are told, was essentially a nation; but the word involves too much to be easily analyzed. That there were and had been from the beginning industrial and social differences between the sections is of course obvious; and that the south had developed a measure of sectional solidarity is equally plain. But of course, fundamentally, the trouble was the "house divided". Despite protestations from the northern political leaders that there was no intention of interfering with slavery in the states, the southerners believed that secession alone could save them from the woe consequent upon emancipation and perhaps even from the horror of black domination.

And still, as far as certain very practical matters went, secession offered no remedy. It did not provide a means of getting back the runaway slave; it isolated the south among the nations of the world; it did not open the territories to the slave-owner. Only one thing could assure the south of development, if it retained its form of labor, viz., expansion, the absorption of more territory. And even then, could the south actually prosper without the slave trade? [35]

be well to devote to slave labor. You want New Mexico, which lies south of this line 36° 30'. New Mexico, you say, belongs to you. Take it! Take it!" January 21. *Congressional Globe*, 36 Cong., 2 sess., appendix, p. 75.

[35] The constitution of the Confederacy declared against the slave trade, and I am not asserting that the south was intent upon opening it. Alexander H. Stephens wrote in 1859, "I have been struck with the various comments that have been made on my speech and the sensation it seems to have produced. On the slave trade question I certainly meant to say nothing except what is clearly expressed—that was that unless we get immigration from abroad we shall have but few more slave states. This great truth seems to take the people by surprise. Some shrink from it as they would from death. Still it is as true as death. On the policy of opening the trade I said nothing, and meant to say nothing. The people must consider that for them-

It is sometimes said that the southern people would not have fought for slavery. Perhaps not; it is reasonable to assume that the slavery cause as a merely moral or abstract matter was not enough, without the passion begotten by the past two decades, without personal pride and resentment, without sectional sentiment, without the ignorance which each section had of the other, and without a sense of injury nourished by politicians. But withal, the south did not condemn slavery; leaders pictured it as a positive moral good; they conscientiously believed they were called upon by the highest sense of duty to protect themselves and even the well-being of the blacks by keeping them in bondage. No one can wonder or accuse. It is foolish in us not to comprehend or attempt to comprehend the pressure of a social system to which men were tied and on which the very foundation of society appeared to rest. How could it be otherwise?

The attempt to show that the south had suffered continuously from the imposition of northern interests, and that the revolt was due to unremitting injustice—an attempt which is especially prominent in Jefferson Davis's *Rise and Fall of the Confederate Government*—has some ground to stand upon; for the tariff was not directly, perhaps not indirectly, helpful to agriculture. But if there is anything to be said for this thesis, it was comparatively inappropriate in 1860. "As a matter of fact," says Rhodes, "both the senators and all the representatives from South Carolina had voted for the existing tariff of 1857; and since 1846 the United States had practically enjoyed a revenue tariff and one of a lower scale of duties than had been in force since 1816." [36] And the notion that the south had been brazenly victimized during two generations will not withstand serious examination.

The truth is, we must go back to slavery and the cause of the slave-owner. The announcement of Stephens cannot be disregarded. Commenting on the position of Thomas Jefferson and "most of the leading statesmen" of an earlier day who believed the enslavement of the African was in violation of the laws of nature and was wrong, Stephens declared, "Our new Government is founded upon exactly

selves." Stephens to J. H. Smith, July 29, 1859, *The Corespondence of Robert Toombs, Alexander H. Stephens, and Howell Cobb*, Am. Hist. Asso. *Report* for 1911, II, pp. 446-447. Professor Boucher points out that while there were strong advocates of reopening the slave trade, "this question served not to unite the South, but to cause bitter controversy in the southern press and the South Carolina legislature." C. S. Boucher, "South Carolina and the South on the Eve of Secession, 1852 to 1860," Washington University *Studies* (Humanistic Series), VI, p. 92.

[36] Rhodes, *History of the United States*, III, p. 204.

the opposite ideas; its foundations are laid, its corner-stone rests, upon the great truth that the negro is not equal to the white man; that slavery, subordination to the superior race, is his natural and moral condition." [37] Why should we shut our eyes to the solemnity and the tragedy of the whole controversy and not see that perennial question which reaches back into the ages of the past—and indeed appears not as yet banished from the horizon—the question not alone of white and black equality, but the question of whether the strong shall inherit the earth and rule it with their strength. All this is more important than the question whether the south or any other region should be politically separate; constitutional history in the ordinary sense falls into the background of obscurity.

No discussion of the cause of the secession is complete without reference to John Brown's raid; that assault upon the safety and peace of the countryside exasperated the southerners from one end of the land to the other. The conservatives who had held back, believing there was no immediate need of breaking the union, and hoping that all might yet be well, could now be taunted by the advocates of secession, who in season and out of season had asserted that lives and property were endangered by fanatics and that further association with Yankees was impossible. Naturally men could not come to the council table in Washington in a mood to consider plans of adjustment in a calm and conciliatory spirit.

It is almost as difficult to say why the north was ready to fly to arms. Why were the people not willing to allow the south to establish a new nation? We can look back now and see what a misfortune it would have been had the north been ready to yield. To-day across three thousand miles of territory from ocean to ocean there is one nation traversed by laws and not by armies. The people of the north were not willing at the beginning to fight for the overthrow of slavery; they were willing to fight with passion for the union, for

[37] Speech at Savannah, Georgia, March 21, 1861. Frank Moore, *The Rebellion Record*, I, doc. 48, p. 45. Italics of the original omitted. Could Jefferson Davis have forgotten the declaration of the Mississippi legislature, November 30, 1860, and of the Mississippi state convention of January 26, 1861? "Our position", says the latter, "is thoroughly identified with the institution of slavery—the greatest material interest in the world." ". . . a blow at slavery is a blow at commerce and civilization." Ames, *State Documents*, no. VI, pp. 71-73, 78-80. Interesting material is in P. M. Hamer, *The Secession Movement in South Carolina, 1847-1852*. "There is Union and Abolition on one hand, and Disunion and Slavery on the other. . . . Give us *SLAVERY or give us death*." E. B. Bryan, "The Rightful Remedy" (1850), quoted in *Ibid.*, p. 67.

their country as one unmutilated whole.[38] They were not willing, when the emergency arose, to accept as wise the plaintive refrain, "Erring sisters, go in peace!" Patriotism, emotion, and indignation pronounced a different decision. A recognition of the southern position as right was a recognition of the fact that there was no "country", north or south.[39]

Though occasionally a northern state had indulged in angry exclamation and appeared to speak in the terms of state sovereignty or of something like state sovereignty,[40] the average northerner did not look upon his state as his country. In the old northwest were many men of southern antecedents who sympathized with the south; but no man could have held that sense of the reality of his state which was so conspicuous in South Carolina and only less so in Virginia. Such thinking was foreign to them, it had no basis in tradition.

What part did party zeal or the folly and ambition of politicians play in the whole sorrowful drama? No one can answer. Both before and after the war, Stephens, whom no one will accuse of dishonest intentions, spoke with some bitterness of the machinations of men who thought they were statesmen. The right and the truth, he said, were not what "secessionists and revolutionists" were after. "Their object is to hide the truth. Personal spite is their aim, and not the public good. They rely upon misleading the people by appeals to their passions and prejudices."[41] The southern people, he maintained, were

[38] The significance of the Civil War and the position of Lincoln I have tried to present briefly in a paper entitled "Lincoln as a World Figure," Lincoln Association Papers (1924).

[39] If the doctrine of state sovereignty as a practical fact should be accepted, "The United States could no longer be considered a nation. . . . The 'country,' hitherto, throughout the North at any rate [and till a few years before throughout the south, on the whole], regarded as unquestionably extending from the Atlantic to the Pacific and from the Great Lakes to the Gulf of Mexico, was, so it now appeared, a dream. It had never really existed. The patriotism directed towards it was in fact nothing but a strong desire for the continuance of an advantageous treaty between the various nations situated within the above-described territory. The great nation, free in its laws and traditions . . . had suddenly disappeared, so it was said, from the face of the earth. What wonder that the Northern people revolted at such conclusions, refused to tolerate the arguments by which they were supported, and determined to put forth all their strength, to crush all opposition, and to re-establish the unquestioned sovereignty of the one only nation throughout the length and breadth of the land?" J. C. Ropes, The Story of the Civil War, I, p. 7.

[40] I have in mind the resolutions of Wisconsin referred to in a previous chapter at the time of the Ableman-Booth affair.

[41] Stephens to J. H. Smith, September 16, 1860, The Correspondence of Robert Toombs, Alexander H. Stephens, and Howell Cobb, Am. Hist. Asso. Report for 1911, II, p. 498.

devoted to principles of self-government established by their ancestors: "It was through their devotion to these principles that the Southern masses were precipitated into the fatal step they took." "The Southern mind was influenced and misguided by a class of public men, politicians not statesmen, newspaper editors, and preachers, who possessed far more ambition and zeal than wisdom and knowledge." [42] If it be true that northern politicians and preachers were equally blind leaders of the blind, there is no use in entering now upon a debate on the subject. A spirit of brotherly love might conceivably have settled the problem without war, but no dove of peace was hovering over the troubled waters of passion.

[42] A. H. Stephens, *Recollections,* pp. 326-327.

CHAPTER XLIV

CONSTITUTIONAL PROBLEMS OF THE CIVIL WAR

Constitutional history of the Civil War period is filled with perplexities, and no adequate treatment can avoid them. The purpose of this chapter is to avoid technicalities, if possible, and to present briefly the prominent facts and principles. No other four years were so crammed with problems, though in some ways, when singled out, they probably loom larger to-day than they did in the mind of the common man during the days of conflict when the masses of men were intent upon winning the war, had confidence in the character of the President, and could not be bothered by abstruse and abstract political questions. Lincoln's general attitude was probably not far different from that of the main body of loyalists: the union must be saved, the Constitution must be defended, and minor encroachments upon constitutional limitations were justified by the necessity of maintaining the life of the nation and preserving its fundamental law.

The main constitutional difficulties arose from, first, the plain fact that the Constitution is peculiarly reticent on the subject of war and the conduct of war; second, from the necessary conflict between provisions calculated to maintain personal liberty and to secure ample and considered justice on the one hand, and the imperious demands for effective warfare on the other; and this latter difficulty is closely connected with the fact that the war was technically an insurrection; the "enemy" were citizens in rebellion; these citizens were using state governments for their purposes; and yet, despite this constitutional theory, the war had in reality many or all of the characteristics of a public war carried on by hostile nations. Had there not been at Washington a serious attempt to follow the dictates of constitutional law, had the Constitution been for the moment deliberately assigned to the dust-heap, no very serious constitutional problems would have been left for the historian's chronicle. The perplexities facing us, therefore, arose from the attempt, partly successful, to reconcile war and law; and the attempt is in itself a matter of great consequence. The very recognition of the problem, the tacit as well as the explicit acknowledgment of the necessity of maintaining civil government instead of sweeping aside all constitutional forms, is the conspicuous matter. A despot would have had no problem and no legal scruples; a battle-mad populace would have laughed in its glee at the absurdity of a contest between law and brute force. The Civil War was a great and influential event in the world's history for many reasons: it affected not America alone, but Europe also; its influence was felt because it gave the final blow to slavery, but chiefly because a democracy survived a devastating civil war, and because during the contest there was recognition of the need for law and constitutional procedure.

The bombardment of Fort Sumter set the north afire. Lincoln issued a proclamation calling for 75,000 of the state militia to suppress combinations "too powerful to be suppressed by the ordinary course of judicial proceedings or by the powers vested in the marshals by law", and "to cause the laws to be duly executed." A few days later he proclaimed a blockade of the ports of seven southern states then members of the Confederacy. In the call for the militia, he was treating the southern uprising as an insurrection which could not be put down by ordinary legal procedure. Presumably he was influenced, and justly so, by the attitude of those slaveholding states that had not as yet seceded but were ready to take umbrage at real or apparent coercion of a state. Probably also he was shrewd enough to take advantage of the sentiments of the northern people outraged by the attack upon national property and the national flag. At all events, his procedure, viewed from either the standpoint of constitutional theory or practical politics, was unquestionably correct.

Technically, the uprising could be held to be a rebellion, and it was so named and so considered. All through the four years of conflict, the government studiously refrained from recognizing the Confederacy as a *de jure* nation or combination of nations. In theory, the Confederate government was without legal existence. Had this theory been actually carried out and not merely depended upon as a theory to justify, on a constitutional basis, the acts of the federal government, then individuals could and would have been held personally responsible for acts of treason. But, as a matter of fact, almost from the beginning there was a state of war, and the armies of the Confederacy in the field were treated as the forces of a belligerent power.[1]

---

[1] Possibly this statement needs modification in one particular. The exchange of prisoners was not carried out with liberality. There was no real need for the ghastly prisons both north and south where scores of thousands suffered.

Practical politics, common sense, and ordinary regard for human rights demanded the recognition of the fact of war; but to acknowledge, in constitutional theory, the right of a combination of states to set up a legal government would be only an acknowledgment that the north was violating constitutional and legal principles and had unlawfully made use of force.

However tenuous the insurrection theory might seem to be to foreign governments, and however much the actual conduct of the war distinguished it from an ordinary suppression of an utterly lawless uprising, there is no great difficulty in recognizing the right of a government, when faced by a powerful opponent, to accord to the opponent the full rights of a belligerent. So the war was of a dual character : in strict theory it was an insurrection; but in the conduct of the war the insurgents were treated as forces of an independent government.

This matter in some of its aspects was presented by the proclamation establishing a blockade of the southern ports. The President of the Confederacy, on April 17, invited all those who were desirous of aiding the Confederate Government "by service in private armed vessels on the high seas" to apply for letters of marque and reprisal—in other words, to take up privateering which was, of course, quite within the proper competence of the government, if it was the head of a sovereign nation or group of sovereigns.[2] Two days later Lincoln, referring to a combination of persons engaged in insurrection and their threat to grant letters of marque, declared a blockade, and announced that any person molesting a vessel of the United States would "be held amenable to the laws of the United States for the prevention and punishment of piracy." A blockade is a war measure; it is of common use in a public war; it necessarily involves the rights and obligations of neutral nations. Two years later the Supreme Court, upholding the legality of Lincoln's proclamation, made this statement: "The parties belligerent in a public war are independent nations. But it is not necessary to constitute war, that both parties should be acknowledged as independent nations or sovereign States. A war may exist where one of the belligerents, claims sovereign rights as against the other. . . . When the party in rebellion occupy and hold in a hostile manner a certain portion of territory; have declared their independence; have cast off their allegiance; have organized armies; have com-

2 Two years later (March 3, 1863) Congress passed an act, and Lincoln signed it, authorizing the issue of letters of marque.

menced hostilities against their former sovereign, the world acknowledges them as belligerents, and the contest a *war*." [3]

The subject discussed by the Court in the Prize Cases involved more than the question whether an insurrection might also constitute a war. When did the war begin? Did the President, without congressional declaration, have the legal right to carry on war? To some extent, if not wholly, the two questions are one. Congress did not meet upon the call of the President until July 4, and in the meantime troops were in the field and hostilities had begun. The Court practically accepted the statement of William M. Evarts, one of the counsel for the government, that "War is, emphatically, a question of actualities." But in speaking of the time when the war began, special attention was paid by the Court to the proclamation of blockade as official and conclusive evidence that war existed.[4] "If a war be made by invasion of a foreign nation," said the Court, "the President is not only authorized but bound to resist force by force. He does not initiate the war, but is bound to accept the challenge without waiting for any special legislative authority. . . . Whether the President in fulfilling his duties, as Commander-in-chief, in suppressing an insurrection, has met with such armed hostile resistance, and a civil war of such alarming proportions as will compel him to accord to them the character of belligerents, is a question to be decided *by him,* and this Court must be governed by the decisions and acts of the political department of the Government to which this power was entrusted." It would have been strange indeed, had the Court decided, months after the war had actually begun, that the President had no such power.

On May 3 Lincoln issued a proclamation summoning 42,034 volunteers to serve for three years; he also called for an increase of the regular army by the addition of 22,714 officers and men, and for the enlistment of 18,000 seamen.[5] These steps were probably entirely justi-

---

[3] Prize Cases, 2 Black 635, 666-667 (1863). For further discussion, see Ford *v.* Surget, 97 U. S. 594 (1878).

[4] Prize Cases, 2 Black 635, 670 (1863). See the statement of the Court in the case of The Protector, 12 Wallace 700, 701-702 (1872): "Acts of hostility by the insurgents occurred at periods so various, and of such different degrees of importance, and in parts of the country so remote from each other, both at the commencement and the close of the late civil war, that it would be difficult, if not impossible, to say on what precise day it began or terminated." Referring to the need of some public act of the political departments, the Court said the proclamation of intended blockade could be assumed as the date of beginning, and the proclamations of the President of 1865 and 1866 as dating the end.

[5] Richardson. *Messages and Papers,* VI, p. 16.

fied by the needs of the situation, if we consider only actual difficulties; no one would deny Lincoln's moral right to break the Constitution in order to save it. But viewed as a constitutional precedent, it bears an ominous look. Can a president of the United States, using his own discretion, build up a large army and even enlarge the standing army? This is not a question of commanding interest, if viewed from the perspective of over half a century; but it presents a general principle not to be answered affirmatively without apprehension for the future. Probably this proclamation was technically beyond presidential authority, more clearly in the enlargement of the regular army than in the call for volunteers.

The sympathy of many citizens in Maryland for the Confederacy made the position of the President and the government embarrassing and dangerous. The President acted with circumspection and his usual common sense. Writing to General Scott, April 25, he said, "The Maryland legislature assembles to-morrow at Annapolis, and not improbably will take action to arm the people of that State against the United States." The question, he said, had been submitted whether it would not be justifiable for the General to arrest or disperse the members of that body. He pointed out the objections to such a course, and concluded "that it is only left to the commanding general to watch and await" the action of the legislature. Should that action be "to arm their people against the United States," the General was to adopt "the most prompt and efficient means to counteract [it], even, if necessary, to the bombardment of their cities, and, in the extremest necessity, the suspension of the writ of *habeas corpus*." Two days later a similar but somewhat more direct authorization was sent to Scott. The President did not suspend the writ but passed on to the officer in charge the authority to do so if necessity arose.

Discussion arose concerning the President's right to take any such action, but before entering upon that question it is desirable to point out that if Washington had been entirely cut off, as indeed it was for a brief interval, if Maryland had swung into the Confederate column, if the threatened disaster had actually occurred, then the President, whose duty it was to save the union and enforce the laws, would have received no credit for neglecting to use every means at all consistent with humanity to establish order and insure public safety.

The validity of the suspension of the privilege of habeas corpus came before Chief Justice Taney when a military officer refused to obey the writ. The venerable Justice denied that the power of suspension belonged to the President; the constitutional declaration concerning it appears in the article dealing with legislative powers and the provisions limiting legislative authority; the prohibition is associated with other prohibitions of congressional action; for this and other reasons, suspension must be considered to be within the power of Congress and of Congress alone.[6] But, we should notice, even Congress cannot legally suspend the privilege unless public safety requires it.[7] The opinion of the Chief Justice was criticized at the time and has been questioned in the calmer years that followed.[8] In reality, the authority to suspend the privilege of the writ is in some respects of much less importance than the right to declare martial law and place the whole region under complete military control. The justification for such a step must be the existence of actual disorder or a condition which seriously threatens civil authority; in other words, justification must rest on *facts*. A portion of Maryland was at that time within the sphere of military operations. Lincoln would have been negligent, had he not proceeded to take such steps as the condition warranted. His own words indicate what the danger appeared to be: "Maryland was made to *seem* against the Union. Our soldiers were assaulted, bridges were burned, and railroads torn up within her limits, and we were many days at one time without the ability to bring a single regiment over her soil to the capital." [9] If the President could properly treat the region as one requiring military control and martial law, it seems difficult to assert that he could not take the comparatively mild step of suspending the privilege of the writ of habeas corpus.

The signal question is the one we have encountered in other connections: who is to judge? Must the court acknowledge the fact and

---

[6] Ex parte Merryman, Federal Cases, no. 9, 487 (1861). Another instance of a similar character arose in October, 1861. See J. G. Randall, *Constitutional Problems Under Lincoln*, pp. 162-163. The statement of the law, it should be noted, was not made by the Court but by the Chief Justice.

[7] The Constitution says, "The privilege of the writ of *habeas corpus* shall not be suspended unless when, in case of rebellion or invasion, the public safety may require it." Art. I, sec. 9, par. 2.

[8] Edward McPherson, *The Political History of the . . . Rebellion*, pp. 154-162, contains the important documents, including the opinion of Chief Justice Taney, the opinion of Attorney-General Bates upholding the authority of the President, an excerpt from the pamphlet by Horace Binney likewise supporting the President, and a summary of an address by Theophilus Parsons taking the same position. "In the light of Civil War experience," says Professor Randall, "it is doubtful whether any clear-cut principle of undisputed legal authority can be said to exist in American jurisprudence with reference to this fundamental point of law." Randall, *op. cit.*, p. 131.

[9] Message of December 3, 1861. Richardson, *Messages and Papers*, VI, p. 55.

the need of martial law or the need of the suspension of the writ whenever the executive so declares? Must the executive yield without delay to the pronouncement of the court and act with all deference to the opinion of some court or some individual justice? Developments of recent years indicate a tendency to recognize "the necessity of giving executive power a free hand in situations of public disorder. . . ."[10] This tendency is illustrated by decisions concerning the state executive authority; but there is no great difference, if there be any, between the principles underlying authority in the state and in the nation. And yet we need not suppose that there is no law and that all is chaotic because the judiciary and the executive are at variance. It is the duty of the courts to protect civil rights and civil law; they need not yield supinely and without protest to the authority of the military or to the order of a martial-minded and dictatorial commander-in-chief.[11] Justification for suspension of the writ or its privilege depends, when all is said, on actual conditions and the extent of the peril.[12]

But the people of a free country, if they wish to remain free, are naturally suspicious of military power. Fundamental in Anglo-American law is the inherited principle, deeply embedded in sentiment, that the army is not superior to the civil arm of government but is subject to legal authority. And the writ of habeas corpus, the most celebrated

[10] E. S. Corwin, "Martial Law, Yesterday and Today," *Pol. Sci. Quart.*, XLVII, p. 104.

[11] It should be noticed that in the instance we are considering the writ was issued. Taney had the opportunity to express his opinion. But the writ was disobeyed; its privilege was suspended.

[12] Important cases have in recent years thrown some light on the question. In the case of In re Boyle, 6 Idaho 609, 611 (1899), the court said, "We are of the opinion that whenever, for the purpose of putting down insurrection or rebellion, the exigencies of the case demanded for the successful accomplishment of this end in view, it is entirely competent for the executive or for the military officer in command, if there be such, either to suspend the writ or disregard it, if issued." Perhaps this statement is better in law than it is in grammatical construction. See also Commonwealth *v.* Shortall, 206 Penn. 165 (1903). In Moyer *v.* Peabody, the question of a military arrest in Colorado by the Governor's order came before the federal Supreme Court. Justice Holmes, giving the opinion of the Court, said, "The facts that we are to assume are that a state of insurrection existed. . . . In such a situation we must assume that he [the Governor] had a right under the state constitution and laws to call out troops, as was held by the Supreme Court of the State. . . . That means that he shall make the ordinary use of the soldiers to that end; that he may kill persons who resist and, of course, that he may use the milder measure of seizing the bodies of those whom he considers to stand in the way of restoring peace. . . . Public danger warrants the substitution of executive process for judicial process." 212 U. S. 78, 84-85 (1909). See also Sterling *v.* Constantin, 287 U. S. 378 (1932). See the discussion by J. W. Burgess, *Political Science and Constitutional Law*, I, p. 248.

writ in English law, gave assurance, as long as it remained inviolate, of the continuance of unarbitrary government and respect for individual rights and personal liberty. The difficulty of preserving orderly government and the supremacy of law during a civil war was a real difficulty; it tested the sanity and political wisdom of the people of the land and of the administration at Washington.

Congress passed an act (signed by the President, August 6, 1861) approving and legalizing "all the acts, proclamations, and orders of the President . . . respecting the Army and Navy . . . and calling out, or relating to the militia or volunteers from the States. . . ." Such an enactment did not definitely decide the legality of what the President had done, and the same can be said of the act of March 3, 1863.[13] Congress cannot legalize retroactively the unconstitutional procedure of the president. The nature of Lincoln's mind and his attitude toward constitutional problems are shown by his defense of what he had done; his statement given July 4, 1861 is characteristic of his reasoning during the course of the war: "The whole of the laws which were required to be faithfully executed were being resisted and failing of execution in nearly one-third of the States. Must they be allowed to finally fail of execution, even had it been perfectly clear that by the use of the means necessary to their execution some single law, made in such extreme tenderness of the citizen's liberty that practically it relieves more of the guilty than of the innocent, should to a very limited extent be violated? To state the question more directly, Are all the laws *but one* to go unexecuted, and the Government itself go to pieces lest that one be violated? . . . But it was not believed that this question was presented. It was not believed that any law was violated."

But more important than the suspension of habeas corpus in certain regions is the whole question of arbitrary arrest and imprisonment. Remembering the fundamental principle which has been already stated—the principle of free government and the subordination of the military to the civil authority except where the civil arm is powerless to protect the state and individual liberty—we can see plainly that any unnecessary encroachment by military forces is unconstitutional; and the question remains, does the necessity exist? We may notice at the outset that the country was not divided accurately into two distinct parts, in one of which the people were in insurrection while in the other

<hr />

[13] For discussion, see G. C. Sellery, "Lincoln's Suspension of Habeas Corpus as Viewed by Congress," Univ. of Wis. *Bulletin* (History Series), I, pp. 234-235, 264-265.

they were loyal and law-abiding. States like Missouri and Kentucky were in a disturbed condition; it was quite impossible to treat them, as the war went on, as if all the people were heartily supporting the union and as if they were not disturbed by Confederates and Confederate sympathizers. But that was not the whole of the difficulty. The states north of the Ohio were not entirely free from plots and conspiracies endangering the union and the success of its armies.

In consequence of these conditions, arbitrary arrests were frequent. They took place not alone in areas where many persons were known to be secretly disloyal and engaged in more or less active conspiracies, but also in regions where there was no evidence of widespread disaffection or of dangerous combinations. While Lincoln was anxious not to carry methods to an extreme and not to cause unnecessary suffering, many of his subordinates—of course and inevitably—were not particularly circumspect or tender in their handling of suspected persons. Every arrest furnished the northern opposition with rallying cries; and objections did not come entirely from the Democratic party or from those who deserve to be called disloyal, but also from timid souls awed by the specter of tyranny. We can scarcely estimate with even an approach to accuracy how many persons were thus arrested beyond the area of actual conflict. The number reached into the thousands, if arrests for all causes be counted; and with this vague statement we may perhaps content ourselves. Competent investigators have found exact enumeration impossible.[14]

Secret societies were formed—the Knights of the Golden Circle and the Order of American Knights, later the Sons of Liberty. How many persons were enrolled among the Knights, no one can say. General H. B. Carrington, who was in the northwest during the war and knew conditions in the most deeply-infected region—the southern portions of Illinois, Indiana, and Ohio—, asserted that there were 70,000 members of the order in Illinois and 87,000 in Indiana.[15] Some of the leaders had plans for freeing southern prisoners and even seizing the state governments; but doubtless the vast majority had no more malicious purpose than to put an end to the war and to reestablish the union with a recognition of slavery and state sovereignty. To

---

[14] Especially see Rhodes, *History of the United States,* IV, p. 230 and note 2; Randall, *op. cit.,* p. 152.

[15] Am. Hist. Asso. *Report* for 1896, I, p. 358. Rhodes estimates the number in the three states above-mentioned may have been 175,000, though Holt, the Judge Advocate General, thought that the total number in the order might be 500,000. Rhodes. *History of the United States,* V, p. 318.

allow all this dark plotting to go along unheeded was naturally quite impossible. The constitutional question, it will be noticed, is not whether persons may be arrested in time of public peril and punished for acts and speeches endangering the welfare of the army and the nation, but whether persons outside the military areas may be legally seized and held by military officials, and tried, if tried at all, by military courts. There is no reason for doubting the elementary principle that, whenever and wherever the public safety permits, arrest and punishment should be left to the civil authorities.

A proclamation issued by the President (September 24, 1862) declared "that during the existing insurrection . . . all rebels and insurgents, their aiders and abettors, within the United States, and all persons discouraging volunteer enlistments, resisting militia drafts, or guilty of any disloyal practice affording aid and comfort to rebels against the authority of the United States, shall be subject to martial law and liable to trial and punishment by courts-martial or military commissions. . . ." The proclamation also declared the writ of habeas corpus suspended in respect to all persons arrested or imprisoned by any military authority or by the sentence of any court-martial or military commission.[16] A congressional act, passed some months later (March 3, 1863), authorized the President to suspend the writ of habeas corpus; it provided for furnishing federal judges with the names of persons held in military custody and for the release of prisoners under certain conditions. It declared that any order of the President, or under his authority, made at any time, should be a defense in all courts to any prosecution civil or criminal. We may well doubt the power of Congress to give immunity to the President's agents chargeable with illegal acts.[17] But the president conducts war, and his acts are to be justified on the ground of the necessities of the case.

[16] Richardson, *Messages and Papers*, VI, pp. 98-99.

[17] Randall (*op. cit.*, pp. 137, 207, 210) discusses the decision of the Supreme Court in Mitchell *v.* Clark, 110 U. S. 633 (1884). Baldwin says, "The State courts disregarded the statute. If, they said, either the common law or martial law justified the order, it justified the act; if neither did, the fiat of Congress cannot make the act a lawful one. The Supreme Court of the United States had this question before them, but did not find it necessary to decide it. Had they done so, it would probably have been answered in the same way." S. E. Baldwin, *The American Judiciary*, p. 302. But see the statement in Mitchell *v.* Clark: "That an act passed after the event, which in effect ratifies what has been done, and declares that no suit shall be sustained against the party acting under color of authority, is valid, so far as Congress could have conferred such authority before, admits of no reasonable doubt." 110 U. S. 633, 640.

At a later time, the Supreme Court announced in the celebrated Milligan case that military tribunals have no legal right to try and punish civilians in a region where the civil courts are open and prepared to try the alleged offender.[18] This decision was rendered after the close of the war by a divided Court, when the time had come to abandon the practices, which, if excusable at all, could be excused only on the ground of imperative necessity. But the Court appears to leave to the judiciary the determination of what is the area of war and of public danger; and the decision has been criticized by competent persons because the full recognition of such a principle in an emergency would be impossible. The principles, already mentioned on preceding pages in connection with the habeas corpus controversy, are, however, plain and of value, even if they leave us in uncertainty concerning their practical application: the courts are not called upon to acquiesce in violation of constitutional rights, but are under obligation to uphold them; they may not find it possible to prevent what in their opinion is unjustifiable encroachment on individual liberty, but they can make their pronouncements with decent regard for executive authority and with a comprehension of the actual situation. No one can plausibly assert that the executive, under the guise of conducting war, can legally harry the peaceful countryside and thrust persons into military prisons; there are limits on the authority of the president in time of war.

The most conspicuous instance of military arrest and punishment arose in the spring of 1863—those dark months before the victories at Gettysburg and Vicksburg. General Burnside had been disastrously beaten at Fredericksburg late in the previous year. In May, Hooker's army met defeat at Chancellorsville. The north was filled with foreboding, though the stalwart loyalists held their heads high despite growing discouragement or alarm. The very night when Lee and Stonewall Jackson were planning their brilliant and successful movement against Hooker, a mass meeting at Mount Vernon, Ohio, was addressed by Clement L. Vallandigham, a brilliant and captivating speaker, who was then seeking nomination by the Democrats for the governorship of the state. The details of his speech are not accurately known, but his words were sufficient to cause his arrest by General Burnside, the commanding General in that area. The General had issued an order announcing that "treason, expressed or implied, will not be tolerated in this department." Vallandigham, turned over to

[18] Ex parte Milligan, 4 Wallace 2 (1866).

the mercies of a military commission, was found guilty and condemned to imprisonment during the continuance of the war. The
President converted the punishment to banishment within the Confederate lines—thus tempering mercy with humor. Vallandigham was
nevertheless nominated and of course badly beaten at the polls. The
arrest and punishment, the failure to ignore the fulminations of acrid
oratory which made the frayed nerves of the loyal northerners tingle
with indignation, probably did more harm than good.[19] Sympathize
as we may with the irritated people who were giving up their sons to
death on the field of battle or to suffer in southern prisons, we must
hold in high esteem a courage which would have upheld free speech
in days of disaster—but it is not for us to pass sentence of condemnation. In the latter part of the war Vallandigham returned to
Ohio and was not troubled by the federal authorities.

In a letter sent by Lincoln in reply to the resolutions of an Albany
assembly, which complained of the military arrests and punishments,
may be found as cogent a defense of his own procedure as can be
found anywhere.[20] But, after all is said, it is the human appeal in the
letter that is most affecting and effective; it gives the reader some
consolation amid the perplexing and insoluble problems of constitutional authority. Speaking of the famous Vallandigham matter which
had especially aroused opposition, Lincoln said, "Long experience has
shown that armies cannot be maintained unless desertion shall be punished by the severe penalty of death. The case requires, and the law
and the Constitution sanction, this punishment. Must I shoot a simple-
minded soldier boy who deserts, while I must not touch a hair of a
wily agitator who induces him to desert? . . . I think that, in such
a case, to silence the agitator and save the boy is not only constitutional, but withal a great mercy." [21]

[19] Rhodes, who made a very careful examination of the Vallandigham affair,
says, "True, he met with defeat by an overwhelming majority; but it was the
victories of Meade and Grant that accomplished his overthrow, and they would have
been potent in taking the sting from his words had he been roaming at will over
his own State." Rhodes, *History of the United States*, IV, p. 252.

[20] Abraham Lincoln, *Complete Works* (J. G. Nicolay and John Hay, editors), II,
pp. 345, 349.

[21] Professor Randall learnedly discusses the subject of confiscation of rebel property, but the subject is for us unimportant except as it strongly illustrates the difficulty of dealing legally with an insurrection which was carried on as a war. Could
all persons within the disaffected area be considered enemies and could their property
be seized without proof that the individuals in question were acting as enemies
or that the property was of service to the enemy's hostile actions? "As there were
hundreds of treason indictments but no punishments, so there were many confiscation

The history of four years of civil war discloses the difficulty of maintaining the principles and practices of peace when peril stalks at midnight and passions are aroused; ordinary constitutional prescriptions are preserved with difficulty and at times appear valueless; but safety from tyranny lies not so much in the technicalities of law as in the constitutional conscience of officials and people and in the intelligence of the voting masses, who, if they use discretion, will seek to place in office men of wisdom and of rectitude rather than greedy graspers for power. That is a simple-minded assertion, but it brings out the basic fact that democracy and civil liberty find their only real security in the mind of a democratic populace cherishing the elements of orderly and responsible government.

It is especially difficult to preserve the freedom of speech and the press in time of war; to mark with precision the line to be drawn between illegal and justifiable suppression is impossible. There was no statutory enactment on which the administration could rely, and once more Lincoln had to do the best he could. He was certainly slow to wrath. No temperamental dictator could have endured the sneers and calumny with which the more truculent newspapers attacked the President and the conduct of the war. These verbal assaults, which were calculated to encourage disaffection, were grievances hard to be borne with patience; and yet, when the publications were suspended, the interference with free, if ruthless, expression of opinion seems on the whole to have done no good. A real and very noteworthy difficulty in carrying on the war was the fear in the minds of many people that tyranny would have them in its grasp; and the wily agitator could take advantage of that very fact.[22]

cases, but only a small amount of property confiscated." Randall, *op. cit.*, p. 288. Professor Randall speaks of the "feeling of irritation and injury on the part of a few despoiled owners"; making war by legislation appears in this case to have been a foolish failure. "The whole experience pertaining to the Civil War confiscations was such as to condemn the policy of promoting war by extreme punitive measures for the coercion of individuals." *Ibid.*, pp. 291-292.

[22] The suppression of the Chicago *Times* (June 1, 1863), the New York *World* (May 18, 1864), and the *Journal of Commerce* (May 18, 1864), aroused discussion and called forth condemnation. The latter two papers acted, or at least asserted that they acted, under a misapprehension in publishing a forged document. The *Times* was a peculiarly bitter sheet directed by a brilliant and spectacular editor who fed the discontented with ample sustenance. The character of his animadversions may be seen from his reflections on Lincoln's "slip-shod", "loose-jointed", second inaugural; "by the side of it," said the gentle critic, "mediocrity is superb." Gideon Welles, the Secretary of the Navy, speaks in his *Diary* of the disadvantage of suppression: "The arrest of Vallandigham and the order to suppress the circulation of the *Chicago Times*

The Conscription Act of March, 1863, aroused opposition and gave the government's opponents another opportunity to portray the lineaments of tyranny. It was immediately met by protests and a flood of constitutional arguments. The politicians, many of them loyal but with strange methods of displaying their devotion, simple-minded souls anxious for constitutional liberty though the heavens fall and the union be destroyed, the weary and the discontented, and certain inflammable elements, as well as the chronic trouble-makers, were all prepared for opposition. Those were months that tried men's souls. Riots broke out in New York City in mid-July, only a few days after Lee had retreated from Gettysburg and Grant had taken Vicksburg. Those victories lifted a load from the heart of the north, but the war was not yet won; disaster in the eastern area had been escaped only by a narrow margin; Lee still led a magnificent army under his superb command. Governor Seymour of New York sympathized with the cause of the rioters, if not with their methods. To question now the right of the government to demand and compel the support of men able to defend it is to assert that a free country, especially a federal republic, cannot, because of certain vague or imaginary constitutional inhibitions, use its power to maintain its life.

The constitutionality of conscription was definitely announced by the Supreme Court passing on the Selective Service Act of 1917.[23] But perhaps Lincoln's words, confided to paper though not published at the time, are quite as telling, and here are more significant: "The case simply is, the Constitution provides that the Congress shall have power to raise and support armies; and by this act the Congress has exercised the power to raise and support armies. This is the whole of it. . . . Do you admit that the power is given . . . and yet insist that by this act Congress has not exercised the power in a constitutional mode?—has not done the thing in the right way? Who is to judge of this? The Constitution gives Congress the power, but it does not prescribe the mode, or expressly declare who shall prescribe it. In such case Congress must prescribe the mode, or relinquish the power. There is no alternative. Congress could not exercise the power to do the thing if it had not the power of providing a way to do it, when

in his military district issued by General Burnside have created much feeling. It should not be otherwise. . . . The President—and I think every member of the Cabinet—regrets what has been done. . . ." *Diary*, I, p. 321. Of the suppression of the *World* and *Journal of Commerce*, he said, "These things are to be regretted. They weaken the administration and strengthen its enemies." *Ibid.*, II, p. 38.

[23] Arver *v.* United States, 245 U. S. 366 (1918).

no way is provided by the Constitution for doing it. In fact, Congress would not have the power to raise and support armies, if even by the Constitution it were left to the option of any other or others to give or withhold the only mode of doing it. . . . The power is given fully, completely, unconditionally. It is not a power to raise armies if State authorities consent; nor if the men to compose the armies are entirely willing; but it is a power to raise and support armies given to Congress by the Constitution, without an 'if.' " [24]

For more than one reason the words above given are of interest. They not only present a forcible argument, perhaps utterly convincing, but they also illustrate the power of the President as a skillful constitutional lawyer. Marshall could not have done better; the argument seems to have the peculiar vigor and the peculiar flavor of Marshall at his best, especially in the simplicity—the adroit simplicity—with which the argument begins and the inexorable steps by which it moves to the conclusion.

In the case of conscription, as in other matters, we get a false perspective if we cast a strong light on the obstacles thrown up by the conscientious or the intriguing opponents of the government. The more important fact is the enforcement of the law, the quiet determination of the people, their readiness to go grimly forward, their confidence in their own strength, a confidence not to be weakened by any apparent, but, in their judgment, imaginary, danger from despotism.

The war, Lincoln believed, was not to free the slaves but to preserve the union, to maintain his country as a living whole. No one knew better than he that slavery caused the war; moreover, he believed the union could not permanently endure half slave and half free. Why then did he not at once proclaim the conflict to be a crusade against slavery? Partly, it would seem, because he knew at the beginning the masses at the north were aroused by disunion, and many were not filled with zeal for the freedom of the slaves; partly because he must hold the border slave states, if possible. Every effort must be made to hold the support of all loyalists whatever be their sentiments concerning slavery. Doubtless he was influenced by constitutional scruples. Did he or others have the right to wage a war primarily to extirpate slavery, which was a state institution subject to state law?

In August, 1862, a few weeks before he issued the emancipation proclamation, Lincoln wrote Horace Greeley: "My paramount object

[24] Lincoln, *Works*, II, p. 389.

in this struggle is to save the Union, and is not either to save or to destroy slavery. If I could save the Union without freeing any slave, I would do it; and if I could save it by freeing all the slaves, I would do it; and if I could save it by freeing some and leaving others alone, I would also do that." [25] This must not be read to imply no disapproval of slavery and no hope of its speedy or ultimate disappearance—of course not. Through those anxious years he must have pondered deeply. If the union were lost, everything would be lost—union, the antislavery cause, democracy; for he believed that America was intrusted with a mission, the mission of demonstrating the capacity of men to govern themselves; if the union were dissolved, slavery as the corner-stone of a great confederacy would be perpetuated. If the union were saved, there would be at least hope of the disappearance of slavery and the development of a democracy freed from the virus of a system of labor already abandoned by most of the civilized world.

Almost from the beginning of the war the existence of slavery in the border states as well as in the confederated states brought many difficulties. [26] Lincoln moved slowly, cautiously, watching the course of things, deciding incidental questions as they arose, seeking, it would seem, to discover the public mind, anxious to act wisely, uncertain of all save the main route he should follow, but determined that not even the antislavery cause should endanger the success of northern armies. Little by little it became plain that slavery must go. Soon after the beginning of hostilities a congressional act (August 6, 1861) declared that if any slave be required to take up arms or to work in military or naval service against the United States, the owner should forfeit his claim to such labor. A year later (July 17, 1862) in the Confiscation Act a further step was taken. All slaves, the act announced, belonging to persons in rebellion, taking refuge within the union lines, and all slaves captured from such owners or found in any place, that had been occupied by the rebel forces, should be deemed

[25] Lincoln, *Works,* II, p. 227. In his annual message to Congress in December, 1862, Lincoln brought out clearly the necessity of national integrity because of the impossibility of disregarding physiographic fact. There was no possibility of severing the "national homestead." "In its adaptations and aptitudes it demands union and abhors separation. In fact, it would ere long force reunion, however much of blood and treasure the separation might have cost." Richardson, *Messages and Papers,* VI, p. 135.

[26] These difficulties are summed up in a telling way in the memorandum of an interview between the President and some border slave state representatives (March, 1862). Lincoln, *Works,* II, pp. 132-136.

captives of war and should be free. How such confiscation could be carried out, if technical regard should be paid to legal rights of the owners who might not be disloyal, is an interesting problem, but in this connection not of supreme importance; the important fact is that Congress acted and its acts pointed to emancipation as an exercise of the power to make war.

In midsummer, after fifteen months of war, during which the north had won some victories and had suffered heart-rending defeats, Lincoln thought the time had come to announce the end of slavery within the Confederate lines. He submitted to the cabinet (July 22, 1862) the draft of a proclamation. It was a bold proposal; McClellan's peninsular campaign was a dismal failure. Was this the moment to take the momentous step? The cabinet members were as a whole not un-favorable, but Seward said, "It may be viewed as the last measure of an exhausted government, a cry for help; the government stretching forth its hands to Ethiopia, instead of Ethiopia stretching forth her hands to the government. It will be considered our last *shriek* on the retreat." Delay appeared advisable, but after the battle of Antietam, and when Lee had withdrawn his forces across the Potomac, the pre-liminary proclamation was issued (dated September 22).[27]

It declared the President's intention to ask Congress to adopt a "practical measure" tendering to the slave states not in rebellion pecuniary aid for the abolition of slavery, and declaring also that the effort to colonize negroes would be continued. It declared that on the first of the succeeding January all persons held as slaves within any state or part of a state in rebellion should be henceforth and forever free. At the appointed time (January 1, 1863) the final proclamation was issued. It designated the states and parts of states which were then in rebellion, and declared all persons held as slaves in those areas to be free. Enjoining the freedmen to abstain from all violence unless in necessary self-defense, it declared that all "such persons of suitable condition" would be received into the armed service of the United States to garrison forts and to man vessels of all sorts. The proclama-tion, it should be noticed, was to apply only to those regions where for the time being the government did *not* possess actual control; it

[27] The tragic conditions of that harrowing summer and the tribulations of Lincoln's own spirit are seen in his words to a committee from the religious denominations of Chicago only ten days before the proclamation was issued: "What good would a proclamation of emancipation from me do, especially as we are now situated? I do not want to issue a document that the whole world will see must necessarily be inoperative, like the Pope's bull against the comet." *Works*, II, p. 234.

proclaimed the freedom of men who could not be made *really* free unless federal armies were victorious. And yet, of course, it pronounced the doom of slavery; such was actually its effect. The nature of the war could no longer be mistaken; everywhere—in Europe, where the struggle was watched with intense attention, and in the north and south alike—men now could see the war as a final desperate struggle to determine whether slavery should perish.

Emancipation was a war measure, proclaimed by the commander-in-chief of the army and navy. Lincoln made no attempt to induce Congress to emancipate the slaves. Such an act would look too much like the presumption that Congress, within its customary field of legislation, possessed control over the subject of slavery, though it had always been held to be a matter for the states alone. The proclamation depended for its justification on the practices of warfare; if property, even if the property be man, is actually used for military purposes by the enemy, an army commander may doubtless properly seize it. Writers on international law commonly now disapprove the confiscation of private property belonging to alien enemies, and the tendency to respect such ownership has been marked in recent decades. But this tendency or practice cannot be looked upon as a principle embodied in the structure of constitutional law. Once again, difficulty arises because the war was something more or something less than a public war; the persons affected might be loyal citizens of the United States and be considered enemies by a forced if necessary construction, only because they lived within areas subject to the Confederacy and not in actual possession of the government of the federal union.

This, more than most problems we have discussed, appears to us now as purely academic and as far away as Genghis Khan; but as an episode in the intensely important movement of the nineteenth century to free civilization from slavery it retains its interest. Did the proclamation have the *legal* effect of destroying slavery within the areas mentioned in the proclamation, or was that famous document in legal purview only a gesture? Did freedom actually wait upon formal constitutional amendment? No one would to-day like to answer the question in peremptory fashion; but on the whole the best decision is probably this: the proclamation could not free the slaves immediately and by its own force within areas not within actual control of the northern army; its legal effect depended upon the progress of the conquering troops; as they extended their actual occupancy, emancipation, as proclaimed by the commander-in-chief, went into effect.[28] Thus freedom literally would follow the flag. Lincoln was fairly certain of the validity and effect of his proclamation, but he saw the advisability of an amendment. For, as we have seen, the proclamation did not even pretend to free the slaves in the border states nor, of course, in the regions of the Confederacy already subdued.

For a considerable time, the President had been intent upon bringing about emancipation, in all the states willing to listen to him, by some plan for federal coöperation and pecuniary aid.[29] In accord with his recommendation Congress passed a resolution (April 10, 1862) which declared that the United States ought to coöperate with any state which should adopt gradual abolishment of slavery, and should give pecuniary aid "to compensate for the inconveniences . . . produced by such a change of system." But the proposal had no effect on the border states. Lincoln, however, did not despair. In December, two months and more after his preliminary proclamation of emanci-

[28] Randall, *op. cit.*, p. 384, quotes a note by R. H. Dana, Jr. in Wheaton, *Elements of International Law*, p. 441. Dana said, ". . . it would seem that, being a military measure by a commander-in-chief who had no general legislative authority over regions . . . not in his possession, it could not operate further than as a military order. From that time, all slaves coming under the control of the forces of the United States in the manner recognized by the law of belligerent occupation, were to be free. If this is the correct view, . . . it became therefore a question of fact, as to each slave and each region of the country, whether the forces of the Union had such possession as to give effect to the proclamation." Dana also says, "all the designated districts did at last come under the military occupation of the armies of the Union, in such sense as to effect the emancipation of all slaves in the strictest view of the law of belligerent occupation. . . ." "These negroes", said a South Carolina court, 'were not made free by the President's proclamation, *in law*, any more than they were *in fact*, because the President had not the right to make them free. . . . Emancipation . . . was, in fact, accomplished by the conquest of the country. . . .'" ". . . slavery . . . ceased to exist in the different parts of the State as they fell into the hands of the conqueror." Pickett *v.* Wilkins, 13 Richardson (S. C.) 366, 367-368 (1867). See Weaver *v.* Lapsley, 42 Alabama 601 (1868) ; Whitfield *v.* Whitfield, 44 Mississippi 254 (1870). There were some fine-drawn distinctions. See H. T. Catterall, *Judicial Cases Concerning American Slavery and the Negro*, III, p. 127.

[29] Lincoln, *Works*, II, pp. 102, 129, 132-135, 137, 204, 270-271. In an interview with border state representatives, March 10, 1862, Lincoln is reported as saying "He thought the institution wrong and ought never to have existed; but yet he recognized the rights of property which had grown out of it, and would respect those rights as fully as similar rights in any other property; that property can exist, and does legally exist. He thought such a law wrong, but the rights of property resulting must be respected; he would get rid of the odious law, not by violating the right, but by encouraging the proposition and offering inducements to give it up." *Ibid.*, p. 135. He is said to have declared in 1864 "that he would be willing to be taxed to remunerate the Southern people for their slaves." A. H. Stephens, *A Constitutional View of the Late War Between the States*, II, p. 617.

pation, he urged Congress to pass a constitutional amendment providing compensation to every state which should abolish slavery before the beginning of the twentieth century. This plan, he said, would shorten the war, perpetuate peace, and preserve the benefits of the union. "Fellow-citizens", he said in the memorable closing passage, "*we* can not escape history. We of this Congress and this Administration will be remembered in spite of ourselves. No personal significance or insignificance can spare one or another of us. The fiery trial through which we pass will light us down in honor or dishonor to the latest generation. We *say* we are for the Union. The world will not forget that we say this. We know how to save the Union. The world knows we do know how to save it. We, even *we here,* hold the power and bear the responsibility. In *giving* freedom to the *slave* we *assure* freedom to the *free*—honorable alike in what we give and what we preserve. We shall nobly save or meanly lose the last best hope of earth. Other means may succeed; this could not fail. The way is plain, peaceful, generous, just—a way which if followed the world will forever applaud and God must forever bless."

Proposals to settle the question for all time by constitutional amendment were offered in Congress at various times after the issuing of Lincoln's final proclamation. The Senate, by a vote of thirty-six to six, adopted a resolution of amendment April 8, 1864; but the House, giving only ninety-five affirmative votes out of a total of one hundred and sixty-one—less than the requisite two-thirds—, refused to take the momentous step. One objection, put forth by Pendleton of Ohio, is of interest because it is an example of the kind of constitutional interpretation which has more than once been vehemently defended: three-fourths of the states, said Pendleton, did not possess the constitutional power to pass the amendment, nor, indeed, all the states save one, because the institution of slavery lay within the dominion reserved entirely to each state for itself.[30] Such an argument implies that the American people do not form one body politic capable of shaping its own destiny. Not forming one people, they are dependent not only on the acquiescence of every state entering the constitutional system at the beginning, but also on the consent of thirty and more states that entered after that time. The argument also rests upon the sup-

---

[30] H. V. Ames, *The Proposed Amendments to the Constitution,* Am. Hist. Asso. *Report* for 1896, II, p. 217. The same kind of argument was used against the validity of the eighteenth and nineteenth amendments. See Rhode Island *v.* Palmer, 253 U. S 350 (1920) ; Leser *v.* Garnett, 258 U. S. 130 (1922).

posed purpose of the men establishing the Constitution: the division of authority between the states and the central government is absolutely unchangeable; only mechanical or incidental alteration of the constitutional system can be made by amendment; any encroachment on the general sphere of the states as provided by the original document is unconstitutional; by amendment additional securities may be given to support the original idea, but no amendment can lessen the force of the original purpose by depriving the states of authority or limiting the scope of their legal competence. This argument against freedom of amendment would scarcely merit refutation were it not that it emerges from obscurity at critical times and has remarkable longevity. It seems peculiarly inappropriate for acceptance by a people who believe they are the embodiment of modernism, whose Constitution has been continuously modified by practice and by interpretation, and who live under conditions so different from those of 1787 that it may be said that greater changes in social and economic life have come since the Constitution was framed than had come in the course of the preceding thousand years.

After the election of Lincoln in the autumn of 1864, and after a summer of success accompanied by horrible slaughter on the battle-fronts, the amendment came once more before the House. It was carried by a vote of 119 to 56—an astonishing result on the whole: after nearly four years of civil strife, a shifting of three votes to the negative would have prevented its passage. It was submitted to the President and signed by him; but such signature, it may be noticed, was unnecessary, if not actually improper.[31] Senator Trumbull immediately proposed and the Senate passed a resolution stating that the approval was unnecessary and should not be taken as a precedent.

In light of the problems of Reconstruction, which are to be considered on succeeding pages, one fact is especially noteworthy. When Secretary Seward announced adoption, December 18, 1865, he counted among the ratifying states which constituted the requisite twenty-seven votes, eight states of the former Confederacy.[32] At that very time congressmen were asserting the incompetence of the states which, by attempting secession, had forfeited their privileges in the union. The wandering commonwealths were, it seems, sufficiently alive to sanction

[31] See Ames, *op. cit.*, p. 296. Hollingsworth *v.* Virginia, 3 Dallas 378 (1798), gives the opinion of the Court to this effect in passing on the validity of the eleventh amendment.

[32] Virginia, Tennessee, Arkansas, South Carolina, Alabama, North Carolina, Georgia, and Louisiana.

formally a constitutional amendment, but not, as yet, far enough revived to be received into full participation in legislative halls. Seward said there were thirty-six states "in the United States", and the number ratifying was twenty-seven. Now if the states of the defunct Confederacy were not in the union, then only nineteen ratifications were necessary—three-fourths of twenty-five; and in fact nineteen of the ratifying states were unquestionably members of the union. It would appear necessary to choose either one horn of the dilemma or the other: if the states of the Confederacy were to be counted as in the union, then their ratification of the amendment was satisfactory; if they were not in the union, then three-fourths of the members who were had ratified the amendment.

The disruption of Virginia and the establishment of a new state within the ancient borders of the Old Dominion present an interesting example of the way in which a constitutional provision [33] can be handled—or mishandled—when political necessity arises. There had long been substantial differences between the western region of Virginia and the old tidewater section. The differences were largely due to the slight hold of slavery on the west, which, moreover, geographically belonged with the states bordering the Ohio River and in large degree with the free states of the old northwest, rather than with the old south or the cotton-raising areas of the new south. The final cleavage is only the most dramatic and conclusive demonstration of sectional diversity and its influence in American history.

The movement for dissolution began soon after the opening of the war. A convention meeting at Wheeling set up a government purporting to be the government of Virginia. The government at Richmond having passed into the hands of men warring against the nation, the people by popular action were entitled—such is the theory, and perhaps it is entirely sound—to bring a loyal government into existence. Francis H. Pierpont was chosen Governor and steps were soon taken to select other state officers. This government, thus strangely begotten, existed as the legitimate government of Virginia during the course of the war—legitimate, that is to say, as far as legal fiction and practical political interest could make it so. A constitutional convention, composed of men desiring the organization of a new state, West Virginia, met at Wheeling in November, 1861, and proceeded to form a constitution. It was submitted to the people and

[33] Constitution, Art. IV, sec. 3, para. 1.

was adopted "by the suspiciously large majority of 20,622 to 440." [34] The legality of this procedure is the critical question; for, if the legality is accepted, the proceedings which follow can be successfully defended as technically sound—even if they seem to rest on a purely legal fiction.[35] The Pierpont government, posing as the government of Virginia, gave its consent to the establishment of the new state; and the deed was done. The provision of the federal Constitution had been accorded formal and ostensible recognition.

Was there any real regard for constitutional behests and restrictions? If a state is ceasing to function as a state in the union, if its government is in the hands of disloyal persons, cannot the loyal citizens act? Can they not proceed on the basis of elementary popular rights and set up a new government willing to perform its legal functions in a state legally acting as a portion of the union? It is rather difficult to deny them that right, even within the domain of strict law.

Lincoln, whose mind normally reacted against mere specious pretense and found open disregard of law obnoxious, had his misgivings; and yet how could he have done otherwise than accept the facts and welcome the effect of the whole situation? The cabinet was divided.[36] Discussions in Congress disclosed wide differences of opinion. One speaker declared that the legislative powers of the people could not be annihilated, and that they reverted to the people when the government at Richmond was overthrown by treason. Another insisted that no person could honestly believe the Pierpont government to be the government of Virginia. Another asserted that to uphold the procedure was merely to trifle with the spirit of the Constitution. Thad-

---

[34] J. C. McGregor, *The Disruption of Virginia,* p. 274. Professor Randall says the vote was 18,862 to 514. Randall, *op. cit.,* p. 452. But the majority is still suspicious, whichever computation be accepted.

[35] I know of no principle in constitutional law which would declare that a people cannot set up a government, when the government formerly theirs had fallen into the hands of insurgents and was no longer acting as the state government in the technical and constitutional sense.

[36] "Chase is strongly for it; Blair and Bates against it, the latter, however, declining to discuss it or give his reasons except in writing. Stanton is with Chase. Seward does not show his hand. My impressions are, under the existing state of things, decidedly adverse. It is a disturbance that might be avoided at this time and has constitutional difficulties." Gideon Welles, *Diary,* I, p. 205 (December 23, 1862). See also *Ibid.,* pp. 206-209. Bates, the Attorney-General, later gave his formal opinion, declaring among other things, that no real legislature of Virginia had given its consent. Randall refers to Bates's manuscript diary which speaks of West Virginia as a "misbegotten, abortive State." Randall, *op. cit.,* p. 459.

deus Stevens expressed his opinion curtly in accord with the philosophy of which he was the chief exponent during the days of Reconstruction: "I say then that we may admit West Virginia as a new state, not by virtue of any provision of the Constitution but under our absolute power which the *laws of war* give us." [37] The new state was finally admitted into the union in the summer of 1863.

Lincoln's final pronouncement was similar in tone and content to his declarations at other times, when necessity or practical common sense appeared to make constitutional refinements and haggling dispute especially unwholesome: "Can this government stand, if it indulges constitutional constructions by which men in open rebellion against it are to be accounted, man for man, the equals of those who maintain their loyalty to it? Are they to be accounted even better citizens, and more worthy of consideration, than those who merely neglect to vote? If so, their treason against the Constitution enhances their constitutional value. Without braving these absurd conclusions, we cannot deny that the body which consents to the admission of West Virginia is the legislature of Virginia." [38] Such a statement may appear to be nothing but traitorous affront to legalism, but it might better be considered as a suitable garment, a garment of good sense, clothing legalistic nakedness. At all events, in the whole course of the war, if highly and finely-drawn constitutional construction had been allowed to impede and hamper the operations of government at every step, one of two results would probably have followed—the union would have been destroyed, or the Constitution and the law would have given way to the mailed fist of a dictator.

Throughout the course of the war, Congress as a general rule coöperated with the President; but the judgment of history must be that, though the legislators were earnest and though some of them were able, they gave little evidence of high-minded and inspiring leadership; at all events, the impressive fact is the way in which Lincoln dominated the scene. The committee on the conduct of the war was active and occasionally troublesome; its most prominent members, brought to the front by the very nature of war, were men of inflexible wills and ruthless determination; such men could not be kept in leading-strings. They sometimes interfered with Lincoln's plans. Critical and inclined to be domineering as some of them were, their criticism or opposition did not on the whole injure the union

---

[37] McGregor, *op. cit.*, pp. 307-311.
[38] Lincoln, *Works*, II, p. 286.

cause to which they were passionately devoted. The absence of a really dangerous conflict between the executive and the legislature is the significant fact. It is impossible to expect several hundred legislators to carry on war in silence.

To reconcile all the orders of the President or the acts of Congress during the war with the constitutional limitations normally operative in time of peace is quite impossible. We may of course avoid the task altogether by asserting that war of itself relieves the government from normal restrictions; and this is much like saying whatever the government finds it necessary to do is constitutionally justified—*inter arma silent leges*. The outstanding fact, however, is not the occasional or frequent breach of particular clauses in the Constitution, but the effort not to disregard them altogether. And even more noticeable is the continuous open discussion and debate. Lincoln did not favor the incarceration of everybody not agreeing with him; he believed it necessary to repress those persons actually endangering the success of the union arms. Most important of all, elections were held, the people expressed their will through the ballotbox, legislatures met, congressmen indulged in prolonged debate, democratic government was not broken down, and democratic public opinion was triumphant.

That a president armed with the "war power" may some day wreck the whole constitutional system is theoretically possible, and the dictator, if he ever appears, may discover precedents for tyranny in the conduct of Lincoln. But one thought continues to force itself upon us and to that thought the reader's attention has already been called: it is not a written constitution, not the slogan a government of laws and not of men, not formulated doctrines, but the spirit of a people which is actually potent; without a democratic-minded people democratic government is at the best a hollow pretense. Despite Lincoln's failure now and again to follow the letter of the law, the sober judgment of history must be that his main purpose was to save democracy, not to ruin it. And the prominent feature of the whole dreadful struggle is not what was done illegally but what was not done at all.[39] The single most important fact in American constitu-

[39] See an illuminating article by J. G. Randall, "Lincoln in the Rôle of Dictator," *South Atlantic Quarterly*, XXVIII, pp. 236-252. "He did not pack his legislature, nor eject his opposition. There was no military 'purging' of Congress. . . . Elections were not forced . . . though military 'protection' was in some few cases supplied. There was no Lincoln party constituting a superstate and visiting vengeance upon political opponents. Criminal violence was not employed *sub rosa* after the fashion of

tional history is that democracy and law survived a desolating and destructive civil war.

Certain congressional measures which were passed during the war and were incidental to the main effort to win victory on the battlefield deserve attention: the establishment of a national banking system, the issuing of national paper currency—the greenbacks—, and the forcing of the state banks to abandon the practice of issuing notes to circulate as currency. The government did not order the state banks to cease the practice, but placed a tax on their notes (1865, 1866), and thus under the guise of using the taxing power the desired result was reached; this act was upheld by the Supreme Court,[40] as was also the greenback act [41] after much tribulation. The national banking act could, of course, find fairly firm footing on the precedents of earlier years. But the important matter is not so much the question of the constitutionality of these measures as the fact that the things were done. The acts illustrate natural expansion of actual governmental activity stimulated by the necessities of war. The government now occupied a wider field than before the war; people looked with equanimity on the activities of the national government; states' rights, a term improperly used as synonymous with state sovereignty, was a term of reproach.

The general constitutional effects of the Civil War are in some respects perfectly evident: slavery was wiped out; the house was no longer divided; the institution which had been the basis of sectionalism in its most dangerous aspects was gone. The nation existed as a political or legal fact, no longer to be threatened by state sovereignty. The actual national character and quality of the union had henceforth opportunity for expression not only in political affairs but also in social and economic development. The active energy of millions of men who were engaged in the struggle to maintain union created a new subconscious sense of national wholeness, long delayed in the

modern dictatorships." pp. 249-250. Professor Randall also states what those who knew America in 1917 and 1918 will probably agree to: ". . . the citizen [during the Civil War] was free to speak his mind against the government, far more so than during the World War." p. 251. Dunning, though bearing rather heavily on the frequent disregard of constitutional limitations, reaches the conclusion that public opinion and not the elaborate devices of the Constitution played the decisive rôle. W. A. Dunning, *Essays on the Civil War and Reconstruction*, p. 59.

[40] Veazie Bank *v.* Fenno, 8 Wallace 533 (1869). Cf. Bailey *v.* Drexel Furniture Co., 259 U. S. 20 (1922).

[41] Legal Tender Cases, 12 Wallace 457 (1871). See the discussion in a later chapter.

south by the pains and penalties of Reconstruction. This common coöperative effort probably prepared men of action and of energy for undertaking extensive corporate enterprises and for the work of integrating the nation industrially as it had been integrated legally

CHAPTER XLV

RECONSTRUCTION

I: EARLY PROBLEMS; RADICAL VICTORY

As we examine the problems of Reconstruction we find them in some respects like those we have considered in treating of the war itself. On the one side was the theory that the states could not secede and that the war was an insurrection; on the other was the fact that the states had ceased to function as states in the union; during four years, claiming independence, they had been joined together in a powerful Confederacy. The union must be restored. But did restoration take place, as a matter of legal right and theory, with the withdrawal of federal arms? As the states could not secede, must they be treated as if they were in the union and possessed of all their rights? Plainly, no amount of legalistic legerdemain could obscure the necessity of readjustment and political reconstruction. The question was how quickly and how thoroughly should the wayward states be once again restored to their normal position in the union. Congress had, on the whole, acquiesced in executive leadership during the war. The President had wielded enormous power; but now that the war was over, reaction was inevitable, and Congress was certain to be less tractable and more determined to have its way.

Before hostilities ceased, Lincoln had taken steps toward reconstruction, and his proposals embraced a policy. On December 8, 1863 he issued a proclamation of amnesty; it included a plan for restoration. Various classes of persons were excepted from the pardon—notably those that had held high rank in the Confederate army or navy and those that had left certain important positions in the federal government or in the military and naval service and had cast in their lot with the Confederacy. The proclamation announced that, if a number of persons in any of the Confederate States (except Virginia, which was in theory under the Pierpont government), not less than one-tenth the number voting in 1860, should take the oath of allegiance and be qualified voters and should reëstablish a state government, republican in form, such a government would be recognized as the true government of the state.

Some months after this, Congress passed an act which differed in some respects from the plan presented by Lincoln, but it was not signed because it was submitted to him less than an hour before the end of the session. With his customary good sense, the President, in a special proclamation, asserted that he was not inflexibly committed to any one plan of restoration, that he was not prepared to declare that constitutions already installed in two of the states should be held for naught, but that he was fully satisfied with the system of restoration contained in the bill.[1] Plainly at this time the President and Congress were not very far apart in their ideas of what should be done. Before the close of the war, constitutional conventions in Tennessee, Louisiana, and Arkansas set up governments. But these governments were rather shadowy affairs, and congressmen from these theoretically reconstructed states did not find their way to seats in the legislative halls at Washington.

The proclamation quoted the constitutional provision concerning a republican form of government.[2] On that provision—if we must find some distinct technical basis—the authority of the national government to restore the union can possibly be based with some degree of assurance. A state government, that is seized by "rebels" and made to do their will, can scarcely be considered a free constitutional government. Technically, a state not in the possession of its loyal citizens is not, constitutionally speaking, republican.[3]

Upon the death of Lincoln, Andrew Johnson assumed the onerous duties of the presidency. The dreary history of Reconstruction during the earlier years is associated with this pathetic figure—pathetic because he was temperamentally not fitted to the peculiarly difficult task, and because upon him was heaped for a time obloquy and the

---

[1] July 8, 1864. The bill provided that the state constitutions should prohibit slavery and declare that no state or Confederate debt should be recognized or paid by the state. In other ways the bill differed from Lincoln's proposals of the previous December. Lincoln expressed his doubts of congressional authority to abolish slavery.

[2] Constitution, Art. IV, sec. 4.

[3] "These new relations imposed new duties upon the United States. The first was that of suppressing the rebellion. The next was that of re-establishing the broken relations of the State with the Union. . . . The authority for the performance of the first has been found in the power to suppress insurrection and carry on war; for the performance of the second, authority was derived from the obligation of the United States to guarantee to every State in the Union a republican form of government." Texas v. White, 7 Wallace 700, 727-728 (1869).

suspicion of millions. It is not for us to attempt an estimate of his gifts and failings, and yet few persons so evidently have a place in constitutional history. His surroundings in early life were not very different from those of Lincoln; but his career as President is proof that more is needed for the highest public service than being born in poverty and reared in adversity. Only within recent years have historians turned to his defense, after candid examination of the evidence; and in these later days if opprobrium is indulged in, it is more likely to be poured out upon the acrid radical partisans than upon the stubborn occupant of the White House.[4] His main fault or misfortune was consistency, a grievous defect in anyone burdened with the duties of statesmanship. His old states' rights theories, his determination to carry on his policy of immediate reconstruction, and his doctrine that states could not secede, with all the utterly logical conclusions from that doctrine, he clung to with undeviating persistence. He did not know when he was beaten, and he believed that truth—his truth—must prevail. Logic and rhetoric, said Bacon, make men able to contend. Johnson's career is a proof of Bacon's wisdom. But in one vital matter he did change. At first, his attitude toward certain southern leaders was as stern and unforgiving as the most violent enemy of the south could desire, but with the subsidence of excitement after Lincoln's death, better counsels prevailed. Lincoln's cabinet, retained by Johnson, appears to have had a quieting influence. Before many months had passed, the President entered upon a policy comparatively mild and free from vindictiveness.

Johnson fell heir to Lincoln's plan of Reconstruction. The Pierpont government was recognized as the government of Virginia (May 9, 1865). The governments set up in the other three southern states already mentioned were assumed to be the legitimate governments.

---

[4] There are many books treating of Johnson and his opponents. Among the recent ones may be mentioned C. G. Bowers, *The Tragic Era;* G. F. Milton, *The Age of Hate;* R. W. Winston, *Andrew Johnson;* L. P. Stryker, *Andrew Johnson.* On the whole, the scales have been held as evenly by W. A. Dunning, *Reconstruction Political and Economic,* as by anyone. "The same integrity of purpose," says Dunning, "force of will, and rude intellectual force, which had raised him from the tailor's bench in a mountain hamlet to leadership in Tennessee, sustained him when he confronted the problems of the national administration. . . . Positive, aggressive, and violent in controversy, fond of the fighting by which his convictions must be maintained, he nevertheless, in the formation of his opinions on great questions of public policy, was as diligent as any man in seeking and weighing the views of all who were competent to aid him." pp. 19-20. These words may be too favorable. The estimate of Rhodes is less so: "Of all men in public life it is difficult to conceive of one so ill-fitted for this delicate work as was Andrew Johnson." *History of the United States,* V, p. 517.

At the end of the month, he issued a new amnesty proclamation, not quite so generous in its provisions as that issued by Lincoln. The required oath of loyalty included a promise to abide by and support all laws and proclamations made during the rebellion with reference to the emancipation of slaves. At the same time he issued pronouncements for the establishment of governments in the states of the Confederacy.[5] For each state a provisional governor was appointed, whose duty it was to prescribe rules for assembling a convention to be composed of delegates chosen by loyal citizens. The convention was to alter or amend the state constitution, take further necessary steps for restoring the state to its constitutional relations, and "present such a republican form of State government" as would entitle the people "to protection by the United States against invasion, insurrection, and domestic violence". A voter must have taken the oath prescribed in the amnesty proclamation, and be qualified to vote under the terms of the constitution and laws of the state in force at the time of attempted secession. The convention or the legislature afterwards assembled was to lay down qualifications for voting—"a power," said the President shrewdly, "the people of the several States . . . have rightfully exercised from the origin of the Government to the present time." [6]

The success of Johnson's policy depended in a measure upon the south's readiness to act with rare discretion. No high-spirited people can be expected even in the hour of utter defeat to confess their sins, when by doing so they acknowledge that all the sacrifices and sufferings of a great war were due to their own blunders and wickedness. But of their readiness to accept the fact of defeat and of their willingness to abandon state sovereignty as a practical doctrine, there is considerable evidence.[7] Among various reports upon southern conditions and attitudes of mind, two important ones were presented to Johnson. General Grant, who made a hasty survey, wrote, "I am satisfied that the mass of thinking men of the south accept the present situation of affairs in good faith." He believed they regarded slavery and the right to secede as "settled forever by the highest tribunal—arms—

---

[5] North Carolina, May 29; Mississippi, June 13; Georgia and Texas, June 17; Alabama, June 21; South Carolina, June 30; and Florida, July 13. Richardson, *Messages,* VI, pp. 312-331.

[6] He also suggested to the Governor of Mississippi the advisability of giving the vote to negroes who could read the Constitution of the United States and could write their own names, and also to negro taxpayers.

[7] Notice a letter from J. L. M. Curry (of Alabama) to Senator Doolittle, quoted in Horace White, *The Life of Lyman Trumbull,* pp. 255-256.

that men can resort to." They would, he thought, carry out in good faith any governmental policy not humiliating to them as citizens. Carl Schurz, on the other hand, while declaring there was no present danger of another insurrection on a large scale, said treason did not appear odious in the south. "The people are not impressed with any sense of its criminality. . . . There is, as yet, among the southern people an *utter absence of national feeling.*" How strange that an able man should remotely expect to find a sense of sin or that a heavy-hearted people should become overnight enthusiastic defenders of the triumphant cause! When all is said, statesmanship should be mixed with common sense. Slavery, he told the President, in its old form, would not be reëstablished, but some species of forced labor would be; and therefore, for the protection of the freedmen, they must be given the suffrage. The states should not be readmitted until this radical step was taken.

In the course of the summer and autumn (1865), the movement for Reconstruction under Johnson's plan went on. Conventions were held in six states.[8] Acts of secession were repealed, and the legislatures of five states ratified the thirteenth amendment, Mississippi refusing, among other reasons, on the ground that slavery was already abolished and that she would not participate in coercing Kentucky and Delaware.[9] Mississippi also passed legislation concerning the freedmen, that was very obnoxious to the northern people and prepared their minds and hearts for stern measures in their treatment of the southern states. Other states took similar steps. The laws in some instances set aside the freedmen as a separate class, commonly designated as "persons of color", who were precluded from enjoying many of the civil privileges belonging to the whites.[10] To the northerners, these "black codes" appeared to be devices for the perpetuation of slavery or something almost as bad. A more charitable spirit would have found in them a serious attempt to solve the problem begotten by the presence of millions of blacks, few of whom were prepared for the duties of freedom. If one seeks to defend the passage of these

[8] South Carolina, Alabama, Florida, North Carolina, Georgia, and Mississippi.

[9] E. P. Oberholtzer, *A History of the United States Since the Civil War*, I, p. 118 ff. Of course that was one of those silly blunders which aroused northern suspicion and helped nobody.

[10] Excerpts from these acts are in Edward McPherson, *The Political History of the United States . . . During the Period of Reconstruction*, pp. 29-44. Acts of a similar character had been on the books of southern states before the war, the purpose being to regulate the free negroes—to deal with the negro problem as distinguished from slavery.

laws because the confusion in the south made them necessary, he must still confess that to pass them was a tactical blunder. And this discrimination against the blacks, which was painted in darkest colors by certain politicians, fired the northern mind.

In considering the whole era of Reconstruction we cannot lose sight of the fact that many northern men cherished the ideals of complete freedom; anything less was anathema; and they pictured to themselves a negro people competent to become immediately self-dependent and capable members of society. Slavery had been denounced from the housetops; and now men could believe the whole trouble had been, not ignorant labor or racial incapacity, but slavery as a system. Freedom would at once have its normal and vivifying effect. We must recognize, too, the instinctive reaction in many minds against a class of persons set aside as a distinctly inferior class, a caste apart, its existence mocking at the theory of democratic equality. To make matters worse, the southern states elected to Congress men who had been prominent in the "rebellion", among them Alexander H. Stephens, who at that very time stood charged with treason and had only recently been released from prison on parole. "There seems", said Johnson, "in many of the elections something like defiance, which is all out of place at this time." [11]

When Congress met in December, 1865, the leaders were in no mood to comply at once with the presidential plans and their results. The admission of southern congressmen would add to the power of the Democratic opposition, and it threatened the hold of the Republicans on the government. When the time should come for a new apportionment of representatives, the southern states, but recently locked in a death struggle with the north, would have more congressmen than before, for with the disappearance of slavery vanished also the three-fifths compromise of the Constitution. This was a situation too grievous to be borne. Had the "rebels" been conquered and slavery banished only to the end that government might be placed in the hands of men who had tried to overthrow it?

The President's message was in many respects statesmanlike. It did not exhale hatred, for Johnson had grown steadily more charitable. He had called upon George Bancroft, the historian, to pen his

[11] The President also telegraphed to Governor Holden of North Carolina, "The results of the recent elections in North Carolina have greatly damaged the prospects of the State in the restoration of its governmental relations." See Rhodes, *History of the United States*, V, pp. 540-541.

message for him,[12] and he had profited by the serene influence of his cabinet—serene, that is to say, in comparison with the tempestuous air of the partisan world without. The message assumed the authority of the President to carry out a plan of Reconstruction, and it announced some of its results. He referred to the desirability, if not the necessity, of expecting the southern states to adopt the thirteenth amendment. But when that step was taken, "it would remain for the States . . . to resume their places in the two branches of the National Legislature. . . ." To Congress, it appears, he would leave only the right to judge of the "elections, returns, and qualifications of your own members."

The Secretary of State announced (December 18, 1865) the adoption of the thirteenth amendment abolishing slavery. But this did not assure immediate recognition of the southern states. Congress was to have its words—its many words. Under the leadership of Thaddeus Stevens, the indomitable "Old Commoner", the House had already refused to admit members from the "so-called Confederate States of America". He also secured the appointment of a joint committee to inquire into the condition of the southern states and report whether any of them were entitled to representation in Congress. Thus was constituted the formidable and effective committee on Reconstruction, with William Pitt Fessenden of the Senate as chairman. There was little hope that Johnson's policies would prevail. If supported by public opinion, the Radicals could carry forward their own purposes; the south could be made to bend to their will in every essential respect.

As the basis of the work to be done, we find various theories, or doctrines. Johnson's theory, sometimes called the presidential theory of Reconstruction, is perhaps better described as the theory of *self-*reconstruction; for he believed that, while the initiative and supervision were his own, the loyal citizens of the states had the right and should be allowed, under such federal protection as might be needed, to restore their governments and bring their states back into their constitutional relations. Three other main theories were advanced, all of them in agreement on one point—that the business of Reconstruc-

---

[12] Dunning, *Reconstruction,* p. 53, note 1; Mass. Hist. Society *Proceedings* for 1905, p. 395 ff. See also, C. R. Fish, "President Johnson's First Annual Message," *Am. Hist. Rev.,* XI, pp. 951-952. Fish points out that a large part of the ideas had been previously announced by Johnson. The message, however, was affected by the general spirit of moderation which Bancroft was able to infuse into the whole.

tion was fundamentally a matter for the legislature and not for the President alone.

The first of these three was the conquered provinces theory promulgated by Thaddeus Stevens. Out of patience with constitutional technicalities, he could see no virtue in theories which denied actual facts. The states had gone out of the union, they had been beaten at the expense of many lives and much treasure, and it was the duty of their conquerors to do what was deemed suitable.[13] "The future condition of the conquered power depends", he said, "on the will of the conqueror. They must come in as new states or remain as conquered provinces." [14]

The second, commonly called the state suicide theory, had been set forth by Charles Sumner during the war: [15] a state attempting secession ceased to be a state, and the region and its people became subject to Congress. This theory differed from that of Stevens in not accepting secession as a fact, but as only destroying the states as bodies politic.[16]

The third theory, known as the theory of forfeited rights, is perhaps more accurately termed the theory of suspended animation; it did hold that the states had temporarily forfeited their rights; they were not, however, as a consequence totally dead, but in a condition of coma; they could be brought to life by the ministrations of a solicitous, if stern, physician whose prescriptions and mandates must be absolutely obeyed. Congress could issue such orders and lay

[13] "The theory that the rebel states, for four years a separate power and without representation in Congress, were all the time here in the Union, is a good deal less ingenious and respectable than the metaphysics of Berkeley which proved that neither the world nor any human being was in existence. . . . After the palpable facts of war, to deny that we have a right to treat them as a conquered belligerent, severed from the Union in fact, is not argument but mockery." Quoted in J. A. Woodburn, *Life of Thaddeus Stevens*, p. 344.

[14] W. L. Fleming, *Documentary History of Reconstruction*, I, p. 148.

[15] See *Ibid.*, I, pp. 144-145. Professor Burgess asserts that the theory of Samuel Shellabarger, a Representative from Ohio, was "sound political science and correct constitutional law." J. W. Burgess, *Reconstruction and the Constitution*, pp. 59-60. This theory was substantially the same as Sumner's. Having complete authority over the region which had lost its status as a state, Congress could erect a new state with the coöperation of loyal inhabitants and admit the state into the union.

[16] Secession sustained by force works abdication of rights under the Constitution, "so that from that time forward the territory falls under the exclusive jurisdiction of Congress as other territory, and the state being according to the language of the law, *felo-de-se*, ceases to exist." Fleming, *Documentary History of Reconstruction*, I. p. 144.

down such conditions as appeared necessary. The state could not spring into full, active existence at the mere word of the President. Which one of these theories predominated in the course of the following years it is not easy to say. But it is probably correct to say that on the whole the idea that the states were utterly wiped out could not and did not prevail. Determined as men were to compel the south to do certain things, the procedure was on the whole that of restoration and reëstablishment. "The Constitution," the Supreme Court declared, "in all its provisions, looks to an indestructible Union, composed of indestructible States. . . . Considered therefore as transactions under the Constitution, the ordinance of secession, adopted by the convention and ratified by a majority of the citizens of Texas, and all the acts of her legislature intended to give effect to that ordinance, were absolutely null. . . . The obligations of the State, as a member of the Union, and of every citizen of the State, as a citizen of the United States, remained perfect and unimpaired. It certainly follows that the State did not cease to be a State, nor her citizens to be citizens of the Union. . . . All admit that, during this condition of civil war, the rights of the State as a member, and of her people as citizens of the Union, were suspended." [17] The President, the Court declared, might, as long as the war continued, institute temporary governments, "But, the power to carry into effect the clause of guaranty is primarily a legislative power, and resides in Congress." [18]

If we could escape from the net and tangle of technicalities, we could content ourselves with Lincoln's words in his last public address. A regret had been expressed, he said, that his mind was not definitely fixed on the question whether the seceded states, "so called", were in the union or out. The question, he declared, had not been and was not at the time "a practically material one. . . ." "As yet, what-

---

[17] Texas v. White, 7 Wallace 700, 725-727 (1869). Justice Grier, dissenting, held that Texas was not a state in the union: "I am not disposed to join in any essay to prove Texas to be a State of the Union, when Congress have decided that she is not." *Ibid.*, 739. Justices Swayne and Miller, accepting the opinion of the Court on the merits of the case, agreed with Grier that Texas then (1869) was incapable as a state to maintain an original suit in the Court. The Court referred with approval to Luther v. Borden, 7 Howard 1, 42, a well-known case growing out of disturbances in Rhode Island nearly thirty years before. It may be that a distinction can be made between the theory of suspended animation and the theory of forfeited rights, but it seems a needless exercise of ingenuity. For a statement of the theories, see W. A. Dunning, *Essays on the Civil War and Reconstruction*, p. 103 ff.; T. C. Smith, "Reconstruction," *Cyclopedia of American Government*, III, p. 164.

[18] Texas v. White, 7 Wallace 700, 730 (1869).

ever it may hereafter become, that question is bad as the basis of a controversy, and good for nothing at all—a merely pernicious abstraction." [19] To the weary searcher after constitutional truth, these words are consoling.

The essentials of the situation are plain. Congress was determined not to accept the President's plans but itself to manage Reconstruction. The leaders, gradually getting recruits from those who had been acquiescent during the summer months of 1865, believed, or sought to believe, that the southern "rebels" were not converted, that the fruits of victory must be garnered, and that something must be done to make the freedmen secure in their freedom; in fact, the states should be kept from participation in the union until Congress had worked its will. The most advanced Radicals were now demanding negro suffrage—some of them doubtless for personal or party reasons; some of them because they believed in the general sanctity of a wide suffrage devoid of class discrimination; others because they believed slavery would in substance continue unless the negroes were given political weapons of defense. Sumner, now insistent upon negro suffrage, had taken up his position some months before the active contest over Reconstruction began. "I insist", he said in a letter to John Bright in the spring of 1865, "that the rebel States shall not come back except on the footing of the Declaration of Independence. . . . Without them [negro votes], the old enemy will re-appear, and under the forms of law take possession of the governments, choose magistrates and officers, and in alliance with the Northern democracy, put us all in peril again. . . ." This sums up the matter: belief in equality of rights, distrust of the "rebels" strengthened by the Democrats of the north, and the consequent need for negro votes. Congress was to come to this position.

It is unfair to charge the Republican leaders with zeal for party supremacy and for that alone. Bitter and vindictive some of them were; but many of them probably, with more than ordinary partisan passion, believed in their duty toward the black men. As partisans— and in their own minds as patriots—they were anxious to maintain their political power. As yet (1866), however, the north was not prepared to take the final step which might ward off the catastrophe of Democratic dominance; enthusiasm for negro suffrage was not

[19] Abraham Lincoln, *Complete Works* (J. G. Nicolay and John Hay, editors), II, pp. 673-674.

widespread.[20] The more Johnson inclined toward leniency, the more he attracted the Democrats of the north as well as the southerners, and the more vehement and determined did the Republican leaders become. This condition and this danger—the danger that the Democrats would irretrievably damage Johnson's cause by supporting it—did not appear at once; but as the months went by, it became plain. He could not prevent the Democrats and, above all, the old-time Copperheads from enlisting under his banner.

There appeared for a time to be a willingness or an inclination to accept the general views of the President. The people-at-large, we may surmise, were aweary. But objections developed; and they were increased by Johnson's veto of the Freedmen's Bureau bill, February 19, 1866. This bill enlarged the scope of an act of the previous year; it provided for issuing food and other supplies to destitute negroes; it imposed on the President the duty of protecting the freedmen; and it declared—here was the heart and center of its offending— that any person, in any region where the ordinary course of judicial procedure had been disturbed by the rebellion, who should subject another, on account of race, color, or previous condition of servitude, to the deprivation of any civil right secured to white people, should be deemed guilty of a misdemeanor. The President vetoed the bill, saying that it referred to certain of the states "as though they had not 'been fully restored in all their constitutional relations to the United States.'" Congress could not accept mildly this assumption that the states could be brought back into full statehood by the wave of the presidential wand. But the Senate failed to pass the bill over the veto; the President was still in a position of authority. But this was his last victory.

On Washington's birthday (1866) Johnson made a speech which reached the height of political impropriety; the old saying, "It was worse than a crime—it was a blunder", can with assurance be said of this. He declared that the country was "almost inaugurated into another rebellion." An attempt was made, he said, to concentrate all

---

[20] Some persons were by this time becoming anxious about the tariff and the conservation of economic interests. H. K. Beale, in *The Critical Year*, discusses this, but shows that the forces of the Radicals were recruited largely by appeals to the people, made by the bitter Radical leaders, who stopped at nothing in their denunciation of Johnson during the critical year, 1866, when hard and unrelenting public opinion was forming. "To keep the economic questions in the background until the Southern problem was settled and their power secure, was therefore essential. A campaign of denunciation and vituperation would accomplish this end by keeping war hatreds alive." *Ibid.*, p. 9.

power in the hands of a few and bring about a consolidation of the republic. He referred to the assumption of power "by an irresponsible central directory. . . ." From the crowd of listeners gathered to congratulate him upon his veto and his victory came a voice asking him to name the culprits threatening the union, and he answered: "I say Thaddeus Stevens, of Pennsylvania; I say Charles Sumner, of Massachusetts; I say Wendell Phillips, of Massachusetts [Great cheering, and a voice, 'Forney!'] I do not waste my fire on dead ducks." Such words illustrate the tone and temper of the harangue. They antagonized Congress and they awakened the antipathy of the people, who, however simple they may be in life and speech, demand dignity and decorum in their higher officials. Though this speech dismayed many of those still believing in Johnson, efforts were made by the less headstrong Republicans to avoid a complete break with the President. Before this unfortunate speech, and immediately after the veto, the House, on the motion of Stevens from the committee on Reconstruction, adopted a concurrent resolution formally declaring that no senator or representative should be admitted to Congress from any state of the former Confederacy until Congress declared the state entitled to representation. The Senate adopted the resolution a few days later. It was scarcely necessary, but it was a direct and emphatic answer to the President.

The Senate had been engaged for some time in framing a Civil Rights bill. Early in February it was passed by the Senate, and some six weeks later by the House—in both houses by large majorities. It was vetoed by the President and passed over the veto.[21] The result showed, however, that if any one of the southern states, whose claims the President was advocating, had been represented in Congress, the Senate could not have voted to override the veto.

The Civil Rights bill disclosed the principles and purposes of Congress concerning the rights of the freedom and the duties of the government. All persons, irrespective of race, color, or previous condition of servitude, were declared entitled to the possession of fundamental civil rights and liberties and to the equal protection of the laws. Anyone, "under color of any law . . . or custom", subjecting another to the deprivation of any right protected by the act, or subjecting him to a punishment different from that prescribed for the

[21] In the Senate the bill was passed over the veto by a vote of thirty-three to fifteen, April 6, 1866; in the House by 122 to 41, April 9. McPherson, *Political History of Reconstruction*, p. 81.

punishment of white people, because such person had been held in slavery or involuntary servitude, should be deemed guilty of a misdemeanor and punished accordingly. The federal district courts were given cognizance of offenses committed against the act; district attorneys, marshals, and certain other officers were required to institute proceedings against violators of the act.

The constitutionality of this act was attacked by the President and by others as a wanton intrusion upon state authority. It assumed the right, until then unheard of, in the central government to protect state citizens against state laws and against officers charged with the execution of such laws. It appeared to set aside or ignore the essential qualities of federalism.[22] The act did not purport to be merely a war measure, and the defense of its constitutionality rested on the thirteenth amendment. The amendment in abolishing slavery gave to Congress the authority to enforce the act by appropriate legislation. Was this appropriate legislation? The answer turns on the question whether discrimination such as that laid down in the "black codes" of the south constituted slavery. Lyman Trumbull, one of the ablest though not the most extreme and vehement of the congressional leaders, strongly defended the act as entirely consistent with the amended Constitution. If people can be deprived of the ordinary rights to life, liberty, and the pursuit of happiness, what is their condition but that of slavery, even though slavery in its cruder form has disappeared? This argument has force; but probably, when the amendment was adopted, the people of the land would have said—if we may paraphrase the words of Polonius—to define true slavery, what is it, but to be nothing else but a slave?[23] Presumably they thought

[22] The details of the bill, said the President, "interfere with the municipal legislation of the States, with the relations existing exclusively between a State and its citizens, or between inhabitants of the same State—an absorption and assumption of power by the General Government which, if acquiesced in, must sap and destroy our federative system of limited powers, and break down the barriers which preserve the rights of the States." *Ibid.,* p. 78.

[23] "Congress . . . by the Civil Rights Bill of 1866, passed in view of the Thirteenth Amendment, before the Fourteenth was adopted, undertook to wipe out these burdens and disabilities, the necessary incidents of slavery, constituting its substance and visible form; and to secure to all citizens . . . the same right to make and enforce contracts, to sue, be parties, give evidence, and to inherit, purchase, lease, sell and convey property, as is enjoyed by white citizens. Whether this legislation was fully authorized by the Thirteenth Amendment alone, without the support which it afterward received from the Fourteenth Amendment, after the adoption of which it was re-enacted with some additions, it is not necessary to inquire." Civil Rights Cases, 109 U. S. 3, 22 (1883). The Civil Rights bill was upheld in the circuit court in two cases, United States *v.* Rhodes (1866), and Matter of Turner (1867). See

the purpose of the amendment was to abolish slavery as it had existed at the south.

Though Congress had its way and the act became law, its constitutionality was doubtful—at least Congress or the courts might at a later time so consider it. Prudence therefore indicated the need of a constitutional amendment embodying the principle of the act, and also various other matters of immense importance to the purposes of the Radical leaders: the sanctity of the public debt, assurance that the Confederate debt would not be assumed or paid, the degree of participation in the government by late "rebels", and, more important than everything else in the minds of eager partisans and philanthropists, negro suffrage, or some way of avoiding the danger that by the increase of southern representation the hold of the Republican party upon the government would be lost and the results of war in part destroyed. Not until June 13, 1866, was the fourteenth amendment passed and submitted to the states for ratification. How affirmative action was obtained in some of the states we shall consider later in connection with the congressional plans for Reconstruction.

Only gradually in the decades after adoption did the full implications and the full consequences of the fourteenth amendment appear, but such consequences and implications were of great importance. No other portion of the Constitution has been the basis of so much litigation, and few portions are of so much political and social consequence. An attempt will be made in later pages to disclose the truth of this assertion, but it is necessary now to examine the amendment without anticipating in any marked degree later interpretations. The first portion of the first section sweeps away the principle announced by Taney in the Dred Scott case, and sets forth briefly the fact of double citizenship.[24] The remaining portions of the first sec-

Abbott's Circuit Court Reports, referred to in White, *Trumbull*, p. 274 and note 2. Professor Burgess, whose opinion on constitutional matters always deserves great weight, considers the bill constitutional, though he has some misgivings about the portion authorizing the President to use military authority. He defends the act as within the province of the thirteenth amendment, and on the ground that the states defeated in the war were no longer states. The terms of the amendment, which speaks of "involuntary servitude", are general enough to apply to more than negro slavery. "If Mexican peonage or the Chinese coolie labor system shall develop slavery of the Mexican or Chinese race within our territory, this amendment may safely be trusted to make it void." Slaughter-House Cases, 16 Wallace 36, 72 (1873). See also Clyatt v. United States, 197 U. S. 207 (1905), upholding a congressional statute against peonage; and Bailey v. Alabama, 219 U. S. 219 (1911).

24 "All persons born or naturalized in the United States, and subject to the jurisdiction thereof, are citizens of the United States and of the State wherein they reside."

tion [25] were quite obviously intended to make illegal henceforth all such acts as those of the southern states denying equality of the races in the possession of civil rights. But the words used were of general rather than only particular application. One profoundly important fact is plain: these clauses of the fourteenth amendment—the only portion really important and of lasting influence—vividly mark the development of the very idea of nationalism in the eighty years after the meeting of the fathers at Philadelphia. The states, and they alone, from the beginning of the government until the ratification of this amendment, were the guardians of the personal liberty of their citizens, and they were free to decide for themselves the extent and character of that liberty. It is true the federal Constitution had placed a few explicit prohibitions upon the authority of the states in dealing with their own citizens, but nothing could have seemed more visionary in 1788 than to dream of charging the national government with defense of personal liberty against encroachment by the states. The fourteenth amendment called upon the central government to protect the citizens of a state against the state itself.

Though the terms of the second section of the amendment were general and did not have reference to negro suffrage alone, the negro vote was then, of course, the chief matter of concern. The purpose of the section was to compel the south to grasp one horn or the other of an embarrassing dilemma: a state might give votes to the negroes, or it might refuse to do so and, in consequence, lose representation in Congress. The alternative prescribed did not satisfy the more eager advocates of negro suffrage, but it did seem to save the Republicans from a flood of southern opponents in Congress. The amazing thing, however, is the slight attention given by the advocates of this amendment to the question of how this section on representation could be made effective.[26] Experience of the coming years presented practically insuperable obstacles to its enforcement. Why, it may be asked, did not the amendment base representation on the actual number of voters? Such a provision might have been enforceable, but the difficulty of determining how many persons were excluded by state action limiting the suffrage is fairly evident. There were several reasons for not making

[25] "No State shall make or enforce any law which shall abridge the privileges or immunities of citizens of the United States; nor shall any State deprive any person of life, liberty, or property, without due process of law, nor deny to any person within its jurisdiction the equal protection of the laws."

[26] See A. C. McLaughlin, "Mississippi and the Negro Question," *Atlantic Monthly,* LXX, p. 828 ff.

voting numbers the basis of representation: one was that it would affect in some degree the representation of the northern states, for the act was not applicable to the south alone; moreover, representation from the beginning of the government had been based on population, not on voters.[27] While the amendment established a new basis of representation, it did not take from the states the primary right to decide upon qualifications for the suffrage.

Of the latter portions of the amendment, little need be said, although at the time a great deal was said. The subject of the third section gave to the debaters in Congress opportunity for fervid and flamboyant declamation, the kind of oratory later known as "waving the bloody shirt". By this third section no person who, having held office under any state or the United States, had taken the oath to support the Constitution and had thereafter engaged in rebellion, could become a member of Congress or hold any office in either the state or the national government. A two-thirds vote of Congress might remove such disability. The most serious consequence of this section of the amendment was the exclusion from state office of men who by experience and by training were or might be most fit to lead. The fourth section, declaring the validity of the public debt and the illegality of the Confederate debt, indicates, once again, the fear or the pretended fear lest the southerners and their northern allies should get control of the government and saddle the southern debt upon the national treasury—a danger which was made much of by the Radical politicians.

An extensive and able report from the committee on Reconstruction was submitted a few days after the amendment was passed by Congress and submitted to the states. It of course declared the reestablishment of the southern states in their constitutional relations to be the duty of Congress and not of the executive. It declared there was no necessity for discussing a "profitless abstraction" and deciding whether or not the states were still states of the union. But it announced the necessity of requiring adequate security "for future peace and safety", and this implied the adoption of the fourteenth amendment. The report did not in so many words declare the necessity of adoption by the southern states before their restoration; that course

[27] If all negroes are by law excluded from the ballot-box, then a census may be conclusive evidence of how many persons are excluded. And there were in later years one or two proposals to gather such evidence. But private citizens might by force prevent negroes from voting, and such action would not subject the state to a loss of representation.

was, however, ultimately followed by Congress.[28] Tennessee ratified the amendment speedily and was admitted into the union. Had Tennessee been long excluded, the medley of constitutional theories would have reached beyond the ridiculous into the sublime, for the President was a citizen of that state. Johnson, in signing the bill for the admission of Tennessee (July 24, 1866), recurred to his former argument; he declared that his signature did not constitute an "acknowledgment of the right of Congress to pass laws preliminary to the admission of duly qualified Representatives from any of the States."

In the spring and summer of 1866 Johnson was plainly losing support in some quarters and gaining in others. After his unfortunate speech on Washington's birthday, many of those who had been acquiescent or had been inclined to give active support, because they longed for peace and were hoping for a speedy reconciliation with the south, began to drift away. In earlier months he had the confidence of former members of the old Democracy who had actively coöperated with the Republican party, which for obvious reasons had adopted the name of National Union party in 1864. He probably continued to retain a considerable portion of that element. Before the summer was well along, he was plainly winning adherents not only in the south, where naturally his stand was applauded, but also from the northern Democrats, the still vigorous supporters of the old party. But, as we have already said, every step taken in his direction by the Democrats endangered his cause and strengthened the hands of the Radicals, who were determined to arouse the combative spirit of the north. Disorder in certain regions of the south, made the most of by Republican politicians and newspapers, aggravated northern suspicion.

And yet, however much we of this generation may lament the violence and the animosities begotten by the policies of that day, it need not be taken for granted that under any circumstances the northern people would have quietly looked on while southern leaders took their places in Congress. It was not altogether pleasant to contemplate the possible ascendancy of the opponents with whom they had been waging a frightful conflict. In a perfect world, there might

---

[28] See act of March 2, 1867. McPherson, *Political History of Reconstruction*, pp. 191-192. The propriety of making adoption by the secession states a condition of restoration is of course debatable—as indeed which one of the many things done is not debatable? If the states as such were not in possession of their powers, if they had lost their status in the union, why not obtain amendment by the existing loyal states and then restore the secession states, which would at that time come in under the Constitution as amended and be bound by it?

have been placid acquiescence; there would have been no rancor; but in a perfect world there would have been no slavery, no war, no heart-burnings and bitterness, which are the deplorable but inevitable products of war.

If there was any well-grounded doubt of Radical success and the downfall of Johnson's policy, he made those results certain by his "swing around the circle". He went to Chicago, where there were ceremonies attending the dedication of a monument to Douglas, and he spoke at various other places. On such occasions the old campaigner was at his worst; like an old war-horse, he was sniffing the fray. He felt as of yore, when he was battling a crowd of heckling parti-sans in the backwoods of Tennessee.[29] The results were disastrous. His speeches, at times undignified and unbecoming, made converts by the thousand to the cause of the Radicals in Congress. It was all pitiable, for beneath the surface of rude and improper speech was in reality a plea for forgiving the vanquished and mistaken south. But he did not see the practical impossibility of cementing the union by his own method, at his own word, and at his own chosen time, or how needless it was to speak of admitting at once to Congress men who had been prominent in the war against the Constitution.

The autumn election of 1866 was a critical one in American his-tory. The supporters of the Radical policy were victorious; hence-forth there would be no dallying with the President's plans; with as-surance of popular support the policy of "thorough" could now be indulged to the full. In the next Congress, which would meet for its first regular session in December, 1867, the Republicans were assured of an overwhelming majority. The Radical leaders now assumed their possession of a popular mandate to work their will.

[29] Referring to Seward, who had been wounded on the night when Lincoln was assassinated, he said, "I would exhibit the bloody garments, saturated with gore from his gushing wounds. Then I would ask you, Why not hang Thad. Stevens and Wendell Phillips? I tell you, my countrymen, I have been fighting the South, and they have been whipped and crushed, and they acknowledge their defeat and accept the terms of the Constitution; and now, as I go around the circle, having fought traitors at the South, I am prepared to fight traitors at the North." McPherson, *Political History of Reconstruction*, p. 135. Some of the speeches are to be found in McPherson; see also, Oberholtzer, *op. cit.*, I, p. 395 ff. Rhodes, *History of the United States*, V, p. 617 ff., is valuable.

CHAPTER XLVI

RECONSTRUCTION

II: CONGRESS HAS ITS WAY; IMPEACHMENT

Johnson's annual message of December (1866) was restrained. but it dwelt on the theme now utterly distasteful to Congress. That body was not to be won over. The day for such hope was past. A bill granting negro suffrage in the District of Columbia was vetoed by the President and immediately passed over the veto (January 8, 1867). A bill establishing negro suffrage in the territories became a law without the President's signature. The hands on the dial were moving steadily toward the enfranchisement of the black man everywhere. The Republicans, desiring the addition of congressmen from states which would support the party's policies and adopt the fourteenth amendment, passed a bill admitting Colorado, but it was vetoed. A similar measure for admitting Nebraska met presidential disapproval, but was passed over his veto. In each bill admission was made conditional upon the acceptance of negro suffrage. Rejection of the fourteenth amendment by the southern states, except of course Tennessee, simply added to the zeal of the Radicals now firmly intrenched in power.

The congressional leaders had by this time reason for being solicitous, not only concerning the President, but concerning the Supreme Court, which, if not submissive, might cause serious trouble. The Milligan case (1866), to which reference has already been made, declaring the illegality of military tribunals for the trial and punishment of civilians when the civil courts were open, might indicate a readiness of the Court to support the President. It made plain that henceforth the north at least was not to be treated as a theater of war. And what of the south? If the doctrine of the case were given full effect, it appeared to endanger plans for keeping the southern states under military control until the congressional will was complied with. But the worst fears of judicial interference with Reconstruction proved unfounded.

Several cases of importance came before the Supreme Court, two of them to test the validity of congressional Reconstruction: Mississippi *v.* Johnson,[1] and Georgia *v.* Stanton.[2] In both cases the Court refused to take jurisdiction. In the first case, the Court declared it had no jurisdiction to entertain a bill to enjoin the President in the performance of his official acts.[3] In the second, the Court said a bill seeking to restrain the Secretary of War and generals acting under him called for the judgment of the Court upon political questions and did not therefore present a case within the proper cognizance of the Court.[4] A state test oath of Missouri, which was intended to keep ex-Confederates and their sympathizers from the exercise of certain professions, was declared by the Court to be an *ex post facto* law;[5] and a federal provision of somewhat similar character was likewise pronounced invalid.[6]

The contemptuous method by which Thad Stevens and his coadjutors now worked their will justified in a measure the charge that

[1] 4 Wallace 475 (1867).

[2] 6 Wallace 50 (1867).

[3] "It will hardly be contended that Congress [the Court] can interpose, in any case, to restrain the enactment of an unconstitutional law; and yet how can the right to judicial interposition to prevent such an enactment . . . be distinguished, in principle, from the right to such interposition against the execution of such a law by the President? . . . Neither can be restrained in its action by the judicial department; though the acts of both, when performed, are, in proper cases, subject to its cognizance." 4 Wallace 475, 500. We should notice that the general principle remains, that, unless the act complained of is distinctly political, the agents of the President may be held responsible for unconstitutional and hence illegal acts. See Little *v.* Barreme, 2 Cranch 170 (1804). "But when he [the president] exceeds his authority, or usurps that which belongs to one of the other departments, his orders, commands, or warrants protect no one, and his agents become personally responsible for their acts. The check of the courts, therefore, consists in their ability to keep the Executive within the sphere of his authority by refusing to give the sanction of law to whatever he may do beyond it, and by holding the agents and instruments of his unlawful action to strict accountability." T. M. Cooley, *The General Principles of Constitutional Law* (4th ed.), p. 203.

[4] Pointing out the argument that the matters in controversy were political and therefore not judicial, the Court said: "This distinction results from the organization of the government into the three great departments . . . and from the assignment and limitation of the powers of each by the Constitution." 6 Wallace 50, 71. Cf. Luther *v.* Borden, 7 Howard 1 (1849), where Taney laid down the principle: "Much of the argument on the part of the plaintiff turned upon political rights and political questions, upon which the court has been urged to express an opinion. We decline doing so." In this connection Kendall *v.* United States, 12 Peters 524 (1838), is of interest, where the Court held that the Postmaster-General, being charged with a purely ministerial duty, could be ordered to perform it.

[5] Cummings *v.* Missouri, 4 Wallace 277 (1867).

[6] Ex parte Garland, 4 Wallace 333 (1867).

the government was in the hands of an "irresponsible . . . directory". Before the end of the thirty-ninth Congress (March 4, 1867) three especially important measures were passed: the Army Appropriation bill, the Tenure of Office Act, and a Reconstruction Act. Particularly obnoxious to any theory of constitutional regularity was a provision of the Army Appropriation bill, which sought to restrict the power of the President as commander-in-chief and directed that the militia in several southern states should not be called into service without the authority of Congress. At least portions of this extraordinary act appear to have been actually dictated by Stanton, Johnson's Secretary of War, who from his seat in the cabinet was prepared to watch the President and protect the interests of the excited and unrelenting coterie in command at the capitol.[7] By the Tenure of Office Act, the President's power to remove officials from office was greatly restricted, and he was thus deprived of the authority to compel obedience to his will. The nature and effect of the act will be discussed in later pages.

The Reconstruction measure, which we shall now consider, not only nullified the President's plans but ignored the decision of the Supreme Court concerning the illegality of military commissions. By this measure Congress put military Reconstruction into operation. If the "rebels" would not behave of their own accord, the federal troops would be on hand to suppress disorder. Five military districts were established; it was made the duty of the President to assign to the command of each district a general of the army with sufficient troops to enforce his authority. The duty of this officer was to protect all persons and their property, to suppress disorder, and, if in his judg-

[7] Though he sent a message of protest, Johnson, not to defeat the appropriation, signed the bill. It provided that all orders and instructions relating to military operations should be issued through the General of the Army; that the General should not be removed or assigned to command elsewhere than at Washington, except at his own request, without the previous approval of the Senate (!). It was necessary, it seems, to have General Grant at Washington, lest the President should misbehave. Johnson, in protest, said the bill virtually deprived the President of his functions as commander-in-chief, and that it denied to the states mentioned the constitutional right to protect themselves in any emergency by means of their own militia. In the former of these two charges, and perhaps in both, his position was unquestionably sound. Johnson's message is in McPherson, *op. cit.*, p. 178. Dunning says Stanton was the source of the legislation obliging the President as commander-in-chief to consult the Senate before issuing certain orders to his subordinate. Dunning speaks of Stanton's "amazing record of duplicity". See Dunning, *Reconstruction,* p. 91, and G. S. Boutwell, *Reminiscences,* II, pp. 107-108.

ment it be necessary, to organize military commissions for the trial and punishment of offenders, with the special provision that no sentence of death be carried into effect without the President's approval.

Though these provisions were a deliberate establishment of military rule, they were thought by Congress to be justified because of disorders in the southern states. The main purpose of the act was to make certain the adoption of the fourteenth amendment and the acceptance of negro suffrage in the south. To this end, elaborate and explicit provision was made in the fifth section. It provided that the previous sections should be inoperative and the states should be admitted to representation when certain things were done: in each state a convention must be chosen and a new constitution framed and ratified by the people; in selecting delegates and in passing upon the constitution submitted, all males twenty-one years of age or older, of "whatever race, color, or previous condition," except such as were disfranchised because they participated in rebellion or were felons at common law, should have the right to vote; and the same basis of suffrage must be laid down in the constitution. But it was specially provided that no person excluded from the privilege of holding office by the proposed amendment should be entitled to vote for members of the convention or be a member of the convention. The constitution, if adopted, must be submitted to Congress, and the fourteenth amendment must be passed by the legislature of each state. This, however, was not all; for not until the amendment had become part of the federal Constitution was the state to be allowed full representation in Congress and the act of Reconstruction to be no longer in force. To make assurance doubly sure, two supplementary acts were passed within a brief time after the passage of the main measure. The first one (March 23, 1867) contained numerous provisions regulating elections and increasing the power of the commanding general of each district. By this method the southern states were to be compelled not only to adopt the amendment but to grant suffrage to the negroes; in other words, though the amendment left to the states the choice of extending the suffrage or, on the other hand, of having representation cut down, the Reconstruction Act forced the adoption of negro suffrage upon the southern states. The act, together with the two supplemental measures, embodied the main principles by which the Reconstruction process was accomplished: the overthrow of the state governments organized under proclamations of the President; the establishment of military government; and congressional determination of the qualifications of voters.[8]

Johnson, helpless, and in the eyes of northern enthusiasts hopelessly discredited, could nevertheless still indulge in powerful if unavailing argument. His message (largely the work of Jeremiah S. Black) vetoing the Reconstruction Act was able and vigorous.[9] "I submit to Congress", the message said, "whether this measure is not in its whole character, scope, and object without precedent and without authority, in palpable conflict with the plainest provisions of the Constitution, and utterly destructive to those great principles of liberty and humanity for which our ancestors on both sides of the Atlantic have shed so much blood and expended so much treasure." It is hardly worth our while to pass upon the constitutionality of this method of Reconstruction; it seems almost a trivial task, because so much more was involved than any question of technical regularity. Congress was determined to force the south to adopt negro suffrage; if anyone can find constitutional justification, that will not help him much in an attempt to find ethical or political justification. No historian now fails to lament the spirit of implacable rancor underlying much of the congressional procedure; and this rancor overtops any question of technical constitutional authority, for it left behind it a sense of bitter injustice which persisted for decades; it postponed the cementing of the real spirit of social union and harmony between the sections.

Conditions and events during the summer of 1867 must be briefly if inadequately summarized: (1) the President issued (September 7) a new and fairly comprehensive proclamation extending pardon, with a few general exceptions, to all persons who had directly or indirectly participated in the rebellion; much as the congressional "directory" might chafe and fume, the President could not be stripped of his pardoning power. (2) The military held sway in the southern states. The officers were faced with great perplexities, especially in deciding how much recognition should be given to the civil authorities and to what extent in ordinary civil and criminal matters state laws should prevail. On the whole, the officers must be credited with commendable restraint, in the light of their great authority which might have been grossly abused.[10] (3) The southern states, under military

---

[8] Cf. Dunning, *Essays*, p. 126.

[9] W. A. Dunning, "More Light on Andrew Johnson," *Am. Hist. Rev.*, XI, p. 585.

[10] Dunning, who certainly holds no brief for the congressional policy of "thorough", says, "It would be hard to deny that. so far as the ordinary civil administration was

supervision, were moving slowly toward the fulfillment of conditions entitling them to reinstatement, while the more respectable whites as a rule were hesitating or refusing to drink the bitter draught that was held out to them. (4) Congressional leaders, now in a state more like hysteria than anything else, were eyeing Johnson with hostility and unending suspicion. They had already been planning impeachment; and they must have been grievously disappointed by the President's failure to resist the Reconstruction Act and thus to make himself guilty of palpable disregard of law. Unremitting watchfulness might still detect in his conduct some ground for the last and conclusive assault.

The President's messages, able and courageous as they were, sometimes were couched in unnecessarily vigorous terms. The annual message of December, 1867, contained at least one unfortunate passage, for the eager watchers were ready to make use of every misstep and to put the worst construction upon his every word. By the beginning of December a dignified protest would have been sufficient; he could make no impression; and he had carried out the measures that had been passed over his veto, or had allowed them to be carried out. Having said that a faithful magistrate would concede much to honest error and not adopt forcible means of opposition, he proceeded in his message to say: "It is true that cases may occur in which the Executive would be compelled to stand on its rights, and maintain them regardless of all consequences. If Congress should pass an act which is not only in palpable conflict with the Constitution, but will certainly, if carried out, produce immediate and irreparable injury to the organic structure of the Government, and if there be neither judicial remedy for the wrongs it inflicts nor power in the people to protect themselves without the official aid of their elected defender—if, for instance, the legislative department should pass an act even through all the forms of law to abolish a coordinate department of the Government—in such a case the President must take the high responsibilities of his office and save the life of the nation at all hazards." He believed the Reconstruction acts, though plainly unconstitutional, not to be of such a character as to justify his using "the high responsibilities of

concerned, the rule of the generals was as just and efficient as it was far-reaching." "Yet equity and sound judgment are sufficiently discernible in their conduct of civil affairs to afford a basis for the view that military government, pure and simple, unaccompanied by the measures for the institution of negro suffrage, might have proved for a time a useful aid to social readjustment in the South, as preliminary to the final solution of political problems." *Essays*, pp. 174-175.

his office". Why, then, did he utter a theoretical assertion, even if it were sound doctrine? Was he threatening to resist forcibly impeachment and removal? If impeachment were successful, it would bring into the presidential office Ben Wade of Ohio, the president *pro tem* of the Senate, one of the crew who were determined to handle the ship; it would come near to the establishment of Congress on the throne. This passage in the message was undoubtedly connected with Johnson's fixed intention, not to resist orderly impeachment, but to oppose any attempt to suspend him, and also to oppose any unconstitutional assaults upon the presidency as a coördinate branch of the government.[11]

Efforts to impeach the President had begun early in the year (1867), but for a time the movement did not meet with success. The diligence of the committee, seeking acts and words that would condemn the culprit, beggars description; the very effort to describe it is humiliating and distasteful.[12] Judged by the precepts of plain common sense, the whole project was as foolish as it proved to be futile. A resolution to impeach was defeated in December, and it looked as if the crisis were passed. But not so. No policy of "thorough" is abandoned until it is finished. Johnson had now only a little over a year to serve; if the ignominy of removal was to be put upon him, there was need for haste. His difficulties in dealing with Stanton, the War Secretary, gave the anxious patriots a chance to win.

We must now return to the Tenure of Office Act passed the preceding March, for upon that act depended in large measure the hopes of those determined upon Johnson's dismissal from office. The act provided in its first and crucial section that "every person holding any civil office to which he has been appointed by and with the advice and consent of the Senate . . . is, and shall be, entitled to hold such office until a successor shall have been in like manner appointed and duly qualified, except as herein otherwise provided: *Provided,* That the

[11] For discussion in the cabinet, see Welles, *Diary,* III, pp. 237-238; Dunning, "More Light on Andrew Johnson," *loc. cit.,* pp. 589-591. Grant was at that time a member of the cabinet. Johnson had polled the cabinet, and Dunning says that it appears "not unlikely that one leading motive in Johnson's project to poll the cabinet was to secure a formal committal of General Grant to the policy of resistance in case an attempt should be made by the radicals to depose the President." The message and the cabinet paper were drafted by Black. *Ibid.,* p. 592.

[12] The nature of the attack may be illustrated by a few words of J. M. Ashley, who asserted that Johnson had come into office "through the door of assassination", was guilty of black and infamous crimes, and was a "loathing [loathsome?] incubus".

Secretaries of State, of the Treasury, of War, of the Navy, and of the Interior, the Postmaster General, and the Attorney General shall hold their offices respectively for and during the term of the President by whom they may have been appointed, and for one month thereafter, subject to removal by and with the advice and consent of the Senate." By the terms of the act the President might, during a recess of the Senate, suspend any officer (except judges) whom he deemed guilty of misconduct or to be incapable, and he might designate another person to perform temporarily the duties of the suspended officer until the next meeting of the Senate and until the Senate acted upon the matter. In case of such suspension the President was to make, within twenty days after the next meeting of the Senate, a report to the Senate, giving the evidence and reasons for his action. If the Senate should not concur, the officer removed must be reinstated. Any person accepting any office or attempting to exercise its powers, contrary to the provisions of the act, should be deemed guilty of a high misdemeanor punishable by fine or imprisonment or both.

This famous act, it is needless to say, ran counter to the practices of the government from the beginning. Constitutional authority for its passage need not here receive long discussion. Possibly it is safe to say that, had it not been for the history of the preceding eighty years and the development of the presidential office during that time, the constitutionality of the act might be open to serious debate; or, let us say, as a purely theoretical problem the authority of the Senate to agree or not agree to removals might be considered defensible, particularly in cases where the act establishing the office provided for the Senate's consent.[13] But history, if not inexorable logic, was arrayed against Congress.

Of chief importance were the express mention of cabinet officers and the words used in the act concerning their terms of office. When the measure was before Congress, the two houses had differed, one from the other, concerning the propriety of taking from the President the power to remove his cabinet members; the result of the controversy was the adoption of the compromise which appears in the proviso quoted in the preceding paragraph. But the compromise, pos-

---

[13] For an argument to the effect that, under some circumstances, an official may not be legally removed from office without the Senate's consent, see especially the dissenting opinion of Justice Holmes in the case of Myers v. U. S., 272 U. S. 52 (1926). The majority of the Court sustained the presidential authority to remove. See the discussion in a preceding chapter of the present volume in regard to Jackson's removal of Duane.

sibly intentionally obscure, does not readily reveal its meaning, for even here we find removal dependent on the Senate's consent. Apparently, however, the clause might be so interpreted as to permit, without the Senate's consent, the removal of the cabinet members who had been appointed by Lincoln and were still in office [14]—an exceedingly important interpretation, as matters turned out.

The presidential veto of the Tenure of Office Act was vigorous and strong. The cabinet unanimously condemned the act. No one was more outspoken than Stanton. He was "very emphatic and seemed glad of an opportunity to be in accord with his colleagues." [15] Seward appears to have written the veto message, with Stanton's assistance.[16]

In midsummer, Johnson asked for Stanton's resignation and the Secretary refused to offer it; evidently by Sherman's definition he was no gentleman. The President then suspended him (August 12) and authorized General Grant to act as Secretary of War *ad interim*. Thereupon Stanton, though denying the right of the President to suspend him, turned over the office to Grant. Soon after the meeting of Congress in December, Johnson transmitted to the Senate his reasons for taking this action; he not only maintained his right on general principles to remove a cabinet officer, but assigned reasons for the suspension of Stanton. The sending of the message could possibly

[14] Some of the Senators persuaded themselves that the clause was unimportant and not worth a controversy. "I have no doubt", said Williams of Oregon, "that any Cabinet minister who has a particle of self respect . . . would decline to remain in the Cabinet after the President had signified to him that his presence was no longer needed." Hendricks, on the contrary, said, "The very person who ought to be turned out is the very person who will stay in. A gentleman, of course, would not." Sherman said the House conferees were "very tenacious" and that "the general purpose of the bill . . . ought not to be endangered by a dispute on a collateral question." "I think that no gentleman, no man with any sense of honor, would hold a position of Cabinet officer after his chief desired his removal. . . ." Sherman maintained that the provision did not apply "to the present President. The Senator [Doolittle] shows that himself, and argues truly that it would not prevent the present President from removing the Secretary of War, the Secretary of the Navy and the Secretary of State." Not all of the Senators at that time knew Stanton as they were to know him. See D. M. Dewitt, *The Impeachment and Trial of Andrew Johnson*, pp. 196-199.

[15] Welles, *Diary*, III, pp. 50-51. "Every member of my Cabinet advised me that the proposed law was unconstitutional. All spoke without doubt or reservation, but Mr. Stanton's condemnation of the law was the most elaborate and emphatic." Johnson's message to the Senate, December 12, 1867. Richardson, *Messages and Papers*, VI, p. 587.

[16] Dewitt, *op. cit.*, p. 203. Dunning says, ". . . it was brought out in the impeachment trial that Seward wrote it. . . ." Dunning, "More Light on Andrew Johnson," *loc. cit.*, XI, p. 583. As to Stanton's participation, see Welles, *Diary*, III, p. 54.

be considered an acknowledgment of the constitutionality and binding force of the Tenure of Office Act. When the Senate refused to concur in the suspension, Grant withdrew (January 14, 1868). Stanton once again assumed office, fully prepared to watch over the destinies of the republic. Some five weeks passed, and Johnson, having decided to test his power, ordered Stanton's removal from the secretaryship and authorized General Lorenzo Thomas to act as Secretary of War *ad interim* (February 21, 1868). Stanton refused to obey, and the Senate declared the President had no power to remove him and appoint another. Stanton continued on guard.

General Thomas, after demanding the office from Stanton, was arrested and released on bail. Excitement ran high. Johnson, on being informed by Thomas of the arrest, said, "Very well, that is the place I want it in—the courts." The question at issue received no judicial determination, however, for the Stanton attorneys did not ask for Thomas's imprisonment, but they consented to his discharge; and thus vanished the opportunity to obtain judicial decision on the constitutionality of the Tenure of Office Act.[17]

Unable longer to endure the contumacious man in the White House, the war gods in Congress were now prepared to strike. A resolution of impeachment passed the House, February 24, 1868, and in the early days of March eleven articles of impeachment were adopted.[18] The first eight articles, with formidable prolixity, charged the President with various high crimes and misdemeanors, especially with violating the Tenure of Office Act, but with other offenses also. The ninth article accused the President of unlawful conversation with a general of the army with intent to induce him to disregard and to violate the act which provided that military orders should issue only from the general of the army—an accusation which in the end proved to be trivial and of no consequence. Article ten, the work of the doughty Ben Butler, whose presence was to darken Republican counsels for some years to come, was a *potpourri* of the foolish things said by

[17] The story, a highly dramatic one, is told in *Trial of Andrew Johnson*, I, especially p. 427 ff. and p. 607 ff. The attorneys for Thomas "directed General Thomas to decline giving any bail for further appearance, and to surrender himself into custody, and announce to the judge that he was in custody, and then presented to the criminal court an application for a writ of *habeas corpus*. The counsel on the other side objected that General Thomas could not put himself into custody, and they did not desire that he should be detained in custody." The Thomas counsel, supposing that the Stanton counsel would not consent, then asked that Thomas be discharged, and he was discharged. *Ibid.*, I, p. 609.

[18] They are to be found in McPherson, *op. cit.*, pp. 266-270; *Trial*, I, pp. 6-10.

Johnson on various public occasions; these "utterances, declarations, threats, and harangues" were pronounced "peculiarly indecent . . . in the Chief Magistrate of the United States," bringing the presidential office "into contempt, ridicule, and disgrace. . . ." The eleventh article, coming from the hand of Stevens, charged Johnson with making various unconstitutional declarations and with attempting to prevent the execution of the Tenure of Office Act and other acts, all of these charges being so woven together as to serve as a blanket indictment.[19]

The charges as a whole appear now to be a decided anticlimax, almost amusing in fact, after all the flurry, the fervid declamation, and the extravagant denunciation in which Congress had indulged. For, unless the disregard of the Tenure of Office Act constituted an impeachable offense, nothing very tangible was set forth. The use of language shocking to Butler—and to far more sensitive souls—, however deplorable such language was (almost as bad indeed as things said by some of the President's accusers), could scarcely be deemed a constitutional misdemeanor; and while the contemptuous references to Congress were reprehensible and in the worst possible taste, they did not reach the stage of absolute illegality. Had the accusers been able to discover actual refusal of the President to carry out the Reconstruction measures, the attack would have had far greater force. On the whole, the refusal to obey the Tenure of Office Act and Johnson's unsuccessful plans to get possession of the office of the Secretary of War formed the burden of the serious charges against him.

The House managers conducting the case against the President were anxious not to countenance anything in the conduct of the trial which would distinctly imply that the Senate was sitting as a judicial tribunal and was bound by the principles of law and the rules of evidence commonly accepted and applied in courts of justice. The question early arose concerning the right of the Chief Justice to pass upon

---

[19] "It will be seen that all of these articles, except the tenth, charge violations either of the Constitution of the United States, of the tenure-of-office act, of the conspiracy act of 1861, of the military appropriation act of 1867, or the of the [sic] reconstruction act of March 2, 1867. The tenth article . . . does not charge a violation either of the Constitution of the United States or of any act of Congress. Five of these articles charge a violation of the Constitution. . . . Seven . . . charge violations of the tenure-of-office act. . . . Two of the articles charge a violation of the conspiracy act of 1861. . . . Two of them charge violations of the appropriation act of March 2, 1867. . . . One only charges a violation of the reconstruction act of March 2, 1867, and that is article eleven." Stanbery, in his address to the Senate, May 2, 1868. *Trial*, II, p. 363.

admissibility of evidence, and in fact whether he was only a presiding officer and in no proper sense a member of the trial body. The accusers of the President did not desire interference. The Senate decided that the "presiding officer" might rule on the admissibility of evidence and that the rule should stand unless there was objection, in which case the question should be passed on by the Senate itself. "We claim and respectfully insist," said Butler in the opening address for the House managers of the prosecution, "that this Tribunal has none of the attributes of a judicial Court as they are commonly received and understood. . . . We suggest, therefore, that we are in the presence of the Senate of the United States convened as a constitutional tribunal, to inquire into and determine whether Andrew Johnson, because of malversation in office, is longer fit to retain the office of President of the United States, or hereafter to hold any office of honor or profit. . . . You are a law unto yourselves, bound only by the natural principles of equity and justice, and that *salus populi suprema est lex.*" [20] According to this reasoning, senators could properly vote on political grounds and decree the removal of Johnson from office because they thought removal would be beneficial and salutary.

The House managers, in order to carry out the theory that the Senate was not sitting as a court and that the proceeding was not a "trial", commonly addressed the presiding officer as "Mr. President". The counsel for the President, on the other hand, attempted to guard and protect the judicial character of the tribunal and to repel the assumption that the Senate was merely a political body. "Mr. Chief Justice," said Benjamin R. Curtis, the distinguished Ex-Justice who had written the famous dissenting opinion in the Dred Scott case, "I am here to speak to the Senate of the United States sitting in its judicial capacity as a court of impeachment, presided over by the Chief Justice of the United States, for the trial of the President of the United States. This statement sufficiently characterizes what I have to say. Here party spirit, political schemes, foregone conclusions, outrageous biases can have no fit operation." This final sentence is sufficient to disclose the proper nature of the proceedings, and it makes clear also the objectionable character of the attack by the President's accusers. The lamentable and shameful fact is that the counsel for the defense found it necessary to make any such announcement. The House managers were intent upon defining an impeachable offense so broadly as to allow them to make charges of impropriety and abuse of discretion

[20] *Ibid.,* I, p. 90.

and not be compelled to show that the President had been guilty of a criminal act or even of distinct disobedience to positive law. "We define, therefore," Butler declared, "an impeachable high crime or misdemeanor to be one in its nature or consequences subversive of some fundamental or essential principle of government, or highly prejudicial to the public interest, and this may consist of a violation of the Constitution, of law, of an official oath, or of duty, by an act committed or omitted, or, without violating a positive law, by the abuse of discretionary powers from improper motives, or for any improper purpose." [21]

The charge of violating the Tenure of Office Act was debated at length. It was in fact the center of the trial; for the other accusations were too flimsy to be relied upon. Johnson's counsel asserted the President's authority to remove officials; they referred to the practices and precedents of preceding decades; they declared that the duty of seeing that laws are faithfully executed involved the duty of removing officials who, in the President's judgment, were not coöperating with him in that imperative obligation. [22]

But did the President have the constitutional authority to refuse obedience to the act? The act, said his accusers, had been passed and it was his duty to obey it; having refused obedience and having acted in open violation of the act, he was a lawbreaker and guilty of a high crime and misdemeanor. Johnson's counsel could not with safety rely openly and frankly on the President's right to disregard the law and treat it as unconstitutional and void; and Curtis, for the defense, announced a doctrine by which he hoped to avoid the difficulty. The President, he said, took no extreme ground: "When a law has been passed through the forms of legislation, either with his assent or without his assent, it is his duty to see that that law is faithfully executed so long as nothing is required of him but ministerial action. He is not to erect himself into a judicial court and decide that the law is unconstitutional, and that therefore he will not execute it; for, if that were done, manifestly there never could be a judicial decision. . . .

[21] *Trial,* I, p. 88. Italics of the original omitted. Before this time there had been five cases of impeachment, all but one of the accused officers being judges. Of one case the Senate had declined to take jurisdiction; in two instances the accused was acquitted. Judge Pickering had been convicted and removed from office, not for any indictable offense but for misconduct on the bench, and as a matter of fact, he was insane. Judge Humphreys was found guilty of serious acts favoring the cause of the Confederacy and was likewise removed (1862).

[22] See especially the final address of Henry Stanbery, *Trial,* II, p. 359 ff.

His idea of his duty is, that if a law is passed over his veto which he believes to be unconstitutional, and that law affects the interests of third persons, those whose interests are affected must take care of them, vindicate them, raise questions concerning them, if they should be so advised. . . .

"But when, senators, a question arises whether a particular law has cut off a power confided to him by the people, through the Constitution, and he alone can raise that question, and he alone can cause a judicial decision to come between the two branches of the government to say which of them is right, and after due deliberation, with the advice of those who are his proper advisers, he settles down firmly upon the opinion that such is the character of the law, it remains to be decided by you whether there is any violation of his duty when he takes the needful steps to raise that question and have it peacefully decided." [23]

This seems to be a practical solution of the problem; and certainly no more extreme position could have been wisely taken by the President's defenders. But it assumes that the Supreme Court is a final arbiter for settling disputes between departments of the government; it shows how far the authority and function of the Court had risen since the early days when courts assumed their right to refuse to respect a law which they deemed unconstitutional. To present an opinion differing from that of the learned Ex-Justice may be rare presumption; but the writer ventures to suggest that the President, in pure theory, can refuse to carry out any unconstitutional law; if, however, a court of impeachment finds the law valid, his refusal to enforce it properly subjects him to the penalty of removal from office. In such a case the Senate, and not the judiciary, is the court. [24] We may even raise the question whether the Senate, sitting as a constitutional tribunal, is technically bound by the decision of the Supreme Court concerning the validity of an act.

Much argument was used by the defense to show that it was at the

---

[23] *Ibid.,* I, p. 387.

[24] Burgess agrees with Curtis and appears to go even further in the way of denying the right of the President to refuse execution of a law: "He must execute the laws passed over his veto upon matters which in his opinion touch his executive prerogatives, just the same as upon all other matters. . . ." *Reconstruction and the Constitution,* p. 183. Curtis said that if after the President has taken competent and proper advice "he finds that he cannot allow the law to operate in the particular case without abandoning a power which he believes has been confided to him by the people, it is his solemn conviction that it is his duty to assert the power and obtain a judicial decision thereon."

best doubtful whether the Tenure of Office Act really protected Stanton in the possession of his office. Johnson, in his answer, declared that on full consideration he had reached the conclusion that the "case of the said Stanton and his tenure of office were not affected" by the act.[25] What was meant by the statement that the cabinet officers should "hold their offices respectively for and during the term of the President by whom they may have been appointed, and for one month thereafter"? Stanton had been appointed by Lincoln. The act might well appear to have for its purpose a recognition of the right of a president to choose his own cabinet and not be bound by the choice of his predecessor. Was Johnson filling Lincoln's term, and was he therefore obliged to retain Lincoln's cabinet, or did Lincoln's term end with his death? If Johnson had found the wrong exit from the obscurity of a perplexing passage, should he be convicted of a high crime or misdemeanor?

After weeks of argument and examination of witnesses, the trial came to an end. The first vote was taken on the eleventh article (May 16, 1868). There were fifty-four senators; thirty-six votes were needed to convict. The ballot showed thirty-five votes for conviction and nineteen for acquittal. Ten days later, the Senate voted on articles two and three; the former declared Johnson guilty of a high misdemeanor in violating the Tenure of Office Act; the latter charged him with a like offense in appointing Thomas Secretary of War *ad interim*. The votes on these articles resulted as before: nineteen senators again voted "not guilty". Whereupon the Senate "sitting as a court of impeachment" adjourned without day. Among the nineteen were seven Republicans, who, though not belonging to the most extreme faction, had been opposed to Johnson and his methods. To them must go the honor— it is now considered an honor—of acting with bravery, resisting public clamor, and facing ostracism and banishment from their party. They were Fessenden of Maine, Fowler of Tennessee, Grimes of Iowa, Henderson of Missouri, Ross of Kansas, Trumbull of Illinois, and Van Winkle of West Virginia. It seems hard indeed, and it marks the depths to which rank partisanship had sunk, that men like Fessenden and Trumbull, able and honest, whose services had been of inestimable value to their party and to the cause of the union, should have to suffer the slings and arrows of petty and ignorant abuse.

Upon the acquittal of Johnson, Stanton "relinquished charge of the War Department". The President nominated General Schofield "in

[25] Answer to Article 1. McPherson, *op. cit.*, p. 273.

place of Edwin M. Stanton, removed". The words quoted are significant of the purposeful tenacity of the two men. But Johnson had the victory. When Grant became President he recommended the total repeal of the Tenure of Office Act, and it was modified by Congress. In Cleveland's term it was finally and totally repealed.

The result of the trial is of great significance in constitutional history. Johnson could be found guilty of no direct violation of law. Stanton must now be adjudged guilty of gross impropriety and of holding office without constitutional authority; and, in light of his whole line of conduct, this is a mild and extra-merciful sentence of condemnation. Had Johnson been engaged in an attempt to seize the war office and order the army to resist Congress and the Reconstruction acts, Stanton's refusal to obey his superior might have been morally justifiable, whether or not it was technically legal; but as he had been closely associated with the President for years, he must have known that to charge Johnson with such purposes was preposterous. If the impeachment had been successful, the result might have been accepted as a precedent of momentous influence on our constitutional system. "Once set the example", said Trumbull, in giving the reasons for his vote, "of impeaching a President for what, when the excitement of the hour shall have subsided, will be regarded as insufficient cause, and no future President will be safe who happens to differ with a majority of the House and two thirds of the Senate on any measure deemed by them important, particularly if of a political character." The trial stands to-day as the most regrettable and shameful exhibition of personal spite and ruthless partisanship in American history.[26]

---

[26] It may be appropriate to quote a few words of Butler's opening address as illustrative of the spirit and the acrimony of the day. He quoted the foolish things which the President had said in the "swing around the circle", and then declared: "We can say *this man* was not the choice of the people for the President of the United States. He was thrown to the surface by the whirlpool of civil war. . . . By murder most foul he succeeded to the Presidency, and is the elect of an assassin to that high office, and not of the people. . . . We can remove him—as we are about to do—from the office he has disgraced by the sure, safe, and constitutional method of impeachment. . . ." *Trial*, I, p. 119.

CHAPTER XLVII

RECONSTRUCTION

III: THE UNION RESTORED; CARPETBAGGERS AND FEDERAL TROOPS

During the summer and autumn of 1868, after the acquittal of the President, the process of Reconstruction—to give it an honorable name—went merrily on. The extremists in Congress were for a time in a very bad temper, but they had everything their own way. Stevens died in August, and for a considerable time Ben Butler stood forth as the conspicuous rebel-hunter in the House, a fact which seems to mark the low tide of congressional history.

The Reconstruction measures had been carefully prepared to make certain the predominance in the states of those persons who would support the congressional plan. In addition to the negroes, absolutely unfamiliar with political matters and most of them utterly uneducated, there were in the south some whites who were eager to take part in the joyous job of carrying out the congressional policy. Some of these men were northerners—the "carpetbaggers"—who had followed in the train of the union army or who after the war had drifted into the south in search of adventure and profit; some of them were by no means without brains and conscience, but there were many not thus encumbered. There were a few southern whites of intelligence and of practical political experience who took active part in constitution-making and appear to have been influential in keeping out of the constitutions some of the more foolish and extravagant proposals. The class most detested by the conservative elements was made up of "turncoat" whites who came to be known as "scalawags", men of southern birth, many of them without either the training or the character to fit them for official tasks. Though a few of the negroes were clever and shrewd, if not wise, and though there was here and there one capable and eloquent, the majority of the freedmen were, of course, ludicrously incompetent. The wonder is that the result of the conventions was not an absolute travesty of anything even masquerading as the work of statesmen; but, as a matter of fact, the constitutions, when framed, were not grotesque, unless a document is grotesque which bestows the suffrage on men of abysmal ignorance.

As the ruthless process of Reconstruction went on, a question arose (1868) which threatened seriously the congressional program. A certain William H. McCardle had been arrested by a military authority and held for trial before a military commission. Having sought release by a writ of habeas corpus, and having failed, he appealed to the Supreme Court. If the Court should adhere to the docrine of the Milligan case, it would in all likelihood announce the unconstitutionality of military tribunals in the south; at least the danger of such a decision was too great to be suffered calmly; and so, to prevent judicial interference with the congressional policy, a bill repealing certain portions of a previous act was passed, withdrawing from the Court the authority to entertain appeals of this sort. The bill was vetoed by Johnson; but the veto was of course futile, and the McCardle case was dismissed by the Court because of want of jurisdiction.[1] The episode is illustrative of the high-handed and arrogant determination of the Radical leaders, and is a conspicuous example of the way in which Congress, with an ample majority in control, may be able to override the other departments and can, if the emergency supply the incentive, cast into the waste-paper basket all inconvenient theories of checks and balances and similar uncomfortable doctrines.

June 22, 1868, a bill admitting Arkansas to representation in Congress was passed over the President's veto. When Congress began in 1865 to oppose Johnson's plans, it relied for its immediate power on its constitutional authority to pass upon the elections and qualifications of its own members; from that position it went forward to prescribe the whole process of Reconstruction. When it came now to the final steps, the recognition or the restoration of the reconstructed states, Congress did not entirely forget its first position. The Arkansas Act said that, as the people, in accordance with the acts of Congress, had adopted a constitution which was republican and the legislature had adopted the fourteenth amendment, the state was "entitled and admitted to representation in Congress, as one of the States of the Union. . . ." Although, as far as affirmative legislation is concerned, this declaration of admission to representation was the substance of the bill, it was nevertheless sent to the President, as if it were an act for the admission of a territory into the union; nothing more clearly exposes the abnormality of the whole process of Reconstruction con-

[1] Ex parte McCardle, 7 Wallace 506 (1869).

stitutionally considered. The Constitution, said Johnson in his veto message—probably not without a certain sardonic satisfaction—, "makes each House 'the judge of the elections, returns, and qualifications of its own members,' and therefore all that is now necessary to restore Arkansas in all its constitutional relations to the Government is a decision by each House upon the eligibility of those who, presenting their credentials, claim seats in the respective Houses of Congress." "If . . . Arkansas is a State in the Union," he also said, "no legislation is necessary to declare it entitled 'to representation in Congress as one of the States of the Union.' "

Arkansas was allowed representation in Congress "upon the following fundamental condition: That the constitution of Arkansas shall never be so amended or changed as to deprive any citizen or class of citizens of the United States of the right to vote who are entitled to vote by the constitution herein recognized". There were minor provisions not here important. Did this condition mean to imply the right or the intention of Congress to cast the state out of the union or to refuse admission of its elected representatives at any time in the future, if the basis of suffrage were altered? Such an intention seems scarcely possible; but if there was to be no penalty for disobedience to the "fundamental condition", the folly of prescribing it is apparent. Shortly after the restoration of Arkansas, the President announced that six other states had fulfilled the requirements prescribed by Congress—North Carolina, South Carolina, Georgia, Alabama, Florida, and Louisiana. New difficulties arose in Georgia, and, as a consequence, that state was not granted full representation until two years later. At this later time also (1870), the remaining states still lying beyond the pale were readmitted or restored—or whatever may be the proper word for describing the whole strange and abnormal process.

On July 20, 1868, Seward issued a preliminary statement declaring the fourteenth amendment had been adopted by twenty-three states. These states were unquestionably exercising their full functions in the union. It also appeared, the proclamation said, that the amendment had been ratified "by newly-constituted and newly-established bodies avowing themselves to be, and acting as, the legislatures, respectively, of the States of Arkansas, Florida, North Carolina, Louisiana, South Carolina, and Alabama. . . ." Two of the states, New Jersey and Ohio, enumerated among the twenty-three states mentioned above, had withdrawn their consent; it was a matter of doubt whether resolutions of withdrawal were valid or not. If the ratifying resolutions of these two states were, notwithstanding their subsequent resolutions of with-drawal, considered in full effect, then the amendment had been ratified by the requisite number.

There is no need of our allowing ourselves to be smothered by the fogs of Reconstruction metaphysics, but can a state, which is not a state and not recognized as such by Congress, perform the supreme duty of ratifying an amendment to the fundamental law? Or does a state—by congressional thinking—cease to be a state for some purposes, but not for others? If the states were no longer states but, as Stevens had asserted, conquered territory, were they competent to amend the Constitution as a *condition* to admission? Or, if they had committed suicide, and had become territories, were they still sufficiently alive to perform this solemn function of statehood? Congress had no qualms, but passed a resolution naming all of the six southern states as well as Ohio and New Jersey, declaring the fourteenth amendment a part of the Constitution, and ordering its promulgation by the Secretary of State. Formal pronouncement of ratification was made by Seward on July 28, 1868.

The action of the federal authorities in denying by direct implication the right of a state to rescind a favorable vote stands as a precedent, and probably is based on good legal grounds. The most substantial basis for asserting the illegality of withdrawal of approval is that, when a state has acted and officially announced its decision, the subject has passed out of its hands; for this particular job its duty is finished. There appears, however, to be reason for acknowledging a state's right to withdraw a vote rejecting an amendment and to substitute a vote of ratification.[2]

The fourteenth amendment and the "fundamental conditions" prescribed at the time of the readmission of the states were not enough to satisfy Congress; the southern whites, determined not to be ruled—if ruling it might be called—by the ignorant blacks and carpetbaggers, might find a way to avoid the conditions and spurn the imposed restrictions. Moreover, suffrage reform was in the air. Woman suffrage was discussed with a new intensity. Some zealots were anxious to go much further; there seemed, indeed, to be a belief occupying otherwise vacant space in many minds that the earth could be purified and

[2] See H. V. Ames, *The Proposed Amendments to the Constitution*, Am. Hist. Asso. *Report* for 1896, II, p. 300; T. M. Cooley, *The General Principles of Constitutional Law* (4th ed.), p. 257 and references there given. Oregon withdrew ratification even after promulgation of the amendment by the Secretary of State. Ames, *op. cit.*, p. 377.

regenerated, if only enough people were allowed to vote; if ignorant freedmen just relieved from bondage could be transformed into competent citizens, why was it not wise to bestow the blessings of the ballot upon everyone?[3] Even at the north there was difference of opinion on the advisability of granting negro suffrage. Some of the states had refused or neglected to alter their constitutional provisions; but Congress decided to act. A constitutional amendment, the fifteenth, was passed (February, 1869) and submitted to the states: "1. The right of citizens of the United States to vote shall not be denied or abridged by the United States or any State on account of race, color, or previous condition of servitude. 2. The Congress shall have power to enforce by appropriate legislation the provisions of this article." March 30, 1870, the Secretary of State announced the ratification of the amendment by twenty-nine states.[4] Three of the states listed as ratifying the amendment were not, in congressional theory, fully restored when they participated in the solemn task of amending the Constitution. The southern states might still keep the negro from voting, but not legally by any provision explicitly directed to that end. That the amendment has at any time been beneficial to the negro at the south may be doubted.

When most of the southern states were restored, conditions were laid down similar in most respects to the conditions prescribed for Arkansas, which we have already mentioned. These conditions were intended to fasten negro suffrage permanently on the reconstructed states; but the terms of the conditions were so sweeping and comprehensive, that, if enforced, they would prevent any and every alteration in the qualifications for voting. Though the fourteenth amendment allowed the states to decide what the basis of suffrage should be—subject to a contingent reduction of representation—the states thus restored were to be perpetually restrained from exercising that very right of determination. Amid all the unnecessary and intemperate measures passed during this dismal decade, no other measures seem so unnecessary or so absurd as these so-called conditions. If congress-

---

[3] The extent to which some enthusiasts were prepared to go is illustrated by an amendment championed by James Brooks of New York in 1869: "The right of any person of the United States to vote shall not be denied or abridged by the United States or any State by reason of his or her race, sex, nativity, or age when over twelve years [!], color or previous condition of slavery. . . ." *Ibid.*, pp. 237-238.

[4] New York, counted among the twenty-nine, repealed her ratification—the repeal being of doubtful validity; and Georgia, not as yet fully in possession of her rights in the union, accepted the amendment—a fact stated by the Secretary in a separate paragraph. The Secretary apparently counted the resolution of repeal as invalid.

men did not know they were both unjust and unconstitutional, their ignorance is not a very satisfactory excuse.

We should notice that the fifteenth amendment did not annul the second section of the fourteenth amendment. There still remained with the individual states the power to modify their suffrage laws, provided that no discrimination was made because of race, color, or previous condition of servitude. Some of the southern states at a later time prescribed qualifications for voting that were in conflict with the terms of the "fundamental conditions", but did not on their face run counter to the fifteenth amendment. No one, presumably, can doubt the right of the states to make such alterations in their suffrage laws. The constitution of Mississippi (1890, 1892), for example, provided that every elector must be able to read any section of the state constitution or he must be able to understand it, when read to him, or give a reasonable interpretation of it.[5] Though these qualifications are applicable to blacks and whites without discrimination, it may be easy enough in practice for election officers to discover the inability of a negro to interpret a passage in the constitution but to discover also remarkable sagacity and legal learning in a white man. However that may be, the effect of these provisions, if honestly and impartially applied, should remove ignorance from the ballot-box. As a consequence, the congressional representation in any state prescribing these qualifications can in theory probably be reduced,[6] if Congress can determine the actual basis for such a reduction. But the subject has been in oblivion for forty years.

No enactment that is obviously intended to avoid the restrictions of the fifteenth amendment can be considered valid. The attempt was made in certain states by inserting in their constitutions a provision commonly called the "grandfather clause", declaring that certain prescribed qualifications for voting should not apply to persons having the right to vote before a specified date or to the descendants of such persons. These provisions would result in admission to the polls of every person who was qualified to vote or whose ancestor was qualified

---

[5] See Williams v. Mississippi, 170 U. S. 213, 225 (1898), where the Court said that the constitution and the statutes of Mississippi do not on their face discriminate between the races, but intimated that "evil" in administration was possible under them. There still remains since the passage of the nineteenth amendment the right to prescribe qualifications for voting, provided there is no discrimination contrary to either the fifteenth amendment or the nineteenth amendment.

[6] Attention should be called to the argument to the effect that the requirement of a capitation tax or of the ability to read is not a denial of the suffrage. See Cooley, op. cit., p. 336.

to vote at a time before the establishment of negro suffrage; they would, therefore, subject negroes to qualifications and restrictions not applicable to many whites. Such enactments were plainly a subterfuge. In pronouncing a provision of the Oklahoma constitution to be unconstitutional, the Court declared its inability to "discover how, unless the prohibitions of the Fifteenth Amendment were considered, the slightest reason was afforded for basing the classification upon a period of time prior to the Fifteenth Amendment. Certainly it cannot be said that there was any peculiar necromancy in the time named which engendered attributes affecting the qualification to vote which would not exist at another and different period unless the Fifteenth Amendment was in view." [7]

After the failure of impeachment, Johnson, though ignored by the men who had sought his overthrow, had charge of his own cabinet, and some things he could do without suffering more than maledictions from his enemies. They might grumble, but he had the power to pardon and this power he exercised. On the fourth of July, 1868, in order to promote and procure complete fraternal reconstruction among the whole people, he issued a proclamation of amnesty, granting pardon to all who directly or indirectly had participated in rebellion, excepting such persons as might be under indictment. On Christmas day, he proclaimed full pardon, without reservation. This pardon could not relieve anyone from the disabilities laid down in the third section of the fourteenth amendment. At sundry times, in later years, Congress passed acts for partial removal of these disabilities, but not until 1898 were they entirely removed.

With the inauguration of Grant (1869), the Republicans were in control of the presidential office. But the election returns, though showing a large electoral majority, did not indicate the unwavering support of a solid north and unqualified readiness to approve the methods of Reconstruction. Out of a total popular vote of 5,716,082, Seymour, the Democratic candidate, received 2,703,249. Among the states casting Republican electoral votes were most of the southern states recently reconstructed. How these states would vote, when once the whites obtained full control, was fairly plain—the emergence of a "solid south", where the people would hold in memory the ignominy

[7] Guinn v. United States, 238 U. S. 347, 365 (1915). See also Myers v. Anderson, 238 U. S. 368 (1915), where a state statute was held void. A state statute excluding negroes from voting in Democratic party primaries was declared a violation of the equality clause of the fourteenth amendment. Nixon v. Herndon, 273 U. S. 536 (1927). See also Nixon v. Condon, 286 U. S. 73 (1932).

of a Reconstruction they detested. Moreover, New York, New Jersey, and Oregon were carried by Seymour, and the vote of Indiana, long to remain a doubtful state, was too close to be comfortable; Connecticut was carried by only 3,000, California by 500. How were the Republicans to be sure of subsequent success unless they held securely in their hands the vote of the reconstructed south? The newly-enfranchised negroes must be protected at the polls.

Unquestionably other matters—the deeds and misdeeds of the party—affected in one way or another the strength of the party in the next few years; the determination to pay the public debt, the preparation for resumption of specie payments, and to some extent the tariff policy strengthened the party's hold upon the country; but more helpful than all else was widespread loyalty to the party that had "saved the union". One of the interesting and significant changes which shows the nature of the party system as an instrument of government is the fact that the Republican party became the conservative party of the nation; it had begun its career in opposition to a powerful and entrenched economic system, slavery, which had its grasp upon interests even beyond the borders of the slave states; Republican policies of the early days were disturbing and productive of anxiety among those not wishing to see the waters of peace agitated. But it had become the natural home of competent and effective business men and men of affairs; a party changes even its character with the passing of time; it is deeply affected by its own successes.

In the years succeeding Grant's accession, it seemed to Republican leaders that the well-being of their party depended on what they termed a fair ballot, an honest count at the south, and an obedience in reality to the new amendments. The process of Reconstruction had antagonized those elements among the southern people who before the war had been most reluctant to break away, and who, perhaps because many of them had been Whigs, had political and social attitudes of mind which might possibly have prevented them from forming a solid block with their old-time political opponents.[8] But now all those wish-

[8] Benjamin H. Hill said in 1871: "I tell you frankly that after the war ended, we, the old whigs and the Union men, expected to take control of affairs down here; that was our expectation, and I think we would have done it if you had allowed us to do so. I will tell you candidly that I think very likely if the republican party had been . . . magnanimous to the old whigs after the war, in extending us privileges, . . . it might have built up a republican party in the South, and given us the control of this country." Quoted in Fleming, *Documentary History of Reconstruction*, II, p. 91.

ing to get possession of the state governments and wrest control from the carpetbaggers belonged to one party; all were Democrats. Probably under any other system of Reconstruction the same results would have followed.

The negro had been given the ballot, partly, no doubt, because of partisan zeal, but also because of a genuine idealism among a large portion of the northern people and because the suffrage provided the freedmen with means of protecting their new-found rights. The south could be ruled by bullets or by ballots, by the federal army or by votes; but to use the army permanently was only theoretically possible, and so Reconstruction was coupled with negro suffrage; ballots were chosen instead of bullets. One of the things difficult to understand is this apparent belief, held by plain citizens and shrewd politicians, that the southern whites would yield supinely to the magic of the ballot in the hands of black men, their former slaves. Hardly had the process of Reconstruction been ended or supposedly ended before it became obvious that voters must be protected by the army. These brief words sum up the history of Grant's administration (1869-1877) as far as that history deals with the south.

Such summing up omits details of stupid, extravagant, and venal state legislatures in the southern states. It omits tales of disorder, riots, and assassinations. It leaves out of consideration the determination of the southern whites not to be governed by ignorance and their determination to have a government and a social order directed and upheld by white men. This story has been often told; it is a sorry and doleful tale. It is a story of the unflinching decision of a competent people to get possession of their own institutions and to manage their own affairs; if this could not be attained except by violation of law, then the law must be violated; civilization, as the south considered civilization, must be made secure despite the cruel and disastrous legislation imposed upon the vanquished by victorious opponents. The fact is, the southerners felt a deep repugnance to negro domination and they did not enjoy being robbed of what substance had been left them; the best of them were not willing, as were many of their compatriots in northern cities, to accept with complacency that species of political banditry which was the humiliating characteristic of American municipal life. They never failed to proclaim undeviating objection to the "lapse of Caucasian civilization into African barbarism"; they denounced the attempt to degrade the Caucasian race and promote the African to authority. And if the south could in its turn be ruthless and vindictive, that is a fact which needs no explanation. The least we can do—and the most we can now do—is to lament the incapacity of those in political authority at Washington to find in conjunction with the best southern leaders a method of reform and restoration which would have helped to make the south politically, socially, and in sentiment an integrant part of an integral nation. Such a nation did not exist for a generation after Appomattox. And so, though the nation was no longer half slave and half free, it continued to be divided against itself.

It is not the historian's business, even when he is drawn into disapproval of a course pursued, to be confident that some other course would have been highly satisfactory in its effects. To a person standing at the forks of a road and questioning which of the two branches of the road he should follow, both routes may appear in most respects free from obstacles, and he chooses the route appearing to be the more convenient and reliable. After he has made his choice and obstacles impede his path, he is likely to think he should have taken the other road; as a matter of plain fact, however, the one road, the one taken, has actually disclosed its troublesome features; of the other he knows little if any more than he knew before he made his choice; its pains and its penalties cannot be known and can with no assurance be imagined. The study of history shows the troubles of a route really followed; it does not let us know what might have happened had the other way been taken. We are entitled, however, to speculate. We have the right to assume as a lesson for political conduct that an attitude of friendly and unvindictive interest in the welfare of others will provide its substantial reward.

Grant's administration began auspiciously. His inaugural address spoke earnestly of a desire to see the union fully restored and the prevalence of good feeling throughout the nation. His conciliatory proposals were helpful in bringing about the restoration of Virginia, Mississippi, and Texas. The troubles in Georgia were especially acute, and, as we have seen, that state, after much tribulation, was not readmitted until the midsummer of 1870. But on the whole there appeared ground for hope that the worst was over and that a new era of good feeling or at least a diminution of the existing suspicion and hostility was at hand. But stormy times were ahead. Conditions in the southern states, where the "carpetbag" governments were wasting the money of communities already impoverished by war, were becoming intolerable. The Loyal Leagues, which had been formed some years earlier to inculcate patriotism and to lead the freedmen in the paths they should follow and were now largely composed of negroes, gave enthusiastic if ignorant support to the "carpetbag" régime. Their processes were not always gentle. By 1869 or 1870, they had been beaten at their own game by the Ku Klux Klan, which stopped at nothing in its determination to crush the "scalawags" and the "carpet-baggers", and to put the negro "in his place".

With the purpose of protecting elections from violence, fraud, and intimidation, Congress passed two "enforcement acts" (May 31, 1870, February 28, 1871). These acts may properly be considered together.[9] They are elaborate and detailed, containing sundry provisions for the protection of the voter and the polls. The first includes a reënactment of the Civil Rights Act of 1866. Any brief discussion is rendered difficult by the complexity of the acts; no general and inclusive judgment is possible because portions were doubtless considered valid and others invalid. These acts were intended to rest upon the enforcement sections of the three amendments, the products of the war and Republican Reconstruction. In considering the question of constitutional validity, we must bear in mind that the construction of the war amendments was worked out only gradually by judicial decisions in the ensuing years. The general principles resulting from the controversies and laid down by the courts are of importance and of continuing interest; a word on that subject is appropriate in this place.

The first section of the fourteenth amendment had been drawn with the purpose of making the provisions of the Civil Rights Act of 1866 unquestionably valid; and that section was intended to protect all persons in the possession of civil rights and of equality under the law. The adoption of the fourteenth amendment did not, however, make the thirteenth entirely valueless and obsolete, for under that amendment the national government may proceed against actual slavery or involuntary servitude, even if unsupported by any state law;[10] but the mis-

---

[9] The acts may be found in Fleming, *Documentary History of Reconstruction*, II, p. 102 ff. "By act of February 8, 1871, a rigorous system of Federal supervision over congressional elections was established. This was designed not only to supplement the weakness and inefficiency of the radical state governments in the South, but also to counteract the fraudulent and violent practices which prevailed in New York and other large cities of the North." Dunning, *Reconstruction*, p. 186.

[10] "We entertain no doubt of the validity of this legislation [referring to federal acts against peonage], or of its applicability to the case of any person holding another in a state of peonage, and this whether there be municipal ordinance or state law sanctioning such holding. It operates directly on every citizen of the Republic, wherever his residence may be." Clyatt *v.* United States, 197 U. S. 207, 218 (1905). "Under the Thirteenth Amendment, the legislation, so far as necessary or proper to

deeds of individuals mentioned in the enforcement acts can scarcely be looked upon as establishing servitude in any proper or improper sense. And as far as these acts were directed against any "person" who should endeavor to deprive another of his civil rights, the legislation cannot be supported by the fourteenth amendment, as later decisions made perfectly plain.

Those sections of the enforcement acts, that were primarily directed against intimidation of voters and corruption at the polls, did not make proper distinction between elections at which representatives to Congress were chosen and those which were solely state elections; and there was no suitable recognition of the limits of congressional power under the fifteenth amendment. The general principles as later announced by the Court may be briefly summarized. Without regard to the war amendments, Congress has authority to legislate for order at the polls and for the sanctity of the ballot when representatives to Congress are chosen. This power has been based in part on the constitutional clause empowering Congress to make regulations concerning the times, places, and manner of holding elections; [11] but the reasoning of the Court points on the whole to the power and the duty of the national government to protect itself, and not merely to a power derived from any specific clause in the Constitution. "The government of the United States", the Court said, "is no less concerned in the transaction than the State government is. It certainly is not bound to stand by as a passive spectator, when duties are violated and outrageous

eradicate all forms and incidents of slavery and involuntary servitude, may be direct and primary, operating upon the acts of individuals, whether sanctioned by State legislation or not. . . ." Civil Rights Cases, 109 U. S. 3, 23 (1883). "The things denounced are slavery and involuntary servitude. . . . All understand by these terms a condition of enforced compulsory service. . . . A freeman has a right to be protected in his person from an assault and battery. He is entitled to hold his property safe from trespass or appropriation, but no personal assault or trespass or appropriation operates to reduce the individual to a condition of slavery." Hodges v. United States, 203 U. S. 1, 16-18 (1906). See also, for an interpretation of the scope of the amendment, Robertson v. Baldwin, 165 U. S. 275 (1897); Bailey v. Alabama, 219 U. S. 219 (1911).

[11] Art. I, sec. 4, par. 1. To take charge to any extent of an election for the choice of presidential electors, if representatives are not chosen at the same time, might in theory be doubted, except as such charge is possible under the fifteenth, and now the nineteenth, amendment. See McPherson v. Blacker, 146 U. S. 1, 35 (1892), where the Court said: "In short, the appointment and mode of appointment of electors belong exclusively to the States. . . . They are, as remarked by Mr. Justice Gray in *In re Green*, 134 U. S. 377, 379, 'no more officers or agents of the United States than are the members of the state legislatures when acting as electors of Federal senators. . . .' "

frauds are committed." The Court went so far as to say, "The objection that the laws and regulations, the violation of which is made punishable by the acts of Congress, are State laws and have not been adopted by Congress, is no sufficient answer to the power of Congress to impose punishment. . . . The imposition of punishment implies a prohibition of the act punished." [12] The fact that state officers are elected at the same time that federal representatives are chosen is no reason for holding federal legislation improper. But the national government has no right to regulate purely state elections, except as far as is appropriate for the enforcement of the fifteenth and nineteenth amendments.[13] And the enforcement justified by these amendments must be directed against state action, that is to say, action provided by state law or action performed by state officials under color of law; for the amendments refer not to individual conduct but place a specific restriction upon the United States and every state.[14]

In April, 1871, the Ku Klux Act was passed. Its purpose was to subdue the disorder in the south and to protect the freedmen from violence and intimidation. In some sections the conditions were intolerable; though the southern whites were prepared to overcome negro domination by any and every available method, the more sub-

[12] Ex parte Siebold, 100 U. S. 371, 388 (1880). Referring to various sections of the revised statutes, and especially to sections 5515 and 5522, the Court said, "These portions of the Revised Statutes are taken from the act commonly known as the Enforcement Act, approved May 31, 1870 . . . and from the supplement of that act, approved February 28, 1871. They relate to elections of members of the House of Representatives, and were an assertion, on the part of Congress, of a power to pass laws for regulating and superintending said elections, and for securing the purity thereof, and the rights of citizens to vote thereat peaceably and without molestation. It must be conceded to be a most important power, and of a fundamental character." *Ibid.,* 382. See also Ex parte Yarbrough, 110 U. S. 651 (1884) ; Wiley *v.* Sinkler, 179 U. S. 58 (1900).

[13] United States *v.* Reese, 92 U. S. 214 (1876) ; Karem *v.* United States, 121 Fed. Reporter 250 (1903) ; United States *v.* Belvin, 46 Fed. Reporter 381 (1891). The power of Congress to legislate at all upon the subject of voting at purely state elections is entirely dependent upon this amendment (fifteenth).

[14] "These authorities show that a statute which purports to punish purely individual action cannot be sustained as an appropriate exercise of the power conferred by the Fifteenth Amendment upon Congress to prevent action by the State through some one or more of its official representatives, and that an indictment which charges no discrimination on account of race, color or previous condition of servitude is likewise destitute of support by such amendment." James *v.* Bowman, 190 U. S. 127, 139 (1903). The amendment "relates solely to action by the United States or by any State and does not contemplate wrongful individual acts. While Congress has ample power in respect to elections of Representatives to Congress, § 5507 cannot be sustained under such general power because Congress did not act in the exercise of such power." *Ibid.* (syllabus).

stantial members of the southern communities were themselves troubled by the disorder.[15] A portion of the act, which doubtless was of supreme importance in the minds of the framers, made it an offense for two or more persons to conspire or go in disguise upon the public highway or upon the premises of another for the purpose of depriving any person or class of persons of the equal protection of the laws, or for the purpose of hindering the authorities of any state from securing to all persons the equal protection of the laws. This portion of the statute was an assumption of unconstitutional power.[16]

But the act also authorized the President to use the army and navy for the suppression of insurrection and domestic violence, and under certain circumstances to suspend the writ of habeas corpus. A method was thus provided for crushing the Ku Klux—but more than this: troops could be used and were used to uphold the carpetbag governments, which had entered upon a drama of extravagance and waste with scrupulous attention to every opportunity for private gain and public discredit. Constitutional or unconstitutional, the law had some considerable effect in checking violence, and the troops succeeded in

[15] Concerning the Ku Klux movement in general, Fleming says: "The first results of the movement were good; the later ones were both good and bad. The early work of the secret orders quieted the negroes, made life and property safer, gave protection to women, stopped burnings, forced the Radical leaders to be more moderate, made the negroes work better, drove the worst of the Radical leaders from the country and started the whites on the way to regain political supremacy. The evil results were those that always follow such movements. . . . The movement lasted under one form or another until the close of Reconstruction, and the lynching habits of today are due largely to conditions, social and legal, growing out of Reconstruction." Fleming, *op. cit.,* II, pp. 328-329. The movement was at its height in its most effective form from 1868 to 1870. *Ibid.,* p. 328. Rhodes calls attention to the fact that in South Carolina there were 1207 cases pending in 1872, and the next year 617. *History of the United States,* VI, p. 318. These numbers give us some idea of the extent of federal action.

[16] "Section 5519 [originally a part of section 2 of the Ku Klux Act of 1871], according to the theory of the prosecution, and as appears by its terms, was framed to protect from invasion by private persons, the equal privileges and immunities under the laws, of all persons and classes of persons. It requires no argument to show that such a law cannot be founded on a clause of the Constitution whose sole object is to protect from denial or abridgment, by the United States or States, on account of race, color, or previous condition of servitude, the right of citizens of the United States to vote." United States *v.* Harris, 106 U. S. 629, 637 (1883). It was asserted by the government in this case that the legislation in question found its warrant in the first and fifth sections of the fourteenth amendment, but the Court pointed out that such contention could not stand, and referred to United States *v.* Cruikshank, 92 U. S. 542 (1876) ; Virginia *v.* Rives, 100 U. S. 313 (1880). In the latter case the Court said, "The provisions of the Fourteenth Amendment . . . we have quoted all have reference to State action exclusively, and not to any action of private individuals." *Ibid.,* 318.

stamping out the more brutal activities and unpleasant enterprises of the Ku Klux.

Throughout the land political conditions in the early seventies presented a dreary picture. The war had left a legacy of corruption and venality. We cannot know, of course, whether the northern people had actually been so affected by bloodshed and by the hatred engendered by Reconstruction that they were no longer sensitive to abuses that should have aroused their anger and moved them to action. Some of them were too busy to be bothered by political corruption. They were engaged in industrial affairs, building railroads, entering on new phases of corporate enterprise. Thousands upon thousands of public-spirited and conscientious men were still certain that the course of Reconstruction had been just and honorable, that the negro must not be left to his fate at the hands of "rebels", and that right and duty pointed to the need for direction and control by the federal government; they believed that the public credit should be made secure and, in general, the country should be saved from disaster which they thought would be brought on by the machinations and incompetence of the Democracy. About the time when Congress was engaged in passing legislation for the crushing of the Klan and was also protecting the corrupt carpetbag governments in the south, New York City, in a spasm of civic righteousness, pounced upon Tweed, who had been gorged to capacity with ill-gotten gain.[17]

The platform of the Liberal Republican party in 1872 demanded the immediate and absolute removal of all disabilities imposed on account of the rebellion, and it announced the belief that universal amnesty would result in peace. It asked for local self-government, with impartial suffrage, which would "guard the rights of all citizens more securely than any centralized power". It declared also for the supremacy of the civil over military authority and the freedom of persons under the protection of the habeas corpus. It demanded "for the individual the largest liberty consistent with public order, for the State self-government, and for the nation a return to the methods of peace and the constitutional limitations of power." The Republican platform declared for the enforcement of the recent amendments and asserted that complete liberty and exact equality in the enjoyment of all civil, political,

---

[17] There was little prospect of reform within the party and little attention given to public corruption when enthusiastic party men would say, "Better the worst Republican than the best Democrat." For conditions in the public service see Oberholtzer, *op. cit.,* II, ch. XVI; III, chs. XVIII-XIX.

and public rights should be maintained by efficient and appropriate state and federal legislation. Congress and the President, it said, deserved the thanks of the nation for the suppression of violent and treasonable organizations in certain lately rebellious regions and for the protection of the ballot-box. On the main question of Reconstruction—or what remained of Reconstruction—the two parties were distinctly opposed.

The Liberal Reform movement was apparently a failure. Greeley was badly beaten. And yet failure it can hardly be called; the outcry against public corruption and the demand for a more conciliatory policy toward the south must have had some effect; at all events, the ruling party lost a considerable number of its most competent members. And events soon showed that members of the old party, though still affected by appeals of the politician and still indignant at southern "atrocities", were growing weary and heartsick, believing that military rule at the south and governments imposed upon the southern people by their conquerors should not continue. So, perhaps, the year 1872 may be looked upon as the beginning of the end. It was high time. Two years later the Republicans suffered a decisive defeat in the congressional elections. Though the defeat was no doubt caused largely by the disastrous panic of 1873, the party must henceforth watch its defenses and study the terrain with care, or it was doomed to defeat in the next presidential campaign.

There was evidence that the war was finished when Charles Sumner declared in the Senate, ". . . it is contrary to the usage of civilized nations to perpetuate the memory of civil war", and proposed that "the names of battles with fellow-citizens" be no longer "continued in the Army Register, or placed on the regimental colors of the United States." And perhaps there was even greater proof of the dying of old animosities when L. Q. C. Lamar of Mississippi, eulogizing Sumner in Congress, said, "Charles Sumner was born with an instinctive love of freedom. . . . To a man thoroughly permeated and imbued with such a creed and animated and constantly actuated by such a spirit of devotion, to behold a human being or a race of human beings restrained of their natural rights to liberty, for no crime by him or them committed, was to feel all the belligerent instincts of his nature roused to combat. The fact was to him a wrong which no logic could justify."

Though the day of new force bills was gone by, Congress did not quite surrender the hope of compelling, by direct legislation, a recognition of the civil rights and, in large measure also, the social equality of the negro. Sumner died in 1874, but, as a memorial to him and his ambitions, Congress passed the Civil Rights Act the next year. It declared all persons within the jurisdiction of the United States entitled to the full and equal enjoyment of the accommodations and privileges of inns, public conveyances, theaters, and other places of public amusement, "subject only to the conditions and limitations established by law, and applicable alike to citizens of every race and color, regardless of any previous condition of servitude." It made the act of any person denying to any citizen such full enjoyment and privilege a misdemeanor punishable by fine or imprisonment, and it allowed the offended party to sue for civil damages. It proved to be an instance of misdirected legislative zeal. Eight years after its passage the essential portions of the act were pronounced unconstitutional by the Supreme Court.[18]

It was held by the Court to assume the existence of federal power unwarranted by either the thirteenth or the fourteenth amendment. "It would be running the slavery argument into the ground," the Court declared, "to make it apply to every act of discrimination which a person may see fit to make as to the guests he will entertain, or as to the people he will take into his coach or cab or car. . . ."[19] And, while positive rights and privileges are undoubtedly secured by the fourteenth amendment, they are secured by way of prohibitions against state laws and state proceedings affecting these rights and privileges. ". . . it is proper to state that civil rights, such as are guaranteed by the Constitution against State aggression, cannot be impaired by the wrongful acts of individuals, unsupported by State authority in the shape of laws, customs, or judicial or executive proceedings."[20]

The principle laid down in the decision was not altogether novel,[21] but it made perfectly clear that the fourteenth amendment was not to be enforced by congressional acts directed against the misconduct of individual citizens unsupported by the authority of the state. The case ranks in importance with the Slaughter-House Cases (1873), an account of which will be given in a succeeding chapter. Worthy of notice, too, is the exercise of the power of the Court to declare a congressional act unconstitutional. By this time there was a consider-

[18] Civil Rights Cases, 109 U. S. 3 (1883).
[19] Ibid., 24.
[20] Ibid., 17.
[21] See, for example, Virginia v. Rives, 100 U. S. 313 (1880).

able body of precedent for the use of that power;[22] but the significance of this case lies in the fact that, had the Court not possessed the power or had the power not been used, the nature of our composite system of government would have been altered—we might almost say destroyed—by a statute based on the supposition that Congress could at will regulate individual conduct and personal relationships. The principle and the practice of judicial review of legislative acts have often been objected to; the courts have been charged with assuming unconstitutional power. But no one has very successfully pointed out how the structure of the federal state can be preserved without judicial determination of legislative limits. These two Court decisions—the Slaughter-House Cases in 1873 and the Civil Rights Cases in 1883—illustrate the way in which judicial power may preserve the essentials of federalism.

The greenback question, which was a matter of great public interest in the years of Grant's administration and, indeed, continued for a time to embarrass politicians and trouble economists after his retirement, was a matter of constitutional as well as economic importance. In 1870 the Supreme Court, three justices dissenting, declared that the acts passed during the war making all United States notes legal tender were invalid in so far as they applied to preëxisting debts.[23] There were many persons not content with the decision; they wished a full recognition of congressional power. At that critical moment, Grant appointed two new justices to the Court—Joseph P. Bradley and William Strong. It would be difficult to question seriously the character or the capacity of these men. But the assertion was made—and the suspicion probably still lingers—that the appointments were made for the express purpose of obtaining a reversal of the Court's decision.

The President was said to have deliberately "packed" the Court. There appears to be no substantial ground for this charge, but it brings to our attention the ease with which the Court can be altered by a president determined to have his way, if a majority of the Senate be with him. And one is tempted to say in addition, that, if Grant had taken that step for the express purpose of bending the Court to his will, it would have been only an extreme and peculiarly obnoxious

[22] Before 1865, there was one case in which the justices of a circuit court had declared an act void—Hayburn's Case, 1792. There were two Supreme Court decisions, Marbury v. Madison, 1803, and the Dred Scott case, 1857. Beginning with 1865 and ending with the Civil Rights Cases, there were fifteen. But in comparison with this decision, all the rest of these fifteen, save perhaps one, are not of vital importance.

[23] Hepburn v. Griswold, 8 Wallace 603 (1870).

example of a practice indulged in, when nominations of judges are under consideration in the Senate. For in those discussions we find many examples of opposition or advocacy, based not upon the character and learning of the person proposed for the bench, but upon the nature of his decisions in a lower court or upon his supposed attitude of mind toward especially significant policies. There is nothing but a high regard for the ethics, an appreciation of the duty of public servants, to restrain them from using the powers of appointment to attain their ends. But this is a delicate and difficult question. We have already seen its appearance in other connections.[24] The present writer is not prepared to deny that circumstances may arise when the composition of the Court and the effect of a particular appointment to its membership may properly be taken into consideration. At all events, such considerations are certain to have weight.

The Court, with its new members, rendered a decision overruling in part the previous decision and upholding the power to make paper money legal tender as applied to contracts made both before and after the passing of the legislation.[25] Justice Strong read the opinion of the Court, in which Justice Bradley concurred though giving an extensive opinion of his own. There was strong and vigorous dissent, and these few words may be taken from the dissent of Justice Field as illustrative of the atmosphere of the court-room: "In the discussions which have attended this subject of legal tender there has been at times what seemed to me to be a covert intimation, that opposition to the measure in question was the expression of a spirit not altogether favorable to the cause, in the interest of which that measure was adopted. All such intimations I repel with all the energy I can express. . . . But I do not admit that a blind approval of every measure which they may have thought essential to put down the rebellion is any evidence of loyalty to the country. The only loyalty which I can admit consists in obedience to the Constitution and laws made in pursuance of it. It is only by obedience that affection and reverence can be shown to a superior having a right to command. So thought our great Master when he said to his disciples: 'If ye love me, keep my commandments.' " [26]

While both Strong and Bradley spoke of the necessities of the times when the acts were passed, the constitutionality was not made to rest on the war power as the distinct basis. Bradley said, "I do not say

---

[24] Notice Lincoln's attitude toward the Court and the Dred Scott case.
[25] Legal Tender Cases (Knox v. Lee), 12 Wallace 457 (1871).
[26] Ibid., 680-681.

that it is a war power, or that it is only to be called into exercise in time of war; for other public exigencies may arise in the history of a nation which may make it expedient and imperative to exercise it." The two opinions were expressive of very decided nationalism and of a broad construction of the Constitution. Thirteen years later (1884) the Court announced the constitutional power to make treasury notes legal tender in time of peace as well as war.[27]

[27] Juilliard v. Greenman, 110 U. S. 421. The power in question was especially associated with the power to borrow money and to provide a national currency.

After the publication of this book an article by Sidney Ratner appeared in the *Political Science Quarterly* (Vol. L, pp. 343-358) : "Was the Supreme Court Packed by President Grant?" This article gives a passage from the manuscript diary of Hamilton Fish, under the date, October 28, 1876. Fish says that at that time Grant said to him, with reference to the charges then being made, "it would be difficult for him to make a statement; that although he required no declaration from Judges Strong and Bradley on the constitutionality of the Legal Tender Act, he knew Judge Strong had on the Bench in Pennsylvania given a decision sustaining its Constitutionality and he had reason to believe Judge Bradley's opinion tended in the same direction; that at that time he felt it important that the Constitutionality of the Law should be sustained, and while he would do nothing to exact anything like a pledge or expression of opinion from the parties he might appoint to the Bench, he had desired that the Constitutionality should be sustained by the Supreme Court; that he believed such had been the opinion of all his Cabinet at the time." To the reader it may appear to be mere quibbling, if the present writer suggests that when anyone, more than six years after an event, declares what he had in mind at the earlier time, his words must be read with at least a glimmer of suspicion. Ratner also calls attention to the assertion in G. S. Boutwell's *Reminiscences* (1902), that Chief Justice Chase, about two weeks before the decision in Hepburn v. Griswold was rendered, had told him what the decision would be. The importance of this fact, if the *Reminiscences* are to be literally believed, is that it tends to discredit the assumption that Grant was ignorant of the character of the decision when he sent the names of the two men to the Senate; for if Boutwell, the Secretary of the Treasury, knew, perhaps he informed Grant. The statement in the *Reminiscences* is not easily reconciled with a statement Boutwell had made to George F. Hoar six years earlier (1896). After saying that in his choice of the two justices Grant was influenced by the belief that they would uphold the Legal Tender Acts, Ratner declares, "Since he did not exact any pledge or expression of opinion from either Bradley or Strong before nominating them, it is not just to say that he 'packed the court,' or that the new judges were 'creatures of the President placed upon the Bench to carry out his instructions.' "

The reader cannot obtain from a brief note like this all the evidence for an opinion; but he is entitled to be informed of the new evidence. My own opinion, put in the shortest possible terms, is that Grant would not have appointed two men who, he believed, would declare the Legal Tender Acts void. At the present writing, I am unwilling to make a more positive statement.

CHAPTER XLVIII

THE ELECTION OF 1876

For the election of 1876, the Republicans nominated Rutherford B. Hayes of Ohio, and the Democrats Samuel J. Tilden of New York. Both were able men. The choice of either would give assurance of an honest and competent administration. It was time that something be done to clear the air, for the vulgarities of partisan strife and the corruption which had penetrated even to the center of the government at Washington were, or should have been, enough to shock the sensibilities of a self-respecting people. If these deplorable conditions are passed over in these pages with brief and insufficient comment, it is not because of an unwillingness to admit their importance even in constitutional history; for the success of a democracy and the maintenance of a reputable constitutional system must depend, not upon cunning partisan strategy, but upon the capacity of the plain people to install honest officials and support decent and honorable government.

The necessity of reform was much discussed in the campaign, and the Democrats made good use of the scandals in Congress and the administration. Many Republicans felt keenly the disrepute that had come to the party because of the misdeeds of public officials. Just how much this issue affected the outcome of the election cannot be said, but there was no return to anything like comparable conditions in the national government until another generation had come and gone.

The campaign did not, however, turn solely on the question of political reform. The panic of 1873 and the ensuing depression naturally weakened the hold of the Republicans on the average voter; the paper money issue was not entirely dead. The Republicans could with justice point with pride to the record of the party in maintaining the public credit and to their determination to resume specie payment. The party thus could rely on the support of the hard-money men. It could still be confident of the loyalty of many thousands who were devoted to the party that had "saved the union". Much of its strength came from its economic and financial conservatism.

The more advanced and radical Republican leaders sought to win support by fervid denunciation of southern lawlessness which had been vehemently denounced before the election by James G. Blaine, a prominent candidate for the presidential nomination and for years thereafter the "Plumed Knight" of the Republican cohorts. The best argument for their opponents, however, was the comparative quiet prevailing in the south.[1] Most of the reconstructed states had passed into the hands of the conservative whites. The feverish anxiety, which had been expended by northern idealists to establish and safeguard negro rights by giving the ballot, and the like anxiety of party politicians to make certain the ascendancy of their party in the nation seemed to have gone for nought. And as a matter of fact, the fruits of Reconstruction appeared to be turning to ashes in the hand.

South Carolina appears to have indulged more freely than other southern states in the grosser and more violent forms of browbeating the negro voter. There the campaign was conducted in a way to merit the name; it was carried on by the determined whites as if it were a combat between life and death.[2] Better, said the South Carolinians, violence for a time than misrule for all time.[3] At the request of Governor Chamberlain, Grant sent troops to the state in October. In the redemption of Mississippi in 1875, the whites had made use of various and effective means of intimidation which as a rule fell short of physical violence and of the more brutal forms of interference at the polls. Suggestion took the place of force in considerable measure—suggestion amplified by visible intent to proceed to realities if a negro were too willful or too stupid to read the writing on the wall. The "Mississippi plan" was hailed as a revelation and imitated, when need be, in other states.[4]

[1] Rhodes, *op. cit.*, VII, p. 224.

[2] D. H. Chamberlain, a Massachusetts man, thus wrote twenty-five years later: "The progress of the canvass developed . . . not only into violence of words and manner, but into breaches of the peace, interference with public meetings called by one party, and latterly into widespread riots. . . . It is not now denied, but admitted and claimed, by the successful party, that the canvass was systematically conducted with the view to find occasions to apply force and violence." "Reconstruction in South Carolina," *The Atlantic Monthly*, LXXXVII, p. 480.

[3] *Ibid.*, p. 481.

[4] "'Intimidation'," says Dunning, ". . . was illegal. But if a party of white men, with ropes conspicuous on their saddlebows, rode up to a polling place and announced that hanging would begin in fifteen minutes, though without any more definite reference to anybody, and a group of blacks who had assembled to vote heard the remark and promptly disappeared, votes were lost, but a conviction on a charge of intimidation was difficult." This is an illustration of the suggestive method. W. A. Dunning, "The Undoing of Reconstruction," *The Atlantic Monthly*, LXXXVIII,

The first announcements of the election indicated a Democratic victory. Tilden had carried four northern states—New York, New Jersey, Connecticut, and Indiana. Without the votes of South Carolina, Florida, and Louisiana, the unredeemed states, he had apparently received 184 votes, one less than the requisite electoral majority. The strategic move for the Republicans was to announce their success in these crucial states, and so the telegraph wires were kept busy sending out to waiting thousands the message from the party headquarters— "Hayes has 185 electoral votes and is elected." The situation was critical; there was actual danger of tumult or more serious social disorder. A people without political discretion or a people not weary of the horrors of civil war might have easily drifted into a temporary condition of anarchy or yielded to the strong arm of a personal dictator.[5]

Conditions were serious enough to test supreme common sense. Partisan spirit ran high. There was no doubt that intimidation and chicanery had been rampant in the election. Indeed, in some of the northern states the purity evinced was nothing to boast of. In the three pivotal states of the south, the votes were so nearly evenly divided that ample opportunity was given for dispute concerning the result. South Carolina appeared to have supported Hayes by a small but probably safe majority. Florida presented its share of anxiety; it needed careful watching. Louisiana offered the most serious problem; the vote might be secured for Hayes, if the Republican officials in charge of the final canvass used their powers with cunning and ruthless determination. To watch proceedings, "visiting statesmen" hurried from the north, the Republicans at the request of President Grant, the Democrats at the request of the chairman of the national committee. The state canvass-

pp. 440-441. Such an incident as this in Louisiana is fairly typical: "Q. Do you know anything about armed bodies of men riding through your parish, or any part of it, during the day or night?—A. Yes, sir. . . . They rode through the parish. I heard them come by my house when I was in the field, afraid to stay in the house, singing,

A charge to keep I have,
A God to glorify;
If a nigger don't vote for us
He shall forever die."

"Louisiana in 1876. Report of the Sub-committee of the United States Senate." *Senate Reports,* 44 Cong., 2 sess., no. 701, p. 19.

[5] The people of that generation knew the realities of war. The south had learned the lesson even more surely than the north. One Kentuckian in Congress said if there should be a war, it would be the work of northern Democrats, "while Benjamin Hill of Georgia referred cuttingly to a section of the party who were 'invincible in peace and invisible in war.'" P. L. Haworth, *The Hayes-Tilden Disputed Presidential Election of 1876,* p. 176.

ing boards, needless to say, were not deficient in acumen or in partisan zeal, but the Republican statesmen believed it unwise to leave them to their unaided devices, and some idea of prevailing conditions needed to be gathered by personal observation. Neither of these groups of visitors went with the express intention of using the grosser means of arranging the count to their own satisfaction, but partisanship is likely to be blind.[6]

In Florida, where the election had passed in comparative quiet, there was dispute concerning which side was ahead on the face of the returns sent to the state canvassing board from the counties. The Republicans claimed a majority of 45, the Democrats a majority of about 100. The state board, two of the three members being Republicans, rejected enough of the county returns to give the election to the Hayes electors by a majority in the neighborhood of 900.[7] The Democrats, however, were not willing to be counted out; and, as a result, conflicting certificates of election were sent to the President of the United States Senate.

To Louisiana must be awarded the prize for displaying the most discreditable condition and the most perplexing problem—the product of years of violence and trickery and of ruthless carpetbag government. In the campaign the "Mississippi plan"—intimidation which in the mind of the expert was not intimidation—had not been too scrupulously followed. On the face of the returns from the localities, the Hayes electors were defeated by apparently conclusive majorities. Such

---

[6] Dunning sums up the situation by saying, ". . . some of the Republican visitors were obliged to ignore or connive at notorious cheating, and some of the Democrats to involve themselves in bargains for bribes. Rumors and charges of these things were incessant during the struggle over the count, but most of the clear evidence about them was revealed only two years later." Dunning, *Reconstruction*, p. 312.

[7] "Florida Election, 1876. Report of the Senate Committee on Privileges and Elections." *Senate Reports,* 44 Cong., 2 sess., no. 611, p. 3; *House Reports,* 44 Cong., 2 sess., no. 143, pt. 1, p. 3, pt. 2, p. 33. "Frauds in the count and return of votes were unquestionably committed on both sides. In this kind of work the Republicans had the advantage of having a small majority of the election officers, but this was probably counter-balanced by the ease with which shrewd Democrats could hoodwink the illiterate negroes who acted as election officers in many places. On the whole, it is not improbable that an unpartisan board, acting on the same theory of its powers as did the actual board, would have held that the returns did not in all cases correspond to the votes in the ballot-boxes, would have thrown out some returns contrary to the interests of each party, but would in the end have found a small majority for Tilden." Haworth, *op. cit.,* pp. 74-75. Haworth says, however, that a *"free election"* might have resulted in a victory for Hayes, while a *"fair count"* might have had the opposite result. *Ibid.,* p. 76.

a state of affairs was alarming; it remained for members of the state canvassing board to show their mettle. They were well fitted for their job. The leader of the board had been described by General Sheridan some years before: "His conduct has been as sinuous as the mark left in the dust by the movement of a snake." [8] It is said that in the meantime his character had deteriorated. At least two of the remaining three members had unenviable records. On the charge of bull-dozing, intimidation, and for other reasons, the returns from various parishes were cast aside with a lavish hand.

The state law gave the board wide power, and there can be little doubt of its legal authority to purge the lists, but in one or two seemingly unimportant matters it quite needlessly ignored the law and its obligations; and these petty irregularities, which might have been avoided by just a little common sense and alertness, proved in the end to be the source of considerable embarrassment to the Republican cause. Probably these cunning politicians were so accustomed to the evasion of law that they could not see the advisability of obeying it when obedience would have been helpful. The result of the board's activities was a return showing, not a Tilden majority of nearly 8,000, but a majority for the Hayes electors of about 3,500.[9] The vote of these electors with the Governor's certificate was sent to Washington. Democratic indignation knew no bounds—indignation was a plentiful commodity in those days. Eight persons claiming to be the legally chosen electors of the state voted for Tilden and Hendricks, and their certificates, accompanied by one from John McEnery, who signed himself Governor of the state, were sent to the President of the Senate.[10] It is not

[8] Rhodes, *op. cit.*, VII, p. 231.

[9] These figures are substantially those given by the Democratic objection presented to Congress. *Electoral Count of 1877*, p. 213. But the exact figures have no special significance. See also Haworth, *op. cit.*, pp. 113-114.

[10] Speaking at a later time of Louisiana and in regard to the decision of the commission, Seelye of Massachusetts, a Republican member of the House, said, ". . . it seems to me perfectly clear that the charges made by each side against the other are, in the main true. No facts were ever proved more conclusively than the fraud and corruption charged on the one side and the intimidation and cruelty charged on the other. Which of the two sides went the farther, did the worst in this wrong-doing, would be very hard to say. The corruption of the one side seems as heinous as the cruelty of the other side is horrible, and on both sides there does not seem to be any limit to the extent they went, save only where the necessities of the case did not permit or the requirements of the case did not call for any more." *Congressional Record*, 44 Cong., 2 sess., V, p. 1685.

An interesting, though possibly extreme, illustration of the feeling animating the impassioned Republican partisans and strongly held by many men of probity is found in a speech delivered after Seelye closed. "Mr. Speaker, since I came into this

necessary to enter upon the task of deciding which side carried the burden of the greater political immorality or to describe all the sordid details. Conditions in Louisiana were intolerable; they mocked at the pretense of constitutional government of a free people. Fortunately for the reader, constitutional history is not compelled to repeat the whole story and to disturb the dust that has settled upon the mire.

The Democrats left no stone unturned in their search for means of winning a victory which they saw slipping away from them because of what they considered high-handed and illegal practices. Although there was little hope of their winning their cause, they decided to test the validity of the Republican returns from South Carolina. The Republican canvassing board was charged with gross fraud. A certificate and the votes of the Tilden electors were forwarded, purporting to be the legitimate result of the popular election. And thus South Carolina offered another critical question to be passed upon.

Oregon rather unexpectedly offered a peculiar opportunity. The Hayes electors had received a majority of about one thousand votes, but one of the electors was at the time of the election a federal officer and was therefore ineligible. The Governor certified to the appointment of one Democratic and two Republican electors. Even if the Democratic elector was not entitled to vote, the loss of one electoral vote, from among the 185 which were claimed for Hayes, was fatal to the Republican cause: the final count would show a tie and the choice of president would devolve upon the Democratic House of Representatives. Two returns were sent from Oregon to the President of the Senate, one with the Governor's certificate showing two votes for Hayes and one for Tilden, the other showing three votes for Hayes.

Concerning the determination of disputes in an election, the Con-

House, one year ago last December, I have continually heard this howl about republican extravagance, republican fraud, and republican corruption. . . . And much of this, sir, I am pained to say, has come from men who now occupy seats in this Hall through the mercy and magnanimity of the party they slander and malign." After referring to the fact that the Republican party saved the country—the inevitable appeal—the orator turned his attention to the fraudulent intent and practices of the Democrats. "The whole scheme to elect the Grand Fraud of Gramercy Park [Tilden] to the Presidency in the late election was a superb democratic cheat. . . . The States of Mississippi, Georgia, and Alabama were carried for Tilden by an organized system of violence and intimidation which shocked humanity and caused cruelty even to blush. And you attempted to carry South Carolina, Florida, and Louisiana in the same way, but you have not succeeded." *Ibid.*, p. 1686. The orator might well have listened to Seelye's reference to the saying of Niebuhr, that no nation ever died except by suicide and that the suicidal poison is engendered by the immoral practices of a people. *Ibid.*, p. 1685.

stitution is reticent. The most important constitutional provisions concerning the election of a president are as follows: "Each State shall appoint, in such manner as the Legislature thereof may direct, a number of electors, equal to the whole number of senators and representatives to which the State may be entitled in the Congress; but no senator or representative, or person holding an office of trust or profit under the United States, shall be appointed an elector." [11] "The President of the Senate shall, in the presence of the Senate and House of Representatives, open all the certificates, and the votes shall then be counted." [12] Congress is authorized to "determine the time of choosing the electors, and the day on which they shall give their votes, which day shall be the same throughout the United States." [13] This last pronouncement is the only plain statement in the Constitution of any power in the central government to control the states' authority to appoint electors; but of course, if the appointment is made by popular election, the fifteenth (and now the nineteenth) amendment affords the government the opportunity to guard against unlawful discrimination.

The right of Congress to prescribe methods and formalities, which will enable the person who is authorized to count the votes to know that the certified votes come from *bona fide* and legally appointed electors is apparently beyond question; and an act prescribing these formalities was passed in 1792. The law named the period within which the electors should be appointed and fixed the day on which the electors should meet and vote. In 1845 a supplementary act fixed definitely the day of appointment and also declared "That each State may by law provide for the filling of any vacancy or vacancies which may occur in its college of electors when such college meets to give its electoral vote". [14] This latter declaration may be an assumption of authority by Congress, because it is not the right of the national government to intrude upon the duty of the state; but in exercising the

---

[11] Art. II, sec. 1, para. 2.
[12] Art. II, sec. 1, para. 3. See also amendment XII.
[13] Art. II, sec. 1, para. 4.
[14] The term "college of electors", we may notice, seems to have been first used officially in 1845; neither that term nor its equivalent is known to the Constitution, but it was in more or less common use from an early day. The words are of significance only as suggesting or implying the organization of the electors into a body, and such organization may indeed be implied by the constitutional obligation to meet and make a list of the persons voted for, "which list they shall sign and certify". The term was used by Abraham Baldwin in 1800, and by John Randolph in 1809. "Counting Electoral Votes," *Miscellaneous Documents of the House of Representatives,* 44 Cong., 2 sess., no. 13, pp. 692, 38.

right to determine the day of appointment Congress may properly provide that vacancies may be filled at a later time.

With conflicting certificates in the hands of the President of the Senate, the question still remained—who had the authority to count the votes? Vice-President Wilson having died, the office of President of the Senate was held in 1877 by Thomas W. Ferry of Michigan, a Republican and by no means a timid partisan. Did he have the right to count the votes and declare the result, while the two houses sat by as competent though silent witnesses that he had done so? The Constitution says, we may remind ourselves again, "The President of the Senate shall . . . open all the certificates, and the votes shall then be counted." But counted by whom? There is nothing intrinsically absurd in assigning to a single officer the counting of votes and announcing the result of an election. Although there is no use in arguing now in behalf of possession of sole power in the hands of the President of the Senate, the claim to such power is by no means preposterous; it seems at least possible to decide that the framers of the Constitution assigned to him the duty and the power in question.[15]

If the two houses are authorized to count the votes, the Constitution gives no hint of how the houses shall be organized. Though occasionally the meeting of the two houses has been called a convention, they have consistently, and probably wisely (for the Constitution speaks of the two houses), refused or neglected to merge themselves into a single body with legislative or administrative authority in which conclusions would be reached by a numerical majority of the whole; rules have been passed, generally of a temporary character; the consequence has been a degree of uncertainty, and in the case of great differences of party opinion or real doubt, the problem has been left to the action of the two separate houses—a method which must be looked upon as the least desirable and feasible method of *counting* a vote.[16] The twenty-second joint rule, which had been adopted in

[15] A study of the history of counting the votes discloses the way in which the houses gradually assumed the power to count, by the appointment of tellers. It discloses also the conditions which resulted in the assumption that they had the right to decide what votes should be counted. The information is contained in "Counting Electoral Votes," *loc. cit.*

[16] Speaking of the counting in 1869, when there was a difference of opinion between the two houses, McKnight says: "To provide that two equal and independent bodies shall canvass the votes, is an absurdity of which the Fathers would never have been guilty; it subverts every political and parliamentary principle, as well as the dictates of common sense." D. A. McKnight, *Electoral System of the United States*, p. 311. "My judgment is that neither House of Congress, nor both

1865, provided that, if any vote were objected to, it should not be counted unless it be accepted by both houses. The rule, however, had not been reënacted in 1876. This complicated the situation.

But of course the pivotal question was not who should do the counting, but what votes should be counted. Past procedure, as we have seen, gave some basis for the assumption that Congress, acting in two chambers, could decide. Are there limits on such authority, or may the decision rest only upon partisan needs and ambitions? There would appear to be in theory only one safe and sane conclusion: each state has the right, free from control, to appoint electors, and if it is unable to send to the President of the Senate a list of the electors, properly certified and to be relied upon, the vote of that state cannot be counted; the vote then is lost. But that Congress can take upon itself the duty of canvassing the popular vote (or investigating the conduct of a legislature, if the legislature were by state law given the duty of appointing electors) appears not only an untenable technical position, but one fraught with difficulty and danger. The development of centralized nationalism has been so marked in the last half century, and the states have lost so much of their own self-respect, that there might now be a complacent acquiescence in congressional control of the state's power to "appoint", specifically announced by the Constitution.

Counsels of wisdom and judgment prevailed in Congress. After the end of an anxious month, an agreement was reached for the selection of a tribunal.[17] In case there were conflicting returns from a state, the "returns and papers" were to be opened and read in a joint meeting of the houses and then turned over to a commission of fifteen, which should have "the same powers, if any", possessed by the two houses, "acting separately or together, and, by a majority of votes, decide whether any and what votes from such State are the votes provided for by the Constitution of the United States, and how many and what persons were duly appointed electors in such State. . . ."

combined, have any right to interfere in the count. It is for the Vice-President to do it all." Hayes to Samuel Shellabarger, December 29, 1876. C. R. Williams, *The Life of Rutherford Birchard Hayes*, I, p. 513, note 1. See also, a letter to John Sherman, January 5, 1877. *Ibid.*, I, p. 522.

[17] The vote in each house showed strong Democratic support. In the Senate 26 Democrats and 21 Republicans voted affirmatively; 16 Republicans and one Democrat voted in the negative. In the House 159 Democrats and 32 Republicans supported the measure, while 18 Democrats and 68 Republicans opposed it. The figures given by different authorities vary slightly.

The decision concerning each one of the disputed states was to be read and entered on the journal of each house, and the counting of the votes should "proceed in conformity therewith," unless the two houses separately should "concur in ordering otherwise. . . ."[18]

The commission was composed of five members from each house and five justices of the Supreme Court. Though there was no explicit provision concerning the party affiliation of the members chosen by the respective houses, the Senate chose three Republicans and two Democrats, the House three Democrats and two Republicans. The justices chosen were named, not personally, but by circuits—the first, third, eighth, and ninth. These four had authority to select a fifth. Of the four, Clifford and Field were Democrats, Strong and Miller Republicans. It was apparent that if the commission, including the justices, proved to be influenced by inclinations resulting from past or present party association, the decision would rest on the shoulders of the fifteenth man, the justice chosen for the unenviable job. When the make-up of the commission was under discussion in Congress, Judge David Davis, it was generally understood or supposed, would be the fifteenth member. But at the critical juncture, just before the bill constituting the commission was passed by the House (January 26), Davis was elected Senator from Illinois and thus could no longer be considered a suitable choice by the four justices. In his place, the four justices selected Justice Joseph P. Bradley; to him, the fifteenth man, was assigned the inconceivably difficult task of decision, for the other judges, though men of honor, might be expected to vote in accord with the interests of party—and such supposition proved in the end well-founded. The selection was, however, the best possible under the circumstances. Bradley had been appointed by Grant, but he was not an extreme partisan; he was a man of high character and, while on the bench, had in the decision of at least one important case shown himself out of sympathy with radical Republican legislation.

The commission met in the Supreme Court room on the last day of January and the next day entered upon its task. There were five prominent problems to be met. (1) Could the commission legally go behind the returns, that is to say, pass upon the correctness of the determination of the state canvassing board which under the law of the state had announced the result of the election? This was the critical but by no means the only troublesome question. (2) What was the effect of the provision of the federal Constitution declaring that no

[18] *Electoral Count of 1877*, pp. 4-5.

person holding any office of trust or profit under the United States should be appointed an elector? (3) Must the action of the legislature of Florida and the quo warranto proceedings in the Florida court, or either of these steps, be accepted by the commission as determinative of the will of the state, despite findings of a contrary character by the canvassing board? (4) Certain questions arose in the interpretation of state laws providing for the make-up and powers of the canvassing board. Was failure to act in strict conformity with the terms of the state statute fatal to the authority of the board and had the state therefore not appointed any electors? (5) Was the governor's certificate final and conclusive or could the commission question it and refuse to be bound by it? The commission, it must be remembered, had no more authority than Congress.

The right of the commission to go behind the returns was elaborately discussed in the Florida case, and the commission by a vote of eight to seven—all of the Republicans on one side and all of the Democrats on the other—refused to investigate the question whether the electors named by the board had actually received the highest number of votes; they refused to question the validity of the decision of the body which under the law of the state had the authority to decide.[19] On this matter the statement of Justice Bradley is especially noteworthy: "Each State has a just right to have the entire and exclusive control of its own vote for the Chief Magistrate and head of the republic, without any interference on the part of any other State, act-

---

[19] The Florida law providing for the canvass said the board "shall canvass the returns of said election, and determine and declare who shall have been elected to any such office, or as such member, as shown by such returns. If any such return shall be shown, or shall appear to be, so irregular, false, or fraudulent, that the board shall be unable to determine the true vote for any such officer or member, they shall so certify, and shall not include such return in their determination and declaration." *Ibid.*, p. 1010. Senator Bayard, a Democrat, a member of the commission, and a man of high character, had made a significant statement in the Senate two years previously (February 25, 1875). Referring to the act of 1792, he said that by this act "the certification, the authentication of the electoral vote, was confided wholly and unreservedly by the Constitution to the States. . . . If the Congress of the United States, either one or both houses, shall assume, under the guise or pretext of telling or counting a vote, to decide the fact of the election of electors who are to form the college by whom the President and Vice-President are to be chosen, then they will have taken upon themselves an authority for which I, for one, can find no warrant in this charter of limited powers. . . . There is no pretext for any cause whatever Congress has any power, or all the other departments of the Government have any power, to refuse to receive and count the result of the action of the voters in the States in that election as certified by the electors whom they have chosen." "Counting Electoral Votes," *loc. cit.*, pp. 472-473.

ing either separately or in Congress with others. If there is any State right of which it is and should be more jealous than of any other, it is this. And such seems to have been the spirit manifested by the framers of the Constitution. . . . The State is a sovereign power within its own jurisdiction, and Congress can no more control or review the exercise of that jurisdiction than it can that of a foreign government. . . . It seems to me to be clear, therefore, that Congress cannot institute a scrutiny into the appointment of electors by a State. . . . While the two Houses of Congress are authorized to canvass the electoral votes, no authority is given them to canvass the election of the electors themselves. . . . It seems to me that the two Houses of Congress, in proceeding with the count, are bound to recognize the determination of the State board of canvassers as the act of the State, and as the most authentic evidence of the appointment made by the State. . . ." [20]

In opposition to this position, the opinion of Justice Field is perhaps the most cogent.[21] He declared the canvassing board had usurped authority; he denied that the state statutes gave the board such authority as it had assumed, and, to sustain him, he quoted the decision of the supreme court of the state, which, he declared, made plain that the powers of the board were purely ministerial, and that "their whole duty consisted, whenever they were enabled to determine the actual vote given for any officer, in simply computing arithmetically the number of votes cast, as shown by the returns [from the counties], and declaring the result by a certificate of the fact over their signatures." [22] He argued at length in behalf of the right to inquire whether the canvassers had made a mistake in addition, had been bribed, had been coerced by physical force, or had in any other way failed to register properly the will of the state; such possibilities, he put forth, not as peculiarly applicable to the Florida case, but as examples of the impropriety of asserting that the decisions of the state canvassing board could not be examined and that its decision, which might be proved to be absolutely false, must nevertheless stand as the will of

[20] *Electoral Count of 1877*, pp. 1020, 1021, 1023. Presidential electors are not federal officers.

[21] *Ibid.*, p. 974 ff.

[22] *Ibid.*, p. 977. Jeremiah S. Black, one of the counsel for the Democratic cause, said in argument, "We are not going behind the action of the State; we are going behind the fraudulent act of an officer of the State whose act had no validity in it whatever." *Ibid.*, p. 98.

the state. Such impropriety and such unwarrantable results, he said, naturally flowed from the denial of the right to go behind the returns.

Though it may be presumptuous to make a positive statement, when highly competent justices differed so radically, it seems evident that the Republican eight held the proper position on this all-important matter.[23] And if we consider, not the technical legality of the commission's decision as then announced, but the practical consequences of adopting the theory that Congress can override the determination of the state board and can itself canvass the vote, or cast out altogether the returns of counties or precincts, we must hold the commission's decision to have been wise and conservative. He would be a bold man who would affirm that, if Congress could exercise the power—which would mean in effect congressional control of presidential elections in the states—there would be no violent partisanship and no chicanery.

The decision of the commission is of importance not alone because of the part it played in the settlement of the dispute of 1876. The spectacle of a Congress in the grasp of a powerful national party exercising the right to thrust in its hand and decide presidential elections as it may choose, is not a pleasant sight to look upon.[24] And, indeed, what was the process of Reconstruction, when it reached its most sordid and lowest stage, but determination on the part of a national party intrenched in Congress to maintain itself and have its way? If the Republicans on the commission were upholding states' rights and if the Democrats were now insisting on an opposite principle, it may appear to be all very amusing; but the fact points to a return of the Republicans to common sense and sound constitutional doctrine. If they were aided in that change by partisan considerations, there is no need in our shedding tears over the prodigals' return.[25]

[23] Field's statement, in which he referred to the decision of the Florida court denying that the canvassing board had the authority it actually exercised, may have had some basis, but the powers granted the board were pretty sweeping.

[24] There is an old story, which appears not improbable, that Thad Stevens, when a contested case involving representatives came before Congress, would pay no attention to evidence or argument, but when the time came for the vote he would go to a colleague and say, "Both of them are rascals. Which is our rascal?"

[25] One of the reasons for not going behind the returns—though that reason did not play a conspicuous rôle—was the impracticability of making an examination of the actual operations at the polls in the various counties of the various states, in other words, of doing the work which the canvassing boards were supposed to do or did do. See the statement of Justice Miller, *Electoral Count of 1877*, pp. 1006-1007. Referring to papers which had been presented in great quantities, he said, "No reference is made to anything by which these papers can be identified. There is nothing to hinder alterations or substitutions among them. They may be *ex parte* affidavits

As we have already pointed out, the Constitution places one distinct restriction upon the state in its appointment of electors: no federal officer can be appointed an elector.[26] Three of the four cases before the commission brought up the necessity of determining the construction and application of this provision. Among the Florida Hayes electors was F. C. Humphreys, who had been United States shipping-commissioner. Whether or not he was a federal officer at the time of the November election was a matter of dispute; and in this instance the commission consented to go behind the certificates. This, of course, they were under constitutional obligation to do. They found that Humphreys had resigned his federal office before he was chosen an elector at the polls. So, for the time being, the perplexing question of eligibility did not create great difficulty. The commission in this instance did not decide on the principle to be followed in case an elector had been actually a federal office-holder when the November election was held. It may be argued that the commission was inconsistent in consenting to go behind the returns of the canvassing board at all, even to discover whether a person appointed was eligible or not. But such inconsistency can scarcely be maintained. It is one thing to claim the general right to examine into and review the decision of a state authority exercising the functions given by state law and clearly assigned to the state by the federal Constitution; and it is another thing to investigate whether the state has observed a restriction definitely prescribed by the federal Constitution. Such an investigation is not an intrusion upon the field of state authority.

The most difficult problem in the Florida case was to decide the effect of the action of the state authorities after the election was held and even after the electoral vote was cast. Quo warranto proceedings were instituted in the circuit court of Florida to test the right of the Hayes electors to act, and the court held that they were not duly elected but on the contrary that the Tilden electors were. The writ was served on the electors before they actually voted;[27] and the Tilden electors as well as the Hayes electors voted on the 6th day of December.[28] The legislature also had passed an act (January 17, 1877) providing for a board of canvassers and ordering a new canvass, which resulted in a statement that the Tilden electors had been chosen at the

taken in the morasses of Florida, the slums of New York, or the private office of retained counsel in this city." *Ibid.*, p. 1007.

[26] Art. II, sec. 1, para. 2.
[27] So asserted, and appears to be the fact. *Electoral Count of 1877*, pp. 50, 78.
[28] *Ibid.*, pp. 13, 25.

November election; an act was also passed (January 26) declaring the original canvassing board had acted illegally and erroneously, that the Tilden electors were duly chosen, and that the Governor was directed to certify to their election. Such a certificate was prepared and was included in the documents presented to Congress.

Did this certificate, the legislative acts, and the decision of the state court constitute the purpose and will of the state? Must a determination thus reached be conclusive upon Congress and the commission? Most troublesome to the Republican cause were the quo warranto proceeding and the finding of the Florida court. If the canvassing board had acted illegally, could anyone assert that its work, if based on fraud, could not be undone by judicial authority? There were no entirely clear constitutional principles to start upon, as the basis of a legal argument, and, in fact, the decision of the commission seems to rest quite as much upon general considerations as upon clear-cut legal theory. At all events, the decision of the majority was based on the declaration that the Hayes electors were in legal possession of their offices; that after they had acted nothing could be done by any state authority of any kind—judicial, legislative, or executive—to annul their act; it was complete and irreversible; any other principle, if adopted as a principle of constitutional law, would involve the right of a state court, even an inferior state court, or the political branches of the state government, weeks or even months after the electors voted, to change the vote of the state, and in this way to change the results of a national election.

But in this instance as in others, the matter is presented best in the words of certain members of the commission, though nothing less than a full statement adequately presents the strength of the argument. Justice Field said: "In this case the State of Florida has furnished evidence in an authentic form and conclusive in its character, that the Hayes electors were never appointed and that the certificate of the governor and of the canvassing-board in this respect is false; and that the Tilden electors were duly appointed." [29] Justice Bradley, on the other hand, said, the action of the board involved more than a mere statement of fact; it was a determination, a decision quasi-judicial; the board, by state law, had power to canvass the returns and to cast out returns appearing to be false or fraudulent. "To controvert the finding of the board, therefore, would not be to correct a mere statement of fact, but to reverse the decision and determination of a

[29] *Ibid.*, p. 982.

tribunal. . . . If the court had had jurisdiction of the subject-matter, and had rendered its decision before the votes of the electors were cast, its judgment, instead of that of the returning-board, would have been the final declaration of the result of the election. But its decision being rendered after the votes were given, it cannot have the operation to change or affect the vote. . . . No tampering with the result can be admitted after the day fixed by Congress for casting the electoral vote, and after it has become manifest where the pinch of the contest for the Presidency lies, and how it may be manipulated. . . . Under the Florida statute, the board had power to cast out returns. They did so." [30]

On February 9 the commission reported in favor of declaring "it is not competent . . . to go into evidence *aliunde* the papers opened by the President of the Senate in the presence of the two Houses, to prove that other persons than those regularly certified to by the governor of the State of Florida, in and according to the determination . . . by the board of State canvassers . . . , had been appointed electors. . . ." The report also asserted that all proceedings of the courts or acts of the legislature after the electors had voted were inadmissible as evidence to show that such electors were not appointed.

Louisiana presented so many serious questions, the whole atmosphere was so charged with miasmic vapors of fraud, cunning, and vulgarity, that the commission might well have felt its job hopeless. What was the use of passing solemnly upon legal questions when the whole situation was characterized by lawlessness? But the problems were seriously discussed and in each instance with a display of legal learning and without outward manifestation of bad temper. To sur-

[30] *Ibid.,* pp. 1024-1025. Miller, objecting to the argument in favor of giving effect to the Florida court decision, said: "In New York there are thirty-two judges of the supreme court of that State, a court which exercises original jurisdiction all over the State. Under the principle asserted any one of these thirty-two judges may issue his writ of *quo warranto,* or of injunction, or other appropriate writ, the day before the votes must by law be cast for President and Vice-President, and by this exercise of his power prevent the 35 votes of the State from being given or counted in the election." *Ibid.,* p. 1008. Justice Strong maintained that the Hayes electors were not merely officers *de facto:* "Neither the action of the legislature, nor a *post hoc* decision of a court, can affect an act rightfully done, when it is done and completed before the legislature and the court attempted to annul the authority for it. . . . The electors of the State of New York cast the votes of the State on the 6th of December last. Can those votes now be nullified by any subsequent action of the New York legislature declaring that the persons who voted were not elected, or creating a new board to make a new canvass, or by the judgment of an inferior court, or any other court, that other persons were entitled to cast the votes of the State?" *Ibid.,* pp. 999-1000.

render in despair would have been the abandonment of good sense and sober statesmanship. When all is said, decisions on the basis of law rather than passion were doubtless of lasting moment.

The problem of eligibility arose sharply in the Louisiana case. Two of the men, who were declared chosen at the election and who voted for Hayes, were at the time of the popular election federal office-holders. They resigned their offices before actually casting their votes for the presidency. The main contention of the Democratic counsel was this: the state of Louisiana was forbidden to appoint a federal office-holder; the time of appointment was the time of the popular election; and such appointment of a disqualified person was illegal and void.[31] With this opinion the majority of the commission did not agree. Justice Bradley summed up the matter in these words: "I still think . . . that it is all one, whether the prohibition is that a Federal officer shall not *be* an elector, or, that he shall not be *appointed* an elector. The spirit and object of the prohibition is to make office-holding under the Federal Government a disqualification. That is all." In the opinion of this justice, the only question was whether a person acting as elector was at the moment of so acting a federal office-holder. This was an important decision, for Hayes could not lose a single vote, and there remained the Oregon case, the last hope of the Democrats, and there, too, a federal office-holder had been chosen at the election. No one can now assert with assurance that the Democratic counsel was wrong and the commission right. But the result of the whole controversy turned on that seemingly trivial point. One thing is obvious; there is one lesson to be learned: even a politician may find it advisable to know something of the Constitution.

The contention that Louisiana did not have a republican form of government,[32] and the assertion that Kellogg, the carpetbag Governor,

---

[31] "The Constitution of the United States," said Senator Trumbull, "in the grant of power has said to the State of Louisiana, 'You may appoint certain persons as electors for President, but you shall not appoint O. H. Brewster.' Now, I say, when the Constitution says that to the State of Louisiana, it is binding upon the legislature and upon every citizen of Louisiana." Justice Bradley asked Trumbull if he intended to prove that Brewster was an office-holder at the time of giving his vote. To this Trumbull answered, "No, sir; at the time of his appointment; he was appointed at the time of the election." *Ibid.*, pp. 336-337.

[32] Notice Thurman's comments upon the assignment of vast power to the canvassing board: "The board is in effect constituted the State—to govern it according to its own arbitrary will and discretion. There is no republican government in Louisiana. There can be no republican government in that State so long as this returning-board is upheld. An oligarchy more corrupt, more odious, more anti-republican, never before existed on this globe." *Ibid.*, p. 837.

was, by law and right, not the governor of the state, were plainly not matters that could be taken up and passed upon by the commission; such a step was impossible unless the commissioners were prepared to cast disrepute upon the series of proceedings taken by the political branches of the national government during the later years of Reconstruction. To assume such an attitude and to make such a pronouncement appear even now to have been a practical impossibility. At least, the relentless eight did not attempt, and perhaps did not desire, to pronounce the whole carpetbag régime a mere vulgar substitute for decent government.

Other serious difficulties of a technical character arose in the Louisiana case in addition to those we have just discussed. The authority of the canvassing board to act at all was strenuously denied by the Democratic counsel. Four members of the board, all of one party, made the canvass and the return, though the law provided there should be five members and that different parties should be represented on the board. As the vacant place was not filled, the board thus constituted, it was contended, was not a legal board and was without authority to act as such. "I do not insist", said Trumbull, one of the Democratic counsel, "that the whole five must have been present; but I do insist that where the authority existed in the four to supply the vacancy they had no authority to go on and make the canvass without supplying the vacancy." [33] The majority of the commission refused to support the validity of this position.

The last substantial hope for Democratic success was offered by Oregon, for, though the South Carolina controversy remained, there was little likelihood of any change in the commission's main position. The Oregon problems were not so confusing or so complicated as those involved in the disputes we have already considered, but there was, or appeared to be, a good fighting chance that the previous decisions of the commission—the determination not to go behind the state returns as certified by the Governor—would make necessary the elimination of at least one Hayes elector. Three days—February 21, 22, 23—were taken up with arguments and with the discussions of the commission. There was no question concerning the result of the popular election. As we have seen, the Governor of the state, how-

---

[33] *Ibid.*, p. 335. Bradley's views on this matter are cogent, perhaps convincing. *Ibid.*, p. 1029. He said, among other things, "Can it be contended that the resignation or death of one of the members, who happened to be alone in his party connections, deprives the remainder of the power to act? I think not."

ever, certified to the election of two Hayes electors and one, Cronin, Tilden elector. The basis for this certificate was the ineligibility of Watts, a Republican, because at the time of the November election he was a federal postmaster. The Governor's conclusion was that Cronin received the vote of the people, the vote cast for Watts being entirely lost. The Republican electors refused to act with Cronin; so, not to be outdone, he appointed two new electors who would deign to act with him; and the electoral college thus constituted cast two votes for Hayes and one for Tilden. Two of the three Hayes electors appointed Watts to fill the vacancy which occurred because of his own disqualification at the time of the election; he had resigned his postmastership and also surrendered his office of elector (by resignation to the electoral college) before the electoral college voted.[34]

Could the commission, with any show of consistency, inspect the validity and question the conclusiveness of the Governor's certificate? It is sometimes said that in this case the commission turned its back upon preceding decisions; but such is not the fact. On several occasions, in the preceding discussions, the right to examine the Governor's certificate, to ascertain whether it correctly presented the decision of the canvassing board (deemed to be the will of the state), had been stated clearly.[35] The distinction between the decision of the returning

[34] *Ibid.*, pp. 459, 641.
[35] For example, Justice Field, supporting the Democratic cause, said in the Florida case, "that in the absence of positive law declaring its effect to be otherwise, a certificate of any officer to a fact is never held conclusive on any question between third parties; it is always open to rebuttal." *Ibid.*, p. 980. Black, arguing for the Tilden electors in the Florida case, came near giving the whole case away: "Therefore, if the governor of the State of Florida, after this appointment of electors was made by the people, undertook to certify that they were not elected and to put somebody else in the place which belonged to them, this act was utterly void and false and fraudulent. We are not going behind the action of the State; we are going behind the fraudulent act of an officer of the State whose act had no validity in it whatever." *Ibid.*, pp. 97-98. Both Field and Black were of course anxious to prove that they could go behind the decision of the canvassing board, and they made no distinction between the pronouncement of the board and the Governor's certificate. The right to go behind the Governor's certificate was distinctly stated by Evarts in the Florida case, *Ibid.*, p. 116, and by Stanley Matthews, *Ibid.*, p. 107. See also pp. 101 and 581. Justice Bradley in the Florida case, said: "But the Houses of Congress may undoubtedly inquire whether the supposed certificate of the executive is genuine; and I think they may also inquire whether it is plainly false, or whether it contains a clear mistake of fact, inasmuch as it is not itself the appointment, nor the ascertainment thereof, but only a certificate of the fact of appointment. . . ." In proceeding "with the count, [the two houses of Congress] are bound to recognize the determination of the State board of canvassers as the act of the State . . . ; and that while they may go behind the governor's certificate, if necessary, they can only do so for

board and the Governor's certificate may be no real distinction (though it appears plain enough), but it was not a new invention when the Oregon case came up for decision.

By the law of Oregon, the Secretary of State was given authority to canvass the vote. There appears no substantial reason for doubting this. The certificate of the Governor naming Cronin and not Watts was attested by the Secretary of State. But the Hayes electors procured from the Secretary of State a statement which showed that the three Hayes electors had actually received the majority at the election; and he accompanied this with a certificate to the effect that the foregoing tabulated statement was the vote "as opened and canvassed in the presence" of the Governor. The commission—once again, by an 8 to 7 vote—decided to ignore the Governor's certificate and to accept the Secretary's statement as to who were in fact the electors chosen, on the ground that he and no one else had the duty under the law of Oregon to canvass the returns, and the act of the Governor in giving Cronin a certificate was without authority of law.[36]

But the defenders of the Democratic cause did not despair, and their most cogent declaration was this—not to the effect that Cronin, the Democratic candidate, was elected because Watts had not been, and not, therefore, that the Governor's certificate declaring Cronin to be an elector was final and valid—but to the effect that inasmuch as Watts was ineligible, only two electors were chosen: "there was a failure on the part of the State to appoint a third elector."[37] Even, however, if

the purpose of ascertaining whether he has truly certified the results to which the board arrived." *Ibid.*, p. 1023. He made statements to the same effect in the Louisiana case. *Ibid.*, p. 1030. Stoughton, one of the counsel for the Republican cause, said in the Florida case, "I have said that the purpose of the testimony offered is to go behind, not merely the governor's certificate—for that undoubtedly, upon questions of forgery, upon questions of mistake, upon many questions, this tribunal could deal with—but, designing to get behind that, the purpose is to get behind the action of that tribunal which the State has set up, and to cancel its finding. . . ." *Ibid.*, p. 112.

[36] *Ibid.*, pp. 455-457, 640-641.

[37] Motion by Field. *Ibid.*, p. 638. See also Field's motion to the effect that, as there was no valid election of a third elector *on the day prescribed by the act of Congress*, only two electors were chosen. *Ibid.*, p. 639. The position of Justice Field, stating one phase of the Democratic case, is as follows: "The question then arises, Watts being ineligible, whether the person receiving the next highest number of votes, he being eligible, was elected. Governor Grover held that such person was elected. . . . In his action in this respect he followed the rule which obtains in England. . . . There are numerous decisions by courts of the highest character in this country to the same effect. . . . But I do not yield my assent to them; they are not in harmony with the spirit of our system of elections. . . . The weight of judicial opinion in this country is, that votes given for an ineligible candidate are merely

there were a failure to choose more than two electors at the popular election, could not the vacancy be filled by these electors legally chosen? Justice Field answered this question in the negative; he declared that while Oregon had by law given the electors authority to fill vacancies, the law referred to filling a vacancy only after the office had once been filled; and inasmuch as the office, in Field's opinion, had not been filled at the election, there was no such vacancy as the Oregon law contemplated. He endeavored to maintain his position by reference to the general law of Oregon, which contained a statement that an office should become vacant under certain circumstances and did not mention ineligibility. But the Oregon law covering the duties of electors read: "If there shall be a vacancy in the office of an elector, occasioned by death, refusal to act, neglect to attend, or *otherwise* [italics not in the original], the electors present shall immediately proceed to fill, by *viva voce* and plurality of votes, such vacancy in the electoral college." [38] Needless to say the stalwart eight did not accede to Field's construction of the Oregon statute; and indeed the law appears to have given the electors ample authority to do just what the Republican electors did. Oregon's three votes were held by the commission to have been cast for Hayes.

South Carolina remained to be considered. Having met with defeat in the three preceding cases, the Democratic counsel could have little or no hope of persuading the commission to change its position. The Republican certificates, as presented, were scrupulously correct in form; to persuade the commission to go behind the returns was a hopeless undertaking. Arguing for the Democratic cause, Montgomery Blair made a powerful though unavailing attack on the political conditions in the state, which showed that the voice of the people had not been freely expressed; he referred to the "criminals", who by military force held South Carolina in thraldom, and made an impassioned plea to the commission to cast out the vote of the state, where only a travesty of popular government had been indulged in: "Can it possibly be a free State authorized to vote and decide a presidential election when the State is covered with deputy marshals and troops, and voters have to pass through files of armed men to the polls? Now I assert that we shall be able to show you they had a deputy marshal for every ten

ineffectual to elect him, and that they are not to be thrown out as blanks, and the election given to the eligible candidate having the next highest number of votes." *Ibid.*, pp. 991-992.
[38] *Ibid.*, p. 993.

negroes, with labels on their shoulders, and marched their squads of ten up before the soldiery and swore them to vote the whole republican ticket, then marched them to the polls and stood by them till they voted. . . . Can you justify yourselves in counting that vote?" [39]

Jeremiah S. Black, presumably without hope of any change in the commission's opinion, indulged in a reckless assault, which probably furnishes an excellent example of the outraged feelings of the Democrats throughout the nation: "We may struggle for justice; we may cry for mercy; we may go down on our knees, and beg and woo for some little recognition of our rights as American citizens; but we might as well put up our prayers to Jupiter, or Mars, as bring suit in the court where Rhadamanthus presides." [40] As in other cases, the commission by the customary majority decided in favor of the Hayes electors: the failure of the legislature to provide a registration system did not render void all elections held under laws otherwise sufficient; there was in the state a government republican in form; the troops were placed there by the President to suppress insurrection at the request of the proper state authorities; there existed no power either in the commission or in Congress to inquire into the circumstances under which the vote for electors was given; the votes to be counted were those of the electors presented by the state.

The results announced by the commission in the four critical cases were of course conclusive. The House refused its consent to counting the votes as reported; the Senate consented; and under the terms of the provision for deciding the controversy, as both houses did not reject the commission's reports, its findings were accepted. On the whole, despite intense feeling and acrid partisanship, the politicians acted as statesmen. The division of the commission reflected, of course, the force of party affiliations; but there is also evident such strong argument on each side, particularly on the more technical questions— and especially on the question arising out of the miasmic morass of Louisiana—that even a faint breeze of unconscious party feeling was sufficient to direct the course of an honest judge. It seems obvious that the refusal to go behind the returns was not a mere subterfuge adopted for purely partisan purposes; nor was that determination reached only in order to escape the necessity of examining actual conditions during the election and actual fraud at the polls; the refusal was good law and good sense. On the very troublesome questions

[39] *Ibid.*, p. 693.
[40] *Ibid.*, p. 696.

which arose in the Louisiana case, the Republican commissioners had at the least a position defended by strong argument. The main decision in the Oregon dispute seems to rest on unquestionable grounds.

As suggested in an earlier page, one constitutional principle appears to be plain: Congress must leave to the state its constitutional authority to appoint electors. But there remains a corollary: the state is under constitutional obligation to certify the appointments and to do so without harassing ambiguity. If a state cannot make a plain law, carry it out and make a conclusive and intelligible announcement of the fact of appointment, there is no reason why its dereliction should embarrass Congress or lead that body into temptation; under such circumstances the state should lose its electoral vote. There is, however, no need of our commenting at length upon what ought to be the law and the accepted principle. Ten years after the disputed election, Congress passed an act covering the subject in considerable detail (February 3, 1887). The act is too long and complex to be fully exposed in these pages, but it gives in most respects substantial recognition of the state's primary responsibility to settle its own disputes in accordance with prescribed state law.

The election of 1876-1877 is commonly spoken of as the stolen election or as the crime of 1876. Comment is unnecessary. The criminality indulged in, notably in Louisiana, like good wine needs no bush. The Republicans throughout the nation pointed to the methods whereby negroes having the constitutional right to vote were prevented by intimidation or violence; and such illegality justified in the minds of the more intense partisans any amount of high-handed procedure, not to say legerdemain, on the part of the returning boards. The Democrats, on the other hand, dwelt on the rascality of the carpetbag politicians and the menace of African domination.

The total product of the whole disagreeable and humiliating controversy was this: the situation, as it really was, had been disclosed in all its nakedness and deformity. The end of the business was at hand. The discussions that had taken place in Congress, the arguments before the commission, and the offers of proof to establish corruption, though much had been said before, were doubtless enlightening and the people were weary of the spectacle. The decisions of the commission are of profound significance, because, by a strange turn of the wheel of fortune, pronouncement of the doctrine of states' rights was made by members of the Republican party. But that was not all: they had given a body blow to the idea that it was proper for a political party holding the reins at Washington to attempt to interfere with certain sacred and presumably untouchable rights of a state; and though the fourteenth and fifteenth amendments still stood, the southern states were left without serious interference to work out the grievous problems begotten by slavery, by racial differences, by the disasters of war, and by the ignominy of Reconstruction.

Before the end of the commission's work, conferences between certain Democratic and Republican leaders in Washington had resulted in an agreement on the one side to go on counting the votes and to refrain from violence in the south; on the other, to induce the administration and, if possible, Grant, to withdraw the troops.[41] On the whole, it appears fortunate that the withdrawal of the troops should have been the act of a Republican President, aware of the impossibility or the unrighteousness of maintaining free government by force. Soon after the inauguration, President Hayes began the process of removing the federal troops and allowing the southern states to manage their own affairs. The era of Reconstruction was over. The negro, we may again remind the reader, had been given the suffrage partly because the ballot was thought a necessary support for his civil liberties; but events proved he could not maintain his hold upon the suffrage without the army; the use of the army was found to be intolerable, pernicious. The courts might still do something. The pronouncements of the first section of the fourteenth amendment were not and are not without meaning even with respect to the negro, for whose sake they were chiefly enacted.

[41] Dunning, *Reconstruction*, p. 339; Haworth, *op. cit.*, pp. 268-270; C. R. Williams, *The Life of Rutherford Birchard Hayes*, I, p. 533 ff. Hayes appears to have come practically, if not wholly and distinctly, to the position that the south should not be ruled by force. Haworth *op. cit.*, p. 268; see also, Williams, *ut supra.*

CHAPTER XLIX

THE FOURTEENTH AMENDMENT

The constitutional history of the decades since the period of Reconstruction is the history of the adaptation of constitutional principles to rapidly-changing economic and social conditions. Such adaptation or development may, of course, be said to be the core of all constitutional history, for changes in the structure and activities of the body politic are brought about by the needs of society continuously undergoing modification. But it is peculiarly and strikingly true of the last quarter of the nineteenth century and the early years of the twentieth. America was for the first time plainly faced with the problems begotten by modern industrialism; though to some extent the issues had appeared before, it is only an exaggeration to say that not until after the Civil War were the people conscious of them, and not until then did the problems come obviously within the sphere of what is now constitutional history. The industrial revolution of the eighteenth century seemed to take effect in America and produce its serious problem of adjustment many decades after the countries of Europe, notably Great Britain, were aware of the task and had entered on efforts of remedial legislation.

This tardiness may be accounted for in sundry ways. One reason doubtless was that the job presented to the people had been to take possession of the continent and to exploit its natural resources; and of that task much remained after the war was over. The main resource was land itself. There were wide stretches of open and unoccupied territory; the west offered its allurement; there was freedom and, mayhap, profit in the farm and the lumber-camp; there was escape from the drudgery of the factory and the tyranny of the machine. The population of the country was predominantly rural or semi-rural. Men were engaged in handling nature's machine, the soil.[1] Railroads

[1] Indeed, if one examines the statistics, he is tempted to say that, despite the rapid and sweeping development of industrial enterprise in the east, the main job of America for two decades and more after the war was to occupy the continent rather than to build up gigantic factories and multiply the products of machinery. Professor Turner

and factories had, it is true, even before the Civil War, affected no small number of people; but life was still comparatively simple and old-fashioned. Household manufacturing was to some extent carried on until after the middle of the century; and there may be men living to-day who can remember seeing their grandfathers or even their fathers as they sat by the fire on a winter evening and carved out with knife or drawshave a new ax-helve or fork-handle. In other words, America had not as yet become industrialized.

And yet we can hazard the guess that, had it not been for the slavery question and the war, the nation would have faced some of the problems of modern industry and labor at an earlier date. The social movements which expressed themselves in politics toward the end of the thirties indicate a partial realization of the new situation and of new social needs. But, as a matter of fact, the people were then beginning the task, not of meeting the new perplexities begotten by machinery, but of getting rid for once and all of the oldest method of industry known to man. Slavery, where the capitalist owned the laborer, presented a labor problem as well as a race problem. The abolition of slavery was viewed as a matter of morality and indeed of religion; clearly enough the real job, which for a generation occupied much of the attention and absorbed the emotional capacity of the people, was thrust upon them by an outworn system of labor. The nation was modernizing itself by casting off a system of labor as old as the pyramids. We probably cannot overemphasize the importance of that fact, accompanied, as it was, with sectional strife, with all the bitterness of war and its aftermath, and with the sordidness which appears to be the inevitable residue of war. We must remember too, keeping the whole epoch in mind, that the nation had been burdened with the task of saving itself from disruption, and to accomplish such a task is quite enough for one generation. People cannot do everything at once or distribute their emotions with a free and easy hand.

If we are interested then, as we must be, in the question of why the problems of very modern life arose so late and why the decades passed without any large view of the changing world and without any conscious preparation for meeting the perplexities that were so soon to come, we answer by pointing to the fact of tardy industrialization and to the tasks which people were actually undertaking. Party strife,

placed the disappearance of the frontier at about the year 1890, and presented impressive figures to show the enormous increase of farm acres and cultivated areas in the years after the war, while the machine age also was rapidly developing.

based in considerable measure upon the old issues of slavery, war and nationalism, continued after the war was finished. To the extent that the slavery question had entered the field of social morality and justice, attention to slavery had naturally brought into clear relief the value of freedom; men were induced to indulge in further glorification of their own freedom and, likewise, to suppose that, if the laborer were not *owned* by the capitalist, he was free. But the truth is, as said on earlier pages of this work, the agitation against slavery was but one of those movements for liberalism and social righteousness—humanitarianism—which were transforming the modern world. If one should desire therefore to deal with the purely speculative, one would expect to find men, upon the extirpation of slavery, also anxious, at the first opportune moment, to reach out the hand of helpfulness to the serfs of the machine and the factory.

Whether such expectations be justified or not, the problems of social control of industry were delayed until slavery was disposed of. After the war was over the politician went merrily ahead; industries grew into giants; wage-earners increased in numbers; corporations occupied strategic positions; but the politician and many a common man seemed not to grow weary of lambasting the rebel or, on the other hand, of pointing to the vulgarities of Reconstruction, and they let the days go by. Passions of the past were fostered rather than forgotten; men did not see the new problems assembling like clouds on the horizon; they waited till the storm had broken. The gift of prophecy, keen appreciation of an impending future, realization of an actual present, are not the possession of most statesmen—or of anyone else.

As long as the country remained rural, or largely so, and retained the sentiments begotten by the frontier and free land, the people were in no state of mind to face the complexities of factory labor or the problems of congested areas. The farmer is proverbially individualistic; and the farm of the olden days was largely self-supporting and self-dependent. The farmer probably felt his isolation to be more than it actually was; and it is significant that the countrymen, in actual fact, were the first class after the war was over to realize their relationship to certain results of modern industrial enterprise. But, using the reaper and raising huge crops of wheat to feed the eastern laborers and the workmen of Europe, the farmer did not for a time see that he was being tied up in a vast economic system and was being enfolded, as were others, in a new and rapidly developing industrial régime. His mind was taken up with visions of new wealth garnered by his own toil from his own wide-flung acres. Awakening to the realities of the new social and industrial world was also delayed and rendered difficult by the common American traditional belief in the virtue of freedom unhampered by regulation or interference; the very essence of Americanism was that the individual should be left alone to fight his way forward and pursue happiness. This sentiment retarded the rise of a sense of social responsibility and a realization of social interdependence long after interdependence of sections and classes was a very actual fact.

The war had established nationalism as a legal fact beyond all questioning; industry had become largely national in scope and character; and by the fourteenth amendment individual liberty was given national protection; local legislation had, in certain vital respects, to be consonant with a national norm, laid down by a central authority, the federal courts. By the subjection of certain types of state action to federal supervision or check, the land lost something of the values of federalism as a system of national organization; perhaps the states might have been treated as so many experiment-stations where devices for meeting new conditions could be tested by experience, by trial and error. But speculations of this kind do not aid us much. The facts are plain.

Before many years, but generally speaking not before the end of the century, some persons were speaking almost contemptuously of a fixed Constitution which placed its barriers in the way of popular legislation or of what passed for popular demand. Why, it was asked, should an intelligent and progressive people be bound by the shackles of an eighteenth-century Constitution? The presence of this sentiment among those eager for change, who advocated the freedom of the people-at-large to act through their governments without hampering restraint, is a matter of considerable significance. The sentiment was commonly expressed with the dogmatic clarity of the self-assured. The fact that the strongest advocates of "democracy" were beginning to look askance at the obstacles set up by a written Constitution shows us the changes wrought by the passing years. In the eighteenth century a fixed constitution was the ideal of men ending or hoping to end the long struggle between superimposed government and personal safety; by the end of the nineteenth century the fixed Constitution, with the balanced system so dear to the men of earlier days, was considered the stronghold of conservatism, which was secured by complexity of the governmental system.

The task of adapting constitutional law to the new conditions rested on the shoulders of justices in the courts. The fourteenth amendment placed new restrictions upon the states, and questions as to the extent and character of these restrictions naturally arose. The limits had to be marked out by the courts, not by the political branches of the government acting by positive legislation. The amendment, though intended at its inception to protect the freedmen, was general in its terms, and the significance of its phrases had to be determined by the courts in passing upon concrete cases. The difficulty involved in working out the scope of the amendment arose out of the fact, that protections were thrown about personal liberty at the very time when there was new need of determining what was the nature or the limits of liberty. Legislation of a drastic character, running counter to older and cherished beliefs, was to many persons a violent wrench, not to be endured without considerable perturbation of spirit. When indicating the respective limits of personal liberty and of governmental control, the courts had to perform their task in legalistic fashion—not by entering upon a complete break with old precepts and principles of law, but by recognizing the reality of new conditions and by adapting old principles to new facts. The task was not an easy one. The nature of this task and some illustrations of how it was accomplished are presented in the following pages.

A few words are needed—and only a few words—concerning the extent to which the negro has been protected and his rights assured by the fourteenth amendment as interpreted by the courts. In cases discussed in a previous chapter, the Supreme Court had declared the amendment to be a guarantee of protection against the act of the state itself and was not intended to restrain or to punish individual offenders.[2] Therefore, if a negro claimed that his rights were invaded, he must be prepared to show that the invasion was by the state or by some officer clothed with state authority and acting under color of such authority.[3] A number of cases arose in which a negro asserted

[2] United States v. Cruikshank, 92 U. S. 542 (1876); Civil Rights Cases, 109 U. S. 3 (1883); Virginia v. Rives, 100 U. S. 313 (1880).
[3] The amendment provides "for a case where one who is in possession of state power uses that power to the doing of the wrongs which the Amendment forbids even although the consummation of the wrong may not be within the powers possessed if the commission of the wrong itself is rendered possible or is efficiently

that he had been deprived of his rights because the jury which tried and convicted him was composed entirely of white men. The first case involved the constitutionality of a West Virginia law which confined the right of jury service to whites; there was a clear-cut instance of state action. The Court held the law unconstitutional inasmuch as the amendment "implies the existence of rights and immunities, prominent among which is an immunity from inequality of legal protection, either for life, liberty, or property." [4] In a similar case arising under a law of Delaware a like principle was announced.[5] So far the negro is assured equality by court decisions. But the assurance is of no substantial value to a negro facing a jury made up entirely of white men, unless it can be shown that there was intentional and quasi-official discrimination; an impaneling officer can, without showing vast and intelligent circumspection, succeed uniformly in summoning a jury of white men.[6] In the Delaware case, however, the Court said that a general practice of excluding negroes raised a presumption of denial of equality, and that, on this ground, the judgment should be set aside.

Of somewhat greater importance is the matter of discrimination in other ways. Does the amendment prohibit setting aside the negroes as a separate class? Does mere classification deprive him of the equal protection of the law? This general subject of equality, whether it bears upon negroes or other persons, presented its difficulties; but the courts have uniformly decided that classification is not by any

aided by state authority lodged in the wrongdoer." Home Tel. and Tel. Co. *v.* Los Angeles, 227 U. S. 278, 287 (1913). See also Ex parte Virginia, 100 U. S. 339, 346-347 (1880). It is an old and well-established principle that the agent of a state, acting under an unconstitutional law, is personally liable; but notice the application of the doctrine to the amendment and the right to prevent a state from using unconstitutional power.

[4] Strauder *v.* West Virginia, 100 U. S. 303, 310 (1880). "Nor", said the Court, "if a law should be passed excluding all naturalized Celtic Irishmen, would there be any doubt of its inconsistency with the spirit of the amendment." *Ibid.,* 308.

[5] Neal *v.* Delaware, 103 U. S. 370 (1881). See also Bush *v.* Kentucky, 107 U. S. 110 (1883); Norris *v.* Alabama, 294 U. S. 587 (1935).

[6] In Virginia *v.* Rives, 100 U. S. 313, 322-323 (1880), the Court commented on the assertion that in a certain county negroes had never been allowed to serve as jurors in any case in which a colored man was interested: "The facts may have been as stated, and yet the jury which indicted them, and the panel summoned to try them, may have been impartially selected. . . . It *is* a right to which every colored man is entitled, that, in the selection of jurors . . . , there shall be no exclusion of his race, and no discrimination against them because of their color. But this is a different thing from the right . . . to have the jury composed in part of colored men." Cf. Ex parte Virginia, 100 U. S. 339 (1880).

means necessarily unlawful; illegality exists where classification has no reasonable basis but is essentially arbitrary.[7]

A case of importance bearing on the right of a state to treat negroes, in their social relations with whites, as a distinct class was the case of Plessy v. Ferguson.[8] The matter at issue was the constitutionality of a Louisiana statute requiring railroad companies to provide separate but equal accommodations for white and colored passengers—commonly called the Jim Crow Car Law. The law was declared to be constitutional. Giving the opinion and decision of the Court, Justice Brown made this significant statement: "The object of the [fourteenth] amendment was undoubtedly to enforce the absolute equality of the two races before the law, but in the nature of things it could not have been intended to abolish distinctions based upon color, or to enforce social, as distinguished from political equality, or a commingling of the two races upon terms unsatisfactory to either. Laws permitting, and even requiring, their separation in places where they are liable to be brought into contact do not necessarily imply the inferiority of either race to the other, and have been generally, if not universally, recognized as within the competency of state legislatures in the exercise of their police power." The opinion referred to the common instance of establishing separate schools for white and colored children, which had been held valid in several northern states by the state judiciary. This sentiment, thus clearly announced by the Court, seems like a far cry from the position taken by Congress twenty-one years earlier in passing the Civil Rights Act, and far from the enthusiastic idealism of the earlier period. Here we find expression of a new, though not entirely new, social philosophy: "If the two races", said the Justice, "are to meet upon terms of social equality, it must be the result of natural affinities, a mutual appreciation of each

---

[7] "The equal protection clause . . . does not take from the State the power to classify in the adoption of police laws" provided the classification has reasonable basis and is not purely arbitrary. "One who assails the classification . . . must carry the burden of showing that it does not rest upon any reasonable basis, but is essentially arbitrary." Lindsley v. Natural Carbonic Gas Co., 220 U. S. 61, 78-79 (1911), and cases cited. In the case of Nixon v. Herndon, 273 U. S. 536 (1927), the Court held a Texas statute invalid, which provided that negroes should not be eligible to participate in Democratic primary elections. The ground of invalidity was that it was denial of equal protection of the laws. "States", said the Court, "may do a good deal of classifying that it is difficult to believe rational, but there are limits, and it is too clear for extended argument that color cannot be made the basis of a statutory classification affecting the right set up in this case". Ibid., 541.

[8] 163 U. S. 537 (1896).

other's merits and a voluntary consent of individuals. . . . If one race be inferior to the other socially, the Constitution of the United States cannot put them upon the same plane." The most expressive phrase in the above quotation is "the nature of things"; the Court was unwilling to enforce an idealistic interpretation and ignore the realities of social facts.

The courts have recognized the validity of classification in the conduct of education. A state may prohibit a private school from educating white and negro students together.[9] Under circumstances justifying the discrimination, a school district may use public money for the maintenance of a high school for white students only.[10] We may perhaps infer in general, therefore, that, though reasonable classification may be made, unfair discrimination in educational privileges will not be upheld; but presumably the fact of unfairness would have to be very evident or the courts would not hold the allotment of public money unconstitutional.

So little has the negro profited by the fourteenth amendment through judicial determination, so signally inoperative has it proved to be in establishing or maintaining social equality, that even such brief consideration as that given in the preceding paragraphs appears unnecessary. One is tempted to say that, for the main purposes in the minds of its originators, the amendment has been a complete failure. But the amendment has probably had moral effect, even when court decisions seemed to be of little or no avail. In all likelihood, without the amendment, legislation like the "black code" of Mississippi would have stood on the state statute books or been placed there; and though some persons may to-day think such enactments wise, the classification thus provided for would not now stand judicial scrutiny for a moment. This fact remains—the essentials of civil liberty are not interfered with by state enactments; and reasonable opportunities for growth and prosperity are checked, if at all, not by formal legal enactments, but by racial barriers and like hindrances which are known full well both north and south of Mason and Dixon's line.

For fifty years or more, the relationship of the freedman to the fourteenth amendment has been practically lost to view. On the other

[9] Berea College v. Kentucky, 211 U. S. 45 (1908).

[10] Cumming v. County Board of Education, 175 U. S. 528 (1899), where it appeared that so few colored children would attend a colored high school that insufficient funds could be used for colored elementary education.

hand its interpretation and its application to social problems have brought scores of cases for judicial decision. The first case in which the essential nature and meaning of the new amendment were discussed by the Supreme Court was decided five years after its adoption.[11] In many ways the problems involved were crucial and critical. The decision was rendered by a divided Court, four to five; and among the four dissenters was Justice Field, of Democratic antecedents, who ranged himself with those asserting the effect of the amendment to be much more sweeping, more destructive of state autonomy, than the majority of the Court admitted. Nevertheless the decision and especially the opinion of the Court as given by Justice Miller appeared to put such a construction upon the amendment that the Court would not in future be troubled by a multitude of controversies. The justices little knew what the future had in store.

The case turned upon the constitutionality of a Louisiana statute which gave to a corporation the exclusive right for a term of years to maintain, within a certain area, a place for slaughtering animals to be sold for meat. In the course of the decision, the Court thought it advisable to place its interpretation on the first sentence of the fourteenth amendment as well as on other portions, though an interpretation of those words was only incidentally germane to the real issue involved. The sentence in question declared: "All persons born or naturalized in the United States, and subject to the jurisdiction thereof, are citizens of the United States and of the State wherein they reside." The purpose, of course, was to overrule the Dred Scott case in so far as that decision denied to negroes the status of citizenship. The Court made plain the existence of double citizenship; the words quoted are a clear indication of a distinction between citizenship in the state and citizenship in the United States.[12] Unless we consider Taney's decision as good law when he announced it, the amendment was, therefore, in its first sentence declaratory and affirmative, intended to allay doubts and not to impose new restrictions;[13] it added

[11] Slaughter-House Cases, 16 Wallace 36 (1873).

[12] "Not only may a man be a citizen of the United States without being a citizen of a State, but an important element is necessary to convert the former into the latter. He must reside within the State to make him a citizen of it, but it is only necessary that he should be born or naturalized in the United States to be a citizen of the Union." *Ibid.*, 74.

[13] "These considerations confirm the view, already expressed in this opinion, that the opening sentence of the Fourteenth Amendment is throughout affirmative and declaratory, intended to allay doubts and to settle controversies which had arisen, and not to impose any new restrictions upon citizenship." United States *v.* Wong

nothing to the body of constitutional law, for when the Constitution came fresh from the hands of its framers it included this idea of double citizenship.

The Court closely associated the opening sentence of the amendment with the sentence immediately following: "No State shall make or enforce any law which shall abridge the privileges or immunities of citizens of the United States". The attention of the majority and of the dissenting justices also was largely directed to the construction of those words. The majority, finding in the amendment a clear distinction between state and United States citizenship, held that the amendment in that clause protected only the rights of the latter. If we assume that, in the framing of this portion of the amendment [14]—the portion referring to privileges and immunities—, the framers and their supporters had in mind conditions in the south and were intent on making unlawful the discriminatory legislation of the southern states (even though the words were of general and not sectional application), they were in this respect unfortunate. One need not expect courts to construe laws so as to accord with legislative intentions, if the law as enacted says something not in accord with those intentions. The amendment plainly prohibits state encroachment upon privileges and immunities of *United States citizenship,* and the question therefore turned upon what these were.

No court has ever attempted strictly to define and enumerate the privileges and immunities belonging either to state or United States citizenship; once and again, general descriptions have been given; and furthermore, it must be said, even in this case the Court was not, to

Kim Ark, 169 U. S. 649, 687-688 (1898). "In this, as in other respects," said the Court, "it must be interpreted in the light of the common law, the principles and history of which were familiarly known to the framers of the Constitution." *Ibid.,* 654.

Without the patient consideration given to other portions of the amendment, the Court, in the Slaughter-House Cases, 16 Wallace 36, 73, said the words, "subject to its jurisdiction" were intended to exclude from the operation of the amendment "children of ministers, consuls, and citizens or subjects of foreign States born within the United States." At a later day the Court declared a Chinaman born in the United States to be an American citizen. United States *v.* Wong Kim Ark, 169 U. S. 649 (1898). In this case the Court refused to accept the definition of "subject to the jurisdiction", as given above, and held that the justices in the Slaughter-House Cases did not in this respect speak with care and exactness, and that the remark was wholly aside from the question in judgment.

[14] Some of the expressions used by congressmen when the amendment was under discussion appear to be distinct pronouncements of the interpretation advocated by the dissenting justices. See *Congressional Globe,* 39 Cong., 1 sess., part III, pp. 2542. 2765-2766.

say the least, over-explicit or pellucid in its exposition.[15] It did emphatically deny that the amendment, by the words in question, swept into the field of federal power the duty to protect the whole catalogue of civil rights and liberties belonging to the citizens of a free state. The amendment, therefore, in this respect was only declaratory; for at no time in the past could anyone properly have asserted a state's right to intrude upon rights inherent in United States citizenship. "If this inhibition", said Justice Field in his dissenting opinion, ". . . only refers, as held by the majority of the court in their opinion, to such privileges and immunities as were before its adoption specially designated in the Constitution or necessarily implied as belonging to citizens of the United States, it was a vain and idle enactment, which accomplished nothing, and most unnecessarily excited Congress and the people on its passage."[16]

In later years there were some persistent though futile attempts to extend this clause of the amendment beyond the limits set by the Court in this critical decision. Attorneys in their arguments sought to have the Court declare that the privileges and immunities included the specific rights provided for in the first eight amendments.[17] This was an interesting example of misdirected acumen; for, as we have already seen, the eight amendments are restrictions on the United

---

[15] The Court did refer to Crandall v. Nevada, 6 Wallace 35 (1868), still a leading case on the subject, and in referring to the privileges and immunities of United States citizenship spoke of their owing "their existence to the Federal government, its National character, its Constitution, or its laws." The privileges and immunities are, we may presume, the corollary of governmental duties and responsibilities. The privileges and immunities of a state citizen flow from the power, duty and obligation of the state and its government; those of a United States citizen flow from the powers, duty, responsibilities of the United States and its government. ". . . those [privileges and immunities of United States citizenship] are privileges and immunities arising out of the nature and essential character of the national government, and granted or secured by the Constitution of the United States." In re Kemmler, 136 U. S. 436, 448 (1890).

[16] Slaughter-House Cases, 16 Wallace 36, 96 (1873). "The amendment [the fourteenth] did not add to the privileges and immunities of a citizen. It simply furnished an additional guaranty for the protection of such as he already had." Minor v. Happersett, 21 Wallace 162, 171 (1875). It was held in this case that the Constitution does not confer the right of suffrage on anyone. A state law conferring suffrage on men alone was valid.

[17] They sought to maintain that the first ten amendments as far as they secure and recognize fundamental rights make them privileges and immunities of the man as a citizen of the United States. See Spies v. Illinois, 123 U. S. 131 (1887). "A trial by jury in suits at common law pending in the State courts is not, therefore, a privilege or immunity of national citizenship, which the States are forbidden by the Fourteenth Amendment to abridge." Walker v. Sauvinet, 92 U. S. 90, 92 (1876).

States government, not on the states; the privilege of a citizen, for example, not to have cruel and unusual punishment inflicted upon him is a privilege which he can claim against any law or process of the United States government. If anyone claims that a punishment provided for by state law is cruel and unusual, he may, perchance, be protected by the later portions of the first section of the fourteenth amendment, but not under the privileges and immunities clause.[18]

In light of later decisions it seems strange that in the Slaughter-House Cases the Court did not discuss at greater length due process of law and the equal protection of the laws. After saying that the argument for the plaintiffs did not much press the contention that they had been deprived of property without due process or had been deprived of equal protection, the Court contented itself with declaring: ". . . under no construction of that provision that we have ever seen, or any that we deem admissible, can the restraint imposed by the State of Louisiana . . . be held to be a deprivation of property within the meaning of that provision."[19] Concerning the equality clause the Court declared, "We doubt very much whether any action of a State

[18] The question so often arises in the minds of students and others, that emphasis seems necessary. Accepting the interpretation of that clause as announced by the Court in the Slaughter-House Cases, the principle is plain enough. Of course no state can deprive any citizen of the privileges of United States citizenship; and one of these privileges is not to be subjected *by the United States* to cruel and unusual punishments. In Maxwell *v.* Dow, 176 U. S. 581 (1900), the question was whether by providing for a proceeding by information and for a trial-jury of less than twelve men the constitution of Utah intrenched upon the privileges and immunities of a citizen of the United States. Even at that late date the Court found it necessary to point to the fact that the early amendments to the Constitution did not bind the states (a decision announced by Chief Justice Marshall more than half a century before—1833, in Barron *v.* Baltimore, 7 Peters 243), and that the provisions of the first eight were not by virtue of the fourteenth amendment made obligatory upon the states. ". . . it is possible that some of the personal rights safeguarded by the first eight Amendments against National action may also be safeguarded against state action, because a denial of them would be a denial of due process of law. . . . If this is so, it is not because those rights are enumerated in the first eight Amendments, but because they are of such a nature that they are included in the conception of due process of law." Justice Moody in Twining *v.* New Jersey, 211 U. S. 78, 99 (1908).

[19] "In view of later decisions of the Court relative to the extent of the State police power over liberty and property, it may well be doubted whether the decision might not have been otherwise, had the case been argued more fully on the point of due process and had the facts been more clearly stressed; for one of the dissenting Judges, Field, always insisted in subsequent cases, that the question whether the statute involved had any real relation whatsoever to the police power had not been properly presented or considered." Charles Warren, *The Supreme Court in United States History*, III, p. 271.

not directed by way of discrimination against the negroes as a class, or on account of their race, will ever be held to come within the purview of this provision." This proved a vain hope.

The decision was indicative of a reaction against the extreme centralizing tendency of the years immediately preceding. Though the opinion of the majority was chiefly directed to the interpretation of "privileges and immunities of citizens of the United States", its attitude toward the whole amendment was decidedly conservative: "And where it is declared that Congress shall have the power to enforce that article, was it intended to bring within the power of Congress the entire domain of civil rights heretofore belonging exclusively to the States?" [20] The answer was in the negative. This at least was clear: the decision left the states, as they were before, in charge of the general field of legislation for controlling and regulating their internal concerns. They were left in charge of the police power, the right to legislate for the health, safety, and well-being of the people. And yet, as we have already seen, the Civil Rights Act, which was passed soon after the decision in the Slaughter-House Cases, assumed the right of Congress to legislate directly for the preservation of equality; and, ten years after the Slaughter-House Cases, the Court found it necessary in the Civil Rights Cases to pronounce the final and conclusive principle so plainly that the dullard could understand.

Only in subsequent years did the full force of the amendment come to light; and, as will appear, the due process of law clause gave basis for continuous and plentiful attacks by litigants alleging the invalidity of state legislation. Many decisions of the Court dealt with matters which the Slaughter-House Cases seemed to have committed finally to the discretion of the states themselves. Five years after Justice Miller gave the opinion in the leading case we have been considering, he commented in another case on the surprising number of cases with which the docket of the Court was "crowded" and in which the Court was asked "to hold that State courts and State legislatures have deprived their own citizens of life, liberty, or property without due

[20] Slaughter-House Cases, 16 Wallace 36, 77 (1873). There was considerable unfavorable as well as favorable comment by the press. "It is important as showing that the Court is recovering from the war fever and is getting ready to abandon sentimental canons of construction." The *Nation*, April 24, 1873, quoted by Warren, *op. cit.*, III, p. 265. Judge Moody, thirty-five years later, said, "Undoubtedly, it gave much less effect to the Fourteenth Amendment than some of the public men active in framing it intended, and disappointed many others. On the other hand, if the views of the minority had prevailed, it is easy to see how far the authority and independence of the States would have been diminished. . . ." *Ibid.*, p. 269.

process of law." [21] The increase in the number of cases was largely due to state enactments in quantity and variety hitherto unknown.

Toward the end of the sixties and at the beginning of the next decade, there was unrest among the people of the agricultural states, especially those states in the upper part of the Mississippi valley. The Granger movement, which was a protest against existing industrial conditions in that region, resulted in the passing of laws to restrict or regulate the rates charged by railroads and elevators. The constitutionality of this legislation was contested before the federal Supreme Court in a series of cases commonly called the "Granger Cases" (1877), which are conspicuous, not to say epochal, in the development of constitutional law. [22] In the railroad cases there was a passing reference to the contract clause of the Constitution and to the effect of provisions in state constitutions declaring the right to alter or repeal corporate charters; and there was some brief discussion also of interference by the states with interstate commerce; but the main point at issue was the right of the state to prescribe rates.

The most significant position of the Court was given in Munn v. Illinois, [23] a case in which there was no question of a charter contract. The case turned upon the validity of an Illinois statute prescribing rates for the elevating and storage of grain. The elevators on the Chicago River held a strategic position. It appeared that fourteen warehouses, though owned by about thirty persons, were controlled by nine business firms, and that rates for storage were annually published in advance. "Thus", said the Court, "it is apparent that all the elevating facilities through which these vast productions 'of seven or eight great States of the West' must pass on the way 'to four or five of the States on the seashore' may be a 'virtual' monopoly." It certainly appeared to the farmer that he and his business were in the

---

[21] Davidson v. New Orleans, 96 U. S. 97, 104 (1878). The same surprise was expressed by Justice Field as late as 1885. Missouri Pacific R. Co. v. Humes, 115 U. S. 512. "Crowded" now appears an ill-chosen word, for the numbers soon increased rapidly. Warren, writing in 1922, says about 800 cases involving state statutes under the due process clause had been brought before the federal Supreme Court since 1873. Op. cit., III, p. 270.

[22] They are all in volume 94 of the Supreme Court reports. In the railroad cases, the counsel for the roads brought up the provision of the fourteenth amendment concerning the depriving a person of his property without due process. But the Court, on the whole, contented itself with referring to the Munn v. Illinois opinion.

[23] 94 U. S. 113 (1877).

grasp of a great combination which left to him the hard work while it reaped the profit.

Could such a condition of things be remedied by state legislation without violating the fourteenth amendment? Although the right to limit or check state legislation of this character could be made to rest only on the due process clause of the amendment, the Court entered upon no searching examination of the phrase.[24] The prohibition of the amendment was held to be as old as civilized government and to be found in Magna Charta—meaning by this, presumably, that due process of law and "law of the land" are of identical import. Until the "adoption of the Fourteenth Amendment, it was not supposed that statutes regulating the use, or even the price of the use, of private property necessarily deprived an owner of his property without due process of law. Under some circumstances they may, but not under all. The amendment does not change the law in this particular: it simply prevents the States from doing that which will operate as such a deprivation." Referring to the common law, "from whence came the right which the Constitution protects," the Court found that when private property is " 'affected with a public interest, it ceases to be *juris privati* only.' " "Property", the Court went on to say, "does become clothed with a public interest when used in a manner to make it of public consequence, and affect the community at large. When, therefore, one devotes his property to a use in which the public has an interest, he, in effect, grants to the public an interest in that use, and must submit to be controlled by the public for the common good, to the extent of the interest he has thus created." The right to regulate the charges of grain elevators was put on the same plane as the right to fix the charges of the common carrier, the miller, the ferryman, the innkeeper, the wharfinger, and other persons pursuing "a public employment" or " 'a sort of public office' ". Such regulation and control were held to be a proper exercise of the police power of the state.

There was strong dissent in the Court. Justice Field wrote a vigorous dissenting opinion in which Justice Strong concurred. "There is no magic", he said, "in the language, though used by a constitu-

---

[24] Logically the "Granger Cases" should be considered in this volume in connection with due process and the police power; but the principle laid down in these cases appears to deserve separate treatment, and I have been influenced by a desire to follow chronology as far as possible and to consider later due process as the doctrine was developed.

tional convention,[25] which can change a private business into a public one, or alter the character of the building in which the business is transacted." If the principles announced by the majority of the Court are sound law, the dissentients declared, there is no constitutional protection for private rights and "all property and all business in the State are held at the mercy of a majority of its legislature." They distinguished between the business thus regulated by the Illinois act and other businesses referred to by the majority of the Court as substantial precedents: "In all these cases [relied on by the majority to support the Illinois act], except that of interest on money, which I shall presently notice, there was some special privilege granted by the State or municipality. . . ."

Outside of the court-room there was approval and dismay. Lawyers of the older school were perturbed and in intellectual rebellion. To the managers of big business, waging commercial warfare and cherishing the principle of *laissez faire,* interference with industry appeared to be nothing short of wanton tyranny, while the public on the other hand came gradually to feel that uncontrolled industry left the common man in fetters, which constantly grew heavier and more burdensome.[26]

The demand for relief by the farmers of the midwest marks the beginning of a contest which ere long entered upon other phases. After the "Granger Cases" there was no doubt of the right of the state to regulate and control certain enterprises, which were as a rule conducted by corporations. Though this general principle was clear, its application, the determination of just how far legislative control could legally go, was not quickly or easily reached. In the Munn case the Court may have been influenced by the extraordinary conditions at Chicago, where the storage of grain was scarcely less than a complete monopoly. But a few years later, an act of the North Dakota legislature, regulating the price of elevating and storing grain, was sus-

---

[25] The constitution of Illinois, adopted in 1870, declared all elevators or storehouses where grain or other property is stored for a compensation to be public warehouses. The act under consideration was passed to carry this declaration into effect, and among other things it prescribed the charges that might be asked.

[26] To the readers of history, the importance of this case is not so much in the technical right to regulate charges and the classification of certain industries as in the rude shock it gave to the very old notion that man could do what he wished with his own. It must be connected also with the multiplication of commissions for regulation and for the fixing of rates. The succeeding decades disclosed the gradual but significant enlargement of governmental control and the adjustment of constitutional principles to social need.

tained, though, it appeared, anyone might build an elevator in that region for a few hundred dollars and be as independent as Robinson Crusoe.[27] The Court thus again justified regulation by placing the business in a certain category.

At no time has there been any attempt to determine with minute exactitude at what stage a business does become thus affected, or with any definiteness to describe its character and thus justify placing it on a certain list.[28] An observer is strongly inclined to say that the whole matter would have been simplified and made intelligible, if the Court had at the beginning said, that, when a business has reached such a stage and assumed such a character that there appeared to be a plain public need for legislative control of rates, enactments to that end would be constitutional. The decision in the "Granger Cases" would then have rested on the same general principle as that on which the Court later based its decisions in passing upon the scope of the police powers of the state. But such a declaration in 1877 would have shocked the conservative sense of the community; and in accord with charac-

[27] "When it is once admitted . . . that it is competent for the legislative power to control the business of elevating and storing grain, whether carried on by individuals or associations, in cities of one size and in some circumstances, it follows that such power may be legally exerted over the same business when carried on in smaller cities and in other circumstances." Brass v. North Dakota, ex rel. Stoeser, 153 U. S. 391, 403 (1894).

[28] In 1914 the Court held insurance to be a business affected with a public interest. "'The underlying principle is that business of certain kinds holds such a peculiar relation to the public interests that there is superinduced upon it the right of public regulation.'" German Alliance Insurance Co. v. Lewis, 233 U. S. 389, 411, quoting People v. Budd, 117 N. Y. 1, 27. In this case, too, the Court announced the need of adjustment to actual conditions of society, as it ha d done in some other cases not involving business affected with a public interest: "It would be a bold thing to say that the principle is fixed, inelastic, in the precedents of the past and cannot be applied though modern economic conditions may make necessary or beneficial its application." Ibid., 411. Stockyards have also been thus classified. Tagg Brothers and Moorhead v. United States, 280 U. S. 420 (1930). In Tyson and Brother v. Banton, 273 U. S. 418 (1927), the question presented was the validity of a New York statute which declared that the price of theater tickets is a matter affected with a public interest and forbade the resale of a ticket at a price in excess of fifty cents in advance of the price printed on its face. A divided Court held the statute void. The Court, striving for a classification, after referring to a number of previous decisions, said, "From the foregoing review it will be seen that each of the decisions of this court upholding governmental price regulation, aside from cases involving legislation to tide over temporary emergencies, has turned upon the existence of conditions, peculiar to the business under consideration, which bore such a substantial and definite relation to the public interest as to justify an indulgence of the legal fiction of a grant by the owner to the public of an interest in the use." Ibid., 438. A classification of sorts is attempted in Wolff Packing Co. v. Court of Industrial Relations, 262 U. S. 522, 535 (1923). See also Rihnik v. McBride, 277 U. S. 350 (1928).

teristic legal method, seeking precedents and practices as grounds for a decision, the Court reached back two hundred years and more and discovered them in Lord Hale's *De Portibus Maris*. Justice Holmes in a dissenting opinion fifty years later (1927) said "that the notion that a business is clothed with a public interest and has been devoted to the public use is little more than a fiction intended to beautify what is disagreeable to the sufferers." [29]

For nearly twenty years after the adoption of the amendment, there appeared no tendency to give the first section any very serious weight. In spite of strenuous opposition of the dissenting justices, the decisions appeared to be, almost literally, reading the amendment out of court. (1) Even before the Civil Rights Cases (1883), the amendment had been interpreted quite inevitably to mean that state action, and state action only, was referred to in the first section. (2) It was made fairly clear in the Slaughter-House Cases that primary legislation by Congress for regulating the internal affairs of the state was not justified by this section. (3) While there were indications of a willingness to protect the negro from discriminatory state legislation, there was no desire so to construe the amendment as to bring industries under the protection of the national government. (4) The privilege and immunity clause, so much relied on, had been interpreted to be in its main effect only an announcement of a principle always inherent in the constitutional system. (5) In the Munn case the Court announced that, if a business was in a certain category, rates for service could be prescribed by the legislature; and legislative discretion, it appeared, was unlimited.

But while it might appear that the amendment was emasculated by judicial interpretation and read out of court, as a matter of fact the courts were soon burdened with responsibility; if no ground for

[29] Tyson and Brother *v.* Banton, 273 U. S. 418, 446 (1927). See also Justice Stone dissenting. *Ibid.,* 451. The paragraph in the text above may stand as a part of constitutional history, but the words were not more than written when the Supreme Court, for the time being in the hands of the "liberals", practically jettisoned by a five to four decision the whole theory that business could be classified or segregated on the basis set down in the "Granger Cases": "It is clear that there is no closed class or category of businesses affected with a public interest. . . . The phrase 'affected with a public interest' can, in the nature of things, mean no more than that an industry, for adequate reason, is subject to control for the public good." Nebbia *v.* New York, March 5, 1934. The case is of interest also because it upheld a state commission's power to fix rates that could be neither lowered nor increased. Nebbia was charged with selling two quarts of milk and a five-cent loaf of bread for eighteen cents, when the commission had set the price of milk at nine cents per quart.

congressional legislation could be found in the general phrases purporting to safeguard life, liberty, property, and equality, then, if these general phrases were to have any marked effect, the responsibility for checking state legislation lay with the courts. In the eighties, judicial duties and obligations began to appear in formidable array, supported by shock troops of ingenious and argumentative counsel. To this matter we may now turn our attention, and first examine, more fully than we have done as yet, the question of equality.

The Court appeared for a time to have less difficulty in applying the principle of equality than that of due process. We have already seen that the Court, in passing upon the rights of negroes and on the question of race discrimination, laid down a leading and basic principle. But the declaration in favor of equality was not interpreted as a defense of negroes alone. The case of Yick Wo v. Hopkins (1886) [30] involved the validity of an ordinance forbidding any person to operate a laundry within the city of San Francisco in frame buildings, unless he should receive permission from the authorities. The decision is important (1) because the Supreme Court recognized an alien as a "person", whose rights are protected by the amendment,[31] and (2) because it recognized the fact that a law, not discriminatory on its face, may be so administered as to work discrimination and deny the equality of persons.[32] But it is well to notice that the Court in an earlier decision had upheld an ordinance of San Francisco which prohibited laundry work, within prescribed areas, during the night;[33] there appeared to be reasonable basis for the classification.

The decisions, coming early in the history of judicial interpretation, are almost sufficient in themselves to mark out the principles on which the Court has stood. Many other cases and decisions followed, but in those just mentioned we find (1) a recognition of the police

[30] 118 U. S. 356 (1886).

[31] "These provisions [for the protection of life, liberty, property and for equality] are universal in their application, to all persons within the territorial jurisdiction, without regard to any differences of race, of color, or of nationality. . . ." Ibid., 369.

[32] In the actual application of the ordinance only Chinese had been denied the required license: "No reason whatever, except the will of the supervisors, is assigned why they should not be permitted to carry on, in the accustomed manner, their harmless and useful occupation, on which they depend for a livelihood." Ibid., 374.

[33] Barbier v. Connolly, 113 U. S. 27 (1885). "The specific regulations for one kind of business, which may be necessary for the protection of the public, can never be the just ground of complaint because like restrictions are not imposed upon other business of a different kind." Soon Hing v. Crowley, 113 U. S. 703, 708-709 (1885).

power of the state to regulate business enterprises and to classify them, and also (2) a plain intimation that the classification must have a basis in reason and must not be founded on willful and unfair distinction.[34] Though a certain number of clear principles were established and fully embodied in well-recognized law, nevertheless what is and what is not discriminatory and unfair legislation, and hence unjust legislation, must depend on the judgment of the justices.

As the readiness of the Court to pass upon the reasonableness of classification appeared in the cases we have just considered, so, in the eighties, we find the beginnings of a determination to pass upon the problem of what was "due process" and whether liberty and property had been unreasonably encroached upon. That not every process which the legislature might prescribe must necessarily be considered due process was announced fairly early in the history of constitutional law. In 1856 the Supreme Court, interpreting the fifth amendment, said, "It is manifest that it was not left to the legislative power to enact any process which might be devised. The article is a restraint on the legislative as well as on the executive and judicial powers of the government. . . ."[35] It was, therefore, the duty of the Court to decide in a given instance whether a process provided for by an act was due process or not; if it were not, then the law was not law because it has been passed in violation of constitutional restriction. The prin-

---

[34] "But it is said that it is not within the scope of the Fourteenth Amendment to withhold from States the power of classification, and that if the law deals alike with all of a certain class it is not obnoxious to the charge of a denial of equal protection. While, as a general proposition, this is undeniably true, . . . yet it is equally true that such classification cannot be made arbitrarily. . . . That [classification] must always rest upon some difference which bears a reasonable and just relation to the act in respect to which the classification is proposed, and can never be made arbitrarily and without any such basis." Gulf, C. & S. F. R. Co. v. Ellis, 165 U. S. 150, 155 (1897). See for further illustration, Atchison, T. and S. F. R. Co. v. Matthews, 174 U. S. 96 (1899); Fidelity Mutual Life Ass'n. Co. v. Mettler, 185 U. S. 308 (1902); St. Louis Consolidated Coal Co. v. Illinois, 185 U. S. 203 (1902); Cotting v. Kansas City Stock Yards Co., 183 U. S. 79 (1901).

[35] Murray's Lessee v. Hoboken Land and Improvement Co., 18 Howard 272, 276 (1856). Webster, arguing in behalf of his alma mater in the Dartmouth College case (1819), said: "By the law of the land is most clearly intended the general law; a law which hears before it condemns; which proceeds upon inquiry, and renders judgment only after trial. The meaning is, that every citizen shall hold his life, liberty, property, and immunities, under the protection of the general rules which govern society. Everything which may pass under the form of an enactment, is not, therefore, to be considered the law of the land." 4 Wheaton 518, 581. For discussion and references to early cases see R. L. Mott, *Due Process of Law*, ch. XII.

ciple, when applied to state statutes and to the prohibitions of the four-teenth amendment, opened up an important field of judicial activity and responsibility.

The Court moved at first rather circumspectly.[36] There was nat-urally and inevitably a desire to test the validity of legislation by the principles and the traditional procedure of the common law. It is im-pressive to see the justices examining the common law procedure of ancient date, referring to Magna Charta and attempting to discover whether certain methods were in vogue or within the purview of the common law in the time of King John or his successors.[37] But this ad-herence to established principles, in the large sense, was soon associated with a readiness to announce the doctrine that, if such fundamental principles were protected, a mere change in procedure would not be sufficient to violate the constitutional restriction; in other words, a new process, however novel, might be considered valid. This prin-ciple was clearly laid down by Justice Matthews in 1884.[38] A pro-vision of the constitution of California which allowed prosecution begun by information after examination by a magistrate, instead of by indictment by a grand jury, was upheld. "The proposition of law we are asked to affirm", said the Court, "is that an indictment or pre-sentment by a grand jury, as known to the common law of England, is essential to that 'due process of law' ", which the Constitution secures and guarantees. This position the Court refused to take; it refused to consider only the antiquity of a form of procedure; the real question was whether the new form was calculated to preserve elementary rights. The opinion quoted with approval the statement made by Justice Johnson in 1819 (Bank of Columbia v. Okely, 4

[36] "Thirty cases were presented involving the validity of state statutes under the due process provision before one was found in which the legislation was considered sufficiently arbitrary to violate it." Mott, *op. cit.*, p. 206.

[37] Take for example a case arising even as late as 1908, where the question arose concerning the right of a trial judge to instruct the jury that they might properly take into consideration the defendant's failure to testify in his own behalf. Twining v. New Jersey, 211 U. S. 78. The Court rejected, as it had in earlier cases, the idea that the procedure of the seventeenth century, brought to this country by the colonists, could not be varied, if substantial justice were secured. Justice Moody in this case gives an especially illuminating statement as to the source of principles of due process and certain essentials of its meaning.

[38] Hurtado v. California, 110 U. S. 516. The Court was able to refer to other cases which supported the doctrine. But the Hurtado case is important because it came at that particular time when the Court was forced by the necessity of adapting con-stitutional law to a changing world. See Davidson v. New Orleans, 96 U. S. 97 (1878).

Wheaton 235, 244) : "As to the words from Magna Charta, incorporated into the Constitution of Maryland, after volumes spoken and written with a view to their exposition, the good sense of mankind has at last settled down to this: that they were intended to secure the individual from the arbitrary exercise of the powers of government, unrestrained by the established principles of private right and distributive justice." [39]

This determination to examine essentials and not mere form, and this willingness to recognize the needs of new governmental methods are in some ways especially indicated by what the courts said about the authority of administrative boards and commissions. The principle appears to be fairly conclusively summarized by Justice Brewer giving the opinion of the Court in the early twentieth century. "Indeed, it not infrequently happens that a full discharge of their duties compels boards, or officers of a purely ministerial character, to consider and determine questions of a legal nature. Due process is not necessarily judicial process." [40] There has been, therefore, a studious effort to maintain the substance of justice and the protection of essential rights, but a recognition also that practical necessity demanded acceptance of the power of an administrative body to act, and often to act conclusively, within the range of its functions and its responsibilities. The courts have, however, by no means surrendered to administrative officers the final right to determine whether their decisions or procedure is due process. [41]

What would be due process—in the sense of method or form of procedure—in one instance would not be due process in another. For example, a dwelling may be demolished on the order of a firewarden,

---

[39] The words of Cooley, in his *Constitutional Limitations,* were also approved: "Administrative and remedial process may be changed from time to time, but only with due regard to the landmarks established for the protection of the citizen." Hurtado *v.* California, 110 U. S. 516, 527-528. The same doctrine was explicitly announced in the same year. "The clause in question [the due process clause of the fourteenth amendment] means, therefore, that there can be no proceeding against life, liberty, or property which may result in the deprivation of either, without the observance of those general rules established in our system of jurisprudence for the security of private rights." Hagar *v.* Reclamation District, 111 U. S. 701, 708 (1884).

[40] Reetz *v.* Michigan, 188 U. S. 505, 507 (1903).

[41] "An appeal on the question of constitutionality of either procedure or result must always be permitted when fundamental rights are involved. . . . Throughout the entire development of administrative law there has been the conflict between administrative necessity and expediency and the innate propensities of the courts to respect and preserve, if possible, the substance of judicial protection, even though in some cases its forms had to be foregone." Mott, *op. cit.,* pp. 239-240.

to stop the spread of a conflagration, and the official is not bound to call the owner into consultation or to have the decision of any tribunal to justify his decision. The courts will however insist, if the question is brought before them, upon the owner's right to a subsequent hearing concerning the necessity or the reasonable ground for the firewarden's order. But though private property may be destroyed because of immediate danger to the community, property cannot be taken for public use without compensation to the owner. In other words, there is a distinction between the proper exercise of two different functions of government—the police power and eminent domain. This elementary distinction, which scarcely needs elaboration, was laid down in a leading case in 1851 by Chief Justice Shaw of Massachusetts: [42] "Rights of property, like all other social and conventional rights, are subject to such reasonable limitations in their enjoyment, as shall prevent them from being injurious, and to such reasonable restraints and regulations established by law, as the legislature, under the governing and controlling power vested in them by the constitution, may think necessary and expedient." Distinguishing eminent domain from the police power, he defined the latter as "the power vested in the legislature by the constitution, to make, ordain and establish all manner of wholesome and reasonable laws, statutes and ordinances, either with penalties or without, not repugnant to the constitution, as they shall judge to be for the good and welfare of the commonwealth, and of the subjects of the same." [43]

Though the words "police power" were used occasionally in the earlier nineteenth century, no very definite connotation was made evident. Taney described the power in general and very comprehensive terms—so general, in fact, that his description can scarcely be called a definition: "But what are the police powers of a State? They are nothing more or less than the powers of government inherent in every sovereignty to the extent of its dominions." [44] But when restrictions were placed upon the states, when the federal government through its judiciary was set up as the guardian of life, liberty, and property, the statement needed clarification. The courts have consistently refused to define the power by such positive and precise terms as definitely to

---

[42] Commonwealth v. Alger, 7 Cushing (Mass.) 53, 85 (1851). For a clear statement see Mugler v. Kansas, 123 U. S. 623 (1887).

[43] The term in its ordinary connotation at the present time is defined by Ernst Freund as "the power of promoting the public welfare by restraining and regulating the use of liberty and property." The Police Power, p. iii.

[44] License Cases, 5 Howard 504, 583 (1847).

circumscribe it; they are willing to describe it in general terms, but prefer to pass upon concrete cases and thus to indicate its scope. They define it by application.

Before the middle of the eighties, as we have seen, the restrictive provisions of the fourteenth amendment, and especially the due process clause of the first section, appeared not very important. The Slaughter-House Cases and the "Granger Cases" seemed to be conclusive barriers against any attempt to subject state legislation to any control that would satisfy the learned counsel who were pestering the Court with ingenious arguments, seeking a decision which would relieve their clients from the burden of uncomfortable statutes. The Court might have grasped a principle out of the air, absorbed it from the nebulous spirit of free institutions as Justice Miller did in the famous case of Loan Association v. Topeka; [45] but the use of such a source presented obvious difficulties. The nature of that opinion is, in fact, an illuminating proof of how far the Court was at that time from any realization that the fourteenth amendment offered concrete grounds upon which the substance and effect of state legislation could be successfully challenged. And the time was still some distance ahead when the Court found itself able to gather the spirit of free institutions and of personal liberty under the protecting wings of "due process".

As early as 1878, Justice Miller, giving the opinion of the Court, said: "In fact, it would seem, from the character of many of the cases before us, and the arguments made in them, that the clause under consideration is looked upon as a means of bringing to the test of the decision of this court the abstract opinions of every unsuccessful litigant in a State court of the justice of the decision against him, and of the merits of the legislation on which such a decision may be founded." [46]

The pressure, however, did not abate. A statement similar to that made by Justice Miller was repeated by Justice Field seven years later,

[45] 20 Wallace 655 (1875). I do not mean to assert that by using the due process clause the Court would have declared the law in question to be unconstitutional. The Court, however, could find or did find no explicit provision in the federal Constitution. As Justice Clifford indicates in dissent, the power assumed by the Court rested upon "a general latent spirit supposed to pervade or underlie the constitution. . . ." In later years so many general principles of elementary rights and justice were brought under the protection of due process that one would hesitate to say what cannot be covered by those words. But this case, coming when it did, and based as it was not on the fourteenth amendment but on the imagination of the Court, is one of the most amazing decisions in the history of a hundred and fifty years.

[46] Davidson v. New Orleans, 96 U. S. 97, 104 (1878).

and he declared in no uncertain terms that the Court was not a "harbor where refuge" could "be found from every act of ill-advised and oppressive State legislation."[47] But the time was rapidly approaching when the Court found itself to be just that kind of a harbor. A turning-point came soon after Field's statement was made. Just why it came at that time, it is difficult to say. But we must take into account the new activities of state administrative boards and the increase of state legislation, the social unrest which though not extreme was real, the activity of the Knights of Labor, and other manifestations of zeal for the abandonment of the old order, all of which may have been instrumental in leading the Court toward a position calculated to protect personal and property interests from what appeared to be unwarranted assault.

In 1887 the Court upheld a Kansas prohibition act.[48] This it could scarcely help doing in light of various previous decisions of the state judiciary. It was necessary in this case to meet the contention that restraint of the individual's right to make, eat, and drink what he might choose was contrary to the most elementary principles of American constitutionalism. Announcing the power of the state to pass legislation of this character, the Court said that the "Power to determine such questions, so as to bind all, must exist somewhere;" and that "Under our system that power is lodged with the legislative branch of the government." Here we find the tendency, which is seen in the Munn case and certain others following that decision, to rely upon legislative discretion and to hesitate about bringing up general statements in the Constitution to restrict legislative competence. But that fact need not detain us now; more significant is the declaration concerning the necessary limits on the police power: "There are, of necessity, limits beyond which the legislation cannot rightfully go. . . . If, therefore, a statute purporting to have been enacted to protect the public health, the public morals, or the public safety, has no real or

---

[47] Missouri Pacific Ry. Co. v. Humes, 115 U. S. 512, 521 (1885). "It is hardly necessary to say, that the hardship, impolicy, or injustice of State laws is not necessarily an objection to their constitutional validity. . . ." *Ibid.*, 520. This date should be noticed—as late as 1885!

[48] Mugler v. Kansas, 123 U. S. 623 (1887). As early as 1874, the Court said that, if it were true that the defendant was the owner of a glass of liquor at the time the state law imposed an absolute prohibition on the sale of such liquor, grave questions would arise: whether the statute would deprive him of property without due process of law and whether it would violate the fourteenth amendment. Bartemeyer v. Iowa, 18 Wallace 129 (1874). This statement has the flavor of Wynehamer v. New York, 13 N. Y. Court of Appeals Reports 378 (1856).

substantial relation to those objects, or is a palpable invasion of rights secured by the fundamental law, it is the duty of the courts to so adjudge, and thereby give effect to the Constitution."

The power of a court to "adjudge" soon proved to be a matter of immense consequence. According to this principle, a state statute cannot be successfully defended simply by saying that it falls within the police power of the state; under the guise of exercising this power, the state cannot arbitrarily deprive a person of life, liberty or property without due process of law; a statute must stand the test of reasonableness, and, as the coming years showed, it must be judged by its actual, and not alone by its ostensible purpose, to promote the public welfare and by its substantial adaptation to that end. More of this will be seen in later pages.

We have seen in a previous chapter a decision by the New York court in 1856 which in substance declared that an act summarily depriving an individual of his property in intoxicating liquor constituted a deprivation of property without due process. The decision did not rest on the nature of the method or the process, but on the substantial effect of the law—the substance of the law not the procedure, was the gist of the matter. This case did not as a rule carry weight in other states, where many decisions were rendered upholding anti-liquor statutes. Taney used the doctrine in the Dred Scott case, but there was no other federal Supreme Court decision of a similar kind until 1870, in the first Legal Tender Case.[49] That case, however, was overruled the next year, and so the precedent was not very valuable. But in the eighties, property rights in railroads were playing much the same rôle as property in intoxicating liquor had played in the days before the war. And, in consequence, the Court began to announce the doctrine that legislative authority was circumscribed and that property could not be confiscated by fixing unreasonably low charges for service.

It is difficult to trace with complete assurance the course of the Court's reasoning, though the result is plain. The following propositions may not be entirely valueless: I. If administrative and remedial processes may be changed, provided the fundamental rules for the security of private rights are observed, it is not a far step to a declaration that fundamental rights, not the process or procedure, are the main thing, and that the Courts therefore have the duty to protect those rights, no matter how precise and elaborate the process may be. The pith and marrow of the due process restriction on legislative power

---

[49] Hepburn v. Griswold, 8 Wallace 603.

were protection of property and liberty, not alone the safeguarding of process, which was only ancillary. II. If a legislature cannot peremptorily transfer the property of A to B and if a person's property cannot be seized except under public necessity or because it is a nuisance, and if it cannot be taken for the public use without compensation,[50] then a statute prescribing confiscatory railroad rates, a statute amounting to a confiscation because it deprives the road of earnings, must be considered a violation of due process and hence void. In the early decisions, when the doctrine was announced or distinctly foreshadowed, there was some consideration of the question of whether procedure had been adequate; the function, the authority and the procedure of commissions received attention; but as we shall see in a moment, the question of procedure became after a time a matter of comparatively little interest. We must now trace out this development in greater detail.

Were there no limits on the power of the state to regulate rates and charges of a business affected with a public interest? A warning came in 1886, the year before the Kansas liquor case which we have already briefly discussed. In this case the Court showed a willingness —though rather a reluctant willingness—to recognize or announce the right of the judiciary to examine the effect of a prescribed rate: the power of limitation or regulation is not without limit; it is not the power to destroy; limitation is not the equivalent of confiscation; under the pretense of regulating rates the state cannot require a railroad company to carry persons or property without reward, nor can it do that which in law amounts to a taking of private property without just compensation, or without due process of law.[51] Neither in this case nor in the prohibition case did the Court actually pronounce a state act invalid; the announcements were rather in the nature of a warn-

[50] Such statements are in Loan Association v. Topeka, 20 Wallace 655 (1875), and in Davidson v. New Orleans, 96 U. S. 97 (1878). As a matter of plain fact, the Court, in Reagan v. Farmers' Loan and Trust Company, 154 U. S. 362 (1894), passed with remarkable ease from discussion of equal protection and of eminent domain to a consideration of the reasonableness of charges: "It has always been a part of the judicial function to determine whether the act of one party (whether that party be a single individual, an organized body, or the public as a whole) operates to divest the other party of any rights of person or property. In every constitution is the guarantee against the taking of private property for public purposes without just compensation. The equal protection of the laws which, by the Fourteenth Amendment, no State can deny to the individual, forbids legislation, in whatever form it may be enacted, by which the property of one individual is, without compensation, wrested from him for the benefit of another, or of the public." Ibid., 399.

[51] Stone v. Farmers' Loan and Trust Company, 116 U. S. 307 (1886).

ing; the Court was safeguarding itself against the supposition that there were no limits. On the whole the reservation thus announced was rather mild; for there may be many steps between regulation or limitation of rates on the one hand and thorough confiscation on the other; but there is evidence of a belief that totally to deprive a road of earnings would be an unconstitutional exercise of authority. In 1890 the Court passed upon a decision by the Supreme Court of Minnesota, which pronounced the determination of rates by a commission to be final and conclusive and declared that the law of the state allowed no inquiry concerning the equality or the reasonableness of the rates.[52] The federal Court refused to accept the principle that the law, thus interpreted, was constitutional: "The question of the reasonableness of a rate of charge . . . is eminently a question for judicial investigation, requiring due process of law for its determination." This opinion and the facts in the case show how close was the connection between process and substance: the legislature could not deprive a corporation of its right to a judicial examination of the reasonableness of a commission's rule or order—and this examination really might be considered in itself a process or procedure; but if the Court should find the rates fixed by the commission to be unreasonable, the decision in practical effect amounted to a protection of the property, despite any amount of elaborate procedure.

Three justices dissenting denied the rightfulness of the Court's position and insisted that a commission, "though not a court, is a proper tribunal for the duties imposed upon it." [53] In this declaration of the powers of the Court and in the opinion of the dissenting justices we find a matter of unusual significance. Are judicial tribunals less likely than commissions to decide justly and reach sound conclusions? Could not a decision by a commission, if it were reached by

[52] Chicago etc. Railway Co. v. Minnesota, 134 U. S. 418, 458 (1890).

[53] "It is complained", said Justice Bradley, in a dissenting opinion concurred in by two justices, "that the decisions of the board are final and without appeal. So are the decisions of the courts in matters within their jurisdiction. There must be a final tribunal somewhere for deciding every question in the world. . . . The important question always is, what is the lawful tribunal for the particular case? In my judgment, in the present case, the proper tribunal was the legislature, or the board of commissioners which it created for the purpose." Justice Bradley admits that there may be a clear case of invasion of rights, and in such instance apparently there may be judicial review of the commission's determinations. But in the case he was considering there was merely a difference of judgment; the board was not charged with fraud. "The board may have erred; but if they did, as the matter was within their rightful jurisdiction, their decision was final and conclusive unless their proceedings could be impeached for fraud."

careful examination of facts, and if it gave reasonable opportunity for protest or discussion, be held to be a decision based on due process? The immense development of administrative law and of administrative tribunals in the last few decades leads one to think that, had conditions been different in the nineties, had there not been so much eagerness for control of corporations and on the other hand so much resentful objection to governmental regulation, the courts might have contented themselves with insisting on reasonable and fair methods · and, in the absence of any showing of willful abuse of power, they might have accepted the conclusions of the commission as final. Had the position of the minority been that of the Court, the courts would have been relieved of immense labor; but as it was, the duty of deciding on the reasonableness of charges was thrown upon the uncomplaining shoulders of federal justices. Justice Brewer, describing the duties of the judiciary, said in 1894 that courts "do not engage in any mere administrative work. . . ." [54] That can scarcely be denied as an abstract principle; but there came to the courts in the course of time difficult and intricate questions concerning the value of property and the effect of rates.

In discussing the right to examine the question of reasonableness of rates and charges the Court seemed inclined for a time to make a distinction between the decision of a commission and the determination by a state legislature. [55] But such a distinction could not be maintained. In 1894 rates fixed by a commission were declared invalid and in the same case the judicial right to examine legislative rates fixed by the legislature was once again announced but not at once acted upon : there is no doubt of the power of the courts "to inquire whether a body of rates prescribed by a legislature or a commission is unjust

[54] Reagan v. Farmers' Loan and Trust Co., 154 U. S. 362, 397. An examination of the opinions in the Reagan case and in Smyth v. Ames, 169 U. S. 466 (1898), will disclose the kind of questions which need to be answered by the judges. Pure questions of law appear to be secondary to the determination of intricate problems of accounting.

[55] Thus in 1892, the Court said, "What was said in the opinion in 134 U. S., as to the question of the reasonableness of the rate of charge being one for judicial investigation, had no reference to a case where the rates are prescribed directly by the legislature." Budd v. New York, 143 U. S. 517, 546. And only four years earlier Justice Gray, delivering the opinion of the Court, quoted with approval the statement made in Peik v. Chicago and N. W. R. R., 94 U. S. 164, 178: "Where property has been clothed with a public interest, the legislature may fix a limit to that which in law shall be reasonable for its use. This limits the courts, as well as the people. If it has been improperly fixed, the legislature, not the courts, must be appealed to for the change." Dow v. Beidelman, 125 U. S. 680, 687-688 (1888).

and unreasonable, and such as to work a practical destruction to rights of property, and if found so to be, to restrain its operation".[56] The whole matter was conclusively settled in 1898, when the Court, saying once again that rates for transportation are primarily to be fixed by the state, declared the question "whether they are so unreasonably low as to deprive the carrier of its property without such compensation as the Constitution secures, and therefore without due process of law, cannot be so conclusively determined by the legislature of the State or by regulations adopted under its authority, that the matter may not become the subject of judicial inquiry."[57]

At a comparatively early day, a corporation was held to be a person as the word is used in the fourteenth amendment. There is no need of our questioning the rightfulness of this position; the courts did not labor over the problem and they had substantial precedent to stand upon;[58] but the appearance of corporation cases in great numbers is nevertheless an important fact, for it brings to our attention the actual, if not the legal, distinction between the old-fashioned belief that a person is entitled to his liberty and to the possession of his property and the newer belief that large capitalistic interests are likewise to be protected. There in reality was the heart of the modern problem.

Toward the end of the century Justice Peckham, giving the Court's opinion, defined liberty in fairly comprehensive terms: "The liberty mentioned in that amendment means not only the right of the citizen to be free from the mere physical restraint of his person, as by incarceration, but the term is deemed to embrace the right of the citizen to be free in the enjoyment of all his faculties; to be free to use them

[56] Reagan v. Farmers' Loan and Trust Co., 154 U. S. 362, 397 (1894). Rates fixed by a commission were declared unreasonable. For further development see St. Louis and S. F. Ry. Co. v. Gill, 156 U. S. 649, 657 (1895). In Covington and Lexington Turnpike Road Co. v. Sandford, 164 U. S. 578 (1896), the Court rendered a decision concerning rates fixed by statute. The Court in this case did not declare the rates to be too low, but did plainly assert its power to do so, and the case was remanded for further proceedings which would allow the parties to make their proofs.

[57] Smyth v. Ames, 169 U. S. 466, 526 (1898).

[58] "A similar provision [against deprivation of life, liberty and property] is found in nearly all of the state constitutions; and everywhere, and at all times, and in all courts, it has been held, either by tacit assent or express adjudication, to extend . . . to corporations". County of San Mateo v. Southern Pac. R. Co., 13 Fed. 722, 746-747 (1882). See also Santa Clara County v. Southern Pac. R. Co., 118 U. S. 394 (1886), the first case in which this position was announced by the Supreme Court.

in all lawful ways; to live and work where he will; to earn his livelihood by any lawful calling; to pursue any livelihood or avocation, and for that purpose to enter into all contracts which may be proper, necessary and essential to his carrying out to a successful conclusion the purposes above mentioned." The Justice, however, went on to say that by giving general definitions the Court did not intend to hold that in no such case can the state exercise its police power; "When and how far such power may be legitimately exercised . . . must be left for determination to each case as it arises." [59] Of significance is the Court's emphatic declaration of the right of an individual to make all proper contracts in relation to his calling or trade. The right to contract was, therefore, a liberty protected by the Constitution; but again the significant word is "proper"; for what may be proper or improper must be a question for judicial determination; and there must arise question of the relationship of legislation to public needs and welfare.

The year after this extensive definition, with the reservation above-mentioned, was given, there arose an important case involving the validity of a Utah statute forbidding the employment for more than eight hours per day of workmen in mines or in smelters for reducing or refining ores.[60] The statute was upheld as a reasonable exercise of power to protect the health of the employees. The Court referred to Allgeyer v. Louisiana, and the doctrine of freedom of contract there laid down, but declared this right to be subject to certain limitations which the state may lawfully impose. This power, the Court said, had been greatly expanded in its application during the past century because of the enormous increase in the number of dangerous occupations or occupations so far detrimental to the health of employees as to demand special precautions for their well-being and protection or for the safety of adjacent property. But of special interest is the Court's recognition of the fact that under certain conditions there is not in reality freedom of contract; proprietors and laborers do not stand upon an equality, and their interests are to a certain extent conflicting. Significant also is the statement that we are not living in

[59] Allgeyer v. Louisiana, 165 U. S. 578, 589, 590 (1897). In 1888, the Court, though not declaring a state statute invalid, had announced its general acquiescence in the principle that one has the right to "his enjoyment upon terms of equality with all others in similar circumstances of the privilege of pursuing an ordinary calling or trade, and of acquiring, holding, and selling property". Powell v. Pennsylvania, 127 U. S. 678, 684. In later years it was declared that liberty in the education of children was protected. Meyer v. Nebraska, 262 U. S. 390 (1923); Pierce v. Society of Sisters, 268 U. S. 510 (1925).

[60] Holden v. Hardy, 169 U. S. 366 (1898).

a static world, and that lawmakers and courts may take that fact into consideration. As we have seen the Court in earlier cases insisting that in matters of procedure there should be no need of clinging obstinately to ancient practices, so now we find a distinct declaration of the necessity of adapting the substance of law [61] to new conditions of society, and, particularly, to the new relations between employers and employees. That was a bold step forward.

In the Utah case which we have just considered, the reasonableness of the regulation of hours rested, in part at least, on the fact that the labor was carried on under peculiarly dangerous conditions. Seven years later, the Court gave a decision which attracted much attention and, in some quarters, condemnation. It declared invalid a New York statute prescribing the number of hours during which work in bakeries could be carried on. The majority of the Court could find no reasonable connection between the health and well-being of the workmen and the limitation of the hours of labor, and no sound reason for interfering with the right of contract and with the right of a laborer to work as long as he might choose.[62] Just why the case should have brought forth so much public discussion, it is difficult to say, certainly, however, the explanation can be gathered chiefly from the conditions of the times, the unusually intense interest in labor problems and labor legislation, and from the general movement toward a bettering of social conditions by legislative regulation. In this case,

[61] The Court made some attempt to associate the principle announced with changes in the forms of procedure; but in reality it was not procedure which was under inspection (except for purposes of suggesting an analogy) but the essential justice of the act.

[62] "Viewed in the light of a purely labor law, with no reference whatever to the question of health, we think that a law like the one before us involves neither the safety, the morals nor the welfare of the public, and that the interest of the public is not in the slightest degree affected by such an act. . . . We think that there can be no fair doubt that the trade of a baker, in and of itself, is not an unhealthy one to that degree which would authorize the legislature to interfere with the right to labor, and with the right of free contract on the part of the individual, either as employer or employé. . . . It is unfortunately true that labor, even in any department, may possibly carry with it the seeds of unhealthiness. But are we all, on that account, at the mercy of legislative majorities? A printer, a tinsmith, a locksmith, a carpenter, a cabinetmaker, a dry goods clerk, a bank's, a lawyer's or a physician's clerk, or a clerk in almost any kind of business, would all come under the power of the legislature, on this assumption." Lochner v. New York, 198 U. S. 45, 57, 59 (1905). "How can the Supreme Court at Washington have conclusive judicial knowledge of the conditions affecting bakeries in New York?" Sir Frederick Pollock, commenting on the Lochner decision in "The New York Labour Law and the Fourteenth Amendment," *Law Quarterly Review*, XXI, p. 212.

as a matter of fact, the doctrine of reasonableness announced in the Kansas liquor case, but not there applied, reached its apogee. Until the outbreak of the World War, progressives and social reformers, finding for a time a champion in President Roosevelt, were zealous in their advocacy of change and often critical of the judiciary.

Could the employment of women be controlled by special regulation? This question was presented to the Court and passed upon in 1908.[63] An Oregon law forbidding the work of women in laundries or factories more than ten hours per day was attacked as a wanton interference with the right to contract, with freedom of the person and with equality. The case aroused public discussion, partly because the position of women in modern industry was then a matter of considerable public interest, and also because an attempt was made by the counsel defending the statute to establish reasonableness by calling the Court's attention to scientific data.[64]

In argument defending the validity of the law, Mr. Brandeis, counsel in the case but afterwards a Justice of the Court, called attention to a list of enactments both in this country and in Europe limiting the working hours of women; and he presented extracts from reports of committees, commissions, inspectors of factories, etc., all tending to show that long hours of work are dangerous for women primarily because of their physical organization. This was an attempt to place judicial decisions upon a scientific basis or upon explicit information, not to leave the matter of the suitability or the necessity of restriction to the unaided judgment of the judges; it could not be presumed that the justices possessed judicial cognizance of matters of physiology, save perhaps the knowledge which might be considered the common possession of all intelligent persons. Upholding the statute, the Court gave some attention to the citations and the information presented by Mr. Brandeis and declared them to be significant of a widespread belief that woman's physical structure and functions justify special legislation; limitations imposed by the act were imposed not alone for the

---

[63] Muller v. Oregon, 208 U. S. 412 (1908).

[64] It is interesting to compare this case with Jacobson v. Massachusetts, 197 U. S. 11 (1905), when the Court upheld a compulsory vaccination statute and referred to the "common belief" in the value of vaccination. "What everybody knows the court must know, and therefore the state court judicially knew, as this court knows, that an opposite theory [i.e. opposite to that held by members of the medical profession who did not believe in vaccination] accords with the common belief and is maintained by high medical authority." Ibid., 30. This is somewhat like the principle that the Court is supposed to have judicial cognizance of history!

benefit of the workers but largely for the benefit of all. Since that time the desirability of finding an informational basis for judicial cognizance of social needs has been variously asserted. The courts, it is said, should have social facts as well as scientific information, not vague personal opinions, upon which to rest their decisions when questions of social conditions and betterment are before them; sociological jurisprudence demands the grasp of realities of social need.[65]

We have seen in the New York bakery case a decision of the Court, denying the validity of an act because, in the judgment of the Court, there was no good ground for limiting hours of labor in such employment. In 1917, an Oregon statute forbidding labor in any mill or factory more than ten hours a day, with certain exceptions, was held valid.[66] In this case there was no attempt to justify the validity upon the peculiarly dangerous or unwholesome character of the employment; the general terms of the statute would make such an attempt futile. The Court sustained the statute on the ground that the legislature and the state supreme court had found such a law necessary for the preservation of health of the employees, and in the absence of facts to support the opposite conclusion, the federal Court would accept the legislative judgment. This obviously was a decided step in advance, and Chief Justice Taft, at a later time, said that he had "supposed that the *Lochner Case* was thus overruled *sub silentio*."[67] For us, the importance of this decision rests in the evidence of a tendency, prompted partly by

[65] "How long we shall continue to blunder along without the aid of unpartisan and authoritative scientific assistance in the administration of justice, no one knows", said Judge Learned Hand a few years ago. Parke-Davis & Co. *v.* Mulford Co., 189 Fed. 95, 115 (1911). He believed there should be a united effort to effect such advance. See also Felix Frankfurter of counsel in Bunting *v.* Oregon, 243 U. S. 426, 432: "'common understanding' is a treacherous criterion". It is well to notice that some state courts had, before the Muller *v.* Oregon decision, taken cognizance of certain physiological and other facts justifying, in the courts' judgment, special legislation for women. See for example, Wenham *v.* State, 65 Neb. 394 (1902); State *v.* Buchanan, 29 Wash. 602 (1902). Noteworthy also is the fact that the Illinois supreme court, which in 1895 had pronounced void an act limiting working hours for women, upheld a statute of that kind two years after the Muller case. Ritchie and Co. *v.* Wayman, 244 Ill. 509 (1910).

[66] Bunting *v.* Oregon, 243 U. S. 426 (1917).

[67] Adkins *v.* Children's Hospital, 261 U. S. 525, 564 (1923). This was the minimum wage case; a congressional act authorizing a commission to fix a minimum wage for women and minors in the District was declared void. Professor Frankfurter, reviewing in 1916 the developments of law in the matters referred to the text, said, "Courts, with increasing measure, deal with legislation affecting industry in the light of a realistic study of the industrial conditions affected" and declared that the emphasis had been shifted to community interests. "Hours of Labor and Realism in Constitutional Law," *Harvard Law Review*, XXIX, pp. 366-367.

social pressure, to move on toward the recognition of a right to legislate in general within a field of regulation, when once a particular piece of legislation, though involving special features, is recognized as valid.[68] We must, it appears, assume that the Court came without much misgiving to accept labor legislation restricting hours, and that common practices, a general acquiescence, a public desire, finally make the justices less hesitant and less wary. We must, however, conclude that the courts, before upholding such legislation as we have been considering, must find or assume some social gain which may be reasonably expected from the invasion of individual liberty of contract.

An interesting example of the way in which changing industrial conditions and developing public sentiment express themselves in legislation and bring critical problems of constitutional law to the decision of courts appears in the workingmen's compensation or employers' liability acts, which began to be passed about the beginning of the twentieth century. By the common law as it was announced and applied by the courts in the absence of statutory modification, the workman under ordinary conditions, even though injured through no fault of his own, was at decided disadvantage when seeking to recover damages from an employer. But there was a growing belief in the public mind that in modern industry the liberty and freedom of contract did not in plain fact exist. It was easy enough to say that if a workingman did not like his employment because it was dangerous, he could give it up and enter another; but such complacency was, of course, serviceable only to those who were not immediately affected by the perils of industry. The prevailing principles of the law, reformers now asserted, were not suited to modern industrial labor; the employer or society as a whole should bear the burden and the expense resulting from accidents in factories; the law should be simplified; the employer should include in cost of production the amount

[68] But are there no limits to which state legislation may go? Before the Bunting case, the Court said, "It is manifestly impossible to say that the mere fact that the statute of California provides for an eight hour day, or a maximum of forty-eight hours a week, instead of ten hours a day or fifty-four hours a week, takes the case out of the domain of legislative discretion. This is not to imply that a limitation of the hours of labor of women might not be pushed to a wholly indefensible extreme. . . ." Miller v. Wilson, 236 U. S. 373, 382 (1915). Are we then, perchance, to find the Court some day passing upon the question whether seven hours a day are reasonable and six and one-half not, or six reasonable and five and three-quarters not? It will be noticed that in the cases already mentioned which dealt with the legislative power to fix rates for service of railroads etc., the Court started with a declaration that the power was within state competence, later said there were limits, and still later found itself examining with critical care the question of exact remuneration.

expended for accident insurance or the amount paid out of his own coffers. American tardiness in entering upon legislation to this end illustrates once more the date at which the country met face to face the problems of the machine age.

In accordance with the established principles of law, commonly prevailing at the end of the nineteenth century, an employer was under no obligation to make compensation to a workman for injury in the course of employment, if the injury had been caused by the negligence of a fellow workman, or if the injured employee had been guilty of contributory negligence even though the employer be also at fault; furthermore, the workman was held, when he entered upon employment, to have assumed the risks of the business—such risks as were naturally incident to the employment. This matter, as we have said, had awakened public attention, and there was much comment, when a compensation act of New York was held invalid by the Court of Appeals of that state.[69]

After the decision the state adopted an amendment to the constitution, and an act based upon the amendment was upheld by the state court.[70] Of course if the act were in violation of the fourteenth amendment, the state constitution could not make it lawful. Though the Court sought to distinguish in some particulars the second act from the previous one, it is probably fair to say that public opinion as to what constituted justice, and what was reasonable interference with the private property and the liberty of contract, really made the second decision all but inevitable. The federal Supreme Court gave a final and conclusive decision in 1917: "The close relation of the rules governing responsibility as between employer and employee to the fundamental rights of liberty and property is of course recognized. But those rules, as guides of conduct, are not beyond alteration by legislation in the public interest. No person has a vested interest in any rule of law entitling him to insist that it shall remain unchanged for his benefit." [71]

[69] Ives *v.* South Buffalo Ry. Co., 201 N. Y. 271 (1911).

[70] Jensen *v.* Southern Pac. Co., 215 N. Y. 514 (1915).

[71] N. Y. Central R. R. Co. *v.* White, 243 U. S. 188, 197-198 (1917). See also Arizona Employers' Liability Cases, 250 U. S. 400 (1919); Hawkins *v.* Bleakly, 243 U. S. 210 (1917). Despite the objection made in the early years of the twentieth century to laws of this character, and despite the opposition to the abandonment of the old doctrines, probably neither employer nor employee has since regretted the change. The whole subject is an interesting example of the fact that laws cannot remain immutable when conditions do not support them, that public sentiment finds its way, and that courts will not continuously uphold the old rules

Indicative of the changed attitude toward the rights of employers in relations with labor are cases dealing with wages, though most of these cases did not attract such wide public interest as the employers' liability cases. The Court upheld a state statute making it unlawful under certain conditions, when wages of workmen in coal mines were determined on a quantity basis, to use screens or other devices to reduce wages; and the Court declared that the legislature being familiar with local conditions, is, primarily, the judge as to the necessity of such enactments.[72] Another act requiring that orders on company stores be redeemable in cash was likewise upheld.[73] To the reader these decisions may appear at the present day to be of no great significance, but they strongly illustrate the disappearance of the old doctrine of *laissez faire*. To the lawyers of the previous generation—the generation in active service in the last quarter of the nineteenth century—anything in the nature of what was called sumptuary legislation was thought to be repugnant to the first principles of American constitutional liberty.

To illustrate with any considerable detail the extent to which courts have been called upon to pass upon the propriety or suitableness of state legislation is not possible for a volume of this scope and purpose. From the point of view of constitutional history, the main facts are evident: the developing social order and the consequent attempts by legislation to regulate and control individual conduct and individual use of property in a degree at variance with older habits; the obligation of the judiciary to carry out the mandate of the fourteenth amendment; the occasional complaint from those demanding immediate recognition of state legislation which they declared to be desirable; the endeavor of the courts to attach judicial decisions to the principles of the past rather than to inaugurate a revolutionary break in the continuity of constitutional law; by giving a new significance and force to the term "due process" the judiciary assumed burdensome obligations; there was and had to be, an acknowledgment of the fact that

---

[72] McLean *v.* Arkansas, 211 U. S. 539 (1909).

[73] Knoxville Iron Co. *v.* Harbison, 183 U. S. 13 (1901). A decision upholding the famous Adamson Act was given during the World War. It dealt with the authority of the national government not the states; and it is state legislation which is being dealt with in the present chapter. The act in question was entitled "An Act to Establish an Eight Hour Day for Employees of Carriers Engaged in Interstate and Foreign Commerce, and for Other Purposes". The Court declared that it amounted to an exertion of congressional power "under the circumstances disclosed to compulsorily arbitrate the dispute between the parties. . . ." Wilson *v.* New, 243 U. S. 332, 351 (1917).

constitutional law was itself a developing science, or at least, that it was not necessary for law to stand forever bound by the conceptions of the eighteenth century. The courts in a certain class of cases shifted their emphasis from a special regard for individual rights to a fuller appreciation of public needs.

It may be that there was in the first quarter of the twentieth century a growing tendency to give greater weight to a legislature's sense of what is just and of what makes for the public well-being, rather than to have the case turn distinctly upon what the Court—or more properly the individual justices—held to be fair and reasonable or the reverse. The Court certainly did not stand still. Those justices of the federal Supreme Court, who were commonly spoken of as the "liberal" justices—perhaps we should say the less conservative—, showed a willingness to recognize, more fully than others, the necessity of taking into consideration public opinion and the changing social order; and more especially were they inclined to question the criteria by which the reasonableness of legislation should be judged.[74] Whatever we may say, however, the duty of passing upon reasonableness was assumed by the Court; and there was no abandonment of its authority to reject as unconstitutional any statute obviously unfair, based on improper discrimination or violation of due process. There was frequent complaint by the laymen to the effect that the conservatives on the bench were retarding social progress.

For a hundred and thirty-five years, criticism of the judiciary has been common, though not quite continuous; and we need not look upon the complaints of the last forty years as unique. In the recent period the Supreme Court had a supremely difficult task. The historian and the jurist are entitled to question the wisdom of its decisions; and they may even go so far as to deplore the whole series of pronouncements which appeared to delay unduly the progress of legis-

[74] The statement of Justice Holmes dissenting in Lochner v. New York, 198 U. S. 45, 75-76 (1905), is especially illustrative. "The Fourteenth Amendment does not enact Mr. Herbert Spencer's Social Statics. . . . But a constitution is not intended to embody a particular economic theory, whether of paternalism and the organic relation of the citizen to the State or of *laissez faire*. . . . I think that the word liberty in the Fourteenth Amendment is perverted when it is held to prevent the natural outcome of a dominant opinion, unless it can be said that a rational and fair man necessarily would admit that the statute proposed would infringe fundamental principles as they have been understood by the traditions of our people and our law." The years made it perfectly plain that the decisions of the Court depended for their character on the personal attitudes of the justices, and that a change, therefore, in the membership would vitally affect the decisions in a certain class of cases. The strengthening of the "liberal" element toward the end of the period is well-known.

lation intended to better social conditions. There has been a renewed attack upon the whole theory of judicial review and more especially upon the extent of its actual exercise. The courts, the critics declared, (and the statement was sometimes made in somewhat similar terms by certain dissenting judges) set up as a standard of constitutionality their own opinions concerning the advisability of legislation; and they sought (under the cover of "due process") either to maintain old-fashioned theories of economic and social order, or to put forth and make effective standards of everlasting right and justice; and thus the justices made declarations not dissimilar in essence to the theories of natural rights so familiar to the ears of men of three or four generations ago. The courts are therefore charged by implication with abandoning their earlier refusal to check legislation by the principles of natural rights and with surrendering their older position and the primary fortress of their actual power—their determination to enforce only the plain mandates of the Constitution. Some such position was naturally the inevitable result of their assuming authority to judge of the propriety and reasonableness of legislation; and the consequence was the tendency to uphold what the judges individually believed right and justice and reasonableness to be.[75] The remedy for this, if we may assume with the critics that a remedy is necessary, is unquestionably a wide, intelligent and sympathetic appreciation of the nature of social processes and of a developing social order. The reader of history need not be told that immutable principles of social competence and rectitude cannot be embodied in any series of decisions, however learned they may be.

The very fact of the Court's setting up "reasonableness" as a standard, by which to judge the constitutionality of social legislation, allows a modification or an accommodation to new conditions of society and to a changing belief concerning the essence of liberty. Such a standard is far better than any rigid definition of right and justice or any highly technical formulas which give no opportunity for development. The great task of the courts is to preserve the valuable and all-important imponderables of constitutional liberty; and until we are ready to sweep aside altogether the judicial power to perform this task, we must depend on the wisdom and integrity of the justices. If, as already said, they sometimes appear to obstruct social progress,

[75] In this connection see the chapter in this volume on Chief Justice Taney and the Supreme Court. Notice also Iredell's statement in Calder v. Bull, 3 Dallas 386, 399 (1798), where the general principles are briefly and admirably stated.

as far as progress can be obtained by legislation, the obstruction cannot be more than temporary. Probably the student of history, though he is justified in positive assurance that society cannot and will not stand still, is likely to think that hasty alteration of constitutional principles is more dangerous than delay and reasoned circumspection.

And yet withal, the declaration that social improvement has been unduly retarded is open to question. It requires no vast amount of critical insight to discern the rapid transformations which have taken place. And there is one thing more to be said: if the courts appear to have been perilously active and too ready to pronounce acts void, this activity was partly induced by a mass of hastily-drawn legislation and by no small number of enactments that appeared to bear no relation to the public good. If "a standing rule to live by" is to have effective meaning, legislators also need to have their share of appreciation of their responsibility in a developing society.

CHAPTER L

THE LATER YEARS OF THE NINETEENTH CENTURY
DEVELOPMENT OF NATIONAL AUTHORITY; THE
PROBLEM OF IMPERIALISM

In the last quarter of the nineteenth century the Republican party was firmly established as a conservative party. The old relics of the Civil War and of Reconstruction clung to the garments in which the faithful could still stand; and men still voted for the party candidates because they or their fathers had voted for Lincoln or had aided in the maintenance of the union, but the interests at stake were economic; the party stood for a protective tariff and cherished the well-being of industry and industrial stability. While industrial and social conditions were rapidly developing, economic interests were especially guarded by a thoroughly-organized and competent political party; and the success of that party did not rest alone upon the interest and activity of men distinctly involved in control of industry or in the safeguarding of vested rights of property, but also upon the allegiance of millions of the common people of the land. It is not necessary to discuss here the controversies between the Republicans and the Democrats on the question of protective duties, though the question sometimes involved what passed for constitutional arguments. There were other matters which proved for constitutional history more significant; there were signs in the sky or rumblings in the earth indicating a movement for social and economic change of a far-reaching character.

In 1884 Benjamin Butler came forth into the broad light of day as a candidate for the presidency—the nominee of two parties, the Anti-Monopoly party and the National or Greenback party. The latter party, representing the demand for paper money, asked also for other measures which, to use a word of later days, were "progressive." The platform of the Anti-Monopoly party, chiefly perhaps because of its brevity, is the more striking of the two; and yet the party and its program—not to speak of its candidate—received scarcely more than a contemptuous glance from its powerful opponents. Both platforms registered in large degree not only the subjects which were to be the source of dispute in the coming decades, but more: they laid down principles and demands which in very large measure actually marked the course of social and constitutional progress in the next forty years. In this rapidly changing world, the demands of the radical of one era may be the possession of the conservative in the next.

The Anti-Monopoly party did not advocate paper money, and its platform is briefer than that of the Greenbackers, but, if we view the two platforms as one, we find the following conspicuous proposals—the rigid inspection of mines and factories, a reduction of the hours of labor in factories, the abolition of child labor, the abandonment of importation of "contracted labor", submission of amendments to the Constitution in favor of suffrage regardless of sex, and on the subject of the liquor traffic, the regulation of interstate commerce, the establishment of bureaus of labor statistics in states and nation, the election of United States senators by popular vote, a graduated income tax. "Give our farmers and manufacturers", said the Greenbackers, "money as cheap as you now give it to our bankers, and they can pay high wages to labor, and compete with all the world."

In the last decade of the century various proposals were made which were indicative of discontent, a feeling that governments, both state and national, were not responsive to public demand, that parties and politicians barred the way, and that popular government was misnamed, if the word were applied to existing conditions. The cure for the evils or misadventures of democracy—it was now emphatically declared—was more democracy (a significant paradox); government must be brought safely within the control of the people. The movement was not unlike that of eighty years before, when old "king caucus" was dethroned and the nominating convention put in its place. The first step of importance, and one of unquestionable value, was the introduction of the Australian ballot, in the place of the party ballot prepared and printed by the party machine or even by the party candidates. Early in the next century came the direct primary as a substitute for the caucus and the convention system of nomination. In some states the referendum and initiative were established, and, symptomatic of the same hope and of a like public mind, was the adoption in some states of elaborate constitutions in which the people were, or thought they were, legislating directly and freely expressing their own will. This procedure expressed a distrust of representative government itself. No one can assert that these efforts to reinstate or invigorate political democracy have been a conspicuous success and have shaken off the hold of the professional politician. And we need not suppose that the great changes, marked by constitutional amendments and social legislation, were the result of party contests, in which issues were sharply presented, fundamental questions were debated, and results were registered at the ballot-box. If some weight must be given to the demands of the minor parties and to the Democratic party after its amalgamation with the Populists—for a party out of power is likely to enlist the discontented—, the fact still remains that changes came because of the slow development of public opinion and of a readiness of the people-at-large, free from distinct party pressure, to visualize the needs of the time. The amendments to the federal Constitution, of which somthing will be said in later pages, were not in any marked degree the product of debate between contending parties.

In 1894 Congress passed an income tax law. It provided for an annual tax of two per cent upon the gains, profits, and income of over four thousand dollars from any kind of property, rents, interest, dividends, salaries or from any profession, trade or employment. The subject naturally attracted much popular interest, and acute attention was given to the arguments concerning the constitutionality of the act, when, the next year, a case was brought to the federal Supreme Court to test its validity.[1] The Constitution gives power to lay and collect taxes, duties, imposts and excises; "but all duties, imposts, and excises" must "be uniform throughout the United States"; and it also provides that "direct taxes shall be apportioned among the several States . . . according to their respective numbers". Objection was raised by counsel to the exemption of incomes under four thousand dollars; and in light of the experience of later years, the objection has especial interest; but it did not give the Court particular trouble or anxiety. In this connection also the counsel pointed out that the payments of the tax would be made chiefly and in undue degree by the citizens of the rich eastern states. The primary question, however, was whether the tax provided for by the act was a direct tax; if it was, then the act was invalid because apportionment among the states was not provided.

That the law would be upheld by the Court appeared to be a reasonable expectation, because of the weight of previous decisions. In the case of Hylton v. United States (1796) [2] the opinion was expressed, without explicit decision, that only a capitation tax and a tax

---

[1] Pollock v. Farmers' Loan and Trust Co., 157 U. S. 429; 158 U. S. 601 (1895).
[2] 3 Dallas 171.

on land were direct taxes. An act of Congress passed in 1864[3] providing for a succession tax had been upheld, and even more important was a later decision which pronounced an income tax valid and definitely accepted the definition of the Hylton case.[4] In no one of these cases was the tax apportioned among the states. The act of 1894 came before the Court twice. In the first decision the Court declared a tax on income from municipal bonds was invalid, and that a tax on income from real estate was a direct tax and that the law in this latter particular was, therefore, unconstitutional, inasmuch as it did not apportion the taxes among the states. Upon other questions the justices were evenly divided and, in consequence, on these points no opinion was expressed. Upon a rehearing six weeks later, the Court declared that not only taxes on incomes from real estate, but also taxes on incomes from personal property were direct taxes. The whole act was declared void, because, though certain portions might be valid, the act constituted "one entire scheme of taxation". Four justices dissented.

The arguments before the Court and the opinions of the justices held the public attention; and the decision was widely criticized. The principle involved was so important that earnest advocates of the income tax and those filled with zeal for industrial and social reform were unwilling to retire from the struggle. Probably no other case, with the exception of the Dred Scott case of forty years before, was so widely discussed or received so much unfavorable comment. The Democratic party declared in 1896 that the Court had sustained constitutional objections, which had previously been overruled by the ablest judges who ever sat on that bench; and the party platform announced the duty of Congress to "use all the constitutional power which remains after that decision, or which may come from its reversal by the court as it may hereafter be constituted, so that the burdens of taxation may be equally and impartially laid. . . ." The end was not in immediate sight, but the desire to curb the expansion of great fortunes and the zeal for what was deemed justice in taxation continued unabated.

[3] Scholey v. Rew, 23 Wallace 331 (1875).
[4] Springer v. United States, 102 U. S. 586 (1881). See also Pacific Ins. Co. v. Soule, 7 Wallace 433 (1869), where the Court laid special emphasis on the opinions in the Hylton case; Veazie Bank v. Fenno, 8 Wallace 533 (1869). Uniformity of taxation means uniformity in every place where the subject of it is to be found. Head Money Cases, 112 U. S. 580 (1884). There was no chance of overthrowing the act because of the fact that some sections would pay more than others or because of exemptions.

Two cases decided by the Supreme Court in the later years of the century deserve special attention because they exposed the development or at least the actual extent of national authority. Only one of them had immediate connection with the social unrest of which we have just spoken; both brought to popular attention the scope of judicial power. The first of these cases was decided in 1890. A United States marshal protecting Justice Field, while on circuit court duty in California, shot a man threatening the life of the Justice. The marshal was arrested by the sheriff of the county and was discharged upon habeas corpus by the federal circuit court. The case was carried to the Supreme Court, where it was held that the marshal acted within his authority and was not answerable in the courts of the state.[5] Only two justices dissented, but the dissent was vigorous; they quoted an opinion of the Court given only six years before: "It is elementary learning that, if a prisoner is in the custody of a State court of competent jurisdiction, not illegally asserted, he cannot be taken from that jurisdiction and discharged on habeas corpus issued by a court of the United States, simply because he is not guilty of the offence. . . ."[6] We need not attempt to impugn the position of the majority of the Court; but the following statement by the minority indicates the historical significance of the whole incident: "We are not unmindful of the fact that in the foregoing remarks we have not discussed the bearings of this decision upon the autonomy of the States, in divesting them of what was once regarded as their exclusive jurisdiction over crimes committed within their own territory, against their own laws, and in enabling a federal

[5] In re Neagle, 135 U. S. 1 (1890).

[6] Ex parte Crouch, 112 U. S. 178, 180 (1884). Five years after the Neagle case, the Court said, ". . . a prisoner in custody under the authority of a State should not, except in a case of peculiar urgency, be discharged by a court or judge of the United States upon a writ of *habeas corpus,* in advance of any proceedings in the courts of the State to test the validity of his arrest and detention." Whitten *v.* Tomlinson, 160 U. S. 231, 247 (1895). Three years after this, the Court, declaring that the discharge of the prisoner was invalid under the circumstances, spoke of the exceedingly delicate jurisdiction given to the federal courts, by which a person under an indictment in a state court might be taken out of the custody of the state upon a writ of habeas corpus. Baker *v.* Grice, 169 U. S. 284 (1898). The judicial code (section 33) now provides (1916) for removal for trial to the federal district court of a civil suit or a criminal prosecution commenced against any federal officer on account of any action done by him under color of his office or in performance of his duties. This, it will be noticed, is quite different from the method of releasing him from state custody under habeas corpus; and it assures a formal trial on the merits of the case. The portion of the judicial code just cited is of importance in the attempted enforcement of the prohibition amendment at a later day.

judge or court, by an order in a *habeas corpus* proceeding, to deprive a State of its power to maintain its own public order. . . ." [7]

The second case of which we have just spoken was the Debs case, which arose out of the great railroad strike of 1894. Under the direction of the Attorney-General of the United States, a bill was filed in the federal circuit court for the northern district of Illinois, complaining of certain persons, officers of the American Railway Union, and declaring that they were interfering with the course of interstate commerce. In response to the prayer of the bill of complaint, the court issued an injunction, commanding the defendants "and all other persons whomsoever" to desist and refrain from interfering with interstate commerce and the carrying of the mails. Charged with violating the injunction, the defendants were found guilty of contempt and sentenced to imprisonment. On their application for a writ of habeas corpus, the Supreme Court, denying the petition, rendered an important decision.[8] "The entire strength of the nation", said the Court, "may be used to enforce in any part of the land the full and free exercise of all national powers and the security of all rights entrusted by the Constitution to its care. The strong arm of the national government may be put forth to brush away all obstructions to the freedom of interstate commerce or the transportation of the mails. If the emergency arises, the army of the Nation, and all its militia, are at the service of the Nation to compel obedience to its laws." [9] Of even greater significance was the statement that the right to use force does not exclude the right of appeal to the courts for the exercise of all their powers of prevention, and that peaceful determination by the judiciary is, or might be, better than the use of clubs and bayonets. Here, then, was announcement of what was stigmatized as "government by injunction", a subject of acute controversy for years. Associated with the Income Tax case, which had been decided only about

[7] In re Neagle, 135 U. S. 1, 99 (1890). I have not attempted in the brief discussion in the text to examine the argument on either side as to whether at that time there was statutory authority for the issue of habeas corpus under the circumstances, or whether the marshal was engaged in executing any "law".

[8] In re Debs et al., 158 U. S. 564 (1895).

[9] It all sounds like Hamilton's statement in *The Federalist,* no. XVI: the federal government "must, in short, possess all the means, and have a right to resort to all the methods, of executing the powers with which it is intrusted, that are possessed and exercised by the governments of the particular states." He also said, "The majesty of the national authority must be manifested through the medium of the court of justice."

a week before, the case was said to be evidence that the courts of the nation were arrayed on the side of property.

The use of the injunction, disobedience to which could be punished as a contempt of court, aroused the opposition of labor leaders. They looked upon the whole procedure as a vulgar and dangerous subterfuge. Others also, though not associated with labor movements and cherishing no sympathy with strikes, were dissatisfied or filled with misgivings; if, they said, property was endangered, it was the duty of the executive of state or nation to protect it, and if it were destroyed, those charged with a penal offense should be tried by a jury and not thrust into prison by a judge.[10] Conservatives of this type were inclined to doubt that respect for law was increased by the use of a summary process rather than by the strong arm of the executive; and some there were who feared lest the dignity and the prestige of the courts be lessened and lest social and class hostilities be augmented rather than reduced.

But of no less interest was the fact that federal troops were sent to Chicago to protect the railroads, the free course of interstate commerce, and the mails. The Governor of Illinois had not asked for troops; he declared that the state forces were able to quell disorder and guard property, and that the national government had therefore no right to encroach upon the states or impugn their authority; to do this was to ignore the elementary principles of local self-government.[11] We need not enter upon a discussion concerning the validity of this argument. Though the issue was not directly presented to the Court, it appears to be by inference thrust aside by the words previously quoted. Of course the critical question was whether this should be considered an instance of "domestic violence" or an uprising against

---

[10] The counsel for the petitioners declared "The suppression of public disorder and tumult is an executive and not a judicial function. . . . But it is equally plain that the only object of a suit by the government for injunction to prohibit what the criminal code has already forbidden is to change the procedure by which the guilt of those charged is to be ascertained and their punishment inflicted." It is not the intention of the present writer to declare the decision rendered by a unanimous Court was incorrect. It was based partly on the fact that the United States has "property in the mails", but the mere fact that an act is criminal does not divest the jurisdiction of equity to prevent it by injunction. If the principle was indubitably sound, it was nevertheless a dramatic exhibition of national authority and judicial power.

[11] "The United States shall guarantee to every State in this Union a republican form of government, and shall protect each of them against invasion; and, on application of the Legislature, or of the executive (when the Legislature cannot be convened), against domestic violence." Constitution, Art. IV, sec. 4.

national authority which the government was under obligation to suppress. No one can seriously contend that the government in the face of a serious insurrection must wait placidly till a governor calls for aid, if the free course of interstate commerce and the mails be obstructed, and the governor be negligent, unwilling, or incompetent. But plainly national authority was marching on; and if the federal authorities were technically justified in law, the fact remained that the government had disclosed its power.

In viewing the manifestation of federal authority in these years, it is desirable to notice the use of an injunction issued by a federal court to prevent a state official or more commonly a board or commission from enforcing a law alleged to be unconstitutional. In these cases the principle which has been mentioned in previous pages—the principle that an officer cannot take refuge behind the authority of the state, if the state has no constitutional power in the matter—is made specially prominent. But also important is the actual exercise of the power to enjoin him, a power extensively used in the succeeding decades. In the Reagan case (1894), already referred to, the Supreme Court sustained an injunction issued by a circuit court restraining a state railroad commission from enforcing rates which the commission had prescribed. Other cases of a similar character followed.[12] And thus it appears that it is not necessary in controversies of this kind to follow the slow processes of the law and to carry the case through the state courts and onward by appeal to the federal Supreme Court to test the validity of the state act or the decision of a state commission.

The leading matter of interest in the closing years of the century was the problem of annexation, the result of the Spanish-American war. There was much vigorous and wholesome public discussion concerning the desirability of annexation, the nature of the union, the ethics of imperial expansion, and the elementary principles which should be respected in the upbuilding of the nation. There was a good deal of wasteful boasting about America's becoming a world power, as if America had not for a hundred years and more been of vast influence in the world for many reasons, among them the very fact of her attempt to give constitutional protection to liberty and democ-

---

[12] Reagan v. Farmers' Loan and Trust Co., 154 U. S. 362; Smyth v. Ames, 169 U. S. 466 (1898). An injunction had been previously used in some cases. In 1911 Congress provided that, as a rule, the injunction should issue from a court of three justices. Judicial Code, sec. 266.

racy. But it remains that at this time the United States was being caught up more and more in the skein of diplomatic controversy and consequent perplexities. The fact that now, more plainly than hitherto, the nation was both a Pacific and an Atlantic power and had corresponding obligations was made plain to the man on the street—who like most men did not take the time to consider all the possible results.

In previous years, if Alaska be left out of consideration, only territory contiguous to the United States had been annexed; and the natural expectation was that the land, thus acquired, would be peopled by American citizens and would ultimately compose a portion of the union. Many persons still held the doctrine, nowhere better stated than by Taney in the Dred Scott case: annexed territory "is acquired to become a State, and not to be held as a colony and governed by Congress with absolute authority". It is an amusing and entertaining fact —this reference to the old slave case to defend the rights of freemen: the Supreme Court, as we shall see later, declared with Taney that absolute and unlimited authority over the territory annexed was not within the scope of governmental powers. In any narrow sense, the annexation of the Philippines and Porto Rico, as a mere fact, does not lie within the field of constitutional history, but in its effects and reverberations it raised the question whether America should in any degree become imperialistic in aim and character. The Democratic platform of 1900 declared this burning question to be the paramount issue of the campaign.

The status of the annexed territory and the bearings of the Constitution upon the extent and character of the rights of the people, who were brought under the American flag, proved a perplexing problem. In the terms of the day, did "the Constitution follow the flag"? Did it carry with it the full blessings of liberty and impose upon the United States all the restrictions which the government must respect when dealing with its own citizens, who were likewise citizens of the states? In the earlier cases, the applicability of tariff duties arose to be solved; but not all the difficulties of that problem need disturb our dreams. In the course of the decisions, certain principles of great importance in a developing empire were gradually determined. In the case of Downes v. Bidwell,[13] the Court, in a five to four decision, announced that the Constitution did not in itself and unaided immediately embrace in its

---

[13] 182 U. S. 244 (1901). The Island of Porto Rico became territory appurtenant to the United States, but not a part of the United States within the revenue clause of the Constitution.

entirety the people of an annexed area, nor did it bestow upon the people all the privileges of United States citizenship.[14] In the opinion rendered by Justice Brown, which in most respects may be considered the opinion of the Court, the only distinction made is that between territories and states; but in a concurring opinion by three justices, with which a fourth largely agreed, we find the declaration that there are three different stages—unincorporated territory, incorporated territory, and states.

This latter classification came in the course of a brief time to be the accepted theory of the Court. Thus, in any given instance, the crucial question is whether Congress, either at the time of annexation or later, expressly or by implication "incorporated" a people. We find in one case (1903) [15] a decision to the effect that certain provisions in the fifth and sixth amendments to the federal Constitution were not made applicable to Hawaii under the joint resolution annexing the Islands: "neither the terms of the resolution nor the situation which arose from it served to incorporate the Hawaiian Islands into the United States and make them an integral part thereof." [16] The next year (1904) the Court, passing upon the question whether right of jury trial was carried by the Constitution to the Philippine Islands, said: "Until Congress shall see fit to incorporate territory ceded by treaty into the United States, we regard it as settled by that decision [Downes v. Bidwell] that the territory is to be governed under the power existing in Congress to make laws for such territories and subject to such constitutional restrictions upon the powers of that body as are applicable to the situation".[17] Next came a case involving the status of Alaska;[18] with only faint protest from Justice Brown and a statement from Justice Harlan, who concurred in the decision but rejected the doctrine of incorporation and non-incorpora-

[14] "We are also of opinion that the power to acquire territory by treaty implies not only the power to govern such territory, but to prescribe upon what terms the United States will receive its inhabitants, and what their *status* shall be in what Chief Justice Marshall termed the 'American empire'. . . . Indeed, it is doubtful if Congress would ever assent to the annexation of territory upon the condition that its inhabitants, however foreign they may be to our habits, traditions and modes of life, shall become at once citizens of the United States." *Ibid., 279.*

[15] Hawaii v. Mankichi, 190 U. S. 197 (1903).

[16] These words are in the concurring opinion of two justices. *Ibid.,* 219. Justice Brown, giving the opinion of the Court, did not make any distinction between incorporated and unincorporated territories. Five justices were in the affirmative; two gave a concurring opinion. Four justices dissented.

[17] Dorr v. United States, 195 U. S. 138, 143 (1904).

[18] Rassmussen v. United States, 197 U. S. 516 (1905).

tion,[19] the Court plainly accepted the theory or the fact of unincorporated and incorporated territories and decided that Alaska belonged in the latter class. But we should especially notice that incorporation and the "organization" of a territory by congressional enactment are distinct processes.

It appeared, therefore, that if the United States desired to become an imperial power—imperial in fact and law if not imperialistic in spirit—, the stage was all set for the process. Dependencies could be kept permanently beyond the pale of the union. But, withal, there were limitations on congressional power: "There are certain principles of natural justice inherent in the Anglo-Saxon character which need no expression in constitutions or statutes to give them effect or to secure dependencies against legislation manifestly hostile to their real interests." [20] These words of Justice Brown were thrown out to calm the "Grave apprehensions of danger" felt by "many eminent men"; but it is specially interesting to notice his reference to "natural justice", his reliance on "Anglo-Saxon character", and his use of the word "dependencies", a term hitherto almost or quite foreign to the American vocabulary. In the opinion there were, however, certain more explicit statements: though declaring that there was no intention to express an opinion how far the bill of rights contained in the first eight amendments was of general and how far of local application, the Court said, "There is a clear distinction between such prohibitions as go to the very root of the power of Congress to act at all, irrespective of time or place, and such as are operative only 'throughout the United States' or among the several states." [21]

---

[19] "I am constrained to say", Harlan had previously declared, "that this idea of 'incorporation' has some occult meaning which my mind does not apprehend." Downes v. Bidwell, 182 U. S. 244, 391. Justice Brown, adhering to his opinion in the earlier case, said the Constitution does not apply to territories acquired by treaty until Congress so declares. The justices all agreed that the sixth amendment was applicable to Alaska.

[20] Downes v. Bidwell, 182 U. S. 244, 280 (1901).

[21] Ibid., 277. The three justices concurring in the decision and giving a separate opinion read by White, said, ". . . even in cases where there is no direct command of the Constitution which applies, there may nevertheless be restrictions of so fundamental a nature that they cannot be transgressed, although not expressed in so many words in the Constitution." Ibid., 291. See also the statement in Hawaii v. Mankichi, 190 U. S. 197, 217-218 (1903).

CHAPTER LI

INTERSTATE COMMERCE; RAILROADS; TRUSTS; AMENDMENTS; THE PRESIDENCY; CONCLUSION

When we examined the Court decisions interpreting and applying the fourteenth amendment, we found the judiciary facing the problems which arose from the establishment of state commissions. Whatever may be said of constitutional theory and all the mists of legal argument, the fact is that the nation and the states, in the later years of the nineteenth century and the early years of the twentieth, were entering upon the commission habit. Amid all the problems which were involved in the development of constitutional law and governmental procedure, that fact stands forth with peculiar distinctness. Commissions were intrusted with extensive power, granted by statutes of a general character. Administration and practical application were in the hands of the commissions. The fact, as in so many other instances, is of more importance than the theory; but constitutional problems inevitably arose; for the whole development, though not utterly without precedent, was essentially new.

Considerable attention was given by the courts to the interpretation of statutes, with intent to discover whether the commissions had transcended the authority granted them; and there was, of course, the perennial question whether they had respected due process. But there was a more elementary problem: had the legislature improperly delegated legislative or judicial authority and thus broken down the traditional separation of the powers or disregarded the elements of constitutional order? And still, every passing day made more obvious the inability of legislative bodies, by plodding along the old route, to meet the tasks produced by the new economic conditions. It was impossible to pass legislation so general, so explicit, and so detailed as to leave no room for judgment in interpretation, application and enforcement.

In the later years of the last century, the courts, as we have seen, were finding barriers against encroachments upon property rights. To condemn and to criticize, to charge the courts with arid and unimaginative conservatism is an easy and comfortable occupation; but it leaves out of consideration the difficulty of the problems of adaptation. And yet, the Supreme Court during those years appears in most ways to have been holding back with what now seems unnecessary persistence.[1] There were, it is true, certain decisions which indicated that there were joints in the defensive armor.[2] But on the whole the conservatism of the supreme bench during that period appeared nearly invulnerable. At the beginning of the period when the courts were or appeared to be resisting a public movement for further social control, Congress entered upon the task which endured for a generation——the task of regulating and properly controlling the railroads. The decisions in the Granger Cases were important but they were not enough. The roads engaged in interstate commerce could not be effectively regulated by state legislation. That fact was daily becoming more evident.

Mere words fail to convey any proper impression of the confusion and the iniquity prevalent in railroad affairs in the eighties. The building of new roads had been going on at a rate hitherto quite unparalleled; in 1886, alone, 12,983 miles of road were laid down.[3] Competition had reached such a state of excess that it was destructive of actual corporate interests or at least of respect for public well-being. Individual shippers were favored at the expense of their rivals; discriminatory rates favored one locality and worked hardship to another; rebates were granted in some instances so excessive and discriminatory as to reach into the realm of the comic opera. Speculation ran riot; and while the big shipper found means of increasing a rapidly swelling fortune, the small shipper and the public paid the

[1] It is not an unimportant fact that the following cases were all decided within a period of five years, 1894-1899; the Sugar case, United States v. E. C. Knight Co., 156 U. S. 1; Reagan v. Farmers' Loan and Trust Co., 154 U. S. 362; the Income Tax case, Pollock v. Farmers' Loan and Trust Co., 157 U. S. 429, 158 U. S. 601; Smyth v. Ames, 169 U. S. 466. And what shall be said about Allgeyer v. Louisiana, 165 U. S. 578? To a student conversant with the constitutional history of England or the history of America for a hundred years after the adoption of the Constitution, it seems strange to point to this case, which staked out the wide field of individual liberty, as an example of judicial conservatism; but in the new conditions, it may perhaps be so listed as the basis of later cases of a conservative character, especially Lochner v. New York.

[2] For example, Holden v. Hardy, 169 U. S. 366 (1898), the hours of labor case, which opened the way for later decisions accepting the validity of state statutes limiting hours of labor.

[3] "The decade of the eighties, so far as common carriers are concerned, was primarily characterized by new railroad construction. Over 70,000 miles of line were built in ten years. . . ." W. Z. Ripley, *Railroad Rates and Regulation*, p. 27.

piper. The whole story is a tale so confusing, so sordid, so wanting in the elements of merit or common sense, that we find it difficult to understand why it took so long to establish, simplify and rationalize the control of railway traffic in the public interest.

In 1886, the Supreme Court, after referring to the Granger Cases, declared that it was not and never had been the deliberate opinion of the majority of the Court that a state statute, which attempted to regulate railroad charges within its limits for a transportation involving a part of commerce among the states, was a valid law.[4] Unless the roads, therefore, were to be left to their own devices in interstate business and allowed to indulge freely in the game they were playing, Congress must act. The next year Congress passed the Interstate Commerce Act and established the Interstate Commerce Commission. The act declared that rates should be reasonable and just. Rebates and discrimination between persons and places were forbidden, as were also pooling and traffic agreements; it was declared unlawful for any carrier to charge more for transportation, under substantially similar conditions, for a shorter than for a longer distance over the same line, in the same direction, "the shorter being included within the longer distance". The Commission was authorized in special cases to relieve the carrier from the operation of this last provision, the justly famous "long and short haul" clause.[5]

The Commission started out bravely and accomplished something. Little by little, however, its power for good was so whittled away by judicial decisions that by the end of the century it had become little more than a body to collect data and make reports. Portions of the act, indeed very essential portions, had from the beginning proved to be difficult of enforcement; and though in 1889 it was provided that a violation of the act was punishable by fine or imprisonment or both, rebates and other discriminations were not easily prevented. In construing the statute, the Court was determined to guard against the exercise of any power not plainly granted the Commission; and in addition the justices feared lest the Commission should so act as to exercise legislative or judicial authority. That regulation could be laid down by Congress to apply in detail to the whole country, and be laid

---

[4] Wabash, St. L. and Pac. Ry. Co. v. Illinois, 118 U. S. 557 (1886).

[5] "In one respect the law of 1887 marks a profound revolution in both commercial theory and practice. Its provisions concerning equality of rates to all classes of shippers denote a great moral uplift in the business standards of the country." Ripley, op. cit., p. 454.

down with such explicitness as to be capable of application to every conceivable situation, was of course no more than an iridescent dream. But as every important rule or order of the Commission was subjected to judicial investigation before it could become effective, the Commission was placed in the position of having to defend itself at every turn. The procedure involved appeals, sometimes years of delay, while every possible obstacle was thrown in the pathway of the body charged by the government with a difficult and perplexing task.

The climax was reached in 1897, when the Court said: "It is one thing to inquire whether the rates which have been charged and collected are reasonable—that is a judicial act; but an entirely different thing to prescribe rates which shall be charged in the future—that is a legislative act." [6] Though the opinion pointed to certain powers which the Commission could properly exercise, this authority was not satisfactory or consoling to the public desirous of seeing a solution of the vexing problem and an end of the iniquities of railroad managers still engaged in ridiculous maneuvers. The people had not surrendered their faith in the virtue of competition; they intended to make it compulsory; but they specially demanded respect for public needs and not merely scramble for booty.

The tide of popular discontent was rising—fear of the money power, the grasp of a few men upon the transportation systems and certain natural resources of the country, indignation against trusts and monopolies, all pointed to the necessity of congressional legislation for curbing unwholesome evils. The chief influence in producing remedial legislation was, of course, the arrogance and the misdirected zeal of the railroad authorities themselves; for it appears to be a rule of life that the extremists defending an outworn fortress batter down their own defenses. Certain changes in the original act were made in 1903, at the request of the railroad managers themselves. In his annual message of 1904, President Roosevelt said that railroad regulation was of prime importance, and he returned to the subject the following year. A new statute was enacted in 1906. In passing on the

---

[6] Maximum Freight Rate case (Interstate Comm. Com. v. Cincinnati, N. O. and T. P. R. Co.), 167 U. S. 479, 499. It should be noticed that the Commission did not pretend to prescribe a general schedule of rates, but it ordered the road to desist from charging certain prices, under certain circumstances, and not to charge more than a named price which the Commission deemed reasonable. It was quite apparent that without some such power the Commission in certain exceedingly important respects would be nearly or quite ineffective. See also the Social Circle case (Cincinnati, N. O. and T. P. R. Co. v. Interstate Comm. Com.), 162 U. S. 184, and especially the remarks, 196-197 (1896).

questions raised by specific complaints, the Commission was given power to prescribe just and reasonable maximum rates. Its conclusions were to have presumption of validity. In other words, the great burden was thrown upon the roads and taken from the shoulders of the Commission. The discussions in Congress when the act was under consideration and, indeed, the whole controversy disclose the essential issue —the extent to which the legislative body can delegate its power. In 1910 an additional act was passed strengthening the Commission's hands in certain respects.

Important judicial decisions upheld the Commission's authority, and the principles were clearly set forth: "One question remains for discussion, the finding of the Commission upon the character of the rate, whether it is unreasonable as decided. Such decision, we have said with tiresome repetition, is peculiarly the province of the Commission to make, and that its findings are fortified by presumptions of truth, 'due to the judgments of a tribunal appointed by law and informed by experience.' " [7] This plainly involved a recognition of the powers of Congress to delegate power to fix rates, and the recognition that rates so fixed would, when subjected to judicial scrutiny, have the presumption of legality and propriety. The Court did not, however, totally abdicate. It reserved the right under certain circumstances not to accept the Commission's findings and rules.[8] In 1912, its position was summed up as follows: the orders of the Commission are final unless beyond the power which it can constitutionally exercise; or beyond its statutory power; or based on mistake of law. An order, regular on its face, may be set aside if it appears that the rate is confiscatory and in violation of the constitutional prohibition against taking property without due process of law; or if the Commission should act arbitrarily and in an unreasonable manner.

Before long, the task of effective regulation was seen to involve more than the mere right of Congress to regulate rates and to control interstate traffic. For the whole process was found to be so inclusive, transportation was so obviously national, that the states even in the management of their own internal commerce were necessarily limited. This fact is illustrated by decisions upholding the power of the federal Commission so to adjust intrastate rates as not to interfere with

[7] Interstate Comm. Com. *v.* Chi., R. I. & Pac. R. Co., 218 U. S. 88, 110 (1910), referring with approval to Ill. Cent. R. Co. *v.* Interstate Comm. Com., 206 U. S. 441, 454 (1907), where the Court said, "And the findings of the Commission are made by law *prima facie* true."

[8] Interstate Comm. Com. *v.* Union Pacific R. R. Co., 222 U. S. 541, 547 (1912).

interstate rates established by federal authority. The existence of such a power was indicated by certain statements made by the Court in 1913;[9] and the next year in the Shreveport case the principle was accepted and applied.[10] At a later date, Chief Justice Taft, giving the opinion of the Court, used these comprehensive and conclusive words: "Commerce is a unit and does not regard state lines, and while, under the Constitution, interstate and intrastate commerce are ordinarily subject to regulation by different sovereignties, yet when they are so mingled together that the supreme authority, the Nation, cannot exercise complete effective control over interstate commerce without incidental regulation of intrastate commerce, such incidental regulation is not an invasion of state authority or a violation of the proviso." [11]

During the later years of the nineteenth century and the first few years of the twentieth, the attempts to control the railroads were not meeting with conspicuous success. Furthermore, another problem, closely associated with the railroads but even more difficult, had forced itself upon public attention. The process of accumulating vast fortunes had been going forward at a rapid rate. Men gifted with shrewdness, business sagacity and a determination to be rich and powerful, took advantage of highly developed transportation systems, the natural resources of the land and the impressive expansion of the nation, to build up a system of industrial control so extensive and so remunerative that the stories of Croesus or Monte-Cristo appear like plaintive tales of penury.

One fact stands forth with especial clearness: the very extensive control in the hands of one man or a single group of men demon-

---

[9] Minnesota Rate Cases, 230 U. S. 352, 399, 420, 433 (1913).

[10] Houston, E. & W. Texas Ry. Co. v. United States, 234 U. S. 342, 354 (1914). "It is manifest that the State cannot fix the relation of the carrier's interstate and intrastate charges without directly interfering with the former, unless it simply follows the standard set by Federal authority." Another interesting illustration of the way in which the national character of commerce was made apparent was the decision of the Court that a state railroad commission could not order through interstate trains to stop at certain stations if local facilities were adequate. Atlantic Coast Line v. Wharton, 207 U. S. 328 (1907).

[11] Wisconsin R. R. Comm. v. C., B. & Q. R. R. Co., 257 U. S. 563, 588 (1922). "In solving the problem of maintaining the efficiency of an interstate commerce railway system which serves both the States and the Nation, Congress is dealing with a unit in which state and interstate operations are often inextricably commingled. When the adequate maintenance of interstate commerce involves and makes necessary on this account the incidental and partial control of intrastate commerce, the power of Congress to exercise such control has been clearly established." Dayton-Goose Creek Ry. Co. v. United States, 263 U. S. 456, 485 (1924).

strated plainly the fact that industry was in some cases so nationalized that only national authority could regulate it. The men who were thus engaged, or beginning to be engaged, in this constructive process, this articulation, this coördination, were creating a structure which by its very nature subjected itself to governmental administration or at least oversight. It used to be said that they were preparing the way for socialism—not by the way of revolt, and of course not intentionally, but as a natural consequence of what they had themselves accomplished in so combining natural resources, transportation and industrial activity as to simplify the task of governmental ownership. Whether that conclusion be sound or not, the development did bring attempts at governmental control and restraint; and the future is to decide whether control is to be expanded and whether restraint is to be followed by ownership. In one way, regulation appears to be a process antagonistic to a further approach toward socialism—or, if the reader wishes a different term, governmental ownership of productive enterprises—because regulation may make complete ownership and complete direction needless. On the other hand, if it fail, it may naturally lead to the forced abandonment of private ownership and control. The main matter of importance to us, as students of history, is, however, that the skill and energy and constructive power of industrial magnates brought into being a high degree of correlation and consolidation, and the onlooker was inevitably led to question whether the nation would be in the hands of a few industrial monarchs or be governed by popular vote.

So, soon after the establishment of the Interstate Commerce Commission, came a demand for the curbing of trusts, a name meaning in common parlance any large industrial enterprise which because of its power was able to crush smaller competitors and subject the public to unreasonable prices.[12] The demand resulted in the passing of the Anti-Trust or Sherman Act in 1890. Naturally the constitutional basis for the act was the interstate commerce clause. It declared every contract or combination or conspiracy in restraint of interstate or foreign

[12] The early conspicuous combination, the Standard Oil trust, was a trust in the technical sense. Centralized control of a number of corporations was established. "Such a 'voting trust', well known to the corporation lawyer, is of course a trust in the technical sense, involving a legal title in trustees who are bound to exercise it for the benefit of the *cestuis qui trustent*. Because the Standard Oil combination was so notorious, and because it appeared for a time as if a large number of great combinations would follow this form of organization, the term "trust" came to be popularly used as a generic term to describe all large combinations." J. A. McLaughlin, *Cases on the Federal Anti-Trust Laws of the United States*, pp. 20-21.

trade or commerce to be illegal. It also declared it illegal to monopolize or attempt to monopolize any part of interstate or foreign commerce. Violation of the act was made a punishable offense. The act lay on the statute book for several years without serious ruffling of its pages.

Most of the numerous decisions of the courts on this matter are not within the field of constitutional law, save as any construction of a statute may be considered as having constitutional significance. Once it has been accepted that the power to regulate interstate commerce involves the power to make combinations and monopolies illegal and to declare certain practices punishable, the main constitutional principle is acknowledged. But the history of the attempt to make the anti-trust legislation effective is of importance; the public criticism of judicial decisions, whether such criticism be technically valid or not, and the difficulties encountered in the application of law are not outside the field of constitutional history. In the whole matter, however, not the technical power to legislate, but the fact of legislation, which was an extension of the former actual activities of the nation, is the crucial matter. Everywhere we turn we find the broadening of national authority and, as a matter of reality, the comparative subordination or submergence of the states.

Five years after the passage of the act, the Supreme Court, in the Sugar case, declared that manufacturing within the limits of a state was not within the field of interstate commerce and that the act did not authorize restraint or prevention of contracts relating exclusively to the acquisition of refineries in a state, the object of which was private gain but not through the control of interstate or foreign commerce.[13] It appeared for a time that in light of this decision it would be impracticable to make anti-trust legislation effective; but not long thereafter, there was a series of decisions which gave the act effect and forecast further results. In the Trans-Missouri Freight case, a contract between competitive railroads, having the effect of restraining trade, was held to be within the provisions of the Sherman Act.[14] That

[13] United States v. E. C. Knight Co., 156 U. S. 1 (1895). "Contracts, combinations, or conspiracies to control domestic enterprise in manufacture, agriculture, mining, production in all its forms . . . might unquestionably tend to restrain external as well as domestic trade, but the restraint would be an indirect result. . . . *Ibid.*, 16. The combination "included 98% of the then existing sugar refining capacity of the country." J. A. McLaughlin, *op. cit.*, p. 25. "Whether or not the blame for this decision is attributable to the Department of Justice, or to the Courts, the fact was that it inhibited practically all prosecutions of industrial combinations during nearly all the remainder of the first decade after the Statute." *Ibid.*, p. 25.

[14] United States v. Trans-Missouri Freight Ass'n., 166 U. S. 290 (1897).

conclusion was of prime importance. In 1899, the Court held illegal an association of pipe manufacturers who had entered into an arrangement whereby there should be no competition between them in certain areas embracing in the aggregate a large portion of the union.[15] This combination presented a condition quite easily distinguishable from that presented in the Sugar case; the association was plainly a contrivance for the elimination of competitive interstate prices. Then came the Northern Securities case,[16] declaring illegal a holding company which, through the ownership of stock of two companies, controlled two railroads which were natural rivals. This was not merely an arrangement for the investment of capital but a plan so to manage two roads as to eliminate uncomfortable competition.

There followed in the next few years the dissolution of certain big combinations—the so-called Beef trust,[17] the Standard Oil trust,[18] and the American Tobacco trust.[19] Whatever may have been the public zeal for drastic action, this at least may be said: the act in question and the important decisions of the Court made plain the fact that Congress could effectively prohibit combinations or conspiracies which, actually within the sphere of interstate commerce, interfered with reasonable competition and freedom of communication. The justices, however, held different opinions concerning the meaning of "restraint of trade" and concerning the application of the prohibitions of the statute. In the Standard Oil case, Chief Justice White, giving the

---

[15] Addyston Pipe & Steel Co. *v.* United States, 175 U. S. 211 (1899).

[16] Northern Securities Co. *v.* United States, 193 U. S. 197 (1904). This was a very important case, and four justices dissented. Justice White, reading a dissenting opinion in behalf of the dissentients, said that Congress was without power to regulate the acquisition and ownership of the stock and declared that if there were any such power in Congress it had not been exercised by the Anti-Trust Act. Justice Holmes also dissenting, with the concurrence of the other three, said he did not expect to hear it maintained that Mr. Morgan could be sent to prison for buying as many shares as he liked in the two railroads; and he also said that if the statute were to be construed with the literalness, which appeared to be asked for, then a partnership between two stage drivers who had been competitors in driving across a state line would be a crime.

[17] Swift and Co. *v.* United States, 196 U. S. 375 (1905).

[18] Standard Oil Co. *v.* United States, 221 U. S. 1 (1911).

[19] United States *v.* American Tobacco Co., 221 U. S. 106 (1911). Notice, however, United States *v.* United States Steel Corp., 251 U. S. 417, 451 (1920), where the Court said, "The Corporation is undoubtedly of impressive size and it takes an effort of resolution not to be affected by it or to exaggerate its influence. But we must adhere to the law and the law does not make mere size an offence or the existence of unexerted power an offence." The Court found neither a monopoly nor the use of improper methods.

opinion, announced the "rule of reason." The same year, in the To-bacco Trust case, the Chief Justice, expounding this doctrine or principle, gave the following explanation: "It was therefore pointed out that the statute did not forbid or restrain the power to make normal and usual contracts to further trade by resorting to all normal methods, whether by agreement or otherwise, to accomplish such purpose. In other words, it was held, not that acts which the statute prohibited could be removed from the control of its prohibitions by a finding that they were reasonable, but that the duty to interpret which inevitably arose from the general character of the term restraint of trade required that the words restraint of trade should be given a meaning which would not destroy the individual right to contract and render difficult if not impossible any movement of trade in the channels of interstate commerce—the free movement of which it was the purpose of the statute to protect." [20]

The rule of reason, which now became a standard principle, caused some leaders of industry to charge that the result was to leave the whole subject in vagueness and uncertainty; and it was also said by other critics that the Court was intent upon reading into the statute its own notions of what was beneficial and what was harmful. Justice Harlan, concurring in part and dissenting in part, said, "After many years of public service at the National Capital, and after a somewhat close observation of the conduct of public affairs, I am impelled to say that there is abroad, in our land, a most harmful tendency to bring about the amending of constitutions and legislative enactments by means alone of judicial construction." He declared that the majority of the Court had in effect said, "You may *now* restrain such commerce, provided you are reasonable about it. . . ." [21] That he pronounced to be a clear instance of judicial legislation.

Two acts passed by Congress (1914)—the Clayton Act and the Federal Trade Commission Act—were additional attempts to compel

[20] United States *v.* American Tobacco Co., 221 U. S. 106, 179-180 (1911). The general terms used in the statute left "it to be determined by the light of reason, guided by the principles of law and the duty to apply and enforce the public policy embodied in the statute, in every given case whether any particular act or contract was within the contemplation of the statute." Standard Oil Co. *v.* United States, 221 U. S. 1, 64 (1911). Fourteen years before this, White, dissenting and supported by three justices, pointed out the distinction between reasonable and unreasonable restraint. United States *v.* Trans-Missouri Freight Ass'n., 166 U. S. 290, 343, 347 ff. (1897).

[21] Standard Oil Co. *v.* United States, 221 U. S. 1, 105, 102 (1911). There was much comment—favorable and unfavorable—in the public press and among legal writers.

the abandonment of unfair methods of competition and to make the anti-trust legislation effective. They embodied President Wilson's theories which aimed to bring in a new industrial order shorn of the abuses of the past. Only a very bold man would try to indicate briefly, or even in many words, the effect of these measures. They are mentioned here only as an indication of the prevailing desire to improve industrial conditions and business practices. At the present writing, the whole subject is undergoing such radical alterations—if not in constitutional law, at least in the public mind—that it is difficult to get a proper perspective; an effort to distinguish the headlands marking out with any clarity the main outlines of historical progress is peculiarly difficult. So futile appear to be the attempts of the past, or at least so far from satisfying the public demand, that it seems as if the whole history of trade-regulation under the interstate commerce power will in the future be looked upon as valuable only because it illustrates the difficulty of the problem, and because the attempts proved to be the forerunners of further and more drastic methods. The whole movement, which purposed to secure social justice and economic freedom by insisting upon competition and by reliance upon the ameliorating effect of compulsory rivalry, appears to be nearing its close. In the public affection, planning seems to be taking the place of compelled competition; restriction is to be supplanted by guidance and, mayhap, control or even public ownership.[22] Nationalism is so real and its realities are so dominant, that any microscopic investigation of the commerce clause of the Constitution is likely to be worthless; and we are probably right in assuming that any method, deemed to be constitutional, will be used if necessary to correct—or seek to correct—what are thought to be the evils of the commercial world. What can be done under the shadow, or in the light, of the commerce clause only the venturesome would dare to predict.

With these few words bearing upon the character and the interpretation of the Interstate Commerce Acts and the Sherman Act, we must be content; but the reader must not be left with the impression that the courts were not busy, without reference to those particular

---

[22] "Students of the Anti-Trust Laws seldom consider them ideal. There is an occasional exception. . . . But economists and legal students are insisting that they represent a certain minimum protection of the public interest subject always to reexamination and modification by legislation or court judgment, which should be retained in the absence of any alternative method of control. Where competition does not work, public control of some sort or public ownership should be substituted." I. A. McLaughlin, *op. cit.*, p. 711.

statutes, in passing upon various phases of interstate commerce law. And yet in a general way the principles laid down by the Court, from the time of Gibbons *v.* Ogden (1824) to and including the Cooley *v.* Port Wardens case (1851), stand on the whole unaffected by the passing of time, in so far as the earlier cases mark out the broad lines of demarcation between intrastate commerce on the one hand and interstate and foreign commerce on the other.[23] The later cases largely involved the application of these principles; fine distinctions were drawn, so fine that the lay reader may at first sight not see them at all.[24] But if distinctions were at all times perfectly obvious, there would be little use for courts.[25]

Congress in recent years has exercised by explicit and affirmative legislation the power of regulating interstate commerce, and has gone so far as to prohibit altogether the transportation of certain articles. In doing so, it has aimed to protect or enhance the well-being of the people and has done this so extensively that it is not uncommon to speak of federal police power; but technically this term must be considered a misnomer; for the powers of legislation must in theory arise from specific or implied grant by the Constitution itself; the Constitution makes no grant of the police power to Congress. The extent of the power in such matters was announced with particular clarity in 1913: that the power over transportation among the several states "is complete in itself, and that Congress, *as an incident to it,* may adopt not only means necessary but convenient to its exercise, and the means may have the *quality* of police regulations." [26] The Court also said,

---

[23] Illustrations are cases bearing on the original package doctrine: Leisy *v.* Hardin, 135 U. S. 100 (1890); May & Co. *v.* New Orleans, 178 U. S. 496 (1900); Austin *v.* Tennessee, 179 U. S. 343 (1900); Askren *v.* Continental Oil Co., 252 U. S. 444 (1920).

[24] Take, for example, two cases, Brennan *v.* Titusville, 153 U. S. 289 (1894), and Emert *v.* Missouri, 156 U. S. 296 (1895). In the former an ordinance requiring a license of any person soliciting in the city orders for goods was held invalid, if applied to a person soliciting orders for goods to be shipped into the state. But in the latter case, if the person carried with him the articles and offered them for sale, demanding a license is not an interference with interstate commerce. See also Howe Machine Co. *v.* Gage, 100 U. S. 676 (1880).

[25] Justice Holmes, giving the opinion of the Court in a case involving the police power, states with his usual succinctness the method by which courts reach conclusions: "With regard to the police power, as elsewhere in the law, lines are pricked out by the gradual approach and contact of decisions on the opposing sides." Noble State Bank *v.* Haskell, 219 U. S. 104, 112 (1911).

[26] Hoke *v.* United States, 227 U. S. 308, 323 (1913), and cases cited. The italics not in the original. Naturally congressional power in the District of Columbia and the territories includes the police power.

"Our dual form of government has its perplexities, . . . but it must be kept in mind that we are one people; and the powers reserved to the States and those conferred on the Nation are adapted to be exercised, whether independently or concurrently, to promote the general welfare, material and moral." It has been held, therefore, that federal legislation may forbid the transportation from one state to another of stolen automobiles, lottery tickets, adulterated articles, obscene literature, prize-fight films, and women for immoral purposes.[27]

So inclusive and extensive was the power of regulation as recognized by the Court, that there was a belief, by no means baseless, that an act excluding from interstate transmission articles made in factories employing child labor would be upheld. But it was declared invalid as a distinct interference with the police power of the states.[28] Four justices dissented—it was one of the four to five decisions which have been made with regrettable frequency in recent decades. Inasmuch, said the dissenters, as the Court had recognized congressional authority to forbid interstate transmission of various articles believed to be harmful, there should be no hesitation about upholding an act directed against an evil generally condemned, "the evil of premature and excessive child labor." The majority, however, made a distinction between the act in question and such other legislation as had been held valid: "In each of these instances the use of interstate transportation was necessary to the accomplishment of harmful results. In other words, although the power over interstate transportation was to regulate, that

[27] Examples of the exercise of "police power," incidental to or growing out of specifically granted power, were cited in a decision in the federal circuit court: "Congress has enacted a safety appliance law for the preservation of life and limb. Congress has enacted the anti-trust statute to prevent immorality in contracts and business affairs. Congress has enacted the live stock sanitation act to prevent cruelty to animals. Congress has enacted the cattle contagious disease act to more effectively suppress and prevent the spread of contagious and infectious diseases of live stock. Congress has enacted a statute to enable the Secretary of Agriculture to establish and maintain quarantine districts. Congress has enacted the meat inspection act. Congress has enacted a second employer's liability act. Congress has enacted the obscene literature act. Congress has enacted the lottery statute above referred to. Congress has enacted (but a year ago) statutes prohibiting the sending of liquors by interstate shipment with the privilege of the vendor to have the liquors delivered c.o.d. . . ." Shawnee Milling Co. v. Temple, 179 Fed. 517, 524 (1910). All these acts can be technically justified on the construction of the interstate commerce clause of the Constitution. Reference has been made in previous pages to the power of Congress over the mails and the power to prohibit the transmission of matter deemed injurious. See Ex parte Jackson, 96 U. S. 727 (1878); Ex parte Rapier, 143 U. S. 110 (1892).

[28] Hammer v. Dagenhart, 247 U. S. 251 (1918).

could only be accomplished by prohibiting the use of the facilities of interstate commerce to effect the evil intended. This element is wanting in the present case."

After the decision announcing the invalidity of the child labor act, ostensibly an exercise of the power to regulate interstate commerce, Congress resolved to use its taxing power for the same purpose. The statute, it seemed, would be more acceptable to the Court than the previous one; for in various cases, tax laws which had the real purpose of prohibition and not revenue had been upheld.[29] But the act like its predecessor was pronounced invalid.[30] The Court found a difference— substantial enough to be visible to those desiring to see it—between the act in question and earlier acts in which the broad scope of the taxing power had been recognized; for the statute, now declared void, appeared to make plain on its very face that its object was repression rather than revenue. The decision therefore did not, in the Court's mind, contravene the principle that the Court would not enter upon an examination of motive or reject an act because there might be a purpose auxiliary to the main intent, if the act on its face and in its general tenor appear to be an exercise of undoubted congressional power.[31] If the justices are to be criticized for their stand and charged with obstructing the extirpation of an evil, something may also be said of the moral impropriety of a government's attempting to accomplish its purpose by a subterfuge; everyone knew that the purpose of the act was to stamp out child labor. In other words, legislative artifice is constitutionally and politically immoral, if there is any force remaining in the old belief that there should be a government of laws and not of men and that governments are to be limited by supreme law, and if federalism as distinguished from centralized nationalism is to survive.

But judicial decision did not end the matter. In the flood of ideas and proposals for the change of laws and the Constitution itself, came a proposed amendment to the Constitution giving Congress power to

---

[29] Notice especially Veazie Bank *v.* Fenno, 8 Wallace 533 (1869); McCray *v.* United States, 195 U. S. 27 (1904); United States *v.* Doremus, 249 U. S. 86 (1919).

[30] Bailey *v.* Drexel Furniture Co., 259 U. S. 20 (1922).

[31] The Court referred to the Doremus case and said, "The court, there, made manifest its view that the provisions of the so-called taxing act must be naturally and reasonably adapted to the collection of the tax and not solely to the achievement of some other purpose plainly within state power." Bailey *v.* Drexel Furniture Co., 259 U. S. 20, 43 (1922). In the Doremus case this statement appears: "The act may not be declared unconstitutional because its effect may be to accomplish another purpose as well as the raising of revenue." United States *v.* Doremus, 249 U. S. 86, 94 (1919).

regulate and to prohibit labor of persons under eighteen years of age (1924). At the present writing the amendment has not been ratified.

It used to be taken for granted that the amending of the federal Constitution was so difficult and the process so elaborate that there could be no reasonable hope of alteration unless it was the consequence of an earth-shaking emergency. Only the thunders of civil war, it was said, had produced any change of vital importance since the beginning of the government. The first third of the twentieth century proved this belief was not well-founded. During that period six amendments were adopted.

The sixteenth amendment gave Congress power to lay and collect taxes on incomes, from whatever source derived, without apportionment among the states (1913). The movement which had been on foot for a generation had reached its goal. Acting upon the authority thus granted, Congress levied a graduated tax, and to this there could be no constitutional objection. The Constitution declares that all duties, excises and imposts shall be uniform throughout the United States, but a tax is held to be uniform when it has the same force and effect in every place where the subject matter is to be found.[32] The various acts passed by virtue of this grant of power are supremely important. The power to tax large incomes and to tax them heavily, as well as to exempt other incomes altogether, is of so much importance and so likely to have influence on economic and social conditions, that the significance of the amendment is apparent without extended comment. As a matter of plain fact, it rivals in importance the first section of the fourteenth amendment; and, indeed, if we consider all its possible effects, it may be considered the most far-reaching addition to the Constitution in the last hundred and forty years. The student of society, viewing our whole taxing system, is inclined to look with misgivings on a policy which has the effect of relieving many millions of people of any consciousness that they are carrying the expense of government. But on the other hand, the amendment furnished one

---

[32] Head Money Cases, 112 U. S. 580 (1884) ; Brushaber v. Union Pac. R. R. Co., 240 U. S. 1 (1916), and references. The sixteenth amendment "does not extend the taxing power to new or excepted subjects". Peck v. Lowe, 247 U. S. 165, 172 (1918). On the basis of this principle, taxes on salaries of state officers and on income from state bonds would still be exempt from taxation. See The Collector v. Day, 11 Wallace 113 (1871). Metcalf v. Mitchell, 269 U. S. 514 (1926), discusses the subject. See specially *Ibid.*, 522. The case holds that consulting engineers under special contracts are not officers.

method, which has been in some degree effective, of remedying the evil of gross inequalities in the distribution of wealth; and without some process directed to that end and reasonably adapted to social well-being and political order, democracy may find difficulty in keeping alive. These comments, however, are directed to questions of legislative policy, not to problems of constitutional power.

The seventeenth amendment provides for the popular election of senators (1913). The purpose was doubtless to deprive political partisans of the opportunity to use corrupt methods of influencing state legislatures and also, perhaps, to make certain the selection of men to the Senate who would immediately represent the public and the public interest. There was probably the further hope of ennobling the character of the Senate by the introduction of men of superior quality. The people were now prepared to reject in toto the remnant of the old trust in the filtering process as a method of setting wisdom on high. The movement producing this amendment was like that which made effective changes in popular government in the Jackson period and the years immediately preceding Jackson. That these aims have all been realized, may well be questioned or passed over without serious discussion. The old-fashioned battles in the legislatures have, of course, disappeared; and thus one scandal, which not infrequently had mocked at popular government, was disposed of. Lifting from the shoulders of state legislatures the burden of electing senators ought in theory to have relieved the legislators from domination by the national parties; men chosen by the people of the state could henceforth divide as they might wish on purely state issues; but there is little evidence of such a result. Allegiance to national parties has proved too strong to be effectively resisted.

The manufacture and transportation of intoxicating liquor was prohibited by the eighteenth amendment (1919). Before its ratification, nearly all the states had enacted prohibition statutes, some of them at a much earlier time. It cannot be said that the amendment was cast into the face of an unsuspecting public. Prohibition had a sorry history. But the amendment presented no very serious trouble to the Court. Able attorneys argued with earnestness and apparent sincerity, but without avail, in attempts to obtain a decision declaring the amendment unconstitutional. Their arguments were based largely on the untenable assertion that there are certain implied limitations on the amending power—practically, therefore, a declaration that the people of the United States would not have adopted the Constitution in 1788, had they imagined that their remote posterity would find a way of changing the structure of the union in any vital particular. In the most important case, the Court disposed of the arguments against the validity of the amendment and did so in a few brief paragraphs, without extensive discussion.[33] The amendment was repealed by the adoption of the twenty-first amendment in 1933, the only amendment, since the formation of the government, which was ratified by state conventions rather than by legislatures. Its second section grants to the national government, not only the power but also, presumably, the duty to see that state prohibition laws or other acts restraining the use and delivery of intoxicating liquors are not impaired or rendered useless by the transportation of the liquors in the course of interstate commerce.

Women were given the suffrage by the nineteenth amendment (1920). The subject had been under periodical discussion for over fifty years. Attorneys had the courage to ask the Court to declare the amendment unconstitutional, once again asserting the existence of an implied restriction on the amending power. But naturally the Court could not accept this doctrine.[34] There is something amusing in this strange situation: for years, there had been insistent criticism and complaint because the Court was not ready to recognize the validity of legislation violating in the opinion of the justices the principle of due process; there had been a demand freely and forcibly expressed to the effect that people, acting through their legislative bodies, should have what they wanted and not be continually held in check by constitutional limitations enforced by courts. And yet, in the cases above referred to, we find persons enthusiastically proclaiming the inability

[33] National Prohibition Cases (Rhode Island v. Palmer, etc.), 253 U. S. 350 (1920). See also Dillon v. Gloss, 256 U. S. 368 (1921). A federal district judge went so far as to declare the amendment had not been constitutionally adopted, because it was of such a character that it ought to have been ratified by conventions and not by legislatures. The Supreme Court, on appeal, paid no prolonged attention to this pretentious position: "The choice, therefore, of the mode of ratification, lies in the sole discretion of Congress." United States v. Sprague, 282 U. S. 716, 730 (1931). The main announcements of the Court are: the requirement of a two-thirds vote in Congress means two-thirds of those present; when a state is acting on the ratification of an amendment, a referendum provision in a state constitution is inapplicable; the amendment was within the power to amend reserved in Article V of the Constitution; concurrent power of Congress and the states does not enable either Congress or the states to defeat or thwart the prohibition, but only to enforce it by appropriate means; the period set by Congress for state action (seven years) was within congressional authority; the amendment became part of the Constitution when the requisite number of states had ratified, i.e., it did not wait upon promulgation by the Secretary of State.

[34] Leser v. Garnett, 258 U. S. 130 (1922).

of the people to change the Constitution itself, if the change be unpleasant or contravene what litigants may think to have been the intention of the men of the eighteenth century.

The twentieth amendment (1933) provides that terms of office of the president and vice-president shall begin on the twentieth day of January, and the terms of members of Congress on the third. The long period of uncertainty between the election of a president and the beginning of his term of office—a period which at times was little less than an interregnum—was thus abandoned. And there was ended also the power of Congress to legislate for several months after a new Congress was chosen by the people. That the inconvenience of the old method—and much more than mere inconvenience—should have lasted for over one hundred and forty years is an indication of the strange conservatism of a progressive people.[35] Of importance also is the provision for filling the presidential office in case of death of the president-elect, and if no president is chosen or has failed to qualify before the beginning of the presidential term.

The most evident fact in the constitutional history of the United States in the last thirty or forty years is the expansion of the actual activities of the national government.[36] The building up of the departments at Washington and their continuous operation present a picture of great interest. It is impossible to describe, and much more difficult to define, the bureaucratic system, or to indicate without minute statement the extent to which the government has taken over what by any earlier conception would have been considered the duty and the power of the states alone. The intrusion of the hand of the central government is plainly seen in the granting of subsidies to the states and in the oversight of expenditures as well as in the enforcement of certain acts.

[35] It is only necessary to remember the months after the defeat of the Federalists in 1800, the retiring attitude of Jefferson some months before his official retirement, and the holding of office by Buchanan four months after the election of Lincoln, to see what the practice involved. For the full text of the amendment, see the appendix.

[36] "The oft-repeated statement that the Federal Government is the greatest business enterprise in the United States needs no elaboration. Its truth, however, can be appreciated only by those who have had occasion to survey in detail the great variety and wide ramification of the functions performed by such establishments, for example, as the United States Veterans' Administration, with expenditures in recent years of about $1,000,000,000, or of such departments as the War and Navy Departments, expending together between seven and eight hundred millions per annum, or the Department of Agriculture, with annual expenditures which have varied in recent years from $150,000,000 to $300,000,000." C. H. Wooddy, *The Growth of the Federal Government 1915-1932*, p. viii.

Most of the congressional measures of this character—if one attempts to find a constitutional basis—appear to rest upon the power of Congress to regulate commerce and the power to appropriate money.[37] The fact of developing centralized control or direction is the main thing. The increase of the annual expenditures is enough in itself to demonstrate the realities of the situation.

In all this expansion of the actual activities of the federal government, we see of course the tendency exhibited by all the governments of the nation to do many things which in earlier years were left to the individual or left undone altogether. Governments both state and national have entered upon undertakings quite beyond the old fields of governmental practice. But the tendency to rely upon the national government to do things which were within the scope of state authority is obvious. The result is that, though federalism still exists as the theoretical structure of the union, it has lost ground in the public consciousness. The desire to get things done, and to get them done quickly, induces people to bring pressure upon the central government rather than rely on the spontaneous action of the states. There has been in recent decades a tendency to look upon doubts of constitutional authority, and especially the constitutional competence of the national government, as mere somber and senile legalistic trifling. Many persons are ready to throw their individual or local responsibilities on the shoulders of a government removed from their very immediate control. The underlying sense or sentiment of the people is in reality national, not local. State pride and state feeling of local authority have greatly diminished.

We must, naturally, take into full consideration the reality of the situation: national industrial unity; the fact that in the modern world neither a state nor an individual can live an isolated life; the states as they now exist are bounded by surveyors' lines; and though there are sectional differences and sectional interests, the particular state, as a rule, has no personality based on its physiography, its peculiar character, or its traditions. Federalism, therefore, as a system of political

[37] No way has appeared or is likely to appear whereby through court action the federal government can be prevented from making such appropriations as it sees fit. See Frothingham v. Mellon (Mass. v. Mellon), 262 U. S. 447 (1923), where a state and a private taxpayer sought to prevent the expenditures authorized by the so-called Maternity Act, which authorized appropriations to be apportioned among such states as should apply for funds and accept and comply with conditions, for the purpose of reducing maternal and infant mortality.

order, has been weakened, perhaps is beyond repair. To the reader such generalizations as these are probably perfectly obvious.

To realize the full significance of what has taken place in the passing decades, we need to look back to earlier times. Jefferson's famous inaugural address, given at that dramatic moment when he took the oath of office administered by John Marshall, contains this passage: "Still one thing more, fellow-citizens—a wise and frugal Government, which shall restrain men from injuring one another, shall leave them otherwise free to regulate their own pursuits of industry and improvement, and shall not take from the mouth of labor the bread it has earned." That was the sentiment of democratic individualism with which the nineteenth century began. Hamilton and Madison, defending the new Constitution when presented to the states for adoption, found it necessary to combat the charge that the new system would result in the consolidation of the union, or, to use the words of recent days, that a unitary state would be ultimately founded on the ruins of the federal state. Both of these statesmen believed that natural tendencies would support the authority and vigor of the individual states: "It will always be far more easy for the state governments to encroach upon the national authorities," said Hamilton, "than for the national government to encroach upon the state authorities. The proof of this proposition turns upon the greater degree of influence which the state governments, if they administer their affairs with uprightness and prudence, will generally possess over the people. . . ." [38] Neither of these statesmen could reckon with the railroad, the telegraph, the automobile, and the radio or with the new *ethos* of the people—that spirit or essence to which governmental forms ultimately adapt themselves, even if the spirit be one of heedlessness.

In the early years of the twentieth century, Theodore Roosevelt expressed by word and deed the belief in the necessity for effective governmental activity and for the exertion of national authority which should be exercised fearlessly. Just what he meant by "new nationalism" is not altogether easily gathered or expressed; but certainly he did not wish to see the welfare of the people—as he conceived that welfare to be—jeopardized by any minute legalistic doctrine concerning the respective fields of state and national power; and he associated his principles with his belief in the duty of the president to act for the public good. In those days there was frequent reference to the "twilight zone"—the area within which the state could not work

[38] *The Federalist*, no. XVII.

effectively and into which the federal government could not or might not enter.[39] In 1910, after retiring from the presidency, he used in a public address the following words: "The state must be made efficient for the work which concerns only the people of the state; and the nation for that which concerns all the people. There must remain no neutral ground to serve as a refuge for lawbreakers, and especially for lawbreakers of great wealth, who can hire the vulpine legal cunning which will teach them how to avoid both jurisdictions. . . . The New Nationalism puts the national need before sectional or personal advantage. It is impatient of the utter confusion that results from local legislatures attempting to treat national issues as local issues. . . . This New Nationalism regards the executive power as the steward of the public welfare. . . ."[40]

In 1907, three years before this speech was made, the Supreme Court had been called upon to meet an argument connected with this general theory of sovereign and inherent power in the national government. This argument, the Court said, was substantially this: "All legislative power must be vested in either the state or the National Government; no legislative powers belong to a state government other than those which affect solely the internal affairs of that State; consequently all powers which are national in their scope must be found vested in the Congress of the United States." This theory was unacceptable: "But the proposition that there are legislative powers affecting the Nation as a whole which belong to, although not expressed in the grant of powers, is in direct conflict with the doctrine that this is a government of enumerated powers."[41]

Mr. Roosevelt, it will be noticed, connected his "new nationalism" with the power and the duty of the president as the steward of the public welfare. In an earlier chapter of this work which dealt with Jackson and the presidential office, reference was made to the theories of Theodore Roosevelt, who acted, as he said, on the Jackson-Lincoln

[39] "The existence of a so-called 'twilight zone,' an ill-defined and hazy territory between state and federal authority, has offered undisturbed opportunity for the operations of the exploiter. Without infringing upon state autonomy the Progressive movement demands the illumination of the 'twilight zone.' It insists that the federal government must have liberty to exercise its function in behalf of the common welfare where the power of the individual state is shown to be insufficient." S. J. Duncan-Clark, *The Progressive Movement,* with an Introduction by Theodore Roosevelt, p. 32 (1913).

[40] In a speech made at Osawatomie, Kansas, on August 31, 1910. T. Roosevelt, *The New Nationalism,* pp. 27-28.

[41] Kansas *v.* Colorado, 206 U. S. 46, 89 (1907).

theory of the presidency. We must consider his position an indication not alone of his personal ideas but also partly of the real, and perhaps we can say inevitable, development of the presidential office. In some respects the development was associated with the increase in national authority, to which we have already pointed. But it is difficult to trace with any degree of accuracy the growth of the office in the last hundred years; the history of the office demands a volume rather than a paragraph. The line of growth was not straight and the upward curve was far from uniform. The extent of actual presidential authority or, more correctly, presidential influence and direction, have varied as different incumbents came into office; actual directive force has been affected or created by circumstances and most of all by the personality of the president himself. At times he has been the center of public attention and even the mainspring of governmental action. At other times, his influence has not been conspicuous. Such additions, however, as are made to the office at one time are not likely to be entirely lost. In the hands of a man capable of wielding the powers normally within his grasp, the office is one of immense power. And still, despite recession and accretion of influence and authority, one fact stands forth fairly clearly: a president's power to shape legislation and to direct the course of government rests on his proper gauging of public opinion, in his ability to appeal skillfully to popular sense and sensibility. To this extent democracy has thus far proved faithful to itself and has battled successfully in its own defense.

The duties of the executive department as a whole increased greatly during the first quarter of the present century, because the national government was entering upon new fields; but we are dealing here chiefly with the president's power to guide or form legislative policy. At times, he has appeared to be assuming the rôle of a prime minister initiating legislation and attaining his purposes. The strength of his position has been maintained by his veto, by his power to appoint and remove officials, by his unique opportunity to appeal for public support, and by the fact, as Jackson's career illustrated a hundred years ago, that he is the single representative of the whole people. A president, with the people behind him, can go far in subjecting Congress to his will.[42]

If we may base a judgment upon the recent experiences of European states, we are justified in assuming that democratic government

[42] The nature of the presidential office and its development have been briefly discussed in chapters XVII, XVIII, XXXII of this work.

is peculiarly endangered, not so much by the intrigues of ambitious leaders hungry for power, as by legislative inefficiency, by interminable debates of which the people grow weary, by the existence of many parties, by petty objections and crafty obstruction, by blocs and factions, by party incoherence and consequent absence of assignable responsibility. The two-party system, which has fairly well maintained itself in our history, may not be the best conceivable system; but the history of the modern world appears to make plain that it is the best arrangement as yet devised for assuring orderly development and reasonable stability of popular government. Many people have criticized parties and have become restless because of the prolonged and often futile debates of party spokesmen in Congress; but we can only with difficulty imagine the condition which would ensue, if there were eight or ten competitive groups, each seeking its own advantage and all of them making systematic legislation nearly impossible. Minor parties, which are commonly composed of enthusiasts for particular reforms, have played at times an important rôle, because they have given definite shape to certain ideas and supported them by organized effort. In some cases they have compelled attention to vital issues, for a third-party platform is intended for use and not merely for exhibition. But so strong has the two-party system been and so tenacious of its own life, that one or both of the major parties were likely to pilfer from the third party portions of its programme—such portions as appeared to be attracting favorable public attention. For a party does not live on sentiment alone, but on the bread of office, and if it wishes to maintain its own vitality, it must absorb strength where it may be found.

As we close this work covering in outline the history of nearly two hundred years, we are led to reflect upon the obvious. The constitutional system, which, when it was established, derived its substance from the experiences and the efforts of previous centuries, has survived. In this modern world, that simple fact is an achievement. Formed for less than four million people living in a narrow area along the coast, it has been adapted to the needs of thirty times that number occupying half a continent. If federalism, democracy, and individual liberty are drowned in the torrent and whirlpool of the future because men are found incompetent to govern themselves, the historical fact remains—for a hundred and fifty years the Constitution lasted as the fundamental law of a successful people. Only the un-historical-minded person, fretted by his present and immediate ills, will underestimate this fact. He may well call to mind the words of Jefferson, who at the opening of the nineteenth century had the boldness to pronounce his faith in America as "the strongest Government on earth. . . . Sometimes it is said that man can not be trusted with the government of himself. Can he, then, be trusted with the government of others? Or have we found angels in the forms of kings to govern him? Let history answer this question." Since these words were spoken, ancient dynasties and old monarchical systems have disappeared; new monarchies have risen and fallen; and the American constitutional system still stands.

APPENDIX

CONSTITUTION

OF THE

UNITED STATES OF AMERICA

WE, the people of the United States, in order to form a more perfect union, establish justice, insure domestic tranquility, provide for the common defence, promote the general welfare, and secure the blessings of liberty to ourselves and our posterity, do ordain and establish this CONSTITUTION for the United States of America.

ARTICLE I

SECT. 1. All legislative powers herein granted shall be vested in a Congress of the United States, which shall consist of a Senate and a House of Representatives.

SECT. 2. The House of Representatives shall be composed of members chosen every second year by the people of the several States, and the electors in each State shall have the qualifications requisite for electors of the most numerous branch of the State Legislature.

No person shall be a Representative who shall not have attained to the age of twenty-five years, and been seven years a citizen of the United States, and who shall not, when elected, be an inhabitant of that State in which he shall be chosen.

Representatives and direct taxes shall be apportioned among the several States which may be included within this Union, according to their respective numbers, which shall be determined by adding to the whole number of free persons, including those bound to service for a term of years, and excluding Indians not taxed, three fifths of all other persons. The actual enumeration shall be made within three years after the first meeting of the Congress of the United States, and within every subsequent term of ten years, in such manner as they shall by law direct. The number of Representatives shall not exceed one for every thirty thousand, but each State shall have at least one representative; and until such enumeration shall be made, the State of New Hampshire shall be entitled to choose three, Massachusetts eight, Rhode Island and Providence

Plantations one, Connecticut five, New York six, New Jersey four, Pennsylvania eight, Delaware one, Maryland six, Virginia ten, North Carolina five, South Carolina five, and Georgia three.

When vacancies happen in the representation from any State, the Executive authority thereof shall issue writs of election to fill such vacancies.

The House of Representatives shall choose their Speaker and other officers; and shall have the sole power of impeachment.

SECT. 3. The Senate of the United States shall be composed of two Senators from each State, chosen by the Legislature thereof, for six years; and each Senator shall have one vote.

Immediately after they shall be assembled in consequence of the first election, they shall be divided as equally as may be into three classes. The seats of the Senators of the first class shall be vacated at the expiration of the second year, of the second class at the expiration of the fourth year, and of the third class at the expiration of the sixth year so that one third may be chosen every second year; and if vacancies happen by resignation, or otherwise, during the recess of the Legislature of any State, the Executive thereof may make temporary appointments until the next meeting of the Legislature, which shall then fill such vacancies.

No person shall be a Senator who shall not have attained to the age of thirty years, and been nine years a citizen of the United States, and who shall not, when elected, be an inhabitant of that State for which he shall be chosen.

The Vice-President of the United States shall be President of the Senate, but shall have no vote, unless they be equally divided.

The Senate shall choose their other officers, and also a president *pro tempore,* in the absence of the Vice-President, or when he shall exercise the office of President of the United States.

The Senate shall have the sole power to try all impeachments. When sitting for that purpose, they shall be on oath or affirmation. When the President of the United States is tried, the Chief Justice shall preside and no person shall be convicted without the concurrence of two thirds of the members present.

Judgment in cases of impeachment shall not extend further than to removal from office, and disqualification to hold and enjoy any office of honor, trust, or profit under the United States: but the party convicted shall nevertheless be liable and subject to indictment, trial, judgment, and punishment, according to law.

SECT. 4. The times, places, and manner of holding elections for Senators and Representatives shall be prescribed in each State by the Legislature thereof; but the Congress may at any time by law make or alter such regulations, except as to the places of choosing Senators.

The Congress shall assemble at least once in every year, and such meeting shall be on the first Monday in December, unless they shall by law appoint a different day.

SECT. 5. Each House shall be the judge of the elections, returns, and qualifications of its own members, and a majority of each shall constitute a quorum to do business; but a smaller number may adjourn from day to day, and may be authorized to compel the attendance of absent members in such manner, and under such penalties, as each House may provide.

Each House may determine the rules of its proceedings, punish its members for disorderly behavior, and, with the concurrence of two thirds, expel a member.

Each House shall keep a journal of its proceedings, and from time to time publish the same, excepting such parts as may in their judgment require secrecy; and the yeas and nays of the members of either House on any question shall, at the desire of one fifth of those present, be entered on the journal.

Neither House, during the session of Congress, shall, without the consent of the other, adjourn for more than three days, nor to any other place than that in which the two Houses shall be sitting.

SECT. 6. The Senators and Representatives shall receive a compensation for their services, to be ascertained by law, and paid out of the Treasury of the United States. They shall in all cases, except treason, felony, and breach of the peace, be privileged from arrest during their attendance at the session of their respective Houses, and in going to and returning from the same; and for any speech or debate in either House they shall not be questioned in any other place.

No Senator or Representative shall, during the time for which he was elected, be appointed to any civil office under the authority of the United States, which shall have been created, or the emoluments whereof shall have been increased, during such time; and no person holding any office under the United States shall be a member of either House during his continuance in office.

SECT. 7. All bills for raising revenue shall originate in the House of Representatives; but the Senate may propose or concur with amendments as on other bills.

Every bill which shall have passed the House of Representatives and the Senate shall, before it becomes a law, be presented to the President of the United States; if he approve he shall sign it, but if not he shall return it with his objections to that House in which it shall have originated, who shall enter the objections at large on their journal, and proceed to reconsider it. If after such reconsideration two thirds of that House shall agree to pass the bill, it shall be sent, together with the objections, to the other House, by which it shall likewise be reconsidered, and, if approved by two thirds of that House, it shall become a law. But in all such cases the votes of both Houses shall be determined by yeas and nays, and the names of the persons voting for and against the bill shall be entered on the journal of each House respectively. If any bill shall not be returned by the President within ten days (Sundays excepted) after it shall have been presented to him, the same shall be a law, in like manner as if he had signed it, unless the Congress by their adjournment prevent its return, in which case it shall not be a law.

Every order, resolution, or vote to which the concurrence of the Senate and House of Representatives may be necessary (except on a question of adjournment) shall be presented to the President of the United States; and, before the same shall take effect, shall be approved by him, or, being disapproved by him, shall be repassed by two thirds of the Senate and House of Representatives, according to the rules and limitations prescribed in the case of a bill.

SECT. 8. The Congress shall have power,—

To lay and collect taxes, duties, imposts, and excises to pay the debts and provide for the common defence and general welfare of the United States; but all duties, imposts, and excises shall be uniform throughout the United States;

To borrow money on the credit of the United States;

To regulate commerce with foreign nations, and among the several States, and with the Indian tribes;

To establish an uniform rule of naturalization, and uniform laws on the subject of bankruptcies throughout the United States;

To coin money, regulate the value thereof, and of foreign coin, and fix the standard of weights and measures;

To provide for the punishment of counterfeiting the securities and current coin of the United States;

To establish post-offices and post-roads;

To promote the progress of science and useful arts, by securing for limited times to authors and inventors the exclusive right to their respective writings and discoveries;

To constitute tribunals inferior to the Supreme Court;

To define and punish piracies and felonies committed on the high seas, and offences against the law of nations;

To declare war, grant letters of marque and reprisal, and make rules concerning captures on land and water;

To raise and support armies, but no appropriation of money to that use shall be for a longer term than two years;

To provide and maintain a navy;

To make rules for the government and regulation of the land and naval forces;

To provide for calling forth the militia to execute the laws of the Union, suppress insurrections, and repel invasions;

To provide for organizing, arming, and disciplining the militia, and for governing such part of them as may be employed in the service of the United States, reserving to the States respectively, the appointment of the officers, and the authority of training the militia according to the discipline prescribed by Congress;

To exercise exclusive legislation, in all cases whatsoever, over such district (not exceeding ten miles square) as may, by cession of particular States, and the acceptance of Congress, become the seat of the government of the United States; and to exercise like authority over all places purchased by the consent of the Legislature of the State in which the same shall be, for the erection of forts, magazines, arsenals, dockyards, and other needful buildings;—and

To make all laws which shall be necessary and proper for carrying into execution the foregoing powers, and all other powers vested by this Constitution in the government of the United States, or in any department or officer thereof.

SECT. 9. The migration or importation of such persons as any of the States now existing shall think proper to admit, shall not be prohibited by the Congress prior to the year one thousand eight hundred and eight, but a tax or duty may be imposed on such importation, not exceeding ten dollars for each person.

The privilege of the writ of *habeas corpus* shall not be suspended, unless when in cases of rebellion or invasion the public safety may require it.

No bill of attainder or *ex post facto* law shall be passed.

No capitation or other direct tax shall be laid, unless in proportion to the census or enumeration herein before directed to be taken.

No tax or duty shall be laid on articles exported from any State.

No preference shall be given by any regulation of commerce or revenue to the ports of one State over those of another; nor shall vessels bound to, or from, one State, be obliged to enter, clear, or pay duties in another.

No money shall be drawn from the treasury, but in consequence of appropriations made by law; and a regular statement and account of the receipts and expenditures of all public money shall be published from time to time.

No title of nobility shall be granted by the United States; and no person holding any office of profit or trust under them shall, without the consent of the Congress, accept of any present, emolument, office, or title, of any kind whatever, from any king, prince, or foreign state.

SECT. 10. No State shall enter into any treaty, alliance, or confederation; grant letters of marque and reprisal; coin money; emit bills of credit; make anything but gold and silver coin a tender in payment of debts; pass any bill of attainder, *ex post facto* law, or law impairing the obligation of contracts, or grant any title of nobility.

No State shall, without the consent of the Congress, lay any imposts or duties on imports or exports, except what may be absolutely necessary for executing its inspection laws; and the net produce of all duties and imposts, laid by any State on imports or exports, shall be for the use of the treasury of the United States; and all such laws shall be subject to the revision and control of the Congress.

No State shall, without the consent of Congress, lay any duty of tonnage, keep troops or ships of war in time of peace, enter into any agreement or compact with another State, or with a foreign power, or engage in war, unless actually invaded, or in such imminent danger as will not admit of delay.

ARTICLE II

SECT. 1. The executive power shall be vested in a President of the United States of America. He shall hold his office during the term of four years, and, together with the Vice-President, chosen for the same term, be elected as follows:—

Each State shall appoint, in such manner as the Legislature thereof may direct, a number of Electors equal to the whole number of Senators and Representatives to which the State may be entitled in the Congress: but no Senator or Representative, or person holding an office of trust or profit under the United States, shall be appointed an Elector.

[The Electors shall meet in their respective States, and vote by ballot for two persons, of whom one at least shall not be an inhabitant of the same State with themselves. And they shall make a list of all the persons voted for, and of the number of votes for each; which list they shall sign and certify, and transmit sealed to the seat of the government of the United States, directed to the President of the Senate. The President of the Senate shall, in the presence of the Senate and House of Representatives, open all the certificates, and the votes shall then be counted. The person having the greatest number of votes shall be the President, if such number be a majority of the whole number of Electors appointed; and if there be more than one who have such majority, and have an equal number of votes, then the House of Representatives shall immediately choose by ballot one of them for President; and if no person have a majority, then from the five highest on the list the said House shall in like manner choose the President. But in choosing the President, the votes shall be taken by States, the representation from each State having one vote; a quorum for this purpose shall consist of a member or members from two thirds of the States, and a majority of all the States shall be necessary to a choice. In every case, after the choice of the President, the person having the greatest number of votes of the Electors shall be the Vice-President. But if there should remain two or more who have equal votes, the Senate shall choose from them by ballot the Vice-President.—*Repealed by Amendment* XII.]

Congress may determine the time of choosing the Electors, and the day on which they shall give their votes; which day shall be the same throughout the United States.

No person except a natural-born citizen, or a citizen of the United States at the time of the adoption of this Constitution, shall be eligible to the office of President; neither shall any person be eligible to that office who shall not have attained to the age of thirty-five years, and been fourteen years a resident within the United States.

In case of the removal of the President from office, or of his death, resignation, or inability to discharge the powers and duties of the said office, the same shall devolve on the Vice-President, and the Congress may by law provide for the case of removal, death, resignation, or inability, both of the President and Vice-President, declaring what officer shall then act as President, and such officer shall act accordingly, until the disability be removed, or a President shall be elected.

The President shall, at stated times, receive for his services a compensation, which shall neither be increased nor diminished during the period for which he shall have been elected, and he shall not receive within that period any other emolument from the United States, or any of them.

Before he enter on the execution of his office, he shall take the following oath or affirmation:—"I do solemnly swear (or affirm) that I will faithfully execute the office of President of the United States, and will, to the best of my ability, preserve, protect, and defend the Constitution of the United States."

SECT. 2. The President shall be commander-in-chief of the army and navy of the United States, and of the militia of the several States, when called into the actual service of the United States; he may require the opinion, in writing, of the principal officer in each of the executive departments, upon any subject relating to the duties of their respective offices, and he shall have power to grant reprieves and pardons for offences against the United States, except in cases of impeachment.

He shall have power, by and with the advice and consent of the Senate, to make treaties, provided two thirds of the Senators present concur; and he shall nominate, and, by and with the advice and consent of the Senate, shall appoint ambassadors, other public ministers, and consuls, judges of the Supreme Court, and all other officers of the United States, whose appointments are not herein otherwise provided for, and which shall be established by law; but the Congress may by law vest the appointment of such inferior officers, as they think proper, in the President alone, in the courts of law, or in the heads of departments.

The President shall have power to fill up all vacancies that may happen during the recess of the Senate, by granting commissions which shall expire at the end of their next session.

SECT. 3. He shall from time to time give to the Congress information of the state of the Union, and recommend to their consideration such measures as he shall judge necessary and expedient; he may, on extraordinary occasions, convene both Houses, or either of them, and in case of disagreement between them, with respect to the time of adjournment, he may adjourn them to such time as he shall think proper; he shall receive ambassadors and other public ministers; he shall take care that the laws be faithfully executed, and shall commission all the officers of the United States.

SECT. 4. The President, Vice-President, and all civil officers of the United States, shall be removed from office on impeachment for, and conviction of, treason, bribery, or other high crimes and misdemeanors.

ARTICLE III

SECT. 1. The judicial power of the United States shall be vested in one Supreme Court, and in such inferior courts as the Congress may from time to time ordain and establish. The judges, both of the Supreme and inferior courts, shall hold their offices during good behavior, and shall, at stated times, receive for their services a compensation, which shall not be diminished during their continuance in office.

SECT. 2. The judicial power shall extend to all cases, in law and equity, arising under this Constitution, the laws of the United States, and treaties made, or which shall be made, under their authority; to all cases affecting ambassadors, other public ministers, and consuls; to all cases of admiralty and maritime jurisdiction; to controversies to which the United States shall be a party; to controversies between two or more States, between a State and citizens of another State, between citizens of different States, between citizens of the same State claiming lands under grants of different States, and between a State, or the citizens thereof, and foreign states, citizens, or subjects.

In all cases affecting ambassadors, other public ministers, and consuls, and those in which a State shall be party, the Supreme Court shall have original jurisdiction. In all the other cases before mentioned, the Supreme Court shall have appellate jurisdiction, both as to law and fact, with such exceptions, and under such regulations, as the Congress shall make.

The trial of all crimes, except in cases of impeachment, shall be by jury; and such trial shall be held in the State where the said crimes shall have been committed; but when not committed within any State, the trial shall be at such place or places as the Congress may by law have directed.

SECT. 3. Treason against the United States shall consist only in levying war against them, or in adhering to their enemies, giving them aid and comfort. No person shall be convicted of treason unless on the testimony of two witnesses to the same overt act, or on confession in open court.

The Congress shall have power to declare the punishment of treason, but no attainder of treason shall work corruption of blood, or forfeiture except during the life of the person attainted.

ARTICLE IV

SECT. 1. Full faith and credit shall be given in each State to the public acts, records, and judicial proceedings of every other State. And the Congress may by general laws prescribe the manner in which such acts, records, and proceedings shall be proved, and the effect thereof.

SECT. 2. The citizens of each State shall be entitled to all privileges and immunities of citizens in the several States.

A person charged in any State with treason, felony, or other crime, who shall flee from justice, and be found in another State, shall, on demand of the executive authority of the State from which he fled, be delivered up, to be removed to the State having jurisdiction of the crime.

No person held to service or labor in one State, under the laws thereof, escaping into another, shall, in consequence of any law or regulation therein, be discharged from such service or labor, but shall be delivered up on claim of the party to whom such service or labor may be due.

SECT. 3. New States may be admitted by the Congress into this Union; but no new State shall be formed or erected within the jurisdiction of any other State; nor any State be formed by the junction of two or more States, or parts of States, without the consent of the Legislatures of the States concerned, as well as of the Congress.

The Congress shall have power to dispose of and make all needful rules and regulations respecting the territory or other property belonging to the United States; and nothing in this Constitution shall be so construed as to prejudice any claims of the United States, or of any particular State.

SECT. 4. The United States shall guarantee to every State in this Union a republican form of government, and shall protect each of them against invasion; and on application of the Legislature, or of the Executive (when the Legislature can not be convened), against domestic violence.

ARTICLE V

The Congress, whenever two thirds of both houses shall deem it necessary, shall propose amendments to this Constitution, or, on the application of the Legislatures of two thirds of the several States, shall call a convention for proposing amendments, which, in either case, shall be valid to all intents and purposes, as part of this Constitution, when ratified by the Legislatures of three fourths of the several States, or by conventions in three fourths thereof, as the one or the other mode of ratification may be proposed by the Congress; provided that no amendment which may be made prior to the year one thousand eight hundred and eight shall in any manner affect the first and fourth clauses in the ninth section of the first article; and that no State, without its consent, shall be deprived of its equal suffrage in the Senate.

ARTICLE VI

All debts contracted and engagements entered into, before the adoption of this Constitution, shall be as valid against the United States under this Constitution as under the Confederation.

This Constitution, and the laws of the United States which shall be made in pursuance thereof, and all treaties made, or which shall be made, under the authority of the United States, shall be the supreme law of the land; and the judges in every State shall be bound thereby, anything in the constitution or laws of any State to the contrary notwithstanding.

The Senators and Representatives before mentioned, and the members of the several State Legislatures, and all executive and judicial officers, both of the United States and of the several States, shall be bound by oath or affirmation to support this Constitution; but no religious test shall ever be required as a qualification to any office or public trust under the United States.

ARTICLE VII

The ratification of the conventions of nine States shall be sufficient for the establishment of this Constitution between the States so ratifying the same.

Done in Convention, by the unanimous consent of the States present, the seventeenth day of September, in the year of our Lord one thousand seven hundred and eighty-seven, and of the Independence of the United States of America the twelfth.

In Witness whereof we have hereunto subscribed our names.[1]

---

[1] The signatures are here omitted.

AMENDMENTS

ARTICLE I

Congress shall make no law respecting an establishment of religion, or prohibiting the free exercise thereof; or abridging the freedom of speech, or of the press, or the right of the people peaceably to assemble, and to petition the government for a redress of grievances.

ARTICLE II

A well regulated militia being necessary to the security of a free state, the right of the people to keep and bear arms shall not be infringed.

ARTICLE III

No soldier shall, in time of peace, be quartered in any house, without the consent of the owner, nor in time of war, but in a manner to be prescribed by law.

ARTICLE IV

The right of the people to be secure in their persons, houses, papers, and effects, against unreasonable searches and seizures, shall not be violated, and no warrants shall issue but upon probable cause, supported by oath or affirmation, and particularly describing the place to be searched, and the persons or things to be seized.

ARTICLE V

No person shall be held to answer for a capital, or otherwise infamous crime, unless on a presentment or indictment of a grand jury, except in cases arising in the land or naval forces, or in the militia, when in actual service in time of war or public danger; nor shall any person be subject for the same offence to be twice put in jeopardy of life and limb; nor shall be compelled in any criminal case to be a witness against himself, nor be deprived of life, liberty, or property, without due process of law; nor shall private property be taken for public use without just compensation.

ARTICLE VI

In all criminal prosecutions, the accused shall enjoy the right to a speedy and public trial, by an impartial jury of the State and district wherein the crime shall have been committed, which district shall have been previously ascertained by law, and to be informed of the nature and cause of the accusation; to be confronted with the witnesses against him; to have compulsory process for obtaining witnesses in his favor, and to have the assistance of counsel for his defence.

ARTICLE VII

In suits at common law, where the value in controversy shall exceed twenty dollars, the right of trial by jury shall be preserved, and no fact tried by a jury shall be otherwise re-examined in any court of the United States, than according to the rules of the common law.

ARTICLE VIII

Excessive bail shall not be required, nor excessive fines imposed, nor cruel and unusual punishments inflicted.

ARTICLE IX

The enumeration in the Constitution, of certain rights, shall not be construed to deny or disparage others retained by the people.

ARTICLE X

The powers not delegated to the United States by the Constitution, nor prohibited by it to the States, are reserved to the States respectively, or to the people.

ARTICLE XI

The judicial power of the United States shall not be construed to extend to any suit in law or equity, commenced or prosecuted against one of the United States by citizens of another State, or by citizens or subjects of any foreign state.

ARTICLE XII

The Electors shall meet in their respective States, and vote by ballot for President and Vice-President, one of whom, at least, shall not be an inhabitant of the same State with themselves; they shall name in their ballots the person voted for as President, and in distinct ballots the person voted for as Vice-President; and they shall make distinct lists of all persons voted for as President, and of all persons voted for as Vice-President, and of the number of votes for each, which lists they shall sign and certify, and transmit sealed to the seat of the government of the United States, directed to the President of the Senate;—the President of the Senate shall, in the presence of the Senate and House of Representatives, open all the certificates, and the votes shall then be counted;—the person having the greatest number of votes for President shall be the President, if such number be a majority of the whole number of Electors appointed; and if no person have such majority, then from the persons having the highest numbers not exceeding three on the list of those voted for as President, the House of Representatives shall choose immediately, by ballot, the President. But in choosing the President, the votes shall be taken by States, the representation from each State having one vote; a quorum for this purpose shall consist of a member or members from two thirds of the States, and a majority of all the States shall be necessary to a choice. And if the House of Representatives shall not choose a President, whenever the right of choice shall devolve upon them, before the fourth day of March next following, then the Vice-President shall act as President, as in the case of the death or other constitutional disability of the President. The person having the greatest number of votes as Vice-President shall be the Vice-President, if such number be a majority of the whole number of Electors appointed, and if no person have a majority, then from the two highest numbers on the list the Senate shall choose the Vice-President; a quorum for the purpose shall consist of two thirds of the whole number of Senators, and a majority of the whole number shall be necessary to a choice. But no person constitutionally ineligible to the office of President shall be eligible to that of Vice-President of the United States.

ARTICLE XIII

Sect. 1. Neither slavery nor involuntary servitude, except as a punishment for crime whereof the party shall have been duly convicted, shall exist within the United States, or any place subject to their jurisdiction.

Sect. 2. Congress shall have power to enforce this article by appropriate legislation.

ARTICLE XIV

Sect. 1. All persons born or naturalized in the United States, and subject to the jurisdiction thereof, are citizens of the United States and of the State wherein they reside. No State shall make or enforce any law which shall abridge the privileges or immunities of citizens of the United States; nor shall any State deprive any person of life, liberty, or property, without due process of law; nor deny to any person within its jurisdiction the equal protection of the laws.

Sect. 2. Representatives shall be apportioned among the several States according to their respective numbers, counting the whole number of persons in each State, excluding Indians not taxed. But when the right to vote at any election for the choice of Electors for President and Vice-President of the United States, Representatives in Congress, the executive and judicial officers of a State, or the members of the Legislature thereof, is denied to any of the male inhabitants of such State, being twenty-one years of age and citizens of the United States, or in any way abridged, except for participation in rebellion or other crime, the basis of representation therein shall be reduced in the proportion which the number of such male citizens shall bear to the whole number of male citizens twenty-one years of age in such State.

Sect. 3. No person shall be a Senator or Representative in Congress, or Elector of President and Vice-President, or hold any office, civil or military, under the United States, or under any State, who, having previously taken an oath, as a member of Congress, or as an officer of the United States, or as a member of any State Legislature, or as an executive or judicial officer of any State, to support the Constitution of the United States, shall have engaged in insurrection or rebellion against the same, or given aid or comfort to the enemies thereof. But Congress may, by a vote of two thirds of each House, remove such disability.

Sect. 4. The validity of the public debt of the United States, authorized by law, including debts incurred for payment of pensions and bounties for services in suppressing insurrection or rebellion, shall not be questioned. But neither the United States, nor any State shall assume or pay any debt or obligation incurred in aid of insurrection or rebellion against the United States, or any claim for the loss or emancipation of any slave; but all such debts, obligations, and claims shall be held illegal and void.

Sect. 5. The Congress shall have power to enforce, by appropriate legislation, the provisions of this article.

ARTICLE XV

Sect. 1. The right of citizens of the United States to vote shall not be denied or abridged by the United States, or by any State, on account of race, color, or previous condition of servitude.

Sect. 2. The Congress shall have power to enforce this article by appropriate legislation.

ARTICLE XVI

The Congress shall have power to lay and collect taxes on incomes, from whatever source derived, without apportionment among the several States, and without regard to any census or enumeration.

ARTICLE XVII

The Senate of the United States shall be composed of two Senators from each State, elected by the people thereof, for six years; and each Senator shall have one vote. The Electors in each State shall have the qualifications requisite for Electors of the most numerous branch of the State legislatures.

When vacancies happen in the representation of any State in the Senate, the executive authority of such State shall issue writs of election to fill such vacancies: *Provided,* That the legislature of any State may empower the executive thereof to make temporary appointments until the people fill the vacancies by election as the legislature may direct.

This amendment shall not be construed as to affect the election or term of any Senator chosen before it becomes valid as part of the Constitution.

ARTICLE XVIII

Sect. 1. After one year from the ratification of this article the manufacture, sale or transportation of intoxicating liquors within, the importation thereof into, or the exportation thereof from the United States and all territories subject to the jurisdiction thereof for beverage purposes is hereby prohibited.

Sect. 2. The Congress and the several States shall have concurrent power to enforce this article by appropriate legislation.

Sect. 3. This article shall be inoperative unless it shall have been ratified as an amendment to the Constitution by the legislatures of the several States, as provided in the Constitution, within seven years from the date of the submission hereof to the States by Congress.

ARTICLE XIX

The right of citizens of the United States to vote shall not be denied or abridged by the United States or by any State on account of sex.

Congress shall have power to enforce this article by appropriate legislation.

ARTICLE XX

Sect. 1. The terms of the President and Vice-President shall end at noon on the 20th day of January, and the terms of Senators and Representatives at noon on the 3d day of January, of the years in which such terms would have ended if this article had not been ratified; and the terms of their successors shall then begin.

Sect. 2. The Congress shall assemble at least once in every year, and such meeting shall begin at noon on the third day of January, unless they shall by law appoint a different day.

SECT. 3. If, at the time fixed for the beginning of the term of the President, the President-elect shall have died, the Vice-President-elect shall become President. If a President shall not have been chosen before the time fixed for the beginning of his term, or if the President-elect shall have failed to qualify, then the Vice-President-elect shall act as President until a President shall have qualified; and the Congress may by law provide for the case wherein neither a President-elect nor a Vice-President-elect shall have qualified, declaring who shall then act as President, or the manner in which one who is to act shall be selected, and such person shall act accordingly until a President or Vice-President shall have qualified.

Sect. 4. The Congress may by law provide for the case of the death of any of the persons from whom the House of Representatives may choose a President whenever the right of choice shall have devolved upon them, and for the case of the death of any of the persons from whom the Senate may choose a Vice-President whenever the right of choice shall have devolved upon them.

Sect. 5. Sections 1 and 2 shall take effect upon the fifteenth day of October following the ratification of this article.

Sect. 6. This article shall be inoperative unless it shall have been ratified as an amendment to the Constitution by the Legislatures of three-fourths of the several States within seven years from the date of its submission.

ARTICLE XXI

Sect. 1. The Eighteenth Amendment to the Constitution of the United States is hereby repealed.

Sect. 2. The transportation or importation into any State, Territory or possession of the United States for delivery or use therein of intoxicating liquors, in violation of the laws thereof, is hereby prohibited.

SECT. 3. This article shall be inoperative unless it shall have been ratified as an amendment to the Constitution by conventions in the several States, as provided in the Constitution, within seven years from the date of the submission hereof to the States by the Congress.

TABLE OF CASES

A

B

C

G

H

I

INDEX

A

Abolitionists, rise and character of, 473-476

Acts: Administration of Justice (1774), 78; Alien, 266; Alien Enemies, 266; Anti-Trust, 777; Army Appropriation, 662; Boston Port (1774), 77; Child Labor, 783-785; Civil Rights (1866), 653-655, 686; Civil Rights (1875), 692; Declaratory, 40; "Enforcement," 686; Enlistment of Minors, 351; Espionage, 270; Excise (1791), 228-229; Fugitive Slave, 534ff.; Interstate Commerce, 773; "Intolerable" (1774), 77-79; Judiciary (1789), 235-237; Judiciary (1801), 288-289; Ku Klux, 688-690; Massachusetts Government (1774), 77; Molasses (West India), 12, 25, 30; National Bank (1791), 229ff., (1863-4), 640; Naturalization, 266-267; Navigation, 12, 25, 29, 30, 31, note 15, 42, 54, 85; Negro Seamen, 471; New England Restraining (1775), 89, note 17; Quartering, 65, 78; Quebec, 79; Reconstruction, 662; Revenue (1764), 28, 30; Sedition, 266, 269; Sherman (*see* Anti-Trust); Stamp, 35ff.; Sugar (1764), 28, 30; Tenure of Office, 662; Townshend, 53

Adams, Charles Francis, nominated for vice-presidency, 512

Adams, John: on writs of assistance, 25-26; and Boston memorial, 47; "Novanglus" papers, 80; theory of empire, 82; on difficulties of Continental Congress (1774), 84-85; on independence, 100; establishment of state governments, 108; checks and balances, 116, 196; on debates in the old Congress, 121; Vice-President, 224, 245; President, 264; conduct of X. Y. Z. controversy, 265

Adams, John Quincy: prepares journal of Federal Convention, 153; describes career of Federalist party, 333-334; constitutional principles, 359; President (1824), 407; presidential candidate (1828), 408; and right of petition, 478-480

Adams, Samuel: power of Parliament (1765), 43; opposition to Townshend Acts, 59; natural rights argument, 59; rights to property, 59; fixed constitution, 59; committees of correspondence, 68-69; contest with Governor Hutchinson, 67-70; and adoption of Constitution, 203, 204; *see also*, Constitution, British; Massachusetts; Rights, natural; Rights, property.

Administrative officers, responsibility of, 392, 393, 767

Admiralty jurisdiction, extent of, 471

Admission of new states, 186, 187, 377-379, 500-505

Alabama: secedes, 603; restored to union, 678

Alaska, 769, 770

Albany Congress and Plan of Union (1754), 20-23

Alien and Sedition Acts, 264 ff., *see also* Virginia and Kentucky resolutions

Amendment, principles of, 634, 635, 786, 787

Amendments of federal Constitution: proposed (1787-1788), 199, 202, 204, 206, 210, 211; proposed (1861), 607; first eight, binding on national government, 225, 730, 731; first ten, 225, 730; eleventh adopted, 302, 303; twelfth adopted, 285; thirteenth proposed and adopted, 634-636; fourteenth proposed, 678; fifteenth adopted, 680; sixteenth, 785; seventeenth, 786; eighteenth, 786, 787; nineteenth, 787; twentieth, 788; twenty-first, 787; child labor, 784, 785; *see also*, Freedom of speech and press; Bill of rights; States, suits against; Fourteenth amendment; Due process of law

American party, 573

Annapolis convention (1786), 147

Annexation: of Louisiana, 294-298; incorporation, 376, 768, 769; of Texas, 496-505; discussed (1898-1900), 767-769; *see also*, Expansion; Imperialism

Anti-Monopoly party, 760, 761

Antislavery: opposition to slavery in the District, 477; position of advocates

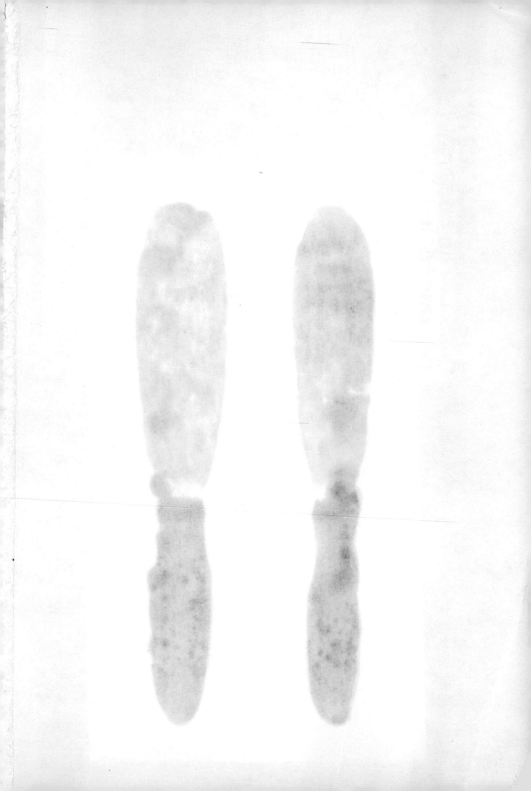